Nineteenth-Century Literature Criticism

Topics Volume

Guide to Gale Literary Criticism Series

For criticism on	Consult these Gale series
Authors now living or who died after December 31, 1959	*CONTEMPORARY LITERARY CRITICISM (CLC)*
Authors who died between 1900 and 1959	*TWENTIETH-CENTURY LITERARY CRITICISM (TCLC)*
Authors who died between 1800 and 1899	*NINETEENTH-CENTURY LITERATURE CRITICISM (NCLC)*
Authors who died between 1400 and 1799	*LITERATURE CRITICISM FROM 1400 TO 1800 (LC)* *SHAKESPEAREAN CRITICISM (SC)*
Authors who died before 1400	*CLASSICAL AND MEDIEVAL LITERATURE CRITICISM (CMLC)*
Authors of books for children and young adults	*CHILDREN'S LITERATURE REVIEW (CLR)*
Dramatists	*DRAMA CRITICISM (DC)*
Poets	*POETRY CRITICISM (PC)*
Short story writers	*SHORT STORY CRITICISM (SSC)*
Black writers of the past two hundred years	*BLACK LITERATURE CRITICISM (BLC)*
Hispanic writers of the late nineteenth and twentieth centuries	*HISPANIC LITERATURE CRITICISM (HLC)*
Native North American writers and orators of the eighteenth, nineteenth, and twentieth centuries	*NATIVE NORTH AMERICAN LITERATURE (NNAL)*
Major authors from the Renaissance to the present	*WORLD LITERATURE CRITICISM, 1500 TO THE PRESENT (WLC)*

ISSN 0732-1864

Volume 76

Nineteenth-Century Literature Criticism

Topics Volume

Excerpts from Criticism of Various Topics in Nineteenth-Century Literature, including Literary and Critical Movements, Prominent Themes and Genres, Anniversary Celebrations, and Surveys of National Literatures

Suzanne Dewsbury
Editor

GALE GROUP

Detroit
San Francisco
London
Boston
Woodbridge, CT

STAFF

This book is printed on acid-free paper that meets the minimum requirements of American National Standard for Information Sciences—Permanent Paper for Printed Library Materials, ANSI Z39.48-1984.

Library of Congress Catalog Card Number 84-643008
ISBN 0-7876-2878-6
ISSN 0732-1864
Printed in the United States of America

10 9 8 7 6 5 4 3 2 1

Contents

Preface

Since its inception in 1981, *Nineteenth-Century Literature Criticism* has been a valuable resource for students and librarians seeking critical commentary on writers of this transitional period in world history. Designated an "Outstanding Reference Source" by the American Library Association with the publication of its first volume, *NCLC* has since been purchased by over 6,000 school, public, and university libraries. The series has covered more than 300 authors representing 29 nationalities and over 17,000 titles. No other reference source has surveyed the critical reaction to nineteenth-century authors and literature as thoroughly as *NCLC*.

Scope of the Series

NCLC is designed to introduce students and advanced readers to the authors of the nineteenth century, and to the most significant interpretations of these authors' works. The great poets, novelists, short story writers, playwrights, and philosophers of this period are frequently studied in high school and college literature courses. By organizing and reprinting commentary written on these authors, *NCLC* helps students develop valuable insight into literary history, promotes a better understanding of the texts, and sparks ideas for papers and assignments. Each entry in *NCLC* presents a comprehensive survey of an author's career or an individual work of literature and provides the user with a multiplicity of interpretations and assessments. Such variety allows students to pursue their own interests; furthermore, it fosters an awareness that literature is dynamic and responsive to many different opinions.

Every fourth volume of *NCLC* is devoted to literary topics that cannot be covered under the author approach used in the rest of the series. Such topics include literary movements, prominent themes in nineteenth-century literature, literary reaction to political and historical events, significant eras in literary history, prominent literary anniversaries, and the literatures of cultures that are often overlooked by English-speaking readers.

NCLC continues the survey of criticism of world literature begun by Gale's *Contemporary Literary Criticism (CLC)* and *Twentieth-Century Literary Criticism (TCLC),* both of which excerpt and reprint commentary on authors of the twentieth century. For additional information about *TCLC, CLC,* and Gale's other criticism series, users should consult the Guide to Gale Literary Criticism Series preceding the title page in this volume.

Coverage

Each volume of *NCLC* is carefully compiled to present:

- criticism of authors, or literary topics, representing a variety of genres and nationalities
- both major and lesser-known writers and literary works of the period
- 4-8 authors or 4-6 topics per volume
- individual entries that survey critical response to an author's work or a topic in literary history, including early criticism to reflect initial reactions, later criticism to represent any rise or decline in reputation, and current retrospective analyses.

Organization

An author entry consists of the following elements: author heading, biographical and critical introduction, list of principal works, excerpts of criticism (each preceded by a bibliographic citation and an annotation), and a bibliography of further reading.

- The **Author Heading** consists of the name under which the author most commonly wrote, followed by birth and death dates. If an author wrote consistently under a pseudonym, the pseudonym will be listed in the author heading and the real name given in parentheses on the first line of the biographical and critical introduction. Also located at the beginning of the introduction to the author entry are any name variations under which an author wrote, including transliterated forms for an author whose language uses a nonroman alphabet.

- The **Biographical and Critical Introduction** outlines the author's life and career, as well as the critical issues surrounding his or her work. References are provided to past volumes of *NCLC* in which further information about the author may be found.

- Most *NCLC* entries include a **Portrait** of the author. Many entries also contain reproductions of materials pertinent to an author's career, including manuscript pages, title pages, dust jackets, letters, and drawings, as well as photographs of important people, places, and events in an author's life.

- The list of **Principal Works** is chronological by date of first publication and identifies the genre of each work. In the case of foreign authors with both foreign-language publications and English translations, the English-language version is given in brackets. Unless otherwise indicated, dramas are dated by first performance, not first publication.

- **Criticism** in each author entry is arranged chronologically to provide a perspective on changes in critical evaluation over the years. All titles of works by the author featured in the entry are printed in boldface type to enable the user to easily locate discussion of particular works. Also for purposes of easier identification, the critic's name and the publication date of the essay are given at the beginning of each piece of criticism. Unsigned criticism is preceded by the title of the journal in which it appeared. Publication information (such as publisher names and book prices) and some parenthetical numerical references (such as page and line references to specific editions of works) have been deleted at the editors' discretion to provide smoother reading of the text. Footnotes that appear with previously published pieces of criticism are reprinted at the end of each essay or excerpt. In the case of excerpted criticism, only those footnotes that pertain to the excerpted text are included.

- A complete **Bibliographic Citation** provides original publication information for each piece of criticism.

- Critical excerpts are prefaced by **Annotations** providing the reader with a summary of the critical intent of the piece. Also included, when appropriate, is information about the critic's reputation, individual approach to literary criticism, and particular expertise in an author's works, as well as information about the relative importance of the critical excerpt. In some cases, the annotations cross-reference excerpts by critics who discuss each other's commentary.

- An annotated list of **Further Reading** appearing at the end of each entry suggests secondary sources on the author. In some cases it includes essays for which the editors could not obtain reprint rights.

Cumulative Indexes

- Each volume of *NCLC* contains a cumulative **Author Index** listing all authors who have appeared in Gale's Literary Criticism Series, along with cross-references to such biographical series as *Contemporary Authors* and *Dictionary of Literary Biography*. Useful for locating authors within the various series, this index is particularly valuable for those authors who are identified with a certain period but who, because of their death dates, are placed in another, or for those authors whose careers span two periods. For example, Fyodor Dostoevsky is found in *NCLC*, yet Leo Tolstoy, another major nineteenth-century Russian novelist, is found in *TCLC* because he died after 1899.

- Each *NCLC* volume includes a cumulative **Nationality Index** which lists all authors who have appeared in *NCLC*, arranged alphabetically under their respective nationalities.

- Each new volume in Gale's Literary Criticism Series includes a cumulative **Topic Index**, which lists all literary topics treated in *NCLC, TCLC, LC 1400-1800*, and the *CLC* Yearbook.

- Each new volume of *NCLC*, with the exception of the Topics volumes, contains a **Title Index** listing the titles of all literary works discussed in the volume. In response to numerous suggestions from librarians, Gale has also produced a **Special Paperbound Edition** of the *NCLC* title index. This annual cumulation lists all titles discussed in the series since its inception. Additional copies of the index are available on request. Librarians and patrons have welcomed this separate index: it saves shelf space, is easy to use, and is recyclable upon receipt of the following year's cumulation. Titles discussed in the Topics volume entries are not included in the *NCLC* cumulative index.

Citing *Nineteenth-Century Literature Criticism*

When writing papers, students who quote directly from any volume in Gale's Literary Criticism Series may use the following general forms to footnote reprinted criticism. The first example pertains to material drawn from periodicals, the second to material reprinted from books:

[1]Kim McQuaid, "William Apes, Pequot: An Indian Reformer in the Jackson Era," *The New England Quarterly*, 50 (December 1977), 605-25; excerpted and reprinted in *Nineteenth-Century Literature Criticism*, Vol. 73, ed. Janet Witalec (Farmington Hills, Mich.: The Gale Group, 1999), pp. 3-4.

[2]Richard Harter Fogle, *The Imagery of Keats and Shelley: A Comparative Study* (Archon Books, 1949); excerpted and reprinted in *Nineteenth-Century Literary Criticism*, Vol. 73, ed. Janet Witalec (Farmington Hills, Mich.: The Gale Group, 1999), pp. 157-69.

Suggestions Are Welcome

In response to suggestions, several features have been added to *NCLC* since the series began, including annotations to excerpted criticism, a cumulative index to authors in all Gale literary criticism series, entries devoted to criticism on a single work by a major author, more illustrations, and a title index listing all literary works discussed in the series.

Readers who wish to suggest authors, single works, or topics to appear in future volumes, or who have other suggestions, are cordially invited to write: The Editors, *Nineteenth-Century Literature Criticism*, The Gale Group, 27500 Drake Rd., Farmington Hills, MI 48331-3535; call toll-free at 1-800-347-GALE.

Acknowledgments

The editors wish to thank the copyright holders of the excerpted criticism included in this volume and the permissions managers of many book and magazine publishing companies for assisting us in securing reproduction rights. We are also grateful to the staffs of the Detroit Public Library, the Library of Congress, the University of Detroit Mercy Library, Wayne State University Purdy/Kresge Library Complex, and the University of Michigan Libraries for making their resources available to us. Following is a list of the copyright holders who have granted us permission to reproduce material in this volume of *NCLC*. Every effort has been made to trace copyright, but if omissions have been made, please let us know.

COPYRIGHTED MATERIAL IN *NCLC,* VOLUME 76, WERE REPRODUCED FROM THE FOLLOWING PERIODICALS:

American Literature, v. 70, June, 1998. Copyright © 1998 Duke University Press, Durham, NC. Reproduced by permission.—*American Studies,* v. XVIII, Spring, 1977 for "Women's Diaries on the Western Frontier" by Lillian Schlissel. Copyright © Mid-American Studies Association, 1977. Reprinted by permission of the publisher and the author.—*Early American Literature,* v. 23, 1988 for "Original Vice: The Political Implications of Incest in the Early American Novel" by Anne Dalke. Copyrighted, 1988, by the Department of English, University of North Carolina at Chapel Hill. Used by permission of the publisher and the author.—*English Studies in Canada,* v. IX, September, 1983 for "Shelley's 'Void Circumference': The Aesthetic of Nihilism" by Ross Woodman. © Association of Canadian University Teachers of English 1983. Reproduced by permission of the publisher and the author.—*Essays in Arts and Sciences,* v. XIV, May, 1985. Copyright © 1985 by the University of New Haven. Reproduced by permission.—*Nineteenth-Century Fiction,* v. 32, December, 1977 for "Incest and Imitation in Cooper's 'Home As Found'" by Eric J. Sundquist; v. 37, December, 1982 for "Business and Bosoms: Some Trollopian Concerns" by Philip Collins. © 1977, 1982 by The Regents of the University of California. Reproduced by permission of the publisher and the respective authors.—*Nineteenth-Century French Studies,* v. 17, Fall, 1988; v. 19, Fall, 1990. © 1988, 1990 by Nineteenth-Century French Studies. Both reproduced by permission.—*Novel: A Forum on Fiction,* v. 29, Winter, 1996. Copyright NOVEL Corp. © 1996. Reproduced with permission.—*Studies in the Novel,* v. XI, Winter, 1979. Copyright 1979 by North Texas State University. Reproduced by permission.

COPYRIGHTED MATERIAL IN *NCLC,* VOLUME 76, WERE REPRODUCED FROM THE FOLLOWING BOOKS:

Barrett, Lindon. From "Self-Knowledge, Law, and African American Autobiography: Lucy A. Delaney's 'From the Darkness Cometh the Light'" in *The Culture of Autobiography: Constructions of Self-Representation.* Edited by Robert Folkenflik. Stanford University Press, 1993. © 1993 by the Board of Trustees of the Leland Stanford Junior University. Reproduced with the permission of the publishers, Stanford University Press.—Baubles, Raymond L., Jr. From "Displaced Persons: The Cost of Speculation in Charles Dickens' *Martin Chuzzlewit*" in *Money: Lure, Lore, and Literature.* Edited by John Louis Di Gaetani. Greenwood Press, 1994. Copyright © 1994 by Hofstra University. All rights reserved. Reproduced by permission of Greenwood Publishing Group, Inc., Westport, CT.—Bottoms, Janet. From "Sisterhood and Self-Censorship in the Nineteenth Century" in *The Uses of Autobiography.* Edited by Julia Swindells. Taylor & Francis, 1995. © Julia Swindells, 1995. All rights reserved. Reproduced by permission.—Burwick, Frederick. From *Poetic Madness and the Romantic Imagination.* Pennsylvania State University Press, 1996. Copyright © 1996 The Pennsylvania State University. All rights reserved. Reproduced by permission.—Colley, Ann C. From *Tennyson and Madness.* University of Georgia Press, 1983. Copyright © 1983 by the University of Georgia Press. All rights reserved. Reproduced by permission.—Crews, Frederick C. From *The Sins of the Fathers: Hawthorne's Psychological Themes.* Oxford University Press, 1966. Copyright © 1966 by Frederick C. Crews. Used by permission of Oxford University Press, Inc.—Dickerson, Vanessa D. From "Feminine Transactions: Money and Nineteenth-Century British Women Writers" in *Money: Lure, Lore, and Literature.* Edited by John Louis Di Gaetani. Greenwood Press, 1994. Copyright © 1994 by Hofstra University. All rights reserved. Reproduced by permission of Greenwood Publishing Group, Inc., Westport, CT.—Faas, Ekbert. From *Retreat into the Mind: Victorian Poetry and the Rise of Psychia-*

Finance and Money as Represented in Nineteenth-Century Literature

INTRODUCTION

The Industrial Revolution in the late eighteenth and nineteenth centuries brought major economic changes to England. One such change appeared in the source of value. Adam Smith, relating pre-industrial economic theory in *The Wealth of Nations* (1776), associated the value of goods and money with labor. However, during the Industrial Revolution, people tended to shift value from labor (i.e., the ability to provide goods and services) to money itself (i.e., the ability to buy such goods, services, and labor). Furthermore, the Industrial Revolution created new economic opportunities and quickened the pace of the economy. For many, especially in the lower and middle classes, money became the primary icon of this economic system. Money was something that people dreamed about, something to be acquired, something that could give power to the powerless. On the other hand, money, in the form of paper, could easily be lost. Moreover, troubling questions accompanied economic opportunities and the quest to take advantage of them. At what cost would the desired power come? How much money and power were enough? Could money, morality, and ethics coexist? Thus, money became the focus of concerns that ranged from hope to fear to guilt. For many people, money became an obsession, and it was given a preeminent place in society in the nineteenth century.

Critics note that the subject of money is one of the most common themes in nineteenth-century writing, although ideas about money and finance vary considerably from author to author. This difference is seen most clearly in the writings of two major thinkers of the time: Immanuel Kant in *Grounding for the Metaphysics of Morals* (1785) and Jeremy Bentham in *Deontology: Or Morality Made Easy* (1834). It is interesting to note also that, in England, the development of the novel paralleled society's debate over proper conduct regarding economic issues. Anthony Trollope's fictional writings, for example, present business in a positive light and the quest for economic success as an enjoyable and fulfilling endeavor. For the most part, though, the portrayal in nineteenth-century literature of the world of money and finance and of its effect on society is negative, despite the popular appeal of rags-to-riches stories.

There are several versions of this negative representation in literature of the world of money and finance. In some works, the pursuit of riches is portrayed as dangerous, as a trap that catches willing victims unaware. In others, the attraction that money holds for the individual can lead to obsession and moral decay. Honoré de Balzac equated spending large sums of money with obsessive behavior. Charles Dickens showed that an obsession with money was akin to selling one's soul to the devil, resulting in the loss of humanity. In *Martin Chuzzlewit* (1843), Dickens's character Montague Tigg lost all sense of moral or social responsibility in his pursuit of wealth. Gustave Flaubert, in *Madame Bovary* (1857), described a society that had been poisoned by wealth and that attached a price to each and every item, including people. Furthermore, two stereotypical literary characters that reveal the degeneration that obsession with money can cause appear with great regularity in the literature. The first type, the miser, is a hoarder of wealth and is usually represented as old, friendless, incoherent, and obsessed. The second type, the spendthrift, is a squanderer of wealth and is usually represented as living recklessly in a world of his or her own with little regard for anyone else. Such representations seem to issue the warning to their readers that the cost of gaining a fortune is too high.

The period of the Industrial Revolution was a time of great change for women in regard to finance. At the beginning of the nineteenth century, a woman's sphere of operations in regard to finances was, for the most part, confined to household business. Women writers of the time who dealt with financial matters in their fiction created female characters whose experience with money was limited to the economizing activities of the household. One such character was Lady Russell in Jane Austen's *Persuasion* (1818). In fiction, as in real life, a woman's rights to control sources of power, land, houses, and money were restricted by law. The real business of women, according to many narratives, was courtship and marriage. With few opportunities to earn money on their own, it was crucial that women find suitable mates, that is, those who could provide for them. A good marriage was often the only avenue available to women for improving their standing, not only financially, but also socially. The sometimes desperate need to marry well while young and desirable was articulated by a character in Anthony Trollope's *The Three Clerks* (1874): "a girl's time is her money . . . a girl like her must make hay while the sun shines." Although an occasional female character was depicted as having a head for business, it was generally in a field that did not grant equality to women. However, toward the end of the nineteenth century, many women writers began to espouse the cause that women should be allowed into the financial world on an equal footing with men.

REPRESENTATIVE WORKS

Jane Austen
  Persuasion (novel) 1818

Honoré de Balzac
  Le Père Goriot (novel) 1835
  The Human Comedy (short stories) 1842-1846; 1848; 1855
  Cousin Betty (novel) 1847
  The Peasants (novel) 1901

Henri Becque
  Les Corbeaux (drama) 1902

Jeremy Bentham
  Deontology: Or Morality Made Easy (philosophy) 1834

Charlotte Bronte
  Jane Eyre (novel) 1847
  Shirley (novel) 1849

Emily Bronte
  Wuthering Heights (novel) 1847

Alphonse Daudet
  Le Nabab (novel) 1895

Charles Dickens
  Oliver Twist (novel) 1826
  Martin Chuzzlewit (novel) 1843
  Little Dorrit (novel) 1847
  Great Expectations (novel) 1861

Fyodor Dostoevsky
  "The Gambler" (short story) 1866

George Eliot
  The Mill on the Floss (novel) 1860
  Daniel Deronda (novel) 1876

Gustave Flaubert
  Madame Bovary (novel) 1857

Andre Gide
  Lafcadio's Adventures (novel) 1928

Immanuel Kant
  Grounding for the Metaphysics of Morals (philosophy) 1785

Eugene Labiche
  La Cagnotte (drama) 1864

Dinah Mulock
  About Money and Other Things (journal) 1886

Guy de Maupassant
  The Necklace (short story) 1884

Gérard de Nerval
  Sylvie (novel) 1895
  La Pandora (novel) 1968
  Promenades et Souvenirs (unfinished novel) 1990

Margaret Oliphant
  Hester: A Story of Contemporary Life (novel) 1883

Anthony Trollope
  The Small House at Allington (novel) 1870
  The Eustace Diamonds (novel) 1872
  Ralph the Heir (novel) 1872
  The Three Clerks (novel) 1874
  The Way We Live Now (novel) 1875

Emile Zola
  Nana (novel) 1879
  Rougon-Macquart (novel) 1879
  Pot-Bouille (novel) 1882
  La Curee (novel) 1887
  Money (novel) 1891

HISTORICAL PERSPECTIVE

John Vernon (essay date 1984)

SOURCE: "Misers and Spendthrifts," in *Money and Fiction: Literary Realism in the Nineteenth and Early Twentieth Centuries,* Cornell University Press, 1984, pp. 27-41.

[*In the following excerpt, Vernon gives an historical overview on the love of money (especially paper money), which led to the comeback of one old literary type (the miser) and to the rise of a new literary type (the spendthrift).*]

Though they weren't necessarily listening to each other, when it came to money nineteenth-century novelists could speak with one voice. "Money is life. Money is all powerful," says Balzac's Père Goriot. The narrator of Dostoevsky's *The Gambler* exclaims, "Money is everything!" In Dickens's *Our Mutual Friend* Bella says, "I have money always in my thoughts and desires," and in Hardy's *The Return of the Native* Diggory Venn echoes her: "Money is all my dream." Dr. Thorne, in Trollope's *Doctor Thorne:* "A rich man can buy anything." Dombey, in Dickens's *Dombey and Son:* "Money, Paul, can do anything."

Bromfield Corey's statement in *The Rise of Silas Lapham* may serve for the entire century: "But there's no doubt but money is to the fore now. It is the romance, the poetry, of our age. It's the thing that chiefly strikes the imagination."

Such comments could be multiplied, and they will be in the course of this and the following chapters. But the question naturally occurs: Couldn't similar remarks be ferreted out of other centuries as well? For example, an eleventh-century Frenchman, cited by Fernand Braudel: "Money, not Caesar, is everything now."[1] Or Francis Bacon in the early seventeenth century: "No man can be ignorant of the idolatry that is generally committed in these degenerate times to money, as if it could do all things public and private."[2] Is the nineteenth century unique, then? Or do we tend to see the worship of money in any period we look at closely, much like J. H. Hexter's description of the historian who sees the rise of the middle class as typical of the period he specializes in?[3]

There are several answers to this question, none of them simple. We might begin by pointing out that from approximately the fifteenth to the nineteenth century the middle class in Europe was steadily and continuously on the rise, so that historians who isolate one century or a portion of a century and note the bulge are in a sense correct; but they are noting a fragment of a continuous curve. The same could be said with regard to money, though there are qualitative differences too in the eighteenth and nineteenth centuries. Braudel sees capitalism as a phenomenon "gradually gaining ground" in Europe from 1400 to 1800.[4] Naturally the love of money would gain ground in this period too, though the consciousness of the idolatry of such love, of course, goes back to Paul's First Epistle to Timothy—and before. In a sense the nineteenth century was the climax to a movement whose slow beginnings reach back to antiquity. The nineteenth century was also "a violent breakthrough, revolution, total upheaval,"[5] as Braudel says—but one whose preparation was long in the making. As Braudel shows in his massive three-volume study, the Industrial Revolution was not the beginning of capitalism, but the final climactic stage of a long process in which its characteristic devices and apparatus—credit, speculation, bills of exchange, banks, investment capital—evolved largely out of international trade. "With the coming of steam," he says, "the pace of the West increased as if by magic. But the magic can be explained: it had been prepared and made possible in advance. To paraphrase a historian (Pierre Léon), first came evolution (a slow rise) and then revolution (an acceleration): two connected movements."[6]

This increased pace of life in the late eighteenth and early nineteenth centuries was something palpably felt, and it certainly contributed to that sense of an economy and society heating up and rushing about, of which money became a chief image. (The other chief image, at least in the second half of the nineteenth century, was the railroad.) For by the nineteenth century money was qualitatively different from money in previous ages: it was symbolic money—paper. Again, the roots of this change go back several hundred years, and it was still in progress in the nineteenth century. The widespread *acceptance* of paper money, however, is unique to the nineteenth century and is one of the major reasons such universals as "everything" and "anything" so often surface in remarks about money. Money was "the thing that chiefly strikes the imagination" because its power to a great extent resided *in* the imagination, in contemplating its power. Of course, its possession entailed unexpected difficulties: once gained, it could be lost, and consequently much of one's energy had to be expended not in exercising that wonderful power, but in turning it to the end of preserving and increasing itself. Particularly in the form of paper, it could easily be lost—as novels like Dickens's *Little Dorrit* and Trollope's *The Way We Live Now* dramatize—so the acceptance of paper money was always qualified by lingering distrust, as we shall see. Dickens and Trollope describe the typical nightmare of speculation: the (largely dishonest) business venture that draws in hordes of investors and turns out to be a bubble. But such nightmares would not be possible without the dream of sudden fortune also made possible by paper money and speculation. In the nineteenth century money came to the fore in part because people had learned what large amounts of it could do, in the form of capital, and because paper money came to symbolize this volatile, expansive force of capital. Paper money is a "circulation like the blood"[7] because without it all that energy would dissipate. It "keeps the land alive"[8] because it touches everyone, rich and poor, and enmeshes society from top to bottom in a common set of values, most of which boil down to the importance of obtaining money.

None of this happened overnight, however. The history of paper money is the history of an ancient institution greeted with distrust by almost everyone except merchants and traders. As Braudel points out, China had paper money as early as the ninth century, though it disappeared by the fourteenth, and Islam had developed most known forms of paper money by the time of the Crusades.[9] In the West—in Europe and England—the "discovery" of paper money in the late seventeenth century was a rediscovery: "As soon as men learnt to write and had coins to handle, they had replaced cash with written documents, notes, promises and orders."[10] But such men were almost exclusively merchants. Others used metal—gold, silver, and copper coins—or paid each other in kind (in produce or commodities), or bartered. In England paper money developed very slowly in the seventeenth century and scarcely was used outside London.[11] Its two chief forms were the goldsmith's note and the bill of exchange. In London and Stockholm in the late seventeenth century, goldsmiths discovered they could retain just a percentage of their depositors' gold in the till and lend out the rest at interest. The receipt or note the goldsmith (or banker) gave his depositor was a promise to pay him cash, but it came to be "passed from hand to hand as a substitute for cash."[12] Even more common a substitute were bills of exchange (bills issued against a consignment of commodities), which merchants often sold to lenders at a discount. According to Braudel, bills of exchange became so widely used in most European countries that by the eighteenth century the sheer volume of paper money—especially bills of exchange—exceeded that of hard currency.[13] I should emphasize again, however, that this was a specialized money, still used almost exclusively by merchants and traders. " 'I propose,' said Mr. Micawber, 'Bills—a convenience to the mercantile world, for which, I believe, we are originally indebted to the Jews, who appear to me to have had a devilish deal too much to do with them ever since—because they are negotiable.' " Micawber is wrong about the Jews—the West learned the practice of issuing bills of exchange from Islam[14]—but otherwise correct: merchants used them, banks and money brokers cashed them, and like bank notes they were negotiable and came to be passed from hand to hand as a substitute for coins, the only currency previously in use. Thus the notes Defoe's Colonel Jack steals from a gentleman's pocket are both goldsmith's notes and bills of exchange.

But the very specialized nature of such forms of paper marks them as distinct from most paper money in the nineteenth century. By the nineteenth century, even workers were often paid in bank notes, especially in England.[15] "From 1797 to 1821," says Robin M. Reeve, "gold coins virtually disappeared from circulation: instead the country relied upon bank notes, about half of which were Bank of England notes while the remainder were issued by country banks."[16] In 1833, Bank of England notes became legal tender; after 1844 no new banks could issue notes, and bank notes other than those issued by the Bank of England gradually disappeared. Money, like capital, became impersonal and mobile. One followed upon the other, and both developments were inseparable from the Industrial Revolution. Of course, as Braudel repeatedly points out, the habit of lending capital for industry (especially mining) and for trade was firmly established before the Industrial Revolution.[17] But in 1760, says T. S. Ashton, "there was nothing that could justly be called a capital market. Lending was still largely a local and personal matter. By 1830 the volume of investable funds had grown beyond measure. Banks, and other institutions, served as pools from which capital, brought by innumerable streams, flowed to industries at home and abroad. . . . Capital was becoming impersonal— 'blind,' as some say—and highly mobile."[18] Statistics bear this out and underline the nineteenth century's

special claim to be the age of money; for example, the increase of banks in England from 280 in 1793 to 626 in 1815.[19]

All this said, it is important to keep in mind that old habits of thought persisted, especially as a refuge against the new. The nineteenth century is characterized not so much by the conquest of paper money as by the long-drawn-out transition, extending back to the previous century, from older forms of wealth to paper. Many still thought of gold as the only real money and land as the only stable and secure form of wealth. We shall look at land in detail in the following chapter; for now I want to concentrate on the psychology of a period in which *both* gold and paper are the things "that chiefly strike the imagination." In the pages that follow I use "gold" in a metonymic sense, to stand for all metal currencies—gold, silver, copper—of which gold was always the most valued.

In the first place, gold and silver coins were commodities as well as a medium of exchange. They were traded, hoarded, and melted down, as Braudel points out.[20] But they were money too, symbolic and material at the same time. As Michel Foucault puts it, money in the sixteenth century not only represented wealth, it was itself wealth.[21] Such a view was still available to the nineteenth century, if chiefly as nostalgia. One who felt threatened by the instability of a society whose middle ranks were swelling, in which wealthy merchants with marriageable daughters were knocking on the doors of the impoverished aristocracy, might well feel inclined to regard gold as the only real form of wealth. Gold conformed to Locke's definition of money: "Some lasting thing that men might keep without spoiling."[22] The grammatical ambiguity here is telling: money is the way *we* keep from spoiling, the way we defer death indefinitely. In a well-known scene in *Dombey and Son* Paul asks his father, "Papa! what's money?" To the answer that money can do anything, Paul counters with the obvious question: "Why didn't money save me my mamma?" Dombey—who by now wants to escape this conversation and perhaps review his assets—acknowledges that money cannot save people whose time has come to die, but very often *can* keep death off for a long time altogether. Even this crumb of comfort, though, is belied by Paul's subsequent death. Indeed, it is this very scene that makes his father suspect the boy is sickly and needs special care.

Though Dombey is not exactly a miser, he is someone who hoards, who keeps things close, who refuses to spend any sympathy on his surviving child, Florence. In fact he exudes such gloom in the novel precisely because he shares the miser's closed personality without availing himself of the miser's source of comfort: poring over his piles of wealth. For misers these piles of wealth are invariably coins, usually gold. We cannot imagine a miser hoarding bills and notes; what he hoards must not perish, because it keeps him alive. Those attracted to paper are speculators and profligates. Gold is material, palpable, valuable in itself, whereas paper is an abstraction, a fiction. The point is that *both* gold and paper were social forces in the nineteenth century; they may have been ships passing, but the passage was slow. Indeed, for most of the century they were linked; England's money was on a gold standard, largely because of the earlier examples on the Continent of floating currencies that turned out to be (in Defoe's term) chimerical: John Law's Mississippi Company notes, and the assignats issued after the 1789 revolution. In France, too, the Bank of France, created in 1800, issued notes convertible to gold and silver, though paper money took longer to catch on in France than in England.[23] Thus Balzac's novels are filled with details of bills being signed, passed back and forth, renewed, discounted, and dishonored; but when Rastignac sends for his sisters' money in *Le Père Goriot,* it arrives as two sacks of gold. In other words, it comes from the provinces, where paper is more suspect than in the city.

Transporting gold in such a manner seems almost anomalous—and clearly is done in *Le Père Goriot* only because of Rastignac's desperation—because gold tends to stay in one place, in contrast to paper, which is inclined to circulate. Gold is hoarded, paper spent, gold is stable and paper unstable, gold attracts misers and paper spendthrifts. In the nineteenth century the miser is still a recognizable literary type, but his portrayal tends to shade into that of the rich merchants and businessmen (like Dombey) who love money and business and nothing else. The attraction of money for the businessman is similar to that of gold for the miser: it insulates against change and decay, is susceptible to tidy manipulation, and centers, even immobilizes, one's life. "His money was never naughty; his money never made noise or litter, and did not spill things on the table at meal times" (Butler, *The Way of All Flesh*). The businessman in novels usually shares the miser's anal-retentive character, though perhaps with less manifest satisfaction.

Behind Dickens's financiers, behind the Dombeys, Merdles, and Podsnaps, lurks the shadow of the miser, who often is presented as a relic of previous centuries, like Fagin in *Oliver Twist*. The nineteenth-century miser, like his literary progenitors, is always old, often babbling, sometimes bordering on second childhood. Sir Pitt Crawley in *Vanity Fair,* Peter Featherstone in *Middlemarch,* Scrooge in *A Christmas Carol,* Silas Marner, old Grandet in *Eugénie Grandet,* old Séchard in *Illusions perdues,* Gobseck in Balzac's "M. Gobseck," Rigou in *Les paysans*—their nostalgia for a past in which the representation of wealth and its material reality were one usually

spills over into a kind of arrested infancy. Boffin, the fake miser in *Our Mutual Friend,* is also a kind of literary miser, and he learns about being a miser (while pretending to have his appetite for it whetted) by paying Wegg to read to him about famous misers of the past. In *Silas Marner,* George Eliot presents the standard picture of the miser, transparent enough in our post-Freudian age: "How the guineas shone as they came pouring out of the dark leather mouths! . . . He spread them out in heaps and bathed his hands in them; then he counted them and set them up in regular piles, and felt their rounded outline between his thumb and fingers, and thought fondly of the guineas that were only half-earned by the work in his loom, as if they had been unborn children."[24] The miser is usually a misanthrope because he cannot live in the present. He longs for the time when a hoard was a hoard, when things, and their value, never changed. *Never changed* means not only that they didn't decrease—the usual justification for a hoard—but that they didn't increase either, as was generally the case in the expanding economy of the nineteenth century. It was this expanding economy and all it represented—change, increase, the unknown, the future—that the nineteenth-century miser deliberately drew back from, longing for a (supposed) earlier and simpler world. For the miser money is time, and time piles up; time is what he hoards and stores, walling himself in against the future. All his desire pours into his hoard in order to harden and kill desire, so he can become, in George Eliot's phrase, "a mere pulsation of desire." Silas Marner's coins are monads, solid and weighty: the essence of material reality, primitive, inert, and immutable.

Paper money, on the other hand, is weightless and flighty—it has wings, cannot stay put. The opposite of the miser is the spendthrift, a literary type for the most part new to the nineteenth century. Mr. Sowerby in Trollope's *Framley Parsonage,* George Vavasor in *Can You Forgive Her?* Felix Carbury in *The Way We Live Now,* Maxime de Trailles in several of Balzac's novels and stories, the Baron Hulot in *La Cousine Bette,* Rosamond Lydgate in *Middlemarch,* Dmitri Karamazov in *The Brothers Karamazov,* Alexis in *The Gambler,* Becky and Rawdon Crawley in *Vanity Fair*—all these characters thrive out on a limb, in a world of their own fiction, spending money they don't even possess ("Borrowing is the best way of sustaining credit," says Rastignac in Balzac's *La peau de chagrin*). In the nineteenth century, paper money represented an explosion of money that took on the quality of a collective fantasy. Around the edges of that explosion, the spendthrift became a kind of holy fool; in *The Brothers Karamazov,* everyone trails behind and gathers around Dmitri as he tosses his money about. Like Dmitri, most spendthrifts are compulsive and asocial. They create an artificial conviviality by buying social energy and companionship. Often they are outcasts or misfits because they fail to understand or have turned away from the traditional male role of earning or managing money. In fact, the spendthrift in the nineteenth-century novel is often a woman—Madame Bovary, Rosamond Lydgate, Becky Crawley—for whom money isn't real. And they are right. It isn't. Money for the spendthrift is the paper image of money. As Defoe says, "Substance is answered by the Shadow. . . . the Name of the thing is made Equivalent to the Thing itself."[25]

On the other hand, paper money possesses the reality of power. It has, if nothing else, exchange value. It can't store value, like gold; its status is the very opposite of the chest of gold and silver coins Robinson Crusoe finds on the wreck and drags to his island, even though he can't spend it. The impotence of Crusoe's money is a little allegory of nascent capitalism in the early eighteenth century, just before banks and credit began to expand. Once that expansion was under way, the power of paper money swelled. We sense it expanding toward the future, swelling credit, swelling capital. This does not happen for the miser, whose desires contract, whose world shrinks. But it happens for the spendthrift, who flees the past and devours the future, who spends money in order not to have it, in order to continuously desire it. The spendthrift spends as quickly as possible to hasten the moment when he has nothing and the future takes on the character of the unknown. One doesn't become a spendthrift by having a store of money to spend. The spendthrift perpetually empties the store before it can become a store. Somehow there's always more to spend. He borrows, gambles, marries into money. His compulsive generosity is really no more generous than a miser's sense of security is secure. Only Balzac could detect an element of calculation in such compulsion. In *La peau de chagrin,* he has Rastignac say, "When a man spends his time squandering his fortune, he's very often onto a good thing: he is investing his capital in friends, pleasures, protectors and acquaintances. . . . If he has the bad luck to lose his capital, he has the good luck to be appointed tax collector, make a good marriage, become the secretary to a minister or an ambassador. He still has friends and reputation, and is never short of money."[26] The last statement is true of all spendthrifts: they are never short of money. Only the miser is short of money. A few notes, a few coins are plenty for the spendthrift—they are no more real than a fortune. The only reality is the lack of money. The more money the spendthrift has, the more he spends, and the less he has. Alexis, in Dostoevsky's *The Gambler,* spends two hundred thousand francs in three weeks. This kind of spending can happen only with paper. Gold possesses a gravitational pull that prevents it from being tossed around. But gold is always there in the background for the spendthrift, defining by contrast the weightlessness of paper.

Indeed, in a certain respect the miser and the spendthrift are two sides of the same coin. They are linked by a historical necessity imperfectly expressed by Gresham's law, that bad money drives out good: in the nineteenth century this meant that gold was hoarded and paper spent. Maxime de Trailles says to the miser and money lender Gobseck (in Balzac's story "M. Gobseck"), "if there were no spendthrifts, what would become of you? The pair of us are like soul and body." The spendthrift Maxime deals primarily with paper—countless notes, some signed by several hands, that he discounts to obtain cash. And Gobseck deals primarily with gold; he distrusts paper, using it only as a means to get his hands on more gold. For both of them, money is not only money but the lack of money. This reciprocal play of money and its lack is contained within money, within its dual nature, and therefore embedded in nineteenth-century society.

Behind all this is a changing conception of the nature of wealth. Misers and spendthrifts are grotesques, parodies of an older and a newer conception of wealth. Etymologically, wealth comes from weal, or well-being. Before the eighteenth century and especially the nineteenth—and surviving in the latter as nostalgia—wealth was thought of as a store of value representing stability and security. In England, as we shall see, its most powerful symbol was not gold, but the landed estate. As Trollope put it in *The Last Chronicle of Barset,* "land is about the only thing that can't fly away." But with the Industrial Revolution and the financial revolution that helped make it possible, wealth gradually came to be thought of as something different, as an active agent, a power. This new sense of wealth meant that money was not only a medium of exchange, but a means of expansion and increase, of augmentation, amplification, multiplication. It became a way to extend one's sphere of influence over nature and society, fuel for the newly discovered voracious ego—which in fact it gave birth to. Especially in the form of paper money, wealth became volatile, unpredictable, patulous. Defoe saw this aspect of money as "meer Air and Shadow, realizing Fancies and Imaginations, Visions and Apparitions,"[27] as indeed it was at times, particularly in the kinds of bubbles Dickens and Trollope portray in *Little Dorrit* and *The Way We Live Now* and to a lesser degree Butler displays in *The Way of All Flesh.*

For this reason, in *Little Dorrit* the irony of Mr. Dorrit's inheriting an estate lies in the context created by the more volatile states of wealth surrounding him—not only Merdle's financial schemes, but also the business debts that have caused Dorrit to spend so much of his life in debtor's prison. The estate is the nineteenth century's link with the past, but for Mr. Dorrit it arrives in the form of a treasure discovered under a rock, of manna from heaven (though of course it turns out to be a curse rather than a blessing). Dickens's juxtaposition of the factors that impoverished and enriched Mr. Dorrit—his business debts and later his inheritance—demonstrates the degree to which by the mid-nineteenth century the domain of the gentry and nobility (landed estates) was being invaded by the middle classes. . . .

Notes

[1] Fernand Braudel, *The Structures of Everyday Life: The Limits of the Possible,* vol. 1 of *Civilization and Capitalism, 15th-18th Century,* trans. Miriam Kochan and Siân Reynolds (New York: Harper and Row, 1981), p. 511.

[2] Cited in L. C. Knights, *Drama and Society in the Age of Jonson* (New York: George W. Stewart, n.d.), p. 123.

[3] See Fernand Braudel, *The Wheels of Commerce,* vol. 2 of *Civilization and Capitalism, 15th-18th Century,* trans. Siân Reynolds (New York: Harper and Row, 1982), p. 479.

[4] Fernand Braudel, *Capitalism and Material Life, 1400-1800,* trans. Miriam Kochan (New York: Harper and Row, 1973), p. xiii. Braudel's *Civilisation matérielle et capitalisme* was first published in France in 1967 and later was revised extensively by the author. The book cited here is the English translation of vol. 1 of the unrevised *Civilisation matérielle et capitalisme; The Structures of Everyday Life* and *The Wheels of Commerce* are the new English translations of volumes 1 and 2 of Braudel's revision (vol. 3 is forthcoming). I am quoting here some comments in the preface to *Capitalism and Material Life* that were dropped in *The Structures of Everyday Life.*

[5] Ibid., p. x.

[6] Braudel, *Structures of Everyday Life,* p. 372.

[7] Thomas Love Peacock, *Paper Money Lyrics,* in *The Works of Thomas Love Peacock* (New York: AMS Press, 1967), p. 115.

[8] Ibid.

[9] Braudel, *Structures of Everyday Life,* pp. 452 and 472.

[10] Ibid., pp. 471-472.

[11] L. A. Clarkson, *The Pre-Industrial Economy in England, 1500-1750* (London: B. T. Batsford, 1974), p. 146.

[12] Charles Wilson, *England's Apprenticeship: 1603-1763* (London: Longman, 1965), p. 208. In addition to the works cited, I have also relied for factual matters in the following pages upon several other books: by

J. H. Clapham, *The Bank of England: A History,* 2 vols. (Cambridge: University Press, 1970); *An Economic History of Modern Britain,* vol. 1, *The Early Railway Age* (Cambridge: University Press, 1950); and *The Economic Development of France and Germany, 1815-1914* (Cambridge: University Press, 1968). Also, Brian Murphy, *A History of the British Economy* (London: Longman, 1973), and P. G. M. Dickson, *The Financial Revolution in England: A Study in the Development of Public Credit, 1688-1756* (London: Macmillan, 1967).

[13] Braudel, *Wheels of Commerce,* p. 113.

[14] Braudel, *Structures of Everyday Life,* p. 472.

[15] Robin M. Reeve, *The Industrial Revolution, 1750-1850* (London: University of London Press, 1971), p. 170.

[16] Ibid., p. 168.

[17] Braudel, *Wheels of Commerce,* pp. 321-325 and 385-395.

[18] T. S. Ashton, *The Industrial Revolution, 1760-1830* (Oxford: Oxford University Press, 1970), p. 87.

[19] Reeve, *Industrial Revolution,* p. 167.

[20] Braudel, *Wheels of Commerce,* pp. 194-204.

[21] Michel Foucault, *The Order of Things: An Archaeology of the Human Sciences* (New York: Pantheon Books, 1970), p. 169.

[22] John Locke, *Of Civil Government* (New York: Dutton, 1924), p. 140.

[23] Braudel, *Structures of Everyday Life,* p. 474.

[24] Compare this with the description of Trina in Norris's *McTeague:* "Trina would play with this money by the hour, piling it and repiling it, or gathering it all into one heap and drawing back to the farthest corner of the room to note the effect, her head on one side. . . . Or, again, she would draw the heap lovingly toward her and bury her face in it, delighted at the smell of it and the feel of the smooth, cool metal on her cheeks. She even put the small gold pieces in her mouth and jingled them there." In Freud's scheme, excrement is aliment. These descriptions of misers find their grotesque culmination in a passage in Beckett's *Malone Dies:* "Yes, a little creature, I shall try and make a little creature, to hold in my arms, a little creature in my image, no matter what I say. And seeing what a poor thing I have made, or how like myself, I shall eat it."

[25] Daniel Defoe, *The Chimera: or, The French Way of Paying National Debts Laid Open* (London: T. Warner,

1720), p. 6. This book was written by Defoe in response to John Law's experiment with paper money in France (the Mississippi Company), apparently just before the bubble burst.

[26] The translation of *La peau de chagrin, The Wild Ass's Skin,* is by Herbert J. Hunt (Harmondsworth: Penguin Books, 1977).

[27] Defoe, *Chimera,* pp. 5-6.

Kevin McLaughlin (essay date 1996)

SOURCE: "The Financial Imp: Ethics and Finance in Nineteenth-Century Fiction," in *Novel: A Forum on Fiction,* Vol. 29. No. 2, Winter, 1996, pp. 165-83.

[*In the following essay, McLaughlin analyzes the conflict between ethics and economics, caused by the economic upheaval of the period and reflected in the literature of the period. McLaughlin focuses on outcome-based actions versus moral absolutes.*]

Economic issues have never been far from British fiction. Indeed, as literary historians have often pointed out, the rise of the novel in Britain in the eighteenth century itself closely paralleled the emergence of the new science of political economy in the period.[1] Similarly, during the Victorian era, while the novel reached new heights of popularity in England, political economy was the main source of philosophical debate. In British philosophy at the time the standing of political economy was quite clear: it marked the sharp separation of moral philosophy into utilitarian and anti-utilitarian schools. The critical point here was the validity of applying the methods of political economy to moral questions, and this point effectively divided moral philosophy into two schools. There were, on the one hand, those advocating the exercise of economic or financial reason in ethical deliberation—the calculation of the moral profitability of an action—and, on the other, those who held that ethics was a matter beyond calculation, the result, not of calculation, but of a human endowment or gift (an "intuition," as they said). The main currents of this debate over political economy in Victorian philosophy can also be discerned in British fiction at the time. Harriet Martineau's decision in her *Illustrations of Political Economy* to use fiction to bring political economy into the British mainstream (xi-xii) and Dickens's efforts two decades later in *Hard Times* to stem the tide of political economism are only two of the most obvious, if ultimately unsatisfying, attempts to produce narratives that would argue for one side or the other in the conflict. Some works of fiction at the time, however, rather than choosing a side in the debate, perceptively confused its entrenched positions and managed to avoid becoming bogged down in the stagnant arguments for and against political economy.

Especially telling in this context, I would argue, was the reflection on the key question of finance, which can be found at the center of certain works of British fiction during the period. What follows here is an attempt to sketch an approach to this reflection on finance in Victorian fiction, first by outlining the importance of finance in the debates dominating moral philosophy at the time and then by considering this question in the fiction of Robert Louis Stevenson, whose contribution to the debate over ethics and economics in the period has yet to be appreciated.

I. Deontology

Moral philosophy has had a long preoccupation with economics. It has even been argued that Western philosophy itself was founded as a reflection on economic issues (Shell, *Money* 2-3; 131-37). Today, some of the most influential recent work in Anglo-American and Continental philosophy has focused on economics and ethics (one thinks of Amartya Sen and Stanley Cavell in the Anglo-American context, and Jacques Derrida in France). Moreover, not only has there been renewed interest in economics in ethical theory, but business schools in the United States and in Europe have also made ethics a required subject for their students. In France, this desire to introduce an ethical dimension into the work of the modern business professional has been expressed by a host of recent books devoted to what the French call "deontology" [*déontologie*].[2] The word "deontology" provides us with a strange, but instructive, link between current discussions of economics and ethics and those of Victorian England. "Deontology" was invented from the Greek root meaning "duty" by Jeremy Bentham in his 1834 *Deontology: Or Morality Made Easy.* Nevertheless, in spite of its English origins in Bentham, French "déontologie" has very little to do with the English word "deontology" as it is currently understood.[3] In English, deontology is a technical term used by philosophers to describe a particular kind of ethical theory: "a deontological theory of ethics," one reference work explains, "is one which holds that at least some acts are morally obligatory regardless of their consequences for human weal or woe . . . the first of the great philosophers emphatically to enunciate the deontological principle was Immanuel Kant" ("Deontological"). In contemporary English philosophy, then, "deontology" is associated, not with Bentham, but with Kant. This is noteworthy, since the names Kant and Bentham are often made to stand for two fundamentally opposed kinds of ethical theories in nineteenth- and twentieth-century philosophy (deontological and utilitarian).

The confusion caused by the different meanings of the word "deontology" in English and in French is thus irritating for students of British philosophy because it seems to collapse the two poles of nineteenth-century ethical theory in England, consequentialism or utilitarianism, on the one hand, and anti-consequentialism or, to use the nineteenth-century term, "intuitionism," on the other (Schneewind, *Backgrounds* 129-42). But the confusion is not merely a matter of mistranslation. Within the British tradition itself the term "deontology" has a complex history. While deontological ethical theories are now understood to be those which consider duty as an imperative to behave in a certain way regardless of the consequences, Bentham coined the word "deontology" to mean something quite different. In fact, in its original sense, "deontology" was used by Bentham to mean more or less what modern ethical theorists call "consequentialism"—the cost/benefit analysis of the consequences of an action. Explaining how "deontology" became severed from its original "consequentialist" meaning, and indeed opposed to it, in British moral philosophy would require a more detailed account than is appropriate here of Anglo-American analytical ethics in the twentieth century. This would involve in particular a study of the influence of W. D. Ross's 1930 *The Right and the Good,* a work which was itself influenced by the philosophy of G. E. Moore's *Principia Ethica.*[4]

But the confusion to which the term "deontology" has been subject, both in English and in its translation into French and German, has had some curious consequences in current discussions of business and ethics. In a recent essay published in French, the British philosopher, Amartya Sen, can be found arguing that business ethicists, particularly those advising the financial professions, not insist too much on a non-consequentialist code of professional conduct—that "déontologie" not be too "deontological" (Sen, "Éthique" 283). In his essay, Sen makes the useful point that consequentialism is in some sense essential to the world of finance and business and that it is therefore senseless to try to impose here an absolute (that is, "deontological") code of ethical conduct. Of course, one could argue—and indeed it has been argued repeatedly in the West for over two millennia—that precisely because the careful calculation of consequences is the very essence of business, and in particular finance, what is needed there is an absolute, non-teleological ethical code.[5] In any case, it would be hard to overestimate the significance of this debate in the history of Western ethical theory. For moral philosophy in the West has been profoundly shaped by attempts to expel financial thinking from ethics, attempts which have arguably had the consequence of also removing ethical thinking from financial consideration. But, as indicated by the word deontology itself, current debates between deontological and consequentialist business ethicists recall in particular those of the nineteenth century, a period which was dominated by the often dogmatic and at times redundant conflict between Benthamite utilitarianism and neo-Kantian "intuitionists." Here too, as at other decisive moments in the history of moral

philosophy, finance proved to be a goad to ethics in a manner that has yet to be fully appreciated.

My contention is that one way of beginning to understand better the role of finance in this ethical conflict—a conflict which is, as I have just suggested, still very much with us—would be to study it carefully in some key works of nineteenth-century literature. Such a study would lead to a more adequate appreciation of how some works of nineteenth-century British fiction may be seen to participate in the ethical debates centering on finance in the period and also how they may in some cases be understood to offer insightful perspectives on the questions that are left unexplored in the more polarized debates of Victorian moral philosophy and cultural criticism. Let us now attempt to outline an approach to the question of ethics and finance in nineteenth-century fiction and to point to some examples. To do so, we must go back briefly to the special role of finance in Bentham and Kant, the two thinkers behind the positions that divided much nineteenth-century ethical discourse in England.

II. Ethics of Finance

Bentham's theory of "deontology" is a clear example of what modern philosophers would call a consequentialist, or teleological, theory of ethics in that it is firmly rooted in the evaluation of the consequences of a particular action. But Bentham's philosophy is not without a certain twist. The emphasis here is to be sure exclusively on moral action as a matter of calculation, but this does not mean that there is no room in Bentham's moral theory for acts of good will to others, just that such acts be subjected to a method of calculation or accounting, a sort of cost/benefit analysis. A good example of this in *Deontology* is the discussion of the relationship between the private and the public as manifested in acts of "benificence," which Bentham defines as "contributing to the comforts of our fellow-creatures" (184). Here I will cite from *Deontology:*

> Over and above any pleasure with which the act may happen to be accompanied, the inducement which a man has for the exercise of benevolence is of the same sort as that which the husbandman has for the sowing of his seed, or that which the frugal man has for the laying up of money. Seed sown is not otherwise of any value than for the crops of which it is productive. Money is of no value than for the services of all sorts which it procures at the hands of other men. . . . By every act of virtuous beneficence which a man exercises, he contributes to a sort of fund—a sort of Saving Bank—a sort of fund of general Good-will, out of which services of all sorts may be looked for as about to flow on occasion out of other hands in to his. . . . (184)

Bentham's "deontology" could not, it seems, be much farther from what modern philosophers call

Jeremy Bentham (1748-1832)

"deontological" ethical theory. By comparing benefi-
cent acts to deposits that will reap future returns,
Bentham is directly opposed to a theory of ethical
imperatives that twentieth-century analytical philosophers trace to Kant ("Deontological"). The German
philosopher, they argue, is precisely concerned to
ground ethical theory beyond such a utilitarian moral
calculus. This view of Kant is questionable, as we
will see in a moment. But this did not prevent a whole
tradition of nineteenth-century anti-utilitarians from
finding their position confirmed in his work. Nor did
it prevent these same anti-utilitarians from failing to
recognize that Bentham's stress on calculation does not
necessarily rule out a rather complex understanding of
"self-interest," or of what Bentham somewhat confusingly calls "hedonism" (See Schneewind, *Sidgwick's*
131).

Given what we have said about the deep link between consequentialism and business or economics,
it is not surprising that Bentham would illustrate his
consequentialist theory with an example from the
realm of finance. But what is perhaps somewhat more
surprising, from a certain point of view at least, is that
despite his supposedly deontological (anti-consequentialist) ethical theory, Kant too chooses a financial example—that of falsely promising to pay back a loan—

in his famous discussion of false promises in the influential *Foundation of the Metaphysics of Morals*.[6] This
financial example is neither isolated nor accidental. It
derives from the deep connection between ethics and
economics—between debt and guilt, as Nietzsche would
later stress—in the tradition within which Kant is
working, a tradition that could be traced to ancient
Greek philosophy, on the one hand, and Christian
doctrine, on the other.[7] Kant's conclusion, it will be
recalled, is that falsely promising to repay a loan is
unethical, or more precisely that it runs counter to
"duty" [*Pflicht*], a fact which emerges when the test of
the "categorical imperative" is administered—in short,
when the *consequences* of universalizing such a false
promise are evaluated.[8] A false promise to repay a
loan would make all promises, genuine and counterfeit, impossible, because, as Kant says, "no one would
believe that something was promised to him, but would
instead laugh at all such utterances as idle pretence"
[*über alle solche Äusserung, als eitles Vorgeben, lachen
würde*] (*Werke* 6: 53; *Grounding* 31).

Ultimately, Kant's purpose in writing the *Foundation
of the Metaphysics of Morals* was of course to establish or ground thinking about ethics beyond the sort of
tallying of costs and benefits that are essential to business and that would become central to Bentham's
Deontology. For Kant, the ethical, in contrast with the
merely moral, is incalculable and, as he says, "sublime" [*erhaben*] (*Werke* 6: 68-69). In this sense, Kant's
approach to ethics is of a piece with his theories of art
and culture: it seeks to demarcate the field of ethics as
apart from the economic realm.[9] Nevertheless, at the
key point in Kant's endeavor to remove economics
from ethics, he decides to invoke the standard of a
financial agreement (of the contractual obligation to
repay a loan). And yet, in spite of Kant's decision to
formulate his ethical theory on the practical basis of a
commercial transaction, a whole tradition of British
ethical theory in the nineteenth century that traced itself to him had little use for commerce and finance.
Instead, these thinkers preferred to conceive of ethics in
terms of the ideal of a gift. This view came to achieve
dominance, by way of Coleridge, in the work of essayists such as Hazlitt, Carlyle, Bulwer-Lytton, and Arnold,
who consistently contrasted the ethical superiority of
the gift to the profit motive they associated with
Bentham's principle of utility.[10] This anti-utilitarian
tradition established itself as one of the two dominant
positions—utilitarian and intuitionist—that would remain
entrenched in English ethical theory until Sidgwick set
about "reconciling" them commonsensically in the 1870s
(in ways that are already anticipated in the more subtle
aspects of Kant and Bentham).[11]

III. Stevenson

The intuitionist criticism of Bentham's moral calculus,
and in particular the argument in favor of gifts as

opposed to loans, of endowments over debts, was of course not limited to the essayists just mentioned. The ideal of the gift can also be found at the center of much Victorian fiction and poetry, though with the difference, I would argue, that here one can find examples of ethical thinking that goes beyond the either/or of much Victorian moral philosophy before Sidgwick. Of particular interest, in my view, are the complications to which some novelists in the period subject the neat opposition between gift and loan, especially as it is related to the central category of the home or the household in the novel. Consider, for example, works such as Eliot's *Mill on the Floss,* Dickens's *Dombey and Son,* and James's *The Golden Bowl* and the ways that each of these novels applies its own particular form of utilitarian pressure to the ideological link between the home and the gift—the category on which the romance of domesticity regularly depends. Think of the image of the mill itself in Eliot's novel—a home, or better an *oikos,* which is both a domestic sight and site of production—of the major preoccupation in the entire first part of the novel with questions of lending and repaying, and of Maggie's ultimate concern in the novel, as she says, with the fact "that we owed ourselves to others, and must conquer every inclination which could make us false to that debt" (601); or of the central question drawn-out by Dickens in *Dombey and Son*—that of the difference between the home and the firm, between children as gifts as opposed to investments or money, between, in a particularly poignant scene, Paul Dombey's offering of a gift and his father's prompt redefinition of it as a loan (197); and also, in James's *The Golden Bowl,* of the strangely utilitarian gift exchanges through which the Verver household establishes itself in the novel. Detailed interpretations of each of these novels along such lines would lead to some important insights into the way novelists in the nineteenth century are specifically concerned to draw attention to the inadequacy of thinking of an ethical community in the stark and equally sterile terms of either the pure gift or what the Victorians often derisively called "commerce." An especially instructive instance of this more complex understanding of the relationship between ethics and finance can be found in the fiction of another leading novelist in the period, Robert Louis Stevenson, specifically in his South Seas tale entitled "The Bottle Imp." If we turn now to Stevenson's story, we can begin to get an idea of some of the consequences of exposing ethical thinking to finance and vice versa.

Let us start by noting that Stevenson's interest in finance was connected to his enthusiasm for America. In light of contemporary attitudes toward America and finance, this point has considerable significance, both for Stevenson's work in general and for the particular perspective on ethics and finance that would evolve in his work. As a young man, Stevenson traveled to California, to San Francisco, on a somewhat risky Ameri-can adventure—a domestic romance of sorts—that involved leaving behind his more cautious Scottish family (a family of lighthouse engineers) and pursuing the then already married woman who would later become his wife. Amid money troubles and threats of disinheritance, Stevenson wrote that what he admired most about America was its sense of aspiration and adventure, a sense he saw expressed in the writing of Whitman and Thoreau.[12] The Scottish writer was particularly taken by the boldness of Thoreau's economic speculations in the first part of *Walden*—by, as he put it, the "sanity of [Thoreau's] view of life, and the insight with which he recognized the position of money" (*Virginibus* 204). Here is Stevenson on Thoreau:

> Prudence, which bids us all go to the ant for wisdom and hoard against the day of sickness, was not a favourite with Thoreau. He preferred that other, whose name is so much misappropriated: Faith. When he had secured the necessaries of the moment, he would not reckon up possible accidents or torment himself with trouble for the future. . . . He would trust himself a little to the world. . . . [Thoreau] describes contemporary mankind in a phrase: "All the day long on the alert, at night we unwillingly say our prayers and commit ourselves to uncertainties." It is not likely that the public will be much affected by Thoreau, when they blink the direct injunctions of the religion they profess; and yet whether we will or no, we make the same hazardous ventures; we back our own health and the honesty of our neighbors for all that we are worth. . . . (Virginibus 202-03)

Significant here is that Stevenson not only identifies and applauds Thoreau's attempt to underline the economic character of our ordinary language and to work out a financial philosophy of "hazardous ventures," he imitaties it. While describing the originality of Thoreau's moral accounting, Stevenson himself employs economic language: he speaks of the misappropriating of faith, the securing of necessities, the reckoning up of possible accidents in the future, trusting to the world, the backing of our own health and the honesty of our neighbors, and so on. Stevenson mimes, in other words, that aspect of *Walden* that has been the subject of important work by the American philosopher, Stanley Cavell and others—what Cavell has described as Thoreau's attempt to call attention in *Walden* to the "network or medium of economic terms [that] serves . . . as an imitation of the horizon and strength both of our assessments of our position and of our connections with one another" (*Senses* 87-88; see also *New* 115).

But Stevenson's comments on Thoreau are telling from another perspective as well, for they suggest a link between the sort of moral economics evoked in the essay and the idea that was to become the source of nearly all of his fiction, namely, that of *adventure* (a word which itself, on the basis of its early signification of fortune, luck or chance, came gradually in the early modern period to be associated with economics or, more specifically, with commerce).[13] If Thoreau's project to think through life as, in Stevenson's words, a "hazardous venture"—as a risky economic and ethical enterprise—elicited the young Scottish writer's admiration, it may also have suggested to him the mingling of ethics and economics in his own experience of adventure—his voyage to America and eventually to the South Seas (the economics of which became the subject of *The Beach of Falsea* and *Ebb Tide*). In any case, Stevenson seems to have begun working out such an idea of adventure in his fiction at this time.[14] In general, I must say, Stevenson's critics have ignored such connections. They have mostly been concerned to point out what they regard as contradictions (ultimately of no importance, they imply) between the fiction writer's critical statements and his own literary practice.[15] There have been a few exceptions, notably Robert Kiely, but even those readers who have recognized the coherence of Stevenson's reflection on adventure in his criticism and fiction have failed to note its connection to the early admiration of Thoreau's economics. A particularly revealing example of this connection from Stevenson's critical writing at the time is an essay on Victor Hugo, in which Hugo's historical novel *Quatre-Vingt Treize* is praised for the way it represents the French Revolution as a national *adventure,* as the sort of "hazardous venture" on a national scale that Stevenson understands Thoreau to be advocating on an individual level in *Walden*. This praise is especially worth singling out because it runs precisely counter to the dominant Burkean view of the French Revolution in nineteenth-century England as a sort of financial farce, as a pseudo-revolution based on the chimera of credit, or as Carlyle said, on "paper."[16] The comment on Hugo in this sense is directly linked to the famous evocation of adventure in the essay "El Dorado," in which Stevenson asserts that the sort of "aspiration" that leads to adventure is "a possession as solid as a landed estate, a fortune which we can never exhaust and which gives us year by year a revenue of pleasurable activity" (*Virginibus* 70-72).[17] This emphasis on the peculiar financial character of adventure separates Stevenson from many of his British contemporaries and attracts him to the Americans Thoreau and Whitman. To see how it figures in Stevenson's fiction, let us turn now to the late tale, "The Bottle Imp."[18]

IV. The Bottle Imp

Like many of Stevenson's stories, "The Bottle Imp" (1891) is a tale of caution. Borrowed from a local legend Stevenson is supposed to have been told during his first two months in Samoa (see Kirtley), the exotic story of the magic bottle containing a wish-granting devil must nevertheless have seemed rather familiar to

a nineteenth-century European and American audience that continued to be fascinated by fantastic tales warning of rags to riches fantasies (see McLynn 371).[19] The narrative of a young and somewhat naive but adventurous young man, a Hawaiian named Keawe, who comes into possession of a talisman that grants every wish but imposes certain conditions, draws on a formula exploited by some of the best and most popular writers of the century, including Goethe and Balzac, both of whom Stevenson knew well and admired.[20] This traditional form provides Stevenson with a way of dealing in "The Bottle Imp" with the relationship between aspiring and possessing that is the focus of the early critical essays just cited. "A man may pay too dearly for his livelihood," Stevenson says in his essay on Thoreau, "by giving . . . his whole life for it, or [by] bartering for it the whole of his available liberty, and becoming a slave till death" (*Virginibus* 201-02). This is exactly what happens in "The Bottle Imp." The young Hawaiian, Keawe, pledges his life for the possession of the magic bottle.

Here is another sense in which "The Bottle Imp" may be described as a tale of caution: not only in that it appears to warn against certain kinds of diabolical pacts, but also because it turns on the deposition of a caution in the sense of a pledge—something given as security in the establishment of a contract or bond (as in caution money).[21] In this case, Keawe offers his life as a caution. He too is in San Francisco, to which he has ventured in order "to have a sight of the great world and foreign cities" ("Bottle" 608). And he too is taken with America, in particular with its houses, a point to which we will return. Immersed in "wonder," Keawe comes upon a house that was "smaller than some others, but all finished and beautiful like a toy" (608)— a reference to Stevenson's essay on toys.[22] Looking into the toy house, he sees there a sorrowful old man, who very quickly sells Keawe the magic bottle, significantly, with little of the sense of foreboding often found in scenes of this kind. The simple terms of the contract have been explained by the old man. Upon purchase of the bottle, one pledges one's life against fulfillment of the following conditions: the bottle's owner is granted by the imp "all that he desires—love, fame, money, houses," provided: 1) that the bottle be sold at some point by the owner; 2) that it be sold "at a loss"; and 3) that it be sold for "coined money" (610-11). Let us examine these conditions briefly. After explaining that prolonging one's life is excluded (the imp does not have this power), the old man goes on: "if a man die before he sells [the bottle], he must burn in hell for ever" (610). This condition makes the exploitation of the bottle a matter of time and, as in all speculative investment, of the timing of the sale. As the old man informs Keawe, "all you have to do is to use the power of the imp in moderation, and then sell it to some one else, as I do to you, and finish your life in comfort" (610). In other words, if buying the bottle means acquiring a source of limitless credit, it also involves accepting the obligation of a debt to a future, as yet undetermined, purchaser to whom the bottle must be sold for a loss (the second condition). In this sense, the bottle is related to money—a substance which represents, as Aristotle says, "a guarantee of exchange in the future for something not given" (30). And indeed, according to the *Oxford English Dictionary,* the noun "bottle" itself can mean money ("a collection or a share of money"). The special qualification here, though, is that in this case the token is of owing, rather than of being owed, something in the future: it is a sign of a negative quantity to its holder.[23] Taking the bottle, in other words, means putting yourself in financial debt to another, putting yourself in another's debt—the minute you take the bottle, you owe someone the difference between the price you paid for the bottle and the necessarily lower price for which you must sell it. The bottle becomes the token of this obligation to pay in the future, an obligation for which your life is pledged as a caution.

The condition requiring that the bottle be sold for "coined money" might at first seem to place a limit on the size of this debt, by establishing some indivisible monetary unit, and thus to destine someone to be the final purchaser.[24] But, we discover, the debt here seems susceptible to division into infinitely smaller parts. As Keawe's resourceful and rather utilitarian wife, Kokua, tells him later in the story, one United States cent can be divided into about two British farthings, one British farthing into about two French centimes, and so on (625-26).[25] And in this story the possibilities of traveling to islands in the South Seas with ever smaller units of currency is, we are led to believe, limitless. In this sense, the debt can hypothetically be resolved into ever smaller amounts in such a way that it remains always possible to pass on the ever-shrinking, but persistent debt (to a new purchaser) and to avoid forfeiture of the caution (the life pledged). The bottle thus betokens an economy that includes a concept, or fiction, of infinitely large and small amounts. A source of potentially infinite credit, it brings with it a debt which is always approaching a fictive absolute zero, as such never to be reached.[26]

The bottle's immediate association with money and finance in the tale is further reinforced by Stevenson's decision to call the demon an "imp." Indeed, Stevenson seems to be reworking, or putting to work, the particular connotations the word "imp" had acquired in English culture at this time. An imp, the *Oxford English Dictionary* informs us, is a "little device or demon" (the *American Heritage Dictionary* gives the additional signification of "a mischievous child"). Imp, however, we are told, again in the *Oxford English Dictionary,* can also be used as a verb meaning "to engraft feathers in the wing of a bird so as to make good losses or deficiencies, and thus to

restore powers of flight—hence, allusively, with reference to 'taking higher flights,' enlarging one's powers." This second meaning is the one that concerns us most here because this use of the word "imp" to describe an operation designed to increase powers of flight intersects precisely with Stevenson's financial understanding of "aspiration" and "adventure." For, it is in this sense that the term "to imp" became associated in English with what many saw as the evil of financial credit and in particular paper money. The *locus classicus* here is Pope's well-known fable about money and wealth, the *Epistle to Bathurst,* which is devoted to the ethical question of "whether the invention of Money has been more commodious, or pernicious to Mankind" (570). The relevant lines from the *Epistle* are as follows:

> Blest paper-credit! last and best supply!
> That lends Corruption lighter wings to fly!
> Gold imp'd by thee, can compass hardest
>   things,
> Can pocket States, can fetch or carry Kings;
> A single leaf shall waft an Army o'er,
> Or ship off Senates to a distant Shore;
> A leaf, like Sybil's, scatter to and fro
> Our fates and fortunes, as the winds shall
>   blow:
> Pregnant with a thousand flits the Scrap
>   unseen,
> And silent sells a King or buys a Queen.
>
> (68-78)

Pope's letter is one of the best-known examples of early eighteenth-century English satires and polemics that ridiculed the new culture of credit and speculation from the pastoral perspective of landed "retirement," to use Maynard Mack's word.[27] Pope thus represents the period's widespread belief in the virtue of land and the fraudulence of financial credit—a belief which has been studied extensively by Pocock and others.[28] The figurative association of credit with flight expressed in Pope's use of the term "imping" would later in the century appear in a substantially modified form in the famous passage from Adam Smith's *Wealth of Nations* on the substitution of paper for gold and silver money in which Smith argues for the cautious use of paper by comparing it to the wings of Daedalus ("The commerce and industry of the country," Smith writes, "cannot be altogether so secure, when they are thus, as it were, suspended upon the Daedalian wings of paper money, as when they travel about upon the solid ground of gold and silver.")[29] What Pope and many other eighteenth-century writers considered fraud and artifice is, in Smith's view, a matter of ends and means, in short of finance—what he calls the "judicious operations of banking."

But in spite of the political economic writing of Smith, and after him of Ricardo and others, financial credit continued to be viewed with deep suspicion, if not superstition, well into the nineteenth century in England. Stevenson, I am suggesting, is different in this regard. Indeed, the difference can already be detected in his admiration for America, which was often viewed as a suspicious financial place for some of the same reasons that elicited Stevenson's praise of Thoreau.[30] But Stevenson's appreciation of the positive powers of financial credit as embodied in the image of America in his early writings is far from unqualified. Indeed, I would argue that in his most important work we also find that admeasure of utilitarianism that accompanied the rise of modern political economy in Britain in the wake of Adam Smith, as we will see if go back again and observe more carefully the workings of the bottle in "The Bottle Imp."

At the beginning of the tale, as we said, there is the enticement of the "new world"—El Dorado—with its promises of riches. Let me quote here from the beginning of the tale: San Francisco is

> a fine town, with a fine harbour, and rich people uncountable; and, in particular, there is one hill which is covered with palaces. . . . "What fine houses there are!" [Keawe] was thinking, "and how happy must these people be who dwell in them, and take no care for the morrow!" (608)

The admiration here, we note, is for a scene from which number and calculation are absent: the "rich people" here are both "uncountable" and unconcerned with future consequences—they "take no care for the morrow." Equally significant, as we indicated earlier, is the focus in the passage on houses—"palaces," as Keawe sees them—and on ways of dwelling. This scene of domestic promise beyond calculation establishes from the start the key link between the home and the bottle in this particular domestic romance. This is precisely, so to speak, where the bottle comes in. In possession of the bottle, Keawe immediately feels free to express his first desire, namely, as he says, "to have a beautiful house and garden on the Kona coast . . . and to live there without care . . ." (613). At this point, however, something happens, which upsets the feeling of freedom. For now there are consequences: the death of an uncle whose estate Keawe is to inherit. The fulfillment of aspirations, as it happens, comes at a price—in this case, the bottle, as Keawe himself notes, serves his domestic aspiration by killing his family (613).

This will be the theme for the rest of the tale: the consequences of the bottle's wish-granting power. "The Bottle Imp" becomes a story of trade-offs. The bottle, we are repeatedly shown, is no gift, unless it is in the sense of the inescapable system of reciprocal debt which, as anthropologists inform us, always accompanies economies of gift exchange (see Mauss). As the

bottle moves through the story, Keawe is made aware of the price to be paid for using its power in a number of contexts, material and spiritual. But the decisive moment comes, as we might expect, in connection with his wife, Kokua, on whom his domestic aspirations depend. At this point, Keawe has managed to sell the bottle but finds that he has contracted a disease that threatens his marriage to Kokua and forces him to recover the bottle. But when he regains it and wishes his illness away, he finds that he has lost his love for Kokua. Here, in other words, according to the same logic we just saw in the case of his desire for a home, in order to preserve his domestic ties to Kokua, he must destroy them—that, in his words, to bind himself to his wife he must be "bound to the bottle imp for time and for eternity" (623). Not because he will be unable to get rid of the bottle, but, on the contrary, because one *must* get rid of it. The bottle must be passed off—this is its fundamental law. It is Keawe's wife, Kokua (significantly the only woman in the tale) who comes closest to a clear understanding of this law—a significant fact given the as yet unappreciated importance of women in the negotiations between utilitarianism and English letters in the nineteenth century. The bottle, Kokua observes late in the story, involves a peculiar ethical responsibility, which she describes as the obligation "to save oneself by the eternal ruin of another" (631).[31]

But is she right? Is it accurate to say that with the bottle self-preservation requires the destruction of another? After all, in the end, Keawe does save himself and preserve his household without exactly ruining someone else. Late in the story, a drunken boatswain emerges to relieve Keawe of the bottle. The bottle is, in other words, passed to the drunk—hence another meaning of the word "bottle"—that is, it is passed to the one least likely to respond to its enticements with the "moderation" recommended to Keawe at the beginning of the story by the old man who sells it to him. Here, in keeping with the utilitarian theme we have been tracing, it is made quite clear that it is certainly not Keawe who ruins the drunk but the drunk who ruins himself. (Indeed, Keawe even offers rather insistently to buy the bottle back from the immoderate boatswain.) Kokua's insight about the bottle's law must, therefore, be qualified—it is not that one ruins others by passing them the bottle, but rather that one *might*, even unintentionally, provide others with the means by which they will ruin themselves. The ethical difficulty of the bottle is the *possibility* of putting into the hands of others something with which they will destroy themselves. "Mate, I wonder are you making a fool of me?" (634), the boatswain asks Keawe. This is the moral question—a question of possibility—to which we are ultimately led by the tale's utilitarian stress on the evaluation of consequences. Keawe's story thus ends appropriately with the departure of the boatswain bottle in hand:

So off [the drunken boatswain] went down the avenue toward town, and there goes the bottle out of the story. But Keawe ran to Kokua light as the wind; and great was their joy that night; and great, since then, has been the peace of all their days in the Bright House. (635)

With this departure of the bottle from the story, "The Bottle Imp" itself goes out. To be consistent, though, not without a final assessment of consequences. In the end, it turns out, Keawe retires to his manor house, the real estate he has derived from "operating judiciously," as Adam Smith would say, with the credit conferred by the bottle. Thus the story of the bottle becomes, like the bottle in the story, the instrument of a particular kind of domestic romance. It affirms that the romance of the home depends upon the utilitarian calculations of means and ends, and in this particular case upon finance (from the Latin *finis* meaning "end"). In other words, the domestic romance of the tale becomes inseparable from the sober calculation of consequences. There is, finally, no escape in this supposedly escapist literature from the evaluation of profit and loss.

But in "The Bottle Imp" domestic romance is not simply wedded to the utilitarian logic of finance. The consequentialist imperative of Stevenson's work extends to the tale itself. It is here, I would argue, that Stevenson's fiction becomes hard to reconcile with the neat oppositions of utilitarian and anti-utilitarian moral philosophy (oppositions which, by the way, the union of the domestic idyll with finance already began to confuse). For, as with the bottle, responsibility for the tale—the narrative medium through which the domestic romance is achieved—lies with those who would make judicious use of the particular way it joins the imp of finance to the idyll of the home.[32] Responsibility for this tale lies, in other words, with those who choose to read the story to their children, recommend it to their friends, or assign it to their students. And the management of effects or consequences in this context will certainly be no easier than it was for Keawe. Who can tell whether, for instance, the romance with its promise of future happiness through the judicious management of financial means and ends will turn out, in retrospect, to be genuine or counterfeit for those into whose hands it falls? One is reminded here, for example, of the case of Maggie Verver in *The Golden Bowl* written by Stevenson's friend and critical adversary, Henry James, and of the utilitarian cunning by which she manages to present her father with the gift of her marriage to the European aristocrat, Prince Amerigo. Does the open secret here of the utilitarian "flaw" in the domestic romance make Maggie's gift a counterfeit?[33] This is the question raised by Stevenson's tale: Who is to say whether the utilitarian domestic romance will become for its readers a magic bottle or, to use the Victorian expression, a "bottle of smoke"—a conventional false-

hood, a lie to which one lent credence? ("Withinsides" the bottle, we are told, "something obscurely moved like a shadow and a fire" [609].) Perhaps the story of "The Bottle Imp" will also turn out to have been for some such "a bottle of smoke," a literary confidence game, passed along, as Dickens puts it in *Little Dorrit*, "to keep up pretense as a labour and a study . . . in short, to pass the bottle of smoke, according to the rule" (Dickens, *Dorrit* 452). The consequences for which we become responsible when we pass along such domestic romances remain relatively unforeseeable. Even when the particular romance happens to urge utilitarian calculation, in the end we pass it along as a sort of gift, if by gift we mean the transmission of something whose exact dimensions are incalculable, something for which precise reciprocation will not be possible—something which is not comparable to a financial transaction because it cannot be paid back. For, as we know, in order for a gift truly to be a gift, we must have in some sense no sure knowledge of what we are giving or being given, or even that something is being given.[34] Otherwise, there is the expectation of reciprocation, and the quidproquo of exchange begins. Thus, if the transmission of Stevenson's utilitarian domestic romance cannot be comprehended within the strict terms of utilitarianism—if its transmission is a gift—then it is a gift of a far less reassuring sort than most nineteenth-century anti-utilitarian proponents of the gift were prepared to acknowledge.

Notes

[1] The locus classicus here is of course Watt (60-74). See also Novak, Meier, Nicholson, and, for a useful recent bibliography, Kibbie.

[2] For a survey of recent writing in France on *déontologie,* see La Bruslerie.

[3] In French, one begins to find the word "déontologie" as early as 1839, in Boiste's *Dictionnaire universel de la langue française,* a mere five years after Bentham's coinage of the term in English. Indeed, a French translation of Bentham's work, evidently made from the manuscript, appeared in 1834 in Paris from the publisher Charpentier under the title *Déontologie, ou Science de la Morale, ouvrage posthume de Jérémie Bentham, revu, mis en ordre et publié par John Bowring, traduit sur le manuscrit par Benjamin Laroche.* On the warmer response Bentham received in France as opposed to England, see Guidi. For a recent overview of the earlier history of the interrelations between English and French ethical theory, see Force. Force's observation of a main current in ethical thought in France, one that defines itself by the refusal of exchange, seems generally accurate. He makes no mention of the important attempts in France in the nineteenth century to join, rather than to separate, ethics from exchange, namely those of the Saint-Simonians

(Enfantin, Rodrigues, Thierry, and others). Benjamin is one of the few thinkers in the twentieth century to have underlined the importance of the Saint-Simonians as social thinkers in nineteenth-century France (708-44).

⁴ For Ross's discussion of Bentham and Moore, the starting points of his approach, and for his defense, against what he calls the French "sociological school" (from which he singles out Durkheim and Lévy-Bruhl) of what might be called an anti-Consequentialist ethical theory, see Ross 7-15.

⁵ A recent example of this long tradition is Pope John Paul II who states in his recently published *Dignity of Work: John Paul II Speaks to Managers and Workers* that "the entrepreneur and manager have a responsibility to promote non-economic values" (1). On this epochal conflict, see Shell, *Art*.

⁶ This discussion opens with the question of promising—a question that runs throughout Kant's work—and in particular with the issue of the "false promise," and he begins by considering this question first from the perspective of whether it is "clever" [*klüg*] to promise falsely. Here, as in Bentham's saving bank example, it is a matter of the short-term as opposed to the long-term consequences of the action. Kant endeavors, in other words, to move the question of the false promise beyond the utilitarian perspective of what he calls mere "cleverness" (i.e., whether it is clever to promise falsely). The aim is to consider the making of false promises with respect to "duty" [*Pflicht*]. And, interestingly enough, it is here that he too decides to use an example taken from the realm of finance. This context requires, Kant says, that I ask myself a different question when I am considering making a false promise. Now the question is not whether it is clever (i.e., whether benefits outweigh costs), but whether I will be happy, be "at peace" (the word here is *zufrieden*), if my practice of falsely promising were to become a universal law. When it comes to questions of duty—of the universalization of a private practice—falsely promising can not at all be desirable, because then there would be no promising possible, not even false promising, since it would be useless for me to declare my intention to do something in the future to those "who would not believe what I professed, or if they over-hastily did believe, would then pay me back later in the same coin [*mit gleicher Münze*]." With respect to duty, a false promise—a promise which I know I will not keep—undermines not just an individual's attempt to derive benefits from a particular contractual agreement, but the existence of contracts as such. It is not just the particular deal, we might say, but the possibility of making deals in general that is compromised by the false promise. See in particular Kant, *Grundlegung zur Metaphysik der Sitte* in *Werke* 6: 52-53; *Grounding* 31.

⁷ Nietzsche's discussion of debt and guilt, both of which translate the German word *Schuld,* can be found in the second part of the *Genealogy of Morals* (195-205).

⁸ Paton draws attention to this "consequentialist" aspect of Kant's reasoning here in his well-known commentary. After commenting on how the false promise to repay a debt "cancels itself out" if universalized as a law, Paton notes: "In another sense, he is taking into account the consequences. He is endeavouring to see the action as it fundamentally and essentially is—that is, as an action destructive of mutual confidence and of any systematic harmony of purposes in a particular sphere (and ultimately in every sphere)" (153).

⁹ The difference between morality and ethics is the difference between "relative value," or "price," and "inner value," or "worth" [*Würde*].

¹⁰ See Hazlitt's *Spirit of the Age* (*Table-Talk* 171-94); Carlyle's *On Heroes, Hero-Worship and the Heroic in History* and "Signs of the Times" (*Heroes* 91-92; "Signs" 472-76); Bulwer-Lytton's *England and the English* (276-83); and Arnold's "The Function of Criticism at the Present Time" and *Culture and Anarchy* (239-46, 409-12). On Kant in England in the nineteenth century, see Wellek.

¹¹ The great exception here of course is Ruskin, as Shell has convincingly demonstrated (*Economy* 129-51). On Sidgwick, see Schneewind (*Sidgwick's* 420) and Donagan. For an example of Sidwick's closeness to Kant on promising, see Sidgwick 313. (In this passage from Sidgwick, communication and society itself is said to depend on the possibility of keeping promises.)

¹² For Stevenson's comments on the "adventurism" of Whitman, see his "Walt Whitman" (*Virginibus* 195-96).

¹³ See the entry "adventure" in the *Oxford English Dictionary*. On the connection between "fortune" and "commerce," see Pocock, *Machiavellian*.

¹⁴ Perhaps Stevenson would have noted a parallel at this point in his career between him and Thoreau. Like Thoreau in *A Week on the Concord and Merrimack River* (1849), Stevenson, before leaving for the United States in 1879, had published *An Inland Voyage,* in which, in a manner not unlike that of Thoreau, he provided an account of his canoe trip through Belgium and France. *Treasure Island* was appearing in serial in 1882 when the Thoreau essay was published. A recent biographer of Stevenson notes: "One of the most disturbing aspects of *Treasure Island* is its lack of a moral center. Money is the ruling principle and even Dr. Livesey and Squire Trelawny are corrupted by it, leave their bucolic

pastures and rush off to the Caribbean with unseemly haste in the hopes of getting rich quick" (McLynn 199).

[15] A recent example of this is McCleary 193-94.

[16] This is, for example, true of Shelley's *Philosophical View of Reform,* even if it was the considerable merit of Shelley's work to conceive of public debt as a sign, not just of finance alone, but of a social contract involving ethical obligations. On Burke, see Pocock, "Introduction."

[17] A source for Stevenson here may be Hazlitt's "On the Spirit of Controversy" (*Table-Talk* 298-99). Hazlitt's importance for Stevenson is suggested by Stevenson's "Books Which Influenced Me" (16: 277).

[18] Ultimately, the link between Stevenson's adventure story and Thoreau's economics would be interesting to consider in light of the kinship Stevenson's work has with the romance tradition in nineteenth-century American literature—the family resemblance that would later in fact put him at odds with his American friend, Henry James.

[19] On Stevenson as a writer of *Bildungsromane,* see Bozetto. The theme of adventure in Stevenson is balanced in a sense by the countervailing prevalence of warnings in his work, even in the theoretical riposte to his friend, Henry James, entitled "A Humble Remonstrance." In this context, it is perhaps worth noting that Stevenson's American adventure and his decision to take up the risky career of professional writer were opposed by his security conscious father, Thomas, who wanted his son to enter the traditional family profession of lighthouse engineer. On this, see McCleary 11-12.

[20] On finance in Goethe's *Faust,* see Shell, *Money;* on this topic in Balzac's *La Peau de chagrin,* see Weber.

[21] According to the *Oxford English Dictionary,* "caution" first meant "security, surety" in English and took on the less specific qualitative sense of "taking heed" in the early modern period.

[22] Keawe is in the realm of "imitations" and "substitutes" described by Stevenson in his early essays collected in *Virginibus Puerisque* (1881): he is at what Stevenson calls the "experimental stage" of confidence, "faith," and "hope"—that stage never "altogether quit"—which is "not only the beginning but the perennial spring of our faculties" (Stevenson, "Child's Play" [*Virginibus* 94] and "Virginibus Puerisque" [*Virginibus* 11-12]).

[23] This phrase is taken from Kant's *Versuch, den Begriff der negative Grössen in die Weltweisheit einzuführen* (*Werke* 2: 775-819). On the question of "negative" debts

and "positive" credits in Kant, see Shell (*Money* 133-37). Also of relevance to the significance of the bottle in Stevenson's story is Benveniste's discussion of a particular meaning of the word "debt" as derived for the Latin *debere:* "The sense of *debere* is different, although it is also translated [from Latin] by 'to owe.' One can 'owe' something without having borrowed it: for instance, one 'owes' rent for a house, although this does not involve the return of a sum borrowed. Because of its formation and construction, *debeo* should be interpreted according to the value which pertains to the prefix *de,* to wit: 'taken, withdrawn from'; hence 'to hold' [*habere*] something which has been taken from [*de*] somebody" (148-49).

[24] This may also reflect contemporary views of coin as the ground for money. Jevons, for example, says "All . . . other commercial property, mortgage deeds, preference shares and bonds, and ordinary shares, resolve themselves into more or less probability of receiving coin at future dates . . ." (249).

[25] Stevenson discusses a system of currency conversion that does not reach equilibrium or relative zero in his remarks on the continued use of the monetary unit of the "bit" in the American West. See his remarks on the "long" and the "short" bit (*Works* 2: 140-42).

[26] In this it brings to mind the passage at the end of "El Dorado" in which Stevenson alludes to certain "Chimaeras" and the narratives of "aspiration" or "adventure" they instigate (*Virginibus* 72).

[27] Also on the *Epistle to Bathurst,* see Wasserman, especially 54.

[28] Pope's letter presents the classic argument against the artificial, fraudulent flights of credit and "fortune" from the landed perspective of the "virtue" of property, to use the terms studied by the historian, Pocock. The reference to the queen in the lines just cited, according to the editor F.W. Bateson, refers to the "rumor that Queen Caroline had accepted a large present from Robert Knght, the cashier of the South Sea Company" (Pope 574 n78). See Pocock (*Machiavellian* 457). "We find reason to suppose," notes Pocock elsewhere with reference to Pope, "that the Apocalyptic triumph of nonsense over language at the end of Pope's *Dunciad* has something to do with a society dominated by speculators in paper promises to repay which will never be made good before the end of time; if property is the foundation of personality, unreal property (in which nothing is owned except meaningless words) makes personalities unreal and their words meaningless" (*Virtue* 247).

[29] Smith's cautious advocacy of credit in *The Wealth of Nations* is of course central to the emergence of modern political economy in Britain, a tradition whose

particular way of linking economics and ethics in fact led to utilitarianism. Smith's advocacy of financial paper is thus appropriately based on the qualification that such paper be used as a means to an end, specifically as a way of "rendering a greater part of [the country's] capital active and productive than would otherwise be so" (1: 483-84).

[30] Think of the American railway ventures of Augustus Melmotte and Hamilton K. Fischer in Trollope's *The Way We Live Now,* a sort of satire of credit; or of the quixotic Martin Chuzzlewit who blindly seeks his fortune in the fraudulent American company, the Eden Land Corporation.

[31] On the basis of this observation, Kokua arranges secretly to purchase the bottle herself from Keawe—to sacrifice or ruin herself, she reasons, to save her husband. An act to which Keawe in turn reciprocates when he discovers his wife's plan: "His wife had given her soul for him," he concludes, "now he must give his for her" (633).

[32] This link between the bottle and the home, between money and domesticity, is suggested in a passage from the influential work of the political economist, W. Stanley Jevons, Stevenson's contemporary. See Jevons 250.

[33] Or, as Maggie's friend Charlotte Stant puts it, "Does one make a present . . . of an object that contains to one's knowledge a flaw?" (James 121).

[34] For some suggestive comments on this, see Derrida, *Donner* 214-15.

Works Cited

Aristotle. *Nichomachean Ethics.* Trans. Terence Irwin. Indianapolis: Hackett, 1985.

Arnold, Matthew. *Poetry and Criticism.* Ed. A. Dwight Culler. Boston: Houghton, 1961.

Benjamin, Walter. *Das Passagen-Werk.* Vol. 2. Frankfurt am Main: Suhrkamp, 1982. 2 vols.

Bentham, Jeremy. *Deontology; together with a Table of the Springs of Action; and The Article on Utilitarianism.* Ed. Amnon Goldworth. Oxford: Oxford UP, 1983.

Benveniste, Émile. *Indo-European Language and Society.* Trans. Elizabeth Palmer. Miami: U of Miami P, 1973.

Bozetto, Roger. "L'île dont le trésor est une aventure." *Europe* 770 (1994): 62-73.

Bulwer-Lytton, Edward. *England and the English.* New York: Routledge, 1874.

Carlyle, Thomas. *On Heroes, Hero-Worship and the Heroic in History.* Berkeley: U of California P, 1993.

———. "Signs of the Times." *The Complete Works of Thomas Carlyle.* Vol. 13. New York: Kelmscott, 1869. 20 vols.

Cavell, Stanley. *This New Yet Unapproachable America.* Albuquerque, NM: Living Batch, 1989.

———. *The Senses of Walden.* New York: Viking, 1972.

Derrida, Jacques. *Donner le temps. 1. La fausse monnaie.* Paris: Galilée, 1991.

———. *Passions.* Paris: Galilée, 1993.

Dickens, Charles. *Dombey and Son.* New York: Penguin, 1985.

———. *Little Dorrit.* New York: Penguin, 1985.

Donagan, Alan. "Sidgwick and Whewellian Intuitionism: Some Enigmas." *Essays on Henry Sidgwick.* Ed. Bart Schultz. Cambridge: Cambridge UP, 1992. 123-42.

Eliot, George. *The Mill on the Floss.* New York: Penguin, 1985.

Edwards, Paul, ed. "Deontological Ethics." *The Encyclopedia of Philosophy.* New York: Macmillan, 1967.

Force, Pierre. *Molière ou le Prix des choses: morale, économie et comédie.* Paris: Nathan, 1994.

Guidi, Marco E. L. "Principe d'utilité et conscience héroïque: La reception de l'œuvre de Bentham au XIXe siècle." *Regards sur Bentham et l'Utilitarisme.* Eds. Kevin Mulligan and Robert Roth. Geneva: Droz, 1993. 27-37.

Hazlitt, William. "Godwin." *Essays.* Everyman Library 459. London: Dent, 1960.

———. *Table-Talk: Original Essays on Men and Manners.* London: Templeman, 1845.

James, Henry. *The Golden Bowl.* New York: Penguin, 1987.

Jevons, W. Stanley. *Money and the Mechanism of Exchange.* New York: Garland, 1983.

John Paul II. *Dignity of Work: John Paul II Speaks to Managers and Workers.* Ed. Robert G. Kennedy. Lanham: UP of America, 1994.

Kant, Immanuel. *Werke in zehn Bänden.* Ed. Wilhelm Weischedel. Darmstadt: Wissenschaftliche, 1983. 10 vols.

————. *Grounding for the Metaphysics of Morals.* Trans. James W. Ellington. Indianapolis: Hackett, 1993.

Kibbie, Ann Louise. "Monstrous Generation: The Birth of Capital in Defoe's *Moll Flanders* and *Roxana.*" *PMLA* 110.5 (1995): 1023-34.

Kirtley, Bacil F. "The Devious Genealogy of the 'Bottle-Imp' Plot." *American Notes and Queries* 9 (1971): 67-70.

La Bruslerie, ed. *Ethique, Déontologie et Gestion de l'Entreprise.* Paris: Economica, 1992.

Mack, Maynard. *The Garden and the City: Retirement and Politics in the Later Poetry of Pope, 1731-1743.* Toronto: U of Toronto P, 1972.

Martineau, Harriet. *Illustrations of Political Economy: No. I. Life in the Wilds. A Tale.* Boston: Bowles, 1832.

Mauss, Marcel. *The Gift: The Form and Reason for Exchange in Archaic Societies.* Trans. W.D. Halls. New York: Routledge, 1990.

McCleary, James. *Le Pays Stevenson.* Courtry: de Bartillat, 1995.

McLynn, Frank. *Robert Louis Stevenson: A Biography.* London: Hutchinson, 1993.

Meier, Thomas Keith. *Defoe and the Defense of Commerce.* English Literary Studies Vol. 38. Victoria, BC: U of Victoria P, 1987.

Nicholson, Colin. *Writing and the Rise of Finance: Capital Satires of the Early Eighteenth Century.* Cambridge: Cambridge UP, 1994.

Nietzsche, Friedrich. *The Birth of Tragedy and The Genealogy of Morals.* Trans. Francis Golffing. New York: Doubleday, 1956.

Novak, Maximillian E. *Economics and the Fiction of Daniel Defoe.* Berkeley: U of California P, 1962.

Paton, H.J. *The Categorical Imperative: A Study in Kant's Moral Philosophy.* London: Hutchinson, 1965.

Pocock, J.G.A. "Introduction." *Reflections on the Revolution in France.* By Edmund Burke. Indianapolis: Hackett, 1987. vii-lvi.

————. *The Machiavellian Moment: Florentine Political Thought and the Atlantic Republican Tradition.* Princeton: Princeton UP, 1975.

————. *Virtue, Commerce and History: Essays on Political Thought Chiefly in the Eighteenth Century.* Cambridge: Cambridge UP, 1985.

Pope, Alexander. *The Poems of Alexander Pope.* Ed. John Butt. New Haven: Yale UP, 1963.

Ross, W.D. *The Right and the Good.* Oxford: Clarendon, 1930.

Schneewind, J.B. *Backgrounds of English Victorian Literature.* New York: Random, 1970.

————. *Sidgwick's Ethics: Victorian Moral Philosophy.* Oxford: Clarendon, 1977.

Sen, Amartya. "Éthique et finance." *Revue d'Économie financière* 20 (1992): 259-85.

————. *On Ethics and Economics.* Oxford: Oxford UP, 1987.

Shell, Marc. *Art and Money.* Chicago: U of Chicago P, 1995.

————. *The Economy of Literature.* Baltimore: Johns Hopkins UP, 1978.

————. *Money, Language, and Thought: Literary and Philosophical Economies from the Medieval to the Modern Era.* Berkeley: U of California P, 1982.

Shelley, Percy Bysshe. *A Philosophical View of Reform. The Complete Works of Percy Bysshe Shelley.* Vol. 7. Ed. Roger Ingpen and Walter E. Peck. New York: Gordian, 1965.

Sidgwick, Henry. *The Methods of Ethics.* Chicago: U of Chicago P, 1962.

Smith, Adam. *An Inquiry into the Nature and Causes of the Wealth of Nations.* 5th ed. Vol. 1. London: Strahan, 1789. 3 vols.

Stevenson. Robert Louis. "Books Which Influenced Me," *The Works of Robert Louis Stevenson.* Vol. 16. London: Chatto and Windus, 1911-25. 25 vols.

————. "The Bottle Imp." *Selected Writings of Robert Louis Stevenson.* The Modern Library. New York: Random House, 1947. 608-35.

————. *Virginibus Puerisque and Familiar Studies of Men and Books.* Everyman Library 765. London: Dent, 1948.

Wasserman, E.R. *Epistle to Bathurst.* Baltimore: Johns Hopkins UP, 1960.

Watt, Ian. *The Rise of the Novel: Studies in Defoe, Richardson, and Fielding.* Berkeley: U of California P, 1957.

Weber, Samuel. *Unwrapping Balzac: A Reading of "La peau de chagrin."* Toronto: Toronto UP, 1979.

Wellek, René. *Immanuel Kant in England, 1793-1838.* Princeton: Princeton UP, 1931.

THE IMAGE OF MONEY

John Vernon (essay date 1984)

SOURCE: "The Revenge of the Material," in *Money and Fiction: Literary Realism in the Nineteenth and Early Twentieth Centuries,* Cornell University Press, 1984, pp. 65-83.

[*In the following excerpt, Vernon discusses money in terms of its physical existence and its existence as an abstraction, a social power which characters will do anything to gain but which novelists usually strip from them in the end.*]

When members of a culture slip easily into the perspective that enables them to recognize that land and great houses, whatever else they may be, are also dirt and wood and stone, literary realism becomes possible. Realism occurs when the social world undergoes a gradual erosion by the material, a process historically set in motion by the Industrial Revolution and the forms of money that accompanied it. In this chapter . . . I shall attempt to approach a definition of literary realism . . . by way of the image of money in novels. . . .

Money is one of the most recurring signs of reality in fiction. As a sign of reality, it takes on an ambivalent physical existence. On the one hand, it is an object among other objects and thus has a material status; in the case of Dickens's dust heaps and "paper currency" (the trash blown down London streets) in *Our Mutual Friend,* or of Mr. Cheesacre's piles of manure (which are money to him) in Trollope's *Can You Forgive Her?* or of the misers' piles of gold in *Silas Marner, Eugénie Grandet,* and *McTeague,* money becomes the image of a kind of prime matter or raw material, the world reduced to lumps and heaps of denuded objects and waste.

On the other hand, money is an abstraction, a social power, and even (or especially) a sign of the appearances and illusions novelists are fond of stripping from their characters. As we shall see, this is more true of Balzac than of almost any other novelist. In Balzac, appearances are always peeling back like wallpaper to reveal the crumbling plaster beneath.

This schizophrenia of money expresses moral attitudes—money is sordid, money gives us wings—and lends itself in particular to novels of social mobility, in which the contrast between the low and the high is crucial. Behind it lies a sense of material reality implicit in the West's binary habits of thought: matter's nature is to *exclude,* and it excludes everything that is not matter—space, the abstract, the immaterial—in order to become what it is. Attitudes like this go all the way back to the Greek atomists (by way of Newton and Descartes)[1] but receive a new emphasis with that massive social and economic change in the late eighteenth and early nineteenth centuries known as the Industrial Revolution. The Industrial Revolution confirmed a growing sense in the West that the physical world consisted of largely inert raw material to be shaped into commodities by human industry. Commodities by definition have price tags. In a customary society, some objects are more valued than others not because of their price, but because of their relation to the past or to various members of the social order, such as the king or clergy. But there can be no hierarchy among objects once they all have price tags, except of course the purely quantitative hierarchy of money. Objects were bought and sold long before the nineteenth century, of course; but more than ever, goods previously made by hand and used by the maker (cloth especially) were now made by machine and sold for cash. The story has been told frequently and is familiar: in the eighteenth and nineteenth centuries the West underwent a dramatic shift from a largely handicraft culture with local markets to a society in which even, or especially, the lowest classes paid with wages for what they consumed, instead of making it themselves, bartering for it, being paid in kind, or all three.

And changes in forms of money expressed this shift. With the growth of paper money, money of account—the notional units of measurement in a currency, such as the pound, the livre, or the sou—became that much more an abstract system of quantification, a means of weighing and measuring the value of commodities. Behind paper money, defined by virtue of its absence, metal currency became reduced to the state of leftover matter. Consequently we see in novels (Balzac is the best example) that objects, clothing, houses, furniture, and flesh all take on a common physical status, all are pieces or fragments of leftover matter, signs of a partial and quantified world. As money becomes more symbolic, reality becomes more reductively material, and in this way a truly physical world first enters literature, a world whose physical existence is actually quite threatening. The sense that Sartre's character Roquentin has in *La nausée* that the world is de trop begins with nineteenth-century realism, especially with Sartre's countrymen Balzac, Flaubert, and Zola. In the realistic novel all objects have price tags, without which they are worthless matter, and conversely money itself is worthless matter with value attached to it by a social contract. In its unstable worthless/valuable state, money is like the dust heaps that produce a fortune in *Our Mutual Friend,* or like the cheap paper made from vegetable pulp in Balzac's *Illusions perdues* that has the potential to earn millions.

With the Industrial Revolution money takes on its own autonomy and power, and so do objects. They are no longer part of a continuum of human existence, a means absorbed into human life. The means has become an end. Dickens's most powerful image of this is Venus's shop in *Our Mutual Friend,* half-dark and cluttered with human parts for sale: hands, eyeballs, legs, skeletons, skulls, fetuses in jars. (The image of the dismembered body part also occurs in later novels dealing with money: McTeague's huge gilded tooth in *McTeague,* or Doctor T. J. Eckleburg's eyes in *The Great Gatsby.* In both cases the body and its parts have become objects, commodities.) The experience of money, especially as gold gives way to paper, is the experience of a desire for a certain end transforming itself into the desire for the means by which all material ends are satisfied. In this way desire fulfills its own secret desire to obliterate itself, and into the vacuum rush those fragmented objects cut off from human life that are in a sense the leftover traces of desire. At the end of Balzac's story "M. Gobseck," Gobseck's rooms are thrown open, and the debris he collected in the final months of his life is revealed: moldy and decayed food, half-eaten by rats and swarming with maggots, along with furniture, bales of cotton, casks of sugar, rum, coffee, and tobacco, lamps and plate, and so forth. The passage is a powerful image of dead matter and waste, and of money's transformation of desire into disgust.[2]

But money is also, as Lionel Trilling says, "the great generator of illusion" in novels.[3] In a world where paper is gradually coming to substitute for gold, money itself is a dream, a fiction. With paper, the representation of wealth itself becomes a form of wealth, so that, as J. Hillis Miller points out, "the appearance of money is as good as really possessing it."[4] So the Lammles in *Our Mutual Friend,* Becky and Rawdon Crawley in *Vanity Fair,* Melmotte in *The Way We Live Now,* or Merdle in *Little Dorrit* live almost entirely upon the credit extended to them because they present the appearance of wealth. But in all cases the bubble bursts. In its double character of the illusory and the real, money has the power to alter appearances by robbing them of their material base; it can turn reality into dream, but it can also turn dream into reality. One of the typical ways reality closes in on appearances in the realistic novel is the seizure and sale of a character's possessions to satisfy creditors. This occurs so often that we may recognize in it one of the collective nightmares of the middle class in the nineteenth century. It happens in *Our Mutual Friend,* *L'éducation sentimentale,* Thackeray's *The History of Samuel Titmarsh* and *Vanity Fair, The Mill on the Floss, David Copperfield, The Mayor of Casterbridge,* and *The Princess Casamassima;* it threatens often in

Balzac; and it is barely averted in *Dombey and Son, Framley Parsonage, Middlemarch,* and *Madame Bovary.* Possessions in such instances become reduced to mere objects, raw material; they are signs no longer of the social but of the physical world. "After that they sold her dresses, then one of her hats with a limp, broken feather, then her furs, then three pairs of shoes; and the distribution of these relics, which vaguely recalled the shape of her limbs, struck him as an atrocity, as if he were watching crows tearing her corpse to pieces" *(L'éducation sentimentale).*[5] A similar scene occurs in Norris's *McTeague.* In both novels, in being displaced from their arrangement in a domestic round of activities and spaces, objects assume their implicit discreteness. They become pieces, atoms, debris, or in the case of Flaubert (ironically, of course) relics.

As a representation of material existence in fiction, money always has this double aspect: it is the dreams and illusions of characters, their world of appearances, and undermining this it is the world of sordid reality. Money encompasses these two poles, but little in between. This split is of course implicit in fiction from the beginning, in *Don Quixote,* but in the nineteenth century it becomes much more pronounced. It is a split between the material and the immaterial worlds, between matter become dense, visible, and inert and all that matter has excluded in order to become so. Thus money becomes an ironic substitute for that discredited spiritual world displaced by matter; it becomes a religion, a god, and it makes one's fortune, in both senses, the way the gods once did. To have money is to be virtuous, respectable, worthy; not to have it is to be base. "An income of a hundred thousand francs provides a very pretty commentary on the catechism and gives us wonderful help for putting a stock-exchange valuation on moral principles!" says Raphael in *La peau de chagrin.* "Vice for me," he continues, "means living in a garret, wearing threadbare clothes, a grey hat in winter and owing money to the concierge." In realistic fiction, the material and the immaterial exist in inverse proportion to each other: as one shrinks the other expands. Of course the material world is far more suited to the novelist's powers of description. Hence genuine virtue often seems shallow and sentimental in Balzac as well as in Dickens. In Balzac it dwells in a world apart, like a nunnery surrounded by gaming houses and brothels.

If money is religion or a substitute for religion, then the split between the material and immaterial worlds, between the low and the high, the sordid and the lofty exists by virtue of the secret link between them: money. Numerous characters in fiction reveal this: Pip in *Great Expectations,* Dorrit in *Little Dorrit,* Emma in *Madame Bovary,* Bulstrode in *Middlemarch,* and any number of characters in Henry James and Balzac.[6] "When the money slides into the young man's pocket," says Balzac in *Le Père Goriot,* "an imaginary column is created for his support. He carries himself better than he did before, he meets your eye directly, his movements are more agile. . . . In short the bird that was wingless has found its powers."[7] This is similar to the language James uses in *The Portrait of a Lady* and *The Wings of the Dove*. "Spread your wings," Ralph says to Isabel Archer. "Rise above the ground." In *The Portrait of a Lady,* money emanates from the sick and old and corrupts the young and innocent. It doesn't matter that the sick and old are themselves innocent and naive (if a bit dangerous, like overgrown children)—money comes from them, and money is sordid. They want Isabel to soar, and instead she lands in the mud. Over and over again nineteenth-century novelists play variations on this theme. Characters soar on wings of money and land in the muck of material reality. For example, the wonderful scene in *Great Expectations* in which Pip, decked out like a gentleman, encounters Trabb's boy on the street:

> Deeming that a serene and unconscious contemplation of him would best beseem me, and would be most likely to quell his evil mind, I advanced with that expression of countenance, and was rather congratulating myself on my success, when suddenly the knees of Trabb's boy smote together, his hair uprose, his cap fell off, he trembled violently in every limb, staggered out into the road, and crying to the populace, "Hold me! I'm so frightened!" feigned to be in a paroxysm of terror and contrition, occasioned by the dignity of my appearance. As I passed him, his teeth loudly chattered in his head, and with every mark of extreme humiliation, he prostrated himself in the dust.

The gap between Pip's "serene and unconscious contemplation" and the dust where Trabb's boy grovels is there from the beginning of *Great Expectations*. It exists in Miss Havisham's house, but Pip doesn't recognize it, being blinded by Estella's beauty. Its most powerful form is in the relationship between Pip and his secret benefactor, Magwitch. Magwitch's money makes Pip a gentleman, and as a gentleman he is by definition worthy and respectable. But when Magwitch turns up, the gap between the high and low is shown for a moment to be a link, and it is a link Pip cannot abide. His rejection of the convict's money as a first act of moral courage is convincing precisely because money has been shown to be touching everything. Still, it is also an act of moral snobbery, since even Magwitch proves to be not what he seems.

Nineteenth-century fiction is filled with Magwitches and Gobsecks, outcasts of society firmly in control of those who blithely or desperately regard money as a privilege. Bulstrode and Raffles in *Middlemarch* are George Eliot's Pip and Magwitch. Money confers power on the powerless, though the limits of such power are also contained within money.[8] The theme of the high and the low is a direct outgrowth of the

two faces of money we have been exploring in this chapter—money as abstract or illusory, and money as matter—and it deserves more attention before we turn to my chief examples, Balzac and Flaubert. Dickens's other great novel on the theme is *Little Dorrit,* whose two-part division (Book the First, *Poverty,* and Book the Second, *Riches*) is intended to establish a contrast between low and high that can repeatedly be exploited as a similarity. For example, in the eyes of Little Dorrit, now wealthy, Venice's tourist society becomes an imitation of her former life in the debtor's prison, the Marshalsea:

> It appeared on the whole, to Little Dorrit herself, that this same society in which they lived, greatly resembled a superior sort of Marshalsea. Numbers of people seemed to come abroad, pretty much as people had come into the prison; through debt, through idleness, relationship, curiosity, and general unfitness for getting on at home. They were brought into these foreign towns in the custody of couriers and local followers, just as the debtors had been brought into the prison. They prowled about the churches and picture-galleries, much in the old, dreary, prison-yard manner. They were usually going away again tomorrow or next week, and rarely knew their own minds, and seldom did what they said they would do, or went where they said they would go: in all this again, like the prison debtors.

Behind the apparent (and sentimental) suggestion here that there is no real difference between poverty and wealth lies a subtler theme: that just as "reality" defines itself with difficulty against dream (Which is real, the Marshalsea or Venice?), so poverty defines itself not against wealth, but against the material appearance of wealth—again, with difficulty. Mrs. General, for example, is hired by Mr. Dorrit to produce in his family the varnished surface of wealth, and her function reminds us of the Veneerings's dining room in *Our Mutual Friend,* or of Pip's pride in his appearance in *Great Expectations.* To have money is to display money, to triumph conspicuously over others (as in Veblen) by means of appearances. But beneath the varnish, the wealthy are just as constrained by their manners and their dreary routines— by the obligations wealth thrusts upon them—as the debtors in the Marshalsea. The suggestion that the forms of wealth under capitalism are imprisoning is clear. Wealthy, the Dorrits become indebted to an image of themselves just as ruthless in its constraints as the walls of the Marshalsea, and far more threatening too, because "good" society turns out to be swarming with people capable of embarrassing them with reminders of their former position.

As in *Great Expectations,* money in *Little Dorrit* serves the purposes of both irony and romance. The novel is "realistic" in the most common sense, as a story of characters who fail (mostly financially), whose lives are a downward curve, but it is also one of those improbable romances of success, of finding, being given, or marrying into a treasure. And, as in *Great Expectations,* the hidden links between poverty and wealth assert themselves all the more forcibly the more the characters attempt to effect an absolute separation between the two states. The dream of poverty is wealth, and the nightmare of wealth is poverty. Because wealth contains its own loss—a kind of trapdoor through which the money may disappear (Merdle's financial bubble is the novel's paradigm of this)—the Dorrits spurn with paranoid desperation all reminders of their former state. They even turn their backs on Clennam, who in a sense is this novel's congenial, more well-bred Magwitch, the one who in assisting their transition from low to high is in their eyes discredited, not elevated, by his efforts—precisely because of his connection with their poverty. All of this finds its climax in one of the great scenes in nineteenth-century fiction, Mr. Dorrit's "Ladies and gentlemen, welcome to the Marshalsea" speech, delivered in his delirium at a formal dinner in high society in Rome (in fact, a farewell dinner for Mrs. Merdle, whose husband's financial schemes are about to collapse in London). In this scene the low finally overtakes the high, and Mr. Dorrit's fear of being embarrassed by someone from his past is confirmed—but the someone turns out to be himself. This image of the low, as it were, appropriating the high from within is subsequently echoed by that of the faceless Merdle, who in death is described as having "an obtuse head, and coarse, mean, common features." Of course we are intended to conclude from this that Merdle was corrupt; but Dickens's metaphor has to do with social class—"common." Dickens's own ambivalence about poverty is reflected in the contradictory valuations of the low in *Little Dorrit.* The low is surely something "common" and sordid, like Merdle's face. But strangely enough, it is also a lost paradise, a lost home—the Marshalsea—a place where Dorrit and his daughter were once affectionate and close. Only in Dickens could such a startling reversal grow so naturally out of the premises of the text: the shades of the prison house are the home we have lost, not the world that closes around us. On the other hand, in the world that closes around us the prison has found its reflection—the world has truly become a prison—in the sham homes we have created with money, the best example of which is Merdle's house in Cavendish Square.

Little Dorrit finds its unlikely echo in the century's last great novel of the high and low, James's *The Princess Casamassima,* in which a prison also plays a significant role. Like Dickens, James discovered that the contrast between high and low provided for his middle-class audience a bold sense of drama: the contrast, for example, between the greasy, murky, festering cockpits of London with which Book Second ends—the worm's eye view of London, to use Braudel's phrase[9]—and the Princess's country estate (Medley Hall) with

which Book Third begins. As in Dickens, the high and the low find their ironic reflections in each other: Hyacinth Robinson, the lowly bookbinder with (possibly) aristocratic blood, becomes attracted to the artistic and architectural wonders of Europe, while his friend the Princess gives her money away to revolutionaries, rents a shabby little house, and fills it with tasteless petit bourgeois bric-a-brac. Hyacinth and the Princess find in each other the qualities each wants to shun but cannot—the low and the high—and as a result they wind up, like Mr. Dorrit before and Mr. Dorrit after, mirroring what each perceives to be his or her own worst side.

The split beween the high and the low was a rich theme for the novel only as long as it could shun Gnosticism, that is, as long as the *links* between high and low could also be revealed. But with the growing sense of physical objects as reductively material, this became less possible. Repeatedly in the nineteenth-century novel we witness the revenge material reality takes upon a morality that regards it as fallen, unredeemed. The final image of Zola's *Nana* is the death blow, not the triumph, of realism, for in this portrait of physical disgust and corruption—the human face not merely as coarse, mean, and common but as rotten meat—the dialectic is stilled, and matter can only decay, can only break down into the "lower" states implicitly present in all its organizations. The trajectory from realism to naturalism completes its course in the theme of entropy, in Beckett and Pynchon in the twentieth century. Of course, we can see the process just beginning in *Persuasion:* the implicit threat of Mr. Elliot's hammer (though never carried out) is that it will break beautiful objects down into chunks of matter. But a better example is perhaps Balzac, in whom objects first explicitly lay siege to the novel's world.

In Balzac there is always a strange world of matter that exists in a sense on either side of reality. It is a series of pictures in a tour guide, a series of economic relationships, but it is also as sordid and cold as clay. It is what is left over when an object's price has been named, the superfluity of matter in its public state, the shell of material appearances: flaking paint on chairs and mantlepieces, threadbare coats, crumbling, worn, and pock-marked friezes and facades. This world of matter is actually abstract, since it usually leaves an aftertaste of reality, a sign of the place where reality used to dwell. It is the shadow of the real world; within it Balzac's characters act out their ambitions and desires. These ambitions and desires alone are real—that is, autonomous, substantial, and in possession of a life, will, and necessity of their own.

Never before and perhaps never since has there been such a sheer abundance of objects in literature, and never have objects been so carefully articulated. Still, they often seem fake, as if the world were papier mâché.

Balzac is always telling us what objects are made of, as though they couldn't be made of themselves. Curtains are made of silk, hinges of brass, dishes of china, floors of wood or tile, and so forth. He is profoundly conscious of materials, as the long digressions on paper manufacture in *Illusions perdues* demonstrate. Objects have a double nature in Balzac: they are a face presented to the world, and they are a material from which the face is shaped. This view of objects is new to literature—again, largely because of the Industrial Revolution—but implicit in Western culture in Aristotle's notions of form and matter and Locke's primary and secondary qualities. Often in Balzac, the face an object presents to the world is wearing away, and the object has begun to assert itself as sheer matter. "Above the arch a long frieze represented the four seasons by figures carved in hard stone but already corroded and blackened." "There, worn and blackened window sills appear, their delicate carvings scarcely visible" (both examples from *Eugénie Grandet*).[10] As objects break down and their faces wear away, their material nature steps forth and they become present, visible, heavy, dense, no longer part of the normal social flow. In *Splendeurs et misères des courtisanes*, Asia deals in splendid gowns that ladies have been forced to sell to obtain money; they are "no longer gowns but are not yet rags."[11] They are illegible—not signs of wealth, but not signs of poverty either. This is a fascinating no-man's-land for Balzac, since objects for him are usually windows through which one views money, or the lack of it ("Paris porters take things in at a glance; they never stop decorated gentlemen of heavy gait who wear blue uniforms. In other words, they recognize money when they see it"—*La Cousine Bette*).[12]

Objects in Balzac are a transparent facade, and they are opaque material reality. "In the drawing room the furniture was upholstered in shabby cotton velvet, plaster statuettes masquerading as Florentine bronzes, a badly carved sconce, merely painted, with molded glass candle-rings, a carpet whose cheapness was belatedly explaining itself in the quantity of cotton used in its manufacture, which had become visible to the naked eye. . . . That horrible room, where everything sagged, where dirty socks hung on the chairs stuffed with horse-hair, whose brown flowers reappeared outlined in dust" *(La Cousine Bette)*. Objects present a face, but at the same time the face is peeling, flaking, worn through, no longer adequate to the job of illusion; thus, objects are emblems both of sham and of the poverty of sheer unredeemed material reality beneath the sham.

In a sense Balzac's world is one in which solid things are breaking down and being replaced by their paper representations, just as gold is being replaced by bank notes. It is a material world emptied of value and becoming an image of itself, a shell. Neither the paper image nor the lost reality has any redeeming qualities. Paper is always unstable in Balzac; bank notes and notes of hand are continually discounted and devalued, and the reader always senses their immanent worthlessness. A variation of this theme is David Séchard's search in *Illusions perdues* for a process to manufacture cheap paper: "He had to invent a cheap paper, and that promptly; he had also to adapt the profits from the discovery to the needs of the household and his business."[13] One feels that he is trying to invent a cheap money, like John Law in the eighteenth century. Similarly, literature in *Illusions perdues* is being replaced by journalism, which Balzac makes clear is nothing more than cheap writing—throwaway words.

Occasionally the paper peels back and we glimpse something underneath. This is a favorite image in Balzac: tarnished or worn or peeling surfaces that show glimpses of objects in their former states. In this sense reality in Balzac is often the nostalgia for reality. Paper representations cover a dense materiality that is a kind of distant lost world, a lost home. Misers hoarding their gold have reverted to that lost world. Gold for the miser actually becomes a kind of manna, in the language of anthropologists, a primitive thriving substance with a magical life of its own. "Really coins live and swarm like men," says old Grandet in *Eugénie Grandet;* "they come and go and sweat and multiply."[14] But of course this is only a short step away from a disgust with matter, since gold for the miser is also excrement.

Such disgust is evident everywhere in Flaubert. Roland Barthes points out in *Writing Degree Zero* that there is a world of difference between Balzac and Flaubert, and I presume he means at least in part that Flaubert is Balzac perfected and become Literature.[15] Still, this world of difference exists only by virtue of the similarities between the two. Both write about characters who victimize themselves by means of money. Madame Bovary's gesture of tossing her last five francs to a blind man while her house and property are being seized is straight out of Balzac, as is the character of Lheureux in that novel, or of Arnoux in *L'éducation sentimentale.*

But above all, Flaubert takes the disgust at material existence that is implicit in Balzac and makes it explicit. Balzac has sufficient energy and even goodwill that such disgust still seems to play a secondary role. In Flaubert it pervades every page and becomes inseparable from the cold light in which his language bathes everything. Material things are usually the sign of material imperfection—grease spots, drops of sweat, moles, pores, stains, patches of raw skin, bad breath, heavy folds of cloth, and so on.

> He tucked the catechism into his pocket and stood swinging the heavy vestry key with his hand.

The setting sun glowing down on his face bleached his woolen cassock. It was shiny at the elbows and frayed at the hem. Grease spots and tobacco followed the line of small buttons down his broad chest. There was a great accumulation of them near his clerical bands, on which the abundant folds of his red skin were resting. His complexion was dotted with yellow blemishes that disappeared under the stubble of his graying beard. He had just had his evening meal and was breathing heavily.[16]

This is realism, but it is also a highly selective vision, like that, for example, in the photographs of Diane Arbus. Its inevitable culmination lies in images of dismemberment and death: the amputation of Hippolyte's leg in *Madame Bovary* after Bovary's farcical operation to correct his clubfoot, the dead baby whose portrait is painted in *L'éducation sentimentale,* the bailiff's fingers "as soft as slugs" in *Madame Bovary,* and the stream of black liquid that flows out of the dead Emma's mouth. As Sartre points out throughout *L'idiot de la famille,* all of this is symptomatic of extreme self-loathing by Flaubert. It is a self-loathing that in Zola finds its echo in Nana's dead face and in the twentieth century is expressed in the climatic moment of Joyce's "Clay," in Beckett's images of bodily disgust, and in Sartre himself by the nausea his character Roquentin feels at the sheer materiality of objects.

Fredric Jameson sees in Flaubert a lack of the Real, of "that which resists desire," because in fact desire has been replaced by *bovarysme,* the "'desire to desire' whose objects have become illusory images."[17] In a sense this is correct, but perhaps it is misleading as stated. In Flaubert the social and the physical worlds have collapsed together, allowing the latter's sordid or "greasy" quality to become not an object of desire but an object of loathing, an occasion for shutting one's eyes and dreaming one's dreams. . . . [This] collapse of the social and material becomes inevitable the further down one goes on the social scale. In Gissing and Zola, for example (as in American society today), most social relations center on the workplace. For Flaubert's bourgeoisie, the case is slightly more ambiguous. Social relations are dominated by hypocrisy because they mask material needs and desires, most of them petty. The material world thus becomes a comment upon the illusory freedom of those who pretend to disregard it, and the social world becomes subject to a downward movement as inevitable as the laws of physics.

"Greasy," by the way, applied to the material, became a favorite word of the naturalists who followed on Flaubert's heels (in French, *graisseux* or *gras*). . . . The word itself contains associations that play variations upon the theme of high and low. Grease reminds us of those who cook their food in grease or oil (hence the American word "greaser") and thus applies to Mediterranean peoples, those darker, poorer, and more idle races who live below the cooler-headed northern Europeans. In Zola's *L'assommoir,* two of the principal characters, Gervaise and Lantier, come from a town near Marseilles. In Norris's *McTeague,* Maria Macapa is described as a greaser. Both novelists, and Gissing too, use the adjective "greasy" to describe physical environments, and in all three the material world becomes what Sartre defines as slime or stickiness *(visqueux):* "the revenge of the In-itself."[18] All of this is implicit in Flaubert, for whom the physical realm is without value and the immaterial or moral realm a matter of the romantic imagination, no more real than knights on white horses.

If Flaubert (as so many assert) is the beginning of modern literature, he also reveals the process by which one strain of realism seeded its own destruction. The gap between the material and immaterial in Flaubert is finally so great that even money cannot act as a link between them. Given such a gap, the novel loses its ability to deal with the very moral issues money raises, and the social world becomes one-dimensional, absorbed into the physical, a kind of machine. For this reason, Flaubert's plots have an overriding sense of necessity that totally excludes the nervous, energetic presence of obsession and chance we find, say, in Balzac or Dostoevsky.

In a sense what we see in Flaubert is a split of self and world so profound that they simply fail to intersect. *Bovarysme,* the desire to desire, makes of the self a monad, contained within the larger but separate monad of physical reality. The social world disappears in between, and money becomes part of the unobtainable not-I that continually recedes beyond Emma's grasp. . . .

Notes

[1] See my *The Garden and the Map: Schizophrenia in Twentieth Century Literature and Culture* (Urbana: University of Illinois Press, 1973), especially chapter 1.

[2] The irony of "M. Gobseck" is also this: that the miser who loves gold because it doesn't perish has also hoarded perishable things, which in fact have begun to decay.

[3] Lionel Trilling, *The Liberal Imagination* (New York: Doubleday, 1953), p. 203.

[4] Afterword to *Our Mutual Friend* (New York: Signet Classics, 1964), p. 904. Compare Trilling: "To appear to be established is one of the ways of becoming established." *Liberal Imagination,* p. 204.

[5] The translation of *L'éducation sentimentale, Sentimental Education,* is by Robert Baldick (Harmondsworth: Penguin Books, 1964).

[6] Cf. Edward Said: "Both Dickens in *Great Expectations* and Flaubert in *Madame Bovary* use money to signify the protagonists' transitory power to shore up their authority to dream and even for a while to be something they cannot long remain being." *Beginnings* (New York: Basic Books, 1975), p. 98.

[7] The translation of *Le Père Goriot* is by E. K. Brown (New York: Modern Library, 1950). Compare these nearly identical passages in Trollope and Gissing. The first is from *The Small House at Allington:* "Moneys in possession or in expectation do give a set to the head, and a confidence to the voice, and an assurance to the man, which will help him much in his walk in life." The second is from *New Grub Street:* "Money is a great fortifier of self-respect. Since she had become really conscious of her position as the owner of five thousand pounds, Marian spoke with a steadier voice, walked with a firmer step."

[8] Cf. Edward Said: "Although the novel itself licenses Pip's expectations, it also mercilessly undercuts them, mainly by showing that these expectations are inherently self-limiting. . . . The more Pip believes he is acting on his own, the more tightly he is drawn into an intricate web of circumstances that weighs him down completely; the plot's progressive revelation of accidents connecting the principal characters is Dickens's method of countering Pip's ideology of free upward progress." *Beginnings,* p. 90.

[9] "The London drama—its festering criminality, its underworld, its difficult biological life—can only really be comprehended from this worm's eye view of the poor." Fernand Braudel, *The Structures of Everyday Life: The Limits of the Possible,* vol. 1 of *Civilization and Capitalism, 15th-18th Century,* trans. Miriam Kochan and Siân Reynolds (New York: Harper and Row, 1981), p. 555.

[10] The translation of *Eugénie Grandet* is by Dorothea Walter and John Watkins (New York: Modern Library, 1950).

[11] The translation of *Splendeurs et misères des courtisanes, A Harlot High and Low,* is by Rayner Heppenstall (Harmondsworth: Penguin Books, 1970).

[12] The translation of *La Cousine Bette, Cousin Bette,* is by Kathleen Raine (New York: Modern Library, 1958).

[13] The translation of *Illusions perdues, Lost Illusions,* is by Herbert J. Hunt (Harmondsworth: Penguin Books, 1971).

[14] According to Marc Shell, *tokos,* the Greek word for biological offspring, also came to mean interest in the economic sense. *The Economy of Literature* (Baltimore: John Hopkins University Press, 1978), pp. 93-94.

[15] Though his first meaning is that 1848 changed everything. Roland Barthes, *Writing Degree Zero,* trans. Annette Lavers (New York: Hill and Wang, 1968), p. 38.

[16] The translation of *Madame Bovary* is by Mildred Marmur (New York: Signet Classics, 1964).

[17] Fredric Jameson, *The Political Unconscious* (Ithaca: Cornell University Press, 1981), p. 184.

[18] Jean-Paul Sartre, *Being and Nothingness,* trans. Hazel E. Barnes (New York: Philosophical Library, 1956), p. 609. A typically sticky description of a physical environment in the naturalists occurs in Gissing's *The Nether World:* "Rain had just begun to fall, and with it descended the smut and grime that darkened above the houses; the pavement was speedily over-smeared with sticky mud, and passing vehicles flung splashes in every direction. Odours of oil and shoddy, and all such things as characterised the town, grew more pungent under the heavy shower."

Patricia Reynaud (essay date 1994)

SOURCE: "Economics as Lure in *Madame Bovary,*" in *Money: Lure, Lore, and Literature,* edited by John Louis DiGaetani, Greenwood Press, 1994, pp. 163-74.

[*In the following essay, Reynaud examines the economic metaphors in Flaubert's* Madame Bovary *that relate to debt, borrowing, investing, and an entire system contaminated by fortune.*]

To read *Madame Bovary* as a novel dealing with political economics, to see how economic metaphors are disseminated in the narrative, seems more to pertain to the category of wager *(gageure)* than to rest on a certainty best symbolized by the gold exchange standard *(gage-or)* as the full convertibility of currency into gold. The play on words (better rendered in French) can appear rather far-fetched and even unreliable, but it will subsequently be justified within the perspective of this chapter, in which falsity is certainly the surest value upon which to rely. When Flaubert's novel was published, the system of the gold exchange standard, although still in existence, was undergoing the first signs of its decline. This system gradually became a wager, a shift that enables me to elaborate the uses of metaphors. If traditionally this figure of speech consists in giving to a thing a name that belongs to another, how is it still possible to adequately convert the meaning? In linguistics and in economics the sign is losing credibility and the security of money, or of the repository of signifieds backing it up, is gradually eroding. Metaphor as a transfer of meaning invests homologous relationships in the prosaic route of transfers of money scattered throughout the book and might lead to abusive uses and to the likelihood of fraud.

The metaphor, however, cannot be bypassed and is a necessary detour claimed as an act of renunciation to the literal in order to apprehend economics in Flaubert's text. Like metaphors, economics is prone to distance itself from the nominal value, which, after all, is a conventional value, to substitute for it with a market price. In this light, the homology between economics and metaphor becomes striking and is portrayed by the logic of the detour of meaning and/or funds. Metaphor is a borrowing of a figurative meaning which is in transit between contexts. Another type of borrowing at the level of the plot makes Emma fall in the economy of loss. Certain episodes of the book are relevant to this logic: an example is the letter from Rodolphe to Emma, breaking off their relationship, which yields a twofold interpretation. Through some words, some clichés, the process of writing acts as the revealing principle of an underlying economic system. For instance, the French term *usure* (usury and erosion) is a metaphor for the writing of the letter since Rodolphe is tired of his involvement, which he sees only as an erosion of feelings; but *usure* also connotes the effigy on a coin which has worn off with time. Illegitimate intercourse is like forged currency in circulation and usury is, in the book, the prohibitive interest rate that Lheureux (a merchant and a usurer) applies to the money he lends to Emma. *Usure* is a result of a too-frequent "use" of partners, feelings, and objects. This concept is in direct opposition to scarcity, according to which the value of a good is so high that it is beyond reach, outside of use. Proliferation of objects and signs from domains so opposed as the sentimental and the monetary conspires and leads to their irremediable devaluation.

Mystification is indeed a problem in this context: the monetary sign represented by the promissory note is autonomous and unchecked in its circulation. Instead of losing value with repeated uses, its value increases even more with each endorsement, each signature. It poses a challenge to the economic law of scarcity and constitutes the keystone upon which surplus value is erected.

One possible interpretation of the letter from Rodolphe to Emma is the portrayal of her lover as a forger, one who writes inflamed but false feelings using *lieux communs* and clichés. This letter is but the epiphenomenon of a generalized piece of trickery, whereby great principles never pass the stage of good intentions. Economics is to be found everywhere in the letter: in various metaphors, in either the comparing or the compared term which relates to precise economic categories such as debt, borrowing, and investing. Econom-

ics is also explicitly present in other episodes such as the ball of La Vaubeyssard, which equates (and trivializes) the aristocratic world with the power of money in an all-too-obvious manner. A dazzled Emma perceives only the deceptive appearance of wealth as she reduces the signs of wealth to their exchange value. Thus she fits into the definition of fetishism as conceived by Marx. The general equivalent of commodities in its money form was first constituted to be a reflection of any possible commodity and therefore to facilitate transactions. But it soon assumes a dominant position as it becomes the reflection of that for which it was originally created, that for which it was playing the role of an equivalent. This general equivalent finally imposes its domination by the enforcement of the law and by the forgetting of its genesis as a supplementary and cultural creation. This alienation proper to the capitalist system is better known as "the ideology of the owner" or an absolute contamination by wealth which attributes a price to everything, human beings included. Even if Emma is contaminated to the point of yielding to the principle of exchange, her relatively free space should not be denied. Because of her ties to the imaginary world, she somehow manages to exceed the principle of exchange. Not having to earn the money she lavishly spends on her lover, she can even afford to spend more than her husband's earnings. That is, for a time, before accounts are settled and she has to pay back society for her debts as much as for her provocative behavior. Her squandering, however, cannot be confused or reconciled with the notion of the total gift seen as the direct negation of a world of bourgeois calculations.

The tangible secret of her spending lies in the signature of promissory notes. The amount of these notes soon becomes uncontrollable and their circulation follows the particular logic of circularity. The monetary standard, or what we have called the general equivalent, originates in a legal decision but eventually acquires a transcendental position resulting in the imposition of its norm on all other commodities, excluding itself from them. It activates the principle of reiteration: the standard is guaranteed by a reserve of gold but what guarantees the gold itself? The spiraling movement proves that gold does not guarantee anything anymore and that the mechanisms of repetition are self-generated without anyone's being accountable. The gold reserve, once safe and reliable is, in the text, shattered in its founding principle by lies and fiction. The mechanisms of the promissory note are just a way to anticipate the necessary evolution toward a script currency whose reserve is no longer actual: such are the instruments of credit when payments are made by simple compensation and when banknotes are unconvertible. But Emma, trapped by the implacable mechanism of borrowing, hangs her only hope of escape on the ethereal mystification of religion. This escape meets economic utilitarianism in a dual fashion: first, she conveniently forgets a pressing need to repay her debts, and second, she only accepts the precious religious objects (she wants to buy a prie-dieu encrusted with emeralds in order to pray properly!). For all her flaws, she refuses to the end to be constituted according to the thematics of detour, a fundamental category in economics which replaces immediate consumption with consumption that is deferred and based on anticipated calculations.

Emma's system can be apprehended as a reflexive deflation, a paralysis in the flow of narration. The heaviness of her dominant mood, the spleen, is then rendered in ways escaping ordinary temporality. But, when economics or calculation is described, directly or metaphorically, the rhythm of the novel accelerates as if inflation were creeping into the plot and prevents further descriptive pauses. At these frantic moments, writing becomes a factual narration with no intervention or value judgment from the narrator, with no mention of intentionality. This symbolically means that surplus value can be calculated without its formation being comprehensible. While being created, surplus value follows a mysterious process of development. According to a similar logic, the careful management of the couple's budget (before Emma starts spending on lovers) and Emma's practical sense, reflecting her bourgeois constitution (which she can never totally overcome, even in her fantastic dream world), are a set of attitudes formally expressed in the lack of interpretative statements, as if the author's strategy were to save his words now, in order to better waste them on gratuitous descriptions, metaphors, or images defying a common logic, the reductive logic based on calculations.

Some microepisodes consist of indirect indictments of Flaubert's society on a global level. Such is the episode of the blind man, who, at the end, is imprisoned. The episode bears witness to the change of perspective of public authorities with respect to the definition of poverty. According to the new mentality (and morality), every individual must be useful, must somehow serve the productive machinery which itself serves the higher purpose of profitability. In another instance, Emma remains utilitarian even when she throws her money to the poor. Her bourgeois character, being used to reduce costs, resurfaces in her most generous gestures. Her gift is thus a disguised loan in which the giver is not the loser in the transaction. The scheme of unproductive spending is reduced to the principle of the balancing of an account, of compensation between profits and loss. For these very reasons, the relationship between debtor and creditor prevails in a book in which everything and everybody have become exchange values. By operating another detour, this time through Hegelian philosophy, we come back to the character Lheureux, the usurer who speculates on the work of others and makes profitable investments while Emma,

seen from an economic perspective, does not accomplish much. All her endeavors are doomed to fail. The reality of a housewife's work was at best imaginary and, at worst, the lot of lower social strata such as Emma's daughter's wet nurse. Thanks to her supposed idleness, however, Emma subverts the classical category of utility. Her (few) grandiose gestures are evidence of her way of overcoming rational economics, a category also called restrictive economics by George Bataille. Her countersystem is diffused and experienced by the reader through sensations of liquidity, lost energies, degradation, and death. Emma re-creates unproductive values, the most subversive being her downfall, which she accepts as the only option offered to her by society. The Hegelian dialectic also applies to Emma's masculine counterpart, Lheureux, who loses in autonomy (with respect to the system) what he gains through speculation as he becomes debtor of a society which uses him to reproduce itself.

Flaubert's novel is a complex book, impossible to read without attributing an array of contradictory meanings to the deeds, thoughts, and words of the characters. As soon as simplification by approximation is applied, falsification can easily be a consequence. Measure, regularity, and norms only provide an ideal case of representation not accountable in terms of residues, discrepancies, and overflow. This appreciation is also another way of rendering the main impression made by this literary work: the real is a considerable impoverishment of the imaginary world. The principle of liquidity, blood as well as meaning, pertains to the era of a defiant economy, an economy that challenges utility, an economy gradually becoming pleasurable. But what are we to do with a meaning which is no longer reducible to its usefulness and whose value henceforth is derived from the price paid for renouncing the affective needs it has previously crushed? The dichotomy between the two economies, between the twofold meaning of liquidity, the restrictive economy as mastery over meaning and general economics as "sovereignty" (in Bataille's words) linked to loss, is struggling throughout Flaubert's novel.

Flaubert seemingly deals with a realistic topic, that of portraying the morals of a French woman living in the provinces during the nineteenth century. In fact, and this fact is corroborated by his correspondence, he denounces the servility of meaning to become the subject of an all-powerful master: style, which he sees as a noncompensated loss, a style through which knowledge and truth disintegrate when faced with the creative impulse in the signifiers, metaphors, and images. Such an attitude leaves the reader with the impossibility of attributing an authoritative meaning to a text lacking any conclusive value or statement. Flaubert's vaunted doctrine of impartiality and formal innovations are partly responsible for the reader's invigorating sense of alienation. His point, claimed in one of his letters, is "to make a mystery of the moral and beneficient meaning of the book" (*Letters* 229). This provocative idea is not as original as it seems. It is an idea flowing in the *air du temps* as it tries to extricate any signs of a detested social anchoring from literary texts. Following the same vein, in the poetic genre, the influence of the movement called "Le Parnasse" touches larger audiences as it defines the beautiful as the negation of the useful, consequently becoming a marketable endeavor but, ironically, one which contests the no less successful theories on the market economy and free enterprise.

This unheard-of superiority of nonmeaning over meaning leads Flaubert to be fascinated by the problem of stupidity made manifest by the massive use of accepted conventions, consumed in abundance by all of the characters in the novels. Using clichés sparingly would contradict Flaubert's perspective, as he bets on stupidity to become a conceptual category which has invaded all relations in his society. Stupidity is also a structural category for his novel, as it touches everyone, regardless of his or her intelligence. Stupidity is a social illness which contaminates first and foremost the bourgeois without respecting privileges due to social hierarchy. Thus the particular (and most insidious) stupidity of the pharmacist Homais is concretized by his adopting a rhetorical discourse inflated with anticlerical statements, in fact a mere reprise of the official discourse of science, one which pays off at the time. Homais is always prone to adopting the fashionable traits reinforcing his image of a modern man emancipated from the obscurantism of the Catholic priests. His critical attitude, however, never questions in depth the sociopolitical and economic order since this order enables him to climb the social ladder (in the end, he is decorated by the state authorities for his alleged contributions to the progress of science). Of a different kind is Emma's stupidity. Hers consists of accepting the forged currency of her society as well as forging it herself in her imagination: "She sees the sentimental world as a market where it is only necessary to pay so that desired realities materialize" (Riggs 258).

The most devastating stupidity is the one wanting to conclude or to close the text. The author categorically refuses to yield to the hackneyed mechanisms of closure, a refusal expressed through the use of formal techniques such as indirect free style, or by assigning an obsessive role to the object, by using provocative narrative tenses which often freeze the plot and dilate durations in an unprecedented manner, and by giving more importance to the musicality of signifiers than to the set meaning of signifieds. For Flaubert knows, by contemplating Emma in her contradictions, that words, when reduced to signifieds, are also traps retaining only an exchange value. As for their use value, it is a

myth. Flaubert's resistance also demonstrates the inscription of his book into modernity, a consequence which leads me into the intricacies of a Derridean analysis as it ill treats logocentrism in the dyad identity-truth.

In his book *Philosophical Perspectives on Metaphor* Marc Johnson examines the semantics of metaphor. His point of departure is the Aristotelian definition according to which metaphor is considered "a deviance from literal usage, since it involves the transfer of a name to some object to which that name does not properly belong" (6). Thus, for Greek philosophers, the separation between literal and figurative meaning had serious consequences since metaphorical use is necessarily inscribed in a subsidiary use of a word challenging its initial definition. This history of metaphors has not been fixed and reduced to this classical interpretation. Recent works by Jacques Derrida, for instance, have aimed to reinsert in its prerogatives that which was previously excluded, the other of a universal definition. These works have enabled new elaboration with respect to the alleged illegitimacy of a transfer of meaning, with a view to reestablishing the analogy in its justified right to existence. As Aristotle would have it, metaphor is a deceptive device, which destroys the identity of the proper meaning since this meaning should not be scattered in derivative tracks. It also privileges feeling over reason, only because metaphors function as a reserve of meaning, a threatening residue capable of subverting an absolute meaning closed onto itself. Modernity has warned us against the arbitrariness of this closure which has to exclude the metaphoric game as well as the notion of exchange to preserve its coherence. The fraud resulting from a literal use supposedly uncompromised can be, in our semantic system, appropriately transferred to the economic detour of production, as well as the circulation of the monetary sign. If a fraud does exist as soon as a metaphor is used to convey a meaning, an easy inference could claim the existence of a premetaphorical thinking as a repository of an integral truth according to the logic that "metaphor is a deviant use of words in other than their proper senses, which accounts for its tendency to confuse and to deceive" (Johnson 13). Such is the argument claimed by empirical philosophers who argued that figurative meaning hinders the adequate expression of the integrity of our thinking. In *Madame Bovary,* I can exemplify this thematics of deceit in various ways and see how it functions in one episode of the book. This episode is narrated at the moment when Rodolphe writes to Emma, letting her know of his decision to put an end to their love affair, thus ruining her dreams of an escape with him. Ironically (irony is the main mode of this passage) Rodolphe adopts for himself the statement on metaphor we have just quoted as the narrator conveys to the readers the total indifference of his character hidden under romantic love clichés.

Approaching the metaphor, in a text which reads as a lie, is a tautology, since the trope, by definition, implies the replacement of a word by another. Furthermore, mystification as a higher form of deception represents the economic metaphor par excellence in Flaubert's book (an array of mystifying forces from the sentimental to the religious, from the value to the semiotic system as a whole). The choice of this episode is thus legitimized as the representative of the metaphor or arch-metaphor, subsumed in the economy of mystification to be inferred from the mystification of economics.

Metaphors also "save" in a literal reading which is sacrificed to a figurative meaning. The homology between this second level of reading and the fiduciary character of currency in which a fictitious value replaces the nominal value is now corroborated. Success depends on making an appropriate use of the metaphor, on not abusing the transfer of meaning that the trope implies, and on not being abused by the underlying economic system as is Emma. "A good metaphor places things in a new light, so that we can see them in a way we have never seen them before" (Johnson 7). The economic metaphor does shed a new light on the opacity of the Flaubertian novel.

Johnson argues that the decline of the metaphor in medieval thought was a consequence of its depreciation since "treated traditionally under rhetoric, it becomes a stylistic device divorced from serious philosophical argument" (9). But how could an economic logic be ignored, a logic still to be interpreted by resorting to the metaphorical thinking of detour and deviation? In this context, nominal would be to literal what real value is to figurative value. The real values still need further investigation in *Madame Bovary*. The point, however, is not to impose on Flaubert intentions alien to his artistic endeavors: Flaubert has not spoken explicitly and literally about economics. Yet, economics is implied all through his book. Thanks to his numerous references such mechanisms as the promissory note, debts, and bankruptcy, the portrayal of a coherent system in the context of a liberal bourgeois society emerges. The interpretive task has to be pursued according to the principle that the reader provides the thesis of the novel and that this task is no longer a privilege reserved for the writer. The references to economics can be found on different levels: in the psychology of the characters (the relationships between Emma and Lheureux, the usurer), in the role of the objects and their proliferation (inflation), and even in the style, which is not exempt from value judgments despite the claimed impartiality of the narrative mode. For instance, the fragmentation of certain passages at times prevents the reader from giving a coherent meaning to some episodes, thus posing the problem of meaning, of property and ownership as well as their credibility.

The classical conception which tries to reduce the metaphor to an elliptical simile is also relevant to our analysis. Metaphors of the diegesis rest upon analogies in Flaubert's style. Here is one selected among many. The context is the following: Charles Bovary's mother comes to pay a visit to the young couple, and she makes known her bitterness now that her son neglects the maternal affection for his devoted love of his new wife, Emma: "and she observed the happiness of her son with a sad silence, like some ruined man who watches through the window-panes people sitting at table in his own old house" (Flaubert 55). A metaphor cannot be reduced to an analogy, but, for my purpose, the elimination of similes in which economics can be read, would have resulted in the denial of valuable information which helps sustain the main argument. This metaphor involves somebody who has gone bankrupt and for whom a window-pane acts as a screen to prevent the unmediated perception of phenomena observed inside his former house. It informs about the analogy between the decay of filial love and the loss of a fortune and is linked to the motive of opacity as the main economic motive of the book. Opacity, as the indirect cause of Emma's bankruptcy, symbolizes the impossibility of making sense of economic calculations as well as, on a larger scale, the mystified relationships of woman to man, objects, and institutions. The quotation is otherwise relevant. In the course of the philosophical tradition, opacity has been associated with a degradation of a prime vision, a solid ground for meaning as if the figurative ground on which metaphors are built is slippery.

Jacques Derrida sets out to deconstruct the contradictory presuppositions of a metaphysics embedded in the Western mythology of the logos and the proper. Since, without resorting to metaphors, the task of reasserting an original and nonmetaphoric meaning is an impossible one, the faulty reasoning has proven its inadequacy and its constructedness is confirmed. There is no original meaning anchored in a presence even through infinite regression. The Derridean logic (or the lack of it) about the impossibility of the proper to be rendered in a total transparency not yet attacked by a metaphor is useful for this chapter in revealing that, if opacity is considered the property of the metaphor, it can also appropriately be considered the property of economics. A conventional image used to describe metaphor is that it is part and parcel of the definition of the trope "as if, so to speak, a word would be in a borrowed house" (Derrida 302). This deceptive definition, combined with the previous one on the obscure character of the trope, thematically corroborates Flaubert's quotation and reasserts my concern to read it following a logic determined by economics. Derrida, in *Margins of Philosophy,* quotes Du Marsais, a French philosopher who, in the seventeenth century, tried to reinstate the argumentation of the classical philosophers. For Du Marsais, the double context of obscurity and dwelling is that which defines the metaphor ontologically, precisely because, as

Derrida points out, the economic value of the house, or the proper, is systematically referred to as soon as the definition of the metaphor is at stake:

> It is a metaphor of the metaphor, expropriation, to be outside of one's own home, but still to be in a dwelling place, outside of one's home but in another metaphoric home where one can find oneself, be oneself, be together outside of oneself in oneself. Such is the philosophical metaphor as a detour in view of reappropriation. (302)

I would like to borrow and play with the presupposition attacked by Derrida according to which "philosophy as a theory of metaphor was at first a metaphor of theory" (303). Literature in the nineteenth century, when read as a means to inform one about Flaubert's unconscious, appears as an economy of metaphors because it is first and foremost an economic metaphor. And since opacity is encouraged by modernity in Flaubert and post-modernity in Derrida, I will suppose that and justify how any permutation of my terms remains adequate. In this way, it is also plausible to read economics as the theory of the metaphor, in that economics deals with exchange mechanisms and, as in the metaphoric transfer of meaning, any exchange can finally result in a dupery. It is also permissible to see an inscription of the metaphor in economics which, like the trope, cannot escape its constitutive premises more than the metaphor escapes its own. And at last, why not consider economics as a metaphor of literature, both fields participating in the process of regulation of exchanges?

Returning to Derrida's metaphor (on dispossession subsequent to the loss of an origin defined in its fullness) leads to further consequences. "To be outside of one's home but still in a dwelling place" could also mean, following a metaphorical logic of substitution, to be in an inn. One of *Madame Bovary*'s critics considers that Emma's somnambulistic journey goes through several inns. He defines it as somnambulistic because "she never meets the real, which is also the one defined by class conflicts" and not only the other of her dream world:

> Fake subsidiaries of her original home, landmarks on a closed-in tour: Lion d'Or-Croix Rouge-Hotel de Boulogne-Croix Rouge-Lion d'Or-home. Each of these places looks like the first one of the Quartier Saint Gervais at which her father stopped with her on the way to the convent and where she had already discovered on painted plates the rudimentary spells keeping her forever prisoner of the dominant ideology. (Picard 94)

With the journey to these inns evolving in a circular way, metaphor as a turn of language is finally evoked, as the last metaphor defining the metaphor. The previous Derridean statement is once more asserted in that it is impossible to return to the original home, or proper

meaning, without resorting to a metaphor, a home temporarily borrowed. This is a difficult statement to prove faulty in our Flaubertian quotation, since the original home henceforth belongs to its new owners and since the transfer of money and title have abolished the initial guarantee of property.

This diegetic metaphor, as we have discussed, deals with an opacity of vision. Max Black studies the image of the screen to describe how metaphors work:

> Suppose I look at the night sky through a piece of heavily smoked glass on which certain lines have been left clear. Then I shall see only the stars that can be made to lie on the lines previously prepared upon the screen, and the stars I do see will be seen as organized by the screen's structures. We can think of a metaphor as such a screen and the system of "associated commonplaces" of the focal work as the network of lines upon the screen. We can say that the principal subject is "seen through" the metaphorical expression—or, if we prefer, that the principle subject is "projected upon" the field of the subsidiary subject. (Johnson 75)

The theory of the metaphor and economic analysis meet in the similarity of their preoccupation with such themes as the proper/property, appropriation or its contrary, exchange, usury and detour. But the notion of metaphor goes beyond the simple analogy of words or syntagmas:

> We use one entire system of commonplaces to filter or organize our conception of some other system. The interaction is a screening of one system of commonplaces by another to generate a new conceptual organization of, a new perspective on, some subject. (Johnson 28)

In Flaubert's case, the one system of commonplaces is the ruined person and the other is the end of the privileged mother/son relationship after the son's marriage. The filter, as the attitude in front of a bankruptcy and the incomprehension of its inner mechanisms, pertains to economics. I regard it as the theoretical way of understanding a possible reading of the novel, one which reveals a new interpretation of a canonical work of literature.[1] Any metaphor is puzzling in dispersing an alleged primary meaning read through a second one, thus inscribing itself as a loan between two series, "a transaction between contexts" according to I. A. Richards (Johnson 40). Just as a black room is necessary to render the image of a normal vision, ideology offers the readers the image of inverted relationships which, thanks to the metaphorical eye, will be able to reappear noninverted. As a conclusive remark, I offer a quotation of M. Black: "If some metaphors are what might be called cognitive instruments indispensable for perceiving connections that, once perceived, are then truly present, the case for the thesis would be made out" (Johnson 41). This statement corroborates my own work on the space of intersection of literature and economics when applied to *Madame Bovary*. The reading strategy offered here would not have been possible without the possibility offered by metaphors of bringing into fruitful relationships new conceptual rapports. If originality is indeed the result (with respect to traditional readings of the well-known novel), it is no longer based on the metaphysics of the proper and property. This reading needed the use of metaphors as a loan in order to exist and can no longer claim to be a creation *ex nihilo,* another common ideology caught in the problematics of logocentric interpretation.

Notes

[1] Certain difficulties arise when a critique of canonical works is at stake. The sacred edifice of Culture has taught us that its authorities monopolize the discourse of truth. Any new interpretation is an adventure and any adventure entails a risk. But, after all, the risk is a basic concept of liberal economics.

Works Cited

Bataille, Georges. *La Part maudite.* Paris: Les Editions de Minuit, 1967.

Derrida, Jacques. *Marges de la philosophie.* Paris: Les Editions de Minuit, 1972.

Flaubert, Gustave. *Madame Bovary.* Trans. W. Blaydes. New York: P. F. Collier and Son, 1902.

————. *The Letters of Gustave Flaubert.* Vol. 2 Trans. Francis Steegmuler. Cambridge: Harvard University Press, 1982.

Johnson, Marc. *Philosophical Perspectives on Metaphor.* Minneapolis: University of Minnesota Press, 1981.

Picard, Michel. "La prodigalité d'Emma Bovary." *Littérature* 10 (mai 1973): 94.

Riggs, Larry. "La Banqueroute des idéaux reçus dans *Madame Bovary.*" *Aimer en France: 1760-1860.* Clermont-Ferrand: Association des Publications de la Faculté des Lettres et Sciences Humaines, 1988.

John A. Frey (essay date 1994)

SOURCE: "Mammon's Finger in the Novels of Balzac, Zola, and Gide," in *Money: Lure, Lore, and Literature,* edited by John Louis DiGaetani, Greenwood Press, 1994, pp. 175-83.

[*In the following essay, Frey discusses money as a metaphor, a medium of exchange, and as a symbol of power and control in the nineteenth-century novel.*]

> No servant can be the slave of two masters; for either he will hate the first and love the second, or he will be devoted to the first and think nothing of the second. You cannot serve God and Money.
>
> Matthew: 6,24

Money is a metaphor, a medium of exchange for goods and services; it is also a symbol of power and control. Images on currency denote intentional metaphorical value. Coins are imprinted with representations of presidents, queens, and kings. Religious and political slogans are presented, such as "In God we Trust" or "Liberty, Equality, and Fraternity." Economics and aesthetics join on script and postage stamps to pay homage to the arts and sciences, to our heroes and heroines. Money language offers positive similes: "he is as good as gold," and negative ones: "as phony as a three-dollar bill"; "not worth a red cent."

In this chapter money is regarded as intrinsic to the narrative structure and to the metaphorical fields accompanying it. The main argument is that focus on money can be seen as a unifying device for the pondering of moral dilemmas of modern societies under the impact of the development of capitalism and the rise of the middle class as a power agent with its own ethical agenda.

Molière's *Miser* (1668) marks the first appearance in France of the modern money problem. Although derived from Plautus, this play does go beyond stock dramatic figuration, suggesting dark personality problems more complex than the simple hoarding of money. On its heels, Lesage's *Turcaret* (1709) develops what is incipient in Molière, that is, the development of the modern money-oriented personality. Turcaret starts out as a lowly lackey, but financial speculation turns him into a powerful financier. At the play's end he is financially ruined, and another lackey replaces him at the top of the financial world.

Lesage's world of servants becoming masters is overshadowed and transformed by the consequences of the French Revolution, and these changes will be first noted fictionally in Balzac's depiction of French society in the first half of the nineteenth century. Zola's depiction of the Second Empire shows the acceleration of forces unleashed by the events of 1789-1815, and by the developing Industrial Revolution. Gide can rightfully be viewed by his dates (1869-1951) as a man of both centuries. He continues the pondering, through fiction, of the meanings of money as found in Balzac and Zola, but in his work there are some fundamental shifts or modifications of the money metaphor.

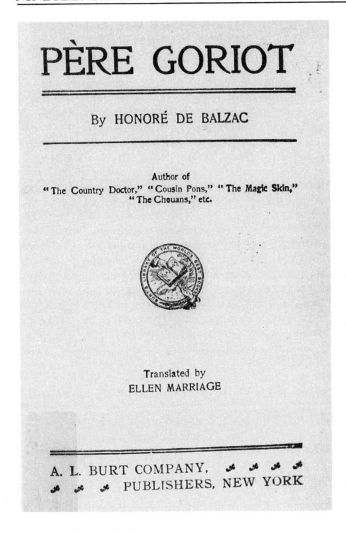

PÈRE GORIOT

By HONORÉ DE BALZAC

Author of
"The Country Doctor," "Cousin Pons," "The Magic Skin,"
"The Chouans," etc.

Translated by
ELLEN MARRIAGE

A. L. BURT COMPANY,
PUBLISHERS, NEW YORK

Balzac's *Human Comedy* depicts the triumph of the bourgeois spirit following the French Revolution. The novel presents a world of moneylenders, bankers, speculators, creditors, and gamblers. It also portrays an underworld of criminals wearing disguises so as to infiltrate, sabotage, and capture the world of money and its facades. Talented crooks, like Balzac's Vautrin, anticipate the world of Gide's adolescent counterfeiters and the swindlers of *Lafcadio's Adventures.*

Money in Balzac's world is a metaphorical code for moral turpitude. Moral flaw is ultimately traced back to obsession with power, be it sexual, political, or religious. Zola's focus is just more intense than that of Balzac. In the *Rougon-Macquart,* money indeed makes the world go round; the stock market is the motor piece of the series, but it implies other moral equivalencies.

Obsessive behavior in the novels of Balzac entails the expenditure of great sums of money, leading to the destruction of stable households (entities). Balzac, expressing a conservative outlook, believes that honesty and the practice of virtue can right financial wrongs. Thus, lascivious males are frequently if only temporarily rescued by redemptive females (angels). In *Search for the Absolute (La Recherche de l'absolu),* the mad alchemist loses the family fortune in his efforts to change raw ores into gold. Virtuous women work with success to reestablish financial stability, only to see it lost again, like the daily ups and downs of the stock exchange. Sexual obsession also leads to moral and financial ruin. *Cousin Betty (La Cousine Bette)* reiterates the sexual perversions of the Baron Hulot. His compulsive sexual behavior persists to the end of the novel, destroying family honor and fortune. Money in the world of Balzac has stolen society's soul; it is the springboard for moral decay.

Figuratively speaking, Balzac and Zola share a metaphorical field in which money as power is seen in terms of bellicose conquest and predatory behavior, wars, battles, attacking, destroying, consuming. Young romantic idealists learn quickly that society is not a realm of virtue but the site for monetary acquisition. Eugène de Rastignac, a young idealistic provincial, comes to Paris to study *(Old Goriot [Le Père Goriot]).* As a witness to the excessive filial devotion of Balzac's Goriot, who increasingly depletes his fortune to give money to his undeserving daughters, he attends the poor man's funeral (where only the daughters' empty carriages attend, for they are too preoccupied with their own affairs, getting their hair fixed, preparing for a ball), and from the heights of Père-Lachaise cemetery realizes the meaning of Paris: one must become an *arriviste* and obtain power through money and sex. Balzac's Restoration Paris is a dog-eat-dog world, and animal comparisons aptly pinpoint the ardent desire for money. To explain the avarice of Monsieur Grandet *(Eugénie Grandet),* the narrator uses a comparison with the predatory habits of cobras and tigers:

> Financially speaking, Mr. Grandet resembled the tiger and the boa: he knew how to stretch out, squat, consider for a long time his prey, and then to leap onto it; then he would open the mouth of his purse, swallowing up a load of coins and then going peacefully to sleep, like the serpent which digests its prey, without feeling, cold, methodical. (Balzac, III, 486; English translations of Balzac and Zola are by Frey)

Consistent metaphorical structures back up the money narrations in Balzac. The color yellow is dominant in *Eugénie Grandet,* relating to the color of gold and Monsieur Grandet's monetary obsessions. The miser's eyes are described as yellow; on his deathbed, as the priest presents a crucifix for his final kiss, it is only the yellow color of Christ's body which he sees.

Zola builds on the money novels of Balzac, amplifying for the Second Empire what Balzac had done for the world of the Restoration. Balzac's world represents the birth of bourgeois power, of nascent mercantilism, the start of the Industrial Revolution and its potential for enrichment. Zola's world of the *Rougon-Macquart* represents the frenzy of acquisition and consumerism. It also underlines the economic extremes of the very rich and the very poor (Furst).

That money relates to power and class ascendancy is poignantly revealed in the plight of Mother Perou of *Pot-Bouille.* This poor old lady is employed by Gourd, the concierge of an apartment building, to sweep the courtyard and do other domestic duties. Her earnings are four cents per hour. Gourd himself had been a servant, but having risen to the rank of concierge, he will take his revenge on what he used to be: "He spoke . . . of old woman Perou with a spirit of brutal domination, the enraged need for revenge of former domestics who in their turn are being waited upon" (Zola, III, 99).

The revenge pattern of former servants persecuting servants echoes class warfare as perceived in Balzac's *The Peasants.* Zola is summarizing what was intuited by the mature Balzac, namely that modern capitalism induces cupidity and the desire for upward mobility (Vernon 147).

Zola's novels explain economic suppression and demonstrate economic power and the lust for it. Such is the world of *La Curée* and *Money (L'argent),* wherein real estate and stock market speculation are the enriching elements of the nouveaux riches of the Second Empire. Zola calls it the "rage to spend" (III, 187), and his novels abound with examples of lurid consumerism, spending for its own sake, vulgarly, without discretion or discrimination. Uncle Bachelard, a minor character in *Pot-Bouille,* likes to eat out in expensive restaurants, ordering meals not from a sense of taste, but from the idea of spending: "He would order whatever was the most expensive, gastronomic curiosities, even the uneatable" (Zola, III, 187).

Au Bonheur des dames, a novel exploring the development of the new idea of the department store, analyzes modern techniques of merchandising. Interpreted in terms of our own society, it could be called the novel of the credit card syndrome. Given the extreme poverty of late nineteenth-century France, the supercilious spending of the rich is morally untenable. The conclusion of *La Curée* describes the death of the heroine, Renée, who leaves behind a bill with her hairdresser, a debt of 257,000 francs (Zola, I, 599).

Money is symbolic of the entire *Rougon-Macquart* series. It reintroduces Aristide Saccard of *La Curée,* husband of Renée, back in Paris trying to rebuild his fortune. Previously Saccard had made a fortune through real estate speculation during the rebuilding of the right bank of Paris by Haussmann. Saccard now plunges into financial speculation. His scheme is simple enough: he asks for investments from pious Catholics for his *banque universelle,* which plans to create a new Christian kingdom of Jerusalem, with the idea of moving the Pope there from Rome. In his financial dealings, Saccard is in financial warfare with the Jewish banking firm of Gundermann, and these two forces of capitalism, associated with two religious cultures, are played out against a third force, that of Sigismond, the scholarly revolutionary and friend of Karl Marx. The elements of socialism and communism, unspoken in Balzac, erupt now in the world of Zola.

As with Balzac, the narrative structure of finance is reinforced with metonymic and metaphorical fields which give the narration its symbolic meaning. *Money*'s narrative hammers away at the idea of an increasing tempo of increase in capital value, the division and subdivision of stocks, increases in growth and national productivity. These inflationary modes are translated into an imagery which suggests relationships with idolatry and conquest, culminating in a major metaphorical field of money.

Balzac and Zola, unlike Gide, represent an argument against capitalism and materialism, based on fundamentally old-fashioned conservative arguments—Balzac, regretting the loss of prerevolutionary France, Zola, seeking an honest bourgeois way of dealing with life, based on a work ethic. Gide will turn the money argument into one of escape from bourgeois restraints.

Zola believed that the materialism of the Second Empire was destroying the very fabric of French society. He saw a new liturgy coming into being in the cult of money. *Nana* tells of the adventures of a sex goddess created by money. Berthe Josserand of *Pot-Bouille* has been raised in a society which recognizes only money as God: "all this religion of money whose cult she had learned in her family" (Zola, III, 243). In *Germinal* the workers do not know for whom they work, but they sense it is some hidden god somewhere in Paris. It is plainly stated in *Money:* "Money, king money, god money" (Zola, V, 220). Money is sacred and will take on the garments of religion, which give it respectability. In *Money,* Saccard supervises the decoration of his new bank. It must have a severe look, should smell like a sacristy, and customers will get the impression that they are entering a devout establishment. Employees are taught to speak in measured tones, and "money is received and given with an entirely clerical discretion" (Zola, V, 139).

Money as warfare, as battle, was noted in Balzac, in Rastignac's challenge to the business world of Paris. This imagery is intensified in Zola with the financial challenges accepted by Saccard. Saccard's Middle East scheme for swindling gullible Catholics of their money involves a curious constellation of images combining echoes back to the Crusades with more recent images of the conquests of Bonaparte. What had not been accomplished by the Crusades, and what Napoleon had failed to do, would now be realized by Saccard's financial enterprise: "What Napoleon could not do with his sword, this conquest of the Orient, a financial company would accomplish it" (Zola, V, 253).

Saccard's financial empire, however, collapses, and instead of conquest we have rout and defeat. The narrator changes Saccard into a Bonaparte, and the floor of the stock market into the battlefield of Waterloo:

> Instead of the expected help, was this a new enemy coming from the neighboring woods? As at Waterloo, Grouchy was not showing up, and it was betrayal which completed the rout. . . . Well, during the last half hour it was debacle, the rout growing and carrying along the crowd. . . . There were no more purchases, the field was strewn with cadavers. . . . But in the hall of the stock market panic had above all been blowing around Saccard, and it was there that the war had done its damage. (Zola, V, 328-30)

The most important metaphorical field in all of Zola's novels is that of variants on money as gold, coin, golden rain, seas of gold. They are found across the series, but specifically in *La Curée* and in *Money*. In the first, Saccard sits at a restaurant from the heights of Montmartre, and he sees the financial possibilities of Paris, a fabulous city transformed into a vision from a *Thousand and One Nights,* a city of gold. Money indeed becomes the central image of Zola's novels:

> "The rain of gold striking against the walls would come down more heavily every day." (Zola, I, 387)

> " . . . this mad dance of millions." (Zola, V, 55)

> " . . . the hail of gold pieces, the dance of millions." (Zola, V, 116)

> " . . . the rain of gold which was to rain on him and around him." (Zola, V, 127)

As in the boa and tiger image of Balzac, there is the fusion of the real world of finance and its metaphorical equivalencies. Money in these nineteenth-century novels is a figure representing moral decay, empowerment, and disenfranchisement. Gide will also explore the meaning of money, but will relate it less in terms of the rich and the poor, and more in terms of moral depravity. He attacks money as a symbol of the moral hypocrisy of the French middle class. This occurs as a product of his Calvinistic upbringing, and his confrontation with his homosexuality. Money will be Gide's metaphor for exploring inauthenticity and sincerity,

enslavement and liberation. A complicated web of personality issues related to society comes into focus in two of his major prose works, *Lafcadio's Adventures* (*Les Caves du Vatican,* 1913), and *The Counterfeiters* (*Les Faux-Monnayeurs,* 1926).

Money is the backdrop for *Lafcadio's Adventures* and acts as symbolic motif for multiple character permutations in *The Counterfeiters.* The complex story of Lafcadio, a modern picaresque hero, is played out against the absurd plot of a so-called kidnapping of Pope Leo XIII by the free masons, and the installation of a fake masonic pope on the papal throne. This is a hoax to get rich pious Catholics to contribute money for the pope's release, a scheme devised by the underworld antihero, Proto. Textually, the plot seems to be a humorous and sardonic continuation of Zola's *Money.* The word *counterfeiters* in the title alludes not only to a novel of the same name being written by one of the main narrators, the novelist Edouard, but also to a ring of small-time crooks at a Protestant boarding school whose ring leader, Strouvilhou, is an underworld anarchist. *Counterfeit* is code in this novel for a variety of artificialities and reversals of moral orders.

In both of these works there exists a tension between what is and what seems to be, between sincerity and hypocrisy, between social conventions and hidden mores, between the world of bourgeois conventions, and a hidden world, a demimonde. Disguise is an important element in both Balzac and Zola. The criminal Vautrin takes on many masks as he tries to hoodwink bourgeois society, and in Zola villains and crooks rise to the heights of power in society. Gide's world seems to be populated by persons who are not what they seem to be; they are fake, they are counterfeit. Gide wants to know how to get beyond that artificiality. Lafcadio has as a basic character trait the dissimulation of his true feelings and nature. This is a lesson he learned from an old school chum, Proto. Lafcadio had once scolded Proto about his ability to imitate anything and everything, and was told in reply that the "important thing in this world was never to look like what one was" (Gide, *Lafcadio,* 90).

Proto is a master of disguise as he sets about his embezzlement schemes. Disguised as a canon of Virmonthal, he gets a huge sum of money from a pious countess. Dressed as a French abbé, he enlists Amedée Fleurissoire into the crusade for the deliverance of the pope. In a final disguise which fools and entraps Lafcadio, he presents himself as a lawyer from the Bordeaux law faculty.

Both Gide texts present a world where moral values are tottering. There is widespread cheating, lying, stealing, snooping, reading other people's journals and letters. In both works illegitimacy becomes a major concern and interrelates with financial survival and inheritance. Lafcadio is illegitimate, as is Bernard Profitendieu. *The Counterfeiters* deals with one of society's deepest social disguises and the metaphors used for it, namely the question of homosexuality. Robert de Passavant is a notorious decadent and contrasts with Edouard the novelist. Both are homosexual and have affairs with young men (Bernard and Olivier). But all is concealed—the code word or metaphor for lover or kept boy is "secretary."

There is in addition the facade of bourgeois morality. In *Lafcadio's Adventures* this inauthentic world is represented by Julius de Baraglioul, whose burning ambition is entrance into the French Academy. *The Counterfeiters* allows Gide to scrutinize the French Protestant middle class from which he is seeking liberation. One example among many is that of Oscar Molinier, a proper father, concerned with the conduct of young people, including his sons, who seem to be engaging the services of prostitutes and also passing counterfeit coins. Trouble is in the air, and Molinier attributes this to the bad influence of Bernard, viewed as a corrupting influence because of his status as bastard.

> I had rather Olivier saw as little as possible of that young fellow. I have heard the most deplorable things about him—not that I'm much astonished at that. We must admit that there are no grounds for expecting any good from a boy who has been born in such unfortunate conditions. I don't mean to say that a natural child mayn't have great qualities—and even virtues; but the fruit of lawlessness and insubordination must necessarily be tainted with the germs of anarchy. (Gide, *Counterfeiters,* 215)

This judgmental attitude of Oscar Molinier is close to the moral hypocrisy found in Zola's novels. Here we have a man worrying about the education of children when he himself has a mistress which could also lead to the birth of a "bastard." Zola and Gide are both concerned with the double standards of society. Money becomes a discourse betraying other social categories: marriages and extramarital affairs, heterosexual love and homosexual liaisons, honest faces and masks, nakedness and disguise, real money and counterfeit.

Lafcadio is a young man who knows many languages and many currencies. Recounting his life story to Julius, the money images pop out of the page. It was his "uncle" Heldenbruck who contributed to his financial education:

> He was, it seems, a distinguished financier. As well as his own language he taught me arithmetic. . . . He made me what he used laughingly to call his "cashier"—that is, he gave into my keeping a whole fortune of petty cash and wherever we went together, it was I who had to do the paying. Whatever he bought . . . he insisted on my adding up the bill in as short a time as it took me to pull the notes or

coins out of my pocket. Sometimes he used to puzzle me with foreign money, so that there were questions of exchange; then of discount, of interest, of brokerage and finally even of speculation. (Gide, *Counterfeiters,* 86)

With such training in money and language, Lafcadio becomes the perfect multinational (another disguise), which for a brief moment leads him down the road to serious crime (the gratuitous murder of Amedée by pushing him off the train), much as the secret society manipulations lead to the suicide of young Boris in *The Counterfeiters.*

Both works, however, indicate a way out of a life of scheming and counterfeiting. Lafcadio is capable of virtue and he practices it by saving children from a burning building. He is also generous. As the work concludes, Lafcadio, who had always taught himself to hate possessions, is a whole person, liberated. We do not know his final decision; we cannot know whether or not he will turn himself over to the police. As for Bernard, having left home because of his discovery of his illegitimacy, he too is capable of generous actions (his feelings and love for the pregnant Laura). In a master stroke, the narrator has Bernard meet an angel from heaven at the Sorbonne; he wrestles with the angel and then returns home to be with the man who is not his real father. The novel announces the beginning of an authentic human relationship.

Gide has given new dimensions to the money question. He has turned the question of bourgeois morality, expressed through a money value system, into a discussion of the meaning of freedom, a freedom he had hoped to find in communism. Gide's quest for a communal society is partly born of his reading of the Acts of the Apostles, and from his recognition that a truly liberated person cannot serve both God and mammon.

In the works herein discussed, money has been viewed as meaning power (Vernon 99) but in the words of Marx, alienated power:

> In the *Grundrisse,* Marx shows how money can appear in the form of collateral. Men place their faith in this collateral because it is an objectified mutual relation between their productive activity. Every other collateral may serve the holder directly in the function of objectified exchange value. Money, however, serves him merely as "the dead pledge or mortgage" of society, but it serves as such only because of its social (symbolic) property; and it can have a social property only because individuals have alienated their own social relationship from themselves so that it takes the form of a thing. (Shell, 126. Shell cites the Marx test)

This alienation is certainly the meaning of money as accurately perceived by Gide in these two works, and it is an amplification of Zola's rage against the bourgeois world of the Second Empire, as well as Balzac's Marxist inclinations, albeit before the fact.

Works Cited

Balzac, Honoré de. *La Comédie humaine.* Paris: Bibliothèque de la Pléiade, 1967, III.

Furst, Lillian R. *L'Assommoir: A Working Woman's Life.* Boston: Twayne Publishers, 1990.

Gide, André. *The Counterfeiters, Les Faux-Monnayeurs,* translated from the French by Dorothy Bussy. New York: Alfred A. Knopf, 1947.

———. *Lafcadio's Adventures, Les Caves du Vatican,* translated from the French by Dorothy Bussy. Garden City, N.Y.: Doubleday and Company, 1953.

Shell, Marc. *Money, Language, and Thought.* Berkeley, Los Angeles, London: University of California Press, 1982.

Vernon, John. *Money and Fiction: Literary Realism in the Nineteenth and Early Twentieth Centuries.* Ithaca and London: Cornell University Press, 1984.

Zola, Emile. *Les Rougon-Macquart.* Paris: Bibliothèque de la Pléiade, 1960, I, III, V.

THE DANGERS OF MONEY

Michael Issacharoff (essay date 1988)

SOURCE: "Phynances," in *Nineteenth-Century French Studies,* Vol. 17, No. 1, Fall, 1988, pp. 208-15.

[*In the following essay, Issacharoff identifies some recurring themes involving money, including sexual exchange, inheritance, deception, humor, and the idea that money is usually not earned but rather either bequeathed, received unexpectedly, or obtained by deception.*]

Money, as Harry Levin put it recently,[1] if not the root of all evil, has been the whetstone of wit. My title, "phynances," is of course designed to suggest just that. But despite the reference to *Ubu,* my paper is *not* on Jarry, nor is it even in French. After all, one of the weapons of wit is surprise—what pleasure would there be in *any* literary text or for that matter in any literary enterprise without an element of the unexpected?

Though I would not make any claims to being a thematicist or thematologist, if the concept of theme still has any validity at all in the late 1980s, it seems to me that its methodological if not its epistemological bases need examining afresh with a critical eye. Why indeed, in the first place, *could* it be significant to focus on X in Y to the exclusion of all or virtually all else? And what precisely is a *theme* anyway? How exactly, supposing for the moment we know what the beast is, does a theme take shape in, say, a novel or in short fiction? Is there any fundamental difference between a theme in fiction and a theme in drama or poetry? Given the basic differences between the literary forms—especially those stemming from the respective channels of communication that are brought into play—it seems appropriate to bear in mind that a theme that takes shape orally and visually (i.e., in the drama) cannot be quite the same beast as the sort of thing that makes itself apparent to us as we thumb through the pages of a novel.

Let us start, then, with the manner in which *theme* has been defined in dictionaries of literary terminology. Todorov and Ducrot, for example, distinguish between *theme* and *motif* and define theme as follows: "une catégorie sémantique qui peut être présente tout au long du texte [. . .] motif et thème se distinguent [. . .] par leur degré d'abstraction et partant, par leur puissance de dénotation [. . .] Il est rare, mais non impossible que le thème soit aussi présenté par un mot dans le texte."[2] As Todorov and Ducrot point out, thematic analyses that use the archetypal typologies proposed by Jung, Bachelard, Northrop Frye and Durand (which have been the main bases for thematic study until recently) entail the risk of neglecting the specificity of literary texts, since they tend to oversimplify and distort. Definitions by many other critics are no less vague or confused—whether it be Richard's "constellation de mots, d'idées, de concepts,"[3] Deleuze's "archétype involontaire,"[4] Mauron's "mythe personnel obsédant,"[5] or Greimas's wordy dictum: "la dissémination des valeurs déjà actualisées par la sémantique narrative";[6] the lack of rigour in all of them is obvious. The problem too, in many cases, is that the actual determination of themes in a text is a highly subjective process that varies considerably from reader to reader.

Northrop Frye even goes as far as to equate *theme* and the Aristotelian concept of *dianoia,* or thought, observing that "the best translation of *dianoia* is, perhaps, 'theme,' and literature with this ideal or conceptual interest may be called thematic."[7]

In more recent years, attempts have been made—especially in the pages of *Poétique,* in a special issue,[8] to outline the fundamentals of what has been called "une nouvelle thématique." More useful, though, than most of what has been written about thematics, even recently, are criteria for "aboutness" suggested by philosophers such as Gilbert Ryle, who distinguishes between *linguistic* aboutness and *referential* aboutness.[9]

My focus in what follows is money as theme in a few obvious instances of nineteenth-century French texts in which it is foregrounded—as much as it is, say, in Shakespeare's *The Merchant of Venice* or in Molière's *L'Avare.* My corpus was selected on the basis of a very simple criterion—cases in which the theme is underscored by titles. Instances such as Dumas fils' play *La Question d'argent*[10] or Octave Mirbeau's turn-of-the-century *Les Affaires sont les affaires*[11] were obvious candidates. Balzac's *Gobseck, Eugénie Grandet* or *La Maison Nucingen,* Zola's *L'Argent,* Daudet's *Le Nabab* provide a wealth of possible examples as do plays such as Henri Becque's *Les Corbeaux* or Labiche's *La Cagnotte,* among others. Instances are thus hardly lacking in nineteenth-century French literature. The problem, though, is not to locate examples as much as to establish some sort of working criteria for suitable selection. The danger of random thematic study is precisely the arbitrariness of the possible results of such an inquiry, if one's purpose is to do more than just study X in Y, given that there are likely to be as many X's as there are Y's.

It seems to me that there are at least two distinct lines of inquiry entailed by a state-of-the-art thematic or thematological analysis. One can either attempt to throw light on the mechanics of thematic meaning by examining the ways in which themes are generated by the text. Alternatively perhaps, a suggestive project could be the semiotic investigation into the hidden meaning(s) of theme X—not just in specific text A, but potentially in any texts. This second line on inquiry—in its generality and in its "scientific" pretensions—is probably somewhat dubious, though, and no more valid, intrinsically, than Durand's enterprise in his *Structures anthropologiques de l'imaginaire.*[12] The pitfall implicit in such a project is the normative grid it is likely to elicit.

A more rigorous result is possible, I think, if one considers theme as a ques[sic] of *reference.*[13] The advantage of such a position is that it helps avoid the subjectivity that characterizes archetype-hunting as well as the pitfalls of the reductive "translation" of text into a roster of themes. It means too that, contrary to Todorov and Ducrot's comments about theme, for an element of a text to qualify as thematic unit, there has to be an explicit mention or mentions in the text. This does not, of course, imply that theme is restricted to *literal* verbal reference—since, obviously, in a literary text, A can always *mean* B. It does, on the other hand, impose the minimum requirement of a textual signal—a referent, in other words—pointing to what may be interpreted as theme X. The consequences of this strategy are (1) a rigorous textual requirement for thematic analysis and (2) a clear distinction that can then be drawn between thematic *signals* and the process of their interpretation.

The method I adopted enabled me to limit my corpus to texts in which the money theme on which I am focusing is central. To determine centrality, I used the commonsense yardstick of the title—not, I hasten to add, for hermeneutic purposes (that would of course be naive), but solely for the purpose of initial selection.

Since it is likely that the treatment of the theme is at least to some extent contingent, as I suggested earlier, on the literary form chosen by the writer, I thought it would be instructive to contrast literary genres, in this instance, fiction and drama. The constant element will be money as the central theme, thus throwing light on the variables that stem from the difference of genre.

With these criteria in mind, then, my first examples are from Maupassant's short stories, eight of which foreground the money theme in their titles: *Les Bijoux, La Parure, La Dot, Le Legs, Un Million, Le Testament, Les Vingt-cinq francs de la supérieure* and *L'Héritage.*[14] In these stories, money takes two forms: it is either jewellery or a legacy. In all eight cases, money either owned, loaned, bemoaned or eagerly awaited, is the principal motivation of the characters and the driving force of fictional action.

Of the four stories that focus on money in the form on inheritance, *Le Legs* is typical. M. and Mme Serbois, learning of the death of their friend Vaudrec, hope that he has remembered them in his will. Money is foregrounded by the title as well as by a mention in the opening exchange between the Serbois:

> "Vraiment, c'est bien étonnant!
> Sa femme demanda: Quoi donc, mon ami?
> —Que Vaudrec ne nous ait rien laissé."
> Mme Serbois rougit; elle rougit brusquement comme si un voile rose se fût étendu tout à coup sur sa peau en montant de la gorge au visage, et elle dit:
> "Il y a peut-être un testament chez le notaire."[15]

In this story the role of money is that of sexual exchange, since the will—Vaudrec leaves a million francs to *Mme* Serbois—is a form of pay-off that, initially, is an embarrassment to M. Serbois, for whom it provides an explicit proof of his wife's infidelity. His honour is at stake, unless he and his wife find some elegant subterfuge to make it appear as if the legacy was intended to be divided equally between them, rather than as a reward for Mme Servois' sexual favours. However, lured by lucre, Serbois is only momentarily troubled by the implications of the legacy with its implicit threat to his honour and self-respect, and convinces his wife that the only honourable solution is for him to accept a half-share. He thus succeeds in cleverly exploiting his wife's sexual guilt, which he turns into cash.

Un Million and *L'Héritage* are very similar. In both, a couple hope to inherit a fortune from a rich aunt. The wealthy aunt leaves a large sum of money, but with strings attached—both couples must have a child within three years of her death if they are to inherit. The two couples, after trying to fulfill the terms of the will in the normal way, fail and resort to an "arrangement" with a friend whose "services," provided at the eleventh hour, rescue the desperate legatees who stand otherwise to lose a fortune.

Whereas in *Le Legs,* the moral issue of conjugal fidelity is glossed over by a husband who is prepared to overlook his wife's infidelity provided that he benefits financially, in *Le Million* and *L'Héritage,* money is used to influence the behaviour of a couple after the death of the legator. However, the donor's intention is, of course, subverted, since the legatees find a convenient way of sidestepping the impasse and of still remaining beneficiaries.

Finally in this cycle of stories about wills, *Le Testament* exemplifies the use of cash as reward. Anne de Courcil leaves all her money to the illegitimate son who had really loved her, and nothing to her legal husband and two other sons whose only interest in her was monetary. The will is thus the manner of revenge open to the legator on her death for the indignity and humiliation suffered during her life.

La Dot, like *Le Legs,* foregrounds money both in the title and in the opening paragraph:

> Personne ne s'étonna du mariage de Me Simon Lebrument avec Mlle Jeanne Cordier. Me Lebrument venait d'acheter l'étude de Me Papillon: il fallait, bien entendu, de l'argent pour la payer; et Mlle Jeanne Cordier avait trois cent mille francs liquides, en billets et en titres au porteur.[16]

Unlike the legacy stories, *La Dot* is about deception, with money as motive. Simon marries Jeanne and then makes off with her dowry. In contrast to the other protagonists who benefit from the wills of wealthy relatives, Simon, an unprincipled fellow, calculates that the quickest means to his end is to make off with the cash just after deceiving his wife into marrying him. Though the strategy is unscrupulous, the manner of his escape is comic—he gives his wife the slip, during their visit to Paris, by pretending to go for a smoke on top of a coach. The beauty of the deception lies in its simplicity.

The two jewellery stories—*La Parure* and *Les Bijoux*—complement each other. Both have an unexpected ending. In *La Parure,* Mme Loisel loses the diamond necklace loaned to her by a friend, and she and her husband spend ten years of their lives earning enough to pay for what turn out to be imitation diamonds. In *Les Bijoux,* on the other hand, the protagonist discovers, after his wife's sudden death, that all her jewellery, that he had assumed was paste, is genuine, and worth a fortune. Thematically, *Les Bijoux* really belongs with the legacy stories, since it is about money as inheritance. The implication too is similar to that of the legacy stories-money as sign of sexual favour. The couple in *Les Bijoux* are too poor to acquire the jewellery by normal means—the wife must therefore have received the jewellery in exchange for sexual favours. The husband, like M. Serbois in *Le Legs,* is thus the financial beneficiary of his wife's infidelity.

Finally, *Les Vingt-cinq francs de la supérieure* is yet another illustration of money as motivating force of an action other than intended by its donor. Père Pavilly, while in hospital with a broken leg, pleases the ward sister by singing hymns in the hospital chapel. On his recovery, the sister gives him 25F for his services. Pavilly, though, decides to go and spend it in the local brothel. Money is thus the direct cause of his new misfortune—he again breaks a leg during a drunken spree, and is taken back to the hospital barely an hour after his discharge. Contrary to the donor's intention, money is thus the direct cause of the protagonist's sexual conduct and its intended purpose is undermined. Hence the *moralité* at the end of the story, which tells us that the nun "ne sut jamais que cette rechute était due à ses vingt-cinq francs."[17]

Before briefly considering my example of our theme in drama, a few preliminary observations about money in Maupassant are now appropriate. My analysis of the Maupassant stories, as the reader will have noticed, was based on Gilbert Ryle's criteria for "aboutness," which stipulate that:

> when we say that something, say Mont Blanc, is the central topic of a conversation, we mean that all or most of the propositions and questions which constitute the conversation are "about" Mont Blanc in the sense which I am investigating and few of them are about some other one subject.[18]

Thus money is the central theme of all the stories, the initial indication of centrality being the title. Though the meaning of money varies slightly from one story to the next, we are nevertheless in a position to formulate a few general conclusions about money in Maupassant's fictional universe:

(1) it is far *less* central than one might think, given that, according to the criteria outlined earlier, it is foregrounded in only eight out of the over 300 stories;

(2) it is *not earned:* it is bequeathed, received unexpectedly, or misappropriated through premeditated deception;

(3) it is primarily *comic:* in none of the stories analyzed does it have the obsessive force that we find in Shakespeare or Molière;

(4) it is *sexual* sign, the coin of sexual exchange, in all cases between unmarried partners. It is, by implication, a sign of frivolity;

(5) Maupassant's *phynance* is in no sense phallic: the power of money is systematically subverted. The control of Maupassant's legators over their respective legatees is minimal—most of the donors' intentions are seriously undermined.

And so on.

Though space does not permit an extended analysis of money as theme in drama, a few short comments on Labiche's *La Cagnotte*[19] will suffice here. It is immediately apparent that the main preoccupation of Labiche's characters (in contrast to Shakespeare's or Molière's) is how to spend cash rather than how to hoard it. Like Maupassant, Labiche uses money as *comic* theme. Though money is the mainspring of the madcap mechanism of Labiche's play—Colladan, Champbourcy, Cordenbois and Co go off on an intended spree in Paris that turns into a fiasco—it provides no more than superficial cohesion for the events that are set in motion.

But if we apply Ryle's "aboutness" criterion to Labiche's *La Cagnotte,* we find that Labiche is a far more anarchistic thematicist than Maupassant. His play, despite the title, is not really "about" money at all. The kitty, or *cagnotte,* does no more than provide specious motivation for talking about the foibles of an ingenuous band of country bumpkins on their visit to Paris and the various tangles that ensue.

We can conclude from this—albeit somewhat hastily—that farce allows a greater measure of thematic and thus referential liberty, or referential anarchy, if you will. At the very least one can conclude that in farce our thematic expectations are inclined to be somewhat different from those we tend to entertain in short fiction. Readers of *En attendant Godot* and *La Cantatrice chauve* know better than to wait around for the referents named in the titles to appear onstage or even be mentioned or discussed at length in the dialogue. Hence the reference, in my title, to Jarry's *Ubu, about* whom I deliberately chose not to speak.[20]

Notes

[1] See Harry Levin, *Playboys and Killjoys. An Essay on the Theory and Practice of Comedy* (New York & Oxford: Oxford University Press, 1987) 47.

[2] Todorov & Ducrot, *Dictionnaire encyclopédique des sciences du langage* (Paris: Seuil, 1972) 241-283.

[3] Jean-Pierre Richard, *L'Univers imaginaire de Mallarmé* (Paris: Seuil, 1961), especially 24-30. Cf. Richard's other definition: "Un thème serait alors un principe concret d'organisation ou un objet fixe, autour duquel aurait tendance à se constituer et à déployer un monde. L'essentiel, en lui, c'est cette 'parenté secrète' dont parle Mallarmé, cette identité cachée qu'il s'agira de déceler sous les enveloppes les plus diverses. . . . Le repérage des thèmes s'effectue le plus ordinairement d'après le critère de récurrence, les thèmes majeurs d'une œuvre . . . sont ceux qui s'y trouvent développés le plus souvent" (24).

[4] Gilles Deleuze & Félix Guattari, *Kafka. Pour une littérature mineure* (Paris: Minuit, 1975) 13-14.

[5] Charles Mauron, *Des Métaphores obsédantes au mythe personnel. Introduction à la psychocritique* (Paris: José Corti, 1962) 9.

[6] A.-J. Greimas & J. Courtès, *Sémiotique. Dictionnaire raisonné de la théorie du langage* (Paris: Hachette, 1979) 394.

[7] Northrop Frye, *Anatomy of Criticism* (Princeton: Princeton Univ. Press, 1957) 52.

[8] 1985, No. 4. See, in particular, the articles by Prince, Bremond and Hamon.

[9] See Gilbert Ryle, "About," in *Collected Papers, 1929-1968* (London: Hutchinson, 1971) 2: 82-84.

[10] Dumas fils, *La Question d'argent* in *Théâtre complet de Alexandre Dumas fils,* vol. 2 (Paris: Michel Lévy frères, 1868).

[11] Octave Mirbeau, *Les Affaires sont les affaires* in Mirbeau, *Œuvres illustrées,* vol. 9 [*Théâtre*] (Paris: Les Editions nationales, 1935). The play was first produced in 1903.

[12] Gilbert Durand, *Les Structures anthropologiques de l'imaginaire* (Paris: Bordas, 1969).

[13] On the problem of reference in literary discourse, see Anna Whiteside & Michael Issacharoff (eds.), *On Referring in Literature* (Bloomington: Indiana University Press, 1987).

[14] Maupassant, *Contes et nouvelles,* 2 vols. (Paris: Gallimard [Bibliothèque de la Pléiade], 1974).

[15] *Contes et nouvelles* 2: 341.

[16] *Contes et nouvelles* 2: 326.

[17] *Contes et nouvelles* 2: 1037.

[18] Gilbert Ryle, *Collected Papers* (London: Hutchinson, 1971) 2: 67.

[19] Eugène Labiche's *La Cagnotte* was first produced in Paris in 1864.

[20] An earlier version of this paper was presented at the Division on Nineteenth-Century French Literature ("L'argent et la littérature française du dix-neuvième siècle," chaired by Thomas H. Goetz) at the MLA Convention, San Francisco, December 1987.

Susan Dunn (essay date 1990)

SOURCE: "Nerval and Money: The Currency of Dreams," in *Nineteenth-Century French Studies,* Vol. 19, No. 1, Fall, 1990, pp. 54-64.

[*In the following essay, Dunn argues that Nerval's fiction reveals the author's contradictory feelings toward money: his desire to live above economics and money conflicts with his desire to prove his self-worth through economic success.*]

Nerval begins *Sylvie* with a portrait of his ideal self, a sensitive, melancholic young man with other-wordly concerns and no concern for money: "un jeune homme correctement vêtu, d'une figure pâle et nerveuse, ayant des manières convenables et des yeux empreints de mélancolie et de douceur. Il jetait de l'or sur une table de whist et le perdait avec indifférence." Among the opening signs of *Promenades et Souvenirs* is also indifference to money: "Il est véritablement difficile de trouver à se loger dans Paris. . . . Évincé du premier (domicile) avec vingt francs de dédommagement, que j'ai négligé, je ne sais pourquoi, d'aller toucher à la Ville . . ." (1: 121).

After Nerval's death, his friends perpetuated the myth of a man detached from money, indifferent to material reality. Gautier, for example, believed that he knew a Nerval who had always been above preoccupations with money: "L'argent était son moindre souci. . . . La richesse lui semblait un embarras. . . . Les louis lui causaient une sorte de malaise et semblaient lui brûler les mains; il ne redevenait tranquille qu'à la dernière pièce de cinq francs" (31-32). Houssaye echoed Gautier: "Gérard n'est pas un homme à s'inquiéter de si peu que de manquer de tout" (Borgal 12). Nerval's biographer, Aristide Marie, agreed that Nerval "n'avait du bohème que le dédain de l'argent et l'insouci des besoins futurs" (351). Although most of his friends insisted that financial difficulties could not have played a role in his suicide, they were well aware that, at the end of his life, he had pawned his over-coat, had no known address, and refused the money they continually urged upon him.

The Nerval they were reluctant to acknowledge was a man anxious about his finances and deeply troubled by debts, a man so scrupulous and obsessive about repaying money that, in the last impoverished weeks of his life, he hesitated to borrow even the most minimal sums, afraid that he would not be able to return them. This Nerval, haunted by financial worries, ultimately located the symptoms of his deteriorating mental state in his inability to manage money. In 1854, he wrote to Dr. Blanche concerning his continuing mental illness: "Le mal est plus grand que vous ne pensez; . . . Le pire est que j'ai dépensé beaucoup d'argent sans nécessité" (1: 1159).

Money was a source of profound emotional ambivalence for Nerval. Disdain for money was a sign of mastery of life, potency, of the superiority of his marginal bohemian existence, and finally of the intangible spiritual value of literature. Texts like *Sylvie* and *Angélique,* which defend a marginal bohemian existence, a life of madness and drifting, place him in opposition to a society that prized economic and social success, a society that, after all, had adopted the slogan, "enrichissez-vous." In Nerval's world, one throws away money for a good reason: economic failure is the happy conditon of literary success. Anxiety about money, on the other hand, was symptomatic of his crippling sense of failure and inability to cope with reality. Money was the barometer of his self-esteem as well as his mental distress.

In Nerval's fiction, money is, for the most part, benign. In *Sylvie, Angélique,* and *Promenades et Souvenirs,* it serves as the initial motor of the plot. In *Sylvie,* the narrator-protagonist, whom I will call Nerval, describes himself as assiduously following stock-market quotations and fluctuations: "Je passai par la salle de lecture, et machinalement je regardai un journal. C'était, je crois, pour y voir le cours de la Bourse . . ." (1: 243). The news of his success in the stock-market inspires him to try to buy his way into the heart of Aurélie. After some reflection, he dismisses that idea and decides that his real desire is to return to the Valois where Sylvie, "si pauvre," might still be waiting. Money is also the pretext for Nerval's adventures in *Promenades et Souvenirs,* in which he searches for an affordable lodging. In *Angélique,* the monetary motor is double, a combination of the narrator's decision not to purchase an expensive book, the *Histoire de l'abbé de Bucquoy,* and his fear of the monetary fines imposed by the amendement Riancey on writers of fiction. In all three cases, money, or the lack of it, sets Nerval on his course, his quest for an intangible ideal: an actress, a non-existent house, or an eternally missing book. Money is the medium through which his dreams and desires could theoretically be realized. But though he is tempted to buy his way into the oneiric world of the past, he ultimately refuses to pay for his dreams, prudently and lucidly realizing that the ideal is contained within himself and within his ability to create literature.

Although Nerval's double, in *Sylvie,* shows no interest in the gold he nonchalantly chooses to lose, the narrator-protagonist himself hopes to gain the actress's affection by offering her money. "La femme aimée si longtemps était à moi si je voulais. Je touchais du doigt mon idéal. La somme gagnée se dressa devant moi comme la statue d'or de Moloch" (1: 244). However, his very sense of himself and his self-respect are at stake, for his next thoughts are not of Aurélie, but rather of her lover, the narrator's double. Nerval dramatizes the conflict between the social self and the ideal personality in the narrator's uncertainty over whether the actress's lover would be envious or contemptuous of him: "Que dirait maintenant, pensais-je, le jeune homme de tout à l'heure, si j'allais prendre sa place près de la femme qu'il a laissée seule? Je frémis de cette pensée, et mon orgueil se révolta" (1: 244). He dismisses his idea of tempting the actress with money, preferring to identify with his double who carelessly discards gold coins. Although pale and melancholic, this double is a figure of potency: not only is he the actress's chosen lover, but he has no need for money to prove his success or power. The ideal self is above or simply removed from material reality. He has the power, freedom, and self-assurance to deny the value of money and treat it with indifference. In addition, there is irony in Nerval's suggestion that the ideal world could be exchanged for money. Although he is tempted by the thought that the object of his desire could find its way, through money, into the quotidian world, he discovers that money is the sign, not of exchange, but rather of the impossibility of commerce between the two worlds of *rêve* and *réalité.*

Having renounced materialism in the quest for love, the narrator's next thought, in *Sylvie,* is a return to the Valois. In a sense, this is a flight from material and economic reality to the lost paradise of childhood. But money also plays a role in the childhood paradise: in the Valois, money is saved, not spent. Nerval fantasizes about Sylvie; with her, he would not have wasted his inheritance. His fortune (luck as well as money) would have lasted and become as timeless as the Valois itself: "Depuis trois ans, je dissipe en seigneur le bien modeste que (mon oncle) m'a laissé et qui pouvait suffire à ma vie. Avec Sylvie, je l'aurais conservé. Le hasard m'en rend une partie. Il est temps encore" (1: 247). He imagines that conserving money would conserve the past; money saved in the Valois rather than spent in Paris would magically enable him to recapture lost time, making him the person he once was: "je redevenais riche" (1: 243). As for Sylvie, guessing that she is still free, he is tempted, for the second time, by

the thought that money might give him power in relation to women: "Qui l'aurait épousée? elle est si pauvre!" (1: 247). But neither money won nor spent nor saved provides an entrance to the ideal world. The narrator learns that money cannot be used to exchange the real for the ideal nor does it have the properties of a fountain of youth.

In *Promenades et Souvenirs,* Nerval associates money with a sense of lost possibilities, of the "trop tard." He laments, again and again, not having spent his money more wisely. Had he done so, the perfect dwelling would have been his; he would have been able to live in a house embodying the old Paris or the ancient *vignobles* of France, one that would have transported him into past time. His regrets over money not spent constitute a leit-motif: "Il y a dix ans, j'aurais pu acquérir (cet humble coteau) au prix de trois mille francs . . . On en demande aujourd'hui trente mille" (1: 122); "Je regrette d'autant plus d'avoir hésité, il y a dix ans, à donner trois mille francs du dernier vignoble de Montmartre" (1: 124). But had he purchased a house, his ideal would have been degraded by contact with banal reality. Nerval's happy inability to afford a suitable dwelling makes him a wanderer, endlessly moving in search of a geographically stable ideal. Dreams of locating his ideal in reality and purchasing it are in vain: "Il n'y faut plus penser. Je ne serai jamais propriétaire" (1: 124). At the end of *Promenades et Souvenirs,* he joins a troup of travelling actors in their van, but he leaves even that protective lodging when the rain stops.

In *Angélique,* once again money is the motor of the plot. The pretext for all his peregrinations and adventures in search of the *Histoire de l'abbé de Bucquoy* was his decision not to buy this charismatic book when he saw it in Frankfurt. The volume, he rationalized, had really been too expensive. The second pretext of *Angélique* is also monetary. When Nerval returns to Paris after his trip to Frankfurt, he discovers that the lives of journalists have been unpleasantly changed by the *amendement Riancey,* the new law prohibiting *romans-feuilletons* and imposing fines on the authors of such fiction. Nerval realizes that he must write articles concerned with "historical reality." And so it is in order to avoid financial penalties that he decides to write a biography of the abbé de Bucquoy. But instead, he writes about his search for the elusive book he refused to purchase. Both pre-texts of *Angélique,* the too-expensive book and the fear of paying fines, create the text, the story of the hunt for the missing book. In *Angélique,* Nerval is not tempted to use money as a medium of exchange for an ideal, as he did in *Sylvie* and *Promenades et Souvenirs.* It is rather the reluctance to spend money that has generative potential. Faced with the situation of not having purchased the coveted *Histoire de l'abbé de Bucquoy,* Nerval is obliged to write his own book. It is the specific absence of money—a kind of monetary void—that has creative power and that, in *Angélique,* generates the text.

Money exists in order to be rejected. Nerval's quests, undertaken because of some association with money, end as flights from pecuniary concerns and transport him into the world of the ideal. Ross Chambers lucidly pointed out to me the mechanism by which Nerval rejects economic value and substitutes literary value in its place. For Professor Chambers, *Sylvie* exemplifies the ascendancy of literature: "In turning away from the world of finance in favor of all that the Valois represents, the protagonist is making an error in hard-nosed terms; but the text demonstrates that this error was a fortunate one because out of it came the man capable of writing *Sylvie* and of using not the "débris" of his fortune but the "débris" of his past to produce a text." In *Angélique* and *Promenades et Souvenirs* as well as in *Sylvie,* Nerval discovered the non-economic, literary value of his peregrinations in the Valois, his most fertile source of literary inspiration. The oneiric Valois existed in opposition to the material and financial reality of Paris. Preferring to produce literature rather than money, Nerval implicitly and explicitly rejected the dominance of economic values during the July Monarchy. In *Paradoxe et Vérité,* he protested the translation into pecuniary terms of all aspects and qualities of human existence: "Il est clair que, dès que vous établissez l'argent comme base de la société, du pouvoir et des honneurs, dès que vous en faites un honneur et une vertu, il n'y a plus d'honneur et de vertu qui ne se compensent par lui. L'or sera le représentant des choses morales, comme il est l'est déjà des choses matérielles; on aura dans la poche la représentation d'une vertu, d'un bienfait, d'un mérite" (1: 437). In his personal economy, he replaced the gold standard with a literary standard; language, not money, was gold and had the real alchemical properties.

In Nerval's 1851 play, *L'Imagier de Harlem,* written with Méry, the primacy of literary value over economic value is the subject of the first three acts. This play is Nerval's version of the Faust legend, although his hero is not Faust, but Laurent Coster, to whom he attributes the invention of printing. Nerval borrowed extensively from Goethe, but his treatment of the issue of paper currency lacks the philosophical complexity of the German *Faust.* In Nerval's play, Coster is in dire need of money to pay for the patent of his printing press and accepts help from the devil (in the incarnation of De Bloksberg) who claims to be an alchemist. Acknowledging the mystery of alchemy, Coster nevertheless prefers the moral purpose of printing: "Mon invention n'est rien peut-être à côté de vos découvertes alchimiques; mais moi, j'ai un but moral. . . . avec la mienne, je veux donner aux hommes la richesse de l'esprit" (38). In fact, Coster's discovery of printing is a new form of alchemy: the transformation of paper

into knowledge and eternal light: "Grâce au levier qui est en mon pouvoir, je distribue ce livre à des millions de mains; je fais rayonner ces pages sur le globe, comme le soleil la lumière; je grave (les lettres) sur un papier fragile qui, à force d'être multiplié, devient éternel" (58-59). The devil and his accomplices, however, discern a different relationship between paper and alchemy. Demanding that Coster make them gold and not books ("faites-nous de l'or, et non des livres" 59), they usurp his invention in order to print paper money, thereby turning paper into the sign of gold: "Nous fondons une chose immense et qui se nommera le crédit! le monde n'a plus besoin d'argent et d'or; le premier des métaux c'est le papier" (65). The implications in the play could hardly be clearer; the artist, genius, or inventor must not yield to the diabolical temptations of money and materialism. Economic values and motives subvert and corrupt the spiritual nature of literature and printing. The final product of the writer's alchemical experiments should be immaterial words, not filthy lucre.

Nerval's idealized self had inner resources that enabled him to rise above concern for money and to associate literary and sometimes even social success with a marginal existence. In a charming early letter, dated November 11, 1834, Nerval described the freedom that temporary poverty granted him to act out his fantasy of being an aristocrat *en voyage,* a prince in the Hôtel des Princes: "Vous croyez, parce que je suis sans argent à Marseille . . . que j'y vis médiocrement: vous vous trompez. Je suis à l'hôtel, où je dîne splendidement à crédit . . . J'avais, en débarquant, cinq sols. J'en ai donné deux pour me faire cirer . . . j'ai trouvé deux gamins et je leur ai promis trois sols pour porter mes effets; . . . et tout bien agrafé, je suis entré sous le vestibule entre mes deux acolytes: j'avais heureusement retrouvé une vieille paire de gants jaunes" (1: 796-7).

His later correspondance, however, reveals a very different person who suffered painfully from the fear of economic and social failure. A lack of money could be the condition of his sense of freedom and superiority, but it finally became the sign of his imprisonment in weakness and illness. In his mysterious work, *La Pandora,* money is associated with dark forms of anxiety. Nerval's protagonist is in despair over his "froide Etoile" who not only insists that he wear an ecclesiastical black suit but who also seems to make financial demands on him: "Et ce n'était pas tant l'habit noir qui me désespérait, mais ma bourse était vide. Quelle honte! vide, hélas! le propre jour de la Saint-Sylvestre!" (1: 349). He describes his hopeful visit to the post office: "Poussé par un fol espoir, je me hâtai de courir à la poste pour voir si mon oncle ne m'avait pas adressé une lettre chargée. O bonheur! on me demande deux florins et l'on me remet une épître qui porte le timbre de France. Un rayon de soleil tombait d'aplomb sur cette lettre insidieuse. . . . Elle ne contenait de toute évidence que des maximes de morale et des conseils d'économie" (1: 349). He returns the useless missive to the post office: "Je la rendis en feignant prudemment une erreur de gilet, et je frappai avec une surprise affectée des poches qui ne rendaient aucun son métallique. . . . " (1: 349). A friend rescues him from financial distress, mentioning that he himself managed to hide some money from his venal mistress: "J'ai sauvé ceci des mains de Dalilah . . . Tiens, voilà deux écus d'Autriche; ménage-les bien et tâche de les garder intacts jusqu'à demain, car c'est le grand jour" (1: 350).

The "grand jour" to which he refers is the New Year, which is here associated not just with return and renewal, but with a full wallet, an obvious symbol of potency, with which to undertake the search for love or adventure. *La Pandora* is populated by the venal women Nerval's uncle had (in *Sylvie*) warned him against. The hero next meets la Kathi with whom he also enters into a negative pecuniary relationship. "Je ne sais trop quelle fleur elle portait à son corsage; je voulais l'obtenir de son amitié. Elle me dit d'un ton que je ne lui avais pas connu encore: Jamais, pour moins de *zehn Gulden Convention-mink*" (1: 350). The mystical flower has been demoted and degraded; Nerval finds himself in the realm of money and materiality which he had mistaken for the ideal. When, at the end of the story, he meets Pandora again, "dans une froide capitale du Nord," and is offered her "boîte fatale," he runs away: "je me pris à fuir à toutes jambes vers la place de la Monnaie" (1; 356). There is no exit from this terrible figure, no liberation from the venal woman in the Place de la Monnaie. Nerval's flight is arrested by material reality. Money blocks the threshold separating *réalité* from *rêve.* Trapped in this hell, symbolized by money, he cries, "O Jupiter! quand finira mon supplice?"

In "Les Amours de Vienne," a source of *La Pandora,* money seems less threatening but is still ambiguous. For example, the association between women and money is formalized, for Austrian paper money bears the resemblance of the country's female symbol: "Un délicieux profil de femme, intitulé Austria, vous inspire le regret le plus vif de vous séparer de ces images, et le désir plus grand d'en acquérir de nouvelles" (2: 49). It is not clear if monetary value is displaced by aesthetic value or if aesthetic value is degraded by materialism and if *les amours de Vienne* are tainted by an association with money and perhaps prostitution. However, in this text, Nerval is not the victim of venal women; on the contrary, "la Katty" insists on paying for her own theatre seat, "déclarant qu'elle n'était pas une *grisette* . . . et qu'elle voulait payer, ou n'entrerait pas" (2: 34).

Even more in Nerval's correspondance than in *La Pandora,* we see his anxiety about money, potency,

and mental illness become progressively more severe. Whereas his ideal self could relish his own marginality, valuing his oppositional stance in relation to the unashamed glorification of materialism, a different self, Nerval the social being, the son and the mental patient, suffered tremendously from guilt associated precisely with this marginality and lack of financial security and success. Especially in relation to his father, Nerval felt compelled to prove his self-worth in terms of worldly and economic success. The bohemian artist had neither time nor patience for money, but the guilt-ridden son was immobilized by the wish for material proof of his literary talent. In his attempt to justify his artistic life, he made pathetic efforts to assure his father that one day he would reap financial rewards from his writing, but these attempts to assert his autonomy ended in severe regression and humiliation.

Although he sought to convince himself and his father of his financial independence and maturity in general, Nerval still hoped for monetary gifts and loans from his father, so many signs of affection and caring, of "la confiante et sympathique amitié qui règnent d'ordinaire entre pères et enfants déjà avancés dans la vie." In November 1839, at the age of 31, he wrote a lengthy letter to his father, explaining, in obsessive detail, his request for a loan of 200 francs. Although he saw his self-esteem at stake ("je m'étais fait une règle de me soutenir entièrement par moi-même"), this did not prevent severe regression: "J'étais à Genève avec 420 francs, à Munich avec 350, . . . à Vienne, enfin, avec 140 francs. . . . Me voilà donc arrivé avec 140 francs. Tu vas voir mon économie: il m'a fallu payer quatre florins (10 fr.) à Vienne pour mon permis de séjour—acheter des gants, des socques, parce qu'il y a beaucoup de boue. Quatre jours à l'hôtel m'ont coûté 30 francs. J'ai loué un logement; j'ai payé 25 francs d'avance. Tu comprends qu'il faut aller jusqu'au 30 avec bien peu—je ne sais même pas si le mois n'a pas 31 jours. . . . Je dois donner 50 francs encore pour mon logement et toutes sortes d'accessoires qu'on m'a fournis, car mes 25 francs ne sont qu'un à compte. Il me faut encore une cravate blanche, des souliers pour les soirées, des gants . . ." (1: 831).

Nerval yearned for this tangible proof of his father's concern: "Je n'ai jamais douté que tu ne fusses toujours disposé à me venir en aide dans un moment important . . . Je connais assez ton affection pour moi pour penser que tu te seras rendu compte de l'importance que peut avoir ce service dans ma position actuelle . . ." (837). In the same letter, he literally begged his father for a loan. But, even more than the money itself, he hoped for a gesture from his father, an act of faith in his future. "Je t'explique tout cela en détail, parce qu'il faut que tu voies qu'il y a là un besoin non pas de ma subsistance, mais de *mon avenir* . . ." (831); "Je tiens à ce que tu ne voies là qu'une aide à *mon avenir* et à mes progrès plutôt qu'à ma subsistance" (832); "Le travail des livres, du théâtre . . . choses lentes, difficiles . . . mais aussi là est *l'avenir,* l'agrandissement, la vieillesse heureuse et honorée" (833); "J'ai maintenant toute confiance, puisque je ne puis plus, pour ainsi dire, douter de *mon avenir*" (834, italics mine).

Nerval attributed so much importance to this loan that strong unconscious feelings must have played a major role. He may have been trying to realize a version of the "family romance" one finds in *Le Prince des Sots* and *Le Marquis de Fayolle,* in which a very young man fantasizes discovering that he is the illegitimate son of a nobleman. Perhaps the gift of money from his father would have given him the sense of being the cherished son of a wealthy, generous, and caring father. In this same letter to his father, he compared himself to the most famous writers of his time, writers whose futures, he believed, were guaranteed by the family fortune. In so doing, he was implicitly criticizing and rejecting his father, who was unable to satisfy his dreams of wealth and nobility. "Les hommes de lettres qui, comme Lamartine, Chateaubriand, Devigny, Casimir Lavigne, Hugo, avaient des rentes, une fortune, enfin la vie assurée d'autre part, sont ceux qui sont arrivés le plus loin . . ." (834). If he had received this loan, he would have been closer to the realization of his family romance, but, in fact, his father never even opened his letter.

In response to his father's criticism of his artistic life in general and his friends in particular, Nerval defended himself by portraying his friendships as important financial relationships, transferring from his father to his friends a willingness to help and sustain him: "C'est Théophile qui m'a fait gagner 250 francs par mois, pendant deux ans, en me faisant, à *la Presse,* le collaborateur de son feuilleton . . . ; c'est Alphone Karr qui m'a fait gagner jusqu'à 400 francs par mois au *Figaro* qu'il dirigeait; c'est M. Victor Hugo qui m'a été utile dix fois . . . C'est Alexandre Dumas, qui m'a fait gagner 6000 francs avec *Piquillo* . . . et depuis 1200 francs avec *l'Alchimiste* . . ." (849).

Although receiving money was charged with emotional meaning, Nerval was scrupulous about paying his debts, and, for this particular loan from his father, he elaborated two alternative repayment schedules, thus oscillating between regression and the need to assert his independence and strength. Nerval had been troubled by debts since 1836, when the magazine he had founded the previous year, *Le Monde dramatique,* failed. Aristide Marie attributes to this financial loss the origin of his future financial worries: "Là gît le secret de son incurable gêne, pendant les années qui vont suivre; car sa droiture s'alarmera toujours d'une obligation non éteinte . . . et il doit rester l'esclave de sa dette" (108).

Nerval associated financial responsibility and the ability to pay debts with being an autonomous and healthy individual, for he was the most conscientious and persistent about his debts when they were linked to his mental health. During his 1841 stay at a clinic, he demanded to know who was subsidizing his hospitalization. Discovering that his father had paid some of his expenses, the embarrassed son insisted on paying him back: "Je te prierai même, lorsque j'aurai pu sortir, de reprendre la somme que tu m'as donnée pour mon séjour dans la maison de Mme Saint-Marcel . . . Reçois donc et mes remerciements sincères et l'espérance qu'à moins d'un coup inattendu, je n'aurais jamais besoin de déranger tes habitudes" (891).

As his mental health deteriorated and as the young Dr. Blanche replaced Dr. Labrunie as a father-figure, the financial relationship between doctor and patient became the object of Nerval's anxiety and confusion: "Il est évident que vous m'avez reçu, traité et obligé à vos dépens, ce qui fait que j'ai eu grand tort de dissiper les premiers fonds qui devaient vous revenir . . . je me croyais en état de gagner tant d'argent que cela ne me paraissait rien" (1108). Nerval struggled to prove to his doctor that he was financially reliable, synonymous for him with being mentally stable. In a letter to Blanche in 1854, which mirrors his 1839 letter to his father, he itemized, in extensive detail, his travel expenses, illustrating his frugality and ability to handle money, important signs of his fortunate "guérison." "Ce qui est encore significatif en fait de guérison, c'est que je suis arrivé à réduire peu à peu mes dépenses . . . J'ai dépensé, depuis un mois, 300 francs . . . cela ne fait pas 200 francs pour nourriture et hôtel, et j'ai été presque toujours dans les bons. J'ai acheté en outre pour environ 25 francs d'effets nécessaires et j'ai fait faire une copie d'un article qui m'a coûté une douzaine de francs . . . j'ai payé pour des monumens (et) musées . . . J'espère que vous penserez comme moi que ce n'est pas de l'argent perdu" (1147). But one month later, he informed Dr. Blanche that he was not well, locating the symptoms of his illness in his mismanagement of money. "Le mal et plus grand que vous ne pensez; cependant je n'ai rien fait qu'on puisse me reprocher et n'ai fait de tort qu'à moi-même . . . le pire est que j'ai dépensé beaucoup d'argent sans nécessité, bien qu'il me reste largement de quoi revenir . . ." (1159). During this most difficult period of his life, he gauged his rationality in relation to his ability to handle money: "J'ai dépensé beaucoup sans doute, mais je pense avoir beaucoup gagné sous d'autres rapports . . . Il fallait que cela fût ainsi; pardonnez–moi ce fatalisme musulman . . ." (1162). But anxiety about his debts to Dr. Blanche was overwhelming, compelling him to leave the Doctor's care. "Je liquide avec le docteur Blanche en lui donnant un à compte et réglant le reste" (1177). One week later, Dr. Blanche implored Nerval to return to his clinic: "J'ai su en même temps que vous attribuiez votre exaltation au chagrin que vous éprouviez de ne pouvoir vous acquitter envers moi. Lorsque vous n'aurez plus de préventions contre moi . . . venez; pour ce qui est de l'argent que vous me devez, puisque vous vous dites mon ami, traitez-moi donc en ami et permettez-moi d'attendre que vos travaux aient produit tout ce que vous en espérez" (1180).

Three months later, the day before his suicide, Nerval visited his friend Méry. Informed that Méry had stepped out, he gave Méry's servant a coin on which he carved a cross. After Nerval's death, Méry said that he felt the coin was "un cri de misère," a sign of distress, even hunger (Marie 351-352). But was the coin the calling-card of a desperate man, down to his last cent? Or was it another occult relic, presented by a poet who had abandoned banal reality, who had given himself over to his world of dreams and hallucinations? Who left the coin for Méry? the other-worldy poet magnetically attracted to dream, or the cold and starving man, struggling to cope with reality, who in one day would be dead.

Works Cited

Borgal, *De Quoi vivait Gérard de Nerval.* Paris: Deux-rives, 1950.

Gautier, Théophile. *Portraits et Souvenirs littéraires* (1875). Paris: Charpentier, 1892.

Marie, Aristide. *Gérard de Nerval.* Paris: Hachette, 1955.

Nerval, *Œuvres.* Paris: Gallimard, volume 1, 1966 and volume 2, 1961. *L'Imagier de Harlem* in *Œuvres complémentaires,* Paris: Lettres Modernes, 1967, vol. 3.

Raymond L. Baubles, Jr. (essay date 1994)

SOURCE: "Displaced Persons: The Cost of Speculation in Charles Dickens' *Martin Chuzzlewit,*" in *Money: Lure, Lore, and Literature,* edited by John Louis DiGaetani, Greenwood Press, 1994, pp. 245-52.

[*In the following essay, Baubles points out Dickens's concerns with the human cost of financial speculation by analyzing the effect of obsession with financial gain on the characters in* Martin Chuzzlewit.]

When Adam Smith in *The Wealth of Nations* addresses the concept of *value,* he locates its source in labor:

> What is bought with money or with goods is purchased with labour. . . . It was not by gold or by silver, but by labour that all the wealth of the world was originally purchased; and its value, to

those who possess it, and who want to exchange it for some new productions, is precisely equal to the quantity of labour which it can enable them to purchase or command. (133)

But a curious phenomenon has taken place since Adam Smith's time. A displacement has occurred which has shifted *value* from the labor, goods, or services acquired by or exchanged for money to the money itself. In other words, my worth is no longer measured by my capacity for labor or by the quality of my goods but by the number of dollars which I generate or possess.

This transmogrification is not a recent one; it began in the late eighteenth and nineteenth centuries. For reasons and through a process too complex to analyze here, financial transactions acquired primary importance and financial entrepreneurs—bankers, stockbrokers, speculators—became more important participants in the economies of nations; money became a commodity in itself, acquiring a life of its own as the concept of profit was disconnected from the products which generated it.

This disembodiment is more than a matter of economics. It has serious social and moral consequences. As money itself becomes the primary commodity, the scramble for dollars or pounds can corrupt social relationships, destroy social responsibility, and lead to a disintegration of moral values and the loss of a sense of self.

The nineteenth-century British novelists were well aware of the terrific power of money and of the insidious effects it could have on the individual caught up by its allure. Time and again, the plot of the Victorian novel hinges upon the acquisition of money or the lack thereof, the misplaced will or its hidden codicil, the real or rumored existence of a natural son, the late second marriage with its threat of renewed fertility—as the various characters watch their anticipated fortunes rise and fall with the rapidity of stock market transactions and speculate on futures as if they were dealing in a commodities market. In many nineteenth-century novels, social relationships are cultivated only insofar as they bring the promise of monetary profit, and moral dilemmas rarely reach the level of consciousness.

Charles Dickens, who well understood the workings of the financial markets, addresses these concerns and illustrates the human cost of financial speculation, of money transactions gone awry, in many of his novels, perhaps most fully in *Martin Chuzzlewit.* Characterized as a novel which "could be defined as Dickens' first elaborate attack on the money worship of commercialized man" (Miller 132), in which "the ugly, disfiguring effect of money as a social force is the central and organizing concern" (Engel 103), *Martin*

Chuzzlewit is predominantly about *self*[1] and "the inherent lunacy of commerce" (G. Smith 47). But it should be noted that it is commerce of a particular sort—the commerce in money rather than in goods, in paper currency detached from any substance whatsoever. And just as the money is disembodied, so too are those who speculate in or deal with it. Ironically, although *self* is a central motif of the novel, the various characters have no self. Altering their identities at whim, chamelionlike in their behaviors, most of Dickens' speculators lack a stable center of identity. What Dickens seems to indicate in this early work is that those who choose to speculate do so at the considerable cost of their humanity. Indeed, they sacrifice their humanity on the altar of mammon, a concern with disembodied profit resulting in a displacement of person.

Emblematic of this disintegration of the human spirit is Montague Tigg, through whom "Dickens is suggesting that there is a fundamental identity between shabby, down-at-the-heel roguery and expansive financial manipulation" (G. Smith 48). Tigg is an unctuous character who adapts his demeanor to the immediate moment. In his third and most significant appearance,[2] now "no longer Montague Tigg but Tigg Montague" (429; ch. 27), he is the chairman of the board of the Anglo-Bengalee Disinterested Loan and Life Assurance Company. In this company, Dickens' most extended and comprehensive analysis of the operations of a bubble enterprise, the reader sees the emptiness and corruption at its core. Little more than a board composed of a chairman and a secretary, "everything else being a light-hearted little fiction" (434; ch. 27),[3] its capital assets amounting to "[a] figure of two, and as many oughts after it as the printer can get into the same line" (429; ch. 27), underwritten by fictional property in Bengal (hence, its name), preying upon small investors who have the most to lose, the Anglo-Bengalee operates in the manner of many of the joint-stock companies of the day,[4] financial bubbles floated by unscrupulous promoters for the sole purpose of gaining other people's money.

In an attempt to seduce Jonas Chuzzlewit to become a partner in the company, Tigg details the duplicity which underlies its operations. When a prospective client approaches the Anglo-Bengalee for a loan to be secured by himself and two others, he is urged to insure his own life for double the amount and to urge his cosigners to purchase policies also. Because the loan is usually desperately needed, Tigg's proposal is more often than not accepted. In addition to charging "the highest lawful interest" (the only instance in which the company operates within the law) to be paid in advance, the amount provided to the borrower is further reduced by the premium on the life assurance policy. As Tigg describes the process,

> We're not exactly soft upon B; for besides charging B the regular interest, we get B's premium, and B's friends' premiums, and we charge B for the bond, and, whether we accept him or not, we charge B for "inquiries" (we keep a man, at a pound a week, to make 'em), and we charge B a trifle for the secretary; and, in short, my good fellow, we stick it into B, up hill and down dale, and make a devilish comfortable little property out of him. (445; ch. 27)

To Tigg, clients are chattel, not people. B, as an individual, is displaced; he becomes the equivalent of the thoroughbred horse pulling Tigg's cabriolet. Other policies are equated with office furniture; in the past, when some of the original ones fell in, Tigg says only that "we had a couple of unlucky deaths that brought us down to a grand piano" (446; ch. 27). He suggests that Jonas, in joining the company, abjure both truth and responsibility; not content to keep his moral bankruptcy private, his counsel, in the event of a recurrence of such a situation, is given "in so low a whisper, that only one disconnected word was audible, and that imperfectly. But it sounded like 'Bolt'" (446; ch. 27). The smarminess which he employs is indicative of his unscrupulousness. If Tigg is willing to help Jonas, it is solely because Tigg will benefit. He baldly states, "We companies are all birds of prey: mere birds of prey. The only question is, whether, in serving our own turn, we can serve yours too: whether in double-lining our own nest, we can put a single lining into yours" (441; ch. 27). A moral bankrupt more than willing to bankrupt others financially for his own ease and comfort, Tigg operates with no other end in mind than the increase of capital. He has no sense of social or moral responsibility. People are property to be exchanged for material possessions; the death of a client is disturbing only because it leads to his own financial loss. There are no grand (or even grandiose) plans for the betterment of society, no investment in capital improvements (for, in this venture, there is little fixed capital), no reinvestment in secondary enterprises for the improvement of the quality of life other than one's own, least of all no intent to honor the policies themselves; there is simply the continuous accumulation of raw capital seemingly for its own sake. About this there is something inherently distasteful since Tigg is promoting a company speculating in human lives. And in the sacrifice of others' humanity in that enterprise, Tigg has sacrificed his own as well.

But he is not alone in such venal behavior nor in the payment of such a price. For the varied plots in the novel all revolve around the contemplated acquisition of someone else's property; all the characters are engaged in speculative ventures of one sort or another, and all lack, as a result, a core identity and moral center. Mere bundles of affections, largely a group of charlatans and *poseurs,* they seek the main chance that will enrich them with the least amount of effort at someone else's expense.

Foremost among them is Seth Pecksniff, a disingenuous schoolmaster-architect and land surveyor who seems never to have worked at his vocations a day in his life.

> Mr. Pecksniff's professional engagements, indeed, were almost, if not entirely, confined to the reception of pupils; for the collection of rents, with which pursuit he occasionally varied and relieved his graver toils, can hardly be said to be a strictly architectural employment. *His genius lay in ensnaring parents and guardians, and pocketing premiums.* (13; ch. 2, my emphasis)

The architectural enterprise is simply a Pecksniffian variation of Tigg's Anglo-Bengalee with one innovation. Pecksniff steals much more than money from his apprentices; he steals their ideas as well. He sets them to the task of drafting original plans, telling them that "it really is in the finishing touches alone, that great experience and long study in these matters tell" (88; ch. 6):

> There were cases on record in which the masterly introduction of an additional back window, or a kitchen-door, or half a dozen steps, or even a water-spout, had made the design of a pupil Mr. Pecksniff's own work, and had brought substantial rewards into the gentleman's pocket. But such is the magic of genius, which changes all it handles into gold! (88; ch. 6)

As bankrupt in morals as he is in ideas (in another context he states, "There is nothing personal in morality" [14; ch. 2] without any comprehension of the ironic applicability of his remark), pharisaical and parasitical, Pecksniff is an even more distasteful, more depraved character than Tigg. Tigg makes no pretense about his treatment of others as objects, openly acknowledging his dishonesty and duplicity to his coconspirators; Pecksniff, however, is far more devious, coyly (but ineffectively) dissembling even when he does not have to do so. With feigned innocence and ingenuousness, Pecksniff tries to mask what is really a mean-spirited brutality toward others. Beneath his smug, self-satisfied air lies a contempt for all humanity; the moralistic platitudes to which he gives voice throughout the novel are belied by his actions.

This disparity between word and deed illustrates an utter disdain for others, a disdain which extends to the very language he uses and which emphasizes his moral vacuity. Like Alice's Humpty Dumpty, "Mr. Pecksniff was in the frequent habit of using any word that occurred to him as having a good sound, and rounding a sentence well, without much care for its meaning" (15; ch. 2). As Sucksmith points out in a most impressive study of Dickensian rhetoric, "[Dickens] deliberately resorts to forced rhetorical figures to betray the insincerity which lies behind the various poses of Pecksniff" (57).

But it is more than mere insincerity and hypocrisy which Pecksniff's use of words reflects; the substitution of manner for matter reveals his lack of an *authentic* personality.[5] This condition is significantly different from and far more demeaning than alienation. As Trilling points out in another context,[6] "[I]t is not the estrangement of the self from the self. . . . Rather, it is the transformation of the self into what is not human" (123). The inauthentic person is, in essence, self-less. For Pecksniff, identity is pose, a continual tailoring of his character and behavior to fit his notions of what others expect or desire of him in order to achieve monetary gain. In shaping himself entirely by external considerations and concerns, in being consistent only in his inconsistency, he becomes inauthentic.

This annihilation of self is motivated by financial reward, either real or anticipated. Pecksniff's emotional life is sterile, superseded by economic considerations. Even his expression of sorrow to Mr. Todgers over the loss of his wife is undercut by the inappropriately appended observation "She had a small property" (149; ch. 9). In this regard, Pecksniff is little different in kind from Tigg; and their enterprises are remarkably similar.

However, Dickens levels his most scathing indictment of speculators and speculation at their American cousins. Renouncing all subtlety in his analysis of the American enterprise, Dickens accuses its operatives of the most meretricious and contemptible behavior. Major Pawkins is the embodiment of all the worst in the American character. His object, no different from that of all Americans, is the acquisition of dollars:

> All their cares, hopes, joys, affections, virtues, and associations seemed to be melted down into dollars. Whatever the chance contributions that fell into the slow cauldron of their talk, they made the gruel thick and slab with dollars. Men were weighed by their dollars, measures gauged by their dollars; life was auctioneered, appraised, put up, and knocked down for its dollars. *The next respectable thing to dollars was any venture having their attainment for its end.* (273; ch. 16, my emphasis)

In this sweeping denunciation of a system that places more value on the accumulation of wealth for its own sake than on any substantial product or labor which that wealth should represent, Dickens maintains that the American character is inherently dehumanized, base, and corrupt. Contrary to their rather sanctimonious attitude, the Americans demonstrate the same moral vacuity as the English, a vacuity which extends to their use of language also; for, like Pecksniff, they use it loosely and casually and frequently with the deliberate intention to mislead and defraud. In *Martin Chuzzlewit,* the emphasis on money on both sides of the Atlantic is capable of engulfing all who would make capital acquisition their ultimate goal, destroying the very fabric of their humanity.

No one escapes ridicule. "Dickens's great fault is his predilection for very mean and despicable characters, out of proportion in number; and, besides, he makes goodness contemptible" (Robinson 645). For the most part, those characters who should function as moral touchstones are themselves monstrous and grotesque. Even Old Martin Chuzzlewit is consumed by his wealth. Obsessed by the desire to protect his fortune, he becomes a thoroughgoing misanthrope and divorces himself from every human impulse; his behavior borders on the reprehensible.

Among the rest of the characters, there is no one who merits the reader's respect or admiration. Indeed, every character in this novel is, like the boarders at Todgers', reduced to a "turn" (144; ch. 9); in no other work does Dickens dehumanize his cast of characters to the extent that he does here. Many of his contemporaries would find themselves in agreement with Henry Crabb Robinson's assessment: "Aug. 24th [1844]. . . . I finished *Chuzzlewit* at night; a book that I do not wish to look into a second time, so generally disgusting are the characters and incidents of the tale" (646). Despite generally favorable reviews (Collins 183), *Martin Chuzzlewit* held little appeal for the reading public, so harsh was its portrait of society and so relentless its bitter tone.

The commercial enterprise, more precisely the commerce in dollars or pounds, does not establish the selfishness and self-centered nature of the characters in this novel so much as it demonstrates their lack of centered selves and their repudiation of all things human. Driven by profit, guided by the principle "Do other men, for they would do you" (181; ch. 11), they reduce themselves and others to mere chattel, valuable only insofar as and to the extent that they can generate profit. Pecksniff berates Mrs. Todgers: "To worship the golden calf of Baal, for eighteen shillings a week! . . . To barter away that precious jewel, self-esteem, and cringe to any mortal creature—for eighteen shillings a week!" (168-69; ch. 10)—but it is not for her betrayal of her humanity that he does so; what offends him is that she does it so cheaply when there was a greater profit to be made.

This will not be the last time that Dickens turns to an examination of these issues and comes to the same conclusions. Ten years later, in *Little Dorrit,* and twenty years later, in *Our Mutual Friend,* he presents far bleaker pictures of the social and moral havoc wrought by financial speculation.

But the message remains the same. In Victorian England, just as, architecturally, main-street facades of respectable houses and shops often conceal an appalling poverty behind them (Marcus 266), so the possession of money frequently masks a moral penury within. In striving for profit for its own sake, disconnected from any commodity produced by labor and, indeed, from labor itself, the financial speculators betray an inner emptiness, a lack of moral values which prevents them from seeing or realizing their own humanity. Because they view their associations in monetary terms, they reduce others to objects, depriving them of their humanity and precluding the development of trust. As a result, the Tiggs and Pecksniffs of the world themselves become objects, commodities to be used and discarded as soon as they have served their purpose.

Notes

[1] Both Steven Marcus in *Dickens from Pickwick to Dombey* (New York: Simon and Schuster, 1965) and J. Hillis Miller in *Charles Dickens: The World of His Novels* (Bloomington: Indiana University Press, 1969) acknowledge this, but their interpretations of Dickens' treatment are significantly different from one another as they are also from my own.

[2] In chapter 27, Tigg, who beforehand seemed a minor character hovering on the fringes of the novel, assumes a larger role in its business, now an essential catalyst in the plot.

[3] Charles Dickens, *Martin Chuzzlewit* (Oxford: Oxford University Press, 1989). Because of the availability of many reliable editions of the text of Dickens' novels, I have included chapter citations as well as page numbers for ease of reference.

[4] That Dickens' portrait is not an exaggerated one is attested to by the fact that "the scandalous activities of a type of promoter personified in *Martin Chuzzlewit* (1843) by one Mr. Tigg Montague . . . were the immediate impetus and occasion of the appointment, in 1841, of a parliamentary committee 'to inquire into the state of the laws respecting joint-stock companies, with a view to the greater security of the public' " (Hunt 90).

[5] I refer here to Lionel Trilling's distinction between authenticity and sincerity. Authenticity, he states, suggests "a more strenuous moral experience than 'sincerity' does, a more exigent conception of the self and of what being true to it consists of, a wider reference to the universe and man's place in it, and a less acceptant and genial view of the social circumstances of life" (11).

[6] Trilling is contrasting Hegelian and Marxist concepts of alienation, but his remarks are apt within the present discussion. It is also interesting to note that he observes

that, according to Marx, "[m]oney, in short, is the principle of the inauthentic in human existence" (124).

Works Cited

Collins, Philip, ed. *Dickens: The Critical Heritage.* New York: Barnes & Noble, 1971.

Dickens, Charles. *Martin Chuzzlewit.* Oxford: Oxford University Press, 1989 (originally published 1843).

Engel, Monroe. *The Maturity of Dickens.* Oxford: Oxford University Press, 1959.

Hunt, Bishop Carleton. *The Development of the Business Corporation in England 1800-67.* Cambridge, Mass.: Harvard University Press, 1936.

Marcus, Steven. "Reading the Illegible." *The Victorian City: Images and Reality.* 2 vols. Ed. H. J. Dyos and Michael Wolff. London: Routledge & Kegan Paul, 1973. 257-76.

Miller, J. Hillis. *Charles Dickens: The World of His Novels.* Bloomington: Indiana University Press, 1969.

Robinson, Henry Crabb. *Henry Crabb Robinson on Books and Their Writers.* Vol. 2. Ed. Edith J. Morley. London: J. M. Dent and Sons, 1938.

Smith, Adam. *The Wealth of Nations Books I-III.* Intro. by Andrew Skinner. New York: Penguin Classics, 1986 (originally published 1776).

Smith, Grahame. *Dickens, Money, and Society.* Berkeley and Los Angeles: University of California Press, 1968.

Sucksmith, Harvey Peter. *The Narrative Art of Charles Dickens: The Rhetoric of Sympathy and Irony in His Novels.* Oxford: The Clarendon Press, 1970.

Trilling, Lionel. *Sincerity and Authenticity.* Cambridge: Harvard University Press, 1972.

WOMEN AND MONEY

Philip Collins (essay date 1982)

SOURCE: "Business and Bosoms: Some Trollopian Concerns," in *Nineteenth-Century Fiction,* Vol. 37, No. 3, December, 1982, pp. 293-315.

[*In the following essay, Collins examines Trollope's use of the financial worries of women—a prominent feature in Trollope's fiction. Collins pays particular attention to the concern of Trollope's female characters with fortune hunting and marrying for money (rather than for love), which was considered the main way in which women could acquire wealth in the nineteenth-century.*]

> . . . my Essays, which of all my other works have been most current; for that, it seems, they come home, to men's business, and bosoms.

>   Francis Bacon, Dedication of *Essays* (1625)

Like an old divine I shall divide my text, dealing first with its context, then in turn with its two substantives, then with the hyphenated concept business-and-bosoms, and finally I shall return to Bacon's sentence about why his *Essays* were "most current."

Blake's splendid epigrammatic comment on the title page of his copy of the *Essays*—"Good advice for Satan's Kingdom"—is, curiously, echoed by one of the marginalia in Trollope's copy. Against "Of Fortune" he wrote: "Very sagacious, but with wisdom all from the Devil."[1] In *Ralph the Heir* he had written of Bacon as "a man who had risen higher and was reported to have fallen lower,—perhaps than any other son of Adam,"[2] and elsewhere he compared him, to his detriment, with Cicero.[3] He regarded the sagacity of the *Essays,* like the integrity of the man, as badly flawed by policy and hypocrisy. Nevertheless Trollope, who much more resembled Bacon than Blake in having a relish for being "current" and for coming home agreeably to men's business and bosoms, was in Blake's sense a denizen of Satan's Kingdom. Though he made his name with stories set in ecclesiastical circumstances, his was a thoroughly secular mind—much more secular and less interested in varieties of religious experience than the agnostic author of *Scenes of Clerical Life* with whom he was, in the late 1850s, briefly and adventitiously linked. In the final pages of the Barsetshire series he enters, of course, a disclaimer: "my object has been to paint the social and not the professional lives of clergymen," and the same phraseology, typical of Trollope, appears in a similar interjection in chapter 42 of *Framley Parsonage* ("I have written much of clergymen, but in doing so I have endeavoured to portray them as they bear on our social life rather than to describe the mode and working of their professional careers"). Being a priest—to use an un-Trollopian locution—is for him a professional career, not a spiritual calling; Escott remarked that, from Trollope's pervadingly official point of view, the Established Church was "a branch of the Civil Service."[4] He took, of course, a similarly low-falutin stance about literature: recall how the first sentence of the *Autobiography* ends with a promise to describe what openings "a literary career offers to men and women for the earning of their bread."[5] Referring to Trollope's clerics, the author of *An Agnostic's Apology,* Leslie Stephen, rightly saw him as being here "in the awkward position of a realist bound to ignore realities" and "to leave gaps in his pictures of life" in what some would call "the only really interesting places." Trollope's view of the clergy was perhaps, Stephen acknowledged,

> a useful corrective to the study of the ordinary lives in which the saintliness of respectable clergymen tends to be a little over-emphasised; still, it omits or attenuates one element—the religious, namely—which must have had some importance in the character of contemporary divines.[6]

Endeavoring, as he says, to describe "such clergymen as I see around me," Trollope "could not venture to be transcendental." His vision and his imagination failed him here; certainly he was never transcendental. George Bertram's religious experience on the Mount of Olives (*The Bertrams,* ch. 7), recalled forty chapters later in the novel's final sentence, is vaguely conceived and thinly presented, as is the more heterodox and skeptical phase of his development.

"For myself," he continues in that penultimate paragraph of *The Last Chronicle of Barset,* "I can only say that I shall always be happy to sit, when allowed to do so, at the table of Archdeacon Grantly." I recall here David Hume's observation that the twelve Apostles were hardly the kind of people one would invite to dinner: just so, but it is not the kind of remark that the finest people make. Trollope never claimed to be among them. He resembles indeed his Archdeacon Grantly, of whom he writes: "His aspirations are of a healthy, if not of the highest kind," his intellect is "sufficient for such a place in the world, but not sufficient to put him in advance of it" (*The Warden,* chs. 20, 21). He was no Biake, far in advance of his world. Civilization, and even Christianity itself, he asserts with dubious historical accuracy, has been made possible by material progress, which is wholly due to "man's desire to do the best he can for himself and those around him," and he is equally sweeping in his moralization that "it is a mistake to suppose that a man is a better man because he despises money. Few do so, and those few in doing so suffer a defect" (*Autobiography,* ch. 6). Well, that puts the saints in their place: "So get you gone, Saint Francis, with few blessings on your head." Still, as Trollope says, "Few do" despise money, and few novels give much space to sainthood; and though his Reverend Josiah Crawley is a convincingly good and upright man, he does "suffer a defect" and is not ennobled by his indigence. Though there are long reaches of human behavior and aspirations beyond Trollope's ken, ample and significant subject matter remains for him. Contrasting him with his freethinking brother Thomas, George Eliot described Anthony as "a Church of England man, clinging to whatever is, *on the whole,*

and without fine distinctions, honest, lovely and of good report."[7] Trollope does not draw his distinctions too fine, nor does he expect too much of fallen human nature; he glimpses no New Jerusalem and would not much have cared for it had he done so. "I have ever," he says, "thought of myself as a preacher of sermons, and my pulpit as one which I could make both salutary and agreeable to my audience" (*Autobiography,* ch. 8), and his sermons—or advice for making the best of things in Satan's Kingdom—are not made disagreeable or innutritious by commending doctrines "too . . . good for human nature's daily food." It was well said, by an early reviewer, that he possessed "an especial talent for drawing what may be called the second-class of good people";[8] and it was characteristic of his art that the first of the Barsetshire novels is a demonstration of what little good is done and how much grief and harm are occasioned by John Bold's righteous passion for "the reform of all abuses" (*The Warden,* ch. 2). *Pas trop de zèle* is implicitly Trollope's motto in social and political, as in moral and spiritual life. No wonder that he found Palmerston so congenial.

Let us turn to "business"—literally—and here I may apply to Trollope two contemporaries' remarks about Dickens. Walter Bagehot praised Dickens for paying adequate attention in his novels to "the pecuniary part of life": "The most remarkable deficiency in modern fiction is its omission of the business of life. . . . In most novels money *grows*"[9]—on trees, as it were. It is much to be regretted that Bagehot—whose affinities with Trollope were noted by Asa Briggs and discussed further and illuminatingly by Ruth apRoberts—never wrote about his novels, which, as I shall be reminding you, were, like Dickens's, eminently innocent of this deficiency. He is manifestly concerned with "the *business* of life," its monetary basis; even his letters, it has been said, read "almost as if [they were] . . . written by his business manager."[10] My other Dickens quotation comes from his son Charley who writes of his father's "system of work" that "no city clerk was ever more methodical or orderly than he. . . . At something before ten he would sit down . . . to his desk . . . and would there remain until lunch time"—though he did not, Charley continues, work on "Mr. Anthony Trollope's plan" of expecting to turn out so much manuscript every day.[11] The two novelists were akin, then, in a businesslike approach to composition; but Trollope had indeed also *been* that "city clerk," and is one of the small band of major authors—surprisingly small, when you tot them up—who over many years of their creative life have held a steady job in an organization remote from letters. And in Trollope's case this mattered to his art, and not only when, as in *The Three Clerks,* he commandeered this experience for fictional purposes, or when, in those regular early-morning writing sessions, at a thousand words an hour with a timetabled schedule to maintain, the solitary author superficially resembled an office worker in an organization. (It comes as no surprise that one of Bacon's sentences which Trollope emphatically marginalized "Good" was this: "In studies, whatsoever a man commandeth upon himself, let him set hours for it.") Deeper down, his extensive experience in a great national concern gave him an ingrained sense, valuable to him as a novelist, that a large and complex society took a lot of running—that "the business of life" preoccupied most men's lives and could be enjoyable and challenging, not just a chore. He had, as Thackeray said, "tossed a good deal about the world"—"banged" about it, you will recall, was the word Froude preferred—with a keen eye for how it wagged and what it cost: witness that illuminating memory of him, in his early Irish days, by the Dublin lady who told Escott that Trollope's "close looking into the commonest objects of daily life always reminded her of a woman in a shop examining the materials for a new dress" (high praise, indeed).[12] This healthy curiosity informs the novels which, on the pecuniary and business aspects of life, have that "air of reality (solidity of specification)" which, for Henry James, constituted "the supreme virtue of a novel—the merit on which all its other merits . . . helplessly and submissively depend."[13]

A simple illustration of this is that, more than any English novelist I know, Trollope almost always, when introducing a character, specifies his or her income or capital. "No other novelist," indeed, said the *Saturday Review* in 1865, "has made the various worries about money so prominent a feature in most of his stories—and this not so much from the comic, but the serious point of view."[14] Harriet Martineau's *Poor-Law Tales* and *Illustrations of Political Economy* have, after their "Finis," a little appendix headed "Summary of Principles illustrated in this Volume," or suchlike. Trollope's novels might similarly carry, as an appendix, a balance sheet or profit-and-loss account, the amounts being duly carried forward in the Barchester and Palliser series. His *Autobiography* indeed, having started in that first sentence with the "earnings" of literature, concludes in its final chapter with that interim statement totaling, so precisely, £68,939.17 *.s.5d.;* and, of his elaborate work schedules for the novels, Mary Hamer has remarked that "the scrupulous arithmetical detail in which his output is planned and recorded owes something to a foible of personality."[15] The foible appears early in his fiction: in chapter 2 of *The Macdermots of Ballycloran* we hear that Thady Macdermot "got himself a wife with two thousand pounds fortune, for which he had to go to law with his brother-in-law." Turn to the first Barchester novel, the plot of which concerns the proper use of funds, and we find that Mr. Harding—himself "as ignorant as a child" about money matters, as he confesses—receives £800 a year as Warden, that he gives to his curate the £80 a year, and glebe, accruing from Crabtree Parva, and that he eventually drops to £75 a year at St. Cuthbert's (*The Warden,* chs. 3, 13, 21). We are told how much Dr. Grantly pays his housekeeper and—at half that salary—his girls' governess, and how well Dr. Vesey Stanhope does out of absenting himself from Crabtree Canonicorum. The next two Barchester novels introduce a long-running Trollope concern with fortune hunting and mercenary marriages, contemplated or consummated: Eleanor Bold, with nearly £1000 a year, and Miss Dunstable the ointment-heiress ("gallipot wench whose money still smells of bad drugs," as old Mr. Gumption is ungallantly to call her [*Framley Parsonage,* ch. 42]) with her fortune of over £200,000, attract appropriately varied and insistent attention. And so one could continue through the Barchester series, to *The Last Chronicle of Barset,* where Johnny Eames is getting £350 a year as against his £80, supplemented by £20 from his mother; in *The Small House at Allington* Conway Dalrymple commands £600 for a painting, the Reverend Mr. Thumble gets paid half-a-crown a service and the Reverend Mr. Crawley £130 a year, Dobbs Broughton is thought to have over £4,000 a year, and Major Grantly, having inherited £6000 from his first wife, can live comfortably on his pension of £600 and can well afford to marry the portionless Grace Crawley provided that his father does not withdraw his annual allowance of £800—this being one of various episodes in the novels where parents or aunts or uncles seek to run the lives of their juniors by threatening to withdraw such allowances: think of Harry Annesley, Hugh Stanbury, Plantagenet Palliser. Or think how another of the earlier novels, *The Three Clerks,* starts by establishing the main characters' incomes: Alaric Tudor and Henry Norman work at the superior Weights and Measures office, where they start at £100 a year, as against the £90 for Internal Navigation men like Charley Tudor; but Charley has received two increments, so now earns £110, and Harry has lately received a comfortable legacy of "some 150*l.* or 200*l.* a-year" (as Trollope says, here with uncustomary inexactitude [chs. 1, 2]). These three pair off, sooner or later, with the daughters of Mrs. Woodward, whose widow's portion brings her £400 a year, though her household fund and her girls' financial prospects when marrying are complicated by the arrival of Captain Cuttwater, able on his half-pay and pension to contribute £200 a year for his board and lodging. Alaric promptly jilts Linda for Gertrude, upon whom Uncle Cuttwater looks with special favor, but had already shown his capacity for financial corruption when he made over £300 by dealing in the mining shares whose price was affected by his official report.

Trollope took pains over these figures: Peter Edwards's edition (1974) of *He Knew He Was Right* discloses that Sir Marmaduke Rowley's salary as Governor of the Mandarin Islands, £3000 a year in the novel's opening paragraph, was originally £5000 but was altered in the manuscript. "Do you ever think what money is?" the Duke of Omnium sternly asks his errant son Gerald (*The Duke's Children,* ch. 65). Trollope often did, and it was a preoccupation of many of his characters. They share his fascination with what people are worth, in this simple monetary sense. Thus all the inhabitants of Guestwick "knew . . . to a penny" what Adolphus Crosbie's income was as Assistant Secretary in the General Committee office (£700, with a patrimony of £100) and rightly surmise that he and Lily Dale will find it hard to live in London on that (*Small House,* ch. 13)—a notion which soon obsesses Adolphus, who had from the start been conscious of "the injustice to which men are subjected in this matter of matrimony. A man has to declare himself before it is fitting that he should make any inquiry about a lady's money; and then, when he has declared himself, any such inquiry is unavailing" (ch. 6). Discovering too late that no money is attached to Lily, he leaves her for Lady Alexandrina De Courcy but soon is disgusted with that bargain too and, having now gained a promotion, finds himself well content to resume his bachelor life on £600 a year while paying her £400 alimony and her brother-in-law £200 a year on the cost of their furniture and fitments. Adolphus had received bad, if frank, advice from Alexandrina's brother, the Honourable George, who had "lately performed a manifest duty, in having married a young woman with money . . . had not been very much— perhaps thirty thousand pounds or so." Marrying, he tells Adolphus, is "the best thing a fellow can do; that is, if he has been careful to look to the main chance,— if he hasn't been caught napping, you know. . . . Yes; I've got something in the scramble" (ch. 17). Many such young men with a title put a price on their matrimonial hand. The amiable Lord Fawn, for instance, having tried for Violet Effingham and proposed thrice to Madame Max, descends to Lizzie Eustace. "Who," Trollope explains, "is to tell a Lord Fawn how much per annum he ought to regard himself as worth? He had [earlier] . . . asked a high price. . . . No doubt he had come down a little in his demand in suggesting a matrimonial arrangement to a widow with a child, and with only four thousand a year," though his mother, in a candid chat, suggests that he check first whether this income is hers in perpetuity or only for life (*The Eustace Diamonds,* ch. 9). Lord Nidderdale, with a future as a Marchioness to offer to his bride, can fly higher and might easily have married £200,000, but he goes all out and offers to take Marie Melmotte "for half a million down." Melmotte niggles about the terms and, later becoming more respectable himself, reckons that he can safely lower his offer to £15,000 a year settled on Marie and her eldest son, the bridegroom to receive, after a probationary period of six months' married life, a personal *bonne bouche* of £20,000, and Nidderdale is willing to settle for that (*The Way We Live Now,* chs. 4, 35).

In the lower reaches of the gentry, a Bernard Dale can name humbler terms for agreeing to propose to Isabella:

"I don't pretend to be very much in love with her [he tells Adolphus Crosbie]. It's not my way, you know. . . . The governor has distinctly promised to allow me eight hundred a year off the estate, and to take us in for three months every year if we wish it. I told him simply that I couldn't do it for less" (*Small House,* ch. 6). But the spirited Isabella, who even wishes she could earn some money "if I knew how," particularly hates those words, "an excellent marriage." In them, she says, "is contained more of wicked worldliness than any other words that one ever hears spoken"; and when eventually she announces to her mother that she is to marry the decent but humble Dr. Crofts, who acknowledges that "we shall not be rich," she interrupts to protest: "I hate to be rich. I hate even to talk about it. I don't think it quite manly even to think about it; and I'm sure it isn't womanly" (chs. 39, 50). Not many of Trollope's characters, even his favored ones, go that far, and in one of his many narratorial discussions of this matter he offers these guidelines:

> That girls should not marry for money we are all agreed. A lady who can sell herself for a title or an estate, for an income or a set of family diamonds, . . . makes hardly more of herself, of her own inner self, . . . than the poor wretch of her own sex who earns her bread in the lowest stage of degradation. But a title, and an estate, and an income, are matters which will weigh in the balance with all Eve's daughters—as they do with all Adam's sons. Pride of place, and the power of living well in front of the world's eye, are dear to us all;—are, doubtless, intended to be dear. [A curious exercise in teleology, one might interject!] Only in acknowledging so much, let us remember that there are prices at which these good things may be too costly. (*Framley Parsonage,* ch. 21)

We shall return to what one Trollope character calls the "profession of matrimony." Courtship is of course the main "business" conducted in his novels, as traditionally it has provided the main plot of most fiction, but in Trollope an unusually high proportion of the young people (and not so young ones) moderate the romantic, or replace it, by the businesslike approach. He does offer pictures, or glimpses, of some other businesses at work—officialdom, politicians, commercial travelers, tailors, moneylenders, lawyers, physicians, clergymen in their organizational rather than their sacerdotal functions—and so on. "Enough!—or Too much" (to cite Blake again) of business. Let us contemplate bosoms.

When, having undertaken to write this essay, I decided upon its title, I naturally wrote to Trollope's latest bibliographical commenter (in the MLA's *Victorian Fiction: A Second Guide to Research*) to inquire about existing studies in this field, and my good friend Ruth apRoberts replied helpfully. I quote here some of her hints on "bosoms": "I know Trollope likes them, but I think he generally calls it *bust,* and the resultant image is a sort of undifferentiated area, the clothed swelling form like a dressmaker's dummy—not discrete protuberances." This, my researches suggest, is just—though who am I to purport to confirm the findings of an accredited Trollopian such as she? The conventions of his day placed limits upon Trollope's descriptions of his heroines' charms: you will recall indeed that he had to delete from the manuscript of *Barchester Towers* "passages marked as being too warm."[16] He permits himself a little extra warmth, however, when writing about the Middle East. Thus a glimpse of "naked shoulders and bosoms nearly bare" occurs in *The Bertrams.* The Jewish washerwomen whom George Bertram and his party observe are "glorious specimens of female creation," and George is so struck by the features of one of these that he is almost prepared to overlook her lack of "feminine softness": " 'If I knew how to set about the bargain, I would take that woman home with me, and mould her to be my wife.' Such was George Bertram's outspoken enthusiasm" (ch. 9). This interesting experiment, however, is not attempted.

Trollope's English scenes depict less bare flesh, and are sexually reticent; so when, reading the episode in which Ned Spooner is having a man-to-man chat with Phineas Finn about his intention of proposing to Adelaide Palliser, my eye lit upon Spooner's remark that "there's nothing like a good screw" (*Phineas Redux,* ch. 19), I momentarily registered, as did Wordsworth on a different occasion, "a gentle shock of mild surprise" (*Prelude,* V.382)—though of course, had I been a horsey academic, I would have known that "a screw" still denotes, in those circles, a horse with imperfections. Trollope didn't intend a double entendre, maybe, though two considerations give me pause. First, Ned Spooner does find it difficult to distinguish between fillies and his intended Adelaide. "She's such a well-built creature!" he exclaims. "There's a look of blood about her I don't see in any of 'em. That sort of breeding is what one wants to get through the mud with" (ch. 29). Secondly, my suspicions are roused by his calling a courting character Mr. Glascock, and the more so because he had that grievous habit of belittling his minor characters by giving them indicatively comic names, and because Trollope was, after all, a worldly-wise man. "Screw" had been sexual slang since the late eighteenth century, "cock" since the early seventeenth, and Trollope must have learned something by attending not just one but two Public Schools.

His descriptions of his heroines often prudently stop at the neckline, having traversed the span from hair to chin, with—for me, who am not specially moved by this anatomical feature—a remarkably frequent pause at the teeth. His first heroine, Feemy Macdermot, has a mouth "half an inch too long; but her teeth were white and good" (*The Macdermots,* ch. 2), and many a heroine afterwards is annotated dentally. Miss

Dunstable—no beauty—has big teeth, Adelaide Palliser's are perfect, Clarissa Underwood's, in the opinion of some caviling critics, *too* perfect, and Caroline Waddington's "were never excelled by any [teeth] that ever graced the face of a woman" (*The Bertrams,* ch. 9). To show one's teeth rarely and sparingly is a big plus-point; Violet Effingham, Madame Max, and Florence Mountjoy are among these modest-toothed ladies. Lizzie Eustace's, predictably, "were without flaw or blemish, even, small, white, and delicate; but perhaps they were shown too often," and Frank Greystock comes to realize that "those teeth would bite" (*The Eustace Diamonds,* chs. 2, 13). Trollope gives the most erotic teeth to Lucy Robarts: small, seldom seen, and white as pearls. "Lucy's teeth!" the narrator exclaims, "it was only now and again . . . that the fine finished lines and dainty pearl-white colour of that perfect set of ivory could be seen." Her sister-in-law is similarly enthusiastic: "You shall get her a husband," she tells Mark; " . . . if I were a man I should fall in love with her at once. Did you ever observe her teeth, Mark?" (*Framley Parsonage,* ch. 10). But he had not. Lucy, however, notices such things: she describes Lord Lufton as having "fine straight legs, and a smooth forehead, and a good-humoured eye, and white teeth" (ch. 26).

I had never thought of Trollope as an especially visual novelist, and he of course groans sometimes when this heroine-describing task occurs again; heroes, of course, are presented less visually, and more in social, professional, and financial terms. "And now looms before me the novelist's great difficulty," he writes in the first chapter of *Framley Parsonage.* "Miss Monsell—or, rather, Mrs. Mark Robarts—must be described": and when, nine chapters later, it is Lucy Robarts's turn, he exclaims, "If one might only go on without these descriptions, how pleasant it would all be!" Sometimes he opts out: "Let each reader . . . fancy [Adela Gauntlet] of any outward shape and colour that he please" (*The Bertrams,* ch. 4, "Our Prima Donna"). Interestingly, however, Michael Irwin begins his book *Picturing* with Trollope's picture of Lucy Morris, in the middle of which the narrator asks, "What else can be said of her face or personal appearance that will interest a reader?" Irwin comments:

> He [Trollope] takes it for granted that we will *want* to form a mental picture of the character after this fashion, that this visual information "will interest a reader." The passage implies that we see a new acquaintance as an aggregation of particular physical features—in this case, hair, eyes, mouth, forehead, nose, dimple, hands and feet.[17]

He remarks, though, that these assumptions or conventions are dubious. Trollope's inventory of physical features does sometimes include the bosom. A medical treatise published in the year of *The Warden* confirmed that "the mammary glands," besides being functional, "by their seat and form constitute the ornaments of the sex,"[18] and Trollope, in that novel, showed his awareness of that "majestic contour that rivets attention," even if only to remark that Eleanor Harding did not have it (ch. 11). Even that reference to "contour" is, however, a little more explicit than Dickens's ingenious evasion when he has David Copperfield exclaim about Dora Spenlow, "What a form she had . . . !"[19] leaving it wholly to the reader to conjure up a thoroughly gratifying outline. Going further in his next novel, Trollope introduces Madame Neroni with the assurance that no "ardent lover of beauty" could resist her: her bust—and yes, her teeth—"were perfect, much more so at twenty-eight than they had been at eighteen" (*Barchester Towers*, ch. 9). Grace Crawley, no doubt somewhat undernourished at first, develops similarly during the action of *The Last Chronicle of Barset*. In chapter 1 she presents "a certain thin, unfledged, unrounded form of person, a want of fulness in the lines of her figure"; by chapter 30 "her figure was . . . full of grace at all points" (an unfortunate pun) and "perfect in symmetry," and a chapter later Lily Dale can say, "I never saw a more lovely figure," though way on in chapter 55 Lady Lufton, who admittedly has cause for reservations, regards her as "downright handsome—or will be when she fills out a little." Better endowed from the start is Emily Rowley "with a bust rather full for her age"—twenty—when she captivates Louis Trevelyan (*He Knew He Was Right*, ch. 1); also Julia Brabazon whose "bust was full, and her whole figure like that of a goddess," to the consternation of Harry Clavering when he compares his memories of her with homely Florence Burton; and when in the end Julia has to part finally with Harry, she cattily—rather like Cleopatra queening it over the absent Octavia—dons a dress so made "as to show off the full perfection of her form" so that, as she says to herself, Harry should "be made to know all that he had lost." Luckily, however, although "Lady Ongar's form, bust, and face were, at this period of her life, almost majestic," Harry has by now decided, after considerable wavering, that "the softness and grace of womanhood" were the charms that he most loves, and Florence does (reputedly) have these (*The Claverings*, chs. 3, 44, 47). Another goddesslike figure—that of "a Juno rather than a Venus"—is Caroline Waddington's: "Her head stood nobly on her shoulders, giving to her bust that ease and grace of which sculptors are so fond, and of which tight-laced stays are so utterly subversive." But her two husbands are to discover that this "sculptor" reference is ominous, as is the "goddess" one; she has the beauty—but also the coldness—"of a marble bust" (*The Bertrams*, chs. 9, 28).

The Baroness Banmann in *Is He Popenjoy?* is a reminder that one can have too much of a good thing: besides possessing a double chin and a considerable moustache she has a bust so "copious" that even the

butch "cloth jacket buttoned up to the neck," which she wears as her feminist uniform, fails to produce "that appearance of manly firmness which the occasion almost required. But the virile collars, budding out over [the jacket], perhaps supplied what was wanting" (ch. 17). Her feminist rival, Doctor Olivia Q. Fleabody, is suitably contrasting: a very thin flat-chested young lady.

With his Lady Eustace, generally excellent in her snaky enticingness, Trollope's anatomical touch momentarily deserts him when, having to allude to that condition—pregnancy—which embarrasses so many Victorian novelists, he remarks that "she bore beneath her bosom the fruit of her husband's love" (*The Eustace Diamonds*, ch. 1), an uncommon place to carry a baby. One final quotation on these exterior views of the bosom: inevitably, *The Way We Live Now* carries Trollope's warning that, in this new world of shabby dishonesty, deception has brought disenchantment to this view too. "In these days," he writes (that phrase which tolls like a bell throughout this novel),

> men regard the form and outward lines of a woman's face and figure more than either the colour or the expression, and women fit themselves to men's eyes. With padding and false hair without limit a figure may be constructed of almost any dimensions. The sculptors who construct them, male and female, hairdressers and milliners, are very skilful, and figures are constructed of noble dimensions, sometimes with voluptuous expansion, sometimes with classic reticence. (ch. 26)

This animadversion, however, is an example of the overinsistence which mars this great novel, for it serves only to lead up to "But Mrs. Hurtle was not a beauty after the present fashion." Whatever her other deficiencies, she is physically genuine, and is so on an ample scale: "Her bust was full and beautifully shaped." But as we are also informed that "her cheeks and lips and neck were full," and so were her nose and chin, it is evident that hers is a decidedly formidable style of beauty (ch. 26).

Femininity, "feminine softness," is one essential for Trollope's heroines, but most of them have some portion of beauty, their bust often being an important element in this, sometimes indeed literally a prominent one. His young ladies were of course generally admired; as Henry James happily put it, he "settled down steadily to the English girl; he took possession of her, and turned her inside out."[20] Some of them, when turned inside out, have seemed rather tame to later readers: but Trollope would doubtless have defended them as he defended Thackeray's Amelia against the charge of insipidity. She was no sillier, he wrote, than "many young ladies whom we who are old have loved in our youth, or than those whom our sons are loving at the present time. . . . I know no trait in Amelia which a man would be ashamed to find in his own daughter"— or daughter-in-law, he may have reflected, with a glint in his eye as he remembered that, not long before this, he was anxiously confiding to G. H. Lewes that his son Harry wanted "to marry a woman of the town" (a species of womankind, incidentally, underrepresented in his fiction).[21] Bosoms, then, have their place in the novels, though, as Ruth apRoberts alerted me, he usually calls the mammary glands "the bust." A heroine is of course permitted to press a loveletter to her "bosom": Clara Amedroz, for instance, does so, and earlier in that narrative Will Belton had yearned "to take her to his bosom and hold her there for always" (*The Belton Estate,* chs. 32, 22). The manly bosom as a receptacle for loving ladies or their tears makes many appearances, at penultimate moments; thus, Lady Glencora weeps upon Plantagenet's when she tells him she is————(that discreet dash which signifies pregnancy) as, suitably enough, "he sat by her on her bedside"—note the "her" (*Can You Forgive Her?,* ch. 73).

The word "bosom" occurs oftenest in Trollope, however, I guess, in its interior or metaphoric sense—that curious but convenient usage which blends the moral sentiments and the emotions. The singular "breast" may be used as a synonym, particularly when a conflict is proceeding: so it is in his breast that Frank Greystock juxtaposes Lizzie and Lucy in *The Eustace Diamonds* (ch. 18) and that Harry Clavering experiences the struggle between his dutiful feelings towards Florence and his amorous and acquisitive ones about Julia, whereas it is in her "bosom" that Julia feels a warm though impermanent "glow of self-sacrifice" (*The Claverings,* chs. 25, 27). Nice anatomical-metaphorical distinctions occur: thus Katie Woodward in *The Three Clerks,* having "probed her young bosom, which now, by a sudden growth, became quick with a woman's impulse," has discovered that she loves Charley Tudor, but soon afterwards discovers that she mustn't, a prohibition in which she acquiesces "with a sad bosom and a broken heart" (chs. 30, 31). But it is not only over affairs of the heart that bosoms get troubled, of course. Arguing the significance of his book on Cicero as a guide to Trollope's thinking, Ruth apRoberts notes his dramatization of the conflicts between the *honestum* and the *turpe,* and the relation of the *honestum* to the *utile*—a relationship, she reminds us, which provides "a recurrent and endlessly interesting theme in Trollope, as he takes up those many cases where principle and expediency seem to be at odds, in sexual selection, in law, in problems of Church and government."[22] Principle and expediency: I am reminded here of Asa Briggs's remark that the political novels "bring to life through illustrative examples Bagehot's notions of responsible power" and that they "explore more sensitively than Bagehot" could

do issues of policy and probity that were "the nineteenth-century equivalent of the problems of Bacon's *Essays*"[23]—a quotation which gratifyingly relates to the allusion in my title. Illustrations here are abundant, but I will confine myself to one bosom troubled by other than courtship questions—Sir Thomas Underwood, that guiltily unproductive Bacon scholar:

> They who know the agonies of an ambitious, indolent, doubting, self-accusing man,—of a man who has a skeleton in his cupboard as to which he can ask for sympathy from no one,—will understand what feelings were at work within the bosom of Sir Thomas when his Percycross friends left him alone in his chamber. (*Ralph the Heir,* ch. 40)

It was of such passages and dramatizations that James was thinking when he made his final claim for Trollope in that obituary essay: he "will remain one of the most trustworthy, though not one of the most eloquent, of the writers who have helped the heart of man to know itself."[24]

I come now, though we have already visited it, to the hyphenated concept "business-and-bosoms"— often a matter of business *versus* bosoms. When Adolphus Crosbie "rather suddenly" says to his fiancée, " 'Lily, . . . I want to say a few words about,—business.' And he gave a little laugh as he spoke the last word, making her fully understand that he was not quite at his ease," we realize that both of them have cause for unease: his concern with "business"—the getting and spending aspect of matrimony—is at odds with the feelings he should have in his bosom for the moral and physical qualities—including the bosom—of his betrothed (*Small House,* ch. 12). Trollope of course explicitly accepted the conventional view that "there must be love in a novel"—"It is admitted," he writes elsewhere, invoking the general will, "that a novel can hardly be made interesting or successful without love"—and he remarks that even when, as in *Phineas Finn,* "I wrote politics for my own sake, I must put in love and intrigue . . . for the sake of my readers" (*Autobiography,* chs. 8, 12, 17). So this conflict between love and money, the dictates of the honest bosom and of an eye to business values, becomes one of his staple subjects. This is of course one of the traditional problems for young people in novels and plays. Recall Elizabeth Bennet's question to Mrs. Gardiner: "Pray, my dear aunt, what is the difference in matrimonial affairs, between the mercenary and the prudent motive? Where does discretion end, and avarice begin?"[25] Or recall that a book has been devoted to *Love and Property in the Novels of Charles Dickens.* Trollope tills this field yet more assiduously and, as we have seen, quantifies the yield more than most. In his stories the matter is sometimes complicated, when, from the male point of view, an eye to business may reasonably look in the same direction as a wandering bosom-admiring eye is looking; thus Julia of *The Claverings* and Lizzie of *The Eustace Diamonds* are sexually more seductive, besides being otherwise better endowed, than their rivals Florence and Lucy. Sometimes the hero's dilemma—for it is usually the hero's—can be reduced to the mnemonically alliterative: "which bride Frank [Gresham] should marry of those two bespoken for him; Mary, namely, or Money?" (*Doctor Thorne*, ch. 31). Trollope of course cheats here, as in *The Claverings* and elsewhere, by ensuring that the hero gets both, through some convenient deaths: and one could make a long list of Trollope characters who die prematurely so that the happy couple can live comfortably, or so that the action can get going (Lord Ongar, Sir Florian Eustace), or so that a series can proceed (John Bold, Mary Finn). It is dangerous, in Trollope's fiction, to possess money or rank and be related, however obscurely, to the hero or heroine. Sometimes a heroine experiences a dilemma and can express it with similar "Mary-or-Money" pointedness. "Oh, Fanny," Lucy Robarts asks, confessing her attraction to Lord Lufton, "is it his legs, think you, or is it his title?"—for Lord Lufton has "fine straight legs" besides a peerage and those white teeth (*Framley Parsonage*, ch. 26). Sometimes it is the woman who adventures after money, with the excuse that a girl's business *is* marrying—besides which, with nothing much else to do, girls can take up love as a full-time occupation. "To be in love, as an absolute, well-marked, acknowledged fact," Trollope reflects in *The Eustace Diamonds* (ch. 4), "is the condition of a woman more frequently and more readily than of a man. Such is not the common theory on the matter" (and Trollope continues with arguments for his contention). Or, in *The Vicar of Bullhampton*, making an anti-feminist point, he remarks that marriage

> is a woman's one career—let women rebel against the edict as they may; and though there may be word-rebellion here and there, women learn the truth early in their lives. . . . Nature prompts the desire, the world acknowledges its ubiquity, circumstances show that it is reasonable, the whole theory of creation requires it. . . . Let men be taught to recognise the same truth as regards themselves, and we shall cease to hear of the necessity of a new career for women. (ch. 37)

This is quoted in an interesting study of Trollope as a sociologist, where it is suggested, with some exaggeration, that it is because there were virtually no careers for genteel girls that "Trollope's novels all divide into two parts, almost two different stories [business-centered and bosom-centered, as we might put it]. Whereas the men in the novels employ themselves in the affairs of their parishes, their country estates, their professions and political careers, the women devote themselves to match-making for others or falling in love themselves. The men hunt foxes; the women hus-

bands."[26] Men can choose their profession, Julia tells Harry Clavering when rejecting him, "but I have had no choice—no choice but to be married well, or to go out like the snuff of a candle"; and, as she walks out of the church, a countess, she tells herself "that she had done right. She had chosen her profession, as Harry Clavering had chosen his . . . Mercenary! Of course she had been mercenary. Were not all men and women mercenary upon whom devolved the necessity of earning their bread?" Lord Ongar had "purchas[ed] her at the price of a brilliant settlement"; later, a not very merry widow but a comfortably rich one, she tries to buy Harry back (*The Claverings*, chs. 1, 3). Another girl tempted to marry money and a title, Nora Rowley, reflects that "she had her fortune to make, and that her beauty and youth were the capital on which she had to found it" (*He Knew He Was Right*, ch. 13), and she determines to accept the future Lord Peterborough, though eventually her honesty triumphs over her self-seeking. Nora's point about her "capital" is made, at a less genteel level, by Mrs. Davis in *The Three Clerks*, putting Charley Tudor on the spot about his intentions with regard to another Norah, Miss Golightly: "A girl's time is her money. She's at her best now, and a girl like her must make her hay while the sun shines. She can't go fal-lalling with you, and then nothing come of it. You mustn't suppose she's to lose her market that way" (ch. 20). Georgiana Longestaffe's sorry adventures on the marriage market show no greater elevation of tone among the gentry; but, as Trollope acknowledges elsewhere, "it is sometimes very hard for young girls to be in the right," for they must not be mercenary, nor marry paupers, nor allow themselves to become old maids, nor "callously resolve to care for nothing but a good income and a good house. There should be some handbook of love, to tell young ladies when they may give way to it without censure" (*The Bertrams*, ch. 10).

The novels are indeed chockablock with adventurers (Phineas Finn gets called that) and adventuresses, with mercenary marriages, and with attempts at them frustrated either by conscience, however tardily, or by inefficiency, bad luck, or bad timing. Bertie Stanhope has been mentioned as an early (and delightful) specimen of these gold diggers: "Eleanor Bold appeared before him, no longer as a beautiful woman, but as a new profession called matrimony. It was a profession indeed requiring but little labour, and one in which an income was insured to him" (*Barchester Towers*, ch. 42)—or so he blithely thinks. He and Mr. Slope are a comic tryout for what later becomes a serious matter, though the later novels sometimes contain, in Shakespearean fashion, comic and often low-life variants on the theme, such as Captain Archie's pursuit of Lady Ongar under Captain Boodle's tutelage in *The Claverings*, or the tiresome Widow Greenow episodes in *Can You Forgive Her?*, the alliterative Prong-Prime affair in *Ralph the Heir*, or Widow

Thoroughbung's businesslike dealings with her suitor Mr. Prosper in *Mr. Scarborough's Family,* or Sir Lionel Bertram's pursuit of Miss Baker, or alternatively Miss Todd, or indeed alternatively Miss Baker. Or there are lower-class gold diggers to balance the higher-class ones, such as Charley Tudor's Norah Golightly or Johnny Eames's Amelia Roper, just as self-consciously "bad" marriages, from a worldly point of view, are sometimes offset against the more money-ridden courtships or temptations in the same novel. Fanny Clavering's eventual acceptance of the unprepossessing and indigent Mr. Saul, or Bell Dale's of Doctor Crofts, are instances of this; similarly, in *The Bertrams* Adela Gauntlet's willingness to marry into poverty contrasts with Caroline Waddington's determination not to do so. "We are much too afraid of what we call beggary," says Adela to Caroline. "Beggary, Caroline, with four hundred pounds a year!" (*The Bertrams,* ch. 17). The marriage-and-money theme, moreover, often gives Trollope, as it gives other novelists, the opportunity to increase the social mix of his books: a version of E. M. Forster's "Only connect . . ." notion. In such impoverished-aristocratic families as Lord Nidderdale's, Trollope sharply remarks.

> it is generally understood that matters shall be put right by an heiress. It has become an institution, like primogeniture, and is almost as serviceable for maintaining the proper order of things. Rank squanders money; trade makes it;—and then trade purchases rank by re-gilding its splendour. The arrangement, as it affects the aristocracy generally, is well understood. (*The Way We Live Now,* ch. 57)

Lord Nidderdale's negotiations for Marie Melmotte have already been mentioned, as has the Honourable George De Courcy's marrying coal; Undy Scott and his relentlessly energetic brothers provide another instance. Some luckier money-seeking suitors can seek titled and thus better-laundered wealth: Burgo Fitzgerald fails, but Plantagenet Palliser succeeds in capturing the Auldreekie fortune: "The heir of the Pallisers had done his duty, and Mr. Fothergill was unfeignedly a happy man" (*Small House,* ch. 55). "Their marriage," we learn in the next book in the series, "in a point of view regarding business, had been a complete success" (*Can You Forgive Her?,* ch. 24), but with further books to go Trollope can make this marriage, along with Lady Glencora's love for Burgo, his most complex exploration of a marriage in which love was not initially the driving force. Another extended study of a young man on the make, but not unscrupulously so, is Phineas Finn. Other more mercenary suitors, who cannot now be discussed in detail, include Miss Mackenzie's, and George Vavasor (who greedily and out of vanity wants Alice's love as well as her cash), and the Reverend Emilius, who can better stomach Lizzie Eustace's duplicity than can Lord George, unfinicky though the

latter had seemed when money was his object. After that brilliant chapter "The Corsair is Afraid" in which Lord George wonders "whether he would take the plunge and ask her to be his wife" and decides otherwise, Lizzie's "dream was over. Lord George was no longer a Corsair, but a brute" (ch. 63)—and, Lord Fawn also having found Lizzie, despite her riches, ultimately ineligible, she gamely turns elsewhere, though not yet having to descend to Mr. Emilius:

> As she practised it before the glass, she thought that she could tell her story in a becoming manner, with becoming tears, to Frank Greystock. . . . Her effort,—her last final effort must be made to secure the hand and heart of her cousin Frank. "Ah, 'tis his heart I want!" she said to herself. . . . Then, after much thinking of it, she resolved upon a scheme, which, of all her schemes, was the wickedest. (ch. 64)

She sends a letter to "Dear Lucy" from "Your affectionate old friend, Lizzie," and, having rehearsed the scene in advance, tells Lucy when she calls that "though he is engaged to you, it is me that he loves. . . . And of whom are you thinking? Are you doing the best for him . . . ? Cannot I do more for him than you can?" (*The Eustace Diamonds,* ch. 64). If, as Henry James says, Trollope "presented the English maiden under innumerable names . . . with every combination of moral and physical qualities"[27]—and Lizzie, though hardly maidenly, is a very striking physical and moral specimen—one must admire the innumerable combinations within which he presents his business-and-bosoms theme.

To conclude, on Bacon's phrase about his *Essays* being "most current; for that . . . they come home, to men's business, and bosoms," Trollope enjoyed—in both senses of the word—currency (and in both senses of that word, too). He took a shameless no-nonsense pleasure in money, but "though the money has been sweet," as he says in the *Autobiography* (ch. 9), "the respect, the friendships, and the mode of life which has been achieved, have been much sweeter." Like most of his great contemporaries in English fiction, he wanted to be, and was, popular; and he was speaking for most of them also when he remarked on the moral responsibility entailed by being "read right and left, above stairs and below," since a novelist "must teach whether he wish to teach or no" and "a vast proportion of the teaching of the day . . . comes from these books, which are in the hands of all readers. It is from them that girls learn what is expected from them"—and he specifies some of these and the "many other lessons also . . . taught" by novelists (*Autobiography,* ch. 12). What Trollope taught, or was conscious of teaching, was unremarkable; he was, as a *Times* reviewer said, "the novelist of common sense"[28]—a quality which the Victorians were happy to discover and praise in their major authors. Dickens's "common sense," wrote one, "had all the force of genius"; "an immense sanity underlay the whole" of Tennyson's work, wrote another, "—the perfection of common sense."[29] This was indeed one of the characteristics, and the strengths, of Victorian literature, and it belonged with the popularity of so many of its major authors; how different, many Victorians would have gratefully added, from the way these things are managed in France. Trollope, the *Times* reviewer continued (and we can assent to much of this),

> . . . writes with a shrewdness and a sobriety, yet with a rush and fullness of thought that satisfies the intellect while seeming but to tickle our curiosity. He is an immense favourite with the most intelligent class of novel readers. He never soars very high, nor digs very deep, but he hardly ever disappoints; we can always rely upon him for a good story well sustained, full of life and not deficient in ideas.[30]

To quote finally from one of the alpha-plus graduates of that "most intelligent class of readers," George Eliot. Trollope endeared himself personally to her by "his straightforward, wholesome *Wesen*," and she similarly praised *Orley Farm* as "admirable in the presentation of even, average life and character" and "thoroughly wholesome-minded." And, writing to thank him for his *Rachel Ray* and praising its construction and naturalness, she continues:

> But there is something else I care yet more about, which has impressed me very happily in all those writings of yours that I know—it is that people are breathing good bracing air in reading them— it is that they (the books) are filled with belief in goodness without the slightest tinge of maudlin. They are like pleasant public gardens, where people go for amusement and, whether they think of it or not, get health as well.

> It seems rather preachy and assuming in me to say that, out of all the other things I might say. But it is what I feel strongly, and I can't help thinking that it is what you care about also, though such things are rather a result of what an author *is* than of what he intends.[31]

It is now, happily, a commonplace that Trollope achieves more than he intends or than he says that he intends; that the *Autobiography* is a very partial guide to the novels; that, as George Eliot discerns, the creative genius was larger than the man of articulated good intentions. Writing novels that were level with life, mostly genial redactions of the familiar, he was well placed, both by "what he was" and by what he was conscious of intending, to come home, heartily and healthily, to men's—and maidens'—business and bosoms.

Notes

[1] See Michael Sadleir, "Trollope and Bacon's Essays," *Trollopian,* 1 (1945), 29.

[2] Anthony Trollope, *Ralph the Heir,* World's Classics, 2 vols. (London: Oxford Univ. Press, 1939), ch. 40. Further references to Trollope's novels which appear in the text are to the Oxford University Press's World's Classics edition, with two exceptions: *The Macdermots of Ballycloran* (London: Chapman and Hall, 1866) and *The Bertrams,* 8th ed., 2 vols. (London: Chapman and Hall, 1869).

[3] *The Life of Cicero,* 2 vols. (New York: Harper, 1881), II, 100, quoted by Ruth apRoberts, *Trollope: Artist and Moralist* (London: Chatto and Windus, 1971), p. 61.

[4] T.H.S. Escott, *Anthony Trollope: His Work, Associates and Literary Originals* (London: John Lane, 1913), p. 227.

[5] *An Autobiography,* ed. Michael Sadleir and Frederick Page, World's Classics (1950; rpt. Oxford: Oxford Univ. Press, 1980), ch. 1; further citations to this edition appear in the text.

[6] *Studies of a Biographer,* Second Series, 4 vols. (1899-1902; rpt. New York: Burt Franklin, 1973), pp. 191, 197.

[7] *The George Eliot Letters,* ed. Gordon S. Haight, 9 vols. (New Haven: Yale Univ. Press, 1954-78), IV, 81-82.

[8] Unsigned Notice, *Saturday Review,* 30 May 1857; rpt. in *Trollope: The Critical Heritage,* ed. Donald Smalley (London: Routledge; New York: Barnes and Noble, 1969), p. 48.

[9] "Charles Dickens," *National Review,* October 1858; rpt. in *Dickens: The Critical Heritage,* ed. Philip Collins (London: Routledge; New York: Barnes and Noble, 1971), pp. 392-93.

[10] Quoted by Donald Smalley in *Victorian Fiction: A Guide to Research,* ed. Lionel Stevenson (Cambridge, Mass.: Harvard Univ. Press, 1964), p. 203.

[11] "Reminiscences of my Father," rpt. in *Dickens: Interviews and Recollections,* ed. Philip Collins, 2 vols. (Totowa, N.J.: Barnes and Noble, 1981), I, 119-20.

[12] Escott, *Anthony Trollope,* pp. 133, 52.

[13] *The Art of Fiction and Other Essays* (New York: Oxford Univ. Press, 1948), p. 12.

[14] Unsigned Notice, *Saturday Review,* 4 Mar. 1865; rpt. in *Trollope: The Critical Heritage,* p. 216.

[15] "Number-length and its Significance in the Novels of Anthony Trollope," *The Yearbook of English Studies,* Vol. 5, ed. T.J.B. Spencer (London: Modern Humanities Research Association, 1975), p. 189.

[16] *The Letters of Anthony Trollope,* ed. Bradford Allen Booth (London: Oxford Univ. Press, 1951), p. 31.

[17] *Picturing: Description and Illusion in the Nineteenth-Century Novel* (London: Allen and Unwin, 1979), pp. 16-17, quoting from *The Eustace Diamonds,* ch. 3.

[18] Eugène Bouchut, *Practical Treatise on Diseases of Children and Infants at the Breast,* trans. Peter Hinckes Bird (London: J. Churchill, 1855), p. 13; rpt. in *Victorian Women,* ed. Erna Olafson Hellerstein, Leslie Parker Hume, and Karen M. Offen (Stanford: Stanford Univ. Press, 1981), p. 228.

[19] *David Copperfield,* ed. Nina Burgis (Oxford: Clarendon Press, 1981), ch. 26.

[20] "Anthony Trollope," *Century Magazine,* July 1883; rpt. In *Trollope: The Critical Heritage,* p. 542.

[21] *Thackeray* (London: Macmillan, 1879), p. 105; *The George Eliot Letters,* V, 357.

[22] apRoberts, *Trollope: Artist and Moralist,* p. 69.

[23] *Victorian People* (London: Odhams Press, 1954), pp. 115-16.

[24] James, "Anthony Trollope," rpt. in *Trollope: The Critical Heritage,* p. 545.

[25] Jane Austen, *Pride and Prejudice,* ed. Frank W. Bradbrook (London: Oxford Univ. Press, 1970), Vol. 2, ch. 4.

[26] Margaret Hewitt, "Anthony Trollope: Historian and Sociologist," *British Journal of Sociology,* 14 (1963), 229. Another sociologist, J. A. Banks, has written effectively about how Trollope's novels may be used as evidence of Victorian assumptions and practices in courtship and marriage; see his *Prosperity and Parenthood* (London: Routledge, 1954), ch. 8, "A Case Study—Anthony Trollope"; and his "The Way They Lived Then: Anthony Trollope and the 1870s," *Victorian Studies,* 12 (1968), 177-200.

[27] James, "Anthony Trollope," rpt. in *Trollope: The Critical Heritage,* p. 542.

[28] Unsigned notice, *Times,* 25 Dec. 1863; rpt. in *Trollope: The Critical Heritage,* p. 190.

[29] W. B. Rands ["Matthew Browne"], *Contemporary Review,* Jan. 1880; rpt. in *Dickens: The Critical Heritage,* p. 593; James Knowles, "Aspects of Tennyson," *Nineteenth Century,* 33 (1893), 165.

[30] *Trollope: The Critical Heritage,* p. 190.

[31] *The George Eliot Letters,* III, 360; IV, 9, 111.

Vanessa D. Dickerson (essay date 1994)

SOURCE: "Feminine Transactions: Money and Nineteenth-Century British Women Writers," in *Money: Lure, Lore, and Literature,* edited by John Louis DiGaetani, Greenwood Press, 1994, pp. 227-43.

[*In the following essay, Dickerson discusses how nineteenth-century women writers depicted women and money. In the early part of the nineteenth-century, female authors confined the financial endeavors of women to the domestic sphere. However, in the later part of the century, female authors espoused the idea of allowing women to participate in the larger economic world.*]

> I had made but about 540 £ at the close of my last affair, and I had wasted some of that. However, I had about 460 £ left, a great many very rich cloaths, a gold watch, and some jewels, tho' of no extraordinary value, and about 30 £ or 40 £ in linnen not dispo'd of.
>
> —*Moll Flanders* (1722)

Few female characters in British fiction have tallied their possessions or counted their pence and pounds with as great a relish as Daniel Defoe's Moll Flanders. This is not to say that money does not figure in works of succeeding writers, or, more specifically in the writings of nineteenth-century British women. Living in a century so preoccupied with "getting and spending" that hell itself, according to Thomas Carlyle, was "equivalent to not making money" (149), Victorian women, who had such limited means of getting and making it, were keenly aware of money.[1] From Jane Marcet's Socratic dialogues on the science of economics to Harriet Martineau's illustrations of political economy to Virginia Woolf's declaration that the woman writer needs money as well as a room of her own, not just the economic but the social and political significance of the sterling pound has proven a subject both open and attractive to women writers. The fiction of such writers as Austen, Brontë, Eliot, and Oliphant shows, however, that even where women appear entrenched in financial affairs and most involved in the business of money, they are rarely accorded direct control of the sovereigns or publicly recognized for their fiscal knowledge. To put it another way, women's relations to money tend to make them the stewards of petty cash, whereas men are the controllers of hard cash.

In *Literary Women* (1977), Ellen Moers says that "money and its making were characteristically female rather than male subjects in English fiction." She points to Jane Austen first and foremost, noting that all Austen's "opening paragraphs, and the best of her first sentences have money in them" (101). While it is true that money means a great deal to Austen and her characters, her young women hardly handle real capital in any official capacity. Women's financial endeavors are always domesticated. Thus in *Persuasion* (1818) when it becomes evident that Sir Walter Eliot "was growing distressed for money," Lady Russell rallies and instigates a "scheme of retrenchment" whereby she "drew up plans of economy . . . made exact calculations, and . . . did what nobody else thought of doing: she consulted [another woman,] Anne" (14, 17). As M. Jeanne Peterson has observed in her case study of "one circle of upper-middle-class women," "women were not isolated from money and the facts of financial life" (125). Lady Russell's and Anne's plans to help rectify the family's grave financial problems highlight this observation. Yet in Austen's novel, the female-engineered rescue is carefully presented. That is, it is kept within the bounds of decorum. The women devise ways of curbing spending and think of economizing activities that fall within or comfortably near their socially prescribed roles of managers and keepers of the household. "While Lady Eliot lived, there had been method, moderation, and economy which had just kept him [Sir Walter] within his income." Anne's "more rigid requisitions" and Lady Russell's gentle reformations do not center in the buying, selling, and trading of the Exchequer, but in the frills and luxuries, as well as the creature comforts, underwritten with household funds. "What every comfort of life knocked off!" cries Sir Walter, presented with the women's financial proposal. "Journeys, London, servants, horses, table—contractions and restrictions everywhere." Finally the women's sally into financial management is "of little consequence" because Sir Walter objects outright to the idea of living "no longer with the decencies even of a private gentleman" and so rejects their economical proposals (18). Overriding the women's fiscal control over the domestic sphere, Sir Walter demonstrates Friedrich Engels' historical contention that man really takes "command in the home also" (189). If Lady Russell and Anne are not to have the ultimate say about domestic spending, then these women are clearly not to have a hand in the nitty-gritty world of money and high finance. They are to "suffer and be still."[2]

In Austen's fiction, not only do women not handle the money, they do not make it. Instead they tend to acquire it through marriage, which, as Moers herself admits, "makes money a serious business in Austen fiction" (102). While "marriage and a husband," as Peterson contends, "far from putting women outside the realm of decision making" may "often [have] widened their realm of financial power" by way of marriage settlements, the fact remains that without the "private legal creations of marriage settlements . . . and trust" (123, 131), the husband was automatically and legally recognized as the owner of money, property, and children. In truth, then, for women the acquisition of money through marriage was at best second-hand. As the American Charlotte Perkins Gilman, who wrote about "sexo-economic relations" near the end of the nineteenth century put it, "The economic status of the human race in any nation, at any time, is governed mainly by the activities of the male: the female obtains her share in the racial advance only through him" (572). Under such circumstances, any woman who sought thus to secure a living was engaged in a risky financial venture. Harriet Martineau would write around 1834 in a sociohistorical review of the marriage compact, "But new difficulties about securing a maintenance have arisen. Marriage is less general and the husbands of the greater number of women are not secure [as in feudal times] of a maintenance from the lords of the soil, any more than women are [made financially secure by] . . . being married" (62). In *Moll Flanders* Defoe had created a lowly female character who maneuvered a succession of marriages to amass a modest fortune; by the turn of the century, Jane Austen depicted genteel female characters ostensibly in search of a cultivated and wise male companion, not a purse. It is fair to say that Austen recognized the financial impact of marriage, but was careful not to reduce that sacrament solely to a principle of feminine economics.

Dorothy Lampen Thompson's study of women's contributions to the development of economics sheds light on Austen's handling of money as an important but delicate matter. Thompson observes that

> early nineteenth-century England was not a propitious time or place for a woman to become an economist. Economics was still neither a scholarly nor a popular study. It had, in fact, only recently gained respectability. In the opinion of the seventeenth century and much of the eighteenth century, the study of trade was beneath the dignity of learning, and the view that "the gentleman does not sully his hands in trade" was one that was slow to be overcome. . . . The prevailing view was that "no gentleman, and especially no self-respecting scholar, would study the profession if he were forced to." (9)

Tradition required that gentlemen maintain a respectable distance between themselves and their money, that it be inherited instead of made. Of course it followed that for a woman, a lady in particular, to concern herself too markedly with the acquisition of money, whether she earned it or sought it through marriage or inheritance, was, if not unthinkable, then as outrageous as Defoe's Moll's and much later Thackeray's Becky Sharpe's financial machinations.[3]

By the mid-nineteenth century, with the growth of manufacturing and the middle class, the Victorians who enjoyed among other things great material and economic progress, did not necessarily feel, like their more fastidious predecessors, that money and the trade that brought it sullied the hands.[4] Still, in the fiction of Austen's British female successors, the treatment of money remains as circumspect as Austen's. In *Jane Eyre* (1847), for example, Jane earns thirty pounds per annum as a governess until she inherits a fortune, then marries the master; Catherine Earnshaw marries the wealthy landowner, Linton, to secure comfort and respectability in *Wuthering Heights* (1847). George Eliot's Gwendolyn Harleth weds the languid and sinister Grandcourt to rescue her financially distressed family in *Daniel Deronda* (1876). In such stories, there is little evidence of female protagonists who go to the bank, finger their coins, or balance the accounts, as the women maintain a commercial "anonymity," to borrow Carolyn Heilbrun's words, "long believed . . . the proper condition of woman" (12). Like the sisters Brown in the Amazonian stronghold of Elizabeth Gaskell's *Cranford,* where "we none of us spoke of money, because that subject savoured of commerce and trade" (41), good strong women represented in these fictions are seldom found in any blatant contact or sustained relation with money that would betray good but vulgar business sense or an undecorous preoccupation with lucre.

By the end of the nineteenth century, Dinah Mulock, later Dinah Craik, would argue that good business sense was exactly what women needed to cultivate. In a volume of essays, *About Money and Other Things* (1886), Mulock declared,

> I know that I shall excite the wrath or contempt of the advocates of the higher education of women, when I say that it is not necessary for every woman to be an accomplished musician, an art-student, a thoroughly educated Girton girl; but it is necessary that she should be a woman of business. From the day when her baby fingers begin to handle pence and shillings, and her infant mind is roused to laudable ambition by the possession of the enormous income of threepence a week, she ought to be taught the true value and wise expenditure of money; to keep accounts and balance them to repay the minutest debt, or, still better, to avoid incurring it; to observe the just proportions of having and spending, and, above all, the golden rule for every one of us, whether our income be sixpence a week or twenty thousand a year—*waste nothing.* (6-7)

Bold as Mulock's observations sound, they finally call for energies that are meant to be channeled back into the domestic sphere. Mulock admonishes women to "observe the just proportions of spending" so that they can be better "helpmeets to the men they marry." For after all, Mulock continues, "very few men know how properly to use money:"

> They can earn it, lavish it, hoard it, waste it; but to deal with it wisely, as a means to an end, and also as a sacred trust, to be made the best of for others as well as themselves, is an education difficult of acquirement by the masculine mind; so difficult that one is led to doubt whether they were meant to acquire it at all, and whether in the just distribution of duties between the sexes it was not intended that the man should earn, the woman keep—he accumulate, and she expend; especially as most women have by nature a quality in which men are often fatally deficient—"the infinite capacity for taking trouble." (4-5)

Even as Mulock questions the male's aptitude for financial management, she describes conditions whereby woman's relation to money is etherealized and so deflated in any real professional or worldly sense. For if woman does handle money, she does so in her angelic role as the keeper of a "sacred trust," as one who traditionally sacrifices and troubles to do her best for others.

In the phrase "just distribution of [economic] duties between the sexes" Mulock does not describe what her American counterpart Charlotte Perkins Gilman calls a partnership. "The comfort a man takes with his wife," writes Gilman, "is not in the nature of a business partnership, nor are her frugality and industry. A housekeeper, in her place, might be as frugal, as industrious, but would not therefore be a partner" (573). While Mulock re-presents the hierarchy that financially subordinates women instead of making them partners, Jane Welsh Carlyle, in a composition which is said to have greatly amused Thomas Carlyle, gives good evidence of woman's economic position in the "just distribution of duties." In "Budget of a Femme Incomprise" (12 February 1855), Jane lightly but sarcastically addresses her husband as "the Noble Lord" as she explains why she must "*speak* again on the money question!" She reminds him that "through six-and-twenty years I have kept house for you at more or less cost according to given circumstances, but always on less than it costs the generality of people living in the same style." As a woman and wife she is put in the uneasy and marginal, if not demeaning, position of having not only to "pester your [Carlyle's] life out about money" but also to account to her modern "lord of the soil" throughout the twenty-six years of marriage for expenditures, "though," as she caustically remarks, "I am not strong in arithmetic." Jane Carlyle sees and states clearly the role of husband and wife in what she terms the "money row": "No, my Lord, it has never been my habit to interfere with your ways of making money, or the rate which you make it at; and if I never did in early years, most unlikely I should do it *now*. My bill of ways and means has nothing to do with making money, only with disposing of the money made" (235-42).

Though not what Gilman calls the "producers of wealth" or for that matter the disposers of substantial sums, middle- and upper-class women like Jane Carlyle contributed "in the final processes of preparation and distribution" (573).[5] Nevertheless, their contributions were not perceived to be as important as those of men. As Gilman wrote, the Mulock too understood, "The labor of women in the house, certainly enables men to produce more wealth than they otherwise could; and in this way women are economic factors in society." However, as Gilman goes on to say, "like the labor of women, the labor of horses [also] enables men to produce more wealth than they otherwise could. The horse is an economic factor in society. But the horse is not economically independent, nor is the woman" (573). In the money row, Jane Carlyle must have certainly felt that she was pulling the plow.

The nineteenth-century British writer Eliza Lynn Linton did not equate the position of middle-class woman with that of a beast of burden; however, she did recognize the servility of a woman in Jane Carlyle's position. She saw that a wife was no more than the servant of her husband:

> an honoured servant if you will, but a servant all the same. . . .
>
> No one but women themselves know how bitter this dependency is to them. Many a wife even after long years of marriage, and when kindly treated by her husband, the mother of his children and used to the manipulation of the housekeeping allowance, many even of this blessed class, feel bitterly that nothing is theirs, that it is not *their own*. It is their husband's. . . .
>
> This is the real meaning of modern revolt—women want to be independent, and to be on terms of monetary equality with men. (227-28)

As domestic guardian of the welfare of others, woman, no better off than a horse or a servant, finds herself a "femme incomprise" whose financial powers are severely qualified.

For a good portion of the nineteenth century most women who dealt with money tended to deal not with pounds but with shillings and pence because, in fiction as in real life, women's acquisition and management of their rights to the real sources of power and governance—land, houses, and, the focus of this chapter, money—were restricted by laws of coverture. Even if a middle- or upper-class woman had property or a fortune, there was a dissociation of her womanliness from cold hard cash. In Charlotte Brontë's *Shirley* (1849), in which Shirley Keeldar has so much money, property, and character that she earns the title of Captain Keeldar, Robert Moore and Shirley's uncle Simpson take charge of the counting houses and manage both the property and financial affairs of the heiress. Shirley proves more an angel of mercy than a captain of industry as she herself finds in her money a sacred trust. Having "money in hand," Shirley feels compelled to "do some good with it": "It is not an immense sum, but I feel responsible for its [her fortune's] disposal; and really this responsibility weighs on my mind more heavily than I could have expected. They say that there are some families almost starving to death in Briarfield: some of my own cottagers are in wretched circumstances: I must and will help them." Money carries with it the responsibility of caring and helping, yet even for Shirley that money is something with which a lady does not directly deal. Caroline, Shirley's sisterly friend, suggests that Shirley let the old maid Miss Ainsley "distribute the cash" since Shirley "will not manage properly" (267-68).[6] Indeed, the old maid Miss Ainsley, Caroline, who fears she is on the way to becoming an old maid, and Robert Moore's spinster cousin Hortense come closer than Captain Keeldar to handling accounts, even if their approach to financial knowledge and experience tends to be by way of the socially sanctioned larders and the sewing boxes got up for charity.

One memorable female character who comes closer than Shirley Keeldar to being a real captain of commerce is George Eliot's Jane Glegg. The proper getting, saving, and disposal of money and material wealth is the business of the oldest Dodson sister Mrs. Glegg in *Mill on the Floss* (1860). The bulwark of the Dodson tradition is so committed to having and saving that she stashes her new dresses and hairpieces away, bringing them out for wear when they are quite moldy and outdated. Adept at putting away and pinching goods and money to amass wealth, Jane Glegg is legally and financially cognizant of how money may lend one authority, get one respect, and create family dependents. Armed with this knowledge, she lords it over weaker-willed and -minded sister Bessy Tulliver, directing that sister how to economize in her own household:

> "It's a pity for you, Bessy, as you haven't got more strength o' mind. It'll be well if your children don't suffer for it. And I hope you've not gone and got a great dinner for us—going to great expenses for your sisters as 'ud sooner eat a crust o' dry bread nor help to ruin you with extravagance— . . . And here you've got two children to provide for, and your husband's spent your fortin i' going to law, and's like to spend his own too. A boiled joint, as

you could make broth of for the kitchen," Mrs. Glegg added, in a tone of emphatic protest, "and a plain pudding with a spoonful o' sugar and no spice, 'ud be far more becoming." (110)

Unlike Mrs. Tulliver, Mrs. Glegg, who has the "strength o' mind" to abhor "extravagance," here shows in that tradition of sacred trust, a fitting and proper concern with money for the children's sake. Interestingly enough, she is critical not only of Mrs. Tulliver, who is so silly as to prepare a financially ruinous "great dinner for us," but also of Mr. Tulliver, who has "spent your fortin 'i going to law." Aware that the man of the house is not taking care of his family as he should, Mrs. Glegg points out her ability to lend financial assistance, if not to fill Tulliver's shoes, as the fiscally responsible individual. As Jane Glegg complains, she reveals her sense of her monetary knowledge and potential: "Well, Bessy, *I* can't leave your children enough out o' my savings, to keep 'em from ruin. And you mustn't look to having any o' Mr. Glegg's money for it's well if I don't go first—he comes of a long willed family—and if he was to die and leave me well for my life, he'd tie all the money up to go back to his own kin" (111). Elsewhere, she comments on a Mrs. Sutton who had died having "left no leggicies, to speak on—left it all in a lump sum to her husband's nevvy":

> There wasn't much good i' being so rich, then . . . if she'd got none but husband's kin to leave it too. It's poor work when that's all you've got to pinch yourself for—not as I'm one o' those as 'ud like to die without leaving more money out at interest than other folks had reckoned. But it's a poor tale when it must go out o' your own family. (114)

Given the limits placed upon women, Mrs. Glegg shrewdly and honestly calculates upon one of the ways in which women could finally own and manage money: the death of a husband meant, of course, widowhood, but it hopefully also meant a will leaving money and material possessions in the hands of the wife.[7] A dowry was a "fortin" that passed from the father to the husband; a will could mean a whole new financial scenario for a woman—a loophole to financial independence and freedom. Mrs. Glegg is well aware of the financial possibilities this legal instrument may offer or withhold when she chides her sister Sophy for bemoaning the death of Mrs. Sutton: "You couldn't fret no more than this, if we'd heared as our cousin Abbot had died sudden without making his will" (114). Finally she gives a great deal of consideration to Mr. Glegg's "handsome provision for her in case of his death." Because "Mr. Glegg, like all men of his stamp, we extremely reticent about his will," Mrs. Glegg worries "in her gloomier moments" that "he might cherish the mean project of heightening her grief at his death by leav-

ing her poorly off" (193). But in her happier moments she dreams of surviving Mr. Glegg to

> talk eulogistically of him, as a man who might have his weaknesses, but who had done the right thing by her notwithstanding his numerous poor relations—to have sums of interest coming in more frequently and secret it in various corners baffling to the most ingenious thieves . . . — finally to be looked up to by her own family and the neighborhood, so as no woman can ever hope to be who has not the praeterite and present dignity comprised in being a "widow well left." (193-94)

To be a "widow well left" is to be left a woman in control of her own resources, to be left a woman with financial autonomy, to be left a woman with the right to go to the bank.

Even without benefit of a will, however, Mrs. Glegg comes to command a part, albeit a small one, in business transactions usually left to men. Indeed, Mrs. Glegg loans money out at 5 percent, secreting her profits in her home, if not taking them to the bank. She even engages in financial speculation with Bob Jakin the packman. However, all of Mrs. Glegg's financial transactions finally go forth more or less under the watchful eye of her noble "lord of the soil," Mr. Glegg, who has condescended to grant his wife some control over her own money. During a conjugal dispute, Mr. Glegg himself points up how unusual it is that a woman have such discretion: " 'Did ever anybody hear the like i' this parish?' said Mr. Glegg, getting hot. 'A woman with everything provided for her, and allowed to keep her own money the same as if it was settled on her, and with a gig new-stuffed and lined at no end o' expense and provided for when I die beyond anything she could expect' " (192).

While Mr. Glegg, who had found in "the eldest Miss Dodson . . . a handsome embodiment of female prudence and thrift" (187), gives his wife control of her money, he remains her adviser, the final financial authority to whom she ultimately listens. Thus, he advises the angry Mrs. Glegg not to "call in her money, when it's safe enough if you let it alone, all because of a bit of a tiff' (191). The emotional female here gets the calming and reasoned professional advice of the experienced man of business and behaves sensibly: "Mrs. Glegg felt there was really something in this [advice]" (190). It is Mr. Glegg who invites and condones Mrs. Glegg's investment in the business venture of Bob Jakin and the Glegg's nephew, Tom Tulliver. " 'What do you say, Mrs. G.?' said Mr. Glegg. 'I've a notion, when I've made a bit more inquiry, as I shall perhaps start Tom here with a bit of nest egg— . . . an' if you've got some little sums lyin' idle twisted up in a stockin' toe' " (416). Though Mrs. Glegg still conducts her business transactions under the paternal umbrella, she is guarded about her money and jealous of her right to make her own decisions about money, though finally Mr. Glegg steers her in a safe direction. Thus when Glegg suggests that his wife add twenty pounds of her own to the money he thinks of handing over to Tom, she replies, "You're not counting on me, Mr. Glegg, I hope, . . . You could do fine things wi' my money, I don't doubt." When an exasperated and tiffed Mr. Glegg invites her to keep her money and stay out of the whole affair, Jane reveals how she at some conscious and unconscious level resents Mr. Glegg's attempts to tell her what to do with her money: "I never said I wouldn't put money into it [the financial venture]— I don't say as it shall be twenty pounds, though you're so ready to say it for me" (417). Later when Mr. Glegg, Tom, and Bob, thinking they have concluded their discussion, prepare to go their several ways, Jane Glegg again feels the need to assert her financial weight:

> "Stop a bit, Mr. Glegg," said the lady, as her husband took his hat, "you never *will* give me the chance o' speaking. You'll go away now, and finish everything about this business, and come back and tell me it's too late for me to speak. As if I wasn't my nevvy's own aunt, and th' head o' the family on his mother's side! and laid by guineas, all full weight for him— as he'll know who to respect when I'm laid in my coffin." (422)

Again Jane Glegg resists what she perceives as her husband's efforts to nudge her into the margins of the financial transaction. She would remind Glegg and particularly her nephew, who has money to gain by her death, that she is a substantive contender for his consideration and respect. Her money exacts inclusion: "I desire as nothing shall be done without my knowing. I don't say as I shan't venture twenty pounds, if you [Mr. Glegg] make out as everything's right and safe. And if I do, Tom,' concluded Mr. Glegg, turning impressively to her nephew, 'I hope you'll always bear it in mind and be grateful for such an aunt' " (422). As one who has some control over her own money, Jane Glegg no doubt feels that she should be able to speak for herself and not be patronized. Her husband as well as Tom and Bob, who are present during this exchange, see what women, economically dependent on men for so long, have known—that persons who have control over their money and therefore have economic independence must sometimes be humored. Having sized up Mrs. Glegg's financial disposition, a winking Bob Jakin outwits her, selling her damaged Laceham goods and thereby seeming to put Jane in her place. But while Jane Glegg's stinginess and flawed business acumen are underscored in the transaction with Bob Jakin, she is no worse off as a woman capable of increasing her capital. For finally, like Mr. Glegg, Tom, and Bob, she too turns a profit.

While Jane Glegg wields some power over her own financial affairs, the rich spinster Catherine Vernon in Margaret Oliphant's *Hester* (1883) manages a commercial concern. Her financial rescue of the failing bank of the Vernons is no small feat in a society where it is remarked that "ladies in this country have nothing to do with business," that "when ladies meddle with business everything goes wrong," and that when women get "mixed up with business they are entirely out of their place. It changes the natural relations—it creates a false position" (46, 54). Margaret Oliphant counters these preconceptions by putting the bank "in the hands of Miss Vernon, who, it turned out, had more than her grandfather's steady power of holding on, and was, indeed, the heir of her great-grandfather's genius for business. The bank throve in her hands as it had done in his days, and everything it touched prospered" (20).

In the hands of men like John Vernon, who embezzles money from the bank, and later of Edward Vernon, who secretly uses the bank's money to engage in speculation for his own personal gain, the Vernon bank is jeopardized. On the one hand, the idea of bank failure, upon which Margaret Oliphant builds the story of Catherine and Hester, was not unique. As John Reed writes in *Victorian Conventions* (1975), "Considering the prevailing economic conditions and attitudes in nineteenth-century England, it is not unusual that financial failure was a major theme in Victorian literature" (176). On the other hand, that the threat of bank failure should become the occasion for a woman to become a financial power broker was not a common theme or story. For while women may have often been presented in fiction as the pawns of what Reed calls "commercial marriages" (108) which could secure money needed to, among other things, save a bank, women were not usually portrayed as individuals in any way capable of directly and nigh singlehandedly reversing a financial calamity of this magnitude and sort.

But in Catherine Vernon, Margaret Oliphant depicts a woman who, to the astonishment and admiration of the head clerk, had a head for business (17) and a fondness, though certainly not Moll's zest, for acquiring and keeping money. At one point, looking back over the days when she was at the helm of the bank, Catherine Vernon comments,

> "For my part, speculation in this wild way is my horror. If you could see the proposals that used to be put before me! Not an undertaking that was not the safest and the surest in the world! The boys are well indoctrinated in my opinions on that subject. They know better, I hope, than to snatch at a high percentage; and love the substance, the good honest capital, which I love. I think," she continued, "there is a little of miser in me or perhaps you will say all women. I love to see my money—to count it over like them—By the way it was the king that did that

[counted his money] while the queen was eating her bread and honey. That goes against my theory." (172)

As Catherine here recognizes, her position as the one who counts the coins reverses the order of the nursery rhyme that has the king or man provide and control, while the queen or woman merely consumes.[8] It is just such a scenario that Catherine's young kinswoman Hester hopes to avoid by having a career. Edward Vernon takes note of Hester's desire to be more than the queen eating honey and bread, commenting

> "but you are a girl, what can you do [but marry Harry]? They would not let you work, and if you could work nothing but daily bread would come of it. And, my dear Hester, you want a great deal more than daily bread. You want triumph, power; you want to be as you are by nature, somebody." (154)

In short, though a jealous Hester resists the notion, she identifies with Catherine, who, as head of the Vernon bank, not only has the power and is recognized as "somebody," but also is a kingly giver of bread:

> People spoke of her, as they sometimes do of a very popular man, by her Christian name. Catherine Vernon did this and that, they said. Catherine Vernon was the first thought when anything was wanted either by the poor who needed help, or the philanthropist who wanted to give it. The Vernon Almshouses, which had been established a hundred years before, but had fallen into great decay till she took them in hand, were always known as Catherine Vernon's Almshouses. Her name was put to everything. Catherine Street, Catherine Square, Catherine places without number. . . . She was, at least, a saint more easily within reach and more likely to lend a favorable ear. (20-21)

Significantly, Catherine's patriarchal role as head of the bank does not render her any less saintly or angelic. "The work of a successful man of business increased, yet softened by all the countless nothings that make business for a woman, had filled her days. She was an old maid to be sure, but an old maid who never was alone" (23). In that tradition of the spinsterish Miss Ainsleys and good housewives, Catherine keeps the sacred trust, reigning "with great benevolence . . . liberality . . . and firmness too" (20) and so realizing on a more sweeping scale the domestic idea.

And yet Margaret Oliphant suggests that the financial but especially the commercial empowerment of a Catherine Vernon is problematic. For one thing, the relations who are "indebted to her [Catherine] for their living, as well as their lodging" (27) are resentful of their rich and powerful kinswoman. For

another, Catherine eventually discovers that Edward Vernon, the young relative whom she favors as the son she never had, despises what he perceives to be his servitude to her. When young Edward tries to explain why he does not want to discuss bank business with Hester, he also accounts indirectly for his aversion to his Aunt Catherine, as he calls her:

> "Hester," he said, "that is not what a man wants in a woman, not to go and explain it all to her with pen and ink, and tables and figures, to make her understand as he would have to do with a man. What he wants, dear, is very different—just to lean upon you—to know that you sympathise, and think of me, and feel for me, and believe in me and that you will share whatever comes." (400)

What Hester unwittingly hears here is Edward's rejection of Catherine, to whom he has on occasion taken "my balance-sheet and my vouchers" (401). What she also hears here is the expression of a society for which, as Linda Hunt declares in *A Woman's Portion* (1988), "the [angelic] female character had become an alternative to the marketplace values that threatened to obliterate the aesthetic, moral, and emotional dimensions of life" (5).

Interestingly enough, while Hester finds Edward's call for "doggish fidelity" and "unreasoning belief," his "calm assertion that such blind adherence was all that was to be looked for from a woman" to be "irritating and offensive," Catherine seems ultimately to concur with Edward's notion that a woman best leave the business of money to men (401, 402). Thus, when as early as the third chapter of the novel, Catherine Vernon has turned sixty-five and decided to find someone to replace her in the bank, she does not think of recruiting a young woman, but instead "selected two hopeful young men to carry on her work," Edward and Harry. Later, when in an act reminiscent of John Vernon's, Edward has stolen money from the bank, sending it into collapse, Catherine disapproves of Hester's desire to follow in her footsteps and conduct the business of the bank:

> "It is a great pity," she said, "a girl like you, that instead of teaching or doing needlework, you should not go to Vernon's, as you have a right to do, and work there."

> "I wish I could," Hester said, with eager eyes.

> "They tell me you wanted to do something like what I had done. Ah! you did not know it was all to be done over again. This life is full of repetitions. People think the same thing does not happen to you twice over, but it does in my experience. You would soon learn. A few years' work, and you would be an excellent man of business; but it can't be."

"Why cannot it be? You did it. I should not be afraid—"

"I was old. I was past my youth. All that sort of thing was over for me." (492-93)

Catherine clearly sees herself as an exception to the rule; moreover, she has been the exceptional woman of business not because of any personal goal but because circumstances required her to rise to the occasion. Instead of the challenge, responsibility, and power she herself has experienced, Catherine holds out for Hester the possibility of marriage to Harry or to Roland Ashton, as "it is better in the end" (493). Catherine's insistence that Hester marry leads the reader along with Hester to the understanding that the commercial empowerment of Catherine Vernon is to remain an anomaly, not the beginning of a new tradition. The angel in the house wins out over the woman in the marketplace.

Jane Lewis writes in *Women in England* (1984) that "the cult of domesticity stressed the sanctity of the home as a refuge from the rapid economic, political and social change outside the home and from the competitive values of the marketplace" (113). While it may well be true that the home was intended to serve as such a refuge, it cannot be denied that even the most angelic of women in the home had some ties to the marketplace if only indirectly as keeper of the budget. As Luce Irigaray has pointed out, in the Western world, woman has been herself to the marketplace as commodity (172). Exemplary of this financial phenomenon is Defoe's Moll Flanders, who commodifies her physical self to survive, to get security, and to gain social standing. That woman could enter the marketplace not as commodity but as an authority and a commercial player, that woman could transact some business other than that of marriage was a revolutionary idea in a society where according to Irigaray men historically "make commerce *of* them [women], but . . . do not enter into any exchanges *with* them" (172). This idea of a woman's participation in the world of money and finance on an equal footing with men was one that a writer like Margaret Oliphant began to imagine. As bread-winner for her and her brother's children, Oliphant perhaps more than some of her contemporaries appreciated the business skills it took to live in a world where money and mammon determine the quality of one's reality and the terms of one's existence. Charlotte Brontë may have helped support her father's household with her teaching and writing, Elizabeth Gaskell may have bought her husband a house, and George Eliot ensured an income for Lewes and his sons, yet for a writer like Oliphant, money and the ability to conduct business were not merely additional feathers in the headdress of the angelic woman. They were becoming a necessity. Though Oliphant and her sister writers may not have been ready either to

educate women or to accept women in the positions of tellers and bankers, they supported the idea that women should, in the words of *Hester*'s narrator, "understand business and be ready for any emergency" (6). Then too, they began to explore the idea of women entering the worlds of business and finance and handling money in ways traditionally exercised exclusively by men.

Notes

[1] The phrase "getting and spending" is taken from William Wordsworth's poem "The World Is Too Much with Us" in *English Romantic Writers,* ed. David Perkins (New York: Harcourt, Brace, and World, 1967), 289. Thomas Carlyle, *Past and Present,* ed. Richard D. Altick (1843; rpt. New York: New York University Press, 1977), 149.

See Norman Russell's very informative *The Novelist and the Mammon: Literary Responses to the World of Commerce in the Nineteenth Century* (Oxford: Clarendon Press, 1986), which "duly acknowledge[s] the importance of prevailing economic theories" and "examines the responses of Victorian novelists to the thriving commercial life of the city, the world, of stockjobbers and brokers, financiers and insurance promoters" (vii). While Russell mentions two or three women writers who focused on banking and commerce in their novels (e.g., Catherine Gore in *The Banker's Wife* [1843], Harriet Martineau in *Berkeley the Banker* [1833], Dinah Mulock Craik in *John Halifax, Gentleman* [1856]) it is very clear in both Russell's book and in the fiction of the women writers he mentions that "the bankers, brokers, insurers, bill-discounters" (1), the purveyors of money and capitalism, were men.

[2] See Martha Vicinus' edition, *Suffer and Be Still: Women in the Victorian Age* (Bloomington: Indiana University Press, 1972). Vicinus herself borrows the phrase from Sara Ellis's *The Daughters of England* (London, 1845).

[3] In *The Lives of Victorian Gentlewomen,* Peterson provides an interesting insight into the relations between gentlewomen and the idea of earning money. Peterson observes that "there were solid practical grounds" for the attitude that earning money was "beneath a lady's dignity":

> A gentlewoman earning her own living fell outside the circle of social activities that would keep her in touch with her own kind. A ball that lasted until 3 A.M., for example, was not conducive to alert employment the following day. More important, the very fact of having to earn a living demonstrated to the world, and to prospective suitors in particular, that a woman had no effective, economically viable family. A good match was one in which each partner brought to the marriage social and economic resources and safeguards . . . that would sustain the new family

being created. The social message of earning a living was the fact of an economically crippled family. In addition, a lady's working would rob of employment those who needed it—those whom it was her social responsibility to aid. (120-21)

Not only her ability to maintain social contacts, but also her role as the consumer bearing witness to her husband's financial powers and her status as the domestic angel who gives instead of depriving others, in this case of needed employment—these might be compromised if the lady earned money.

4 Writers like Carlyle and Dickens did, however, worry that relationships were getting to be based upon the artificial and unfulfilling cash nexus.

5 Lower- and upper-middle- and upper-class women in some cases exercised significant economic power. Though Elizabeth Roberts focuses on the years 1890-1940, she describes a working-class tradition in which women had significant control over family finances and were in fact "financial controllers." Thus, "all earning children gave their wages to their mother for her to dispose of as she thought best. Similarly, 'good' husbands were expected to hand over their wages without any deductions having been made. There were variations in the operation of this custom. Some wives were so strict that their husbands received no pocket money at all. One worked as a waiter at the local pub, and was expected to rely on his tips for pocket money; another was allowed to keep his overtime pay, but not a penny of his wages," *A Woman's Place: An Oral History of Working-Class Women 1890-1940* (Oxford: Basil Blackwell, 1984), 110-11.

M. Jeanne Peterson in *Family, Love, and Work in the Lives of Victorian Gentlewomen* (Bloomington: Indiana University Press, 1989) asserts that "money, its ownership, and its management were a fact" in the case of "one circle of upper-middle-class women" she studies, the Pagets. Dwelling on such legal arrangements as the wills and marriage settlements that set these women apart, Peterson contends that "in the upper-middle-class family a gentlewoman was usually empowered by the private legal creations of marriage settlements, wills, and trusts. As a consequence, the Victorian gentlewoman had a sphere of power, a realm of autonomous existence, based on the financial resources inherited from parents, settled on her at marriage, and made available to her as a widow. The world of money . . . was not forbidden to gentlewomen" (131).

6 Because Miss Ainsley is an old maid without the protection of brother, father, or husband she is accustomed to fending for herself economically. As one who by unfortunate necessity transacts many of her own financial affairs, the old maid is in part exempt from the socioeconomic requirement that women not engage in significant monetary transactions. Here though, Miss Ainsley's role is suitably angelic because charitable.

7 M. Jeanne Peterson does a fine job of demonstrating how a gentlewoman could be "empowered by the private legal creations of marriage settlements, wills, and trusts in *Lives of Victorian Gentlewomen.* As Peterson points out,

wills and marriage settlements gave women power over marriage portions and legacies. Such monies gave women a separate financial sphere. She was not subject to a husband's control in these matters, but neither did she, by these arrangements, have any direct influence over him or the family's finances. It is important to look to the "family purse" for a measure of women's role in money matters. Women's roles in family financial management included both the mundane household matters that were part of middle-class women's lives and major responsibilities related to family finance. (124)

8 In *The Feminization of American Culture* (New York: Avon Books, 1977), Ann Douglas gives an interesting analysis of woman's role as consumer in the United States, where

the ideal woman whom the counselors and educators wished to shape was to exert moral pressure on a society in whose operations she had little part, and to spend money—or have it spent on her—in an economy she could not comprehend. She was in embryo both a saint and a consumer. Naturally the lady and her advisors underplayed her status as consumer and overplayed her status as saint. They were largely ignorant of the developing economic situation of which they were a part; they were more aware of the sincerity of their conscious religious motivations than of the reality of the economic forces which partially determined them. . . . In actual fact . . . the two roles, saint and consumer, were interlocked and mutually dependent; the lady's function in a capitalist society was to appropriate and preserve both the values and the commodities which her competitive husband, father, and son had little time to honor or enjoy; she was to provide an antidote and a purpose for their labor. (69-70)

As Douglas herself comments, in the roles of angel and consumer the American woman in the nineteenth century may well have out-Victorianed the Victorians (3).

Works Cited

Austen, Jane. *Persuasion.* New York: Signet, 1965.

Brontë, Charlotte. *Shirley.* New York: Penguin, 1974.

Carlyle, Jane Welsh. "Budget of a Femme Incomprise." *Life of Jane Welsh Carlyle* by Mrs. Alexander Ireland. New York: Charles L. Webster, 1891.

Carlyle, Thomas. *Past and Present.* 1848. Ed. Richard D. Altick. New York: New York University Press, 1977.

Defoe, Daniel. *Moll Flanders.* Ed. James Sutherland. Boston: Houghton Mifflin, 1959.

Eliot, George. *The Mill on the Floss.* New York: Penguin, 1974 (originally published 1860).

Engels, Friedrich. "The Origins of the Family, Private Property, and the State." *Feminism: The Essential Historical Writings.* Ed. Miriam Schneir. New York: Random House (Vintage), 1972.

Gaskell, Elizabeth. *Cranford and Cousin Phillis.* Ed. Peter Keating. Middlesex, England: Penguin, 1976.

Gilman, Charlotte Perkins. *Women and Economics. The Feminist Papers: From Adams to de Beauvoir.* Ed. Alice S. Rossi. New York: Columbia University Press, 1973.

Heilbrun, Carolyn G. *Writing a Woman's Life.* New York: Norton, 1988.

Hunt, Linda C. *A Woman's Portion: Ideology, Culture, and the British Female Novel Tradition.* New York: Garland, 1988.

Irigaray, Luce. *This Sex Which Is Not One.* Trans. Catherine Porter with Carolyn Burke. Ithaca, N.Y.: Cornell University Press, 1977.

Lewis, Jane. *Women in England 1870-1950: Sexual Divisions and Social Changes.* Bloomington: Indiana University Press, 1984.

Linton, Eliza Lynn. *Ourselves.* London: Chatto and Windus, 1884.

Martineau, Harriet. "On Marriage." *Harriet Martineau on Women.* Ed. Gayle Graham Yates. New Brunswick, N. J.: Rutgers University Press, 1985.

Moers, Ellen. *Literary Women.* Garden City, N. Y.: Doubleday (Anchor), 1977.

Mulock, Dinah. *About Money and Other Things: A Gift Book.* New York: Harper, 1887.

Oliphant, Margaret. *Hester: A Story of Contemporary Life.* New York: Penguin (Virago), 1984 (originally published 1883).

Peterson, M. Jeanne. *Family, Love, and Work in the Lives of Victorian Gentlewomen.* Bloomington: Indiana University Press, 1989.

Reed, John R. *Victorian Conventions.* Athens, Ohio: Ohio University Press, 1975.

Thompson, Dorothy Lampen. *Adam Smith's Daughters.* New York: Exposition Press, 1973.

Vicinus, Martha. *Suffer and Be Still: Women in the Victorian Age.* Bloomington: Indiana University Press, 1972.

Wordsworth, William. "The World Is Too Much with Us." *English Romantic Writers.* Ed. David Perkins. New York: Harcourt, Brace, and World, 1967.

FURTHER READING

Vernon, John. *Money and Fiction: Literary Realism in the Nineteenth and Early Twentieth Centuries.* Ithaca and London: Cornell University Press, 1984, 213 p.

> Explores money as one of the most common themes in nineteenth-century fiction and whether or not novelists of that time period depict it realistically.

DiGaetani, John Louis, ed. *Money: Lure, Lore, and Literature.* Westport, Conn. and London: Greenwood Press, 1994, 268 p.

> Contains essays examining money in the context of Russian, American, French, and English literature from the seventeenth to the twentieth century.

Russell, Norman. *The Novelist and the Mammon: Literary Responses to the World of Commerce in the Nineteenth Century.* Oxford: Clarendon Press, 1986, 226 p.

> Examines how Victorian novelists responded to the growing commercial life in society during their lifetimes.

Incest in Nineteenth-Century American Literature

INTRODUCTION

In spite of, or perhaps because of, the force of the social and moral prohibitions against it, incest was a relatively common motif in early American literature, occurring most frequently in novels of the time. The fascination with incest was associated strongly with a call for a social order proper to the newly independent and still largely "uncivilized" nation. The frequent and diverse use of this theme suggests its symbolic power both in sentimental novels toward the beginning of the century and in gothic novels later on. The most common form of actual or potential incest occurs between siblings, whose sexual union typically is narrowly averted as the truth is revealed at the last possible moment. Early American novels assumed a stern tone with regard to incest: In works such as William Hill Brown's *The Power of Sympathy* (1789), neither party involved is granted forgiveness, even if the actions are a result of ignorance. Instead, both parties either succumb to tragic deaths from shock, suicide, or other violent means; they fall victim to such afflictions as madness; or they are punished by exile or ostracism. Toward the mid-nineteenth century, as the family unit stabilized within larger population centers and a greater proportion of society found themselves with both the time and the financial security to enjoy the luxury of reading, sensationalistic, or pulp, fiction rose in popularity. Plots revolving around internal family dynamics, particularly those about the "mentionable unmentionable"—incest—quickly became thrilling favorites.

A central preoccupation of many works of literature in nineteenth-century America was the stability of the social order. The incest theme illuminated the danger of fragmentation of the family, the basic unit of social order. In nineteenth-century literature, the incestuous family is often motherless, and includes a male member who violates a sister or daughter. Typically, the incestuous situation originates with the sexual indiscretions of the father, who begets an illegitimate daughter, casts her off, and thus unknowingly sets up his son's potential incestuous connection with his own half-sister. The experience is so catastrophic—usually concluding with the deaths of those involved—that it literally destroys the family. And often the destruction is blamed on the father. According to Anne Dalke (1988), the "early American father is not only prime sufferer in his children's misfortune, but prime cause of their suffering as well." At times, the father, too, is haunted by his sins, as he finds himself involved in an incestuous relationship with his own daughter.

In many gothic nineteenth-century works, including those of Edgar Allan Poe, this destruction of the family is often literal. In Poe's short story "The Fall of the House of Usher" (1839), for example, the incestuous family is doomed by its geographic isolation; the house is literally "closed in" by the surrounding lake. Secluded in this way, according to James B. Twitchell (1987), the Usher siblings "are hermetically sealed in the cocoon of family. For them there can be no sexual excursions beyond the family border and so they must collapse in on themselves." This literal destruction is also found in Charles Brockden Brown's novel *Wieland* (1798), in which the father carries a mysterious curse out of Europe into the New World and then dies, leaving his son and daughter orphans. In time, Theodore, perhaps having inherited the curse, begins confusing his new wife with his sister. He ultimately murders his wife, placing the body in his sister's bed, then kills himself.

This concern with the destruction of the family—and more specifically, with paternal authority—was firmly tied to a deep anxiety over the instability of America's social hierarchy. Many early writers feared the ease with which Americans moved between social strata, and related these fears in sexual terms. In fiction, this usually took one of two forms: in one, a male character chooses to marry a poor woman from a lower class, and she invariably turns out to be his illegitimate half-sister; in another, an older man attempts to seduce a poor, young woman, and she eventually is revealed as his illegitimate daughter. Many critics see these scenarios as metaphoric pleas for a return to a time when the elder males of society—members of the established upper class—understood and maintained their roles as benevolent protectors of their inferiors, and thus ensured a stable and secure hierarchical social structure. At the same time, however, some writers viewed the past as corrupt and questioned whether or not inhabitants of America were doomed to pay throughout eternity for the sins of their fathers. Responding to their country's rejection of England and its attempts to establish an independent culture and society, many writers, including Nathaniel Hawthorne and Herman Melville, treated incest as the inability to escape the wrongs of the past in order to forge an unsullied future. For instance, Hawthorne's story "Alice Doane's Appeal" (1835) treats the deep affection a brother feels for his sister. Some critics claim that by treating these possibly incestuous feelings, coupled with another plotline involving a long-lost brother and his sexual interest in the same sister, Hawthorne attempted to instill in his readers feelings of guilt and shame over the past and the need for a sense of moral responsibility for the future. In addition, critics claim, Hawthorne went one step further by bringing into the story his own family's involvement in the past: Hawthorne includes a scene in which a ghostly pageant features the founding fathers of Salem represented as demons and damned souls. As Frederick C. Crews (1966) states: The "idea of past generations here is in keeping with the story's theme; in some tentative, unformulated sense, ancestry is associated with incestry."

The uniquely nineteenth-century American treatment of incest thus most often concerns itself with social issues—whether personal, such as the desires within an individual family—or political, including the hierarchical structure of society. Few novels or short stories of the time feature female narrators relating the incident or danger of incest, and even fewer question the gender roles that dominated the century and that, to some extent, cultivated and idealized the incestuous relationship. Still, the use of incest as a particularly dangerous form of human relation illuminates the extent to which nineteenth-century authors focused on the interaction of authority and desire in relationships between men and women.

REPRESENTATIVE WORKS

Charles Brockden Brown
Wieland; or, The Transformation (novel) 1798

William Hill Brown
The Power of Sympathy: or, The Triumph of Nature (novel) 1789
Ira and Isabella: or, The Natural Children (novel) 1807

James Fenimore Cooper
Home as Found (novel) 1838

Nathaniel Hawthorne
"Alice Doane's Appeal" (short story) 1835

Herman Melville
Pierre; or, the Ambiguities (novel) 1852

Edgar Allan Poe
"The Fall of the House of Usher" (short story) 1839

Susanna Haswell Rowson
"Marian and Lydia" (short story) 1791
Charlotte's Daughter (novel) 1828

Susan Warner
The Wide, Wide World (novel) 1892

Sarah Sayward Wood
Julia and the Illuminated Baron (novel) 1800

OVERVIEW

James B. Twitchell (essay date 1987)

SOURCE: "'The Disease of the Last of the Ushers': Incest in Nineteenth-Century American Culture," in *Forbidden Partners: The Incest Taboo in Modern Culture,* Columbia University Press, 1987, pp. 185-219.

[*In the following essay, Twitchell examines the incest taboo in the context of a developing American social order, which chronologically coincided with the rise of the gothic novel.*]

> Thus the basic question becomes: *Why, by and large, don't human beings like it* [incest] *much?* Why, in the vast majority of societies, do they take *some* trouble, however vague, to discourage incestuous unions, even though most human beings are probably not going to indulge in such unions? . . . *Unease* and *avoidance* seem to be the common denominators—not fierce desire held in check by even fiercer sanctions or lust reined in by the power of taboo. The universal root phenomenon appears to be the *ease with which it rouses our unease.*—Robin Fox, *The Red Lamp of Incest*

If the unease we feel in contemplating incest is partially cultural, and if culture carries these feelings from generation to generation through the creation of a shared grammar, will different verbal texts from different cultures betray different methods of avoidance? If the taboo is ideological, will different political and economic systems generate different expressions? Will there even be observable variances within similar cultures as to how unease is communicated? Will stories of family romance be different, characteristic of their culture? More specifically, if we look at early modern American culture, will it differ from the English culture of the same period in how incest behavior is coded?

Toward the end of Chateaubriand's *René,* the eponymic protagonist sets out to the new world full of melancholy hope that he may find temporary palliative for his suicidal depression. He has fallen in love with his sister, Amelia, who has been locked away forever in a convent. René heads westward to the land of starting over, the land of dreams, the land where everything can be forgiven, and almost everything forgotten, the land where there is no personal, national, or racial past. He heads off into the American wilderness. And what does he find? He finds Chactas, an Indian chief, as natural a man as Rousseau could ever have imagined, living as pastoral a life as any poet could have desired, and Father Souel, a missionary who has come to the Mississippi lands to teach the Indians how to live the European way. René tells the old chief and the wise Father his story of woe. Instead of comforting the lad, these wise men scold him, tell him he has been a fool, and assure him he will find no comfort here. Father Souel makes it clear to his young countryman that this land of manifold opportunities is not the land of infinite alternatives. He tells René to pack his things and go home:

> Nothing in your story deserves the pity you are now being shown. I see a young man infatuated with illusions, satisfied with nothing, withdrawn from the burdens of society, and wrapped up in idle dreams. . . . Your sister has atoned for her sin, but if I must speak frankly, I fear that through some terrible justice, that confession, emerging from the depths of the tomb, has in turn stirred up your own soul. What do you do all alone in the woods using up your days and neglecting all your duties? You will tell me that saints have retired to the wilderness. Yes, but they were there weeping and subduing their passions, while you seem to be wasting your time inflaming your own. . . . Whoever has been endowed with talent must devote it to serving his fellow men, for if he does not make use of it, he is first punished by an inner misery, and sooner or later Heaven visits on him a fearful retribution.

The wise chief tells the young European the mixed message of the new world: its tolerance is matched only by its abomination of aberration.

> My son, he [Father Souel] speaks severely to both of us; he is reprimanding the old man and the young, and he is right. Yes, you must give up this strange life, which holds nothing but care. Happiness can be found only in the common paths. (pp. 112-113)

René returns home to France and to his wife and unhappiness. Thus, the literary work that introduced incest as a subject of romantic inquiry into Europe ends with the final American response, "You can't do that on our shores."

It may be ironic, but not unpredictable, that American culture, which for the better part of two hundred years has prided itself, even boasted, of its independence from oppressive ancestral traditions, has been in many instances the most supportive of the traditional forms it spurned. Nowhere is this better seen than in family matters. American concepts of domestic relations are often contradictory and short-lived. On the one hand we have stressed the importance of individual choice, of "breaking away," of each generation bettering the previous, of melting-pot diversity. On the other hand

we have enforced role behavior, prolonged adolescence, partially abetted the generation gap, fueled xenophobia, and tolerated, at times encouraged, racial and religious barriers we professed to have abolished. The paradox of the last few decades in which beatniks, hippies, and now punks live side by side with "togetherness," the Jesus movement, and jingoism, characterized nineteenth-century culture as well. All Western heterogeneous societies have such diversities and contradictions. The degrees, however, are different.

American domestic boundaries may have occasioned such concern both to maintain and to violate because, with no past and with the clear and present danger of the wilderness before us, we were tempted to exaggerate what we had and did not have. At first this struggle took the form of the bizarre confrontation between Roger Williams and John Cotton over, among other things, family patterns and rights. It would later unfold in the movement west, in race relations, and now in our sense of the nuclear family. As long as there was plenty of room to go around, if you disapproved of your neighbor's conduct, or your own family's, you could move on. By the nineteenth century, however, new land east of the Appalachians had run out. The Renés were sent home, or far across the Mississippi.

For the most part, the struggle over social boundaries had less to do with inherited patterns or with ecclesiastical polity than with economic necessity. The financial panic of 1837 and the transformation from an agrarian to an industrial state had dislocated families, forcing them west or back into population centers. The political upheaval of Jacksonian democracy was extending the concept of nation over state over family and was having profound implications, as we see in the reactionary prose of Thoreau, Emerson, and even Cooper. The industrial revolution was having its impact on what held families together. Separation anxiety, parental love, habit, tradition, and mutual fears were now joined by the possibility of economic gain. American families were different. Those who were not born to wealth could *become* rich.

In a sense, the promise of organizing the family anew in order to achieve wealth continued the debate between Salem and Provincetown, except that economics replaced religion and the geography of conflict had moved. By the 1830s the literal confrontation was between the axis of Boston and southern New England on the one hand, and, on the other, familylike communities scattered on the near frontier of Pennsylvania and Ohio to the west, and upper New York and southern Vermont to the north. Not by happenstance did Coleridge and Robert Southey intend to head to the banks of the Susquehanna River in Pennsylvania to start their Pantisocracy based on the communal ownership of everything including each other, for they knew of the experiments in family living that were occurring on the near frontier. As the California coast has become to us today, so the rolling hills of the upper New England states and the eastern Midwest were to the early nineteenth century—a place sufficiently far away to be safe, yet close enough to be noticed.[1] With the exception of the Mormons, experimental American communities rarely headed out into the real wilderness. What they did was best done *almost* in private. They did, after all, have a point to make, and that point almost always had to do with showing both their financial success and the corruption of their neighbors.[2]

A two-day trek north of Boston in the early nineteenth century would have taken you close to one of the most interesting attempts to deal with the domestic and economic problems of the disease of modern life—an attempt to literally establish the fictional family designs of English romanticism. Of all the utopian communities that sprang up along the periphery, such as the Shakers, Amish, and Hutterites, none was more important in reconfiguring the modern family than the Putney, Vermont, commune of John Humphrey Noyes. Noyes had seen the problem of the fracturing family and he proposed the obvious return to pure forms. If God was the father of man, and if we were all his precious children, then our relationships should be those of siblings—all our relationships. Noyes was one of the few to confront the specific sexual ramifications of the argument, which has the elegance of the Elizabethan world picture, that our little human world reflects His larger and perfect one.

The Perfectionists, as Noyes humbly called his group, were not the first to learn that propagation à la the angels was difficult. His immediate predecessors in resolving this prickly matter, the Shakers, had already learned what reproductive problems were engendered by *literally* being in the family of God. Celibacy was their answer, not so much as the result of logic as of the sexual phobias and inhibitions of their founder, Ann Lee. Still, it was clear that for any "little family" to evolve it somehow would have to gain members. The conjugal bed might be "made of embers," as Mrs. Lee reported of her own, but in the frontier commune the alternative to embers was to be frozen forever in one nonreproducing family.

So, literally like the angels, the Shakers added to their family horizontally. They adopted family members, be they orphans or converts. As many modern communes have discovered, the family hierarchy is too strong to subvert, so it must be built upon. Mother was Mrs. Lee, still called "Mother Ann," and "Father" was her own brother William—a substitution that was in no literal way sexual, but nevertheless must have posed a psychological problem. For all the members were their "children." Mixed into this was the mythic older brother, temporarily missing in the flesh but alive in the spirit, Jesus Christ, whose rela-

tionship to Mother Ann must have given the family, as both followers and children, another moment of confusion.

It was just this kind of confusion that John Humphrey Noyes wanted to resolve. From the romantics he found inspiration, from Christianity he drew the outlines, and from the Shakers he observed an invaluable example. Noyes adopted many of their organizational practices. After all, he was going to apply the most modern methods of efficiency to communal life and would not make the Shaker mistake of planned anachronism. When it came to the problem of siblings breeding, he resolved the dilemma by fiat.[3] He proposed "universal marriage"—all men henceforth would be married to all women, and, it should be stressed, all women married to all men, at least initially. Charmingly, he called the process "omnigamy." Noyes explains:

> In a holy community there is no more reason why sexual intercourse should be restrained by love, than why eating and drinking should be, and there is as little occasion for shame in the one case as in the other. . . . The guests of the marriage supper may have each his favourite dish, each a dish of his own procuring, and that without the jealousy of exclusiveness. I call a certain woman my wife; she is yours; she is Christ's; and in Him she is the bride of all saints. She is dear in the hands of a stranger, and according to my promise to her I rejoice.[4]

Having Christ as the buffering agent intellectually detoxified any threat of forbidden encounters, but Noyes was sensitive enough to realize that intellectual explanations only satisfy intellectuals. What happens when thinking turns to doing? His method of deflecting the psychological inhibitions as well as the physical threat of inbreeding was accomplished by his self-touted system of "male continence." Males would be allowed to treat all women like sisters, and all sisters like women, only after they had proved themselves able to treat no woman as a wife. In other words, he proposed sex without orgasm. Although Noyes claimed his success was achieved by the conscious constriction of the seminal ducts, it seems more likely that coitus interruptus was simply given new emphasis.

Whether or not sibling incest occurred within the intrepid band that Noyes collected in the southern Vermont woods is now beside the point. At the time, however, this was the only point. One of the reasons the people around Putney were so eager to rid themselves of the Perfectionists was that they could not countenance such sexual deviance so close by. In the first small commune of some twenty people were Noyes's own brother and two sisters, and two brothers-in-law. The probabilities of inbreeding were too great to be overlooked. Noyes's explanation of "complex marriage," of "omnigamy," and of "male continence" may have satisfied commune members. They may have believed him when he said: "The only plausible objection to amative intercourse between near relations, founded on the supposed law of nature that 'breeding in and in' deteriorates offspring [thus had been] removed."[5] But the neighbors needed convincing. The Noyes Bible Group was driven out—the proffered charge was adultery; the implied charge was incest.

The Perfectionists went deeper into the hinterlands, into upstate New York, where in relative peace they turned their prodigious energies away from explaining to others and to themselves, and started to behave like Americans. They first manufactured animal traps and then formed a joint stock company to produce flat silverware. How ironic that today we should remember them only by the trade name of the flatware (Oneida) we usually give to celebrate the one institution Noyes abhorred above all—marriage.

Whatever their differences, the romantic movement and fundamental Christianity were similar in almost demanding adult mimicry of childlike relationships. Both stressed the model of idealized childhood as the centerpiece of faith. The success, limited as it now seems, both of the Shakers and the Perfectionists testifies to the profound desire of people under stress to return to simpler states of familial interaction. Here in nineteenth-century America the spirit of Shelleyan romanticism was made flesh. Not only was the language of recognition full of "brothers" and "sisters," but the dress (bloomers, frocks, pantalets) as well as the diurnal habits of sleeping and eating separately, imitated the idealized family of childhood memories. To a psycho-historian these may seem regressionary methods of coping, but to an economist they can be remarkably efficient. If only sex had not become mixed up in family relationships Noyes's vision might have proved prophetic. Even now his words retain their peculiar logic:

> Love between the children of God, is exalted and developed by a motive similar to that which produces ordinary *family affection* . . . the exciting cause is not sexuality . . . but the fact that the parties have one Father. . . . The sons and daughters of God, must have even a stronger sense of blood-relationship than ordinary brothers and sisters, because the Spirit of the Father . . . is always renewing their consciousness of unity with him and with each other. Marriage, in the world, requires a man to "leave father and mother and cleave unto his wife." But the sons and daughters of God can never leave *their* Father and Mother. Of course, the paramount sexual affection, required by the law of marriage, can have no place among them. They live as children with their Father forever, and the paramount affection of the household is . . . *brotherly* love, an affection that grows directly out of the common relationship to the Father, and of course is as

universal as that relationship. . . . This affection as it exists between the different sexes is necessarily unlimited as to number. A brother may love ten sisters, or a sister ten brothers, according to the customs of the world. The exclusiveness of marriage does not enter the family circle. But heaven is a family circle; and . . . brotherly love . . . takes the place of supremacy which their matrimonial affection occupies in this world.[6]

But sex did become involved; incest was a threat, and, when confronted, Noyes had to admit its clear and present danger. Pressed, as he was in his *Essay on Scientific Propagation,* he attempted to transform this supposed weakness into a strength. Noyes argued, almost forgetting his vaunted prophylactic method of "male continence," that although

> it must be conceded that, in the present state of human passions and institutions, there are many and great difficulties in the way of our going back to the natural simplicity of the Hebrew fathers or forward to the scientific simplicity of the cattle-breeders, yet it is important to know and remember that these difficulties are not physiological, but sentimental . . . in the pure races, such as the European aristocracies and the Jews . . . vital power and beauty have been the result of close interbreeding.[7]

Argue as he might, the threat still remained. And that threat, together with encroaching "civilization," forced these utopians (numbering now about two hundred) to once again disband. If Noyes had followed his fellow Vermonter Joseph Smith out into the real wilderness of Utah, he might have been able to stabilize his community and perhaps to survive. However, the Latter Day Saints never restructured the family in such a way as to make sibling intercourse a possibility. Polygamy is tame compared to the "complex families" envisioned by Percy Bysshe Shelley and John Humphrey Noyes.

If Noyes had had to depend on the American intellectual community for support of his "errand into the wilderness," he would have been in still more desperate straits—quite possibly he never would have made it out of Vermont. Had his "city upon the hill," his American Eden, been outside Boston, he most probably would have been arrested. Note that Brook Farm was almost closed down by its neighbors, even though the Institute for Agriculture and Education had presented no sexual ambiguities; in fact, there was little sexual activity at all. Although the more intense battle of individual versus state freedoms was to be fought throughout the century, the battle over family organization was short-lived. The patriarchs clearly won.

As with their English counterparts, the radical spokesmen of American romanticism—Thoreau, Whitman, and Emerson—were men who had little or no family of their own. It is of more than passing interest that the American intellectuals who advocated the most sweeping rearrangement of the family were a self-advertised recluse, a homosexual, and a man who was an extremely passive parent and distant husband. In revolutionizing family matters often those with the least family were the most confident in deciding how others should live. They spoke with the confidence of inexperience.[8]

The American artists who did indeed concentrate on family interactions were not philosophers, not the transcendental stockholders of the "Brook Farm Institute for Agriculture and Culture," but were rather the emotional and intellectual descendants of John Cotton— modern Puritans. For them the family was the anchor of self and thus the center of their fiction. The introspective impulse was vitalized in the fiction of the first American novelist, William Hill Brown; it continued through the first important early gothicist, Charles Brockden Brown, and then unfolded in the central works of nineteenth-century American literature—works by Poe, Hawthorne, and Melville. These Americans were all family men and they all took the family as a central subject of their fiction. In their make-believe families it is clear that they would tolerate little aberrant behavior. If experimentation did occur, it would be quickly suppressed. Fundamental codes would be enforced at the expense of individual freedom. In an economic sense, good business practices would prevail. The "new man," the corporate man, backed by a stable family, would make sure that the John Humphrey Noyeses of the world stay not just on the frontier, but far off in the deepest woods.

To see how this strain of American Puritanism energized, subverted, and finally repressed family romance, I will return to the central prohibition of family life, incest, and trace how it functions from the first native novel, William Hill Brown's *The Power of Sympathy,* through the *Schauerromans,* to temporarily play itself out in the works of Hawthorne, Poe, and Melville. Although I will only briefly discuss the incest theme in modern American literature, I do not argue that this is *the* dominant theme of American letters, but it certainly is one of the most dynamic and, until recently, one of the most neglected. To a considerable extent the frisson of incest inspired many of the greatest works of American romanticism as well as some of the most awkward.

The transformation of the European romance tradition first into the gothic, and then into the hybrid of the American gothic, was of degree rather than kind. The story remained the same—young people under sexual stress. Viewpoints, participants, and conclusions were just shifted by crucial degrees. Although many critics have argued that "the American experience" led to a unique view of family life more informed by capital-

ism, or the frontier, or puritanism, or narcissism, than by biology, such singularity is not borne out.[9] These are mitigating factors, to be sure, but the peculiar shade cast on the family romance by the "dark" introspective American romantics from Brown to O'Neill was not as much the result of their personal perceptions as it was the gradual evolution in Western culture toward greater concentration on intrafamilial dynamics. One need only read the works of Schiller, De Sade, Müllner, Tieck, Alfieri, and later Wagner, to realize that the situation on the Continent was in many respects like that in America. The industrial revolution that allowed a quick economic escape from family often produced just the opposite result. Families needed to stay close together to consolidate their gains, but not too close. Literature, both serious and popular, reflected this need. The sentimental tradition gave way to the budding gothic, which in turn carried the macabre. The family matrix, cemented for generations by the inability of members to get loose, now risked collapsing in upon itself.

Montague Summers, one of the first catalogers of the gothic, once slyly commented that to make a sentimental tale gothic, all an author need do was substitute a castle for a house, a snarling baron for a father, a knight for a boyfriend, a ghost for an attorney, a witch for a housekeeper, and a midnight murder for marriage. A slight exaggeration here, a minor change there, and tears could be changed into shivers. The only constant was the role of the central protagonist—the young female. The heroine remains forever the center of concentration, for it is always the violation of her privacy that charges our response.[10] In the transformation of the sentimental into the "low" gothic, the violator need only be changed from boyfriend to baron to brother. However, for the macabre, the "high" gothic, the shift must be made from brother to father.

What the Americans did to this story line was to compress the nuclear family and excise all the satellite characters. The witch/housekeeper, ghost/attorney, and all the supernumeraries are removed to lesser, or nonexistent roles. The "home" or castle is isolated by surrounding wilderness, and the internal pressure is increased until matters, and occasionally even characters, spontaneously combust. Call it Mettingen, Saddle Meadows, Usher, Yoknapatawpha, the centrifugal forces placed on a usually motherless family as the male sexual violation of daughter/sister is no longer threatened, but often realized, caused a catastrophe so complete that finally nothing of the family remains. Let the English mythologize incest as did Byron, or metaphysicalize it as did Shelley, the nineteenth-century American experience is uniformly horrible, irrepressibly gothic, maybe even characteristically pragmatic.

But not always. Because the exception, while not always proving the rule, at least shows where the rule is supposed to apply, I should like to examine first an overlooked work by a central nineteenth-century American artist—a short story by Edgar Allan Poe, *The Spectacles*. Although ostensibly *The Spectacles* satirizes the sentimental tradition of "love at first sight," it shows as well those aspects of human behavior usually only exposed under the dark cloud of the gothic. The plot of *The Spectacles* was not original with Poe; it had a history as an American tall tale. Clearly, Poe was drawn to expanding its salty humor as a potboiler for the Philadelphia *Dollar Newspaper*. Just as clearly, judging from his lengthy revisions, once he became involved, he could not let it go until he had touched a nerve, a rather particular nerve.

The Spectacles is told to us by a foppish man-about-town who is attempting to enter fashionable society. First, he has changed his name in order to inherit a small fortune from a distant relative. Once "Napoleon Buonaparte Froissart," a respectable enough French name even in the Colonies, he has become simply Mr. "Simpson."[11] Still, the exchange was certainly worth it, for what he might have sacrificed in presumptuous name, he more than made up for not just in his current bank account, but in future economic expectations as well. After all, in this country money makes money.

All Mr. Simpson now lacks is the proper lady friend to help him consolidate the gain via matrimony and, at the opera, he thinks he has found one. He spies the aristocratic Eugenie Lalande sitting off at a distance; it is love at first sight. She is the very essence of polite society, complete with sequined gown, a young female companion and opera glasses. Both Simpson and Mme. Lalande are terribly nearsighted. Mme. Lalande solves her problem by bringing her opera glasses; he is too proud to do so. As their myopic eyes meet, he is enraptured: "This was my *first* love—so I felt it to be. It was love supreme—indescribable. It was 'love at first sight'; and at first sight too, it had been appreciated and *returned*" (p. 895). What is returned, of course, is only her dim vision of him, but like a Platonic lover gone berserk, that is all the encouragement he needs. Simpson has become "possessed" and is as monomaniacal in his devotion to her vision as his brother narrators in *Morella, Bernice,* and *Ligeia* would be toward their inamoratas.

Unlike his other fictional incarnations, however, Simpson keeps his distance, first from diffidence and then from bashfulness. Finally when Eugenie takes a trip out of town he is convinced he must act. After loving her from afar, he approaches and gushes a proposal of marriage. She is literally aghast, asks him to please reconsider, to step back and have another look, but he will have none of it. He will not be restrained:

> "My sweetest Eugenie," I cried, "what is all this about which you are discoursing? Your years surpass

in some measure my own. But what then? The customs of the world are so many conventional follies. To those who love as ourselves, in what respect differs a year from an hour? I am twenty-two, you say; granted: indeed you may as well call me, at once twenty-three. Now you yourself, my dearest Eugenie, can have numbered no more than—can have numbered no more than—no more than—than—than—than—." (p. 903)

Simpson obviously hopes she will interrupt to tell him her age, but she doesn't. Instead, she only asks if he will please use her opera glasses, her "little ocular assistant," to be sure his vision is clear. But no, his vision is clear enough. Again, she entreats; he refuses. Rather like the narrator of *The Cask of Amontillado* leading dumb Fortunato down the stairs asking him at every landing if he wishes to continue, Mme. Lalande repeats her offer. In desperation she forces him to take the glasses. He puts them aside until too late.

Almost too late; after all, this is not a horror story but a tall tale. Simpson waits until his wedding day to use the glasses and only then when almost at the altar does he realize his fiancée is an elderly matron. The sight is, in his own words, *"horrific"*: "'You wretch!' said I catching my breath—'you—you—you villainous old hag!'" To which she exclaims that she may be old (in fact, 82 years old), but "hag" she is not. She is the grand dame of a prestigious family, the Froissarts. Dumbfounded, Simpson, aka Froissart, screams hysterically, as he now realizes that he has married his great-great-grand-mother!

The marriage is mysteriously annulled. The materfamilias is understanding if not forgiving, and offers him instead the hand of her lovely young consort: "a distant and exceedingly lovely relative of her second husband's—a Madame Stephanie Lalande" (p. 914). This is the marriage to be consummated with the complete blessing of the family. Any possible horror has been dissipated and the sentimental resolution has carried the day. Or has it? Look again, for as Daniel Hoffman noted Foissart

> doesn't have to marry his great, great, grandmother. He married his cousin. Even if we smile at Poe's impostor, aren't we struck by the consanguinity which afflicts his suitor? How curious that his faulty vision leads so precipitously toward incest! And the happy resolution only mitigates somewhat the closeness of the attachment of his heart for a member of his mother's blood.[12]

Even keeping in mind that Stephanie is not really consanguineous because she is from the great, great, grandmother's *husband*'s family, the point is still well taken. For all the posturing and punning, for all the folderol and foppery, the focus of the story returns us again to the magnetic attraction, the blind attraction, of a young man and his love of/at first sight, his mother, or, in this case, his barely displaced mother. Yes, he will "marry" Stephanie, but his heart is elsewhere. Admittedly, he finally ends with his cousin, his "mother's" consort, in a sense, his sister. Little wonder that Poe should have revised and diluted the relationships, but for all the sublimation and effacement, certain family relationships cannot be erased. After all, it is just these currents that provide the frisson, that excite our interest. *The Spectacles* concludes when our Hero accepts both his proper Leander, as well as his proper economic and social place in the family—the Froissart family:

> Nevertheless I am *not* the husband of my great, great, grandmother; and this is a reflection which affords me infinite relief;—but I *am* the husband of Madame Lalande—of Madame Stephanie Lalande—with whom my good old relative, besides making me her sole heir when she dies—if she ever does—has been at the trouble of concocting me a match. In conclusion: I am done forever with *billets doux*, and am never to be met without SPECTACLES. (p. 916)

When Poe wrote this *jeu d'esprit* in the 1840s, he was well aware of the melodrama that lurked within his subject especially when the tale was played out in the New World. The mistake of a newly minted American of distinct European background, who allows his ardor to settle on a member of his own family, would be told again and again. It would be told more than a century later in a work Poe himself would surely have been proud of—Vladimir Nabokov's *Lolita*. Although we usually think that this theme was only exploited after Poe, actually, other American writers had already pulled back the curtains of family life. What they saw was always shocking. In fact, in the first extended American novel, William Hill Brown's *The Power of Sympathy; or the Triumph of Nature,* published in 1789 just at the appearance of English gothicism, there is a sibling relationship that ushers in what, with Poe, will become the most famous family implosion.

At the commencement of American prose fiction, William Hill Brown inadvertently shows how much of the nascent American gothic was informed by Richardsonian romance. The central subplot of *The Power of Sympathy* traces the ill-fated love of a Lovelacean Harrington and his almost-Clarissa, Harriot. Harrington is a rogue whose plan is "to take this beautiful sprig [Harriot], and transplant it to a more favorable soil, where it shall flourish and blossom under my own auspices. In a word, I mean to remove this fine girl into an elegant apartment, of which she herself is to be the sole mistress" (1, letter #3, p. 17).[13] However well laid his plans of sexual exploitation may have been, her beauty soon transforms his sexual lust

into domestic desire. He proposes marriage—the conqueror has been conquered, the victimizer has become victim. Although she is an orphan and destitute, he will make her a place in the world, give her a name, father her a family.

But just as the happy couple are about to stroll altarward, they meet plot complication number three, which turns the sentimental into the gothic. They learn that, because of a paternal indiscretion, they are brother and sister. Drawn together by "the Power of Sympathy" they are now split asunder by "the Triumph of Nature." Although Harriot had earlier assured us that the *"link of Nature"* had drawn them together, they now learn that Nature will not tolerate this particular "link" (2, letter #50, p. 113). They should have known what they could not have known. Too late Harrington blurts: "'Had I known her to be my sister, my love would have been more regular—I should have loved her as a sister—I should have marked her beauty—I should have delighted in protecting it'" (2, letter #55, p. 127). And too late Harriot confesses, "'O! I sink, I die, when I reflect—when I find in my Harrington a brother—I am penetrated with inexpressible grief—I experience uncommon sensations—I start with horror at the idea of incest—of ruin—of perdition'" (2, letter #50, pp. 109-110). The curtain has fallen: Harriot dies from shock; Harrington by his own hand.

Viewed in the context of the burgeoning English tradition of the gothic novel, *The Power of Sympathy* is notable primarily for the artlessness of its prose style, the desultory manipulation of events, and the surplus of extraneous plot. But viewed from the perspective of the particular treatment of incest in early modern American culture, *The Power of Sympathy* is important for just those deficiencies. Its very flatness becomes its importance. No chances are taken with the plot or with the style, no "let's just try it once," no experimentation or titillation as in the English novel. To spin this roulette wheel is to invite disaster. Note that *both* parties must die rather than be forgiven for ignorance. William Hill Brown took his task with utmost seriousness. He told just what he announced on the original title page.

This same dispassionate tone and stern voice is echoed in the eight or so subsequent works before the 1830s in which, with only one exception, incest is actual, not implied, and the penalty is not diffused but final. When the incestuous act, or its threat, occurs in the sentimental works of mid-century as it did in the now almost forgotten, but once vastly popular writers like Susanna Rowson or Sara Wood, it is severely countered with death, exile, or permanent stigma.[14] As opposed to what was happening to René and his Amelia, Laon and his Cythna, or even Manfred and his Astarte, American fictional siblings were finding not temporary solace, or purposeful inspiration, but destruction and death. "Do it and die" is the clear American message. In this respect the early American gothic more nearly resembles the austerity of the folk ballad than the tender mercy of the English novel. If this part of American culture had to be aligned with a Western tradition, it would not be with the English or the French, but with the German.[15]

Perhaps as a tribute to its Northern European counterparts, Charles Brockden Brown's *Wieland* specifically emphasizes Germanic ancestry to supply badly needed motivation. To make incest properly gothic much must be made of family background—witness the familial patterns established in *Otranto, The Monk, Melmoth,* or *Frankenstein.* In *Wieland* the circle is even more elaborately spun out and then more abruptly contracted. Early on we are introduced to the mysterious old prophet Wieland who has left his fatherland, Germany, to expunge some unexplained sin. As an apostle of some mysterious truth, he is compelled to minister to the heathen Indians not so much to save them as to save himself. From what he flees we don't know, but we do know the escape drives him insane. If we are to believe the cloyingly semi-omniscient narrator, the pressure of the nameless sin builds inside the elder Wieland until he literally explodes; he spontaneously combusts; he burns up from within. The curse, however, is not destroyed; it is passed on to his son Theodore. Here, for all practical purposes, the novel really begins, but that Brown should think it necessary to provide the European causality may intimate his need to tie his bizarre tale into an appropriate context.

We are never told the exact nature of the curse carried out of Germany to the New World. Probably it is, as Fred Lewis Patee and others have contended, "the destruction of the family."[16] But how and why? What kind of behavior can cause a family to be blown apart from within? Is it the same process that spontaneously combusted the family father? Are these the sins of the father that are literally visited upon the son? Judging from what little has preceded *Wieland* in American cultural history, we may already be able to guess. In this almost classic tale of nineteenth-century family tragedy, the destruction proceeds apace with mechanical rigor. What is striking in Brown's version is that there is so much hesitating and rethinking as the awful denouement approaches, even though we are continually told that inevitable disaster looms ahead.[17]

After the elder Wieland's death the mother dies, leaving Theodore and his sister Clara alone, orphaned in the New World with no one to keep them company or to trust. They soon find another sibling pair (Henry and Catherine), as well as a "mysterious" older man, Carwin. As expected, the youngsters fall in love with their counterparts of the opposite sex. This is a con-figuration common enough in the English and German novels of the time in which sibling pairs multiply the prospects for pathos. We are assured that all would be well except that this Carwin insinuates himself so completely into the mind of Theodore that the young man has no idea what any of the relationships mean. Are they brothers and sisters, future in-laws, or lovers? He is not the only one who has lost control of role placement in this little family drama. During her parallel love affair, sister Clara dreams such interpretively helpful dreams as:

> I at length imagined myself walking, in the evening twilight, to my brother's habitation. A pit, methought, had been dug in the path I had taken, of which I was not aware. As I carelessly pursued my walk, I thought I saw my brother, standing at some distance before me, beckoning and calling me to make haste. He stood on the opposite edge of the gulf. I mended my pace, and one step more would have plunged me into this abyss." (p. 62)

Theodore does marry Catherine, but his sister's marriage to Henry is postponed; Henry happens to have a German fiancée. If we think we are confused, poor Theodore has so confounded the roles of the women surrounding him that he imagines his sister to have been sexually tainted and settles the "punishment" of her on his *wife.* In a crescendo of chaos, he literally drags his wife to his sister's house, kills her in his sister's bed, and then leaves her corpse there ostensibly as his sister's. Brown exercises no subtlety in this *Doppelgänger* transference; it is presented almost without affect. Now that Theodore has removed any impediment to his "real" sister, now that he has removed the surrogate, can he confront the real personage of repressed desire? No, not at all. Rather like Victor Frankenstein, or even like Dr. Jekyll, he can approach only just so close and then the realization of his real repressed sexual interest causes him to replay the father's finale. He ends his life, not in spontaneous combustion as did his father, but in a self-inflicted destruction reminiscent of the folk ballad. He stabs himself to death with his sister's penknife.

Clara now safely finishes the sublimated exchange by returning to Germany and marrying Henry, who has conveniently settled affairs with his fiancée. As with the seemingly unconscious social coda at the end of *The Spectacles,* in which a proper family member (a cousin for a "mother") is substituted, Clara marries her brother-in-law, her barely displaced "brother." What distinguishes her behavior from her brother's, from what her father possibly had been cursed for, is that the displacement is removed two layers from reality. In addition, her action occurs far from the boundaries of the New World. Remember that Clara leaves America, and its acute sensitivity and swift punishment, for the Old World of Northern Europe. Little wonder that

Wieland was subtitled *The Transformation,* for what we have seen are the changes wrought by a frontier family who wishes to, or is cursed to, rearrange their roles. The further sub-subtitle even specifies where such a price will be paid—it is *An American Tale.*

Although I have earlier (Chapter 2) discussed the sibling incest in Edgar Allan Poe's *Fall of the House of Usher,* it should be noted that one of its more perplexing aspects is that the eerie *mise en scène* is probably *not* in America. As a matter of fact, the House of Usher seems to be located in the Stygian lands of Annabel Lee or in some distant Ulalume which, if anything, is Germanic in the pictorial mode of Von Schwind, Richter, Friedrich, or Runge. All we know of its geography is that the house is surrounded not by a swamp, which might have given a misty air of the American South, but by a "tarn," which usually refers to an Alpine lake. Poe was not haphazard with descriptive terms, and he may well have chosen "tarn" very carefully. As contrasted with swamp, bog, fen or, better yet for the Ushers, quagmire, a tarn is specifically "a body of water that does not participate in the exchange of waters and keeps itself to itself."[18] Just as the tarn allows no entry or exit of itself, so the Ushers, brother and sister, are hermetically sealed in the cocoon of family. For them there can be no sexual excursions beyond the family border and so they must collapse in on themselves.

This geographic isolation seems a peculiarly American treatment of incest. The Wielands are sealed off in Mettingen, Pierre Glendinning and Isabel are initially confined to Saddle Meadows, the crazed Poe narrators are stuck in manor houses with their Morellas or Ligeias. Even the Faulkner and O'Neill families are mired in the South or frozen in New England. As opposed to the English tradition where incest may "open up" relationships with the proximate world, in the American milieu incest almost invariably closes it down. The family circle constricts until, as in the case of the Ushers, it consumes what is left of the family. Although critics such as Leslie Fiedler claim that this collapse into the self represents Poe's real-life focus on his nubile cousin, whom he called "Sis," and hence that "incest in Poe is too personal and pathological to shed much light on the general meaning of the latter theme in American literature and life," such is not the case.[19] The incest motif is so pervasive in Poe's other works, as well as so embedded in the American nineteenth-century *Zeitgeist,* that one suspects it is more closely tied to cultural anxieties than to personal eccentricities.

In *Berenice* and *Eleanora,* for instance, crazed narrators attempt to explain away the forbidden attraction of a cousin. In the more dense *Morella* and *Ligeia* the same libidinous energies are directed first to a seemingly proper exogamous mate but then swung back to

concentrate on the tabooed issue of their sexual union. Daughter is confused with mother, who, in turn, is confused with wife. Within this core father-daughter relationship, the now fully berserk narrator proposes a physical closeness that generates palpable horror. In *The Living Dead,* I argued that to generate this frisson Poe superimposed the vampire myth on the incestuous interaction so that the forbidden transfer of sexual energy from narrator to proper mate, then to improper mate, is mythologized and thus distanced from our conscious understanding.

The one activity that is conspicuously missing from Poe's fictional father-daughter dyad is the one activity that creates their relationship and the one behavior that horrifies us in the audience: sex. Sex is never mentioned, never even directly implied; instead we know only that certain women are enervated by the narrator's presence and that when one is mysteriously pushed aside, he commences courtship in earnest with her younger, innocent double. In contradistinction to *Usher,* where the participants are coevals, in these other tales the male narrator is first a child suitor to an older woman, then is a father to the child of their mysterious union, then suitor to this child.

The collision of these intrafamilial roles and relationships is the magnet that first holds fictional chaos together and then lets it fly apart. In each retelling, the price of these pseudo-sexual liaisons is first the unbalancing of a once attractive, but now totally maniacal, narrator, and then the collapse of his fledgling family. This demise is not simply the result of concentric narcissism or class struggle. It is a more generalized, a more sociobiological description of how human consciousness, if you will, refuses to countenance certain reproductive strategies.[20]

With this more generalized interpretation in mind, we might well conclude with Fiedler that there is nothing particularly *American* about Poe's treatment. But then notice how Hawthorne develops the same motif at approximately the same time.[21] In *Alice Doane's Appeal,* written just as Poe was starting his series of incest tales, Hawthorne set the specifically American stage for his own rendition of sibling entanglement:

> On a pleasant afternoon of June, it was my good fortune to be the companion of two young ladies in a walk. The direction of our course being left to me, I led them neither to Legge's Hill, nor to the Cold Spring, nor to the rude shores and old batteries of the Neck nor yet to Paradise; though if the latter place were rightly named, my fair friends would have been at home there. We reached the outskirts of the town, and turning aside from a street of tanners and curriers, began to ascend a hill . . . [upon which] the curious wanderer . . . will perceive

that all the grass, and every thing that should nourish man, or beast, has been destroyed by this vile and ineradicable weed: its tufted roots make the soil their own, and permit nothing else to vegetate among them; so that a physical curse may be said to have blasted the spot, where guilt and phrenzy consummated the most execrable scene, that our history blushes to record. For this was the field where superstition won her darkest triumph; the high place where our fathers set up their shame, to the mournful gaze of generations far remote. (pp. 266-67)

This specifically New England locale is "curst" by Nature in a typically romantic way. Its barrenness is a singularly Wordsworthean image. Think only of the "curse poems" like *Hart Leap Well, Peter Bell, The Thorn, The Danish Boy,* or even *Michael,* in which a sentient Nature, Mother Nature, has refused to share her bounty with man because of some particularly loathsome act of natural subversion. As with Wordsworth, in Hawthorne and Poe natural infecundity is also the result of a human act of atrocity. Beneath this dirt lies the body of a man whose story will explain why this patch of ground on Gallows Hill has been, and shall always be, barren. Even in America there is a force stronger than the force that drives up the green grass, a force so powerful that it can never be removed or overcome.

Many years ago, during the Puritan sway, a young man, Leonard Doane, "characterized by a diseased imagination and morbid feelings . . . with a deep taint of his nature," lived alone with his "beautiful and virtuous" sister. They were the last of their family save for a phantasmagoric brother, Walter, who mysteriously has been separated from them and whose surname is "Brome." All we know about this darkly enigmatic sibling is what we glean from Leonard's notebooks. It seems that Leonard suspects some "secret sympathy" has developed between his sister and Walter, for he writes:

> Searching into the breast of Walter Brome, I at length found a cause why Alice must inevitably love him. For he was my very counterpart! I compared his mind by each individual portion, and as a whole, with mine. There was a resemblance from which I shrank with sickness, and loathing, and horror, as if my own features had come and stared upon me in a solitary place, or had met me in struggling through a crowd. Nay! the very same thoughts would often express themselves in the same words from our lips, proving a hateful sympathy in our secret souls. (p. 271)

The doubling motif, so much a staple of barely sublimated incestuous desire, is invoked. A man just like Leonard loves Alice in a forbidden way, in a way a brother should not love his sister. The narrator now enters to help explain:

Leonard Doane went on to describe the insane hatred that had kindled his heart into a volume of hellish flame. It appeared, indeed, that his jealousy had grounds, so far as that Walter Brome had actually sought the love of Alice, who also had betrayed an undefinable, but powerful interest in the unknown youth. The latter, in spite of his passion for Alice, seemed to return the loathful antipathy of her brother; the similarity of their dispositions made them like joint possessors of an individual nature, which could not become wholly the property of one, unless by the extinction of the other. At last, with the same devil in each bosom, they chanced to meet, they two on a lonely road. (p. 272)

Indeed they meet, and rather like Victor Frankenstein and his monster, or Dr. Jekyll and his Mr. Hyde, or a host of other *Doppelgängers* driven by the self-destructive nature of a buried desire to do what should not be done, Leonard throttles his alter ego, Walter. Almost immediately Leonard regresses into childhood and now, for the first time, the inner dynamics are played out on the surface. In Leonard's own words:

> Methought I stood a weeping infant by my father's hearth; by the cold and blood-stained hearth where he lay dead. I heard the childish wail of Alice, and my own cry arose with hers, as we beheld the features of our parent, fierce with the strife and distorted with the pain, in which his spirit had passed away. As I gazed, a cold wind whistled by, and waved my father's hair. Immediately, I stood again in the lonesome road, no more a sinless child but a man of blood, whose tears were falling fast over the face of his dead enemy. But the delusion was not wholly gone; that face still wore a likeness of my father; and because my soul shrank from the fixed glare of the eyes, I bore the body [of Walter] to the lake. . . . (p. 273)

Did Walter really exist? Did Leonard really kill him? Was Walter the violator of his sister's virtue? Or was it Leonard? As if to make sure we never quite phrase, let alone answer, these questions, Hawthorne has the inner story of Leonard being told to a wizard. The function of this sorcerer is clearly to sidetrack us away from the Leonard-Walter-father triad. All we know for sure from the story's frame is that under a patch of barren ground lies the body of someone who did something so horrible that Nature herself is repulsed and will issue forth no new life.

The narrator, really a wizard manqué, now continues the game, but raises the stakes.

> I dare not give the remainder of the scene, except in a very brief epitome. This company of devils and condemned souls had come on a holiday, to revel in the discovery of a complicated crime; as foul a one as ever was imagined in their dreadful abode.

In the course of the tale, the reader had been permitted to discover, that all the incidents were results of the machinations of the wizard, who had cunningly devised that Walter Brome should tempt his unknown sister to guilt and shame, and himself perish by the hand of his twin-brother. I described the glee of the fiends, at this hideous conception, and their eagerness to know if it were consummated. The story concluded with the Appeal of Alice to the spectre of Walter Brome; his reply, absolving her from every stain; and the trembling awe with which ghost and evil fled, as from the sinless presence of an angel. (p. 277)

As Byron reportedly said of Coleridge's metaphysics, "I wish he would explain this explanation," for this gloss serves both to deflect still further the hideous act, while at the same time to categorize the crime. For most readers the distance now is simply too much. We have been deceived too often. However, the fact that Hawthorne should feel the need of still another buffer shows how cautious most authors, especially American bourgeois authors, thought they should be if they were to describe familial interactions that their English brethren, admittedly aristocratic brethren, were enacting with comparative impunity. The lessons of Oneida had to be remembered. To approach the subject of incest in *this* country, at least in front of *this* audience of young women, Hawthorne has had to adopt a fairy-tale "once upon a time" format; tell the story by word of mouth many times removed from the "here and now"; quote copiously from Leonard's diary; and, finally, turn his back on the verifiability of the tale and claim it was caused by the machinations of a wizard. All that we finally know for certain is that whatever happened here in New England, whatever the "black horror and deep woe," it has left Nature unwilling to bring forth new life. The outer tale finally concludes as the narrator and his young lady friends leave the barren and infertile patch and return to the world of community.

We slowly descended, watching the lights as they twinkled gradually through the town, and listening to the distant mirth of boys at play, and to the voice of a young girl, warbling somewhere in the dusk, a pleasant sound to wanderers from old witch times. Yet ere we left the hill, we could not but regret, that there is nothing on its barren summit, no relic of old, nor lettered stone of later days, to assist the imagination in appealing to the heart. We build the memorial column on the height which our fathers made sacred with their blood, poured out in a holy cause. And here in dark, funereal stone, should rise another monument, sadly commemorative of the errors of an earlier race, and not to be cast down, while the human heart has one infirmity that may result in crime. (p. 280)

" . . . the human heart has one infirmity that may result in crime"—hardly are the words read than one won-

ders about all the other equally mysterious crimes in the Hawthorne canon that have stubbornly remained cloaked in the mist of uncertain explanations. I would not venture to assume an overly incestuous relationship between Rappachini and his daughter, or in the deflected adultery of *The Scarlet Letter,* or even such a reading of the strangely childlike interaction of Holgrave and Phoebe in *The House of Seven Gables.* I do believe, however, and some critics have also suggested, that the possibility of incestuous relationships was one of the recurring subjects of Hawthorne's art.[22] Granted that such sexual constellations of family members may simply be an occupational hazard if a writer is going to deal with "the secrets of the human heart," as Hawthorne contended. But if the self-same heart holds the "one infirmity that is criminal," then the subject of incest seems destined to be overtly, or covertly, exposed. What separates Hawthorne's treatment is not just that he needs to distance himself from expressly acknowledging incest, but that it seems so irredeemable an act on American soil. The stigma of incest is a brand not worn like the "A," but instead burned into the everlasting soul of Nature.

There is never anything titillating about incest in Hawthorne's work—it is sad, irredeemable, and tragic. Not so, however, in the sensationalist fiction of the mid-century. Here, in pulp novels, incest became one of the staples, the mentionable unmentionable, the *almost*-consummated forbidden act. By 1850 the increasing stability of the family, thanks to the clustering of population centers, the rise of large-scale industry, and the receding of the frontier with all its attendant physical and psychological demands, not only allowed family introspection, but occasionally demanded it. Women who read at home and men who read on the railroad wanted more than thrills, they wanted to know specifically who they were and where they were going. Cheap pulp, massive steam-driven presses, permanent ink, and the likes of Maria Susannah Cummins, Augusta Jane Evans, Miriam Coles Harris, Mary Jane Holmes, Mrs. E. D. E. N. Southworth, Harriet Beecher Stowe, and Susan Warner were as ready to inform women as were Emerson Bennett, Osgood Bradbury, "Ned Buntline," F. A. Durivage, Henri Foster, Joseph Holt Ingraham, George Lippard, and George Thompson were to inform their husbands.[23]

Whether the setting be city life or country habitat, the titillation caused by brothers who treat wives as sisters and sisters as wives (which, after all, was the Victorian ideal taken literally) formed the donnée of inappropriate seduction. No longer were these dynamics only embedded in the gothic where trembling was sanctioned by the genre. A literary format was being revived here as it was in England, where the trembling was an end in itself. The gothic romance was recharged as it now told of the middle-class family under specific and identifiable sexual pressure. This form is still popular, as a glance at any best seller list or a trip to the drug store book display will attest. A curious audience eager to witness the excitement and horrors of "home sweet home" is still in place.

The bourgeois American audience, financially able and irrepressibly eager for this scenario of families run amok, was so powerful a force in the literary market-place that by midcentury it was demanding reams of its own sentimental pulp. Reader-response critics, who contend that audiences create works of art by forcing artists to address specific topics, will find no better situation to observe how economic and social pressures were brought to bear on storytellers. Readers make writers write, just as movie viewers make moviemakers make movies.

Melville, whose greatest novel, *Moby-Dick,* was written at roughly the same time as his *Pierre,* demonstrates the struggle both for and against the market. *Moby-Dick* is an intricate, dense, intellectually turbid vision of the world as seen by men without families. It took, even at Melville's prodigious speed, years to write and almost as long to publish. It found no market and, I daresay, without academics who provide a scholarly market, this book would still not be widely read. However, while waiting for *Moby-Dick* to appear in print, Melville started the first draft of *Pierre,* finished it, found a publisher who rushed it to print just as *Moby-Dick* was slowly being introduced. *Pierre* had middling success, but at least it had good prospects. Melville was optimistic about *Pierre;* he knew what would happen to *Moby-Dick.* Yet, *Pierre* is a careless work, sloppily written, about a sentimental protagonist and the maudlin destruction of his family which results from specific sexual confusion. Ironically, in spite of all the artistic blunders, we can learn much about survival on the high seas of family life from the land-locked *Pierre.*

I suppose the kindest comment made by critics about *Pierre* is that it is a parody, a send-up of the hundreds of fictional genealogies that were spewed forth from the maw of the steam presses and avidly consumed by newly literate Americans.[24] Indeed, it is clear in the first fifty pages that Melville is scoffing at the pomposity of his little fictional family, the Glendinnings, as they play out the fantasies of silver-fork fiction. Secluded in the edenic world of Saddle Meadows, the foppish Pierre lives with his doting mother in nectarine innocence. The father/husband has long since died, leaving only his fortune and two portraits behind. Pierre calls his mother "sister" and "sis"; she calls him "love": it is clearly a hothouse of family romance deep in the Berkshires. Here is a sample:

> This romantic filial love of Pierre seemed fully returned by the triumphant maternal pride of the widow, who in the clearcut lineaments and noble air of the son, saw her own graces strangely translated into the opposite sex. There was a striking personal resemblance between them; and as the mother seemed to have long stood still in her beauty, heedless of the passing years; so Pierre seemed to meet her half-way, and by a splendid precocity of form and feature, almost advanced himself to that mature stand-point in Time, where his pedestaled mother so long had stood. In the playfulness of their unclouded love, and with that strange license which a perfect confidence and mutual understanding at all points, had long bred between them, they were wont to call each other brother and sister. Both in public and private this was their usage; not when thrown among strangers, was this mode of address ever suspected for a sportful assumption; since the amaranthiness of Mrs. Glendinning fully sustained this youthful pretension.—Thus freely and lightsomely for mother and son flowed on the pure joined current of life. But as yet the fair river had not borne its waves to those sideways rebelling rocks, where it was thenceforth destined to be forever divided into two unmixing streams. (p. 25)

At the age of sixteen Pierre all but "marries" his mother; they partake of the holy sacrament of communion not so much with Christ as with each other. What is missing in the little Glendinning family, we are repeatedly told, is a sister/daughter. The bemused narrator opines, "So perfect to Pierre had long seemed the illuminated scroll of his life so far, that only one hiatus was discoverable by him in that sweetly-writ manuscript. A sister had been omitted from the text" (p. 27). To which Pierre blurts out, "Oh, had my father but had a daughter! . . . someone whom I might love, and protect, and fight for, if need be. It must be a glorious thing to engage in a mortal quarrel on a real sweet sister's behalf! Now, of all things, would to heaven, I had a sister" (p. 27)!

Sisters were, after all, central in chivalric romance because they could be fought for without the embarrassment and debasement of sexual desire. No sooner is a sister requested than she is delivered. Into this dwindling family the sister *must* come, and indeed she does in the person of Lucy Tartan. Bright, vivacious, the only daughter of a "most cherished friend of Pierre's father," also now conveniently deceased, also raised by a widowed mother, Lucy is the "light" the Glendinnings need to find their way to familial happiness. Pierre will make this girl his wife and then make his wife a sister, then make this sister his mother's daughter, and then all will live happily ever after. The circle will be closed. Eden will be reconstituted in upstate Massachusetts just across the state line from the Oneida community, which was also plodding toward perfection by condensing the family.

Dull black clouds swag across the heavenly skies of Saddle Meadows, or, in the novel's terms, ocean waves foam over the cliffs of Glendinning harbor. Both Lucy and Pierre feel "some nameless sadness" coming on. "Foretaste I feel of endless dreariness," says Lucy, and Pierre counters, "God help thee, and God help me, Lucy. I can not think that in this most mild and dulcet air, the invisible agencies are plotting treasons against our loves" (p. 61). As might be expected, neither Pierre nor Lucy can understand their sense of unease, this mysterious harbinger of the sad irreconcilability of ordinary life. We do not have to wait long to find out, for who should appear but the "real" sister, Isabel Glendinning, natural child of Pierre's father's youthful indiscretion, a child who, above all else, is the single object of Pierre's eternal quest. Why should he treat his mother like a sister when he has Lucy, and now why should he treat Lucy like a sister when he has his very own sister or, at least, his very own half-sister?

The introduction of the image of actual incest is laid on with a sticky hand, and yet, for all the sentimental parody, one senses that halfway through this inevitable plot development Melville realized that for all its ridiculousness there was a real story struggling to get out. Critics who have been able to trudge through the first half of *Pierre* have been quick to comment that once the constellation of mother-son and brother-pretend sister links with real brother-real sister, it sets up a vibration that even Melville couldn't slow down.[25] The novel now takes hold as the real sister replaces imagined sister who has replaced mother-as-sister. In the process we come to realize that the subtitle of *Pierre, or the Ambiguities* is indeed about liberating family characters from predefined family roles. No one knows who is who, especially not Pierre and, even more important, not the reader.

For these sins of confusion, not for his misplaced ardor, Pierre is cast out of the family. His mother disinherits him and in doing so she pushes him still closer to the only family he has left—into the waiting arms of his sister. As his vision of controlling the family fades, Pierre is forced to recognize that this is the result of the other side of paternalism: you cannot be a master unless you have servants. This knowledge comes too late to stop the fall from grace, yet Pierre wants to sanctify all he can. Ostensibly to assure Isabel her place in the family, Pierre proposes marriage. A marriage, mind you, Pierre proudly asserts, without sex. Isabel responds to this "glorious ideal" by

> lean[ing] closer to him, with an inexpressible strangeness of intense love, new and inexplicable. Over the face of Pierre there shot a terrible self-revelation; he imprinted repeated burning kisses upon her; pressed hard her hand; would not let go her sweet and awful passiveness.

> Then they changed; they coiled together and entangledly stood mute. (pp. 225-226)

Asexual relationships, as Pierre will discover, are best left to parthenogenetic species. Exiled from Eden, Pierre goes to the city with Isabel, still determined to make her not only a part of the family but part of his intimate life. He has already lost his mother; losing his sister would destroy him.

Meanwhile his mother, who has already disowned Pierre, dies, leaving the Glendinning fortune to a priggish cousin, who having inherited Pierre's lands, also wants to acquire his erstwhile fiancée, Lucy. Slowly it dawns on Pierre that his charity for Isabel is really only mistaken Eros; altruistic aims disguising carnal desire; vice parading as virtue. In one of the book's more extraordinary passages, Pierre, who has earlier seen himself as the martyred Christ, now dreams of himself as the withered Titan Enceladus, who in ancient times propagated his family through the body of his mother and sister. Pierre wakes in horror as he realizes he is living out that myth. Here the narrator, no longer bemused by his posturing protagonist, enters the text to make certain the point is well taken, although in slightly muddied form:

> Old Titan's self was the son of incestuous Coelus and Terra, the son of incestuous Heaven and Earth. And Titan married his mother Terra, another and accumulatively incestuous match. And thereof Enceladus was one issue. So Enceladus was both the son and grandson of incest; and even thus, there had been born from the organic blended heavenliness and earthliness of Pierre, another mixed, uncertain, heaven-aspiring, but still not wholly earth-emancipated mood; which again, by its terrestrial taint held down to its terrestrial mother, generated there the present doubly incestuous Enceladus within him; so that the present mood of Pierre—that reckless sky-assaulting mood of his, was nevertheless on the side the grandson of the sky.

> Recovered somewhat from the after-spell of this wild vision folded in his trance, Pierre composed his front as best he might, and straightway left his fatal closet. Concentrating all the remaining stuff in him, he resolved by an entire and violent change, and by a willful act against his own most habitual inclinations, to wrestle with the strange malady of his eyes, this new death-fiend of the trance, and this Inferno of his Titanic vision. (pp. 388-389)

Knowing what he now knows about the mythic past, Pierre realizes his demise is close at hand. He has, after all, been raised in the sentimental tradition, nurtured on its myths, has even attempted to write out its truths in an abortive Melvillean novel. Now he has to be, like Enceladus, consumed in its foregone conclusion. Having undermined all authority of roles, having placed the Glendinning family at the edge of destruction, Pierre is reunited in the last scenes with his Lucy and his Isabel. Pierre, now destitute in prison, is fi-

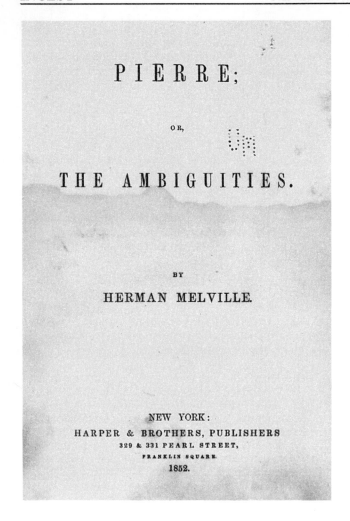

PIERRE;

OR,

THE AMBIGUITIES.

BY

HERMAN MELVILLE.

NEW YORK:
HARPER & BROTHERS, PUBLISHERS
329 & 331 PEARL STREET,
FRANKLIN SQUARE.
1852.

In a sense, Pierre's death ends the romanticizing of family sexual relations. As Shelley had been for English romantic poetry, Melville was now for American romantic prose. No one could, or really wanted to, rewrite their texts. The first unfolding of family sexual dynamics was over. What had begun with the zealous transportation of revolution over the very doorstep of the bourgeoisie, what had energized some of the greatest poetry of romanticism, what had stimulated prose fiction almost to the point of supporting the gothic as the dominant genre, what had occasioned some of the most adventuresome utopian experiments in the wilderness as well as some of the most repressive American responses, had here run out of steam. The first of the modern conversations, so to speak, on the subject of forbidden relations was over. The taboo was firmly in place and interests, literary and other, moved elsewhere.

We are now entering the second of these conversations, a revival of interest. As I mentioned in the first chapter, this has often become a strident and shrill debate as certain interests have turned into supposed advocacy just as happened in the first blush of romanticism. Exactly how our current discourse will end is anyone's guess. Perhaps our interests will lead us to the desultory plottings of another Pierre, or maybe to the sublime rejoicings of another Laon. Perhaps the family knot will be untied as kinship patterns are reevaluated and reformed. In any case, I hope I have shown that we are not the first to address these secret anxieties, and not the first to be confused and startled and upset when they are made public. Although all scholars dream of resolving such confusion in an eleventh-hour conclusion, let me venture into the current thicket still attempting to follow the same trail, albeit now unmarked and unbeaten, of more current literary fictions and speculations. For if artists are indeed the first apprehenders of unarticulated truths, it may prove that we are indeed revising the taboo in ways as yet unknown to most of us.

Notes

[1] Whatever it is in the American culture that prompts this behavior, has yet to be resolved. Witness the Rajneeshpurham in Oregon, a settlement on what is left of our frontier based on the subversion of contemporary capitalistic culture. It is clearly important to parade the Bhagwan Shree Rajneesh about in one of his forty-six Rolls-Royces to show how decadence itself can be perverted and just as important to show how much more compassionate to the poor they can be than the "outside" world is. Also of interest is their rearrangement of the family under "father" Bhagwan and "mother" Ma Anand Sheela, for, we are told, the incest taboo has been "set aside." Honest sex needs no "complications." It may not be happenstance that the commune fell apart after Ma Anand left the family.

[2] In the last two decades the frontier community has been a subject of considerable academic interest; see, for a

nally visited by the sister who is a sister, and the sister who just pretends to be a sister. As these "sisters" enter his cell, Pierre cries out:

> "Ye two pale ghosts, were this the other world, ye were not welcome. Away!—Good Angel and Bad Angel both!—For Pierre is neuter now!" . . .

> At these wailed words from Isabel, Lucy shrunk up like a scroll, and noiselessly fell at the feet of Pierre.

> He touched her heart.—"Dead!—Girl! wife or sister, saint or fiend!"—seizing Isabel in his grasp—"in thy breasts, life for infants lodgeth not, but death-milk for thee and me!—The drug!" and tearing her bosom loose, he seized the secret vial nestling there. (p. 403)

Pierre dies, poisoned, drinking the metaphoric death from her breast. To complete the triad, Lucy drains what is left, and the novel ends, " . . . her whole form sloped sideways, and she fell upon Pierre's heart, and her long hair ran over him, and arbored him in ebon vines" (p. 405).

general view, A. N. Kaul, *The American Vision.* There are a plethora of specific studies, for instance, Laurence Foster, *Religion and Sexuality: Three American Communal Experiments of the Nineteenth Century;* Diane Barthel, *Amana: From Pietist Sect to American Community;* Raymond Muncy, *Sex and Marriage in Utopian Communities;* Arthur Bestor, *Backwoods Utopias;* John Chandler, "The Communitarian Quest for Perfection"; and William Bridges, "Family Patterns and Social Values in America 1825-1875." I am particularly indebted to Anne Dalke, "'Had I Known Her to be my Sister': Incest in Nineteenth-Century American Fiction" for making many provocative connections between the literary establishment of the nineteenth century, the reading public, and the frontier experiments.

[3] Noyes himself came from a family known for their inability to effectively breed out; in fact, according to the family biography, *A Yankee Saint,* by Robert Allerton Parker, the Atkinson/Noyes family was "said to be so bashful that they could not pop the question to anybody but cousins. This became known as the 'Atkinson difficulty.' "

[4] Noyes to David Harrison, January 15, 1837. In Dixon, *Spiritual Wives,* 2: 55-56.

[5] Oneida Association, *Bible Communism,* p. 53.

[6] *Ibid.,* pp. 27-28.

[7] Noyes, *Essay on Scientific Propagation,* p. 17, 21.

[8] The Transcendentalists were clearly in the avant garde in these matters, of which they knew little, even though they had an experimental family at Brook Farm near Boston. Recent study of this commune questions the Transcendental Club's high social concerns as Hawthorne's *Blithedale Romance* first intimated. The "brotherly co-operation" of the farm was more to ensure George Ripley's leisure than to revolutionize family dynamics. Although Brook Farm was primarily an economic experiment, the fact that the institution of marriage was never really discussed gives some indication of a dedication to matters other than to concepts of family life. When the Farm disbanded in the mid-1840s, it was not because of dissension from the nearby citizens of West Roxbury but from within the group.

[9] For example, Henri Petter, *The Early American Novel,* believes that "near incest" was an American imitation of an English "fashion"; Alexander Cowie, *The Rise of the American Novel,* contends that incest appears as a desire to edify the young; Edward Wagenknecht, *Calvalcade of the American Novel,* and Leslie Fiedler, *Love and Death in the American Novel,* see it as a reaction to Puritanism; Anne Dalke, "'Had I Known Her to be my Sister . . .'" interprets

incest as an outgrowth of paternalism, and James Wilson, "Incest and American Romantic Fiction," sees it as the extension of romantic solipsism. I am oversimplifying, to be sure, but I do it to show the range of possible interpretations. I think it is clear that all apply in varying degrees.

[10] Summers, *The Gothic Quest,* p. 35.

[11] Poe may well have been aware of the nineteenth-century belief that Napoleon had incestuous relations with his sister. Poe's knowledge of the continental literary tradition of incest is documented by Anne Dalke, "'Had I Known Her to Be My Sister. . . . '"

[12] Hoffman, *Poe, Poe, Poe, Poe, Poe, Poe, Poe,* p. 243.

[13] Because of the confusion over editions, I will cite the book and letter numbers as well as the page.

[14] Here, as with other comments on nineteenth-century American literature, I an indebted to the scholarship of Anne Dalke, "'Had I Known Her to Be My Sister. . . . '" In Chapter 2 she details the reading audience of popular fiction.

[15] In his chapter "Incest and American Fiction" in *The Heroic Romantic Ideal,* James D. Wilson has pointed out, "America more closely resembled Germany, which was also at the time a loose collection of city-states lacking the literary, political, or religious cohesiveness characteristic of its more prosperous neighbors. Like their American counterparts, German artists too gave incest harsh treatment: Tieck's *Der blonde Eckbert,* Schiller's *Die Braut von Messina,* and Grillparzer's *Die Abnfrau* all portrayed incest as an unconscious act—as in *Oedipus*—the recognition of which invariably led to dementia and death (p. 139).

[16] Patee, "Introduction," *Wieland, or the Transformation,* p. xi. Scholars are at odds as to whether incest actually occurs: Bredahl, "Transformation in *Wieland*"; Fiedler, *Love and Death;* Ziff, "A Reading of *Wieland*"; and Wilson, "Incest and American Romantic Fiction," say yes; but Manley, "The Importance of Point of View in Brockden Brown's *Wieland,*" says that "obviously" no sexual assault occurs; it is simple homicide.

[17] Harry Warfel, "Charles Brockden Brown's German Sources," makes a convincing case that Brown's hesitancy is partly uneasiness with his German sources, most specifically Cajetan Tschink's *Geisterserer.*

[18] Renata Wasserman, "The Self, the Mirror, the Other: *The Fall of the House of Usher,*" details the specific significance of the "tarn" in terms of the exchange

theory of Lévi-Strauss. She argues that just as the tarn will allow no movement of water and therefore turns stagnant, so will human families if they do not over-flow into others.

[19] Fiedler, *Love and Death,* pp. 415-416. It should be noted that Fiedler is not alone in believing Poe was independent of American cultural tradition. From Vernon Parrington, *Main Currents in American Thought,* onward, Poe has been viewed as a "private" author who was thus not in the main "current of American thought," but this view is by no means unanimous and, in fact, no longer seems as standard as it once did. In his implicit condemnation of incest Poe is certainly a mainstream American romanticist.

[20] Here is D. H. Lawrence, *Selected Literary Criticism,* on Poe's incestuous, vampiric lovers: " . . . the secondary law of all organic life is that each organism only lives through contact with other matter, assimilation, and contact with other life, which means assimilation of new vibrations, non-material. Each individual organism is vivified by intimate contact with fellow organisms. . . . In spiritual love, the contact is purely nervous. The nerves in the lovers are set vibrating in unison like two instruments. The pitch can rise higher and higher. But carry this too far, and the nerves begin to break, to bleed, as it were, and a form of death sets in. . . . It is easy to see why each man kills the things he loves. To *know* a living thing is to kill it. You have to kill a thing to know it satisfactorily. For this reason, the desirous consciousness, the SPIRIT, is a vampire" (pp. 331-335). This view is also reiterated by Allen Tate, "Our Cousin, Mr. Poe."

[21] *Alice Doane's Appeal* was published anonymously in 1835 and was subsequently ignored by Hawthorne. He never republished it, or even mentioned it again. Why? Philip Young, *Hawthorne's Secret,* claims this neglect was purposeful, for in this short story Hawthorne came to grips with his own guilt, a guilt that also figures in his stories of the same time—*My Kinsman, Major Molineux, Young Goodman Brown,* and *Roger Malvin's Burial.* Although these stories do not overtly deal with incest, they are closely related in theme, spirit, and especially tone. For more on this argument, see the subsequent note.

[22] See Fiedler, *Love and Death,* pp. 229-230; Crews, *The Sins of the Fathers,* p. 37; and Loggins, *The Hawthornes,* p. 279. Recently Erlich, *Family Themes and Hawthorne's Fiction: The Tenacious Web,* and Young, *Hawthorne's Secret: An Un-Told Tale,* have breathed new life into the biographical interpretation by contending that incest not only figured in relations between the Mannings (Margaret, Anstice, and their brother Nicholas) who were maternal ancestors, but also occurred between the author and his sister. Pro-

fessor Young does not call it "incest"—his unfortunate phrase is "something happened"—but the implication is clear. These two books are especially important, for it is one thing to make intuitive guesses, as do Fiedler and Crews, but it is quite another to provide the connections between biographical fact and literary text.

[23] The American sentimental novel has not been as well studied as its English counterpart, but Frank Mott, *Golden Multitudes,* and Herbert Ross Brown, *The Sentimental Novel in America, 1789-1860,* as well as chapter 5 of Dalke, "'Had I Known . . . '" survey the genre, and the latter concentrates specifically on those novels overtly detailing incestuous configurations.

[24] Critics have been kinder to *Pierre* than have readers. From constructive S. Foster Damon, "Pierre the Ambiguous," to deconstructive Eric Sundquist, *Home as Found,* scholars have been able to overlook desultory prose and tedious plotting en route to profundities be they philosophical or psychological. *Pierre* even has the mark of ultimate authority as canonical text: Ralph Willell, ed., *The Merrill Studies in "Pierre"*—a collection of critical essays.

[25] There have been a number of incest-centered interpretations of *Pierre* from George Homans, "The Dark Angel," in the 1930s to the affective criticism of the present like Brook Thomas, "The Writer's Procreative Urge in *Pierre.*" Recently there has been renewed interest in comparing the use of the Cenci motif in American romanticism: R.L. Carothers, "Melville's 'Cenci,'" and Diane Hoeveler, "La Cenci: The Incest Motif in Hawthorne and Melville."

Works Cited

Barthel, Diane L. *Amana: From Pietist Sect to American Community.* Lincoln: University of Nebraska Press, 1984.

Bestor, Arthur. *Backwoods Utopias: The Sectarian Origins and the Owenite Phase of Communitarian Socialism in America, 1663-1829.* Philadelphia: University of Pennsylvania Press, 1970.

Bredahl, Carl A. Jr. "Transformation in *Wieland.*" *Early American Literature* (1977) 12:177-192.

Bridges, William E. "Family Patterns and Social Values in America 1825-1875." *American Quarterly* (1965), 17:3-11.

Brown, Herbert Ross. *The Sentimental Novel in America 1789-1860.* 1940; reprint. Freeport, N.Y.: Books for Libraries, 1970.

Brown, William Hill. *The Power of Sympathy:* or, *The Triumph of Nature. Founded in Truth. In Two Volumes.* Boston: Isaiah Thomas, 1789.

Carothers, R. L. "Melville's 'Cenci'": A Portrait of *Pierre. Ball State University Forum* (1969), 10:53-59.

Chandler, John W. "The Communitarian Quest for Perfection." In Stuart C. Henry, ed., *A Miscellany of American Christianity.* Durham, N.C.: Duke University Press, 1963.

Cowie, Alexander. *The Rise of the American Novel.* New York: American Book Co., 1951.

Crews, Frederick C. *The Sins of the Fathers: Hawthorne's Psychological Themes.* New York: Oxford University Press, 1966.

Dalke, Anne F. "'Had I Known Her to be my Sister, My Love Would have been More Regular': Incest in Nineteenth-Century American Fiction." PhD dissertation, University of Pennsylvania, 1982.

Damon, S. Foster. "Pierre the Ambiguous." *The Hound and Horn* (1929), 2:115-117.

Dixon, William H. *Spiritual Wives.* 2 vols. London: Hurst and Blackett, 1868.

Erlich, Gloria C. *Family Themes and Hawthorne's Fiction: The Tenacious Web.* New Brunswick, N.J.: Rutgers University Press, 1984.

Fiedler, Leslie. *Love and Death in the American Novel.* New York: Stein and Day, 1966.

Foster, Laurence. *Religion and Sexuality: Three American Communal Experiments of the Nineteenth Century.* New York: Oxford University Press, 1981.

Hawthorne, Nathaniel. "Alice Doane's Appeal." In *The Snow-Image and Uncollected Tales.* The Centenary Edition, vol. 11. Columbus: Ohio State University Press, 1974.

Hoeveler, Diane L. "La Cenci: The Incest Motif in Hawthorne and Melville." *American Transcendental Quarterly* (1977), 44:247-259.

Hoffman, Daniel. *Poe, Poe, Poe, Poe, Poe, Poe, Poe.* Garden City, N.Y.: Doubleday, 1972.

Homans, George C. "The Dark Angel: The Tragedy of Herman Melville." *New England Quarterly* (1932) 5:699-730.

Lawrence, D. H. *Selected Literary Criticism.* 1932; reprint. New York: Viking, 1966.

Loggins, Vernon. *The Hawthornes: The Story of Seven Generations of an American Family.* New York: Columbia University Press, 1951.

Manley, William. "The Importance of Point of View in Brockden Brown's *Wieland." American Literature* (1963), 34:311-321.

Melville, Herman. *Pierre, or the Ambiguities.* Introduction by Laurance Thompson. New York: New American Library, 1964.

Mott, Frank L. *Golden Multitudes: The Story of Best Sellers in the United States.* 1947; reprint. New York: Bowker, 1966.

Muncy, Raymond L. *Sex and Marriage in Utopian Communities; Nineteenth-Century America.* Bloomington: Indiana University Press, 1975.

Noyes, John Humphrey. *Essay on Scientific Propagation, with an Appendix Concerning a Health Report of the Oneida Community,* by Theodore R. Noyes, M.D. 1875; reprint. New York: AMS, 1974.

Oneida Association. *Bible Communism: A Compilation of the Annual Reports and Other Publications of the Oneida Association and Its Branches.* Brooklyn, N.Y.: Office of *The Circular,* 1853.

Parrington, Vernon. *Main Currents in American Thought: Romantic Revolution in America 1800-1860.* vol. 2. New York: Harcourt Brace, 1958.

Patee, Fred Lewis. "Introduction" to Charles Brockden Brown, *Wieland or The Transformation Together with Memoirs of Carwin the Biloquist: A Fragment.* New York: Harcourt Brace, 1926.

Petter, Henri. *The Early American Novel.* Columbus: Ohio State University Press, 1971.

Poe, Edgar Allan. "The Spectacles." In Thomas O. Mabbott, ed. *Tales and Sketches 1843-1849. Collected Works.* vol. 3. Cambridge: Harvard University Press, 1978.

Summers, Montague. *The Gothic Quest: A History of the Gothic Novel.* London: Fortune, 1938.

Sundquist, Eric J. *Home as Found: Authority and Genealogy in Nineteenth-Century America.* Baltimore, Md.: Johns Hopkins University Press, 1979.

Tate, Allen. "Our Cousin, Mr. Poe." In Allen Tate, ed., *The Forlorn Demon: Didactic and Critical Essays.* Chicago: Regnery, 1953.

Thomas, Brook. "The Writer's Procreative Urge in *Pierre:* Fictional Freedom or Convoluted Incest?" *Studies in the Novel* (1979), 11:416-430.

Wagenknecht, Edward. *Cavalcade of the American Novel.* New York: Holt, Rinehart, and Winston, 1952.

Warfel, Harry. "Charles Brockden Brown's German Sources." *Modern Language Quarterly.* (1940) 1:357-365.

Wasserman, Renata R. "The Self, the Mirror, the Other: *The Fall of the House of Usher*." *Poe Studies* (1977), 10:33-35.

Willell, Ralph, ed. *The Merrill Studies in "Pierre."* Columbus, Ohio: Charles E. Merrill, 1971.

Wilson, James D. "Incest and American Romantic Fiction." *Studies in the Literary Imagination* (1974), 7:31-50. Reprinted as ch. 6 of *The Romantic Heroic Ideal.* Baton Rouge: Louisiana State University Press, 1982.

Young, Philip. *Hawthorne's Secret: An Un-Told Tale.* Boston: David R. Godine, 1984.

Ziff, Larzer. "A Reading of *Wieland*." *PMLA* (1962), 77:51-57.

THE CONCERN FOR SOCIAL ORDER

Anne Dalke (essay date 1988)

SOURCE: "Original Vice: The Political Implications of Incest in the Early American Novel," in *Early American Literature,* Vol. XXIII, No. 2, 1988, pp. 188-201.

[*In the essay that follows, Dalke argues that the incidents of unconscious incest in early American novels indicate a concern with social instability.*]

The first American novel and many of its most popular successors incorporate a striking motif: that of unconscious incest. Eight times before 1830, the early American novel raises the possibility of unwitting incest. The discovery usually results in madness or suicide; only once does the threat prove specious. By dwelling on such disastrous consequences, the earliest American novelists expressed no literal fear of widespread incest, but rather a fear of the dreadful condition incest symbolizes: the absence of a well-defined social system. They used a story of thwarted love to express, obliquely, deep anxiety about ease of social movement.

The first American novelist, William Hill Brown, the first best-selling American novelist, Susanna Rowson, and the first American gothicist, Sarah Sayward Wood, as well as a medley of less known writers (some of them anonymous), demanded in their fiction the careful establishment, and as careful maintenance, of social and economic difference and responsibility. Those

hierarchical distinctions were repeatedly expressed in sexual terms. The fictional couples who exemplify such principles are little known: little known to us today, of course, but also unknown to one another. They all contemplate incest unawares. Theoretically, in the flexible social arrangements of this new republic, a man could chose his sexual partner from any class. In the early fiction, however, when he selects a wife from a class beneath his own, his decision is often thwarted by the discovery that his choice is his bastard half-sister; when he seeks a lower-class mistress, she is as often his unacknowledged daughter.

The typical grouping of kin in early American fiction is most often a profligate father, a dead mother, an illegitimate daughter, and a legitimate son and heir. The family unit is not dissolved by incest, but is rather fragmented even before incest occurs. Indeed, it is precisely this fragmentation that leads to the unwitting commission of the deed. With the mother absent, usually dead, only the father can hold together the disjointed community that is the early American fictional family. But his misbehavior destroys the group entirely. Early American fiction depicts young men and more particularly young women entangled in the ties of family, their social mobility hampered by the sexual sins of their fathers.

This fiction suggests not only attitudes about proper sexual and familial conduct, but attitudes about larger social arrangements as well. The disasters that occur in early American fiction cannot all be laid to parental lapses. Even the best of fictional fathers cannot avert misfortune for the young man who attempts marriage below and the young woman who attempts it above the station in which they are placed by birth. The characters of these novels long, not merely for fathers who will perform their duties more prudently, but for a benevolent, protective upper class, for a clearly defined and clearly responsible social structure that will minimize the effects of misbehavior and the disruption it causes.

The early American novelists deal with accidental incest of two varieties. In the first version, a well-to-do young gentleman, acting on republican sentiments, proposes marriage to a poor young girl. The threat of incest intercedes to prevent their union. In the second plot, the lascivious career of an older man is halted when he seduces a poor young woman who proves to be his cast-off daughter. The anonymous novel *The History of Albert and Eliza* (1812), Brown's first and second novels, *The Power of Sympathy* (1789) and *Ira and Isabella* (1807), Rowson's posthumous *Charlotte's Daughter* (1828), and Wood's *Julia and the Illuminated Baron* (1800) all tell the first story; the anonymous *Margaretta* (1807) and two of Rowson's earlier works, *Mentoria* (1794) and *The Trials of the Human Heart* (1795), tell the second.

The History of Albert and Eliza presents the most abbreviated version of the first plot motif. The incest is limited to minor characters, whose story is briefly summarized by their author: "a nobleman had been illicitly connected with a woman . . . by whom he had . . . a daughter. He afterwards married." His legitimate son marries in turn and brings home his wife: "his father found her to be his own daughter, by the woman before mentioned" (48). The sister's family relationship to her lover grants her no membership in his social class, but points paradoxically to the great gulf in status that separates them. Although she is her brother's equal in birth and parentage, when she attempts to marry him she is considered merely a usurper of his class privilege.

In such turn-of-the-century American fiction, the "brother" is the legitimate heir, the "sister" poor and illegitimate. Such an arrangement heightens the social implications of the incest taboo. The legitimate son passes on the family name and would degrade it by marriage beneath him. The existence of the father's bastard daughter thus poses less a threat to the family's social standing than does her intention to engage the heir in a lower-class marriage. That intention leads to the damnation of both brother and sister; their attempt to subvert the distinctions of class is roundly condemned.

In its development of the first incest plot, Brown's novel *The Power of Sympathy* is as extensive as *The History of Albert and Eliza* is brief. Brown actually presents a series of four seductions, culminating in the revelation of brother-sister incest. In three of these cases, it is the wrong done the fathers, not the seduced girls, that receives the most attention.

The emphasis placed on the fathers' intense suffering in such situations calls attention to the mutual obligations inherent in the family system portrayed in this novel. The personal deprivations suffered by the children are not as important as the loss of the services they provide for their parents. The focus is the privation of the father, rather than that of those whose primary function is to make his life comfortable.

As Fliegelman has demonstrated, a new parental idea dominated mid-eighteenth-century America: the concept of an affectionate and equalitarian relationship with one's child. But the emphasis on parental solicitude and emotional commitment contributed to the development of "affectional authoritarianism": because so heavily invested in the child, the parental heart was vulnerable; filial disobedience thus became a heartbreaking betrayal of love, even a "species of parricide" (1, 260).

Such a concept is clearly demonstrated in *The Power of Sympathy,* in which Fidelia's story is actually pieced together from her father's "painful recollection." His poor child was kidnapped by a seducer; in despair over her loss, her fiancé committed suicide. She herself subsequently went mad. But the father portrays his sufferings as more extensive than those of either his daughter or her lover. He dwells on his deprivations in great detail and Biblical language:

> "In her disordered state . . . she knows me not as a father. . . . she forgets the sound of my voice— she is no longer unto me as a daughter. She who hath so often said, she would support me with her arm, and lead me about, when I should be old and decriped—to her I call, but she returns me no answer. Is not the cause of my woe, a melancholy instance of the baleful art of the SEDUCER? . . . I am doubly burdened with her affliction, and the accumulated misfortune of immature decripitude. . . . *They have taken away my staff in my old age."* (1: 137-38; letter 28)

In this passage, Fidelia's father laments not so much his daughter's loss of virginity or sanity as the loss of her aid and support for his own infirmity. He presents himself as the wronged party, the seducer's ultimate victim. Fidelia's seducer divests a young girl of her virtue; more importantly, he thereby disrupts a familial contract, which places the obligations of children to parents foremost.

Ophelia's seducer does the same, although his means of destroying his family is to take his sister-in-law as his mistress. The primary party wronged in this case is, of course, the wife of the seducer and the sister of his victim, but her distress is mentioned only in passing. The calamity overwhelms her father. The injury to his pride and disruption of his solace are displayed as greater sufferings: "This event was a severe mortification to [his] proud spirit. . . . His resentment to his daughter was implacable, and his revenge of the injury . . . not to be satiated" (1: 95-96; letter 21). The loss of her father's esteem, rather than the loss of her sister's love, or even of her lover's affection, most distresses the hapless Ophelia. She poisons herself, explaining in her suicide note that she dies for the lack of a father's love, and that she hopes for forgiveness from him and from a Parent more understanding than he.

Ophelia's father is undoubtedly wronged by her seduction. But he is also primarily responsible for her subsequent suicide. As the seducer himself reminds him, in language that sounds legalistic, heavy-handed abuse of his power as a father has manifestly contributed to his daughter's death:

> "a straying, but penitent child, [was] driven to despair and suicide by a severe use of paternal power, and a vain attempt to resent an injury, for which it was impossible the accused party could make compensation[.]" (1: 109-10; letter 23)

Couched in the complaint of Fidelia's father is a lament for the failure of the patriarchal form of family organization. But the indictment of Ophelia's father points to an opposing danger, the possible abuses of strong parental power. For the bourgeois American family of the late eighteenth century, as Rogin has demonstrated, the authority of the English patriarch had given way to the Lockean ideal of the "natural family," in which the mutual rights and obligations of mother and children were balanced against those of the father. Ideal family relations were contractual, based on reason and experience. The formal equality of the bourgeois family meant both that the father could not, or at least should not, stand against the independent action of his children, and that children possessed the right to protest parental misconduct (20-21, 28, 49).

If Brown portrays one father as victim, he gives us two who are criminal, two who have failed less as patriarchs than as benefactors to their children. Fidelia's father is unmistakably the party most wronged by her fall. Ophelia's father, also wronged by his daughter's seduction, contributes in his despair to her suicide. But for the final seduction and death portrayed in the novel the father is directly and solely responsible. Mr. Harrington is more lascivious than his children, and more reckless in pursuing the object of his lust than are they. His libertinism has disastrous consequences for them both.

Mr. Harrington seduced a lower-class woman, then cast off both her and her child. By consigning his illegitimate daughter to oblivion, in a country where men may take wives from all walks of life, he creates a potentially incestuous situation for his legitimate son.

At the beginning of the novel, young Harrington shares with his father a sense of the sexual prerogatives of the upper-class male. He reports to a friend that Harriot, although sexually attractive, is a social nobody, and so undeserving of his respect:

> "I suppose you will be ready to ask, why . . . I do not marry her. . . . But *who* shall I marry? . . . Harriot has not . . . kindred of any degree who claim any kind of relationship to her. I am not so much of a republican as formally to wed any person of this class. How laughable would my conduct appear, were I . . . to be heard openly acknowledging for my bosom companion, any daughter of the democratik empire of virtue!" (1: 15-17; letter 3)

The "humanity and goodness" on which Harrington prides himself are the condescensions of a superior class to an inferior one; his sentiments, as he himself acknowledges, are anything but republican.

But Harriot is an effective advocate of her rights: "'Is the crime of dependence to be expiated by the sacrifice of virtue?'" she demands. "'And because I am a poor, unfortunate girl, must the little I have be taken from me?'" (1: 23; letter 6). Won over by her eloquence, Harrington determines to continue his addresses to her on just and honorable principles.

Harriot converts Harrington to virtue of a decidedly republican stamp. His newly acquired principles are illustrated not only in his re-ordered relations with his mistress, but in a larger social forum. He records in great detail his preference for a "democratical" kind of government, speaks approvingly of "independence and equal liberty," and imagines a commonwealth free of "distinction of rank": "Why . . . should those distinctions arise which are inimical to domestick quietude?" (1: 82-84; letter 17). But as soon as Harrington converts from upper-class rapist to democratically minded fiancé, Harriot is revealed as his sister. For the first of many times in American literature, the threat of incest intercedes to prevent the marriage of a wealthy man to a poor young woman. Put into practice in this fiction, republican sentiments lead to disaster.

Both Harriot and Harrington declare their abhorrence of incest. Yet the language of the young girl's declaration is strikingly erotic. The loss for her seems to be primarily a sexual one: "'O! I sink, I die, when I reflect—when I find in my Harrington a brother—I am penetrated with inexpressible grief—I experience uncommon sensations—I start with horrour at the idea of incest—of ruin—of perdition'" (2: 109-10; letter 50). She dies from the shock of the discovery.

Harrington's response is at first less charged, more philosophical: "'Had I known her to be my sister, my love would have been more regular—I should have loved her as a sister—I should have marked her beauty—I should have delighted in protecting it'" (2: 127; letter 55). Had their blood relation only been explained to him in time, he thinks he could have ordered his affections accordingly. But Harrington proves unable to accept with equanimity the belated revelation that his love is his sister; he commits suicide.

Mr. Harrington survives his children. The "rude spoiler," as he calls himself, "has his share of remorse" (2: 57; letter 39). He upbraids himself for being the author of his own misfortune and berates his libertinism and his adultery. "'Spare your reflections, my friend,'" he begs, "'my heart is monitor enough—I am strangely agitated!'" (2: 83-84; letter 42). Here the illicit sexual activity of the parent is roundly condemned as generally inappropriate for a new age, and as specific cause of his children's woe.

This early American father is not only prime sufferer in his children's misfortune, but prime cause of their suffering as well.

Fathers misbehave even more egregiously, if possible, in Brown's second novel. But in *Ira and Isabella* the fathers' wide-ranging sexual activity enables their offspring, both illegitimate, to marry one another. The subtitle of the novel proclaims that it is "Founded in Fiction"; Brown explains in his preface that the fictitious element is the happy ending. The book cheerfully dissolves the threat of incest that is viewed so soberly in other early American fiction. Indeed, *Ira and Isabella* is the only American novel of its period that portrays the incest threat as specious, and so allows a man and woman to marry who have been accused of being brother and sister. Yet Brown's second novel still views the possibility of marriage between different classes seriously and anxiously. Although Isabella is illegitimate, her father does not want her to marry the bastard Ira; he hopes she will rise, by marriage, above the station of her birth. But women in early American fiction are time and again denied that mobility. Because her lover's father was as profligate as her own, Isabella blithely remains within the class to which her parent's sexual misconduct has condemned her. The marriage of the title characters is finally allowed in this novel only because both are illegitimate and so unworthy of concern. They share the same lowly class.

The responsibility for both these bastard children is assumed not by their proven parents, their mothers, but by their fathers. The men do not at first openly acknowledge their offspring, but they do support them from infancy. Mothers are even less in evidence in *Ira and Isabella* than they are in *The Power of Sympathy*. The letters of Harriot's dead mother are at least read in the first novel, but Ira's and Isabella's mothers are voiceless. The fathers choose their children's nurse; their sexual partners are granted no opinion in the distribution, or in the subsequent upbringing, of their children.

Brown's novels dispose of both home and mother; they offer not a closed family pattern, but a world filled with illicit sexual activity. This representative family is composed of a single parent and children who are the result of various affairs with different partners. Because the woman who engages in one extramarital affair normally does not live to participate in another (at the very least she fades away, sobbing, into poverty), the surviving single parent is the child's father. The mother is obliterated entirely, destroyed by the adulterous activity that carries no penalty for her sexual partner.

If Brown's novels are nightmares of fathers gone astray, Rowson presents in *Charlotte's Daughter* their complement: an encomium to perfect fatherhood. The

Rev. Matthews assumes the father's role by adoption. *The Three Orphans* of the novel's subtitle, whom he raises, all come to him through their own fathers' neglect, but he fills the void assiduously, "endeavoring to cultivate the understandings, fortify the principles, and . . . invigorate the frames of his fair wards" (65; chap. 5). These orphans run the gamut of the American social system: one is a "splendid heiress," one has a "genteel independence," and the third is an orphan of unknown family and no fortune (68; chap. 5). The Rev. Matthews attempts to equalize the differences among them.

His own marriage had effected a similar leveling. The youngest son of an "honorable but reduced" family, the Rev. Matthews married a noble woman who soon after lost her fortune (33; chap. 2). Distinctions between classes are repeatedly invalidated in *Charlotte's Daughter*. The rich and the poor, those with stature and those without, are seemingly interchangeable. Class boundaries, seldom observed, prove false when they are acknowledged, illusory when acted upon. The Rev. Matthews' "orphan of quality" is flattered by the attentions of a baronet who courts her for her supposed wealth (37; chap. 2). Both hope to improve their social and financial station by marriage; such hopes prove unfounded, and their elopement is a bitter disappointment to both.

In *Charlotte's Daughter*, marriages occur across class boundaries, effecting a leveling in wealth and status. Those marriages are attended, however, by loss of fortune. The society of Rowson's novel is highly mobile—but in the negative sense. Numerous opportunities are offered young women to lose their wealth. Those who seek money or stature in marriage fail to find it; others forfeit what they do possess. In this novel, marriage lowers quite a few. The wheel of fortune seems always headed down.

Rich Lucy Blakeney, for example, is thought a poor orphan. Delighted at the prospect of raising such a lovely young women "from dependence to a state of comparative affluence" (70-72; chap. 5), her suitor is disappointed to discover that she is a wealthy heiress. The role of benefactor that he covets is finally denied him, however, not by her wealth, but by the discovery that she is his sister. His father shrieks from his death bed: "'The woman you would marry is my own daughter! . . . the record of your father's shame'" (147; chap. 11). Fleeing to join the army, Lucy's suitor is wounded in battle and dies barbarously soon after. His death is ignominious and swift. Lucy declines more slowly.

Yet the third of Rev. Matthews' charges does marry successfully. Like Lucy, poor Aura Melville is courted by a man who hopes to improve her condition. Receiving a large inheritance, he vows to become a "useful, benevolent, and religious country gentleman" (160; chap. 15). His first act of benevolence is his proposal to Aura.

Her easy move into prosperity does not, however, signal a society without class distinctions. The patronage expressed in Aura's marriage is extended by both her and her husband to all their neighbors, at their wedding feast. Rowson announces, with some exultation, that the marriage is "celebrated after the fashion of the good old time, when the poor not only looked to the gentry for protection and friendship, but took a lively interest in their domestic affairs" (177; chap. 19).

The novel thus closes with an approving nod at the benevolence of the upper class. *Charlotte's Daughter* insists not on equality but on hierarchy. This final scene expresses as vividly as does the insistent repetition of the incest theme in these early novels a longing for the restoration of an illusory "good old time" when all classes, and the women of those classes in particular, knew their proper place, and for a time when benevolent protection, both of sexual partners and of social inferiors, was expected of the well-to-do male.

Incest in Wood's gothic romance, *Julia and the Illuminated Baron,* follows the same pattern as it does in Brown's novels of sensibility and Rowson's sentimental fiction: a rich man attempts to seduce a penniless young girl, unaware that she is his sister. The title character of Wood's first novel is discovered, destitute, in a cottage, by a gentleman of wealth and standing. He adopts her, introducing her to his son with the joking admonition to "think of her only as a sister." The baron begins immediately, of course, to treat Julia as his prospective wife. When his wooing proves unsuccessful, he kidnaps her and proposes while she is under guard: "'give me your hand and you are from this moment free, the mistress of my hand, my heart, my fortune, the sharer of my titles, my honour'" (65; chap. 6; 202, chap. 19).

Harrington begins as an upper-class seducer and ends as a republican suitor converted to a belief in the American ideal of mobility. The Count reverses that order and follows an honest proposal with a threat: "'either conclude to be my wife, by laws that custom has rendered respectable; and that you consider as holy; or else be mine upon terms less honorable'" (206; chap. 19).

The joyous discovery at the conclusion of the novel that Julia's adoptive father is her real one is simultaneously the discovery of her near incest with her brother. As the daughter of the Marquis, Julia is half-sister to the baron who has threatened to rape her.

As for so many other fictional brothers, wealth confers on the baron the power to threaten his sister sexually. *Droit de seigneur* asserts the power of a wealthy man to take poor women, with no legal responsibility. His prerogative confirms the abusive power structures of both class and gender. With his wealth also comes the license to perform numerous other evils. The illuminated baron not only attempts to rape his sister, but successfully murders his stepmother, and in conjunction with a group of other freethinkers, seems also to have brought about the French Revolution. Wood explains in her preface that her equanimity has been disturbed by "infidels who have thrown off religion": the secret society of the Illuminati whom she sees as dedicated to the belief that humanity should free itself "from petty principles of religion, marriage, property rights, and other negligible conventions" (Cowie 24). To expose their misbehavior, which is expressed in revolution, murder, and attempted incest, she wrote this novel.

Wood's fear of the disturbing effects of the order of the Illuminati was widespread among the conservatives of her day. As Stauffer has shown in his study of *New England and the Bavarian Illuminati,* the orthodox clergy and the Federalist party joined forces in charging the Illuminati with responsibility for a radical plot to overwhelm the institutions of both the old world and the new. Wood ascribed to this theory that the changes of the late eighteenth century were brought about by a vast secret conspiracy. The threat to Julia's virginity is accompanied in the novel by the coming of the French Revolution: "it was necessary for every friend to order, for every lover of peace and religion, to leave that ill-fated nation. The principles of the Illuminati triumphed; anarchy, confusion, cruelty, and bloodshed succeeded" (284; chap. 36).

Julia escapes her brother's clutches, marries and flees France with her new husband. They give up their rank for "the title of plain Mr. and Mrs." (285; chap. 36). But their gesture scarcely makes them democrats. They seek in America a social system even more structured than the one they left behind, and are disappointed to discover that the institutions of their adopted country are as disordered as those in France: "'this new world imitates the old so well, that it would be difficult to say which is the original'" (80; chap. 8).

Those characters who flee Europe hoping to escape its disorders are doomed to failure. Or so early American novelists and the readers who made their books popular feared. The use of the incest theme in early American fiction expressed deep anxieties about class upheaval. The authors' longing for a stratified class system was shared by the large audience who read and approved their examinations of the contractual form of family government, which placed particularly stringent demands on the duty of fathers. The overwhelming class consciousness of these novelists was expressed by the most gothic of them in a paranoic fear of a secret society that would overturn the old order they hoped to see perpetuated in the new country.

In arguing for rigidly hierarchical class and sexual structures, however, these early American novelists did not countenance abuses of the prerogatives of either class or gender. By showing the larger social repercussions of rich men seducing poor women, by having such crimes come back to haunt the men themselves, these early American novels demand benevolent protectionism of the well-to-do and invoke a sense of protective responsibility toward inferiors, both the lower classes and one's own children. The second version of the unwitting incest motif makes this clear.

The wide-ranging sexual activity of the father is eventually condemned, and eventually halted, whenever it appears. In *The Power of Sympathy, Ira and Isabella, Charlotte's Daughter,* and *Julia and the Illuminated Baron,* fathers follow their extramarital affairs with legitimate marriages. The consequences of their early sexual misbehavior are potentially incestuous connections between their offspring. The lascivious careers of three other early American fathers are unabated by marriage and untroubled by the discovery of brother-sister incest in the next generation. Their sexual engagements with lower-class women are finally arrested, however, by the ultimate sexual encounter: they seduce poor young women who prove to be their daughters.

The title character of the anonymous novel *Margaretta; or the Intricacies of the Heart* is, like Harriot, courted by a wealthy man who does not plan to marry her. William De Burling explains that he is not "romantic enough to consign myself as a sacrifice to a little rustic. . . . Many belles of fashion have attractions more suitable to my ambitious views in life. I must marry a fortune" (28, 14). A marriage has been arranged for him, with the daughter of his father's business partner.

De Burling's concern for his father's financial standing is slowly overwhelmed, however, by his affection for Margaretta. The gradual loss of his pride results, not only in an honorable declaration of marriage, but in an eulogy to her heritage:

> "But she was of low extraction! What would the world say to such an unequal match? How should I not be condemned for allying myself with a family whose father, grandfather, and great-grandfather had been, from the remotest period, nothing but humble farmers. . . . With honesty enough to make all ends meet at the close of the year, and nobility of spirit to exert their right to the common claim of liberty and independence; too upright in mind calmly to yield to oppression, and too just and too humane to oppress the oppressed." (172)

Like Harrington, De Burling is converted to virtue of a decidedly republican hue; like Harrington, he is also punished for wanting to marry a poor girl and raise her to his social level. Furious at De Burling's "palpable devotion to a girl of the lowest orders" (130), his

fiancée ruins him. Margaretta is left prey to the "vicious libertinism" (343) of two men old enough to be her father. The suit of the first is replaced by that of the second, and that of the second halted only by the discovery that he is, indeed, her parent.

The eventual revelation of Margaretta's birth, and the belated discovery that her father has inherited a barony "with all its emoluments" (350), elevate her from "the lowest rank of life . . . to one of the greatest distinction," from which she can "bid defiance alike, to the assaults of vicious libertinism, and the grasp of chilling poverty" (343). She remains only briefly beyond the reach of the plain Mr. De Burling; impressed by the young man's democratic convictions, her father grants him enough wealth to marry his daughter as a peer. Margaretta praises her parent as a "true republican . . . whose political principles are founded upon a system of united federalism" (398).

Margaretta's father demonstrates his republicanism by refusing the name he inherits with his barony. His daughter and son-in-law, like Julia and her husband before them, likewise take a "plain appellation," "laying their title on the altar of liberty, as a sacrifice to equality, peace and independence" (417). Despite Margaretta's frequent use of the word, however, neither her father nor her husband believes in "equality." They champion no obliteration of social and economic distinctions, but only movement within a fairly rigid hierarchical system. When both generations settle in America, they do not abandon the gradations of English social organization, but just remake them slightly. They judge one another not by title, rank or breeding, but solely on the basis of wealth. In the world of *Margaretta,* such revision scarcely qualifies as republicanism. For opportunity is open in this novel only to those already well-to-do. No man rises here by his own efforts: De Burling's failure in trade is marked, and he and his father-in-law both succeed finally by means of inherited wealth.

Upward mobility is possible in this book only through inheritance. Like young men, young women can experience a change in status solely by parental fiat. In the world of *Margaretta,* as in *The Power of Sympathy,* a woman's social standing is determined by her father. If her birth, like Harriot's, is illegitimate, or if her father, like Margaretta's, deserts her, the heroine's chance of bettering her condition is limited to her father's discovery and public acknowledgment of her as his daughter. Without his benevolent protection, she is even prohibited from raising her social standing by her own efforts, through marriage with a man of higher rank. She must succeed socially through the grace of her father or not at all.

She often does not succeed. Commonly, a father fails to accept his parental responsibility and is punished for his negligence, not only by bringing his daughter to the brink of incest, but by observing her subsequent death. Such is the pattern, for instance, in Rowson's *Mentoria*. In one of the loosely connected tales that compose that book, "Marion and Lydia," a father propositions his daughter, unconscious of her identity, and thereby is condemned both for parental neglect and for the lascivious behavior that is the underlying cause of that negligence. His desertion of his family is the original cause of his daughter's decline; his near seduction of her only just fails to complete her fall. His pride and profligacy initiates a disaster that engulfs his child. Fiedler presents incest as "the offense against the father" (129), but in these early American novels it is a further consequence of the father's original vice. The sins of the father are visited upon the daughters with a vengeance, as the fathers seek to possess them sexually.

Fictional children are hampered in their movement across class lines by the freedom with which their fathers engaged in precisely the same activity. By seducing and discarding a lower-class woman, these fictional early American fathers prevent their sons from marrying below them and their daughters from marrying above. The father's early sexual sins, fundamentally transgressions against the responsibilities of rank, are of paramount importance in limiting the mobility of their offspring.

In a fictional world that repeatedly condemns the parent for his failure to establish and maintain an affectionate, egalitarian relationship with his children, the father's sexual abuse of his daughter is presented, of course, as an even greater sin. *The Trials of the Human Heart* portrays yet another profligate and negligent father. Mr. Howard pursues Meriel for his own pleasure: he kisses her, propositions her, twice enters her room at night. She finds a strangely exaggerated relief, three volumes later, in the revelation that what she thought incest was only an attempt at rape. Meriel is jubilant to discover not only that Mr. Howard is not her father, but that her real father is alive and virtuous: "'That I should live to say I have a father!—a noble! honorable! father!'" (4: 139-40; letter 66).

Actual parent-child incest never occurs in early American fiction; the crime is too unspeakable. But the same revelation which releases Meriel from the onus of her "one secret sorrow" (4: 135; letter 66) implicates Mr. Howard's son in a form of incest by now familiar to us: the unconscious attraction of brother and sister. Like the Illuminated Baron, Howard Jr. has dallied with and plans to marry a young woman of low standing and repute. But when all relationships are made clear in the finale of the novel, this young woman, like so many others of her day, proves to be her lover's sister, "the natural daughter of his

father" (4: 141; letter 66). Meriel announces their relationship with a shudder, and the observation, "'to what sins are mortals led, as it were blindfold; by the vices of their parents'" (4: 142; letter 66). Once again, the misconduct of a profligate father is responsible for his child's unwitting brush with incest. Young Howard's near miss with unconscious incest, no less than the specious "incest" that Howard Sr. attempts, brands the parent a villain.

More importantly, it points with loathing to a form of social structure—flexible, mobile, classless—in which the consequences of such villainy were so great. These cautionary tales of parental excess express a decided attitude about the social order: at the same time that they charge fathers with a failure of benevolence, they charge the social structure with a failure to maintain the hierarchy of established distinctions between classes, a distinction that demands of the well-to-do a similar benevolent protectionism. These authors approved established patterns of familial and social deference and responsibility. They did so by inversion, in their display of the dreadful consequences of neglecting such obligations.

Works Cited

Brown, William Hill. *Ira and Isabella: or the Natural Children. A Novel, Founded in Fiction.* Boston: Belcher and Armstrong, 1807.

———. *The Power of Sympathy: or, the Triumph of Nature. Founded in Truth. In Two Volumes.* Boston: Isaiah Thomas, 1789.

Cowie, Alexander. *The Rise of the American Novel.* New York: American Book Company, 1951.

Fiedler, Leslie. *Love and Death in the American Novel.* New York: Stein and Day, 1966.

Fliegelman, Jay. *Prodigals and Pilgrims: The American Revolution Against Patriarchal Authority, 1750-1800.* Cambridge: Cambridge Univ. Press, 1982.

Ladd, Russell, comp. *The History of Albert and Eliza.* Philadelphia: R. Ladd, 1812.

Margaretta: or the Intricacies of the Heart. A Novel. Philadelphia: Samuel Bradford, 1807.

Rogin, Michael Paul. *Fathers and Children: Andrew Jackson and the Subjugation of the American Indian.* New York: Knopf, 1975.

Rowson, Susanna. *Charlotte's Daughter: or, The Three Orphans. A Sequel to Charlotte Temple.* Boston: Richardson and Lord, 1828.

————. "Marion and Lydia." *Mentoria; or the Young Lady's Friend. In Two Volumes.* Philadelphia: Samuel Harrison Smith, 1794.

————. *The Trials of the Human Heart: A Novel.* 4 vols. Philadelphia: Wrigley and Berriman, 1795.

Stauffer, Vernon. *New England and the Bavarian Illuminati.* 1918. New York: Russell and Russell, 1967.

Wood, Sarah Sayward. *Julia, and the Illuminated Baron. A Novel: Founded on Recent Facts, which have transpired in the course of the late Revolution of Moral Principles in France. By a Lady of Massachusetts.* Portsmouth, N.H.: Orade, 1800.

G. M. Goshgarian (essay date 1992)

SOURCE: "His Sister's Keeper: Susan Warner's *The Wide, Wide World*," in *To Kiss the Chastening Rod: Domestic Fiction and Sexual Ideology in the American Renaissance,* Cornell University Press, 1992, pp. 76-120.

[*In the following essay, Goshgarian contends that the plot of Susan Warner's* The Wide, Wide World *exemplifies the structure of male authority and female submission, a structure that idealizes the incestuous relationship.*]

> Being natural self-knowledge, knowledge of self on the basis of nature and not on that of ethical life, [the relationship of husband and wife] merely represents and typifies in a figure the life of spirit, and is not spirit itself actually realized. Figurative representation, however, has its reality in an other than it is . . .

> The feminine element, therefore, in the form of the sister, premonizes and foreshadows most completely the nature of ethical life. She does not become conscious of it, and does not actualize it, because the law of the family is her inherent implicit inward nature, which does not lie open to the daylight of consciousness, but remains inner feeling and the divine element exempt from actuality. The relationships of mother and wife, however, are individualized partly in the form of something natural, which brings pleasure; partly in the form of something negative, which finds simply its own evanescence in those relationships . . . In a household of the ethical kind, a woman's relationships are not based on a reference to this particular husband, this particular child, but to *a* husband, to children *in general,*— not to feeling, but to the univeral. The distinction between her ethical life . . . and that of her husband consists just in this, that it has always a directly universal significance for her, and is quite alien to the impulsive condition of mere particular desire. . . .

> The brother, however, is in the eyes of the sister a being whose nature is unperturbed by desire and is ethically like her own; her recognition in him is pure and unmixed with any sexual relation . . . This relationship at the same time is the limit, at which the circumscribed life of the family is broken up, and passes beyond itself.

—G. W. F. Hegel

Heroines of domestic fiction suffer horribly, as a rule. Sooner or later, they start to wonder why one should have to. Somebody is always on hand to tell them. Gerty Amory, protagonist of Maria Susanna Cummins's *The Lamplighter,* raises the issue early on, after just barely emerging from the rigors of a childhood that makes David Copperfield's look like fun. Gerty is about fifteen when she pauses to review her catastrophic past. When she was eight, her wicked stepmother gorily boiled her pet kitten alive, felicitously summing up the first chapter of a cataclysmic career spanning malarial Rio, the London underworld, and the Boston slums. Her impecunious guardian Trueman Flint and her bosom friend/quasi-lover Willie Sullivan have recently put a categorical point to chapter two, Trueman by expiring after a debilitating illness, Willie by weighing anchor for India. Readers uninitiated into the Stygian world of scribblerdom might suppose that picking her way through this catalog of horrors would have won Gerty the right to complain some. Cognoscenti will know better. For, by prevailing standards, Gerty's represents an entirely unexceptional coming of age, which is why it is fitting that, after caterwauling briefly over her own "childish griefs,"[1] the heroine shapes up and shifts her plaint into the third person—the more fitting as the unfortunate whose shoulder she is crying on, the saintly Miss Emily, has suffered far more spectacularly than Gerty, having, for example, been tragically blinded by a former lover (Gerty's long-lost father, as it turns out) who reached for the acid instead of the smelling salts at the cathartic moment of an always dramatic relationship. Here, then, are Emily and Gerty putting female troubles in perspective, in a recital of *The Lamplighter*'s version of what might be called the scribbler catechism:

> "And so, Miss Emily, since I see that you and Willie have troubles, and that tears will come, though you try to keep them back, I think the world is full of trials, and that everybody gets a share."

> "It *is* the lot of humanity, Gertrude, and we must not expect it to be otherwise."

> "Then who can be happy, Miss Emily?"

> "Those only, my child, who have learned submission; those who, in the severest affliction, see the hand of a loving Father, and, obedient to his will, kiss the chastening rod."

> "It is very hard, Miss Emily."[2]

No one will ever state more succinctly than these two the central issues in the mid-century mass novel. Indeed, it is scarcely an exaggeration to say that the whole corpus of scribbler scholarship boils down to the handful of arguments contained in Gerty's and Emily's chat. Traditionalists contend, in essence, that the scribblers were of Emily's party; revisionists counter that they adhered secretly to Gerty's; the dialectically minded consider that they were of both parties at once. But not only do Emily and Gerty give us half a century of proper criticism in embryo; more to our purposes, they also stake out the embryo's phylogenetic limits. The critics may be at loggerheads as to what domestic fiction means, but they are in perfect and so unspoken agreement with Gerty, Emily, and one another as to what it does *not* mean: for example, that the hard, chastening rod Emily's theodicy attributes to the loving Father is the sacred equivalent of that other hard, chastening rod biology and the gender system conjointly bestow upon father. Briefly, not-saying this non-meaning is what makes scribbler criticism proper. Nina Baym, whom we will continue to cite whenever we need to pull things back into proper perspective, decants all the commentary in which the Father's rod is just the Father's rod: "in woman's fiction . . . purity was so taken for granted that it was ignored."[3] Indeed; that Miss Emily can deliver her homily without once smirking at Gerty proves it. And as anyone who has read *The Lamplighter* knows, it is easier to imagine the Virgin Mother smirking at the archangel than it is to imagine Miss Emily smirking at anybody.

It would, however, be a bit hasty to conclude that in domestic fiction "[God's] nature . . . transcended gender," much less that the scribblers "produce[d] a feminist theology in which the godhead is refashioned into an image of maternal authority."[4] For the chastening rod en-gendered the Father even if "woman's fiction," Emily-like, turned a blind eye to His sex. More: it was precisely through its pure blindness to God's sex that domestic fiction granted itself the purity it took for granted. The true woman's fiction—the fiction of the true woman—consisted in neither seeing nor saying what "woman's fiction" fairly flaunted: the reciprocal relation between woman's suffering and her sexuality, the unholy alliance between the female animal and her highly sexed Maker.

Emphatically, this is not to suggest that purity was an artful blind for a shameful sexual insight. Miss Emily would be indignant—and rightly so—if she heard that what she was "really" talking about was sex. The opposite is the case: sex was precisely what she was *not-talking* about. Still more precisely: what she was not-talking about was incest. In all probability, incest was the furthest thing from her mind when she exhorted Gerty to love their common Father, or when, years later, she married her (Gerty's) beloved father, the searing but maladroit lover of her (Miss Emily's)

youth. For the improper critic, that purblind love stands as a trenchant warning: it cuts short all speculation to the effect that woman's fiction has secretly appropriated its own impropriety, that it is ridden with a guilty awareness of its own incestuous underside. But if this necessitates treating the scribblers' ignorance with the profoundest respect, it by no means obliges one to adopt Miss Emily's vision of things.[5] Improper criticism, at any rate, tries not to: scrutinizing textual functions the novels and their critics quite properly scotomize, it asks how woman's fiction managed to cohabit with the impurity it shut out, how the loving rod could be *both* the sexless Father's *and* the sexy father's. For the mid-century reading formation (whose [de]forming presence we will be taking for granted from now on) did indeed take the scribblers' unmanning purity for granted: in the 1850s, domestic fiction was as pure as it was purely incestuous. The resulting pure duplicity is the object of the practical criticism that follows.

Mothers, Old Gentlemen, and Better Friends

To the two principal offenses solicited and refused by domestic ideology—incest and onanism—there correspond, broadly, two character types in domestic fiction. The first is the congenitally flawed child-woman who commutes passion into passion(lessness) at the prodding of God and a man. The second is the debilitated yet potentially masterful male who conquers an unmanly habit with the help of a sovereign and subordinate child-woman. Improperly regarded, the simpler scribbler texts attend only to the etiology of passion(lessness), while the more complicated treat both woman's primal fault and man's derivative failing. Since woman's fault *is* primal, it seems appropriate to begin an examination of domestic fiction by analyzing a novel in the first category first. None is more instructive than the tearjerker heading up the parade of 1850s bestsellers: Susan Warner's *The Wide, Wide World.*

Like all the best-selling novels of the decade (with the partial exception of *Uncle Tom*), *The Wide, Wide World* is dedicated to the proposition that kowtowing to authority makes for happiness in this world and bliss in the next. It develops the idea in a domestic Bildungsroman that chronicles the chastening of its heroine, Ellen Montgomery, by a representative assortment of authority figures, chief among them the hero, Ellen's "adopted brother," John Humphreys. For hundreds of pages, God and/or John give Ellen a rough time: after a wrenching separation from her mother, she is treated hardly by her crotchety Aunt Fortune, adopted by a saintly young lady who dies, subjected to a severe if salutary drilling by John, and then, after she falls in love with her drillmaster, forced to leave him for British relatives who manhandle her à la Aunt Fortune. According to a familiar pattern, Ellen's submission to all this purgatorial unpleasantness fits her for the paradisal pleasures of religion's happy reign. But bending to the Father's will also yields her "un-speakable joy" of an earth(l)ier sort. As the novel closes, it is delicately intimated that, after "three or four more years of . . . discipline"—significantly, after the end of *The Wide, Wide World*—the lucky heroine gets to marry her "brother."[6]

Discourses commending docility generally feature rebels, and Warner's is no exception. But Ellen's rebelliousness is of a cast rarely encountered out-side scribblerdom; it bears a confusing resemblance to excruciating obedience. The confusion sets in with the novel's opening scene. The prepubescent hero-ine has just learned that her bankrupt father will be sailing off to Europe in hopes of recouping his for-tune. On doctor's orders, his invalid wife will reluc-tantly go with him. Ellen is to be left behind in the United States. Deprived at a blow of parents and prospects, the dutiful orphan designate utters not a word of protest. She cannot, however, keep from crying, and "passionately" at that. But not for long. Upbraided by her mother, the heroine quickly reins in her childish passions: "Ellen was immediately brought to herself by these words [of reproof]. She arose, sorry and ashamed that she should have given occasion for them; and tenderly kissing her mother, assured her most sincerely and resolutely that she would not do so again. In a few minutes she was calm enough to finish making the tea." (14)

The next day, the devoted daughter declares herself even more plainly:

> "Why mamma:—in the first place I trust every word you say—entirely—I know nothing could be truer; if you were to tell me black is white, mamma, I should think my eyes had been mistaken. Then everything you tell or advise me to do, I know it is right, perfectly. And I always feel safe when you are near me, because I know you'll take care of me. And I am glad to think I belong to you, and you have the management of me entirely, and I needn't manage myself, because I know I can't; and if I could, I'd rather you would, mamma."
> (18)

This is as perfect a pledge of allegiance as ever model heroine spoke. But, like every instance of female perfection in the scribblers, it has the defect of its virtues: it glows with the same misplaced passion that makes a girl cry over losing her mother.[7] Mrs. Montgomery's restrained reception of Ellen's filial loyalty oath indicates why her daughter's atti-tude is both just right and all wrong: "My daughter, it is just so;—it is *just* so:—that I wish you to trust in God. He is truer, wiser, stronger, kinder, by far, than I am, even if I could be always with you; and what will you do when I am away from you?" (18)

Here, in few, is the semi-orthodox lesson the further course of *The Wide, Wide World* will impress upon us: Ellen must forsake mother and follow Him. Her will to impotence must be retained, yet reoriented. But how are her childish affections to be transferred from mother to the Father? The Sovereign she owes fealty to has always been "with" her; Mrs. Montgomery has surely been true, wise, and kind enough to enjoin her daugh-ter to seek Him; yet this paragon of a parent, though armed with the Christian truth, has not succeeded in breaking and beating down the instincts alienating Ellen from God. Even her unflinching declaration of her own preferences for the Father fails to wean Ellen of her powerful weakness for her mother:

> "Mamma," said Ellen . . . with an indescribable expression, "do *you* love him *better than you do me?*"
>
> She knew her mother loved the Saviour, but she thought it scarcely possible that herself could have but the second place in her heart; she ventured a bold question to prove whether her mother's practice would not contradict her theory.
>
> But Mrs. Montgomery answered steadily, "I do, my daughter." (38-39)

Just as steadily, Mrs. Montgomery names the evil power she is impotent to overcome. It is because her daughter's heart is "hardened by sin" that Ellen ada-mantly prefers her mother to her Savior. Heir to Eve's fault, with "passions . . . by nature very strong" (11), the child-woman is naturally incapable of "loving him *best*" (38).

Or so it seems to her anxious parent. But Mrs. Montgomery's is perhaps a one-sided view of the prim-Eval passion agitating Ellen's bosom. The very heart that so obdurately spurns the Father may yet be softly yearning for its true Lord and master, and merely marking time with a maternal substitute for some paternal object it knows not what (cf. p. 60). If so—if Ellen's spontaneously "feminist theology" is only an infantile error—then her mother can safely consign her to the wide world's mercies, trusting precisely to her child's maligned passion to find the strait way to one "truer, wiser, stronger, [and] kinder." Because Mrs. Montgomery is true, wise, kind, and infirm, we have reason to suppose that such emotion as may tip Ellen toward Him will be stirred to life by what her invalid mother manifestly lacks: muscle. Should that turn out to be the case, Mrs. Montgomery's imminent (and, we feel sure, permanent) departure from the scene will have been, for her daughter, pre-cisely a point of spiritual departure: a sign that Provi-dence sunders little girls from mothers the better to acquaint them with woman's natural part. That part, and its (im)proper counterpart—in Miss Emily's muscular metaphor, the Father's chastening rod.

As if to test the hypothesis, Mrs. Montgomery dispatches Ellen on a dry run into the wide, wide world, represented, in this instance, by the nearest dry goods store. Fighting nameless fears and forebodings, "confused, and almost confounded" by the "moving crowd" all around her, the heroine promptly encounters a personage who gives her nebulous anxiety terrifyingly solid form. It is the bold, ill-bred, and ill-humoured clerk Saunders. A glance at his disagreeable eyes convinces Ellen that "she need not expect either kindness or politeness from him," and her child-woman's intuition is right on the mark: refusing to do his clerkly duty by Ellen, Saunders tricks, mocks, insults, and finally abandons her, leaving his victim "struggling with her feelings of mortification," "her face . . . on fire, her head . . . dizzy." She stands there traumatized, unable to stir. Fortunately, a kindly old gentleman happens along, and, after acquainting himself with the mistreated girl's tale, gives her no longer so cocky tormentor the tongue-lashing he so richly deserves. Because the miscreant knows this is "a person that must not be offended," he complies, crest-fallen, with the order to serve Ellen as he ought. The heroine melts with gratitude toward the kindly old gentleman. Joyously she goes forth from the store with her protector, who sees her straight home (45-49). There, over the child-lady's uncomprehending head, he declares meaningfully to her mother: "I assure you, ma'am, if I had had no kindness in my composition to feel for the *child,* my honour as a gentleman would have made me interfere for the *lady.*" And he draws the ominous moral: "There are all sorts of people in this world, and a little one alone in a crowd is in danger of being' trampled upon." (50-51)

With these words the old gentleman unwittingly echoes his author, who entitles the chapter recounting Ellen's maiden mishap "A peep into the wide world." We have had a preview of *The Wide, Wide World,* cast as a premonitory review of "this world" and what it holds in store for "little ones" like Ellen; notably, monsters like Saunders, ready and willing to "trample upon" the *lady* in a *child.* But if that fate, as the "Peep" shows primly but grimly, attends the child-woman just around the corner, so too does the surest means of warding it off: with the proper sort of bodyguard, Ellen may yet negotiate little-ladyhood intact. The Saunders affair is thus an inauspicious beginning and the foretaste of a happy end; John Hart knew what he was doing when he picked it to represent Warner in his anthology of U.S. women's fiction.[8] Yet these hair-raising pages promise us Warner's finale as much by differing from as by anticipating it—better, anticipate it *by* differing from it. As climax, the Saunders episode would be sadly defective; and, though he saves the day, the defect lies with Ellen's savior. His insufficiency is that he is insufficiently like the savage he saves her from. For the shopman offers to perform the cruelly necessary task whose needfulness Mrs. Mont-

gomery has freshly impressed upon Ellen. *Saunders sunders*—or, rather, he would if he could. The old gentleman, in contrast, reattaches Ellen to her mother; through his protective person, *incest insists.* The miracle to be wrought by a Better Friend will consist in overcoming the difference between these two operations. The old gentleman is not the man for the job: he is not made of stern enough stuff to "confound" the passions allusively exposed in the "Peep." We cannot, however, flesh out that point before examining other of the men in Ellen's life. For the moment, then, let us simply say that her first champion is too old. For readers schooled in scribbler nuance, the description that introduces him suffices to trace his limits: "It was an old gentleman— an odd old gentleman too, [Ellen] thought; one she certainly would have been rather shy of if she had seen him under other circumstances. But though his face was odd, it looked kindly upon her." (48)
Odd, old, and kindly: together, the adjectives neuter Ellen's benefactor, clearly no match for the worst the wide world has to offer. The Saunders episode confirms this, despite appearances. Tactfully, it signals that the old gentleman speaks too loudly, and does not (even when in a great passion) carry a big enough stick. He rages at Saunders—"'You know better, you scoundrel!' retorted the old gentleman, who was in a great passion"—where the truly potent hero would, bridling his rage, dispassionately dispatch the brutal bully,[9] and, while he plies the chastening rod stoutly enough to scotch the snake, he fails to quash him, as appears years later when this inveterate enemy of womankind is resurrected to work further evil. The situation, of course, precludes his administering a more thoroughgoing humiliation, but that is part of the point. Real heroes find themselves in different situations.

In short, our dry-goods store savior is a surrogate. Mrs. Montgomery has steeled us for that disappointment by declaring, in words that acquire their full resonance only in the wake of Ellen's misadventure, who all surrogate saviors are surrogates for: "him without whom you can do nothing" (22). Supplementing her sanctioned view of matters with another, the "Peep" discretely hints that the old gentleman is also doubling for a manlier Messiah, one equipped—let us provisionally say—permanently to suspend the sexual threat old gentlemen can only fend off. The Omnipotent, one gathers, is incapable of guaranteeing Ellen safe conduct without more potent male help. Praising "Him," we begin to suspect, Mrs. Montgomery said more than she knew. Or else she knew more than she said.

Certainly she said more than that a Christian girl's patrimony entails matrimony. In the improper context the Saunders episode begins to weave, Ellen's mother's hymn to Him evokes something one might better call patrimatrimony. What that is, Mrs. Montgomery, the old gentleman, and Ellen's vile tormentor cooperate to show us—by showing us, from a standpoint the young heroine cannot yet share, what it *will not have been*. It will not have been more perfect union with mother. Looking prophetically toward Ellen's future, perfect guardian, the "Peep" also draws the eye back toward the congenital imperfections of his aboriginal stand-in, inviting one to notice that (invalid) mothers are even less qualified than old gentlemen to take His place. It is, we cannot but conclude, tragically appropriate that Ellen's is going away to die. In her own sanctified idiom, Mrs. Montgomery says just that: "'O, my child, my child! if losing your mother might be the means of finding you that better friend, I should be quite willing—and glad to go—for ever.'" (23) Going forever, the Better Friend's locum tenens trails the obvious question in her wake. What about father? Father leaves much to be desired. His glaring absence from the Saunders scene suggests as much; as if this called for prompt clarification, the next chapter trains the spotlight on Ellen's should-be protector. It is, appropriately, the only chapter in which he figures; appropriately, because, as the chapter is there to show, Captain Montgomery is AWOL even when he reports for action. Like his wife or the old gentleman—but with considerably less excuse—Ellen's father defines a space he cannot fill. We already know that he has plunged his womenfolk into their present woe by going bankrupt. Now it is hinted that his failure stems from unmanly self-indulgence: "Captain Montgomery was abroad [on *Sunday*]; and he had been so,—according to custom,—or in bed, the whole day." (56) Even solvent, a man enfeebled by such vitiating practices is hardly likely to make a satisfactory husband or father. Without delay, the Captain demonstrates that he is neither. Breaking in at 10 P.M. on his ailing wife's Sabbath repose, he discloses that he has unilaterally arranged for Ellen to be shipped off at six the next morning, forbids Mrs. Montgomery to wake and bolster her for the shock of their imminent parting, and then falls callously asleep: "The captain, in happy unconsciousness of his wife's distress and utter inability to sympathize with it, was soon in a sound sleep, and his heavy breathing was an aggravation of her trouble; it kept repeating, what indeed she knew already, that the only one in the world who ought to have shared and soothed her grief was not capable of doing either." (60)

Even more conspicuously than the old gentleman, then, Captain Montgomery is standing—or lying—in for an absent "only one in the world." His wife's emotional deprivation is also his daughter's. The immediate indication is that this paternal zero can move Ellen neither to tears nor to spontaneous confession, which is to say, according to a protocol Warner has already begun to lay down, that he can play no positive part in shaping her soul. In the presence of soul-shapers,

friendly or otherwise, the heroine is given to weeping.[10] As to her confessional urge, we have the evidence of her relationship with the old gentleman, in whose company "her tongue ran very freely, for her heart was completely opened to him. He seemed as pleased to listen as she was to talk; and by little and little Ellen told him all her history." (51)

With the Captain, in contrast, Ellen is tight-lipped:

> "How did she bear it [the news of her impending departure]?" asked Mrs. Montgomery when he returned.
>
> "Like a little hero. She didn't say a word, or shed a tear. . . . "
>
> Mrs. Montgomery sighed deeply. She understood far better than her husband what Ellen's feelings were. (62)

The as yet absent "only one" will, evidently, find no rival for Ellen's affections in her father. But that does not diminish the Captain's importance, it grounds it. For the Captain engenders his daughter's desire precisely by leaving so much to be desired. His happy unconsciousness, fruit of his spiritual bankruptcy, feeds her passion for her mother in ways the little girl can hardly appreciate, but that we can hardly fail to: unable to open Ellen's heart or loosen her tongue, the Captain compels her to solicit her mother for the satisfaction of all her natural needs. The family threatens, in consequence, to escape the command of the fatherly, and Ellen's rebel heart the loving correction of the Father; mother and daughter are menaced with a liberation no true woman can want. Because she *is* a true woman, Mrs. Montgomery responds valiantly, battling like a Trojan to keep the paternal front from caving in. That she is debarred by her own true-womanly logic from manning the post the Captain deserts does not make her any less formidable a Christian soldier; her heroism consists precisely in leaving his position perilously undefended, while begging Ellen to beg Heaven to leap into the breach. The Captain's gaping breaches thus become a pivotal factor in Ellen's spiritual odyssey, and this at the critical moment when her journey through the wide world is about to begin. Looking back, as it were, through them, we see that the Captain has been pivotal from the first; absent center of the practice pilgrimage that has already led Ellen from one father-manqué to the next, his nullity founds the series that promises to converge on the Infinite. That, perhaps, is why *The Wide, Wide World* opens by almost reverently (un)veiling papa's failings. "'Mamma,'" Ellen launches the novel by asking, "'what was that I heard papa saying to you this morning about his lawsuit?'" The reply images the doom the Captain's appalling negligence hastens: "'I cannot tell you just now. Ellen, pick up that shawl, and spread it over me.'" (9) Yet when the invalid finally does put a caption under her morbid tableau, she spurns the easy chance to damn her husband for prematurely digging her grave—to say nothing of the temptation to give fatherhood as such a bad name. Her tendency is rather to exculpate her worst enemy on the grounds that he is but her Better Friend's accomplice: "'You know, my dear, that I am not apt to concern myself overmuch about the gain or the loss of money. I believe my Heavenly Father will give me what is good for me.'" (11)

Who, then, is the Better Friend better than? Should we say, with recent critics, that Mrs. Montgomery is her own Best Friend, that she conceives her "Heavenly Father" as a superlative version of her matronly self? The suicidal logic she espouses tends toward a different conclusion. She points to it when she sells her mother's ring to buy her daughter a Bible. Cashing in the maternal legacy to promote the Father's Word, she symbolically converts her mother as she would hope to convert her daughter; liquidating her mother's "trinket" (29) to cover her husband's liabilities, she becomes her own Better Friend . . . by championing the Friend Who liquidates *her*. In the process, she willy-nilly identifies Him with His earthly travesty: the "holy alliance" that weds her to "the source of all power" annuls her invalid self, while aligning the *Captain*'s murderous impotence with the doings of the Omnipotent.[11] To be sure, Captain Montgomery is at best an accessory to murder; after all, it is his heavenly Ally Who sends his wife to her final reward. But that, of course, is the point. The Better Friend is not merely better than Mrs. Montgomery; nor is He nonspecifically—uncomparatively—better. The Better Friend is a *better friend than His bumbling lieutenant, the Captain;* He is a General Signifier of the fatherly, Who, as its overarching, infinite limit, integrates even the most negligible and negligent of papas into the paternal army. Thus it is that Warner engenders Ellen's (other)worldly savior, deriving Him without Whom she can do nothing from an invalid mother and a paternal cipher. Her next task is to bring Him into *The Wide, Wide World.*

She claims to do so against the resistance put up by Ellen's natural passion. It is a perplexing claim. For if the first fruit of Ellen's passion—her all-absorbing love for her mother—is indeed "natural," then the love that will bind her to her Better Friend must be less so. Naturally the narrative does not want to concede this. Nor does it have to, directly, since it can tacitly refer Ellen's excesses to the Captain's deficiencies: if father were worthy of his archetype, Ellen would not love mother to distraction. This, however, only bares a deeper dilemma, implying that if the Captain had properly secured the affections of his family, Ellen's passion would have chained her to him, its natural male object.

By a logic Sigmund Freud was to make notorious, unperverted natural passions produce perverse results.

It is therefore good—indeed, providential—that Ellen's family circle is so unnaturally breached. Her father's failings force a kind of fortunate fall from the familial Eden, driving the future orphan out into the world in quest of her natural liege Lord. Does this make the love she will eventually bear Him natural or unnatural? The answer is both, and in a double sense. Insofar as it fulfills her patrimatrimonial desire for (a) father, it will be natural, and therefore, like incest, unnatural; but it will be unnatural, and therefore, like true religion, natural, to the extent that it *supplements* her desire for father with a *super*natural desire for the Father. It is this natural unnaturalness, the shifting foundation of female passion(lessness) as of patrimatrimony, that constitutes the improper burden of *The Wide, Wide World*— and Ellen's burden in it.

Strange Familiar Gentlemen and the Commutation of Passion

The Wide, Wide World puts the theoretical question of Ellen's relations to the Father in the down-to-earth terms of evangelical practice: how is the child-woman to be made to love Him? It answers, with apparent ingenuousness, that she was made to love *him*—and then proceeds, as we will see in a moment, to elevate the homonym into a synonym. But it also shows, as we saw a moment ago, that she loves mother with a depraved passion that threatens to deprive her eternally of Him. The relation between these two moments is the riddle of *The Wide, Wide World.* If Ellen's devotion to the Father derived naturally from her attachment to mother, redemption would emerge as the baseborn child of sin. If the Father displaced Ellen's mother by fanning the flames of a competing congenital passion—a parallel, but more powerful, desire for Him—then sin and redemption would be as sister and brother. Both alternatives are unthinkable. There is only one other. Ellen must be denatured in order to be saved.

But, rejoins natural religion, she must be denatured *naturally.* Ellen is accordingly subjected to a natural conversion process whose effect is less to denature her than to endow her with a second nature: patiently, her passion is written over by Scripture until she desires the Only One capable of delivering her from her desire. This obscures the family tie between sin and salvation; it fails to obliterate it. For if the power to rewrite her now comes from without, still, she must desire to be righted by it; if the rectified version of Ellen is to be a version, precisely, of *Ellen,* something of her original desire must survive its conversion. What makes the simultaneous repetition and redemption of her prim-Eval self possible? What reconciles the necessity that her passion perish with the equally urgent necessity that it persist?

In principle, the answer is grace. In practice, it is a sexually stimulating regime of Christian nurture: Christian com-mutation. Com-mutation gracefully mobilizes the logic of the constraint of love: it brings the child-woman round to loving the Father only insofar as he (re)rights her congenital fault. But only her fault inspires her love of Him. She cannot, in consequence, properly love Him at all: Christian com-mutation is, strictly speaking, impossible. That impossibility begets *The Wide, Wide World.* Prolonging the climactic moment of Ellen's conversion forever, it ensures (pace St. Paul) that *her* master's charge will never be at an end. With good reason: should the master ever stop righting—should Ellen come to love the Father con-genitally—the wide world itself would end, and end most abominably. Here, then, are the elements of Ellen's coming of age: eternal writing and abomination, incest and the Word. The Better Friend's sacred mission is to forge their (un)holy alliance.

Incest first meets the Word on the symbolic boat that transports the (un)fortunate Ellen to her paternal Aunt Fortune's.[12] Hardly has she embarked than her unmotherly chaperone Mrs. Dunscombe (oblivious, despite the name, to the deficiencies of her own God-given headgear) pokes fun at Ellen's perfectly decent, if mildly frumpish bonnet. Dunscombe's gratuitous sadism sends the "lightning of passion" crackling through her temporary charge's "every vein" (66). Devastated, the little girl shoots off, and buries herself below decks. Hours later she is still disconsolately alone, lost in imaginary intercourse with her mother ("'Who is there to teach me now? O! what shall I do without you?'" [68]). It seems as though the whole wide world were against her; but, if only because we have seen the chapter heading—"'Strangers walk as friends'" (5)—we know better. *Salvation is coming in the person of the stranger.*

The stranger in some sense caps the sequence Mrs. Montgomery initiates by going forever. In some sense, because he is not quite man enough to master Ellen in the end; he does not (perhaps only for lack of time) confound her as thoroughly as he ought. Otherwise he is everything a better friend should be, and prefigures in his few hours with the fledgling heroine her interminable relation with her main mentor and master John. Which is to say, above all, that he prefigures the fusion of *The Wide, Wide World's* religious and sexual dynamics, just as both are beginning to gather head. The operation is effected simply enough. The stranger's charms plead his cause; he pleads the Father's; his pleading the Father's cause is passed off as the greatest of his charms. Schematically, it is just what will transpire between Ellen and John, with a single difference immediately apparent but hard to pin down: let us call it the more

thorough (de)sexualization of Ellen's encounter with the stranger. It is unimaginable that the prepubescent heroine should enter into an erotic relation with this model "gentleman," doubtless old enough to be her father.[13] Because it is unimaginable, it can happen before our very eyes: expertly, the strange gentleman seduces Ellen for Christ. Her passionate grief provides him his opening:

> At length, a gentleman . . . happened to look, as he passed, at [Ellen's] little pale face. . . . he stopped just in front of her, and bending down his face towards hers, said—"What is the matter with you, my little friend?" . . . There was no mistaking the look of kindness in the eyes that met hers, nor the gentleness and grave truthfulness of the whole countenance. It won her confidence immediately. All the floodgates of Ellen's heart were at once opened. She could not speak, but . . . burst into one of those uncontrollable agonies of weeping. . . . He gently . . . drew her to a retired part of the deck . . . then taking her in his arms he endeavored by many kind and soothing words to stay the torrent of her grief. (68-69)

This overture sounds the eternal themes of Warneresque romance. First, the child-woman, forlorn, vulnerable—a figure marking the perpetual possibility of her possession by another, a standing, or rather sitting, invitation to a seduction. Then, a strange gentleman. The word itself signals that Ellen's invitation is about to be taken up, for in Warner's lexicon "gentleman" automatically carries a sexual charge (the proof is that elsewhere it has to be carried off with modifiers like "odd" or "old"). Between the child-woman and the gentleman, a mating ritual that immediately finds its essential form, that of the *examination.* Examination in a double sense: inspection ("bending down his face towards hers"), but also interrogation ("What is the matter with you, my little friend?"). The ambiguity of the question bespeaks the ambiguity of the gaze that prefaces it. Solicitous/inquisitive/inquisitorial, the stranger will set things to rights (what is the matter with you, what is your trouble) by ferreting out what is wrong with Ellen (what is the matter with you, what is your fault). But, in *The Wide, Wide World,* these two tasks are one. Hence the *un*ambiguity of the gaze and the question that articulates it: as plainly as Saunders's vile eyes declare his evil intent, so there is "no mistaking" the "truthfulness" of the stranger's "whole countenance." The effect too is as unmistakable in the one case as in the other. Indeed, it is more or less the same. The examination overpowers and opens (here, "the floodgates of Ellen's heart"), leaving its subject in "uncontrollable agonies" before her examiner. With a look and a penetrating question, the stranger becomes a familiar.

He exploits this instant intimacy to reright Ellen according to Scripture:

> "You love your mother better than you do the Saviour?"

"O yes, sir," said Ellen, "how can I help it?"

"Then if he had left you your mother, Ellen, you would never have cared or thought about him?"

Ellen was silent.

"Is it so?—would you, do you think?"

"I don't know, Sir," said Ellen, weeping again—"o, sir! how can I help it?"

"Then Ellen, can you not see the love of your heavenly Father in this trial? He saw that his little child was in danger of forgetting him, and he loved you, Ellen; and so he has taken your dear mother, and sent you away where you will have no one to look to but him: and now he says to you, 'My daughter, give *me* thy heart.'—Will you do it, Ellen?" (70)

"Will you do it, Ellen?"—there is the question *The Wide, Wide World* turns on. It is definitively answered only at the other end of the novel, when Ellen eagerly agrees to "do it" for her "brother" John. The strange familiar gentleman's preliminary plea names the major condition for John's eventual victory: the loving Father must "hinder" His daughter's "enjoyment" of her mother (70), must lure the sinfully passionate girl-child into the Paternal arms. The familial metaphor shades off into another; masterfully articulating the desire of the Father, the stranger slips naturally into the role of the father. The familiar tone of his discourse would by itself suggest the analogy, but the text tactfully insists on it, now calling the stranger Ellen's "grave protector," now arranging for him to call her "my child" after repeating that she is Christ's:

"And were there ever sweeter words of kindness than these?—'Suffer the little children to come unto me, and forbid them not'. . . . Do you wish to be his child, Ellen?"

"O yes, sir—if I could."

"I know, my child, that sinful heart of yours is in the way." (73)

"I know, my child . . .": leagued with One Who knows Ellen's inmost self even better than she does ("he is here, close to you, and knows every wish and throb of your heart"), her deputy father questions her not to procure information, but to procure Ellen—to confirm his natural right to plumb the depths of her soul. It is a penetration she ardently desires, or, rather, desires to desire. Only the flesh is weak (Ellen's, but perhaps also the stranger's):

"Shall I put you in mind, Ellen, of some things about Christ that ought to make you love him with all your heart?"

"O yes, sir! if you please." (71)

This commendable will to submission convinces the stranger that "his little friend" is not simply leading Christ on ("and he thought he saw that she was in earnest"). Heartened, he presses His suit with a hymn to Him:

"Open my heart, Lord, enter in;
Slay every foe, and conquer sin.
Here now to thee I all resign,—
My body, soul, and all are thine." (75)

The hymn brings the Father only partial success, since Ellen, though she "long[s] to," cannot quite assent to the last couplet: her "completely melted" heart still somehow resists the passage of the Word. But the "father" fares better: we are given an earnest of the eventual triumph of the Former in Ellen's unconditional surrender to the latter. Hardly has the familiar gentleman begun to examine her than he "takes her in his arms"; as he plies his probing questions, she perches on his knees; after some further evangelical exhortation, she sleeps with him: "She dropped her head against the arm of her friend and fell fast asleep. He smiled at first, but one look at the very pale little face changed the expression of his own. He gently put his arm round her and drew her head to a better resting-place than it had chosen." (77) The pair's physical and spiritual communion crests in a thrilling embrace:

"I must go," said Ellen, standing up and extending her hand;—"Good-bye Sir."

She could hardly say it. He drew her towards him and kissed her cheek once or twice: it was well he did; for it sent a thrill of pleasure to Ellen's heart that she did not get over that evening, nor all the next day. (82)

In fact, Ellen never gets over that thrill of pleasure, the ambivalent joy of yielding to the Lord and master who purges her of one (un)natural passion by awakening another still more (un)natural. The kiss is prologue; it gives her the taste of a consummation she most devoutly wishes ("Shall I . . . ?" "O yes, sir! if you please") but is as yet incapable of accomplishing ("O, if I could!—but I don't know how"). Poor Ellen will never quite learn how: hence the abiding thrill of that aporistic embrace, whose irresolvability it is the improper business of the rest of *The Wide, Wide World* to draw out. But her gentleman friends have already intimated what sort of drama is coming: the odd old one obscurely, the strange familiar one oscularly. *The Wide, Wide World,* their foreplay foretells, will revolve around com-muting her incestuous passion; and commuting it will be a matter of soliciting and refusing a daughterly kiss—forever and ever.

Brothers and Sisters and Something Superadded

The air of romance that wafts enticingly through *The Wide, Wide World's* hundred pages of prologue grows considerably thicker in its central episodes, dominated by Warner's hero John. We meet him toward the middle of the novel and instantly recognize him for the savior Ellen has long sought unawares: the no longer absent "only one in the world," the secular authority nonpareil, the hyperpotent protector with a privileged relation to Omnipotence. Mrs. Montgomery could wish her daughter no better (worldly) friend. One could hardly blame her for wishing something more.

Or could one? John is, after all, Ellen's brother, or rather "brother." The novel takes pains over this "fraternal" relationship. It is established even before John makes his entrance, when his unsullied sister Alice adopts Ellen as her "sister." It is pointedly reestablished when Ellen meets John:

"John," said Alice, "this is my little sister that I wrote you about—Ellen Montgomery. Ellen, this is your brother as well as mine, you know."

"Stop! stop!" said her brother. "Miss Ellen, this sister of mine is giving us away to each other at a great rate,—I should like to know first what you say to it. Are you willing to take a strange brother upon her recommendation?"

Half inclined to laugh, Ellen glanced at the speaker's face, but meeting the grave though somewhat comical look of two very keen eyes, she looked down again, and merely answered "yes."

"Then if I am to be your brother you must give me a brother's right, you know," said he, drawing her gently to him, and kissing her gravely on the lips. (274)

From this moment forward we are relentlessly reminded of Ellen's and John's "consanguinity" ("I will not let you forget that I am your brother, Ellie," vows John on p. 348, proving in this, as in all else, as good as his word). The last reminder comes in the novel's penultimate paragraph, the one that—"for the gratification of those who are never satisfied"—coquettishly publishes our siblings' banns. Grown to womanhood, we gratifiedly read there, "Ellen did in no wise disappoint her brother's wishes" (569).

What it means to be John's sister we can deduce from his relationship with Alice. It is, to put it mildly, intense. Here is how she receives the budding divine when he comes home from divinity school at, significantly, Christmastime:

Alice started to her feet with a slight scream, and in another minute had thrown her arms round the stranger and was locked in his. Ellen knew what it meant now very well. She turned away as if she had nothing to do with what was going on there. . . . And then she stood with her back to the brother and sister, looking into the fire, as if she was determined not to see them till she couldn't help it. But what she was thinking of, Ellen could not have told, then or afterwards . . . [Alice's] usually calm, sweet face was quivering and sparkling now,—lit up as Ellen had never seen it,—oh, how bright! (273-74)

Brother and sister locked in one another's arms, with a supernumerary "sister" (not) looking on: this is *The Wide, Wide World's* primal scene. If Ellen turns shamefacedly away from it, "as if she had nothing to do with what was going on there," it is because she really *is* locked out of the fraternal embrace: she can never ever become John's sister. The fact that she becomes his "sister" insists on the exclusion. It serves as a nagging reminder that *her* relation to John rests on an "as if" that makes it a simulacrum of the connatural bond between John and Alice, an imitation that must forever fall short of the real thing. But the real thing is an imitation too: Alice can quiver in John's arms to her heart's content, but that is all she will ever get to do there. The potential for full and natural union between brother and sister can only be realized via the *un*natural union of "brother" and "sister." The novel's primal scene thus derives from a scene that derives from *it:* John and Alice's prefatory embrace rehearses the future coupling of John and Ellen, which rehearses the impossible coupling of Alice and John. The Warneresque ménage à trois is a pair of counterfeit pairs in search of their real—and impossible—original.

Relations in this unstable triad are derivative in another sense: they reduplicate—with "something superadded"—the ménage à trois that was the Montgomery household. This calls attention to itself above all through Alice:

"Miss Alice," said Ellen after a long time—"I wish you would talk over a hymn with me."

"How do you mean my dear?" said Alice rousing herself.

"I mean, read it over and explain it. Mamma used to do it sometimes . . ."

"I am afraid I shall be a poor substitute for your mother Ellen. What hymn shall we take?" (238)

The suggestion that Ellen's "sister" is substituting for her mother encourages us to read her "brother" as her ersatz father. No doubt innocently, Alice invites us to notice how Ellen's facsimile family repeats and completes its defective model. The contrast, no less than the similarity, speaks for itself. The novel never tells whether Alice outdid Mrs. Montgomery at talking over a hymn; it is too busy demonstrating how much more serviceable she can be when it comes to taking over a him. Plainly, Ellen's second mother's advantage is her John: first, because Ellen can share him; second, because he is worth the sharing.

Ellen must feel the difference from the moment John takes his sister in his arms. That initial eye-opening embrace between her future foster parents contrasts poignantly with the Captain's snoring indifference to his sighing spouse, his "happy unconsciousness" of her deepest conjugal needs: John plays out with Alice a domestic scene Ellen missed at home. By identifying with her "sister" and second mother, then, Ellen can vicariously couple with a lovable version of the Captain. Her (non)relation with her dormant father is retroactively made over into a kind of incest degree zero, an effect amplified by the symbolic damping of the distinctions between Ellen, Alice, and Mrs. Montgomery. The patrimatrimonial undertones swell to a crescendo with the emergence of a final parallel between Ellen's families old and new: both disintegrate. Having consoled her over the definitive departure of Mrs. Montgomery, Ellen's second mother follows her prototype to the grave.

Exiting, she bequeaths Ellen John ("dear Miss Alice said Miss Ellen was to take her place" [448]). But the continuing existence of the flesh-and-blood Captain threatens drastically to devalue the bequest. As long as her father is bifurcated into a repulsively real and a seductively symbolic variant, Ellen's relation to her spiritual "brother" must remain imperfectly patrimatrimonial. If God awards her only a "brother" in compensation for a dead mother—while leaving her saddled with a fatherly dud—He will hardly have "ma[d]e up to [her] more than all [she] has lost." (57) She must *lose* her father in order to gain him; nothing else can prevent the qualitative difference between the godly "brother" and the all-too-human father from rupturing the continuity of *The Wide, Wide World*'s male line. This, perhaps, is why Warner now reduces her defective father figure to the absolute zero he always potentially was. In the thick of the Alice-John drama, Ellen's surviving biological parent fades insubstantially away, disappearing, we are casually informed, at sea. Yet, though Warner remorselessly drowns father, she also tosses him a life preserver: he is sea-changed into something that can be superadded, as a kind of enriching paternal strain, to "brother." The defunct Captain thus raised to a pure paternal function, one masterfully assured by John, Ellen can regale the patrifratrimatrimonial desire she will never suspect she had: she can take her first rival's place in her rejuvenated father's arms by taking her second rival's place in her "brother's."

The Wide, Wide World hands her the victory without making the slightest allusion to the fray. Dying the ethereal death reserved for the saintliest scribbler virgins, Alice sweetly clears the field for John and his "sister" while the latter hovers decently in the background. This is Warner's second and final take of the primal scene:

"Are you happy, Alice?" whispered her brother.

"Perfectly. This [John's last-minute arrival on the scene] was all I wanted. Kiss me, dear John!"

As he did so, again and again, she felt his tears on her cheek . . . kissed him then, and then once again laid her head on his breast. They remained so a little while without stirring; except that some whispers were exchanged too low for others to hear, and once more she raised her face to kiss him. A few minutes after those who could look saw his color change, he felt the arms unclasp their hold; and, as he laid her gently back on the pillow they fell languidly down; the will and the power that had sustained them were gone. *Alice* was gone. (440-41)

Her going unites the symbolic siblings in an embrace that presages their coming union, while recalling that introductory clinch between John and his sister:

With an indescribable air of mingled tenderness, weariness, and sorrow, [Ellen] slowly rose from her seat and put both her arms round [John's] neck. Neither said a word; but to Ellen the arm that held her was more than all words; it was the dividing line between her and the world—on this side everything, on that nothing . . . he held her still, and looking for a moment at the tokens of watching and grief and care in her countenance, he gently kissed the pale little face, adding a word of endearment which almost broke Ellen's heart again. Then taking her hand they went down the mountain together. (443-44)

Patrifratrimatrimonially considered, Alice's conclusion is eminently logical. Her death eliminates the impossible possibility that she might couple with her brother; it also realizes it, and that twice over. First, Alice's unilateral *Liebestod* transports her to realms where nothing will ever again sunder her from John ("'we have,'" he once prophetically consoles her, "'an eternity to spend together!'" [406]). That she dies a *sister* but not a *wife* means, then, not only that she dies forever secured against the possibility of incest, but also that the possibility of incest is forever secured by her dying; no bothersome brother-in-law will be vying with brother for Alice's attentions in heaven. But this eternal suspension of the forbidden passion is attended by obvious impracticalities. Ellen's convoluted relations to her relations provide the down-to-earth alternative. Coupling with his "sister," John couples with his sister this side the grave; shielded by those invisible inverted commas, Ellen embraces the father she never really had. Alice's supreme sacrifice seals an unspoken covenant: it promises an authorized transgression of the interdict on whose inviolability *The Wide, Wide World* turns. The siblings' deathbed embrace is the dress rehearsal for the unplayable scene Mrs. Montgomery, the Captain, the strange gentleman, even Saunders have, each in his/her own way, taught Ellen—and us—(not) to look for.

The Sister's Seduction

John and Ellen having gone down the mountain together, one might expect that Warner would precipitously marry them off. Instead, one finds John protractedly chastening his charge. Since well before his sister's (un)timely demise, the young divine has been drilling her understudy; indefatigably, he keeps it up afterwards, fixing chastening as the sole mode of intercourse between "brother" and "sister." We must, then, renouncing romance, satisfy ourselves with pedagogy—and this to the very end of *The Wide, Wide World.*

There is an easy explanation for the exclusion of eros from Warner's tale. John's "sister" is scarcely thirteen when his sister breathes her last; to become a true woman, she needs more "time, 'that rider that breaks youth'" (11). In orthodox perspective, then, the second stage of our passionate pilgrim's progress simply gives her the time she needs. And, of course, the training. Mrs. Montgomery and Alice have schooled Ellen in the rudiments of Christian theology; John will now initiate her into its practical applications. But the continuity masks a quiet revolution. The infantile instinct binding Ellen to her mother(s) had to be unambiguously rechanneled toward the Better Friend. In contrast, the passion that makes John's "arm" mean more "than all words" will be dammed up without being diverted, quelled and yet retained in its original intensity. Prolonging Ellen's Christian education, her last mentor simultaneously reverses it: transferring her affections to the next world, he transfixes them to their (im)proper object in this one. There is no constraint like that of love; John Humphreys wields living proof of Heman Humphrey's dictum.

The constraint of love, as the strange familiar gentleman has shown, is imposed principally by the masterful gaze. John deploys his the moment he lays eyes on his "sister":

> Meeting the grave though somewhat comical look of two very keen eyes, she looked down again, and merely answered "yes" . . . Ellen's eyes sought the stranger as if by fascination. At first she was in doubt what to think of him; she was quite sure from that one look into his eyes that he was a person to be feared;—there was no doubt of that; as to the rest she didn't know. (274-75)

About the potency that shoots from those fearsome orbs, Warner wants us to be quite as sure as Ellen. She therefore lets us eavesdrop on this exchange between a man who knows John and a woman who obviously doesn't:

> "I do not know precisely," he went on to the lady he was walking with, "what it takes to rouse John Humphreys, but when he *is* roused he seems to me to have strength enough for twice his bone and muscle. I have seen him do curious things once or twice!"
>
> "That quiet Mr. Humphreys?"
>
> "Humph," said Mr. Howard,—"gunpowder is pretty quiet stuff so long as it keeps cool." (318)

Indubitably potent, then: Ellen did not miss her guess, the mastering gaze never lies. But potency has many faces; small wonder that Ellen, after facing Saunders, should be wary of the gunpowder in her He-man's glance. Her suspicions are, however, promptly allayed—or lulled—by a second overpowering look, "the look of love" John shoots at his (then still hale) sister Alice. Though aimed at his sister rather than his "sister," it wins the latter's undying regard at first sight: "from that minute Ellen's mind was made up as to the doubt which had troubled her" (279). She is never once tempted to change it.

John sees to that. Reassuringly, he presses his optical might into the service of the pedagogy of surveillance, lovingly devoting his super-vision to comprehensive supervision. It is comprehensive indeed. One can hardly exaggerate the divine's clairvoyance. There is no hiding from big brother: "Of one thing [Ellen] was perfectly sure, whatever [John] might be doing,—that he saw and heard her; and equally sure that if anything were not right she should sooner or later hear of it." (461) There is no hiding one's thoughts from him either:

> Ellen blushed exceedingly. "I do believe, Mr. John," said she, stammering, "that you know everything I am thinking about." (317)
>
> "Why," said Ellen, laughing and blushing,—"how *could* you guess what I was thinking about, Mr. John?" (321)
>
> "[John] always knows what I am thinking of," [Ellen said], "just as well as if I told him." (414)

This preternatural prescience makes it unnecessary for John to pry. Like the strange familiar gentleman, he nevertheless pries with a vengeance. Though he has all the answers, John is forever questioning Ellen. His aim, like his predecessor's, is to make her see that she is *questionable*. He begins in earnest at a Christmas party at which Ellen, succumbing to a momentary temptation, cheats at a children's game. A public confession notwithstanding, she remains oppressed by the onus of her sin, and steals off to an empty room to grieve over it unassisted. But she is not alone. Hardly has she shut the door behind her than she senses a panoptical presence. It is John, who proceeds to conduct *The Wide, Wide World*'s first full-length examination:

> "Running away from your brother, Ellie!" said he kindly; "what is the matter?"
>
> Ellen shrank from meeting his eye and was silent. "I know all Ellie," said he, still very kindly,—"I have seen all;—why do you shun me?"
>
> Ellen said nothing; the big tears began to run down her face and frock. (295-96)

Eve would have recognized the scene. But it takes a turn that would have pleasantly surprised her. Quite unlike Jehovah, John queries his quarry solicitously, not punitively:

> "I want to talk to you a little about this," said he. . . . " Will you let me ask you a question or two?"
>
> "O yes. . . . " (296)

"O yes": having lovingly constrained that pledge of full cooperation, John sets out to extract the confession of unworthiness that is "all the answer he wishe[s]" (297). To expedite matters, he hands down this mild but damning verdict, unwittingly sustaining the strange familiar gentleman's: "'You will wonder at me perhaps, Ellie,' said John, 'but I am not very sorry this has happened. You are no worse than before;—it has only made you see what you are—very, very weak,— quite unable to keep yourself right without constant help.'" (296) And he goes on to pronounce this chastening sentence: "'Be humbled in the dust before him— the more the better; but whenever we are greatly concerned, for our own sakes, about other people's opinion, we may be sure we are thinking too little of God and what will please him.'" (297)

There is no need to spell out that what pleases God pleases John, that he has taught Ellen how to please him in teaching her how to please Him. She responds by signifying that she is eager to please, that is, to be humbled in the dust before her "brother": "'I am very sorry,' said poor Ellen, 'I am very wrong.'" According to the established pattern, she should now reap a token of the ultimate earthly reward for her self-abnegation: her master should afford her "the thrill of pleasure"

that his acknowledgement of her tractability would bring. But here John breaks precedent, affording the miscreant no opportunity to embrace her one-man judge and jury. It falls to his sister to bring the scene to its climax: "As Alice came up with a quick step and knelt down before her, Ellen sprang to her neck, and they held each other very fast indeed. John walked up and down the room" (297).

The constraint of love, it appears, mandates the restraint of love. To say so is to only to repeat our frustrated question: why should *The Wide, Wide World*, instead of galloping toward its patrifratrimatrimonial climax, insist on incessantly chastening its nubile childwoman? But we are champing at the bit, proving only that we too deserve a "strong check" (416) of the sort John periodically administers his "sister." To be sure, what he *says* in defense of his permanent arraignment of Ellen is hardly enough to bridle our impatience. Where is the logic, he spurs us rather to ask, of humbling a little girl in the dust because she is "very, very weak"? John, however, sees more than he says. Indeed, he sees all. He does not need to read *The Wide, Wide World* to know that Ellen's weakness is yoked to "passions . . . by nature very strong." Nor does he need to say that the mightiest of those animal passions is a very, very strong weakness for her "brother." The novel's elementary structures say it for him, in accordance with a principle he helpfully explains: "When two things have been in the mind together, and made any impression, the mind *associates* them; and you cannot see or think of the one without bringing back the remembrance or the feeling of the other." (479)

We cannot, for example, see or think of Ellen's chastening without bringing back the remembrance of the family affair. That the two are so memorably *associated* is an accident of the child-woman's experience, an accident which yet constitutes the main axis of *The Wide, Wide World:* the examination illuminates, as Fichte might have put it, her family history's divine pedagogy, while her family history, in turn, illuminates the pedagogy of her divine. Against the backdrop of the family affair, the immoral impulse curbed in the examination emerges as the female animal's rampant con-genital passion. Taming her with question and gaze, John enacts Warner's rendition of the incest taboo; harrying instead of marrying her, he acts out the deferral of love that is the law of *The Wide, Wide World.* Not by accident· is it his chastening rod that forestalls the unseemly hastening of our "siblings'" nuptials. Sisterly deference to the rod and the deferral of fratrimatrimony are different versions of the same chastening thing.

Yet woman is not chastened by discipline alone. Only love can constrain her to defer to the rod that restrains her. John has firmly grasped this (Heman) Humphreyesque truth: *his* rod is a "happy mixture of pointedness and kindness" (415). Hardly has he begun to wield it than it "has wound round Ellen's heart, and constrained her to answer immediately" (477) all the humbling questions he puts to her. Indeed, her "brother's" loving strictures—unlike, say, her "sister's"—carry the irresistible authority of *natural law:* "what [Alice] asked of her Ellen indeed *tried* to do; what John told her *was done*" (351). The heart that, "hardened by sin," has rebuffed her heavenly Father joyfully embraces the living Word as proffered by John. Only under *his* rod does she come to cry "'O how love I thy law,'" does she learn to love with her whole sin-hardened heart the power that denies her her heart's desire:[14] "Of one thing [Ellen] was perfectly sure, whatever [John] might be doing,— that he saw and heard her; and equally sure that if anything were not right she should sooner or later hear of it. But this was a censorship Ellen rather loved than feared." (461)

What makes her love it so? It is that John does ocularly what the strange familiar gentleman did oscularly: he thrillingly indulges the lawless impulse he checks. The Law-Man's all-seeing gaze is double-barreled. To penalize Ellen, John looks her down, as here: "'Why?' said Ellen, the crimson of her cheeks mounting to her forehead. But her eye sunk immediately at the answering glance of [John's]." (415) This "reproof," we are told, "went to the quick." But not cuttingly: though it makes Ellen cry for an hour, she "join[s] with it no thought of harshness or severity." For John commutes every sentence he executes in the very act of executing it; looking Ellen down, he also looks lovingly *into* her. The gaze that enforces the law effects a coupling outside the law: the penetration the child-woman provokes by being bad is the optical version of incest. Forever stemming his patient's passion, Ellen's spiritual physician is also forever pandering to it; the pedagogy of surveillance *is* the family affair. What has been said about Ellen's brewing her mother's tea therefore applies nicely to John's sensual censorship too: "this ritual does not merely promise fulfillment; it offers consummation in the present moment."[15]

But, if the punishment of Ellen's desire doubles as its accomplishment, John risks being hoist by his own petard. One need only invoke his *associative* law to implicate him in incest: as one who "always knows" what is in Ellen's mind, is the Law-Man not guilty of countenancing—more, of instigating—the female lawlessness he so emphatically interdicts? Without, of course, acknowledging the accusation, Warner does her best to rule it out of court. John, she shows us, censures Ellen only because Ellen wants him (to); moreover, the passion that makes Ellen want him (to) is precisely what he censures. But such evidence damns the divine quite as definitively as it exonerates him. The ocular firepower that "completely subdues" the little girl's frailty (415), the penetrating interrogatories

she "never [thinks] of trying to evade" (469), the "higher style of authority" that "reach[es] where [others] could never attain" (538)—are these so many manifestations of the constraint of love, or so many proofs of an act of prior restraint? Reaching Ellen's unattainable place, does John's irresistible authority— by virtue of its very irresistibility—not constrain his "sister's" love in the most forceful sense of the word? And how, indeed, must we judge the divine Word, if incest meets with the secret sanction of the divine who meets it with such stringent sanctions?

There is a line of questioning that threatens to turn the wide world upside down. But the higher authorities have no easy way of quashing it. The sensual/censorious question is too valuable a disciplinary tool to be scrapped for the sake of sheltering the Law-Man from evil imputation; the Warneresque Grand Inquisitor can no more relinquish the prerogative of the interrogative than he can admit that his pedagogy amounts to child molestation. As if in response to this fundamental dilemma, the novel compulsively rehearses its traumatic beginnings; it sends Ellen out on a second solitary sally into the wide, wide world. There, in a stormy replay of the Saunders scene, Warner not only reopens the question of Ellen's questionability; she also reads it back into the very origins of *The Wide, Wide World.* It is the Law-Man's main chance to abrogate his own *associative* law. He turns it to violent advantage.

Chiding, Chastening, Chastising

We now know how much is riding on John's repression of his sinfully passionate "sister": he staves off nothing less than incestuous apocalypse by staving Ellen off. But it hardly seems that he needs the rod to do it. In a pedagogical program founded on the constraint of love, muscular chastening ought to yield to a gentle motherly chiding, the human powder keg to that "image of maternal authority" bestsellerdom's more sanguine critics discern in the scribblers. Why, then, does John's distinctly paternal-fraternal "bone and muscle" (318) remain so salient a feature of Warner's anatomy of power? *Why doesn't the chastening rod wither away?*

The answer is that only heroic prowess can keep girlish weakness from becoming woman's—and the wide world's—ruin. *The Wide, Wide World* rams that lesson home in an episode in which potency bares its other face: violence. Potent violence finds its pendant in something that, one might think, should have perished with the Puritans: breathless child-womanly terror.

Two men in *The Wide, Wide World* inspire that chastening emotion: Saunders, the villain, but also John, the hero. Saunders's beastly behavior in the dry goods store indicates well enough what makes *him* so frightful. Thus, though one may be shocked, one can hardly be surprised when, (un)expectedly resurfacing years after his inaugural humiliation, the rebarbative shopman waylays Ellen and falls to molesting her pony: "His best way of distressing Ellen, he found, was through her horse; he had almost satisfied himself [by whipping it a little]: but very naturally his feeling of spite had grown stronger and blunter with indulgence, and he meant to wind up with such a treatment of her pony, real or seeming, as he knew would give great pain to the pony's mistress." (400)

If Saunders's villainy comes as no surprise, neither does the fate he is meted out: one knows, after all, about the gunpowder in John's soul. Now the militant Christian explodes into action. Riding up out of nowhere, he catches the recreant flagrante delicto, demands that he unhand Ellen's mount, and, when the impassioned blackguard offers to resist by brandishing the "club end" of his "sapling whip," collars and sends him sailing "quite over into the gulley at the side of the road" (401). With this the snake is foiled for good. But it takes his retraumatized victim an age to recover her aplomb:

> She had no words, but as [John] gently took one of her hands, the convulsive squeeze it gave him shewed the state of nervous excitement she was in. It was very long before his utmost efforts could soothe her, or she could command herself enough to tell him her story. When at last told, it was with many tears. "Oh how could he! how could he!" said poor Ellen;—"how could he do so!—it was very hard!" (401)

It is a time-honored tableau: the villain quavering at his rival's feet, the virgin quivering in her savior's arms. One might regard it as sufficient justification of the hero's muscle: Saunders's recrudescence, in that perspective, would be potency's best defense. It is an eminently proper reading: heroic violence vanquishes villainous vileness, preserving the virgin from violation.

But John's law of *association* authorizes less conventional arrangements of the figures in this group portrait. One can, for example, associate the antagonists with a view to highlighting the *resemblance* between them. Saunders's eyes, in particular, look like John's: the second Saunders scene, glancing back at the first across the grueling interval of the examination, insists on the affinity between the master's gaze and the monster's glare. The common feature that puts them "in the mind together" is the confounding "impression" both leave on Ellen: fear dwells in her response to being pedagogically eyeballed by John (she "shrank from meeting his eye"; "her eyes sunk immediately at the answering glance of John's") as to being sadistically sized up by Saunders ("the most disagreeable pair of eyes she had ever beheld . . . she could not bear

to meet them, and cast down her own"). We have seen enough of John's pedagogy to appreciate the associative logic of Ellen's anxieties. What the vicious clerk tries to do to her on the road, the virtuous clergyman does to her at home: John too penetrates her, punishes her, works his will on her weakness. Indeed—a circumstance his detractors have eagerly seized on—John has even anticipated Saunders by "chastising" (376) a defenseless horse.[16] Warding off the rapacious shopman, in a by now standard view, Ellen's protector shields her from a version of himself; the energy informing both the hero's heroism and the villain's villainy appears to alternate between saving the heroine and savaging her. The reason benevolent male violence crushes malevolence, it would seem to follow, is to maintain a precarious distinction between itself and its dark double.

Warner would not have endorsed the suggestion. Yet it is not, in our sense, an improper one. Standing helplessly to one side while the mighty vie to work their will on her, shrinking back from the vi(ri)le eyeballing minister and monster both treat her to, Ellen quails conventionally before a conventionally generalized male lust. Secret sharer in Saunders's crime, John helps set off the child-woman's lustrous purity by making part of its naturally lascivious male foil.

But the luster is deceptive: Ellen embodies a purity that is also the sheerest duplicity. Innocent, she is also guilty as sin. We will, then, reshuffle our trio once more, putting Ellen in the mind together with Saunders in token of her unlawful association with her fellow sinner. She herself confesses her collusion in the crime attempted against her. As her savior prepares to hurl Saunders into the pit, his gathering wrath puts the fear of the Lord into *her*. Breathlessly, she betrays her identification with the reprobate:

> "We will dispense with your further attendance," said John coolly. "Do you hear me?—Do as I order you!"
>
> The speaker did not put himself in a passion, and Mr. Saunders, accustomed for his own part to make bluster serve instead of prowess, despised a command so calmly given.—Ellen, who knew the voice, and still better could read the eye, drew conclusions very different. She was almost breathless with terror. (400)

The point of John's deterrent strike is plainly not lost on Ellen. Her breathless terror testifies to her intuition that the chastising of churls carries out the chastening of little girls by other means. Doubtless, her spontaneous sympathy with her mortal foe is only a kind of prim-Eval tic; but the reflex reflects, precisely, an ancient affinity. It is rooted in natural rebelliousness against the Law-Man. Victim and victimizer are associated in their (un)natural desire to break the law: Ellen, by violating the incest taboo; Saunders, by violating Ellen. But it is a condition of *The Wide, Wide World* that Ellen's desire never surface. Her fellow feeling for the outlaw she abhors must therefore be met with *prophylactic* terror, token of an anti-incestuous violence that, given her manifest innocence, is always in excess. Saunders is there to absorb the excess. That is what makes him crucial and negligible at once: theme of a trifling ten pages out of some six hundred, and an ubiquitous, eternal presence in the wide, wide world. The nugatory shopman represents a menace of the first order because he threatens to breach the social citadel at its most vulnerable point—or, rather, to slink in where it is always already breached: at the portal of female sexuality. Ellen is why Saunders must be so terrifyingly chastised.

But if Ellen is a version of Saunders who is a version of John, then John too stands convicted of clamoring at the incestuous gates; the second Saunders incident would only seem to confirm the suspicions we have already laid at the Law-Man's door. Yet there is less John to Saunders than meets the eye. This "brother" (as Saunders dares suggest: "'Not for you, brother,' said Mr. Saunders sneeringly; 'I'll walk with any lady I've a mind to.'" [400]) of Ellen's "brother" can offer her no more than a mock chastening and a travesty of fratrimatrimony; exposed, he turns out to be almost comically short on "prowess." Indeed, the pitiful contrast with John's storied potence all but reduces the masquerader to a version of the con-genitally defective child-woman. It thereby points to the factor distinguishing his bogus prowess from the real thing: namely, his acceptance of the invitation his "brother's" "sister" embodies. The essential difference between John and his fellow horse-beater is that the one curbs, while the other whips up, woman's animal passion. Saunders is the unmale malefactor the Law-Man would become if he yielded to the blandishments his "sister's" weakness proffers. It follows that, in snapping the blusterer's "sapling whip" in two, Ellen's savior scores a double victory: casting out woman's old enemy, he routs the prim-Eval sin whose notorious consequence is the fall of man. Protecting the vulnerable virgin from the villain's seeming strength, he protects *himself*—and the wide world— from the child-woman's lethal weakness.

That her weakness is not defenseless innocence but defenseless guilt we have all the evidence of the family affair to show. But, as if to prevent Saunders's more spectacular delinquency from putting that evidence out of mind, the second Saunders incident is prefaced by a supplementary reminder of Ellen's moral frailty. It comes in the person of her naughty playmate Nancy Vawse. Jane Tompkins has recently heaped praise on Nancy's impoverished, widowed grandmother, celebrating her husbandless self-sufficiency as a worldly emblem of scribbler "Heaven"; she commends the sprightly separatist for achieving fulfillment "without the dependency

of childhood, or of most Victorian women."[17] But there is trouble in this paradise; what may be Heaven for the post-menopausal widow is Hell for the prenubile Nancy, an orphan the unendowed dowager has to raise without a John. One can imagine what must become of the unchastened creature. Warner, however, spares one the effort. Whenever Ellen goes out to play with her father- and brotherless alter ego, she comes home sopping, sobbing, and/or soiled. In time, the good girl learns to àvoid such contamination; the bad one continues to besmirch herself. Ellen moves Heaven and earth to persuade Nancy to read the Bible and reform, but Ellen is not a John any more than Mrs. Vawse is. Hence one is anything but certain that her blackest visions do not materialize after Nancy permanently and ominously vanishes: "'But Nancy—before you begin to read the Bible you may have to go where you never can read it, nor be happy nor good neither.'" (334)

That unnamed tomb of all feminine hope, Ellen innocently reminds us, is where all girlish waywardness tends. Bound, one fears, for Hell via the whorehouse, naughty Nancy stands as a warning of the mor(t)al risks of autonomous female development. The warning is intended, not least, for the one who issues it. That it unfolds in counterpoint with the drama of John, Ellen, and Alice encourages us to elaborate on Nancy's bad example: the vector that extends from Nancy's actual insubordination toward some unnamed horror has an invisible extension that connects Ellen's potential insurgency to the nameless horror of incest. But for the severe, severing grace of God and John, Ellen would be mired in a morass even fouler than the one her playmate must disappear in.[18]

The events that blaze the way for Saunders's assault prove it. Ellen exposes herself to him while trying to help Mr. Van Brunt, her aunt's benevolent but benighted farmhand. She does to Van Brunt what John does to her, and more or less simultaneously: she chastens him until he takes Christ into his heart. This is at once eminently desirable, and problematic in the extreme. On the one hand, God's moral agent-in-training is duty-bound to evangelize, and, concomitantly, to chasten. On the other hand, whenever she does, there arises the intrinsically perverse possibility of the rod's passing to the distaff side. Sexual order can, therefore, only be maintained (as well appear more fully in the next chapter) if the chastened male, or a proxy, simultaneously chastens his chastener. But Van Brunt, however truehearted, remains a blunt and brutish hired hand; he is in no position to apply the rod to so delicate a creature as Ellen, or to be represented in that disciplinary capacity by so refined a personage as John. Indeed, he is in no position to apply the rod at all. On the day Saunders is resurrected, he indicates as much by breaking his leg—by "us[ing] himself up," as Nancy characteristically puts it, bawdily insisting on his incapacitation.[19]

Van Brunt's fracture is in keeping with his humble social status; that Ellen should take one "sickened" (386) look at his leg, and then boldly ride off for help, is therefore no more unseemly than the fact that she makes him "fit to go to heaven" (389).[20] But this is, for the reasons just noted, vaguely unseemly. To be sure, the indiscretion involved is trifling. But it is not therefore inconsequential; for, as John observes, Hamlet-like, right after vanquishing Saunders: "'Little things often draw after them long trains of circumstances . . . and that shows the folly of those people who think that God does not stoop to concern himself about trifles.'" (401)

The trifle in question, Ellen's temerarious assumption of the rod, takes *its* weighty significance from the long train of circumstances that precede it. *Their* significance has been spelled out by Saunders's assorted "brothers." When Ellen's shipboard savior asked his little friend, "what is the matter with you," he posed, we recall, two questions at once: "how have you been wronged," but also "what is wrong with you." John's Christmas party verdict sustained the negative note: this "has only made you see what you are—very, very weak—quite unable to keep yourself right without constant help." The sentence John pronounces after extracting Ellen from Saunders's clutches is only superficially different: "But Ellen, you must ride no more alone." (401) In fact, *she must ride no more alone because she is quite unable to keep herself right.* Without the help of him without whom she can do nothing, even her efforts to save a Van Brunt can drive her straight into the skulking Saunders's arms— or, what is the same thing but worse, prematurely into his "brother's."

In the end, then, Saunders is Ellen's fault: she is weak because she is very, very weak. As her powerful weakness solicits her "brother's" sensual censorship, so too does it secretly long for her "brother's" "brother" to flagellate her mount. No wonder Ellen is "wrought up to a terrible pitch of excitement and fear" as Saunders's ersatz whip flicks over her filly (398). If the fear does not blind us to the excitement, we will find it no more surprising that, as her tormentor "fashion[s] a very good imitation of an ox-whip" out of his sapling, Ellen watches "in an ecstasy of apprehension" (397). Always already relinquished by Van Brunt, the chastening rod has momentarily slipped from the Law-Man's grip, passing into the hands of his lawless twin. Ellen's terrified delight springs from her intuition that the usurpation portends a violation of the sexual order. That it also portends a violation of *her,* one she carves as much as she dreads, is the logic of sensual censorship and the indelible mark of John's and Saunders's fraternity: with the one horse-beater as with the other, Ellen craves the censorship for the sake of the fratrimatrimonial sensuousness. Shadowing the image of the virgin writhing in the

embrace of a fiend is another, more blurred but more basic, that portrays her as her vicious tormentor's ecstatically Vawsian victim.

She was similarly victimized the day of her maiden venture into the wide world. In retrospect, one may perhaps be pardoned for wondering if a little secret doubtfulness does not also attend her role in that introductory engagement with male malevolence. She is, we recall, "confused, and almost confounded" even before approaching the shopman: might this be our initial clue that she cannot keep herself right without constant help? Effortlessly, Saunders works her up to a terrible pitch of excitement and fear: is this complex emotion a precocious, negative manifestation of that trembly girlish instinct that seeks some object it knows not what? If so, the foreboding Ellen feels the first time she sallies forth without him without whom she can do nothing ought not to be pooh-poohed: "But at the very bottom of Ellen's heart there was a little secret doubtfulness respecting her undertaking." (44) Magnified, that trifling doubt suggests that the passionate prepubescent who stands with face on fire under Saunders's mortifying glare is the same doubtful creature who blushes crimson at a chastening frown of John's, the same creature who thrills as the familiar gentleman bares her weakness or burns with ecstatic apprehension as Saunders makes ready to flog her filly. In short, the pattern of Ellen's responses to the vi(ri)le is retroactively invested with its (im)moral meaning by her post-preadolescent encounter with John's bastard "brother." If Saunders is Ellen's fault in the end, he is—so the highly improper verdict—her fault in the beginning too.

The point of blaming the victim is, of course, to exculpate the victimizer(s): if Saunders is Ellen's fault, then her passion cannot be John's. The second Saunders scene thus provides a recapitulative reading of the family affair: it reads the suspicions generated by the examination out of textual court. But those suspicions, we have been saying, color the second Saunders scene itself. John eliminates them with coldblooded violence. Without "put[ting] himself in a passion," he sunders Saunders from Ellen. He sunders himself, that is, both from the naturally (com)passionate child-woman and her impassioned companion in sin. Dispassionately chastising the malevolence that would prey on Ellen's con-genital weakness, he retroactively secures his license to chasten his future bride: the impassive, *chastising* rod proclaims that the *chastening* rod was always unincestuous. The gunpowder in John's soul explodes the blasphemous notion that his "sister's" incestuous self is made in his godly image.

But does Ellen accept her spiritual physician's interpretation? Does she now appreciate the enormity of riding alone, and has she been suitably chastened by the chastising of Saunders? For once, John seems uncertain. He therefore falls back on the admonitory technique that made up the major part of Ellen's Christmas party· punishment: he restates his text in *negative oscular terms.* Already, in the person of his unholy "brother," Ellen has been offered the fraternal kiss whose suspended possibility has long held her in an ecstasy of apprehension. That offer was violently revoked, only to be replaced by another not so different; John's victory once in hand, it is his own "brotherly" kiss that comes within Ellen's purview. But he seems not to want to bestow it. Waiting for her reward, the heroine is, for a memorable moment, made to stand with "swimming eyes and a trembling lip . . . Mr. John had forgotten the kiss he always gave her on going or coming." We know why it is so important: "Ellen was jealous of it as a pledge of sistership." And we can guess why John has "forgotten" it: withholding his affection, he gives his "sister" time to remember how close she has come to putting her precious "sistership" at risk. In that chastening interval, the chastisement visited upon Saunders humbles the only miscreant who matters in the dust. Having duly deposited her there, John can bring the episode to its real climax: chastened, expectant, Ellen garners the fraternal kiss "the want of which she had been lamenting" (402-3). She had been lamenting the want of it since the Captain. Now that she has secured it, one can be fairly certain she will ride no more alone.

The Defiles of the Defiling Signifier: The Incestuous Union of Nature and the Word

Writing alone was like riding alone. Warner religiously avoided it: she wrote with God. Indeed, she went so far as to suggest that He, not she, had composed *The Wide, Wide World.* "Thank him for it," she wrote her admirer Dorothea Dix, "I wash my hands of all desert in the matter." Such (un)pretentiousness characterizes scribblerdom from top to bottom.[21] As the domestic heroines efface themselves before their Johns, so their authors efface themselves before their Author. Nor is the gesture confined to the margins of their work; it is enacted *in* their fiction, *as* their fiction. Scribbler novels are self-effacing artifacts: recounting their heroines' self-effacement, they simultaneously recount their own. Thus the story of the righting of Ellen doubles as one about the righting of writing. But Ellen's education involves more than righting alone. It is also, and not fortuitously, a matter of riding. The critics are quite right to insist on Ellen's spontaneous identification with John's chastened horse: her horse-beater of a "brother" gives her too "a regular [riding] lesson" (341) in more than one sense of the word. To put it bluntly, he rides her—or, more precisely, rides the female animal *in* her. That she "rather love[s]" it links riding, via righting, to (re)writing: Ellen's craving for a riding master all but spells out her author's for a writing master. As the one child-woman loves being overridden by her sensually censorious "brother," so the other longs to

be written over by her celestial Father. Warner's magisterial pun, then, conjugates more than the taming of equine and child-womanly passion; it whispers that textual desire too can only be satiated under "religion's happy reign" (553).

Let none accuse our author of verbal excess. However powerful her passion for words, Warner's overriding impulse was to surrender her will to the Word's.[22] She had been trained to it by a long tradition, that of the *typos* or *figura.* Typology, it will be recalled, "establishes a connection between two events or persons in such a way that the first signifies not only itself but also the second, while the second involves or fulfills the first."[23] Invented mainly to facilitate rewriting the Old Testament in the light of the New, the hermeneutics of the *figura* also served, from the Church Fathers to Dante, as a tool for assimilating *post*-Biblical events to the Master Writing of Scripture: "what Dante does, in his journey, Christ *has* done. Dante's descent into Hell, and his release from it, is a typological repetition, a 'subfulfillment' of Christ's."[24] The Puritan divines in whose writings Warner was steeped exploited the *figura*'s "post-Scriptural" potential to the full, above all to write their own history as a "subfulfillment" of the Word. From here it was a short step to finding typological correspondences in natural history too. In a "world slickt up in types" (Edward Taylor), God's cross-references graced every page of the book of His creation.

The Wide, Wide World is slickt up in stereotypes. Here is Warner's *typos,* the mark of her covenant to write, like Dante, "in imitation of God's way of writing."[25] Lest we miss its significance, exemplary characters regularly affirm the wide world's stereotypicality, chiefly by assimilating Ellen's history to the canonical texts it "subfulfills." Showing her that her experience has already been had, they show *us* the aesthetic function of the ugly fault that sets its immutable course: Ellen, they make one see, is a throwback to our first Mother. Taking her Scripturally pre-scripted place in the story of sin prim-Eval, she enters her author's claim to have written a *fiction non-novel.*

It is a problematic claim. Even as he validated it, John Hart pinpointed the problem. *The Wide, Wide World,* he exclaimed in his *Female Prose Writers,* was "one of the most original and beautiful works of fiction of which American literature can boast . . . the only professed novel in which real religion, at least as understood by evangelical Christians, is exhibited with truth."[26] An original fiction that faithfully recites the eternal verities: the formula goes straight to the paradoxical heart of Warner's aesthetic. If the archetypicality of her pilgrim's progress implies the timeless validity of Holy Writ, the mere existence of a *Wide, Wide World* implies that Holy Writ has to be wholly rewritten. "One book like it is not written in an age," declaimed *The New York Times*[27]; this was, whatever the reviewer's intentions, equivocal praise. Had Warner authentically imitated God's way of writing? Or had she impiously foisted off an original as a copy?

Her misgivings over what she (or God) had wrought crystalized as a problem of genre: the novel Hart called a "professed novel" did not in fact profess to be a novel. Like all Warner's novels, it professed to be a "story." Caroline Kirkland might contrast *The Wide, Wide World*'s "respectability" with the degeneracy of earlier novels;[28] Warner knew, like generations of Calvinists before her, that her genre was innately depraved.[29] Small wonder that her sister Anna turned a look of "troubled surprise" on a friend indiscreet enough to call Susan's "novels" by their proper name.[30] But we can cite higher authority than Susan's sister's. At the end of *The Wide, Wide World*, Ellen's "brother" secures her promise to "read no novels" (564). He does not trouble to name his reason.

He does not have to: the reason lies in the name. The novel's *novelty*, precisely, challenges "real religion's" timelessness. Yet the "post-Scriptural" extension of typology implies a capacity to engage novelty that is fully exploited only *by* the novel. The problem was that, by Warner's day, the novel was threatening to put the typological cart before the spiritual horse. Once one pole of the *figura* was planted outside Scripture, in human or natural history, the Biblical letter itself sank inexorably toward the level of the postscriptural. A "world slickt up in types" authorized a "potential symbolization of all natural phenomena" that must ultimately put spiritualized nature on the same footing as the Scripture it verified.[31] The implications, celebrated by Emerson, tormented his sometime student Beulah Benton, a fictional scribbler fashioned in the image of the real ones: "She was perplexed to draw the exact line of demarcation between myths and realities; then followed doubts as to the necessity, and finally, as to the probability and possibility of an external, verbal revelation."[32]

Warner sought to sidestep such pitfalls by carrying the effacement of the scribbler signifier to the limit, by practicing a textual self-abnegation without reserve. Since novel writing, by its nature, blurs the "line of demarcation" between Scripture and scribbling,[33] the *figuras* of the (non)novel must be relentlessly denatured; to present the wide world *sub specie aeternitatis*, and no mistake, the stereotypical had to perform *on its own substance* the act of converting ephemeral nature into enduring spirit. Only by that sacrifice of its own natural part could the scribbler text approach the pure immanence of (if one may be forgiven the pun) a Divine Enunciation. But, as a fiction purged of the dross of its natural signifiers is no fiction at all, this amounts to saying that Divine Enunciation portends obliteration of *The Wide, Wide World*. John says no less. "'I know,'" he tells Ellen, "'that a day is to come when those heavens shall be wrapped up together as a scroll—they shall vanish away like smoke, and the earth shall wax old like a garment;—and it and all the works that are therein shall be burned up.'" (312)

This is, as it were, a self-effacing prophecy. For the John citing John citing Jesus citing His Father[34] is not exactly quoting; *he is the quotation.* "Typologically repeating" the John whose revelations he reveals to Ellen, the divine proclaims the nullity of the (non)novel writing that (re)produces him; recalling the impending annihilation of the wide world and its works, he symbolically undoes the (non)work which is *The Wide, Wide World*. Through her *typos*'s representative and redeeming self-sacrifice, Warner offers to absolve herself of the sin of originality.

Yet John *Humphreys* remains his author's creature, *The Wide, Wide World* her creation; the day when they shall vanish away like smoke is not yet. If Warner is to avoid even provisionally impersonating her Creator, the relationship between the author and her creation must be inverted: her creature has somehow to make her *his*. *John* must stand godfather to Warner's (re)production of the Word, and hence, not least, of John. He does so by preserving what he prophetically destroys; he redeems the very nature Divine Enunciation spirits away.

That he can is owing to his status as a doubly privileged *figura*. For John recalls not only the John who comes after Jesus (the John of Revelation, traditionally identified with the John who became a second son to Jesus' mother), but also the John who goes before Him; he thus (ex post facto) prefigures Christ. Especially for Ellen: his are "the hands," Warner says, "of all the most successful" in tending the divine "seed" implanted in her (569). They assume their sacerdotal task, as we have noted, at Christmas, seizing the reins of a plot against Ellen's passion until then conducted by . . . whom? By (representative of all the others) Ellen's stern (aunt) Fortune; by "time, 'that rider that breaks youth'"; by the Writer who pens "the great book of [Ellen's] fate."[35] Nominally, that book is Warner's; by rights, it is the Divine Author's. But not even He writes alone. His text is time's and Fortune's: it is collectively written by all those whose youth-breaking power is summed up and surpassed in John—the rider who rights Ellen's original fault, and thus the writer who (re)writes the great book of her fate. In a word, coming into *The Wide, Wide World* to go about his Father's business, John also takes over his author's. Relieved, under the new dispensation, of the "anxiety of authorship,"[36] Warner authorizes herself to create *The Wide, Wide World* by *de-authorizing* herself. *John* writes in imitation of God's way of writing; his putative author trails after time's rider.

Ellen is what John writes on. He reworks her nature as he reworks his horse's; with a "judicious use of the whip and spur" (377), he forms her into the *typos* she was born to become. Chastening is thus erected into a *figura* of figuration. This is what makes Ellen, in her turn, a privileged *figura*. A type in the making, *she types the (non)novel*—and hence the wide world as well as *The Wide, Wide World*.

Yet the world Ellen types is more than an inert vessel for the Word. The child-woman does not passively reflect the Father; she actively reproduces him. "'There is a friend,'" quotes Alice, after exhorting Ellen to bear with her (aunt) Fortune "manfully," "'that sticketh closer than a brother.'" This delicate allusion (whose immediate source is Widow Vawse, p. 189) to our *imitatio Christi's* limits also stakes out those of the fiction he figures in: it says that scribbling is to Scripture as John's rod is to the Lord's scepter. But has Ellen truly grasped the imitation's limitations? Her response to her "sister" suggests quite the opposite. "'How soon,'" anxiously inquires the heroine, "'is Mr. John going away?'" (321).[37] To be sure, a glimpse into the little lady's fantasy life partially dispels the impression this creates:

> "What was your little head busied upon a while ago?" [John asked Ellen] . . ."Well?"—
>
> "I was thinking—do you want me to tell you? . . . I was thinking about Jesus Christ," said Ellen in a low tone. (407)

Alongside this soulful confession, however, honesty compels us to range another. It is wrested from Ellen by Mr. Lindsay, a natural relation who, since he himself aspires to become Ellen's father, equally disapproves her devotion to God and to John:[38]

> "What was the matter with you this afternoon?" . . .
>
> "Must I tell you all, sir? . . . I wish you wouldn't ask me further; please do not!—I shall displease you again."
>
> "I will not be displeased."
>
> "I was thinking of Mr. Humphreys," said Ellen in a low tone. (534)

Is the pattern of Ellen's low-toned musings symptomatic? Does she take all too literally Alice's advice to parry Fortune's blows "manfully"? If she "'do[es] sometimes seek [the Divinity's] face very much when [she] cannot find it'" (471), is it because her divine's keeps getting in the way? Doubtless. But to claim that, for Ellen, it is *John* who sticketh closer than a brother would be to claim both too little and too much. It is Jesus Christ, *and* Ellen's "brother."

That is, the child-woman (to spill a secret evident since John began to keep her right at the Christmas party) yokes the Divinity and her divine in a natural *figura* of godhead; she "beholds [God] with reverent desire in the mirrors that reveal him."[39] Thus, even while being written on, Ellen sustains the rider who (re)rights her; (mis)conceiving Jesus as her John, she brings God into the world. (Child-womanly) nature forges the instrument of its chastening: Ellen *makes* her chastener into time's rider. Associating her hero and her Author by prostrating herself before both, she associates herself with her author in (re)creating her Creator.

One might take John's law of *association* as the law of this association. That, however, would be to place *The Wide, Wide World* under the sign of the contingent, and thus the novel. Not accidentally, Warner launches her version of gospel by evoking the perversions this can breed. Had Ellen's mother had better doctors, might her depraved daughter not have forged godhead into an image of maternal authority? But what would become of the (stereo)typological if one's mother came to type the Father? What, on the other hand, ensures that she will not, in the realm of the novel writing that naturally deviates from Holy Writ?

Child-womanly nature does. By the miracle of commutation, Ellen is *instinctively* constrained to associate God with familial gentlemen. For her, the Father is, precisely, a father, and His beloved Son a "brother"; she embraces the saving Word because she adores the family member it is figured by. Her girlish weakness motivates the apparently arbitrary bond between the transcendental Signified and its worldly signifier. "'There is something wrong then with you, Ellie,'" says John, when she confesses a chronic inability to find God's face (471). Need we add that, if there were not, her "brother" could never become time's rider? That it is because the child-woman wants him to right her that she embraces the Master Writing of Scripture? That, consequently, her weakness underwrites both religion's happy reign *and* the reigning scribbler aesthetic?

And yet there *is* something wrong with Ellen. She rewrites the supernatural as the familiar/familial because hers are the narrow limits of the wide, wide world; so rewriting it, she inevitably *wrongs* it. Not that she thereby *misrepresents* the otherworldly: the family, Warner knows better than Hegel, "represents and typifies in a figure the life of spirit." But if this familiar figure is not a defective representation, it nevertheless has the defect of being a *representation:* between it and the pure immanence of godhead stands the barrier of "natural relation."[40] The demerit of the child-woman as of the *figura* is to erect that barrier.

Is it Ellen's glory, or her shame, that she can bring down what she erects? Everything rides on the answer—one's assessment, not only of the child-woman, but of the (non)novel too. For the latter, as everybody knows, is preeminently her genre. Indeed, one might go so far as to say that it is her *gender,* rewrought as an aesthetic. Naturally relating the life of spirit, the novel enacts the child-woman's inmost wish to relate naturally to the life of spirit; figuring God as a natural relation, it enables her to engage Him in barrier-breaking natural relations. "'Do not fancy he is away up in heaven out of reach of hearing,'" her gentleman friend once admonished Ellen; " 'he is here, close to you . . . and knows every wish and throb of your heart'" (73). It is because He sticketh as closely as this that His daughter can relate to her "brother" as to her Father's Son. And it is because he sticketh *closer* than a brother—as closely as the John the gentleman only prefigures—that she can eventually rise from the rank of "sister" to that of bride of Christ. Which is to say—by a logic in which typology, theogony, and aesthetics coincide—that she can envision one day *becoming her Father's mother.*[41] Warner's, in short, is a natural imitation of God's way of writing, a child-womanly and yet divinely authorized conception of the living Word. The ultimate stake of *The Wide, Wide World* is imaginary Holy Patrifratrimatrimony.

Or else it is incest on the grandest conceivable scale.

What demarcates the improper from the immaculate conception of Divine Enunciation? How is Scripture to be discriminated from the foulest scribbling, the all-embracing Word from the (un)naturally proliferating word, a natural relation to godhead from apocalyptically unnatural relations? Plainly, the Father cannot sequester Himself up in Heaven out of worldly passion's reach, dooming the d———d mob to write alone. Is His sole remaining option to entice woman's fiction toward the thin line of demarcation between the ethereal and the venereal—only to hurl it back into the chastening nothingness figured by Alice's anti-incestuous death? Must scribblerdom join the Humphreys (John and Heman) in deriding womanly writing? Does woman's fiction have no choice but to image its "holy alliance" with the Word as that necrophiliac revel John seems to promise his moribund sister?

Happily, Warner holds out a practical alternative. For her as for Hegel, there exists a natural relation untainted by natural relations: *one* familial figure straddles the line of demarcation between the Word and the world. No need to open the *Phenomenology* to say which one it is. "The brother," Warner has proclaimed the length and breadth of *The Wide, Wide World,* "is in the eyes of the sister a being whose nature is unperturbed by desire," "her recognition in him . . . pure and unmixed with any sexual relation."[42] That the sister can mingle with her father's son in "pure," "unmixed" and yet natural union is nature's way of saving the scribbler aesthetic; "un-

perturbed by desire," *this* (un)natural bond, than which "no relationship is more pure," guarantees that the *figura* of the *figura* can reproduce God without prejudice to the rod.[43] Cast in its matrix, every *typos* bears the stamp of Divine Enunciation. The irreproachability of woman's fiction's conception of God is figured by the chaste passion which welds Ellen to her "brother"; that of the spiritual power which fecundates the figural, in the chaste chastening rod with which John rights his "sister." Heaven can boast nothing holier than the natural relation between natural relations at the heart of the fiction non-novel's natural relation of the Word.

The *Phenomenology* leaves it at that. *The Wide, Wide World* takes a more dialectical view of the affair. It is encapsulated in the invisible inverted commas that distinguish Warner's siblings from Hegel's: her natural relations are "natural relations." "'This person you call your brother—'" Mr. Lindsay jealously demands of Ellen, "'do you mean to say you have the same regard for him as if he had been born so?'" Replies the heroine, passionately: "'No . . . but a thousand times more!'" (530). John, in other words, sticketh a thousand times closer than a brother. But is this because he is a thousand times the brother, or because he is, after all, only a "brother"? The little lines of demarcation are conspicuously absent from Warner's text; the way she writes it, Ellen's "'brother'" is simply a "brother." Could one ask for a clearer sign that the sole difference between super-natural relations and supernatural relations is, in the final analysis, writing alone?

But writing, in Warner, makes a *double* difference. The (anti)incestuous writing which is *The Wide, Wide World* is also the rerighting which makes incest (im)possible by deferring it to the end of the wide, wide world. To abolish the novel, then, would be to collapse back into the (im)purity of the undifferentiated Word. The worldly *typos* of that preverbal fusion is familiar: it is the unhallowed alliance of the child-woman and her mother. Its otherworldly *typos* is familiar too; it is the (un)holy alliance of the child-woman and her Father. One had better not, then, deride writing: for the duration of *The Wide, Wide World,* it is the only available means of suspending Unholy Patrimatrimony. Yet the cunning of incestuous reason derides writing from within the very scene of righting. What, if not writing alone, breeds the textual perversion that equates the Father's *righting* Ellen with her brother's *riding* her? What, if not the perverse word, permits that conning of reason which—whether the fault be one of genre, or gender, or both—conjugates proper and improper from one end of woman's fiction to the other? Like the child-womanly teapot (cf. p. 103) or the Paternal-fraternal rod, the word too offers consummation in the present moment—even as it defers it to an all-consuming moment that never comes. Womanly fiction's *figuras* disfigure what they figure; the line of demarcation that sunders "brother" from brother, and Father from lover, is effaced by each stroke of the pen that traces it.

But it is also traced by each stroke of the pen that effaces it. That is why one so badly wants *The Wide, Wide World* to end: in the hope that what comes after will indeed "transcend gender," that a merciful God will at last erase the line so frustratingly effaced and retraced by His rod. Is this prospect of liberation John's ultimate Revelation? Or does he simply promise Ellen more of the same, forever? He has "no doubt," he tells her, that people who "love each other" in this world "will know each other again" in the next. This glimpse of the post-apocalyptic throws him and his "sister" into a "long musing fit," prolonged a great while after Alice joins them (313). Is our trio musing about a happier place than scribblerdom, and do they eventually get there all three? One likes to think so. But writing alone will never tell. Nor will anything else in the wide, wide world. . . .

Notes

[1] Susanna Maria Cummins, *The Lamplighter,* in Donald Koch, ed., *The Lamplighter by Maria Susanna Cummins and Tempest and Sunshine by Mary Jane Holmes* (New York, 1968), p. 239.

[2] Ibid., p. 297.

[3] Baym, *Woman's Fiction: A Guide to Novels by and about Women in America, 1820-1870* (Ithaca, N.Y., 1978), p. 313.

[4] Ibid., p. 44; Jane Tompkins, *Sensational Designs: The Cultural Work of American Fiction, 1790-1860* (New York, 1985), p. 163.

[5] Taking *The Wide, Wide World* as his/her text, someone shows us what happens when one does: "The fact is that Warner cannot *imagine* what it would mean for such a little girl as Ellen Montgomery to be totally depraved." Myers, "The Canonization of Susan Warner," *The New Criterion* (December 1988): 76. As we will see, this is absolutely correct. Venturing even further than D. G. Myers, we will hazard the assertion that *Ellen herself* couldn't imagine what it would be like for Ellen to be totally depraved. But there is more in *The Wide, Wide World* than is contained in Warner's, Ellen's, or Miss Emily's philosophy. There might even be more there than is contained in D. G. Myers's.

[6] Susan Warner, *The Wide, Wide World* (1892; New York, 1987), p. 569. Further references, included in the text, are to the 1987 edition, though the slightly different punctuation of the first edition has been retained. The 1987 publication includes a thitherto wisely suppressed final chapter on Ellen's wedded life, here ignored.

[7] The tension between girlish perfection and girlish passion leaves its mark even on *The Wide, Wide World*'s lexicon; "perfect" and "passionate," William Veeder reports, are Warner's favorite intensifiers. See *Henry James: The Lessons of the Master: Popular Fiction and Personal Style in the Nineteenth Century* (Chicago, 1975), p. 240.

[8] See Elizabeth Wetherell [the pseudonym under which Warner published *The Wide, Wide World*], "Little Ellen and the Shopman," in *The Female Prose Writers of America* (Philadelphia, 1852), pp. 388-95.

[9] Cf. Heman Humphrey, *Domestic Education* (Amherst, Mass., 1840), p. 59: "Never use the rod when you are in a passion."

[10] Two hundred forty-five times before *The Wide, Wide World* ends, according to one F.S.D., "Tears, Idle Tears," *The Critic* (New York), 29 October 1892, pp. 236-37. F.S.D. lists alphabetically every passage in which Ellen breaks down.

[11] Tompkins, *Sensational Designs,* p. 163. As the quoted phrases suggest, Tompkins makes a radically different argument, but we can roundly endorse her conclusion: "It is no accident that [Montgomery] uses her own mother's ring to make the purchase."

[12] Unsurprisingly, Ellen's beloved *maternal* aunt has recently died.

[13] In fact, as we learn 264 pages later, he is Ellen's maternal uncle. The Ellen in question, however, is not *our* Ellen, but a younger admirer of Ellen's a lot *like* Ellen. Ellen seems to have something of an identity problem; she once asks Ellen, "'We have both got the same name . . . how shall we know which is which?'" (284).

[14] In this connection Tompkins, *Sensational Designs,* p. 182, draws a suggestive parallel between *The Wide, Wide World* and *The Story of O.*

[15] Tompkins, *Sensational Designs,* p. 170.

[16] Mary Hiatt, "Susan Warner's Subtext: The Other Side of Piety," *Journal of Evolutionary Psychology* 8 (1987): 257; Tompkins, "Afterword," *Sensational Designs,* p. 600. Joanne Dobson, "The Hidden Hand: Subversion of Cultural Ideology in Three Mid-Nineteenth-Century American Women's Novels," *American Quarterly* 38 (1986): 232, seizes on the fact that Ellen questions John for manhandling his mount, but

omits to mention that it is this very beast, now splendidly disciplined, that carries him to Alice's deathbed as well as to Ellen's rescue. "'Sometimes,'" Alice comments on John's apparent cruelty to animals, it "'is necessary to do such things'" (377). For more on the link between horsewhipping and female education, see the last section of the present chapter.

[17] Tompkins, *Sensational Designs,* p. 167.

[18] For a sympathetic discussion of Nancy's naughtiness, see Hiatt, "Susan Warner's Subtext," pp. 254-55.

[19] The unmistakable allusion to Poe's "The Man That Was Used Up" shows well enough how Nancy has been squandering the time she should have been devoting to her Bible.

[20] Ellen is not the only scribbler heroine to cast a "sickened" look at a fractured member, and then take energetic measures to save it. For another instance, see p. 142 below.

[21] Kelley, [Mary] *Private Woman,* [*Public Stage: Literary Domesticity in Nineteenth-Century America* (Oxford, 1984),] p. 293.

[22] For an extended treatment of mid-century women writers' guilt-ridden attitudes toward writing, see Kelley, *Private Woman,* pp. 180-214. For a different evaluation of female horsemanship (and, therefore, sexuality) in the domestic novel, see Frances Cogan, *All-American Girl: The Ideal of Real Womanhood in Mid-Nineteenth-Century America* (Athens, Ga., 1989), pp. 50-51.

[23] Erich Auerbach, *Mimesis: The Representation of Reality in Western Literature,* trans. Willard Trask (Princeton, 1953), p. 73.

[24] A. C. Charity, *Events and Their Afterlife* (Cambridge, Eng., 1966), p. 245.

[25] Robert Hollander, *Allegory in Dante's Commedia* (Princeton, 1969), p. 62, cited in Sacvan Bercovitch, ed., *Typology and Early American Literature* (Boston, 1972), p. 60.

[26] John Hart, ed., *The Female Prose Writers of America* (Philadelphia, 1852), p. 387.

[27] Quoted in Edward Halsey Foster, *Susan and Anna Warner* (Boston, 1978), Twayne's United States Author Series, vol. 312, p. 119.

[28] Caroline Kirkland, Review of *Queechy* by Susan Warner and *Dollars and Cents* by Anna and Susan Warner, *North American Review* 76 (1853): 109.

[29] No lesser an authority than Humphrey, writing in 1840, concluded—reluctantly, to be sure—that even religious novels worked more harm than good. "What confirms me still more in the opinion," he declared on p. 102 of *Domestic Education,* "is, that even many fathers and mothers in our Israel, who were brought up on the substantial aliment of the old Puritans, are now regaling themselves with the condiments of the nursery, instead of adhering to the meat."

[30] Olivia Stokes, *Letters and Memories of Susan and Anna Bartlett Warner* (New York, 1925), p. 14, cited in Foster, *Susan and Anna Warner,* p. 33.

[31] Ursula Brumm, *American Thought and Religious Typology,* trans. John Hooglund (New Brunswick, N.J., 1970), p. 60.

[32] Augusta Jane Evans [Wilson], *Beulah* (1859; London, n.d. [c. 1861]), p. 271. Beulah, it will be recalled, is the heroine of the best-seller *Beulah,* and an author in her own right.

[33] By mid-century, a male scribbler and professor of theology at Williams could embolden a heroine of his to exclaim: "Fiction! what else are the parables of the New and Old Testament, and probably the whole book of Job?" Joseph Alden, *Elizabeth Benton; or, Religion in Connection with Fashionable Life* (New York, 1846), p. 145, cited in David Reynolds, *Faith in Fiction: The Emergence of Religious Literature in America* (Cambridge, Mass., 1981), p. 93.

[34] Revelations, 1:1-2; Revelations 6:13-15; 2 Peter 3:10; Psalms 102:26; etc. John Humphreys is also, in a sense, citing *his* father, who, like John, is a preacher of the Word—and, incidentally, adores and is adored by his "little girl" (448) Ellen.

[35] Caroline Lee Hentz, *Ernest Linwood* (1856; Boston, 1857), p. 69.

[36] For a discussion of the English variant, see Sandra Gilbert and Susan Gubar, *The Madwoman in the Attic: The Woman Writer and the Nineteenth-Century Literary Imagination* (New Haven, 1979).

[37] Has Ellen been reading Orson Fowler on the sly? He glosses this ambiguous verse as follows: "But, there *is* a 'friend that sticketh closer than a brother.' There is a tie stronger than life. It is that oneness of soul 'which binds two willing hearts' indissolubly together, and makes 'of them twain, one flesh.' Connubial love! . . . Oh, God, we thank thee for emotions thus holy; for bliss thus divine!" *Love and Parentage* (c. 1844; London, n.d.), p. 2.

[38] For more on Ellen's relation with Lindsay and her other natural relations in the United Kingdom, see Hiatt, "Susan Warner's Subtext," pp. 257-59.

[39] Horace Bushnell, "Our Gospel a Gift to the Imagination," in *Horace Bushnell: Sermons* (New York, 1985), ed. Conrad Cherry, p. 114.

[40] *The Phenomenology of Spirit,* trans. James Baillie (Evanston, Ill., 1967), p. 475. For a fuller statement of Hegel's thoughts on this subject in its relation to sister-and-brotherhood, consult the epigraph to this chapter.

[41] It is perhaps unnecessary to point out that we have here the supreme guarantee that the child is father to the woman, hence of the identity between man-child and Law-Man, and so between maternal and daughterly incest.

[42] Hegel, *Phenomenology,* p. 477. On the multiple links between the Immaculate Conception, the Virgin Birth, Hegel, and sisterhood, see Jacques Derrida, *Glas,* trans. John P. Leavey, Jr. and Richard Rand (Lincoln, Nebr., 1986), pp. 177-84, 222-23.

[43] William G. Eliot, *Lectures to Young Women,* 3d ed. (Boston, 1854), p. 85.

Sally Allen McNall on the incest motif in American fiction:

The model of salvation as a regression to simple variations on parent-child relationships is underscored over and over in [American women's] books by a theme of almost-incest. When not marrying men they have always previously thought of as fathers or brothers, women nearly marry their brothers (*Violet*), spend years believing they have done so (*Allworth Abbey*), are suspected of infidelity when found embracing long-lost brothers (*The Forsaken Bride, Ernest Linwood*) or father (*Lena Rivers*). Such plot devices were by no means new to popular fiction of this period; indeed they formed a staple item in the French romances of previous centuries. Yet in this body of American fiction, so obsessively concerned with the fragmentation and re-creation of family relationships, such a plot formula is given new meaning. In the first place, incest was a favorite theme of the Romantic writers of the early and middle part of the century, including such Americans as Melville and Hawthorne. It was characteristic of the Romantic attitude to give new significance to what we would call unconscious desires. . . . We have seen that American women writers enjoyed a somewhat different repertoire of symbolic devices, to much the same end. In Jungian terms, however, both these women and the English Romantic poets may be seen as literary examples of the contrasexual self, as both employ the incest motif.

Sally Allen McNall, in Who is in the House?: A Psychological Study of Two Centuries of Women's Fiction in America, 1795 to the Present, *Elsevier, 1981.*

AUTHORITY AND AUTHORSHIP

Frederick C. Crews (essay date 1966)

SOURCE: "Brotherly Love," in *The Sins of the Fathers: Hawthorne's Psychological Themes,* Oxford University Press, 1966, pp. 44-60.

[*In the following essay, Crews argues that Hawthorne's short story "Alice Doane's Appeal" manifests a narrative tone that reflects simultaneous fascination with and repugnance toward the issue of incest.*]

> "Incest is, like many other incorrect things, a very poetical circumstance."
>
> —Shelley

At the very beginning and very end of his career Hawthorne produced halting, fragmentary works of fiction which are of peculiar interest for their revelation of essential themes. What is subtle and even problematical in his more polished writing leaps plainly into view in these otherwise incoherent works; we can watch him first trying to subdue, and later trying to fend away from consciousness, obsessive attitudes that are successfully sublimated elsewhere. In a psychologically oriented study we must ask the reader to be more patient with such works than their aesthetic value might warrant; like other ruins, they offer special opportunities for knowledge *because* their inmost structure is directly exposed to us.

The chief example of such a work before the late romances is "Alice Doane's Appeal," one of the two surviving narratives from Hawthorne's first collection, "Seven Tales of My Native Land."[1] The story as we have it is not the original version, which Hawthorne tells us escaped burning only because it "chanced to be in kinder custody" (XII, 282) when he destroyed his early works. Rather, it is a reworking and probably an incorporation of that version into an autobiographical framework, so that we are now reading a story within a story. Indeed, three distinct plot-strands, ineptly and confusingly joined, need to be distinguished in the surviving tale. There is a legend of murder and confession in early Salem; an historical pageant of the Salem witch hangings, presented by the Hawthornian narrator as the final scene of his evocation of the past; and finally, the story of the narrator's relating these episodes to two modern young ladies on a tour of Salem's Gallows Hill.[2]

Of the three components, the narrator's modern plot has received the least critical attention; and even the murder plot has been dismissed as "unimportant, an incidental means to a large end."[3] This end, according to one theory, is to communicate to present readers a sense of inherited historical guilt, so that they may "assume the moral responsibilities, the guilt and righteousness," stemming from our national past.[4] If this was Hawthorne's aim, however, some bosom serpent compelled him to thwart it at nearly every point. His own generation of readers is represented only by the narrator and the two ladies who, he assures us gallantly, would have been at home in Paradise (XII, 279). All the emphasis in the "storytelling" part of the plot falls on the inapplicability of the historical material to the sentimental and complacent nineteenth century; the narrator is hard put to keep the ladies' attention, indeed to keep them from giggling at his efforts to move them. The comic wistfulness of *The House of the Seven Gables* and the self-critical irony of *The Blithedale Romance* are thus already discernible, and these qualities undermine any moralistic lesson. Hawthorne is ultimately less interested in his story's moral effect than in the narrator's private reasons for wanting to produce such an effect. It is true that the narrator, like one side of Hawthorne, wants us to be horrified by recalling the spot "where guilt and frenzy consummated the most execrable scene that our history blushes to record" (XII, 280); but it is also true that another side of Hawthorne seems embarrassed by this rhetoric and anxious to neutralize it.

We may begin to see why such embarrassment is called for by examining the atmosphere of the historical pageant at the end of the tale. As we might anticipate by now, Hawthorne's depiction of an injustice in which his own great-great-grandfather was implicated is full of anxiety and disgust. The narrator strives to communicate "the deep, unutterable loathing and horror, the indignation, the affrighted wonder, that wrinkled every brow, and filled the universal heart" (XII, 293). As he introduces the alleged witches he stresses the vicious fantasy and projection behind the charges, which are nevertheless effective in intimidating the accused. One condemned woman does not even know why she is being marched off to execution; a once-proud man is "so broken down by the intolerable hatred heaped upon him" (XII, 293) that he yearns for death; and another woman is "distracted by the universal madness, till feverish dreams were remembered as realities, and she almost believed her guilt" (XII, 293). Again, a mother "groaned inwardly yet with bitterest anguish, for there was her little son among the accusers" (XII, 293). As in Hawthorne's scenes of accusation generally, victims and persecutors are caught up in a collective shame, a cringing before the human spirit's war upon itself.

Such scenes are never dispassionately recounted in Hawthorne's fiction; there is, invariably, a surplus of uneasiness and cruelty that spills over into the narrative tone. Whether or not the narrator is a created character, he always gets seized by the combined fear and contempt that Hawthorne customarily shows toward Puritan tyrants—especially ancestral ones. In the present case John Hathorne does not appear in person, but another figure may be said to stand in his place. Here is the climax of the procession:

> Behind their victims came the afflicted, a guilty and miserable band; villains who had thus avenged themselves on their enemies, and viler wretches, whose cowardice had destroyed their friends; lunatics, whose ravings had chimed in with the madness of the land; and children, who had played a game that the imps of darkness might have envied them, since it disgraced an age, and dipped a people's hands in blood. In the rear of the procession rode a figure on horseback, so darkly conspicuous, so sternly triumphant, that my hearers mistook him for the visible presence of the fiend himself; but it was only his good friend, Cotton Mather, proud of his well-won dignity, as the representative of all the hateful features of his time; the one bloodthirsty man, in whom were concentrated those vices of spirit and errors of opinion that sufficed to madden the whole surrounding multitude. (XIII, 294)

Surely the bitterness of this paragraph was not inspired by an objective study of Cotton Mather's peripheral role in the Salem trials. This Mather is a scapegoat, an object of all the undischarged emotion that has accumulated through the episode. As a figure of tyrannical authority, he of course resembles Endicott in "Endicott and the Red Cross"; but here there is no ambiguity of patriotism, no ironic balancing-off of rival tyrannies. Rather, there is a concentrated outburst of hatred against the arch-tormentor. And the loss of control over thematic material is evidenced by the next development. The narrator, who has hitherto failed to engage the emotions of his two auditors, "plunged into my imagination for a blacker horror, and a deeper woe, and pictured the scaffold—" (XII, 294). But at this moment the two ladies begin to tremble and weep, and the historical evocation abruptly stops. The narrator has finally succeeded in his effort to find "whether truth were more powerful than fiction" (XII, 292), but the kind of truth that has reduced both him and his two friends to near-hysteria is psychological, not historical. It is the faithful reflection of repressed hostility, whatever the real object of that hostility may be.

This fact, I think, provides us with a reason—admittedly a vague one—for most of the contradictions and false starts in "Alice Doane's Appeal." Far from tutoring us about the moral meaning of our past, Hawthorne is wholly occupied in mastering an imaginative over-involvement in that past. But it is not "history" *per se* that upsets him; exactly the same emotions that color the Cotton Mather scene are apparent in the one that precedes it, ending the "Alice Doane" segment of the tale. It seems reasonable to ask whether both plots may not hold the same inner significance for Hawthorne—whether the emotional imbalance of one may not be explained by the thematic emphasis of the other. Instead of being "incidental" to the moral about history, the main plot of "Alice Doane's Appeal" suggests an explanation for Hawthorne's furtiveness about history—not just here, I would add, but everywhere in his fiction.

Here is a summary of this main plot, much of which is itself hastily summarized by the narrator. Leonard Doane, a young Salemite who as a child has been orphaned by an Indian raid, conceives a wild hatred for a stranger, Walter Brome. The cause is an affection that the wicked sophisticate Walter feels for Leonard's beautiful and virtuous sister Alice. When Walter taunts Leonard "with indubitable proofs of the shame of Alice" (XII, 286), Leonard murders him. Leonard confesses the deed to an old wizard who, it transpires, had prearranged everything that has happened thus far. In the shadowy company of the wizard, Alice and Walter make a midnight visit to a graveyard containing all the dead in Salem's history, and are treated to a spectral pageant. The sinful souls of the damned are joined by "fiends counterfeiting the likeness of departed saints" (XII, 290). The whole evil group, we learn, is assembled to revel in the wizard's successful machinations, which become doubly horrible when Walter Brome is revealed to have been Leonard's long-lost brother. But the story ends on a note of triumphant virtue: Alice gets Walter's ghost to absolve her from guilt, and the bad spirits flee "as from the sinless presence of an angel" (XII, 292).

It takes very little reflection to see that these Gothic clichés of plotting are tied to a concern with incest. Most obviously, Alice Doane may have committed incest with Walter Brome, her brother. Understandably, though, the question is thickly cloaked in ambiguity. Hawthorne assures us of Alice's spotless virtue, but then hints at her "undefinable, but powerful interest in the unknown youth" (XII, 286). Next come the "indubitable proofs of shame," but they turn out to be less than indubitable; Leonard is "now tortured by the idea of his sister's guilt, yet sometimes yielding to a conviction of her purity" (XII, 287). The wizard's fiendish laughter at Leonard's story of revenge suggests that perhaps Alice was innocent after all. Then, however, we discover that the wizard had "cunningly devised that Walter Brome should tempt his unknown sister to guilt and shame" (XII, 291f.)—seemingly a plain indication that the act took place. Yet in the very next sentence the graveyard fiends are described as eager to learn whether the wizard's plan was really consummated; and we are finally left to infer, not without misgiving, that the ghost's "absolving her from every stain" (XII, 292) includes not only a disavowal of Alice's *willingness* to commit incest, but a rejection of the idea that the act occurred at all.

However much this vacillation may be due to Hawthorne's own discomfort with the subject of incest, its immediate reference in the story is to Leonard Doane's mind. His intense affection for his sister, which he likes to think of as a "consecrated fervor" (XII, 284), verges into sexual passion, and his no less intense hatred for Walter Brome is composed at least in part of sexual jealousy. These facts are established in Leonard's confession to the wizard, which we must quote at length:

> "Searching," continued Leonard, "into the breast of Walter Brome, I at length found a cause why Alice must inevitably love him. For he was my very counterpart! I compared his mind by each individual portion, and as a whole, with mine. There was a resemblance from which I shrunk with sickness, and loathing, and horror, as if my own features had come and stared upon me in a solitary place, or had met me in struggling through a crowd. Nay! the very same thoughts would often express themselves in the same words from our lips, proving a hateful sympathy in our secret souls. His education, indeed, in the cities of the old world, and mine in this rude wilderness, had wrought a superficial difference. The evil of his character, also, had been strengthened and rendered prominent by a reckless and ungoverned life, while mine had been softened and purified by the gentle and holy nature of Alice. But my soul had been conscious of the germ of all the fierce and deep passions, and of all the many varieties of wickedness, which accident had brought to their full maturity in him. Nor will I deny that, in the accursed one, I could see the withered blossom of every virtue, which, by a happier culture, had been made to bring forth fruit in me. Now, here was a man whom Alice might love with all the strength of sisterly affection, added to that impure passion which alone engrosses all the heart. The stranger would have more than the love which had been gathered to me from the many graves of our household—and I be desolate!" (XII, 285)

Only the most gullible reader could take Leonard's reasoning at the end of this passage at face value. He tries to discriminate between "sisterly affection," whose appropriate object is himself, and "impure passion," which can be directed only to a stranger like Walter; yet Walter is his "very counterpart"! In effect he attributes incestuous feelings to his sister by saying that she must be attracted to Walter *because* Walter resembles him. The reason Leonard shrinks from the resemblance "with sickness, and loathing, and horror" is that his counterpart's frankly sexual interest in Alice points up his own surreptitious one. The alter ego to whom all vices are permitted has boasted of enacting Leonard's most secret wish. As so often happens in nineteenth-century plots,[5] and as we see most clearly in Hawthorne's own unfinished romances, incestuous desire is thinly masked by a "fortuitous" discovery of kin relationship. The plot itself, we might say, has committed incest.

Leonard's recognition of the incestuous basis of his hatred for Walter is not quite explicit; yet he *acts as if* he understood this basis, and Hawthorne ensures that we too will understand it. The brothers, he says, are "like joint possessors of an individual nature, which could not become wholly the property of one, unless by the extinction of the other" (XII, 286). This is to say that in murdering Walter, Leonard *becomes* Walter, and that he has nurtured a "Walter" component of himself all along. Indeed, the first mention of Leonard is that he is a young man "characterized by a diseased imagination and morbid feelings" (XII, 284). Alice's excellent influence is said to be "not enough to cure the deep taint of his nature" (XII, 284)—a mordant irony, for Alice's influence is precisely Leonard's problem. His buried passion for her turns his otherwise just indignation at Walter's villainy into an "insane hatred that had kindled his heart into a volume of hellish flame" (XII, 285f.). And most significantly, when he has killed Walter he feels guilty not just for the murder but for something less easily formulated. He finds himself "shuddering with a deeper sense of some unutterable crime, perpetrated, as he imagined, in madness or a dream" (XII, 287). Can there be any question of what crime Hawthorne has in mind?

It appears, then, that at the outset of his effort to "open an intercourse with the world" (I, 17) Hawthorne felt impelled to treat the most shameful of subjects, and to do so in a spirit of turbulent agitation—surely a strange fact if we regard him as a gentle moralist whose essence is repose. That he was not being sufficiently euphemistic about his theme is registered for us by that touchstone of popular taste, Samuel Goodrich, who wrote him in 1830 that while "The Gentle Boy" and "My Kinsman, Major Molineux" could appear in *The Token,* "about 'Alice Doane' I should be more doubtful as to the public approbation."[6] Hawthorne himself never collected or even acknowledged the story, despite his padding-out of the *Twice-Told Tales,* the *Mosses,* and *The Snow-Image* with inferior work. Not until 1883 did "Alice Doane's Appeal" get publicly linked with Hawthorne's name. As Seymour L. Gross has argued, the incest theme must have been especially prominent in the earlier version of the tale, necessitating the addition of the storyteller framework and the summarizing of overly vivid scenes.[7] Everything indicates that Hawthorne was consciously aware that he had hit upon dangerously unmanageable material.[8]

This brings us to consider the chief technical feature of "Alice Doane's Appeal," its displacement of attention from its implicit center of interest. Part of this displacement takes the form of factual obfuscation as to whether Alice really committed incest. Another part consists in the narrator's efforts to make the story palatable to his empty-headed lady friends; and indeed, the ladies seem untroubled by the most troublesome scenes. This in turn is made possible by a convenient

ambiguity within the main plot. Hawthorne enables the casual reader to see Leonard in perfectly conventional terms, as the virtuous brother who avenges his sister's honor. It is only by paying attention to innuendoes that we begin to see the appropriateness of his rage against Walter to his own compromised relationship with Alice. And thus we can say that the very presence of Walter Brome as a stereotyped villain is a further instance of displacement in the story. It is convenient for both Leonard and Hawthorne that Walter is so dastardly, for—so goes the popular logic—only a fiendish cad would relish the idea of seducing his sister. If, to the psychologically minded reader, Leonard has in effect murdered his personified incest wish, to every other reader he has simply been driven to rashness by a noble fraternal impulse.

The principle of displacement also helps us to grasp the role of the wizard, which is far from admirable on aesthetic grounds. Every reader must feel cheated when he is told that the wizard has prearranged the greater part of the plot; with one blow Hawthorne thus cancels all the personal motivation he has so carefully established. Yet this strikes me as exactly why the wizard is useful. He acts as a *deus ex machina* who relieves the other characters of responsibility for their compulsions. At the same time—and this is typical of Hawthorne's circular flights from his themes— his description of the wizard shows us that he has been thinking of unconscious compulsion all along. Though fiendishly evil, the wizard is "senseless as an idiot and feebler than a child to all better purposes" (XII, 284). Under certain conditions, we learn, he "had no power to withhold his aid in unravelling the mystery" (XII, 288). He personifies that portion of the mind which drives men to do things they find abhorrent, and if we confront him honestly he will reveal his machinations.

Lastly, but most revealingly, we must examine a displacement at the very heart of the main plot—a symbolic substitution of one family figure for another. In an extraordinary passage Leonard recounts to the wizard a vision that struck him as Walter Brome lay dead at his feet:

> But it seemed to me that the irrevocable years since childhood had rolled back, and a scene, that had long been confused and broken in my memory, arrayed itself with all its first distinctness. Methought I stood a weeping infant by my father's hearth; by the cold and bloodstained hearth where he lay dead. I heard the childish wail of Alice, and my own cry arose with hers, as we beheld the features of our parent, fierce with the strife and distorted with the pain, in which his spirit had passed away. As I gazed, a cold wind whistled by, and waved my father's hair. Immediately I stood again in the lonesome road, no more a sinless child, but a man of blood, whose tears were falling fast over the

face of his dead enemy. But the delusion was not wholly gone; that face still wore a likeness of my father; and because my soul shrank from the fixed glare of the eyes, I bore the body to the lake . . . (XII, 287)

We must thank Hyatt Waggoner for stressing the power of these lines—and we must question his belief that they have no relevance to the rest of the story.[9] They are irrelevant only in the sense of reaching a level of ultimate motivation that supersedes Leonard's conscious reasoning. Leonard shows us in this moment of vision that by killing Walter he is symbolically reliving the murder of a prior "dead enemy," his father. To be sure, it was an Indian raiding party that performed the first crime; but Leonard's fantasy ambiguously casts himself in the Indians' place. The open murder of Walter becomes horrible to him by virtue of Walter's resemblance to his father, and we may surmise that this resemblance had something to do with the urge to kill him. Leonard has seen in Walter a reincarnation of the dead parent toward whom, we perceive, he has continued to harbor both hostility and penitence. When he has acted upon his hostility he is free to weep tears of remorse—tears that are inappropriate to the despicable Walter but not to the dimly remembered father for whom he stands.

No one who is acquainted with psychoanalytic theory will be astonished by these inferences. Leonard's evident self-blame for a murder he did not commit is paralleled by any number of case-histories in which the accidental death of a consciously revered person—most often a parent—has touched off fantasies of guilt and symptoms of neurosis.[10] Nor should we be surprised at the emergence, under great strain, of a patricidal obsession in Leonard's case. If we recognize, as Hawthorne obliges us to, that Leonard's "diseased imagination and morbid feelings" are focused upon incest wishes, we must find his unresolved filial hatred entirely appropriate. That his morbidity is directed toward a sister rather than a mother is immaterial, for—again following psychoanalytic dogma—this is the expected pattern of deflection. Just as Leonard's brother has become psychologically identical with his father, so, we might infer, Alice Doane is the recipient of feelings whose first object was her mother. The reader is entitled to reject this latter inference as extraneous to the text; yet he can hardly deny that the story's twin themes of incest and murder are connected by Leonard's classically Oedipal feelings toward a father, a brother, and a sister. There is also, of course, room for disagreement as to whether such complexity of motivation can be ascribed to so imperfectly rendered a character as Leonard. As we found in "The Maypole of Merry Mount," the implied motivation resides rather in imagery and plot-configuration than in direct authorial statements; we are free to choose between attaching it to Leonard and calling it self-revelation on Hawthorne's part.[11] Either view is acceptable so long as we recognize the nature of the feelings that govern the general atmosphere of the tale.

Given the emergence of an actual fantasy of patricide in the main plot, we are now in a better position to understand the spirit of the concluding, and supposedly irrelevant, witch-hanging scene. For it is no exaggeration to say that Hawthorne ends his tale on a patricidal note. The arch-villain Cotton Mather is blamed for all the false incrimination of the time, including, we might repeat, the accusation of a "little son" against his mother (XII, 293). Just as Leonard Doane's dead father apparently survives in repressed fantasy, even after remorseful tears have been shed over his surrogate, so the tale abruptly ends in the shadow of a wicked tyrant, unmurdered and newly deserving of that fate. An irrational impulse of vengeance thus connects the "fictitious" part of the story to the "antiquarian" part. It would be far-fetched, of course, to say that the "deep, unutterable loathing and horror" (XII, 293) of the witch-hanging scene are really evoked by the "unutterable crime" (XII, 287) of Leonard's thoughts; the literal situation is sufficient to account for any degree of agony. What we *can* say is that Hawthorne or the narrator treats the two parts of the story in the same spirit—that the fantasy which is fairly explicit in one plot-fragment has not been wholly subdued in the narration of the other.

This fact is made especially clear by the transitional scene that separates the two fragments. We may recall that Alice is finally absolved from guilt by the ghost of Walter Brome, who appears at a midnight convocation of fiends and damned souls, representing all the early founders of Salem. Such a scene is clearly meant as fiction, yet it must also draw upon Hawthorne's sense of his early ancestors. The most striking feature of the ghostly pageant is that nearly every personage is described in terms of family relationship—"the gray ancestor," "the aged mother," "the children," "husbands and wives," "young mothers" and "their first babes" (XII, 289f.). In the place of real fathers there are seemingly admirable authorities: "old defenders of the infant colony," "pastors of the church, famous among the New England clergy" (XII, 290). When the narrator suddenly confesses that all these shapes, many of which were loved and respected in life, are really lost souls, the nature of their damnation is hinted:

> The countenances of those venerable men, whose very features had been hallowed by lives of piety, were contorted now by intolerable pain or hellish passion, and now by an unearthly and derisive merriment. Had the pastors prayed, all saintlike as they seemed, it had been blasphemy. The chaste matrons, too, and the maidens with untasted lips, who had slept in their virgin graves apart from all other dust, now wore a look from which the two trembling mortals shrank, as if the unimaginable sin of twenty worlds were collected there. The faces

of fond lovers, even of such as had pined into the tomb, because there their treasure was, were bent on one another with glances of hatred and smiles of bitter scorn, passions that are to devils what love is to the blest. (XII, 290f.)

This is the first of many such scenes in Hawthorne's fiction, where the entire population of a town will be accused of some undefined wickedness of heart. Here the customary circumlocution—"the unimaginable sin of twenty worlds"—seems less euphemistic in view of the similar language that has been applied to Leonard Doane's sense of guilt. We must consider, as well, that the main emphasis of the passage falls on guilty sexual thoughts; that Leonard and Alice, the embodiments of incestuous love, are shrinking from the spectacle; and that all these damned spectres turn out to have gathered in order to delight in Walter and Alice's incest. Thus the idea of past generations here is in keeping with the story's theme; in some tentative, unformulated sense, ancestry is associated with incestry.

We may note in passing that a similar argument could be drawn from certain images which link one part of the tale to another. Gallows Hill, for example, where the narrator tells his story to the giddy maidens, is said to be covered with wood-wax, a "deceitful verdure" (XII, 279) that simulates grass and in one season puts forth glorious yellow blossoms. From a distance the effect is quite lovely. "But the curious wanderer on the hill," says the narrator portentously, "will perceive that all the grass, and everything that should nourish man or beast, has been destroyed by this vile and ineradicable weed: its tufted roots make the soil their own, and permit nothing else to vegetate among them; so that a physical curse may be said to have blasted the spot, where guilt and frenzy consummated the most execrable scene that our history blushes to record" (XII, 280). The wood-wax bears a symbolic relevance to the story that is about to be told in its midst. Leonard's helpless subjection to incestuous feeling, resting on the apparent purity of his affection for Alice, is comparable to the usurpation of everything natural by the speciously beautiful weed; only on close inspection, Hawthorne implies, do we see that certain growths and blossoms of the personality have exacted a terrible sacrifice. But the immediate reference of the image is, of course, to the witch trials. Probably without conscious intention, Hawthorne blames his ancestors not just for theological error, but for a "guilt and frenzy" whose sources lie deep in unnatural feeling; Leonard Doane's murder of a man who shares his own motives is a psychological counterpart to what the New England magistrates did in 1692. The vile and ineradicable weed of incestuous obsession has done its utmost to choke off every rival theme in Hawthorne's tale.

No wonder, then, that Hawthorne's narrator hesitates to begin his story, backs away in disgust from his own descriptions, and vacillates between erotic insinuation, sarcasm, and apology. Hawthorne himself, we must suppose, shares his narrator's "dread of renewing my acquaintance with fantasies that had lost their charm in the ceaseless flux of mind" (XII, 283). "Alice Doane's Appeal" is striking evidence that Hawthorne's own sense of guilt, rooted in the twin themes of incest and patricide, informs his idea of history and sabotages his efforts at moral objectivity. For Hawthorne, as we shall continue to show, the sense of the past is nothing other than the sense of symbolic family conflict writ large.[12]

Notes

[1] See Adkins, [Nelson F. "The Early Projected Works of Nathaniel Hawthorne,"] *Papers of the Bibliographical Society of America*, XXXIX, [(Second Quarter, 1945),] 121-6. The other conjectured survivor, "The Hollow of the Three Hills," is better controlled than "Alice Doane's Appeal" but highly similar in theme and atmosphere.

[2] However fictional this outer frame of the tale may be, it is clear that Hawthorne wants us to think of himself as the narrating "I." He speaks of his Salem ancestry and the burning of his early works, and alludes to his role as a contributor to *The Token*—which is further grounds for believing that the narrator's part was added at some point after the tale was submitted to *The Token* in 1830 and before it was published there in 1835.

[3] Pearce, [Roy Harvey. "Hawthorne and the Sense of the Past, or, The Immortality of Major Molineux." *ELH*, XXI, [(December 1954),] 337f.

[4] *Ibid.*, 337. Cf. Leslie Fiedler's theory that "Alice Doane's Appeal" is a Gothic "parable of the American Revolution" (*Love and Death in the American Novel*, [(New York, 1960),] p. 43).

[5] See Mario Praz, *The Romantic Agony*, tr. Angus Davidson (New York, 1951), *passim*. This study, first published in 1930, remains a valuable guide to the less sublime side of Romantic self-revelation.

[6] Quoted by Adkins, *Papers of the Bibliographical Society of America*, XXXIX, 128.

[7] "Hawthorne's 'Alice Doane's Appeal,'" *Nineteenth-Century Fiction*, X (December 1955), 232-6.

[8] We know, by the way, that Hawthorne's sister Elizabeth had an unusually frank curiosity about incest, and that she investigated the question of Byron's alleged incest with his sister (see Loggins, *The Hawthornes*, pp. 301f.). Elizabeth is conjectured to have been the person who rescued "Alice Doane's Appeal" from burning, and according to Lathrop she still "retained

some recollection of the story" (XII, 9) in her last years, over half a century after its publication.

[9] *Hawthorne* [:*A Critical Study*] ([Cambridge, Mass.,] 1963 ed.), pp. 52f.

[10] . . . the plot of "Roger Malvin's Burial" turns upon exactly this principle of unconscious logic.

[11] This is Waggoner's view; the death-memory is coherent, he says, only in the light of such circumstances as "the death of Hawthorne's own father when Hawthorne was four, the neuroticism of his mother and his elder sister, his own years of unhappy seclusion, his feeling that he had been 'saved' by his marriage, his lifelong restlessness . . ." (*Hawthorne*, p. 52). I agree with the spirit of this statement, and would only add that the whole of "Alice Doane's Appeal," not just one passage, reveals the same unresolved conflict.

[12] Cf. Ernest Jones: " . . . forefathers are psychologically nothing but fathers at a slight remove." (*Essays in Applied Psycho-Analysis*, Vol. II: *Essays in Folklore, Anthropology, and Religion* [London, 1951], p. 163.)

Eric J. Sundquist (essay date 1977)

SOURCE: "Incest and Imitation in Cooper's *Home As Found*," in *Nineteenth-Century Fiction*, Vol. XXXII, No. 3, December, 1977, pp. 261-84.

[*In the essay that follows, Sundquist claims that the interaction between authority and imitation structures the plot of* Home as Found.]

Cooper is best known for exploring in the Leatherstocking tales that "area of possibility," in the words of R. W. B. Lewis, represented by the American frontier.[1] Still, no one would deny that his dramatizations can be both penetrating and ludicrous on the same page, that the frontier can at times become an area of impossibility populated by stick figures mouthing stylized handbook creeds. In the case of the Leatherstocking novels we quietly utter the word "romance" and tend to forgive, if only to salvage Natty Bumppo as the totem of our literature. What to do with Cooper's "Silk-Stocking Tales,"[2] as Arvid Schulenberger calls *Homeward Bound* (1838) and *Home As Found* (1838), is another thing altogether. It is precisely the point of the second and third Effingham novels, *The Pioneers* (1823) being the first, that Natty Bumppo has vanished over the western horizon and that the area of possibility has become a scene of both chaos and constriction. What was once in *The Pioneers* a difficult tension between the natural virtue of Natty and the civic virtue of Marmaduke Temple has become an inflexible stand-

off between the unharnessed democracy of language and manners in Steadfast Dodge, Aristabulus Bragg, and the general population of Templeton on the one hand, and the inbred self-importance of the socially aristocratic Effinghams on the other. David W. Noble has convincingly argued that in the long run Judge Temple in *The Pioneers* is Cooper's truly intended archetypal hero and that the aim of the Leatherstocking series is finally to depict the collapse and passage of the nostalgic Adamic myth represented by Natty Bumppo.[3] One must add to this that *Home As Found* portrays the consequent near failure of the Judge Temple myth, the myth, that is, of the public leader whose authority is resolute and just, both civically responsible and privately compassionate.

Whatever is wooden in the Judge's character or harsh in his policies in *The Pioneers,* Cooper exaggerates, if in part unintentionally, in the later generations of Effinghams. As abstractions they show up quite well against the uncouth puppet of public opinion, editor Dodge, and the fawning, unmannered land agent Bragg; but in the flesh the Effinghams seem finally, as James Grossman puts it, to be little more than "trained mechanisms of recoil from the vulgar."[4] The rancorous pride which they display is a transparent substitute for Cooper's own, and the family thus occupies a somewhat privileged position among Cooper's automatons. *Home As Found* is not only a biting social satire—one of the best, despite disastrous sections, in American writing—but also an absorbing exhibition and defense of Cooper's own psychological vagaries and social tastes. To this end, D. H. Lawrence's observation that the "Effinghams are like men buried naked to the chin in ant-heaps, to be bitten into extinction by a myriad ants" which secrete "the formic acid of democratic poisoning,"[5] is, though overblown, more indicative of the drastic situation Cooper portrays under the cover of a novel of manners.

The strangulated self-esteem of the Effinghams is, in an important sense, just as much the object of Cooper's ridicule as the Templeton populace, though in an intensely covert and sublimated fashion. What is generally brushed aside as one more piece of rather obtrusive machinery—the disclosure of the mysterious identity of Paul Effingham and his fairy-tale marriage to his cousin Eve—is the very heart of the book, not only because the resolution of the plot hinges upon it, but because aristocratic incest and inbreeding is the last, and most extreme, bulwark against the mob rule which Cooper found threatening himself and his country. We will see too that his treatment of incest is intimately tied to the peculiarly American question of imitation and its relation to social and literary authority. Yet if incest and imitation are part of Cooper's defensive posture, that defense also has the marks of a repression which cannot be sustained but bursts into violent self-parody.

While the degree to which *Home As Found* is auto-biographical has often been presented, it may be well to summarize the pertinent parallels.[6] The Effinghams, like Cooper's own family who resided abroad from 1826 to 1833, return to find their homeland intoxi-cated by wildcat speculation and an inflated faith in democratic "go-aheadism," their ancestors' language degenerating into a discordant medley of cant phrase and barbarous slang, and their fondly remembered Templeton populated by "birds of passage" for whom "'always' means eighteen months, and . . . 'time immemorial' is only since the last general crisis in the money market!" and who consider anything not nailed down to be public property.[7] John Effingham characterizes the home Cooper found on his return when he tells his own family that

> "the whole country is in such a constant state of mutation, that I can only liken it to the game of children, in which, as one quits his corner another runs into it, and he that finds no corner to get into, is the laughing-stock of the others. Fancy that dwelling the residence of one man from childhood to old age; let him then quit it for a year or two, and on his return he would find another in possession, who would treat him as an impertinent intruder, because he had been absent two years." (118)

The trigger for Cooper's satire is the controversy over Three-Mile Point, a picnic area on Lake Otsego, which by law belongs to the Effinghams, but which in their absence the "public" has claimed as its own, upon the authority of a universally acknowledged rumor that from "time immemorial," and by right of the will of Edward Effingham's father, the Point has been owned by the public. Though the will specifically names the Effingham family as heirs, Edward's publication of a warning against trespassing is greeted by a town as-sembly in which resolutions are passed condemning the Effinghams as aristocratic snobs and denouncing their claim to ownership.

Cooper lifted the incident almost directly from his own life, and *Home As Found* is in some respects but the second installment of his vendetta with Cooperstown, the first being his letters that appeared in the *Freeman's Journal* after the Point controversy, explaining the ac-tual ownership and attacking the public. Judge Cooper's will had left the land in his son's trust, designating that it remain the mutual property of the Cooper family until 1850, when it would pass solely to the youngest descendant bearing the name of Cooper. Since his father's will bears directly on the central issues of *Home As Found*, it is worth examining one of Cooper's news-paper letters in detail:

> In 1850, there will be descendants of Judge Cooper in the fifth generation. The family tie, even, is broken by time, and the connexion between these children would be getting to be remote. Intermarriages and females would interpose other names between that of the family of the testator and those of these descendants, and it is only in the direct line that feelings of the sort I have described are long continued. The testator would seem to have foreseen this, and that the tradition and feelings of other families might take the place of his own. He makes a remainder, therefore; and with what intention? To abandon the Point to the public? So far from this, he recalls it to his name and blood, bringing it as near himself, again, as circumstances will at all allow. He even bestows it on the *youngest* of his name, as if expressly to keep it as long as possible in his direct line. In short, he made one of these dispositions of this spot, that men are apt to make, who desire to associate themselves with their remote posterity.[8]

What is at stake here personally for Cooper is the in-tention and honor of his father; what he sees to be at stake publicly is whether or not a man's will shall be respected and his family and property safe from the rapacious democratic fever sweeping the nation. But Cooper's letter reveals too a protective, even obses-sive, regard for the sacrosanct family *name,* as though insuring that the authority of Judge Cooper would prevail from beyond the grave. More important, though, is the fact that it is Cooper's attention to the letter of his father's will which is responsible in *Home As Found* for the elaborate ruse by which Paul Powis becomes an Effingham, thus protecting the continuance of the patriarchal name.

The affair of Three-Mile Point does not dominate *Home As Found,* yet the issues it raises about the authority of the past in America, and how it affects present and future settlement, pervade the book, ei-ther in recognizable displacements of Cooper's per-sonal conflicts or in more general inquiries into American customs and manners. When, for example, Bragg upbraids Sir George Templemore over the fact that in England "industry and enterprise are con-stantly impeded by obstacles that grow out of its recollections" (23) and goes on to "rejoice in being a native of a country in which as few impediments as possible exist to onward impulses" (24), the sat-ire on American progress at the expense of a usable past is hardly exceptional. After Bragg continues by adding that a "man who should resist an improvement in our part of the country, on account of his forefa-thers, would fare badly among his contemporaries" (24), Cooper's hand is beginning to show. But when Cooper plants a question about preference in trees to which Bragg can reply, "the pleasantest tree I can remember was one of my own, out of which the sawyers made a thousand feet of clear stuff, to say nothing of mid-dlings" (25), Cooper's muted rage is getting uncom-fortably close to home. The figure of the tree not only embraces the overall desecration of the wilderness which American settlement entailed, but for Cooper it has a profoundly personal significance: one of the incidents that finally brought him to issue the trespassing warning for the Point was that along with damage done to several cabins on the property, a certain tree, which, Cooper enigmatically reported, "had a *peculiar association connected with my father*,"[9] had been flagrantly cut down. Bragg goes on to say, "the house I was born in was pulled down shortly after my birth, as indeed has been its successor" (25). We have only to recall Henry James's remark, upon returning from abroad to find his birthplace demolished, that the effect "was of having been amputated of half my history,"[10] to gauge the anxiety Cooper has funneled into a relatively innocuous piece of dialogue and into the simple symbols of house and tree which, as we will see, recur in the book in more dramatic roles.

The emblem of the severed tree stands at a personal level for the repudiation of the past that seems to govern the country at a national level. For Cooper, the fact that Americans have no "social capital" and thus "possess no standard for opinion, manners, social maxims, or even language"[11] is directly responsible for the cultural breach which has opened between him and his countrymen, and which has permitted the name and authority of his father to be sullied by a mindless mob. The disrespect for private property, the wrenching daily changes in language, and the blind financial fury of "Western fever" (22) are the most manifest signs of a general "mania of mutations" (130) infecting American life at every juncture. The country is bloated by false ostentation, by the strutting language of Bragg and Dodge, and by mad speculation. Cooper's vignette of New York finance is as penetrating a critique of commerce as sheer game as anything in Emerson or Dreiser. John Effingham takes a somewhat cynical glee in showing Sir George how the increases in value have no foundation whatever, but are "all fancy," all based on the "imaginary estimate" of the auctioneer. Property value, like all other standards, is at the whim of the current owner and increases exponentially with each new buyer. All that matters is to get the property *on paper,* to get it mapped, so that it will rise to its "just value." As the broker informs them, there is "a good deal of the bottom of the sea that brings fair prices in consequence of being well mapped" (101, 102). Cooper is not as handy with the kind of philosophical teasing that would later allow Thoreau to turn the bottom of Walden Pond into a metaphor for America's unsettled foundation; for him the country is demonstrably plunging, like a vehicle careening out of control, "towards the bottom" of its social and economic "institutions" (57).

While Templeton, a virtual replica of Cooperstown, is not exactly consumed by the financial lusts of New York, it is hardly better off. Templeton society has reached and begun to pass through the second of Cooper's cycle of three stages, which is "perhaps the least inviting condition of society that belongs to any country that can claim to be free, and removed from barbarism." In this period following initial settlement, struggles for position begin, but "tastes are too uncultivated to exercise any essential influence," and any manners that do exist "are exposed to the rudest assaults of the coarse-minded and vulgar" (163-64). The memory of the first stage, that of Judge Temple and *The Pioneers,* is "already passing into tradition," and set dead against the few remaining "relics of the olden time [are] the birds of passage so often named, a numerous and restless class, that of themselves are almost sufficient to destroy whatever there is of poetry or of local attachment in any region where they resort." The only hope lies with those who, like the Effinghams, believe "the temple in which their fathers had worshipped more hallowed than strange altars; the sods that [cover] their fathers' heads, more sacred than the clods that [are] upturned by the plough; and the places of their childhood and childish sports dearer than the highway trodden by a nameless multitude" (165-66).

Critics have labeled the Effingham family variously and located their beliefs at different distances from a line running between Jefferson and Jackson. While John's republican cynicism and Edward's more idealized and calculated defiance of the town can be read as two sides of Cooper himself, the latter is obviously supposed to prevail as Cooper's truest voice. Yet their particular creeds, which are never very clear in the book (they are more clearly put in *The American Democrat*), are not so important as their joint attempt at a stolid representation of correct form in the face of rampant social disintegration. The wall of manners and breeding thrown up by the Effinghams barely keeps out the surrounding chaos, however, and it does so only by cutting them off into a restricted world where purity comes to equal artificiality in the most disturbing fashion. In *Home As Found,* as in all his fiction, Cooper is concerned with social clashes and the barriers that keep one group clean and cast out another. Natty Bumppo is the most obvious example of the tragedy which the legitimization of society entails. What continually haunts Cooper, though, is that too far outside of society is lawlessness and anarchy, but too deep inside it is denial of freedom, if not outright suffocation; Natty can survive only on the outside, beyond the fringes, while the Effinghams can only survive, though deadeningly, at the very core. Living at the center of Templeton, they are the fixed standard, while the surrounding riff-raff are the human equivalent of that deceitful network of "opinion always vibrating around the centre of truth" (374). The Effinghams stand still, or attempt to, but America gyrates wildly about them.

One way to stand still is to repeat; one thing that gains a particular power by repetition is a name. As we have seen, the desire of Cooper's father to perpetuate the yoke of his *name* and his *land* is what governs from the start his son's interest in the issue. Cooper understood as well as Whitman that "all the greatness of any land, at any time, lies folded in its names," that "names are the turning point of who shall be master."[12] The problem of giving names, of keeping them, and of making them respectable is for Cooper intimately bound up with the backsliding of American values, the rampaging commercialism, and the decay of language. The Effinghams find on their return that "even the names of a place undergo periodical mutations, as well as everything else" (117) and that those "who have flocked into the Middle States within the last thirty years . . . are not satisfied with permitting any family or thing to possess the name it originally enjoyed, if there exists the least opportunity to change it" (51).

Names have ceased to mean anything in America (or perhaps have not yet begun to mean anything) and function merely as badges of convenience. The nadir of linguistic democracy, one imagines, is reached in the scene in which Ordeal Bumgrum wants to borrow Mrs. Abbott's name for his mother's use on a trip to Utica; Mrs. Bumgrum complains that "folks don't treat her half as well when she is called Bumgrum as when she has another name," and she decides to try Mrs. Abbott's this time (232). This is ludicrous enough, especially in view of the fact that Mrs. Abbott spends the day sending her children around town to borrow one utensil or another as a pretext to cull the current gossip. In divesting Mrs. Abbott of her name, though, Cooper is setting up a specific effect, as is revealed soon after when Dodge and Mrs. Abbott debate Edward Effingham's ownership of Three-Mile Point:

> "But he does not own it," interrupted Mrs. Abbott. "Ever since I have known Templeton the public has owned it. The public, moreover, says it owns it, and what the public says in this happy country is law."

> "But, allowing that the public does not own—"

> "It does own it, Mr. Dodge," the nameless repeated positively. (237)

This is an irritatingly effective example of Cooper's contention in *The American Democrat* that "'THEY say' is the monarch of this country."[13] It intimates as well that in Cooper's America legal rights threaten not to issue from an identifiable authority but to arise almost magically from a nameless repetition of rumor and hearsay.

Just as ridiculous as Mrs. Bumgrum's borrowed name are the mock hybrid names of the Abbott children—Orlando Furioso, Bianca-Alzuma-Ann, Roger-Demetrius-Benjamin, and Rinaldo-Rinaldini-Timothy (229-31). Cooper's satire is not without problems though, for who, after all, is his hero?—a character who is first

identified by the townspeople as a poet because he has no name at all (133), who admits in his marriage proposal to Eve that he bears "a name to which I have no legal title" (349), and who must, when all is told, carry around the ponderous appellation of Paul Blunt-Powis-Assheton-Effingham, the first surname being his disguise in *Homeward Bound,* the second his stepfather's name, the third his real father's false married name, and the last his father's true name. The Abbotts violate decorum by a corrupt imitation of age-old European names, while they at the same time represent the grafting so integral to American naming. Paul Effingham fulfills his function as hero precisely by escaping a tangle of names and assuming the name with a history of respect; but he at the same time exists perilously close, if not to burlesque, at least to taboo, for his role is to imitate *exactly,* to bind and secure the sacred family name by incest. How important this problem is for Cooper appears in the most tossed off but unnerving speech in the book, that delivered by Eve when she is playfully miffed to discover that her almost husband is also her blood cousin: "You abridge me of my rights, in denying me a change of name. . . . What a happy lot is mine! . . . finding my married home the same as the home of my childhood!" (396). This is *home as found* with a vengeance.

The problem of naming and of the right to a name is always a central one for Cooper. Natty's reply in *The Deerslayer* when Hetty Hutter asks his name is the famous example: "That's a question more easily asked than it is answered." It is a question answered with difficulty because Natty, as he proves, has "borne more names than some of the greatest chiefs in all America."[14] Natty's name changes with his prowess as he undergoes an extended initiation ritual reaching a preliminary climax at "Deerslayer," a process Richard Slotkin has described as a totemistic marriage of hunter and beast whereby the hunter takes on the powers and name of his prey.[15] Since *The Deerslayer* was written three years after *Home As Found* and can be read at least in part as a last desperate recuperation of the Leatherstocking myth, the emphasis Cooper puts on Natty's names not only romanticizes him as a mysterious patriarchal figure, but also opens an enormous ironic rift between the nostalgic wilderness and the settled Templeton. Natty's string of names, gained by ordeal, is juxtaposed to the foolish hybrids of the Abbott children; but more significantly it highlights the trap Cooper lays with Paul's palimpsest of names. A perplexing distance arises between Natty's totemic name, earned by wilderness trial and consecrated in a symbolic marriage to nature, and Paul's final name, earned by the sublimated hunt for an identity which turns out to mimic that of his prey and consecrated in an incestuous marriage. Something drastic has occurred in the interval between Natty's chaste marriage to "nature" and the bond of Paul and Eve, who first by blood and now by sacred ceremony are one another's "natural heirs" (444).

Lewis Leary has maintained that "it would be monstrous to suspect that [Cooper] considered the possibility that a union between two young people, so closely kin and so much of a kind, might lead to sterility. In advance of his time or behind it, Cooper did not maneuver well within conscious subtleties."[16] What must be said about Leary's assessment is that, aside from its probable accuracy regarding Cooper's knowledge of physiology, it plainly skirts the issue. Cooper may be clumsy at times, but the question of incest in *Home As Found* cannot be dismissed so lightly. If nothing else, Leary's own allusion to *Hamlet* ("A little more than kin, and less than kind!") should have led him to ponder one of the book's strangest scenes and to reflect on the fact that both Shakespeare's play and Cooper's novel are concerned with revenge on behalf of a wronged father.[17] The relevance of the scene in question—actually it is not a scene at all, but a two-line epigraph—is not immediately evident. What is crucial is the acting off stage, that is, Cooper's own acting marginally unveiled in the few terse words from *Hamlet* that form the epigraph for chapter 27: "What's Hecuba to him, or he to Hecuba, / That he should weep for her" (395). Hamlet, in the soliloquy closing the second act, refers to the player who has just delivered Aeneas's tale of Priam's slaughter. Hamlet's speech mocks his own balked motivation and speculates on how convincing the player would be if he only had Hamlet's reasons for despair. Cooper's point is not so clear. The action of the chapter includes John Effingham's confession of his dark past—that he is Paul's father—and Paul's and Eve's congratulation of themselves on the fact that Paul has turned out to be an Effingham. There is little of Hecuba in this. But a glance at Hamlet's speech at greater length brings to the surface Cooper's fullest intentions:

Is it not monstrous that this player here,
But in a fiction, in a dream of passion,
Could force his soul so to his own conceit
That, from her working, all his visage wann'd,
Tears in his eyes, distraction in's aspect,
A broken voice, an' his whole function suiting
With forms to his conceit? And all for
  nothing,
For Hecuba!
What's Hecuba to him, or he to Hecuba,
That he should weep for her? What would he
  do
Had he the motive and the cue for passion
That I have? . . .

    . . . . .

                            Yet I,
A dull and muddy-mettled rascal, peak
Like John-a-dreams, unpregnant of my cause,
And can say nothing; no, not for a king,

Upon whose property and most dear life
A damn'd defeat was made. . . .

    . . . . .

Why, what an ass am I! This is most brave,
That I, the son of a dear father murthered,
Prompted to my revenge by heaven and hell,
Must like a whore unpack my heart with
  words,
And fall a-cursing like a very drab . . .

(II.ii.551-62, 566-71, 582-86)[18]

Hamlet goes on, of course, to plan the entrapping play within the play and closes with the lines, "The play's the thing / Wherein I'll catch the conscience of the King" (II.ii.604-5).

The epigraph in context becomes a startling revelation of Cooper's own anxiety and self-consciousness about his novel and the actions it portrays, for it raises pointedly the specters of incest and paternity which haunt *Home As Found*. Behind Cooper's invocation of Hamlet's speech is the affair of Three-Mile Point and Cooper's sense of the violation done his father, so much so that he might well have amended Hamlet's lines to read, "The novel's the thing wherein I'll catch the conscience of the town." Of course Cooper did catch the conscience of the town, was harshly rebuked in the Whig newspapers, counterattacked on his own with libel suits, and spent years in court with barely more gains than losses. What is important to note, though, is Cooper's recognition of his own Hamlet-like impotence and, moreover, of the degree to which his players, like *Hamlet*'s player or even Hamlet himself, have become but strutting actors, figures geared up in a fiction, yet painfully far removed from his own "motive and cue for passion." And it is exactly at the point where the plot of Cooper's novel, with the unraveling of Paul's identity, has become most stupefying and nakedly contrived, that he calls attention to it as an elaborate charade, a tale which in its preposterousness is nearly like the harangue of Aeneas spoken by the player.

Cooper's stark plunge into incest as a means of saving the honor of Paul and Eve's marriage is not strictly necessary; any honorable past would have done for Paul. Turning him into an Effingham is Cooper's desperate ploy, conscious or not, for guarding, even in fiction, his father's desire to perpetuate the bond between his name and his property. More than a mere trick of plot on Cooper's part, as may be the case when Oliver Edwards turns out to be an Effingham in *The Pioneers*, the discovery of Paul's identity in *Home As Found* is a last-ditch effort at *founding* a true and lasting home that will withstand the turmoil of mob democracy. The weight Cooper places on the family bond could not be clearer than it is in the proposal scene of chapters 22 and 23, where a bizarre ritual is played out to secure the marriage. During the waning hours of the Fourth of July celebration, the "Fun of Fire," Eve and Paul walk leisurely through the mazelike, carefully landscaped (though unfinished) garden grounds surrounding the Effingham "Wigwam." After several interruptions and his own hopelessly stylized stammering, Paul gets out what amounts to a proposal, which Eve of course accepts. Paul, elated, continues, "But your father?"—at which point Edward Effingham emerges from the shrubbery, where he has been listening to their conversation, and announces he "is here to confirm what his daughter has just declared" (350). When Edward later refers to the marriage as a "treaty" of which he was the "negotiator" (383), we are hardly surprised, so candidly, even stiltedly, ritualized has the marriage become, the father handling the daughter like property or the stake in a game.

We may be tempted to dismiss the scene as one more bit of heavy-handed staging on Cooper's part. But the staging of the scene is very much to the point. The Effingham grounds stand at the center of Templeton, a weird labyrinth in which the family entourage promenade in two's and three's, crisscrossing each other's paths and watching or listening to one another from behind the bushes, while outside the celebration of independence sputters to an end. It is no more an accident that Cooper's proposal scene is enacted on the Fourth of July than it is that Thoreau took up his abode at Walden that day; both play out the meaning of independence by making desperate statements to their audiences. But if Thoreau's pure democrat would break out of the constricted circle of Concord, Cooper's would draw the circle, in the face of the Templeton populace, ever more snugly about him. For Cooper, marriage is as much a contract as is government; both are intended to be indissoluble. One protects the family, the other the nation, against the common tyranny of the public; and in this respect the drama of incest performed by the Effinghams is as much a political as a social statement. It would be straining reason to suggest that Cooper had in mind a sort of familial suicide on the part of the Effinghams, a deliberate last hurrah in the midst of what they found to be a crumbling aristocratic fortress. But the effect—given Cooper's highly self-conscious staging of the marriage chapters and the ridiculously blatant fairy-tale ending, where Nanny pronounces the marriage a fulfillment of a dream she had four years prior in which Eve marries a prince and all live happily ever after (446-47)—is both comic and grotesque.

Still more intriguing, though, is the fact that the prince Nanny has Eve married to is a "Denmarker." Has Eve married Hamlet? But Cooper is Hamlet. Has she, then, married Cooper? Before the reader objects to this seem-

ingly rash invention, it will be well to remember that Cooper was often accused of rendering his elder sister Hannah, who was killed in a fall from a horse in 1800, in the character of Elizabeth Temple in *The Pioneers*. Though Cooper's own footnote to the scene in which Elizabeth nearly falls from her horse ambiguously confirms the identification and even describes the dead sister as a "second mother,"[19] he was thrown into an uncomfortable position after the publication of *Home As Found*. Since the Whig papers crucified Cooper for presuming, so they thought, to draw his own portrait in the figure of the noble and refined Edward Effingham, Cooper, even though the portrait *is* a piece of dreamy self-flattery, needed a convincing rebuttal. The tack he chose is hardly convincing, but it explodes his motives and desires before our eyes: "I have an interest in clearing up this matter, since, if Elizabeth Temple was Miss Cooper, and I am Edward Effingham, the latter being distinctly stated to be descended from the former, I am left in the awkward predicament of being the son, or grandson, of my own sister!"[20] Cooper's additional disclaimer that "the image [Hannah] has left on my mind is any thing but that which would create a desire to disturb her ashes to form a heroine of a novel. A lapse of forty years has not removed the pain with which I allude to this subject at all"[21] is certainly more moving, but no more convincing; if anything, Cooper's inability to come to terms after forty years with the loss of his motherly sister is in itself enough to require us to plumb more deeply the Effingham dynasty and particularly the union of Paul and Eve. And since Cooper's father is undeniably represented by the testator of the Effingham will, it is not far-fetched to suppose Cooper displaced his own devotion to his sister to the equally dangerous and fantastic affair of the two cousins. That is as close to a representation of incest as Cooper could reasonably come; it is left only for Mrs. Abbott to exclaim that "in a country of laws" this kind of union—whether between Eve and John, whom she first thinks are to be married, or, as it turns out, between Paul and Eve—ought not be permitted (234, 413). Cooper permits it, but his raising it as a legal issue only accentuates his alertness to its full implications, whether cultural or autobiographical.

The garden scene, then, is a kind of spectacle, a ritual action. It takes its place in the long list of representations of the garden which pervade American writing from the Puritans to the present. And if Paul is not named Adam, it is only because Eve's name carries enough force by itself. Yet there are things rank and gross in the nature of this garden. It is still a type of the enclosed garden—almost perversely so an echo of that literary favorite in *Song of Songs* (Song of Sol. 4.12): "A garden enclosed *is* my sister, *my* spouse; A spring shut up, a fountain sealed."[22] But Cooper's aristocratic settlers are no longer exactly in a wilderness, and they must protect themselves not from satanic Indians but from their own mad countrymen. The risk they run, however, is of a suffocating inbreeding. Cooper's American garden is perhaps most like the nightmarish Eden Hawthorne offers in "Rappaccini's Daughter," father and daughter conspiring to trap the new Adam in a poisonous family web. To be sure, Cooper is hardly this blunt, but the upshot of his romance is no less startling.

Blake Nevius has remarked in his admirable study of Cooper's use of landscape how intensely Cooper anticipates Hawthorne's need, "for the purposes of psychological drama, to exploit the possibilities of the close circumscription of space."[23] The limitation of space may reach beyond the obvious clashes entailed by settlement to an even more basic trauma acted out in the imposition of civilization on the wilderness. Cooper's use of the Glenn's Falls cavern in *The Last of the Mohicans,* which Annette Kolodny has analyzed as a womblike enclosure whose protection is shattered by the futile explosion of Duncan Heyward's gun, comes immediately to mind.[24] The Effingham garden, a tilled and cultivated protective fortress of domesticity, performs a similar function. Cooper's vision of the American Eve in *Home As Found* still reflects the more optimistic attitude he entertained about America when he wrote in 1828 in *Notions of the Americans* that America is a virtual "Paradise of woman," a place where she fulfills "the very station for which she was designed by nature. . . . Retired within the sacred precincts of her own abode, she is preserved from the destroying taint of excessive intercourse with the world."[25] In Cooper's case, the natural mythology of America was inflamed by his own familial attachments, however contradictory that may in fact seem. As clearly as Natty's primitive wilderness, the virgin territory defiled by settlement, the Effingham garden stands for a nostalgic protection and a sentimental view of possession. Cooper, like Melville's Pierre, was haunted by the fact that "a sister had been omitted from the text";[26] his recourse was to reinsert her at the center of a quirkily personal myth of the American paradise. The mazelike garden which encloses the Effinghams and structures the marriage pact of the next heirs enacts geographically the circumscription that is occurring genealogically. Order and artifice are opposed to the surrounding moral chaos of Templeton, but the artifice is so severe as to be stunted by its own self-defeating imitation.

Yet *Home As Found* is precisely concerned with the problem of imitation and concomitantly with the disappearance of the American garden, or at least its dream as represented by Natty Bumppo. Old Leatherstocking was on his way out in *The Pioneers;* in *Home As Found* he has become a virtual myth, the land on which his hut once stood a spot to be pointed out during a tour of the countryside and his voice at best a mocking echo. Along with Washington he is one of the van-

ished fathers (200) who have taken with them the possibility of settlement based on natural virtue. The inland journey which the Effinghams make on their return to Templeton illustrates how different the topography of the American dream now is. Though Eve judges favorably the scenic bluffs along the Hudson, her standards are continually European (114-15); and her final pronouncement on Lake Otsego during the view from Mount Vision is as full of panting for antiquities as anything in James's *Hawthorne:* "'Fancy the shores of this lake lined with villas,' said Eve, 'church-towers raising their dark heads among these hills; each mountain crowned with a castle or a crumbling ruin, and all the other accessories of an old state of society, and what would then be the charms of the view!'" (136). Yet this view from the Vision, to which John Effingham cunningly leads the party on their way home, is as deliberately staged as the garden scene. When Cooper announces—after what seems at first a "void" becomes "a *coup d'œil* that was almost Swiss in character and beauty"—that the "whole artifice of the surprise was exposed," the word "artifice" rings with a calculated irony (125). Cooper's chance to display the wild thrills of American landscape falters before both a changed terrain and the strictures of taste he gained in the years abroad. Cultivation in both senses has now forced the view to resemble "the scenery of a vast park or a royal pleasure-ground," "teeming with the fruits of human labor" and such "signs of life" as the network of roads which reproduces on a grand scale the mazed garden surrounding the Wigwam (125-26). Perry Miller has pointed out that the "sublimity of our national backdrop" once "relieved us of having to apologize for a deficiency of picturesque ruins and hoary legends" and guaranteed that the country would "never be contaminated by artificiality."[27] The Cooper of the early Leatherstocking tales would no doubt have agreed; but after his residence abroad, the choice between natural American sublimity and European artifice could never be so simple.

The question of landscape provides a narrower focus on the general problem of originality versus imitation which Cooper ponders continually in *Home As Found,* whether with regard to the maladies of American architecture, social decorum, financial speculation, or his own literary enterprise. On the one hand Cooper denigrates his countrymen for their aping of European social customs, but on the other he recoils in disgust from their most original acts—their reckless abuse of the language, for example, or the public's appropriation of Three-Mile Point. He mocks America's quasi-Grecian dwellings as "whited sepulchres" on the outside which are wasted by "deformity within" (119). Yet his own ideal home, the Effinghams' Wigwam, which is more or less a copy of Cooper's own house, is decorated with a swarm of cheap plaster busts of Shakespeare, Caesar, Milton, Dryden, and Locke, purchased in a New York shop to replace the worn-out Parisian busts of *The Pioneers* (152). Like so many of the seemingly symbolic constructs in *Home As Found,* the collection of venerable heads teeters on the verge of the ridiculous without quite committing itself; one can easily enough imagine Cooper's admiration for the names in question, yet mutely lodged in an American home barely past Cooper's second stage of settlement, the figures rapidly approach the dimensions of travesty.

The busts are a crucial part of Cooper's parodic attack on American imitation, a deliberate "deformity within"; but like his adherence to landscape conventions, they are also a sign of homage and protection—they are Cooper's cultural authorities. One has not, moreover, to look far to find further traces of these revered fathers: we have seen what use Cooper made of two lines from *Hamlet.* Cooper was always fascinated by the authority of written documents; *The Pioneers,* for example, is built on the tension between Natty's natural spirit and the letter of Judge Temple's law. In *Home As Found* the Effingham will, the letters revealing Paul's identity, the family prayerbook, the United States Constitution, and even *The Pioneers* itself are all called on to provide the authority of a text, which is noticeably lacking in America. Cooper makes his characters speak as though from prepared social and political texts precisely to the degree that he feels none exists or that the ones which do are threatened with molestation or destruction. The question of his own literary authority would seem to have become equally acute for Cooper by the time of *Home As Found.* The primarily European epigraphs which stud nearly all his novels are often somewhat buffoonish, particularly in the Leatherstocking· tales, where one would suppose a completely original American myth was being generated. But in *Home As Found,* at least, the epigraphs seem more clearly an integral part of Cooper's defense of all he holds sacred and dear. Like the busts, they are a strange flourish of classicism in what for Cooper was worse than a wilderness. Yet their authority is often equally ironic: the sudden self-flagellation of Hamlet's speech turns the realistic illusion of Cooper's drama into a mock show, unmistakably linking together the revered father and the literary tradition as objects of imitation.

Cooper is running a risk with his epigraphic quotations. It was, after all, only in the 1834 *Letter to His Countrymen,* an attack on the corrosion which the Constitution was suffering through American subservience to and imitation of European handling of governmental affairs, that Cooper denounced the American journalistic "practice of quoting the opinions of foreign nations, by way of helping to make up its own estimate of the degree of merit that belongs to its public men," as one "destructive of those sentiments of self-respect, and of that manliness and independence of thought, that are necessary to render a people great, or a nation respectable."[28] It may be that Cooper spoke so

eloquently against quotation because he had repressed and internalized his own practice so thoroughly. As much as the journalism of the day, Cooper's epigraphs indicate his own submission to European authority, and since his overwhelming concern in *Home As Found* is imitation, they reveal his ambivalence as certainly as the Effingham marriage. Edward W. Said has contended that "quotation is a constant reminder that writing is a form of displacement," that it "symbolizes other writing as encroachment, as a disturbing force moving potentially to take over what is presently being written."[29] If this is the case in *Home As Found,* it is only half the case. The epigraphs are also protection and control; they authorize Cooper's book by their very presence. Since what Cooper is fighting ideologically in his novel is the kind of radical originality and displacement represented by the Templeton populace, his falling back on quotation is more than a literary convention; it is also the signature of his anxious bid for the paternal security of tradition. Shakespeare's name is as talismanic in one sense as Judge Cooper's is in another.

The problems of imitation and authority come together also in Cooper's treatment of Paul Blunt-Powis-Assheton-Effingham. That Paul appears in the book first as a poet, so identified on the basis of the singular fact that he has no name, is no more an accident than the Fourth of July marriage proposal. He is verified as a poet in the eyes of Templeton when he copies the opening couplet of Pope's *Essay on Man*—"which, fortunately, having an allusion to the 'pride of kings,' would pass for original, as well as excellent, in nineteen villages in twenty in America, in these piping times of ultra-republicanism"—and drops it where it is sure to be found by Bragg. As Paul admits to the Effinghams, though, he is no poet at all, merely "a rank plagiarist" (143). The episode indicates Cooper's worry about his own craft; yet since the uncovering of Paul's true name is of crucial importance to Cooper's vision of authority, the gross irony of Paul's feigned career is made clear only when he turns out to be but a *ficelle* for the Effingham family's own "rank plagiarism" of itself.

The Effinghams' incest keeps the family secure in name and blood by erecting a copy, by in effect quoting and repeating its own authority. Paul's role points up the extreme tenuousness not only of authority in America but concurrently of Cooper's desperate groping after it. Especially significant is the fact that *Home As Found* to a certain extent repeats *The Pioneers;* but it does so by way of proving that in fact *The Pioneers* cannot be repeated, that the first imitation of Cooper's home town, presided over by the figure of his father in the guise of Judge Temple, has been trampled down by a herd of fortune-seekers and demagogues. The scene which could not accommodate Natty Bumppo, but shuttled him deeper into the West, is now threatened itself; the

Effinghams' natural aristocracy has contracted into an enclosed camp. Cooper's most effective extension of the problem of imitation shows up in the dialogue between the two books, for his testimony to the vanished past of Natty takes the form of an echo which derides at the same time it honors. The references to Natty in *Home As Found* are, as Kay Seymour House suggests, "thoroughly classical,"[30] since Natty stands for the heroic age past; but Cooper's invocations of the venerable spirit are answered not by sage advice but by grotesque repetition. The echoes which the Effingham party delights in at the Speaking Rocks are though to "come from the spirit of the Leather-Stocking, which keeps about its old haunts, and repeats everything we say, in mockery of the invasion of the woods" (200). The mocking echoes reveal that settlement itself is repetition, a fact which it is Natty's horror continually to realize, since he acts as the harbinger of a process which repeats itself westward across the continent. Cooper could not have found a more chilling way to frame the Effinghams' dynasty than by deriding them with the voice of the very dream their ancestors drove away in the original act of settlement.

As though to make perfectly clear the power that has swept aside the romantic wilderness and opened the way for rapacious progress, Cooper allows the Effinghams to entertain themselves by firing the field artillery stored at Lake Otsego. While the gun-house purports to be a "speaking picture of the entire security of the country, from foes within as well as from foes without" (204), it is only one page later that the Effingham security begins to disintegrate, as John reveals the public's claim to Three-Mile Point (205). Inserted between is the firing of the gun; three times repeated, the reverberations roll down the valley "always with the same magnificent effect, the western hills actually echoing the echoes of the eastern mountains, like the dying strains of some falling music" (204). The progress of the echoes from east to west may be incidental, but the show of power built on copy is an impressive display in the midst of nature—until, that is, the allusion to *Twelfth Night* ("That strain again! it had a dying fall") underlines the military echoes with a literary one and calls ironic attention to their fading force. Paul ensures our recognition that the firing is a show designed to exhibit mock potency when the echoes prompt him to remark that this "locality would be a treasure in the vicinity of a melodramatic theatre . . . for certainly no artificial thunder I have ever heard has equalled this" (205). The echoes which began as a demonstration of security and power have created an enclosure of theatrical artifice that measures the attainment of the Effinghams as accurately as do Natty's mocking echoes. The very center of artifice and convention, it is the Effinghams who are on stage; it is they who are fading echoes. If Natty's Killdeer is the weapon of chastity, the Effinghams' field guns are the ineffectual equipment of failed power and imitation.

In haunting contrast to the echoing rocks and guns, however, stands the "Silent Pine," rising "in solitary glory, a memorial of what the mountains which were yet so rich in vegetation had really been in their days of nature and pride." This "tall, column-like tree," reputed to have a catalytic effect on those of poetic persuasion, is a true "American antiquity." But its age and grandeur alone are not what makes it peculiarly American; what sets it off as an authentic native is the fact that, as poet-plagiarist Paul recognizes, "its silence is, after all, its eloquence" (201-3). This silence can be read several ways, though, as can the highly symbolic tree itself. Its power stems not only from the sublime beauty of the lacuna which was, more or less, American history, but also from its probable link with the severed Point tree which Cooper, as we have seen, intimately connected with his father. The Silent Pine is split between proud defiance and stifled potency. But whether it represents the virile bachelor, isolated in his mistress woods, or the lapsed paternal voice, the upshot is the same: the patriarchal authority is stymied and the echo of generation closed off into either faltering myth or the desperate self-parody of incest.

The Pine's silence belongs on the one hand to the vanishing mythology of Leatherstocking's echoes and the commodore's "patriarchal" but nonsensically named fish, the mythical "sogdollager," yet another American totem like Melville's whale or Faulkner's bear to be married and murdered at the same time (198, 280); but it belongs equally to Paul's missing past. The irony of the fact that it is Paul who names the Pine's eloquence lies in Cooper's need to vocalize the silence of Paul's past by giving him the Effingham name, by giving him a history which will allow him to found an American home by incest and repetition. The names "Effingham" and "sogdollager" stand finally in strange contrast and kinship in *Home As Found.* One is loaded with a history of respect and authority; the other is completely mythical, part of an archetypal fish story. Set alongside the totem animal is the ancestral father; both live by repetition and imitation, the totem by tale and worship, the father by regeneration of his name and blood.

Cooper wrote in his preface to *Notions of the Americans* that he was "not without some of the yearnings of paternity in committing the offspring of his brain to the world."[31] American authors have, of course, been particularly obsessed with *fathering* a tradition which will stand alone. In this respect, Cooper laid the solidest of foundations with the Leatherstocking tales. What he did of equal importance, in *Home As Found* for example, was to call into question the possibility of complete originality. The last Effingham novel is not only Cooper's defense of himself and an attack on his countrymen, it is also a terse exposure of his own precarious position—as a democrat and as a writer; for though he stingingly burlesques America's indulgence in servile social imitation, Cooper's own embracing of incest, his inquiry into the mystery of names, the many self-consciously parodic moments in his narrative, and not least his use of the setting and events of his own life, all combine to expose his own anxiety about both cultural and authorial paternity. *Home As Found* acts out a crucial chapter in the history of American society, but it does so in an arcanely autobiographical and artificial fashion. Precisely because Cooper pursued his revenge on Cooperstown in the public forum of fiction, the book's stylized rituals do not flounder in sentiment. His indulgence in romance, indeed in family romance, both honors and mocks its own commitment, which is to found a home. If the home Cooper found is surprisingly uncanny, *unheimlich*, it is because his one sure locus of authority lay in a sullied name which could be redeemed only by echo.

Notes

[1] *The American Adam: Innocence, Tragedy and Tradition in the Nineteenth Century* (1955; rpt. Chicago: Univ. of Chicago Press, 1971), p. 99.

[2] *Cooper's Theory of Fiction: His Prefaces and Their Relation to His Novels* (Lawrence, Ks.: Univ. of Kansas Press, 1955), p. 50.

[3] "Cooper, Leatherstocking, and the Death of the American Adam," *American Quarterly,* 16 (1964), 419-31.

[4] *James Fenimore Cooper* (New York: William Sloane, 1949), p. 116.

[5] *Studies in Classic American Literature* (1923; New York: Viking Press, 1969). p. 41.

[6] *Home As Found* has too seldom been treated seriously as literature, though there have been several discussions of it as social satire and autobiographical tirade. The most useful and generous are John P. McWilliams, Jr., *Political Justice in a Republic: James Fenimore Cooper's America* (Berkeley: Univ. of California Press, 1972), pp. 216-36; George Dekker, *James Fenimore Cooper: The American Scott* (New York: Barnes and Noble, 1967), pp. 153-60; Marvin Meyers, *The Jacksonian Persuasion: Politics and Belief* (1957; rpt. New York: Vintage, 1960), pp. 74-97; and Lewis Leary's introduction to *Home As Found* (New York: Capricorn Books, 1961).

[7] *Home As Found,* the Mohawk Edition of *The Works of James Fenimore Cooper* (New York: G. P. Putnam's, 1896), pp. 165, 212. Parenthetical page references in my text are to this edition; pagination is the same in the Capricorn paperback edition, except for the preface.

[8] *The Letters and Journals of James Fenimore Cooper,* ed. James Franklin Beard (Cambridge, Mass.: Harvard Univ. Press, 1964), III, 278-79.

[9] *Letters and Journals,* IV, 271.

[10] *The American Scene,* introd. Leon Edel (Bloomington: Indiana Univ. Press, 1968), p. 91.

[11] Cooper's Preface, *Home As Found,* p. iv (Mohawk Edition); p. xxviii (Capricorn Edition).

[12] *An American Primer,* ed. Horace Traubel (Boston: Small, Maynard, 1904), pp. 31, 34.

[13] *The American Democrat,* ed. H. L. Mencken (New York: Knopf, 1931), p. 175. *The American Democrat* and *The Chronicles of Cooperstown,* both published in 1838, the same year as *Home As Found,* were influenced to a certain extent by the Point controversy, and though the latter alludes to it in a general way, the facts and names are not specified. The two books provide, however, an intellectual framework for the more personalized attack Cooper pursued in his novel.

[14] *The Deerslayer,* Red Rover Edition of *The Works of James Fenimore Cooper* (New York: George Putnam's Sons, n.d.), p. 55.

[15] *Regeneration Through Violence: The Mythology of the American Frontier, 1600-1800* (Middletown, Conn.: Wesleyan Univ. Press, 1973), p. 499. "Deerslayer" is not, of course, the end of Natty's name changes, even in that novel. He must yet slay a man and thus become "Hawkeye."

[16] Leary, Introduction, *Home As Found,* p. xix. "Sterility should perhaps be "deformity," for the latter would make clearer the irony inherent in Cooper's indecision as to whether it is aristocracy or democracy which is based on "accidents" of birth and circumstance (pp. 30, 35, 56, 313), and his consequent obsession with proving that Paul himself is not an "accident," that is, illegitimate.

[17] Judge Cooper died in 1809 from pneumonia, which he apparently contracted after being struck on the head from behind by a political opponent, someone whom Cooper could no doubt easily associate years later with the demagoguery plaguing Cooperstown-Templeton and the town's ignorant response to Judge Cooper's will. See *Letters and Journals,* I, 16, n. 1. That Cooper had *Hamlet* on the brain is evident in a veiled allusion in *The American Democrat,* where he remarks that "in a democracy, the delusion that would elsewhere be poured into the ears of the prince, is poured into those of the people" (p. viii).

[18] *The Riverside Shakespeare,* text ed. G. Blakemore Evans (Boston: Houghton Mifflin, 1974); two sets of brackets have been silently removed.

[19] *The Pioneers,* Red Rover Edition of *The Works of James Fenimore Cooper* (New York: George Putnam's Sons, n.d.), p. 236, n. 1.

[20] *Letters and Journals,* IV, 76. It is also worth recalling that *Home As Found* was published in England under the title *Eve Effingham,* which further emphasizes Cooper's sense of her centrality.

[21] Ibid., p. 256.

[22] For the English tradition of the enclosed garden, see Stanley Stewart, *The Enclosed Garden: The Tradition and the Image in Seventeenth-Century Poetry* (Madison: Univ. of Wisconsin Press, 1966); for the enclosed garden in the Puritan tradition, see Peter N. Carroll, *Puritanism and the Wilderness: The Intellectual Significance of the New England Frontier 1629-1700* (New York: Columbia Univ. Press, 1969) and George H. Williams, *Wilderness and Paradise in Christian Thought* (New York: Harper, 1962).

[23] *Cooper's Landscapes: An Essay on the Picturesque Vision* (Berkeley: Univ. of California Press, 1976), pp. 99-100.

[24] *The Lay of the Land: Metaphor as Experience and History in American Life and Letters* (Chapel Hill: Univ. of North Carolina Press, 1975), pp. 97-98.

[25] *Notions of the Americans, Picked Up By a Travelling Bachelor,* 2 vols. (Philadelphia: Carey, Lea, and Carey, 1828), I, 104-5.

[26] Herman Melville, *Pierre; or, The Ambiguities,* ed. Harrison Hayford, Hershel Parker, and G. Thomas Tanselle (Evanston: Northwestern Univ. Press, 1971), p. 7. The parallel is not exact, of course, but a comparison of Cooper's and Melville's treatments of incest is worthwhile. Cooper, it should be noted, remained quite close to his surviving sister, Anne, as his letters to her indicate.

[27] "The Romantic Dilemma in American Nationalism and the Concept of Nature," *Harvard Theological Review,* 48 (1955), 247. For discussions of Cooper's changing attitudes towards and uses of landscape, see Nevius, *Cooper's Landscapes,* and Donald A. Ringe, *The Pictorial Mode: Space and Time in the Art of Bryant, Irving, and Cooper* (Lexington: Univ. Press of Kentucky, 1971).

[28] Quoted in Robert E. Spiller, *Fenimore Cooper: Critic of His Times* (New York: Minton, Balch, 1931), p. 227.

[29] *Beginnings: Intention and Method* (New York: Basic Books, 1975), p. 22.

[30] *Cooper's Americans* (Columbus: Ohio State Univ. Press, 1965), p. 160.

[31] *Notions of the Americans,* I, vii.

Brook Thomas (essay date 1979)

SOURCE: "The Writer's Procreative Urge in *Pierre:* Fictional Freedom or Convoluted Incest?" in *Studies in the Novel,* Vol. XI, No. 4, Winter, 1979, pp. 416-30.

[*In the essay that follows, Thomas studies the significance of human procreation as a figure for writing in Melville's* Pierre; *the title character's unsuccessful attempt to free himself of his family's past reveals the extent to which the authority of a text's author is fictional.*]

One need not subscribe to Edward Said's implied historical schema, which seeks to establish the possibility for a new beginning because of, rather than in spite of, a doubt about origins, to agree with him that much narrative fiction in the nineteenth century is linked intimately with an attempt to reproduce in language the mysteries of human procreation. By no means does Said argue that the attempted metaphoric link between human and artistic procreation is confined to either the novel or the nineteenth century. What he has done is to show a particular manifestation of the metaphor. For Said nineteenth-century narrative sequences reflect an adulterous subversion of the eighteenth century's attempt to create, "by wedding a mimetic, verbal intention to time." The nineteenth century brings about "the substitution of irresponsible celibacy for fruitful marriage." Said enriches his argument by referring to Marx and showing how money is often the seductive force luring the protagonist "from natural procreation to a novelistic enterprise, to living with great expectations."[1]

As Said knows, however, more than money is at stake. Recent critics, most notably Jacques Derrida and Jacques Lacan, have argued that the human/artistic procreation metaphor, in the West at least, is conditioned by a system of patriarchal authority, a system based on a myth giving authority to the Logos; God, the Father; the Word of the Father and the sacred text embodying his Word. Societies in which legitimate political and familial authority is based on the myth of fatherhood may eventually be forced to question the origin of that authority because of a biological fact about fatherhood: a male can never be certain that he has sired his son or daughter. Unlike a female, who carries her child within her for nine months and is still connected to it by the umbilical cord at birth, after conception a male is totally cut off from his child and life's cord. The child no longer needs him to be born or exist. As a result, even though in a patriarchal society the father is given authority over the family, the father's authority is always subject to doubt.[2] Because the father has no connection to his child at birth, because his presence is no longer necessary, the father's claim to authority could be a counterfeit claim.

When we explore the human /artistic procreation metaphor, we find the same questions about origins and authority. The uncertainty of a father's authority over his child is reflected in the uncertainty of an author's authority over his text. Just as after conception a child is totally cut off from his father, so after conception a text is cut off from an author. As soon as an author commits his work to paper, it can live without him. It continues to exist despite the author's absence or even death. Derrida, therefore, defines writing as "a structure of repetition, a structure cut off from any absolute responsibility or from consciousness as ultimate authority, orphaned and separated since birth from the support of the father."[3] According to Derrida it is writing's lack of an incarnated logos that leads Plato to condemn it in the *Phaedrus*. The myth that gives the father authority over the family also seems to give the author authority over his text. In both cases the claim is for the legitimate presence of an authority figure when what we really have is a possible absence.

With this in mind I would like to turn to Melville, one of the nineteenth-century writers whom Said mentions, to show that the questioning of the human procreation metaphor for writing undertaken by today's critics occurs equally exhaustively in the texts of self-conscious writers of fiction. Rather than choosing *Moby-Dick* as Said does, I will choose *Pierre*—a more appropriate text because *Pierre* is Melville's attempt to write a domestic novel. A bizarre companion piece to *Moby-Dick*, which was intended to appeal to a male audience, *Pierre* was directed at the growing female audience for fiction. Furthermore, questions about fatherhood would have been on Melville's mind, because he wrote *Pierre* soon after becoming a father for the second time.[4] Perhaps it is no accident that in exploring the workings of the patriarchal domestic family Melville produces one of his most reflexive novels. Or is it vice-versa? In either case the patriarchal structure of the family and of writing is scrutinized and we are forced to entertain, although not necessarily accept, the possibility that the authority of the father is a fictional creation. Perhaps Said's claim that contemporary American fiction questions its own authority could be extended to the entire reflexive strain of the novel.[5]

For instance, early in *Pierre* the narrator explicitly links the act of writing with the mysterious relationships of the domestic family. Only one hiatus is discoverable by Pierre in the "sweetly-writ manuscript" of his life.

"A sister had been omitted from the text" (p. 7). But Melville's text shortly remedies the situation by providing Pierre with a sister—Isabel. Or at least Isabel is probably his sister. Illegitimate, she is never publicly acknowledged by Pierre's father and she learns of her connection to Pierre only through a series of mysterious coincidences. In fact because of the incertitude of fatherhood, the connection may not be a connection at all. The only two clues establishing Isabel's link to Pierre are, appropriately, a work of art and a name. The work of art, which I will come back to later, is a portrait of Pierre's father as a young bachelor, referred to as the chair portrait. The name, of course, is also the name of Pierre's father: Glendenning.

Denied her father's name because of her illegitimacy, Bell, nonetheless, hears the family she lives with call an occasional visitor her father, and she too refers to him by this word. But the word "father" for Bell did not contain

> all those peculiar associations which the term ordinarily inspires in children. The word father only seemed a word of general love and endearment to me—little or nothing more; it did not seem to involve any claims of any sort, one way or the other. I did not ask the name of my father; for I could have had no motive to hear him named, except to individualize the person who was so peculiarly kind to me (p. 145).

Yet in a patriarchal society it is the father's *name* that exerts a claim on a child, that gives legitimacy to a child, just as the author's signature gives legitimacy to a text. So it is that Isabel learns her father's name when she deciphers the writing embroidered on a handkerchief that he accidentally leaves behind during one of his visits. Although when she first receives the handkerchief Bell cannot read, she intuits that the embroidery conceals some important meaning. Therefore, she treats the handkerchief as if it were a sacred relic of her father. After she learns of his death it becomes a sacred text in need of deciphering.

> But when the impression of his death became a fixed thing to me, then again I washed and dried and ironed the precious memorial of him, and put it away where none should find it but myself, and resolved never more to soil it with my tears; and I folded it in such a manner, that the name was invisibly buried in the heart of it, and it was like opening a book and turning over many blank leaves before I came to the mysterious writing, which I knew should be one day read by me, without direct help from any one. Now I resolved to learn my letters, and learn to read, in order that of myself I might learn the meaning of those faded characters (p. 146).

Thus, it is learning to read a text left behind by her father that allows Bell to establish lines of communication with her kin.[6]

It is almost certain, however, that Pierre's father did not write the "sacred text" himself. Chances are that Pierre's aunt, who had embroidered the initials on the neckcloth Pierre's father wears in the chair portrait, had also embroidered "Glendenning" on his handkerchief. If so, a spinster sister, rather than a male, passes on the family name by inscribing it in the text of a handkerchief. In fact Aunt Dorothea, who has a thinly veiled incestuous love for her dear brother, seems to be identified by a linen/sewing motif. (One of the Fates?) When she sets little Pierre down to tell him the story of the chair portrait, she reaches into her pocket, causing Pierre to cry,

> "Why, aunt, the story of the picture is not in any little book, is it, that you are going to take out and read to me" "My handkerchief, my child" (p. 74).

Her only child is indeed a handkerchief, knitted with incestuous love, and Isabel's reading of a handkerchief/text does help tell the story of the chair portrait. Furthermore, as the narrator reminds us through the introduction of "Wonder and Wen," the "two young men, recently abandoning the ignoble pursuit of tailoring for the more honorable trade of the publisher" (p. 246), books are made of cloth and paper.

So from the beginning of the novel, the name of the father holding authority to legitimize the family is connected with the writing of fictional texts and illegitimate incestuous desires. The way in which families are held together by the fictional authority of the father's name helps account for the early digression in comparing the longevity of families in America and England. At first look, families in England seem to last longer than in America, where "the democratic element operates as a subtile acid among us; forever producing new things by corroding the old" (p. 9). But we find that the longevity of families in England is, like a novel, an artificial creation of words. Although the bloodline of a family may have died out, the name can be bought by a commoner with enough money. "In England this day, twenty-five hundred peerages are extinct; but the names survive. So that the empty air of a name is more endurable than a man, or than dynasties of men; the air fills man's lungs and puts life into a man, but man fills not the air, nor puts life into that" (p. 10). Names, "which are . . . but air," account for England's "endless descendedness." Similarly, Pierre, thinking he lacks a blood sister, bestows the name of sister on his mother. But Pierre is not given the arbitrary power delegated to English lawyers who can nominally manufacture a peer. "The fictitious title, which he so often lavished upon his mother," could not "at all supply the absent reality" (p. 7).

Yet Pierre is destined to become a novelist, and a novelist's task is precisely to create absent realities

through bestowing upon them a fictitious title of words, which are but air. As Shakespeare knows:

> The poet's eye, in a fine frenzy rolling,
> Doth glance from heaven to earth, from earth
>   to heaven,
> And as imagination bodies forth
> The forms of things unknown, the poet's pen
> Turns them to shapes, and gives to airy
>   nothing
> A local habitation and a name.
>
> [*MND* v. i. 12-17.]

Pierre's growing awareness of the basic counterfeit nature of writing eventually causes him to despair about writing and call it a cheat and a lie. A writer becomes a party to "those impostor philosophers" who pretend somehow to get an answer from "that divinest thing without a name" (p. 208). This can be manifested in two ways. On one hand, the writer can take "the solid land of veritable reality" (p. 49) and fictionalize it by turning it into the airy nothing of language. On the other hand, he can take the disembodied "mystery, underlying all the surfaces of visible time and space" (p. 52) and distort it by exposing it "to the miserable written attempt at embodying it" (p. 273). Therefore, true philosophers seem to reject writing. For instance, Plotinus Plinlimmon, who like Isabel before she knew how to read, "seemed to have no family or blood ties of any sort. . . . never was known to work with his hands; never to write with his hands (he would not even write a letter); he never was known to open a book" (p. 290). The copies of his works are not written by him but by disciples (just as Aunt Dorothea wrote Pierre's father's initials on the text of a neckcloth) and are, therefore, a distortion of his true beliefs. At the same time, because he does not test his ideas by writing them down Plotinus could very well be a fraud himself.

Pierre, on the other hand, decides to risk becoming a fraud through writing rather than, like Plotinus, a possible fraud through silence. Pursuing his "novelistic" enterprise involves forsaking the beloved bonds of domestic happiness to embrace a world of airy words.

> There is a dark, mad mystery in some human hearts, which, sometimes, during the tyranny of a usurper mood, leads them to be all eagerness to cast off the most intense beloved bond, as a hindrance to the attainment of whatever transcendental object that usurper mood so tyrannically suggests. Then the beloved bond seems to hold us to no essential good; lifted to exalted mounts, we can dispense with all the vale; endearments we spurn; kisses are blisters to us; and forsaking the palpitating forms of mortal love, we emptily embrace the boundless and the unbodied air. We think we are not human; we become as immortal bachelors and gods; but again, like the Greek gods themselves, prone we descend

to earth; glad to be uxorious once more; glad to hide these god-like heads within the bosoms made of too-seducing clay (p. 180).

For Melville, the novelist's task is a bachelor's quest. The writer gives up the tranquility of domestic life at Saddle Meadows ("earth's saddle"), and seeks transcendence by vaulting "over to the other saddle awhile" (p. 348). He is like Ahab, who refuses to return to wife and child, and instead continues on his mad quest of Moby Dick.

> Weary with the invariable earth, the restless sailor breaks from every enfolding arm, and puts to sea in height of tempest that blows off shore. But in long night-watches at the antipodes, how heavily that ocean gloom lies in vast bales upon the deck; thinking that that very moment in his deserted hamlet-home the household sun is high, and many a sun-eyed maiden meridian as the sun. He curses Fate; himself he curses; his senseless madness, which is himself. For whoso once has known this sweet knowledge, and then fled it; in absence, to him the avenging dream will come.
>
> Pierre was now this vulnerable god; this self-upbraiding sailor; this dreamer of the avenging dream (p. 181).

His attempt to become a god haunts him in his dream about Enceladus, the son of the Titan born from the incestuous coupling of Heaven and Earth who later married his mother, the Earth. Like Enceladus, Pierre too is heaven aspiring, but not wholly earth-emancipated. Even so Pierre, in his "sky-assaulting mood," tries to regain his paternal birthright by giving up marriage to the earth for the universe. "The great men are all bachelors, you know. Their family is the universe" (p. 281).

But the bachelor's transcendental quest is continually undercut. The last quotation, for instance, comes from Charlie Millthorpe, an obvious incompetent. Furthermore, it is the essence of the bachelor's quest to be original, to avoid life's ordinary generative process which involves him in genetic reduplication.[7] His novelistic hope is to create without being conditioned by his earthly past, to create ex nihilo. The narrator knows all too well, however, that "The world is forever babbling of originality; but there never yet was an original man, in the sense intended by the world; the first man himself—who according to the Rabbins was also the first author—not being an original; the only original author being God" (p. 259).

In an attempt to avoid the Titan's path of incestuous marriage with his mother, the Earth, Pierre is led on a transcendental quest which involves him in an equally incestuous marriage with an offspring of his father. Pierre, the novelist, is caught in this impasse because,

in Melville's eyes, the creative process itself is incestuous. Hoping to write a purely transcendental work Pierre learns that it is impossible.

> For though the naked soul of man doth assuredly contain one latent element of intellectual productiveness; yet never was there a child born solely from one parent; the visible world of experience being that procreative thing which impregnates the muses; self-reciprocally efficient hermaphrodites being but a fable (p. 259).

The incestuous mating of Heaven (the father because not physically connected to the child at birth) and Earth (the mother because physically bound to the child at birth) is repeated by every novelist, who marries spiritual imagination with realistic detail from the visible world of experience. If the novelist tries to escape his ties to mother earth (the realistic pole of the novel) in order to write disembodied transcendental truths, he finds himself face to face with a solipsistic image of himself (the pole of the novel exploring man's inner subjectivity), reminding him of his paternal origins. The novelist Pierre comes to believe that the "mystic and transcendental persuasions" convincing him that Isabel is his sister were "originally born, . . . purely of an intense procreative enthusiasm." Artistic procreation is incestuous. The metaphor of incest accounts for both the difference necessary for the creative act and the continual reduplication of personality (repetition) that no artist can avoid, for in incest we make love to someone of the opposite sex in whom we see ourselves mirrored.

The bachelor's quest, however, can be worse still. It can end by denying difference and embracing purely an image of the self. This can, in the case of Ahab, for instance, become a self-indulgent, solipsistic, and exploitative act, leading to the sterility of an entire society. To see how exploitative it can become we need to turn to Melville's short work, "The Paradise of Bachelors and Tartarus of Maids." The bachelors, similar to the Apostles in *Pierre,* have abandoned their transcendental quest for a life of material ease. Although they retain the name of the holy order of Knights-Templar, these bachelors no longer serve a transcendental God. Instead they are lawyers seeking secular profit. They want the comfort of domestic life without the responsibilities of engendering life. Their paradise, located in the Temples of London, owes its comfort to the exploitation of virgins in a paper factory in Vermont. (Remember that in *Pierre* speculators considered starting a paper mill at Saddle Meadows "expressly for the great author, and so monopolize his stationery dealings" [p. 264].) In a perversion of human procreation the bachelors are wedded to the virgins through the intermediary of a machine. The offspring of this machine, with its "erected" swords, are blank sheets of paper which represent the sterility of this economic and sexually exploitative act. The exploitation is consumed when the blank pieces of paper are filled with ink from the bachelor lawyers' one-handed quills. These quills, we learn, have replaced the bachelor knights' long two-handed swords, thus changing the traditional sword/penis metaphor to a pen/penis metaphor and allowing the exploitative lawyers to do all of their screwing on paper. The bachelor's transcendental quest, always a suspect quest in search of airy nothings, has been reduced to the novelist's quest to create a counterfeit world by filling up blank pages with the self-indulgent "effusions" (pp. 246, 253) of his pen.

Indeed it is during his life as a "brisk, unentangled, young bachelor" (p. 73) that Pierre's father seems to have engendered Bell. (Just as another male has left Delly Ulver pregnant, abandoned, and living above Bell.) It is the mystery of Bell's paternity that is at the crux of the book and the crux of the metaphor between artistic and human procreation. Pierre intuits that "In her life there was an unraveled plot; and he felt that unraveled it would eternally remain to him" (p. 141). Yet, Pierre's "novelistic" enterprise is an attempt to understand no less a mystery than the mystery of fatherhood. If, however, Pierre tries to unravel the plot of Isabel's life by locating her origins, by determining if his father really were her father, by interrogating the remaining relatives on his father's side to "rake forth some few small grains of dubious and most unsatisfactory things," his quest would only "serve the more hopelessly to cripple him in his practical resolves" (p. 141). This is because the "intuitively certain, however, literally unproven fact of Isabel's sisterhood to him" links him to an "unimagined and endless chain of wondering" (p. 139). As Said says, the novelistic quest of trying to reproduce in language the mysteries of the chain of human procreation renders the protagonist impotent. Even in his youth Pierre had distrusted novels' "false, inverted attempts at systematizing eternally unsystemizable elements; their audacious, *intermeddling impotency,* in trying to unravel, and spread out, and classify, the more thin than gossamer threads which make up the complex web of life" (p. 141, my emphasis).

In abandoning himself to his quest Pierre forsakes a marriage approved by a mother with incestuous love and involves himself in a false marriage and possible incest with his sister/wife Isabel. Because of the mystery of fatherhood the question will always remain as to whether the cause Pierre embraces is based on a true blood relationship or grows out of Pierre's attempt to fabricate a cause to fill the void he feels because of the lack of a sister.

> "Oh, had my father but had a daughter!" cried Pierre; "some one whom I might love, and protect, and fight for, if need be. It must be a glorious thing to engage in a mortal quarrel on a sweet sister's behalf! Now, of all things, would to heaven, I had a sister" (p. 7).

"He who is sisterless," we are told, "is as a bachelor before his time" (p. 7).

At the end of the book, having been granted a sister, Pierre searches for something "*legitimately* conclusive" (my emphasis) to prove his link to her. But he can only come up with evidence that is possibly counterfeit. The letter announcing her sisterhood could easily have been forged. Upon receiving it he cries, "This is some accursed dream!—nay, but this paper thing is forged,—a base and malicious forgery" (p. 65). Then when he overcomes his doubt and believes the letter, the narrator chides him.

> Such a note as thine can be easily enough written, Pierre; imposters are not unknown in this curious world; or the brisk novelist, Pierre, will write thee fifty such notes, and so steal gushing tears from his reader's eyes; even as *thy* note so strangely made thine own manly eyes so arid; so glazed, and so arid, Pierre—foolish Pierre! (pp. 69-70).

Furthermore, Isabel's story, as well as Aunt Dorothea's, is nebulous and shadowy. Even if we accept the story of the handkerchief, we might ask, with Shakespeare, "What's in a name?" The fact that the man Isabel called "father" accidentally left behind a handkerchief with Glendenning written on it does not prove that his name is Glendenning, and even so that he is necessarily Pierre's father.

Finally, "the entire sum and substance of all possible, rakable, downright presumptive evidence" (p. 353) is the chair portrait. It is this "portrait's painted *self,*" stolen by cousin Ralph against Pierre's father's will, unacknowledged by Pierre's mother, but confirmed by an aunt who harbors incestuous feelings for her brother, that seems "the real father of Isabel" (p. 197). The resemblance between this portrait "with its noiseless, ever-nameless, and ambiguous, unchanging smile" (p. 196) and Isabel causes Pierre to believe in his vital link to Isabel.

But the chair portrait, like any work of art, is a possible counterfeit. Indeed Pierre's final doubts are provoked by the appearance of a painting almost identical to the chair portrait in a display of counterfeit paintings from Europe. This portrait, the only painting of value in the entire show, is painted by an anonymous artist. For Pierre,

> the original of this second portrait was as much the father of Isabel as the original of the chair-portrait. But perhaps there was no original at all to this second portrait; it might have been a pure fancy piece; to which conceit, indeed, the uncharacterizing style of the filling-up seemed to furnish no small testimony (p. 353).

In other words, we are being reminded that the "real father" of Isabel could be "a pure fancy piece," a counterfeit work of art (the novel we are reading) by an anonymous author. (Melville had written his publisher suggesting "it might not prove unadvisable to publish this present book anonymously, or under an assumed name" [p. 367].) The inexplicable web that we are caught in may be merely the enclosed world of incestuous, convoluted fiction created by an author trying to fill his own lack or void, "the uncharacterized style of the filling up."

At the same time, the mystery of the web may be caused by the real mystery of human creation. The thread linking Pierre and Isabel may be the umbilical cord, "life's cord," which inevitably points to artifice, those "Cretan labyrinths" (p. 176). For while early in the book Pierre believes that it is the human imagination that makes the mystery so mysterious ("Seek not to mystify the mystery so" [p. 53].), later we are told that it "was not so much Isabel who had by her wild idiosyncrasies mystified the narration of her history, as it was the essential and unavoidable mystery of her history itself" (p. 138). Whether the mystery of her history is real or fabricated is the ultimate, unresolved ambiguity surrounding Isabel. "Always in me, the solidest things melt into dreams, and dreams into solidities" (p. 117). This same ambiguity surrounds all of Melville's major fiction. Is it merely a piece of involuted fiction or is it linking us to the invisible mysteries of life itself?[8]

It is exactly the closeness between the mystery surrounding the creation of works of art and the mystery surrounding the creation of human life that accounts for the exploration of one while exploring the other. But this resemblance can turn into a trap. In reading we are perpetually doomed to confuse the two sides of the metaphor, a metaphor held together in this case by the name and portrait of the father. We continually take the fact for fiction and the fiction for fact because they seem to melt into one another. Most reflexive works of fiction account for the necessity of their own misreading by including misreaders within their pages. The normal misreader of fiction within fiction (Quixote, Bovary, Tom Sawyer) reads fiction as if it were real. Pierre, on the other hand, reads the real as if it were fiction. Captivated by the possibility that "Fatherhood may be a legal fiction,"[9] that life's origin is no more than a counterfeit work of art, Pierre reduces the ambiguity by operating under the assumption that fatherhood *is* a legal fiction.

If the mysterious labyrinth of life is merely a work of fiction, then it can be rewritten.[10] This is the essence of Pierre's novelistic/bachelor enterprise. He tries verbally to transform the world in order to make it conform to his own sense of what is right and wrong. ("With the priest it was a matter, whether certain bodiless thoughts of his were true or false, but with Pierre it was a question whether certain vital acts of his were right or wrong" [p. 205].) By embracing Isabel's cause, Pierre hopes to deny those "arbitrary lines of conduct" created by the fiction of the patriarchal structure of the domestic family. If the laws of the world are merely created by airy words, in the same manner that English families are perpetuated through name rather than blood, then Pierre can make Isabel a legitimate heir to his (her) father by performing "the nominal conversion of a sister into a wife" (p. 177).

But Pierre's belief that the world is merely a fiction, capable of being rewritten, is tested in "one of the closest domestic relations of life" (p. 177). Perhaps he can no more transform sister into wife than he could mother into sister. His verbal effort to create reality flies directly in the face of the incest taboo. So it is that when Pierre and Isabel are possibly about to commit possible incest, Isabel claims that all, including Virtue and Vice, is a dream, mere words, nothing. Catching Bell's arm Pierre exclaims,

> "From nothing proceeds nothing, Isabel! How can one sin in a dream?"
>
> "First what is sin, Pierre?"
>
> "Another name for the other name, Isabel."
>
> "For Virtue, Pierre?"
>
> "No, for Vice."
>
> "Let us sit down again, my brother."
>
> "I am Pierre" (p. 274).

Pierre nominally converts sin into nothing and brother into possible lover.

It is no accident that in order to wed himself to his "sister's" cause Pierre must commit symbolic parricide in an effort to free himself from the burden of "hereditary forms and world usages" (p. 89). Feeling that "in his deepest soul, lurked an indefinite but potential faith, which could rule in the interregnum of all hereditary beliefs" (p. 87), Pierre strives "to banish the least trace of his altered father." Announcing "I will no more have a father," he conceals the chair portrait from his sight by reversing the picture on the wall, leaving of course a blank nothingness. Still not satisfied, Pierre later tries to cut all ties with his father by burning the portrait along with "repeated packages of family letters, and all sorts of miscellaneous memorials in paper" (p. 198). "'Henceforth, cast-out Pierre hath no paternity, and no past; and since the Future is one blank to all; therefore, twice-disinherited Pierre stands untrammeledly his ever-present self!—free to do his own self-will and present fancy to whatever end!'" (p. 199).[11]

By disinheriting himself from the past, Pierre hopes to write the blank page of the future in total freedom. Pierre's belief that he can liberate himself by rejecting what seems to be the fictional authority created in the name of the father is a belief necessary to any liberation movement, which tries to reject the influence of the past in a patriarchal society.[12] In the United States, a country created by declaring its independence in a text and populated by immigrants trying to rewrite the text of their lives from scratch, the rejection of the past is almost an obsession.[13] Yet Melville gives us hints that the break with the past, even through parricide, may not be possible. Though absent through death, the father continues to leave traces of his presence in his son and possible daughter. (Notice the textual terms used to describe Pierre's memory of his father: "tracings out" [p. 67], "impression" [p. 68], "stamped," "engraves" [p. 69].)

Similarly the American break with its European and aboriginal past is questioned. "Hundreds of unobtrusive families in New England . . . might easily trace their uninterrupted English lineage to a time before Charles the Blade: not to speak of the old and oriental-like English planter families of Virginia and the South" (p. 10). Furthermore, royal blood is mixed with democratic American blood in a family like the Randolphs, "one of whose ancestors, in King James' time, married Pocahontas the Indian Princess, and in whose blood therefore an underived aboriginal royalty was flowing over two hundred years ago" (p. 10). "However we may wonder at [these families] thus surviving, like Indian mounds, the Revolutionary flood: yet survive and exist they do" (p. 11).

Perhaps recalling the United States's illicit wedding to the French monarchy in order to gain its independence, Melville suggests that Isabel herself has a French mother of possible noble birth, and Isabel may have been raised in France, where she recalls originally speaking in two childish languages. Finally, if the chair portrait is Isabel's "real father," then its close duplicate with an anonymous European origin could also be Isabel's father. A new beginning denying the paternalistic authority of Western history and writing as a form of repetition may not be possible.

Yet, if we are to rely on empirical evidence alone, it seems as if Pierre should be able to rewrite society's "arbitrary lines of conduct," including the sin of incest, at least with a sister whose only tie to him is a father, not a mother. While the mother is physically connected to life's mysterious cord, the father is cut off from it. Isabel and Pierre can only be proven brother and sister by proving that Isabel's father is Pierre's and, as we have seen, the only available evidence is the fictional authority of an absent father. His authority is founded on the void of absence, not the plenitude of presence. Similarly, the author of a text is cut off

from his text. There is no empirical means of proving his connection to it. He is not incarnated in the words of his text, yet just as the father whom Pierre tries to reject leaves his traces in Pierre, so the author seems to leave traces of his presence in the text.

The power of the mystery persists. Though physically cut off from life's cord, the father seems invisibly connected to it. Isabel may really be Pierre's sister. Her mystery may be real, rather than her or Pierre's fabrication based on a counterfeit work of art.

The text remains ambiguous to the end. Its ambiguity is caused by the very metaphor of human and artistic procreation that it explores. We are left pondering whether this metaphor is real or fictional, whether it is just one of those wonderful coincidences as Pierre will have it, or whether "coincidence" is a word by which we "vainly seek to explain the inexplicable" (p. 352). Does Isabel represent a world of pure freedom in which "all words are thine, Isabel; words and worlds with all their containings, shall be slaves to thee, Isabel"? (p. 313). Or, like her face, does she represent a world inextricably connecting past to future, "vaguely historic and prophetic; backward hinting of some irrevocable sin: forward, pointing to some inevitable ill"? (p. 43). Is the dying out of the Glendenning family a precursor to a new life and order? "For the most mighty of nature's laws is this, that out of Death she brings Life" (p. 9). Or is the death of the family a warning to those who would try to deny the past and transcend it? Finally, is the patriarchal system of authority a pure fiction that can be rewritten at will or do we live in an historical continuity in which, unable to disinherit ourselves from the past (no matter how absent it may be), we must continue to pay for the bachelor sins of our fathers?

Notes

[1] Edward W. Said, *Beginnings* (New York: Basic Books, 1975), p. 145.

[2] A classic statement on the incertitude of fatherhood is made by Stephen Dedalus as he tries to explain Shakespeare's artistic creation.

> Fatherhood, in the sense of conscious begetting, is unknown to man. It is a mystical estate, an apostolic succession, from only begetter to only begotten. On that mystery and not on the madonna which the cunning Italian intellect flung to the mob of Europe the church is founded and founded irremovably because founded, like the world, macro- and microcosm, upon the void. Upon incertitude, upon likelihood. *Amor matris,* subjective and objective genetive, may be the only true thing in life. Paternity may be a legal fiction. Who is the father of any son that any son should love him or he any son? James Joyce, *Ulysses* [New York: Random House, 1961], p. 207).

Another example of the pervasiveness of the fatherhood/authorship metaphor comes in Gabriel Marcel's definition of fatherhood. In order to explain the essence of fatherhood Marcel is forced to rely on aesthetic terminology. See Gabriel Marcel, "The Creative Vow as Essence of Fatherhood" in *Homo Viator,* trans. Emma Craufurd (London: Camelot Press, 1951), pp. 98-124.

[3] Jacques Derrida, *Marges de la philosophie,* p. 376, quoted in *Structuralist Poetics* by Jonathan Culler (Ithaca: Cornell Univ. Press, 1975), p. 132.

[4] Herman Melville, *Pierre or The Ambiguities,* ed. Harrison Hayford, Hershel Parker, G. Thomas Tanselle (Evanston: Northwestern Univ. Press, 1971), p. 366. From here on, references to *Pierre* are from this edition and will be noted parenthetically.

[5] Edward Said, "Contemporary Fiction and Criticism," *Tri Quarterly,* 33 (Spring 1975), 255.

[6] See Edgar Dryden, *Melville's Thematics of Form* (Baltimore: The Johns Hopkins Univ. Press, 1968), p. 140. Dryden's entire discussion of *Pierre* is useful for my argument. Professor Dryden informs me that he is at work on a new study of *Pierre* which focuses on the problem of representation and its relationship to the genealogical and reading metaphors.

[7] Again Said's discussion of this quest in *Beginnings* (pp. 137-53) is enlightening. John T. Irwin provides a provocative exploration of this issue in the works of William Faulkner (*Doubling and Incest/Repetition and Revenge* [Baltimore: The Johns Hopkins Univ. Press, 1975]).

[8] Another self-reflexive American novelist whose work raises the same question, Thomas Pynchon, has this to say about the truth of metaphor. The act of metaphor is "a thrust at truth and a lie, depending on where you [are]: inside, safe, or outside, lost" (Thomas Pynchon, *The Crying of Lot 49* [New York: Bantam Books, 1967], p. 95).

[9] The phrase is Stephen Dedalus's. See n. 2.

[10] Yet another self-reflexive American novelist, John Barth, has taken as a theme the novelist's ability to rewrite history and mythology. For instance, in *Chimera,* Barth takes three of the West's most male-chauvinistic myths, the *Arabian Nights' Entertainment,* the Medusa, and the Chimera (in which with a sword/pen/penis the male tries to destroy a female monster), and rewrites them, just as feminist Anteia in "Bellerophoniad," who derides "the male-supremist character of the great body of our classic myths," plans to do. "You're a lie!" she says to the male hero. "We're going to rewrite you" (John Barth, *Chimera* [New York: Random House, 1972], p. 278).

[11] See Guy Rosolato, "The Voice and the Literary Myth" in *The Structuralist Controversy* (Baltimore: The Johns Hopkins Univ. Press, 1970), pp. 201-17, for another discussion of the role of the dead father in writing.

[12] Thus the exposure of the fatherhood myth is of extreme importance for Said in his attempt to establish a new "beginning." It also gives him a starting point for his study of colonial writing, which, although forced to use the language of the occupying country, attempts to undermine the paternal dominance of that country.

But perhaps the current liberation movement most affected by the deconstruction of the fatherhood myth is the women's liberation movement. Here Hélène Cixous is an interesting case. Cixous argues that the free space opened up by Derrida's exposé of the logocentric (or as she calls it "phallologocentric"), paternalistic myth at the foundation of Western writing can now be filled by "feminine writing," writing which, rather than trying to do away with difference by seeking an origin, will eternally resist definition, enclosure, and coding. Because feminine writing is not conditioned by the past in any sense of the word, Cixous announces that writing can bring about a new beginning "The future must no longer be determined by the past." "Beware my friend of the signifier that would take you back to the authority of the signified!" "The fact that this period extends into the present doesn't prevent woman from starting the history of life somewhere else" (Hélène Cixous, "The Laugh of Medusa," in *Signs,* 1 [Summer 1976], 875-93).

[13] Numerous studies have dealt with the antiauthoritarian character of the American people. Perhaps the most interesting in terms of my argument is Geoffrey Gorer's *American People* (New York: W. W. Norton, 1964). Gorer links Americans' hatred of authority to the second generation American's individual rejection of the European father and his language as a model and moral authority. This act of rejection was given more significance by its similarity to the rejection of England by which America became an independent nation.

FURTHER READING

Barnett, Louise K. "American Novelists and the 'Portrait of Beatrice Cenci'." *The New England Quarterly* 53, No. 2 (June 1980): 168-83.

> Traces the use of the portrait and narrative of Beatrice Cenci— "the embodiment of victimization and crime on the level of the most ancient and absolute taboos, those against incest and parricide"—in the work of Hawthorne, Melville and Edith Wharton.

Becker, Allienne R. "'Alice Doane's Appeal': A Literary Double of Hoffman's *Die Elixiere des Teufels.*" *Comparative Literature Studies* 23, No. 1 (Spring 1986): 1-11.

Examines the similarities between Hawthorne's "Alice Doane's Appeal" and E. T. A. Hoffman's novel.

Carothers, R. L. "Melville's 'Cenci': A Portrait of *Pierre.*" *Ball State University Forum* 10, No. 1 (Winter 1969): 53-59.

Analyzes the father-son relationship in *Pierre,* contending that the association between the two has its roots in a "curious blending of Christian mythology and a sort of pre-Freudian-Jungian psychoanalysis of the unconscious."

Cory, Donald Webster, and R. E. L. Masters. *Violation of Taboo: Incest in the Great Literature of the Past and Present.* New York: The Julian Press, 1963, 422 p.

Offers a variety of perspectives on incest, "one of the most ancient of human problems and preoccupations," including chapters on Hawthorne and Melville.

Egan, Phillip J. "Isabel's Story: The Voice of the Dark Woman in Melville's *Pierre.*" *American Transcendental Quarterly* 1, No. 2 (June 1987): 99-110.

Argues that the character of Isabel in Melville's *Pierre* is a figure of the subconscious imagination.

Higgins, Brian, and Hershel Parker. "The Flawed Grandeur of Melville's *Pierre.*" In *Herman Melville: A Collection of Critical Essays*, edited by Myra Jehlen, pp. 126-38. Englewood Cliffs, N.J.: Prentice Hall, 1994.

Contends that Melville's psychological drama *Pierre*, which followed the metaphysical narrative of *Moby Dick*, contains serious internal tensions.

Hoeveler, Diane Long. "La Cenci: the Incest Motif in Hawthorne and Melville." *American Transcendental Quarterly,* No. 44 (Fall 1979): 247-59.

Examines how both Melville and Hawthorne used the "Cenci" motif to reveal their lack of faith in America?s ability to rise from its corrupted past and become a nation of promise and hope.

McLennan, Karen Jacobson. *Nature's Ban: Women's Incest Literature.* Boston: Northeastern University Press, 1996, 394 p.

An anthology of women's literature on incest from a variety of historical periods and cultures.

Petter, Henri. "Illegitimate Love." In his *The Early American Novel*, pp. 242-56. Columbus: Ohio State University Press, 1971.

Discusses the incest motif in the novels of William H. Brown.

Post-Lauria, Sheila. "Genre and Ideology: The French Sensational Romance and Melville's *Pierre.*" *Journal of American Culture* 15, No. 3 (Fall 1992): 1-8.

Distinguishes the genre of the sensational romance from that of the sentimental or Gothic novel, and argues that *Pierre* belongs to the former category.

Wasserman, Renata R. Mautner. "The Self, the Mirror, the Other: 'The Fall of the House of Usher'." *Poe Studies* 10, No. 2 (December 1977): 33-35.

Claims that Poe's short story illuminates the tension between the desire for self-containment (or to remain with the familiar), and the social need for a relationship with the "Other," or something outside the House of Usher.

Wilson, James D. "Incest and American Romantic Fiction." In his *The Romantic Heroic Ideal*, pp. 133-67. Baton Rouge and London: Louisiana State University Press, 1982.

Contends that the preoccupying interest with incest in early American literature reflects a concern with social order and the relation to paternal authority.

Madness in Nineteenth-Century Literature

INTRODUCTION

The prevalence of depictions of madness in nineteenth-century literature in England and America paralleled the growth of the scientific and medical study of insanity. Increasingly in the nineteenth century, madness was seen more as a social and medical problem, compared to the eighteenth century, when madness was feared as the absence of reason, and therefore, evil. Whereas eighteenth-century rationalists viewed madness as a result of overindulgence of the imagination, nineteenth-century romanticists embraced imaginative excess. Romantic poets, such as Percy Bysshe Shelley, explored the relationship between the creative imagination and madness, and some poets, including John Clare, were thought to be truly mad and were confined to insane asylums. The condition of life in insane asylums was reported in autobiographies by those who had been consigned there. In fiction, madness was treated in a variety of ways. Some authors attempted to portray mental "aberrations" in a realistic manner, while others sensationalized the symptoms of and reaction to a character's insanity. Such sensation fiction often portrayed characters who were wrongfully accused of insanity. The multitude of ways insanity was treated in literature reflects nineteenth-century society's fascination—bordering on obsession—with madness.

In 1867, Elizabeth Packard published her account of life in an Illinois insane asylum. Packard was committed in 1860 by her husband, who claimed that in Bible study groups organized and led by Elizabeth, she questioned Calvinist doctrine and encouraged those in the groups to interpret the Bible on their own. Elizabeth's husband maintained that these activities demonstrated that her mind was unbalanced. Elizabeth was released in 1863. Mary Elene Wood analyzes Packard's *The Prisoner's Hidden Life; or, Insane Asylums Unveiled*, in which Packard recounts the abuses suffered by the women in the asylum, including beatings and punishment by dunking in cold water. Wood notes the ways in which Packard's account both conforms to and challenges the conventions of the sentimental novel and the slave narrative.

Many Romantic poets explored the relationship between art and madness, and Shelley was no exception. In his examination of Shelley's views on this matter, as expressed in his poetry and in *The Defense of Poetry* (1821), Ross Woodman argues that while Shelley viewed poetry as a means of mastering the "inner world"—that is, the realm of creativity and of madness—Shelley's poetic career reveals the poet's frustration with art's inability to truly represent the visions of that inner world. Alfred, Lord Tennyson approached the issue of madness from an entirely different angle, not wishing to embrace it as Shelley seemed to want to, but seeking to analyze it and fearing its encroachment upon society, as many of his contemporaries did. Ann C. Colley studies the way Tennyson, in *Idylls of the King* (1859-85; 1891), uses the madness of Camelot, brought about by excesses of sexuality and ambition, as a metaphor for the madness of Tennyson's England. Colley argues that Tennyson, in *Idylls* and in *Maud* (1855), skillfully demonstrated the way madness attacks the mind, and that the poet used this knowledge to further explore how madness attacks the health of the nation. When Tennyson wrote about sexually explicit, "morally insane" themes such as necrophelia, Ekbert Faas explains, it was within an accepted framework in which it was clear that the madman was an object being analyzed. Faas argues that Algernon Charles Swinburne's poetry was condemned as depraved because it lured the reader into sadomasochistic, anti-Christian fantasies, without any objective framing device. Faas observes that many poets were judged in biographies written by "alienists" (physicians who studied mental disorders) as insane or suffering from a "disposition to mental aberration." While many poets were condemned in this manner, John Clare was actually committed. Frederick Burwick speculates as to the nature and depth of Clare's mental problems, but states there is no way to ascertain whether or not Clare was truly insane. In studying the poetry Clare composed while confined to asylums, Burwick observes a shift from Clare's earlier, Wordsworthian tone to a more ironic, introspective, Byronic tone.

In fiction, there were two basic trends in the way madness was represented: authors strove either for psychological realism, or they sensationalized madness, using it as a tool to bring about a certain effect on characterization or plot. In 1866, an anonymous critic in *The Spectator* chastized this latter trend, arguing that madness was used to disguise the lack of art in such novels. In 1993, Sally Shuttleworth examined the same trend, maintaining that sensation novels used madness to challenge the male-controlled society of Victorian England by celebrating female "sensation," often wrongly diagnosed by males in the novels as insanity. Several critics have analyzed the representation of madness in the works of prominent nineteenth-century writers. Barbara Hill Rigney suggests that in *Jane Eyre* (1847), Charlotte Bronte correlates chastity with sanity. Rigney argues that Bronte continually associates sexuality with death throughout the novel, emphasizing the message that a woman will lose her identity and therefore her sanity by engaging in sexual activity. Edgar Allan Poe's depictions of madness are well known, yet the means by which Poe brings forth the almost tactile quality in his work are less frequently studied. Leonard W. Engel takes a closer look at "The Fall of the House of Usher" (1840), focusing in particular on the way in which Poe uses the language and imagery of enclosure to follow the narrator on his journey from reason to insanity. Donald A. Ringe traces Nathaniel Hawthorne's portrayal of insanity in short stories and in novels. Ringe demonstrates Hawthorne's desire to accurately portray the abnormal psychology of certain characters, noting that Hawthorne's portrayals are supported by contemporary psychological studies. In examining the function of madness in Hawthorne's work, specifically *The Scarlet Letter* (1850), Ringe indicates that Hawthorne associates madness in this world with damnation after death, and that the author similarly links sanity and salvation. Like Bronte and Hawthorne, Herman Melville attempted realistic psychological portrayals in the characters of his novels. Paul McCarthy studies Melville's achievement in this area in *Moby-Dick, or, The Whale* (1851). McCarthy finds madness everywhere in this novel—in animals, in humans, and in the universe itself. Examining in particular the forms of madness of the characters aboard the ship, McCarthy studies the way mental aberration is revealed through characters' speeches and traces the development of Ahab's madness.

REPRESENTATIVE WORKS

George Borrow
Lavengro (novel) 1851

Mary Braddon
Lady Audley's Secret (novel) 1862

Charlotte Bronte
Jane Eyre (novel) 1847

Charles Brockden Brown
Wieland (novel) 1798
Edgar Huntly (novel) 1799

Henry Cockton
The Life and Adventures of Valentine Vox, the Ventriloquist (novel) 1840

Wilkie Collins
The Woman in White (novel) 1859

Nathaniel Hawthorne
"Hollow of the Three Hills" (short story) 1830
"The Prophetic Pictures" (short story) 1837
The Scarlet Letter (novel) 1850

Herman Melville
Moby-Dick, or, The Whale (novel) 1851

Elizabeth Packard
The Prisoner's Hidden Life; or, Insane Asylums Unveiled (autobiography) 1867

Edgar Allan Poe
"The Fall of the House of Usher" (short story) 1840

T. P. Prest
The Maniac Father (novel) 1844

Charles Reade
Hard Cash (novel) 1863

Algernon Charles Swinburne
*"Dolores" (poem) 1866
*"Hymn to Prosperine" (poem) 1866

Alfred, Lord Tennyson
Maud (poem) 1855
Idylls of the King (poem) 1859-85; 1891

Mrs. Henry Wood
St. Martin's Eve (novel) 1866

*Published in *Poems and Ballads* in 1866.

OVERVIEW

John R. Reed (essay date 1975)

SOURCE: "Madness," in *Victorian Conventions*, Ohio University Press, 1975, pp. 193-215.

[*In the following essay, Reed traces the connection between the growth of the Romantic movement in the early nineteenth century and the changing opinions among the medical community and the public regarding madness.*]

Insanity: An Overview

In *Madness and Civilization*, Michel Foucault described the signal transformation that occurred in Western civilization's conception of madness as a shift from a philosophical to a pathological outlook; "that is, the reduction of the classical experience of unreason to a strictly moral perception of madness, which would secretly serve as a nucleus for all the concepts that the nineteenth century would subsequently vindicate as scientific, positive, and experimental."[1] In Foucault's view, the eighteenth-century attitude toward madness depended upon the assumption that it was "the negation of reason." It is a philosophical paradox which itself would be agreeable to the classical taste for order and balance:

> For madness, if it is nothing, can manifest itself only by departing from itself, by assuming an appearance in the order of reason and thus becoming the contrary of itself. Which illuminates the paradoxes of the classical experience: madness is always absent, in a perpetual retreat where it is inaccessible, without phenomenal or positive character; and yet it is present and perfectly visible in the singular evidence of the madman.[2]

This attitude ultimately engendered a fear of madness. What was unlike reason, if left uncontrolled, became evil. Earlier, madness had its acknowledged, if eccentric, place in the pattern of social existence, being treated openly. But by the eighteenth century, it had become a feature of human nature to be hidden and confined. The secrecy surrounding madness helped to cultivate the belief that it was a moral pollutant. "Moral condemnation of the mentally abnormal was as strong a component of eighteenth-century rationalist theology as it was of medical thought, or the inarticulate beliefs of the labouring classes."[3] Only an age that admired the complete order of the mind through reason could so deeply fear what it had defined as the principal threat to reason. Samuel Johnson was not alone in his belief that madness was occasioned by too great an indulgence of the imagination; nor was he peculiar in his conviction that the exercise of reason was the means to restrain imagination's whimsy.[4]

Nigel Walker, concerned with insanity in relation to English law, observed that, since there were no provisions for housing the insane in the eighteenth century, madmen were necessarily confined in jails which "was neither as unjust nor as inhumane as it sounds to modern ears. Private madhouses were few until the end of the eighteenth century, and in any case were beyond the means of all but the well-to-do."[5] These madhouses were custodial rather than remedial; haphazardly employing old and new techniques for curing inmates such as surprise baths, emetics, and restraints. About 1755-69 notable changes occurred in the treatment of the insane because of an increased public awareness of social problems raised by the mentally disordered.[6] The first real successes with pleas of insanity in court trials began at this time, and voluntary subscription hospitals for the insane were founded.

The only official institution for the insane in England, from 1547, when it was given to the city of London as a hospital for poor lunatics, until 1751, when St. Luke's Hospital for Lunaticks opened, was Bethlehem Hospital. Conditions at Bethlehem had been brutal, but St. Luke's, proposed and operated by William Battie, was to be of a new character. In his *A Treatise on Madness* (1758) Battie defined madness as "deluded imagination," and distinguished two basic forms of the malady; original madness, which he felt was owing to disorders of the nervous substance, and Consequential Madness, which he attributed "to some remote and accidental cause." He noted that a medical man should not ignore the stomach, intestines or uterus as seats of madness, because of their effect upon the nervous fiber. Battie's innovations were little more than assertions that human beings suffering from madness were much like those afflicted with other diseases, and, though he objected to devices such as opium and induced vomiting to treat madness, he agreed that much madness was as unmanageable as other illnesses. James Monro, who was the physician at Bethlehem, disputed Battie's assumptions and, in his *Remarks on Dr. Battie's Treatise on Madness* (1758), asserted that madness would be forever incurable and never understood. He defended the time-honored practices of bleeding, purging, and evacuation by vomiting, as means of treating the insane. Despite Monro's response, Battie's book "came to have a considerable influence, especially on nineteenth-century judges."[7]

The *Gentleman's Magazine* of January, 1763, published an influential article which criticized the abuses suffered by the insane under confinement,[8] and in 1774 an Act for Regulating Private Madhouses was passed though it had little effect. By 1789, "the nature of the King's [George III] illness became generally known, and the topic of insanity was widely discussed in a context which excluded the attitude of moral condemnation."[9] With the model of the Retreat, run by the Tuke family at York, lunacy reform began on a national scale with the establishment of county asylums following the Act of 1808.[10]

Nineteenth-century England was given to superstitions and strange theories about madness, but unlike the eighteenth century it did not so much fear madness as pity it. Moreover, the Romantic movement was in large part a reaction against rationalism.[11] If Johnson's contemporaries feared excesses of the imagination, the Romantics exalted them. The ordered existence proposed and desired by neoclassical minds had little appeal for those who sought to emphasize the uniqueness and multiplicity of the individual and the mutability of all existence. The Romantics plunged eagerly into the subjectivism their predecessors had so warily skirted.

Too much of what the Romantics admired smacked of mental imbalance and melancholia for them to feel alien toward the insane. Much of Romanticism was a flirtation with all that had formerly been deemed madness. It is appropriate that the great encyclopedist, Diderot's, subversive sketch, *Rameau's Nephew,* should have been brought to light by the most classical of Romantics, Goethe, who translated the work and saw it published in 1805. The character of Rameau's nephew represented forces of disorder, immorality and subversion in a society that valued order, and marked a decisive change in attitude toward madness and unreason. It is not so great a step as one might imagine from Diderot's exchange to the nineteenth-century dialogue of the mind with itself that concludes with the mind finding itself disintegrating into antagonistic parts. From Diderot and Rameau's nephew to Byron's Manfred, to Dr. Jekyll and Mr. Hyde, Dorian Gray, or Conrad's Secret Sharer, is not a long, nor a complex journey.

By the eighteen thirties, English medicine viewed madness not as a manifestation of evil but as a consequence of social conditions, all too likely to strike nearby and unexpectedly. In *A General View of the Present State of Lunatics and Lunatic Asylums, in Great Britain and Ireland, and in some other Kingdoms* (1828), Sir Andrew Halliday declared that insanity was a result of the refinement of the organs. "The finer the organs of the mind have become by their greater development, or their better cultivation, if health is not made a part of the process," he averred, "the more easily are they disordered."[12] At the same time, George Burrows suggested, in *Commentaries on the Causes, Forms, Symptoms and Treatment, Moral and Medical, of Insanity* (1828), that intellectual derangements were induced mainly by society at large. "The vices of civilization, of course, must conduce to their increase," he said, "but even the moral virtues, religion, politics, nay philosophy itself, and all the best feelings of our nature, if too enthusiastically incited, class among the causes producing intellectual disorders."[13] For Burrows, as for Battie before him, madness was both constitutional and educational. It was no longer the simple result of too much scholarship or precarious religious convictions, it was now another aberration of a humanity that was, more and more, emerging as multiple and mysterious.

John Conolly wrote in his study, *An Inquiry Concerning the Indications of Insanity with suggestions for the better protection and care of the insane* (1830):

> Insanity is often but a mere aggravation of little weaknesses, or a prolongation of transient varieties and moods of mind, which all men now and then experience; an exaggeration of common passions and emotions, such as fear, suspicion, admiration; or a perpetuation of absurdities of thought or action, or of irregularities of volition, or of mere sensation, which may occur in all minds, or be indulged in by all men, but which are cherished and dwelt upon only by a mind diseased. (pp. 166-67)

Allowing that mental disorders were ascribable to "corporeal disease," Conolly nonetheless admitted that there was no clear relationship. And he declared that the error, thus far, of medical men was that they "sought for, and imagined, a strong and definable boundary between sanity and insanity, which has not only been imaginary, and arbitrarily placed," but hurtful to those so segregated. (pp. 295-96) No longer was madness in a realm clearly discrete from that of reason. Reason and unreason could abide together in a constantly changing climate of human unpredictability. The extraordinary having become attractive, it was no longer necessary to fear the outrageous or unusual in human behavior. It was only necessary to appreciate it and correctly estimate its effect. "Every man is interested in this subject," Conolly says, "for no man can confidently reckon on the continuance of his perfect reason." Any departure from sound mind might occasion the loss of property and liberty, and subject the individual to sufferings and wrongs, passing "his melancholy days among the idiotic and the mad." (pp. 8-9) It was an ominous possibility that was, as we shall see, too often enacted.[14] But, if madness was now no stranger to the community, but a near companion of simple eccentricity, it remained to distinguish just what the difference was. For Conolly, and many in his time, insanity became "the impairment of any one or more of the faculties of the mind, accompanied with, or inducing, a defect in the comparing faculty." (p. 300) From this point on, consideration of the insane was in the realm of the positivists, or, as we have them today, the clinical psychologists, the behaviorists.

Among the first who sought to apply clinical methods to the understanding of aberrant states of mind, were the phrenologists. Foremost among these was Johann Christoph Spurzheim, who, in *Phrenology, or the Doctrine of the Mind; and of the Relations between Its Manifestations and the Body* (1825), set forth his theory concerning the parts of the brain and their influence upon human behavior. More directly concerned with the problem of madness was his later study, *Observations on the Deranged Manifestations of The Mind, or Insanity* (1833), where he argued for improved training of medical men to treat insanity. Although Spurzheim was largely concerned with derangements of external functions of the mind, he believed that "no branch of medicine is so intimately connected with the philosophy of the mind as insanity." (p. 49) He was fully convinced that the causes of insanity were corporeal and declared that, "The soul cannot fall sick, any more than it can die." (p. 75) In his opinion, "*the incapacity of distinguishing the diseased functions of the mind,* and the irresistibility of our actions," constituted insanity. (p. 53) Spurzheim's views of the various causes of insanity became common in the nineteenth century. Affections and passions, or intense study were popularly accepted as causes of insanity. The crime of seduction, Spurzheim said, was also a fertile source of insanity, as were religion and intemperance. He declared women more inclined to madness than men, and added that "the greatest number of insane females are the victims of amativeness." (p. 126) He attributed the high proportion of insane people in England and Ireland, compared with other countries, to the excessive indulgence in "the sentiment of self-esteem and independency." (p. 124) He proposed, therefore, that the treatment of the insane was primarily moral.

Concern for the problem of madness coupled with a suspicion that insanity was on the increase, led to the establishment of the Metropolitan Commission in Lunacy, which issued an impressive series of reports between 1829-1844, at which time their report acknowledged "that insanity comprises a complex of causes and effects—not merely one disease with a single cause."[15] The stringent Lunacy Act of 1845 followed; and, thereafter, insanity was increasingly viewed as a social and medical, not a moral problem. In 1859, a Select Committee under the guidance of Lord Shaftesbury was formed to study the lunacy laws, and it found many instances of abuse, particularly in workhouses. But despite these advances, treatment of the insane was a difficult issue and a controversial subject preceding the Lunacy Act of 1890.

Madness in Literature

In the literature of the nineteenth century, the subject of madness was gradually liberated from its frightening associations, and was treated with interest, and in some cases, even admiration. In Gothic fiction, insanity had enhanced supernatural effects and was primarily a terrible prospect, a curse imposed by gods or devils. With the Romantics, a new notion appeared, indicated benignly in Wordsworth's "The Idiot Boy." But beyond acceptance, admiration was possible.

In Byron's "The Dream," for example, an unhappy marriage and frustrated love lead to madness. But this disturbance of normal intellectual life hardly seems, in the circumstances, so terrible. Of the distracted lady, Byron writes:

> oh! she was changed,
> As by the sickness of the soul; her mind
> Had wander'd from its dwelling, and her eyes,
> They had not their own lustre, but the look
> Which is not of the earth; she was become
> The queen of a fantastic realm; her thoughts
> Were combinations of disjointed things;
> And forms impalpable and unperceiv'd
> Of others' sight familiar were to hers.
> And this the world calls phrenzy; but the wise
> Have a far deeper madness, and the glance
> Of melancholy is a fearful gift;
> What is it but the telescope of truth?

> Which strips the distance of its fantasies,
> And brings life near in utter nakedness,
> Making the cold reality too real!

There is no fear of the insane here, only pity and respect. To have been driven mad through the frustration of a passionate love was not among the crimes or offenses of the nineteenth century.

Likewise, it was not shameful to have had one's reason unseated by other severe shocks. Hence, the pious and cordial Mrs. Aubrey in Samuel Warren's *Ten Thousand A-Year* loses her reason when she learns that her family must abandon the family estate, Yatton. Her reason returns just in time for her to die a peaceful death. In the same novel, however, Warren draws a picture of a despicable form of lunacy. The ludicrous central character, Tittlebat Titmouse, who is constantly provoked by minor annoyances to exclaim that he shall go mad, eventually does lapse into lunacy after having indulged in various debaucheries and having been deprived of Yatton. In the end, he is "admitted an inmate of a private lunatic asylum." (Vol. 3, ch. 12) This use of lunacy in fiction was, of course, a cautionary device. A relationship between dissipation and madness is frequently assumed, as in Thackeray's early work, *The Adventures of Barry Lyndon*. Graphic works such as Hogarth's "The Rake's Progress," or Cruikshank's "The Bottle," offered similar warnings and paralleled later medical caveats, such as those Walter describes in *My Secret Life,* that masturbation would surely result in madness.

Dissipation and debauchery were not the only deviations that might lead to madness. The innocent might also suffer as Mrs. Aubrey's case suggests. Duels were frequently presented as sources of madness, especially for the bereaved survivors. If the historians of duelling can be trusted, there seems to have been a good deal of truth in such portrayals. Lorenzo Sabine quotes one such event, "Duelling: A Tale of Woe," in his *Notes on Duels and Duelling* (1856), and Andrew Steinmetz, in recounting the details of a duel between a Mr. McLean and a Mr. Cameron in Scotland in 1772, in which Mr. McLean was killed, says that "His mother hearing of this melancholy event, was instantly deprived of her senses, and Miss McLeod, a young lady to whom McLean was soon to be married, was seized with fits and died three days later."[16] Such historical incidents make Lucy's madness at the end of *The Ordeal of Richard Feverel* more credible.

In *Lavengro*, George Borrow relates the history of a gentleman who, through his and his family's foolish attraction to the Roman Catholic faith, ended in lunacy. (ch. 100) Clearly any folly might devolve into madness. The folly need not be one's own. The father in T. P. Prest's novel, *The Maniac Father* (1844), was not an unfamiliar type. His madness was consequent upon his daughter's loss of virtue.[17] Prest used the same figure in *Vice and Its Victims: Or, Phoebe, the Peasant's Daughter,* in which Mr. Mayfield goes insane when his daughter, Phoebe, elopes with a profligate lord. Mayfield recovers abruptly, however, when he learns that Phoebe's marriage was legal. Loss of virtue could occasion madness in the violated party as well. In Bulwer-Lytton's popular novel, *Pelham* (1828), Gertrude Douglas, beloved by Reginald Glanville, is driven mad as a consequence of being raped by the unscrupulous Tyrrell. Fortunately, she dies. Glanville, in his grief and revenge, comes close to madness himself, but never is this excess criticized. It is clear in the novel that this authentic insanity and near-madness follow from an excess of admirable qualities.[18] When a noble mind is faced with insupportable emotions, it cannot bend or wheedle; it cracks. Throughout the century, madness took one of two fundamental literary routes: either it was the result of a sinful, ruined life, or it was the necessary consequence of a passionate nature trapped in unbearable circumstances.

Among the earliest and most memorable instances of madness resulting from offended virtue was Scott's Lucy Ashton in *The Bride of Lammermoor* (1819). The sensitive but too highly susceptible imagination of young Lucy leads her to the violent and tragic loss of reason that a stronger but less passionate nature might have overcome. Lucy goes mad on her wedding night, when her unwanted husband enters her bedchamber. The theme of offended love begetting madness was persistent, but Scott provided other memorable models of insanity as well. The innocent madness of Davie Gellatley in *Waverley* or Madge Wildfire in *The Heart of Midlothian* reappeared in Dickens' innocently haunted Barnaby Rudge, whose simple-mindedness results directly from the criminal violence of his vicious father. And the insane Bertha Mason's death in the blazing destruction of Thornfield Hall in Charlotte Brontë's *Jane Eyre* had as its model a similar death of a maniac in a burning tower in Scott's *Ivanhoe.* Kathleen Jones finds Bertha Mason thoroughly conventional, describing her as Charlotte Brontë's "figment of the imagination stimulated by the horror novels of the late eighteenth century. Mrs. Rochester is a figure from *The Castle of Otranto* or the later 'penny dreadfuls'—not a personification of an existing social problem."[19] But the public would have been far more prepared to accept this conventional view than any realistic social characterization. Still, in utilizing the conventional type, Charlotte Brontë implied psychological realities that social comment might not have explored. The hidden Bertha is a symbol of confined passion, representing the powerful and destructive urges in man that Jane Eyre's self-control promises to remedy. Images of fire and violence prepare for the final destruction of Rochester's guilty secret, after which, a subdued man, he is fit to share his life more temperately with the disciplined Jane.

Madness for Scott was a means of advancing and complicating his plots; he rarely stopped to preach or offer symbolic overtones. His practices were imitated in much of the popular literature of the nineteenth century where certain stereotyped situations recurred regularly. Dickens' "A Madman's Manuscript," one of the interpolated tales of *Pickwick Papers,* offers splendid examples of all of the conventions. There is a history of madness in the narrator's family, though an editorial note to the manuscript describes this history as the narrator's "delusion." The madman himself is described as "a melancholy instance of the baneful results of energies misdirected in early life, and excesses prolonged until their consequences could never be repaired. The thoughtless riot, dissipation, and debauchery of his younger days, produced fever and delirium." (ch. 11) The predictable moral is not lacking, nor is the customary inclusion of an unfortunate romance. There is an echo of Scott's *Bride of Lammermoor* in the madman's account of his relationship with a young lady who eventually becomes his wife and dies by his hand. This young lady is, like Lucy Ashton, a victim of family interests, but unlike Lucy, is the target for insane violence rather than its vehicle. After his homicidal outbreak, the madman ends where all who permit their appetites unbridled sway are in danger of ending, in an asylum, haunted by a spectre of his crimes.

This crude tale is thoroughly in the conventional mold but Dickens attempted other modifications of madness in other novels.[20] Barnaby Rudge, who, as Poe was quick to observe, was hardly a successful character, recalled, as Kathleen Tillotson put it, "the theatrical stereotypes of lunacy."[21] Gordon, in the same novel, is more plausible but so much more subtle as to constitute less an example of madness than of eccentricity or deviation. Dickens does, however, manage to equate the madness of society with Gordon's deviation and indicates how different it is from Barnaby's innocent symptoms. It is a segment of society that is mad in this novel, and it is this lunacy that is more aptly depicted by Dickens than any specific individual instance. Moreover, this madness is itself associated with forces long restrained that must, after all, break loose in wild abandon. For Dickens, madness becomes a form of social infection that must be lanced before it can be cured.

Less conventional, but also less clearly related to what may genuinely be considered madness are Mr. Dick in *David Copperfield,* and Mr. Dorrit in *Little Dorrit.* In Mr. Dick, Dickens is able to present an amusing, if not medically convincing picture of benign lunacy growing out of a shock to a good man's sensitive nature and resulting in an *idée fixe,* both pathetic and diverting. Mr. Dorrit's case, on the other hand, demonstrates the way in which a mind, unused to the burdens of liberty, relapses into the comforting familiarity of strictly defined regulations. If the public madness of *Barnaby Rudge* indicated a festering illness demanding release, the mental collapse of Mr. Dorrit indicates a central vacuity, too long preserved by a surrounding shell, that must, in normal conditions, give way. Mr. Dorrit's breakdown signifies a physical decay as much as a mental failure, and his death follows close after it. Clearly Dickens was mainly concerned with madness as a metaphor for aspects of the human condition. He made no more attempt at precise delineation than did Scott or Charlotte Brontë. But more suggestively than either, he implied through the convention of madness some monstrous consequences of conduct that violated a natural moral order. Still, Dickens never was persuasive in his descriptions of madness, which seemed related to theatrical and literary sources. This is all the stranger with him since he was acquainted with the famous Dr. John Conolly. Moreover Dickens' close friend and professional adviser, John Forster, was himself an official of the Lunacy Commission, and an article entitled "The Treatment of the Insane" appeared in *Household Words* in 1852. Despite these connections with the practical details of insanity, Dickens' use of the subject remained primarily suggestive and evocative rather than descriptive and realistic.

Exploitation of the Theme

If, for the most part, Dickens failed to exploit madness as a theme, his contemporaries made good use of it. In Henry Cookton's *The Life and Adventures of Valentine Vox, the Ventriloquist* (1840), Grimwood Goodman is falsely confined in a private lunatic asylum by his brother and nephew, who have designs upon his money and property. There is no problem in getting corrupt medical men to sign the necessary papers and once Grimwood is confined, escape is almost impossible. In addition to brutal restraint, Dr. Holdem and his cohorts change Grimwood's name and transfer him to a different asylum to keep him hidden. Ultimately Grimwood is rescued from the asylum, but his health is so reduced that he dies soon after. Meanwhile retribution is visited upon his conscience-stricken brother who goes mad and commits suicide. Vox introduced this novel with a preface denouncing the system of private lunatic asylums as pernicious and cruel, emphasizing the ease with which sane men might be confined and kept isolated from any suitable source of assistance.

In 1859, Wilkie Collins began the serial publication of his novel, *The Woman in White,* which called attention to the abuses practiced by owners of private lunatic asylums. Although there was no elaborate examination in this novel of what constituted madness, Collins, like Vox, clearly signified that the sane might easily be taken for insane on the assertion of persons scarcely qualified to determine such an important issue. Collins made no profound statement about madness, and he only implied that society itself was not free from de-

lusion if it could be so duped and deceived by men such as Glyde and Count Fosco. In *Armadale,* Collins repeated his point about illegal confinement. The disreputable Dr. Downward changes his name to Dr. Le Doux and establishes a private asylum subject to no inspection or control, despite his lack of any professional skill. In this novel, as in *The Woman in White,* the asylum, designed for the assistance of the mentally deranged, serves as an illegal prison to confine an innocent individual likely to upset mischievous plots. In neither of these novels did Collins deal with absolute insanity, for he was more concerned with abuses of the law which permitted sane individuals to be confined.[22] Moreover, he tried subtly to demonstrate the tenuous distinction between sanity and madness that prevailed in his time.

Charles Reade was even more determined to reveal the unjust and outrageous practices allowed under the heading of treatment for the insane in his novel, *Hard Cash* (1863). Kathleen Jones suggests that the book "was probably inspired by the Report of the Select Committee of 1859-60. It was published at a time when public feeling on these issues ran high; and it enjoyed considerable financial success."[23] Reade satirized the respectable John Conolly as Dr. Wycherley, a man of little intelligence and less scruple. Dr. Wycherley, at the dishonest Mr. Hardie's request, has the banker's son, Alfred Hardie, confined in an asylum as supposedly suffering from "Incubation of Insanity." Wycherley has not even met or interviewed Alfred, and the symptoms described—headache, insomnia, melancholy—would fit any sane but temporarily distressed individual. Yet Alfred is forcibly detained in the madhouse; and, the government inspectors remain unconvinced of his sanity since they themselves are either senile or totally prejudiced by the madhouse keepers.

Alfred is not the only sane individual restrained in the asylum managed by the lascivious Mrs. Archbold. David Dodd, a victim of Richard Hardie's chicanery, is another. Both ultimately escape from their confinement, but not before Reade delivers a lecture on how easily unsuspecting individuals may be committed. Later, when Alfred has an opportunity to denounce the regulations governing such confinements, he explains to his solicitor that he was not even permitted to see the certificates that occasioned his confinement:

> "Not I," said Alfred. "I have begged and prayed for a sight of them, and never could get one. That is one of the galling iniquities of the system; I call it 'THE DOUBLE SHUFFLE.' Just bring your mind to bear on this, sir: The prisoner whose wits and liberty have been signed away behind his back is not allowed to see the order and certificate on which he is confined—until *after* his release: that release he is to obtain by combating the statements in the order and certificates. So to get out he must first see and contradict the lies that put him in; but to

see the lies that put him in, he must first get out. So runs the circle of Iniquity. Now, is that the injustice of Earth or the injustice of Hell?" (ch. 44)

It is all too easy for a modern reader to understand this dilemma, but for a Victorian audience, the moral impact was appalling. Reade sought to increase the impact of his tale by a large dose of irony. The genuinely unbalanced James Maxley cannot persuade Hardie to have him committed to an asylum and later Maxley beats Hardie's beloved daughter, Jane, to death. Moreover, it is eventually Richard Hardie himself—the avaricious and unscrupulous money monger—who declines into semi-madness. He dies believing that he is on the verge of ruin, though he is, in fact, wealthy.

Although here, as in his later novel, *A Terrible Temptation* (1870-71), Reade is more concerned with demonstrating abuses in the treatment of the insane than he is with the problem of insanity itself, his novels, like those of Collins, do indicate the degree of interest expressed during the mid-Victorian period in the social and practical problems of madness. A passage from *Lady Audley's Secret* (1862) indicates how glibly the subject of confinement for insanity could be tossed about. When Robert Audley openly challenges Lady Audley with deceiving her husband about her past, she responds by threatening to charge him with madness. That such a threat could be seriously entertained shows how far fiction had gone to accept the contemporary social concern about the mismanagement of the laws dealing with the insane. It is both fitting and melodramatic that later in this popular sensation novel, Lady Audley confesses her own fear that she might have inherited madness from her mother. (ch. 34)

Anthony Trollope, in *He Knew He Was Right* (1868-69), also described the unjust circumstances which permitted the confinement of a man supposed mad; but, in the development of his character, Louis Trevelyan, failed to convey a plausible madness. Trevelyan's aberration proceeded from his jealousy and willfulness. In effect, madness, for Trollope, is what happens to people who cannot resolve the various demands of their passional natures. In the background of Trollope's story there always hovers the amiable or aggressive eccentricity of a Miss Jemima Stanbury or a Wallachie Petrie. Madness is only a further stage of such eccentricity— a stage which is frightening only insofar as it concerns the innocent.

Unjust confinement is a melodramatic device in Joseph Sheridan LeFanu's *The Rose and the Key* (1871), where Maud Vernon is confined at the avaricious Dr. Antomarchi's asylum, Glarewoods, by means of a ruse and for motives of her mother's which are never fully explained. Maud is unable to communicate with anyone outside the asylum and is warned not to make trouble, being forced to witness another inmate's sub-

jection to a monstrous showerbath for thirty-five minutes, followed by the administration of an emetic. This incident, Le Fanu explains, was taken from a documented case. (ch. 74) Before the Lunacy Commissioners, Maud is too overwrought to respond properly, and they see no reason to release her. This is subtler than Cockton's description in *Valentine Vox* of attendants tickling Grimwood's feet until he becomes hysterical just before the Commissioners make their visit. Maud is finally freed through Dr. Damian, Antomarchi's superior, and an honest man.

Meredith

For many Victorian writers, like Meredith, madness was more clearly a literary convention and less of a social consideration. In *The Ordeal of Richard Feverel* (1859), the impulsive Richard's behavior leads not only to his own temporary madness, but also to that of his wife Lucy. "The shock," Lady Blandish explains to Austin Wentworth, referring to Richard's injury in a duel, "had utterly deranged her." (ch. 49) For Meredith, mental imbalance is a dreadful, yet likely possibility when men are so slow to learn the value of genuine self-discipline. How easy the disintegration of the mind can be is illustrated in *Rhoda Fleming* (1865). Dahlia Fleming's two great passions meet in her illicit love for Edward Blancove; both her physical desires and her proud ambitions are temporarily gratified and then destroyed in the progress of her painful romance. The result is that Dahlia sinks into a "semi-lunatic" state, feeling that she is "a living body buried." (ch. 41) Her frenzy declines into stupor, her passion to melancholy. After an attempted suicide and a renunciation of her lover, she settles down to a calm life devoted to caring for her sister's children. "She had gone through fire, as few women had done in like manner, to leave their hearts among the ashes; but with that human heart she left regrets behind her." (ch. 48)

Dahlia's obsessions led her close to insanity and back through its purging fire to a saner existence. Meredith, to intensify his point and establish a certain parallelism in his novel, describes a similar pattern in the character of Anthony Hackbut, the uncle of the Fleming girls. Uncle Anthony has deceived his brother-in-law, Farmer Fleming, into believing that he is a wealthy and influential representative of a London bank, whereas he is merely a bank porter. Nonetheless, his whole preoccupation is with money, and, after a long career in which his honesty and dependability have been his major acquisitions, he unaccountably carries off money belonging to the bank. He has, for too long a time, permitted his imagination to fabricate this scene; finally, the event transpires and he crumbles under the realization of it.

Uncle Anthony's collapse immediately precedes the chapter entitled "Dahlia's Frenzy," in which Dahlia affirms her passion for Edward Blancove, reemphasizing both that Dahlia and Anthony have allowed their central preoccupations to overcome them and that the consequence is mental collapse. Only through self-government and self-abnegation can the valuable experiences of life be assured and preserved.

The association of madness and excess is more clearly drawn in *One of Our Conquerors,* in the character of Victor Radnor. Radnor is a successful and contented man, but beneath his happy home life and his public position is an early "error"—marriage to an elderly woman now hateful to him—which has resulted in a life of bigamy and necessary disguise. This is the tension of his life, but what is more important is that his ambitions for influence, social position, and wealth have caused him to underrate the significance of small details of his own behavior. At the opening of the novel, Radnor slips on a piece of fruit or vegetable and falls. The "sly strip of slipperiness" that has thus overthrown him, is emblematic of the way in which all of his great plans are overthrown by small details.[24] Just as Radnor refuses to acknowledge the true nature of his early slips, he now ignores the nature of his fall, for, as Meredith remarks, "Sanity does not allow the infinitely little to disturb us." (ch. 2) In this case, however, the infinitely little upsets Radnor's sanity, for at the climax of all his ambitions, he is forced to realize that "there had been a moral fall, fully to the level of the physical" along the way. (ch. 41) And ultimately, he is left "the wreck of a splendid intelligence," when his beloved companion, Nataly, dies, and his schemes fail. (ch. 42)

Meredith employed madness in his novels not as a medical reality, but as a sign of moral qualities. Yet, in the time at which he wrote, it was not uncommon to view madness as the result of lost moral control. William B. Carpenter wrote, in his *Principles of Mental Physiology* (1874), that "It is, in fact, in the *persistence* and *exaggeration* of some emotional tendency, leading to an erroneous interpretation of everything that may be in any way related to it, that Insanity very frequently commences; and it is in this stage that a strong effort at self-control may be exerted with effect, not merely in keeping down the exaggerated emotion, but in determinately directing the thoughts into another channel."[25] For Meredith and his contemporaries, this would have seemed a sound explanation. Carpenter explained that early discipline would strengthen the will to resist the chaotic impulses leading on to madness. In a sense, madness was the punishment for an unregulated will; it was the necessary moral collapse fully predictable through the indulgence of the emotions. To let the emotions run unbridled was the first "slip" toward an imbalance that might end in lunacy.

Numerous uses of the convention of madness near the close of the century can be found, varying from Boldwood's rage in *Far From the Madding Crowd,* to Winifred Wynne's hysteria upon learning of her father's crime in Watts-Dunton's *Aylwin,*[26] to the amazing case of Renfield's madness, caused by Count Dracula's vampirism in Bram Stoker's *Dracula.* In most such cases, madness served mainly as a convenience of plot, a way of providing a natural retribution, a probable or improbable shock to the mind involving complications of narrative, and so on. In this way, the usage resembled the modern convention of amnesia. It is difficult to believe that so many subjects of private investigation could suffer partial or total amnesia from a blow to the head or a shock to the sensibilities, and yet, the numbers of these amnesia victims does not decrease, and the convention continues to flourish in fiction, film and television drama of the lower order. To the Victorian novelist, madness served, at its most rudimentary level, just this purpose.

But there was another more profound, side of the Victorian attitude toward madness. In the first volume of *Passages from the Diary of a Late Physician,* Samuel Warren included a story entitled, "Intriguing and Madness" which recounted the history of a Mr. Warningham, who, becoming infatuated with a popular actress, pursues her passionately, though he is already the accepted suitor of another lady. Upon the presentation of an emerald ring, Mr. Warningham is received at breakfast by the actress, but her lover, a military man, appears, quarrels with Warningham, and beats him. This physical punishment, combined with his frenzy, leaves Warningham in a dangerously unhealthy mental state. A doctor finds Warningham in a "state of madness" and deals with him cautiously, noting that a madman is never to be contradicted. Gradually Warningham's fit abates and his ravings end; he is disgusted with himself and with his past dissipations and resolves to lead a virtuous life. The doctor then observes that "These salutory thoughts led to a permanent reformation; his illness, in short, had produced its effect." (ch. 7)

Although his story makes familiar employment of the convention of madness, what is different is that the madness resulting from reckless conduct actually operates as a cure for the victim's moral obliquity. It is as though madness were still conceivable as an accumulated humor which, having been afforded release, leaves the body and mind purified. But in the nineteenth century it is an energy of the spirit not a humor of the body that is involved. In a way, immorality acquires a materiality affecting the self, independent of physical causes. Madness is brought on by physical conditions, but not only by physical conditions. In certain cases, madness is a malady of the soul. So often associated with evil, crime and sin, it becomes a means of curing and controlling the very condition that it has engendered. So Julius and Augustus Hare, in their *Guesses at Truth by Two Brothers* (1827) could suggest,

"Temporary madness may perhaps be necessary in some cases, to cleanse and renovate the mind; just as a fit of illness is to carry off the humours of the body."[27] The notion that an outburst of madness could serve as a purgative found broader applications. The madness of Bertha Mason, which represents the recklessness of mankind—and of Rochester in particular—leads to the blazing end of Thornfield in *Jane Eyre,* and with it the extermination of its begetting madness. Similarly, the mad outbreak of the Gordon Riots in *Barnaby Rudge* expends the accumulated pressure of the society there described, and a more moderate climate prevails. Other outbreaks and holocausts serve similar purposes throughout the literature of the period.

Later in the century, the notion that madness could be beneficial led to a further recognition that it might, in a mad world, be necessary to feign madness in order to do good. So Frank Vanecourt concludes in Laurence Oliphant's *Piccadilly* (1870). At the end of this work, Vanecourt decides that the world in its present form is a madhouse, mainly because people do not act in accordance with their stated beliefs, and therefore are in a state of hallucination.[28] His recommended cure is a conversion to genuine faith which most men are unable to achieve because "they can't face the severe training which the perfection of self-sacrifice involves." (ch. 6) Oliphant's expression of this sentiment was by no means the first, nor the last. Earlier in the century, the poet laureate had produced a poem, troubling to many of his contemporaries, which summarized in a superior artistic manner the several functions of the theme of madness.

Tennyson

In a review of Tennyson's *Maud* (1855), in *The Asylum Journal of Mental Science,* of which he was the editor, John Charles Bucknill, M.D., described the poem as "the history of a madman depicted by the hand of a master."[29] Bucknill praised Tennyson's accuracy in such details as hereditary tendency, misanthropic opinions, early hallucinations, and foreknowledge of possible madness. In the doctor's view, "the common medley of reason and unreason is truthfully given. A less skillful artist would have left this portion of the picture without any light, and would thus have missed the truth."[30]

Although Tennyson might have been pleased to have his poem praised for psychological accuracy, he would probably have urged other features of the poem as more central to his purpose. He was intimately acquainted with madness, since his father was surely unstable and one of his brothers went insane. Moreover, he had used the convention of insanity elsewhere in his poetry. Edith, in "The Sisters," goes mad from frustrated love, and Sir Aylmer Aylmer ("Aylmer's Field") after driving his daughter to death by his resistance to her love for Leolin Averill, lapses into madness ("the man became / Imbecile") and later commits suicide. Obviously, Tennyson used the madness convention with full awareness of its literary function. But in *Maud* he sought to elevate that function.

The narrator in *Maud* does not differ much in outline from common types in the literature of the time. Dickens' madman, for example, has a roughly similar career.[31] For Tennyson, however, madness serves a larger purpose as his own familiar summary indicates. He says of the narrator:

> He is the heir of madness, an egotist with the makings of a cynic, raised to sanity by a pure and holy love which elevates his whole nature, passing from the height of triumph to the lowest depth of misery, driven to madness by the loss of her whom he has loved, and, when he has at length recovered his reason, giving himself up to work for the good of mankind through the unselfishness born of his great passion.[32]

Tennyson demonstrates in his poem several uses of the madness convention. The most obvious is that of plot: a frustrated love leads to madness, which that love, enduring, cures. This is a far more sophisticated form of the model proposed by Samuel Warren in "Intriguing and Madness." But Tennyson's madman does not merely purge his mind of an unhealthy lust. Instead, a mind preoccupied with strong but morbid emotions manages to transfer its passions to a nobler object. The temporary insanity caused by the loss of that object is a form of purgation since it fastens the victim's mind upon the lost but elevated love. The madman's attention focusses more surely on his lost love, his mind regains its balance, and he is brought from morbid inaction "to fight for the good" as he sees it. William B. Carpenter was to explain the medical significance of this transfer of attention and the subsequent reassertion of the healthy will in his standard study, *Principles of Mental Physiology* (1874), where he wrote that many men were saved from an attack of Insanity by "the direction of the Mental activity towards any subject that has a healthful attraction for it."[33] But the moral significance of the events in *Maud* scarcely requires expression, since it is fundamental to Christianity—redemption through love and escape from the confinement of the self.

The world of *Maud* is, like that described in *Piccadilly,* characterized by false seemings and maddening offenses. The motif of madness in the poem, although indicating the condition of the narrator, implies as well some cause in society that makes insanity a predictable end for engaged feelings. If, for example, young women can be sold to high bidders despite their feelings, then love is indeed a "cruel madness." Thus, when the narrator of *Maud* emerges finally from "cells of madness, haunts of horror and fear," and awakes "as it seems, to the better mind," he fulfills a pattern which the nation also seems to be following as it unites itself to prove, in what appears to be a just war, that "we have hearts in a cause, we are noble still."

In this poem, which Tennyson had considered entitling *Maud, or the Madness,* the convention of insanity is used in a factual, accurate way, as a convenience of plot, as an agent of moral recovery, and as an emblem of a diseased and endangered society. Tennyson was thus able to convey meaning without producing a mere tract or sermon, because, understanding the convention for what it was, he used it with precision and effect.

Later Uses of the Convention

Late into the century madness continued to be utilized traditionally; hence, Mary Backhouse, in Mrs. Humphry Ward's *Robert Elsmere* (1888), loses her mind after losing her virtue. But apparent madness came to be associated as well with spiritual states. Lady Alice, in George MacDonald's *The Portent* (1860), is considered a lunatic, though she is simply in a waking trance for twelve years. Similarly, Lilian Ashleigh, in Bulwer-Lytton's *A Strange Story* (1862), loses her senses and lapses into a state of suspended consciousness resembling madness, after reading a letter imputing dissolute behavior to her. During her apparent madness, Lilian lives in her imagination, dwelling close to the world of spirit. Recovering from her malady, she exclaims, "in the awful affliction that darkened my reason, my soul has been made more clear." (ch. 78) As in Tennyson's *Maud,* madness serves as a beneficial cleansing of error. It is, like the salubrious illness described earlier, an automatic indication of the limits of human expectation.

Not all writers felt that the consequences of ambitious human expectation were totally reprehensible. The many new and challenging ideas that became inescapable by the late nineteenth century called up certain predictable responses. Most prevalent of these, according to John A. Lester, Jr., was that of pessimism.[34] Among those who sought more positive escapes from the threatening revelations in science and philosophy, there was a spirited interest in examining nonlogical faculties of cognition through psychical research or exotic forms of religious belief. There was a profound desire to find a source of certainty within the human mind. In art this desire led mainly to an exaltation of the imagination and the more "esthetic" qualities of artistic production. But whether in art or in life, the escape into the mind brought the individual closer to the state of insanity than men had been willing to acknowledge for some time. Dryden could remark, "Genius and Madness are near allied, / And thin partitions do the bounds divide"; but this view had been largely dormant during the nineteenth century, though admiration for poets such as Blake and Chatterton indicated a simmering recognition of the notion.

Late in the century, the desire for escape became pronounced enough to make the madman's case almost enviable. In George du Maurier's *Peter Ibbetson* (1892), Ibbetson himself is considered mad because of his curious behavior and his strange assertions, but we quickly learn that his contempt for the madmen with whom he is confined is justifiable—if his experiences are true. For Ibbetson believes that he has lived a substantial life with the woman he loves in his dreams, and the more prominent features of his madness are merely signs of his impatience as he awaits his "translation to another sphere," that is, to existence in eternity beyond death. (Part 6) If Ibbetson's dreams are true, he is not mad and knows a life far richer even than the most remarkable imagination might attain. If they are not, he is mad, but his experiences have been none the richer for that, since he believes them. In any case, real or reputed madness provides experiences beyond the humdrum existence of most men. The intensity and beauty of the experience, even if it is ultimately false, is more pleasurable to the madman than ordinary life is to the monotonously sane.

Perhaps the most succinct and moving statement of this attitude occurs in Ernest Dowson's elegant poem, "To One in Bedlam." The lunatic's "delicate, mad hands" are more appealing than "the dull world" that stares at him. "Oh, how his rapt gaze wars / With their stupidity!" The madman's world, though actually miserable, does not seem so to him. His world is more alluring than that of all the crude and unfeeling multitude considered sane.

> Know they what dreams divine
> Lift his long, laughing reveries like
>   enchaunted wine,
> And make his melancholy germane to the
>   stars'?

Sadder yet for the poet who speaks is the recognition that his portion is even less attractive than the unenlightened mass, since he can yearn like the madman for the ideal. Like his "lamentable brother," he can imagine exquisite beauty. But he can have only "Half a fool's kingdom," because he is sane and must always know that the madman holds "scentless wisps of straw" not "posies" in his hands. Nonetheless, for one forced to live in a region between dreams and the vanity of the world, the madman's case seems best.

> Better than mortal flowers,
> Thy moon-kissed roses seem: better than love
>   or sleep,
> The star-crowned solitude of thine oblivious
>   hours!

Summary

Throughout the nineteenth century madness was a real part of every man's consciousness. There were extraordinary historical cases, such as Madame Lavalette's loss of reason after the ordeal of managing her husband's escape from a French prison and the death sentence in 1815; or Georgiana Weldon's escape from confinement for insanity in 1884, which became a popular issue, containing all the ingredients of a *cause célèbre*: "the society background, the wealthy and beautiful lady under threat of duress, the dramatic escape in disguise."[35] Literary minds too could scarcely forget that such luminaries as William Cowper, Christopher Smart, and William Collins had not been entirely sane. Some, like Hazlitt, knew madness in their own families, and others, like John Clare or Arthur Symons, in themselves.

In literature, madness had first served primarily as a device to provide sensation, drama and intense climaxes. It was a convenience of plot, a quick way to explain reckless or imprudent behavior. It served the moral purpose of indicating the just termination of a dissolute life. Gradually, however, it came also to serve as a convenient emblem of more than individual madness. As insanity figured more and more readily not as evil, but as purgative good—a necessary trial by fire— it came to refer to society at large, also hopefully susceptible to cure by some species of brain fever. This hope proving vain, one last service was left to the mad. They could stand as lonely, outcast figures who preserved in their mad kingdoms the riches of the imagination so wantonly abandoned by the world about them. Although in society itself the madman, like the gypsy, was undergoing a steady domestication; in literature, like the gypsy, the madman came to represent an unreal, but earnestly desired, preserve of values no one hoped to see so purely again. The literary convention departed from social reality, creating a new, enhanced region of experience, which with the discoveries of Freud and other investigators of the human psyche, seemed even more necessary. As human nature became more and more the subject of scientific analysis, writers ventured more and more to sentimentalize and ennoble a state that men still feared, but which seemed as attractive as the alternatives facing them in a world of growing ugliness and declining values.

Notes

[1] Michel Foucault, *Madness and Civilization: A History of Insanity in the Age of Reason,* trans. Richard Howard (New York, 1967), p. 161.

[2] Ibid., p. 93.

[3] Kathleen Jones, *Lunacy, Law, and Conscience 1744-1845* (London, 1955), p. 7.

[4] See W. B. C. Watkins' discussion of this subject in *Perilous Balance: The Tragic Genius of Swift, Johnson, & Sterne* (Cambridge, 1960), pp. 90ff.

[5] Nigel Walker, *Crime and Insanity in England: Volume One: The Historical Perspective* (Edinburgh, 1968), p. 43.

[6] Ibid., p. 70. This subject is also treated in William Ll. Parry-Jones' *The Trade in Lunacy. A Study of Private Madhouses in the Eighteenth and Nineteenth Centuries* (London, 1972).

[7] Walker, *Crime and Insanity,* p. 71.

[8] Jones, *Lunacy, Law,* p. 32.

[9] Ibid., p. 26.

[10] Ibid., p. 66. William Ll. Parry-Jones discusses the growth and function of the private lunatic asylums thoroughly.

[11] In *The Mind of the European Romantic* (Garden City, 1969), H. G. Schenk has written that the explosion of irrational or subconscious behavior associated with the French Revolution "was the signal for the Romantic battle against Reason." (p. 3) Mental aberration may also, he argues, be attributed to the stress of a philosophy of "nihilistic subjectivism," and he points out that artists such as Nikolaus Lenau, Gerard de Nerval, and Caspar David Friedrich died mad. (p. 52) E. T. A. Hoffmann maintained that "some measure of madness, or folly, is so deeply rooted in human nature that one cannot come to know human nature better than through a careful study of the insane and the mentally deficient" (Quoted in Harvey W. Hewett-Thayer's *Hoffmann: Author of the Tales* [New York, 1971], p. 185).

[12] Quoted in George Rosen's *Madness in Society: Chapters in the Historical Sociology of Mental Illness* (Chicago, 1968), p. 183.

[13] Quoted in ibid.

[14] Parry-Jones insists more than once in his book that there was actually very little evidence presented to justify charges of false incarceration in mental institutions being a practice in any way common.

[15] Jones, *Lunacy, Law,* p. 183. In an article entitled "Commissions of Lunacy," which appeared in the *Cornhill Magazine* for February, 1862, madness is defined as "an insensibility to the general principles of human nature caused by disease." The article asserts that madness is not merely advanced eccentricity, and occupies itself with the legal aspects of insanity. The article was prompted by the famous Windham Case.

[16] Lorenzo Sabine, *Notes on Duels and Duelling* (Boston, 1856), 2, p. 15. In fiction, Jack Sheppard's mother, in William Harrison Ainsworth's *Jack Sheppard,* is driven insane by her son's crimes and confined to Bedlam.

[17] This novel was based upon Mrs. Opie's play, *Father and Daughter* (1802). See Louis James, *Fiction for the Working Man 1830-1850* (London, 1963), p. 100.

[18] Bulwer-Lytton was driven at one point in his quarrels with his wife to have her certified insane and detained with medical attention. The same doctor, however, conveniently certified her as fit to travel with her son, whom she abused mercilessly. This illustrates not only Bulwer-Lytton's familiarity with aberrant behavior later in his career, but also the ease with which individuals could be confined and classified as lunatics (V. A. G. R. Lytton, *The Life of Edward Bulwer, First Lord Lytton* [London, 1913], 2, pp. 273-74).

[19] Kathleen Jones, *Mental Health and Social Policy 1845-1959* (London, 1960), p. 21. In the *Cornhill Magazine* for July, 1900, Andrew Lang suggested that the hidden mad wife in Jane Eyre was borrowed from Mrs. Radcliffe's *A Sicilian Romance.*

[20] See George H. Ford, *Dickens and His Readers: Aspects of Novel-Criticism Since 1836* (New York, 1965), p. 18.

[21] Kathleen Tillotson, "Introduction," *Barnaby Rudge: A Tale of the Riots of 'Eighty* (London, 1954), New Oxford Illustrated Edition, p. xii.

[22] The Medical Registration Act of 1858 prescribed examinations for medical men to treat the insane. Kathleen Jones concludes that, in the early part of the century, there were many cases of illegal detention, in which patients' names were changed and they were forbidden to communicate with the outside world. Often such patients were victims of greedy relatives. The madhouse keeper, meanwhile, "had a vested interest in the continuation of the "illness," since he was able to charge a high fee for his doubtful "care"; it was scarcely in his interest to discharge a patient while the relatives were willing to pay for his confinement" (*Mental Health,* p. 11). But Parry-Jones contends that, whatever abuses may have occurred early on, by the mid-nineteenth century there was little evidence of false confinement (*Trade in Lunacy,* pp. 26, 222, etc.).

[23] Jones, *Mental Health,* p. 20.

[24] Jack Lindsay discusses the motif of the fall in *George Meredith: His Life and Works* (London, 1956), pp. 284ff.

[25] William B. Carpenter, *Principles of Mental Physiology, with their applications to the training and discipline of the mind, and the study of its morbid conditions* (New York, 1896), p. 671.

[26] Winifred's madness is cured by being transferred to the healthier Sinfi Lovell by magnetic means, a practice that Watts-Dunton defended as medically performable.

[27] Julius and Augustus Hare, *Guesses at Truth by Two Brothers* (London, 1889), p. 159.

[28] In his memoir, *Episodes in A Life of Adventure, or, Moss from a Rolling Stone* (1887), Oliphant said that "The world, with its bloody wars, its political intrigues, its social evils, its religious cant, its financial frauds, and its glaring anomalies, assumed in my eyes more and more the aspect of a gigantic lunatic asylum. And the question occurred to me whether there might not be latent forces in nature, by the application of which this profound moral malady might be reached." (p. 342) See Robert Lee Wolff's *Strange Stories: And Other Explorations in Victorian Fiction* (New York, 1972) for an interesting account of Oliphant and his religious views.

[29] John Charles Bucknill, M.D., review of *Maud and Other Poems* in *The Asylum Journal of Mental Science,* no. 15 (Oct., 1855), p. 96.

[30] Ibid., p. 103.

[31] See *The Poems of Tennyson,* ed. Christopher Ricks (London, 1969), p. 1038, for notes on similarities of plot and so forth.

[32] Hallam Tennyson, *Alfred Lord Tennyson: A Memoir by His Son,* 2 vols. (New York, 1905) 1, p. 396.

[33] Carpenter, *Mental Physiology,* p. 673.

[34] John A. Lester, Jr., *Journey Through Despair: 1880-1914. Transformations in British Literary Culture* (Princeton, 1968), p. 59.

[35] Jones, *Mental Health,* p. 26.

AUTOBIOGRAPHY

Mary Elene Wood (essay date 1994)

SOURCE: "Elizabeth Packard and Versions of Sanity," in *The Writing on the Wall: Women's Autobiography and the Asylum,* University of Illinois Press, 1994, pp. 25-47.

[*In the following essay, Wood examines Elizabeth Packard's account of her experience in an insane asylum. In particular, Wood studies the parallels between Packard's story and both slave narratives and sentimental novels.*]

In 1860, Theophilus Packard forced his wife Elizabeth from their home and committed her to the state insane asylum at Jacksonville, Illinois. According to her own account, she had long been battling with Theophilus, a Presbyterian minister, over the validity of what she considered the outdated and repressive concept of innate depravity. Elizabeth held her own Bible discussion groups, where she encouraged church members, mostly women, to question the traditional Calvinist doctrine and develop personal interpretations of biblical passages. Her husband and certain church elders considered her preaching subversive and indicative of an unbalanced mind. With the signature of a doctor and the corroboration of Andrew McFarland, the asylum superintendent, Elizabeth Packard was separated from her four sons and her daughter and made a prisoner of the institution. She would not be released until 1863, after which she would become an active and successful lobbyer for the rights of married women and the mentally ill. To raise money to support herself and her campaign, she published several pamphlets and books, the first of which was her autobiography, originally published in 1867, then reissued a year later as *The Prisoner's Hidden Life; or, Insane Asylums Unveiled.*[1]

She based her autobiography largely on writings she kept hidden in the backing of her mirror in the asylum, out of the sight of asylum authorities, who would examine and confiscate any writing materials they found in inmates' quarters. As Packard introduces her book: "the working of this Institution is so carefully covered up, and so artfully concealed from the public eye, that the external world knows nothing of the 'hidden life of the prisoner,' within. Therefore the journal of an eye witness taken on the spot, is now presented to the public, as the mirror in which to behold its actual operations" (p. 125). Packard does not fail to note the significance of the place in which she chooses to hide her asylum writings; the mirror that she brings with her from home and preserves throughout her imprisonment comes to represent her maintenance of a sense of sanity and selfhood. She can look into it and see the person she has always known, maintaining her need to look as well as be looked at, resisting the attempts of asylum authorities to deny her position as subject and identify her as an insane woman and an object of study.

As her asylum stay lengthens and she begins to record her experiences in journal entries and letters, she comes to identify her writing with the mirror; her journal reflects the "actual operations" of the asylum. By presenting her journal as a record of fact, she tries to separate her work from the "insane" woman whose credibility as a witness would be questioned by her mid-nineteenth-century audience. She hopes that if, by holding up her mirror, she can convince her readers that her experience is objective fact, they will see not only the asylum world but also their own image superimposed on her portrayal of the asylum. She seeks to establish her own sanity as a woman labeled insane and to show that an asylum community of insane women can reflect a world that smugly considers itself sane.

In trying to discover how a woman incarcerated as insane can speak her own experience, Elizabeth Packard engages in the nineteenth-century debate in the United States over what constitutes valid evidence and authority and to what extent women could be considered rational beings. Packard's text questions the growing scientific monopoly on knowledge and cultivates the idea that a woman's personal observation and testimony are sufficient evidence in themselves, proof of a reality whose existence must be respected and recognized. She thus challenges the dominant nineteenth-century American belief that middle-class women are only reasonable, if at all, within the domestic sphere and rarely able to observe and describe the world with the same accuracy with which men can.[2]

An asylum autobiography is the appropriate place for Packard to formulate a redefinition of the female subject, given that in the discourse on insanity and on the nature of the asylum, power distinctions within the larger culture emerge in extreme form. Packard's autobiography shows that in nineteenth-century discussions of insanity, much more is at stake than the good of the suffering patient. Both alienists and patients struggle to define "sanity" and "rationality" and the ways these terms help construct gender and class distinctions. In so doing, the actors in what Packard refers to as "The Great Drama" argue over who has authority to enforce logical systems, not only in the asylum itself but in the legal codes and social mores that intersect the asylum world.

In crafting her autobiography, Packard taps into several generic traditions that establish the authority of a speaking subject. In particular, her text invokes the strategies of spiritual autobiography, captivity narrative, and slave narrative (which itself draws on spiritual autobiography), strategies in which the writing voice presents itself as coherent and sane even as it occasionally disappears into selflessness before the story it tells and the spiritual power it invokes. By comparing her own situation to that of the slave, however erroneous and self-serving that comparison may be, Packard connects her narrative to an autobiographical tradition in which personal experience provides grounds for argument against injustice. By simultaneously drawing on the American version of the sentimental novel tradition, in which a virtuous woman is victimized by an unfeeling rake, Packard's text reaffirms the middle-class womanhood of the writer, whose public presence threatens to identify her as someone who has stepped outside her proper sphere. By drawing on forms familiar to her middle-class readers, Packard recreates and uses the ideology of middle-class femaleness, stressing her piety and maternal feeling, even as she calls that ideology into question. This asylum autobiography thus calls upon and reformulates a variety of forms and strategies that weave themselves throughout the text in an effort to create a speaking female subject— Elizabeth Packard—who is rational yet "feminine," authoritative yet victimized, autonomous yet selfless, politically-minded yet maternal.

Packard's work follows the pattern described by autobiography theorist Estelle Jelinek, who claims that in writing the stories of their lives, women tend to create forms that are often nonlinear and fragmentary (Jelinek, p. 12). At first, Packard's form seems scattered and disorganized as she alternates between telling her story in the past tense, offering present-tense journal entries, telling the stories of other inmates, expounding her views on morality and religion, and introducing letters she wrote while in the asylum.

The fragmented nature of the work is complicated by the fact that Packard presents other women's histories along with her own, offering chapter after chapter titled with other women's names as well as several first-person narratives that she appends to her own writings. The longest and most important of these is by Sophie Olsen, who entered the asylum as a voluntary patient in 1862 under pressure from her husband. Packard clearly intended that the works should be read as a whole. In fact, in a later edition of her autobiography, *Modern Persecution,* Packard incorporated Olsen's narrative, which appears in an appendix in the first edition, as a chapter of her book, eliminating the appendix of the first edition. The first-person narratives of other inmates are also important to Packard's autobiography because they provide complementary, alternative visions that rarely duplicate Packard's story but help create a multi-voiced narrative about life within the asylum.

The variety of strategies put into play within the text indicates that what is at issue for Packard is who wields power over writing itself, who has the right to tell whose story. She writes that upon arriving at the asylum she is allowed substantial privileges, probably because she begins as a paying patient with an educated background. She soon becomes aware of the abuses exercised against the other patients and resolves to take up their cause, writing a letter of complaint to the superintendent that "depicted their wrongs, oppression and received cruelties, in the most expressive terms

I could command" (p. 87). This is the first time she puts pen to paper in the asylum for the purpose of expressing wrongs, and she soon discovers that her words really have no power at all to elicit changes by the establishment.

Throughout, Packard expresses her fear that McFarland's silencing does more than leave a blank void where her words might have been; it also allows the blank to be filled by others' assumptions or his own words. Her indignation at being deprived of her "post-office rights" is always tied to her indictment of the doctor's "dictation." After a long exposition on McFarland's injustice in not allowing her to write freely, Packard says she knows "that all my favors, rights and privileges, were suspended entirely upon the will of the Superintendent, and therefore entirely subject to his dictation" (pp. 86-87). She associates the censorship of her writing with dictation in both meanings of the word: the "dictator," the despot, is one who tells her what to write. Packard feels that McFarland's dictatorship gives him the power to write history. She is continually frustrated by the fact that those who look at the asylum from the outside never see it informed by her insider's perception. She makes the plea, "O, Illinois! State of my adoption, when, when will you look intelligently, with your own eyes, into the practical operation of your Insane Asylum system, as it is now being practiced in your State Institution at Jacksonville? Never, never, will you see it as it is, until you can look at it through some other medium than Dr. McFarland or his Reports" (p. 159). McFarland's reports were published regularly in the *American Journal of Insanity,* while the letters of Packard and other inmates rarely reached the outside world. Given that McFarland was an established alienist who was both a respected landowner in the town of Jacksonville, where he was superintendent of the state asylum from 1854 to 1870, and president for a time of the Association of Medical Superintendents of American Institutions of the Insane, his accounts of asylum life held authority in both the public and professional eye. As a result, a single version of asylum reality was transmitted to the world; McFarland's asylum was considered to be the only one that existed.[3]

According to her narrative, from the first time she tries to write within the asylum about her experiences, she suffers the consequences of speaking out against such asylum abuses as the prohibition of writing materials, interception of letters to the outside, use of physical restraint and beatings, punishments by dunking in cold water, threats of violence or removal to the worst wards, transfer of patients from ward to ward without warning, denial of patients' simplest requests: "This document cast the die for my future destiny. The transition time had fully come, when comfort, attention, respect, privilege, all, all, were in the dead past, and discomfort, inattention, disrespect, contempt, wrong and deprivation are to mark the future of my prison life" (p. 87).

Elizabeth Parsons Ware Packard, c.1864

Here, as throughout the work, she emphasizes her own subjectivity by claiming the authority of the historian. By so doing, she violates the nature of women's sphere not so much in asserting her subjectivity, which has a place within that sphere, but by asserting it within the context of philosophical and psychological discourse. In the nineteenth-century world of separate male and female spheres, writing that created a personal world was gendered as feminine, while writing that presented itself as impersonal discussion of ideas related to the political realm was gendered as masculine. Packard's writing challenges this separation by blending personal narrative with psychological and political theory.

Yet Packard's text never abandons the feminized forms that would be expected of her. Woven into the fragments of political treatises, stories, letters, and journal entries in Packard's autobiography is a progression of events that in many ways repeats that of most nineteenth-century domestic fiction, which dominated literary sales from the 1820s until after 1870. However, Packard ultimately deviates from the standard formula in a way that reminds her reader that she is writing autobiography, not fiction, and that popular literary forms cannot contain her experience. Where domestic novels usually end with marriage and the reform of cruel men, Packard's story ends with a call for reforms in laws related to marriage and institutionalization of women.

Nina Baym has pointed out that most women's novels of this period follow a standard plot line: a poor lonely orphan or disinherited heiress is thrown out into the world alone, where she learns to make her own way and develop an independent identity before she inevitably settles down and marries a good man (p. 35). The primary message of these novels for the largely female reading public was that a woman should escape from those who abused their power over her (usually fathers, uncles, or guardians), establish her own sense of self, take responsibility for her life, and use her then well-founded moral strength to educate those around her. If she fell in love and was swept away by a man before she established her independence, she was destined to learn her lesson the hard way and be forced to begin anew (Baym, pp. 40-41). In E. D. E. N. Southworth's *The Curse of Clifton,* for example, when young Zuleime clandestinely marries Frank Fairfax while still under her father's thumb, she is destined to suffer as a consequence through widowhood, extreme poverty, and the humiliation of becoming an actress to support herself. Only after the heroine has established a strong sense of self, can she then marry a good man and settle down.

Just as these novels begin when a young woman is thrown from an oppressive domestic situation out into the cruel world, Packard's history of her asylum life opens when she is being removed from a home char-acterized by conflict with her husband to an asylum where she, "his constant companion of twenty-one years, was entrusted to the hands of my prison keeper to be led by him to find my bed and lodging, he knew not where, and to be subject to insults, he knew not what" (p. 59). Her husband, with his "brute force claims upon my personal liberty" (p. 44), denies her ability and desire to act independently, just as the cruel father of the domestic novel allows his daughter little control over her life. This battle for power continues in the asylum. Like the fictional heroine, Packard draws on her moral strength to fight for independence. She makes mistakes along the way, such as trusting the superintendent to protect her, but, like the heroine, she begins again, relying more and more on her own resources. Just as most domestic fiction centers on the heroine's involvement with a tyrannical male character, Packard's autobiography focuses on her struggle with the asylum superintendent, Andrew McFarland, and the power he represents, a struggle that revolves primarily around her attempts—as well as those of other women—to speak and write their thoughts and experiences. Her story recalls the epistolary sentimental novel, precursor to the American domestic novel. In Richardson's *Clarissa,* Lovelace controls the letters of the kidnapped heroine. He writes them, signs them, and sends them, just as he controls and violates her body. Like Harriet Jacobs, who, in *Incidents in the Life of a Slave Girl,* engineers her escape from slavery by writing and sending letters, Packard revises Richardson's form to give women control over writing.

Ultimately, the book itself becomes the most powerful character in its own story, the chronicle of her attempts, finally successful, to gain access to writing. The narrative describes her transfer to one of the worst wards, where she is denied writing implements, and forbidden to obtain paper on her own. She claims that because McFarland knows she holds influence among both the staff and the inmates, he tells her at various times that she must not speak with anyone, nor may the other inmates speak to her. At one point she is instructed "to hold no more prayer-meetings, lend no more books, and those she has lent must be immediately returned" (pp. 74-75). Much of her narrative describes her attempts to avoid these mandates by obtaining paper clandestinely, hiding copies of everything she writes, communicating with the other inmates, or turning to the staff for help denied her by the superintendent.

Packard finally appeals to the asylum's board of trustees and obtains her release. The board forces her back into her husband's custody, however, denying her request to stay on at the asylum voluntarily, with freedom to come and go, so that she can finish her book and begin to support herself financially. She ends her story by describing her successful efforts to gain her freedom from her husband and have her sanity legally revindicated, concluding that she has established herself as an independent, financially solvent writer who is now willing and able to take responsibility for her family "in order that society and their friends be relieved of the burden of their support and education" (p. 315).

Thus while in the fictional conventions of domestic fiction the heroine's marriage ends her tale, Packard's story ends with her separation not only from the asylum but from her husband and children. She writes, "At about fifty years of age I have been compelled, in consequence of the unreasonable position the law assigns me as a married woman, to begin life's struggle alone, and unaided, having no other capital to depend upon, but my good health and education. With the aid of this capital alone, I have paid the entire expense of printing and selling eighteen thousand books, by my own efforts entirely" (p. 344). The fact that her book ends differently from most domestic fiction suggests that Packard has worked to develop a concept of female subjectivity quite different from that of the dominant culture and of contemporary women novelists. For, as Baym points out, while nineteenth-century popular women novelists espoused a kind of domestic feminism based in a woman's strong sense of her self and her ability to influence the world around her through her moral purity and sacrifice, in the end these novelists usually portrayed the married heroine as reconciled to the social order, performing a difficult balancing act in marriage between submission and "suicidal defiance" (Baym, p. 37). In the real-life experience after the storybook ending, perhaps, these middle-class women would tend to fulfill Tocqueville's characterization of American women as independent young ladies and submissive wives. The novels may well end at marriage precisely because it would be difficult for the writers to carry the self-dependence established by their characters into a portrait of married life.

Packard counterposes her own ending to the expected marriage and anticipated life of happiness. In order to maintain her belief in her status as creative subject she must remain apart from the familial hierarchy or at least redefine her relation to it. Unlike the fictional heroine, who supposedly holds her own once she comes to know herself, Packard feels she can never be certain that the independence and respect she has worked so hard to establish and maintain is a permanent state. Moreover, she comes to believe that if she wishes to be regarded as a creative, rational person, she must reject the identity of wife.

Packard turns away from marriage largely because, given her asylum experiences, she sees it as linked to the powerlessness she felt when incarcerated. She writes that McFarland kept women in the asylum "until they begged to be sent home. This led me to suspect that there was a secret understanding between the husband and the Doctor; that the subjection of the wife was the cure the husband was seeking to effect under the specious plea of insanity; and when they began to express a wish to go home, the Doctor would encourage these tyrannical husbands that they were 'improving'" (p. 81). She claims McFarland deliberately exercises power over her in order to keep her in her place: forbids her to meet with the other inmates, confiscates her personal belongings, and, most importantly, restricts what she calls her "post-office rights," which guarantee she can send and receive letters.

As Packard challenges McFarland's claims to authority she draws parallels between what she sees as her minister husband's unreasonable authoritarianism and that of the doctor. The domestic novel genre enables her to portray both men as part of a family drama in which, in addition to proving themselves to be weak debating partners, they inappropriately seek to exert power over her. That Packard sees an intimate connection between the authority of husband and doctor corresponds with the historian Nancy Tomes's assertion that asylum superintendents tended to adapt themselves to the definitions of insanity understood by a patient's family. Packard's case reinforces Tomes's contention that "the only party likely to challenge the doctor-family consensus, that is, the patient, had little power to dispute the decision" (pp. 121, 127-28). The link Packard sees between doctor and husband is their shared belief in men's mental superiority and naturally endowed authority over women. When she asks McFarland for "liberty to support myself, as other wives do who cannot live with their husband," he replies, "'The only right course for you is to return to your husband, and do as a true woman should do; be to him a true and loving wife, as you promised to be by your marriage vow, unto death, and until you do consent to do so, there is no prospect of your getting out of this place! For until you will give up this insane unreasonable notion of your duty forbidding it, I consider this institution the proper place for you to spend your days in'" (p. 134). In chapter after chapter, she reports similar confrontations with the doctor, emphasizing the hopelessness of her appeals to him and stressing that she is doubly bound by the authority of doctor over patient and man over woman.[4]

It is this sense of a double oppression that leads Packard to link reform of insanity laws to advocacy of laws reforming and protecting the rights of married women. She points out in her later work *Modern Persecution* that the law under which she was incarcerated, passed February 15, 1851, held that married women and children judged insane by the medical superintendent of the state hospital could be committed at the request of the husband without further evidence. Writes Packard,

"Thus I learned my first lesson in that chapter of woman law, which denies to married women a legal right to her own identity or individuality" (*Modern Persecution,* p. 55).

Packard's insistence that a link existed between the unreasonable authority of physician and husband is telling in the light of Elaine Showalter's finding that asylum life simply exaggerated the home lives of many nineteenth-century women.[5] Indeed, the interrelationships between family and other societal institutions often become startlingly clear in the language of superintendents themselves. In the same 1869 article in the *American Journal of Insanity* that describes McFarland's persecution before the Illinois State Legislature by "a handsome and talkative crazy woman" ("Illinois Legislature," p. 204)—namely, Elizabeth Packard—the writer explicitly compares the asylum director to a father:

> No father of a household allows of interference with his private and domestic arrangements or discipline; and he is not responsible to the community except for some criminal abuse or neglect. His domestic affairs are his own, and are not properly liable to any general inquisition; and he may defy any impertinent intrusion simply to gratify curiosity or for obtruding advice as to management and discipline. So of the great households committed by the State to the charge of such as are intrusted with them, and who stand to them *in loco parentis.* ("Illinois Legislation," pp. 214-15)

The asylum becomes the place where the contradictions inherent in the separation of spheres and the rhetoric of democracy are made explicit. If the "private," "domestic" sphere belongs to women, it is also the place where male law is sovereign and the democratic rule of the public realm has no place. The asylum represents that point at which women, while they may hold a certain amount of moral power within the home, are reminded of where the power really lies. Both the name and the use of the notorious and controversial restraining device, the Utica crib, a box in which the patient was locked beneath wooden slats, reinforce the infantilization of women in these surrogate, often motherless homes in which father-superintendents seek to exert absolute control.[6]

If the "household" metaphor is not a strong enough reminder, the *American Journal of Insanity* narrative reinforces it with another metaphor—that of a military ship. After one writer warns, "not more assuredly can the small worm that riots in the massive timbers of the ship becalmed in the tropics, send her with all her rich freight to the bottom, than can a troop of ill selected and ill disciplined hospital attendants wreck the reputation of any institution in which they find lodgment," he admonishes, "certainly, the stern necessities of mili-

tary service do not require any more prompt compliances than our own" ("Annual Meeting," pp. 54-55). The conflation of family metaphors with military ones exposes the intersection of these two institutions in which white male dominance is supposed to reign supreme. Such a conflation makes it virtually impossible for Packard's narrative to end with a return to marriage and family.

Unlike the domestic novel, Packard's narrative is meant to persuade her audience to take political action. Her efforts to persuade are both subject matter and form in her autobiography. The reader, like McFarland, must be convinced that she is sane. Packard must show that she *can* reason as much as she must persuade her readers with the content of her arguments. For a woman, let alone an "insane" one, this effort to persuade is itself suspect. Packard holds that "even [a married woman's] right of self-defense on the plane of argument is denied her, for when she *reasons,* then she is insane! and if her reasons are wielded potently, and with irresistible logic, she is then exposed to hopeless imprisonment, as the response of her opponent" (p.126). First as a wife and then as an asylum inmate, she is deprived of her ability to be accepted as a reasoning being. The fact that her husband committed her already cast such doubt on her sanity that everything she says in her own defense is seen merely as a symptom to be analyzed and examined.

Packard's focus on persuading her reader both to believe her story and to take action for legal reform invokes the slave narrative alongside her domestic romance tale.[7] Packard's narrative clearly borrows from slave narratives the use of legitimating documentation to support her tale of personal experience. *Insane Asylums Unveiled* is structured much like what critic Robert Burns Stepto refers to as a "first phase" slave narrative. In this early version of slave narrative the writer creates an "*eclectic narrative* form,*" in which authenticating documents are appended to the central tale, so that "the documents collectively create something close to a dialogue—of forms as well as voices" (p.225). By appropriating a form that would help give her credence in the eyes of white antislavery readers, Packard obscures significant differences between her own position and that of most slave narrative writers (her white middle-class upbringing, her preasylum access to literacy, her connections, however tenuous, to white middle-class legislators outside the asylum). Still, Packard connects her story to an autobiographical tradition in which personal experience and the documents used to verify it provide grounds for argument against injustice directed at an oppressed group.

Like many slave narratives, Packard's text uses Christian rhetoric to establish her right to speak and be considered a legitimate subject. Her views on Christianity are consistent with the movement in the nineteenth-century United States away from Calvinism toward forms of Christianity that rejected the concept of natural depravity. She knew that in her struggle against Theophilus Packard's religion, she would have supporters among her readers, as she did among the jurors who eventually declared her sane after her release. Many would agree with the words she reports speaking to her Bible class, "the religion of authority has had its day—a reasonable religion, such as will bear the infallible tests of truth, based on arguments drawn from God's word and works is the religion for us" (p. 19). Many of her contemporaries had long since adopted a Christianity that allowed each of them to analyze the Bible and argue theology without fear of being thought heretics.

She knew that she would find less sympathy, however, when she went beyond discussing "a reasonable religion" to advocating a reasonable legal system that would recognize a married woman's separate identity and reasonable belief system that would grant women's ability to decide their own fate. She realizes that she may have been imprisoned and declared insane by an outdated Calvinism but what keeps her in the asylum is less her husband's religion than the strength of his legally-sanctioned authority over her. It is for this reason that she opens her book with a plea not against Calvinism but against "the legalized usurpation of human rights" as manifested in the absence of laws protecting married women from their husbands' authority (iii).

Still, once institutionalized, Packard feels she must assert and support her own right to religious choice. She describes a confrontation with McFarland in which she argues that her anti-Calvinist religious opinions cannot be used as evidence of her insanity. Comparing herself to a sighted woman declared blind by the superintendent of a "Blind Institution," Packard first asks, "Must not the individual herself be tested, in order to settle this controverted question?" (pp. 292-93). She then asks the doctor,

> "But supposing he should admit that the lady can see, but she don't see *right*; for instance, she contends that the moon looks to her as large as a cart wheel, while he says it should look only as large as a saucer. Now the common people, or the public tribunal, more than ever, see their Superintendent's folly; for the very fact that it looks to her as large as a cart wheel, demonstrates that she is not blind, and that her organ of vision, too, is not peculiar, for there is just this difference in the size of the same object, as seen through different organizations. Now, Dr. McFarland, tell me, is reason, which is the eye of the Soul, extinct, while the individual gives every evidence that it is in full and healthy exercise?"

He replied, "There is a certain kind of disease of the eye which can not be detected by common people; it takes great learning and the highest kind of professional skill to detect it; and besides, this kind of optical disease is hopeless—there is no cure for this kind of blindness." (p. 293)

Here, as she blends personal narrative with rhetorical skill, Packard denies that there can be an external measure of whether someone is rational or not. The symbols that Packard uses tie this discussion of rationality to her insistence that women are equal to men in their credibility. As both the "blind" woman and the doctor look at the moon, traditional symbol of female power, the woman compares it to a cart wheel, symbol of locomotion, travel, freedom. The doctor, on the other hand, compares it to a saucer, an object from a woman's domestic life. Packard implies here that the doctor and his patient see differently depending upon the subject position of each. The doctor insists that what she sees should remind her of the domestic sphere; the "blind" woman wishes for power to decide the course of her own life. By using this example of the moon "as seen through different organizations," Packard implies that the interpretation of the image depends upon the position and desires of the observer rather than upon an absolute external reality identifiable only by an expert.

By the time Packard was writing, scientists in the United States both claimed that they could describe a solid external reality and expressed a profound distrust of the "reality" perceived by the senses, a distrust that went back on the one hand to Locke's ambivalence about the verifiability of external reality and on the other to Calvinist doubts about signs of sainthood. In addition, white middle-class Americans in the 1860s were in search of categories, hierarchies, ways of ordering their unstable and all-too-democratic post–Civil War world. As medicine and psychology became more professionalized, experts encouraged the average citizen to depend more and more on their ability to interpret the "facts" of human behavior and the human mind. Experience itself—the individual interpretation of perception, essential to the constitution of the Lockean self—was increasingly seen as untrustworthy, unless it was accompanied by expert training and knowledge. A decade or so after Packard was writing, prominent neurologist George Beard expressed this growing suspicion of uninformed observation. According to Beard,

> On the principles of evidence as drawn from the testimony of human beings, it has thus far been undenied that the senses are worthy of trust, that the first quality of an observer and reporter is not expertness but honesty, and that what is good evidence for one class of claims is equally good for any class. These three assumptions—the common

basis of law and logic—the neurology of the future must push utterly aside; and in their place it will be established that in science or organized knowledge only the testimony of experts can be of value, and that the quality and amount of evidence needful to establish any claim must vary with, and be relative to the nature of that claim (p. 70).

The growing specialization of the age is evident here in Beard's insistence that claims be divided into classes, each of which requires a separate body of evidence identifiable only by a certain category of experts. The "testimony of human beings" based on information gathered through the senses, the kind of testimony Packard wishes to give, must be replaced in both the classroom and the courtroom by the "testimony of experts" (here differentiated from "human beings"), who, like McFarland, have a special kind of vision.

Beard's words reverberate with the claim to authority of medical superintendents who battled throughout the century with state legislatures intent on monitoring their institutions. After Packard brought superintendent Andrew McFarland to the attention of the State under suspicion of mismanagement and abuse of power in late 1867, the editors of the *American Journal of Insanity* defended his autonomy and attacked the state investigating committee by claiming, "It is this exposure to open general observation and criticism which, with all its obvious security to the public, is the most apt to lead to suspicions and distrust, and to annoying and idle examinations. Many details of management and discipline cannot be accurately judged of by an undiscriminating' populace, and undue publicity would also destroy their purpose and effect" ("Illinois Legislation," p. 214).

Packard continually shows that within the asylum the doctor's authority, his ability to decide whether the vision is diseased or not, takes precedence over her own. Yet while she challenges this authority, she does not reject science altogether. Since she advocates a science redefined to admit the reasoning power of every individual, she supports the primacy of evidence, of fact, but what she calls fact or evidence is different from McFarland's concept of the same terms. "Fact" in her view is inseparable from subjective experience. For her, personal narrative is itself a kind of science, in which the voice of the narrator is a necessary correlate of the "data" collected and reported.

In the preface of her book, she defines her personal experiences as "data": "In disclosing to the blinded public the real character of their Insane Asylums, the author has relied mainly upon her own personal observation, and three years experience, as data from which to draw her own conclusions; and if from this data her conclusions are not legitimate, she asks the reader to be the judge" (v). She does not draw the classic

Baconian distinction here between herself as observer and that which she studies.[8] Even as she provides her reader with legitimating documents, she ignores the question of how objective she is or is not. She claims the right to report her own experience in her own words and have it be accepted as legitimate evidence.

When Packard reports her own experience as acceptable data, she both gives her narrative the legitimacy of the researcher's perspective and maintains that a human mind cannot be observed as an object of science. There will always be subjectivity and context to take into account, both that of alienist and that of patient. This belief naturally undermines what she sees as a major premise of McFarland's authority—that he may observe and pass judgment on the asylum inmates without actually interacting with them.

> "Now if you, Doctor, or any other individual, will bring forward one act of my own, showing lack of reason in it, I will own you have a right to call me insane."
>
> After waiting a long time, he said, "was it not an insane act for you to fall down stairs, and then to be carried back to you ward?"
>
> "That was not *my act* in being carried back to my ward. It was your own act, and my falling down stairs, was an accident, caused too, by *your* ungentlemanly interference; and the object I had in view by asserting my rights, was a rational one, for I had good reasons for doing so."
>
> "O, no, no, the *reasons* are nothing."
>
> "Yes they are; for unless you know the reasons which influence the actions of others, many acts would appear insane, that would not, if we knew the reasons which prompted the act." (pp. 251-52)

Packard is interested in going beyond the observed behavior that serves as evidence in the doctor's eyes. As Foucault has shown, "under observation madness is constantly required, at the surface of itself, to deny its dissimulation. It is judged only by its acts, it is not accused of intentions, nor are its secrets to be fathomed. Madness is responsible only for that part of itself which is visible. All the rest is reduced to silence. Madness no longer exists except as *seen*" (p. 250). Inherent in the nineteenth-century definition of madness is the idea that it exists beyond dialogue, beyond interaction. Observed and interpreted by the expert's inner eye, madness is an object of study, doubly so for women, who are already regarded as objects of study by the medical profession.[9]

Foucault's statement finds resonance in McFarland's own idea that mental illness assumes a deceptive surface that must be read by the psychiatrist. In an article warning physicians untrained in mental illness about how easily they may be deceived by a patient's physical ailments, McFarland writes, "The history of cases of insanity presented for treatment often reminds us how frequently the disease has commenced with some delusion upon the subject of health; and the time spent in the treatment of a disease wholly imaginary, and the number of practitioners who will be successively deceived by the same case, is a matter of continual surprise. The forms which such imaginary diseases assume are truly Protean, and practitioners are much to blame for their readiness to give a name for the thousand shifting and transient sensations to which all persons of ill-regulated sensibilities are more or less subject" ("Minor Maladies," pp. 14-15). The patient's language, like his or her behavior, is also liable to be deceptive, so that "the terms applied by different individuals to the same degree of personal suffering vary to the widest extremes; and the physician should be carefully on his guard against those whose minds conceive such a state only in the superlative degree" ("Minor Maladies," p. 13). The patient's description of his or her own condition should fall under the physician's discerning gaze as do body and behavior. If the diagnosis is indeed mental illness, the patient's mind comes even more readily under the microscope.

Packard is concerned throughout the narrative with showing that if someone's self-expression is treated only as symptom or ignored altogether it becomes impossible for that person to behave in ways considered normal. She claims that McFarland not only stops communication between inmates, but rebuffs her attempts—and those of many others also—to speak to him personally. In one case, after he has transferred her to the Eighth Ward, the "maniacs' ward," she appeals to him to separate her from the more violent inmates. She remarks: "I have sometimes thought the Doctor put me there for the very purpose of getting me killed by these maniacs. I have been nearly killed several times, and I have appealed most earnestly to Dr. McFarland to save my life, but he would simply turn speechless away from me!" (p. 91). She tells us that this is not the only time he "turns speechless away" from her or from another inmate appealing to him for help or criticizing his actions and policies. For Packard, his refusal to respond is a refusal to acknowledge that she has even spoken, has the ability to speak. It is a way of denying her stance as subject and using his authoritative position to define her language itself as an object to be observed or ignored, not as the medium of communication of a rational mind. Packard becomes frustrated again and again as she musters her thoughts, puts them into reasonable words, then speaks into a void.

In reaction against the contemporary idea that madness is to be observed and interpreted by an expert, Packard struggles to develop a kind of evidence based on sympathy and the assumption that each patient has a story to tell. Here Packard uses a supposedly innate quality of nineteenth-century middle-class femininity—sympathy—to cross over into the masculine discourses of medicine and psychology, in which "data," "evidence," and "conclusions" are integral to legitimate science. Packard's stories become a litany of her fellow inmates' experiences as she presents the "data" necessary for an indictment of the asylum. All these stories provide evidence the superintendent has neglected to mention in his reports, which chronicle supposed cure rates and detail physical improvements to the asylum buildings.

Thus after speaking with a man who says he is Jesus Christ, Packard finds that by his own logic the claim makes sense. In her chapter on Mrs. Bridgman—one of many sections describing other patients—she tells how asylum attendants fail to understand her friend's disease and consequently can only make it worse. According to Packard, Mrs. Bridgman's

> appearance of restless uneasiness, would seek vent from the ends of her fingers by nervous twitches upon something tangible, which effort seemed to be an almost instinctive act of self-defense from the overflowings of her pent up mental agonies. I could not blame her any more than I could blame a drowning man for catching at a straw as a reliance of self-defense. Although the drowning man's act is in itself an unreasonable act of self dependence, yet we do not call it an insane act under his surrounding. (pp. 242-43)

Packard attaches as much importance to the internal reasons for a patient's behavior as she does to the appearance of that behavior itself. Like the drowning man, the so-called insane person may have logical reasons for his or her seemingly nonsensical behavior. Even as Packard occasionally distinguishes herself from the "maniacs" in the asylum, she calls into question the distinction between sanity and insanity that is integral to nineteenth-century American discourse on the human mind.

As Packard herself points out, for her to engage in debate on the subject of madness is to risk being seen as inappropriately outside a middle-class woman's proper sphere. The challenge with which Elizabeth Packard struggles in her narrative is to present herself finally as rational and independent while still maintaining enough "femininity" to qualify as sane. She must overcome the fact that, within the dominant culture, to identify as sane she must be rational, but to identify too vehemently as rational can also place her outside her proper sphere. Female rationality, by definition, was applicable only to domestic concerns. The institution of middle-class motherhood provides her with a discourse with which she can expand what counts as "domestic." Motherhood is one area of women's sphere where middle-class women were expected to exercise reason and strength of mind, despite the conflicting ideology that described them as incapable of these qualities.[10] The autobiography is in a sense the chronicle of her changing relationship to the ideology of motherhood as she comes to see it as connected to her incarceration.

The issue of personal liberty comes to inform her definition of true maternal duty, "How can a mother defend her children, unless she can defend herself? I must defend myself not only for their sake, but also for the sake of society where I belong" (p. 141). Using strategically the discourse of pious maternity, she claims it is God's will that she not give into her husband's demands only so that she may return to her children. By claiming that she is making a mother's best possible decision, she gives legitimacy to her choice to become a reformer over returning to her husband and children: "If I could only feel as some undeveloped women do, that it is right to give up the responsibility of their own actions to their husbands, I could then say 'I will do and think as he please, since I am a nonentity after marriage!' If God regarded me as the law does, in this respect, I could willingly yield my conscience to get my children. But he does not. He holds me as an entity, subject to his own laws equally with my husband" (*Insane Asylums,* pp. 192-93). Christian attention to conscience here becomes the only avenue to proper maternal action, which in this case means the abdication of her children's care.[11] Self-dependence becomes a woman's first priority and the necessary prerequisite to true motherhood. In a key incident in which McFarland and two other men allow Packard to fall unaided, she comes to see that she can depend on no one but herself: "The fall had so stunned me, that for a few moments I hardly knew whether I could rise or not, but when I saw the three men who ought to be my protectors, and helpers, under such circumstances forsake me, I began to try my powers of self-dependence, and found I could not only rise myself, but could also stand alone too, without a man to lean upon!" (p. 212).

At one point Packard berates herself for trusting McFarland to help publish her manuscript of *The Great Drama,* the first version of her autobiography, which she wrote while in the asylum. She learns through this experience and the reactions of the other women inmates that she has been naive to count on connections of class and education that tend to dissolve within the institution. She relates that after the superintendent took her book away, "from every part of this spacious house I could hear that the wail of pity for me was being expressed in language as various as the sources whence it came—I received many of the most tender messages of sympathy suited to the emergency. But in one particular all agreed that I

would never see my book again" (p. 323).[12] According to Packard, every woman in the asylum expresses pity in her own way because she has in her own way experienced this sense of trust betrayed. The very fact that these women are in the asylum means that they have lost their children, if they had any, as well as their ability to express themselves and be heard. In a way their "wail of pity" is a maternal wail that would have evoked the sympathy of Packard's readers, themselves well-versed in an ideology that revered the connections of middle-class women to their children.

The significance of Packard's stolen book is made clear when she explains that, "like Abraham, I felt that my darling book would in some way be saved, as was his darling Isaac" (p. 323). The child, who to a large extent reflected and thus defined the identity of a nineteenth-century woman, has here become a metaphor for writing. The metaphor is especially interesting in Packard's case, since one of her sons is actually named Isaac; like Abraham, she must offer him up to a higher cause. The figure of mothering allows her to present herself as a legitimate author, extending the sphere of women, as did many women writers of her period.[13]

Yet ultimately, in the context of the asylum, the metaphor undermines the ideology of motherhood that brought it into being. The grieving voices of the other inmates reveal to Packard that her trust of the superintendent has been based on illusions about the power of her class-based connections to him. Even as it draws her readers into the scene, the ideology of motherhood dissolves before the image of women locked up "for their own good," mourning for their literal and metaphorical children.

By the end of Packard's book, the bond with her writing and her political work has clearly taken precedence over that with her children. Significantly, in the dedication of a later edition of her autobiography (*Modern Persecution*), she tells her children, "Every earthly love has died within me—but oh! the death agonies of the *maternal love* well nigh rent soul and body asunder. Yes, the mother has died! But she has risen again—the mother of her country—and her sons and daughters are *The American Republic*" (*Modern Persecution,* dedication). Here Packard transforms the concept of the "republican mother"—the mother who educates her children according to the ideals of the republic—to mean a mother who educates not the children within her own family but everyone—adult and child alike—within the country defined now as her larger community.[14]

In the chapter called "My Journey," she describes her passage from her home and family to the Jacksonville Asylum. On the train ride she contemplates her fate and the choices before her, deciding that she must accept the separation from her children, since she can do nothing about it, and redefine her duty as the restoration of her own liberty. Immediately on deciding this, she writes,

> After exchanging a few remarks respecting the beauty of the country through which we were passing, and the delightfully calm and clear atmosphere, so tranquilizing in its influence over one's disturbed feelings, I looked about to see who were my companions, when I met the eye of a young lady, a stranger to me, whose eyes seemed to fasten upon me with such a penetrating look, that I could hardly withdraw my own without bestowing upon her a smile of recognition. Upon this she bent forward and spoke to me, and extended to me her hand, saying,

> "I am very sorry for you. I see they are carrying you to the Insane Asylum, and you do not wish to go." (p. 54)

The "penetrating look" of her companion and her own "smile of recognition" suggest that her plight is one potentially shared by other middle-class women. Packard's companion here acts as a figure for the middle-class reader who sees in Packard's predicament the tenuousness of her own class privilege. Through the smile, Packard also suggests that she will gain a new sense of identity—throughout her struggle, and especially within the asylum itself— that will upset any complacency she may have had with her middle-class existence, a complacency revealed in her enjoyment of the scenery as if she were out for a Sunday carriage ride. "The Journey" is a spiritual and emotional one, in which Packard relinquishes, however partially and reluctantly, a traditional middle-class sense of entitlement to material comfort and privacy.

Toward the end of her experience in the asylum, then, she comes to define herself less in relation to the family she has left behind and more in relation to her emotional and intellectual interactions with the others in the asylum and with those who either hinder or help efforts to reform the asylum and improve the rights of married women. In the course of the autobiography, she relates having learned to distrust the legal and medical systems that she previously believed to be on her side. Her privileged place in relation to state and familial power has been exposed as an illusion. She has learned to communicate with the outside world not by handing her manuscript to the asylum superintendent but by sending clandestine letters, written on anything available and secreted out of the asylum: "As all communication with my children was cut off by the authority of Dr. McFarland, I was led to resort to strategy to secure this end. Therefore I procured some nicely dressed bleached cotton, and embroidered my daughter some double underwaists, on which I could easily and legibly pencil a long communication, such as my feelings prompted, hoping thus to bring myself to their recollection, so that I might not become an object of indifference to them" (p. 116).

As she tells how she secretly communicates with her daughter, Packard reveals her discovery that the sacred status of the maternal and of familial relations that she might have experienced as real in her preasylum life disappears once she has been deprived of her property and civil rights. In this "journey," the narrative rewrites the captivity version of American spiritual autobiography. Where Mary Rowlandson tells that she was captured by Indians, removed to increasingly remote locations, and redeemed by God back into her Puritan community, Packard relates that she was delivered into captivity by those she trusted in her own community, removed to increasingly remote asylum wards, and then redeemed into a new life through her own efforts and those of asylum reform activists. In her new world, the private sphere she was supposed to inhabit as a middle-class woman has slipped into the male public sphere of institutions, revealing that it was there all along. Her survival strategies must shift accordingly.

As she develops new ways of writing—penciling her messages in cloth, inserting her writing behind her mirror, and keeping her journal "all rolled up in small separate portions in the different articles of my wardrobe" (p. 321)—she grounds her creativity and her sense of self in her female world. As she sews messages into her daughter's underclothing, she passes on to her not only her own secrets but the idea of female secrecy itself, hidden away beneath the outer clothing seen by men's eyes. Indeed, it is by keeping her writing linked to women's things—clothing, embroidery, mirrors—that she outwits McFarland, watching him pass unsuspectingly over her hiding places again and again.

By always keeping some of her writing beyond his grasp, Packard makes clear that she ultimately has overcome his power to dictate. She thinks about her hidden journal after McFarland confiscates the diary he had allowed her to keep openly: "I begged that he would return [the diary] without tearing it. But he heeded nothing I said, either in defence of its truth, or of my claim to it, as by his consent I had obtained it. But instead, put it into his vest pocket, and walked off with it. This is the last I ever saw of this part of my Asylum diary. My journal covering this period is complete" (p. 121). By following her statement that the diary has been lost with her assertion that the journal is complete, she reaffirms her ascendancy over the superintendent. Whatever he tries to destroy of her writing and thus of her sense of identity—here especially represented in her personal diary—there will always be more writing, more self-creation that she has kept hidden beyond his grasp. Packard's hidden writing comes to represent, then, a part of herself that is beyond his power to destroy or co-opt.

Even while Packard reconstructs class distinctions in her narrative of her asylum experience, she has learned new strategies within the asylum and has learned to distrust the privilege upon which she used to depend. Throughout her autobiography, she struggles to appropriate the terms of the dominant discourses available to her—motherhood, paternal authority, Christianity, sanity/insanity—and to reveal those terms as parts of the carriage that bore her to the asylum.

Notes

[1] Himelhoch and Shaffer point out that until recently, most historians accepted the case history of Andrew McFarland, the Jacksonville Asylum superintendent at the time Packard was an inmate, as the best account of Packard's story. Himelhoch and Shaffer undertake "a comprehensive review of her contributions" to legislative reform. As they point out, Dorothea Dix received both praise from contemporaries and a place in history for supporting the supposedly benevolent asylum system. In contrast, Packard was villified by the medical profession of her era and was virtually unheard of until her reform work was rediscovered by historian Albert Deutsch in the 1930s (Himelhoch and Shaffer, p. 346). Since then, Packard has also been discussed by Thomas Szasz, in *The Manufacture of Madness,* and Phyllis Chesler, in *Women and Madness,* pp. 33-34. Packard published several versions of her autobiography, which she sold primarily by subscription (Himelhoch and Shaffer, p. 359).

[2] Many nineteenth-century American advice writers and physicians saw the acquisition of knowledge or any kind of intellectual activity as dangerous for women. See Haller and Haller, *The Physician and Sexuality,* pp. 37, 38, and Smith-Rosenberg, *Disorderly Conduct,* pp. 187-92, on the nineteenth-century concept that education was dangerous to women's reproductive systems. Also see Showalter, *Female Malady* (p. 55) and Scull, "Psychiatry in the Victorian Era" (pp. 23-24), on insanity and women's reproductive systems.

[3] On Andrew McFarland's term as superintendent of the state asylum at Jacksonville, see Hurd, *The Institutional Care of the Insane,* p. 453.

[4] See Smith-Rosenberg, *Disorderly Conduct,* pp. 197-216, on physicians' perceptions of their female patients. See also Douglas, "The Fashionable Diseases," p. 7, on doctors' common belief that women pretended illness, and Barker-Benfield, "Spermatic Economy," pp. 355-56, on the use of female castration to control rebelliousness later in the century.

[5] See Elaine Showalter, "Victorian Women and Insanity": "as the Victorian asylum became more overtly benign, protective, and custodial, it also became an environment grotesquely like the one in which women normally functioned. Such factors of asylum life as strict chaperonage, restriction of movement, limited occupation, enforced sexlessness, and constant subjugation to authority were closer to the 'normal' lives of women than of men" (p. 169). See also *The Female Malady,* pp. 17, 28, on the "homelike" nature of the asylum.

[6] The Utica crib was not only infamous among patients (it is mentioned by all three nineteenth-century autobiographers in this study) but was an object of debate among alienists themselves. In an 1885 study of American asylums, noted British alienist Daniel Tuke writes that, despite some of the crib's uses, it "inevitably suggests, when occupied, that you are looking at an animal in a cage. Moreover it is so temptingly facile a mode of restraint, and is on that account so certain to be abused, that I hope it will not be introduced into this country among the useful American inventions we are so glad to possess. That whatever its occasional utility may be, it may be abused, will be admitted when I say I counted fifty in use in a single asylum, and that a very good institution in most respects. At the celebrated Utica Asylum, under Dr. Gray, where a suicidal woman was preserved from harm by this wooden enclosure, my companion, Dr. Baker, of the York Retreat, allowed himself to be shut up in one of these beds, but preferred not remaining there" (p. 55).

[7] William L. Andrews discusses the way that slave narratives developed within the context of a particular rhetorical situation in which African-American writers needed to persuade white readers of their selfhood (p. 17). While Packard is writing within a context of power relations connected to defining sanity and insanity, rather than within the context of race relations, she adopts strategies of persuasion modeled in slave narratives. Whether or not she actually read these narratives, which is unclear from her writing, they emerge in her own narrative. Her numerous references to the abolitionist movement suggest that she was at least familiar with such stories.

[8] In her reading of Bacon's "Masculine Birth of Time" (1602-3), Evelyn Fox Keller shows that Bacon separated the inquiring mind from the objectified body and used a language of sexual domination to describe the masculine scientist's analysis of his always feminized object of study. According to Bacon, the scientist must enact "'a chaste and lawful marriage between mind and Nature'" in which Nature was perceived as a subduable feminine object. At the same time that Bacon denied "that truth is, as it were, the native inhabitant of the human mind and need not come in from outside to take up its abode there," he characterized

the object of scientific inquiry as female; truth was both separated from the (male) scientific mind and feminized (Keller, pp. 44-59, 36, 39).

⁹ This rendering of madness and the mad into object is nowhere more evident than in alienists' use of photography in their practice. British psychiatrist Hugh Diamond celebrated the use of photography in the observation and cure of the mad in his 1856 paper, "On the Application of Photography to the Physiognomic and Mental Phenomena of Insanity." He writes, "I may particularly refer to the four portraits which represent different phases of the case of the same young person commencing with that state of Mania which is marked by the bustled hair, the wrinkled brow, the fixed unquiet eye, and the lips apart as if from painful respiration, but passing, not to a state in which no man could tame her, but happily through less excited stages to the *perfect* cure—In the third portrait the expression is tranquil and accompanied with the smile of sadness instead of the hideous laugh of frenzy—the hair falls naturally and the forehead alone retains traces, tho' slight ones, of mental agitation. In the fourth there is a perfect calm—the poor maniac is cured. This patient could scarcely believe that her last portrait representing her as clothed and in her right mind, would even have been preceded by anything so fearful; and she will never cease, with those faithful monitors in her hand, to express the most lively feelings of gratitude for a recovery so marked and unexpected" (quoted in Gilman, pp. 164-65). Here the photograph is truly the "perilous mirror" that Packard seeks to destroy. Diamond links the photographic proof and record of her cure to his own fear that she might have worsened, might have regressed "to a state in which no man could tame her."

¹⁰ On the contradictory role conflicts experienced by nineteenth-century American women, see Smith-Rosenberg on the hysterical woman, *Disorderly Conduct,* esp. pp. 198-208.

¹¹ Interestingly enough, in her later version of this work, *Modern Persecution,* Packard reasserts her claim to motherhood, stating, "To my mind the claims of the public are secondary at least to those of maternity. Never primary when her children's training is at stake. Could I have prevented it my children would never have been separated from their mother" (p. 381). I think at this point, Packard had come to see maternal rights as inseparable from the other reforms she sought. Even here, however, she continues to support her family by selling her books, "which took me from them about three months in a year" (p. 381).

¹² McFarland later returned this manuscript to Packard. She continued to work on it after she left the asylum and published it as *The Prisoner's Hidden Life* in 1868, including, among other added sections, the appended narrative of Sophie Olsen. *Modern Persecution,* which she published in 1873, was another expanded version of her original story, including more testimony by friends and acquaintances and a general revision of the previous work. She published *The Great Drama* in book form in 1892. While this shows some differences from *The Prisoner's Hidden Life,* I'm not sure whether it reflects completely the earlier manuscript that she composed primarily from within the asylum.

¹³ On women reformers' use of the rhetoric of maternity and domesticity, see Ryan, p. 208.

¹⁴ Linda Kerber has described the ways the "republican mother" was supposed to use her domestic function in the early United States to create virtuous citizens for the new republic. See Kerber, *Women of the Republic.*

Works Cited

. . . Andrews, William L. *To Tell a Free Story: The First Century of Afro-American Autobiography, 1760-1865.* Urbana: University of Illinois Press, 1986. . . .

Barker-Benfield, G. J. "The Spermatic Economy: A Nineteenth-Century View of Sexuality." In *The American Family in Social-Historical Perspective.* Ed. Michael Gordon. New York: St. Martin's Press, 1973. Pp. 336-72. . . .

Chesler, Phyllis. *Women and Madness.* New York: Avon Books, 1972. . . .

Douglas, Ann. "'The Fashionable Diseases': Women's Complaints and Their Treatment in Nineteenth-Century America." In *Clio's Consciousness Raised: New Perspectives on the History of Women.* Ed. Mary Hartman and Lois W. Banner. New York: Harper Colophon Books, 1974. Pp. 179-91. . . .

Gilman, Charlotte Perkins. *The Living of Charlotte Perkins Gilman.* New York: Appleton-Century, 1935. . . .

Haller, John S., Jr., and Robin M. Haller, *The Physician and Sexuality in Victorian America.* Urbana: University of Illinois Press, 1974. . . .

Himelhoch, Myra Samuels, with Arthur H. Shaffer. "Elizabeth Packard: Nineteenth-Century Crusader for the Rights of Mental Patients." *American Studies* 13 (1979): 343-75. . . .

Henry M. Hurd. *The Institutional Care of the Insane in the United States and Canada, Vol. IV.* New York: Arno Press, 1973. . . .

Keller, Evelyn Fox. *Reflections on Gender and Science.* New Haven: Yale University Press, 1985. . . .

Kerber, Linda. *Women of the Republic: Intellect and Ideology in Revolutionary America.* Chapel Hill: University of North Carolina Press, 1980. . . .

Packard, Elizabeth Parsons Ware. *The Great Drama; or, the Millenial Harbinger.* Hartford: Author, 1892. . . .

———. *Modern Persecution, or Insane Asylums Unveiled.* Hartford: Author, 1873. . . .

———. *The Prisoner's Hidden Life; or, Insane Asylums Unveiled.* Chicago: Author, 1868. . . .

Scull, Andrew. "The Social History of Psychiatry in the Victorian Era." In *Madhouses, Mad-Doctors, and Madmen: The Social History of Psychiatry in the Victorian Era.* Ed. Andrew Scull. Philadelphia: University of Pennsylvania Press, 1981. Pp. 5-32. . . .

Showalter, Elaine. *The Female Malady: Women, Madness, and English Culture, 1830-1980.* New York: Pantheon Books, 1985.

———. "Victorian Women and Insanity." *Victorian Studies* 23 (1979): 157-82. . . .

Smith-Rosenberg, Carroll. *Disorderly Conduct: Visions of Gender in Victorian America.* New York: Oxford University Press, 1985. . . .

Szasz, Thomas. *The Manufacture of Madness.* New York: Harper and Row, 1977. . . .

Tuke, Daniel Hack. *The Insane in the United States and Canada.* Repr. London: H. K. Lewis, 1885. New York: Arno Press, 1973. . . .

POETRY

Ross Woodman (essay date 1983)

SOURCE: "Shelley's 'Void Circumference': The Aesthetic of Nihilism," *English Studies in Canada,* Vol. IX, No. 3, September, 1983, pp. 272-93.

[*In the following essay, Woodman analyzes Percy Bysshe Shelley's views regarding the relationship between artistic creativity and "divine insanity." Woodman demonstrates how Shelley's career reveals the poet's frustration with the inability of art to truly represent divinely inspired vision.*]

I

Since Plato banished the poets from his Republic many have rushed to their defence in an attempt to reinstate them. Among the English poets, Shelley remains the foremost apologist for the divine insanity of which Plato accused the poets and for which he sent them into exile as unfit for citizenship in a rational society governed by logos rather than mythos, philosophy rather than religion. Shelley in his apology, particularly his *Defence of Poetry*, meets Plato on his own ground. He too rejects the role of religion in society, substituting for it what he calls in his essay, *On Life*, the "intellectual philosophy" (p. 477).[1] More than that, his objection is Plato's: the superstitious acceptance of the probable or mythical account of ultimate reality turns it into a true account supported by institutional and priestly sanction. Plato rejected the poets because as myth-makers they were the founders of religion. Shelley, following in Plato's footsteps, was determined that poets would no longer assume this role. Because "the deep truth is imageless" (*Prometheus Unbound,* II.IV.116), all poetry as poetry is a fiction. Like Plato, Shelley argues that the poet works by spell and incantation. However, because the poet now knows this, he is no longer (as Shelley describes him in the preface to *Alastor*) "deluded" or "duped" by his "generous error," "doubtful knowledge," and "illustrious superstition" (p. 69). So long as he remains true to his own experience, he will dissolve or abjure his "rough magic" in bringing the creative process, "always arising unforeseen and departing unbidden" (*Defence of Poetry,* p. 504), to an end. He will in the name of poetic truth take every precaution to remind his auditors that what they have just suspended their disbelief in is a spell the true object of which remains unknowable, poetry for Shelley being the true voice of scepticism:[2]

> No voice from some sublimer world hath ever
>   To sage or poet these responses given—
>   Therefore the name of God and ghosts and Heaven,
> Remain the records of their vain endeavour,
> Frail spells—whose uttered charm might not avail to sever,
>   From all we hear, and all we see,
>   Doubt, chance and mutability.

("Hymn to Intellectual Beauty," 25-31)

Though poetry has its limitations, it nevertheless assists man to become the master rather than the slave of "Doubt, chance and mutability" by rendering them answerable to that harmony among the various parts of the tripartite soul (imagination, intellect, and sense, for Shelley) which Plato argued it was the function of dialectic to achieve. And here again Shelley agrees with Plato. The function of dialectic, he suggests, is to bring into consciousness among the various parts of the soul that intuitive harmony "beyond and above consciousness" (*Defence of Poetry,* p. 486) which poetry mimetically represents. Plato in *The Republic* is, as Shelley reminds the reader, also a poet.[3] The myths he constructs, however, are placed at the service of a dialectical process that cannot function without them. Shelley is equally concerned that his own mythopoeia be used in somewhat the same way, which is to say, copied by legislators and moral reformers into what in his *Defence* he calls "the book of common life" (p. 501).

What, however, most distinguishes Shelley from Plato is his attempt as a poet to explore "the mind in creation" (*Defence of Poetry*, pp. 503-04) by making the subject of the poem the creative process itself. In this way he hoped to render that process not something separate from, but an integral part of, the functioning consciousness of men, a consciousness that would render them the masters of the inner world even as science was rendering them the masters of the outer. Plato himself had attempted something like this in his integration of dialectic and myth-making in such a way that myth propelled the dialectic toward an enlargement of consciousness even to the point of granting it some direct knowledge of the "imageless" world to which the archetypes belong. Plato in the *Ion* seems to have believed that the poets in a state of divine possession had in some direct, immediate, and outrageously short-circuited way gained a direct revelation of the Forms without, however, having any idea of how or why that experience took place. "For the authors of those great poems which we admire," he writes in *Ion* (Shelley's translation),

> do not attain to excellence through the rules of any art, but they utter their beautiful melodies of verse in a state of inspiration, and, as it were, *possessed* by a spirit not their own. Thus the composers of lyrical poetry create those admired songs of theirs in a state of divine insanity, like the Corybantes, who lose all control over their reason in the enthusiasm of the sacred dance; and, during this supernatural possession, are excited to the rhythm and harmony which they communicate to men. Like the Bacchantes who, when possessed by the God, draw honey and milk from the rivers, in which, when they come to their senses, they find nothing but simple water. . . . For a poet is indeed a thing ethereally light, winged, and sacred, nor can he compose anything worth calling poetry until he becomes inspired, and as it were, mad, or whilst any reason remains to him. For whilst a man retains any portion of the thing called reason, he is utterly incompetent to produce poetry or to vaticinate. . . . The God seems purposely to have deprived all poets, prophets, and soothsayers of every particle of reason and understanding, the better to adapt them to their employment as his ministers and interpreters; and that we, their auditors, may acknowledge that those who write so beautifully, are possessed, and address us, inspired by the God.[4]

Plato, I suspect, is here identifying the poet with a sacred disease to which considerable superstition is attached. Many who are not afflicted by possession would pretend to be in order to gain the kind of control or power traditionally attached to prophets, shamans, and soothsayers. The Romantics were conscious of the fact that in an enlightened society governed by reason and natural law, the poets had still to defend themselves against the accusations of madness that were continually raised against them. Shelley's *Defence of Poetry,* for example, was a reply to Peacock's satirical attack in *The Four Ages of Poetry.* Characteristically, the Romantics provided a natural or psychological explanation of the supernatural phenomena Plato critically, even mockingly, dismissed. Thus they identified the world of supernatural possession with the fantasy world of the infant—even as Peacock identified the poet with the infancy of society— and the naturalizing of it with the process of growing up. Where the process of growth remained blocked, the poet becoming the prisoner of the infant's world, unable to put to creative use his reason, consciousness, and will, the poet projects the image of a traumatized infant bound to tyrannical gods (possessive parents) from which he struggles in vain to escape. Blake's "Infant Sorrow" reveals the dangers of innocence, though in a manner that Shelley, as we shall see, failed to grasp in *Prometheus Unbound:*

> Struggling in my father's hands:
> Striving against my swadling bands:
> Bound and weary I thought best
> To sulk upon my mothers breast.

Romanticism does not idealize innocence; it seeks, rather, to rescue the psyche from imprisonment within it, while at the same time lamenting the fact that consciousness cannot completely absorb or transform it. The limitless domain of the gods, identified with the oceanic world of the unconscious, cannot be contained within the finite world of consciousness. The fancy, therefore, is a "deceiving elf" (74) if it deludes the poet into believing that he can arrest the nightingale's "full-throated ease" (10) or capture the "profuse strains" of the skylark's "unpremediated art" (5). The bird's unconscious ecstacy becomes "high requiem" (60) and "plaintive anthem" (75) in Keats's conscious song, its "sweetest songs" inevitably telling Shelley's "saddest thought" (90). The Romantic poet advancing toward maturity, Keats's "sole self" (72), weeps in his poetry of process for the divinity he must leave behind. With the single exception of Blake, the elegiac mode dominates Romanticism, Wordsworth's "Intimations of Immortality Ode" providing a paradigm or model. What, however, the poet laments is not the loss of innocence, but the inability of poetry adequately to transform it. It laments the limitations of consciousness which, as Shelley argues in his *Defence,* renders the actual poem "a feeble shadow of the original conception of the poet" (p. 504). The Romantic elegy mourns its own limited reality, the "fading coal" that is the "mind in creation." Plato's divine madness might be attributed to the nightingale's song; it cannot be attributed to the poet's. "Does the Eagle know what is in the pit?" asks Blake in his motto to *The Book of Thel*,

> Or wilt thou go ask the Mole:
> Can Wisdom be put in a silver rod?
> Or Love in a golden bowl?

Keats's *Fall of Hyperion* contains one of the most outspoken attacks upon the poet as dreamer creating a "paradise for a sect" (2) in an unconscious state resembling sleep. With his own *Endymion* in mind, he condemns the poet who takes up residence in "the bosom of a leafy world" ("Sleep and Poetry," 119), as, for example, Prometheus finally does in Shelley's lyrical drama. Keats's Narrator in *The Fall of Hyperion* finds himself in the ruins of that world. Overcome by an "appetite / More yearning than on earth [he] ever felt" (38-39), he eats deliciously of a feast that "seem'd refuse of a meal / By Angel tasted or our Mother Eve" (30-31). He is, after the fall, back in the now forbidden garden feasting at the breast of the "mighty Mother" who induces oblivion as surely as does the Urania of *Adonais*. To extricate himself from "the recesses of a pearly shell" ("Sleep and Poetry," 121) where, like an embryo in the womb of the Great Mother he lies "upcurl'd" (which is Prometheus's fate at the conclusion of Shelley's third act), the poet-narrator must give birth to himself. In response to Moneta's command either to mount the steps or die upon the pavement, Keats's Narrator describes his own labour pains which are the contractions of "Soul-making" or "Spirit creation" (14 February-3 May 1819):

> I heard, I look'd: two senses both at once
> So fine, so subtle, felt the tyranny
> Of that fierce threat, and the hard task
>   proposed.
> Prodigious seem'd the toil, the leaves were yet
> Burning,—when suddenly a palsied chill
> Struck from the paved level up my limbs,
> And was ascending quick to put cold grasp
> Upon those streams that pulse beside the
>   throat:
> I shriek'd; and the sharp anguish of my shriek
> Stung my own ears—I strove hard to escape
> The numbness; strove to gain the lowest step.
> Slow, heavy, deadly was my pace: the cold
> Grew stifling, suffocating, at the heart;
> And when I clasp'd my hands I felt them not.
> One minute before death, my iced foot
>   touch'd
> The lowest stair; and as it touch'd, life seem'd
> To pour in at the toes: I mounted up,
> As once fair angels on a ladder flew
> From the green turf to heaven.

> (I, 118-36)

It is this particular agony of "Soul-making," which is of course for Keats poetry-making, that led Keats to be critical of Shelley's poetry which struck him as possessed by a divinity not his own because he had not earned it. Thus he writes to Shelley (16 August 1820) in reply to his invitation to join him in what for Keats was a false paradise: "A modern work it is said must have a purpose, which may be the God—*an artist* must serve Mammon—he must have 'self-concentration' selfishness perhaps." Having recommended that Shelley "curb his magnanimity and be more of an artist," he continues: "The thought of such discipline must fall like cold chains upon you, who perhaps never sat with your wings furl'd for six Months together." Though in daily expectation of Shelley's Prometheus, he points out that he is not particularly looking forward to receiving it. Not knowing what Shelley had done with the myth, he could nevertheless anticipate the treatment: the unbinding would come far too swiftly and far too easily, as spontaneously, indeed, as a wandering thought. "I am in expectation of Prometheus every day," he writes. "Could I have my own wish for its interest effected you would have it still in manuscript—or be but now putting an end to the second act. I remember your advising me not to publish my first-blights, on Hampstead heath—I am returning advice upon your hands." Keats, in short, is accusing Shelley in advance of abandoning himself to the divine madness that only Mammon could cure. The radically different postures of Keats's Moneta and Shelley's Asia reveal at once everything Keats rejected in Shelley.

Not surprisingly, Keats, unlike Shelley, greatly admired Wordsworth's *Excursion*. While, for Shelley, Wordsworth had in *The Excursion* proven himself one of "those meaner spirits" described in the preface to *Alastor* who had dared to abjure the dominion of "that Power which strikes the luminaries of the world." Keats, as he wrote to his brothers (13, 19 January 1818), considered the poem one of the "three things superior in the modern world," the other two being "Haydon's pictures" and "Hazlitts depth of Taste." Wordsworth had earlier exploited Plato's notion of divine madness by applying it to his vision of the child as "Mighty Prophet! Seer blest!" Having, however, deified the child, as indeed in *The Prelude* he deifies his first seventeen years by rendering them an account "Of genius, power, / Creation and divinity itself" (III, 170-71), Wordsworth in "Resolution and Independence" recognized that the imagination subjects the poet to a dangerous delusion. "By our own spirits are we deified," he writes;

> We Poets in our youth begin in gladness;
> But thereof come in the end despondency and
>   madness.

> (47-49)

The divine madness of the poet, which Wordsworth celebrates in his visionary account of his first seventeen years, becomes in the end mere madness if not chastened and subdued by "the still, sad music of humanity" ("Tintern Abbey," 91). The poet, he argues, cannot separate the "divinity in man" (*Defence of Poetry,* p. 505) from the humanity it must ultimately serve if that divinity is to remain sane. The poet cannot isolate himself from society, nor poetry from moral reform. He must in the construction of his artefacts bridge the two worlds, though in the very process of construction the "radiance which was once so bright" is "forever taken from [the poet's] sight" ("Intimations of Immortality Ode," 180), inspiration declining even as composition begins. Blake's divine child, having invoked the poet's song, immediately disappears, leaving the poet to pluck a hollow reed, make a rural pen and stain the water clear. Vision, Blake insists, must descend to the "Printing house in Hell" (*Marriage of Heaven and Hell,* Plate 15). In the loss of innocence or divine possession resides not only the poet's humanity, but his sanity as well. The coming to terms with loss constitutes the poet's release from divine madness, a release that provides the Romantic answer to Plato's attack upon the poets as well as the cure for the sacred disease he describes.

The chief danger of Romanticism, which Blake alone managed creatively to circumvent during a long and arduous career, is the Romantic poet's tendency to focus in his poetry of process upon a one-sided struggle between the son and his "mighty Mother," a struggle in which he must overcome the lyrical or narcissistic temptation to remain forever an infant feeding upon "honey dew" and drinking "the milk of paradise." For that infantile world, described by Wordsworth in *The Prelude* as "the eagerness of infantine desire" (II, 26), he must substitute the epic hero's task which demands that he leave behind the world of the mothers to seek at-one-ment with the world of the fathers. In moving from the lyric to the epic, he must substitute for Dionysian frenzy Apollonian calm, without however rendering that calm lifeless. He must, in Coleridge's phrase, "carry on the feelings of childhood into the powers of manhood." Plato attacks the poet's apparent failure to fuse them, the Dionysian or oceanic feelings which the Romantics identified with childhood overcoming the Apollonian rationality of manhood which they identified with loss. He attacks, that is, the excesses to which the Romantic spirit is prone, a spirit which, through reason and dialectic, he had in himself managed to subdue.

While Shelley was thoroughly conscious of the grounds of Plato's attack upon the poets in *The Republic* (part of which he translated) and made every effort to accommodate that attack by focusing upon the dangers of fiction if embraced as truth, he nevertheless images himself in *Adonais* as the victim of the very dangers he, even within the elegy, warns against. Having by stanza 47 of *Adonais* been "lured . . . to the brink" of suicide by the fictional world he had constructed for Keats out of the Adonis myth, Shelley's Narrator, as if aware of what was happening, instructs himself to "Clasp . . . the pendulous Earth" and to "keep [his] heart light" (417, 422). Yet he cannot stop the creative process that has taken over with what would appear to be a will and a direction of its own. The poem dialectically, rhetorically, imagistically ascends to meet the suicidal stance that in the guise of "The One" (460) propels it toward itself. Struggling as a man to protect himself against the possession that has overcome him as a myth-making poet, the Narrator tries centripetally to "shrink / Even to a point within our day and night" in an effort to resist the centrifugal force of his "spirit's light" which left to itself defies gravity and darts "Beyond all world's" to "Satiate the void void circumference" (418-20). This centripetal shrinking, like an interval of inspiration in which for Shelley "a poet becomes a man" (*Defence,* p. 507), becomes briefly a shelter "in the shadow of [Keats's] tomb" where he finds momentary refuge from "the world's bitter wind" (457-58) as if he were mad Lear upon the heath. "What Adonais is, why fear we to become?" (459), he asks, the question dissolving in him "the last clouds of cold mortality" (486). The ego (Keats's Mammon) destroyed, the poet continues:

Why linger, why turn back, why shrink, my Heart?

Thy hopes are gone before: from all things here

They have departed; thou shouldst now depart!

(469-71)

As if tempting him, the "world's bitter wind" now becomes "the low wind [whispering] near" (475). "'Tis Adonais calls!," he cries, "oh, hasten thither, / No more let Life divide what Death can join together" (476-77). *Adonais* ends with its Narrator "darkly, fearfully" possessed by his own fiction as he is "borne" toward an "abode" that had for Shelley, the man, no objective existence (493-96). The "point" within his night and day finally bursts as "the massy earth and spheréd skies are riven" (491), leaving the poet to that "one annihilation" (587) with which *Epipsychidion* breaks off. The irony at work in *Adonais* extends even beyond Earl Wasserman's brilliant analysis of it,[5] the death of Keats becoming the death of Shelley now seen as the proper subject of his own elegy. The elegy as tomb, however, lies empty. Shelley has explored an aesthetic of nihilism to affirm a "void circumference" that makes the action of mind the action of a Quixote striking at windmills. The poet "in mad trance, strike[s] with

[his] spirit's knife / Invulnerable nothings" (347-48). After reading Peacock's "anathemas against poetry," Shelley wrote to him good humouredly (15 February 1820) to say that they had excited him "to a sacred rage, or *caloëthes scribenti* of vindicating the insulted Muses." "I had the greatest possible desire to break a lance with you, within the lists of a magazine, in honour of my mistress Urania," he continues with Don Quixote in mind,

> but God willed that I should be too lazy, and wrested the victory from your hope; since first having unhorsed poetry, and the universal sense of the wisest in all ages, an easy conquest would have remained to you in me, the knight of the shield of shadow and the lance of gossamere.

II

In *Alastor,* Shelley's Wordsworthian Narrator enacts in his tale of the Visionary his own frustrated attempts to consummate his love for the "Mother of this unfathomable world" (18) by penetrating her "inmost sanctuary" (38). Fully eroticizing in the Visionary's dream and the Narrator's "strange tears" and "breathless kisses" (34-35) Wordsworth's intellectual love for this "goodly universe," Shelley implies that Wordsworth's Christian orthodoxy in *The Excursion* had betrayed his earlier vision. Instead of celebrating the marriage announced in his Prospectus, Wordsworth contemplates his own poetic corpse with the "pale despair" of the Solitary and the "cold tranquillity" (718) of the Wanderer. The "wedding garment" had become a "shroud" ("Dejection: an Ode," 49).

Shelley's response to the spectacle of Wordsworth's "poisonous decay" can be seen in his attitude to the Visionary. As he points out in his sonnet, "To Wordsworth" (published in the *Alastor* volume), Shelley identified himself with Wordsworth's loss of the "visionary gleam." Unlike Wordsworth, however, he alone deplored it. "One loss is mine," he writes in the sonnet, "Which thou too feel'st, yet I alone deplore" (5-6). "Deserting these ["Songs consecrate to truth and liberty"]," he concludes, "thou leavest me to grieve, / Thus having been, that thou shouldst cease to be." Wordsworth had substituted the "truths" of the Christian religion for the fictions of the imagination. He was the victim rather than the maker of myth.

If Wordsworth refused to grieve for his own death as a poet why should Shelley weep for him? Shelley raises the question both in the poem (which he refuses to call an elegy) and in the preface. Perhaps nothing better reveals the apparently impenetrable complexity of Shelley's *Alastor* than the Narrator's response to the death of what is essentially his own "visionary gleam":

> Upon those pallid lips
> So sweet even in their silence, on those eyes
> That image sleep in death, upon that form
> Yet safe from the worm's outrage, let no tear
> Be shed—not even in thought. Nor, when those hues
> Are gone, and those divinest lineaments,
> Worn by the senseless wind, shall live alone
> In the frail pauses of this simple strain,
> Let not high verse, mourning the memory
> Of that which is no more, or painting's woe
> Or sculpture, speak in feeble imagery
> Their own cold powers. Art and eloquence,
> And all the shews o' the world are frail and vain
> To weep a loss that turns their lights to shade.

(699-712)

Shelley, it would appear, is here deconstructing the elegy he has just composed by questioning the ability of "high verse" (as opposed to his "simple strain") to deal with the larger issues of life and death. All art, whether sculpture or painting or poetry, is "cold," "feeble," "frail and vain" when measured by the human aspiration it attempts to encompass or contain. The artist, as artist, is doomed because the "divinest lineaments" of his insatiable desire are themselves "worn by the senseless wind" of inspiration. The "feeble imagery" of art testifies finally to its "own cold powers." What then is left to the Wordsworthian Narrator who, subject to the capricious, even "senseless," waxing and waning of creative power, must continue to deal with his "incommunicable dream, / And twilight phantasms, and deep noon-day thought" (39-40)? Wasserman offers what may be the definitive answer:

> For in his opening invocation the Narrator had prayed that the inspiring
> breath of the Great Mother sweep over him, moveless as a long-forgotten lyre
> Suspended in the solitary dome
> Of some mysterious and deserted fane.

(42-44)

His later management of the same image reveals that for man to be but a passive lyre totally submissive to the forces of nature is actually to be a corpse, senseless, motionless, soulless, and gradually eroded by nature's forces. Now the Narrator's original comparison of himself as poet to the "long-forgotten" lyre in the "solitary" dome of a "deserted" fane, so casually brushed over in a first reading of the invocation, gains its full ironic horror in retrospect: despite his belief that he is of the community of nature, he is, as merely a child of the World Mother, just as solitary as the Visionary, as alone as the incarnate death of the Wandering Jew.[6]

The psychic setting of *Alastor* is the empty skull of the Narrator, imaged as a "moveless" lyre suspended in the "solitary dome" of a "deserted fane" (Locke's *tabula rasa*) and briefly stirred to illusory life, even as in *Adonais* "Life's pale light" (220) flashes through the dead limbs of Keats as Death, invoked by Urania, rises to meet her "vain caress" (225). Poetry, Shelley suggests, is the futile attempt to animate a corpse; the poet is a necrophiliac whose eternal lot is the "LIFE-IN-DEATH" of Coleridge's Mariner. The irony of the Narrator's hope resides in the death it contains. The irony of Shelley's poem is that the process of its construction is at the same time the process of its deconstruction. Composition and decomposition are both in nature and in the mind one and the same. Shelley in *Alstor* is exploring an aesthetic of nihilism.

At the same time, however, Shelley in his preface is critical of the nihilism his poem enacts. In his critical reaction to the Visionary's "self-centred seclusion" (which the Narrator shares through his identification with the sub-human brotherhood of nature), Shelley resists the temptation to make his poem answerable only to itself, mirroring as artefact the process of its making. The self-centred seclusion of his Visionary is mirrored in the self-centred seclusion of the poem. Standing back from it, Shelley, as critic, addresses in his preface the Visionary of the poem, imposing upon him values which, if alien to poetry, are nevertheless necessary to human life. He judges the poem on moral grounds and finds it wanting. The "Poet's self-centred seclusion" becomes an "instruction to actual men" (p. 69). All men, he argues, who refuse to be "deluded" by "generous error" or "duped" by an "illustrious superstition" are "morally dead." By rendering his vision of the veiled maid answerable to the "beloved brotherhood" of "Earth, ocean and air" (I) to which the Narrator attaches himself, she simply dissolves into the elements to become, like Wordsworth's Lucy, nothing at all. Narrator and Visionary are the victims of natural religion. "Wordsworth must know that what he Writes Valuable is Not to be found in Nature," writes Blake in his annotations to the 1815 edition of Wordsworth's poems (p. 655). If, however, the veiled maid "is not to be found in Nature," nature must be "found" in her if nature is to be awakened from her subhuman world where his only "kindred" are birds, beasts, and insects. In his discovery that natural objects lack "an intelligence" similar to his own, he encounters the resistance of the Great Mother to his entirely human demands, though not before gaining in sleep a vision of her emerging human form. His failure to sustain awake his vision of her in sleep, to affirm as "waking dream" the "spousal" vision capable of transforming the "simple produce of the common day" into "Paradise and groves / Elysian" (*Recluse,* I, 47-55), constitutes his (or Wordsworth's) "moral" failure. Thus, for the Shelley of the preface the "sudden darkness and extinction" of the Visionary is preferable to the "slow and poisonous decay" of the Narrator as Wordsworth himself witnessed it in *The Excursion.*

Confronted by the spectacle of Wordsworth's ruin, which he poetically explores in *Alastor* (finally to identify with it in *The Triumph of Life*), Shelley in his preface makes a futile attempt to resolve the impasse confronting the Narrator. That resolution resides in the human uses of the Visionary's discovery of "strange truths in undiscovered lands" (77) among "secret caves / Rugged and dark" (87-88) that record "the Zodiac's brazen mystery" (119). What, Shelley asks in his preface, is the Visionary to make of the flashes of meaning which work upon him like "strong inspiration" (127) to reveal "thrilling secrets" (128) "inaccessible / To avarice and pride" (89-90)? If he is not to be struck "by sudden darkness and extinction" because his perception is "too exquisite" or "dare to abjure its dominion" in order to preserve his life, what stance or attitude must he assume? Shelley's answer owes something to Coleridge: he must willingly "suspend his disbelief for the moment." He must affirm in the name of "poetic faith" everything that his reason would otherwise reject. He must, in short, allow the "strong inspiration" working in flashes to usurp his intellect and dupe him into the working acceptance of "illustrious superstition." He must, as Coleridge does in "The Ancient Mariner," work with the protagonist's "delusion" in an attempt to discover the poetic or dramatic truth which it reveals. Shelley's answer to the fate of both the Visionary and the Narrator, tentatively suggested in his preface, is fully explored in "Mont Blanc" and "Hymn to Intellectual Beauty" which he wrote the following year.

In "Mont Blanc" and "Hymn to Intellectual Beauty" Shelley releases the poet from the "NIGHTMARE LIFE-IN-DEATH" constellated in *Alastor* by affirming the supreme fiction which constitutes the "delusion" without which human life is both devoid of meaning and "morally dead." The poet's task, he argues, is to construct a myth that is answerable to human desire, a myth which gives birth to itself "in the still cave of the witch Poesy" ("Mont Blanc," 44). He must, at the same time, acknowledge its source so that what issues from its "secret springs" is never separated from its origins to become other than what it is: an "illustrious superstition" whose life resides in "spells" and "incantation." The poet, according to Shelley in 1816, constructs for the psyche in those inspired "uncertain moments" images that may suffice. Confronting once again in "Mont Blanc" the Narrator's "beloved brotherhood" of "Earth, ocean and air," on the one hand, and the Visionary's corpse, on the other, he asks:

> And what were thou, and earth, and stars, and sea,
> If to the human mind's imaginings
> Silence and solitude were vacancy?

Shelley answers:

> a long-forgotten lyre
> Suspended in the solitary dome
> Of some mysterious and deserted fare.

III

The realization that "the dream / Of dark magician in his visioned cave"—"the still cave of the witch Poesy"—is not "the true law / Of this so lovely world" (681-86) defeats the Narrator in *Alastor* and conducts his Visionary "to a speedy ruin." "Natural piety" prevents him from affirming the psychic or poetic truth of delusion. In *Prometheus Unbound,* on the other hand, Shelley releases the imagination from Wordsworth's "natural piety," rendering it answerable to what he calls in his *Defence* man's "diviner nature" (p. 504) that operates "beyond and above consciousness." Shelley in *Prometheus Unbound* is at liberty to consummate the marriage denied to the Visionary in *Alastor* because of the Wordsworthian moral fetters imposed upon his creative desire. The "impulse" that "rolled back . . . on [the Visionary's] vacant brain" (191-92) is carried in *Prometheus Unbound* to its apocalyptic conclusion because Prometheus in the first act is released from the precipice upon which his moral will has been impaled for three thousand years. Shelley's Narrator in *Alastor* is a bound Prometheus unable through and in the Visionary to break free of Jupiter's natural religion. Though union with the Great Mother is his apocalyptic theme, "natural piety" dictates against it. Thus Shelley, satirizing Wordsworth while at work on *Prometheus Unbound,* describes him as "a kind of moral ennuch" who

> touched the hem of Nature's shift,
> Felt faint—and never dared uplift
> The closest, all-concealing tunic.

> ("Peter Bell the Third," 314-17)

The Great Mother of *Alastor* has "ne-er yet / . . . unveil'd [her] inmost sanctuary" despite the attempts of the Narrator, "like an inspired and desperate alchymist," to penetrate her mystery (31-38).

Shelley's transformation of the nightmare vision of *Alastor* into "the spousal verse / Of this great consummation" can be seen in Shelley's treatment of the relations among Prometheus, Asia, and Earth. The psychic action of Shelley's drama traces the gradual process by which Prometheus, morally bound to Jupiter, making his "agony" the sole barrier to Jupiter's complete conquest of nature and man, is reunited with Asia, thereby releasing the recreated universe and man from the last vestiges of Jupiter's rule. Though Asia herself does not appear until the second act, her transforming

presence, "beyond and above" the consciousness of the bound Prometheus, is already at work in him during the first act, the second being the internal type of the external events of the first. Asia's journey with Panthea to the cave of Demogorgon is her own "interpenetration" of Prometheus's soul in answer to Prometheus's longing. Initially, therefore, Prometheus, determined to recall the curse, is bewildered; the "awful whisper" that is rising up appears less to be the now forgotten sound of his own earlier curse than the voice of love:

> for I would hear that curse again. . . .
> Ha, what an awful whisper rises up!
> 'Tis scarce like sound, it tingles through the
>   frame
> As lightning tingles, hovering ere it strike.—
> Speak Spirit! from thine inorganic voice
> I only know that thou art moving near
> And love.

> (I, 131-37)

The "awful whisper" that he hears is the "melancholy Voice" of his mother which he does not yet recognize. "Obscurely through my brain like shadows dim," he says,

> Sweep awful thoughts, rapid and thick.—I feel
> Faint, like one mingled in entwining love,
> Yet 'tis not pleasure.

> (I, 146-49)

The Earth then identifies herself.

> I am the Earth,
> Thy mother; she within whose stony veins
> To the last fibre of the loftiest tree
> Whose thin leaves trembled in the frozen air
> Joy ran, as blood within a living frame,
> When thou didst from her bosom, like a cloud
> Of glory, arise, a spirit of keen joy!
> And at thy voice her pining sons uplifted
> Their prostrate brows from the polluting dust
> And our almight Tyrant with fierce dread
> Grew pale, until his thunder chained thee here.

> (I, 152-62)

Reuniting with his mother, Prometheus, as one of "her pining sons," is gradually undergoing a new birth. Unlike the Great Mother of *Alastor,* Earth is unveiling to him her "inmost sanctuary," thereby opening the way to that reunion with Asia who is the Great Mother herself now seen as bride, which is to say, the Venus Genetrix who in *Adonais* is both the mother and mistress of the poet. The "inorganic voice" that rises up within Prometheus, tingling "through [his] frame / As lightning tingles, hovering ere it strike" and "entwining" him in a love that is not yet pleasure, becomes in the second act Asia herself descending from her long exile to the cave of Demogorgon, that teeming womb of creation which is the proper scene of Shelley's action. Thus, after his unbinding, Prometheus's reunion with Asia is imaged as a sexual union with his mother now transfigured to become Asia, his bride. When he addresses her, bending down to kiss the earth, the Earth replies:

> I hear.—I feel.—
> Thy lips are on me, and their touch runs down
> Even to the adamantine central gloom
> Along the marble nerves—'tis life, 'tis joy,
> And through my withered, old and icy frame
> The warmth of an immortal youth shoots
>   down
> Circling.
>
> (III, 84-90)

Prometheus embracing the transfigured earth, the Venus Genetrix, is fathering himself to become, like the poet, his own creator. Man through his creative faculty gives birth to himself. In the son's sexual consummation with the "Mother of this unfathomable world" which confronts and rejects the social taboo that would bind the poet to a fixed moral order, Shelley celebrates Wordsworth's intended incestuous marriage to "this goodly universe / In love and holy passion," a marriage which renders "Paradise and groves / Elysian" the "simple produce of the common day."

So long as Prometheus, bound to the rock of morality which governs Jupiter's reign, is denied his incestuous union with the Great Mother, nature itself remains a "God / Profuse of poisons" which in the likeness of a "green serpent" drives the Visionary of *Alastor*, as it drove Wordsworth, to "a slow and poisonous decay." Prometheus's reunion with his Mother, creating himself anew in her "inmost sanctuary," purifies nature to make it once more what Wordsworth in a state of noble rapture would in his Prospectus boldly declare it to be:

> —I, long before the blissful hour arrives,
> Would chant, in lonely peace, the spousal
>   verse
> Of this great consummation:—and, by words
> Which speak of nothing more than what we
>   are,
> Would I arouse the sensual from their sleep
> Of Death, and win the vacant and the vain
> To noble raptures; while my voice proclaims
> How exquisitely the individual Mind
> (And the progressive powers perhaps no less
> Of the whole species) to the external World
> Is fitted:—and how exquisitely, too—
> Theme this but little heard of among men—

> The external World is fitted to the Mind;
> And the creation (by no lower name
> Can it be called) which they with blended
>   might
> Accomplish:—this is our high argument.
>
> (56-71)

It is precisely this "high argument," the "dominion" of which Wordsworth "dare[d] to abjure," that Shelley's Earth Mother now proclaims:

> There is a Cavern where my spirit
> Was panted forth in anguish whilst thy pain
> Made my heart mad, and those who did inhale
>   it
> Became mad too, and built a Temple there
> And spoke and were oracular, and lured
> The erring nations round to mutual war
> And faithless faith, such as Jove kept with
>   thee;
> Which breath now rises, as among tall weeds
> A violet's exhalation, and it fills
> With a serener light and crimson air
> Intense yet soft the rocks and woods around;
> It feeds the quick growth of the serpent vine
> And the dark lined ivy tangling wild
> And budding, blown, or odour-faded blooms
> Which star the winds with points of coloured
>   light
> As they rain through them, and bright, golden
>   globes
> Of fruit, suspended in their own green heaven;
> And, through their veined leaves and amber
>   stems,
> The flowers whose purple and translucid
>   bowls
> Stand ever mantling with aereal dew,
> The drink of spirits; and it circles round
> Like the soft waving wings of noonday
>   dreams,
> Inspiring calm and happy thoughts, like mine
> Now thou art thus restored. This cave is thine.
>
> (III.iii.124-48)

Earth is here addressing Asia who is the "Lamp of Earth," or Earth itself restored through reunion with her son to its original "celestial" form. The cave in which she will dwell forever in androgynous union with Prometheus is the womb of the Earth Mother purged now of its poisonous vapours to become everything that Wordsworth originally believed it to be before submitting his insatiable desire to the binding restrictions of Jupiter's rule. Wordsworth's divine child who, as a "Mighty Prophet! Seer blest!" lives in a nature that is "apparelled in celestial light" becomes in *Prometheus Unbound* Asia and Prometheus living forever in an enchanted cave "Like human babes in their brief innocence" (III.iii.33).

To suggest that Shelley in his lyrical drama transcends what in his preface he calls "the moral interest of the fable" by releasing his imagination to "ascend to bring light and fire from those eternal regions where the owl-winged faculty of calculation dare not ever soar" (*Defence*, p. 503) is not to argue that he abandons the moral interest. Shelley insists in his lyrical drama, as he insists in his *Defence of Poetry*, that the only way to sustain the moral interest is to offer men a vision of hope which makes it possible for them "to suffer woes," "to forgive wrongs," and "to defy Power" (IV, 570-72). The man who remains after Demogorgon Prospero-like dissolves the spell is a bound Prometheus who is able, like the Prometheus of the first act, to suffer, forgive, and defy because he can now also "love," "bear," and "hope" (IV, 574), creating in his imagination, if not on earth, the very thing his hope contemplates. Shelley's drama, like Shakespeare's *Tempest*, has taught its audience the power of "rough magic," shown it how to weave a spell by encouraging it to shape rather than suppress its own insatiable longings which, as Wordsworth argues, are "in most, abated or suppressed," while "in some, / Through every change of growth and of decay," they remain "pre-eminent till death" (*Prelude*, II, 263-65). Shelley's apocalyptic vision in *Prometheus Unbound*, like the vision that in Wordsworth failed to materialize, resides in the son's incestuous union with the Great Mother, a union that drives Shelley's earthly ideal toward a revolutionary anarchism that leaves man "Sceptreless, free, uncircumscribed— . . . / Equal, unclassed, tribeless, and nationless, / Exempt from awe, worship, degree,—the King / Over himself" (III.iv.194-97).

Over this vision of liberated man Asia presides as its reigning goddess, threatening in her radical reversal of the patriarchal despotism of Jupiter's reign to reduce Prometheus to the passive recipient of her redemptive grace. The last act of Shelley's drama is very close to Blake's world of innocence, chimney sweeps released from their coffins to "rise upon clouds, and sport in the wind" ("The Chimney Sweeper," 18) and the children released from the charity schools, "like a mighty wind" raising "to heaven the voice of song" ("Holy Thursday," 9). The fact that their freedom is in some sense a dream, that Tom will still have to rise in the dark and get with his bags and brushes to work or that the "grey headed beadles" are still in control is, partly at least, the warning of Demogorgon as he dissolves his spell, though not, as in Blake's satirical lyrics, with the sinister advice to "cherish pity" or to do one's duty in order to escape harm. Shelley appears to be far less aware of the dangers of innocence than Blake, at least in *Prometheus Unbound*. By making Asia the active agent of Prometheus's unbinding, which then takes place in a stage instruction ("Hercules *unbinds* Prometheus *who descends*"), Shelley tends to trivialize the "suffering

and endurance" of the first act by effectively isolating them from the apocalyptic action of the drama proper. Prometheus finds Hercules's "gentle words . . . sweeter even than freedom long desired / And long delayed" (III.ii.4-6). Addressing Asia and her "Fair sister nymphs," he tells them that they "made long years of pain / Sweet to remember, through [their] love and care" (III.ii.8-10). Pain having been eclipsed by pleasure, never to appear again, Prometheus immediately begins his long account of the enchanted cave "all overgrown with trailing odourous plants, / Which curtain out the day with leaves and flowers." By obliterating even the memory of Jupiter, Prometheus has in effect regressed to something very like Blake's Beulah rather than advanced through ceaseless "mental fight" to Jerusalem. He has ceased even to be, as he was in the first act, "the king / Over himself;" kingship in any guise, psychic or political, is finally alien to Shelley's poetic nihilism, governed by a pursuit of the "void circumference" or "intense inane." Like Wordsworth in the first book of *The Prelude* who, "baffled and plagued by a mind that every hour / Turns recreant to her task," Prometheus has regressed to infancy to find both release and renewal in

> those lovely forms
> And sweet sensations that throw back our life,
> And almost make remotest infancy
> A visible scene, on which the sun is shining.

> (*Prelude*, I, 632-35)

Prometheus tells Asia that they

> will sit and talk of time and change
> As the world ebbs and flows, ourselves unchanged—
> What can hide man from mutability?—
> And if ye sigh, then I will smile, and thou
> Ione, shall chant fragments of sea-music,
> Until I weep, when ye shall smile away
> The tears she brought, which yet were sweet to shed;
> We will tangle buds and flowers, and beams
> Which twinkle on the fountain brims, and make
> Strange combinations out of common things—
> Like human babes in their brief innocence.

> (III.iii.8-18)

The echoes here of Lear's "Come, let's away to prison" reinforce the unfortunate impact of Prometheus's vision of life in the enchanted cave from which, according to Shelley, man's future Utopian life on earth will eventually emanate. Prometheus, it would appear, has been released from three thousand years of unending torture only to enter again his mother's womb, there, united with Asia, to become androgynous and render nature henceforth man's perpetual bride. Shelley's Prometheus inherits the fate that might have been Wordworth's had the first book of *The Recluse* ("Home at Grasmere") remained the "great consummation" of his powers, or indeed the fate of Lear had not Shakespeare conferred upon his hero the dignity of tragedy. Prometheus's retreat to the vales of Har suggests that in Shelley's lyrical drama divine madness is the final resolution of pain. Between these two opposing extremes, both of them humanly uninhabitable, the "Man," declares Shelley, "remains." The struggle to keep him there, even though the poet's divine madness lures him to the brink, is the tension that Shelley brings to its apocalyptic breaking point in *Adonais.*

IV

In the added fourth act of *Prometheus Unbound,* Shelley distances himself from the divine madness of the poet by identifying his "spousal verse" or epithalamion with a magical spell similar to the one that Prospero stages as a wedding gift for Miranda and Ferdinand. When the masque is complete, Demogorgon steps forward to dissolve it and in that dissolution the Shelleyan poet again becomes a man "abandoned to the sudden reflux of the influences under which others habitually live" (*Defence,* p. 507). The abandonment of the poet to this "sudden reflux" is at once a defeat of the poet's "divinity" and an affirmation of his humanity, the man emerging as the gods retreat, though leaving behind a glimpse of "something evermore about to be" that arises from the poet's "effort, and expectation, and desire" (*Prelude,* VI, 607-08). The constellation of that paradox without at the same time arresting it into a dogmatic formulation that reduces a mystery to a creed is the achievement of Wordsworth's "Intimations of Immortality Ode" that, according to Shelley, Wordsworth "dare[d] to abjure" in *The Excursion.* That the paradox itself imposes upon the human psyche an insupportable burden would appear to be at least one of the inviting perspectives open to the reader of *A Triumph of Life,* though it is not an invitation that Shelley himself extended, there being no available evidence that he wished the poem to be published in its fragmentary form, unless, of course, his actual drowning was intended as the completion of a poem described in his *Defence* as "wind over a sea, which the coming calm erases, and whose traces remain only as on the wrinkled sand which paves it" (p. 504).

In *Prometheus Unbound,* Shelley celebrates the transfiguration of Asia after her experience in the cave of Demogorgon in a series of lyrics that have for their theme the movement of language toward silence or the "intense inane." "How thou art changed!" cries Panthea:

> I dare not look on thee;
> I feel, but see thee not. I scarce endure
> The radiance of thy beauty. Some good change
> Is working in the elements which suffer
> Thy presence thus unveiled.—

> (II.v.16-20)

For nature so radically to change as to suffer the "unveiled" presence of Asia is for nature as nature to disappear altogether, the poet, as it were, having penetrated to its "inmost sanctuary" there to experience in the "flash" that reveals "the invisible world" a going out of sense. Asia compares herself to "an enchanted Boat" floating "upon the silver waves" of sound issuing from the singing air. The boat itself "seems to float ever-forever—,"

> Till like one in slumber bound—
> Borne to the Ocean, [Asia's soul] floats down, around,
> Into a Sea profound, of ever-spreading sound.—

> (II.v.73-84)

The lyric is a metaphorical enactment of drowning; language reaches beyond meaning to pure sound and sound itself becomes so pervasive that it approximates silence.[7] "So far as he is serious," writes Susan Sontag in "The Aesthetics of Silence,"

> the artist is continually tempted to sever the dialogue he has with an audience. Silence is the furthest extension of that reluctance to communicate, that ambivalence about making contact with the audience which is a leading motif of modern art, with its tireless commitment to the "new" and/or the "esoteric." Silence is the artist's ultimate other-worldly gesture: by silence, he frees himself from servile bondage to the world, which appears as patron, client, consumer, antagonist, arbiter, and distorter of his work.[8]

One can witness in Shelley's development the gradually ridding himself of an audience. "Still," Sontag continues,

> one cannot fail to perceive in this renunciation of "society" a highly social gesture. The cues for the artist's eventual liberation from the need to practice his vocation comes from observing his fellow artists and measuring himself against them. An exemplary decision of this sort can be made only after the artist has demonstrated that he possesses genius and exercised that genius authoritatively. Once he has surpassed his peers by the standards which he acknowledges, his pride has only one place left to go. For, to be a victim of the craving for silence is to be, in still a further sense, superior to everyone

else. It suggests that the artist has had the wit to ask more questions than other people, and that he possesses stronger nerves and higher standards of excellence.[9]

The strategy of *Adonais,* moving relentlessly toward the extinction of the poet, gives to his presence within the poem a precariousness that intensifies rather than lessens its impact. When the decision is whether to cross a "t" or jump off the cliff, the crossing of the "t" assumes an unearthly radiance that makes the word itself burn not merely with the energy of a man's earthly power but with a fire that would consume "the last clouds of cold mortality" (186). Shelley thus becomes "the last cloud of an expiring storm / Whose thunder is its knell," "a dying lamp, a falling shower, / A breaking billow" (273-75) which is broken in the very act of utterance. Words, struggling to articulate silence, must finally be abandoned altogether because the articulation mocks its own intention. "Woe is me!" he cries at the end of *Epipsychidion,*

> The winged words on which my soul would
>   pierce
> Into the height of Love's rare Universe,
> Are chains of lead around its flight of fire.—
> I pant, I sink, I tremble, I expire!

> (587-91)

Shelley's suicidal stance, it would appear, was necessary to the perfecting of his work which attempts to give form to a vision of liberty so complete that it involves, again in Sontag's words, "the liberation of the artist from himself, of art from the particular art work, of art from history, of spirit from matter, of the mind from its perceptual and intellectual limitations."[10] Thus, *Adonais,* by enacting its own dissolution as well as the dissolution of the poet, became in Shelley's description of it (5 June 1821) "better in point of composition than anything I have written" (p. 628). A suicidal stance is a "highly wrought" (p. 628) dying into art, like Keats's Apollo dying into life. Beyond that, it is, of course, the "void circumference" that the poet in pursuing must as a poet momentarily subdue.

Shelley, I suggest, is the only Romantic poet fully to inhabit the post-Miltonic universe the author of which is Milton's Satan. Confronting it as the limit of opacity, Blake, who enacts the Romantic struggle to reverse the natural bent of creation as an endless fall into division, sought to give the opacity a visible form so that poets, himself included, might have something for the imagination to build on. Shelley's "fullness" is paradoxically the void of Blake's Satan, a void emptied of consciousness, being "beyond and above" it. Shelley's Platonic dialectic carried him "darkly, fearfully afar" toward the death of art itself, a death that only his visionary suicide could sublimely enact,

though, by remaining visionary, denying for itself the reality which it perhaps sought to embrace. The Visionary who in *Alastor* confronts the "blackness" of his "vacant brain" as the "veiled maid" folds him in her dissolving arms is fundamentally the Narrator of *Adonais* who confronts that same "blackness" and "vacancy" as it bears him "darkly, fearfully afar." Shelley's actual drowning thus becomes the poem he never wrote, arrived at only by that progressive revelation offered by the ones he did.

Notes

[1] All quotations from Shelley's poetry and prose are from *Shelley's Poetry and Prose,* ed. D. H. Reiman and S. B. Powers (New York: W. W. Norton & Co. Inc., 1977). Quotations from Shelley's letters are from *The Letters of Percy Bysshe Shelley,* 2 vols., ed. F. L. Jones (Oxford: Clarendon Press, 1964). Quotations from Blake's poetry and prose are from *The Poetry and Prose of William Blake,* ed. David Erdman (Garden City: Doubleday & Co., Inc., 1965). Quotations from Wordsworth's poetry are from *The Poetical Works of Wordsworth,* ed. Thomas Hutchinson, revised E. de Selincourt (London: Oxford University Press, 1960). Quotations from Coleridge's poetry are from *The Poems of Samuel Taylor Coleridge,* ed. E. H. Coleridge (London: Oxford University Press, 1960). Quotations from *Biographia Literaria* are from the edition edited by George Watson (London: J. M. Dent & Sons, Ltd., 1975). Quotations from Keats's poetry are from *The Poetical Works of John Keats,* ed. H. W. Garrod (Oxford: Clarendon Press, 1958). Quotations from Keats's letters are from *Letters of John Keats,* ed. Robert Gittings (London: Oxford University Press, 1975).

[2] The best study of Shelley's scepticism remains C. E. Pulos, *The Deep Truth: A Study of Shelley's Skepticism* (Lincoln: University of Nebraska Press, 1954). For a systematic application of Pulos's thesis to Shelley's poetry, see Lloyd Abbey, *Destroyer and Preserver: Shelley's Poetic Skepticism* (Lincoln: University of Nebraska Press, 1979).

[3] "Plato was essentially a poet—the truth and splendour of his imagery and the melody of his language is the most intense that it is possible to conceive. He rejected the measure of the epic, dramatic, and lyrical forms, because he sought to kindle a *harmony in thoughts divested of shape and action* . . . (*Defence of Poetry,* p. 484, italics mine). The "harmony in thoughts divested of shape and action," as will be seen, is what Shelley means in part by "void circumference." "Harmony," when "divested of shape and action," releases the word (or signifier) from the meaning that is asserted by binding the word to what is signified by it. It provides it with what Hartman in the preface to *Deconstruction and Criticism* (New York: Continuum,

1979) calls "a certain absence or indeterminacy of meaning" that renders literary language "something not reducible to meaning" (p. viii). More than any other English poet, Shelley's art lends itself to deconstructive criticism. Indeed it might be argued that deconstructive criticism had succeeded in unsealing the meaning which earlier criticism sealed in.

[4] *The Complete Works of Percy Bysshe Shelley*, 10 vols., ed. R. Ingpen and W. Peck (London: Ernest Benn Ltd., 1927), VII, 238-39.

Plato's notion of "divine madness" offers a veiled attack upon the poet who would, like the deconstructionist critic, release the language of poetry from the prison house of meaning. Shelley ironically affirms in Plato precisely what Plato himself rejects, as indeed he affirms in Milton's *Paradise Lost* what Milton's reason rejects. Thus, in the absence of Freud, Plato's notion of "divine madness" provided Shelley with a justification for exploring in his art a realm "beyond and above consciousness" in which language enjoys a suspension of meaning in a realm approximating pure sound.

Thus release of Shelley's poetry from logocentric or incarnationist perspectives is explored in *Reconstruction and Criticism* as, indeed, it is explored (with reservations) by Tillotama Rajan in *Dark Interpreter: The Discourse of Romanticism* (Ithaca: Cornell University Press, 1980). Professor Rajan's rejection of the logocentric reading of Shelley offered by Wasserman and others (including myself), while a valuable corrective, particularly in bringing the sub-text into focus, tends, I think, not to recognize the extent to which the visibility of that sub-text depends upon a logocentric perspective. Certainly my own reading of *Adonais* in particular stresses the sub-text which is set within the logocentric reading which I, following Wasserman, present in "Shelley's Urania," *Studies in Romanticism* (Winter 1978), pp. 61-75.

[5] *Shelley: A Critical Reading* (Baltimore: The Johns Hopkins Press, 1971), pp. 462-502. For a more deconstructive reading of Shelley's *Adonais* intended, in part, as a corrective to Wasserman's metaphysical interpretation, see my article, "Shelley's Urania," cited in n. 4.

[6] Ibid., p. 38. The narrator "as alone as the incarnate death of the Wandering Jew" is the fate of the poet who believes that literary language is bound to nature. In *The Triumph of Life*, Rousseau warns the poet that the signifier operates without a signified. "Rousseau's history," writes Paul DeMan in "Shelley Disfigured" (*Deconstruction and Criticism*, p. 50), "as he looks back upon his existence from the 'April prime' of his early years to the present, tells of a specific experience that is certainly not a simple one but that can be des-

ignated by a single verb: the experience is that of forgetting." Forgetting, as DeMan "interprets" it is not the absence of what was once known or remembered. It is the not known, that which is not knowable. It is the absence of meaning. The "meaning" of *Alastor*, I suggest, is its absence of meaning. The "elegy" is the elegy Shelley refuses to write. It is present in its announced absence. *Alastor*, like *The Triumph of Life*, explores the experience of forgetting.

[7] Particularly in the lyrics that celebrate the transfiguration of Asia, Shelley avoids the dangers of a incarnationist theory of poetry that would assign meaning to the word thereby rendering it didactic, which is to say, abhorrent. In "Shelley Disfigured," DeMan speaks of "the madness of words" which is "the endless prosopoeia by which the dead are made to have a face and a voice which tells the allegory of their demise and allows us to apostrophize them in our turn" (p. 68). Asia transfigured is also Ophelia drowning in the madness of her words, even as in *Adonais* it is Shelley's narrator drowning in the poetic act of being "borne."

[8] *Styles of Radical Will* (New York: Farrar, Straus and Giroux, 1969), p. 6.

[9] Ibid., pp. 6-7.

[10] Ibid., p. 18.

Ann C. Colley (essay date 1983)

SOURCE: "Madness as Metaphor and the *Idylls of the King*," in *Tennyson and Madness*, University of Georgia Press, 1983, pp. 87-116.

[*In the following essay, Colley argues that Alfred, Lord Tennyson's* Idylls of the King *reflects the commonly held view among Victorians that their society was particularly afflicted by madness. Colley shows that Tennyson used madness as a metaphor in order to emphasize the relationship between excess, particularly sexual excess, and insanity.*]

Many of Tennyson's contemporaries were convinced that they were living in a country and in an age literally madder than all others. In the popular mind England and insanity were all too frequent companions. The physician Alfred Beaumont Maddock was one of many to register alarm. In 1854 he wrote that "in no other country, compared with England, do we find such numerous and formidable examples of this extensive scourge."[1] Later Tennyson's Dr. Matthew Allen also remarked on the nation's poor health. Alluding to the common belief, he wrote: "It need scarcely be mentioned, that the present constitution of society is not in a healthy state. . . . Discord and disseverment prevail to an extent which seem to threaten its decomposition and destruction."[2] For all of these believers the metaphor of madness touched a sensitive spot and must have seemed as much a reality as a poetic device.

Of all the poems demonstrating Tennyson's sensitivity to his contemporaries' sense of England's unhealthy state, none illustrates it more thoroughly and indeed more anxiously than the *Idylls of the King.* Here Tennyson resurrects the legendary Camelot to expose simultaneously the forces threatening contemporary England's moral fiber and the excesses enslaving the minds of the nation's inhabitants. Because of the link he sees between personal and national aberrations, Tennyson deliberately chooses not to reproduce any of the king's twelve grand battles. Rather, he chooses to reconstruct the smaller, grittier, nastier, internal battles that propel Arthur's kingdom toward destruction. The blows of these battles are blows to the head, to the mind. The battles are personal and internal as well as national.[3] Throughout the poem, therefore, Tennyson confronts those excesses that created the monomaniacal lovers, the obsessive and tyrannical fathers, the revolutionary mobs, and, worst of all, civilizations mastered by lust. Also before him is his understanding of madness and how it attacks the mind. That knowledge serves as a paradigm for analyzing the collapse of the nation's health. Camelot is, in fact, a macrocosm of a mind laboring under the tyranny of one idea. Conversely, the morbid mind is a microcosm of a diseased England.

To describe England's unhealthy state Tennyson does not depend only on his scientific understanding of madness. He is also aware of the heritage of the madness metaphor. This metaphor and this heritage give him a means of addressing his fears and of writing about sexual excesses, wild enthusiasts, and people driven mad by ambition. Moreover, the metaphor reinforces the tragedy of the fall of Camelot and exposes those responsible for it. These are the people who are not only subject to their passions but also subject to their deceitful dreams, which cause them to misapprehend the world. Finally, the metaphor of madness serves as a vivid emblem of the nation's increasing moral inadequacy.

It is not surprising that when writing the *Idylls* Tennyson utilized the metaphor of madness as well as his clinical knowledge of it, for as we have seen Tennyson could never regard madness solely from a clinical perspective. Throughout his poetry madness is literary as well as clinical. For example, in *Maud* the hero is at once a patient belonging to a nineteenth-century case study and a mad lover belonging to a literary tradition that often featured those who suffer from a thwarted, single-minded adoration. Because Tennyson was familiar with literary portraits of madness, he could not overlook

their metaphoric function. Even in a poem as clinically accurate as *Maud*, the madness is not merely present for its own sake; rather, it allows Tennyson to describe the horrors resulting from the nation's unhealthy regard for Mammon and the travesties attached to the sheer "lunacy" of sacrificing children, love, and moral principles to greed. And, as it had for innumerable writers in preceding generations, madness underscores the hero's tragic confusion.

Maud, of course, is not the only poem in which Tennyson shows his sensitivity to madness as a literary metaphor. In "The Flight" (1836), "The Wreck" (1855), and in "Aylmer's Field" (1862), for instance, madness functions metaphorically to expose and heighten the suffering of those tyrannized by Mammon-worshipping parents, who for the sake of an economically and socially advantageous marriage deny their children love and disrupt the moral order. Before going on to discuss at length the function of madness in the *Idylls,* it will be helpful to review Tennyson's use of the metaphor of madness in these shorter poems. In "The Flight" and "The Wreck" Tennyson demonstrates the wickedness of arranged, mercenary marriages by letting their victims speak of the immorality and suffering that result. They speak of mercenary fathers who are tyrant vassals "of a tyrant vice" ("The Flight," l. 25), and they speak of their own madness, their burning temples and their "oft-wandering mind" ("The Wreck," l. 130). The madness in these poems not only magnifies the tragic consequences of the parents' failings but also punishes those parents for their immorality. The most extreme and melodramatic example of this madness comes in "Aylmer's Field" when Tennyson uses insanity to dramatize and damn Sir Aylmer's greed, a greed that drives his daughter Edith mad, causes Lionel, her socially inferior lover, to commit suicide, turns his wife into an hysteric "confined to a couch of fire," and in the end drives himself, raving, into an asylum—a fitting punishment given the metaphorical context and the continuing literary tradition that prompted many of Tennyson's contemporaries to castigate such offenders by driving them mad.[4]

The metaphor in these poems, however, has a value for Tennyson beyond its conventional task of mirroring despair and disorder and of doling out punishment. The metaphor also offers Tennyson the opportunity of safely encountering reality. In the poems mentioned above, for instance, it allows him to speak of his own traumas suffered at the hands of those who discriminated against him because of their regard for Mammon. And it also allows him to speak of these matters without risking writing a poem that is either too autobiographical or too removed from his readers' experiences. The metaphor diffuses the private nature of the poem by attaching his experiences to those of many who were familiar with the metaphor and who, like

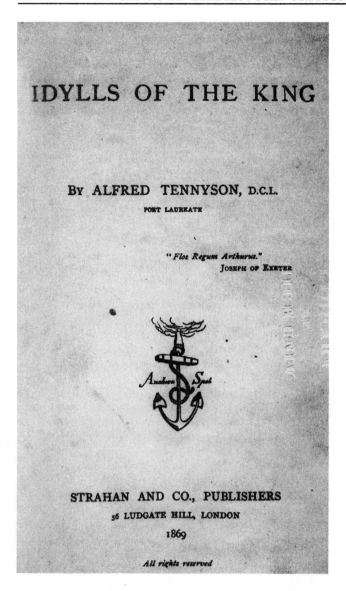

Carlyle, felt threatened by a pervasive and inordinate regard for wealth at the expense of moral principles.

That these poems are personal should be clear from earlier discussions of Tennyson's emotional difficulties. Because of the circumstances surrounding his father's disinheritance, Tennyson, at times, felt as desperate and as thwarted, and indeed as maddened, as the confused lovers in these poems. He, like his father, was affected by the disinheritance. Because he lacked position and wealth, he too was subjected to those who champion Mammon. For example, as Ralph Rader and, more recently, Robert Martin have pointed out, Tennyson suffered considerably when Rosa Baring's father put an end to their relationship because of the Tennysons' inferior financial and social status.[5] In addition, there is evidence that Tennyson also felt angry and chaotic when Arthur Henry Hallam's father opposed his family's relationship with the less prosperous Tennysons. Experiences like these, especially in the early 1840s, brought Tennyson close to a breakdown. These traumas were so pressing that they necessarily formed the subject matter of these poems about greedy parents, thwarted love, and subsequent breakdowns. Since Rader's discussion of *Maud,* for example, it is clear that Tennyson's frustrations over his affair with Rosa Baring served as a nucleus of that poem and, by extension, "The Flight" and "The Wreck." The affair and the Barings' resistance to the union, though, are only implicit in these poems. The metaphor protects the privacy by offering Tennyson a ready-made vocabulary and structure in which to address the affair and to encounter the subsequent periods of depression and hysteria. Moreover, the very conventional nature of the metaphor allows him to move these intimate and painful interludes into the public arena with little fear of exposing his personal difficulties with the Barings or his own chaotic state of mind. Paradoxically, then, the metaphor simultaneously exposes the personal instability and shelters it. Personae emerge which originate in Tennyson's own traumas but which, because they are transposed into the familiar by the metaphor, cease to be purely personal. They are instead a unique blend of scientific fact, literary convention, and personal and national traumas.

Naturally, madness as it functions metaphorically in Tennyson's poetry addresses more than his impatience with people's dangerous regard for Mammon. Building on perhaps the most familiar and certainly the most tenacious of the literary conventions associated with madness, Tennyson often couples insanity with "unbridled passion" and lust. "Lucretius" (1868), a poem based on the legend of Lucretius's death, offers an example of this coupling. In this poem Tennyson charts in detail the deterioration of Lucretius's mind after his frustrated wife gives him a love potion that is more powerful than she expects. It arouses the beast within him and kills any power he might possess to subdue or rule the resulting sexual passion. In the end, disgusted and unbalanced by his overwhelming lust and believing he can never find "passionless tranquility," Lucretius commits suicide. Even though there are moments in the poem when Tennyson satisfies his need to be clinical and consequently describes how the wife's love potion "confused the chemic labour of the blood" and "made havock among those tender cells" (ll. 20-23), there are many more moments when Tennyson satisfies his compulsion to explore the metaphorical function of Lucretius's instability. Tennyson uses madness so he can dramatically display Lucretius's fall and the rise of the unchecked brute brain. He uses madness to express his utter disgust at the power of the bestial nature to overthrow the noble Lucretius. As it had for him in *Maud,* the metaphor allows him to express his disgust in a public and acceptable idiom. His contemporaries, of course, were well versed in the ancient image of "unbridled passion" and immersed in their own practice of linking dissipation to madness and suicide. Victorian novels and melodramas were all too well populated with characters in a frenzy or a stupor because of an overwhelming, reckless passion.[6]

It is important that Tennyson have this metaphor, for sexual passion, particularly for him, was fraught with an anxiety far surpassing that attached to his fears concerning Mammon worship. As several critics have noted, one of the most active forces governing Tennyson's life and work is his distrust of the flesh, of human sexuality, a distrust so strong that in the guise of Lucretius he can do little more than gasp at the sight of the lustful satyr, "I hate, abhor, spit, sicken at him." Tennyson was convinced that given an opportunity, the bestial nature would rise to the surface and quickly disturb a person's equilibrium. He was all too willing to equate the satyr with sexuality and madness. Because of these fears, throughout his life he found it difficult to feel comfortable with any sort of passion or sensual pleasure. For example, as a youth he wrote "The Passions" (1827) and uneasily explored the passions' power to enslave and destroy. That uneasiness never disappeared, for later he dramatized the decline of victims of sensual excess like the sailors in "The Lotos-Eaters" (1832) and the dissolute company in "The Vision of Sin" (1842). Much later he couched his unease in the comical "Spinster's Sweet-Arts" (1885) by creating the portrait of a happy, eccentric spinster who, because she has not given in to her "brute brain," has avoided the tragic end that the passionate and sinful "Black Sal" met.

With this sensibility it is not surprising that Tennyson was so often attracted to the moralistic melodramas and novels of his period and to Ann Radcliffe's cautionary words from *The Mysteries of Udolpho,* words that would stick in his mind and preface his early poem "The Passions": "You have passions in your heart—scorpions; they sleep now—beware how you awaken them! they will sting you even to death." Tennyson must have remembered these words when a series of national acts exacerbated his anxiety and verified his sense of a growing, unhealthy sexual freedom. These acts authorized the establishment of the divorce courts in 1857 and the attempts, beginning in 1866, to legalize marriage with a deceased wife's sister. These acts went hand in hand with numerous studies on prostitution in the 1830s, with the success of Swinburne's sex-centered *Poems and Ballads* (1866), and with the popularity (beginning in the 1830s) of what was known as "the literature of prostitution." This literature had caught the attention of those anxious about "unprofitable reading" and those whom Walter E. Houghton identifies as being acutely aware of "unbridled sensu-

ality."[7] Tennyson referred to that literature as "the thoughts of Zolaism" ("Locksley Hall Sixty Years After," l. 145).

As might be expected, because the metaphor of madness helps Tennyson address moral dilemmas, it also aids him in writing his political poems. The phenomenon is not surprising. As can be discovered in a survey of literary madness, throughout the history of literature writers have often called on madness and its accompanying confusion to capture the chaos of civil strife, the frenzy of battle, the lawlessness of revolution, and the foolishness of lawmakers and leaders. Consequently, when Tennyson injects phrases like war's "mad blasts" into his poems and when he speaks of the "maddening strife" and "maddening shouts" of battle, he is participating in a well-practiced convention. However, there is a difference, for he is employing the metaphor at a time when his reading public is more sensitive than usual to its truth. Well versed in the classical tradition with its practice of equating war and political chaos with madness, and all too familiar with Swift's use of madness to satirize political follies, Tennyson's contemporaries were already attracted to the metaphor and used it to address their growing concern over their nation's faltering mental health. In fact, such was the metaphor's popularity that cartoons in *Punch* and newspaper accounts of disturbing national events and deviations from the status quo frequently drew on it.

Tennyson shared fears about the nation's health, and, like others, tended to blame much of the nation's insanity on the behavior of individuals. Convinced that one could not exist without the other, he stressed the interrelation between personal and national aberrations. Part of his willingness to see this connection came from the support he received from those like Maddock and Allen, but much of it also came from the literary metaphor that set a precedent for it. The Jacobean drama, for instance, to which Tennyson was attracted, is full of examples of intertwined personal and national madness. Tennyson had only to recall the madness and mad masques in *The Duchess of Malfi, 'Tis Pity She's a Whore,* and *The Changeling* to find examples.

Because Tennyson is sensitive to the interrelation between personal and national aberrations, he sees the mad excesses of the French Revolution and the wild behavior of the rick-burning peasants terrorizing the Cambridge countryside as extensions of personal appetites which have not been checked but have been allowed to gain the upper hand. In a manner that finds its parallel in the equation of political chaos and madness in Charles Dickens's *Barnaby Rudge* and in Thomas Carlyle's *The French Revolution,* Tennyson in "The Vision of Sin" parallels the company's sensual liberties and destructive actions with the frenzied actions of the civil libertarians who are "roaring" for freedom. In "Aylmer's Field" he suggests a similar parallel when he equates the tyrannical personality of Sir Aylmer and the resulting horrors of the chaos and tragedy during the reign of terror: Sir Aylmer with his "hoary" hair and ravenous greed is as much a wolf as those wolves said to have prowled on the shores of France, eating the revolution's victims. The parallel continues when Tennyson writes that the only marriage left to the dead Edith and Lionel is one similar to those shocking unions left to dead men and women who during the Reign of Terror were tied naked together and wrapped in "ghastly" sacks. "Lucretius" also draws a parallel between personal and public excesses. In this poem, Tennyson asks the reader to regard the wife's action and its effect on Lucretius as being similar to those vile actions of an undisciplined democracy. Both bring anarchy and madness. The inferior wife's careless act and her wish to master the noble Lucretius are analogous to a frightening democracy in which the base "crowds that in an hour of civic tumult" overthrow "the best and stateliest of the land."[8]

Not only did Tennyson find precedents for the parallels in the literary metaphor of madness, but also in his preoccupation with and the Victorians' fear of monomania, a fear that also complemented the metaphor. In Tennyson's mind England is similar to those fictional lovers and sinners who are tyrannized by a mastering passion. England is just as clogged by its tyrannical passions and accumulated poisons. The mad city or kingdom and the mad man are inseparable. For example, in the germ of *Maud*, "Oh That 'twere Possible!" the city's yellow choking vapors are more than a picture of the smoke coming from the factories—the monuments to Mammon. They are also those internal vapors (associated with melancholy in Burton's *Anatomy*) which clog people's organs and pollute their minds, trapping them in a "yellow" or melancholic mood—a mood, of course, which quickly alters its character and becomes monomaniacal.

Tennyson's sense of a nation suffering from monomania was encouraged not only by the definitions of madness but also by the increasing interest of psychiatrists and the informed public in mob psychology. They were fascinated with epidemics of madness and the power of the mob or violence to capture the mind. They translated French studies on the epidemics of the Middle Ages and they investigated the revolutions of their own time. At the turn of the eighteenth century, Benjamin Rush's studies on the behavioral consequences of the American Revolution and Philippe Pinel's studies on the excesses of the French Revolution caught people's interest.[9] More and more people agreed with their conclusion that revolution and political upheaval caused insanity. They agreed with Pinel that the storm of revolution stirred up the "corresponding tempests in the passions of men, and overwhelmed not a few in total ruin of their distinguished birthright as rational beings."[10] By 1828 these conclusions were acceptable enough for George Man Burrows to announce confidently: "Great political or civil revolutions in states are always productive of great enthusiasm in the people, and correspondent vicissitudes in their moral condition; and as all extremes in society are exciting causes, it will occur, that in proportion as the feelings are acted upon, so will insanity be more or less frequent."[11]

Because Tennyson shared in the public's fear that England and its subjects had lost control and had become slaves to their passions, it is not surprising that when he wrote the *Idylls* he made use of madness in his characters, and its infectious spread through the kingdom, as a metaphor for the breakdown of order and as the fatal genesis of that collapse. Madness is to be expected in a poem that anxiously explores the ruin of the nation's morality and, thus, its sanity. It is also not surprising that in the *Idylls* he uses madness as he does in his other poetry to mirror despair, disorder, inordinate passion, and civil chaos. Indeed the metaphor of madness is most appropriate, for not only is there precedent for it in Tennyson's poetry and in the treatises concerning the nation's "insanity," but also in the public's familiarity with the metaphor. For them as well as for Tennyson madness was familiar as a metaphor of disorder and as a real threat. Madness is a most appropriate gauge of the fall of Camelot.

Because madness plays such a vital role in Tennyson's vision of the fall, and because it allows him to link his fears to his sense of the nation's distress, it emerges as a binding, central force in the *Idylls*.[12] As a result, the *Idylls* is Tennyson's most extensive inquiry into madness as a reality and madness as a metaphor. With such a concentrated use of the metaphor, contrary to what many might expect, the *Idylls* exceeds even *Maud* in its exploration of madness. The madness in the poem as it appeared in its final, published form (1883) should be considered at length.[13]

Significantly, when the *Idylls* opens, madness belongs to the past. For the moment, it is conquered, and all is held in balance. Soon, however, as the realm begins to deteriorate, all kinds of madness appear and infect the inhabitants of Camelot. The insanity extends far beyond that usually associated with Lancelot, Balin, and Pelleas. In the end it seems even to reach King Arthur. He leaves Camelot in "confusion."

The first idyll, "The Coming of Arthur," opens with multiple and conflicting accounts of the king's birth, the variety of which immediately suggests that the king is born with a multiple inheritance: he is born of anger, passion, bitterness, sweetness, nobility, and love.[14] With this inheritance, he emerges as a person who contains within him the bestial and the noble passions. He is at once baseborn and sublime or "more than man." Initially as king he unites and controls these warring elements so that he and his kingdom are balanced. He and "his knighthood for a space / Were all one will" (ll. 514-15). They draw in "the petty princedoms" so that all function harmoniously. Moreover, because he can balance these passions, he is able to transform the "great tracts of wilderness / Wherein the beast was ever more and more, / But men less and less" (ll. 10-12) into an orderly society. No longer do the wolves roam his land and devour children; no longer do the children fall victim to the beastly and excessive passions of their forebears. To complete the harmony, Arthur marries, an act that is necessary in the minds of Tennyson and his contemporaries who, despite certain fears for those with a predisposition to madness, maintain that few are whole without marriage and without uniting the masculine and feminine elements of their character.[15] The marriage as a representation of this wholeness, however, cannot last long in the *Idylls,* for already the seething passions are surfacing and tyrannizing the kingdom and the citizens. Even in this first idyllic section there are hints of the evil lurking below and the madness waiting to break out, for Gawain bursts into song and wildly dashes about while Modred eavesdrops hoping to find a means of overthrowing the king (ll. 319-24).

In the second idyll, "Gareth and Lynette," order continues to dominate, but the challenge posed to that order or sanity by the bestial passions becomes slightly more visible. As yet, though, neither the individual inhabitants of Camelot nor Camelot itself is overwhelmed and maddened by the baser instincts as Lucretius was. The mood throughout the idyll is idealistic. It is replete with allusions to a fairy-tale world where wishes come true and with proclamations or evidence of Gareth's faith in King Arthur's court. Gareth's innocence within such a world allows him to overcome potentially treacherous moments. Later, however, Tennyson will tip Gareth's innocence upside down and place his faith within the context of a fallen world that does not even have the benefit of the virtues and illusions belonging to the fairy tale.

This second idyll opens with affectionate banter between Gareth and his mother and with his telling the story of the goose and the golden eggs. Through the telling of the story, Gareth disarms his mother's objections to his leaving home for Camelot. In leaving, Gareth turns his back on a life of idleness (his weak father's life), always so dangerous in Tennyson's mind, and goes forward. When Gareth comes to the gates of Camelot his companions are frightened. Armed with his innocence and idealistic faith, Gareth is not bothered by the shadowy, illusory movements that meet him as he enters Camelot, or by the riddle of the king's birth that has no answer (ll. 184-231). He enters "with

all good cheer." Believing in Arthur's order of the Knights of the Round Table, he willingly takes the difficult vows "Of utter hardihood, utter gentleness, / And, loving, utter faithfulness in love, / And uttermost obedience to the King" (ll. 542-44). By believing in and becoming a vassal to Arthur's order, he is able to combat the excessively proud and nasty prodding of Lynette, to overcome the four destructive knights, to survive his journey through the maddening mire, to save the baron, and, in the end, with Lancelot's help, to save the "blooming boy" from a death in life. He controls pride, despair, savagery, doubt, peril, lawlessness, insanity, the passions, and the temptations met in the various stages of life. His victories over the "wronger of the Realm" are the conquests of Arthur's ideal soul. They mirror the king's judicious hold over the realm which Gareth has witnessed in Arthur's court. Gareth's victories are analogous to Arthur's victories over himself, for even he must control his base inheritance (he is "baseborn") which periodically threatens to unseat him. For example, when the widow of Arthur's enemy requests his aid, the king's tense reply reflects his inner turmoil. Control, however, wins:

> "We sit King, to help the wronged
> Through all our realm. The woman loves her
>   lord.
> Peace to thee, woman, with thy loves and
>   hates!
> The kings of old had doomed thee to the
>   flames,
> Aurelius Emrys would have scourged thee
>   dead,
> And Uther slit thy tongue: but get thee
>   hence—
> Lest that rough humour of the kings of old
> Return upon me!"

> [ll. 363-70]

This power, though, is possible only in an innocent, fairyland setting. As Tennyson knew only too well, the shadows and riddles of one's inheritance always threatened to disrupt even the best situations.

Beginning in the next idyll, "The Marriage of Geraint," the ideal state begins to totter. The wise Merlin's warning that Gareth is passing into a city where "the King / Will bind thee by such vows, as is a shame / A man should not be bound by, yet that which / No man can keep" ("Gareth and Lynette," ll. 265-67) contains truth. These vows are the ideal, and, in reality, they are impossible. People are normally more vulnerable than Gareth was. As people and a nation progress in life, from their morning to their evening, they are going to meet with conflict; they fall into battle with the mire of despair, lust, pride, anger, and anarchy; and many are going to become victims of these vices. It will not always be possible to rescue the child from death or madness; to save the innocent or nobler self from the darker, deadlier self. It will not always be possible to fall and laugh as Gareth has done:

> And Gareth crying pricked against the cry;
> But when they closed—in a moment—at one touch
> Of that skilled spear, the wonder of the world—
> Went sliding down so easily, and fell,
> That when he found the grass within his hands
> He laughed.

["Gareth and Lynette," ll. 1191-95]

In the future idylls madness will become a more immediate and ominous threat. It will not be dismissed as quickly as it is in this second idyll, where madness is a word used lightly and where it is as illusory as the knight who is the Star of Evening. Gareth's fight with that "madman" is long, but Gareth wins. In the future such struggles with madness will be harder. Once a person is touched by its lawlessness, rarely will he regain order. Balin will return to the court and be reprieved, but his sanity is only to be temporary. The nation too will not recover from its infliction. From "The Marriage of Geraint" on, Tennyson describes how many lose these battles, how many tumble and become lost in the mire of their tyrannizing passions. Neither the people nor the nation can break their habits and release their saner selves.

The long, hot summer, the season for madness and the heat of excessive passion, begins in the next two idylls, "The Marriage of Geraint" and "Geraint and Enid," when Lancelot's and Guinevere's sexual passion for one another has begun to gain control. No longer can their affair be kept secret. Rumors spread, and with those rumors corruption extends from the two lovers to many in Arthur's court. Their effect on the court is very much tied to Tennyson's discomfort with and distrust of sexual passion. No passion is as contaminating as theirs; it too easily destroys the mind's and the nation's delicate balance, too frequently rouses the monster madness from its sleep. Because Lancelot and Guinevere have not repressed their lust, they and others will weaken and become more vulnerable to other excesses. Geraint is the first to be sullied and victimized by their affair. Before learning of their "guilty love" (ll. 24-28) Geraint has exhibited "exceeding manfulness / And pure nobility of temperament" (ll. 211-12), but afterward he fears he is effeminate, dashes madly into the wilderness, and distorts what he hears. He has lost control of the delicate relation between his masculine and feminine qualities, which, of course, the ideal King Arthur exhibits. Now the knowledge of Guinevere's and Lancelot's passion transforms Geraint's moments of splenetic behavior (as when he shouted at the armorer and "flashed into sudden spleen") into a prolonged, mad fury; it transforms his effeminate tendencies (his wearing of the long purple scarf with the gold apple dangling from it) into impotency; and it turns his scrupulous attention to his wife's deportment and clothing into a dangerous obsession, and, finally, into a sexual fantasy. Because of Guinevere's sin, the fear envelops him "lest his gentle wife, / Through that great tenderness for Guinevere" (ll. 29-30) become as tainted as she. Like the mad lovers in case studies and those belonging to the literary convention, Geraint's mind is seized by one mastering thought, causing him to distort all that goes on around him. To give a sense of just how deeply Geraint is trapped by his unhealthy obsession, Tennyson repeats phrases and locks them into an obsessive pattern. For example, when Geraint madly refuses to leave Enid's side, Tennyson uses the trapped syntax to speak of the consequences. Geraint grows

> Forgetful of his promise to the king,
> Forgetful of the falcon and the hunt,
> Forgetful of the tilt and tournament,
> Forgetful of his glory and his name,
> Forgetful of his princedom and its cares.

[ll. 48-54]

The consequences of Geraint's monomania are almost fatal. His excessive anger, pride, jealousy, and fear fight to rule him. Under their domain, losing his grip on reality, Geraint mistakes his wife's motives, deceives King Arthur, talks to himself, and babbles to others. He is an example of those who "Do forge a life-long trouble for [themselves], / By taking true for false, or false for true" ("Geraint and Enid," ll. 3-4). Geraint's excesses lead him to those "Gray swamps and pools, waste places of the hern, / And wildernesses, perilous paths" (ll. 31-32)—wild places that complement the chaos, danger, and barrenness of his sick mind. Like any truly sick person he vacillates between wrath and despair, between irrationality and rationality. In the more rational moments, Geraint and Enid come to a smoother landscape, a meadow cared for by mowers. But even there Geraint displays excessive behavior—an indication of his continuing unbalanced state. Without realizing it he ravenously consumes all the mowers' food; and then, when he understands what he has done, he overpays them "fifty fold." Later he pays the host with "five horses and their armours," a payment that the amazed host admits is equal to five times the cost of a room at his inn.

Geraint's appetite and payments are as out of proportion as his judgment. His monomania affects not only his "appetite" but also his sense of the world around him. He rides "as if he heard not"; he hears only half, as when waking from his sleep to catch the last few words of his wife's speech. Sometimes he neither hears nor sees. Enid must do that for him. She says: "I hear the violent threats you do not hear, / I see the danger which you cannot see" ("Geraint and Enid," ll. 420-21). In the end, lawlessness nearly overwhelms Geraint. His excesses lead him to the Earl of Doorm's wasteland. Here the "wild Limours" attacks "all in a passion uttering a dry shriek." Although Geraint stuns this mad lover, he receives a terrible wound. He totters. Losing his balance, he falls from his horse. The struggle with Limours, though, is a turning point for Geraint. He begins to find a way out of his living death, to release himself from the lawless lord's estate—a realm resembling an asylum. Among its inhabitants are a man-at-arms "half whistling and half singing a coarse song" and another "flying from the wrath of Doorm / Before an ever-fancied arrow" (ll. 522-32).

It is logical that Limours unbalances Geraint, for Limours's excessive passion for Enid mirrors Geraint's and, furthermore, comments on Guinevere and Lancelot's affair. His fate mirrors what Geraint's might have been if Enid had not kept her husband in touch with reality. Limours has become "wild" because he is completely subjected to his own sensations. There is no one to help him hear or see, he says, except "Enid, the pilot star of my lone life, / Enid, my early and my only love, / Enid, the loss of whom hath turned me wild—" (ll. 306-8). Geraint survives only because he is cared for by Enid, a person who shields her head from the sinful sun and the fires of madness, who shuns "the wild ways of the lawless tribe." Governed by moderation, she refuses to eat and participate in Geraint's lawless appetite, and can therefore protect him. Eventually with Enid's help Geraint's manliness and balance return. The earl slaps Enid, and her cries for help awaken and arouse Geraint's masculinity. He takes his sword, an emblem of Arthur's order, and "with a sweep of it / Shore through the swarthy neck" of the Earl of Doorm. The taking of the sword is an act by which Geraint simultaneously regains his sanity and his masculinity.

With harmony restored, Geraint and Enid can now mount the same horse and ride together back to King Arthur's court, where the king's reigning order promises to nurse Geraint back to health. In the court an image of restored inner harmony awaits them. Edyrn, who had believed himself "well-nigh mad," is now, in Arthur's words, "One of the noblest, our most Valorous, / Sanest and most obedient" knights (ll. 909-10). Unfortunately, though, the court is no longer a perfect place. The restored harmony is not secure. Experience has broken the innocence, and Enid realizes that governed passion may soon erupt to tyrannize once more. When she meets Edyrn and remembers his former,

destructive self, she cannot help shrinking "a little." As Tennyson adds: "In a hollow land, / From which old fires have broken, men may fear / Fresh fire and ruin" (ll. 820-22)—an autobiographical statement from Tennyson, who periodically had seen madness break out and threaten to consume him and his family; and, moreover, a poignant statement for his contemporaries, who had feared that the horrors of the French Revolution and the chaos of brutal democracy might break out on English soil and upset the nation's delicate balance.

Enid fears more than Edyrn. She also lives in horror of the "bandits scattered in the field." Although Geraint seems to be whole again, and although the Earl of Doorm is dead, the earl's lawless followers, like the rumors of Guinevere and Lancelot's affair, are very much alive, although scattered. Geraint too is suspicious. He can "never take again / That comfort from" Enid's and Guinevere's "converse which he took / Before the Queen's fair name was breathed upon" (ll. 948-50). Shadows also hover over the king's justice. There is still a belief that man and nation can "repent," but now that belief is qualified. Significantly, Arthur is not blind to the difficulties:

> "The world will not believe a man repents:
> And this wise world of ours is mainly right.
> Full seldom doth a man repent, or use
> Both grace and will to pick the vicious quitch
> Of blood and custom wholly out of him,
> And make all clean, and plant himself afresh.
>
> [ll. 899-904]

All these fears, suspicions, shadows, and qualifications seem to be Tennyson's attempt to show how easy it is to doubt. Like Arthur, Tennyson worries about that doubt. He wants people to hold on to their idealism and beliefs, for without them the Limours and the lawless bandits of Doorm will turn civilization into a wild place. Doubting brings people closer to their madness. It causes people to neglect the task of weeding out their evil passions. Like Yniol, Enid's father, they stand idly by allowing their kingdoms to topple over from disuse; they stand there in old and rusty arms, tyrannized like Edyrn, who if only given the chance to live under Arthur's order can be made sane again.

The hot summer and the fevers of madness continue to blast through "Balin and Balan." They bring with them a confusion more perilous than that in the previous idylls. People's doubts, wrath, pride, and lust are more lethal than ever. Moreover, what Enid and Tennyson had feared comes true. The old fires break out afresh and consume. Only for a while does Balin find inner harmony, but all too soon the anger and "outer fiends," which his brother Balan had begged him to control, rage. He cannot recover his sanity as Edyrn and Geraint had. In "middle May," the season of madness, Balin fights "hard with himself" to repress his moods but cannot. He vows, "I will be gentle," but fails. He kills his brother and falls into despair, crying "My violences, my violences!"

Throughout this idyll Balin's struggle to control his violence is his quest. He desperately wants to heed his brother's warning, so he accepts Arthur's invitation to "walk with me, and move / To music with thine Order and the King" (ll. 72-74), and he tries to "learn what Arthur meant by courtesy, / Manhood, and knighthood" (ll. 155-56). Neither the invitation nor the lesson is strong enough to destroy the disorder threatening Balin's stability. Already the king's order is slipping away. Balin ends up going on a journey that takes him the very opposite of where he wishes to go. Ironically, instead of keeping him within Arthur's promised order, Balin's quest leads him away from Camelot into the chaotic wilderness filled with hallucinations—a sure sign of insanity. His flight from court horrifyingly echoes the maddened figure in the previous idyll, who stumbled through the lawless woods "flying from the wrath of Doorm / Before an ever-fancied arrow" ("Geraint and Enid," ll. 530-31). Balin's madness is similar:

> He felt the hollow-beaten mosses thud
> And tremble, and then the shadow of a spear,
> Shot from behind him, ran along the ground.
> Sideways he started from the path, and saw,
> With pointed lance as if to pierce, a shape,
> A light of armour by him flash, and pass
> And vanish in the woods; and followed this,
> But all so blind in rage that unawares
> He burst his lance against a forest bough,
> Dishorsed himself, and rose again.

> [ll. 316-25]

Eventually he falls under the power of King Pellam, the enemy of order, who will not pay tribute to Arthur's court. Balin can no longer bridle his passion, so his horse does not carry him back to Camelot as Gareth and Enid's had. Instead it crushes him. When Balin falls from his horse there is no laughter. That was possible only in Geraint's fairy-tale world. Death replaces not only laughter, but also marriage and the future promise concluding the previous idylls. Balin and Balan die tyrannized by madness. As Balin admits, "My madness all thy life has been thy doom, / Thy curse, and darkened all thy day; and now / The night has come" (ll. 608-10).

Once more Guinevere's and Lancelot's lust has tipped the balance, for Balin lost control after the shock of overhearing the queen and her lover's amorous conversation in the garden. The shock of his discovery unleashes his madness. He gives in to its fury, blaming his inheritance from an angry father, and turns his back on Arthur's court.

The queen's guilty passion, however, is not the only root of Balin's madness. Despair and unwillingness to have complete faith in Arthur's order also unbalance him. Both conspire to destroy his trust. Balin fears: "Too high this mount of Camelot for me: / These high-set courtesies are not for me" (ll. 221-22). Like his anger, his doubts distort his judgment. He chooses to follow not only shadows, as Geraint did, but also shadows of shadows. Believing that to become one of Arthur's knights is "beyond *my* reach," he mistakenly and single-mindedly champions Guinevere as an image of purity and order: "'No shadow' said Sir Balin 'O my Queen, / But light to me! no shadow, O my King, / But golden earnest of a gentler life!'" (ll. 202-4). His delusion and his single-mindedness bring their own madness, creating more confusion. Despite Sir Garlon's scorn of Guinevere's purity, Balin insists she is the "fairest, best and purest." Later, despite Vivien's blatant distortion of Guinevere and Lancelot's garden conversation, Balin believes her account is the truth. Vivien's "truth" is yet another blow to his chaotic mind. Once more the shock excites his madness. Emitting a "weird yell, / Unearthlier than all shriek of bird or beast" (ll. 535-36), Balin goes wild. His brother believes the shriek to be that of the "wood-devil I came to quell." In a moment of utter chaos the brothers do not recognize each other and attack. Indeed Balin has momentarily turned into a wood-devil: "his evil spirit upon him leapt, / He ground his teeth together, sprang with a yell, / Tore from the branch, and cast on earth, the shield" (ll. 529-31). But his death is not the death of the demon in the woods. The real demons are left to scatter like the lawless lords, "to dwell among the woods" and bring destruction and madness closer to the center of Arthur's order. Vivien with her "truth" is the real wood-devil, not Balin. From this moment on, the survivors are the destroyers.

In the next idyll, "Merlin and Vivien," Balin's disorderly world creeps closer to Camelot, for despair, passion, and madness attack Merlin, the very architect of the order. Like a cancer, the warring passions are multiplying and gradually overtaking the individual's healthy soul and that of the nation. In this idyll Vivien is a demon driven by her lust and pride. She pursues Merlin into the woods, where she wears down his resistance to her sensuous touch and entangles him in his own lust and weaknesses. She leaves him trapped within the walls of a hollow tower, locked within the cells of madness, useless, and tyrannized by his passion. Merlin has allowed "the meanest" to have power "upon the highest." In the end, Merlin is "lost to life and use and name and fame." His end is prophetic of Guinevere's. She too will be locked within the convent's hollow walls, useless and barren.

Merlin's fall comes because he is first melancholy's victim.

> Then fell on Merlin a great melancholy;
> He walked with dreams and darkness, and he
>   found
> A doom that ever poised itself to fall,
> An ever-moaning battle in the mist,
> World-war of dying flesh against the life,
> Death in all life and lying in all love,
> The meanest having power upon the highest,
> And the high purpose broken by the worm.

> [ll. 187-94]

In this warped state he is most vulnerable. He has little power to resist Vivien's wiles. He despairs too easily; therefore he gives in too easily. His fall is a pessimistic image of what Tennyson considers is happening to his country, and it is also a reminder that the wisest and the cleverest are as vulnerable as their inferiors. As Tennyson once commented, "Some loyal souls are wrought to madness against the world. Others, and some among the highest intellects become the slaves of the evil which is at first half disdained."[16]

As the heat of summer continues, so madness continues to gauge the passions' assault on the ideal order. In "Lancelot and Elaine," madness comes to and from those whose minds are as trapped as Merlin's. They too are held in hollow towers, tyrannized by their lust. The story in this idyll centers on Elaine, who, like her family, lives apart from Arthur's realm and is therefore unsullied by its moral erosion. Corruption comes, however. This time it is neither Guinevere nor Vivien whose sensuous touch destroys; it is Lancelot's which brings death and confusion.

Before Lancelot's arrival in her father's kingdom of Astolat, Elaine is an innocent "lily maid." After he comes, however, and she catches a glimpse of his guilty love, Elaine's innocence disappears. Lancelot's "mellow voice" arouses her and unbalances her mind. Immediately her infatuation distorts her perception and sets her off on a destructive quest to gain Lancelot's love. She begins by misinterpreting his courteous ways, mistakenly thinking "all was nature, all perchance, for her." Then, in a manner reminiscent of Tennyson's tyrannized and maddened lovers, she dwells "all night long" on Lancelot's face. Sudden flashes of wild desire govern her, and she impetuously offers her red sleeve, a symbol of her passion, as a favor to Lancelot to carry with him to the tournament he has left Camelot to attend. Foolishly Lancelot accepts and gives her his shield. So wrapped up is he in his passion for Guinevere that he is not sensitive to Elaine's. After he leaves for the tournament, Elaine climbs to her tower, takes the shield, and "there kept it, and so lived in fantasy." She is now like all those before her whose passion has possessed them and trapped them in a hollow, barren world. Nothing now exists for her but her passion and her false idea of Lancelot's intentions. After the tournament, when she is nursing the wounded Lancelot, she immoderately exclaims: "I have gone mad. I love you: Let me die." Lancelot will not and, worse, cannot give his love, for he is bound by his passion for the queen. Therefore, denied his presence and his love, Elaine once more retreats to that mad tower and mixes "Her fancies with the sallow-rifted glooms / Of evening, and the moanings of the wind" (ll. 995-96). Now, so lost is she in her delusion, that she cannot recognize truth. Her self-deception echoes Balin's, for she does not believe the rumors her father tells her about Lancelot's affair.

> "Sweet father, all too faint and sick am I
> For anger: these are slanders: never yet
> Was noble man but made ignoble talk.
> He makes no friend who never made a foe.
> But now it is my glory to have loved
> One peerless, without stain.

> [ll. 1079-84]

In the end, like a hysteric, she wills her death. As she dies, so separated is she from her true and saner self that her father barely recognizes her: "So dwelt the father on her face, and thought / 'Is this Elaine?'" [ll. 1023-24].

Elaine's loss of self parallels Lancelot's. Because he cannot break the hold of his lust, he too loses his way and himself. Angry with himself, yet still drawn by his desire for Guinevere, he decides to attend the king's tournament rather than remain in Camelot pretending to the king to be suffering from an unhealed wound (ll. 88-159). His journey to the jousts, like his warring mind, is not straightforward. It is impetuous and chaotic.

> Then got Sir Lancelot suddenly to horse,
> Wroth at himself. Not willing to be known,
> He left the barren-beaten thoroughfare,
> Chose the green path that showed the rarer
>   foot,
> And there among the solitary downs,
> Full oft lost in fancy, lost his way.

> [ll. 158-63]

Lancelot is as lost in his fancy as Elaine is in hers.

Throughout the rest of the idyll Lancelot progressively loses his grasp on his sanity. Periodically the anxieties stemming from his divided loyalty to Guinevere and to Arthur, his battle between his sense and his conscience, spur the madness seething within him. At times he appears very much like Balin, for he becomes another demon of the woods: "His mood was often like a fiend, and rose / And drove him into wastes and solitudes / For agony, who was yet a living soul" (ll. 250-52). Lancelot's disguise at the tournament is yet another manifestation of this loss of self. By pretending to be a "stranger knight," he is acting out, maybe even acknowledging, this loss; furthermore, he is courting death. After the tournament he lies almost fatally wounded. Like his madness, his existence is a living death. The disguise and the wound at once echo and reverse Gareth's harmless, innocent, and advantageous charade as the kitchen knave. In that early idyll, before corruption had spread, Gareth's noble nature showed through the disguise. The charade did not bury his true self. Indeed it permitted Gareth to find himself. Now, however, in a disorderly and maddening climate, deception is evil. It is a means by which Lancelot strays further from his nobler nature. In fact, that nobler nature is so weakened that people at the tournament do not, at first, see through his disguise. After the tournament Lancelot has so little moral strength that he is unable to rescue Elaine, to help her "from herself." Moreover, he has little drive to save himself. While he is recovering from his wound he resolves to give up Guinevere. But, as the narrator knows too well, after Lancelot's physical health returns, his passion will also revive to war with and tyrannize his conscience once more.

> Yet the great knight in his mid-sickness made
> Full many a holy vow and pure resolve.
> These, as but born of sickness, could not live:
> For when the blood ran lustier in him again,
> Full often the bright image of one face,
> Making a treacherous quiet in his heart,
> Dispersed his resolution like a cloud.

[ll. 873-79]

Elaine's and Lancelot's lust and their resulting loss of self find their parallels among other figures in this idyll. Gawain and Guinevere are two examples. Gawain comes to Astolat on a quest to find Lancelot and give him the tournament prize, but being more enthralled with Elaine and lost in his desire for her, he forgets his mission. Elaine asks him:

> "O loyal nephew of our noble King
> Why ask you not to see the shield he left,
> Whence you might learn his name? Why
>   slight your King,
> And lose the quest he sent you on, and prove
> No surer than our falcon yesterday,
> Who lost the hern we slipt her at, and went
> To all the winds?"

[ll. 648-54]

Gawain's lust crowds out any remaining loyalty to the king's order. Guinevere's passion distorts her judgment and turns her into "the wild Queen." She cannot recognize the truth, that Arthur is human, that he has "a touch of earth." Her jealousy when she learns of Elaine is completely out of proportion, and she acts rashly, throwing the tournament's prize into the water.

In all cases this madness is barren, a living death. The king's description of Lancelot at the end of the idyll as "a lonely" person and "heirless" is also true for Elaine, Guinevere, and Gawain. All are lost to their passion and consequently themselves. Arthur, whose personal order is ideally balanced and whose will controls his passion, knows better than those whose lives become a living death, and he realizes that freedom can come only with control, with limits. As Arthur tells Lancelot, "Free love, so bound, were freest." Excess binds rather than liberates. It locks people into hollow towers.

As in "Lancelot and Elaine," much of the emphasis in the first half of the *Idylls* is on the destructive excesses of pride, anger, despair, jealousy, and desire, and on their challenge to the individual's as well as to the nation's sanity. Throughout this half, those excesses have spread and have come close to overwhelming Camelot. They have surfaced as madness, an emblem of the order's unbalance, but for the most part that madness has remained outside the kingdom's gates. Given Tennyson's and his contemporaries' concern for England's sanity and their fear of immoderation, however, it is inevitable that this chaos enters those gates. In the idyll "The Holy Grail," the madness that had once been held outside the realm in exile—like Balin— is now within. Arthur's absence in this idyll signals the entrance of disorder, and perhaps more significantly the people's growing disbelief in his order.

In "The Holy Grail" Tennyson concentrates on the distortion and insanity found in the quest for the spiritual and nonmaterial, a quest that held Tennyson's close attention. This idyll reflects his anxiety concerning England's religious crisis. Like England, Camelot is an unbalanced state suffering from a loss of faith. Tennyson watches nervously as its subjects, damaged by doubt, worn down by the excesses of the previous idylls, and lacking the benefit of any clear vision, attempt to fill the existing void with a meaning and a faith which in his mind, take people further and further away from religious faith. These attempts send them on quests that increasingly distort their understanding and allow them to fall deeper into their personal quagmires. As Tennyson said to his son Hallam: "Faith declines, religion turns from practical goodness and holiness to superstition. These seek relief in selfish spiritual excitement."[17]

Tennyson's concern for false religious visions was topical as well as personal. In the nineteenth century not only were these numerous investigations into the physical and emotional sources of apparitions, but there was also a clinical interest in religious enthusiasm and hysteria. With few exceptions physicians easily linked these apparitions of "delusions" with insanity. In 1824, for instance, Alexander Morison talked about an insanity that comes from "excessive devotion, and contrition or remorse of conscience," and he identified doubt in religious doctrines "previously professed" as one source of madness.[18] Four years later George Man Burrows recognized, as most Victorians did, the danger of "exuberance of zeal on any subject," and he, like many others, found religious enthusiasm the most dangerous exuberance of all. He writes: "excess of religious enthusiasm, unless tempered by an habitual command over the affective passions, usually and readily degenerates into fanaticism."[19] To this distrust was added the fear of mass hysteria. Sensitive to the contagious nature of passion, people were all too aware that religious experiences can be no more than a form of hysteria. Mesmerism also undermined the validity of religious enthusiasm, for it had popularly demonstrated the power of suggestion and the power of one individual over another.[20]

Tennyson has these concerns very much in mind throughout "The Holy Grail." He parades one false vision after another. Time and time again he illustrates how the defining qualities of character and people's expectations and excesses trap and deceive them.[21] He also demonstrates how dangerous such religious delusions are; how they can, as the physicians claimed, quickly arouse hysteria or insanity, spread from person to person, and tyrannize not only minds but nations.

The first to see the Holy Grail is the nun. She is a religious hysteric,[22] a figure familiar to nineteenth-century readers. In the past, frustrated by "blunted" love, she had thrown all her "fervent flame," her thwarted passion, into religion and had given herself "to fast and alms." Now, in this idyll, news of Guinevere and Lancelot's affair arouses in her that frustrated lust and excites her zealousness. After denying herself food and following a strict regime of prayers, she suddenly awakes in the "dead of night" to a vision. The combination of her thwarted passion, zealous fasting and praying, and the delusive night would be enough to warn most of how erroneous her vision of the Holy Grail is. Her description of the cup, however, confirms just how impure and deceptive this revelation is. The cup is "rose-red with beatings in it, as if alive." Her frustration colored and shaped it.

The nun's hysteria is contagious, for it soon entangles the whole court. First it mesmerizes Sir Galahad. Sir Percivale watches, fascinated, as "this Galahad, when he heard / My sister's vision, filled me with amaze; / His eyes became so like her own, they seemed / Hers, and himself her brother more than I" ("The Holy Grail,"

ll. 139-42). When she speaks to Sir Galahad, her words are sensuous and hypnotic. She weaves her words in the way she had woven her belt with crimson threads. His will soon becomes her servant, as Merlin's had become Vivien's: "and as she spake / She sent the deathless passion in her eyes / Through him, and made him hers, and laid her mind / On him, and he believed in her belief" (ll. 163-65). Not heeding Merlin's example, he sits in the fallen wizard's seat, whose inscription warns, "No man could sit but he should lose himself." Thus, contrary to his belief that by becoming the nun's disciple he will "save himself," he, like those before, falls. Possessed, he cannot speak, except "in a voice shrilling." The deluded knight now held in the hysteric's control sees visions of the Holy Grail as crimson as the nun's lust. Caught in her hysteria, he tells Percivale:

> "And never yet
> Hath what thy sister taught me first to see,
> This Holy Thing, failed from my side, nor come
> Covered, but moving with me night and day,
> Fainter by day, but always in the night
> Blood-red, and sliding down the blackened marsh
> Blood-red, and on the naked mountain top
> Blood-red, and in the sleeping mere below
> Blood-red."
>
> [ll. 468-76]

Sir Galahad is overwhelmed by his enthusiasm. Hence, he cannot find his way back to Camelot. His eyes, now as mesmeric as the nun's, capture Percivale. Percivale speaks: "While thus he spake, his eyes, dwelling on mine, / Drew me, with power upon me, till I grew / One with him, to believe as he believed" (ll. 485-87). These lines frighteningly echo those describing the nun's hold over Galahad. Wanting to see the Holy Grail too, Percivale follows Galahad. Percivale's ensuing vision is colored by the nun's and Galahad's hysterical, crimson passion. The vessel he sees hanging over his head is "redder than any rose." Its hue gives "a rose-red sparkle to the city." Percivale, though, is not as blindly zealous as either of them. Doubts tug at his mind to prevent him from coming as close to the spiritual city as they do. Subject to the absent king's warning, "This Quest is not for thee" and fearing he was following "wandering fires," Percivale cannot make Galahad's spiritual leaps. The bridges that knight crosses to reach the spiritual city crumble before Percivale. Beneath, Percivale sees a quagmire filled with his doubts. He fears them as much as the unconditional belief waiting for him on the other side. He is one of many in the nineteenth century caught between the sensuous and the spiritual worlds, comfortable in niether. He lacks what the monk recognizes as "the warmth of double life." He literally cannot bridge the two. Thus, when Percivale sees the vision it is at a distance.

Once more, state of mind has shaped the vision. The experience has had little to do with spiritual reality. Rather, the appearance of the Holy Grail is nothing more than a mirror of the person's expectations and a measure of his own weaknesses. Lancelot's inability to see the Grail clearly or to benefit from its healing qualities is similar. His "grief and love" block his journey to the spiritual heights. To begin with he has "small heart" to pursue the quest. Then, when he sees the Grail, it reflects nothing of a true spiritual world. Its heat reflects only his own madness and the sordidness of his excessive lust.

> "Then in my madness I essayed the door;
> It gave; and through a stormy glare, a heat
> As from a seventimes-heated furnace, I,
> Blasted and burnt, and blinded as I was,
> With such a fierceness that I swooned away—
> O, yet methought I saw the Holy Grail,
> All palled in crimson samite, and around
> Great angels, awful shapes, and wings and
> eyes.

[ll. 838-45]

Frightened and perhaps knowing better, he leaves, exclaiming, "this Quest was not for me." Sir Bors also sees the Holy Grail "according to" his "sight." To Bors, who is more selfless, who "scarce had prayed or asked it for myself," an unexpected, sweeter, more delicate vision comes. This time the crimson and the rose-red tint of the vision is pink: "—O grace to me—/ In colour like the fingers of a hand / Before a burning taper, the sweet Grail / Glided and past" (ll. 689-92). Yet another knight in search of the Grail falls prey to his character. Following his nature, Sir Gawain predictably forgets the quest. He is the very antithesis of Galahad who loses himself in a false, spiritual world and cannot find his way back to Camelot. Gawain is so weighed down by his sensuous concerns, that he cannot even move from the silken pavilion with its "merry maidens" to search for a spiritual light.

Each of these knights has sadly proved King Arthur correct.[23] They have followed "wandering fires" and have become lost in the quagmires of themselves. Their hysteria has taken them away from Camelot and allowed them to indulge in their weaknesses and to maintain neither personal nor national order. The resurgence of their personal disorder is reflected in the ruin and waste of their kingdom. On their return to Camelot the wearied knights find "horses stumbling as they trode / On heaps of ruin, hornless unicorns, / Cracked basilisks, and splintered cockatrices, / And shattered talbots, which had left the stones / Raw, that

they fell from" (ll. 713-17). England's traditional symbols of order have fallen. Moreover, the city with its four zones, each representing progress from the bestial toward the spiritual ideal, has crumbled. The cracks in the city's foundations are the consequences of the inhabitants' passions, untempered by Arthur, who if he had not had to quell the spreading evil would have moderated these passions and prevented the knights' hysteria. The closing description of Camelot reflects Tennyson's fears that England is a country cracking under the weight of such enthusiasms, excesses, doubts, and materialistic concerns; that it has lost sight of the true spiritual values; and that it is filled with those who, like Percivale, are caught by their doubts and cannot make the spiritual leap.

The remaining idylls follow the cracks as they spread through and shatter the foundations of Arthur's realm. In two short idylls, "Pelleas and Ettarre" and "The Last Tournament," the fall comes quickly. These two idylls reverse all that Camelot has ideally represented.[24] A new generation of knights reigns and revives the ascendancy of bestiality which Arthur had fought and controlled. Pelleas, a new knight "to fill the gap / Left by the Holy Quest," and Tristram are among this new generation. They are the inheritors of the unhealthy state. They move about in a kingdom where the sensuous Gawain and the evil Modred are becoming more visible. Until now this evil pair has been lurking in the background.

To illustrate this reversal, Tennyson continues to use the image of madness. Pelleas's madness is a sad image of the breakdown of any control or law. The supremacy of the will, desired so by the nineteenth century, is not his. Deluded by false splendor, deceptive dreams, and his passion (which he mistakes for true love), and a slave to "the pleasure of the blood," Pelleas becomes a vassal to the proud, deceitful, and lustful Ettarre. Blindly he rejoices: "Behold me, Lady, / A prisoner, and the vassal of thy will" (ll. 232-33). He is now held by yet another demon of the woods, a woman who is more willing to dally with the sensuous Gawain than with Pelleas, a knight who aspires to be Arthur's true follower, and a demon whose excesses attack her until she loses herself in her "ever-veering fancy."

Because Pelleas's will is possessed by a demon, any self-control he might have easily evaporates. Such is the case when he discovers Gawain and Ettarre sleeping together. In a manner reminiscent of the maddening King Lear reviling his eldest daughter, Pelleas loses all control and screams maniacally at Ettarre:

> "O towers so strong,
> Huge, solid, would that even while I gaze
> The crack of earthquake shivering to your
> base
> Split you, and Hell burst your harlot roofs

Bellowing, and charred you through and
    through within,
Black as the harlot's heart—hollow as a skull!
Let the fierce east scream through your
    eyelet-holes,
And whirl the dust of harlots round and round
In dung and nettles! hiss, snake—I saw him
    there—
Let the fox bark, let the wolf yell. Who yells
Here in the still sweet summer night, but I—"

["Pelleas and Ettarre," ll. 454-64]

He continues his harangue by echoing the maddening
speaker of "Locksley Hall," who longs for a savage
nation where there is no insanity and lust: "O great
and sane and simple race of brutes / That own no lust
because they have no law!" (ll. 471-72). Pelleas's
breakdown is complete after he learns of Guinevere
and Lancelot's impurity. He falls into a deep depression and loses not only his faith in the order, but also
all sense of self—he has "no name." Now suicidal, he
asks Lancelot to slay him. His sword, which had been
for Pelleas an image of his belief in Arthur's vows
and a symbol of the king's order, is also no longer
with him. Those idealistic values and the sanity it
represents are gone. Like the sword Pelleas has left
lying on the sleeping bodies of Gawain and Ettarre,
those values and that harmony are now mingled with
and overwhelmed by the bestial passions. Leaving
the lawless realm, the broken knight returns to Camelot
with no will, no name, and no sword. He goes into
darkness.

    And he, hissing "I have no sword,"
Sprang from the door into the dark. The
    Queen
Looked hard upon her lover, he on her;
And each foresaw the dolorous day to be:
And all talk died, as in a grove all song
Beneath the shadow of some bird of prey;
Then a long silence came upon the hall.

[ll. 590-96]

This silence signals that Modred's time to upset the
order has come.

This idyll has reversed the action of the second idyll,
"Gareth and Lynette." In that earlier, healthier time,
Lynette's scorn of Gareth, the new knight, was not
destructive. When Arthur's order was more secure,
and Guinevere and Lancelot's sin had not upset its
balance, Gareth's power to counteract the evil forces
remained with him. He could conquer Lynette's taunt-
ing; he could master her pride, battle the four knights,
and travel through the mire. There Gareth can defeat
death and "a blooming boy / Fresh as a flower
new-born" can step out of darkness (ll. 1371-74).

In "The Last Tournament" any semblance of order has
disappeared. There are no knights who even hope to
follow Arthur's example. Passion, violence, and discord predominate. Red colors all. Freedom is lawlessness; fools are wise; the mad fight the mad; Lancelot,
the sinner, rules, and not the king; and the lustful
Tristram, not the pure knight, wins the tournament
(appropriately called "The Tournament of the Dead
Innocence"). Throughout this idyll Tennyson emphasizes Lancelot's madness to give a sense of this horrifying disorder now tyrannizing the center of Camelot.
Trapped and worn down by his lust, Lancelot is powerless to stop the lawless tournament. Paralleling those
idle and useless leaders who have watched their kingdoms fall apart, Lancelot listlessly officiates.

    But when the morning of a tournament,
    By these in earnest those in mockery called
    The Tournament of the Dead Innocence,
    Brake with a wet wind blowing, Lancelot,
    Round whose sick head all night, like birds of
        prey,
    The words of Arthur flying shrieked, arose,
    And down a streetway hung with folds of
        pure
    White samite, and by fountains running wine,
    Where children sat in white with cups of gold,
    Moved to the lists, and there, with slow sad
        steps
    Ascending, filled his double-dragoned chair.

["The Last Tournament," ll. 134-44]

Once more disorder and madness reign because Arthur
is not there to control them. As in "The Holy Grail,"
the king is outside his city attempting to block this
spreading evil. He is pursuing his former champion,
Pelleas, now named the red knight because Pelleas's
madness and rage so inflame him. In the ensuing
struggle Arthur, ever in control of himself, allows
Pelleas to defeat himself, as madness will. But, even
though Arthur remains unscathed, his company does
not. The discord is now as pervasive and as infectious as the religious hysteria. Arthur cannot restore
harmony. In a terrifying scene Arthur's knights, excited by Pelleas, turn manic and destroy Pelleas
and the village. Their conduct mirrors the horrible
disorder.

    Thus he [Pelleas] fell
    Head-heavy; then the knights, who watched
        him, roared
    And shouted and leapt down upon the fallen;
    There trampled out his face from being
        known,
    And sank his head in mire, and slimed
        themselves:
    Nor heard the King for their own cries, but
        sprang

Through open doors, and swording right and
  left
Men, women, on their sodden faces, hurled
The tables over and the wines, and slew
Till all the rafters rang with woman-yells,
And all the pavement streamed with massacre.

[ll. 466-76]

The anarchy is national and personal, for at the same time, Tristram is dallying with Queen Isolt—an adulterous relationship full of blatant disloyalties and excesses that magnify Guinevere and Lancelot's sin. Arthur sees the massacre and returns to see his "Queen's bower was dark." He knows the end has come.

The end comes rapidly in two short idylls: "Guinevere" and "The Passing of Arthur." From this moment on, Vivien and Modred are more powerful than ever before, for the evil that was lurking in the background has come to the front. There is no longer enough will to battle Vivien's wiles and Modred's sins. The madness has spread too far. Weakened by his bestial passion, Lancelot can now do little more than "pluck" the scheming Modred by the heels and throw him into the dust. Weakened by his knights who have either defected or lost themselves, King Arthur cannot survive. In "The Passing of Arthur" the king has enough strength left to kill Modred but not enough to withstand Modred's final blow to his head. Arthur's life begins to slip away. Camelot is no more. Before the king dies, however, he asks Sir Bedivere to return Excalibur to the lake, and he pleads with Sir Bedivere to take him to "the level lake"; to take him beyond the chaotic landscape that surrounds him.

"My end draws nigh; 'tis time that I were
  gone.
Make broad thy shoulders to receive my
  weight,
And bear me to the margin; yet I fear
My wound hath taken cold, and I shall die."

    . . . . .

But, as he [Sir Bedivere] walked, King
  Arthur panted hard,
Like one that feels a nightmare on his bed
When all the house is mute. So sighed the
  King,
Muttering and murmuring at his ear, "Quick,
  quick!
I fear it is too late, and I shall die."

[ll. 331-34, 344-48]

The urgency of the second request is significant, for it shows how fearful Arthur is of dying among the "barren chasms" and "bare black cliffs" that "clung" around him. His urgency suggests how closely the ideal soul comes to losing itself, as the king's knights have done, in that chaotic landscape. In fact, so powerful is the chaos at the end that the king barely escapes it. Eventually, though, with Sir Bedivere's help, the king does reach the smooth way and dies on the barge as it travels down the peaceful waters.

And the barge with oar and sail
Moved from the brink, like some full-breasted
  swan
That, fluting a wild carol ere her death,
Ruffles her pure cold plume, and takes the
  flood
With swarthy webs. Long stood Sir Bedivere
Revolving many memories, till the hull
Looked one black dot against the verge of
  dawn,
And on the mere the wailing died away.

[ll. 433-40]

Throughout the *Idylls* King Arthur has seldom spoken—even though his presence has always been felt. In "Guinevere," however, Tennyson does give Arthur his chance. For 165 lines the king lectures the queen, reminding her of his humanity, his love for her, the need for moderation, and, of course, her sins. The lecture is a curious mixture of compassion and severity, and a powerful one. Many readers, especially twentieth-century readers, have experienced difficulties with the king's speech. Many have been annoyed by its self-righteous tone.[25] They find his words too high-minded. They are annoyed with his moralistic posture because they claim that he has no right to be so critical. They claim that he is not "blameless." These readers want to blame "the blameless King" for Camelot's fall. Certainly the many references scattered throughout the *Idylls* to the impossibility of the king's vows encourage such thoughts. However, the blame does not lie with him or with his naïveté. It rests with the individuals, the citizens of Camelot, and not with the king. As Tennyson once said, "Take away the sense of individual responsibility and men sink into pessimism and madness."[26] Such is the problem in the *Idylls*. The fall belongs to those individuals who are unwilling to believe in or to follow the king's vows. Camelot would have survived had people not only continued to believe in the ideal, but had they also, through moderation, maintained a harmonious balance.

Tennyson's contemporaries would have had little difficulty with the king's lecture. They would have found him "blameless," for they too believed in moderation, and they too were involved in the battles of the *Idylls*. They knew that to keep order they must fight their bestial forces; that they must not lose sight of order and must exercise their wills. For a public that felt threatened by the passions and constantly searched for new ways in which to govern themselves and their nation, the effects of madness in Tennyson's *Idylls* were all too familiar. For these reasons the public would have also been most sensitive to Tennyson's praise of Prince Albert in the dedication preceding the *Idylls.* Tennyson lauds the prince for many qualities:

> And indeed He seems to me
> Scarce other than my king's ideal knight,
> "Who reverenced his conscience as his king;
> Whose glory was, redressing human wrong;
> Who spake no slander, no, nor listened to it;
> Who loved one only and who clave to her—"
> Her—over all whose realms to their last isle,
> Commingled with the gloom of imminent war,
> The shadow of His loss drew like eclipse,
> Darkening the world. We have lost him: he is
>   gone:
> We know him now: all narrow jealousies
> Are silent; and we see him as he moved,
> How modest, kindly, all-accomplished, wise,
> With what sublime repression of himself,
> And in what limits, and how tenderly;
> Not swaying to this faction or to that;
> Not making his high place the lawless perch
> Of winged ambitions, nor a vantage-ground
> For pleasure; but through all this tract of
>   years
> Wearing the white flower of a blameless life,
> Before a thousand peering littlenesses,
> In that fierce light which beats upon a throne,
> And blackens every blot.

> [ll. 5-27]

The praise mirrors Arthur's speech to Guinevere and suggests an equation between Arthur and Prince Albert. Both "loved one only" and more important, both exercised moderation—both were "blameless."

Buried among the praise is the curious phrase "sublime repression"—a phrase that has puzzled many.[27] However, in the light of the public's fears and the *Idylls*'s concerns, the phrase is not so puzzling, but is clearly appropriate. To survive personally and to survive as a healthy nation, people must repress their doubts and their excesses. And in Tennyson's mind, given the necessity and the difficulty of this task, this repression is indeed "sublime." Tennyson suggests that his audience follow Albert's and Arthur's example: the audience must themselves exercise "sublime repression." They must be more aware of how the bestial forces constantly bombard and erode the will, upsetting the delicate balance, sending them and their nation headlong into madness. The *Idylls* is indeed an example not only of the sublime nature of repression, but of its necessity. The fall of Camelot is the fall of "sublime repression."

Notes

[1] Alfred Beaumont Maddock, *Practical Observations on Mental and Nervous Disorders* (London: Simpkin, Marshall, 1854), p. 13.

[2] Matthew Allen, *Essay on the Classification of the Insane* (London: John Taylor, [1837]), p. 18.

[3] John D. Rosenberg, *The Fall of Camelot: A Study of Tennyson's "Idylls of the King"* (Cambridge: Harvard University Press, 1973), p. 24. See also Rosenberg, "Tennyson and the Landscape of Consciousness," *Victorian Poetry* 12 (1974): 303-10. Other critics following Rosenberg's lead speak of the *Idylls'* emphasis on psychological experience. Donald S. Hair in *Domestic and Heroic in Tennyson's Poetry* (Toronto: University of Toronto Press, 1981) writes, for example, of the "emphasis on inner psychological experience in the second idyll" (p. 166), and Robert Pattison in *Tennyson and Tradition* (Cambridge: Harvard University Press, 1979) thinks of the *Idylls* as "a series of portraits of the Arthurian characters, not in the process of action, but in the throes of internal debate" (p. 137).

[4] See for example Penelope B. R. Doob, *Nebuchadnezzar's Children: Conventions of Madness in Middle English Literature* (New Haven: Yale University Press, 1974), p. 154. Doob argues that Merlin's madness is not merely the result of "excessive grief and melancholia," but it is also a consequence of his "disgust at human sinfulness masquerading as virtue." She points out that this larger concern for human sinfulness also influences Lancelot's and Tristram's madness, a concern that not only colors the Arthurian legends, but also other medieval pieces. Doob concludes that in medieval literature madness is a symbol of the deformity of the soul and tangible proof of sin. This understanding of madness had its equivalent in Tennyson's *Idylls.* Here too madness becomes an emblem of the continuing assault of the passions on Arthur and his kingdom, the "Ideal Soul." Furthermore, madness erupts from those like Guinevere and Lancelot who are caught in a "masquerade." They appear to be virtuous, but in reality they are symbols of "human sinfulness."

[5] Robert Martin, *Tennyson: The Unquiet Heart* (Oxford: Clarendon Press, 1980), pp. 215-21.

[6] For discussions of literary madness in the nineteenth century see, for example, Sandra M. Gilbert and Susan

Gubar, *The Madwoman in the Attic: The Woman Writer and the Nineteenth-Century Literary Imagination* (New Haven: Yale University Press, 1979).

[7] Walter E. Houghton, *The Victorian Frame of Mind, 1830-1870* (New Haven: Yale University Press, 1975), p. 368. In *Alfred Tennyson* (New York: Macmillan, 1949) Charles Tennyson writes that Tennyson "had a deep-seated loathing for recent tendencies in French politics and art. 'The frightful corruption of their literature makes me fear that they are going straight to Hell,' he said" (p. 390). Tennyson also thought it upsetting that Swinburne wrote a sonnet in praise of Mademoiselle de Maupin.

[8] Paul Turner, *Tennyson,* Routledge Author Guides, ed. B. C. Southam (London: Routledge and Kegan Paul, 1976), p. 176. In discussing Tennyson's political poems of the early fifties, Henry Kozicki states that they "were occasioned by his concern that the nation was falling into anarchy on the plane of ordinary providence as a result of its failure to engage the historically formative power of active providence. More specifically, man microcosmically . . . was failing to make base passions (selfishness, sensuality, covetousness) subservient to the nobler conditions of selfishness, struggle, and sacrifice" (*Tennyson and Clio: History in the Major Poems* [Baltimore: Johns Hopkins University Press, 1979], pp. 98-99).

[9] One example of the popular interest in epidemics of madness is the publication of Charles Mackay's *Memoirs of Extraordinary Popular Delusions,* 3 vols. (London: R. Bentley, 1841). Another example is B. G. Babington's translation of J. F. C. Hecker's *The Epidemics of the Middle Ages* (London: Sydenham Society, 1846). For a lengthier treatment of the interest in political or social revolution as a cause of insanity see Richard Hunter and Ida Macalpine, *Three Hundred Years of Psychiatry, 1535-1860* (London: Oxford University Press, 1963), pp. 821-22. See also Richard Robert Madden, "Epidemic Insanity," ibid., pp. 1040-42.

[10] As quoted in introduction to "Amariah Brigham," in *Three Hundred Years of Psychiatry,* p. 821.

[11] George Man Burrows, *Commentaries on Insanity* (London: Underwood, 1828), p. 20.

[12] E. D. H. Johnson recognizes the fact that madness is an important motif in the *Idylls of the King.* See *The Alien Vision of Victorian Poetry,* Princeton Studies in English, no. 34 (Princeton: Princeton University Press, 1952), p. 42.

[13] For a discussion of the *Idylls of the King* and its serial evolution see J. M. Gray, *Thro' the Vision of the Night* (Edinburgh: Edinburgh University Press, 1980),

pp. 3-9, and for a discussion of the *Idylls* in chronological sequence see J. Philip Eggers, *King Arthur's Laureate: A Study of Tennyson's "Idylls of the King"* (New York: New York University Press, 1971), pp. 139-84.

[14] There are numerous explanations of Arthur's multiple birth. Paul Turner, for example, links the multiple birth to the theme of "truth" and "falsehood" which runs throughout the *Idylls of the King* (*Tennyson,* p. 167). A. Dwight Culler sees the multiple birth as a means of questioning and establishing Arthur as a "spiritual absolute" (*The Poetry of Tennyson* [New Haven: Yale University Press, 1977], pp. 214-15). James R. Kincaid relates the multiple birth to the question, "how do we know, what is the nature of knowledge, what sort of knowledge is authentic? The question is Arthur himself: who is he, where does he come from, how does he operate?" See *Tennyson's Major Poems: The Comic and Ironic Patterns* (New Haven: Yale University Press, 1975), p. 158.

[15] In *Domestic and Heroic in Tennyson's Poetry,* Donald S. Hair emphasizes the importance of marriage in the *Idylls.* He writes "the central action is his [Arthur's] marriage, and on that marriage the fate of civilization depends. The link between an individual and the state is thus much more than just an analogy" (p. 217).

[16] Hallam Tennyson, 2 vols. *Alfred, Lord Tennyson: A Memoir* (London: Macmillan, 1897), 2: 131.

[17] Ibid.

[18] Alexander Morison, *Outlines of Moral Diseases* (Edinburgh: MacLachlan and Stewart, 1824), pp. 70-71.

[19] George Man Burrows, *Commentaries on Insanity,* p. 33.

[20] The number of articles on mesmerism seems endless and indicates just how mesmerized the nineteenth-century public was. For a good account of the popular interest in mesmerism see Fred Kaplan, "The Mesmeric Mania," in *Dickens and Mesmerism: The Hidden Springs of Fiction* (Princeton: Princeton University Press, 1975), pp. 3-33.

[21] Tennyson's sensitivity to those whose expectations deceive them and lead them into false beliefs must have been encouraged not only by those who were doing studies in popular delusions, but also by those like Samuel Hibbert (1824) who "concluded that whatever their exciting cause apparitions, that is illusions and hallucinations, resulted from the recall of forgotten memories which being emotionally charged attained a vividness exceeding that of external sensory impressions." As quoted in "Samuel Hibbert," in *Three Hun-*

dred Years of Psychiatry, pp. 760-63. Tennyson must also have been influenced by W. B. Carpenter's doctrine of unconscious cerebration or muscular action— a doctrine receiving much attention while Tennyson was at work on "The Holy Grail." It is helpful to recall what Tennyson said about the visions of the Holy Grail—that "the differences between the five visions of the Grail" are dependent on the nun's and the knights' "peculiar natures and circumstances, their selflessness, and the perfection or imperfection of their Christianity" (Hallam Tennyson, *Memoir,* 2: 63 [originally an 1869 entry in Emily Tennyson's journal]).

[22] A. Dwight Culler has stated, "Tennyson treats the quest for the Holy Grail as an example of mass hysteria. The whole thing originated, he makes perfectly clear, in the frustrated sexual desires of a young woman who had been disappointed in love and gone into a nunnery" (*The Poetry of Tennyson,* p. 228). Donald S. Hair writes that when the nun "does have a vision of the Grail, it is hard to distinguish the Grail from the phallus and her ecstasy from sexual orgasm" (*Domestic and Heroic in Tennyson's Poetry,* pp. 191-92).

[23] Critics tend to think that Galahad's vision is the exception to that of the others. For instance Donald S. Hair in his discussion of the *Idylls* writes that "Nonetheless, Galahad is genuine. He alone of all the knights is suited for the Grail quest, and he alone is successful" (*Domestic and Heroic in Tennyson's Poetry,* p. 192).

[24] The idea of the last idyll being a reversal of Arthur's order can be found in Donald S. Hair's study. He writes, "When we look back over these four idylls [the last four], we can see that parody is one of Tennyson's main techniques. Men and women are still attracted to each other; the Order of the Round Table still exists; and quests are undertaken. But the character of all these has dwindled from the original, or become uneven. If James R. Kincaid is right in arguing that *Gareth and Lynette* provides 'the standard against which all else is measured' . . . then we can say these four idylls are parodies of this one" (*Domestic and Heroic in Tennyson's Poetry,* p. 210).

[25] A typical response to Arthur's lecture to Guinevere is in Ward Hellstrom, *On the Poems of Tennyson* (Gainesville: University of Florida Press, 1972): "Arthur, in a rather self-righteous tone of moral superiority which is at once priggish and quite human, makes Guinevere's culpability paramount" (p. 132). Another version of that response can be seen in James R. Kincaid's *Tennyson's Major Poems:* "'Guinevere' apparently had quite a spectacular effect on many Victorians. It seems astonishing, for instance, that the idyll 'made George Eliot weep when Tennyson read it.' These days the idyll is more likely to seem an unaccountable lapse on Tennyson's part. Less

open about our emotions and also less struck by the novelty of domestic realism, we are prone to blame the whole episode on sexual prudery. In any case, it seems thematically narrow, generically and tonally inappropriate" (pp. 206-7). I agree with J. M. Gray, who in *Thro' the Vision of the Night* writes, "One class of criticism condemns the cold, passionless Arthur. . . . The proper critical question to ask is whether Arthur's conduct at this point is consistent with his character and with the spirit of Tennyson's Arthurian world. There is not a single passage to suggest that Arthur's condemnation of Guinevere is out of character" (pp. 133-34).

[26] Hallam Tennyson, *Memoir,* I: 317.

[27] Most readers have trouble with the phrase because they feel separated from Victorian values. I agree with Ward Hellstrom when he writes, "The tendency of modern audiences is, I think, to concur with [John] Sterling's criticism of the *Idylls,* that 'the miraculous legend of "Excalibur" does not come very near to us'" (*On the Poems of Tennyson,* p. 133).

Ekbert Faas (essay date 1988)

SOURCE: "Swinburne, or the Psychopathology of Poetic Creation," in *Retreat into the Mind: Victorian Poetry and the Rise of Psychiatry,* Princeton University Press, 1988, pp. 184-98.

[*In the following essay, Faas investigates the negative reaction of Victorian critics to Algernon Charles Swinburne's poetry, which often focused on sadomasochistic, anti-Christian, or other "morbid" themes. Faas notes that Swinburne, like other poets of his time, was criticized as being "morally insane."*]

In one sense, the Victorian reading public was surprisingly open-minded. While balking at Browning's obscurity, it hardly objected when the poet spoke through the mouth of, say, Johannes Agricola as he gloats over those who, despite their good will or innocence, are predestined to eternal damnation—"the broken-hearted nun, / The martyr, the wan acolyte, / The incense-swinging child" (54-56). Nor did it take offense at Porphyria's lover who strangles his mistress with her own hair in order to preserve pure the moment of her abandon to him and then proceeds to lavish upon the corpse the affectionate attention he could not muster for the live woman.

> As a shut bud that holds a bee,
> I warily oped her lids: again
> Laughed the blue eyes without a stain.
> And I untightened next the tress
> About her neck; her cheek once more
> Blushed bright beneath my burning kiss:

I propped her head up as before,
Only, this time my shoulder bore
  Her head, which droops upon it still

                                    (43-51)

Rather than criticize the poet for his morbid interests, readers clamored for more of the same, praising him for analyzing "the minds of men as deftly as a surgeon can dissect their bodies."[1]

But there were definite limits to this open-mindedness. By and large, reviewers tolerated the portrayal of mental perversion only as long as it was done the way in which an alienist would diagnose a morally insane delinquent so as to have him hospitalized for further observation and treatment. Whether insane morally or otherwise, a madman, after all, was a madman, to be pitied, analyzed, and, if possible, cured, but hardly to be let loose upon "normal" society. Like Victorian asylums, dramatic monologues in this sense are a means of sequestration, particularly of their authors' own morbidities. Wherever they deal with mental aberrations, they are "madhouse cells" like "Porphyria's Lover" and "Johannes Agricola in Meditation."

Tennyson and Browning, in their early years, had come up against these limits, and both made the concessions requested by society. Browning, who in *Pauline* has the speaker wonder how he "might kill" his mistress "and be loved for it" (902), received J. S. Mill's rebuke for dealing with "this morbid state" without suggesting a convincing mode of recovery—"for *he* is hardly convalescent, and 'what should we speak of but that which we know?'"[2] We know how the poet reacted by declaring *Pauline* to be his first dramatic monologue. The young Tennyson, when suspected of indulging in "sick writing," responded in similar fashion.[3] This is most obvious from *The Lover's Tale*, whose protagonist fantasizes about forcing the woman he loves, but who loves another, to drown with him:

  Aloud she shrieked;
  My heart was cloven with pain; I wound my
      arms
  About her: we whirled giddily; the wind
  Sung; but I clasped her without fear: her
      weight
  Shrank in my grasp, and over my dim eyes,
  And parted lips which drank her breath,
      down-hung
  The jaws of Death.

                                    (II, 196-202)

As we know, Tennyson withdrew the already typeset poem from inclusion in his 1832 *Poems,* and, when he finally published it in 1869, provided the autobiographical ramblings of the poet narrator Julian with a case-history-type framework. A friend of Julian's continues the story by describing the protagonist as simply "crazed, / Though not with such a craziness as needs / A cell and keeper" (IV, 162-164). Within these new safeguards Tennyson even ventured to explore the hero's necrophiliac tendencies. His beloved is thought to be dead and Julian, stirred by his fancy to "kiss her on the lips," "To kiss the dead," duly proceeds to the vault where he finds "His lady with the moonlight on her face; / Her breast as in a shadow-prison":

  He softly put his arm about her neck
  And kissed her more than once, till helpless
      death
  And silence made him bold—

                            (IV, 48, 50, 56-57, 70-73)

Julian, after all, is a declared maniac. Victorians therefore found no reason to reprove the poet for poetically analyzing his aberration the way alienists scrutinized comparable cases in asylums all across the country.

Dramatizations of the Perverse

From this perspective, one has difficulty understanding the uproar over Swinburne's *Poems and Ballads,* or why Victorians should tolerate, for instance, "Porphyria's Lover" while denouncing "The Leper." Was not Swinburne's poem, just like Browning's, simply another case study in necrophilic erotomania? In one sense "Porphyria's Lover" strikes one as even more horrible than "The Leper" for combining necrophilia with homicide, a tendency the younger poet has his speaker fantasize about but not perpetrate. To take another instance, there is Swinburne's "Les Noyades" whose protagonist rejoices at the prospect of being drowned tied breast to breast to the lady he loves but who despises him: "I shall drown with her, laughing for love; and she / Mix with me, touching me, lips and eyes" (55-56). Long before Swinburne, Tennyson made Julian indulge in similar, or worse, fantasies in *The Lover's Tale.*

But where post-Freudian critics notice parallels, contemporary reviewers only saw contrasts. With the same extravagance with which they had praised Browning and Tennyson for exploring the most aberrant manifestations of the human mind, they denounced Swinburne for being "publicly obscene," "unclean for the sake of uncleanness" and for writing poems that were "utterly revolting," "depressing and misbegotten," ravingly blasphemous, or mere deifications of incontinence.[4] Where most critics had learned to distinguish between, say, Browning and his personae, they quickly shed such practices with Swinburne. Along with his speakers, the author was counted among the "lecherous priests of Venus"; he was called the "libidinous laureate of a pack of satyrs,"[5] or simply a "Swine-born."[6] Where Tennyson had been praised for giving readers a "remarkable sketch of poetic mental pathology" in *Maud,*[7] the author of "Anactoria" or "Dolores" was declared insane himself. "There are many passages," commented the *Pall Mall Gazette,* "which bring before the mind the image of a mere madman, one who has got maudlin drunk on lewd ideas and lascivious thoughts."[8] The worst of it perhaps was that Swinburne might drive his readers insane as well. To read him long, wrote Henry Morley, would either "make you mad" or moral.[9]

It was to little avail that Swinburne, in response, tried to defend his poems the way Browning had defended *Pauline. Poems and Ballads,* he protested in *Notes on Poems and Reviews,* is "dramatic, many-faced, multifarious; and no utterance of enjoyment or despair, belief or unbelief, can properly be assumed as the assertion of [the author's] personal feeling or faith."[10] Reviewers then and now remained unconvinced. According to *Punch,* Swinburne's *Notes* simply added a "prurient poetics" to filthy poetry.[11] If the poems were indeed dramatic, what was the justification for dramatizing such subject matter, wondered the *London Review.*[12] But *were* the poems really dramatic? Even where Swinburne in "Hymn to Proserpine," for instance, adopts the masque of a Roman devotee of the ancient divinity, he hardly makes us assume the critical distance that, in most dramatic monologues, tempers our sympathy for the speaker. For one, the ideas put into the mouth of the Roman, as Robert Buchanan pointed out rightly, imply "precisely the same conditions of thought as we find expressed in the lyrical poems elsewhere."[13] Futhermore, Swinburne's mesmerizing prosody and rhetoric, here and elsewhere, constantly lure the reader into identifying with the persona. It is not surprising to learn that young men at Cambridge, as Edmund Gosse reports, joined hands and marched along chanting "Dolores."

Private comments by Swinburne reinforce the impression that there was, as Clyde K. Hyder puts it, "more logic than candour" in his protests that his poems were essentially dramatic.[14] According to Swinburne's *Notes,* "Dolores," for instance, was meant to express "that transient state of spirit through which a man may be supposed to pass, foiled in love and weary of loving, but not yet in sight of rest; seeking refuge in those 'violent delights' which 'have violent ends.'"[15] But, as far as we know, the genesis of neither the poem nor of *Notes* bears out these pious sentiments. Swinburne clearly had as much fun in writing "Dolores" as his student proselytes at Cambridge had in chanting it. Eight recently added lines (173-80), as he bragged to Charles Augustus Howell, contained "une vérité que ne comprendront jamais les sots idolateurs de la vertu." Another ten lines, which came to him while writing the same letter, struck their author as equally successful—"très infâmes et très bien tournés. 'Oh! monsieur—

peut-on prendre du plaisir à telles horreurs?' Tu le vois, Justine, je bande—oh! putain, que tu vas souffrir'—."[16] The defense of this (to quote the *London Review*) "especially horrible"[17] poem was conducted in similar tongue-in-cheek high-handedness. "I have proved Dolores to be little less than a second Sermon on the Mount, and Anactoria than an archdeacon's charge," Swinburne wrote to W. M. Rossetti.[18]

Of course, some poems were more fictitious than others, but the critics, as Swinburne recalled gleefully over three decades later, had failed to identify them. "There are photographs from life in the book," he wrote, "and there are sketches from imagination. Some which keen-sighted criticism has dismissed with a smile as ideal or imaginary were as real and actual as they well could be: others which have been taken for obvious transcripts from memory were utterly fantastic or dramatic."[19] Swinburne identified at least one of his more autobiographical poems. "Félise," particularly on account of the speaker's "antitheism," he confessed to W. M. Rossetti, represents "a mood of mind and phase of though not unfamiliar to me."[20]

Somewhat confusingly, Swinburne nonetheless insists on the poem's "dramatic" character. "No reader (*as a reader*)," he argued, "has a right (whatever he may conjecture) to assert that this is *my* faith and that the faith expressed in such things as the 'Litany' or 'Carol' or 'Dorothy' is not. Of course it is a more serious expression of feeling; and of course this is evident; but it is not less formally dramatic than the others."[21] "Félise" suggests the peculiar nature of such formal dramatization, which, though imaginary in terms of concrete detail, simply embodies the poet's own yearnings and beliefs. Félise, who attracted the speaker for being "subtly warm, and half perverse" (102), is given a lecture evincing the speaker's predilection for polymorphous perversity, which, if unsatisfied by reality, can always be supplemented by the poetic imagination:

> For many loves are good to see;
>   Mutable loves, and loves perverse;
> But there is nothing, nor shall be,
>   So sweet, so wicked, but my verse
> Can dream of worse.

(161-65)

Readers, then, had good reason for identifying Swinburne with his personae. For with a few exceptions like "The Leper," his speakers are dramatic merely in the way in which even deliberately confessional poets cannot fully reveal themselves (to quote E. Johnson) "without resorting to some oblique, objective, or dramatic mode of expression."[22] It is true that Swinburne is not confessional in the sense that Wordsworth is in the

Prelude. In other words, he does not communicate, but rather withholds, facts from his personal life. But he is confessional in expressing, even dramatizing, his opinions, emotional idiosyncracies, and favorite fantasies. The speaker in "Hymn to Proserpine" may be a Roman, but the anti-Christian sentiments he expresses are the author's.

Swinburne's relation to this and other of his personae is neither critical nor empathic. Or where it is, such distance or closeness is circumscribed by the ways with which one views one's own emotional penchants and convictions. Swinburne wanted to shock and he did. Blasphemy and sensuality had been his aims at least since 1858 when he meant to say so publicly, by reviewing himself.[23] Even his closest friends and admirers like the Rossettis, Meredith, and Ruskin had advised him not to publish or at least to "play savagely with a knife among the proofs for the sake of" his fame.[24] But Swinburne defied both enemies and friends and paid the expected price.

In short, where Browning and Tennyson had opted for the disguise, Swinburne spoke out more directly. This is not to say that what the older poets chose to hide was of the same kind as what their younger successor preferred to reveal. But one wonders what might have happened to literary history if Tennyson, for one, had decided to openly draw upon his trances and hallucinations for poetic inspiration instead of suppressing poems like "Hark! the dogs howl!" and passing off others like "See what a lovely shell" as the musings of a madman in embryo. A poet of his stature, undisguisedly writing about his spectral visions, would no doubt have stirred up an uproar similar to that which Swinburne caused with his sadomasochistic and anti-Christian fantasies.

The different between them, in other words, was not so much one of the respective poet's greater or lesser "morbidity," but of his attitude toward it in relation to the public. Browning and Tennyson had turned against themselves in making their pact with Victorian propriety. Hence, both were predictably aghast at discovering this younger poet of unquestionable genius who refused to make the same concessions. To Browning, Swinburne's poems were "moral mistakes, redeemed by much intellectual ability." Swinburne undoubtedly "had genius," but he "wrote verses in which to [Browning's] mind there was no good at all."[25] Even more negative was Tennyson's attitude, partly no doubt because in "condemning some of Swinburne's proclivities," as Leonard M. Findlay puts it, "he would be reminded of the unflattering circumstances behind his abandoning similar themes."[26] The Laureate hardly had to await the publication of *Poems and Ballads* to make up his mind about this poet. When some of the critics fell foul of the "sensuality and materialism" of *Chastelard*, Tennyson "emphati-

cally shared their views, saying that although he thought the poem very fine, his objections to it were as deep as Heaven and Hell."[27]

Whatever poets and critics read of the writings by psychologists about art and artists must have reinforced them in this damnatory attitude. In fact, the diagnostic eagerness of Victorian alienists increasingly encroached upon the reviewers' task. We have already seen how the early psychiatrists mapped out their proper domain of critical analysis in showing how Shakespeare's, Tennyson's, and other poets' works revealed an understanding of the human mind ignored by the literati but paralleling their recent discoveries. A second new critical genre developed by Victorian alienists was that of short psychoanalytic biographies usually based upon larger works written by the standard biographers. Its typical method of applying the "modern insights" of mental science in this area was, as J. F. Nisbet points out in *The Insanity of Genius,* "not unlike that of the family doctor who is called in to examine a patient": "With the help of the biographer I ask the great man, figuratively speaking, to stand up; I look at his tongue, feel his pulse, and inquire into his family history. By this means a wholly different view of genius is obtained from that generally current. The biographer, unfortunately, is too often as troublesome a person to deal with as the family nurse."[28]

Insane Artists and Alienist Biographers

One of the first to write this "sort of microscopic biography" was R. R. Madden whose *Infirmities of Genius* of 1833 purports to solve the psychological mysteries surrounding Burns, Byron, Cowper, Dr. Johnson, Pope, and Scott.[29] As Madden keeps reminding us, previous biographers, with the possible exception of Robert Burns's J. Currie, simply could not account for what really motivated these men.[30] Thus T. Moore, for instance, fails to trace the origin of Byron's "morbid sensibility" to its "true cause; we are simply told that his temperament was a poetic one, and that it was unfavorable to the due performance of his social and domestic duties."[31] By contrast, Madden himself, rather than detailing the poet's eccentricities, peccadilloes, or hysterical affections in the gossipy manner of this biographer, simply traces them to their allegedly common root. To him, the "simple fact is" that Byron "laboured under an epileptic diathesis": "If feelings of delicacy induced his biographers to conceal a truth they were aware of, or deemed it better to withold their motive was unquestionably a good one; but it was nevertheless a mistaken delicacy; for there are no infirmities so humiliating to humanity as those irregularities of conduct in eminent individuals; and the only palliation they admit of is often precluded by our ignorance of the bodily disorders under which they may have laboured."[32]

Madden, then, largely tries to find extenuating psychiatric circumstances for what might otherwise shock the public's sense of normalcy and moral propriety. But such liberal-mindedness often changed into a more judgmental attitude as the notion of moral insanity—according to J. C. Prichard a "morbid perversion of the feelings, affections, habits, without any hallucination or erroneous conviction impressed upon the understanding"—gained widespread currency.[33] Poets and artists who previously might have escaped the charge of insanity altogether, came in for the severest censure. The *Autobiography of Benjamin Robert Haydon,* for instance, gave the anonymous reviewer of the *Journal of Psychological Medicine and Mental Pathology* "ample materials for a psychological study of genius" in terms of the new category.[34] Essentially, this study, like many similar ones, is an indictment of the artist for his moral turpitude and hence self-inflicted psychopathological dilemmas. Haydon is charged with "wondrous folly" and "inextinguishable vanity and self-will"; he is found to be dishonest, unjust, "thoroughly obstinate," "morbidly proud," and "irremediably egotistical." Worst of all, his autobiography revealed, even bragged about, his lack of self-control. Haydon's "undisciplined will" was at the core of most of his problems, and, most notably, vitiated his art.

> He "dashes at his canvas like an inspired devil," he "drives" at it, he "flies" at it. This constantly. He continually "races" into the city for money; and if his earliest, his kindest, his very judicious friend hesitates a moment to minister to his wildly incurred necessities, he "pours forth a dreadful torrent of sarcasm" and shakes the unfortunate man "to death." This activity he called "virtuous industry;" it was more nearly allied to the delirious activity of insanity; it had its source in self-gratification—not self-denial.[35]

What post-Freudian psychiatrists tend to trace to repression, their Victorian predecessors largely attributed to the lack of it, and artists were allowed no exception. The verdict passed on Haydon is only typical of what alienist biographers had to say about many of the painter's peers and superiors. Rousseau, for instance, was found "destitute of the power to repress . . . his carnal nature"[36] and "deplorably subject to the hallucinations of erotic insanity."[37] Another alienist speaks of his "erotomania" as one of several symptoms of this "morally mad" genius.[38] Rousseau, in this view, lacked all notion "of truth, rectitude, honesty, in short, of the sense of right and wrong." Who else would have preferred "the foul, brutal, sanguinary wild man of the woods to the finest examples of virtue?"[39] Another favorite target of such diagnostic zeal was Edgar Allen Poe whose moral insanity resulted in a "profligacy in intemperance" as well as in bouts of "distempered fancy and unhealthy poetry."[40] Many others, like George Morland, James Gates Percival, and Richard Savage,[41] were found subject to similar "morbidity of the moral

sense." Torquato Tasso was said to suffer from "erotic mania,"[42] Swift from "morbid acrimony of temper" and "evil genius,"[43] Friedrich Schiller from dipsomania, not to mention dozens of other artists who were diagnosed for religious melancholia, mania errabunda, "folie circulaire," paraxysmal and suicidal melancholia, delusions and hallucinations.[44]

Even artists who traditionally had been held in high esteem for their respectability or idealism were retroactively diagnosed as victims of moral insanity. A reviewer of the *Journal of Mental Science,* after reading Dowden's biography of Shelley,[45] found "evidence of an insane temperament" in the poet's "altogether disproportionate regard for the questions arising out of the relations of the sexes." Although not actually insane, Shelley had "an insane diathesis, a strong disposition to mental aberration."[46] Another alienist writing for the *Journal of Psychological Medicine* claimed to have found the key to an understanding of Turner's bizarre existence, a mystery that he claimed eluded the authors of all six of the then existing memoirs of the famous artist. Friends and foes alike, he writes, "failed to discover the key to the mystery, to apply the true solvent to that compound of crudities and jewels which constituted the nature of the man with whom they were dealing. That key and solvent are to be found in unhealth and unsoundness of mind pervading his whole career, but becoming more prominent and palpable at certain periods and under certain influences."[47] Even Carlyle, the wise man of Chelsea, was subjected to a post-mortem analysis of his "lifelong mental condition."[48] In sum, reviewers denouncing Swinburne as an infectious madman drunk with "lewd ideas and lascivious thoughts,"[49] were in basic agreement with Victorian alienists pronouncing similar judgment on a large number of poets and artists.

A Poetics of Madness and Revolt

One of the few to actively try to stem the tide of such denunciatory tirades was Swinburne himself. In this he began by defending others and, in doing so, hammered out his cause several years before making his debut with *Atlanta in Calydon.* The first occasion arose when R. H. Hutton attacked Meredith's *Modern Love* in the *Spectator.* There "is a deep vein of muddy sentiment in most men," Hutton argued, accusing Meredith of not letting "the mud settle," and for boasting of it to the world instead.[50] *Modern Love,* in Hutton's view, should be renamed *Modern Lust.* While dealing with "a deep and painful subject," Meredith had "no convictions to express" regarding it.[51] Ignoring Hutton's abusive tirades, Swinburne, in a letter to the editor, simply takes issue with the reviewer's didactic understanding of poetry: "There are pulpits enough for all preachers in prose; the business of verse-writing is hardly to express convictions. . . . As to subject, it is too much to expect that all schools of poetry are to be for ever subordinate to the one just now so much in request with us, whose scope of sight is bounded by the nursery walls."[52]

Even more prophetic of his own future was Swinburne's pioneering review of Baudelaire's *Les fleurs du mal* whose first edition had been subjected to the prosecution that *Poems and Ballads* was to be threatened with later. Here the English poet found a subject matter that, while akin to his own poetic interests, was strenuously repressed by the censors of his age—"the weariness of pain and the bitterness of pleasure—the perverse happiness and wayward sorrows of exceptional people."[53] Baudelaire's response to the review must have further strengthened Swinburne's evolving "l'art pour l'art" aesthetic. The English poet had tried to prove that "this poetry of strange disease and sin" and of "hideous violence wrought by a shameless and senseless love" has an implicit "background of morality to it."[54] "Je ne suis pas si *moraliste* que vous feignez obligeamment de le croire," Baudelaire wrote Swinburne in a letter: "Je crois simplement 'comme vous sans doute' que tout poème, tout objet d'art *bien fait* suggère naturellement et forcément une *morale.* C'est l'affaire du lecteur. J'ai même une haine très décidée contre toute *intention* morale exclusive dans un poème."[55]

Swinburne took Baudelaire's advice in his influential *William Blake,* most of which was written during 1863 and 1864, again before he began publishing his major poetry.[56] The book, as finally printed in 1867, opens with a motto from Baudelaire's essay on Richard Wagner. It draws on the French poet once again when Swinburne, in Part Two, presses Blake into the service of his by now more radical "l'art pour l'art" doctrine. Those who would like to appreciate Blake, he argues, have to abandon "the heresy of instruction," so denounced by Baudelaire, this "living critic of incomparably delicate insights."[57] However, if Swinburne (to quote Cecil Y. Lang) "rescued Blake"[58] from previous critical contempt or neglect, it was merely by substituting one "heresy of instruction" with another. Swinburne is deeply concerned with Blake's own kind of didacticism or "philosophy" as suppressed by "the abject and faithless and blasphemous timidity of our wretched English literary society."[59]

This was said at a time when Gilchrist's biography had already managed to persuade most readers and reviewers that, contrary to previous allegations, Blake had not been a lunatic after all. Nonetheless, Swinburne found reason for his own crusade. Gilchrist's defense had mainly focused on Blake's hallucinations or "visitors," which the biographer carefully distinguishes from ghosts and other "gross" phenomena invoked by contemporary spiritists.[60] Rather than having "external, or (in German slang) . . . *objective* existence," these visions were simply projections of his imagination,

Gilchrist argued. In short, Blake was "an enthusiast, not an *insane* man."[61] As a result of his biography, Blake, overnight, became one of the most cherished figures of the Victorian imagination. As Deborah Dorfman puts it, people "relinquished mad Blake and took to their hearts the gentle and frugal engraver who chanted hymns on his deathbed and died with his debts paid."[62]

Almost as quickly as it arose, this picture of Blake as the prototype of angelic, though eccentric, innocence and respectability was destroyed by Swinburne's book. Hardly acquitted from the charge of insanity, the Romantic poet reappeared under some new form of madness. "Blake . . . whose life . . . was as pure and blameless as one of the winged messengers," complained one critic, "comes out of Mr. Swinburne's crucible with the attributes and aspects of a satyr."[63] The reason for this was that Swinburne praised precisely those aspects of Blake's person and writing which even Gilchrist, echoing current psychiatric notions of the time, put down to eccentricity, irritableness, or even deliberate perversity.[64] Typical of such deplorable extravagance to the biographer were the Proverbs of Hell, which had left Palmer, another Blake devotee and adviser of the biographer, shuddering "like a child for the first time in Madame Tussaud's 'Chamber of Horrors.'"[65] Palmer advised Mrs. Gilchrist, who finalized Blake's biography upon her husband's death, to eliminate the Proverbs from *The Marriage of Heaven and Hell,* and she duly followed his advice; otherwise the book would revolt "every drawing-room . . . in England."[66]

No one could have disagreed more than Swinburne, who once transcribed *The Marriage of Heaven and Hell* from a copy in Richard Monckton Milnes's private library of rare and forbidden books.[67] To him, *The Marriage* was simply "the greatest work of its century"[68] precisely for being centered on the notorious Proverbs. Like Baudelaire's "Litanies de Satan"—"one of the noblest lyrics ever written" and "the key-note to this whole complicated tune" of *Les fleurs du mal*—Blake's poem,[69] to Swinburne's delight, derived its inspiration from "hell instead of heaven." This predilection for the satanic had recently been sharpened by another treasure trove of infernal inspiration thrown open by Lord Houghton's private library: the works of the "Divine" Marquis de Sade. A long annotation to his *William Blake,* illustrating the poet's rebellion against God, directly echoes various of the Marquis' most basic creeds in a universe ruled by crime and destruction:

> Nature averse to crime? I tell you, nature lives and breathes by it; hungers at all her pores for bloodshed, aches in all her nerves for the help of sin, yearns with all her heart for the furtherance of cruelty. . . . Friends, if we would be one with

nature, let us continually do evil with all our might . . . for nature would fain have it so, that she might create a world of new things; for she is weary of the ancient life: her eyes are sick of seeing and her ears are heavy with hearing; with the lust of creation she is burnt up, and rent in twain with travail until she bring forth change; she would fain create afresh, and cannot, except it be by destroying: in all her energies she is athirst for mortal food, and with all her forces she labours in desire of death.[70]

Unlike Gilchrist's gentle engraver, Swinburne's Blake, then, was the prophet of infernal wisdom walking arm in arm with the Marquis de Sade. For who else but a man of the most trenchant insights could have written proverbs such as "The lust of the goat is the bounty of God."[71] In turn, the reasons for the suppression of Blake and of the Divine Marquis were analogous. Society ostracized both by declaring them mad, actually institutionalizing the one and ridiculing the other. To Swinburne, the parallel was obvious. Whenever a man like Blake or de Sade devoted himself "to the benefit of humanity and the upsetting of its idols (notamment 'cette chimère méprisable qu'on appelle la Vertu, et cette chimère éxécrable qu'on appelle Dieu') . . . humanity rewards their supreme benefactor with a madhouse or a gaol."[72] In short, Gilchrist had missed the point in acquitting Blake from the charge of insanity by staying too close to the arguments of Blake's denunciators. To do so was like proving the innocence of the accused without releasing him from jail. All the "chatter about 'madness' and such-like . . . even when well-meaning and not offensive,"[73] simply obscured the true issue.

For Swinburne the true issue was to vindicate not Blake, the allegedly insane visionary, but Blake, the supposedly deranged artist, whose works, according to an 1809 reviewer were "the wild effusions of a distempered brain."[74] Even Gilchrist, as we remember, had dismissed Blake's religious and moral opinions by attributing both to a perverted creative impulse.[75] But to Swinburne, the "apparent madness of final absurdity"[76] manifest in, say, the Prophetic Books, had "its root in the deepest and soundest part of Blake's mind and faith." If *The Marriage of Heaven and Hell* was "the greatest of all his books" as well as "about the greatest" of its century "in the line of high poetry and spiritual speculation," it was precisely because of its "cool insanity of manner."[77]

No doubt, Blake, as Swinburne confessed in private, was not "always wholly sane, or sound in mind, in the . . . vulgar sense."[78] But such hyperexcitability bordering on a definite "*dérèglement* de *tous les sens*"[79] was precisely what gave him his uniquely "subtle, trenchant and profound" insights.[80] Without it, the poet might never have been able to perpetrate the complete "transvaluation of values" current at his time. Swinburne does not use Nietzsche's terminology but clearly interprets *The Marriage* and other work along these lines. As Ruskin was to argue later, Blake's poems were "the words of a great and wise mind, disturbed, but not deceived, by its sickness; nay, partly exalted by it";[81] in fact, it may well be that Swinburne, in evolving his image of Blake the revolutionary poet-prophet of near-psychotic hypersensitivity, was influenced by what Ruskin said about *Poems and Ballads*.

Of course, there were other influences as well. Thus *William Blake* is Swinburne's partial self-portrait as the Baudelairian *poète maudit* preaching liberation from the crippling constraints of Christian morality in "sudden cries of melodious revolt."[82] From Baudelaire Swinburne also borrowed the idea of how our instinctual nature is demonized by repression; for instance, Venus, to him, grows "diabolic among ages that would not accept her as divine,"[83] while love turns "perverse passion" and "annihilat[ing] all else, falls at last to feed upon itself, to seek out strange things and barren ways."[84] But Ruskin more clearly even than Baudelaire must have impressed upon Swinburne the conviction that only someone who shares such sickness can become its poetic analyst. "There is assuredly something wrong with you," he wrote the young poet,

> awful in proportion to the great power it affects, and renders (nationally) at present useless. So it was with Turner, so with Byron. It seems to be the peculiar judgment-curse of modern days that all their greatest men shall be plague-struck. But the truth and majesty which is in their greatest, causes the plague which is underneath, in the hearts of meaner people, smooth outwardly, to be in them visible outside while there is purity within. The rest are like graves which appear not—and you are rose grafting set in dung.[85]

Of all the critics of *Poems and Ballads,* Ruskin stood out by reversing the consensus of his day, by accusing the reviewers of precisely the moral perversion they purported to find in the poet. No doubt, Swinburne's work was "diseased";[86] but hardly in the ignoble way that marked the sickness of his detractors. Theirs was a disease they misconstructed as normalcy, while the poet's contained its own cure. "There is hardly a piece of music written now in Europe," Ruskin assured Swinburne's father, "hardly a spectacle on any European stage—which is not more or less guilty and vile in a sense in which no thought of your son's ever could be—and it is the people who indulge in this continued viciousness who will most attack his work. The more I read it— the nobler I think it is. It *is* diseased—no question— but—as the blight is most [?] on the moss-rose—and does not touch—however terrible—the inner nature of the flower."[87] But such pre-Laingian insight, which

Swinburne in turn applied to Blake, found itself pitted against the consensus of those whose self-righteous claims in determining what was sick and sound in the arts had recently gained fresh support from the newly developed mental science.

Notes

1 *Browning: Critical Heritage,* p. 368.

2 J. S. Mill, *Autobiography and Literary Essays,* p. 597.

3 See L. Hunt in A. Tennyson, *Poems,* ed. C. Ricks, p. 186.

4 Quoted in *Swinburne: Critical Heritage,* pp. xix, xx.

5 Quoted in *Swinburne Replies,* p. 1.

6 Quoted by C. K. Hyder, *Swinburne's Literary Career,* p. 61.

7 [J. C. Bucknill], *Asylum Journal of Mental Science* 2 (1855-56), pp. 95-104, p. 102.

8 Quoted in *Swinburne: Critical Heritage,* p. xx.

9 H. Morley, in ibid., p. xxi.

10 *Swinburne Replies,* p. 18.

11 Quoted ibid., p. 5.

12 Quoted ibid., p. 4.

13 R. W. Buchanan, in *Swinburne: Critical Heritage,* p. 32. For a more recent discussion of the same issue, see D. G. Riede, *Swinburne,* pp. 43f.

14 C. K. Hyder, ed., *Swinburne: Critical Heritage,* p. xxi.

15 *Swinburne Replies,* p. 22.

16 *Swinburne Letters,* I: 123.

17 *Swinburne: Critical Heritage,* p. xix.

18 *Swinburne Letters,* I: 186.

19 *Swinburne Replies,* p. 92.

20 *Swinburne Letters,* I: 193.

21 Ibid.

22 E. Johnson, *Browning Society's Papers,* I: 354.

23 See *Swinburne: Critical Heritage,* p. xiii.

24 Quoted ibid., p. xviii; see also ibid., p. xix.

25 R. Browning, *Swinburne Letters,* I: 84.

26 L. M. Findlay, *VP* 9 (1971), p. 222. See also K. McSweeney, *VS* 22 (1978-79), pp. 5-28; and C. B. Stevenson, *VP* 19 (1981), pp. 185-95.

27 A. Tennyson, *Swinburne Letters,* I: 218. As we know, Tennyson later wrote "Lucretius" as a model of "how an indelicate subject might be treated delicately." (See O. Browning, *Memories,* p. 117.) "Happy: The Leper's Bride" was written in similar competition with Swinburne. "[As] he was reading it to me," reports Oscar Browning, he exclaimed: "'What a mess little Swinburne would have made of this!'" Ibid.

28 J. F. Nisbet, *Insanity of Genius,* p. xvi. For a more general study of *The Mad Genius Controversy,* see G. Becker's recent study of that title.

29 R. R. Madden, *Infirmities of Genius,* I: 9.

30 Ibid., 2: 281.

31 Ibid., p. 113.

32 Ibid., pp. 129, 130. See also *Quarterly Review* 50 (October 1833—January 1834), pp. 34-56; W. Newnham, *Essay,* passim; *British and Foreign Medical Review* 3 (January-April 1837), pp. 197-98.

33 J. C. Prichard, in *Cyclopaedia of Practical Medicine,* ed. J. Forbes et al., 3: 28.

34 *Journal of Psychological Medicine* 6 (1853), pp. 501-27, p. 501.

35 Ibid., pp. 516, 502, 513, 519, 513, 524.

36 *Journal of Mental Science* 20 (1874-75), pp. 60-74, p. 63.

37 Ibid., p. 69.

38 *Journal of Psychological Medicine* n.s. 5 (1879), pp. 30-90, pp. 68, 69.

39 Ibid., pp. 68, 69.

40 Ibid., pp. 52, 53. See also H. Maudsley, *Journal of Mental Science* 6 (1859-60), pp. 328-69. Maudsley's Poe is "Angry and envious, malignant and cynical, without sense of honour or love" (p. 367), an individual who barely escaped madness (p. 361) and whose poetry, as a result, lacks real emotion as found in Tennyson's (pp. 356ff.).

41 Cf. *Journal of Psychological Medicine* n.s. 6 (1880), pp. 33-75, pp. 61ff.; ibid. n.s. 5 (1879), pp. 30-90, pp. 47ff., 69ff.

[42] Ibid., pp. 85ff.

[43] *Journal of Psychological Medicine* 2 (1849), pp. 349-72, pp. 361, 358. See also ibid. n.s. 5 (1879), pp. 30-90, pp. 78ff.; *American Journal of Insanity* 5 (1848-49), pp. 206-14; *Fraser's Magazine* 10 (July-December 1834), pp. 18-32.

[44] *Journal of Psychological Medicine* n.s. 5 (1879), pp. 30-90, pp. 73ff., 30ff., 34ff., 36ff., 44ff., 82ff., 85ff.

[45] *Journal of Mental Science* 33 (1887-88), pp. 113-26, 303-10, 409-17; ibid. 34 (1888-89), pp. 98-113, 242-56.

[46] Ibid. 34 (1888-89), pp. 108, 251.

[47] *Journal of Psychological Medicine* n.s. 6 (1880), pp. 33-75, p. 68.

[48] Ibid., n.s. 7 (1881), pp. 157-73, p. 157. See also I. Ray, "Illustrations of Insanity by Distinguished English Writers," *American Journal of Insanity* 4 (1847-48), pp. 97-112; "Charlotte Corday," ibid., pp. 359-68; C. Mackay, "Want of Sleep, the Real Cause of Southey's Insanity and Death," ibid., pp. 273-75; "Insanity in . . . Sir Isaac Newton, Charles Lamb, and his sister, Mary Lamb," ibid. 5 (1848-49), pp. 65-78; "Insanity of Dean Swift and His Hospital for the Insane," ibid., pp. 206-14; on J. Swift see also *Journal of Psychological Medicine* 2 (1849), pp. 349-72; "The Wear and Tear of Literary Life; or, The Last Days of Robert Southey," ibid., 5 (1852), pp. 1-41; "The Overworked Mind," ibid., pp. 257-76; "The Insanity of William Cowper," *American Journal of Insanity* 14 (1857-58), pp. 215-40; "Charlotte Brontë—A Psychological Study," *Journal of Psychological Medicine* 11 (1858), pp. 295-317; "Dante: A Psychological Study," ibid. 12 (1859), pp. 413-28; "The Madness of Rousseau," *Journal of Mental Science* 19 (1873-74), pp. 256-59.

[49] *Swinburne: Critical Heritage,* p. xx.

[50] R. H. Hutton, in *Meredith: Critical Heritage,* p. 96.

[51] Ibid., p. 95.

[52] A. C. Swinburne, in ibid., p. 98.

[53] *Swinburne as Critic,* pp. 28-29.

[54] Ibid., pp. 33, 32.

[55] C. Baudelaire, in *Swinburne Letters,* 1: 88.

[56] See D. Dorfman, *Blake,* p. 90.

[57] A. C. Swinburne, *Complete Works,* 16: 138. See also D. Dorfman, *Blake,* p. 91; and J. J. McGann, *Swinburne,* p. 51.

[58] C. Y. Lang, ed., *Swinburne Letters,* 1: xviii.

[59] Ibid., pp. 208-209.

[60] See D. Dorfman, *Blake,* p. 75.

[61] Ibid., p. 75.

[62] Ibid., p. 83.

[63] Quoted ibid., p. 88. See also M. D. Conway, *Fortnightly Review* n.s. 3 (January-June 1868), pp. 216-20.

[64] See D. Dorfman, *Blake,* p. 73.

[65] Quoted ibid., p. 71.

[66] Quoted ibid., p. 72.

[67] Cf. *Swinburne Letters,* 1: lxvi, 206.

[68] Ibid., p. 102.

[69] *Swinburne as Critic,* p. 34.

[70] A. C. Swinburne, *Complete Works,* 16: 202-203. See also G. Lafourcade, *La Jeunesse de Swinburne,* 2: 354ff.

[71] W. Blake, *Poetry and Prose,* p. 36.

[72] *Swinburne Letters,* 1: 86.

[73] A. C. Swinburne, *Complete Works,* 16: 60.

[74] *Blake: Critical Heritage,* p. 66.

[75] See D. Dorfman, *Blake,* pp. 72, 73.

[76] A. C. Swinburne, *Complete Works,* 16: 239.

[77] Ibid., pp. 246, 247.

[78] *Swinburne Letters,* 2: 348.

[79] A. Rimbaud, *Oeuvres complètes,* p. 251.

[80] A. C. Swinburne, *Complete Works,* 16: 260.

[81] J. Ruskin, quoted in D. Dorfman, *Blake,* p. 39.

[82] A. C. Swinburne, *Complete Works,* 16: 181.

[83] *Swinburne Replies,* p. 26.

[84] A. C. Swinburne, *Complete Works,* 16: 222.

[85] J. Ruskin, in *Swinburne Letters,* 1: 182.

[86] Ibid., p. 185. For a recent neuro- and psychopathological assessment of Swinburne's masochism and general psychological problems, see W. B. Ober, *BMC* 39, 6 (November 1975), pp. 501-55.

Frederick Burwick (essay date 1996)

SOURCE: "Clare's 'Child Harold,'" in *Poetic Madness and the Romantic Imagination,* Pennsylvania State University Press, 1996, pp. 254-75.

[*In the following essay, Burwick studies the poetry written by John Clare during the years he spent in insane asylums. While acknowledging that it is impossible to ascertain whether or not Clare was truly mad, Burwick traces the shift in the tone in Clare's poetry from a Wordsworthian one to a Byronic one.*]

When Thomas De Quincey wrote on John Clare for the *Edinburgh Review,* he assumed the role of apologist. The fits of severe depression that Clare had suffered in 1824 De Quincey readily diagnosed as an "affection of the liver," a morbid reaction to the tumultuous and licentious habits of London, a mode of life for which the "Peasant Poet" was ill-prepared. As De Quincey saw it, Clare was a Wordsworthian poet of nature, who thrived upon "his own humble opportunities of enjoyment in the country."[1] The artificial excitements of London were detrimental to his mental health.

De Quincey, of course, had strong preconceptions about the susceptibility of the creative mind to bouts of madness. His long-time friend, Charles Lloyd, best known for his fictionalized account of Coleridge in *Edmund Oliver,* had been in and out of institutions before he was permanently consigned to the asylum in Chaillot where he had died just the year before. De Quincey had not only cared for Lloyd in his delirium, he had also struggled with his own frightening hallucinations wrought by his opium addiction. With Coleridge he had discussed the problems of medical treatment of mental disturbances, and in his periodical essays, he not only deliberated on the affinities of genius and madness, he also wrote psychological portraits of such idiosyncratic characters as Walking Stewart. It is not surprising, then, that De Quincey should turn his attention to John Clare who, since 1837, had been sequestered in the asylum at Epping Forest as a patient of Dr. Matthew Allen.

Although fits of melancholy had troubled Clare when they first met in London, De Quincey recollects that the "Peasant Poet" had found a therapeutic relief in the poetry of Wordsworth. "Even in this season of dejection," wrote De Quincey, Clare "would uniformly become animated when anybody spoke to him of Wordsworth—animated with the most hearty and almost rapturous spirit of admiration" (*DQ* 3:145). From *Poems Descriptive of Rural Life and Scenery* (1820) and *The Village Minstrel* (1821) through *The Shepherd's Calendar* (1827) and *The Rural Muse* (1835), Clare continued to inform his lyric with precise botanical descriptions of nature. Whatever Wordsworthian attributes Clare might seem to display in his early poetry, he resisted the mold into which he felt he was being cast by his publishers. Edward Drury warned his cousin, the publisher John Taylor, in a letter of 2 January 1820, that they must be patient with Clare: "It is to be feared that the man will be afflicted with insanity if his talent continues to be forced as it has been these 4 months past; he has no other mode of easing the fever that oppresses him after a tremendous fit of rhyming except by getting tipsy." Requesting books of Chaucer and the "old poets," Clare asserted that he "must have Poetry to read otherwise I cannot rhyme; & these Wordsworth's, Bowles &c that Mr Gilchrist lends do me no good" (Storey, *Critical Heritage,* 34). Taylor was, for a time, a patient publisher, and Clare promptly had his copy of Chaucer.

Twenty years later, after long "fits of rhyming" and many more bouts of "getting tipsy," Clare was indeed "afflicted with insanity." When Cyrus Redding visited him in Dr. Allen's asylum, he still wanted books: not Chaucer now, but Byron. In much of the poetry Clare produced in the asylum he adopted a deliberate and self-conscious Byronic pose. De Quincey, of course, had no notion of this belated, perhaps benighted, turn to Byron. No less than Edward Drury, however, he observed the symptoms of mental duress threatening Clare's sanity. Drury hinted that alcohol was Clare's bane. De Quincey, too, noted that Clare suffered "from an affection of the liver." As one who had recorded his own chaste cohabitation with "Ann of Oxford Street," De Quincey saw Clare's downfall abetted by an ardent attraction to London prostitutes.

Once the "brilliant parties" and "glittering theatres" had "made his rural life but too insupportable to his mind," Clare went in quest of stimulation. "It is singular that what most fascinated his rustic English eye was not the gorgeous display of English beauty," De Quincey recalls, "but the French style of beauty, as he saw it amongst the French actresses of Tottenham Court Road" (*DQ* 3:145). Clare's Wordsworthian sensibility was finely tuned to nature, according to De Quincey's diagnosis, but too easily distracted and debauched by the wanton enticements of the city. De Quincey's appraisal is confirmed by Clare himself in brooding over his sins in "Child Harold" and in jesting about the whorehouses of London in "Don Juan." Such matters, to be sure, are well suited to his Byronic identity in these poems. But there is no sense that the poet has simply invented remorse and self-recrimination for the sake of the pose.

When they first met, Clare may well have recognized in De Quincey a kindred spirit, one who seemed just as overwhelmed and ill at ease amidst the social whirl as himself. At the gala dinners hosted by Taylor and Hessey, Clare met the London literati and contributors to the *London Magazine:* Reynolds, Lamb, Coleridge, and Hazlitt. The author of the "Confessions of an English Opium-Eater," which had appeared in the issues of September and October 1821, was also among the company. Clare describes him as friendly yet not unlike a little boy lost: "A little artless simple-seeming body something of a child overgrown in a blue coat & black neckerchief for his dress is singular with his hat in his hand steals gently among the company with a smile turning timidly around the room It is De Quincey the Opium Eater & that abstruse thinker in logic & metaphysic X.Y.Z." (*Prose*, 91). Clare read the "Confessions" and followed the articles by "X.Y.Z." in the *London Magazine.* When a second printing of *The Village Minstrel* was called for in 1823, Clare wrote to Hessey asking that copies be given to the other contributors to *London Magazine.* He also requested "a copy of the Opium Eater he is a great favorite of mine" (April 1823). De Quincey's review of Goethe's *Wilhelm Meister* (August 1824) he considered "excellent" and, along with an essay by Elia in the same issue, "sufficient to make a bad no. interesting" (Journal, 11 September 1824; also letter to C. A. Elton, 18 December 1824). Readily granting that De Quincey had "contended right enough that women had an inferior genius to men," Clare observed that De Quincey's essay "False Distinctions" (June 1824) stirred a debate in subsequent numbers of the *Surrey* and the *Lion's Head* (Journal, 6 October 1824). Clare followed, too, the controversy over *Walladmor,* the German forgery of a Scott novel that De Quincey not only reviewed (October 1824) but also translated in a two-volume edition published by Taylor and Hessey. Conceding that "some parts of the novel" were "alive with action," Clare added the wish that "De Quincey had better subjects for his genius" (Journal, 13 October 1824).

By this time, after submitting several pieces on natural history, Clare had abandoned his effort to write for the *London Magazine.* Hessey began to sound more patronizing than supportive, and Taylor did not hesitate to ridicule both his poetry and his prose (Clare, *Natural History* [= *NH*], xxxvi-xxxviii). Both were well aware of Clare's precarious mental health. When he wrote Taylor to report that Dr. Arnold (of Stamford) had helped quiet his fits, Clare complained that he still felt "a numbness all over just as I should suppose a person to feel when bitten by a serpent" (August 1824). Worried about this reaction to Dr. Arnold's treatment, he wrote to Hessey asking him to secure the advice of Dr. G. Darling, the physician who had subjected Keats to "copious bleedings."

> I have gave up doctoring save the taking of opening pills occasionally I am as stupid as ever & blood comes from me often my insides feels sinking & dead & my memory is worse & worse nearly lost the sensation as if cold water was creeping all about my head . . . I feel desirous Hessey of having Dr. Darlings advice & would feign get to London if I could. (20 August 1824)

As Clare recorded in his autobiography, Dr. Darling was successful in allaying temporarily "the complaint . . . in my head & chest." But his visit to London in 1824 was also an occasion of willed and unwilled fantasies, illusions that slipped into delusions. "I amused my illness by catching the most beautiful women faces in the crowd as I passed on in it," he wrote, "till I was satiated as it were with the variety & the multitude & my mind lost its memory in the eternity of beautys successions & was glad to glide on in vacancy with the living stream." But the beauties of daytime perception were replaced by the terrors of night. Although he declared himself "a stubborn disbeliever" of the supernatural, he confessed an utter failure in resisting his fears:

> At night their terrors came upon me tenfold & my head was as full of the terrible as a gossip's thin death-like shadows & goblins with saucer eyes were continually shaping on the darkness from my haunted imagination & when I saw anyone of a spare figure in the dark passing or going on by my side my blood curdled cold at the foolish apprehension of his being a supernatural agent whose errand might be to carry me at the first dark alley we came to. (*Prose* 94)

Because he was painfully conscious of his own mental debilities, it may be a deliberate omission that he made no mention of De Quincey's "Madness" (June 1824), which, like "False Distinctions," appeared in the "Notes from the Pocket-Book of a late Opium-Eater." Whatever the cause of Clare's "affection of the liver," De Quincey presumed that it was directly to blame for Clare's mental condition. In his account for the *London Magazine,* he confidently postulated that "all madness, or nearly all, takes its rise in some part of the apparatus connected with the digestive organs, most probably the liver." The brain is merely the organ that through a sympathetic response to disruptions in the stomach or liver, produces those symptoms of irrationality. The fact that the brain of a lunatic might, upon dissection, reveal "some lesion or disorganization" does not mean the disease originated in the brain itself. A lesion in the brain may merely mark the ravages that commenced, most probably, in a diseased liver. Because opium had played havoc with his own digestive tract, De Quincey was particularly sensitive to the powerful influence the inner organs could work upon the mind. He therefore takes as the primary ground of his argument on the cause of madness the evidence of his own experience:

> For some years opium had simply affected the tone of my stomach; but, as this went off, and the stomach, by medicine and exercise, &c., began to recover its strength, I observed that the liver began to suffer. Under the affection of this organ, I was sensible that the genial spirits decayed far more rapidly and deeply, and that with this decay the intellectual faculties had a much closer sympathy. Upon this I tried some scores of experiments, raising or lowering alternately for periods of 48, 60, 72, or 84 hours, the quantity of opium. The result I may perhaps describe more particularly elsewhere; in substance, it amounted to this,—that, as the opium began to take effect, the whole living principle of the intellectual motions began to lose its elasticity, and, as it were, to petrify; I began to comprehend the tendency of madness to eddy about one idea; and the loss of power to abstract—to hold abstractions steadily before me—or to exercise many other intellectual acts, was in due proportion to the degree in which the biliary system seemed to suffer. (*DQ* 10:446-47)

Through his opium addiction, De Quincey had come to experience the conditions of madness. He fought its awful hold on his mind, yet endeavored to document all the symptoms, physical and mental, that the addiction had imposed upon him.

If there is some truth in De Quincey's insistence on the salubrious effects of Wordsworth, it may well be possible that in his turn to Byron, notorious as prodigy turned prodigal of Regency London, Clare indulged a hazardous mode of homeopathic therapy. In writing his "new cantos" for "Child Harold" and "Don Juan," he developed his own version of the Byronic identity. The poems of Clare's madness use this Byronic identity to explore the dark interiors of desire and guilt. These interiors, however, also resemble the haunted realms of De Quincey's nightmare visions. As Mark Storey has noticed, Clare had begun to imitate De Quincey in "The Dream" and "The Nightmare," and he returned to the De Quinceyan bifurcation of self in the recurring apocalyptic visions of "Child Harold" (*Critical Introduction* 167, 216). The sense of Clare reading Byron is subordinate to Clare adopting and transforming Childe Harold as his own *alter ego*. Clare, to be sure, was fully aware that Byron's poetic strategy involved a subtle in-and-out relationship of narrator and character. If this is parody, it is desperately earnest and

far more complex than a mere appropriation of a Byronic "self." The tormented dreams of the Opium-Eater also inform the intertextuality. Nor has Clare abandoned his former habits as the "Peasant Poet" who could lose himself in act of observing the "minute particulars," as Blake would say, of a wayside weed.

As in Hölderlin's "Patmos" and Nerval's "Le Christ aux Oliviers," Clare writes his text by reading himself into another text. An outcast from the society of the London *beau monde* where he had been feted for a season, Clare no doubt felt a certain sympathy with the poet who left England amid scandal. He recognized too, and appropriated, the ironic displacement of self that Byron accomplished in engendering his poetic persona. Most critical commentary on Clare's "Don Juan" and "Child Harold" has been preoccupied with the mimicking of Byron. In line with the preceding investigation of Hölderlin and Nerval, I stress instead Clare's hermeneutic penetration into Byron's text where he recovers the "wandering outlaw of his own dark mind" and engenders his own "being more intense" (canto 3, stanzas 3 and 6). This is Clare's poem, not Byron's. Clare's Spenserian stanza is more roughshod (often ignoring the convention of a final Alexandrine),[2] and his Child Harold is the form of his own fancy, the image of his own life, as its opening stanza tells us.

> Many are the poets—though they use no pen
> To show their labours to the shuffling age
> Real poets must be truly honest men
> Tied to no mongrel laws on flatterys page
> No zeal have they for wrong or party rage
> —The life of labor is a rural song
> That hurts no cause—nor warfare tries to wage
> Toil like the brook in music wears along—
> Great little minds claim right to act the wrong.

Clare stubbornly insists on his right to be a poet. Reared among the hovels of farm laborers, he is an "honest" man who has heard a song amid the sweat and toil. During the 1820s he won acclaim, but soon discovered that he had been received as little more than a curiosity and a freak, a minstrel plowboy. His early poems are notable for their keen observation of nature; his asylum poems are introspective and tinged with irony and defiance. With this shift from a Wordsworthian to a Byronic mode, Clare denies the ideological contests of the established parties. He champions the voice of the marginalized working class: "Great little minds claim right to act the wrong."

Undercutting the posturing of his poetic self-projection, Clare's "honest" persona does not conceal the squalor of his existence and the sad confrontation with the futility of his ideals and ambitions:

My life hath been one of love—no blot it out
My life hath been one chain of contradictions
Madhouses Prisons wh-reshops—never doubt
But that my life hath had some strong
   convictions
That such was wrong—religion makes
   restrictions
I would have followed—but life turned a
   bubble

                              (145-50)

Clare's Child Harold does not range across the nations of Europe; he travels the lonely backroads, a man abandoned and betrayed.

Life is to me a dream that never wakes
Night finds me on this lengthening road alone
Love is to me a thought that never aches
A frost bound thought that freezes life to
   stone

                              (255-58)

His Child-Harold self, in the stanzas just quoted, seems to confess some sexual disorder. The cause of Clare's debility has been variously attributed to epilepsy or alcoholism. Although medical records at the Northampton General Lunatic Asylum typically made note of such evidence, the certification of his insanity, signed by Dr. William Page and Dr. Fenwick Skimshire, mentions neither epilepsy nor veneral infection. When Patty's "temper or injudicious conduct" drove him away from home in 1826, he had a brief affair with another woman. His guilt in the aftermath of this episode grew into the conviction that he had contracted a disease (letter from Eliza Emmerson, 1826; letter from James Hessey, 18 June 1828; in Tibble and Tibble 305). Although his symptoms were not manifest in lesions of the flesh, they were real enough to provide a recurrent motif of "Child Harold," in which the retribution for his sins is manifest as the freezing blight that "fell in youths mayday" (32-33).

Because the cottage in Helpston was overcrowded after their seventh child was born, Lord Milton arranged for Clare and his family to move into a house with some five acres in Northborough in 1832. Unsettled by the move, Clare complained to Dr. Darling that he could no longer concentrate: "I cannot sleep for I am asleep as it were with my eyes open & I feel chills come over me & a sort of nightmare awake. . . . I cannot keep my mind right as it were for I wish to read & cannot—there is a sort of numbing through my private parts which I cannot describe" (Autumn 1835; *Letters* 183). He told Thomas Inskip that an "appoplectic fit" had left "a numbing pain" in his head and "an acking void at the pit of my stomach" (10 August 1824). Such "fits," Clare thought, had

commenced when, as a child, he witnessed a man break his neck in a fall from a wagon (*Sketches* 70). He also suffered, by his own account, periods of severe melancholy. His letters contain detailed descriptions of a numbness penetrating his head and a lethargy overwhelming his body. "A tottering trembling state of nerves & . . . sickly sensibility" were the symptoms he described to Taylor (March-April 1821). During the next ten years Clare's recurrent agonies became more severe. He told Eliza Emmerson that "my very brains seemed to boil up almost into madness & my arms & legs burnt as it were with a listless feebleness" (13 November 1832).[3]

Eliza Emmerson had advised him to avoid "anything that may affect your *Head*" (December 1825). As the torment of mind and body increased, Clare curtailed his drinking. Answering Taylor's suspicion that he might be lapsing into former habits and probably had too much to drink as a guest of the mayor of Boston (in Lincolnshire), Clare explained that he had merely indulged an incautious enthusiasm when "a lady of the table talked so ladily of the Poets that I drank off my glass very often without knowing." He felt the influence of the wine, precisely because "I was not used to the drink." He then adds: "I dont think I have drank a pint of ale together these two years in fact I can drink nothing strong now in any quantity & as to spirits I never touch them & yet without them I feel hearty & hale & have quite recovered from my last ailments & hope to prolong the lease of life for a good season" (3 January 1829).

Clare was never long free of his ailments. The "fits" of melancholy were also accompanied by hallucinations. Clare's letter to Dr. Darling (Autumn 1835) is filled with fear that he is losing his mind; he declares desperately that he "can scarcely bear up against my fancys or feelings." When Taylor, accompanied by a doctor, visited him in December 1836, they found Clare enfeebled by delusion and able to speak only in repetitious babbling (Grigson 6). At Taylor's recommendation, Clare was sent to Dr. Allen's asylum in Epping Forest (near Enfield, Essex).

De Quincey, we recall, was certain that madness arose from an "affection of the liver." Dr. Allen argued that there was a link between kidney function and certain forms of insanity. He consequently advocated regular observation of the color and clarity of the urine (*Classification of the Insane* 36). Clare's portrait of "Doctor Bottle imp" confirms that Dr. Allen put his theory into practice at his High Beech asylum:

There is Doctor Bottle imp who deals in urine
A keeper of state prisons for the queen
As great a man as is the Doge of Turin
And save in London is but seldom seen
Yclep'd old A-ll-n—mad brained ladies curing

Some p-x-d like Flora and but seldom clean
The new road oer the forest is the right one
To see red hell and further on the white one

("Don Juan," 223-30)

By calling attention only to the female patients under Dr. Allen's care, Clare seems to detach himself from confinement, to stand some distance from Epping Forest, and merely to point the way to the "red hell and . . . the white one" (the lodge and clinic at High Beech).[4] The reference to the "mad brained ladies" might echo some persisting gossip among the attendants about the court case over Dr. Allen's treatment of one of the women patients four years before Clare's arrival at the asylum.[5]

In spite of Dr. Allen's advocacy of proper medical and moral treatment (*Cases of Insanity,* part 1, vol. 1), the attendants did not always act with the prescribed benevolence. Indeed, records at other asylums during this period reveal that brutality to the patients was all too common (Digby 140-70). After his escape, Clare wrote to Dr. Allen that the "servants & stupid keepers" had made life in the asylum unbearable:

> I can be miserably happy in any situation & in any place & could have staid in yours in the Forest if any of my friends had noticed me or come to see me but the greatest annoyance in such places as yours are those servants & stupid keepers who often assumed as much authority over me as if I had been their prisoner & not liking to quarrel I put up with it till I was weary of the place altogether so I heard the voice of freedom & started (August 1841; *Letters* 294)

The only belongings abandoned in his escape which he wished to have forwarded were his volumes of Byron's poetry. His journey home from Epping Forest to Northborough, a distance of 100 miles, would have been less arduous if Clare had a proper pair of shoes and some food. As it was, he arrived on the road north from Petersborough limping and hungry. Two nights he slept in fields, one night he took shelter on the porch of a cottage, and he chewed grass and tobacco to allay the hunger pangs. Just a few miles from his home, he was met by a woman in a cart. "When nearing me the woman got out & caught fast hold of my hands & wished me to get into the cart but I refused & thought her either drunk or mad" (*Prose* 247). It was his wife Patty.

His failure to recognize his wife may have been the consequence of having long dwelt upon his fantasy of Mary Joyce, his first love. "Young as my heart was," he recollected in his autobiography, "it would turn chill when I touched her & tremble & I fancyd her feelings were the same for as I gazd earnestly in her face a fear

would hang in her eye & she would turn to wipe it away." Even in its inception, the relationship was "romantic or Platonic" and nourished in Clare's own fancy. "I fancyd her eyes told me her affections," he wrote of those days when "we walked together as school-companions." Whatever her eyes may have told him, they soon ceased to look upon him. "When she grew to womanhood she felt her station above mine at least I felt that she thought so for her parents were farmers, & farmers had great pretensions to something then" (*Prose* 44).

In later years, he began to elaborate this "fancyd" love into an almost mystical ideal. From Epping Forest, he addressed letters to "My dear Wife Patty" and "My dear Wife Mary." After his escape from the asylum, he was informed that Mary Joyce had died in 1838, one year after his confinement. "Mary has been dead eight years," he wrote to Dr. Allen. The lapse of time is garbled—three years became six or eight—and the very fact of her death is challenged. In the account of his escape, "The Journey from Essex," he scoffs at "the old story of her being dead six years ago." Such a tale "might be taken from a bran new old newspaper printed a dozen years ago but I took no notice of the blarney having seen her myself about a twelvemonth ago alive & well & as young as ever" (*Prose* 250). Indeed, she came to him in a dream and lay at his side on that very journey homeward.

The love affair with Mary blossomed in the poet's imagination at High Beech. It is her image, not Patty's, that becomes his muse and mental companion:

> Here where Mary loved to be
> And here are flowers she planted
> Here are books she loved to see
> And here the kiss she granted

(125-28)

In the very next quatrain of this song from "Child Harold" Clare recognizes that Mary's haunting presence is expelled and eradicated by the physical evidence of absence. Not even her picture remains, "Both walls and rooms are naked now / No Marys nigh to hear me."

In the asylum version of their childhood love, Mary had been his bride and, only after she was taken from him amid "maledictions," had he "made the error double" by wedding a second wife. His imprisonment in the madhouse enforces his separation from both:

> Yet absence claims them both and keeps them too
> And locks me in a shop in spite of law
> Among a low lived set and dirty crew
> Here let the Muse oblivions curtains draw

And let man think—for God hath often saw
Things here too dirty for the light of day
For in a madhouse there exists no law—
Now stagnant grows my too refined clay
I envy birds their wings to flye away

(154-62)

Byron's "Prisoner of Chillon," after the death of his
two brothers, falls into madness, a dark despair of
"no thought" and "stagnant idleness." When the song
of a bird "broke in upon my brain," rather than envy
its freedom to fly, he is glad that it is not caged like
him. Byron's prisoner, his mind and will broken, made
friends with spiders and mice and "my very chains."

Clare, too, may have gradually resigned himself to cap-
tivity during his twenty-two years as an inmate at the
Northampton General Lunatic Asylum. But at Epping
Forest he continued to protest: "No one knows how sick
I am of this confinement"; "If I was in prison for felony
I could not be served worse"; "Having been cooped up
in this Hell of a Madhouse till I seem to be disowned
& even forgot by my enemies. . . . I am almost mad in
waiting for a better place & better company"; "It Would
Seem By Keeping Me Here One Year After Another
That I Was Destined For The Same Fate Agen & I
Would Sooner Be Packed On A Slave Ship For Africa
Than Belong To The Destiny of Mock Friends & Real
Enemies" (*Letters* 290-92). Some of the letters that he
drafted in his High Beech notebook may well have been
intended for the eyes of his keepers, who no doubt also
had occasion to peruse the satirical diatribe against the
Madhouse in Clare's "Don Juan" as well as the spiritual
meditations of his "Child Harold." Although he had been
meeting "with some gipseys one of whom offered to
assist in my escape from the madhouse," Clare was
careful not to reveal the plan in his notebook. But he did
leave a broad hint in the small High Beech notebook,
when he drafted a letter to "My Dearest Mary": "This
Will Be My Last Letter To You Or Any One Else—Let
My Stay In Prison Be As Long Or As Short As It May"
(*Letters* 293). Five nights before his escape, he inserted
into his "Child Harold" the lines "Written in a Thunder
storm July 15th 1841":

> My soul is apathy—a ruin vast
> Time cannot clear the ruined mass away
> My life is hell—the hopeless die is cast
> And manhoods prime is premature decay
>
> Roll on ye wrath of thunders—peal on peal
> Till worlds are ruins and myself alone
> Melt heart and soul cased in obdurate steel
> Till I can feel that nature is my throne
>
> . . . . .
>
> Smile on ye elements of earth and sky
> Or frown in thunders as ye frown on me

Bid earth and its delusions pass away
But leave the mind as its creator free

(221-28; 233-36)

It would be clutching at straws to relate Clare's language to specific passages from Byron; nevertheless,
his rhetoric and rhythms are not without Byronic resonance. While Grigson had more ample warrant to see
in "Maid of Walkherd" Clare's indigenous version of
Byron's "Maid of Athens" (Grigson 9), the opening
line of "Written in a Thunder storm" echoes the agony
of the mad Saul in "My Soul is Dark," and the apostrophe to the "wrath of thunders" celebrates the power
of the elements much in the manner of Byron's Childe
Harold when looking down upon the sea from Alban
Mount: "Roll on, thou deep and dark blue Ocean—
roll!" (stanza 4, line 174). And the final quatrain anticipates the ultimate liberty of mind in terms similar
to Childe Harold's when he imagines that moment
"when, at length the mind shall be all free / From
what it hates in this degraded form" (stanza 3, line
74).

In his asylum poetry, Clare sings of an anguish which
has long fermented in his bouts of dark depression:
"My Mind Is Dark and Fathomless And Wears / The
Hues Of Hopeless Agony" (1011-12). Byron's heroic
personae—the exile, the outlaw, the madman—have
been seen as projections of the poet's own troubled
mind. Byron may have empathically identified with
the madman in his cell in "Prisoner of Chillon" or
"Lament of Tasso," but the experience was never his
own. Clare's "Child Harold" speaks of real confinement, not imaginary, when he cries out, "I'm not an
outlaw in this midnight deep" (266), and laments that
in his imprisonment, "Day seems my night and night
seems blackest hell" (272).

Clare did not think that he was Byron in residence at
Epping Forrest, but he may well have enjoyed the ruse
to baffle his madhouse attendants.[6] In "Don Juan" he
dons and doffs his Byronic identity with the alacrity of
Charles Mathews in one of his "polymonologues."
"Now this day is the eleventh of July / And being
sunday I will seek no flaw / In man or woman," he
declares a the beginning of stanza 29. Satire is unsuited for the sabbath, and all modes of irony and humor
are unsuited for the madhouse. Because his keepers
have no sense of humor, he declares that "In a madhouse I can find no mirth pay." The odd phrasing of
"mirth pay" serves to call forth the rhyming line: "—
Next Tuesday used to be Lord Byron's birthday." The
rhyme is forced, the date is wrong. Wrong, at least,
from one mode of reckoning. "Next Tuesday," July
13, was Clare's birthday.

So there is one Byron, a historical figure who happened to be born on January 22, and whose funeral

procession Clare had witnessed in London. And there is another Byron, who persists in dispelling lies through his poetry. And yet another Byron, among the fools "still in Allens madhouse caged and living":

> Lord Byron poh—the man wot rites the
>   werses
> And is just what he is and nothing more
> Who with his pen lies like the mist disperses
> And makes all nothing as it was before
> Who wed two wives and oft the truth
>   rehearses
> And might have had some twenty thousand
>   more
> Who has been dead so fools their lies are
>   giving
> And still in Allens madhouse caged and living
>
> ("Don Juan," 263-70)

In the notoriety of Byron, Clare saw justification of his own troubled lot. Byron, like Clare, had been pampered then rejected by the fickle society of London. Eliza Emmerson and Lord Radstock had sought to squelch Clare's satirical voice. Byron defied the disapproval of the Regency and wielded his pen as weapon against hypocrisy and corruption. Byron, too, had "wed two wives . . . / And might have had some twenty thousand more." Embalmed in spirits the body of Byron had been brought back from Greece. As the coffin was carried from the London Docks through Oxford Street, Clare had watched in awe. Not the death of the poet, but the adulation of the onlookers is what most impressed Clare: "A young girl that stood beside me gave a deep sigh & uttered 'Poor Lord Byron' I looked up at the young girl's face it was dark & beautiful & I could almost feel in love with her for the sigh she had uttered" (Autobiography, July 1824, in *Prose* 99).

Clare respected Byron's reputation and poetic accomplishment, yet he knew he was no Byron. He could, however, adapt a Byronic pose to his own homely manner. The rhetorical flourishes of the exiled aristocrat, the noble outlaw, were too bold to be absorbed with ease into Clare's native idiom. Rather than abandoning or suppressing the Wordsworthian strain that had come into his poetry in the 1820s, Clare returned in his asylum poetry to the Wordsworthian strategies of recollecting the exuberant self of the past and mocking the myopic self of the present. In his Journal, Clare described a conversation with "a sensible & well informed man" who "talkd much of the poets but did not like Wordsworth": "When I told him I did he instantly asked me wether I did not like Byron better I don't like these comparisons to knock your opinions on the head when I told him I read Wordsworth oftener than I did Byron & he seemd to express his surprise at it by observing that he could not read Wordsworth at all" (Journal, 3 April 1825, in *Prose* 142). He was fasci-

nated by the grand manner of Byron, but Wordsworth was a poet whom he could read and reread. Clare confessed that he had originally resisted the efforts of Drury and Hessey to push him into a Wordsworthian mode. To his surprise, once he began to explore Wordsworth's poetry he found himself enthralled:

> Read some poems of Wordsworth his 'Lucy Gray' or Solitude 'The Pet Lamb' 'We Are Seven' the Oak & Broom 'the Eglantine & the Fountain' Two April Mornings are some of my favorites When I first began to read poetry I dislikd Wordsworth because I heard he was dislikd & I was astonishd when I lookd into him to find my mistaken pleasure in being delighted & finding him so natural & beautiful in his 'White Doe of Rylstone' there is some of the sweetest poetry I ever met with tho full of his mysteries. (Journal, 29 October 1824, in *Prose*, 118)

A Wordsworthian communion with nature was never as important to Clare as the simpler modes of observation and description. In the asylum, however, Wordsworthian evocations of childhood memories become increasingly important. His "Child Harold" often pauses to reaffirm the mind's capacity to revisit scenes from the otherwise inaccessible landscape of the past:

> Dull must that being live who sees unmoved
> The scenes and objects that his childhood
>   knew
> The school yard and the maid he early loved
> The sunny wall where long the old Elms grew
> The grass that e'en till noon retains the dew
> Beneath the wallnut shade I see them still
> Though not such fancy's do I now pursue
> Yet still the picture turns my bosom chill
> And leaves a void—nor love nor hope may
>   fill
>
> (603-11)

When Byron calls upon memories of the past, his purpose is show how past joys have been blighted. The pattern, as in *Hours of Idleness* or the first two cantos of *Childe Harold,* is to conjure a memory even in the declared act of abjuring it. Recollections of the past, for Byron, are strangely imageless, dominated by feelings rather than perceptions. The painful opposition of joy and loss prompts the Byronic hero to call for oblivion and forgetfulness. Clare, tempering the Byronic tensions with Wordsworthian tranquillity, continues to cherish images of the past even if they ultimately leave him all the more forlorn in a bleak and hopeless present.

> After long abscence how the mind recalls
> Pleasing associations of the past
> Haunts of his youth—thorn hedges and old
>   walls

And hollow trees that sheltered from the blast
And all that map of boyhood overcast
With glooms and wrongs and sorrows not his
    own
That oer his brow like the scathed lightning
    past
That turned his spring to winter and alone
Wrecked name and fame and all—to solitude
    unknown

                                    (612-20)

While such "associations of the past" in "Child Harold" turn from the Byronic to the Wordsworthian, Clare's rapt attention to nature remains as selflessly unWordsworthian as it had been in *Poems Descriptive of Rural Life and Scenery* (1820) and *The Village Minstrel* (1821).

The blackbird startles from the homestead
    hedge
Raindrops and leaves fall yellow as he springs
Such images are natures sweetest pledge
To me there's music in his rustling wings
'Prink prink' he cries and loud the robin sings
The small hawk like a shot drops from the
    sky
Close to my feet for mice and creeping things
Then swift as thought again he suthers bye
And hides among the clouds from the
    pursuing eye

                                    (770-78)

In his solitary walks around the asylum grounds, he is still alert to the sights and sounds of nature. If this lonely stance, as observer rather than as participant, is Wordsworthian, it is a Wordsworth in anguish over his own sense of isolation and numbness: "The things which I have seen I now can see no more" ("Intimations of Immortality," 9). As Clare put it, "nature to me seems dead & her very pulse seems frozen to an icicle in the summer sun" (letter to "My Dear Wife Mary," 1841).

Isolation and estrangement were conditions that Clare, from the time he wrote his first poems, found inescapable. "I always felt anxiety to control my scribbling," Clare said of the necessary stealth, "& woud as leave have confessed to be a robber as a rhymer." A would-be poet could expect no sympathy or encouragement, only envy and hostility. His illiterate fellow laborers hated him for his learning, and his employers condemned him as a lazy shirker or as a pretentious upstart (*Prose* 30-33, 48, 60, 62, 66-67). Even Drury, who claimed to have "discovered" Clare's talent, did not hesitate in his letter to Taylor to mention his lethargy and his affectations (Storey, *Critical Introduction,* 3). It was Clare's folly, according to many of his contemporar-

ies, to struggle against his place in society, to oppose the labors proper to his class. Much the same judgment was recorded on the medical papers consigning Clare, five months after his escape from Epping Forest, to the General Lunatic Hospital in Northampton. His employment, the doctors recorded, was gardening, and his present mental condition was attributed to "years of Poetical prosing" (Grigson 22).

Robert Southey, in *Our Uneducated Poets* (1831), sought to put a kinder light on the poetic efforts of those among the lower classes. But his kindness is condescending, a smug and patronizing *noblesse oblige:*

When we are told that the thresher [Stephen Duck],
the milkwoman [Ann Yearsley], and the tobacco-
pipe-maker [John Frederick Bryant] did not deserve
the patronage they found,—when it is laid down
as a maxim of philosophical criticism that poetry
ought never to be encouraged unless it is excellent
in its kind,—that it is an art in which inferior
execution is not to be tolerated,—a luxury, and
must therefore be rejected unless it is of the very
best,—such reasoning may be addressed with
success to cockered and sickly intellect, but it
will never impose upon a healthy understanding, a
generous spirit, or a good heart. (164)

What Southey expects of "a generous spirit" is a tolerance for "bad poetry," which "can do no harm, unless it passes for good, becomes fashionable, and so tends to deprave still further a vitiated public taste, and still further to debase a corrupted language." He grants that "mediocres have long been a numerous and increasing race," but he insists that it can be no "offence against the public, to publish verses no one is obliged either to purchase or to read." The benevolent motives of "a healthy understanding" in forwarding the cause of one of "our uneducated poets," is not "the hope of rearing a great poet, but for the sake of placing a worthy man in a station more suited to his intellectual endowment, than that in which he was born" (165-66). The class system remains intact. The aspiring poet, thus co-opted by the benevolent establishment, is allowed to ascend a rung or two up the ladder of privilege.

Arrogance disguised as patronage was not new to Clare. In a letter to Taylor, he expressed his anger: "Mr Southey seems to hold uneducated poets in very little estimation & talks about the march of mind in a sneering way—as to education it aids very little in bringing forth that which is called poetry—& if it means [a] humble station in life is to be the toleration for people to praise him I should say much admiration is worth but little" (7 March 1831). Those who enjoyed the advantages of education and who deigned to admire his works, Clare learned early in his career, were seldom to be trusted. His letters and journal record many false promises. Worse, a patron could assume the right to dictate and to censor what the poet should write.

Lord Radstock felt particularly incensed that Clare should rail against the poor conditions of field laborers. Why, the world might think that there was such exploitation on his own estates! Eliza Emmerson is called upon to bring Clare to his senses. He must "expunge certain highly objectionable passages":

> Passages, wherein, his then depressed state hurried him not only into error, but into the most flagrant acts of injustice; by accusing those of pride, cruelty, vices, and ill-directed passions—who, are the very persons, by whose truly generous and noble exertions he had been raised from misery and despondency. . . . It has been my anxious desire of late, to establish our poets character, as that, of an honest and upright man—as a man feeling the strongest sense of gratitude for the encouragement he has received—but how is it possible I can continue to do this if he suffers another Edition of his poems to appear with those vile, unjust, and now would be ungrateful passages in them?—no, he must cut them out . . . he must give me unquestionable *proofs,* of being that man I would have him to be—he *must expunge!* (11 May 1820, in Storey, *Critical Heritage,* 61)

Eliza Emmerson thus reports the benefactors command, and she adds her own request that he remove the "*Radical* and *ungrateful* sentiments" from his poetry (she has marked the passages for him). Lord Radstock had his way. Grudgingly, Clare informed Taylor that he must "leave out the 8 lines in 'Helpstone' beginning 'Accursed wealth' and two under 'when ease and plenty'—and one in 'Dawning of Genius' 'That necessary tool' leave it out and put ***** to fill up the blank this will let em see I do it as negligent as possible D—n that canting way of being for to please I say—I cant abide it and one day or other I will show my Independence more strongly than ever" (16 May 1820). When the new edition was brought out, Clare was angry to find that Taylor had taken even further liberties in rendering the poetry acceptable. He wrote to Hessey, in whom he thought he had an ally:

> I have seen the third Edition I am cursed mad about it the Judgement of T. is a button hole lower in my opinion—it is good—but too subject to be tained by medlars *false delicasy* damn it I hate it beyond everything those frumpt up misses brought up in those seminaries of mysterious wickedness (Boarding Schools) what will please em? why we well know—but while their heart and soul loves to extravagance (what we dare not mention) false delicasy's seriousness muscles up the mouth and condemns it. (July 1820)

Hessey wrote back to placate their "vexed" poet. The changes were made, he insists, in the "firm conviction that your own Interest would be most essentially served" (11 July 1820, in Storey, *Critical Heritage,*

63). Editors were worse than patrons: the latter demanded "gratitude," the former enforced propriety. "Editors are troubled with nice amendings," Clare asserted, "& if Doctors were as fond of amputation as they are of altering & correcting the world woud have nothing but cripples" (Journal, 30 April 1825, in *Prose* 146).

After his literary career had been effectively frustrated and stifled, Clare grew increasingly despondent. The editors and the doctors had indeed left him a cripple. His Byronic stance at the asylum in Epping Forest allowed him the only "Independence" and the only "honest" poetic voice that he could muster: the irony of an honest confession that he had capitulated to a world of deception.

> This life is made of lying and grimace
> This world is filled with whoring and
>   decieving
> Hypocrisy ne'er masks an honest face
> Story's are told—but seeing is believing
> And I've seen much from which there's no
>   retrieving
> I've seen deception take the place of truth
> I've seen knaves flourish—and the country
>   grieving
> Lies was the current gospel in my youth
> And now a man—I'm further off from truth
>
>   (526-34)

The truth that he had dared to tell was only a momentary light. It passed and the poet was left to a world of darkness and blighted hope.

> Fame blazed upon me like a comets glare
> Fame waned and left me like a fallen star
> Because I told the evil of what they are
>   (426-28)

More than either Hölderlin or Nerval, Clare turns within the precincts of his hermit-crab text to shake his fist at the society that rejected and incarcerated him.

In spite of the profound and disturbing insights that emerge from the poetry of Hölderlin, Nerval, and Clare, their debilitating sickness progressively destroyed their creativity. Nerval's condition was brought about by ergotism; Hölderlin most probably suffered from schizophrenia; Clare, too, may have been a victim of schizophrenia, but the diagnosis of his case is less certain. Schizophrenia may be a more precise term than madness, but its symptoms and manifestations are various, as are its causes. Even after the rise of psychology as a science, the boundaries between idiosyncracy and insanity, neurosis and psychosis, have often been shifted and redefined. Although the relation between various mental aberrations and artistic creativity still seems uncertain, substantial progress has been made in the treatment of manic-depressive illness. Thomas Caramagno, in *The Flight of the Mind: Virginia Woolf's Art and Manic-Depressive Illness* (1992), argues that a Freudian diagnosis of Woolf's disorder as a neurosis subjected her to an onus of blame, as if the biological imbalance had been caused by some deliberate quirk in her personal character. The drug therapy currently available could have prevented the periods of dark suffering that plagued her career. The advent of psychiatric medicine, to be sure, has been accompanied by many false promises. What restores psychological equilibrium to one patient, may produce dangerous side effects in another and lead to chemical abuse in a third.

Nevertheless, the clinical research of Nancy Andreasen, Kay Redfield Jamison, and others has provided a much better understanding of the relationship between bipolar affective disorders and artistic creativity. In responding to the problems I have been addressing . . . Dr. Nancy Andreasen emphasized the importance in recognizing the difference between schizophrenia and manic-depressive illness. "In general," she wrote, "schizophrenia is not very compatible with creativity, since people with this illness for some reason tend to deteriorate rather badly and in particular to lose volition, drive, and richness of thought. People with mania, on the other hand, tend to be very intact between episodes, and they are often very clever and interesting while in the midst of an episode" (letter to author, 23 November 1992).

The epigrams from Plato, Aristotle, and Seneca . . . come from an age that could not appeal to Freudian psychology and psychiatric medicine in formulating its concepts about the creative process. This does not mean that Seneca's declaration, "There is no genius without some touch of madness" (*De tranquillitate*), is without truth. It does mean, however, that we must be careful how we interpret references to "madness." It has often become a term leveled by authority against a voice of insurgency. Any assertion of the imaginary, as Luiz Costa Lima has argued, may be deemed a threat to the established order. Dryden hoists the banner of "Reason" on behalf of Charles II when he condemns the Earl of Shaftesbury in the well-known couplet from *Absalom and Achitophel:* "Great wits are sure to madness near allied, / And thin partitions do their bounds divide" (163-64). Franciscus Junius also writes on the side of "Reason" when he denounces Sir William Draper for the "vipers" that "dance through your letters in all the mazes of metaphorical confusion." These "vipers," Junius declares, "are the gloomy companions of a disturbed imagination; the melancholy madness of poetry, without the inspiration" (3 March 1769). Emily Dickinson, although she is ready to acknowledge her place on the wrong side of the partition, refers to "madness" in much the same in sense:

Much madness is divinest sense
To a discerning eye;
Much sense the starkest madness.
'Tis the majority
In this, as all, prevails.
Assent, and you are sane;
Demur,—you're straightway dangerous,
And handled with a chain.

(No. 435, *Poems,* 209)

The mad rhapsodist, at various moments in history, has been revered as a prophet, tolerated as harmless lunatic, condemned as dangerous conspirator. The age of Junius and Sir William Draper was also the age of William Cowper and Christopher Smart, poets whose madness was not merely conjured by antagonists but arose within their own being, an internal source of persecution and agony. The "viper thoughts" that Coleridge felt "coil around my mind" (*Dejection: An Ode,* 94), stifling the last efforts of creativity, are very different from those metaphorical "vipers" condemned by Junius. When Wordsworth fears that the poet will lose the "gladness" of youth and end his days in "despondency and madness" (*Resolution and Independence,* 48-49), he, too, refers to a real loss of vitality brought about by progressively enervating and enfeebling depression.

The dilemma of the mad rhapsodist results, in part, from the irrational wellings that accompany the creative process, whether or not the artist endeavors to reassert rational order. The very endeavor rationally to contain the irrational . . . results in an paradox of representation. The literary representation of madness is further confounded by the multiple meanings of madness. Shelley, who meant one thing by "madness" in *Julian and Maddalo,* clearly meant something very different when he asked, in *To a Skylark,* for the bird's gladness so that he, too, might sing forth in "harmonious madness" (stanza 21). "Madness" may mean liberation, yet it may also mean persecution. Whether Shelley is talking about the "madness" of Torquato Tasso's resistance to his exploitation and torment, the hallucinations of Laon or Cythna, or his own lyrical flight, the word "madness" retains in its manifold connotations Shelley's sense of opposition to the oppression of reason, an opposition that may end in agony or in freedom.

For Hölderlin, Nerval, and Clare, "madness" was by no means merely metaphorical or imaginary. It was an insidious invader of the mind and body that relentlessly destroyed the being that it conquered. Yet it also aroused its victim to a valiant struggle, and to a creative endeavor that, because of its intertextuality, unwinds a thread of reason as it wanders through the dark labyrinth of irrationality. It maintains its literary integrity as poetry of the interior realm of experience.

While the poetry of irrationality may baffle literary critic and psychologist alike, it nevertheless exercises a powerful appeal precisely because the "unknown" is hauntingly familiar. The mad rhapsodist exposes a dark side of the mind that is as intimate as the shadows of our own repressed consciousness.

Bibliography

. . . Allen versus Dutton. Published at the request of the friends of Dr Allen. London, 1833. . . .

Clare, John. *The Letters of John Clare.* Ed. J. W. Tibble and Anne Tibble. London: Routledge & Kegan Paul, 1951. . . .

De Quincey, Thomas. *The Collected Writings of Thomas De Quincey* (= *DQ*). 14 vols. Ed. David Masson. Edinburgh, 1889-90. . . .

Grigson, Geoffrey, ed. *Poems of John Clare's Madness.* London: Routledge & Kegan Paul, 1949. . . .

Storey, Mark. ed. *Clare: The Critical Heritage.* London: Routledge & Kegan Paul, 1973. . . .

Notes

[1] Thomas De Quincey, "Sketches of Life and Manners," Tait's *Edinburgh Magazine*, December 1840, 771-72; in *DQ* 3:144-45.

[2] Clare had used the Spenserian stanza in "The Village Minstrel" (the title poem of the 1821 collection) as well as in many of the poems of *The Shepherd's Calendar* (which owes more to Spenser than stanza and title).

[3] John Clare, *Letters,* 73, 85, 135, 136, 147, 175, 110, 147, 157-58, 165, 208.

[4] Referring to the three separate buildings at High Beech, Geoffrey Grigson, *Poems of John Clare's Madness,* 363, reports that "Leppit's Hill Lodge housed the incipients, the convalescents, and the partially deranged."

[5] *Allen versus Dutton* documents the suit brought by Dr. Matthew Allen to vindicate himself against Richard Dutton who had alleged malpractice in the treatment of Mrs. Frances Louise Dutton during her stay as a patient in his asylum.

[6] When Cyril Redding visited Clare in May 1841, he found him lucid and "communicative." The only sign of "mental eccentricity," Redding reported, was his mention of an engagement as a prize-fighter, which was "brought in abruptly, and abandoned with equal suddenness" (Storey, *Critical Heritage,* 248) Later, at Northampton, February 1847, Clare told his visitors that Byron had written a lengthy review of *Poems Descriptive of Rural Life* (it had been reviewed by Octavius Gilchrist). By 1850, according to the account of G. J. de Wilde, Clare was quoting from *Childe Harold* and Shakespeare passages which he declared to be his own (Grigson 35, 42-43; Storey, *Critical Heritage,* 266).

FICTION

The Spectator (essay date 1866)

SOURCE: "Madness in Novels," in *The Spectator,* Vol. 39, Feb. 3, 1866, pp. 134-35.

[*In the following essay, the anonymous critic examines the trend of depicting madness in novels. The critic maintains that in novels such as* St. Martin's Eve *and* The Clyffards of Clyffe, *madness is used as a tool to disguise the lack of art in the novel.*]

The hint given by Miss Braddon has been very quickly taken. For her purpose it was necessary to strengthen the old machinery of novel-writing, to introduce changes more frequent, acts more unaccountable, catastrophes more violent and appalling. She did not wish, being artist after her kind, to introduce these things absolutely without explanation, and yet where was the explanation to be found? The world, strangely tolerant of supernatural machinery in real life, half inclined to believe in instructions from the dead and messages from above, in people who can float through the air and people for whose sake the souls of the just are willing to proclaim themselves arrant fools, is nevertheless very intolerant of the supernatural in novels. If any young lady kills somebody because an angel told her to do it, which, granted the angelic command, might not be an unnatural proceeding, we simply shut the book, and refuse to read anything its author may subsequently have to produce. On the other hand, the author cannot avail himself of the old instrument, self-will as developed among those who never felt any external restraint. Gilles de Retz would simply be disgusting in a modern novel. If the tyrannous baron in a story sends retainers to kill his daughter's low-born lover, we unconsciously inquire why the lover does not apply to the police. Even the machinery of passion must be kept within due bounds. The nineteenth century believes in love and jealousy, and in a feeble way even in hate, but it is aware nevertheless that the mental concentrativeness out of which these passions spring is in this age rare, that it is hard for John to hate Thomas up to the point of killing him if John reads the *Times* every morning at breakfast, that when there are ten Jills for one Jack love can hardly be intensely individual, that jealousy, of all passions, dies amid a multiplicity of interests and pursuits. It believes in fact in Trollope rather than in Mrs. Radcliffe. The sensationalist was at fault, for to make a sensational novel "harrowing" there must be motive, impulse, human act, and human suffering, as well as mere incident. To "bring your 'art to your mouth" there must be a soul as well as a life in peril. A tumble down a well is nothing, a wife who throws her husband down one is much. One does not tumble down wells, but in the murder one may, if it is only artistically told, recognize the undeveloped wild beast in one's own heart. Miss Braddon perceived this, and it is to her credit that she discerned a mode of restoring the lost sensational effect to character. Madness may intensify any quality, courage, or hate, or jealousy, or wickedness, and she made Lady Audley mad. Thenceforward she was released from the irksome *régime* of the probable. Nobody could say that a yellow-haired goddess, surrounded with every luxury, and delighting in them all, fond of dress, and furniture, and high feeding, with intense appreciation of art, and of art in its domesticated form, would not for very refinement push her husband down a well or burn a village inn. Who knows what a mad woman would or would not do? Who realizes her impulses, or those wild temptations which are not impulses, which so far from developing the character, are so unlike it that the Oriental world to this day holds madness and possession synonymous, and reverences the mad. Probability became unnecessary, *vraisemblance* a burden, naturalness a mistake in art, everything was possible, and the less possible the emotion the greater the surprise and pleasure.

It was a great discovery, and novelists have not been slow to seize it. Here is Mrs. H. Wood in want of a strongly sensational machinery. She wants to paint jealousy in its extreme forms, and she has not of course the power to create Othello, or the art to paint, as Thackeray or Trollope might have done, the morbid passion in its naturalistic nineteenth-century dress. She could not paint the being who should commit murder before the eyes of his audience and seem not only natural but even noble, and still less could she draw the figure of to-day, in whom all passions ought to be lukewarm, yet who can be made by this feeling murderous in purpose, can be provoked to taunt, and bite, and starve, and slander the victim of his animosity, who can think murder and do it provided only he or she is not called on to use the dagger—the spurting blood would spoil her dress—or offer the bowl—Herapath would say what it was made of. But Mrs. Wood can, being familiar with medical lore, make a mad woman do anything. If any ordinary novelist made an ordinary woman do what Charlotte Norris does in *St. Martin's Eve*,—fascinate the man she loves, then hate his child, and then either burn to death the

poor infant of four years old who loves her, or seeing him on fire leave him to burn, we should condemn her as ignorant of the first truths of the human heart, and her story as a meaningless tissue of improbabilities. But then Charlotte Norris is mad, secretly mad, and an access of jealousy brings out homicidal mania. She has been born just after her father has gone mad, and displayed his madness in a fit of raging jealousy, and her mother has striven through life to keep her from marrying at all. The idea of her congenital insanity—which, by the way, in a physiological point of view is badly put, the father having been sane till just before her birth—is kept carefully before the reader, and he throughout expects from it some such crime as he is barely aware throughout the last volume has been committed. All therefore seems to him natural,—the horrible hatred of the stepchild, the equally horrible detestation of the nurse who in delirious ravings has declared her suspicious of her mistress's crime, and the calm worldly demeanour through it all. We say it is natural, but at all events the unnaturalness disappears, for no one except Dr. Forbes Winslow knows what is natural in a patient with intermittent lunacy taking the form of jealousy on behalf of another. Granted her data, Mrs. Wood has worked out her story well, but then her data exclude art as much as the data of the novelists who used to employ ghosts, and revengeful Italians, and secret passages, and all the rest of it, to produce impossible or exaggerated results. As a picture of a mad woman cursed with an invisible form of madness *St. Martin's Eve* is not good, as a story of crime dictated by undiscovered mania it seems natural, and that being the one quality it would otherwise lack, it may be pronounced a good novel. It curdles the blood without exciting the feeling of contempt.

The author of *The Clyffards of Clyffe* has gone farther. In his story everybody is mad except the first hero and his betrothed. The chief sufferer is insane evidently, and the second hero, the bad heroine has helped to keep a madhouse, and has insanity lurking in her veins, and both the bad villains are mad doctors, and make a trade of torture. A lurid horror is thrown over the drama, such as a Greek tragedian would have obtained from the presence of his inevitable [*Ananke*, necessity] the remorseless fate pressing equally upon the evil and the good. Every one either is mad, or fears he may be mad, or is sought in love in order to keep away madness, or drives a debasing trade in the sufferings of the mad, and of course everything is possible. It is possible that a man might believe his own wife the haunting spirit of his ancestral home, possible that his mad son might hunt by night as a wild eccentricity, possible that the stepmother might, with insanity lurking in her, plot or carry out any extent of murders. It is possible that a madhouse-keeper given to torture might taunt his victim as he hung from the cliff, possible to the excited reader that he might hate a crab till he dug for him in the sand in such a position that a rock fell on his arm and held him fast to die of exposure and starvation. What *is* impossible in an asylum, and Clyffe is merely an asylum without apparent keepers? Such incidents told by a strong pen of course attract, just as a horrible newspaper report attracts, and *The Clyffards* will have readers. We do not object, except when we are told that there is high art in such books. There is not, for the very object of using such a machinery is to conceal the absence of art, the inability to invest human motives, and natural impulses, and acts, and incidents such as we see around us with sufficient interest to enchain the reader. The infinite majority of civilized persons are not mad, very few of them are murderers. Not many of them are adulterers, or haters, or madly jealous, or permeated with any passion save that of getting on, and being in their different ways reasonably happy. True art, as it seems to us, would depict this majority and interest us in them, make us see the differences of pale colours, and follow the feeble *nuances* of gesture, and appreciate the chasms created by apparently faint disparities of culture, and we have artists among us who can do all this. But then we do not deny that there is an art in depicting the unnatural, an art shown in conceptions like Fuseli's, an art which may rivet the spectator not in what it sees, but in the thought of what it would see were all the conditions of art reversed. There is power in *Vathek* as well as *Hamlet,* and we complain only when the one is raised by false criticism to the level of the other. Granted an atmosphere in which light does not elicit colour, and *St. Martin's Eve* and *The Clyffards of Clyffe* are singularly well painted.

Barbara Hill Rigney (essay date 1978)

SOURCE: "'The Frenzied Moment': Sex and Insanity in *Jane Eyre,*" in *Madness and Sexual Politics in the Feminist Novel,* University of Wisconsin Press, 1978, pp. 13-37.

[*In the following essay, Rigney maintains that in Charlotte Bronte's* Jane Eyre, *Bronte suggests an association between sexuality and the loss of one's identity, and consequently, one's sanity.*]

. . . the lunatic asylum is yellow.

On the first floor there were
women sitting, sewing;
they looked at us sadly, gently,
answered questions.

On the second floor there were
women crouching, thrashing,
tearing off their clothes, screaming;
to us they paid little attention.

On the third floor
I went through a glass-panelled
door into a different kind of room.
It was a hill, with boulders, trees, no houses.

. . . the air
was about to tell me
all kinds of answers.

Margaret Atwood's "Visit to Toronto with
Companions," *The Journals of Susanna Moodie*

> In the deep shade, at the further end of the room, a figure ran backwards and forwards. What it was, whether beast or human being, one could not, at first sight, tell: it grovelled, seemingly on all fours; it snatched and growled like some strange wild animal: but it was covered with clothing; and a quantity of dark, grizzled hair, wild as a mane, hid its head and face.[1]

Charlotte Brontë presents this vision of desexed and dehumanized insanity in *Jane Eyre* as Bertha Mason, Rochester's lunatic wife. For ten years, she has been hidden and confined in a denlike room in the attic of Thornfield Hall, where she paces and snarls and howls her tragic and preternatural laugh. Her form is grotesque; her eyes are "red balls," her face "bloated" and "purple" (370). Madness has caused this metamorphosis from human into animal, for Bertha was once "the boast of Spanish Town for her beauty" (389).

Critical interpretations of Bertha's symbolic functions in *Jane Eyre* are varied and sometimes contradictory. For traditional critics who see the novel as a form of religious allegory, the mad woman represents the evil in Rochester's soul from which he must be purified by purgatorial fires and the ministrations of a devout woman in the archetypal pattern of sin, suffering, and redemption.[2] In Freudian terms, Bertha is the evil-mother figure who prevents Jane's sexual union with the fatherlike Rochester,[3] or she is seen to embody the idlike aspects of Rochester's psyche for which he suffers symbolic castration, blindness being the punishment for sexual crime since Oedipus.[4]

However, Bertha is as much a doppelgänger for Jane as for Rochester: she serves as a distorted mirror image of Jane's own dangerous propensities toward "passion," Brontë's frequent euphemism for sexuality. Bertha embodies the moral example which is the core of Brontë's novel—in a society which itself exhibits a form of psychosis in its oppression of women, the price paid for love and sexual commitment is insanity and death, the loss of self. Female ontological security and psychological survival in a patriarchal Victorian age, Brontë maintains, can be achieved only through a strong feminist consciousness and the affirmation of such interdependent values as chastity and independence.

Many modern psychologists, like R. D. Laing, state that societies themselves can manifest symptoms of psychosis.[5] The Victorian social system, as described by Helene Moglen in her biography of Brontë, reflects a collusive madness in its sexual politics:

> The advent of industrialization and growth of the middle class was accompanied by a more diffuse yet more virulent form of patriarchy than any that had existed before. As men became uniquely responsible for the support of the family, women became "possessions," identified with their "master's" wealth. The status of the male owner derived from the extent of his woman's leisure time and the degree of her emotional and physical dependence upon him. Sexual relationships followed a similar pattern of dominance and submission. Male power was affirmed through an egoistic, agressive, even violent sexuality. Female sexuality was passive and self-denying. The woman, by wilfully defining herself as "the exploited," as "victim," by seeing herself as she was reflected in the male's perception of her, achieved the only kind of control available to her. Mutuality was extraordinarily difficult, if not impossible, to achieve.[6]

All male characters in *Jane Eyre,* to a greater or lesser extent depending on their area of influence, are agents of such a sexually oppressive system. John Reed, the Reverend Brocklehurst, Rochester, and St. John Rivers, each of whom is dominant in one of the successive landscapes which make up the novel's progress, become a single symbol of tyranny as they share a common conscious or subconscious desire to render Jane an object, a Bertha, something less than a human being. Brontë indicates that, were Jane to succumb, to allow her will to be usurped, she as a sexual and human identity would cease to exist, just as Bertha Mason has ceased to exist in both human and sexual terms.

Jane first learns about female powerlessness from her guardian's son, who is also her cousin, John Reed. Like most of Brontë's male characters, he is the sole male in a female community, the members of which accept the role of self-abnegation deemed rational for women by society, and accordingly pamper and indulge their male relative. Jane, for a time, grudgingly assumes the traditional role, as John summons her to receive punishment for an imagined crime:

> Habitually obedient to John, I came up to his chair: he spent some three minutes in thrusting out his tongue at me as far as he could without damaging the roots: I knew he would soon strike, and while

dreading the blow, I mused on the disgusting and ugly appearance of him who would presently deal it. . . . (7)

But Jane is not always "rational" and must retaliate against such obvious sexual threats: "Wicked and cruel boy! . . . You are like a murderer—you are like a slave driver—you are like the roman emperors!" (8) She bloodies John's nose and is punished, just as Bertha is later to be punished for analogous acts of revenge, by confinement. During her imprisonment in "the red room," significantly a color associated with passion and a place associated with her uncle's death, Jane experiences a "species of fit" (16), a temporary madness and loss of consciousness. Jane's own reflection in the great mirror which dominates the room contributes to her hysteria.

Moglen describes this episode as one in which "the principle of irrationality is given concrete form,"[7] and in which Jane "loses her sense of the boundaries of her identity."[8] Mrs. Reed tells Jane that she can be liberated only "on the condition of perfect submission and stillness" (16), that is, on the condition of "sane" behavior.

Reverend Brocklehurst is also a lone male oppressor in a female society, that of Lowood Institution. Jane's first impression of him is one of tremendous phallic impact: he was "a black pillar . . . a straight, narrow, sable-clad shape standing erect on the rug: the grim face at the top was like a carved mask, placed above the shaft by way of capital" (33). For the second time, Brontë associates male sexuality with cruelty and even death. But unlike John Reed, who only seems to Jane to be a murderer, Brocklehurst is in fact guilty of indirectly causing the deaths of numbers of his charges at the school. He starves their bodies, chastizes their souls with threats of damnation and hellfire, symbolically desexes them by cutting their hair, and generally forces them into submission. Jane escapes the contagious typhoid which kills many of the debilitated inmates of Lowood by a self-imposed isolation in the surrounding woods and valleys.

An analogous withdrawal, and also self-imposed, will again save Jane from annihilation, this time psychological, in the next phase of the novel. Thornfield Hall is dominated by the Byronic figure of Rochester, again the only male in residence. In spite of the fact that Rochester is at times gratuitously cruel in his attempts to provoke Jane's jealousy, that he lies on a number of occasions, and that he is attempting the social and religious crime of bigamy, Jane is profoundly tempted to surrender her very self to the magnetism, the sexuality, the male charisma that is Rochester. Brontë has frequently indicated that Jane's longing for love is so intense as to be self-destructive. Jane has confided to her friend Helen Burns:

. . . if others don't love me, I would rather die than live—I cannot bear to be solitary and hated, Helen. Look here; to gain some real affection from you, or Miss Temple, or any other whom I truly love, I would willingly submit to have the bone of my arm broken, or to let a bull toss me, or to stand behind a kicking horse, and let it dash its hoof at my chest. . . . (80)

Brontë's own letter to the beloved Monsieur Heger bespeaks a painfully similar state of emotion.

I know that you will be irritated when you read this letter. You will say once more that I am hysterical (or neurotic)—that I have black thoughts, etc. So be it, monsieur, I do not seek to justify myself; I submit to every sort of reproach. All I know is, that I cannot, that I will not, resign myself to lose wholly the friendship of my master. I would rather suffer the greatest physical pain than always have my heart lacerated by smarting regrets. If my master withdraws his friendship from me entirely I shall be altogether without hope; if he gives me a little—just a little—I shall be satisfied—happy; I shall have a reason for living on, for working.

Monsieur, the poor have not need of much to sustain them—they ask only for the crumbs that fall from the rich man's table. But if they are refused the crumbs they die of hunger.[9]

Similar images of hunger and starvation recur throughout *Jane Eyre.* Margot Peters, in *Charlotte Brontë: Style in the Novel,* sees such references as indicative of Jane's sexual and emotional deprivation.[10] Frequent references to cold and the desire for warmth serve the same function. But the fire that is Rochester's passion, and Jane's as well, becomes volcanic in its intensity: like Brocklehurst's hellfire, it consumes rather than warms and is thus perceived by Brontë as ultimately dangerous.

Brontë's frequent use of fire symbolism to represent passion and sexuality also has psychological significance. Laing has written in *The Divided Self* that ontologically insecure people are in constant dread of what he calls "engulfment," the sense that one may lose one's self in the identity of another. This fear, writes Laing, is often expressed in images of both burning and drowning: "Some psychotics say in the acute phase that they are on fire, that their bodies are being burned up . . . [they] will be engulfed by the fire or the water, and either way be destroyed."[11] It is significant that both Brocklehurst and St. John Rivers threaten Jane with the fires of damnation, that Helen *Burns* dies an early and sacrificial death, and that Rochester frequently invites Jane to sit with him by the fire where both his touch and his glance burn like coals. Bertha Mason dies as the result of a conflagration she herself has set. Drowning, too, is a concern of

Jane's: " . . . the waters came into my soul; I sank in deep mire: I felt no standing; I came into deep waters: the floods overflowed me" (375). Among Jane's paintings displayed to Rochester, presumably revelations of her inner feelings, is one in which "a drowned corpse glanced through the green water" (153).

It becomes increasingly apparent that what Brontë fears for Jane is that marriage with Rochester will not be a union of equals, but rather a loss of self, an engulfment in the identity of another, just as it was for Bertha Mason. Laing describes a similar fear, which he again attributes to the psychotic personality:

If one experiences the other as a free agent, one is open to the possibility of experiencing oneself as an *object* of his experience and thereby of feeling one's own subjectivity drained away. One is threatened with the possibility of becoming no more than a thing in the world of the other, without any life for oneself, without any being for oneself. In terms of such anxiety, the very act of experiencing the other as a person is felt as virtually suicidal.[12]

Jane's extreme sense of ontological insecurity, however, need not necessarily be labeled psychotic, as it is surely justified by Rochester's behavior during their courtship period. On hearing from Rochester that she is to become "Jane Rochester," to lose her very name, Jane states that "the feeling, the announcement sent through me, was something stronger than was consistent with joy—something that smote and stunned: it was, I think, almost fear" (325). Rochester becomes progressively more possessive, less cognizant of Jane as a human being with individual tastes and preferences. Despite Jane's remonstrances, he insists on extravagant gifts which serve to emphasize her economic powerlessness: "The more he bought me, the more my cheek burned with a sense of annoyance and degradation" (338).

The image of the slave, notable in Jane's encounter with John Reed, recurs frequently in her relationship with Rochester: "I thought his smile was such as a sultan might, in a blissful and fond moment, bestow on a slave his gold and gems had enriched. . . . " (339) Rochester threatens in response to Jane's withdrawal: " . . . it is your time now, little tyrant, but it will be mine presently: and once I have fairly seized you, to have and to hold, I'll just—figuratively speaking—attach you to a chain, like this (touching his watch guard)" (341). In the next chapters, Jane will witness Rochester seizing a violent Bertha and binding her with rope.

And, as in Jane's encounters with John Reed and Brocklehurst, Brontë again makes the association of sex and literal death. Rochester's love song to Jane intimates they will die together. Jane replies, "What did he mean by such a pagan idea? *I* had no intention of dying with him—he might depend on that" (344). Bertha's fate will confirm Jane's fear: Rochester paradoxically becomes both rescuer and killer as, in his very efforts to save Bertha, he precipitates her suicidal leap into the flames.

Virginia Woolf, too, saw Rochester as a figure of devastation, attributing his characterization to Brontë's own personal suffering. Woolf writes in *A Room of One's Own:*

> The portrait of Rochester is drawn in the dark. We feel the influence of fear in it; just as we constantly feel an acidity [in Brontë] which is the result of oppression, a buried suffering smouldering beneath her passion, a rancour which contracts these books, splendid as they are, with a spasm of pain.[13]

Brontë fears for Jane's psychological survival as she apparently feared for her own, as is indicated in a letter written to her friend Ellen Nussey:

> My good girl, "une grande passion" is "une grande folie" . . . no young lady should fall in love till the offer has been made, accepted—the marriage ceremony performed and the first half year of wedded life has passed away—a woman may then begin to love, but with great precaution—very coldly—very moderately—very rationally—if she ever loves so much that a harsh word or a cold look from her husband cuts her to the heart—she is a fool—if ever she loves so much that her husband's will is her law—and that she has got into the habit of watching his looks in order that she may anticipate his wishes, she will soon be a neglected fool.[14]

It is possible that Rochester's need to reduce Jane to the state of object indicates an insecurity of his own. Jane's very virginity and inexperience are perhaps the qualities which most attract Rochester because he perceives them to be those most opposite to Bertha's. Bertha's sexuality, her capacity for passion, apparently presented Rochester with real difficulties. Bertha possessed, Rochester tells Jane, "neither modesty, nor benevolence, nor candour, nor refinement in her mind or manners" (389). She was "coarse and trite, perverse and imbecile" (390). "Her vices sprang up fast and rank," and she demonstrated "giant propensities," being "intemperate and unchaste." Her nature was "the most gross, impure, depraved I ever saw" (391). Rochester comes to despise Bertha's very geographical origin, its lush, tropical refulgence being associated with her sexual personality.

Adrienne Rich, in an article entitled "*Jane Eyre:* Temptations of a Motherless Woman," provides a possible explanation for Rochester's attitude toward his wife:

The 19th century loose woman might have sexual feelings, but the 19th century *wife* did not and must not. Rochester's loathing of Bertha is described repeatedly in terms of her physical strength and her violent will—both unacceptable qualities in the 19th century female, raised to the nth degree and embodied in a monster.[15]

Rochester further inadvertently reveals what might be seen as his own sexual inadequacy as he explains to Jane his chain of mistresses: "I tried dissipation—never debauchery: that I hated, and hate" (397). Moglen's psychosexual analysis of the Byronic hero in general is illuminating in Rochester's case: "Always intrinsically connected to man's insecurity concerning his own sexuality, the fear of women is particularly pronounced in the psychology of the Byronic hero whose need to prove his masculinity by sexual conquest drives him to extremes of behavior."[16]

To preserve his own sexual identity, Rochester must rob Jane of hers. He insists on associating Jane with the supernatural rather than with the natural, that is, the sexual. He refers to her repeatedly as "angel," "fairy," "elf," "spirit," and tells little Adele that he will take Mademoiselle to the moon to live in an alabaster cave. Even Adele is skeptical, knowing that a real Jane is preferable to an idealized image. Rochester also emphasizes the contrast between Jane and Bertha, the purity of one and what he sees as the result of gross sexuality in the other, as he calls upon assembled wedding guests to witness his justification for bigamy:

> That is *my wife*. . . . And *this* is what I wished to have . . . this young girl, who stands so grave and quiet at the mouth of hell, looking collectedly at the gambols of a demon. I wanted her just as a change after that fierce ragout . . . look at the difference! Compare these clear eyes with the red balls yonder—this face with that mask—this form with that bulk. . . . (371)

Bertha at this point, however, can hardly be seen as a sexual being, her very sexual identity having been lost with her claim to humanity. Jane later accuses Rochester: "You are inexorable for that unfortunate lady: you speak of her with hate—with vindictive antipathy. It is cruel—she cannot help being mad." Rochester counters, "If you were mad, do you think I should hate you?" and Jane responds, "I do indeed, sir" (384).

Nearly as complex and dangerous as Rochester is St. John Rivers, the clergyman master of Moor's End, yet another female community. St. John's masculine attractiveness, like Rochester's, poses a temptation for a sexually deprived Jane:

> I can imagine the possibility of conceiving an inevitable, strange, torturing kind of love for him:

because he is so talented; and there is often a certain heroic grandeur in his look, manner, and conversation (531).

But she also knows, from previous experience and from intuition, that love threatens the self:

> In that case, my lot would become unspeakably wretched. He would not want me to love him; and if I showed the feeling, he would make me sensible that it was a superfluity. . . . It is better, therefore, for the insignificant to keep out of his way; lest, in his progress, he should trample them down (531).

St. John, like his predecessors, is seen as a potential murderer, both of the mind and of the body. On a literal level, St. John seeks to lead Jane to a missionary life in India, a place of such extreme climate, Jane feels, as to assure her an early death. "God did not give me my life to throw away," she tells St. John, "and to do as you wish me would, I begin to think, be almost equivalent to committing suicide" (528).

At the same time that he wishes to burn her body in India, St. John wishes to freeze her soul by denying her physical love. In his stern Calvinism, reminiscent of Brocklehurst's, St. John would deny Jane's sexual and human self by binding her in a loveless and presumably sexless marriage. "Would it not be strange," Jane asks herself, "to be chained for life to a man who regarded one but as a useful tool?" (531) As the predominant image for Rochester is fire, so St. John is associated with ice—both extremes threaten death or the loss of identity, sexual and psychological.

The slave image becomes associated with St. John as it has with other male characters. "His kiss was like a seal affixed to my fetters," Jane says (509). And again: "By degrees, he acquired a certain influence over me that took away my liberty of mind" (508). St. John, like Rochester, is seen in fact as threatening the self with engulfment:

> I was tempted to cease struggling with him—to rush down the torrent of his will into the gulf of his existence, and there lose my own. I was almost as hard beset by him now as I had been once before, in a different way, by another. I was a fool both times (534).

Pushed to the extreme by St. John's insistence on marriage, Jane cries out, "If I were to marry you, you would kill me. You are killing me now" (526). St. John, reflecting his society's attitude that woman's role is to surrender to the male will, reproves Jane: "Your words are such as ought not to be used—they are violent, unfeminine. . . . " (526-27)

These very charges are those brought repeatedly against Bertha Mason. Critics have frequently seen her as "unfeminine"—as either androgynous or as a kind of parody of masculinity. Terry Eagleton in his study of the Brontës, for example, sees Bertha partly as a projection of Jane's psyche, yet, "since Bertha is masculine, black-visaged and almost the same height as her husband, she appears also as a repulsive symbol of Rochester's sexual drive."[17] Moglen, for another, describes Bertha in this way: " . . . an androgynous figure, she is also the violent lover who destroys the integrity of the self; who offers the corruption of sexual knowledge and power—essentially male in its opposition to purity and innocence."[18]

Certainly Bertha's violent behavior—rending male antagonists with her very teeth—can be called "unfeminine." She has not, however, been masculinized, but rather desexed altogether, symbolically castrated in the same way that Jane's sexual self has been repeatedly threatened by Rochester and others. Bertha's opposition to "purity and innocence," too, is questionable. It is worthy of note that she attacks male figures, never her female keeper, Grace Poole, or Jane, though she enters Jane's room and leans above her sleeping form. It is on this night that Bertha tears Jane's wedding veil, which Jane herself has said is a symbol of "nothing save Fairfax Rochester's pride" (355). Finally, Bertha is the agent for Rochester's purification as well as his fall.

Perhaps Bertha's madness quite literally has a method, and, as Grace Poole has said, "it is not in mortal discretion to fathom her craft" (370). She behaves in such an "unfeminine" manner as many "feminine" people, like Jane herself, might find possible only in fantasy. Perhaps Brontë even suggests, with the depiction of the ebony crucifix on the cabinet door which hides the entrance to Bertha's den, an identification with the scapegoat aspect of the dying Christ (264).

But such an identification for Bertha is, at best, tenuous and possibly subconscious on Brontë's part. The figure of Bertha is, after all, a warning and not a model. A more sympathetic view of Bertha and a reinterpretation of her insanity occur in Jean Rhys's novel *Wide Sargasso Sea*.[19] Rhys has rewritten the mad sequences from *Jane Eyre* from Bertha's point of view, allowing her to tell her own story from the account of her childhood in the West Indies through her marriage to Rochester and her eventual breakdown and confinement at Thornfield Hall. Rhys's Bertha, unlike Brontë's, is delicate in her appearance and feminine in her behavior. Even the name "Bertha," declared to be solely Rochester's appellation for her, is changed to the more musical "Antoinette." Rhys also dismisses the allegations made by Brontë's Rochester that Bertha's insanity is hereditary, and provides excellent alternative causes for both Antoinette's and her mother's psychoses. The mother has suffered a series of atrocities during a native uprising; Antoinette has undergone Rochester's prudish and cruel rejection of her passion for him. Rhys's Rochester is the unmitigated villain as he consciously inflicts the most insidious forms of mental torture.

In her imprisonment at Thornfield Hall, Antoinette is more pathetic than bestial, her periods of violence clouded by amnesia so that we never see her at her worst. She becomes more and more the lost child, the wronged innocent. Her fault, however, is the same as that of Brontë's Bertha—she has unreservedly surrendered to her passion for Rochester. Rhys's character, then, shares with Brontë's this basic similarity: they are both vehicles for the essentially feminist message that, whatever the sexual ethos, there is a danger of the loss of self when self-love and self-preservation become secondary to love for another.

In Brontë's novel Jane first sees Bertha's face reflected in a mirror, and a wall, after all, is all that separates Jane from Bertha in the setting for one of Brontë's most overtly feminist and didactic statements. Jane, like her double, paces the third floor of Thornfield Hall, longing for some unnameable form of liberty, experiencing a "restlessness" which would be deemed improper, even irrational, for the Victorian woman:

> Who blames me? Many no doubt; and I shall be called discontented. I could not help it: the restlessness was in my nature; it agitated me to pain sometimes. Then my sole relief was to walk along the corridor of the third story, backwards and forwards. . . .

> It is vain to say human beings ought to be satisfied with tranquility: they must have action; and they will make it if they cannot find it. Millions are condemned to a stiller doom than mine, and millions are in silent revolt against their lot. Nobody knows how many rebellions besides political rebellions ferment in the masses of life which people earth. Women are supposed to be very calm generally: but women feel just as men feel; they need exercise for their faculties, and a field for their efforts as much as their brothers do; they suffer from too rigid a restraint, too absolute a stagnation, precisely as men would suffer; and it is narrow-minded in their more privileged fellow-creatures to say that they ought to confine themselves to making purses and knitting stockings, to playing on the piano and embroidering bags. It is thoughtless to condemn them, or laugh at them, if they seek to do more or learn more than custom has pronounced necessary for their sex (132-33).

The next lines, which so disturbed Virginia Woolf in her reading of *Jane Eyre* and left her at a loss for explanation,[20] describe the laugh of the lunatic in close proximity: "the same peal, the same low, slow ha! ha! which, when first heard, had thrilled me" (133). Ber-

tha, herself one of the "millions fermenting rebellion," longing for "action," and quite obviously suffering from "too rigid a restraint," perhaps laughs, along with Brontë herself, at Jane's naive understatement.

It is a similar kind of undefined restlessness to that Jane experiences which precipitates the temporary insanity of Lucy Snowe, the protagonist of Brontë's *Villette,* a novel which Kate Millett in *Sexual Politics* describes as "too subversive to be popular."[21] Lucy is alone in a girls' school which has been abandoned for the summer vacation when she begins to experience extreme depression, "the conviction that fate was of stone, and Hope a false idol—blind, bloodless, and of granite core."[22] Terrible dreams, Lucy says, "wring my whole frame with unknown anguish" and provide "a nameless experience that had the hue, the mien, the terror, the very tone of a visitation from eternity." Such dreams lead her to the realization that "my mind has suffered somewhat too much; a malady is growing upon it—what shall I do? How shall I keep well?"[23] Lucy, like Jane, does keep well, but only by an exertion of will and an affirmation of the self as indomitable. Kate Millett describes her in this way: "In Lucy one may perceive what effects her life in a male-supremacist society has upon the psyche of a woman. She is bitter and she is honest; a neurotic revolutionary full of conflict, back-sliding, anger, terrible self-doubt, and an unconquerable determination to win through."[24]

Like Lucy, and like Bertha, Jane is, when driven, capable of "unfeminine" outbursts of temper and even of violence, and in these acts, at least partly, lie her survival. The Victorian adjuration to the female, "suffer and be still," is to Brontë's mind yet another weapon of patriarchal domination. Jane has, after all, punched John Reed, and she has told the subservient Helen Burns:

> If people were always kind and obedient to those who are cruel and unjust, the wicked people would have it all their own way: they would never feel afraid, and so they would never alter, but would grow worse and worse. When we are struck at without reason, we should strike back again very hard; I am sure we should—so hard as to teach the person who struck us never to do it again (65).

The adult Jane has hardly changed:

> I know no medium: I never in my life have known any medium in my dealings with positive, hard characters, antagonistic to my own, between absolute submission and determined revolt. I have always faithfully observed the one, up to the very moment of bursting, sometimes with volcanic vehemence, into the other. . . . (511)

Laing's observations on the feelings of the ontologically threatened person are perhaps relevant here. Hate, says

Laing, can be a less disturbing relationship than love because it is somehow less engulfing. Liking a person, Laing writes in *The Divided Self*, can be equal to being *like* that person, or even being the *same* as that person, thus with losing one's own identity. Hating and being hated may therefore be interpreted as less threatening to the sense of self.[25]

Margot Peters, in her biography, remarks on Brontë's own capacity for intense resentment and hatred. Peters quotes Brontë's self-description written in a letter to Ellen Nussey: "I am a hearty hater."[26] Certainly, within the scope of her novel, Brontë is capable of great vengeance. In order to preserve Jane's self from annihilation, Brontë annihilates the oppressors, systematically and thoroughly. John Reed dies a suicide as a result of his own excesses; Brocklehurst is socially discredited and disappears; and St. John, at the novel's end, is soon to find his martyrdom in death. These characters have been rendered strawmen by Jane's assertion of self.

Perhaps the greatest victory is that achieved over Rochester. Jane clearly surpasses her statement (which is also something of a threat) made earlier in the novel:

> I have as much soul as you,—and full as much heart! And if God had gifted me with some beauty, and much wealth, I should have made it as hard for you to leave me, as it is now for me to leave you . . . it is my spirit that addresses your spirit; just as if both had passed through the grave, and we stood at God's feet, equal,—as we are! (318)

Such a claim to equality, addressed in the Victorian age to a male and a male employer at that, is surely insurrection.

Ultimately, however, as Jane seeks out Rochester in the final chapters to find his house in ruins, his body crippled and blinded, his worst fears realized in the depletion of his powers of masculinity, she finds herself his superior rather than his equal. Rochester has leaned on Jane before: at their first meeting when he falls from his horse, later when Bertha sets fire to his bed, and at other intervals of crisis. Now he must formally avow his dependence, "just as if a royal eagle, chained to a perch, should be forced to entreat a sparrow to become its purveyor" (562). Significantly, Rochester now bestows on Jane his watch and chain, that very chain to which he had threatened to attach her during their earlier relationship.

Moglen maintains that, like Brontë's own blinded father whom she nursed as she wrote *Jane Eyre*, Rochester, at the end of the novel, is in need of a mother—not a lover. Jane can assume the role of what Moglen terms "the virginal daughter who has been magically transformed—without the mediation of sexual contact—into the noble figure of the nurturing mother."[27]

Carolyn Heilbrun in *Toward a Recognition of Androgyny* provides a purely political interpretation of Rochester's fall:

> Jane Eyre's demand for autonomy or some measure of freedom echoes politically in the cries of all powerless individuals whether the victims of industrialization, racial discrimination or political disenfranchisement. So we today begin to see that Rochester undergoes, not sexual mutilation as the Freudians claim, but the inevitable sufferings necessary when those in power are forced to release some of their power to those who previously had none.[28]

Whether sexual, political, or psychological, it is a terrible justice which Brontë calls down upon Rochester. "My master" has become "my Edward" and Jane can aggressively announce, "Reader, I married him" (574).

More important than the victories over the male oppressors, and more difficult for Brontë, is the annihilation of the insane doppelgänger, the potential Jane-as-victim. She must be done away with both physically and as a shadow in the mind. Metaphors associating passion with madness, both of which Brontë sees as a loss of self and sexual identity, recur throughout the novel. Early in her relationship with Rochester, Jane warns herself that

> it is madness in all women to let a secret love kindle within them, which, if unreturned and unknown, must devour the life that feeds it; and if discovered and responded to, must lead, *ignis fatuus*-like, into miry wilds whence there is no extrication (201).

In a world so dangerous to the sanity, so oppressive to the sense of self, one means of survival lies in being inaccessible; and chastity is a form of inaccessibility. Jane thus rejects the temptation to become Rochester's mistress:

> I will keep the law given by God; sanctioned by man. I will hold to the principles received by men when I was sane, and not mad—as I am now. . . . If I cannot believe it now, it is because I am insane—quite insane: with my veins running fire, and my heart beating faster than I can count its throbs. Preconceived opinions, foregone determinations, are all I have at this hour to stand by: there I plant my foot (404-5).

Peters describes Jane's chastity as "the source of that self-esteem which can keep her alive."[29] Jane celebrates her own physical and psychological survival:

> . . . let me ask myself one question—which is better?—to have surrendered to temptation; listened to passion; made no painful effort—no struggle;—but to have sunk down in the silken snare; fallen

asleep on the flowers covering it . . . Whether is it better, I ask, to be a slave in a fool's paradise at Marseilles—fevered with delusive bliss one hour— suffocating with the bitterest tears of remorse and shame the next—or to be a village-schoolmistress, free and honest, in a breezy mountain nook in the healthy heart of England?

Yes; I feel now that I was right when I adhered to principle and law, and scorned and crushed the insane promptings of a frenzied moment (459).

Chastity, which Brontë often euphemizes as the "unmined treasure" of the body, and sanity, the mind's treasure, thus become synonomous.

In thus asserting chastity and self, rejecting the self-abnegating role traditional for women, Jane also rejects the authority of the male power structure. She seeks, throughout the novel, another kind of authority—that of the female. Adrienne Rich has suggested that *Jane Eyre* is the story of a search for a literal mother:

Many of the great mothers have not been biological. The novel *Jane Eyre* . . . can be read as a woman-pilgrim's progress along a path of classic female temptation, in which the motherless Jane time after time finds women who protect, solace, teach, challenge, and nourish her in self-respect. For centuries, daughters have been strengthened and energized by nonbiological mothers, who have combined a care for the practical values of survival with an incitement toward further horizons, a compassion for vulnerability with an insistence on our buried strengths. It is precisely this that has allowed us to survive. . . . [30]

The fact that Brontë, like Jane, was motherless lends a poignancy to this search for an actual, literal mother figure. However, unlike Rich, I feel that, within the scope of the novel, such a search is doomed to disappointment. There is hardly a female character in Jane's acquaintance who has not conformed in some way to social expectations for the female. Mrs. Reed, whose energies are consumed in pampering her son, rejects Jane and chooses to assume the role of evil stepmother rather than provide Jane with the nurturing love she longs for. On the occasion of Mrs. Reed's death, later in the novel, Jane reveals: "Many a time, as a little child, I should have been glad to love you if you would have let me" (300). Jane finds some grudging affection, motivated undoubtedly by pity, in the person of Bessie, the maid, whose song of "The Poor Orphan Child," however, serves only to confirm Jane's sense of loss. At Lowood Institution, Jane seeks love and tenderness with Helen Burns, but Helen is solipsistically caught up in her own vision of Christian stoicism and dies a martyr of self-denial, an act which Jane's strong survival instincts would never permit her to emulate.

Miss Temple, the beloved teacher, also in effect abandons Jane when she leaves Lowood to marry a respectable clergyman. Diana and Mary Rivers, the sisters of St. John, arrive on the scene only after they are no longer needed as mother figures, and they too marry and are lost to Jane.

The only mother available to Jane is thus a metaphoric mother, virtually a cosmic force, who lives both in the universe and in the self. Jane sees her clearly for the first time on the night of her abortive wedding to Rochester. She lies alone in her room at Thornfield, as desperately unhappy as she had been in the red room at Gateshead, where there also occurred revelations of a quasi-supernatural nature. Now Jane communicates with the moon itself:

She broke forth as never moon yet burst from cloud: a hand first penetrated the sable folds and waved them away; then, not a moon, but a white human form shone in the azure, inclining a glorious brow earthward. It gazed and gazed on me. It spoke to my spirit: immeasurably distant was the tone, yet so near, it whispered in my heart—

"My daughter, flee temptation!"

"Mother, I will" (407).

The moon here undoubtedly represents, in accordance with long literary tradition, primarily chastity. Yet Brontë's images are never quite so simple. For example, a similar moon often precedes the apparition of the nun in *Villette* whose mysterious life had included some sin, presumably sexual, against her vows. Perhaps Brontë would be more in accord with the Jungian psychologist M. Esther Harding, who devotes her study *Woman's Mysteries* to an analysis of the moon-mother in ancient and modern cultures. Various moon goddesses, says Harding, have represented fertility as well as chastity; they are universally autoerotic, "one-in-themselves," belonging only to themselves.[31] If we can assume such a complexity for Brontë's image, it is possible to conclude that the moon-mother is the voice of the feminist consciousness, a kind of inner voice of sanity which, unlike the traditional patriarchal God to whom Jane frequently pays lip service, affirms self-respect and not self-denial, sexual or otherwise.

Again, as Jane wanders the moors in flight from Rochester, she finds affinity with the cosmic mother rather than with the male God. This time the mother-goddess is represented by the earth rather than by the moon:

I have no relative but the universal mother, Nature: I will seek her breast and ask repose. . . . Nature seemed to me benign and good; I thought she loved me, outcast as I was; and I, who from man could anticipate only mistrust, rejection, insult, clung to her with filial fondness. Tonight, at least, I would be her guest—as I was her child: my mother would lodge me without money and without price (412-13).

Jane is thus so absorbed in her own search for the mother that she at least subconsciously rejects the role of motherhood for herself as being yet another threat to autonomy. Though the novel abounds in images of pregnancy and conception, as Peters has pointed out in *Style in the Novel,*[32] Brontë spares but a few lines for the birth of Jane's own child. We know only that it is a male child who has inherited Rochester's black eyes. Jane's attitude toward Adele has been one of professional indulgence rather than sincere affection, and shortly after Jane's marriage to Rochester Adele is unceremoniously shipped off to school. Also reflective of Jane's reluctance to assume the role of mother herself is her recurring dream of the wailing infant which clings to her neck, strangles her at times, poses a terrifying responsibility in the form of a burden which she is not permitted to lay down, and always forbodes disaster. That which at least partly contributes to Lucy Snowe's mental crisis in *Villette* is her onerous duty as sole caretaker of an idiot child. Moglen attributes such feelings of obvious antipathy to the fact that Brontë's own mother died very probably as the result of excessive child bearing.[33] Ironically, Brontë herself was to die of complications of pregnancy.

Thus, Jane wishes only to be a mother to her *self,* and the authority she has sought in the moon and in the earth is after all but the mother within. Jane, at a moment of severe temptation, asks herself, "Who in the world cares for *you?*" Her immediate recognition is, "*I* care for myself. The more solitary, the more friendless, the more unsustained I am, the more I will respect myself" (404). The female self, for Brontë, is an idea of psychological order; its preservation lies in the sanity of the feminist consciousness.

Notes

[1] Charlotte Brontë, *Jane Eyre,* ed. Jane Jack and Margaret Smith (London: Oxford University Press, 1969), p. 370. All subsequent references are to pages in this edition.

[2] W. A. Craig, *The Brontë Novels* (London: Methuen, 1968), p. 81.

[3] David Smith, "Incest Patterns in Two Victorian Novels," pt. 1, "Her Master's Voice: *Jane Eyre* and the Incest Taboo," *Literature and Psychology* 15 (Summer 1965), 136-44.

[4] Richard Chase, "The Brontës: A Centennial Observance," in *The Brontës: A Collection of Critical Essays,* ed. Ian Gregor (Englewood Cliffs, N.J.: Prentice Hall, 1970), p. 25.

[5] R. D. Laing, *The Politics of Experience* (New York: Random House, 1967), p. 12.

[6] Helene Moglen, *Charlotte Brontë: The Self Conceived* (New York: Norton, 1976), p. 30.

[7] Ibid., p. 110.

[8] Ibid., p. 111.

[9] Winifred Gerin, *Charlotte Brontë: The Evolution of Genius* (London: Oxford University Press, 1967), p. 278.

[10] Margot Peters, *Charlotte Brontë: Style in the Novel* (Madison: University of Wisconsin Press, 1973), p. 108.

[11] R. D. Laing, *The Divided Self* (New York: Random House, 1969), p. 47.

[12] Ibid., p. 49.

[13] Virginia Woolf, *A Room of One's Own* (New York: Harcourt, Brace and World, 1957), p. 76.

[14] Margot Peters, *Unquiet Soul: A Biography of Charlotte Brontë* (New York: Doubleday, 1975), p. 95.

[15] Adrienne Rich, "*Jane Eyre:* Temptations of a Motherless Woman," *MS.* 2, no. 4 (October 1973), p. 98.

[16] Moglen, *Self Conceived,* p. 128.

[17] Terry Eagleton, *Myths of Power: A Marxist Study of the Brontës* (London: Macmillan, 1975), p. 32.

[18] Moglen, *Self Conceived,* pp. 126-27.

[19] Jean Rhys, *Wide Sargasso Sea* (New York: Norton, 1966).

[20] Woolf, *Room,* p. 72.

[21] Kate Millett, *Sexual Politics* (New York: Doubleday, 1969), p. 140.

[22] Charlotte Brontë, *Villette* (New York: Harper & Row, 1972), p. 154.

[23] Ibid., p. 200.

[24] Millett, *Sexual Politics,* p. 192.

[25] Laing, *Divided Self,* p. 47.

[26] Peters, *Unquiet Soul,* p. 19.

[27] Moglen, *Self Conceived,* p. 143.

28 Carolyn Heilbrun, *Toward a Recognition of Androgyny* (New York: Alfred A. Knopf, 1973), p. 59.

29 Peters, *Style in the Novel,* p. 107.

30 Adrienne Rich, *Of Woman Born: Motherhood as Experience and Institution* (New York: Norton, 1976), pp. 252-53.

31 M. Esther Harding, *Woman's Mysteries, Ancient and Modern* (New York: Bantam, 1973), p. 70.

32 Peters, *Style in the Novel,* p. 153.

33 Moglen, *Self Conceived,* p. 21.

Allan Gardner Smith (essay date 1980)

SOURCE: "Charles Brockden Brown," in *The Analysis of Motives: Early American Psychology and Fiction,* Rodopi, 1980, pp. 1-37.

[*In the following essay, Smith studies the manner in which Charles Brockden Brown portrayed madness in his novels. Smith observes that Brown was intensely interested in science and psychology and that through his novels, Brown achieved a deeper understanding of the human mind than that which was offered by contemporary psychology.*]

Scientific Terror

Charles Brockden Brown's *Wieland* begins with an "Advertisement" to the reader. The incidents related, it claims, "are extraordinary and rare. Some of them, perhaps, approach as nearly to the nature of miracles as can be done by that which is not truly miraculous. It is hoped that intelligent readers will not disapprove of the manner in which appearances are solved, but that the solution will be found to correspond with the known principles of human nature."[1] The mysterious power of ventriloquism, Brown said, was extremely rare but well supported by historical evidence. The peculiar conduct of young Wieland he defended by an appeal to "physicians, and to men conversant with the latent springs and occasional perversions of the human mind." One parallel fact in history, he continued, would be a sufficient vindication of the writer, but "most readers will probably recollect an authentic case, remarkably similar to that of Wieland." (This "case" is probably that of James Yates, who murdered his entire family in December 1791; it was reported in the New York *Weekly Magazine* of July 20, 1796.)[2]

Brown's defence is very like that of Edgar Allan Poe in his "Preface" to *Tales of the Grotesque and Arabesque:* "If in many of my productions terror has been the thesis, I maintain that terror is not of Germany, but of the soul—that I have deduced this terror only from its legitimate sources, and urged it only to its legitimate results."[3] From each of these prefaces a question arises: Why are these "gothic" writers so concerned to establish a naturalistic basis for their fictions?

One answer might be that such stances are taken in response to scathing criticism of the "German school" and that they express a genuine desire on the part of the author to illustrate, as Brown suggested in the "Advertisement" to *Wieland,* some important branches of the moral constitution of man, and thus prove useful, instead of merely amusing. But neither the importance of these motives nor the difficulty American writers felt in escaping them fully accounts for the claim to legitimacy.[4]

A more positive answer, which seems to me valid for Brown and Poe, is that scientific progress was intensely interesting to men of this time. One informed person might hope to perform usefully in a number of different areas, as did Benjamin Franklin or Benjamin Rush, and if he did not actually contribute as much as these two, he might at least hope to understand and share in the excitement of new developments. Henry Adams later found the price of this sharing a high one to pay, but for Poe or Brown the sense of being able to join in scientific progress could be stimulating. In a world where, the catch phrase went, it must be allowed that all is wonderful, or nothing is wonderful, science is as interesting as magic. One popularizer of "science" expressed his sense of participation: "Discovery may be nearer to us than we suppose. The enigma in which every point seems to contradict the other, may be rendered clear, perhaps, by one word alone."[5]

[Poe's "one word" was Unity.]

Brown's enthusiasm for science is indicated by his address to the newly formed Belles Lettres Club in 1789 when he enjoined the group to comprehend "science and art within the same circle." His long friendship with Dr. Elihu H. Smith, and the extensive coverage given to scientific developments in Brown's *Monthly Magazine* provide further illustration.[6] W.H. Prescott observed in his *Memoir* of Brown the effect of this penchant in his fiction:

> He may rather be called a philosophical than a poetical writer; for, although he has that intensity of feeling which constitutes one of the distinguishing attributes of the latter, yet in his most tumultuous bursts of passion we frequently find him pausing to analyse and coolly speculate on the elements which have raised it. This intrusion, indeed, of reason, *la raison froide,* into scenes of the greatest interest and emotion, has sometimes the unhappy effect of chilling them altogether.[7]

Prescott's reservation is justified, but Brown's "intrusions" are of great interest as psychological and scientific observations based on considerable information. He was familiar with the writings of Locke and Hume, and he seems to have read the French *Encyclopédie* in the original.[8] In *Wieland* he refers the curious to Erasmus Darwin's *Zoonomia* and Dr. Burney's *Musical Travels,* and in *Ormond* to Count Rumford's *Essays.* For instances of spontaneous combustion Brown sends the reader to the *Journal de Médicine* of February and May, 1783, to the researches of Maffei and Fontana, and to a journal of Florence.[9]

A letter to the Philadelphia *Weekly Magazine,* probably written by Brown as an advertisement to *Sky-Walk* (1798), summed up his ambitions for the use of such erudition:

> A contexture of facts capable of suspending the faculties of every soul in curiosity may be joined with depth of views into human nature and all the subtleties of reasoning. Whether these properties be wedded in the present performance the impartial reader must judge.[10]

In such ambitions we have an explanation of Brown's preference for the peculiar and bizarre in human experience and the dry rationalism which underlies its presentation. (*Sky-Walk* was based upon Indian atrocities and upon somnambulism, themes which he later fashioned into the story of *Edgar Huntley.*)

Wieland's Madness

In *Wieland* (1798), Brown's ambitions were achieved through the use of ventriloquism ("biloquism", as he called it), religious mania, and manipulation of the conventions of the sentimental novel as exemplified in Richardson, Holcroft, Bage, and Godwin.[11]

Wieland's religious mania is foreshadowed by that of his father, whose excessive zeal led to spontaneous combustion and subsequent death. Later we learn that Wieland's maternal grandfather also died through the promptings of maniacal delusion. As Brown claims in a footnote, these instances of hallucination are in line with contemporary medical teaching, in their circumstances and in their hereditary origins. The reference to Erasmus Darwin's *Zoonomia* is more than a mere bolstering of the text with occasional scientific evidence, since in the light of Darwin's study the whole of Wieland's situation is conducive to the particular kind of madness which Carwin's ventriloquism precipitates.

Early in the novel, Clara describes Wieland as of an "ardent and melancholy character." She continues:

> Those ideas which, in others, are casual or obscure, which are entertained in moments of abstraction

and solitude and easily escape when the scene is changed, have obtained an immovable hold upon his mind. The conclusions which long habit have rendered familiar and, in some sort, palpable to his intellect, are drawn from the deepest sources. All his actions and practical sentiments are linked with long and abstruse deductions from the system of divine government and the laws of our intellectual constitution. He is in some respects an enthusiast, but is fortified in his belief by innumerable arguments and subtleties.[12]

In education, Clara noted, Wieland was allowed to follow the guidance of his own understanding, so far as religion was concerned. Darwin had stressed the perils of such freedom, saying that "the violence of action accompanying insanity depends much on the education of the person; those who have been proudly educated with unrestrained passions, are liable to greater fury."[13] Those most liable to insanity, he speculated, "are such as have excess of sensibility."

Darwin's section on "Mania Mutabilis," to which Brown's footnote refers, offers numerous instances of mania, but none of these are hereditary and only some are religious. The most frequent cause of insanity, Darwin says, "arises from the pain of some imaginary or mistaken ideas; which may be termed hallucinatio maniacalis." He offers several examples, of which this one is the most pertinent:

> Miss———, a sensible and ingenious lady, about thirty, said she has seen an angel; who told her, that she need not eat, though all others were under the necessity of supporting their earthly existence by food. After fruitless persuasions to take food, she starved herself to death.—It was proposed to send an angel of a higher order to tell her, that she must begin to eat and drink again. . . . [14]

Brown's footnote, in fact, refers us to the wrong part of Darwin's work. Darwin does argue elsewhere that the disposition to insanity is hereditary and therefore to be induced in some families more easily than others,[15] and his comments on religious mania or "superstitious hope" are those most appropriate to Brown's story. This "maniacal hallucination," says Darwin, "in its milder state produces, like sentimental love, an agreeable reverie, but when joined with works of supererogation, it has occasioned many enormities" such as self-tortures, flagellations, and cruel martyrdoms.[16]

In *Wieland,* the protagonist is driven to murder his wife and children by the following succession of ideas; he has gone to look for his sister Clara whose return is expected at her house and on the way Wieland has what amounts to a revelation of joy:

> The series of my thoughts is easily traced. At first every vein beat with raptures known only to the

man whose parental and conjugal love is without limits, and the cup of whose desires, immense as it is, overflows with gratification. I know not why emotions that were perpetual visitants should now have recurred with unusual energy. The transition was not new from sensations of joy to a consciousness of gratitude. The Author of my being was likewise the dispenser of every gift with which that being was embellished. The service to which a benefactor like this was entitled could not be circumscribed . . .

Wieland's sense of his fortune leads him into a prayer for further enlightenment:

For a time my contemplations soared above earth and its inhabitants. I stretched forth my hands; I lifted my eyes, and exclaimed, "Oh that I might be admitted to thy presence! That mine were the supreme delight of knowing thy will, and of performing it! The blissful privilege of direct communication with thee, and of listening to the audible enunciation of thy pleasure!"

Wishing that some unambiguous token of God's presence would "salute his senses," Wieland enters his sister's house. He is dazzled by an indescribable vision of a heavenly being who intones; "Thy prayers are heard. In proof of thy faith, render me thy wife. This is the victim I choose."[17] After great internal struggle, Wieland rallies his "rebellious heart" and strangles his wife, Catherine.

Brown's account of Wieland's vision is close to Darwin's description of the process involved in a "pleasurable insanity" such as religious fanaticism:

When agreeable ideas excite into motion the sensorial power of sensation, and this again causes other trains of agreeable ideas, a constant stream of pleasurable ideas succeeds, and produces pleasurable delirium. So when the sensorial power of volition excites agreeable ideas, and the pleasure thus produced excites more volition in its turn, a constant flow of agreeable voluntary ideas succeeds; which when thus exerted in the extreme constitutes insanity.[18]

Wieland's suggestibility has been aroused by strange voices and perhaps also by the new book he has received (which, "according to German custom . . . was minute and diffuse, and dictated by an adventurous and lawless fancy"). His thoughts lead him from joy into gratitude, and the pleasure of these sensations induce him to increase his mental efforts, until he wills himself into an hallucinatory state and has his vision. At this point his pleasure subsides and is succeeded by despair, but his delusion is abetted by his extraordinary moral strength. A man with less self-control and power of will would perhaps be unable to hold to his conviction as Wieland does. But his faith in his powers of observation and his rational habits of mind now trap him.

Dr. Benjamin Rush observed that mental derangement could take the form of "murdering impulses." He listed a number of such cases, with the comment that such behaviour is usually unprovoked and sudden, and that the victims are commonly relatives or friends of their killer. Some cases included the murder of children by their parent, and some were committed by persons holding delusive opinions in religion. He added that circumstances of greater and more deliberate cruelty appear here than in common murders, and that it is usual for the action to be followed by confession and the desire for the utmost rigor of punishment.[20]

Brown's description of Wieland and his murderous delusion, so far, is completely in accordance with the current teachings of physicians, and even Wieland's reaction to his deed is in keeping with these opinions, as he passes from ecstasy into despair:

'I lifted the corpse in my arms and laid it on the bed. I gazed upon it with delight. Such was the elation of my thoughts, that I even broke into laughter. . . . '

'For a while I thus soared above frailty. I imagined I had set myself forever beyond the reach of selfishness; but my imaginations were false. This rapture quickly subsided.'

He looks at the body of his wife, but it is no longer the beautiful woman he has loved, and he is overcome by the "livid stains" and hideous deformity he sees: "Alas! these were the traces of agony; the gripe of the assassin had been here!" Wieland now moves into horrified remorse, as his faith deserts him:

"I will not dwell upon my lapse into desperate and outrageous sorrow. The breath of heaven that sustained me was withdrawn, and I sunk into *mere* man. I leaped from the floor; I dashed my head against the wall; I uttered screams of horror; I panted after torment and pain."[21]

However, Wieland is raised again to his supernatural mission: next he murders his children and his faith seems for a time secure. He does not, like those murderers described by Rush, implore the severest penalty. On the contrary, he claims that he will do his best to evade punishment because he has done good, not evil, and he accuses his judges of his own mistake: "You say that I am guilty. Impious and rash! thus to usurp the prerogatives of your Maker! to set up your bounded views and halting reason as the measure of truth!"[22] All men are limited by their need to believe the evidence of their senses—an important theme in *Wieland.*

Clara Wieland also goes mad in the course of the novel and her madness, like Wieland's, agrees with the observations of the physicians. She becomes delirious, understandably enough, after the killings, believing Carwin to be the murderer:

> Carwin was the phantom that pursued my dreams, the giant oppressor under whose arm I was forever on the point of being crushed. Strenuous muscles were required to hinder my flight, and hearts of steel to withstand the eloquence of my fears. In vain I called upon them to look upward, to mark his sparkling rage and scowling contempt. All I sought was to fly from the stroke that was lifted. Then I heaped upon my guards the most vehement reproaches, or betook myself to wailings on the helplessness of my condition.[23]

Contemporary theorists would have missed the note of sexual attraction which underlies Clara's fear of Carwin and is skilfully exploited by Brown to upset the expectations of conventional novel readers, but they were aware that "immoderate suspicion is generally the first symptom" of madness.[24] The idea which causes such madness is generally untrue, a "delirious idea," Darwin calls it, which "cannot be conquered by reason; because it continues to be excited by painful sensation, which is a stronger stimulus than volition."[25] Poor Clara is fated to have her delirious idea replaced by a still worse perception; that her brother is the murderer. This new shock brings her "once more to the brink of the grave." Then the fact that she also has heard the voices, with her knowledge of the family inheritance of madness leads her to despair in the fear that she too might become a killer. She sinks into an inactive and morbid state, which Darwin would have called "melancholia."[26] . . .

Dreams

Much of Brown's writing is concerned with the questions aroused by sleep and dreaming. His characters are often disturbed by horrific or prophetic dreams and, in some cases, by sleep-walking. The narrator of *Edgar Huntly* observes:

> The incapacity of sound sleep denotes a mind sorely wounded. It is thus that atrocious criminals denote the possession of some dreadful secret. The thoughts, which considerations of safety enable them to suppress or disguise during wakefulness, operate without impediment, and exhibit their genuine effects, when the notices of sense are partly excluded and they are shut out from a knowledge of their entire condition.[34]

For the novelist, such a perception may be useful because it allows him to present insights for which the waking consciousness of his characters would not provide justification. It also allows him a degree of subtle

anticipation of the plot. A good example of this device occurs in Clara Wieland's dream, which is interrupted by the mysterious voice. "In my dream," she says, "he that tempted me to my destruction was my brother. . . . What monstrous conception is this? My brother?" She attempts to repress the idea: "No; protection, and not injury, is his province. Strange and terrible chimera! Yet it would not be suddenly dismissed. It was surely no vulgar agency that gave this form to my fears. . . . Ideas exist in our minds that can be accounted for by no established laws."[35]

But Brown knows that ideas existing in the mind can indeed be accounted for by established laws. This dream of Clara's, while perhaps occasioned by "uneasiness of posture, or some slight indisposition," is significant because of the intrusion of ideas which would not be permitted by her waking mind. Her sense of impending danger has been awakened by the phenomenon of the voices, first heard by her brother, and by his dangerously calm acceptance of them. In a conversation Clara had attempted to investigate the state of his thoughts on the matter through indirect enquiry. ' "Why," she said, "must the Divine Will address its precepts to the eye?" He smiled significantly. "True," said he, "the understanding has other avenues." ' Then Wieland suggests that there are "twenty suppositions" more probable than deception, but will not elaborate further on the matter. Here is cause for Clara's concern, but she is not able to admit it to herself and it finds expression through the dreams. Rush describes the process:

> there are cases in which the change that is produced in the state of the brain, by means of sleep, affects the moral faculty likewise: hence we sometimes dream of doing and saying things, when asleep, which we shudder at, as soon as we awake.[36]

How is it that Carwin's injunction: "Hold! Hold!" becomes a part of Clara's dream at such a strategic time, when she is at the brink of the gulf? An answer may be found in the work of both Rush and Darwin. Rush says, "the intellects act here without order but they act with uncommon celerity," and thus a day may pass in the course of a minute. Darwin suggests that the reason for this is the absence of volition, which prevents the mind from comparing one thought with another and thus speeds up the succession while disturbing, on Lockean principles, the sense of time. Thus the injunction of "Hold!" finds an appropriate place in the sequence of her thoughts, on the principle of association.

Darwin had a fairly sophisticated theory of the difference caused in the sleeping mind by the lack of the power of volition. Normally, the mind follows trains of association which are quite well established and incorporate some acts of volition within them, as we compare our passing trains of thought with our acquired knowledge of nature. But in sleep the lack of volition causes these habitual connections to be dissevered, and to fall into new "catenations." Therefore dreams display the kind of inconsequence that Brown describes so frequently, often in the form of nightmare. "Incubus," as Darwin calls it, is accounted for by a combination of uneasy sensations and profound sleep. The desire of moving the body is "painfully exerted," but the power of so doing is absent. Clara has such a nightmare during a fire at her home. She dreams that she has been "transported to some ridge of Etna, and made a terrified spectator of its fiery torrents and its pillars of smoke." Clara describes her feeling of powerlessness due to the lack of volition: "However strange it may seem, I was conscious, even during my dream, of my real situation. I knew myself to be asleep, and struggled to break the spell by muscular exertions. These did not avail. . . . "[37]

Sky-Walk was to have been based upon Indian atrocities and somnambulism, ideas later used by Brown in the ingenious plot of *Edgar Huntly*. There are *two* somnambulists in *Edgar Huntly,* and one of them, to the reader's confusion, is the narrator. Although the early psychologists did not claim that somnambulism was quite so common as it seems to be in Brown's "Norwalk", they did describe its features in some detail:

> In this malady the patients have only the general appearance of being asleep in respect of their inattention to the stimulus of external objects, but, like the epilepsies . . . , it consists in voluntary exertions to relieve pain. The muscles are subservient to the will, as appears by the patient's walking about, and sometimes doing the common offices of life. The ideas of the mind are also obedient to the will, because their discourse is consistent, although they answer imaginary questions. The irritative ideas of external objects continue in this malady, because the patients do not run against the furniture of their room; and when they apply their volition to their organs of sense, they become sensible of the objects they attend to, but not otherwise, as general sensation is destroyed by the violence of their voluntary exertions.[38]

Brown's sleepwalkers behave in this manner, and they agree with Darwin's descriptions in another important particular. An interesting aspect of Darwin's model of the mind is his perception of rhythms in physical and (because of his sensationalist theory) mental processes. In fevers, for example, a diurnal rhythm is common; the patient feeling weak at the same time each day. Darwin's theory is that there are two patterns of association of mental and physical actions: *trains* of associated actions, which are progressive, and *circles,* which are repetitive. These trains he compares to the linear epic poem as against the song, with its repeated choruses.[39] All "animal motions," including the motions of

the sense organs, which have occurred at the same time, or in immediate succession, become connected in such a way that when one of them is reproduced, the other has a tendency to accompany or to succeed it.[40] But,

> if any circle of actions is dissevered, either by omission of some of the links, as in sleep, or by an insertion of other links, as in surprise, new catenations take place in a greater or less degree. The last link of the broken chain of actions becomes connected with the new motion which has broken it, or with that which was nearest the link omitted; and these new catenations proceed instead of the old ones. Hence the periodic return of ague fits, and the chimeras of our dreams.[41]

We need not anachronistically invoke theories of neurosis, then, to explain Clithero's regular nightly rambles or his attraction to the site of the elm, and Huntly's nighttime terrors similarly fall into place as a part of the broken circle: "Solitude and sleep are now no more than the signals to summon up a tribe of ugly phantoms. . . . If, by any chance, I should awake and find myself immersed in darkness, I know not what act of desperation I might be suddenly impelled to commit."[42] The fact that Norwalk itself is circular may be a reflection of Darwinist theory, and it is surely no accident that Clithero and Huntly's nightly rambles are also circular. Huntly's adventures bring him around in a geographical circle, back to his starting point where he finds that he himself hid the letters he has been seeking. Thus the relationship established in the early pages of the book between the narrator's mind and the scenes about him develops into a topographical expression of *self-returning, introverted,* and *ineffectual* mental action. Donald Ringe is correct in seeing Huntly's wilderness as a version of a mental labyrinth, and the cave as a metaphor for mental unbalance, but he misses the essential shape of both and thus some of the force of Brown's attack on the desire for knowledge.[43]

Brockden Brown's Extension of Sensationalist Psychology

Brown's method is psychological realism—an attempt to render interior experience as accurately as external actions. I have shown that he knew the principles of contemporary psychology and that he based some key points in his plots upon them, yet it is virtually impossible to convey the intensity with which he focused upon the mental life of his characters and the vast quantity of psychological reference in his novels; to examine his characters in terms of their mental life and to express that life in the language of eighteenth century psychology seems his first principle of fiction. It is time then, to examine some of the broader implications of the psychology that Brown used as they emerge in his novels.

Henry Warfel says that although Brown "drew his incidents and persons as much from books as from life, his emphasis on psychopathic traits adds depth to characters whose range of action is narrow in the physical world."[44] His concentration on the inner world is like Poe's in its focus on brooding and tormented minds. But Brown's own attitude is, as Warfel says, essentially rationalistic and inquisitive, a response to the observation that human life "abounds in mysterious appearances" and that the mind has only its perceptions to prepare its judgments.

Donald Ringe says further that Brown does not accept sensationalist psychology uncritically but uses it rather as a convenient tool. He notices that in *Wieland* the chief problem for the characters is of "discerning the truth that lies behind the appearance of things," and that the action of the novel demonstrates the difficulty they find in drawing correct inferences from the evidence of their senses. Their problem is not simply due to Carwin's ventriloquism because Pleyel, a sane rationalist, draws the wrong conclusions from Clara's journal and her expression as well as from the voices that he hears in the summer house.[45] The rationalist theory fails to take sufficient account of the fallibility of minds and the power of passions; Pleyel is misled by his own strong feelings and is unable to recognise his distortion. In a similar and more disturbing way, Wieland trusts to his own sensations rather than his long knowledge of Clara. He argues that his hearing and vision would be sufficient to persuade him that Clara had fallen into wickedness. In his mania, he accepts his hallucinations as valid sensory evidence, failing to see that these may be as fallible as other sources of knowledge.

Clara Wieland's experience, Ringe argues, is another variation on the theme of sensationalist psychology. She is more willing than Pleyel to accept a supernatural explanation for events, but she is less systematic than Wieland in religious matters and does not brood on them. Her brooding is on the problems of psychology and the difficulty of interpreting sensations correctly. Clara finds that she is unable to provide rational explanations for the dream of her brother and the abyss, the cry of "Hold!", the whispered voices in her closet, and the warning away from the door. She realises that her "actions and persuasions" are at war, that she is somehow made aware of danger while her actions and sensations are those of one wholly unacquainted with it.[46] Correctly, but without any evidence from her senses, she feels that the threat is from Wieland, and she can only conclude that "ideas exist in our minds that can be accounted for by no established laws."[47] The removal of the rational foundation of her consciousness and the consequent lack of security in her relation to the world causes her descent into madness—this, and the powerful stimulus of fear.

The problems of the rationalist-sensationalist view, then, Ringe says, are expressed in two related directions in *Wieland*. Sensations are not reliable, since some characters misinterpret true sensations or are unable to distinguish between true and false sensations. The rationalist is prone to rationalization, the justification of actions inspired by passions through the use of fallacious reasoning. But although Brown is engaged in an attack on the rationalist principles which he adopted in his youth, his probing does not reveal any alternative moral or religious system. Hence, Ringe decides, *Wieland* must be considered "an intellectually truncated book."[48]

But my argument is that although Brown does not offer any alternative "system," he is nonetheless attempting to postulate alternative insights, whereby we see that the more deeply hidden motives of Brown's characters appear to themselves, and to some extent to others, only in the form of dimly felt intuitions, which are often wrong in specific details but correct in general principle. Clara is wrong to be convinced that Wieland is in her closet, but right in fearing that he will be the instrument of impending evil. She is wrong in her later belief that Carwin must be the murderer, but right in feeling that he is instrumental in the Wielands' tragedy. Pleyel is wrong in his suspicions of Clara's behaviour, but somewhat correct in his opinion that Clara is much attracted to Carwin.[49] The problem for Brown, and for other writers who attempted to convey such an insight, was the lack of a systematised vocabulary for conveying information about the deeper processes of mind, and the embarrassing availability of a psychological vocabulary which implied their non-existence. From this follows the juxtaposition of gothic elements with precise scientific language in the fiction of Brown and Poe.

An alternative to the opinion that all human knowledge is reached through the senses and the reason is what used to be called the ideal view. This antithesis emerges derogatively in the preface of a novel which has been shown to be a source for *Wieland*, Cajetan Tschink's *Geisterseher,* translated as *The Victim of Magical Delusion* (1795). The preface reads, in part:

> The sources from which we derive the knowledge of what is good and true, originate from Sensation, Experience, Reflection, Reasoning, and from the genuine accounts we receive of the observations and the experience of others; and we cannot miss the road leading to the Sanctuary of Truth, if we make a proper use of *all* these different sources of knowledge. If we, however, conceive an exclusive attachment to *one* of them, and, for instance, confine ourselves merely to sensation and experience, if we desire to *see* and *feel* those things which cannot be perceived by the senses, but are known to us only through the medium of our understanding; if we, for example, are not satisfied with what

the contemplation of nature, and the gospel teach us of God, but desire to have an immediate, and physical communion with the invisible; we then cannot avoid the deviations of fanaticism, and are easily led to confound our *feelings* and *ideas* with external effects; the effects of our soul with effects produced by superior beings; we believe that we see, hear, and perceive what exists no where but in the imagination; we stray from ourselves and the objects around us, to a world of ideas which is the workmanship of our fancy, and are misled by the vivacity and strength of our feelings, and mistake for *reality* what is merely *ideal.* Thus we dream while we are awake, and sooner or later find ourselves woefully deceived.[50]

This passage, which might be matched by accounts in a score of textbooks, indicates very well the sort of strait-jacket fashioned by eighteenth century Rationalists to deny validity to non-reasoning aspects of the mind. Clara's claim that the will is the tool of the understanding, which is based on the senses, and thus "if the senses be depraved it is impossible to calculate the evils that may flow" is derived from such opinions, and of course, Wieland's religious fanaticism exemplifies them.[51]

But while he accepted such arguments on the surface level, Brown attempted to go beyond them and express covertly the kind of validity which should be assigned to alternative intimations of "reality." In Larzer Ziff's words, Brown and his heroine, Clara, "discover that human behaviour is not what they take, and, in a sense, want it to be, but springs from far dimmer and more turbulent sources."[52] However, Ziff argues that the finale of the story demonstrates the correctness, in the end, of the conventional psychology: senses *are* the initial guides to conduct and the mysterious events have a natural explanation. Ziff thinks that Brown's deviation from the conventional psychology lies in his idea that there may exist not merely *delusion* of the senses but also *depravity* of the senses, as Clara suggests. The idea of depravity is Clara's response to the horrors she vaguely anticipates but cannot rationalize. "The horrors of incest," Ziff writes, and the

> inherited depravity which Clara forces back from the threshold of her consciousness by turning away to think about thinking are not to be explained away by the *tabula rasa.* . . . Wieland's homicidal actions result, finally from causes which are inexplicable scientifically.[53]

Ziff sees Brown's criticism of the *tabula rasa* formulation as a rejection of Lockean and sensationalist "optimism," and a movement towards restatement of the doctrine of original sin, exemplified in Wieland's inherited depravity. Therefore, he claims, Brown "ends his journey by approaching the outskirts of Edward's camp."[54]

It is not here, however, that Brown deviates from the conventional psychology. Such cases as Wieland's had been quite adequately assimilated into the body of psychological knowledge of the time, without disturbing the Lockean foundations. Wieland's is, after all, an extreme case. In any event, the enlightened psychology could, in its extreme determinism, be quite a reasonable basis for a doctrine of original sin working through inherited disposition and environment. In this respect it might be considered a "pessimistic" psychology because of its tendency to undermine theories of free will. Brown's deviation from the conventional psychology lies not in Wieland's delusions but rather in Clara's half-conscious intimation of his mania, in Pleyel's accurate insight into Clara's deep inclinations towards Carwin, and in the description of Carwin's curiosity and will to power over others, together with his ability to rationalise his strange behaviour.

The Limits of Rationality

The model of the mind implicit in Brown's fictional characters and made explicit in statements by them and by their author is one in which the senses are very important but not reliable because they are susceptible to illusions, ill health and the state of the affections.[55] However, most of the characters while aware of the defects of sensory information find themselves unable to do other than believe in the evidence of their own eyes and ears rather than in the testimony of others or in their own past experience. Clara Wieland asks: "Could the long series of my actions and sentiments grant me no exemption from suspicions so foul? Was it not more rational to infer that Carwin's designs had been illicit?" It would have been more rational, and Theodore Wieland claims that he is ready to question his own senses if they should plead against her: but he contradicts this by saying, "Nothing less than my own hearing and vision would convince me, in opposition to her own assertions, that my sister had fallen into wickedness like this.[56] So it seems that the understanding must, as Clara asserts, "fashion its conclusions on the notices of sense."[57] Exactly how this process works Brown never specifies. On the one hand all his characters feel it imperative to think and act in a rational manner by reflecting on the materials supplied by sensation. The rules for this activity are laid down in such popular works as William Brattle's *Logic* (1735) (which was widely used in American schools): "first, nothing is to be admitted as true so long as it includes anything of doubt; second, we should beware of trusting too much to the senses; third, what we perceive we perceive by the mind alone; and fourth, that is true which we perceive clearly and distinctly."[58] Most of Brown's characters seem to subscribe to such a creed. But on the other hand, they seem to lay more stress on the confused thronging of images in their minds than upon the processes of logical thought. Thus Clara: "My mind was thronged by vivid but confused images, and no effort that I made was sufficient to drive them away." And Arthur Mervyn: "I stretched myself on the mattress and put out the light; but the swarm of new images that rushed on my mind set me again instantly in motion. All was rapid, vague, and undefined, wearying and distracting my attention." Henry Colden is similarly afflicted: "Not a moment of undisturbed repose have I enjoyed for the last two months. If awake, omens and conjectures, menacing fears, and half-formed hopes, have haunted and harassed me. If asleep, dreams of agonizing forms and ever-varying hues have thronged my fancy and driven away peace."[59] These minds are victims, not masters, of their thought processes.

Brown's model of the mind implies that association of ideas is the central principle. This process, however, is not shown to be subject to the control of the individual but rather as an autonomous activity which directs the individual. Wieland, for example, is lost in a maze of confused reflection when, "speedily this train was broken. A beam appeared to be darted into his mind which gave a purpose to his efforts," and he realizes the possibility of killing himself.[60] We have already examined the lengthy process of association which leads him to imagine a divine injunction to sacrifice his family; again, he has no power to control the sequence or to deny its conclusions. Most of Clara's reflection consists of following such trains of ideas.[61] In one of the most interesting of these she muses over Pleyel's lateness, then begins to worry that he might have met a violent end, like that of her father. The combination of the images of her lover and her dead father leads her to "a significant association which combines the two notions, that of her brother and the fantasy she has had about him."[62] The direction of a character's thoughts is rather at the mercy of deeply motivated associations than under the conscious control of the will.

At the mercy of its images and associations, the rational mind has a hard time of it. But it is also subject to the "hurricane of passions" and the distortions inherent in introspection. As Henry Colden laments: "Yet, though I have a fuller view of myself than any other can have of me, my imperfect *sight*—that is, my erring judgment—is continually blundering."[63] And illness also has a tremendous effect in engendering mental confusion, delirium or gloomy meditations.[64]

The conjunction of these hazards in the path of reason frequently results in the condition of madness, which is experienced by a remarkably large number of Brown's characters. The roll-call of those who succumb, if only temporarily, to mental derangement includes the elder and younger Wielands, Clara Wieland, Constantia Dudley and Sophia Westwyn's mother in *Ormond,* Watson's father, Susan Hadwin and Arthur Mervyn, Clithero and Edgar Huntley, Philip Stanley in *Clara Howard,* and Henry Colden in *Jane Talbot.* If

the mind is not driven into madness, it is frequently afflicted by a Poe-like inclination to be perverse. Arthur Marvyn notices this trait in himself: "The constitution of my mind," he says," is doubtless singular and perverse; yet that opinion, perhaps, is the fruit of my ignorance. It may by no means be uncommon for men to *fashion* their conclusions in opposition to evidence and *probability,* and so as to feed their malice and subvert their happiness. Thus it was, in an eminent degree, in my case."[65] (This is also the secret motto of *Edgar Huntly.*) Henry Colden is another sufferer from this malady: "And whence," he asks, "this incurable folly?—this rooted incapacity of acting as every motive, generous and selfish, combine to recommend? Constitution; habit; insanity; the dominion of some evil spirit, who insinuates his baneful power between the *will* and the *act.*" Brown is certainly aware of the criticisms which might be levelled at the sensationalist psychology of the Enlightenment.[66] The consequences of this perversity are, for these characters, more or less private, but the figures of Carwin and Ormond develop the idea into a full analysis of the impossibility of rationalist right thinking.

In *Ormond,* "considerations of justice and pity were made, by a fatal perverseness of reasoning, champions and bulwarks of Ormond's most atrocious mistakes."[67] Along with Carwin, who demonstrates a similar ability to arrive at apparently logical but severely misguided conclusions, Ormond is the fullest embodiment of the Godwinian ideas by which Brown is said to have been greatly influenced. Comparison demonstrates the influence very well: Ormond distinguished "between men in the abstract and men as they are. The former were beings to be impelled, by the breath of accident, in a right or wrong road; but whatever direction they should receive, it was the property of their nature to persist in it." Godwin says, in his Preface to *Thoughts on Man:* "We act from motives apprehended by the judgment, but we do not stop at them. Once set in motion, it will not seldom happen that we proceed beyond our original mark."[68] Ormond believes that a man is merely a cog in the social system, activated by external causes: "Man could not be otherwise than a cause of perpetual operation and efficacy. He was part of a machine, and as such had not power to withhold his agency." Again, Godwin is probably the source of this opinion in his argument that: "We shall however unquestionably, as our minds grow enlarged, be brought to the entire and unreserved conviction, that man is a machine, that he is governed by external impulses, and is to be regarded as the medium only through the intervention of which previously existing causes are enabled to produce certain effects."[69]

Ormond shares Godwin's convictions, but through "a fatal perverseness of reasoning" common to many of Brown's characters he distorts their application until he might claim, with Welbeck—"One tissue of iniquity and folly has been my life; while my thoughts have been familiar with enlightened and disinterested principles."[70]

Most of Brown's rationalists are mistaken rather than evil in their attempts to use reason as the sole guide to action. Pleyel and Wieland try to make rational inferences from incorrect information, although their reasoning is fallacious. Pleyel should have given more credit to Clara's history, and Wieland is illogical in his response to Carwin's "biloquism" because "He reflected not that credit should be as reasonably denied to the last as to any former intimation; that one might as justly be ascribed to erring or diseased senses as the other."[71] Wieland ought to have been aware of the perils of religious fanaticism made evident in the death of his father. So he is wrong when he claims that "if I erred, it was not my judgment that deceived me, but my senses."[72]

A contrast to this pattern appears in Constantia Dudley. She is the most rational of the women described in Brown's fiction, for, despite their attempts to behave only as their understanding dictates, Brown's other heroines, like Clara Wieland or Clara Howard, are motivated as much by emotion as by reason. In contrast Constantia claims that she can only love where her understanding affirms her emotions. Her gratitude to Ormond "created no bias on her judgment."[73] In fact, her thinking is paradigmatic of the rational process:

> Constantia did not form her resolutions in haste; but, when once formed, they were exempt from fluctuation. She reflected before she acted, and therefore acted with consistency and vigour.[74]

She is such a paragon in this respect that her friend Sophia describes her in Constantia's own words as a person in whom "the female was absorbed, so to speak, in the rational creature, and the emotions most apt to be excited in the gazer partook less of love than of reverence."[75]

It is odd to find this "rational creature" so admired in a novel which devotes much effort to the demonstration that reason alone is not enough for proper action. If Ormond is led astray by thinking so freely, would not Constantia also fall into error? Sophia warns that Constantia is unguarded where she might be most secure, that is, in religious faith. This would protect her from the danger of seduction by Ormond. Still, we find that this is not a real danger, because Constantia is steeped in the tradition wherein "death, untimely and violent, was better than the loss of honour."[76]

Constantia's weakness is that she is unable to perceive Ormond's compulsion to deceive. Despite his treatment of Helena and the careful ambiguity in his state-

ments about his political designs she still believes him honest and open, saying, "All you know, all you wish, and all you purpose, are known to others as soon as yourself."[77] The less credulous Sophia holds that Ormond is bad enough to have been a killer of Constantia's father:

> The enormity of this deed appeared by no means incongruous with the sentiments of Ormond. Human life is momentous or trivial in our eyes, according to the course which our habits and opinions have taken. Passion greedily accepts, and habit readily offers, the sacrifice of another's life, and reason obeys the impulse of education and desire.[78]

Sophia's better knowledge is based upon European experience and a greater acquaintance with Ormond's history, which is not available to Constantia. Constantia's rationalism is only as competent as her limited information and experience permits. Rationality needs to be assisted either by greater experience and knowledge or by the traditions of organized religion and institutionalized morality. With such guidance, Constantia would not have risked her lonely stay in the house in Jersey, with all its tragic consequences.

We have seen that, in Brown's fiction, the extremes of rationalism, given the imperfections of the human mind, inevitably lead to error, while even the balanced and moderate mind needs guidance beyond its own abilities. Most minds need this guidance because Brown demonstrates that they are driven by motives inaccessible to their conscious selves. Wieland's case is the best example; the next section documents two less obvious cases of unconscious compulsion.

Unconscious Compulsions

Arthur Mervyn adds to the convictions of rationalism his belief that benevolence is the proper motive for action. He can see the difficulties of his position but is sure that they are not insuperable: "Good intentions, unaided by knowledge, will, perhaps, produce more injury than benefit, and therefore knowledge must be gained, but the acquisition is not momentary; is not bestowed unasked and unlooked for. Meanwhile we must not be inactive because we are ignorant."[79] This seems a reasonable credo, or would seem so, had he not admitted just previously that "I choose the obvious path, and pursue it with headlong expedition." Mervyn constantly places himself in compromising situations and becomes comic in his protestations of innocence and beneficence as he meddles in the affairs of others. His benevolent intentions rarely lead to the effect he desires, and the reader slowly becomes aware of a self-seeking quality in his aspirations.

The young men of American fiction, like Robin in Hawthorne's "My Kinsman, Major Molineux," or

Melville's Whitejacket, are often engaged in a search for a father; Arthur Mervyn is distinguished by his deep drive to find a mother.[80] He finds her in the youngish Mrs. Ascha Fielding, whose "superior age, sedateness and prudence" give his deportment a "filial freedom and affection." He is, he tells us, "fond of calling her "mamma.""[81]

In a dream, Arthur finds Mr. Fielding returning to claim his wife; it is an interesting sequence which points to the incest taboo. On that night, Arthur has been told that Ascha Fielding loves him, and he has considered for the first time the possibility of a sexual relationship with her. But when he attempts to sleep, a swarm of images assails him:

> What chiefly occupied me was a nameless sort of terror. What shall I compare it to? Methinks that one falling from a tree overhanging a torrent, plunged into the whirling eddy, and gasping and struggling while he sinks to rise no more, would feel just as I did then. . . . These were all the tokens of a mind lost to itself; bewildered; unhinged; plunged into a drear insanity.[81]

When Fielding appears in his dream, Arthur shudders. "Fielding changed his countenance into rage and fury. He called me villain . . . and drew a shining steel from his bosom with which he stabbed me to the heart."[82] Arthur's sense of incestuous guilt finds expression in the dream of the terrible plunge and the avenging "father" and later drives him to gloomy wanderings in the devious paths around Stedman's villa.

Arthur is not able to interpret this dream, but its meaning is sensed by Mrs. Fielding who pales when she hears of it and says: "I hate your dream. It is a horrid thought. Would to God it had never occurred to you." She dreads disappointment in this affair, but says, "Indeed I know not what to do. I believe I ought still to retract—ought at least to postpone an act so irrevocable."[83] Such a use of dreams does not in fact require that Mrs. Fielding or even Brown should be aware of the full implications of them, but the novelist at least must have a profound sense of the undercurrents of human motivation and the ability to intimate them in a suitable image.

In *Edgar Huntly* we are made aware from the beginning of the story that Huntly's sanity is not to be trusted. He tells of the "insanity" of vengeance and grief into which he was driven by the murder of his friend Waldegrave, and his many distracted wanderings and reveries at the fatal spot, an elm tree. Eventually we find that the intensity of Huntly's grief is dictated by a secret guilt which he is unable to admit to himself and is expressed in the most circuitous fashion. Clues are given early in the narrative that we are to witness a further development of the "insanity"

which has apparently been subdued. In a nocturnal ramble "the impulse was gradually awakened that bade me once more to seek the elm; once more to explore the ground; to scrutinize its trunk. . . . Lately I had viewed this conduct with shame and regret," Huntly continues, "but in the present state of my mind it assumed the appearance of conformity with prudence."[84] In retrospect he resorts to a common psychological theory to explain his "relapse into folly":

> My return, after an absence of some duration, into the scenes of these transactions and sufferings, the time of night, the glimmering of the stars, the obscurity in which external objects were wrapped, and which, consequently, did not draw my attention from the images of fancy, may in some degree account for the revival of those sentiments and resolutions which immediately succeeded the death of Waldegrave. . . . [85]

But the reason for the revival of Huntly's previous sentiments is really his guilt at having benefitted financially by his friend's mysterious death; that and the sense of a duty undone in failing to destroy some of his friend's early letters. (These letters contained Rationalist theorising, since renounced by Waldegrave. Huntly planned to transcribe them for his future wife, Waldegrave's sister, contrary to his explicit instructions.)

Most of Huntly's comments on Clithero, whom he finds digging under the elm in a somnambulist state, reflect back on Huntly himself, just as Clithero's story of false guilt parallels Huntly's assumption of guilt over an action he did not commit. Huntly muses on Clithero: "The incapacity of sound sleep denotes a mind sorely wounded. It is thus that atrocious criminals denote the possession of some dreadful secret. The thoughts, which considerations of safety enable them to suppress or disguise during wakefulness, operate without impediment, and exhibit their genuine effects, when the notices of sense are partly excluded and they are shut out from a knowledge of their entire condition."[86] Clithero was acting out "some fantastic drama in which his mind was busy. . . . an incoherent conception of his concern in the murder bewitches him hither."[87] A parallel emerges in that Huntly, too, has been driven to seek the elm, a hundred times,[88] and he too ponders so much on the murder that he is incapable of sleep.[89] In fact he spends the whole of the next day in contemplation and rejoices at the arrival of night.

Huntly resolves to accost the stranger, overcoming his fears of an excessive desire for vengeance by the rationalization that, "Having found my ancient fortifications insufficient to withstand the enemy, what should I learn from thence but that it becomes me to strengthen and enlarge them."[90] In following Clithero, he is led into a maze of valleys and fens, along the verge of a precipice above a "dreary vale", which is "embarrassed with the leafless stocks of bushes, and encumbered with rugged and pointed rocks." The pursuit ends with the disappearance of Clithero into a cavern. The clue is given in *Arthur Mervyn* that wanderings in the wilderness may be an indication of severe mental disturbance. On Arthur's night of distress, when he contemplates marriage with Mrs. Fielding, he also wanders through "embarrassed and obscure paths," and he comments that "it was certainly a temporary loss of reason; nothing less than madness could lead into such devious tracks, drag me down to so hopeless, helpless, panicful a depth, and drag me down so suddenly; lay waste, as at a signal, all my flourishing structures, and reduce them in a moment to a scene of confusion and horror."[91] It is, then, obvious that Clithero is here portrayed as deranged. Donald Ringe extends the analogy to apply also to Huntly:

> Seen in this light, the journey of Huntly into the region of Norwalk bespeaks the developing madness in a man who has left his normal path to satisfy his irrational compulsions. . . . Later one learns that the cavern has often served Clithero as a place to brood over his sorrows (IV, 85), so that it comes to be a symbol of a mind possessed; but, even without this clue to its interpretation, one could still recognise the cave as the external expression of an obsessive mental state and the journey into the wilderness as movement through an intellectual labyrinth that can only terminate in such a place.[92]

Huntly thinks that his motives in seeking out Clithero are benevolent, but, like Arthur Mervyn and the characters in *Wieland,* he is misguided in this. He is also incorrect in his inference that Clithero must be Waldegrave's killer. Clithero points out to him that, like most others, he is blind to the consequences of his own actions, for his "misguided zeal and random efforts" have brought Clithero's life to a miserable end and put the seal to his perdition.

Clithero's complicated and unlikely story is an extreme version of Huntly's own assumption of guilt. In youth, Clithero was adopted by a woman named Mrs. Lorimer, to whose ward, Clarice, he became engaged. The father of Clarice, Wiatte, is Mrs. Lorimer's brother and she believes that her fate is supernaturally intertwined with his. Wiatte, however, is a renegade, who assaults Clithero for his money. In self-defence Clithero kills Wiatte without realising his identity. Perhaps significantly, Clithero says "had the assailant been my father, the consequence would have been the same."[93] The impulse here is strikingly similar to that in Arthur Mervyn's dream about Mr. Fielding. The feelings of ingratitude and unworthiness that have already tormented Clithero rush now upon him with renewed force, throwing his mind off balance. "My fancy," he says, "began to be infected with the errors of my understanding. . . . all within me was tempestuous and

dark."[94] He fears that in killing Wiatte he has ensured the death of Mrs. Lorimer, because of her superstition of connected fates, and is relieved to find that she sleeps tranquilly. But at once "the madness to whose black suggestions" the interval of lucidity offered so strong a contrast afflicts him, and he reflects that although she now lives, the news will kill her when she wakes. In this pass, it seems to Clithero that the only way to serve her is to prevent a return to consciousness, and so he strikes at her with a dagger. The blow is intercepted from behind. Now Clithero discovers that the sleeping figure is Clarice, and that Mrs. Lorimer has held back his arm. Mrs. Lorimer sinks to the floor and Clithero flees, assuming that she is now dead. His frequent visiting of the elm is due, he says, to the "distant resemblance which the death of this man bore to that of which I was the perpetrator."[95]

David Davis has suggested a concealed Oedipal fantasy logic in this attempt to kill Mrs. Lorimer. In killing Wiatte (the father figure), Clithero has assumed Oedipal guilt. To disprove such intentions, he *must* also kill Mrs. Lorimer (the mother figure). This perhaps accounts for the feature of Clithero's madness which Brown does not explain, his continuing intention to kill Mrs. Lorimer when he discovers that she is still alive.[96]

Huntly's response to Clithero's story is to absolve him from guilt because his intentions were good. Huntly's own disturbance of mind takes the form of misguided and intrusive benevolence, which is another parallel between the two men. In fact he assures Clithero that Mrs. Lorimer is well and in New York, thus enabling the homicidal maniac to set off on another attempt to kill her. Thus Huntly is blind to the dangers of a mental disturbance similar to his own. Yet another similarity rests in the fact that both men have documents about which they feel guilty (Clithero's document is a defence by Mrs. Lorimer of Wiatte's character), both hide them in intricately locked receptacles, and both conceal them again while sleepwalking.

The neurosis under which Huntly has been suffering is resolved by the appearance of Weymouth, a legitimate claimant of the money found in Waldegrave's possession. This money would have made possible Huntly's marriage and was therefore of great importance to him, but he feels guilty because it makes his friend's death a benefit to him. Weymouth's claim removes the benefit but impinges directly on the unadmitted cause of Huntly's neurosis, and, in doing so precipitates a tremendous psychic disturbance. Huntly wanders in his sleep until he falls into the cave. The final movement of the book begins at this stage.

After his fall into the cave, Huntly's movements are largely dictated not be compulsion but by the need to survive in hostile territory during Indian raids on the settlements. Donald Ringe claims that Huntly is still possessed by madness because he continues to leap to faulty conclusions on slight evidence; he decides that his uncle's house has been pillaged and his relatives murdered because he sees his uncle's musket in an Indian's hands. However, the conclusion is not absurd as Ringe would have it, because his uncle *is* actually dead, although the house has not been attacked. Nor is Ringe fair in his statement that "Huntly is thus as driven by compulsion to make his way home as he had been to seek Waldegrave's murderer or to pursue Clithero in order to help him." In such circumstances, an eagerness to get home can hardly be called compulsive. Actually, Huntly's actions from the time of his fall into the cave are quite sane, if a little faulty in judgment. His leap into the river is a prudent response to the danger his senses indicate, and his rashness in informing Clithero that Mrs. Lorimer lives cannot be construed as insane, although it does demonstrate the kind of weakness he is prone to. The deep cause of his disturbance has been removed by Weymouth's claim to the money, and the immediate mental disturbance and sleepwalking mark both the cause of his problems and the turning point in his return to sanity. This inarticulate understanding by Huntly of the cause of his trauma provides an answer to the problem noted by Leslie Fielder: that Huntly's statement of his experience is too extreme to be justified by the surface events. Huntly says, "What light has burst upon my ignorance of myself and of mankind! How sudden and enormous the transition from uncertainty to knowledge!"[97] We expect some radical understanding of the mind to justify such an assertion, and I think that Brown provides it in his exploration of irrational guilt.

The Final Answer

Brown's last novels, *Jane Talbot* and *Clara Howard,* are comedies of manners, safely inside the sentimental conventions. Their plots are contrived and rather absurd: *Clara Howard,* for example, depends upon the unwillingness of the heroine to marry Philip Stanley because the girl to whom he was engaged, Mary Wilmot, has a prior claim on his affections. Mary is poor, which inspires Clara's capacity for enthusiastic self-sacrifice to such an extent that she insists Philip use all his persuasive power to induce Mary to marry him. This would be an arbitrary choice, as Philip lucidly points out, of one person's supposed happiness at the expense of two others.

Jane Talbot is more interesting, because it provides an answer to the problem which engages Brown in all his novels: on what basis is it possible to behave correctly? Jane has religious faith, but lacks a rational basis for her beliefs. Henry Colden, on the other hand, is unable to believe because he is convinced by the rationalist critique of religion. But he has been impressed by the dying injunctions of his friend Thompson, who did find faith. The difference between Henry and Jane in relation to faith is the real core of the novel, rather than the contrived plot of slander and misinformation which directs the surface action. Henry is finally able to believe through a mysterious sea change during his absence of four years in America:

> The incidents of a long voyage, the vicissitudes through which I have passed, have given strength to my frame, while the opportunities for wisdom which these have afforded me have made *my mind whole.* I have awakened from my dreams of doubt and misery, not to the cold and vague belief, but to the living and delightful consciousness, of every tie that can bind man to his Divine Parent and Judge.[99]

Philosophy in Brown's fiction is inseparable from psychology, as we see in this statement. It is natural that we should not be given an account of the basis for Henry's new-found faith because the basis is revelatory, a matter of wholeness of mind, or psychic health. Passing references in *Wieland* and *Ormond* indicate that this conclusion was always in Brown's mind, but not fully accepted, and therefore we might suspect the sincerity of his resolution of the problem here. But since this was Brown's last novel, we may take it as a statement of his final position as a novelist. It is inimical to engaging fiction, of course, which may explain his unwillingness to advance it earlier. Balanced religious faith and psychic wholeness would have solved his characters' problems rather too effectively. His interest lay rather in their sensational failures than in their comfortable successes.

Even these weak last novels are replete with detailed psychological observation of internal response. Jane, for example, acknowledges in a peculiar way the forged paragraph of a letter which purports to implicate her and Colden in a sexual impropriety: "Methinks I then felt as I should have felt if the charge had been true. I shuddered as if to look back would only furnish me with proofs of a guilt of which I had not hitherto been conscious." She acknowledges the letter because it represents the truth of what she wanted to do rather than what she actually did. Her experience is of a piece with Clara Wieland's prophetic dream, Mervyn's nightmare of Mr. Fielding, or Pleyel's assumption of Clara's association with Carwin. These descriptions add depth to Brown's characters and an undertone to his plots. The effect of the incessant reflection on possibilities indulged in by most of Brown's characters is to increase the complexity and the suspense of their situation. They muse upon all possible actions and eventualities, neglecting no intimations of terror or horror.[100] Such intensity of mental life makes credible the foreshadowing of danger in *Wieland* and *Ormond*, it vivifies quite ordinary existence into a dramatic series of crises, and it encourages the reader to participate in the mistakes of perception which Brown's protagonists so frequently make. Above all, it enables Brown to transcend the rather limited and mechanical version of the mind afforded by contemporary psychologies in the creation of a complex web of versions of external and internal realities.

Notes

[1] *Charles Brockden Brown's Novels,* (1887, Mckay; facsimile rpt. New York: Kennikat Press, 1963). I, 23. Hereafter cited as *Works.*

[2] Noted in Henry R. Warfel, *Charles Brockden Brown: American Gothic Novelist* (University of Florida Press, Gainsville, Florida, 1969).

[3] *The Complete Works of Edgar Allan Poe,* edited by James A. Harrison, 17 vols. (New York, Crowell and Co. 1902), I. 151.

[4] See Terence Martin, *The Instructed Vision: Scottish Common Sense Philosophy and the Origins of American Fiction* (Bloomington, Indiana University Humanities Series no. 48, 1961)

[5] Rev. Chauncy Hare Townshend, *Facts in Mesmerism, or, Animal Magnetism* (Boston, Little and Brown, 1841), p.29.

[6] David Lee Clark, *Charles Brockden Brown, Pioneer Voice of America* (Durham, N.C., Duke University Press, 1952), pp.45, 146-7, 291, 22.

[7] *Works,* III (Memoir), 35-6.

[8] Clark, pp. 43, 69. See also Ernest Marchand's "Introduction" to *Ormond* (New York, Hafner, 1962), pp.xviii, xxi.

[9] *Works,* I. 39. See also Clark, p.167.

[10] Quoted in Warfel, p.89.

[11] As Larzer Ziff has demonstrated in "A Reading of *Wieland,*" *PMLA* LXXVII (1962), pp.51-57.

[12] *Works,* I, 55.

[13] Erasmus Darwin, *Zoonomia: or, The Laws of Organic Life,* 2nd ed. (London, 1796), II. 353.

[14] *Darwin,* II, 354, II, 357-8.

[15] *Darwin,* II, 354.

[16] *Darwin,* II, 367.

[17] *Works,* I, 186-7.

[18] *Darwin,* I, 438.

[19] *Works,* I, 97.

[20] Benjamin Rush, *Sixteen Introductory Lectures* (Philadelphia, Bradford and Inskeep, 1811), p.386. These lectures were delivered earlier at the University of Pennsylvania and it is likely that Brown knew of them through his friend Smith.

[21] *Works,* I, 191-2.

[22] *Works,* I, 195.

[23] *Works,* I, 176-7.

[24] *Darwin,* I, 437.

[25] *Darwin,* II, 351, 352.

[26] *Darwin,* II, 350. . . .

[34] *Works,* IV, 13.

[35] *Works,* I, 106.

[36] Benjamin Rush, "The Influence of Physical Causes on the Moral Faculty," *Selected Writings of Benjamin Rush,* ed. Dagobert Runes (New York, New York Philosophical Library, 1947), p.188.

[37] *Darwin,* I, 209. 205 Brown, *Works,* I, 255.

[38] *Darwin,* II, 336.

[39] *Darwin,* I, 190.

[40] *Darwin,* I, 30.

[41] *Darwin,* I, 193, Sleepwalking: I, 441-2.

[42] *Works,* IV, 151.

[43] Donald Ringe, *Charles Brockden Brown* (New York, Twayne, 1966). p.90.

[44] Warfel continues: "Quite apparent is Brown's indebtedness to contemporary sensationalist psychology, to Erasmus Darwin's chapter on "Mania Mutabilis" in *Zoonomia,* and to other writings on insanity. Dr. Cambridge's lecture to Clara echoes Dr. Benjamin Rush. Not until the advent of Poe and Hawthorne does another fictionist create characters tormented by brooding minds." p. 107.

[45] Ringe, pp. 27, 31.

[46] *Works,* I, 105.

[47] *Works,* I, 106. . . .

[48] Ringe, p. 42.

[49] *Works,* I, 106-7; I, 73-4. See also Ziff, p.54.

[50] Quoted in Henry Warfel, "Charles Brockden Brown's German Sources," *MLQ* I (1940) pp.361-65, p.365.

[51] *Works,* I, 55. Of course the difficulty of deciding between perceptions and projections by the self has been a major theme in American fiction, even to the present day. See, for example, Tony Tanner, *City of Words* (London, Cape, 1971), p.252.

[52] Ziff, p. 53.

[53] Ziff, p. 54. See also Leslie Fielder, *Love and Death in the American Novel,* (Delta, 1967), pp.150-1, and David Davis, *Homicide in American Fiction,* (Cornell, Cornell University Press, 1968), pp.90-1.

[54] Ziff, p. 54.

[55] *Works,* I, 55, 94, 124, 133, 138.

[56] *Works,* I, 124, 128.

[57] *Works,* I, 55.

[58] Quoted in Fay, p.20.

[59] *Works,* I, 75; III, 220, V, 229.

[60] *Works,* I, 250.

[61] *Works,* I, 75, 83-4.

[62] See Ziff, p.54.

[63] *Works,* V, 137.

[64] *Works,* VI, 57.

[65] *Works,* II, 77.

[66] *Works,* V, 199. (Poe made a more explicit issue of it, in "The Imp of the Perverse.")

[67] *Works,* VI, 275.

[68] *Works,* VI, 110. William Godwin, *Thoughts on Man* (Preface) (1831; rpt. N.Y. Augustus M. Kelley, 1969).

[69] Godwin, *Thoughts,* p. 240. See also *Caleb Williams* (1794).

[70] *Works,* II, 86.

[71] *Works,* I, 249.

[72] *Works,* I, 243.

[73] *Works,* IV, 172.

[74] *Works,* VI, 142.

[75] *Works,* VI, 75.

[76] *Works,* VI, 275.

[77] *Works,* VI, 248.

[78] *Works,* VI, 255.

[79] *Works,* III, 107.

[80] As are Brown's other heroes from this point on. Fiedler calls them "dependent boys in search of motherly wives." *Love and Death,* p.151.

[81] *Works,* III, 220.

[82] *Works,* III, 221.

[83] *Works,* III, 229.

[84] *Works,* IV, 8.

[85] *Works,* IV, 9.

[86] *Works,* IV, 13.

[87] *Works,* IV, 13.

[88] *Works,* IV, 8.

[89] *Works,* IV, 16.

[90] *Works,* IV, 14.

[91] *Works,* III, 225.

[92] Ringe, p. 88. Ringe's account is valuable; at times, however it seems rather stretched. It *is* reasonable for Huntly to assume that the mysterious stranger digging in the night under the elm where Waldegrave was murdered will have some connection with the killing; therefore in investigating Huntly is not "giving in to strange compulsions that have hitherto moved him." Still, his later pursuit of Clithero may be properly described in these terms.

[93] *Works,* IV, 70.

[94] *Works,* IV, 73.

[95] *Works,* IV, 85.

[96] Davis, *Homicide in American Fiction* (Cornell, Cornell University Press, 1968)

[97] *Works,* IV, 6.

[98] *Works*, V, 234.

[99] *Works*, V, 82.

[100] See Warfel, *Charles Brockden Brown*, p. 158.

Leonard W. Engel (essay date 1985)

SOURCE: "The Journey from Reason to Madness: Edgar Allan Poe's 'The Fall of the House of Usher,'" *Essays in Arts and Sciences*, Vol. XIV, May, 1985, pp. 23-31.

[*In the following essay, Engel argues that in "The Fall of the House of Usher," Edgar Allan Poe uses language and imagery relating to enclosure as a means of tracing the journey of the narrator from reason to insanity.*]

In an essay some years ago, David Hirsch remarked that in many of Poe's tales houses were symbols of the mind, and in "The Fall of the House of Usher," in particular, Roderick's "strangely furnished chamber is symbolic of his strangely furnished mind."[1] Hirsch noted how Poe's language expressed "a modern sense of alienation and disintegration."[2] This fact, among others, has, no doubt, made "Usher" extremely popular not only among critics and scholars of Poe but among students, especially college students, and general readers as well. And although "Usher" has been the object of much critical attention and interpretation, no extensive analysis has been made of the enclosure, the "strangely furnished chamber," in the tale, though physical enclosures, imagery and metaphor of enclosure, and the language of confinement and entrapment are crucial artistic devices in the tale. In point of fact, the delicate connection between the chamber and the mind that Hirsch so deftly points out has not been explored.

That Poe realized the potency of the enclosure in fiction is clear from his essay "'The Philosophy of Composition," where he refers to it as a "close *circumscription of space*." It is, he writes, "absolutely necessary to the effect of insulated incident;—it has the force of a frame to a picture."[3] Decidedly, Poe is speaking of the importance of an enclosure on the plot, or incident, of a narrative, but I believe it has a significant influence on character in his tales as well. For one thing, it serves to separate the character from the real world, isolate him physically, and intensify his mental experience. For example, in "The Fall of the House of Usher," the series of enclosures obvious from the opening scene in the tale to its conclusion, contributes to the mood of gloom pervading the narrator's consciousness and leads directly to the dominant enclosure—the House itself, which the narrator will soon enter and from which he will barely escape. In short, Poe's use of the enclosure device chronicles the narrator's journey from reason to madness in addition to providing the artistic focus and unity of impression that were such a fundamental part of his theory of the short story.

Poe's particular use of enclosure in this tale is not unique. In *The Narrative of Arthur Gordon Pym*, he uses the device to influence Pym's physical and psychological crises and to affect his behavior. Other Poe characters who experience horrifying enclosures, for example, the narrator in "A Descent into the Maelström" and to a degree the narrator of "MS. Found in a Bottle," emerge from their confinements markedly changed, often revealing traces of a new psychic identity. In another tale, "The Premature Burial," the narrator is severely claustrophobic; he is deathly afraid of being buried alive—he is obsessed with the thought—but, ironically, his symbolic "burial and resurrection" are the means by which he is finally cured of his fear and allowed to become "a new man."[4] In "Usher" Poe employs a variation of this theme through a careful and systematic use of the language and imagery of enclosure.

The first sentence, "During the whole of a dull, dark, and soundless day in the autumn of the year, when the clouds hung oppressively low in the heavens, I had been passing alone, on horseback, through a singularly dreary tract of country, and, at length found myself, as the shades of the evening drew on, within view of the melancholy House of Usher,"[5] and the description that follows are highly suggestive of a tightly closed, virtually airtight box. The narrator's next words, " . . . with the first glimpse of the building, a sense of unsufferable gloom pervaded my spirit," a masterful stroke by Poe, emphasize not only the dominance of the House and the mood of gloom, but deepen the effect of confinement on the narrator, as though he were on the verge of suffocation. Thus in the first two sentences, Poe artfully describes, in the following order, the climatic conditions, the time of year, the countryside, the time of day, and finally the House itself. The movement is from the general to the particular, culminating with the House, and leaving the narrator with powerful and ominous feelings.

A sensitive man of reason, he makes a concerted effort to dispel the gloom by trying to objectify the scene, to detach himself from it and describe it logically, perhaps even reduce the House to a mere house, but he is unsuccessful. He rearranges the particulars of the scene, descending from his horse to gaze into a black tarn by the house. What he sees shocks him more because all the images are now grotesquely inverted. The "lurid" black water, of course, foreshadows the dramatic conclusion of the tale. Despite his disturbing feelings, however, the narrator faces the inevitable, " . . . in this mansion of gloom I now proposed to myself a sojourn of some weeks," (p. 398). Clearly, he is a man whose head rules his heart, and he is able to put his feelings of depression aside and accept his situation, at least for the present.

After this lengthy introduction, uncommon in most of Poe's tales but quintessential in this one, establishing the mood of gloom, Poe has the narrator ride over a short causeway—the threshold of the House—and enter the Gothic archway. "A valet, of stealthy step," he relates "thence conducted me, in silence, through many dark and intricate passages in my progress to the *studio* of his master," (p. 400). From this point on, the narrator's sense of responsibility, sense of self, diminishes, and his actions are more and more controlled by those around him. For example, he is "conducted" by the valet "through many dark and intricate passages" and is "ushered . . . into the presence of his master." This description, consistent with the singular mood of gloom, has about it a sense of further isolation from the world the narrator has recently left. He is entering a labyrinthine unknown, symbolized, of course, by the House. As Roy Male has remarked, "The narrator is 'ushered into' Roderick's room." "The name of the house and its occupants," Male concludes, "is in keeping with the story's province: the threshold between mind and matter, reason and madness, life and death."[6]

The narrator's journey *does* symbolically suggest a movement from "reason to madness." Daniel Hoffman has astutely pointed out that "Usher" is a terrifying tale of the protagonist's journey into the darkest, most hidden regions of himself.[7] I believe that Poe uses the House, with its numerous chambers and passageways, to reinforce the mysteriousness of this journey and to dramatize the stages or levels of awareness he passes through, or loses touch with, as he moves from the rational, safe, secure world to the irrational world of Roderick and Madeline.

The narrator's description of Roderick's room, with its remote angles and recesses and "air of stern, deep, and irredeemable gloom," (p. 401) substantiates this view, and the changes he sees in Roderick are shocking. "Surely, man had never before so terribly altered," the narrator exclaims, "in so brief a period, as had Roderick Usher! It was with difficulty that I could bring myself to admit the identity of the wan being before me with the companion of my early boyhood," (p. 401).

In the following passage, Poe reveals the changes in Roderick's psychological identity through his "struggle with the grim phantasm, FEAR." Roderick, the narrator relates,

> . . . was enchained by certain superstitious impressions in regard to the dwelling which he tenanted, and whence, for many years, he had never ventured forth—in regard to an influence whose suppositious

force was conveyed in terms too shadowy here to be re-stated—an influence which some peculiarities in the mere form and substance of his family mansion, had, by dint of long sufferance, he said, obtained over his spirit—an effect which the *physique* of the gray walls and turrets, and of the dim tarn into which they all looked down, had, at length, brought about upon the *morale* of his existence (p. 403).

The key words here connote confinement and point toward the concluding phrase, "the *morale* of his existence." Not only has Roderick's physical identity been affected by the atmosphere of the House, these images suggest deeper, more complex changes as well. In effect, Usher's psychological identity is in the grip of "FEAR," and the enclosure has provided the impetus for his obsession.

Even Roderick's art is filled with images of enclosure. An oppressive sense of entombment pervades the narrator's description of one of the pictures Usher has painted, "A small picture presented the interior of an immensely long and rectangular vault. . . . this excavation lay at an exceeding depth below the surface of the earth. No outlet was observed in any portion of its vast extent, and no torch . . . was discernable; yet a flood of intense rays . . . bathed the whole in a ghastly and inappropriate splendour," (pp. 405-406). Undoubtedly, this passage describing Roderick's picture foreshadows Lady Madeline's premature burial in the vault beneath the House. Furthermore, in one of Roderick's poems, "The Haunted Palace," the narrator notes a reference to past glories being " . . . but a dim-remembered story / Of the old time entombed," (p. 407).

Enclosures are everywhere, and the more the narrator immerses himself in Roderick's life, the more he senses the overwhelming gloom he noted in the initial paragraph. In "The Haunted Palace," he relates, "I was . . . the more forcibly impressed with it . . . because I perceived, and for the first time, a full consciousness on the part of Usher, of the tottering of his lofty reason upon her throne," (p. 406). The narrator perceives Usher's awareness of his own irrationality, and the line "Of the old time entombed," might symbolize Roderick's perception of the entombment of his reason.

Remarkably, what the narrator *fails* to perceive is the beginning of his own psychological deterioration. When Roderick tells him of Madeline's death and of his intention to preserve her corpse, "(previously to its final interment) in one of the numerous vaults within the main walls of the building," the narrator regards it "as at best but a harmless, and by no means an unnatural, precaution," (p. 409), especially since the family burial ground is at a distance from the house and exposed to grave robbers.

The body having been encoffined, we two alone bore it to its rest. The vault in which we placed it (and which had been so long unopened that our torches, half smothered in its oppressive atmosphere, gave us little opportunity for investigation) was small, damp, and entirely without means of admission for light; lying, at great depth, immediately beneath that portion of the building in which was my own sleeping apartment, (pp. 409-410).

Before leaving the vault, they have a last look at the deceased. "The disease which had thus entombed the lady in the maturity of youth, had left, as usual in all maladies of a strictly cataleptical character, the mockery of a faint blush upon the bosom and the face, and that suspiciously lingering smile upon the lip which is so terrible in death. We replaced and screwed down the lid, and . . . made our way, with toil, into the scarcely less gloomy apartments of the upper portion of the house," (p. 410). Poe clearly indicates they are burying a living person, but the narrator for all his astute reasoning elsewhere in the tale fails to discern this most crucial of facts.

Poe has from the beginning used enclosures as a means of creating setting, influencing the mood of the narrator, and intensifying the mystery, and the cumulative effect of them on the narrator results in an increasing awareness of Usher's situation. But, at the same time, the narrator appears to lose perspective in other areas, such as the mystery surrounding Madeline. After his initial glimpse of her on the evening of the day he arrived, he does not see her again until he and Roderick convey her to the vault and seal her up. His lack of curiosity about her is amazing; he does not ask to see her while she is ill, nor does he mention her name to Roderick, and he unhesitatingly accepts Roderick's explanation for temporarily entombing her. One would, at the very least, expect some sort of ceremony accompanying Madeline's death; after all, she was held in respect in the region for she was known as "Lady Madeline." But the narrator apparently sees nothing wrong with the proceedings and does not even question the "faint blush" upon her bosom and face. One wonders if this sane man from the outside world, this model of objectivity and rationalism, Roderick's touchstone with reality, is not beginning to lose his own bearings.

I believe this is exactly what Poe wants his readers to infer, and he indicates this change most forcibly when the narrator is gazing at the face of the living Madeline and rationalizing about her appearance and the nature of the malady in pseudo-scientific jargon. The climactic loss of his old self in this scene, in point of fact, his identity, what Sam Girgus calls his "separation of self from his body—" his disembodiment or transcendence,[8] occurs while the narrator is in a vault under the House; this seems to be the major event toward which Poe's language and imagery have been directed.

In the days following Madeline's burial, the narrator's continuing loss of self is evident as he absorbs more of Roderick's mood. He states, "It was no wonder that his [Roderick's] condition terrified—that it infected me. I felt creeping upon me, by slow yet certain degrees, the wild influences of his own fantastic yet impressive superstitions," (p. 411). In the final awful scene, Poe intensifies the narrator's mental and emotional deterioration almost entirely in terms of physical enclosure. About a week after the burial, the narrator relates, he experiences "the full power" of these wild influences. He cannot sleep and, struggling up, peers "within the intense darkness of the chamber [listening] . . . to certain low and indefinite sounds," (p. 411).

Rationally, the narrator knows there is no cause for alarm, but emotionally he is terrified. He tries, unsuccessfully, to attribute his feelings to the room with its strange trappings and thus explain them away. It then crosses his mind that the room may be affecting him in some unknown way and thereby be a possible explanation for his emotional confusion. But because of his scientific bias, he dismisses this as unreasonable, and he is left with an inexplicable situation, which further agitates him because he is unaccustomed to it. The room thus serves as a continuing metaphor for his breakdown, but Poe skillfully keeps that breakdown in the shadow of Roderick's, which, indeed, is climaxed by the return of Madeline.

Poe further intensifies the moment by describing the unnatural weather conditions and metaphorically correlating the mind of the narrator with the tempest outside. He had done this in the opening scene, it will be recalled, when he suggested the narrator's vacillating mental state by describing the low hanging clouds. Now he describes the storm in all its fury as Roderick, who has run to the narrator's apartment in an extremely distracted state, hurries to one of the casements and throws it open: "The impetuous fury of the entering gust nearly lifted us from our feet. . . . the exceeding density of the clouds . . . hung so low as to press upon the turrets of the house. . . . . . . [and] gaseous exhalation . . . hung about and enshrouded the mansion," (p. 412). Thus the storm outside mirrors the turmoil and confusion in the minds of Roderick and the narrator.

This passage also suggests that Roderick, who has not moved from the interior of the house, has not even gone near a window since the narrator arrived, now wishes to be released from its influence. Ironically, it is the narrator who closes the window and induces Roderick to sit and listen to one of his favorite romances, the Gothic "Mad Trist," which the narrator begins to read. This is a reversal; up to this point Roderick has been the initiator of the action, first requesting the narrator to visit him, then gradually leading him into deeper involvement with his activities.

Significantly, the events of the eerie narrative the narrator reads, foreshadow those which will occur in the room very shortly. More important, the act of reading the emotionally explosive "Mad Trist" to the highly unstable Roderick at this critical moment is either to overlook or become so desensitized to present reality that his own thinking and feeling processes are dangerously disconnected. It indicates the narrator's further withdrawal from self, for he seems to sense no incongruity between his action and the reality around him. Even mad Roderick recognizes the gravity of the situation for just before Madeline appears, he jumps to his feet and shouts at the narrator—*"Madman! I tell you that she now stands without the door!"* (p. 416).

It seems certain Roderick has been tacitly pleading with the narrator for some kind of recognition, some understanding of the seriousness of their plight. He has come to the narrator's chamber at a late hour and in a disturbed state and has thrown open the window in the middle of a raging storm not merely to be soothed, sat down, and read to as though he were a child. His frustration is reflected by his shrieking at the narrator and twice calling him *"Madman!"*

As I have argued, I believe that Poe has used the enclosure to indicate the levels of awareness the narrator is no longer capable of perceiving. The device chronicles the stripping away of the narrator's old, controlled, self where his finely honed mind has been dulled by the exigencies of the moment, becoming less aware of crucial, empirical facts. However, at the climatic moment of the tale the device also awakens him to the horror of what he has been witnessing. When he sees the "enshrouded" figure of Madeline, "trembling and reeling," enter the room and fall on Roderick, enclosing him under her and bearing him "to the floor a corpse, and a victim to the terrors he had anticipated," (pp. 416-417), he finally comes to himself as though awakening from a bad dream:

> From that chamber, and from that mansion, I fled aghast. The storm was still abroad in all its wrath as I found myself crossing the old causeway. Suddenly there shot along the path a white light, and I turned to see whence a gleam so unusual could have issued, for the vast house and its shadows were alone behind me. The radiance was that of the full, setting, and blood-red moon, which now shone vividly through that once barely discernible fissure, of which I have before spoken as extending from the roof of the building, in zigzag direction, to the base. While I gazed, this fissure rapidly widened—there came a fierce breath of the whirlwind—the entire orb of the satellite burst at once upon my sight—my brain reeled as I saw the mighty wall rushing asunder—there was a long tumultuous shouting sound like the voice of a thousand waters—and the deep and dark tarn at my feet closed sullenly and silently over the fragments of the "House of Usher," (p. 417).

The narrator leaves the chamber, flees the house, crosses the causeway, removes himself from the shadow of the house, which is so sharply defined by the light from the "blood-red moon," and apparently feels no oppressive clouds, as he had in the first scene, for they have been dispelled by the change in climatic conditions. In other words, he extricates himself from all the enclosures to which he has been systematically and inevitably drawn. In point of fact, the entire "House of Usher" is at once destroyed, enclosed so to speak, by "the deep and dank tarn" at his feet.

These events have suggested a number of interpretations,[9] but to me one thing they undoubtedly imply is that the attempt to lose oneself, or bury one's identity and assume an identity foreign to one's nature, must prove an extremely dangerous undertaking. Fatally fascinated with the language and imagery of enclosure, the narrator finally recognizes that he cannot lose contact with his deeper self, cannot separate his thoughts and feelings, and still remain sane. This sudden revelation comes just in time to allow him to make a harrowing escape from the house with his identity relatively intact. In effect, what he experiences is a symbolic "burial"—a journey to the edge of madness, to the brink of destruction—and a "resurrection," a "rebirth" of sorts and a chance for another life.

Similar to his other tales where the enclosure plays a dominant role—in "William Wilson," for example, Poe marks the narrator's journey to self-revelation, which in this story means self destruction, with a series of carefully wrought enclosures—the device provides dramatic focus for both plot and character, greatly heightening the artistic merit of "The Fall of the House of Usher."

Notes

[1] David H. Hirsch, "The Pit and the Apocalypse," *Sewanee Review,* 76 (Autumn 1968), 644.

[2] *Ibid.,* p. 651.

[3] *The Complete Works of Edgar Allan Poe,* vol. XIV, ed. James A. Harrison (New York: AMS Press, 1965; rpt. of the 1902 ed. pub. by Crowell, New York), p. 204.

[4] Edgar Allan Poe, "The Premature Burial," *Collected Works of Edgar Allan Poe,* vol. III, ed. Thomas Ollive Mabbott (Cambridge, Mass.: The Belknap Press of Harvard Univ. Press, 1978), p. 969.

[5] Edgar Allan Poe, "The Fall of the House of Usher," *Collected Works of Edgar Allan Poe,* vol. 11, ed. Thomas Ollive Mabbott (Cambridge, Mass.: The Belknap Press of Harvard Univ. Press, 1978), p. 397. All other references to this tale will be cited in parentheses immediately following the quote.

⁶ Roy Male, "Introduction to Poe," in *American Literary Masters* (New York: Holt, Rinehart, & Winston, 1965), pp. 16-17.

⁷ Daniel Hoffman, *Poe Poe Poe Poe Poe Poe Poe* (Garden City, N.Y.: Doubleday, 1972), p. 302.

⁸ Sam B. Girgus, "Poe and the Transcendent Self," in *The Law of the Heart* (Austin: Univ. of Texas Press, 1979), p. 27.

⁹ See D. H. Lawrence, "Poe," in *Studies in Classic American Literature* (London: Seltzer, 1924; rpt. New York: Viking, 1964), p. 89, who claims that "The Ushers, brother and sister, betrayed the Holy Ghost in themselves. They would love, love, love, without resistance. They would love, they would merge, they would be as one thing. So they dragged each other down into death."

Lyle H. Kendall, Jr., "The Vampire Motif in 'The Fall of the House of Usher,'" *CE,* 24 (March 1963), 450-53; rpt. *Twentieth Century Interpretations of "The Fall of the House of Usher,"* ed. Thomas Woodson (Englewood Cliffs: Prentice-Hall, 1969), 104. Kendall sees Madeline as a "vampire to the finish." "Evil in the long run feeds incestuously upon itself, and it is self-defeating, self-consuming, self-annihilating."

John L. Marsh, "The Psycho-Sexual Reading of 'The House of Usher,'" *Poe Studies,* 5 (June 1972), 9. Marsh comments that "Madeline may or may not be a Gothic vampire, but in the final embrace of brother and sister there is implied not a reunion with supernal beauty but a final meeting of those dark and irrational forces that have conspired to destroy the last of the Ushers."

Colin Martindale, "Archetype and Reality in 'The Fall of the House of Usher,'" *Poe Studies,* 5 (June 1972), 10. Martindale sees Usher as being "overwhelmed and destroyed by the unconscious. With the union in death comes the dissolution of the whole personality and its sinking into the unconscious as symbolized by the sinking of the house into the black tarn."

Sam Girgus, "Poe and the Transcendent Self," in *The Law of the Heart* (Austin: Univ. of Texas Press, 1979), 24-36. Girgus sees Madeline as the ultimate symbol of the existential dilemma at the heart of the story—the attempt of the self to preserve its being through its own death. The existential conflict between life and death runs through the tale (pp. 33-34).

Donald A. Ringe (essay date 1987)

SOURCE: "Madness in Hawthorne's Fiction," in *The Cast of Consciousness: Concepts of the Mind in British and American Romanticism,* edited by Beverly Taylor and Robert Bain, Greenwood Press, 1987, pp. 125-40.

[*In the following essay, Ringe reviews Nathaniel Hawthorne's treatment of insanity throughout his short stories and novels. Ringe argues that Hawthorne attempted to accurately portray the mental disorders of his characters, and demonstrates how Hawthorne's understanding of such disorders concurred with documentation by contemporary medical authorities. Additionally, Ringe studies the function of insanity in Hawthorne's characters, noting that madness is not always a negative trait, as mad characters may serve as "agents of truth."*]

Although much has been written about the psychology of Hawthorne's fiction, little attention has been paid to the pervasive theme of madness in his tales and romances.[1] From the early "Hollow of the Three Hills" (1830), where, through auditory images, he describes the horrors of a madhouse, to *The Marble Faun* (1860), where Miriam's insane model precipitates the tragedy that transforms Donatello, Hawthorne explores the problem of madness through the actions of many different characters. Some, like Jervase Helwyse in "Lady Eleanore's Mantle" (1838) are completely insane; others, like the Reverend Mr. Hooper in "The Minister's Black Veil" (1836) perform bizarre acts, but are not necessarily mad. Some, like Arthur Dimmesdale when he returns from the forest in *The Scarlet Letter* (1850), question their own sanity; others, like Roderick Elliston in "Egotism; or, The Bosom-Serpent" (1843) are called insane by those they meet. Hawthorne's interest in madness was deep and lasting, and he sought to make his insane characters convincing. A number of them, in fact, conform so well to the various types of madness described by contemporary medicine that the mental disorders from which they suffer can be accurately labeled.

The most easily identified of Hawthorne's madmen is probably Walter Ludlow in "The Prophetic Pictures" (1837). Although this enthusiastic young man appears at first to be sane, there are signs that all is not right with him. Elinor, his betrothed, has observed a disquieting look in his face, and though she tries to dismiss the perception as only an idle fancy, it continues to trouble her. The artist who paints their portraits, moreover, sees even deeper into Walter's character, perceives his incipient madness, and draws a sketch portraying what he believes will be the couple's eventual fate. So skilled is he, indeed, in taking their likenesses that both the pictures reflect the developing emotional drama in which Walter and Elinor are engaged; when the painter returns after a trip to the wilderness to see the paintings and their subjects again, the event his sketch foreshadowed comes into being. As Walter stands absorbed before his own portrait, his eyes kindle, his face grows increasingly wild, and he howls, "Our fate is upon us!"[2] Drawing a knife, he tries to drive it into Elinor's bosom. Only the painter's intercession prevents the murder.

In presenting this picture of homicidal mania, Hawthorne was faithful to contemporary thinking about this form of insanity.[3] Though we do not know if he read the work of Benjamin Rush,[4] a leading medical authority in the United States during the early years of the nineteenth century, Hawthorne's depiction of Walter Ludlow's madness is consistent with Rush's views. In *Sixteen Introductory Lectures* (1811), the famous doctor discussed just such an impulse to murder, presented a number of cases, and showed that such unprovoked attacks are usually made on the murderer's relatives and friends.[5] Indeed, in his major work on insanity, *Medical Inquiries and Observations, upon the Diseases of the Mind* (1812), Rush even suggested that in the advanced state of mania, or general mental derangement, "the hostility of the [madman] is confined to his friends and relatives only, and this is frequently great in proportion to the nearness of the connection, and the extent of the obligations he owes to them. Its intensity cannot be conceived of by persons who have observed that passion only in ordinary life."[6] Walter Ludlow's attack on Elinor, who, despite his assault, still loves him, is soundly based in recent medical thought.

There was precedent, too, in literature for Walter Ludlow's insanity. By the time "The Prophetic Pictures" appeared, a number of similar madmen had been depicted in American fiction. Best known, of course, is Charles Brockden Brown's Theodore Wieland, who murders his wife and children at the command of a mysterious voice and later attempts to kill his sister Clara, in *Wieland* (1798), but similar characters appear in the works of other American writers who much admired and were influenced by Brown's fiction. Richard Henry Dana's Paul Felton, driven by an insane jealousy, plunges a knife into the heart of his sleeping wife in "Paul Felton" (1822), and James Kirke Paulding's Dudley Rainsford, under the influence of a religious mania that leads him to believe he is doing her an important service, almost kills his beloved Virginia Dangerfield in *Westward Ho!* (1832). Though Hawthorne includes in his story none of the motivation—the insane jealousy, inherited madness, or religious obsession—that drives these characters to murder those they love, Walter Ludlow shares with them a total derangement of mind which, whatever its cause, impels him to a similar crime.

Walter Ludlow is not, however, Hawthorne's typical madman. Hawthorne was much more interested in the subtler forms of insanity and usually explored types of madness that are not so easily recognized by the world at large. The painter in "The Prophetic Pictures" provides a good example. Driven by his passion for art, he is perhaps even more of an enthusiast than his unfortunate subject, but he does not recognize the failing in himself. When he returns from the wilderness, his mind is filled with fervent thoughts on the power of his art, and he hurries toward Walter and Elinor's house with an obsessive desire to see the portraits again. "Thus," Hawthorne comments, "with a proud, yet melancholy fervor, did he almost cry aloud, as he passed through the toilsome street, among people that knew not of his reveries, nor could understand nor care for them. It is not good for man to cherish a solitary ambition. Unless there be those around him, by whose example he may regulate himself, his thoughts, desires, and hopes will become extravagant, and he the semblance, perhaps the reality, of a madman" (vol. IX, p. 180). The painter is dangerously close to becoming one.

There are many characters like the painter in Hawthorne's fiction, people who are not totally deranged, but whose minds have taken them so far from the normal in at least one area of their lives as to justify their being called mad. The Seeker in "The Great Carbuncle" (1837), for example, is one who in "early youth" had been smitten by the legendary gem "with a peculiar madness" (vol. IX, p. 150), a state of mind shared by most of those who seek it. Each of them, however, smiles "scornfully at the madness of" all the others "in anticipating better fortune" in the present quest than they had had before, yet each maintains "a scarcely hidden conviction, that he would himself be the favoured one" (vol. IX, p. 153). A similar madness may afflict religious persons, such as the Quakers, for example, in "The Gentle Boy" (1832), whose "enthusiasm [is] heightened almost to madness by the treatment which they received" at the hands of the Puritans (vol. IX, p. 69), or even the irreligious, like the merrymakers in "The May-Pole of Merry Mount" (1836), many of whom "had been maddened by their previous troubles into a gay despair," while others, like the Lord and Lady of May, "were as madly gay in the flush of youth" (vol. IX, p. 59).

Persons afflicted with this mental disorder may function perfectly well in all other phases of their lives. Their madness is limited to one particular idea with which they become obsessed. Old Esther Dudley in Hawthorne's story of 1839 epitomizes the type. Given the key to Province House by Sir William Howe when the British withdraw from Boston in 1776, and told to return it to himself or to some new Royal Governor who should succeed him when the British troops return, Esther Dudley remains in Province House throughout the Revolution. Her mind becomes affected by the experience. "Living so continually in her own circle of ideas," Hawthorne writes, "and never regulating her mind by a proper reference to present things, Esther Dudley appears to have grown partially crazed" (vol. IX, p. 298). So strong is her faith in the triumph of the Crown that she transforms every battle into a British victory and even acts at times as if the British triumph were already complete. When at the end of the war, John Hancock comes to occupy Province House, Esther Dudley thinks at first that the Royal Governor has returned. She dies when informed of the truth.

This kind of madness was widely recognized by contemporary medical authorities. Philippe Pinel, the French physician still noted today for his radical reform of asylums for the insane, discusses the illness as "delirium upon one subject exclusively" in *A Treatise on Insanity* (1806),[7] a British translation of the French edition of 1801. Drawing on both Pinel and his own medical experience, Benjamin Rush describes the illness as "Partial Intellectual Derangement," or "error in opinion, and conduct, upon some one subject only, with soundness of mind upon all, or nearly all other subjects," in his *Medical Inquiries and Observations, upon the Diseases of the Mind.*[8] Thomas C. Upham, the Bowdoin College philosopher who taught Hawthorne in his senior year, follows the medical men in his chapter on "Mental Alienation" in *Elements of Intellectual Philosophy* (1827). He too describes "Partial mental alienation" as one of the diseases that can afflict the mind.[9] The agreement among these men is not surprising since each drew on the works of his predecessors. Rush cites Pinel in his book, and Upham drew on both not only for his *Elements,* but also for his much more extensive *Outlines of Imperfect and Disordered Mental Action* (1840).

We do not know that Hawthorne read any of these works, but it seems logical to assume that he could have become acquainted with the mental disorder through his association with Upham at Bowdoin College. Speculation aside, we can observe that Hawthorne's treatment of partial insanity closely resembles Rush's description of the disease. Rush divides the illness into two kinds: "When it relates to the persons, affairs, or condition of the patient only, and is attended with distress, it has been called hypochondriasis. When it extends to objects external to the patient, and is attended with pleasure, or the absence of distress, it has been called melancholia. They are different grades only, of the same morbid actions in the brain, and they now and then blend their symptoms with each other."[10] Rush considered both the terms misleading and suggested tristimania as perhaps a better term for the former, amenomania as a more proper term for the latter. For our purposes, the names are not significant. It is rather the state of mind they denote that is most pertinent to Hawthorne's tales and romances.

The best example of hypochondriasis in Hawthorne's fiction is undoubtedly Roderick Elliston in "Egotism; or, The Bosom-Serpent." According to Rush, a hypochondriac may believe "that he has a living animal in his body," or may imagine that he is "converted into an animal" himself. "In this case he adopts the noises and gestures of the animals into which he supposes himself to be transformed."[11] Elliston, of course, thinks he has a serpent in his bosom, and is deeply distressed by the pain he feels gnawing within. He also seems "to imitate the motion of a snake; for, instead of walking straight forward with open front, he [undulates] along the pavement in a curved line," and "an audible hiss" comes from his lips when he speaks (vol. X, pp. 268-69). So disturbed—and disturbing to others—does Elliston become that he is placed for a time "in a private asylum for the insane" (vol. X, p. 278), but the medical doctors who care for him finally decide "that his mental disease did not amount to insanity." Though he was without question eccentric and had made himself a pest to others, "the world was not, without surer ground, entitled to treat him as a madman" (vol. IX, p. 280). Roderick Elliston is, in other words, not totally deranged.

Most of Hawthorne's partially mad characters, however, suffer not from hypochondriasis, like Roderick Elliston, but from melancholia, or, as Rush would have it, amenomania, like Esther Dudley. Her madness extends to objects outside herself, and she feels not distress but rather pleasure in her delusion that British arms will triumph during the Revolution. Many who suffer from this disease, according to Rush, are "enthusiastic votaries" of some idea, cause, or pursuit, and though perfectly sane on other subjects, seek the perpetual motion, the elixir of life, the philosopher's stone, perfection through human reason, or some other much desired goal.[12] An amusing example of this kind of delusion is Peter Goldthwaite's pursuit of wealth through a number of impractical schemes in "Peter Goldthwaite's Treasure" (1838). When all his projects fail, he becomes obsessed with the belief that a fortune lies concealed within his house, and he takes the building apart room by room until nothing is left but the frame and the kitchen. Throughout the search, the crackbrained but harmless Peter remains completely happy; even when the treasure he finds turns out to be worthless, he is ready to speculate again with the money he can obtain from the sale of what remains of his house and lot.

A much more serious form of melancholia or amenomania, is that which afflicts Richard Digby, the religious enthusiast in "The Man of Adamant" (1837). In his firm belief "that Providence had entrusted him, alone of mortals, with the treasure of a true faith" (vol. XI, p. 161), he illustrates perfectly a form of the disease described by Rush. According to the physician, amenomania is "most frequently [seen] in the enthusiasts in religion, in whom it discovers itself in a variety of ways," among them "in a belief that they are the peculiar favourites of heaven, and exclusively possessed of just opinions of the divine will, as revealed in the Scriptures."[13] Digby is, without question, a fine example of the type. Convinced that he alone has found the truth, he refuses to hold communion with his fellows, and, expecting the wrath of God to shower them with fire and brimstone, he withdraws from society lest the boon that he was granted be revoked and he too perish. Guided, he believes, by Providence, he finds a dark cave in the wilderness where he can pray undisturbed, and he congratulates himself that through its "narrow entrance" lies "the only way to Heaven" (vol. XI, p. 163). Here he lives alone in "the sole and constant enjoyment of his happy fortune" (vol. XI, p. 161).

The kind of mental derangement found in Esther Dudley, Peter Goldthwaite, and Richard Digby seems to have held a particular interest for Hawthorne, and he returns to it again and again in his fiction. It forms the very basis of *The Blithedale Romance* (1852), where the plans of enthusiastic projectors are revealed as a kind of insanity.[14] Hollingsworth's obsession with the one idea that moves him—the reform of criminals through "moral, intellectual, and industrial" methods (vol. III, p. 131)—is so described by Coverdale. "It is my private opinion," he writes, "that, at this period of his life, Hollingsworth was fast going mad." Coverdale cites his "prolonged fiddling upon one string; [his] multiform presentation of one idea!" (vol. III, p. 56). Hollingsworth is not alone, however. Blithedale itself is "a kind of Bedlam"—for the time, at least, a madhouse where Coverdale feels himself "getting quite out of [his] reckoning, with regard to the existing state of the world" and losing "the sense of what kind of a world it was, among innumerable schemes of what it might or ought to be" (vol. III, p. 140). Seen in these terms, Blithedale is in no sense an ideal community, but a place of collective insanity—a fitting backdrop for the mad dream of Hollingsworth and its tragic consequences.

Not all Hawthorne's partially deranged characters can be so easily classified. Some exhibit, as Rush maintains in his description of the disease, a blend of the symptoms of both types of madness. The hypochondriac in "The Christmas Banquet" (1844) seems to be such a one, for his delusion not only concerns himself, but is also projected into the external world. His "imagination," Hawthorne writes, "wrought necromancy in his outward and inward world, and caused him to see monstrous faces in the household fire, and dragons in the clouds of sunset, and fiends in the guise of beautiful women, and something ugly or wicked beneath all the pleasant surfaces of nature" (vol. X, p. 288). Another guest at the banquet has the sense of mission typical of the melancholic, but he takes no pleasure in his delusion. In attempting to deliver his message to the world, he "had found either no voice or form of speech, or else no ears to listen." He constantly questions himself, therefore, wondering if he is perhaps "a self-deluding fool," and during the course of the evening, "he quaffed frequent draughts from the sepulchral urn of wine, hoping thus to quench the celes-

tial fire that tortured his own breast, and could not benefit his race" (vol. X, pp. 288-89).

Some of Hawthorne's best-known characters are men of this type. Ethan Brand, in Hawthorne's story of 1850, thinks he has committed the unpardonable sin, a belief that, according to Rush, is typical of some hypochondriacs,[15] but instead of being distressed by the thought, as persons with the delusion usually are, he accepts it calmly and even asserts his willingness to incur the guilt again. On the other hand, Aylmer, the scientist in "The Birth-mark" (1843), is a projector of the melancholic type, but his pursuit of human perfection is not without distress, largely because of the horror he feels at the mark itself and what it represents. Perhaps even Owen Warland in "The Artist of the Beautiful" (1844) may be included in this category. His pursuit of ideal beauty is fraught with personal distress. Both Robert Danforth and Peter Hovenden almost drive him to madness, and his townsmen at one point consider him insane. "In Owen Warland's case," Hawthorne writes, "the judgment of his townspeople may have been correct. Perhaps he was mad. The lack of sympathy—that contrast between himself and his neighbors, which took away the restraint of example— was enough to make him so" (vol. X, p. 462).

There is, of course, a great deal more to all these characters than merely the kind of madness they exhibit. After all, Hawthorne was not concerned with writing case histories of the insane, but with creating works of art through which he could express deeply pondered themes. That he made so many characters the victims of madness is nonetheless significant. They range from the comic Peter Goldthwaite to the somber Ethan Brand, from the physically powerful Hollingsworth to the delicate Owen Warland, and from the pathetic Esther Dudley to the forbidding Richard Digby. They include the self-consumed Roderick Elliston and the aspiring Aylmer, and are concerned with philanthropy, science, philosophy, art, and religion. They include both the social reformer and the defender of the status quo, both colonial figures and contemporary men and women. Hawthorne seems to be saying that the partial derangement they suffer is a common affliction of human nature. It distorts the attitudes of the most well-meaning of men and often leads to results that they do not anticipate. It is, therefore, a primary force in the motivation of character and a major element in the revelation of theme.

Its function, however, is not always negative. Even at his most deranged, tortured by jealousy and severely judgmental of others, Roderick Elliston is an agent of truth. He correctly points out that other people too harbor serpents in their bosoms. Old Mr. Ellenwood serves a similar purpose in "The Wedding-Knell" (1836). He is introduced as a character whose "diseased sensibility" had caused him to shrink from public notice, yet whose "wild eccentricity of conduct" had led people to search "his lineage for an hereditary taint of insanity" (vol. IX, p. 28). When he comes to marry the twice-widowed Mrs. Dabney dressed in a shroud and accompanied by a funereal train, he seems to confirm his derangement, yet the point he makes is valid. The worldly old woman has clung desperately to youth, has dressed and adorned herself like a young girl, and is surrounded at her wedding by youthful attendants. In other words, her appearance is even less appropriate than his. The madness of her struggle against time is at last brought home to her by the truth-revealing madness of her aged lover, and the two, finally in their right minds, marry in their old age, not for this world but for eternity.

A related use of madness appears in *The House of the Seven Gables* (1851). Like old Mr. Ellenwood, Hepzibah and Clifford Pyncheon are presented as partially mad. Hepzibah has lived alone for many years in the dark old house, and "though she [has] her valuable and redeeming traits, [she has] grown to be a kind of lunatic, by imprisoning herself so long in one place, with no other company than a single series of ideas, and but one affection, and one bitter sense of wrong" (vol. II, p. 174). She takes pride in her Pyncheon past, shrinks from contact with the townspeople, and dotes on her brother Clifford. He has been driven to near imbecility by the wrong that was done him—his imprisonment for a crime he did not commit—and his mind, ruined by the experience, is "without force or volition" (vol. II, p. 224). But if Clifford is "partly imbecile," he is also "partly crazy" (vol. II, pp. 157-58). On one occasion he almost leaps from the arched window on the second story of the house into a procession that is passing in the street. To the people below, the "wild, haggard figure, [with] his gray locks floating in the wind" (vol. II, p. 166) must seem deranged.

On the other hand, Judge Jaffrey Pyncheon, Clifford and Hepzibah's cousin, appears to all the world an eminently sane person, concerned as he is with the solid realities of life: business and politics. His offer of help to his cousins seems only kind and Hepzibah's refusal seems mad, yet when Jaffrey threatens to put Clifford into an asylum for the insane if he does not tell him the secret of their deceased uncle's wealth—a secret which Jaffrey is sure Clifford possesses—the Judge's own mental state is revealed. Hepzibah tells him correctly that it is he who is "diseased in mind." He already has more than enough money to keep him in luxury for the rest of his life and pass on riches to his only son, yet he would do "so mad a thing" as persecute his cousin only to acquire more. With his "hard and grasping spirit," he is committing once again "in another shape" the sin of their original ancestor, "and sending down to [his] posterity the curse inherited from him." Though Jaffrey tells her to "talk sense,"

it is clear that the half-mad Hepzibah has in fact done so (vol. II, pp. 236-37). She has discerned the hidden madness in the ambitious Judge.

A more complex version of the same theme appears in "The Minister's Black Veil." When the Reverend Mr. Hooper places a piece of crape over his face one Sunday morning to preach a sermon on secret sin, he is immediately labeled mad by a member of his congregation, and the village physician concludes that "something must surely be amiss with Mr. Hooper's intellects" (vol. IX, p. 41). As time goes on, even Elizabeth, "his plighted wife," thinks that his dark fantasy might be "a symptom of mental disease" (vol. IX, pp. 45, 47). But if people suspect him of madness, the severity of his affliction remains an open question. "By persons who claimed a superiority to popular prejudice," the veil is "reckoned merely an eccentric whim, such as often mingles with the sober actions of men otherwise rational, and tinges them all with its own semblance of insanity." To the multitude, however, the minister is "a bugbear," an object of both curiosity and dread. Indeed, the minister himself seems to share in their attitude, for he fears to look into a mirror or "drink at a still fountain," and he admits to Elizabeth that he is lonely and frightened in the "miserable obscurity" of the black veil (vol. IX, pp. 47-48).

Whatever his mental state, the minister is another of Hawthorne's revealers of truth. The point he repeatedly makes is that all men refuse to show their real selves to others. He can smile, therefore, at the reactions of those who, terrified by the symbol he uses to reveal this ruth, are not appalled by the reality it represents. Even in his grief when Elizabeth parts from him, he smiles "to think that only a material emblem [separates] him from happiness, though the horrors which it shadowed forth, must be drawn darkly between the fondest of lovers" (vol. IX, p. 47). Yet if Hooper perceives this truth, he himself may err in the way he tries to express it. The veil darkens the world to his perception and prevents him from seeing as clearly as he might. It throws its obscurity on the pages of Scripture when he tries to read, and it even lies between him and God when he raises his eyes to heaven. Perhaps Mr. Hooper is indeed mad in the dark view he takes of reality. Such madness, however, would not invalidate the truth he has tried to express, that there is on every face an unacknowledged black veil.

One type of madness in Hawthorne's fiction remains to be mentioned, the cases of demonic possession that he occasionally depicted. In "Young Goodman Brown" (1835), for example, Brown is depicted as "maddened with despair" when, well along his journey into the forest, he sees the pink ribbons belonging to Faith, his wife. Convinced that his "Faith is gone" and the world has been given to the devil, Brown breaks into hideous laughter and rushes through the trackless wilderness "with the instinct that guides mortal man to evil." Though the forest is "peopled with frightful sounds," Brown is "himself the chief horror of the scene," and indeed there is nothing in the forest more frightful than he. As he flies through the dark woods, he brandishes "his staff with frenzied gestures, now giving vent to an inspiration of horrid blasphemy, and now shouting forth such laughter, as set all the echoes of the forest laughing like demons around him. The fiend in his own shape," Hawthorne comments, "is less hideous, than when he rages in the breast of man." The image of Brown is that of a man possessed. He has become, as Hawthorne calls him, a demoniac in his headlong flight toward the Satanic meeting (vol. X, pp. 83-84).

Miriam's model, the spectral character who haunts the unfortunate girl in *The Marble Faun,* is another example of this kind of madness. When the character is first introduced, Hawthorne offers a number of explanations to account for his presence in the Catacomb of St. Calixtus. Some explanations are matter-of-fact: he might have been merely a Roman beggar, a political offender, a robber, a thief, or an assassin hiding from the police. Other explanations are more suggestive. He might also "have been a lunatic" who makes "it his dark pleasure to dwell among the tombs, like" the Gerasene demoniac, "whose awful cry echoes afar to us from Scripture times" (vol. IV, p. 35).[16] He is even associated with the legendary Memmius, the "man, or demon, or Man-Demon," who spied on the early Christians and was therefore condemned to haunt the catacomb seeking "to beguile new victims into his own misery" (vol. IV, pp. 32-33). The demonic aspect of the character is maintained throughout the book. He is seen as the model for the demon in Guido Reni's preparatory sketch for his painting of the Archangel Michael, he is a creature who must be exorcised by Miriam with water from the Trevi fountain, and he is the evil spirit that inhabited the body of Brother Antonio, the Capuchin monk.

Contemporary medical practice allowed no room, of course, for this kind of madness. Though Philippe Pinel included a brief section on "demoniacal possession" in his *Treatise on Insanity,* this son of the French Revolution dismissed the possessed as merely "extravagant maniacs." One "need only visit a lunatic asylum in order to appreciate justly the nature of their pretended inspiration. In a word, demoniacs of all descriptions are to be classed either with maniacs or melancholics."[17] Benjamin Rush, the physician, did not mention demonic possession in his *Medical Inquiries and Observations, upon the Diseases of the Mind,* nor did the philosopher Thomas C. Upham in his discussions of mental alienation and disordered mental action. Why then, one may ask, did Hawthorne, the artist, include it in his fiction? Part of the answer lies in his theory of the romance, outlined in his preface to *The House*

of the Seven Gables. There he justified the inclusion of the marvelous, so long as it was treated delicately, to create the kind of atmosphere that he deemed necessary for presenting in the most effective manner the truths of the human heart. Wherever it appears in Hawthorne's fiction, demonic possession was certainly included with this artistic purpose in mind.

There were also thematic reasons for its use. It enabled him to suggest the relation between the psychological and the moral. Both Goodman Brown and Miriam's model are motivated by evil. Deliberately seeking it in the forest, Goodman Brown falls into a moral and mental trap from which he cannot extricate himself; he ends with a vision of reality that is neither sane nor morally sound. Miriam's model undergoes a similar but more complex development. His original character "betrayed traits so evil, so treacherous, so wild, and yet so strangely subtle, as could only be accounted for by . . . insanity" (vol. IV, pp. 430-31). His madness, moreover, was "developed by those very acts of depravity which it suggested, and still more intensified by the remorse that ultimately followed them" (vol. IV, p. 432). He is at once both mad and wicked, and each element in his nature influences the other. Because they exemplify so unusual a degree of moral and psychological obliquity, one that transcends the experience of more commonplace sinners and madmen, Hawthorne needed some unusual means for revealing the moral and mental condition of both Brown and the model. He found it in the suggestion of the demonic.

One aspect of the model's experience was accounted for in contemporary medical practice—the relation between guilt and madness. In his discussion "of the *remote* and *exciting causes* of intellectual derangement," Benjamin Rush had observed: "The understanding is sometimes deranged through the medium of the moral faculties. A conscience burdened with guilt, whether real or imaginary, is a frequent cause of madness. The latter produces it much oftener than the former." Rush was aware that "a morbid sensibility" of conscience predisposed some "to madness from the most trifling causes,"[18] perhaps like Mr. Hooper in "The Minister's Black Veil," who suffered from "so painful a degree of self-distrust, that even the mildest censure would lead him to consider an indifferent action as a crime" (vol. IX, p. 44). But "the most distressing grade of derangement under this head," Rush goes on to say, "is, where real guilt, and a diseased imagination, concur in producing it," and he cites "the occasional acts of self-mutilation which deranged patients sometimes inflict upon themselves, and the painful and protracted austerities voluntarily imposed upon the body in Catholic countries."[19] Miriam's model acts in this manner in his penitential phase: "his severe and self-inflicted penances had even acquired him the reputation of unusual sanctity" among his brother monks (vol. IV, p. 432).

The relation of madness to guilt is especially important in Hawthorne's fiction, for it informs his best and most profound works, *The Scarlet Letter* and *The Marble Faun*. In the latter book, the demonic model has a baneful influence on most of the other characters. His persecution of Miriam makes it clear that there is some dark secret in their background, and though she is apparently innocent of any wrongdoing herself, her involvement with the model drives her toward madness. A hint of mental unbalance appears in the drawings she shows Donatello, each depicting a scene of bloodshed in which a woman has destroyed a man. Miriam tries to dismiss the pictures as "ugly phantoms that stole out of my mind; not things that I created, but things that haunt me" (vol. IV, p. 45). They are nonetheless unmistakable signs of psychological trouble. Moreover, when she visits Kenyon in his studio she tries to reveal the source of her problem. "There is a secret in my heart," she confesses, "that burns me!—that tortures me! Sometimes, I fear to go mad of it!" (vol. IV, p. 128). Unfortunately, Kenyon turns her aside with a cold reply, and Miriam must keep her dreadful secret bottled up within her.

What she fears, however, does happen the following evening when the group of artists takes a moonlight ramble through Rome. In the shadows of the Coliseum, they see the model going about the shrines on his knees and praying at each. Miriam withdraws and, throwing off her self-control, concentrates "the elements of a long insanity into" a single moment. Unaware that Donatello has followed her, "and fancying herself wholly unseen, the beautiful Miriam began to gesticulate extravagantly, gnashing her teeth, flinging her arms wildly abroad, stamping with her foot. It was as if she had stept aside, for an instant, solely to snatch the relief of a brief fit of madness." Angered when she perceives Donatello watching her, she warns him away, "speaking low, but still with the almost insanity of the moment vibrating in her voice" (vol. IV, pp. 157-58). A terrible evil, she says, hangs over her, and if he ever expects to live the long and happy life for which he seems most fitted, he must cast her off. Miriam's madness has reached the point of almost demonic intensity, and a short time later it leads to a fatal consequence.

Alone together on the Tarpeian Rock after their companions have departed, Miriam and Donatello see the model approach them out of the shadows, and at one brief but meaningful glance from Miriam, Donatello hurls him to his death. A horror or ecstasy, or both, Hawthorne writes, had flamed up in Miriam's heart, and "be the emotion what it might, it had blazed up more madly, when Donatello flung his victim off the cliff, and more and more, while his shriek went quivering downward" (vol. IV, p. 173). The initial reaction of both is a kind of insanity. "Guilt has its moment of rapture," Hawthorne observes. "The foremost result of

a broken law is ever an ecstatic sense of freedom. And thus there exhaled upward (out of their dark sympathy, at the base of which lay a human corpse) a bliss, or an insanity, which the unhappy pair imagined to be well-worth the sleepy innocence that was forever lost to them." Their spirits rise "to the solemn madness of the occasion" (vol. IV, p. 176), and they wander without remorse or purpose through the streets of Rome. Only the next morning, when the "strong madness that hurried [them] into guilt" is gone (vol. IV, p. 178), do they return to a more sober view of their situation.

The experience transforms them both. Miriam is awakened to love for Donatello, and the Faun becomes a man as a result of his sin and suffering. But they also go through a second kind of madness after the elation deserts them and Miriam realizes that they must part. When she visits Hilda the day after the crime and is cruelly rejected by her erstwhile friend, "her trouble [seeks] relief in a half-frenzied raillery," and she is filled with a "wild emotion" that she cannot suppress (vol. IV, p. 209). Donatello, at her urging, retires to his ancestral home among the Apennines. When Kenyon visits him there, Donatello describes what it must be like to fall from a great height, and Kenyon is "aghast at the passionate horrour which was betrayed in the Count's words, and still more in his wild gestures and ghastly look" (vol. IV, p. 261). Both Miriam and Donatello are driven toward madness by their crime, and each suffers alone at this stage of the experience. Only when they are brought together at Perugia do they return to sanity, but then their new state entails a final separation of the lovers: prison for Donatello and penitence for Miriam.

But Miriam and Donatello are not the only ones affected by their crime. Guilt and madness also visit the innocent Hilda, who is an accidental witness to the murder. Horrified by what she has seen, Hilda almost feels it "a crime to know of such a thing, and to keep it to" herself (vol. IV, p. 210). She cannot endure the burden. As she tells the priest in the confessional at St. Peter's, she felt herself cut off from God. "I groped for Him in the darkness, as it were, and found Him not—found nothing but a dreadful solitude, and this crime in the midst of it! I could not bear it. It seemed as if I made the awful guilt my own, by keeping it hidden in my heart. I grew a fearful thing to myself. I was going mad!" (vol. IV, p. 359). By means of her confession, Hilda is restored to sanity. As she tells the shocked Kenyon, who had seen her enter the confessional, her talk with the priest has saved her reason. "It was the sin of others that drove me thither; not my own, though it almost seemed so. Being what I am, I must either have done what you saw me doing, or have gone mad" (vol. IV, pp. 367-68).

Hilda is last in a chain of cause and effect initiated by the demonic acts of Miriam's model, the final victim of a process that ensues when evil is loosed in the world. The relation of madness to guilt is thus treated sequentially in *The Marble Faun.* The evil spreads from character to character as each, deeply affected by the crimes of others, is driven towards insanity. In *The Scarlet Letter,* on the other hand, Hawthorne treats the relation differently. He focuses more sharply on the inner lives of his characters, probing their emotional responses as each struggles with guilt and madness over a period of some seven years. When *The Scarlet Letter* opens, the act of adultery, which in seventeenth-century Boston was both a sin and a crime, has already taken place. It has been revealed through Hester's pregnancy and the birth of Pearl, and the only known partner has been brought to justice. All that remains, therefore, is to explore the effects of guilt on Hester Prynne, the publicly exposed sinner, and Arthur Dimmesdale, the secret one, as each attempts to come to terms with the act and its consequences.

Both are afflicted with madness. When Hester mounts the scaffold in the opening scene and faces the "unrelenting eyes" of the people, she feels "as if she must needs shriek out with the full power of her lungs, and cast herself from the scaffold down upon the ground, or else go mad at once." She retains her self-control, however, by letting her mind wander over the past as "phantasmagoric forms" from her childhood and maiden years come "swarming back upon her" (vol. I, p. 57). Hester is relieved from this state by the appearance of Roger Chillingworth and her firm resistance to the ministers' command that she reveal her partner in sin. Then, exhausted by her ordeal, Hester sinks into insensibility when the Reverend Mr. Wilson preaches. But on her return to prison, Hester breaks down completely. In her "state of nervous excitement," she has to be watched constantly lest she harm herself "or do some half-frenzied mischief to" her child (vol. I, p. 70), and when night approaches, she becomes impossible to control. The jailer summons the physician, Roger Chillingworth, and reports that she "hath been like a possessed one." The doctor finds her "in no reasonable state of mind," but he does succeed in quieting her (vol. I, pp. 71-73).

Though Hester recovers from this paroxysm, her mental state remains unhealthy. There are several manifestations of her condition: her partial self-delusion concerning her reasons for remaining in New England; a "morbid meddling of conscience with an immaterial matter" (vol. I, p. 84)—her pleasure in sewing, for example, which she interprets as sin; and her attitude toward others. Hester is troubled with the same evil that afflicts Roderick Elliston and overwhelms Goodman Brown. "She felt or fancied . . . that the scarlet letter had endowed her with a new sense. She shuddered to believe, yet could not help believing, that it gave her a sympathetic knowledge of the hidden sin in other

hearts." Unlike Roderick Elliston, however, she does not openly accuse others of sin, and unlike Goodman Brown, she does not fall under the shadow of perpetual gloom. Instead, she is "terror-stricken by the revelations that were thus made" (vol. I, p. 86). Though she feels that evil lurks in magistrate and minister, in proper matron and in blushing maiden, she nonetheless struggles "to believe that no fellow–mortal was guilty like herself," a proof, Hawthorne suggests, that despite her unbalance, "all was not corrupt in this poor victim of her own frailty, and man's hard law" (vol. II, p. 87).

Because she must care for her daughter Pearl, Hester is able to maintain a degree of equanimity in her difficult situation, but when the authorities consider taking the child from her, Hester again approaches madness. She hurries to the Governor's Hall, ostensibly to deliver a pair of gloves but actually to assert her own rights to the child. When it seems as if they do intend to take Pearl away from her, Hester reacts with great emotion. She raises "her voice almost to a shriek" and with a "wild and singular appeal" which shows that her "situation had provoked her to little less than madness," she turns to Arthur Dimmesdale and charges him to speak for her (vol. I, p. 113). Dimmesdale succeeds in persuading the Governor to let her retain the little girl, but the aftermath of the scene reveals how much has hung in the balance for Hester Prynne. Had they taken the child, she tells Mistress Hibbens, the reputed witch, "I would willingly have gone with thee into the forest, and signed my name in the Black Man's book too, and that with mine own blood!" (vol. I, p. 117). Because the child is not taken from her, Hester is saved from both madness and sin.

The unfortunate Arthur Dimmesdale has no Pearl to save him. He lives instead with his relentless but unknown enemy, Roger Chillingworth, who probes his very soul to learn if he was indeed Hester's partner in the adultery, and who exults like a devil incarnate when he discovers the mark on the minister's breast. Beset on one side, then, by the demonic Chillingworth, yet venerated on the other by his parishioners, who treat him as if he were a saint on earth, Dimmesdale is driven to madness. His madness takes a form well recognized by the medical theory of the time and later exemplified by Miriam's model and, indeed, even Donatello. Like the model, Dimmesdale indulges in self-inflicted acts of penance, here more clearly specified as the "bloody scourge" which "this Protestant and Puritan divine [applies to] his own shoulders; laughing bitterly at himself the while, and smiting so much the more pitilessly, because of that bitter laugh." He engages in rigorous fasts, and like Donatello, keeps long vigils in the night. He even views his own face in the mirror under a strong light, typifying thereby "the constant introspection wherewith he tortured, but could not purify, himself" (vol. I, pp. 144-45).

Dimmesdale's madness is so intense that he suffers mental delusions. During his vigils visions seem "to flit before him; perhaps seen doubtfully, and by a faint light of their own, in the remote dimness of the chamber, or more vividly, and close beside him, within the looking-glass." Some are "diabolic shapes" that mock him, some "shining angels" that fly upward filled with sorrow. "The dead friends of his youth" appear, as do "his white-bearded father, with a saint-like frown, and his mother, turning her face away as she" passes. Even a spectral Hester Prynne glides by, leading Pearl "and pointing her forefinger, first, at the scarlet letter on her bosom, and then at the clergyman's own breast." Dimmesdale is never totally deluded by these visions. "At any moment, by an effort of his will, he could discern substances through their misty lack of substance, and convince himself that they were not solid in their nature" like an oaken table or a "volume of divinity." So false has he become, however, that these visions are, "in one sense," at least, "the truest and most substantial things" in the life of the guilt-ridden minister (vol. I, p. 145).

On one of these terrible nights, Dimmesdale performs his maddest act of all. He dresses himself carefully, as if for public worship, and "walking in the shadow of a dream, as it were, and perhaps actually under the influence of a species of somnambulism" (vol. I, p. 147), he goes out to stand on the scaffold. There his acts bespeak his mental state. He thinks that he shrieks aloud, but no one hears him. He smiles at the conceits that enter his mind when he sees the Reverend Mr. Wilson approach with a lantern, and he wonders if he is going mad. He speaks to the old minister as he passes—or thinks he does, for the words "were uttered only within his imagination." His mind even makes "an involuntary effort to relieve itself by a kind of lurid playfulness," and a "grisly sense of the humorous [steals] in among the solemn phantoms of his thought" (vol. I, p. 151). Finally, when a meteor flashes across the sky, "his guilty imagination" makes him interpret it as a red letter A. In his "highly disordered mental state," he extends "his egotism over the whole expanse of nature, until the firmament itself [appears] no more than a fitting page for his soul's history and fate" (vol. I, p. 155).

Dimmesdale is unable to help himself. Though he feels a surge of life course through his veins when he joins hands with Hester and Pearl on the scaffold, his "dread of public exposure" (vol. I, p. 153) maintains its grip on him, and when Chillingworth comes upon them, Dimmesdale places himself again in the old man's power. Hester, on her part, is horrified at the minister's condition. "She saw that he stood on the verge of lunacy, if he had not already stepped across it" (vol. I, p. 166), and she knows the cause. He has been in the hands of a physician who used his opportunities for a cruel purpose. Chillingworth kept "the sufferer's con-

science . . . in an irritated state, the tendency of which was, not to cure by wholesome pain, but to disorganize and corrupt his spiritual being. Its result, on earth, could hardly fail to be insanity, and hereafter, that eternal alienation from the Good and True, of which madness is perhaps the early type" (vol. I, p. 193). Insane on earth and damned in the afterlife, Dimmesdale must doubly perish unless Hester can help him. Her attempt, however, leads to a result that she does not anticipate when she meets him in the forest.

Hester reveals to Dimmesdale that Chillingworth was her husband, hoping thereby to free the minister from the old man's control. Unfortunately, Dimmesdale is too weak to act on his own, and when Hester offers escape from the torment he has been suffering, Dimmesdale consents to go with her to Europe, fully aware that he will be entering an adulterous union. The decision seems to give him relief, but after the brief interlude with Hester and Pearl, strange things begin to happen. He hurries back to town with feelings so excited as to lend "him unaccustomed physical energy." He leaps "across the plashy places," pushes through the underbrush, climbs the hills, and plunges into hollows "with an unweariable activity that astonished him" (vol. I, p. 216). Dimmesdale's reaction here is the counterpart of Miriam and Donatello's, when, after murdering the model, they feel the insane elation that comes from having committed a crime.[20] Now Dimmesdale has sinned in the forests more culpably perhaps than he had previously done even in his passionate union with Hester. "Tempted by a dream of happiness," Hawthorne writes, "he had yielded himself with deliberate choice, as he had never done before, to what he knew was deadly sin" (vol. I, p. 222).

Out of the guilt comes madness, manifest first in the unusual physical activity and then in the frightening thoughts that enter his mind. Dimmesdale feels a desire to corrupt the people he meets: to utter some "blasphemous suggestions [about] the communion-supper" to one of his deacons; to whisper an "argument against . . . immortality" into an old woman's ear; to plant licentious thoughts in a young girl's mind; and even to "teach some very wicked words to a knot of little Puritan children" (vol. I, pp. 218-20). So appalled is he by these compulsions that Dimmesdale questions his sanity, and well he might. His actions resemble a manifestation of madness described by Benjamin Rush. Though Rush observed that "the ravings and conduct of mad people" corresponded in general to "their natural tempers and dispositions," he noted an exception: "All those cases in which persons of exemplary piety and purity of character utter profane, or impious, or indelicate language, and behave in other respects contrary to their moral habits."[21] Though Dimmesdale has suffered long from hidden guilt, he has always been faithful in fulfilling his ministerial duties, and his public life has been exemplary. The compulsions he feels when he leaves the forest, therefore, are utterly out of character and must be considered aberrations.

Yet Dimmesdale returns to sanity—and almost at once. He has left the man he used to be in the forest, and when he arrives in town, he frees himself from the power of Chillingworth. Dimmesdale believes he has little to do with the change that occurs, however. He feels himself acted on by an external force. He rewrites the Election Sermon "with such an impulsive flow of thought and emotion, that he [fancies] himself inspired" (vol. I, p. 225), an opinion shared by those who hear him deliver it. When he walks to the meeting house in the public procession, he exhibits a spiritual energy that seems to carry his feeble body and all but converts it to spirit itself. After the sermon, however, the inspiration leaves him, and Dimmesdale must summon a reluctant Hester to help him up the steps of the scaffold. Even here, however, he believes that the grace of God alone gives him the will to resist the evil physician and take his rightful place where she had been punished seven years before. Though Hester may question his decision and Chillingworth call him a madman, Dimmesdale is acting his sanest when, following the spirit that moves him, he makes his public confession.

If madness, as Hawthorne suggests, is the counterpart in this world of damnation in the hereafter, sanity and salvation must also stand in a similar relation. Such certainly seems to be the case with Arthur Dimmesdale, whose alienation from God is greatest when his insanity is at its height and whose hope for a future life returns when his madness fades. Because he is also without question one of the most fully and sympathetically developed madmen in Hawthorne's fiction, his experience must be considered critical in any interpretation of the other characters in the tales and romances who also suffer from some degree of insanity. Though they may differ from him and from each other in their culpability and degree of sinfulness, all illustrate the complexity of the human being in whom the moral and psychological elements so mix that each has a vital influence on the other. Seen in these terms, madness is a major element in Hawthorne's fiction. It signals a moral as well as a psychological unbalance in the characters it afflicts, and an alienation from God and isolation from their fellows that manifests itself in the derangement of their minds.

Notes

1 A recent discussion of psychology in Hawthorne's fiction is Allan Gardner Smith, *The Analysis of Motives: Early American Psychology and Fiction* (Amsterdam: Editions Rodopi N. V., 1980), pp. 76-119, where he discusses topics such as: "The Disordered Mind," pp. 82-86; "The Haunted Mind," pp. 87-94; "Guilt and Identity," pp. 95-99; "Obsession," pp. 100-05; and "Isolation," pp. 106-10. There is also a chapter on mental alienation in John Thomas McKiernan, "The Psychology of Nathaniel Hawthorne," unpublished dissertation, Pennsylvania State University, 1957, pp. 127-69. McKiernan deals not so much with madness, as with psychological aberration. He discusses the causes (pp. 128-34) and treatment (pp. 161-69) of mental alienation, and he presents as symptoms: "Disorders of Perception, Associations, or Imagination," pp. 135-46; "Hyperactivity," pp. 146-49; "Disorganized Behavior," pp. 149-50; "Mechanisms of Adjustment," pp. 150-58; and "Dreams," pp. 158-60. Neither Smith nor McKiernan, however, treats the subject as I have here.

2 Nathaniel Hawthorne, *Twice-told Tales,* The Centenary Edition of the Works of Nathaniel Hawthorne (Columbus: Ohio State Univ. Press, 1974), vol. IX, p. 181. All citations of Hawthorne's works in my text refer to volume and page numbers in the Centenary Edition.

3 Although Hawthorne cites as his source for this story an anecdote of Gilbert Stuart recounted in William Dunlap, *History of the Rise and Progress of the Arts of Design in the United States,* the madman in the anecdote commits suicide. The homicidal mania of Walter Ludlow is thus Hawthorne's own invention. See Dunlap, *History* (New York, 1834), vol. I, p. 187.

4 Hawthorne could have learned about Rush's work on insanity from Thomas C. Upham, who taught at Bowdoin College during Hawthorne's senior year. Upham cites both Rush and Philippe Pinel, the well-known French authority on madness, in his own discussion of mental alienation. See, for example, Thomas C. Upham, *Elements of Intellectual Philosophy,* 2nd ed. (Portland, 1828), pp. 513-15, 517-18.

5 Benjamin Rush, "On the Study of Medical Jurisprudence," *Sixteen Introductory Lectures* (Philadelphia, 1811), pp. 380-88. The lecture was delivered November 5, 1810. Though Smith cites this lecture in his discussion of Charles Brockden Brown (*Analysis of Motives,* p. 7), he does not apply it to Hawthorne's tale.

6 Benjamin Rush, *Medical Inquiries and Observations, upon the Diseases of the Mind* (Philadelphia, 1812), p. 152.

7 Philippe Pinel, *A Treatise on Insanity* (Sheffield, 1806), p. 136.

8 Rush, *Medical Inquiries,* p. 74.

9 Upham, *Elements,* pp. 518ff.

10 Rush, *Medical Inquiries,* p. 74.

[11] Rush, *Medical Inquiries,* p. 80.

[12] Rush, *Medical Inquiries,* pp. 136-37.

[13] Rush, *Medical Inquiries,* pp. 137-38.

[14] Hawthorne's attitude toward reformers is also revealed in an entry of 1835 in *The American Notebooks.* Hawthorne wrote: "A sketch to be given of a modern reformer—a type of the extreme doctrines on the subject of slaves, cold-water, and all that. He goes about the streets haranguing most eloquently, and is on the point of making many converts, when his labors are suddenly interrupted by the appearance of a keeper of a mad-house, whence he has escaped." *Hawthorne's Lost Notebook 1835-1841* (University Park: Pennsylvania State Univ. Press, 1978), p. 12. A slightly altered version, probably edited by Sophia Hawthorne for her edition of the *Notebooks,* may be found in the Centenary Edition, vol. VIII, p. 10.

[15] Rush, *Medical Inquiries,* p. 116.

[16] For the Biblical source, see Mark 5:1-20. Hawthorne also refers to the incident in an entry of 1835 in *The American Notebooks.* See *Hawthorne's Lost Notebook,* p. 5. The entry, probably deleted by Sophia Hawthorne when she prepared her edition of the *Notebooks,* does not appear in the Centenary Edition.

[17] Pinel, *Treatise on Insanity,* pp. 237-38.

[18] Rush, *Medical Inquiries,* pp. 30, 44.

[19] Rush, *Medical Inquiries,* p. 44.

[20] Dimmesdale's experience seems to be related also to Goodman Brown's mad rush toward the Satanic meeting in the forest.

[21] Rush, *Medical Inquiries,* p. 160.

Paul McCarthy (essay date 1990)

SOURCE: "The World is Mad: *Moby-Dick,*" in *"The Twisted Mind": Madness in Herman Melville's Fiction,* University of Iowa Press, 1990, pp. 50-73.

[*In the following essay, McCarthy studies Herman Melville's depiction of madness in* Moby-Dick, *arguing that "madness is all but ubiquitous" in this novel. McCarthy contends that madness is found in animals and humans, that the universe itself appears to be mad. Furthermore, McCarthy analyzes the distinct manifestations of insanity in the characters on board the ship and demonstrates the progression of madness in Ahab.*]

After five strenous months writing *Redburn* and *White-Jacket* in the crowded house at 103 Fourth Street in New York City, Melville was a tired, somewhat disillusioned man in need of rest and a change of scene. With blessings of his concerned family and others and financial assistance from Judge Shaw, Melville boarded the *Southampton,* a British liner, on 11 October 1849 for an extended trip to England and the Continent. He took along proof sheets of *White-Jacket* with the hope of gaining a better contract in England. The trip proved to be beneficial and eventful. Melville visited a number of noteworthy places, met interesting people, discovered to his surprise that *Redburn* was selling well, and secured a good arrangement for the publication of *White-Jacket.* One passenger on the *Southampton* was George J. Adler, a professor of German and linguistics at New York University, who, like Melville, had just completed exhausting intellectual labors and was going abroad to regain his health. As he confessed to Melville shortly after they met, he "was almost crazy . . . for a time."[1]

The traditional view of the Melville-Adler relationship has been that the learned Adler stimulated Melville's interest in philosophic ideas, including those of Kant and Swedenborg, that were to appear in his writing and thinking for some years. In an excellent 1986 study of the meeting and relationship, Marovitz explains that Melville's main benefit from the friendship was not philosophic but psychological: Melville discovered that the other man had tensions and difficulties resembling his own. "The German philologist simultaneously reflected an image of Melville's present psychological state and represented to him as well a portentous confrontation with his own fears and intellectual aspirations." During their many meetings aboard ship Melville's "subliminal fear" of insanity was usually in his conscious mind. Melville's encounters early in the journey with two crazy male passengers, one of whom he unsuccessfully attempted to save from drowning, would be a reminder of his own vulnerability.[2] This appears sound. It is likely though that such fears were close to the surface before Melville came aboard ship, for after months of intense writing, some of it on difficult youthful experiences and scenes of poverty and abnormality, he was fatigued.

Although there is no evidence that the two friends met again after parting in Paris, the interest was certainly there. Back in this country, Melville inquired of Adler in four letters to their mutual friend Evert Duyckinck, two written in the fall of 1850 and two early in 1851.[3] In January 1851, Adler sent to Melville in Pittsfield a copy of his recent translation of Goethe's *Iphigenia in Tauris.* Although evidence of Melville's response has not been found, it is hard to believe that he would not respond. In 1853, after a violent outbreak of hallucinations and delusions, perhaps in the form of monomania or agoraphobia, Adler was committed to the private

Bloomingdale asylum in New York City, from which he wrote to Duyckinck on 10 October 1853, asking for his assistance and that of "my literary confederates" in obtaining his freedom. Adler had described his situation and complaints in September letters to the president of New York University and the New York mayor.[4] There is no known record of responses or replies to Adler's complaints or to his pleas for support. If Melville had been aware of Adler's situation, he would undoubtedly have written to his friend. The hiatus in the Melville-Duyckinck relationship between 1852 and 1856 may possibly account for lack of evidence of Melville's response to Adler and, conceivably, of his ignorance as well of Adler's stay at Bloomingdale, but that, too, is difficult to believe, for Melville corresponded with others in New York, especially with his brother Allan, who as a lawyer and interested bystander might have learned of Adler's situation and informed Melville. At any rate, Melville did not forget Adler, for he was among the very few to attend Adler's funeral in 1868.

When Melville left on the *Southampton* for England, he took along a copy of *Old Wine in New Bottles: or, Spare Hours of a Student in Paris* (1848), a collection of letters describing typical Paris scenes and also accounts of insane asylums, patients, prisons, inmates, morgues, and the like.[5] According to his journal, Melville stopped in at least a morgue and an abattoir. He also stayed in a place recommended by the author of the book, Dr. Augustus Kinsley Gardner, a friend and fellow contributor to Duyckinck's *Literary World.* Dr. Gardner was a young physician described by Leon Howard as "perhaps the most stimulating of all the young author's acquaintances at the time; and he, with other literary lights . . . in the Duyckinck circle, kept Melville's mind in a simple state of excitement too strong to be relieved by a simple whaling story."[6] During Melville's productive years he and Dr. Gardner probably talked about one topic of interest to both—the nature and effects of insanity. Although Dr. Gardner's practice was primarily in obstetrics and diseases of women and children, his preference was "in the direction of diseases of the brain." He had received psychiatric training at the Poor House Lunatic Asylum in Boston and for several years was in charge of an asylum near Bloomingdale. After Melville returned to New York City in February 1850, Gardner apparently became the family physician; he was in attendance at the time of Malcolm Melville's suicide in 1867.[7] For someone like Melville, the spirited doctor would seem to be a natural source of information on questions of mental aberration.

Another man indirectly connected with Melville's trip to England and perhaps the individual who most kindled his interest in insanity during these years was his father-in-law, Judge Lemuel Shaw, who was knowledgeable about legal aspects of insanity. Melville was on close terms with Shaw, a family friend for many years and chief justice of the Supreme Judicial Court of Massachusetts. Judge Shaw presided over many important cases, including several involving insanity.

A hallmark case in January 1844 centered on Abner Rogers, an inmate of the Massachusetts State Prison charged with the murder of the asylum warden. Rogers claimed that he had heard voices stating that the warden would kill him. He therefore acted to protect himself. A defense attorney during the 1844 trial in Boston entered a plea of not guilty by reason of insanity. In that day, no single interpretation or definition of insanity prevailed, but the McNaghten decision reached in England in 1843 "supposedly set the pattern in the United States." According to the decision or the rules therein, a person was judged insane if the individual was unable to distinguish right from wrong and suffered from a defect of reason. An insane person would not understand that his or her criminal or illegal act was wrong. The McNaghten rules were applied for the first time in the United States in the Rogers case, but authorities then and now differ as to the extent of Judge Shaw's knowledge of the rules and the extent also of his application of the rules in the trial proceedings. According to a modern legal authority, Leonard W. Levy, Shaw was not only influenced by the McNaghten rules but in effect strengthened them. According to a modern medical authority, Jacques M. Quen, M.D., Shaw was not aware during the trial of the McNaghten rules. Whatever the case, Judge Shaw was apparently influenced by American psychiatrists testifying at the trial, including Isaac Ray, author of a major work on insanity and an asylum director. Ray agreed with the testimony of two other experts that Rogers was insane at the time of the crime because he was suffering from delusions and because, in addition, he was driven to commit the crime by "an uncontrollable impulse to violence" or an "irresistible impulse."[8]

In the formal charge to the jury, and according to one interpretation, Judge Shaw went beyond the interpretations of the McNaghten rules in that he related will or volition, emotions, and mens rea in any assessment of insane or sane behavior. In his charge, Shaw clarified the nature of monomania and the accompanying delusion: "The character of the mental disease relied upon to excuse the accused in this case, is partial insanity, consisting of melancholy, accompanied by delusion. The conduct may be in many respects regular, the mind acute, and the conduct apparently governed by the rules of propriety, and at the same time there may be insane delusion by which the mind is perverted."[9] The most significant statements in the charge clarified a related element of Rogers's insanity: "that the act was the result of the disease, and not of a mind capable of choosing: in short that it was the result of uncontrollable impulse, and not of a person acted upon by motives, and governed by the will."[10]

Though the Rogers trial occurred in January 1844 while Melville was at sea, it received wide attention in both the popular press, especially in Boston and New York, and in professional journals.[11] The crime was violent, Abner Rogers was obviously demented, and the idea of "uncontrollable impulse" and the larger concept of moral insanity were both controversial. It would seem natural that Melville, with his background and curiosity, would talk with Judge Shaw about issues in the trial, including the nature of the two diseases.

Arriving back in this country on 1 February 1850, after sixteen weeks of travel in Europe, an invigorated Melville was soon making progress on his sixth work, which was not to be a book of adventures involving one Israel Potter but a whaling novel that on 1 May, as he informed Richard Henry Dana, Jr., was half finished. To obtain whaling information, he had applied earlier that spring for a new membership in the New York Society Library. However, after working several months in the crowded house at 103 Fourth Street and remembering all too well the previous summer, Melville decided to look elsewhere for a quieter house and area. Elizabeth was in complete agreement. With something different in mind, Melville took his family in mid-July to stay at his cousin Robert Melvill's large farmhouse near Pittsfield, Massachusetts.

A short time later, in early August, occurred the historic picnic in the nearby Berkshires and the unique meeting with Nathaniel Hawthorne, whose stories in *Mosses from an Old Manse* Melville had begun reading only a few weeks before. The meeting proved to be a great one for Melville, who soon became inspired by Hawthorne and his writings. In Robert Melvill's farmhouse a few weeks later, after reviewing stories in *Mosses* and *Twice-Told Tales,* Melville began writing his anonymous "Hawthorne and His Mosses" in which he praised Hawthorne for his great brain and heart, a "touch of Puritanic gloom," awareness of a "blackness, ten times black," and his probings into the "very axis of reality," a depth penetrable for only great writers like Shakespeare and the American Hawthorne.[12]

Only the previous year in Boston and New York City, after finishing *Mardi,* Melville had for the first time read Shakespeare's plays with care. He read several again in 1850, recognizing, perhaps before the fateful meeting with Hawthorne, that the captain of an American whaler need not be an ordinary whaling captain but could be a remarkable one, perhaps a heroic or a tragic figure. Hamlet and King Lear in particular provided Melville with insights into the workings of troubled or abnormal minds of the mighty, of characters who speak "the sane madness of vital truth."[13] Such characters and Coleridge's views of Shakespearean tragic heroes would figure importantly in portrayals of Ahab, the sea captain whose obsessions would in time make

monomania a literary as well as psychological byword. Shakespeare's "fool," in Melville's treatment, would influence the behavior of cabin boy Pip, who at sea exchanges his sanity for a divine insanity. From Milton's *Paradise Lost,* the Bible, Carlyle's *Sartor Resartus,* Byron's *Manfred,* and others, including Gothic romances and five books on whaling, Melville drew materials and ideas enabling him to transform experiences chasing whales and living on grubby whaling ships with castoffs and dreamers into high adventure and vigorous art. Of the various influences at work on the writer during this period the most important would be Shakespeare and Hawthorne.

The benefits of Hawthorne's friendship, periods of intense reading and writing, the peaceful farm, and visitors were to some extent countered by the drab realities of house routines, burdens of several kinds, and worries.

The chief burden and worry was likely money. "Dollars damn me," Melville explained to Hawthorne on 1 June 1851, when the big book was almost finished.[14] The complaint had been a familiar one since at least 1847. Only the previous September Melville had borrowed $3,000 from Judge Shaw so that he could make a partial payment of $1,500 on the 160-acre Brewster farm he had named Arrowhead. Only a year or so before, Melville had borrowed money from Judge Shaw for the 1849 trip to Europe, and in 1847 he had paid his share for the house in New York City with a $2,000 loan from Judge Shaw. Even with *Redburn* and *White-Jacket* selling fairly well in 1850, the royalties could hardly cover family expenses, debts, and interest payments the next year on the farm. Before writing to Hawthorne in June, Melville asked the Harpers on 1 April for an advance on the whaling book but was turned down 29 April because he owed the firm $695.65. He was indeed damned. On 1 May he borrowed $2,050 at 9 percent from one "T.D.S."; the amount and terms would come back to haunt him. If Melville had no fear of poverty at this time, the possibility may have made him apprehensive (JL 1:410).

There were other concerns and worries as well. The newly acquired Arrowhead was a source of pride, for it provided a measure of independence and freedom and also the status of ownership. But the farmhouse itself was not sizable. With eight people living there, including Melville's mother and four sisters, the house was crowded. As there was no room to write on the first two floors, Melville wrote in the attic, which would be too hot in the summer, too cold in the winter, and hardly isolated from noises of activities in rooms below. Melville had to ignore the sounds and other distractions and bury himself in his writing. He had to ignore also tensions that would naturally arise in a house with seven adults,

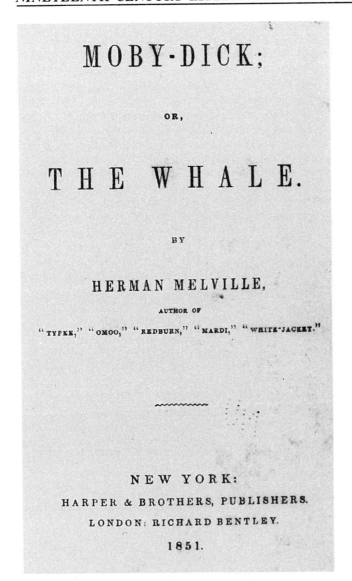

Writing of Ahab, Gabriel, and others, Melville was well aware of peculiarities, including those of the insane. He was well aware also in 1850 and 1851 that some family members and friends regarded him as peculiar or strange. By 1855, several family members were certain that something was wrong with him. During work on *Moby-Dick,* Melville's tendencies toward depression and irascibility may have been less noticeable because of his long hours upstairs writing. When he needed to get away, he could do farm chores, look around the barn, or walk to the village. Hawthorne lived in Lenox, only six miles away. A talk with him would dispel gloom or moodiness. His family was supportive or attempted to cater to his needs when Elizabeth was busy. But sometimes disturbances while he was writing could not be forgotten or simply walked off outside. His mother's habitual moralizing or someone's remarks at the dinner table could bring back recollections of earlier years, of the family house in Albany, of his father and his final illness. Fears of the twisted mind must have been lurking somewhere in Melville's mind as he wrote of Ahab, Elijah, Pip, and Ishmael. There would be other troubling reminders in those months: the 5 October notice in Pittsfield of the sale of the estate of his cousin "Henry D. Melvill, 'an insane person'"; the arrival that fall of a shipmate from the *Acushnet* and their compilation of a list of twenty-two men aboard that ship of whom four "went ashore . . . half dead," one committed suicide, one was killed, and three—not including Melville and Toby Greene—ran away; the arrival in January 1851 of George Adler's translation of Goethe's book—Adler had his own fears of insanity (JL 1:397, 399-400, 403).

In a February 1851 letter to Evert Duyckinck, Melville, in a crotchety mood, rejected Duyckinck's request for a daguerreotype of himself to be used in a new series of biographies in the *Literary World* of "Distinguished American(s) in Public Life." Melville explained that, as "almost everybody is having his 'mug' engraved nowadays," a copy of a portrait is "presumptive evidence that he's a nobody." Perhaps realizing that his explanations may have seemed a little odd, he offered the following comment: "We all are queer customers, Mr. Duycknk [*sic*], you, I, & every body else in the world. So if I here seem queer to you, be sure, I am not alone in my queerness, tho' it present itself at a different port, perhaps, from other people, since every one has his own distinct peculiarity."[16]

All such matters at Arrowhead the first year—recollections of Adler and others, letters, the friendship with Hawthorne, farm work, visits and social activities, the big burdens or concerns like money and family activities, Melville's own problematic stability—provided a background for the writing of *Moby-Dick.* They provide as well clues for the prominence of insanity in the book.

at least five of them rather talkative females. The long hours and concentration would wear away at his sensibilities. Some years later in her memoirs Elizabeth described her husband's regimen that year: "Wrote White Whale or Moby Dick under unfavorable circumstances—would sit at his desk all day not eating any thing till four or five oclock—then ride to the village after dark—would be up early and out walking before breakfast—sometimes splitting wood for exercise" (JL 1:412). In the evening, because of eyes weakened by childhood scarlet fever, Melville refrained from writing, but he might skim over a book with large type or spend "the evening 'in a sort of mesmeric state' in his room," thinking about the present work or future projects. Howard points out that the others in the house, "knowing nothing of the normal state of excitement produced by intellectual activity . . . may have begun to fear that winter that Herman—like his father, during the last weeks of life, before him—was 'peculiar.'"[15]

Resembling the white whale in at least one respect, madness is all but ubiquitous in *Moby-Dick*. It can be found in some form almost anywhere—aboard ships, in towns and cities, in the sea. Manhattan itself may not be mad, but conditions in the city appear harassing, even maddening. The city is described in terms of its insularity, its "lanes and alleys, streets and avenues," its Bowery and wharves toward which come thousands on Sunday afternoon to stand and gaze at the water. They are pressured, coerced individuals, "tied to counters, nailed to benches, clinched to desks,"[17] seeking freedom as well as answers. Ishmael and others like him want to escape by going to sea. New Bedford, with its "dreary streets! blocks of blackness," provides an escape route. The town may not be the best place to stay for long, however—it has queer qualities and Spouter Inn is described as queer.

The chief places in the novel, and perhaps the most conducive to the growth of insanity, are the ships and the sea itself. The whaling ship, with its irregular, hard life, provides a natural place for abnormality. The *Pequod* is described as a "tranced ship," a "most melancholy ship," a "noble craft but somehow most melancholy," and as the "material counterpart of her monomaniac commander's soul" (p. 423). The whaler is engaged in a journey that is at least questionable and may be mad in view of Ahab's "grand, monomaniac object" (p. 292).

Madness is to be found in *Moby-Dick* in both animals and humans. In Chapter 1, Ishmael writes, "Why is almost every robust healthy boy with a robust healthy soul in him, at some time or other crazy to go to sea?" (p. 5). The pun may be at least partly serious. As we will see, a number of men aboard the *Pequod* appear disturbed in some manner. Others afflicted are found on ships like the *Jeroboam* or on shore like Elijah after years at sea. Various sea animals are not exempt from the disease. The white whale can be viewed as mad, for it is the "monomaniac incarnation of all those malicious agencies . . . some deep men feel eating in them" (p. 184). During the three-day chase, Moby Dick displays a "demoniac indifference" and is described as "maddened by yesterday's fresh irons" (p. 567). Nor is Moby Dick the only whale afflicted with a form of mammalian insanity. One whale, flaying about with a harpoon embedded in its side, is "tormented to madness," and another, suffering from infection, is driven to madness (p. 389). The sharks gorging themselves on dead whales moored to the *Pequod* are engaged in a wild, mad activity.

The dominant place or environment in the novel is of course the sea, described in various passages as beautiful or beneficial. It contains myriad forms of life, some of which are essential to man. The sea has also its ugly, dangerous side. Storms and typhoons can destroy man or drive him mad. On one occasion, Ahab addresses the sea as "mad," and, in a scene involving Gabriel, "the crazy sea . . . seemed leagued with him" (p. 316). The collective seas provide a natural environment for the mad whale. The mad seas and animals appear indicative of a reality which Ishmael examines in terms of its whiteness. After considering the bewildering range of meanings of whiteness, Ishmael concludes that the universe itself is essentially corruptive, destructive, or meaningless. That is to say, the universe may be without reason, or "mad." If Ishmael's imaginative assessment makes sense, is there any wonder that so many things in the universe or whaling world manifest one degree or another of mental imbalance?

The *Pequod* crew and officers comprise, of course, the main group in the novel. Other groups include natives from the South Seas, town or country people, city folks, and ex-whalers. All are or become landmen. One showing signs of disturbance is Bildad, a former sea captain with the "reputation of . . . incorrigible old hunks . . . a bitter, hard taskmaster." Bildad appears inflexible if not rigid. Ishmael describes him as "the Queerest old Quaker I ever saw" (pp. 74, 75). Bildad's religious and business obsessions are evident in his remarks that Peleg is doomed to hell. Bildad delivers views in a pontifical, righteous manner, another indication that inflexibility is part of a possible mental problem. The old man appears near the thin red line separating the sane from the insane.

During Ishmael's stay in the Try Pots Inn in Nantucket, he learns of the unfortunate Stiggs, a sailor who had stopped at the inn a few years before. After four years at sea, Stiggs returned with his ship to Nantucket and committed suicide at Mrs. Hussey's Try Pots Inn. The facts are few. Presumably, the years at sea and desperately poor results of the whaling effort—three barrels of oil—adversely affected Stiggs and led to his death. His suicide may not be the only one in the novel, for much later at sea aboard the *Pequod* a crewman, perhaps sleepy or careless, falls from the masthead into the sea and is seen no more. Radney, the *Town-Ho* mate, is not a suicide, but he courts death in relations with Steelkit. Ugly, a fanatic worker, and part owner of the ship with worries on that count, Radney hates the handsome, bold, "wild ocean-born" Steelkit. Obsessed with hatred, Radney acts in "a most domineering and outrageous manner" and is described as "doomed and made mad" (pp. 244-45). In his last days, Radney all but loses control in his brutal treatment of Steelkit. Signs of monomania appear evident.

The "tranced" *Pequod* carries a number of quite sane and rational figures and a few like the ship's carpenter with questionable sanity. "No duplicate," the carpenter is clearly different. For an experienced, skillful man who works with others aboard ship, he is surprisingly oblivious to them, isolated as he is by "an all-ramifying heartlessness." Possessing "a certain impersonal stolidity," "a half-horrible stolidity," he tends to regard whalers as things. The carpenter's general attitude suggests possible inroads of a form of moral insanity. Not feeling as others do, he does not relate to them in "normal" ways. He lives "without premeditated reference to this world or the next." The carpenter is accordingly a "pure manipulator," relying not on reason or even instinct but on "a kind of deaf and dumb, spontaneous literal process." Immersed in the inanimate materials of his calling, he is saved from the distractions of moral insanity by a "wheezing humorousness" and a "certain grizzled wittiness" (pp. 467, 468).

Perth, the ship's blacksmith, is another matter. He shows definite signs of monomania. Yet fellow monomaniac Ahab does not regard him as mad, telling him that he should go mad—"Say, why dost thou not go mad?" (p. 487). For once eagle-eyed Ahab does not see clearly. He may not be able to because Perth hides his troubles in his work. "Silent, slow, and solemn; bowing over . . . he toiled away, as if toil were life itself" (p. 484). Perth works to forget alcoholism and deaths caused by it. Such memories cannot be forgotten. Years of alcoholism, hardship, and sorrow have left marks of a profound melancholy: Perth is one of Melville's most deeply sad characters. He is sadness, saddened—to paraphrase the description of Ahab as "madness, maddened" (p. 168). Having punished himself by going to sea (referred to as a form of suicide), he punishes himself further by unmitigated work and separation from others. This "most miserable" character, with no evidences of irrationality, likely suffered earlier from effects of moral insanity. Prichard's 1835 account of aspects of monomania appears noticeably pertinent to the blacksmith's condition and situation: "An individual of melancholic temperament, who has long been under the influence of circumstances calculated to impair his health and call into play the morbid tendencies of his constitution, sustains some unexpected misfortune, or is subjected to causes of anxiety; he becomes dejected in spirits, desponds, broods over his feelings till all the prospects of life appear to him dark and comfortless."[18]

Melville's portrayals in *Moby-Dick* of such figures are clearly superior to earlier ones in his fiction. Qualities of sane and insane figures alike are described with greater precision and relevance. Appearance and mannerisms are more concretely portrayed. Melville's familiar technique of combining realistic and romantic details is shown to excellent advantage in portrayals of the carpenter and others. The blacksmith's skills, habitual drinking, family life, and failures are recorded with an intensity and focus that make for an unforgettable and highly individualized life history.

The writer's superb control and technical skill are evident also in characterizations of three major figures, each illustrating the importance of monomania in the whaling world and each pointing toward the classic monomaniac, Ahab. The three are Elijah, a former whaler now on land in Nantucket; Gabriel, a Shaker from the New York village of "Neskyeuna," and Pip, a young crewman from "Tolland County in Connecticut" (pp. 314, 412).

Elijah first appears in Chapter 19 as a fairly typical, aging, seemingly poor ex-whaler. Initial observations of him emphasize the concrete and ordinary. "He was but shabbily apparelled in faded jacket and patched trowsers; a rag of black handkerchief investing his neck" (p. 91). His speech—to be discussed later—is in some respects routine. Elijah appears, then, despite eccentric mannerisms, to be more or less normal. As Ishmael discovers, however, Elijah's behavior and remarks quickly raise serious doubts as to his stability. Prichard refers to "reputed persons of a singular, wayward, and eccentric character . . . [with] something remarkable in their manners and habits . . . [leaving] doubts as to their entire sanity."[19] Ishmael describes Elijah as "broken loose from somewhere . . . a little damaged in the head . . . this crazy man . . . cracked" (pp. 92, 93, 99). Impatient and suspicious of the other man, Ishmael exaggerates. Elijah's preoccupation with his past, however, makes him indifferent to routine life. The general consequence is a loss of sensibilities noticeable in friendship and social relations, a diminution of normal social emotions. After a time, Elijah's tattered appearance, strange remarks, and pertinacity suggest a form of moral insanity. His obsessive thoughts of Ahab and his expectations that strangers will heed his warnings indicate a possibility of monomania, but in the scientific vocabulary of the time, Elijah is not a monomaniac. Prichard's 1842 study of insanity and jurisprudence makes clear that in monomania the hallucination or obsession centers primarily on the individual's self. "The predominate feeling . . . is always a selfish desire or apprehension, and the illusory ideas relate to the personal state, and circumstances of the individual."[20] This conception applies to Ahab or Gabriel but not to Elijah, whose obsessive concerns are with others but not with himself. He remains a strange, slightly "touched" but pathetic figure, one of the first victims of Ahab's obsession.

The wild Gabriel aboard the *Jeroboam* is not without typical or ordinary qualities if the terms are stretched a little. He is described as "a small, short, youngish man, sprinkled all over his face with freckles, and wearing redundant yellow hair"; he possesses on occasion a plain exterior. But unlike Elijah, Gabriel hides a deep, chronic mental derangement. Even when calm and rational, Gabriel shows "a deep, settled, fanatic delirium . . . in his eyes." He is complex. To get aboard the *Jeroboam,* Gabriel, strengthened by "that cunning peculiar to craziness," "assumed a steady, common sense exterior, and offered himself as a green-hand candidate for the . . . voyage" (pp. 314-15). Once aboard ship, he is sometimes the conventional madman—highly eccentric and potentially violent. Yet his melodramatic actions reveal Melville's sharp, hardheaded insights. Gabriel suffers from a form of complex monomania. Ray explains that in simple monomania the individual focuses on one point. In another class of monomania, an individual may have "a train of morbid ideas."[21] Gabriel is an example. He regards himself as the arch-angel Gabriel, as the "deliverer of the isle of the sea, and vicar-general of all Oceanica," as the controller of the *Jeroboam* itself, and as an archangel at the call of the "Shaker God incarnated"; that is, Moby Dick. While the general course of Gabriel's insanity may be pre-dictable, particulars of his monomania are not. He may be peaceful or violent, humble or arrogant, an archan-gel or a crewman. As expected in such a profound monomania, Gabriel's reason has been affected: flaws of conception and logic are obvious. Causes lie in large part in his family and religious background. Gabriel was "originally nurtured among the crazy society of Neskyeuna Shakers, where he had been a great prophet," trained in their "cracked, secret meetings," and involved in many cultish practices, including descent "from heaven by way of a trap-door" and possession of a replica of the seventh vial (pp. 315, 316, 314).

With the exception of Ahab, Pip is the most strik-ingly mad figure aboard the *Pequod.* The young cabin boy is more intricately mad than Elijah and Gabriel, for he can be profound as well as silly. Likely causes of his abnormality appeared first in his Connecticut boyhood: the peaceful village and family life would hardly prepare him for the whaling environment of tough shipmates and dangers. He received little en-couragement from shipmates and little reassurance from memories of home. He felt lonely, then moody, and as months passed fearful. Signs of moral insanity likely appeared. Most disturbing of all activities would be whale lowerings, the worst part of the "panic-striking business in which he had somehow unaccountably become entrapped." In his first lowering for a whale, Pip evinces "much nervousness." In the second, he jumps from the whaleboat. In the third lowering, unable to control fear or imagination, Pip jumps for the last time. The consequences are profound. Left alone "in the middle of such a heartless immensity," Pip is overwhelmed by a form of monomania. The comparable effects of Pip's abandonment and Ahab's loss of his leg can be expressed in terms of soul. After Ahab's loss of his leg, his body and soul inter-mingle, with insanity as a likely consequence. After Pip's submersion, his body remains intact but his soul is drowned. "Not drowned entirely, though" (pp. 412, 414), Ishmael adds. Thereafter, Pip appears increas-ingly eccentric, incomprehensible, or "crazy."

Pip's monomania centers, on the one hand, on his seeming awareness of God. When Pip descends into the ocean, he sees or believes that he sees "God's foot on the treadle of the loom" and evidence of God's mighty creations. In the sense that the book is a ro-mantic creation, Pip does see these unique things. Although he may need to be insane to see them, he perceives them as entities. On the pragmatic level, Pip is hallucinating. In this sense—the one stressed in this study—Prichard's explanation of a hallucina-tion is pertinent. A hallucination is the consequence of a "very intense . . . morbid reverie . . . [which] produces . . . false impressions . . . [of] unreal objects as actually present."[22] Pip's belief in his own death is hallucinatory. At other times Pip explores profoundly if erratically—perhaps in illustration of Starbuck's ex-planation in Chapter 110—aspects of resurrection, the ship's fate, and perspective. Profound himself, Ahab is well aware that Pip draws upon deep sources for his "wondrous philosophies" (p. 433). Only Ahab and possibly Ishmael can understand Pip at such times. Unlike Gabriel, Pip is not physically driven to express religious or philosophic truths. His expression and insight are natural and instinctive.

On the other hand, Pip's monomania centers at times on his alleged cowardice and physical absence re-ferred to above. This obsession dwells on self, but, unlike Gabriel's, Pip's obsession is usually self-depreciatory. In wandering about on the *Pequod* deck, he proclaims his cowardice by repeatedly cry-ing out "Shame" and "Coward." This conception of self contrasts most significantly with Ahab's grandi-ose conception of self. A related obsession is Pip's belief that he is not Pip. Pip has drowned and is therefore dead; or, Pip, a coward, has run away. Yet as the real Pip is aboard ship, he must be someone else: he is, therefore, the bell-boy, the ship's crier who identifies himself with the refrain, "Ding, dong, ding" (p. 522). These views of identity and Pip's jump from the whale boat manifest a profound self-hatred. Not until Pip is befriended by Ahab does he become aware of his own individuality or his need for someone else or of Ahab's need for him. Other-wise, his only positive sense of self comes when, paradoxically, he denies the self in order to express profound truths.

One indicator in *Moby-Dick* of Melville's greater under-standing of effects of mental aberration is the treatment of insane speech. The occasional examples of Jackson's dialogue in *Redburn* and of Surgeon Cuticle's ridicu-lous formalisms in *White-Jacket* provide interesting il-lustrations of the troubled mind. But the association of speech and mental upset in *Moby-Dick* goes deeper and may represent advances not evident to American scien-tists then.[23] The carpenter, standing before his bench talking to himself, reveals something of the abstract quality of a form of incipient moral insanity.

More revealing is the speech of major figures, particularly Elijah, Gabriel, and Pip. Ishmael regards Elijah's speech as "ambiguous, half-hinting, half-revealing, shrouded sort of talk." Elijah refers mysteriously to "souls," the signing of articles, and "soul's a sort of fifth wheel to a wagon." Part of Ishmael's confusion about Elijah and his speech is due to his own ignorance. Part may be due to Elijah's obession with the past. His meandering around in a private world is suggested in the rather puzzling remark, "Well, well, what's signed, is signed; and what's to be, will be; and then again, perhaps it won't be, after all. Any how, it's all fixed and arranged a'ready" (pp. 93, 91, 93).

Gabriel's speech is not as distinctive as it might be had the writer used speech or dialogue more often. When Gabriel's speech is described, the intent and tone come through nonetheless. As he arrives aboard the *Jeroboam* Gabriel no doubt speaks with relative calmness. Later, as his insanity breaks out, he commands the captain to jump overboard and proclaims himself "the deliverer of the isles of the sea and vicar-general of all Oceanica" (p. 315). "The unflinching earnestness with which he declared these things" indicates the depth of his obsessions. After warning Captain Mayhew against attacking the white whale, Gabriel pronounced his truths in "gibbering insanity". Webster defines gibberish as "rapid and inarticulate talk; unintelligible language; unmeaning words."[24] A year or two later, furious that the whale has been attacked, Gabriel from the top mast tosses an "arm in frantic gestures, and hurls forth prophecies. of speedy doom" to the attackers. Later, the *Jeroboam* and the *Pequod* cross paths. Because of the epidemic aboard his ship, Captain Mayhew is rowed in a boat alongside the *Pequod* to communicate with Ahab. One of the crewmen in the boat is Gabriel, who believes he controls the epidemic and most everything else. When Ahab shouts down to the captain that he has no fear of the epidemic, Gabriel gets to his feet and shouts, "Think, think of the fevers, yellow and bilious! Beware of the horrible plague" (p. 315). In delivering two other warnings to Ahab and all who can hear him, Gabriel repeats the basic sentence pattern. On the last occasion, "Gabriel once more started to his feet, glaring upon the old man and vehemently explained, with downward-pointed finger—'Think, think of the blasphemer—dead, and down there!—beware of the blasphemer's end!'" (pp. 316, 317).

Of these three monomaniac figures, Pip speaks in the most revealing and distinctive manner. Bright, sensitive, and spirited before the submersion, Pip shows the same qualities after he is struck with insanity. But having witnessed "God's foot on the treadle of the loom," Pip is so upset and confused that he must play games with himself and others and act silly much of the time. Sometimes Pip's riddles and puzzles take on philosophic form, as in the quarterdeck scene in Chapter 99. As Pip and others take turns observing the doubloon

nailed to the masthead, Pip points out in professorial manner, "Here's the ship's navel, this doubloon here, and they are all on fire to unscrew it. But, unscrew your navel, and what's the consequence?" The language is suitably concrete and specific, but the meaning is elusive. He expresses other paradoxes. Pip does not often refer to his obsession with God. But as the central one, it shapes his wit. Possessing remarkable insights, Pip shows a breadth of speech unmatched by any other character except Ishmael. He repeats the "I look, you look, he looks" refrain three times with noticeable variations, including references to bats and crows. While the schoolboy recitation includes serious philosophic overtones, it exhibits a bizzare silliness reflective of both instability and wisdom. His disturbing thoughts of self or nonself can be countered by a form of dissemblance as when he creates a silly rhyme or word like "Hish." He can also speak in a bantering way of cowardice, drowning, or running away. As Queequeg lies ill, Pip sings of his own other self, the lost Pip: "Seek out one Pip, who's now been missing long: I think he's in those far Antilles. If ye find him, then comfort him; for he must be very sad; for look! he's left his tambourine behind:—I found it. Rig-a-dig!" (pp. 435, 434, 479). At other times, when he turns to matters of origins, death, and resurrection, the tone becomes speculative and the language serious.

The dominant figures in the *Moby-Dick* society are of course Ishmael and Ahab. Ishmael as narrator no longer feels like following funerals or knocking off people's hats. He has managed to cope with moods and hostilities, although he retains much of his earlier skepticism. As character, Ishmael is pessimistic and discontented. He is noticeably disturbed by city restraints and confinements and critical of the "dreary" New Bedford streets and houses, finds the black church depressing, and at one point regards Queequeg as mad and the Spouter-Inn as "a queer sort of place." In Nantucket, Ishmael is contemptuous of Elijah's mentality and irritated by his incoherence.

The character has obvious problems, for his "hypos" indicate in modern terms a "state of depression somewhat more chronic and morbid than our 'blues.'" That condition may be regarded as a form of hypochondriasis, which may "appear . . . [as] a specific neurosis . . . [or] in association with such disorders as anxiety neurosis, obsessive-compulsive neurosis, and most often with the initial states of any psychosis."[25] One of the few critics beside Henry Nash Smith to consider characters in *Moby-Dick* in mid-nineteenth-century terminology, the German critic Armin Staats places Ishmael and Ahab in a taxonomy based on James Prichard's *A Treatise.* In this interpretation, according to Smith's translation, Ishmael is in the first or introductory stage, his "melancholy" representing a "neurotic" or apparently a moral insanity stage which leads to Ahab's psychotic or monomaniac stage. Staats explains that in both stages, moral insanity and monomania, disturbances occur in emotions and in cognition. Explanations in the *Penny Cyclopaedia* article and in Prichard's *Treatise,* however, indicate that theoretically disturbances in moral insanity occur in only the emotions, not in cognition; actually, moral insanity may or may not include failures in cognition.[26] The distinction is important, for although Ishmael can be suspicious, depressed, and occasionally confused, his mental processes do not appear to be actually affected.

During the many months at sea, the touchy, imaginative Ishmael manages to keep his equilibrium. Queequeg is a major factor. The native's friendship and presence diminish Ishmael's sense of alienation. His example and strong character reinforce Ishmael's faltering sense of self and enable him to get along better with others. But it is Ishmael's decisions and actions during the long journey that largely account for a gradual maturation or for significant changes in attitudes. Ishmael learns to control his fear when a storm lashes the ship or a whale plunges alongside a whaling boat. As a crewman he must regularly climb the rigging, furl canvas, pull an oar in a boat, and scrub decks. Such duties allow little time for moody introspections.

What Ishmael must finally learn nonetheless is to resist his natural tendency to daydream or to place too much importance on intangibles. The narrator tells of a boyhood experience when he was sent to bed by his stepmother to fall "into a troubled nightmare of a doze" and then awaken "half steeped in dreams" to feel "a shock running through all my frame," and then "a supernatural hand seemed placed in mine." He lies there for some time, "frozen with the most awful fears" (p. 26). This suggests the possibility of a hypnagogic trance[27] or a cataleptic condition found in some mental illnesses. This is not to say that Ishmael was ill at the time but that he may have become somewhat disoriented. Years later aboard the *Pequod,* as a "lad with lean brow and hollow eye; given to unseasonable meditativeness" (p. 158), Ishmael, on the masthead, risks losing hold of reality, of deluding himself as to what is real and what is not.

Somewhat later in the remarkable try-pots scene, Ishmael loses contact briefly with reality and almost capsizes the ship. He had been standing for hours at the tiller guiding the *Pequod* and watching the try-pots activity. The nighttime scene—the darting fires, the hissing blubber, the "Tartarean shapes of the pagan harpooners" dancing around—gradually mesmerizes him until the "rushing *Pequod* freighted with savages, and laden with fire . . . seemed the material counterpart of her monomaniac commander's soul." As Ishmael grows drowsy, the Gothic scene before him "at last begat kindred visions in my soul." The visions may be occurring during a hypnagogic trance. During this time of approaching unconsciousness, Ishmael turns around to face the stern. When he awakens, "I was horribly conscious of something wrong" (p. 354). Aware now of only blackness with occasional flashes of red, he is certain that the tiller has been inverted. At the time he is not suffering from an "unnatural hallucination," as the narrator explains, for a hallucination is created by the mind independent of external conditions, but from an illusion or mistaken perception of external conditions. Because the condition is temporary and Ishmael recognizes his failures, he appears to be in modern terms neurotic, not psychotic. In other words, he is suffering from a form of moral insanity. Having been frightened out of his wits, Ishmael will avoid similar circumstances in the future or react differently if he has to confront the nighttime scene again.

In contrast, Ahab at fifty-eight has lived a lifetime of comparable experiences, some overwhelming, and has survived all of them. An account of the experiences is a testament to his courage, adaptability, and integrity. He survived the early loss of both parents, one of them insane. In the tough occupation of whaling, he advanced rapidly, perhaps gaining his own ship before he was thirty, a not unusual feat in the mid-nineteenth century. Knowledgeable and pragmatic, he proved to be an efficient, brave leader. In the course of many years, Ahab survived the attack of a whale, a bolt of lightning, a deadly skirmish with a Spaniard,[28] rebellious sailors, sea storms.

But such an account gives little idea of the price Ahab had to pay; it does not clarify the harmful effects of the life on him mentally and emotionally. Ahab's psychological difficulties began not with his loss of leg to the whale but many years earlier during what the captain describes as "forty years of privation, and peril" (p. 543). Early in this period appeared the first signs of emotional stress or of moral insanity. Physical dangers and hardships, monotonous daily routines, almost endless whale watches, leadership responsibilities, the necessity of privacy and periods of thought and introspection gradually wore down his emotional strength and reserves, turned him inward; relationships with others suffered. At forty the captain had become crotchety, aloof, only occasionally communicative, with deep angers and resentments directed at owners, crewmen, whales, the weather. Whaling was no longer challenging or fulfilling.

Ahab's marriage "at past fifty" marks the approximate beginning of a second stage of mental difficulty identifiable as a settled condition of moral insanity. Ahab married to forget the hardships and loneliness of whaling and to find affection and companionship. He lost them the day after the wedding as he embarked on another long whaling adventure. He missed his wife and son very much. After admitting to Starbuck that in marrying the girl he had widowed her, Ahab immediately adds, "And then, the madness, the frenzy, the boiling blood and the smoking brow, with which, for a thousand lowerings old Ahab has furiously, foamingly chased his prey—more a demon than a human" (p. 544). The "thousand lowerings" may be a hyperbole for dramatic effect, a reference to the career of forty years, to the years after he became "old Ahab," to the years since his marriage, or to the few since the leg mutilation. Whatever the case, Ahab describes no sane man or recent madness. It is likely that the "thousand lowerings" extend over a period of ten to twenty years. If so, the lowerings cannot refer to a period of monomania, a comparatively recent condition, but to periods of moody detachment, to strong hatreds and angers, all controlled by a "broad mentality," a strong, firm intelligence. The condition remains one of moral insanity.

A third and final stage in Ahab's madness begins with the traumatic loss of his leg. The most documented and involved, this stage includes early monomaniac hates and angers precipitated by the great "corporal animosity" (p. 184) arising from the loss, which, as Smith points out, is a physical cause or "external shock" contributing to insanity.[29] This stage includes also months of suffering. The "final monomania" strikes Ahab as the *Pequod* rounds Cape Horn and his "torn body and gashed soul [bleed] . . . into one another; and so interfusing [make] . . . him mad" (p. 185). This conception of the relationship of body and soul was neither original nor the received view in the mid-1800s, when most psychiatrists regarded the two, body and mind, as separate. The latter represented the traditional Christian view of the nonmaterial soul or mind as separate from the physical brain. As the soul or mind was regarded as eternal, diseases of brain or body could not affect it. Whether or not he pondered the matter, Ray doubted this immaterialist-materialist dichotomy, explaining that the mind and brain were inter-dependent and made for a "single, individual man" so that the mind, "which was the mortal brain functioning, would be diseased." This fairly advanced interpretation seems to have expressed Melville's general conception of the "interfusing" of body and soul.[30] In the months following the amputation, Ahab's physical suffering clearly affected his mental faculties.

The "final monomania" in the third stage includes not only physical violence and raving—similar to an acute attack of mania—but a deceptive calmness that misleads the *Pequod* crew into believing that Ahab's delirium has been left behind with the Cape Horn winds. The calmness resembles Gabriel's. In Ahab's case, however, the delirium or "full lunacy" has turned inward and is not ordinarily discernible, certainly not to crew members.

The paragraphs in Chapter 41 on Ahab's monomania and "bodily dismemberment" can be best described as an example of "poetic analysis" because they combine figurative language and precise explanation, poetic imagery and careful analysis. The passages reveal not only Melville's perceptive insights into complexities of monomania but his powerful and dramatic exposition of insights. Concrete, realistic words are combined with figurative words in a dramatic analysis and definition of Ahab's delirium. Melville uses three synonyms for insanity, "lunacy," "madness," and "monomania," combines them with contrasting adjectives, "broad," "full," "narrow," and "special," and proceeds to trace the process of insanity from "broad madness," or moral insanity, through a "full lunacy," or violent monomania, through the "narrow–flowing monomania," or somewhat constricted insanity, to the "special lunacy," or sharply obsessed monomania, which "stormed his general sanity." Referring to "human madness," Ishmael pointedly admits, "When you think it fled, it may have but become transfigured into some still subtler form" (p. 185). The obsessed stage is accelerated by Ahab's second physical injury—the severe groin wound suffered in Nantucket, which constitutes a second physical cause. In his "monomaniac mind" (p. 463), Ahab regards the subsequent torment as supernaturally related to the torment following the leg loss. The groin injury makes him even more determined to exact revenge. Tragic dimensions of the "final monomania" take final shape as Ahab draws upon disappointments of early years, the deepening troubles of middle years, or second stage, to regard the whale at last as "the sum of all the general rage and hate felt by his whole race from Adam down" (p. 184). Conceived in terms of evil, God, a whale, and a whaling captain, Ahab's delusion is created by a mind both coldly sane and furiously mad.

In James Prichard's taxonomy, Ahab's delusions and general illness show symptoms of a grandiose monomania far more conceptualized and focused than Surgeon Cuticle's. Except under the greatest strain, Ahab thinks rationally on any subject, including his own obsession; such a portrayal of monomania ran counter to the received opinion.[31]

Melville's treatment of Ahab's monomania is innovative in another sense. It shows for the first time in Melville's fiction a lengthy, detailed dramatization of unconscious levels of the mind. In this area he advanced beyond the concerns and studies of scientists of the time, specifically Esquirol, Ray, and Prichard, and in depth beyond accounts of Brown, Poe, and Hawthorne as well.[32] The quarterdeck scenes in *Moby-Dick* are notable for dramatic revelations of areas of Ahab's mind. The deepest probings, however, of unconscious areas of his mind appear in expository accounts in Chapters 41 and 44. A passage in Chapter 41 contains a cryptic metaphor suggestive of Ahab's unconscious or his "larger, darker, deeper part" (p. 185). The passage includes the following: "Far beneath the fantastic towers of man's upper earth, his root of grandeur, his whole awful essence sits in bearded state; an antique buried beneath antiquities, and throned on torsoes! . . . He patient sits, upholding on his *frozen* brow the piled entablatures of ages" (p. 185, my italics). Although the metaphor may be literary and political rather than psychological, "his root of grandeur, his whole awful essence" suggest elemental forces in Ahab's unconscious mind, which are suggested also by images of burial and death and by the reference to "frozen brow," a phrase possibly anticipating descriptions of mind in *Pierre:* "Those barbarous hordes which Truth ever nourishes in the loins of her frozen, yet teeming North."[33] Ahab's own "hyperborean regions of the mind" would be implied in this remarkable metaphor. Such images lack the fluidity and brilliance, however, of the "strange shapes of the unwarped primal world . . . glid[ing] to and fro" and awaiting Pip in his own psychological descent into oceans of the mind. Such figures as "joyous, heartless, ever-juvenile eternities" and "God-omnipresent, coral insects," although referring primarily to mundane eternities, convey a sense of the uncharted depths of Pip's mind (p. 414). In turn, descriptions in the Ahab passage convey a sense of colossal forces in the mind, not to be understood or eluded, not even by Ahab. Both sets of descriptions can be regarded as Jungian archetypes originating in the collective unconscious. Similar ones of Ishmael also indicate something of the nature of the unconscious.

The boldest explorations of a troubled mind and unconscious appear in Chapter 44 descriptions of Ahab's monomaniac nightmares. Praised for its brilliance, the last paragraph of the chapter is nonetheless faulted for complex abstractions, reliance on coined terms, and other devices for creating a model of Ahab's mind.[34] Such terms as "life-spot," "living principle," "common vitality," and the "spiritual throes" figure have been regarded as imprecise. These terms and metaphors nonetheless succeed in creating a sense of Ahab's mental turbulence. The "intolerably vivid dreams of the night" may refer to monomaniac nightmares too extreme to be accepted on a cognitive level. They are evidently too extreme in emotional terms as well, for they occur during a "clashing of phrensies" and concentrate finally in the "throbbing of his life-spot." The last phrase may be, as Feidelson asserts, a reference to the heart.[35] It seems more likely that the phrase refers to the area of both head and heart, to intense pressures Ahab feels in his head and chest. A key metaphor in the Chapter 44 passage begins, "These spiritual throes in him heaved his being up from its base, and a chasm seemed opening in him, from which forked flames and lightnings shot up, and accursed fiends beckoned him to leap down among them . . . [into] this hell—yawn[ing] beneath him" (p. 202). Despite the confused visualization, it effectively dramatizes traumatic effects of Ahab's insane fury. During this period,

Ahab's unconscious mind figuratively opens, releasing into the conscious hitherto hidden forces—raging guilts, hates, fears—suggested by the flames and lightning and by the "accursed fiends." Both personal and collective forces of the unconscious are on the verge of overpowering the conscious Ahab, who, in the search for the whale, has deluded himself into believing that he is equal to any confrontation on earth, whether it be with man, beast, or a manifestation of the supernatural.

The portrayal in Chapter 44 of Ahab's mental processes contains a somewhat cumbersome structure of faculties. This four-part paradigm follows naturally from the two-part paradigm of body and soul illustrated in Chapter 7, as Ishmael thinks of the soul as eternal and separate, and also from the account in Chapter 41, as he describes the interfusing of body and soul that brings on monomania. Although the soul-mind-will-brain paradigm is mechanical, it clarifies the tortured workings of Ahab's powerful mind. After Ahab bursts from his cabin, his soul in effect flees from his mind. Brodtkorb explains that when the narrator Ishmael realized that the mind and soul could not exist apart he created a grand purpose, a vulturelike creature which drives off the "common vitality," or "soul plus mind." Zoellner keeps the separation of soul and mind intact by positing two Ahabs: a daytime Ahab directed or vitalized by this creature and a nighttime Ahab with a soul.[36] It appears, however, that the description refers not to an actual separation but to a metaphoric one. Ordinarily, the mind is "leagued with the soul"; the soul is an "integral" of the mind. Under the great emotional stress of a monomaniac nightmare, the soul or spiritual elements are subjugated or, in a sense, nullified by the union of mind and will. This union is the "unbidden and unfathered birth" from which the "eternal, living principle," or soul, flees "horror-striken" (p. 175). This union appears to be the crux of Ahab's "special lunacy," the sharply focused monomania which marks the most radical upset of Ahab's tormented mentality. During this period the soul is present but subjugated or dormant. The paradigm is vitalized by remarkable imagery which organically relates conscious and unconscious forces of Ahab's mind. Despite confusions of language and ideas, the long passage in Chapter 44 provides a more convincing portrayal of deep mental anguish and upset than do case studies of Ray or Prichard dealing with comparable conditions.[37]

Shakespeare's plays and heroes no doubt influenced Melville's conception of Ahab's will, and accounts of religious and dramatic figures by Bayle and Carlyle may have contributed to that conception. The conception may have derived something also from Thomas Upham's scientific *Outlines of Imperfect and Disordered Mental Action,* a copy of which was available in the New York Society Library and also likely available, Wilson Heflin explains, in the enlisted men's library of the *United States* on which Melville sailed in

1843-44.[38] A professor of psychology, Upham regarded the mind as consisting of the intellect, sensibilities, and will. An important aspect of the will is power, which is not a faculty but an attribute suffused throughout the mind and concentrated in the will. Any decision or action of the will is based on power, which becomes a factor therefore in any "disordered action" of the will.[39] A disordered action or "insanity of the will" is more likely to come from insane aspects of other parts of the mind than from internal defect of the will. Upham's simplistic explanations clarify Ishmael's complex accounts.

Ahab's rationality, or mind, driven by monomaniac conceptions of self and power, nullifies the effects of the soul and, in aligning itself with the disordered will, creates the delusions of a global mind. In such a development the will has power and is also powerless. Upham's description of the effects of a "deep-rooted and permanent melancholy" upon the will also clarifies the powerful account of Ahab's midnight upset.[40] Upham's scientific accounts and Melville's dramatic exposition cannot be lengthily compared because of different purposes and audiences. But only Melville's fictional account creates a credible sense of the ineluctable mysteries and complexities of the deeply troubled mind.

Although the portrayal of Ahab's consciousness is a highlight of *Moby-Dick*, Ishmael's psychology and the aberrations of Elijah, Gabriel, Pip, and others are depicted with similar brilliance if with perhaps somewhat less depth. These and other characters illustrate the distance Melville had traveled in trying to understand his own complex mentality and consciousness. What he learned from his introspections no doubt helped clarify dramatic treatments of Ahab and others and indicated possibilities for later psychological explorations. These occurred a short time later as he turned to thoughts about another obsessed character. . . .

Notes

[1] Herman Melville, *Journal of a Visit to London and the Continent By Herman Melville 1849-1850*, p. 4.

[2] Sanford E. Marovitz, "More Chartless Voyaging: Melville and Adler at Sea," pp. 376, 377.

[3] Davis and Gilman, eds., *Letters*, pp. 115, 118, 122, 123.

[4] Leyda, *Melville Log*, 1:403. Longfellow wrote in his journal on 17 April 1853 of a visit by Adler. "He has overworked his brain; and has a monomania. . . . Crowds look him [*sic*] strangely in the street, and voices under his window at night cry, 'Go home! Go home'" (1:468). Howard, *Herman Melville*, p. 208, explains that in 1853 Adler "had developed such a severe case

of agoraphobia that he was to be confined in the Bloomingdale Asylum in October." Agoraphobia has been defined in this century as "the dread of open spaces. The patient becomes panic-stricken, sometimes at the thought of, but more often at the impending visit to an open space." The patient generally prefers to remain indoors and near "a kind, helpful, guiding influence." Campbell, *Psychiatric Dictionary*, p. 19. For George J. Adler's opinions, see his *Letters of a Lunatic, or a Brief Exposition of My University Life, During the Years 1853-1854*, pp. 5-10.

[5] Augustus Kinsley Gardner, M.D., *Old Wine in New Bottles: or, Spare Hours of a Student in Paris*.

[6] Howard, *Herman Melville*, p. 110.

[7] Samuel W. Francis, "Augustus Kinsley Gardner, M.D.," in *Biographical Sketches of Distinguished Living New York Physicians*, pp. 124-27; Howard, *Herman Melville*, p. 7.

[8] Leonard W. Levy, *The Law of the Commonwealth and Chief Justice Shaw*, pp. 211-18; H.A.B. (H. Amariah Brigham), "Medical Jurisprudence of Insanity," *American Journal of Insanity* 1 (June, 1845):258-74. For a different view of Shaw's understanding, see Quen, "Introduction," p. x. For Isaac Ray's understanding, see ibid. For Ray's 1861 discussion of the "uncontrollable impulse" or "irresistible impulse," see "Objections to Moral Insanity Considered" in ibid., pp. 102-3.

[9] Brigham, "Medical Jurisprudence," pp. 268-69. The second sentence is quoted by Smith, "The Madness of Ahab," p. 38. Smith also discusses the McNaghten decision and Brigham's 1848 views on pp. 38-39 and refers to an October 1844 article by Brigham on p. 175.

[10] Brigham, "Medical Jurisprudence," p. 269.

[11] See ibid.; Thomas M. McDade, comp., *The Annals of Murder: A Bibliography of Books and Pamphlets on American Murders from Colonial Times to 1900*, pp. 246-47.

[12] Herman Melville, "Hawthorne and His Mosses," in *The Piazza Tales and Other Prose Pieces 1839-1860*, pp. 243, 244.

[13] Ibid., p. 244.

[14] Davis and Gilman, *Letters*, p. 128.

[15] Howard, *Herman Melville*, p. 173.

[16] Davis and Gilman, *Letters*, p. 121.

[17] Melville, *Moby-Dick*, p. 4. Hereafter, all page references to this edition will appear in the text.

[18] Prichard, *Treatise,* p. 28.

[19] Ibid., p. 12.

[20] James Prichard, *On the Different Forms of Insanity in Relation to Jurisprudence,* p. 69.

[21] Ray, *Treatise,* p. 164.

[22] Prichard, *Treatise,* p. 115.

[23] A check of primary works by Ray and the Englishman Prichard discloses little comment on speech as such in discussions of insane patients. See, for example, Prichard's discussion in *A Treatise* of representative cases of moral insanity. Speech is seldom referred to and is not analyzed.

[24] *Webster's Third New International Dictionary, . . . Unabridged,* p. 1055.

[25] Melville, *Moby-Dick,* p. 12; Campbell, *Psychiatric Dictionary,* p. 295.

[26] Smith, "The Madness of Ahab," p. 174, explains ideas expressed by Armin Staats, "Melville—*Moby-Dick,*" p. 123; Prichard, *Treatise,* p. 12; "Insanity," in Knight, ed., *Penny Cyclopaedia,* p. 484.

[27] For a detailed discussion in Freudian terms of the counterpane, tryworks, and other episodes involving Ishmael, see Harold Hellenbrand, "Behind Closed Doors: Ishmael's Dreams & Hypnagogic Trances in *Moby-Dick,*" *American Transcendental Quarterly* 61 (October 1986): 47-71.

[28] Nathalia Wright, *Melville's Use of the Bible.*

[29] Smith, "The Madness of Ahab," p. 40.

[30] Ray, *Treatise,* p. 135. Edward F. Edinger, *Melville's Moby Dick: A Jungian Commentary,* provides a Jungian interpretation of the "torn body . . . soul" image: "The body bleeds into the soul; that is, the collective unconscious with its archetypal images streams into consciousness. Instead of relating to these images meaningfully, however, Ahab becomes identified with them, succumbs to inflation, and thus to madness" (p. 56).

[31] Prichard, *Treatise,* pp. 26, 31.

[32] To my knowledge Ray, Prichard, Brigham, Conolly, and Esquirol were not engaged in the mid 1800s in attempts to understand the nature of the unconscious, although European scientists, notably German, had been active by studying that area for some time. See Henri F. Ellenberger, *The Discovery of the Unconscious: The History and Evolution of Dynamic Psychiatry,* pp. 205-10, passim.

[33] Melville, *Pierre,* p. 167; see Murray, "In Nomine Diaboli," pp. 6-7, 8.

[34] Smith, "The Madness of Ahab," p. 47, discusses interpretations by Paul Brodtkorb, Jr., *Ishmael's White World: A Phenomenological Reading of Moby-Dick;* and by Robert Zoellner, *The Salt-Sea Mastodon: A Reading of Moby-Dick,* p. 127.

[35] Charles Fiedelson, Jr., ed., Herman Melville, *Moby-Dick, or the Whale,* p. 271.

[36] Brodtkorb, *Ishmael's White World,* p. 63; Zoellner, *Salt-Sea Mastodon,* pp. 98-101.

[37] See Ray, *Treatise,* pp. 162-66; Prichard, *Treatise,* pp. 36-44.

[38] Howard, *Herman Melville,* pp. 60, 166, 171-72. Millicent Bell, "Pierre Bayle and *Moby Dick,*" *PMLA* 66 (September 1951):626-48, explains that Melville's conception of Ahab owes something to Bayle's essay on Zoroaster. This figure's unusual powers and views of good and evil would suggest something of the will. Wilson Heflin kindly informed me of this in a 25 July 1981 letter.

[39] Upham, *Outlines,* p. 384.

[40] Ibid., pp. 396-97.

Bibliography

. . . Bell, Millicent. "Pierre Bayle and *Moby Dick.*" *PMLA* 66 (September 1951):626-48. . . .

[Brigham, Amariah, M.D.]. "Medical Jurisprudence of Insanity." *American Journal of Insanity* 1 (January 1845): 258-74.

Brodtkorb, Paul, Jr. *Ishmael's White World: A Phenomenological Reading of Moby-Dick.* New Haven: Yale University Press, 1965. . . .

Davis, Merrell R., and William H. Gilman, eds. *The Letters of Herman Melville.* New Haven: Yale University Press, 1960. . . .

Ellenberger, Henri F. *The Discovery of the Unconscious: The History and Evolution of Dynamic Psychiatry.* New York: Basic Books, 1970. . . .

Feidelson, Charles, Jr., ed. Herman Melville, *Moby-Dick, or the Whale.* Indianapolis: Bobbs-Merrill Company, 1964. . . .

Francis, Samuel W. *Biographical Sketches of Distinguished Living New York Physicians.* New York: George P. Putnam and Son, 1867. . . .

Gardner, Augustus Kinsley, M.D. *Old Wine in New Bottles: or, Spare Hours of a Student in Paris.* New York: C. S. Francis and Company, 1848. . . .

Hellenbrand, Harold. "Behind Closed Doors: Ishmael's Dreams and Hypnagogic Trances in *Moby-Dick*." *American Transcendental Quarterly* 61 (October 1986): 47-71. . . .

Howard, Leon. *Herman Melville: A Biography.* Berkeley: University of California Press, 1951. . . .

Levy, Leonard W. *The Law of the Commonwealth and Chief Justice Shaw.* Cambridge: Harvard University Press, 1957. . . .

[Leyda, Jay]. *The Melville Log: A Documentary Life of Herman Melville 1819-1891.* 2 vols. New York: Gordian Press, 1969. . . .

McDade, Thomas M., comp. *The Annals of Murder: A Bibliography of Books and Pamphlets on American Murders from Colonial Times to 1900.* Norman: University of Oklahoma Press, 1961. . . .

Marovitz, Sanford E. "More Chartless Voyaging: Melville and Adler at Sea." In *Studies in the American Renaissance 1986.* Ed. Joel Myerson. . . .

[Melville, Herman]. *Journal of a Visit to London and the Continent By Herman Melville 1849-1850.* Ed. Eleanor Melville Metcalf. Cambridge: Harvard University Press, 1948. . . .

———. *Moby-Dick: or the Whale.* Ed. Hayford, Parker, and Tanselle. Evanston and Chicago: Northwestern University Press and the Newberry Library, 1988. . . .

———. *The Piazza Tales and Other Prose Pieces, 1839-1860.* Ed. Hayford, Parker, and Tanselle. Evanston and Chicago: Northwestern University Press and the Newberry Library, 1987.

———. *Pierre, or the Ambiguities.* Ed. Hayford, Parker, and Tanselle. Evanston and Chicago: Northwestern University Press and the Newberry Library, 1971. . . .

Prichard, James Cowles. *A Treatise on Insanity and Other Disorders Affecting the Mind.* London: Sherwood, Gilbert and Piper, 1835.

———. *On the Different Forms of Insanity in Relation to Jurisprudence.* London: Hippolyte Bailliere, 1842. . . .

[Ray, Isaac]. *A Treatise on the Medical Jurisprudence of Insanity.* Boston: Charles C. Little and James Brown, 1838. . . .

[Smith, Henry Nash]. "The Madness of Ahab." In *Democracy and the Novel: Popular Resistance to Classic American Writers.* New York: Oxford University Press, 1978. . . .

Upham, Thomas C. *Outlines of Imperfect and Disordered Mental Action.* New York: Harper and Brothers, 1840. . . .

Webster's Third New International Dictionary of the English Language Unabridged. Springfield: Mass.: Merriam-Webster, 1981. . . .

[Wright, Nathalia]. *Melville's Use of the Bible.* Durham, N.C.: Duke University Press, 1949. . . .

Zoellner, Robert. *The Salt-Sea Mastodon: A Reading of Moby-Dick.* Berkeley: University of California Press, 1973.

Sally Shuttleworth (essay date 1993)

SOURCE: "'Preaching to the Nerves': Psychological Disorder in Sensation Fiction," in *A Question of Identity: Women, Science, and Literature,* edited by Marina Benjamin, Rutgers University Press, 1993, pp. 192-222.

[*In the following essay, Shuttleworth examines how Victorian sensation fiction exploited the language and concepts of psychology, and why the novels were so heavily criticized. Shuttleworth maintains that the novels challenged the Victorian "culture of control" by emphasizing the value of "feminine 'sensation'" over the often faulty "masculine reason."*]

The sensation fiction of the 1860s shared with the emerging science of Victorian psychiatry a preoccupation with psychological excess. Authors such as Mary Braddon, Wilkie Collins, and Mrs. Henry Wood focused their attention on forms of action and feeling that violated the rules of normative social behavior. The novels of the sensationalists (a loose term that embraced a wide variety of authors) were ones of high incident and passion: murderous impulses, throbbing sexuality, and dark secrets abound. For contemporary reviewers, the scandal of these works lay in their suggestion, and indeed often in their overt claims, that such forms of thought and behavior were not aberrant but rather mimetic of contemporary life. While Victorian psychiatry sought to demarcate the boundaries of sanity and insanity, of pathological and acceptable behavior, thus conferring the authority of science on bourgeois norms of respectability, the sensationalists seemed to privilege pathology, to locate normality not in the realm of psychological control and socially disciplined behavior, but rather in the sphere of turbulent excess.

Victorian fears that insanity was increasing at an alarming rate reached a crescendo in the late 1850s and 1860s. Sensation fiction was one of the more remarkable expressions of this fear: madness was a well-nigh obligatory element of any text. Threats of committal to an asylum furnished a dominant plot line, whose genesis and contemporary reregistration lay in the hands of psychiatric practice. Law, psychiatry, and sensation fiction had a strong intertextual relation in this period. Celebrated legal cases contesting the validity of psychiatric committals captured the popular imagination, focusing attention on the authoritative powers invested in the medical profession and the whole problematic issue of differentiating sane from insane behavior. Sensation novelists drew explicitly on the vocabulary and diagnoses of psychiatric discourse for the diverse forms of male and female madness they depicted. But, writing from a very different position within the cultural spectrum, and following very different generic rules, they did so to very different effect. This . . . explores the relationship between these two discursive formations, examining the different social effects they produce, and the subtle reregisterings that occur when language and concepts are transposed from the high culture of medical science to the popular domain of sensation fiction.

The discursive transposition is implicitly a gendered one: high patriarchal culture is assimilated into a subversive generic form whose traits, as delineated by Victorian critics, mirrored medical projections of disruptive femininity. Masculine reason and control are implicitly set against female sensation and nervousness and bodily disorder. Gender itself is in turn one of the central sites of rewriting in the sensation text. Although sensation novels seem, at one level, to support the psychiatric framing of the female body, at another level they expose the instability of such diagnoses by revealing the relational interdependence of male and female insanity. The texts work to demystify male medical authority by highlighting structurally the alignment of the respective economic and psychiatric positions offered to the male and female subject.

In some cases the transpositions between medical and fictional texts are not subtle in their effects but quite blatant and aggressive. In Charles Reade's *Hard Cash* (1863), for example, John Conolly, the hero of moral management and champion of humane systems of treatment, is depicted as Dr. Wycherley, a figure who, in all good faith, diagnoses monomania in the hero, whom the reader knows to be sane. Although Wycherley's words are drawn directly from Conolly's writings, their effects are radically altered by context, becoming both sinister and intrusive.[1] Doctors figure frequently in these texts, giving textbook diagnoses of protagonists, but their authority is often undermined by other textual factors at work. Even where the language of psychia-

try is employed by an impersonal narrative voice it does not carry the same weight, but opens itself to interpretation in ways that psychiatric texts themselves do not. Few statements can be taken at face value. Strong formal dislocations frame the propositional ambivalences of these texts.

Sensation fiction is a literature not only of psychological but also of formal excess. In structuring their works, novelists were deliberately pushing at the bounds of both psychological and literary respectability, as incarnated in the principles of realist fiction. The transgressive power of such texts demands an equivalent alteration of our reading codes and modes of interpretation. By incorporating in their formal structure the disruptive qualities attached by male medicine to the female body and psyche, sensation texts self-reflexively foreground the relationship between generic form and gender.

The relationship between sensation fiction and psychiatry cannot be charted along a simple course of mimetic transmission, for the disruptive formal qualities of these novels ensure that they are often challenging the very authorities they seem to enshrine. Thus the male detective figure might fulfil the role of psychiatric authority in pursuing and unveiling female madness, but he does so within a novelistic framework that inverts the gendered hierarchy of patriarchal science exposing female nature. The psychiatric pursuit of inner truth is figured in several texts as itself a form of madness.

The medical discourse of female pathology was invoked in contemporary responses to sensation fiction.[2] Outraged Victorian reviewers depicted the sensation novel as both source and symptom of emergent forms of social disease. According to H. L. Mansel in the *Quarterly Review,* such "morbid" works were "indications of a wide-spread corruption, of which they are in part both the effect and the cause; called into existence to supply the cravings of a diseased appetite, and contributing themselves to foster the disease, and to stimulate the want which they supply." Drawing a direct homology between the health of the social body and that of individual readers, he concludes that these works, looked at as "an eruption indicative of the state of health of the body in which they appear . . . are by no means favourable symptoms of the body of society."[3] References to lurking disease and poison (which draw on precisely the same forms of rhetoric as the despised novels themselves) litter the pages of hostile reviews. For Margaret Oliphant, the English novel had always held a high reputation for "a certain sanity, wholesomeness and cleanness" until the advent of sensation fiction. Her model for such psychological cleanliness is Trollope, whose works are taken here as the epitome of English respectability and realistic representation. "It is not he," she comments, "who makes us ashamed of our girls."[4] The observation exposes the relation between critical conceptions of realism and the gendered norms of bourgeois propriety.

The sin committed by the sensationalists was not simply to include new spheres of subject matter, for crime and sexuality have always been the staple of English fiction, albeit in less sensually explicit terms. Such indiscretions might have been forgiven if the novels had not also violated the sacred tenets of realism. Criticism of the sensation novel focused on both its subject matter and its form, revealing in the process the ideological assumptions underpinning critical conceptions of realism. Not only should the realist novel proffer an acceptable image of social life, it should also obey the formal rules of coherence and continuity, which were themselves predicated on specific notions of psychology. In the hands of writers such as George Eliot or Trollope, the realist novel, with its cumulative movement toward greater social understanding and self-awareness, established a literature whose keynotes were continuity and responsibility. Gradual, cumulative action revealed the continuity of the psyche; all actions were explicable, even the apparently irrational (such as Hetty Sorel's abandonment of her child in *Adam Bede*), in terms of the individual's history and psychological makeup. The self, such novels suggested, was a unified entity; all actions had inescapable consequences, and the process of self-development was one of learning to take responsibility for one's own actions.

Sensation novels, by contrast, explicitly violated realism's formal rules of coherence and continuity and the psychological models of self-hood on which those works were founded. Disorder, discontinuity, and irresponsibility are the hallmarks of these feminine texts. Structurally, the plots play with elements of surprise and discontinuity. The reader is not placed in a position of calm knowledge superior to that of the characters but is rather continually startled by events and actions into states of extreme sensation. Such novels, H. L. Mansel maintained, were "preaching to the nerves," hence situating their readers in the feminine position of nervousness while inviting vicarious, sensual participation in the thrills of the unexpected, the inexplicable, and the forbidden.[5] Rhoda Broughton, for example, flagrantly disobeyed the rules of dramatic closure in *Red as a Rose Is She* (1870) in order to permit her readers the sensual gratification of improper embraces, sanctified by the deathbed. The opening of the following chapter miraculously resuscitates the heroine, however: "Lifeless! Yes! But there are two kinds of lifelessness: one from which there is no back-coming—one from which there is. Esther's is the latter."[6] Such dramatic transformations necessarily challenge realist patterns of psychological representation. In Mrs. Henry Wood's *St. Martin's Eve* (1866) it appears as if the textual climax

has been reached: the heroine's incipient madness finally bursts out beyond all bounds of control. Yet the next time she appears, she is once more calm and collected, calculatedly pursuing her own economic interests in the shape of another marriage.

Victorian critics were infuriated by these seemingly gross inconsistencies in sensation fiction plots, the ways in which characters could be restored to life or sanity with seeming impunity, attributing them entirely to lack of artistic skill. Such dramatic disjunctures in textual and psychological continuity are, however, part of the sensationalists' tactical assault on the social, psychological, and gendered certainties of bourgeois realism. Margaret Oliphant tellingly attributed the rise of sensation fiction to the demise of the imperial complacency typified by the Great Exhibition of 1851, and to the ensuing wars and loss of social direction manifested in English society. Ten years ago, Oliphant observed, "the age was lost in self-admiration," but peace and industry had since been displaced by war: "We who once did, and made, and declared ourselves masters of all things, have relapsed into the natural size of humanity before the great events which have given a new character to the age." People had come to enjoy the thrills of war, and sensation fiction now pandered to the emergent need for "a supply of new shocks and wonders."[7] With the loss of phallic "mastery," the culture of control is undermined from within as the populace increasingly seeks out the bodily, and hence feminized, shocks of sensation. Sensation fiction both responded and contributed to this fracturing of social certainties, whose effects are registered in the texts' insistent ambiguity and in their preoccupation with the symbolically central issue of gender identity. Uncertainties of gender positioning occur throughout the genre, whether in the male/female duality of the characters in *The Woman in White,* or in the ambiguous relation to gender stereotypes incarnated in that "beautiful fiend" Lady Audley, whose outer form and inner self seem so totally at odds. Sensation fiction highlights the uncertain relation between the outer and inner forms of selfhood, but there is no possibility, as in realist fiction, of pursuing a course of revelation until the "true" self is unveiled.[8] The very category of selfhood is itself subject to interrogation. To try to determine, for example, whether Lady Audley was really mad, is to misunderstand the radical workings of the text—its challenge of certainty. The critical controversies provoked by the question of her psychological status are themselves eloquent testimony to the ambiguity of the text.[9]

Although the sensation novel frequently employs the framework of a detective hunt, where the secret in question is often the sanity of the female protagonist, the results are never conclusive. The texts do not move toward an ultimate revelation by masculine science of the hidden truths of femininity. The final disclosure can raise more questions than it answers, while the male detective himself is usually tainted by his quest. Walter Hartright, hero of Wilkie Collins's *The Woman in White,* sets his narrative up as a quasi-legal document, following the proceedings of a court of law, but the effect is only to highlight the impossibility of objective knowledge. This is a novel where even tombstones can lie, and where the key to all the layers of secrecy lies not in tangible evidence but in absence: the lack of an entry in the parish register to record the marriage of Sir Percival Glyde's parents: "That space told the whole story!"[10] Upon this blank space Hartright imaginatively transcribes an entire history, which leads directly to his own empowerment and the overthrow of his enemy. At one stroke, which itself mirrors the central crime of the novel, their identities and status are exchanged. Sir Percival loses his baronetcy, and the way is cleared for Hartright's own social ascent into the landed gentry. In its foregrounding of the instability of identity, manifested preeminently in the central plot whereby Fosco takes from the heiress Laura her rank and name and installs her in the identity of Anne Catherick, a lower-class inmate of an asylum, *The Woman in White* self-consciously addresses many of the issues and problems that mark the genre of sensation fiction. Discontinuities, absences, uncertainties, both structural and thematic, define these works, and in the central ambiguity of madness they find a convenient locus for their challenge to the ordered, gendered certainties of much realist fiction.

For the Victorian critics, sensation novels were themselves a form of madness, "feverish productions" that, in "preaching to the nerves," exacerbated the decline of self-control, that hallmark of masculinity, which was held to be essential for the psychic and economic health of the nation.[11] The madness of which the novelists themselves stood accused, however, formed one of the central subjects of their fiction. As the jaundiced author of an article entitled "Madness in Novels" remarked, everyone in the anonymous *The Clyffords of Clyffe* "is either mad, or fears he may be mad, or is sought in love in order to keep away madness, or drives a debasing trade in the sufferings of the mad."[12] Such a text is of course extreme, but it does suggest the ways in which concerns with madness enter into every level of sensation fiction. As I suggested, the sensationalists mirrored the concerns of Victorian psychiatry in their preoccupation with the domain of psychological excess, but the sense of a stabilizing normative vision is missing in their work. In William Gilbert's novel *Shirley Hall Asylum; or, Memoirs of a Monomaniac* (1863), for example, the asylum seems to stand as a microcosm of society, where keeper and kept alike exhibit symptoms of multitudinous forms of insanity. At one level, the sensationalists' preoccupation with insanity can be seen in terms of its usefulness as a plot device that allows them to transgress realist conventions of character and probability with impunity (the

view held by the author of the *Spectator* article "Madness in Novels")—nothing is improbable if the character is defined as mad.[13] But at a deeper level, the sensationalists' fascination with insanity responds to profound cultural uncertainties of the era. We can best appreciate these connections and their social significance if we place the novels in the cultural context of Victorian psychiatry.

The nineteenth century witnessed the rise of medicine as a socially authoritative profession, and the specific emergence of psychiatry as a medical discipline. It became a truism in the midcentury that the physician now occupied the role of the priest: repository of all the inner secrets of the self, and sole arbiter of physical and mental health.[14] As the hero of Mary Braddon's *Lady Audley's Secret* observes, on summoning a physician in the hopes of getting Lady Audley committed, "physicians and lawyers are the confessors of this prosaic nineteenth century."[15] Commentators stressed with alarm the power that now seemed to reside in the figure of the doctor: "No one possesses such absolute power as the medical man over his patient; that which the veriest despot in the world exercises over his slave does not equal it."[16] This sense of power was intensified by the changes in attitudes toward insanity that underpinned the rise of medical psychiatry. Insanity became a distinct medical condition, and one that, according to the theorists of moral management in the first half of the century, was susceptible to treatment.[17] Both the physiology and psychiatry of the nineteenth century broke down earlier absolute divides between the normal and the pathological, insisting that disease arose merely from an excess or deficency of elements integral to normal functioning.[18] The mad were no longer "other," to be locked away with criminals or the insane: anyone, the theory implied, could become insane by the slight movement into imbalance of his or her physiological and mental system. As Braddon again remarks, "Who has not been, or is not to be, mad in some lonely hour of life? Who is quite safe from the trembling of the balance?"[19]

In the eighteenth century "nervousness" was deemed a "success tax," the price to be paid for the advances in civilization, and it could be borne with a certain degree of pride.[20] At the opening of the nineteenth, the tone had already changed. Thomas Trotter warned ominously that England's "commercial greatness" was at risk from "the increasing prevalence of nervous disorders; which, if not restrained soon, must inevitably sap our physical strength of constitution; make us an easy conquest to our invaders; and ultimately convert us into a nation of slaves and idiots."[21] Mental health is here tied directly to the economic progress of the nation, illuminating the ways in which psychiatric and economic ideologies were intertwined in the nineteenth century. In an industrial culture devoted to the domination of markets and the maximization of labor efficiency, the dominant ethos was one of transformative control. Within psychiatric discourse this ethos was manifested in the moral managers' emphasis on the powers of the individual will, as exemplified in John Barlow's popular work *Man's Power over Himself to Prevent or Control Insanity* (1843). While drawing on economic ideologies of self-control and self-help, this work also, paradoxically, drew attention to its own sense of the omnipresence of insanity. The difference between sanity and insanity, Barlow argued, consisted entirely "in the degree of self-control exercised." He advises the reader who remains unconvinced to "note for a short time the thoughts that pass through his mind, and the feelings that agitate him: and he will find that, were they expressed and indulged, they would be as wild, and perhaps as frightful in their consequences as those of any madman."[22] The state of insanity, in other words, is that of acting out the hidden desires we all possess. Psychiatric discourse itself unwittingly supplied the subversive plot line of much sensation fiction.

Psychiatric texts fostered fears of an ever-lurking threat of insanity. As John Conolly, one of the preeminent theorists and practitioners of moral management, observed in his introduction to *An Inquiry Concerning the Indications of Insanity* (1830), "every man is interested in this subject; for no man can confidently reckon on the continuance of his perfect reason."[23] Studies, widely reported in the popular press, that suggested an alarming increase in the incidence of insanity further fueled fears of social epidemics of madness.[24] Although the statistics were misleading, relating more to changing modes of classification and patterns of institutionalization than to any actual increases in insanity, the responses they evoked constitute a very telling self-portrait of Victorian Britain.[25] The ever-present threat of insanity formed the subtext of the culture of self-control.

Professional self-interest on the part of members of the burgeoning psychiatric profession led to alarming pronouncements on the state of the nation's health. Conolly observed that without the aid of medical men, the influences to which men and women were subjected in the pressurized climate of industrial England would soon "render the greater part of mankind helpless and miserable."[26] Articles in periodicals of the time paint a picture of a general populace paralyzed by fear of possible insanity. "A Plea for Physicians" in *Fraser's Magazine* outlines a hypothetical scenario:

> A person—say a young female, say a mother—is haunted with the fear of hereditary insanity. If she feel low-spirited, she dreads it; if she feel more than ordinarily happy, in the midst of her joy the thought strikes her that perhaps her merriment is morbid; if her children gambol, and laugh, and shout, more than usual, she trembles lest each ebullition of joy be not the first symptom of the object of her

dread, or they may retire from their rougher sports, and she again apprehends the worst.[27]

This hypothetical case, in focusing on a young mother, takes a subject whose insanity is overdetermined in contemporary discourse, and exposes the gendered power dynamics that reside in the relationship between male medicine and its female subjects. Once fear is established, any slight deviation from normal behavior can be construed as a symptom of insanity. The woman is at the mercy of her own fears, and of the physician who is alone empowered to pronounce definitively on the constitution of normality. The scenario painted is a familiar one in the sensation fiction of the 1860s, where latent female insanity can lie dormant for years before suddenly bursting forth to disrupt the calm surface of familial and social life. Mrs. Henry Wood's *St. Martin's Eve,* for example, portrays an anxious mother, desperately watching her married daughter for signs of inherited insanity, while the family doctor, who has kept the heroine under surveillance since childhood, waits in the wings to sign the committal forms once his early prognosis has been confirmed by subsequent behavior.

From the 1860s onward, medical emphasis on hereditary and latent insanity increased, as England's decline in economic prosperity and confidence was shadowed forth in the evolutionary pessimism of Maudsley and other post-Darwinian theorists. Andrew Wynter pointed out in *The Borderlands of Insanity* (1875) that there was "an immense amount of latent brain disease in the community, only awaiting a sufficient exciting cause to make itself patent to the world."[28] The sensationalists, writing at a transitional period, drew both on these biologically deterministic theories of madness and on the theories of moral management of the earlier part of the century, which, with their emphasis on the powers of the will and the possibilities of recuperation, belonged to a more optimistic cultural and economic climate. For the moral managers, insanity was not necessarily an inescapable biological given; it could be partial, and it could be cured. While avoiding the oppressive determinism of later theories, these conceptions also had their negative side, which the sensationalists were quick to exploit. The threat of insanity hung over all, not merely the biologically selected few, and its presence was compatible with an apparently normal lifestyle within the community.

The two primary forms of partial insanity, as formulated in early nineteenth-century psychiatric theory, were moral insanity and monomania, both developed from the theories of Pinel and Esquirol in France. According to J. C. Prichard, moral insanity consisted in

> a morbid perversion of the natural feelings, affections, inclinations, temper, habits, moral dispositions, and natural impulses, without any remarkable disorder

or defect of the intellect or knowing and reasoning faculties, and particularly without any insane illusion or hallucination.[29]

The definition dispenses with all the traditional outward signs of lunacy; madness is compatible with a total absence of illusion, and an ability to reason without any discernible flaws in logic or understanding. Monomania seems an even more circumscribed form of insanity; it is a mode of intellectual insanity "in which the understanding is partially disordered or under the influence of some particular illusion, referring to one subject, and involving one train of ideas, while the intellectual powers appear, when exercised on other subjects, to be in a great measure unimpaired."[30] While moral insanity can transform all affective behavior, monomania can refer simply to an intellectual obsession. Both terms quickly caught the public imagination and became common currency in the journalism of the day. In line with the increasingly rigidified social codes of Victorian England, these formulations suggested that behavior could be defined as insane if, on the moral and emotional front, it exceeded the highly gendered definitions of the "natural," or, on the intellectual front, it sprang from firmly held convictions that ran counter to normative social expectations. Thus in *Hard Cash,* for example, the hero is diagnosed as suffering from monomania and is placed against his will in an asylum because he, quite rightly, accused his father of theft. The physicians' powers of forcible committal, to either private asylums or the public asylums set up after the two 1845 Lunatic Acts, were cause for great concern in the newspapers of the day, and they feature repeatedly in sensation novels. One of the most famous cases was that of the wealthy heiress Eliza Nottridge, who was confined by her mother and brother-in-law in an asylum for seventeen months on the grounds of her membership of a millennial sect. On her escape she sued for wrongful confinement and won. The *Leeds Mercury* commented on the unsatisfactory role played by physicians with reference to committals: "In lieu of the simple intelligible principles which should govern determinations regarding the imputedly insane, medical men have erected themselves into metaphysical censors of the movements of the human mind, and their oracular *dicta* take effect in the shape of committals to lunatic asylums!" Miss Nottridge's case, the paper suggests, gives rise to the suspicion "that many other persons may be incarcerated on grounds equally untenable, and whose cases, except through some fortunate escape, are likely to be hidden from public justice" (14 July 1849). Charles Reade's *Hard Cash* was specifically designed to draw the public's attention to the possibilities of wrongful confinement, while Wilkie Collins claimed that *The Woman in White* was based on a contemporary case.[31] General public unease had led to the setting up in 1858 of the Parliamentary Select Committee into the Care and Treatment of Lunatics and Their Property.

Part of the mystique and threatening nature of the physicians' authority sprang from the sheer invisibility of insanity to the untrained eye. Psychiatric texts stressed repeatedly that only the highly trained eye of the medical expert could detect the outward signs of insanity, so skilled were the insane at dissembling, and, one could add, so subtle were the distinctions at stake.[32] Esquirol is said to have watched his patients during their sleep, convinced that they would reveal the telltale signs of insanity when off guard, while Pinel managed to persuade a man that his wife had been insane, not just for the past six months, but for the previous fifteen years.[33] The English translator of Esquirol inserted a footnote into the text to warn readers that "insanity is sometimes so insidious in its attack as to escape the notice of even the nearest relatives for a considerable period. As a general rule, any change from the usual habits of the individual should excite suspicion."[34] Such incitements to vigilance are bred within and help perpetuate an atmosphere of self-distrust and mutual suspicion, producing a nation of watchful readers and interpreters, ever ready to detect outward signs of insanity, either in the self or others.

Mid-Victorian psychiatry was preeminently a science of interpretation and detection. According to Conolly, the fully trained physician should be able to read through surface plausibility, and to detect madness even in the way a man wore his hat.[35] Not only is latent insanity at issue: partial states of insanity such as monomania and moral insanity can be transient, lasting only as long as the impulse itself.[36] The physician must learn to read the signs not only of buried, dormant hereditary characteristics, but also of forms of behavior that, if only for an instant, exceed the bounds of social acceptability. Sensation fiction was quick to capitalize on the narrative potential of this dimension of medical psychiatry. Physicians are frequently wheeled in to attest to the insanity of a heroine who, according to traditional conceptions of insanity, is far from mad. But the primary role of detecting and interpreting the signs of insanity generally falls to the male hero, as in Braddon's *Lady Audley's Secret,* or Mrs. Henry Wood's *St. Martin's Eve.* Detection in these cases ceases to be a neutral activity and becomes instead a site of ambiguity and of male contagion.

While sensation fiction follows psychiatry in foregrounding the practices of interpretation and detection, it questions the authority vested both in the medical profession and in the interpretative process itself. Walter Hartright in *The Woman in White* stops to ask whether he is really following a train of villainy, or whether all the connections he sees are symptoms of his own disordered mind: "It seemed almost like a monomania to be tracing back everything that happened, everything unexpected that was said, always to the same hidden source and the same sinister influence."[37] We as readers, busily interpreting the trail of signs Walter lays before us, are similarly afflicted.[38] Is the desire to impose interpretative coherence itself the product of an obsessional mind? *Lady Audley's Secret* raises the same issue in even more explicit terms. Robert, the detective-figure hero, asks early on in his quest whether his own doubts and suspicions "may grow upon me till I become a monomaniac."[39] His self-doubt intensifies as he pursues his detective work. Why should he see such a mystery in his friend's disappearance?

> Was it a monition or a monomania? What if I am wrong after all? What if this chain of evidence which I have constructed link by link is woven out of my own folly? What if this edifice of horror and suspicion is a mere collection of crotchets—the nervous fancies of a hypochondriacal bachelor? . . . Oh, my God, if it should be in myself all this time that the mystery lies! (217-218)

Robert rejects his doubts because he believes he has hard evidence, suggestively situated in his pocket, but events reveal that the initial premise lying behind his investigations and pursuit of Lady Audley, that his friend was murdered, is unfounded. Can a false premise lead to a correct conclusion, or are all his connections and surmises therefore tainted and misguided? In drawing attention to his own position as a bachelor, Robert locates himself in one of the prime categories for male nervous disorder, a position intensified by his idle life. (Male insanity, contemporary theorists argued, could be caused both by sexual continence and by failure to exert oneself in professional life). The tale ends with the incarceration of the woman who had initially aroused his illicit sexual desire and with his own dual reward of domestic, marital bliss and the successful launching of his professional career.[40] The structure of the novel suggests that the affirmation of male sanity and social normality is dependent upon the social placement of woman in a position of insanity.

Recent work on insanity in the Victorian novel has focused largely on female insanity.[41] If the sensation novelists' preoccupation with male insanity is taken into account, however, a complex network is revealed in which male and female insanity are relationally interdependent. In novels that take the detective form, the stakes involved in the quest to determine which party is insane are both economic and psychological. For the woman, her economic independence is usually at issue, while for the man it is nothing less than the assurance of his own masculinity and the improvement of his own economic and social status and prospects. In their representations of insanity the sensation novelists worked both within and against Victorian psychiatric discourse, using the categories and vocabulary, but in the process raising questions as to both its validity and its social functions. The sensationalists' preoccupation with male insanity strikes at the roots of the patriarchal foundations of Victorian culture: if insanity is indeed a relative term, and male sanity is assured only by the successful certification of female insanity, then notions of masculinity, and dependent ideologies of domestic and social order, are destabilized, while the very possiblity of authoritative interpretation is set at risk.

The male detective figure in these fictions is usually of precarious masculinity and social status. Walter Hartright in *The Woman in White* is a penniless drawing master, occupying a social position of even more than feminine dependency: he is admitted among his pupils not as a man but as a "harmless domestic animal" (89). Robert Audley is a "lazy, care-for-nothing fellow" (27) who fails to practice his profession, and prefers to spend his time on the feminized occupation of novel reading. Frederick St. John in *St. Martin's Eve* has run through his patrimony yet occupies his time in the dilettantish, and again feminized, activity of painting. The sexual politics involved are most starkly depicted in *Lady Audley's Secret* and *St. Martin's Eve,* where male and female careers follow an inverse trajectory: the ambitious (and hence masculinized) female who has sought to gain economic security is pursued by a feminized male whose interests are threatened. Both novels end with the incarceration of the deviant woman in a lunatic asylum (a testimony to her physiologically flawed, female status), and the confirmation of the hero's masculinity and social normality through his marriage. The fall of the female marks the rise of the male. Robert starts to practice his profession, while Frederick, in successfully getting Charlotte certified as insane, has blocked his brother's possible marriage and ensured his own succession to the St. John fortune.

This gendered pattern of ascent and fall highlights the different positioning of men and women in the economic and social order. Heroines who are marked out by insanity are usually also economically disadvantaged. We are told explicitly in *St. Martin's Eve* that Charlotte would have inherited her father's fortune if she had been a boy. As it is, she and mother are turned out of Norris Court on her father's death (which coincides with her own birth). This secondary status is reinforced by her marriage; as a widow she remains in her own home only as guardian of her stepson, and loses all when first her stepson and then her own son die. The steps she takes to ensure her economic independence (which do, admittedly, include such sensational tactics as locking the young heir in a room and leaving him to burn to death) lead to her committal. Similarly, the steps Lady Audley takes (which also involve the attempted burning of someone in a locked room) to preserve her wealth and social status when they are threatened by the return of her first husband provide the ground for her certification.

The women's negative economic placement is also inscribed on them physiologically. As Lady Audley declares in her speech of exculpation, she learned early on that "the only inheritance I had to expect from my mother was—insanity!" (296). Passed through the female line, and excited in her mother's case by giving birth, this form of inheritance appears as a symbolic encapsulation of the condition of femininity—of economic and social powerlessness. Lady Audley's mother was not, she carefully points out, a "distraught, violent creature" (295); her madness took the form rather of the childish innocence that was the ideologically preferred model of Victorian womanhood. Charlotte's only form of inheritance is also a physiological one. She inherits from her father his fits of jealousy, which in her case start to manifest themselves when her economic interests are threatened. Her jealous passions are directed toward her stepson the heir, who has cut off her own child's prospects, and the girl who, she believes, is preventing her from making the marriage that will restore her fortunes.

While the women tend to be defined by negative economic and physiological inheritance, the men are placed in positions of economic possibility; either they stand in line for a title and wealth, or they are permitted to marry money, like Walter Hartright, without having their motives or their sanity impugned. The threat of insanity that hangs over them is rarely an inescapable physiological destiny, but rather a partial, temporary form, which can be shaken off through self-discipline and a transformation of life-style. The details offered of female insanity in these texts are all in accordance with contemporary psychiatric accounts, which stressed that, physiologically, women were far more prone to insanity than men.[42] But while the novelists take pains to follow the vocabulary and categories of contemporary psychiatric discourse in their depictions of female insanity, the structural functions of this insanity in their works, and specifically its relations to economic inheritance, suggest that they were using insanity as a device to raise questions about a culture whose legal and medical institutions worked in harness to proclaim and enforce women's physiological and economic inferiority.

Although the heroes of these tales are always presented as perfect, unimpeachable gentlemen, the suspicions roused as to their sanity, and the actual structuring of the text, often suggest a rather more subversive reading. Frederick in *St. Martin's Eve* is introduced to us as a "true gentleman at heart" even though he is almost immediately arrested for debt. His subsequent career is far from glorious. He pursues an angelic creature who is already betrothed to another, fails to trust in the truth of her love when appearances seem against her, and turns his back on her in anger, leading her to burst a blood vessel and thus die, literally, of a broken heart. This plot line provides perhaps the most sensational of all scenes in sensation novels. Frederick returns, not knowing of Adeline's death, and is taken to her house, where she appears, clad in bridal attire, to be holding a reception. It is only when he stands opposite her and gazes into her face that "with a rushing sensation of sickening awe and terror, the terrible truth burst upon his brain. That it was not Adeline de Castella, but her CORPSE which stood there."[43] Wood makes great play, through a footnote address to the reader, of the factual authenticity of such practices of displaying the dead, but the scene is literally unwritable in realist terms. With its flagrant violation of realist proprieties, the scene constitutes the ultimate transgression of the boundaries that had defined the realist body. It offers a ghastly temporal parody of a spiritual reawakening, which, in its insistent physicality, turns death itself into an erotic exchange. Symbolically, furthermore, it functions as an ironic comment on the optimistic trajectory of realism. As embalmed bride, the cold and lifeless Adeline is the literal figuration of the conventional ending of the realist novel.

The scene's sensational effects have their primary impact on the nervous system of the reader, and not on our hero. Despite this shock to the system, he nonetheless reflects at Adeline's funeral that it was best that she had died, since had they married she would have passed on to their children "her fragility of constitution" (374). While not the bearer of insanity, she would pass on as her legacy an equally flawed physiological state.[44] By a process of association, Frederick's thoughts then turn immediately to the hints he has picked up as to Charlotte's insanity. The rest of the novel is devoted to the battle between himself and Charlotte as he attempts to find enough evidence of her insanity to get her committed and thus prevent her marriage to his brother.

The narrative draws attention to Frederick's detective role and the difficulties of interpreting signs. Although apparently idle, Frederick was "secretly busy as ever was a London detective" watching Charlotte until he "persuaded himself that he did detect signs of incipient madness" (386-387). The text highlights the self-persuasion involved in diagnoses of insanity. The signs Frederick detects are so intangible—nothing more than a transient look, followed immediately by such charm—that "had all the doctors connected with Bethlehem hospital come forward to declare her mad, people would have laughed at them for their pains" (391). Frederick determinedly ups the stakes, installing the doctor, Mr. Pym, in the role of "a very private-detective" (439), but Charlotte, unlike Lady Audley, takes no evasive action. She remains outwardly impassive, watching the surgeon "just as keenly as he did her" (443). It is a game she cannot win, however; relying solely on her own cleverness and self-control, she has failed to take into account the fact that Mr. Pym and Frederick hold the trump card of patriarchal medical authority. The text covertly indicts psychiatric diagnostic practices that rely on the constant surveillance of the chosen subject until the desired signs of insanity are displayed. Mr. Pym informs Charlotte's mother that he could never come to the conclusion that there was nothing wrong with her daughter: "Were I to remain in the house a month, and see no proof whatever of insanity, I could not be sure that it did not exist. We know how cunning these people are." (437). Once a presupposition of insanity has been established, there is no escape. The statement encapsulates the position held by women within psychiatric discourse: in a reversal of the legal code, they are deemed potentially insane until proven otherwise. Like *Lady Audley's Secret,* the text stresses that the act of detection in and of itself produces the symptoms it seeks to detect. Charlotte's first outbreak of anger, brought on by being told that she is being removed for her own good, leads to her being placed in an asylum "from which she can never more be released in safety" (447).

The narrative of *St. Martin's Eve* abides by the rules of psychiatric discourse: Charlotte is depicted as a real threat, violent and demonic in her anger when roused, and Frederick and the doctor bide their time, waiting until an outbreak of violence will justify her committal. It also highlights, however, the questionable nature of detection and the presuppositions that direct its patriarchal pursuit. Double standards are clearly in operation. Frederick, for all his attractive manner and unimpugned integrity, was, like Charlotte, responsible for the death of another through an uncontrolled fit of anger. His economic future also hinges on his ability to demonstrate Charlotte's insanity. As in *Lady Audley's Secret,* the defeat of the mad woman ensures the hero's accession to true manhood; Frederick fulfils his brother's dearest wishes and marries, taking on the mantle of heir. The final scene, however, is unsettling, hardly a celebration of marital bliss. Rose, Charlotte's sister, draws attention to the transitory nature of Frederick's love by reminding his wife of Adeline. She also questions whether Charlotte is kindly treated in the asylum, and is told by Frederick that it "could not be well" for her to visit. While Lady Audley is conveniently driven to her death by boredom, Charlotte remains alive, a presence who must be forcibly forgotten and ignored if the facades of domestic and social order are to be maintained.

While the threat of incarceration works only one way in *St. Martin's Eve,* in *Lady Audley's Secret* it is double-edged. Lady Audley herself initially tries to convince Sir Michael that Robert is a monomaniac. Her arguments are drawn straight from the psychiatry of the day: madness can be a "mere illness of the brain" to which anyone is subject; and "people are insane for years and years before their insanity is found out" (245). The specific cause she adduces for Robert's monomania, his mental stagnation, is again in line with psychi-

atric theory. For young men, failure to show enterprise in their profession or commerce was judged sufficient evidence of insanity. Conolly cited the example of men who had talents but failed to show ambition: "They have no violent desires nor perturbations, and they never ripen. Neither ambition nor pride can rouse them to sustained efforts."[45] The passivity so desirable in women becomes pathological in men. While Lady Audley's active ambitions leave her open to charges of insanity, Robert's lack of ambition and failure to pursue his profession conversely place him under the same threat. His "sustained effort" in his pursuit of Lady Audley becomes, however, the vehicle of his redemption.

Although Robert wheels in the physician to attest to Lady Audley's madness, the initial diagnosis comes from Lady Audley herself. She invalidates Robert's victory by proclaiming that all his "cool calculating intellect" has been exercised only to conquer a "MADWOMAN!" (293). Her self-exculpation, which shows how thoroughly she has internalized the doctrines of psychiatry, draws on two different strands of theory: she is mad because of inheritance, "the hidden taint that I had sucked in with my mother's milk" (332), but also, as she repeatedly claims, because she has "crossed that invisible line which separates reason from madness" (299). While the first claim belongs to theories of physiological determinism, and hence incurable insanity, the second belongs to the rhetoric of moral management, which suggested that insanity could be a transient, curable state, and one to which all were susceptible.

The verdict on Lady Audley's insanity is left open. For both the physician and Robert, her incarceration in an asylum is an expedient that, in effectively "burying her alive," removes any threat she might still represent to the Audley name and family. The physician diagnoses her not as mad but as dangerous, and on those grounds signs the certificate for her committal. The text's preoccupation with insanity is not removed with her presence, however. Indeed, most of the discussion of insanity has a male focus in the figure of Robert. His own fears about his possible monomania are reinforced in the text by explicit narrative commentary that makes him the vehicle of speculation as to whether we might all, like Lady Audley, cross the thin dividing line between madness and sanity. Robert's sense of powerlessness and disorientation after meeting Clara leads the narrator to observe:

> Madhouses are large and only too numerous; yet surely it is strange they are not larger, when we think of how many helpless wretches must beat their brains against this hopeless persistency of the orderly outward world, as compared with the storm and tempest, the riot and confusion within;— when we remember how many minds must tremble upon the narrow boundary between reason and unreason, mad to-day and sane tomorrow, mad yesterday and sane to-day. (175-176)

The madness of unreason, the passage suggests, is the normal state of our psyches: we live in a constant state of imbalance, trying to suppress and disguise the rage within while we fulfil our expected roles in the outer mechanisms of social life. Madness, as Conolly and Barlow suggested, is the state that occurs when we let the social mask slip, and the inner self disrupts surface social performance.

The incarceration of Lady Audley does not ensure Robert's immediate recovery; indeed his nervousness intensifies, and the narrator again intervenes to remind us that "there is nothing so delicate, so fragile, as that invisible balance upon which the mind is always trembling; mad to-day and sane to-morrow" (341). A dramatic picture of Dr. Johnson, reduced to childish terror, is invoked to reinforce the message: "Who has not been, or is not to be, mad in some lonely hour of life? Who is quite safe from the trembling of the balance?" (341). While underscoring Robert's own fragile hold on sanity, the question necessarily reverberates to include Lady Audley who, for acting out her inner desires, has been imprisoned not for some lonely hour but for life. Lady Audley constitutes for Robert the demon he must exorcise before he can marry his angel Clara and enter those ideologically prescribed arenas of masculine sanity: domestic and professional life.

Braddon seems to reverse standard stereotypes with her "beautiful fiend," the golden-haired Lady Audley, and the dark-eyed angel, Clara. But the true picture is by no means so simple. Clara herself is depicted in terms drawn straight from psychiatric accounts of female hysteria. Her unnatural calmness is broken when she runs after Robert in a feverish passion, stating that she will go mad unless she can avenge her brother's death. Her self-diagnosis quickly follows: "'I have grown up in an atmosphere of suppression,' she said quietly: 'I have stifled and dwarfed the natural feelings of my heart, until they have become unnatural in their intensity. I have been allowed neither friends nor lovers'" (171). Writers on female hysteria in the midcentury repeatedly stressed that the outward calm demanded of women led to a damaging suppression of feeling and consequent outbursts of insanity. As J. G. Millingen records in *The Passions; or, Mind and Matter* (1848):

> In woman, the concentration of her feelings (a concentration that her social position renders indispensable) adds to their intensity; and like a smouldering fire that has at last got vent, her passions, when no longer trammelled by conventional propriety, burst forth in unquenchable violence.[46]

To Robert's clouded judgment Clara, in her violent declarations of vengeance, seems "elevated into sublimity" (171), but the descriptions of her impact upon him suggest something altogether more sinister. He perceives this "noble" creature to be a merciless force, trampling down all who stand in her way and forcing himself "upon the loathsome path, the crooked bye-way of watchfulness and suspicion" (175). Clara takes on demonic, vampirelike qualities: "This woman knows half my secret; she will soon possess herself of the rest; and then—and then—" (175). Clara violates Robert's self-possession, the very grounding, in Victorian ideology, of manhood and sanity. Under her scrutiny he is once more feminized, placed in exactly the same position in which he himself locates Lady Audley. It is he who is now the possessor of a secret that he wishes to hide from prying eyes. In his relations with Lady Audley, Robert had placed himself in the role of the Victorian physicians who sought to unveil the secrets of the female mind and body, revealing the dark inner side of that which was outwardly so fair.[47] His early loss of self-control precipitated by his involuntary sexual attraction was to be sternly extirpated through this exercise of patriarchal authority. But when he meets Clara, the tables seem reversed. He is reduced to feelings of utter helplessness as Clara's gaze takes on a psychiatrist's power to pluck out "the innermost secrets of his mind" (221). Although the novel seems to portray the victory of male reason over female madness, and Robert's ascent to true masculinity, it shows in fact his complete overthrow and loss of self-possession. The reiterated statement that Clara has his lost friend's face reinforces the sense that he is actively feminized by Clara, and intensifies our sense of unease with the conclusion of the novel, where Clara, George, and Robert (and the inevitable signifier of heterosexual normality, a baby) are portrayed as existing in perfect domestic bliss.[48] Just as at the beginning of the novel, outward order masks inner disarray. Imprisoning Lady Audley has done little to restore sanity to a world in which the balance of social and psychological order is so finely poised.

The endings of sensation novels invariably seem to exacerbate rather than resolve the tensions and problems addressed in the text. Collins's *The Woman in White* is no exception. Although it has a detective framework and is preoccupied with madness, it does not, as do Braddon's and Wood's later treatment of this theme, portray the hero hunting down threatening female insanity. This is a novel that seems to undercut all sureties of identity, of gender, class and sanity. The dualism of Anne and Laura, with its staging of the radical uncertainties of class and sanity, functions as the central site of ambiguity around which all other questionable boundaries of identity are clustered. Few characters seem to possess an unproblematic gender identity. While Marian, with her voluptuous female figure and mannish face, is the key figure of gender duality, many of the other major characters transgress gender lines, although in less startling physical form. Laura's uncle, Frederick Fairlie, purposefully installs himself in the female role of nervous helplessness, while

Count Fosco combines ruthless, aggressive intelligence with the soft stealthy movements of a woman (not to mention his love of cakes and his pet mice). His partner in villainy, Sir Percival Glyde, exhibits masculine calm and sadistic authority coupled with nervous excitability and loss of self-control, passions that lead in the end to his very feminine demise: he is, like Brontë's mad wife in *Jane Eyre,* consumed in flames as he seeks to preserve the secret of his identity.[49]

Gender transgression, as in the case of Percival, is repeatedly linked to questions of psychological disorder and hence of insanity. (Marian's statement that she is "mad" when she thinks of the ways in which men enchain women [203] should not be taken solely as a figure of speech.) Our hero, Walter Hartright, starts off, as I suggested, in the feminized position of drawing master, and he has to undergo fears of loss of self and monomania and be sent off to prove himself in the primeval jungles of South America before returning to display his newly acquired masculinity in the defeat of Percival and Fosco. Initially his position seems similar to that of Anne Catherick, the escaped inmate of an asylum, who is racked with hatred of Sir Percival and states repeatedly that she will "forget" and "lose" herself if she speaks of him (51, 128). Walter admits that the feelings that fueled him in his relations with Sir Percival "began and ended in reckless, vindictive, hopeless hatred" (106). It is an admission that reinforces our credence in his own fears of monomania and undermines the validity of the entire narrative he has so painstakingly constructed. Anne's fears that she will lose herself, lose her tenuous grip on her own memories and sense of selfhood, are echoed in Walter's thoughts as he approaches Limmeridge when he experiences a "confused sensation of having suddenly lost my familiarity with the past" (57). Just as Laura, after her incarceration, loses her firm sense of the past, so Walter has his identity obliterated as he enters the world of Limmeridge. While Anne Catherick's entanglement with the secrets of Limmeridge is to lead literally to her loss of self in death, however, Walter loses self only to emerge as the epitome of the self-made man. Percival is toppled from his rank, name, and wealth, and Walter moves up the social ladder to take his place, as husband of Laura and member of the landed gentry. The dualism signified by the figure of Anne/Laura, penniless imbecile and perfect lady, is duplicated both in the figure of Sir Percival, who is at once pauper and baronet, psychologically disordered (as his nervous cough reveals) and yet controlled, and in the history of Walter, who moves from poverty to wealth, from psychological insecurity to assertive manhood.

The central device of the novel whereby Laura is installed within the social and psychological identity of her lower-class half-sister attests to the total relativity both of ascriptions of insanity and of identity itself. Fosco has no need to draw in accomplices either in the external world or in the asylum. All act in perfectly good faith in accepting Laura as the inmate Anne and rejecting her claims to be Lady Glyde. Laura's own state is hinted at by Walter, in accordance with the warp of his gender biases: "Faculties less delicately balanced, constitution less tenderly organised, must have suffered under such an ordeal as this. No man could have gone through it and come out of it unchanged" (449). Laura can only be restored to her previous identity when the official inscription marking her death is erased and she is publicly recognized by the tenants. Given the ambiguity of the text, however, can we be absolutely sure that this figure is Laura? Anne Catherick was said to have had a tenacious memory, and Laura is nursed back to identity by Walter and Marian rehearsing with her the details of her early life. Like the gap in the marriage register that exposes the sham of Sir Percival's identity, the absolute proof of Laura's identity rests on the shaky grounds of absence: the loss of a day. All hinges on the memories of a string of witnesses, each of whom reveals himself or herself to be highly fallible, and on the "confession" of that arch-deceiver Fosco. Such ambiguity reinforces our sense that identity, both social and psychological, is inherently unstable and fragile.

Our understanding of the two figures of Anne and Laura is transmitted preeminently through the testimony of Walter. On meeting Laura he is struck by the fact that there is "something wanting" (76), either in her or in himself. Although it appears that this "something" is her resemblance to Anne Catherick, the fact that he feels the absence to be within himself as well is significant. The "something wanting" could be the frisson of sexual desire he experienced when Anne Catherick laid her hand on his arm: "Remember that I was young; remember that the hand which touched me was a woman's" (50). Compared with his responses to Marian, Walter's reactions to Laura seem desexualized. Like Petrarch's Laura, she is a neoplatonic figure whom the reader is invited to take as "the visionary nursling of your own fancy" (76).[50] For Walter to emerge into a state of unproblematized masculinity, the threateningly sexualized, mannish Marian has to be laid low (raped, as Miller argues, by Fosco) and Laura has to be placed in the sexually provocative position of utter helplessness in which he first encountered Anne Catherick. Although Walter depicts himself as "heart-right," his actions, like those of the other detective heroes in sensation fiction, carry disturbing overtones. Confronted with Laura, "her beauty faded, her mind clouded—robbed of her station in the world," he lauches into rapturous statements of possessiveness: "Mine. . . . Mine. . . . Mine" (435). Earlier in the narrative Walter has referred in mysterious terms to "the woman who has possessed herself of all my energies" (37) and to "the veiled woman [who] had possession of me, body and soul" (431). The vocabulary and sense of menace are those later employed by

Braddon to depict Robert's relations with Clara. But in Collins's text there is no doubt as to who is ultimately in possession. Walter marries Laura (or Anne) when she is still in a state of childish imbecility, and concludes his narrative with the creation of a new aristocratic version of himself. Walter returns from a trip to Ireland and is introduced by Marian to his own son: "'Let me make two eminent personages known to one another: Mr Walter Hartright—the Heir of Limmeridge'" (646). The wording is deliberately ambiguous, suggesting that father and son are elided into the single figure of heir, completely erasing Laura's maternal role. Laura's second marriage constitutes yet one more effacement of her identity, an effacement that, as Fosco testifies, is actively demanded of and enforced on wives by English law and custom.[51] Fosco boasts that he could have taken Laura's life, but he took her identity instead. Walter's heroic rescue of Laura is but a duplication of the main plot.

The final text I wish to consider, Braddon's *John Marchmont's Legacy* (1863), draws together many of the ingredients of the other texts but treats insanity in a rather different light; it is neither the physiological destiny portrayed in *St. Martin's Eve* and *Lady Audley's Secret,* nor the totally open, relative term of *The Woman in White.* As the title suggests, this text also foregrounds questions of inheritance, both physiological and economic. The legacy in question could be the unexpected wealth John Marchmont himself inherits and later bequeaths, or the physiological inheritance of morbid sensitivity he entails on his daughter. Equally, it could refer to the way in which Mary herself is treated as a commodity to be entrusted to the care of Edward Arundel and her ill-chosen stepmother, Olivia. As in *St. Martin's Eve,* and *The Woman in White,* the female role is divided into two. The docility of the angelic heiress, Laura, in the latter text is explicitly contrasted with the decisive, mannish qualities of the penniless Marian; while in *St. Martin's Eve* the two halves of the story offer two different heroines, the equally docile heiress, Adeline, who actually dies from a weak constitution breaking under the strain of self-suppression, and the fiery, aggressive, and dowerless Charlotte. In *John Marchmont's Legacy,* the role of heroine is split between the childlike heiress, Mary, and the fiercely intelligent but penniless Olivia. Within this genre it seems that economic inheritance necessarily entails a correlative weakness of physiological constitution.

John Marchmont's love for his daughter is described as "almost morbid in its intensity" and is reciprocated by his daughter, who "loved her father *too much,*" so much so that on the night he dies she becomes "mad"; although she recovers, her morbid sensitivity and weakness render her "submissive to the will of others."[52] She unquestioningly accepts her stepmother's verdict that her fiancé, Edward Arundel, cannot love her, and passively allows herself to be imprisoned in the boat-house while the presumptive heir, Paul Marchmont, takes over her property. Her condition, diagnosed by the doctor as "morbid sensitivity," seems to be a form of insanity brought on by too much femininity; she adheres so rigidly to Victorian female roles that her own identity and desires are entirely obliterated. Olivia, by contrast, seems to suffer from an insanity produced by too much masculinity. She is the result of a female pen taking up Marian's impassioned statement that she is mad when she thinks of the self-sacrifice demanded of women and the imprisoning conditions of their lives. Olivia in similar vein revolts against the narrow round of social duty that is her lot: "The powerful intellect revolted against the fetters that bound and galled it. The proud heart beat with murderous violence against the bonds that kept it captive" (1:135-136). Whereas the "something wanting" in Laura Fairlie was a sense of physical sexuality, in Olivia it is precisely those soft characteristics of womanhood that define Mary Marchmont and Laura Fairlie:

> The thick bands of raven-black hair were drawn tightly off a square forehead, which was the brow of an intellectual and determined man rather than of a woman. Yes; womanhood was the something wanted in Olivia Arundel's face. Intellect, resolution, courage, are rare gifts; but they are not the gifts whose tokens we look for most anxiously in a woman's face. (1:125-126)

Olivia's problem, Braddon repeatedly informs us, is that her biological endowment is too great, misplaced in a woman: "She ought to have been a great man. Nature makes these mistakes now and then, and the victim expiates the error" (3:54).

Olivia is a fascinating revision of Lady Audley; she too marries for money and is guilty of ambition and cruelty. Whereas the narrative commentary in the earlier text seems to endorse demonic representations of Lady Audley, leaving more subversive interpretations to the reader, the later novel gives a very sympathetic portrait of its madwoman. Her madness is not foisted onto a hereditary taint but is made explicitly the product of a clash between great gifts and narrow, constraining circumstances. As in George Eliot's *The Mill on the Floss,* our heroine is endowed with the intellect and energy applauded in a man but positively harmful for a Victorian woman, given the social conventions of the era. Like that other "mistake of nature" Maggie Tulliver, Olivia is also endowed with a passionate sexuality, but it leads not to drowning by water, but the volcanic eruptions of madness.[53] In contrast to Olivia, Mary, who is depicted as the archetype of womanliness, is explicitly desexualized; she is womanly as a child, and childlike as a woman (2:83). Womanliness and sexuality are defined as mutually exclusive. Braddon's text highlights the contortions of Victorian ideology: the social accolade of womanliness can only be achieved by the complete extirpation of the physiological marks of feminity. Olivia, who is repeatedly described as wanting womanliness, is afflicted with an explicitly sexual desire for her cousin, Edward Arundel. This desire is quite beyond her control and, exacerbated by the narrow conditions of her life, turns into a form of madness: "All the volcanic forces of an impetuous nature, concentrated into one narrow focus, wasted themselves upon this one feeling, until that which should have been a sentiment became a madness" (1:74-75).

Olivia's sexuality distinguishes her from the other heroines considered in this piece; their primary demonic characteristics come from ambition rather than sexuality.[54] Yet in endowing her with such violent impulses, Braddon was not running counter to Victorian ideology, but rather following the line of Victorian medical theory, which stressed the ungovernable nature of female sexual desire. Far from being presented as asexual beings, women in physiological and psychiatric texts were presented as creatures of sexual excess, endowed with strong bodily urges, which they controlled only with great difficulty and often at the cost of their own sanity. Amid the disparaging accounts of female hysteria arising from contained sexuality, there were many that recognized, like Braddon's text, the role played by social convention in producing female breakdowns. Conolly, for example, quotes the French physician Georget in an encyclopedia article on hysteria:

> "The social position of women," observes M. Georget, "renders the sex, already subjected to peculiar ills from their organisation, the victims of the most acute and painful moral affections. Their moral existence is entirely opposed to their faculties; they possess a will, and are constantly oppressed by the yoke of prejudices and social arrangements in their infancy and early life. . . . Sensible and loving, they must only love when the master orders them: they are for ever constrained to concentrate within themselves the most powerful of passions and the gentlest of desires; to dissemble their desires; to feign a calmness and indifference when an inward fire devours them, and their whole organization is in tumult; and to sacrifice to a sense of duty, or rather for the happiness of others, the happiness and tranquillity of a whole life."[55]

Braddon develops this theory of the crippling effects of female containment, exposing as a sham the whole ideology of duty and self-effacement that governed Victorian female lives. Her heroine, however, is not the gentle, loving victim of Georget's depiction; it is sexuality, not love, that drives Olivia, a force of passion she hates but cannot control: "Love to her had been a dark and terrible passion, a thing to be concealed, as monomaniacs have sometimes contrived to keep the secret of their mania, until it burst forth at last, fatal and irrepressible, in some direful work of wreck and ruin" (1:298-299). Braddon draws on the contemporary discourse of psychiatry to depict the destructive impact of sexuality on Olivia. This is not some unexplained monomania, however, but the explicit product of the limited conditions of her life and her willed adherence to ideologies of female self-negation. Female violence and evil, the text asserts, are not the result of physiological aberrations but are directly produced by the social conventions governing Victorian femininity. The meek and submissive, like Mary, bow down and negate themselves; those endowed with any force of character are warped and corrupted.

A midcentury medical article, "Woman in her Psychological Relations," spoke of the "enchantment" exercised by a soldier's uniform on young females, "predisposed to the allurement by an excess of reproductive energy."[56] Olivia similarly feels herself to be "possessed"; Braddon comments that in an earlier century she would have accused a witch of being the "author of her misery" (1:100). Yet this is no simple portrait of a woman's powerlessness to control the forces of her own body, as recurs repeatedly in the medical texts; the strength of Braddon's representation comes from the ways in which she depicts Olivia's forceful intelligence battling against her "madness," whose object, Edward, she scorns intellectually. Braddon renders explicit the social subtext of much sensation fiction when, in a passionate oration, she traces Olivia's sexual obsession and consequent insanity to the lack of social opportunities for women:

> The narrow life to which she doomed herself, the self-immolation which she called her duty, left her a prey to this one thought. Her work was not enough for her. Her powerful mind wasted and shrivelled for want of worthy employment. It was like one vast roll of parchment whereon half the wisdom of the world might have been inscribed, but on which was only written over and over again, in maddening repetition, the name of Edward Arundel. If Olivia Marchmont could have gone to America, and entered herself amongst the feminine professors of law or medicine,—if she could have turned field preacher, like simple Dinah Morris, or set up a printing-press in Bloomsbury, or even written a novel,—I think she might have been saved. The superabundant energy of her mind would have found a new object. As it was, she did none of these things. She had only dreamt one dream, and by force of perpetual repetition the dream had become a madness. (1:279)

As the reference to Dinah Morris of *Adam Bede* suggests, Braddon is exploring the same terrain as George Eliot. Whereas Eliot's heroines tend to rise above the social pettiness that constrains them, however, Olivia is dragged down and perverted, her nobility turned to violent hatred and madness. In speaking of the entrapment of Olivia's energies, Braddon is employing the same vocabulary and discourse of physiological psychology to be found in Eliot's works. But whereas Dorothea's energy in *Middlemarch* is allowed to find channels of dispersal, Olivia's remains trapped in the labyrinths of thwarted desire.[57] Eliot permits Dorothea to find redemption through her love of that creature of brightness Will Ladislaw.[58] Braddon's text, although it predates Eliot's by seven years, is the more radical of the two. The conventional marriage ending is not an option for Olivia, who is destroyed by her love for this "bright-haired boy" (1:173). It is work she requires, not further self-sacrifice on the altar of love.

The hero of the text and object of Olivia's misplaced desire fulfils a role similar to that of the other heroes considered in this piece. Handsome, and a true gentleman, he is without immediate prospects, being a second son who has entered the army, but by the end of the novel he has acquired the Marchmont wealth and land. Mary, the conduit of this wealth, is allowed to expire so that Edward can marry a less fragile and childlike bride. The central plot is similar to that of *The Woman in White:* Mary's identity is taken. She is locked away by the presumptive heir, Paul, who declares she has committed suicide. Edward is cast in the detective role, but is not tainted by the quest because he proves to be such an incompetent investigator. Although he has married Mary he fails to protect her, and he mouches around under the very boathouse where she and his son are hidden, without once suspecting the truth. The dual role of Frederick in *St. Martin's Eve* of both heir and detective is here split between Edward and the villain Paul, who, like Frederick and Walter Hartright, occupies the dubious position of artist. The psychiatric science of detection in this text becomes explicitly an agency of evil control. Paul takes his "dissecting knife" and conducts an "intellectual autopsy" of Olivia: "He anatomised the wretched woman's soul. He made her tell her secret, and bare her tortured breast before him. . . . He *made* her reveal herself to him" (2:105). Like Robert Audley, Paul tries to read this madwoman's inner secrets from the slightest of signs of face or gesture. His motives, however, are unequivocally corrupt; his aim is to control Olivia, to enforce her participation in his plot against her rival and stepdaughter, Mary.

The last section of the novel depicts Olivia falling into imbecility, as her hopeless love again devours her. Imbecility is not solely confined to the sphere of feminity, however. Edward is also threatened by imbecility, but, as with other forms of masculine madness in these texts, the genesis is external rather than internal, and the effects shortlived. His imbecility is produced mechanically, by a train accident that wipes out his memory and threatens to leave him mindless for life. Patriarchal science, however, redeems rather than condemns him; he is not locked away in an asylum but operated on by a skilled physician who repairs all his faculties. Free now to play the hero, to find his

wife and expose the villainous plot against her, he embarks on his inglorious career as detective. He is only too ready to believe in his wife's madness and concur with the official pronouncement of suicide. Like Walter in *The Woman in White,* he had married his childlike bride when her wits were severely shaken, and seems both to treasure and endorse her helplessness, confirming once more the ideological alignment between Victorian prescriptions for femininity and insanity. Edward is also, significantly, the author of a plot line the novel does not take up: he suggests that Paul might take out a commission of lunacy against Mary in order to take control of her property. The actual plot whereby Paul, acting the role of Count Fosco, robs Mary of her official identity only succeeds due to the willingness of all concerned to believe in Mary's incipient madness.

Like Frederick in *St. Martin's Eve,* Edward proves fairly faithless and quickly falls in love again. The announcement of his impending marriage, which marks his reinstatement into full masculinity, has a correlative impact on Olivia, arresting her descent into total madness. Galvanized by jealousy, she gathers her faculties and bursts sensationally into the church to disrupt the ceremony, proclaiming the supreme impediment: Edward has a wife and child already. Paul once more uses the weapon of madness in an attempt to discredit her testimony, but Olivia scornfully rejects such allegations with the wonderful line "'Mad until to-day,' she cried; 'but not mad to-day'" (3:193). The text playfully underscores both the instability of insanity as a diagnostic category and the social parameters within which it is deployed. The final verdict on Olivia's madness remains open. While Lady Audley, who is clearly in possession of her faculties, is locked away, Olivia is arguably consigned to an even worse fate. She resumes the deadening round of social duties in her father's parish, accompanied always by a faithful servant since it is said she forgets where she is and what she is doing. In fulfilling the conventional role of Victorian middle-class womanhood she has become, as Braddon earlier suggested, "a human automaton" (3:137). *John Marchmont's Legacy* uses the diagnostic language of contemporary psychiatry but inverts its categories: the loss of self that constitutes true madness springs not from the instabilities of the female physiological system, but from social adherence to the medically sanctioned patterns of normative female behavior. True womanhood is synonymous with the emptiness of madness.

Victorian psychiatry and sensation fiction addressed similar issues, but from very different cultural positions, and to very different effect. While psychiatric discourse claimed the high ground of medical authority, sensation fiction was reviled as trash, proof of an endemic social disease. Both were working in a cultural climate in which the dominant economic ideologies of control were shadowed by increasing fears of social and psychological disruption. For the medical professionals, such fears helped solidify their claims to social authority, as they charted the innumerable ways in which insanity might manifest itself in even the best-run households. The sensation writers seized on the narrative potential vested in this psychiatric discourse: insanity might be latent, hiding behind calm, orderly exteriors, or partial and transient, flashing out only at rare intervals, and signaled by the merest flicker of a facial gesture. In a self-reflexive move, sensation fiction installed reading of the bodily text at its very heart. The psychiatric dictum that only a thin line divides sanity from insanity becomes the ground for textual play. Socially, the effects of this dictum are uniformly repressive: the medical word becomes law, in a very direct and literal fashion, with the signing of committal decrees. The fears generated as to psychological status also act to intensify the forces of social convention: the only proof an individual can possess of his or her own sanity is adherence to normative patterns of behavior. Taken out of their framing context within psychiatric discourse, however, these ideas take on a more subversive function, as manifested in sensation texts, where the boundaries of normality are no longer held in place. The psychiatric science of detection, of reading the outer bodily signs of an inner soul, ceases to be authoritative and appears instead as arbitrary, motivated by patriarchal designs, and always open to contagion by that which it seeks to detect. Detection itself becomes, indeed, a sign of the pathological. The gendered hierarchy of male science exposing female secrets is subject to inversion during the pursuit, and male and female insanity are exposed as relationally interdependent terms. Although the sensation authors draw directly on psychiatric accounts of female instability and bodily vulnerability, the paradigmatic alliance of economic and physiological inheritance in their texts calls attention to the sociolegal functions of such diagnostic practices and their role in consolidating the patriarchal foundations of Victorian culture. Playful and excessive, sensation texts make obeisance to dominant ideological formations while simultaneously challenging and undermining their authority.

While psychiatric discourse fostered a climate of fear, sensation fiction was altogether more subversive in spirit and effect. In deliberately flouting the formal constraints of realism, it also transgressed dominant models of social and psychological order. The heiresses might be weak, and the strong women punished or marginalized and disarmed by the main plot lines, but through their form these texts tell a very different story. The self is neither biologically given, nor fixed and unified: one can go mad, or die, and live to fight again. The fears and hostility aroused by the genre of sensation fiction focused on the ways in which these texts were "preaching to the nerves." As Victorian critics were quick to realize, the textual experience they offered was a celebration of feminine "sensation," not masculine reason. In their form they carried the ultimate challenge to the culture of control.

Notes

[1] Even in this text the relationship between the fictional and psychiatric discourse is not straightforward, as Reade then employs the selfsame psychiatric diagnosis of monomania in order to punish his villain. Although the abuses of the system are criticized, the categories of insanity remain unchallenged.

[2] For discussion of Victorian theories of female bodily disorder, disease, and corruption, see Elaine Showalter, *The Female Malady: Women, Madness, and English Culture, 1830-1980* (New York: Pantheon, 1985), and S. Shuttleworth, "Female Circulation: Medical Discourse and Popular Advertising in the Mid-Victorian Era," in *Body/Politics: Women and the Discourses of Science,* ed. M. Jacobus, E. Fox Keller, and S. Shuttleworth (New York: Routledge, 1990), 47-68.

[3] H. L. Mansel, "Sensation Fiction," *Quarterly Review* 113 (April 1863): 482-483, 512.

[4] Margaret Oliphant, "Novels," *Blackwood's Edinburgh Magazine* 102 (September 1867): 257, 277.

[5] Mansel, "Sensation Fiction," 482.

[6] Rhoda Broughton, *Red as a Rose Is She* (1870), 12th ed. (London: Richard Bentley, 1895), 443.

[7] Margaret Oliphant, "Sensation Novels," *Blackwood's Edinburgh Magazine* 91 (May 1862): 564-584. Ten years ago, Oliphant observes, "the age was lost in self-admiration," but peace and industry had since been displaced by war: "We who once did, and made, and declared ourselves masters of all things, have relapsed into the natural size of humanity before the great events which have given a new character to the age." People had come to enjoy the thrills of war, and sensation fiction now pandered in the emergent need for "a supply of new shocks and wonders" (564).

[8] As Jenny Taylor observes in *In the Secret Theatre of Home: Wilkie Collins, Sensation Narrative, and Nineteenth-century Psychology* (London: Routledge, 1988): "In sensation fiction masks are rarely stripped off to reveal an inner truth, for the mask is both the transformed expression of the 'true' self and the means of disclosing its incoherence" (8).

[9] Elaine Showalter reversed earlier readings of the text in *A Literature of Their Own: British Women Novelists from Brontë to Lessing* (Princeton: Princeton University Press, 1977), when she declared that "as every

woman reader must have sensed, Lady Audley's real secret is that she is *Sane* and, moreover, representative" (162). To assume, however, that there is one fundamental truth, and that sanity can be clearly demarcated from insanity, is to override the ambiguity of the text, where the very possiblity of definitive judgment is called into question.

[10] Wilkie Collins, *The Woman in White* (1861), ed. J. Symons (Harmondsworth: Penguin, 1974), 529.

[11] Oliphant, "Novels," 275.

[12] "Madness in Novels," *The Spectator,* 3 February 1866, 135.

[13] The author of "Madness in Novels" (cited in note 12) argues that the reader is forced to accept the behavior of the heroine of *St. Martin's Eve* as natural, since she is represented as mad: "We say it is natural, but at all events the unnaturalness disappears, for no one except Dr. Forbes Winslow knows what is natural in a patient with intermittent lunacy taking the form of jealousy on behalf of another" (135). (Dr. Forbes Winslow was editor of *The Journal of Psychological Medicine and Mental Pathology.*)

[14] See, for example, "Moral Physiology; or, the Priest and the Physician," *Journal of Psychological Medicine and Mental Pathology* 1 (1848): 557-571.

[15] Mary Braddon, *Lady Audley's Secret* (1862; London: Virago, 1985), 125.

[16] "A Plea for Physicians," *Fraser's Magazine* 37 (March 1848): 293.

[17] For a short summary of the theories of moral management, see Vieda Skultans, *English Madness: Ideas on Insanity, 1580-1890* (London: Routledge, Kegan and Paul, 1979), and her edited collection of texts *Madness and Morals: Ideas on Insanity in the Nineteenth Century* (London: Routledge, Kegan and Paul, 1975).

[18] For an excellent discussion of this issue with reference to physiology, see Georges Canguilhem, *Essai sur quelques problèmes concernant le normal et le pathologique* (Paris: Publication de la Faculté des Lettres de l'Université de Strasbourg 100, 1950).

[19] *Lady Audley's Secret,* 341.

[20] Roy Porter, "The Rage of Party: A Glorious Revolution in English Psychiatry?" *Medical History 27* (1983): 43.

[21] Thomas Trotter, *A View of the Nervous Temperament; Being a Practical Enquiry into the Increas-* ing *Prevalence, Prevention, and Treatment of Those Diseases* (1807; New York: Arno Press, 1976), xi.

[22] Reverend John Barlow, *On Man's Power over Himself to Prevent or Control Insanity* (London: William Pickering, 1843); 45.

[23] John Conolly, *An Inquiry Concerning the Indications of Insanity, with Suggestions for the Better Protection and Care of the Insane,* ed. Richard Hunter and Ida Macalpine (1830; London: Dawsons, 1964), 8.

[24] Barlow, for example, observes, "The cases of insanity, we are told, have nearly tripled within the last twenty years" (*On Man's Power,* 49).

[25] See Andrew Scull, *Museums of Madness: The Social Organization of Insanity in Nineteenth-century England* (London: Allen Lane, 1979).

[26] Conolly, *Indications of Insanity,* 496.

[27] "A Plea for Physicians," 294.

[28] Andrew Wynter, *The Borderlands of Insanity and Other Allied Papers* (London: Robert Hardwicke, 1875), 1.

[29] J. C. Prichard, *A Treatise on Insanity and Other Disorders Affecting the Mind* (1837; New York: Arno Press, 1973), 16.

[30] Prichard, 16.

[31] See Barbara Fass Leavy, "Wilkie Collins's Cinderella: The History of Psychology and *The Woman in White,*" *Dickens Studies Annual* 10 (1982): 91-141.

[32] See, for example, J. C. Bucknill and D. H. Tuke, *A Manual of Psychological Medicine,* 3d ed. (London: J. and A. Churchill, 1874), 415.

[33] A. Brierre de Boismont, *On Hallucinations: A History and Explanations of Apparitions, Visions, Dreams, Ecstasy, Magnetism, and Somnabulism,* trans. Robert T. Hulme (London: Henry Renshaw, 1859), 191; J. C. Prichard, "Insanity," in J. Forbes, A. Tweedie, and J. Conolly, *The Cyclopaedia of Practical Medicine,* 4 vols. (London: Sherwood, 1833), 2:327.

[34] J.E.D. Esquirol, *Observations on the Illusions of the Insane, and on the Medico-Legal Question of Confinement,* ed. William Liddell (London: Renshaw and Rush, 1833), 35.

[35] Conolly, *Indications of Insanity,* 379.

[36] According to Conolly, "it is only when the passion so impairs one or more faculties of the mind as to

prevent the exercise of comparison, that the reason is overturned; and then the man is mad. He is mad only while this state continues" (*Indications of Insanity,* 227).

[37] Collins, *Woman in White,* 105. All further references to this work will be given in the text.

[38] As D. A. Miller argues in *"Cages aux folles:* Sensation and Gender in Wilkie Collins's *The Woman in White,"* *Representations* 14 (Spring 1986), the reader becomes paranoid (115).

[39] Braddon, *Lady Audley's Secret,* 125. All further references to this work will be given in the text.

[40] Robert is initially roused from his customary languor to enthusiastic praise of Lady Audley. He concludes, "I am falling in love with my aunt" (48).

[41] The main study in this area is Showalter, *Female Malady.*

[42] For accounts of theories of female vulnerability to insanity see Showalter, *Female Malady,* and Shuttleworth, "Female Circulation."

[43] Mrs. Henry Wood, *St. Martin's Eve* (1866; London: Macmillan, 1905), 364. All further references to this edition will be given in the text.

[44] For further discussion of this point, see S. Shuttleworth, "Demonic Mothers: Ideologies of Bourgeois Motherhood in the Mid-Victorian Era," in *Rewriting the Victorians: Theory, History, and the Politics of Gender,* ed. Linda Shires (New York: Routledge, 1992).

[45] John Conolly, *The Croonian Lectures. On Some of the Forms of Insanity* (London, 1849), 68-69.

[46] J. G. Millingen, *The Passions; or, Mind and Matter* (London: J. and D. Darling, 1848), 157-158. Similar arguments are offered in Robert Brudenell Carter, *On the Pathology and Treatment of Hysteria* (London: John Churchill, 1853), 33.

[47] See Shuttleworth, "Female Circulation."

[48] D. A. Miller's intricate study of gender and sexuality in *The Woman in White* ("Cage aux folles") similarly locates a strong homosexual element in that work. While I do not agree entirely with his reading of that text, his arguments have clear significance for *Lady Audley's Secret* and Robert's involvement with the dual figure of George/Helen.

[49] I am indebted for this point to Abeer Zahra, "The Construction of Womanhood in Victorian Sensation Fiction, 1860-70," (Ph.D. diss., University of Leeds, 1990).

[50] My reading here differs from that of Miller, who sees Walter moving from homosexual identification with Anne to heterosexual desire for Laura.

[51] In his testimony Fosco explains the mystery of his wife's submissive devotion: "I remember that I was married in England, and I ask if a woman's marriage obligations in this country provide for her private opinion of her husband's principles? No! They charge her unreservedly to love, honour, and obey him. That is exactly what my wife has done" (632).

[52] Mary Braddon, *John Marchmont's Legacy,* 3 vols. (London: Tinsley Brothers, 1863), 1:32, 227, 228. All further references to this edition will be given in the text.

[53] George Eliot, *The Mill on the Floss,* cabinet ed., 2 vols. (Edinburgh: Wm. Blackwood, 1878-1880), 1:14.

[54] Elaine Showalter argues in "Family Secrets and Domestic Subversion: Rebellion in the Novels of the 1860s," in *The Victorian Family: Structure and Stresses,* ed. A. Wohl (London: Croom Helm, 1978), that "the escape from sexual bonds and family networks rather than sexual gratification or frustration was the real subject of female sensationalism" (104). Sexual desire, however, is dominant in some of the texts, particularly those by Rhoda Broughton, whose heroines are all awash with desire.

[55] John Conolly, "Hysteria," in *The Cyclopaedia of Practical Medicine,* ed. John Forbes, A. Tweedie, and J. Conolly (London: Sherwood, 1833) 1:572.

[56] "Woman in Her Psychological Relations," *Journal of Psychological Medicine and Mental Pathology* 4 (1851): 25.

[57] See Sally Shuttleworth, *George Eliot and Nineteenth-century Science: The Make-Believe of a Beginning* (Cambridge: Cambridge University Press, 1984), chap. 7.

[58] "The first impression on seeing Will was one of sunny brightness. . . . His hair seemed to shake out light" (George Eliot, *Middlemarch,* cabinet ed., 3 vols. (Edinburgh: Wm. Blackwood, 1878-1880), 1:320-321.

FURTHER READING

Felman, Shoshana. "Gustave Flaubert: Living Writing, or Madness as Cliché." In *Writing and Madness,* translated by Martha Noel Evans and the author, with the assistance of Brian Massumi, pp. 78-100. Ithaca, N.Y.: Cornell University Press, 1978.

Studies Flaubert's early work, *Memoirs of a Madman,* demonstrating the ways in which the various readings of the text contradict themselves, but that in doing so, these interpretations "reveal the dynamics of the production of meaning in the text as inseparable from such questions of approach and from a general problematic of reading."

Lougy, Robert E. "The Sounds and Silence of Madness: Language as Theme in Tennyson's *Maud." Victorian Poetry* 22, No. 4 (Winter 1984): 407-26.

Examines the way in which madness pervades *Maud,* in terms of content, language, and form.

Martin, Ellen E. "The Madness of Jane Austen: Metonymic Style and Literature's Resistance to Interpretation." In *Jane Austen's Beginnings: The Juvenilia and* Lady Susan, edited by J. David Grey, pp. 83-94. Ann Arbor, Mich.: UMI Research Press, 1989.

Analyzes the juvenilia of Austen, arguing that in these works Austen's narrative does not depend on causation or plot but that the author reduces "causality and common sense into the metonymic names and objects we use to figure our desires. . . . " In this manner, Martin maintains, we as readers are able to interpret the apparent madness of the characters.

Matus, Jill L. "Disclosure as 'Cover-up': The Discourse of Madness in *Lady Audley's Secret." University of Toronto Quarterly* 62, No. 3 (Spring 1993): 334-55.

Suggests that Mary Braddon uses the revelation of Lady Audley's madness at the end of the novel to offset the "uncomfortable implications" of issues related to economics and class that have earlier been raised in the story.

McCarthy, Paul. "Fact, Opinions, and Possibilities: Melville's Treatment of Insanity Through *White-Jacket." Studies in the Novel* XVI, No. 2 (Summer 1984): 167-81.

Surveys the range and depth of insanity in the characters in Melville's *White-Jacket,* attributing the portrayals in part to Melville's readings of psychological studies and articles.

Oberhelman, David D. "Trollope's Insanity Defense: Narrative Alienation in *He Knew He Was Right." Studies in English Literature 1500-1900* 35, No. 4 (Autumn 1995): 789-806.

Maintains that Trollope relates the depiction of madness to "the questions of personal identity" which form the basis of the contemporary legal doctrine related to criminal insanity, a doctrine defining insanity as the inability to distinguish right from wrong.

Petrey, Sandy. "Balzac's Empire: History, Insanity, and the Realist Text." In *Historical Criticism and the Challenge of Theory,* edited by Janet Levarie Smarr, pp. 25-41. Urbana: University of Illinois Press, 1993.

Uses Balzac's novella *Adieu* to study the way critics approach the analysis of Balzac's work.

Small, Helen. "*The Woman in White, Great Expectations,* and the Limits of Medicine." In *Love's Madness: Medicine, the Novel, and Female Insanity 1800-1865,* pp. 179-220. Oxford: Clarendon Press, 1996.

Examines the positions of Wilkie Collins and Charles Dickens—both "credited with inventing the sensation form"—regarding the debate over the asylum laws in Britain and the way insanity and its treatment should be represented in fiction.

Wiesenthal, Chris. *Figuring Madness in Nineteenth-Century Fiction.* London: Macmillan Press Ltd., 1997, 202 p.

Analysis of the representation of insanity in fiction, exploring this depiction "from both historical and psychoanalytic perspectives." The authors studied include Charlotte Perkins Gilman, Jane Austen, Anthony Trollope, and Herman Melville.

Nineteenth-Century Women's Autobiography

INTRODUCTION

The autobiography genre has received serious scholarly attention only in the last fifty years and much of this work has focused on the writings of men rather than women. Early scholars focused almost exclusively on the lifestyle and the perceived moral state of the author and not on the form and style of the genre itself. As Estelle C. Jelinek writes, "Even when women's autobiographies are given some scant attention in studies, social bias against the condition or the delineation of their lives seems to predominate over critical objectivity." However, recent scholarship suggests that women possessed a unique mode of self-representation and set of justifications for their self-histories and that these perceptions have evolved from the eighteenth century to the twentieth century. Other scholars have focused on what nineteenth century women's autobiographies reveal about how women perceived themselves, their self-defined gender ideology, the issues of particular concern in their lives, and factual information about their accomplishments and lifestyles. Few women published autobiographies until the end of the nineteenth century; among the most famous are Margaret Oliphant, Harriet Martineau, Annie Besant, and Elizabeth Cady Stanton.

Recent scholarship has focused on the style and structure of autobiographies written by women, the way in which the writers order and relate the events of their lives, the way the women interpret the events, and the tone of their narration. Sidonie Smith discusses the way in which nineteenth century women created a "self" within their writings and the way in which Victorian ideology limited women's conceptualization of themselves. Jelinek describes how Stanton's determination to convert readers to the suffrage cause led her to emphasize only the positive aspects of her life, even when this created a simplified and even paradoxical narrative. Ruth A. Symes disagrees with earlier critics who see Catharine Cappe's *Memoir* (1822) as an aberration from the typical flowery prose of the period. Symes argues that Cappe writes in educational voice because her middle class Unitarian background led her to believe that her most important duty was to teach children and instruct parents. Elizabeth Winston states that nineteenth-century women's autobiographies were conciliatory, and the authors' "need to assure readers of their womanliness results in apologies, disclaimers, and words of self-depreciation." Genaro Padilla gives rise to another question of form, that is, whether autobiographical accounts that were collected by a scholar rather than recorded solely by the source

are valid. Padilla refers to the more than forty autobiographical recollections of Hispanic women living in California recorded by Hubert Bancroft in the 1870s. Padilla argues that even though these women did not initiate the autobiographical process nor control it, they still articulated their identities and experiences. In addition, he argues that a sense of representing their culture or experiences as a group was as important to these Hispanic autobiographers as relating their individual experiences.

Critics agree that women's autobiographical writing differed from men's in several regards. First, women authors felt that they had to defend their decision to write about themselves. Particularly in the early nineteenth century, society believed that women should not call attention to themselves, in their lives or deeds. Women autobiographers often attempted to assure readers of their ordinary lives, filled with domestic duties and service to their families. The authors justified their writing as a moral obligation, either to educate others or to entertain other women. Women autobiographers differed from men in their focus, often de-emphasizing the role of men in their lives and writing mostly about themselves and other women. Stanton barely mentions her husband, and the diaries of women pioneers focus on their own experiences and hardships, and on those of other women. As Padilla explains, the Hispanic women involved in the Bancroft history project often sought opportunities to discuss their experiences and their struggles for autonomy in a patriarchal society where women seldom enjoyed a public voice. Anna Julia Cooper in *A Voice from the South* (1892), states that only African-American women can speak for themselves and that it is futile for men to attempt to speak of women's experiences. In addition, women writers reflect the cultural ideologies and assumptions of their period. Often, they emphasize the aspects of life that were considered in the women's sphere in the nineteenth century: childcare, housekeeping, nursing, marriage and family. Critics note that these women's autobiographies provide information about the private family sphere which is often unavailable in other official sources.

REPRESENTATIVE WORKS

Mary E. Ackley
Crossing the Plains and Early Days in California (autobiography)   1925

Leila Ada
Leila Ada, the Jewish Convert. An Authentic Memoir (autobiography) c. 1840

Maria de las Angustias de la Guerra
Ocurrencias en California [Occurrences in California] (autobiography) 1878

Maria Inocente Pico de Avila
"Cosas de California" (autobiography) 1876

Elizabeth Barrett Browning
Glimpses into My Own Life and Literary Character (diary) 1820

Catharine Cappe
Memoir of the Life of the Late Mrs Catharine Cappe (autobiography) 1822

Mary Boykin Chesnut
A Diary from Dixie (diary) 1905

Anna Julia Cooper
A Voice from the South by a Black Woman of the South (essays) 1892

Miriam Colt Davis
Went to Kansas (autobiography) 1862

Lucy A. Delaney
From the Darkness Cometh the Light (autobiography) 1844

Abigail Scott Duniway
Path Breaking: An Autobiographical History of the Equal Suffrage Movement in Pacific Coast States (autobiography) 1914

Ann Lady Fanshawe
Memoirs of Ann Lady Fanshawe (autobiography) 1829

Lodisa Frizzell
Across the Plains to California in 1852 (autobiography) 1915

Anne Lady Halkett
The Autobiography of Anne Lady Halkett (autobiography) 1875

Alice Hayes
A Legacy, or Widow's Mite, Left by Alice Hayes to Her Children and Others (autobiography) 1836

Adrietta Applegate Hixon
On to Oregon! A True Story of a Young Girl's Journey into the West (autobiography) 1947

Alice James
Alice James, her brothers—her journal (diary) 1934

Apolinaria Lorenzana
"Memorias de la Beata" ["Memories of the Pious Woman"] (autobiography) 1878

Harriet Martineau
Harriet Martineau's Autobiography 2 Vols. (autobiography) 1877

Mary Jane Megquier
Apron Full of Gold: Letters from San Francisco, 1819-1856 (autobiography) 1949

Mary Mitford
Recollections of a Literary Life (autobiography) 1852

Lady Sydney Morgan
Passages from My Autobiography (autobiography) 1859
Memoirs (autobiography) 1862

Margaret Oliphant
Autobiography and Letters (autobiography) 1899

Eulalia Perez
"Una Vieja y Sus Recuerdos" ["The Memories of an Old Lady"] (autobiography) 1877

George Sand
Histoire de ma Vie [Story of My Life] (autobiography) 1846-54

Mollie Dorsey Sanford
Journal in Nebraska and Colorado Territories 1857-1866 (autobiography) 1958

Elizabeth M. Sewell
The Autobiography of Elizabeth M. Sewell (autobiography) 1907

Amanda Smith
An Autobiography: The Story of the Lord's Dealings with Mrs. Amanda Smith the Colored Evangelist (autobiography) 1893

Elizabeth Cady Stanton
Eighty Years and More: Reminiscences, 1815-1897 (autobiography) 1898

Alice Thornton
The Autobiography of Mrs. Alice Thornton (autobiography) 1875

Mrs. Humphrey Ward
A Writer's Recollections 2 Vols. (autobiography) 1918

Mary Countess of Warwick
Autobiography of Mary Countess of Warwick (autobiography) 1848

OVERVIEWS

Elizabeth Winston (essay date 1980)

SOURCE: "The Autobiographer and Her Readers: From Apology to Affirmation," in *Women's Autobiography: Essays in Criticism*, edited by Estelle C. Jelinek, Indiana University Press, 1980, pp. 93-111.

[*In the following excerpt, Winston argues that nineteenth-century women autobiographers were more self-conscious and conciliatory than women of the twentieth century.*]

From the seventeenth century into the twentieth, women writers have shown an acute self-consciousness of the criticism they often aroused simply because they were female. One finds an interesting pattern of response to this criticism in the autobiographies of professional women writers, British and American, who were born in the last century. Those whose autobiographies were published before 1920 tended to establish a conciliatory relationship to their readers, by this means attempting to justify their untraditional ways of living and writing so as to gain the audience's sympathy and acceptance. Women who published autobiographies after 1920, however, no longer apologized for their careers and successes, though a few still showed signs of uneasiness at having violated cultural expectations for women. These more recently published writers openly asserted their intellectual and aesthetic gifts and their serious commitment to the literary life.

This change in the autobiographer's relation to her readers reflects an important change in the writer's self-image and in the kinds of autobiographical intentions she exhibited. That is, the more confident these women became of the legitimacy of their way of life, the more freely they used autobiography for explicitly personal and, thus, more self-validating reasons—to express strongly held beliefs, explore and understand the self, or experiment with the conventions of the genre. A sample of fourteen autobiographies of professional women writers, published between 1852 and 1965, demonstrates this progression in self-image and intentions. Women writing between 1850 and 1920—Lady Sydney Morgan, Mary Mitford, Margaret Oliphant, and to a lesser extent, Mrs. Humphry Ward, youngest of the four—show ambivalence about being professional writers at a time when the usual pattern for a female was immersion in domesticity. Their need to assure readers of their womanliness results in apologies, disclaimers, and words of self-deprecation. These autobiographers express their desire to interest and entertain their readers, defend past actions, or leave a record for their children—intentions directed mainly toward satisfying others.

Harriet Martineau, who rightfully belongs in this early group (the autobiography came out in 1877), is a transitional figure, somewhat ahead of her time. She is the only woman among the autobiographers in this early period who sometimes assumes a didactic role in telling her story, an act which reflects her sense of authority vis-à-vis her readers. Yet she does resemble other women writing at this time in that though she never apologizes for the record of her life, she minimizes her "selfish" needs to write the autobiography by stressing the moral obligations which prompted her. At the beginning of the narrative she says she felt it a "duty" to record her personal history—it was a way of repaying other autobiographers for the pleasure and benefit they had given her. By invoking duty as her reason for writing, she transforms the fundamentally self-assertive autobiographical act into what she viewed as a commendable gesture of gratitude appropriate to a lady.

The women who published autobiographies after 1920 show a stronger professional commitment and belief in the value of their work than the earlier women writers, though a few still offer somewhat defensive explanations for their divergence from traditional female roles. Among their reasons for writing autobiography are the desire to present and recommend the ideas for which they have lived (Charlotte Perkins Gilman and Harriet Monroe), to show the improvement in women's lives since Victorian days (Elizabeth Haldane), to pay tribute to a way of life that has vanished (Edith Wharton and Edna Ferber), and to achieve self-understanding (Ellen Glasgow). The most confident writers in this later group—Edith Sitwell, Mary Austin, and Gertrude Stein—openly affirm their achievements, in tones ranging from the playful self-advertisement of Stein in *The Autobiography of Alice B. Toklas* (1933) to the defiant emphasis of Sitwell in *Taken Care Of* (1965). Not only do they use their autobiographies to inform and exhort their readers or to clarify the past for themselves, but also to assert their personal superiority (Stein and Sitwell) and to experiment with the autobiographical form (Austin and Stein). Yet even in these vigorously self-affirming narratives, especially in Sitwell's angry autobiography, one detects the signs of struggle, the force spent in challenging criticism and fighting restrictions. One gets a glimpse, in other words, of the price of success for a woman writing.

All of the women in this sample had succeeded in their careers. Even the early writers (Morgan, Mitford, and Oliphant), though little known today, enjoyed an enthusiastic reception during their lifetimes and were thus able to support themselves and their families through writing. That these successful women should have felt the need to justify their actions is a measure of the strong pressures on women to fulfill cultural expectations for their sex. The feminine stereotypes were pervasive: women were not autonomous individuals but dependents of their fathers and husbands, whether these men really "provided" for them or not; women were intellectually inferior to men and born to express their limited creativity through reproduction rather than through art; a "true woman" was modest and self-effacing and would never invite unseemly publicity by writing for publication. Given these limiting expectations, even highly gifted women would have had difficulty sustaining their self-confidence as artists. They needed continual confirmation of their work from people whose opinions they respected, to quiet the doubts within and to challenge the negative voices without. It is not surprising, then, that in autobiography—that most self-assertive and self-revealing of genres—these professional women writers should feel particularly vulnerable to criticism.

Women have traditionally experienced a conflict of values in deciding whether or not to write autobiographies. In *The Female Imagination,* Patricia Meyer Spacks refers to Margaret Cavendish, Duchess of Newcastle, whose autobiography of 1656 reveals its author's intense struggle with opposing inner demands: the desire to uphold traditional "feminine" values of self-effacement and suppression and the compelling need to assert herself in writing. In seventeenth-century Britain, says Spacks, "the propriety of feminine autobiography is dubious."[1]

Two centuries later, in Lady Sydney Morgan's *Memoirs* of 1862, one can still discern that writing an autobiography is for a woman a distinctly political act requiring careful justification. Though as a novelist and popular historian Lady Morgan has chosen a life that in some ways deviates sharply from the traditional feminine pattern, she projects the image of a woman who accepts the stereotypes and socially sanctioned roles for women. She justifies the writing of her memoirs by offering herself to her "dear, kind, fair-judging public" as an example of a female who has managed to realize her literary ambitions while at the same time fulfilling her desire "to be *every inch a woman*."[2] For Lady Morgan this meant being a devoted daughter, an attentive wife and hostess, but—surprisingly for her time—not necessarily a mother.[3]

In *Passages from My Autobiography* (1859), Lady Morgan reinforces the conventional belief in women's intellectual inferiority to men when she compares her husband's "clear Anglo-Saxon intellect and profound reflection" with her own "flimsy, fussy, flirty Celtic temperament, by courtesy called Mind."[4] In her 1862 *Memoirs,* she assures her audience that

> ambition and vanity, and social tastes have led me much into that chaos of folly and insincerity called the world, but domestic life is my vocation—unfortunately, my high organisation, and my husband's character of mind, our love of art, and all that is best worth knowing renders *la vie domestique* impossible. (II, 417)

Here Lady Morgan reveals her dilemma regarding her identity as a woman. She seems to pay lip service to traditional feminine stereo-types and social expectations for women, but at the same time she recognizes and rejects the severe limitations inherent in the orthodox female's existence.

At least Lady Morgan was able to earn money by publishing her works. The Duchess of Newcastle's remuneration came in the form of psychological release, distraction from cares, and the admiration of some of her readers. Lady Morgan, writing at a time when literary women were no longer limited to the status of amateurs, commanded good prices for her novels and histories.

Yet in the two hundred six years between the publication of the duchess's and Lady Morgan's autobiographies, although many women in Britain and America began to support themselves through writing, they seem to have made slow progress in accepting the legitimacy of their new public and professional roles.[5] As Ann Douglas Wood points out, most of the American "scribbling women" (so named by Hawthorne) followed the advice of ministers, male reviewers, and certain influential writers of their own sex and used their talents to uphold the current limited notions about woman's nature and proper sphere. They published mainly in ladies' magazines and annuals, satisfying the demand for sentimental fiction and pious, imitative verse. They took pains to show their subordination of literary activities to domestic tasks and their unconcern for literary style or for recognition. In other words, says Wood, these women writers assuaged their guilt at succeeding in the "masculine" roles of breadwinner and public person and enjoying this success, "by hiding behind a conventional 'feminine' facade." In this way they avoided viewing themselves as serious professionals. Writing was simply a means to express themselves or to earn money in one of the few occupations open to educated women at the time.[6]

Lady Morgan took herself more seriously as a writer than these women apparently did. The editor of her *Memoirs,* Geraldine Jewsbury, notes that Morgan was a hard bargainer with her publishers and never sold herself short. In contrast to the "scribbling women" Wood describes, who tried to fulfill the feminine ideal of domesticity and self-effacement, Morgan took an active interest in liberal politics and championed the cause of oppressed people—the Irish and the Greeks—in some of her novels. She certainly believed herself superior to the nonliterary wives whose less finely nerved "organisations" allowed them to tolerate *la vie domestique.* But she was still ambivalent enough about what constituted the appropriate female vocation to use what could be called a "rhetoric of justification" to charm and placate those people of both sexes who might find her behavior audacious.

Like Lady Morgan, other women autobiographers writing before 1920 address their readers in conciliatory tones. In *Autobiography and Letters* (1899), Margaret Oliphant explains that she was prompted to make "a little try at the autobiography" after reading a biography of George Eliot. Ruefully comparing her achievements with Eliot's, she admits that her practice of always subordinating her career to maternal duties and family interests has negatively affected the quality of her work, and she reasons that since probably no one will want to write her biography, she will write it herself. Thus, the initial motive for the autobiography is what Oliphant calls "self-compassion" and "self-defence": showing the hardships she has endured and the financial burdens under which she has constantly labored in order to educate her own and her brother's children. Nine years later, Oliphant cites another motive for the autobiography: she had meant to leave it for her sons, and now, in 1894, both are dead. She apologizes for her frequent expressions of grief and eventually breaks off without completing the narrative.

Many readers of Oliphant's *Autobiography* would surely have approved her sacrifice of literary excellence to the claims of family and friends and her wish to leave an account of her life for her sons. These same readers also would have deemed appropriate the modest way in which Mary Mitford and Mrs. Humphry Ward referred to their professional achievements in their autobiographical volumes. Mitford says almost nothing about her career in *Recollections of a Literary Life* (1852), and when she does occasionally speak on this subject, her tone is self-deprecating. For example, she gratefully records receiving encouragement from a Mr. and Mrs. Kenyon, whose patronage of her "poor writings" has enabled her to support her improvident father and herself. Generally we learn about her writing indirectly, through the literary extracts she includes and the criticism she gives of these works.

In her two-volumed memoir, *A Writer's Recollections* (1918), Ward declares her intention of treating events "broadly" and "with as much detachment as possible," so as to maintain interest in her narrative. Accordingly, she devotes most of the first volume to descriptions of famous relatives and their friends (her grandfather, Dr. Arnold of Rugby; her uncle Matthew Arnold; William Wordsworth) and prominent people she knew at Oxford (the Mark Pattisons, Walter Pater, Benjamin Jowett). Yet when she comes to the point in her story where she should describe the writing of the novel with which *she* first achieved national prominence, Ward apologizes beforehand:

> If these are to be the recollections of a writer, in which perhaps other writers by profession, as well as the more general public, may take some interest, I shall perhaps be forgiven if I give some account

of the processes of thought and work which led to the writing of my first successful novel, *Robert Elsmere*.[7]

It is difficult to imagine such a statement coming from a man! For years, male novelists have described the genesis of their writing in great detail (Henry James, a contemporary of Ward, comes to mind), automatically assuming that this material was both interesting and important. Ward does focus more attention on her novels in the second volume of the *Recollections,* but always with the proper feminine modesty.

Harriet Martineau is modest, too, about her successes as a political economist and writer. In *Autobiography* (1877) she rejects any claim to genius, saying that what "facility" she possesses was developed through discipline and years of translating. Nor does she emphasize her special status as a professional woman. At one point she admits to having been "provided with what is the bane of single life in ordinary cases to want— substantial, laborious and serious occupation."[8] But the passive construction of this statement conveys her characteristic reserve in referring to her literary vocation.

To explain her divergence from the feminine ideal of marriage, Martineau says she was "unfit" to marry because of a personal "disability"—her lack of the self-respect needed to fulfill familial duties without encroaching on her husband's and children's freedom (I, 132). Thus, she justifies her choice by pleading her own unsuitability to marriage and family life rather than by criticizing the institutions themselves.

When she turns to the issue of justice for oppressed people, however, Martineau exhibits a more positive sense of self. At these times she speaks authoritatively, revealing a didactic purpose. She voices particular concern for children, describing her childhood sufferings (her gradual loss of hearing) in order to alert parents to conditions about which they might otherwise remain ignorant. And she champions the cause of Catholics, American slaves, and women. Like her sister novelists, Harriet Beecher Stowe and Elizabeth Gaskell, who spoke out against the oppression of slaves and factory workers, Martineau had "access, via a sense of personal injustice," to collective problems of economic and religious discrimination.[9]

Martineau also seeks justice specifically for herself in the autobiography, giving her version of some controversial acts. She defends her participation in antislavery activities in America, justifies her refusal of a governmental pension, and defends her authorship with H. G. Atkinson of the *Letters on Man's Nature and Development.* This collaboration caused her to be called, rightly, an atheist and, wrongly, a victim of her male coauthor. (People did not seem able to accept the idea that a man and woman with similar philosophical views would freely enter into a cooperative publishing venture.) On the whole, her work of self-vindication is convincing. . . .

Women autobiographers writing before 1920 consciously worked to establish a special relation to their audience. They sought primarily to justify their ways of living and the fact of their writing. The particular acts they felt compelled to defend reflect the cultural stereotypes which inhibit women from fully realizing their potentialities. Reacting to the prevailing belief that women found their true vocation as wives and mothers, these women defended their choice of a career or their deviation from the traditional marital and maternal roles. In response to the notion that "good" women were modest and self-effacing, they understated their achievements, disclaimed interest in personal recognition, or stressed the broad historical value of their life stories. Generally, it was only later in this century, as stereotypes became less rigid and women writers began to experience fewer negative reactions to their untraditional assertive behavior, that female autobiographers acknowledged more personal reasons for writing and affirmed their achievements without apology.

Contemporary writers like Mary McCarthy, Lillian Hellman, and Maya Angelou have exhibited even greater self-confidence in their autobiographical works. Their self-assertive, gender-affirming narratives are encouraging models for female readers and give promise of a future in which a woman's right to write will be assured.

Notes

[1] Patricia Meyer Spacks, *The Female Imagination* (New York: Knopf, 1975), p. 194.

[2] *Lady Morgan's Memoirs,* ed. W. H. Dixon, 3 vols. (London: William H. Allen, 1862), I, 230.

[3] Perhaps Lady Morgan rejected motherhood partly because she had seen its negative effect on her younger sister Olivia. Olivia married four years before Lady Morgan and immediately began producing babies—too many of them in Lady Morgan's view. Olivia was "all over morbid maternity." Lady Morgan's husband, Sir Charles, playfully advised Olivia to read "three thick volumes of Malthus on Population." See Lady Morgan, *Passages from My Autobiography* (London: Richard Bentley, 1859), pp. 60, 92-93, 102-03.

[4] Ibid., p. 318.

[5] J. M. S. Tompkins writes that by the end of the eighteenth century, a host of young women in England had been forced by poverty to "market" their literary talents. They wrote mainly epistolary domestic novels—sentimental, didactic, occasionally satirical. See *The Popular Novel in England, 1770-1800* (1961; rpt. Westport, Conn.: Greenwood Press, 1976). For the situation in the United States, see Helen Waite Papashvily, *All the Happy Endings* (New York: Harper Brothers, 1956).

[6] Ann Douglas Wood, "The 'Scribbling Women' and Fanny Fern: Why Women Wrote," *American Quarterly,* 23 (Spring 1971), 3-24. George Eliot deplored a similar lack of professional commitment and aesthetic integrity among "lady novelists" in England. See "Silly Novels by Lady Novelists," *Westminster Review,* 46 (October 1856), 442-61, reprinted in *Essays,* ed. Thomas Pinney (London: Routledge & Kegan Paul, 1968), pp. 300-24.

[7] Mrs. Humphry Ward, *A Writer's Recollections* (New York and London: Harper Brothers, 1918), I, 216. See also I, 202, where Ward asks permission to repeat a compliment she received for her work for the *Dictionary of Christian Biography,* and II, 18-19, for her response to Henry James's assessment of her first novel.

[8] Harriet Martineau, *Autobiography,* 3 vols. (London: Smith, Elder, 1877), I, 101. Subsequent references appear in the text.

Linda H. Peterson (essay date 1993)

SOURCE: "Institutionalizing Women's Autobiography: Nineteenth-Century Editors and the Shaping of an Autobiographical Tradition," in *The Culture of Autobiography: Constructions of Self-Representation*, edited by Robert Folkenflik, Stanford University Press, 1993, pp. 80-103.

[*In the excerpt below, Peterson explores the structure and subject matter of women's autobiographies and notes the differences between women's and men's writings.*]

What is women's autobiography, and when was it first written? Answers are difficult to give. We do not know what English-woman produced the first piece of self-writing; what women's texts we have lost from the mid-seventeenth century, the moment that seems to mark the beginning of an unbroken English autobiographical tradition; or what texts we have lost—or lost sight of—from centuries before and after the seventeenth. Despite such lacunae, feminist scholarship of the last decade has attempted to delineate a tradition of women's autobiography. Beginning with Mary G. Mason's "The Other Voice" (1980) and continuing with Estelle C. Jelinek's *The Tradition of Women's Autobiography* (1986), Sidonie Smith's *A Poetics of Women's Autobiography* (1987), and Carolyn G. Heilbrun's *Writing a Woman's Life* (1988), the agenda has been to (re)discover a tradition of women's own.[1]

That agenda has included more specific goals: the (re)discovery of lost or forgotten women's texts, the posing of literary questions about gender and genre, the posing of more general questions about women's self-representation, whether it has always been different from men's or whether women's writings show certain fundamental "human" patterns of development. Whatever the specific goals, as versions of literary history, critical studies of the 1980's have assumed a common argument: that women's autobiography represents a separate and distinct tradition, a genre or subgenre different from autobiographical writing produced by men. In Jelinek's words, "contemporary women are writing out of and continuing to create a wholly different autobiographical tradition from that delineated in studies of male autobiography."[2]

That women's autobiography represents "a wholly different autobiographical tradition" has been a practical, even necessary critical assumption. Prior to 1980 major critical studies of autobiography excluded serious consideration of women's texts. The fact of exclusion seemed to call for new approaches to, and new theories about, women's forms of self-representation.[3] Nonetheless, the argument about a separate women's tradition is worth reexamining—not simply because, as I believe, it misrepresents a significant number of women's texts, but because it involves a blindness about the writing of literary history. To oversimplify, recent studies of women's autobiography have tended to read women's texts as if gender were the hermeneutic key to authorial intention and textual production; they have assumed that gender determines the form of women's autobiography or, at least, that it motivates women writers to seek a separate autobiographical tradition. Other possibilities—that gender may not be a crucial factor in some autobiographical writing, that some women autobiographers may deliberately avoid a female literary tradition, or that a woman's autobiography may self-consciously invoke multiple literary traditions—have been overlooked or avoided. So, too, have possibilities that implicate editors and critics in the process of defining what constitutes "women's autobiography." The desire to define a women's tradition has, in other words, shaped the writing of literary history and practical criticism. I want, therefore, to reconsider the question of women's autobiography not by presupposing the existence of a tradition but instead by asking about possible traditions available to, acknowledged, or created by women writers. And I want to begin not by posing an alternate version of literary history, but by looking at early attempts to define "women's autobiography"—because as it turns out, modern literary critics are not the first to construct a tradition of women's autobiographical writing.

The effort to construct a literary past, a tradition of English autobiography that accounts for women's texts as well as men's, originated in the nineteenth century. By 1797 English literary critics had coined the term *autobiography* for a "new" genre.[4] Within three decades Victorian antiquarians, scholars, and critics had begun to resurrect and publish the texts we cite today when we write about the "emergence" or "origins" of women's autobiography: the *Memoirs of Ann Lady Fanshawe* (1829); *A Legacy, or Widow's Mite, Left by Alice Hayes* (1836); the *Autobiography of Mary Countess of Warwick* (1848); *The Autobiography of Mrs. Alice Thornton* (1875); *The Autobiography of Anne Lady Halkett* (1875); and numerous spiritual accounts written by Nonconformist women. Indeed, except for the autobiography of Margaret Cavendish, Duchess of Newcastle, which first appeared as part of her *Natures Pictures Drawn by Fancies Pencil to the Life* (1656), these seminal women's autobiographies would be lost to literary history were it not for the editorial efforts of the Victorians.

The Victorians rescued and wrote about these texts for reasons similar to our own: for their historical interest, for the social and familial information they contained, for their contribution to literary discussions of the "new" genre, for their relevance to their own lives. Thus nineteenth-century efforts at reconstructing literary history can illuminate our own contemporary efforts at delineating traditions of autobiography, whether men's, women's, or both. They can be used to challenge or affirm critical claims that the "male" tradition of autobiography excludes or misrepresents women's lives; that women's self-representation assumes a form different from men's, one that is "relational" or "contextual" rather than "positional" or "linear"; or that the traditions of male and female autobiography have developed separately—and, by implication, that critics do best to treat them separately.

The important nineteenth-century reconstructions of autobiographical traditions that I shall consider are these: (1) a tradition of spiritual autobiography, embodied in the documents of *The Friends' Library* (1837—1850), a collection that includes more than twenty accounts by Quaker women; (2) a tradition of domestic memoirs, represented not by a single collection but by the publications of various antiquarian societies (1829—1875); and (3) the women's texts chosen for Hunt and Clarke's ground-breaking *Autobiography* series (1826-1833), the first known attempt to create a literary collection of autobiographical writing. As we shall see, the question of "women's autobiography" has been vexed from its origins, with neither writers nor editors agreeing on the relevance of gender to genre.

Has women's autobiography been, from its origins, fundamentally different from men's? A great deal hangs on what one means by "origins." In her survey of "archetypal" women's autobiographies, Mary Mason argues this position categorically: "Nowhere in women's autobiographies do we find the patterns established by the two prototypical male autobiographers, Augustine and Rousseau." Augustine's use of a dramatic structure of conversion, where the "self is presented as the stage for a battle of opposing forces" and where "a climatic victory of one force—spirit defeating flesh—completes the drama of the self," is, according to Mason, essentially alien to women's self-conception; so, too, is Rousseau's "unfolding self-discovery where the characters and events are little more than aspects of the author's evolving consciousness."[5] Such an argument assumes that gender determines generic production—and not, as the late Paul de Man proposed, that what the autobiographer does is "governed by the technical demands of self-portraiture and thus determined, in all its aspects, by the resources of [the] medium."[6] In fact, one early nineteenth-century reconstruction of an autobiographical tradition suggests a view of self-construction quite different from Mason's and more compatible with de Man's; it used women's autobiographies to suggest that gender was an almost negligible concern of (or influence on) life writing.

Between 1837 and 1850 the Quaker historians William and Thomas Evans published a series of spiritual memoirs and journals that included both men's and women's texts, English and American. Their series, called *The Friends' Library,* had a non-literary agenda: it was meant to preserve the seminal texts of Quakerism and, through its representative auto/biographies,[7] set the standard for Quaker self-presentation in life and in print. As the prospectus explained, "It is both our duty and our interest to be intimately conversant with [the early Friends'] writings; to imitate their piety and devotedness, and to strive to be imbued with that fervour and heavenly mindedness which so conspicuously marked their example." The editors assumed, as was generally true for spiritual autobiography, that subsequent writers would imitate these autobiographical models, exemplary as they were in their "heavenly mindedness." They seem also to have assumed that women's and men's texts were equally suitable for institutionalizing as autobiography, equally based on seminal forms (like George Fox's *Journal*) and thus equally imitable by subsequent writers.[8]

Quite apart from stated intentions, what the women's autobiographies in *The Friends' Library* demonstrate is that seventeenth-century women writers readily engaged the traditional model of spiritual autobiography. They treated their lives as a struggle between opposing forces; they delineated a pattern of spiritual progress from bondage in sin to enlightenment and victory over the world, flesh, and devil; most importantly, they composed their lives without a sense that they were appropriating a "male" tradition or that their experiences were radically different from men's. These

women's accounts belie the label of the Augustinian or Bunyanesque form as prototypically "male."[9] When, for example, Elizabeth Stirredge wrote *Strength in Weakness Manifest* (1711), included in the Evans collection as her *Life and Christian Testimony* (1838), she followed the general formula for Quaker autobiography, beginning with her earliest recollections of religious seriousness and her "dread and terror" in the contemplation of death. Her autobiography describes at great length her temptations to sin (the most serious being a hankering after "fine clothes"), her wanderings without spiritual guidance (like the children of Israel in the wilderness), her conviction of sin and conversion under Quaker preaching, and finally her persecutions for religious conscience.[10] Formally, Stirredge's account differs little from the male autobiographies included in the same volume. *A Brief Account of the Life and Travels of Thomas Wilson* contains the same testimony to youthful "hungerings and thirstings," the same prolonged conviction under Quaker preaching, the same detailing of religious persecution and perseverance.[11] Equally for the male Wilson and the female Stirredge, the structure of autobiography follows from the Quaker belief that spiritual reality is all-encompassing. Both their accounts rely heavily on the literary models provided by other Quaker accounts and, as Richard T. Vann has shown, on the Puritan literary heritage that many Quakers drew upon as they remembered and inscribed their religious pasts.[12]

Within the autobiographical tradition constructed by *The Friends' Library,* variations in form reveal little correlation with gender. Both men and women may report rebellious episodes (Elizabeth Ashbridge disobediently elopes at age fourteen, Joseph Pike confesses his delight in the company of "wild boys" so that he may digress on the importance of parental supervision). Either gender may incorporate dialogues that record serious clashes with worldly authority (Alice Hayes and Benjamin Bangs recapitulate doctrinal disputes with Anglican priests, Thomas Wilson harangues the Baptists). Both men and women recount their journeys as Quaker ministers (Jane Hoskens subtitles her life, *A Minister of The Gospel,* a claim possible for most of the autobiographers in the collection because Quakers expected the public testimony of both men and women).[13] Such formal homogeneity was encouraged within Quakerism, where a similarity in the representation of experience gave assurance of genuine conversion.

A stylistic homogeneity also marks *The Friend's Library*—in part because of the practice of the writers themselves, in part because of the editorial policies of William and Thomas Evans. Quaker autobiographers, like other Protestant writers, relied heavily on the language of scripture to recount their lives, the ideal being to merge the words of their texts with the divinely inspired words of the Bible. Thus Alice

Hayes's multimetaphoric sentence: "Now was the refiner's fire very hot, in order to burn up the dross and the tin," which echoes the words of Malachi and Ezekiel to describe her trials under conviction of sin.[14] This stylistic practice was exacerbated (or improved, it depends on one's perspective) by an editorial decision to modernize and regularize the original documents. Because the Evanses felt that early Quaker texts were often "prolix and redundant," they made "a judicious selection and abridgment," thereby presenting the series "in a more attractive form, [its] intrinsic value enhanced."[15] Or so they claimed. While abridging, they also moderated extremes of style, thus eradicating many telling, individualistic features of style we today associate with autobiographical writing.

The point here is not to lament Quaker stylistics or editorial practice, but rather to stress the virtually genderless form of many early English autobiographies. In its first five volumes alone, *The Friends' Library* reproduces eight examples of women's autobiography, all of them showing women writers who worked comfortably within what today is identified as a masculine form. If these women perceived the world differently from men, they did not register their perceptions in the shape or style of their spiritual accounts.

Nor was their gender registered in special thematic concerns. Modern literary criticism assumes that women autobiographers will show a special facility or predilection for domestic themes, for the exploration of matters relating to marriage, children, or housewifery.[16] This assumption, complemented by modern psychological theories of women's "relational" approach to self-definition,[17] often predisposes critics to foreground those autobiographical episodes in which women writers touch on familial matters or domestic details. Of course such details appear, but no more frequently in women's spiritual accounts than in men's.

If we compare men's and women's autobiographies in *The Friends' Library* on the themes of marriage and the family, we discover that neither develops such themes, although occasionally they appear in the accounts of both. We know that Elizabeth Stirredge was married, for instance, only because the editors preface her account with "testimonies" from acquaintances who refer to her husband James. Stirredge herself gives no account of courtship or marriage; her husband appears incidentally (if effectually) in an episode about persecution, where the king's officers attempt to confiscate their personal goods and James protests with her against the action.[18] Jane Hoskens refers to her marriage in a subordinate clause, written to explain why she left the care of Quaker mentors in 1738; after the reference, she continues her narrative as if nothing special has occurred.[19] Another autobiographer, Mary Pennington, discusses her first and second marriages

at some length, but primarily to explain her long search for religious truth.[20] So, too, for male autobiographers. Like Pennington, Joseph Pike gives some account of his marriage, though his interest lies in the "instruction and information" he can pass on: after naming his wife and listing their fourteen children, he goes on to cite several paragraphs of scriptural texts that stress the importance of seeking God's light in marriage. And it may be only coincidental that we read details of courtship in a male autobiography, Benjamin Bangs's *Life and Convincement.* Bangs's encounters with Mary Lowe, his future wife, occur as interstices between records of his journeys as a Quaker minister. "Although we had often met together before in our Journeys," he comments, "I never so much as mention'd, one Word of Courtship to her; though my Spirit was closely united in a divine Fellowship with her."[21] One does not question his silence, given the tendency of Quaker accounts to efface such moments. The repression of romance becomes even more complete in *The Friends' Library* version, where the editors eliminate Bangs's reference to courtship and summarize his word to Mary Lowe as an "impart[ation]" of his mind.[22] Perhaps the editors wished to lift Bangs's account to the same level of heavenly-mindedness that George Fox demanded in his teaching on marriage: "as it was in the beginning, before sin and defilement was."[23]

Whatever the editorial motive, the tendency to efface details of romance and domesticity demonstrates the powerful operation of generic conventions and editorial practice on the autobiographer's self-construction—whether the writer is male or female, whether we understand that operation to occur as the writer lives her life or as she later converts it into textual form. The spiritual autobiography, unlike the domestic memoir, does not concern itself with marriage and the family.

Such generic power asserts itself most peculiarly in the spiritual autobiographer's treatment of children, ultimately to the point of obscuring meaning. One might think that women autobiographers would devote more space to children and childrearing than men, that they would stress their maternal concerns even as they detail their inner struggles or report their travels in the ministry. Indeed, the best female autobiographer in the Quaker tradition titled her autobiography *A Legacy, or Widow's Mite, Left by Alice Hayes to Her Children and Others,* and she rationalizes her authorship by explaining that it is "for the encouragement of the young to faithfulness and continual trust and confidence in the Lord." But this rationalization was equally common among male writers: Joseph Pike similarly writes "for the benefit and instruction of my children" and "for others also," while Joseph Oxley prefaces his journal with an address to his children, admonishing them "to follow me, in like manner, only in greater degrees of purity."[24] If we label Hayes's autobiographical stance "maternal," then Pike's and Oxley's must be also.

More perplexing is the indeterminacy of the word *Children* in the titles of many such autobiographies. Does Hayes refer to her own children or to spiritual offspring, including the reader, left to her care? Perhaps both, for Hayes mentions that her first husband, Daniel Smith, was "an indulgent father to our children," but she also frames her text with prayers for "all the babes and lambs of God."[25] Yet in Elizabeth Stirredge's autobiography the reader can never determine if the "children" are anything other than Quakers under spiritual guidance. When she warns "my dear children" of the "subtle devices" of "the enemy of your immortal soul," she may refer to either natural or spiritual offspring. When she later recounts her testimony before King Charles II, including a plea for the end "of persecuting and shedding the blood of my dear children," she refers to all Quakers. Within the text the referent is never fixed. Stirredge's "maternal" stance becomes a function of her writerly role. This stance demands—for male and female autobiographer alike—the nurturing of a spiritual community.[26]

The minimizing of romantic and domestic concerns in the spiritual autobiography—or, more specifically, in the autobiographical tradition that *The Friends' Library* reconstructs—should challenge the modern critical assumption that gender is always the operative force in self-writing. It should lead us to ask whether theory and criticism of women's autobiography proceeds most perceptively when it emphasizes sexual difference. One might, of course, interpret the documents in the Evans collection and the construction of literary history they represent in different ways. One might argue that the women who wrote such accounts were exceptional or anomalous, or that gender was necessarily a secondary issue among radical English sects under persecution, or that spiritual accounts allow only limited views of human experience. These interpretations—psychological, sociological, literary—have a certain validity, but the existence of such a large body of women's documents contradicts categorical assertions about a distinctively gender-linked origin and history of women's autobiography. More likely, as Nancy Armstrong has argued in *Desire and Domestic Fiction,* "gender" is a category of modern invention, subsuming and even denying the relevance of older categories such as class, status, or religion.[27] In *The Friends' Library* the Evans brothers meant to reassert the importance of one of those older categories by preserving autobiographical texts in which the religious was all-important and by editing out details that might hint of other means by which to interpret life experiences.

If *The Friends' Library* institutionalized a form of women's autobiography that avoided or minimized issues of gender, a different editorial trend helped to authorize a form that was explicitly feminine. This trend was the publication of archival materials that came with no generic label but that increasingly came to be called "autobiography" by their editors. The form they reproduced was, in today's terms, the domestic (or family) memoir, a *res gestae* account rooted not in a conception of an individual self or a religious soul but in the autobiographer as recorder of communal history.

As a form of women's writing, the domestic memoir dates back to the seventeenth century, the earliest examples emerging contemporaneously with the earliest spiritual autobiographies (1654 for Anna Trapnel's *Legacy for Saints,* 1656 for Margaret Cavendish's *True Relation of My Birth, Breeding, and Life*). The domestic memoir placed great emphasis on social continuity and family service in public causes, thus revealing its essentially upper-class origins and modes of self-definition. Indeed, the use of the word *legacy* in the title of many spiritual autobiographies suggests that some lower- and middle-class writers were consciously echoing their secular, aristocratic counterparts but offering a spiritual inheritance instead of a corruptible earthly one of status and wealth. While the forms of the spiritual autobiography and domestic memoir may be historically linked, however, they represent radically different ways of representing subjectivity. The spiritual autobiography focuses on the individual writer's progress or regress, whereas the memoir tends to stress the writer's place in an extended family unit and to make her (since most such writers were female) the repository of its significant accomplishments, more likely those of a husband or a father than her own.

Ann Lady Fanshawe's *Memoirs* (1829) delineates the typical pattern and its conventional features.[28] Lady Fanshawe's account originates in a desire to pass on both her personal and the familial history to children. She addresses her words to her "most dear and only son," beginning not with memories from her own childhood but instead with several paragraphs of Polonius-like advice (pp. 2-4) and a hagiographic character sketch of her late husband, the boy's father (pp. 5-9). She includes two long segments of genealogy, one tracing the paternal line (pp. 9-25), the other the maternal (pp. 25-32), both giving details of the family estates, finances, and public honors. When the narrative proper gets underway, the *Memoirs* follows the career of Lady Fanshawe's husband, who served as Secretary of War to Charles II (then Prince of Wales), later as ambassador to Portugal and Spain.

Because Ann Fanshawe witnessed foreign court life in its official pomp and its unofficial details, her account records many political events from a "feminine" perspective. She takes particular note, for instance, of the perquisites she receives as ambassador's wife, right down to the large silver chocolate pot, twelve fine filigree cups, two large silver salvers, and twelve fine saceret napkins that the English merchants of Seville presented to her and her husband on their arrival from England (p. 204). Because the account is also a domestic memorial, she includes many intimate stories about her marriage, including her husband's tears on their first separation (p. 45), her secret visits while he was imprisoned in Whitehall (pp. 116-17), and even her assumption of cabin boy's garb so that she could fight by his side when pirates attacked their ship (pp. 91-93). In its structure, Fanshawe's· is a typically seventeenth-century account: it ends when Sir Richard's life ends. Fanshawe finds it within her power (or desire) only to describe his funeral and then her father's death before she breaks off the narrative.

Despite the autobiographical elements of this and other such documents, and despite their early emergence in the history of self-writing, the domestic memoir was not recognized as an autobiographical form until the nineteenth century. Certainly it was not considered a public or publishable form until then. With the exception of Margaret Cavendish's *True Relation* (1656), all the now-famous memoirs of seventeenth-century women, including Fanshawe's, were kept privately within family archives and published only two centuries later by descendants or antiquarians. When published, the accounts increasingly came to include "autobiography" in the title or editorial preface, as the following chronological listing suggests: the *Life of Mrs. Lucy Hutchinson* (1806), *A Pairt of the Life of Lady Margaret Cunninghame* (1827), the *Memoirs of Lady Fanshawe* (1829), the *Autobiography of Mary Countess of Warwick* (1848), the *Autobiography of Mrs. Alice Thornton* (1875), the *Autobiography of Anne Lady Halkett* (1875). Even Cavendish's account, published during her lifetime in *Natures Pictures Drawn by Fancies Pencil to the Life,* was issued separately only in 1814 by Sir Egerton Brydges, who attached the label "auto-biography" that has stayed with it ever since.

It is worth asking why these texts were published first and in such numbers in the nineteenth century and why they were then given the literary designation of *autobiography* (rather than, say, *history*).[29] A simple answer would note, of course, that the term *autobiography* did not become established until the nineteenth century, along with rising interest in the genre; thus, not until the nineteenth century were these older texts likely to attract literary attention or fashionable terminology. A more complicated answer would point to the cultural cultural conditions—and contradictions—that authorized these forms as "women's autobiography"; it would include consideration of what critics and editors said about such women's texts, what they praised and blamed, what they sanctioned and omitted.

Nineteenth-century editors seem to have been uncommonly nervous about publishing women's private documents, but they nevertheless articulated the case for doing so and, in the process, authorized certain kinds of life writing as legitimately feminine. Charles Jackson, editor of Alice Thornton's autobiography, expresses a common rationale for going public when he states that such specimens, "hid among the archives of many of our ancient houses," deserve to be shared with the English nation; "from their intrinsic merit, [they] have a right to be considered *publici* as well as *privati juris*."[30] What does he mean by "intrinsic merit"? One criterion for merit was historical. Like Charles Jackson, Lady Halkett's editor stresses "the value of the historical information which she actually imparts"; Lady Warwick's, the "great historical value" of such records of "the domestic occurrences of the period, soon after the restoration of Charles II"; the preface to Lady Fanshawe's *Memoirs* claims that, whether the work "be read for the historical information which it contains, or with no higher motive than for amusement," it will "more than amply gratify either object"; Lucy Hutchinson's editor praises the ability of the work to make the reader feel "a party in the transactions which are recounted."[31]

Amplifying the claims of these last two editors, both nineteenth- and twentieth-century scholars have added appeals to literary merit to assertions of historical value, praising the works as lively, imaginative examples of an evolving genre or arguing for them as "contributions to the early development of the English secular autobiography."[32] Despite the defensibility of the historical and aesthetic claims, the evidence for literary influence is dubious—at least as formulated by twentieth-century critics. Few (virtually none) of these domestic memoirs were published until the Victorian period, at which point the secular tradition of autobiography had already been shaped by male writers. We need another explanation for the Victorian publication of these seventeenth-century accounts and the promotion of their nineteenth-century equivalents, a promotion that did, subsequently, influence a tradition of autobiography.

These documents represent, I think, a literary manifestation of the doctrine of separate spheres—at best a form of commitment to the private and domestic, at worst a form of compensation for loss of the public and professional. The seventeenth-century women who wrote family memoirs stayed, as writers, safely within the domestic realm. Their texts were thus exemplary for would-be Victorian women writers. The memoir—domestic in its focus, relational in its mode of self-construction—allowed women to write as mothers, daughters, and wives. It allowed them to represent their lives in terms of "good" feminine plots. It did not, however, allow women writers to develop—or disturb—the primary male traditions of autobiography: the public, *res gestae* account of professional life or the more introspective form of spiritual confession.

That there is a cultural link between the publication of seventeenth-century memoirs and the remarkable increase of nineteenth-century domestic memoirs is suggested by the bibliographical records. Whereas women wrote and published significant numbers of spiritual autobiographies from the mid-seventeenth century to the early eighteenth, by the nineteenth century such women autobiographers had virtually disappeared.[33] Instead, women with religious inclinations turned inward to spiritual diaries or outward to what William Matthews categorizes as autobiographies of "clergymen's wives"—actually domestic memoirs of life in a vicarage or on the mission field.[34] At the same time, in the secular arena, editors resurrected memoirs by diplomats' and soldiers' wives like Ann Fanshawe and Lucy Hutchinson and encouraged nineteenth-century equivalents written by women who traveled with their husbands to India, Egypt, the West Indies, and the Far East, published under such titles as *Foreign Courts and Foreign Homes, Our Home in Cyprus, At Home in India,* or *Garden of Fidelity.*[35] So, too, in the memoirs of Anne Halkett and Alice Thornton, the Victorians edited women's perspectives on the disruptions of the Interregnum, just as they published books by their own politicians' and diplomats' wives on domestic conditions during colonial and internal crises. And they published numerous examples of what William Matthews calls simply "domestic and family life," accounts in which women recorded their memories and the social mores of Victorian Britain.[36] Thus was the domestic memoir institutionalized as an appropriately feminine form of autobiography, as a model for female subjectivity and self-representation.

We should not lose sight of the fact, however, that it was Victorian editors and critics who authorized these works as "women's" autobiography. Had the texts come to light at a different cultural moment, they might not have been labeled "autobiography" at all. But because a feminine sensibility and certain nascent structures seemed evident in seventeenth-century women's self-writing, literary history—in the form of ancient manuscripts and modern critical commentary—seemed to validate the notion of a separate autobiographical sphere and the development of a female autobiographical tradition. After all, didn't the memoirs of these female predecessors represent the origins of women's autobiography? Didn't these original and originating texts add historical weight to the enterprise of writing domestic memoirs and give a sense of a female tradition that women needed?[37]

As I have been arguing, origins are created, not found; traditions constructed, not discovered. The fact that

the Victorians created—or, rather, believed they had discovered—a generic link between seventeenth-century women's texts and those of their own era is the significant point. In fact, the texts they resuscitated did not represent a unified feminine tradition or a coherent genre. If we relinquish the nineteenth-century perspective, we can see that Lady Halkett's account reads like a historical romance; Lady Cunninghame's, a legal deposition; Lady Warwick's, a spiritual confession but without the religious ecstasies or hermeneutic vagaries of sectarian practitioners. Alice Thornton's autobiography was compiled from four discrete books of record, its basic structure (so far as we can tell) suggesting a spiritual diary with meditations following each entry.[38] Even within a single autobiography, we can find different modes of self-expression—as in Lady Cunninghame's, which uses a plain, factual style in the primary text but shifts to highly abstract, typological discourse in an extended address to her husband.[39] Despite such diversity, Victorians treated these accounts as a generic unit, as part of a continuous literary tradition. And they gave the texts and the tradition coherence by stressing a fundamental quality: a feminine mode of self-conception.

This mode I shall designate, following modern psychological terminology, as relational. According to theorists like Nancy Chodorow and Carol Gilligan, women's ways of conceiving the self focus on relationships with another person or group. In Chodorow's terms, "the basic feminine sense of self is connected to the world; the basic masculine sense of self is separate." Girls emerge from childhood "with a basis for 'empathy' built into their primary definition of self in a way that boys do not"; they "come to define and experience themselves as continuous with others; their experience of self contains more flexible and permeable ego boundaries." In contrast, boys have "engaged, or been required to engage, in a more emphatic individuation and a more defensive firming of experienced ego boundaries"; hence, their self-conceptions tend to be "positional" rather than "relational."[40] Nineteenth-century editors did not, of course, refer to modern psychology when they characterized seventeenth-century women's texts. But judging from editorial prefaces and critical reviews, we can recognize a comparable language for interpreting women's experience. For virtually every text, the critical commentary and rhetorical weight fall on the woman writer's achievements as daughter, wife, and mother.

Editors viewed these early women autobiographers—and believed these women viewed themselves—in relational terms, in their connections with fathers and mothers, husbands and children. For example, Ann Lady Fanshawe's editor characterizes his authoress as "a beautiful example of female devotion" (p. xxxiv). Although he notes her "literary merits" (p. ix) and frequently remarks on the fascinating historical information she conveys, the self he conceives for his subject is that of wife and mother—as in his descriptive sequence, "an accomplished and clever woman, the wife of one of the most faithful servants of Charles the First and Charles the Second" (p. vi). His emphasis in analyzing her autobiography lies on Lady Fanshawe's feminine virtues, those "instances of conjugal devotion, of maternal excellence, and of enduring fortitude under calamities, which render her a bright example to posterity" (p. ix).

Certainly these seventeenth-century women understood their lives in relation to others. Lucy Hutchinson composed her autobiography (a fragment, never finished) to accompany her massive biographical memorial, the *Memoirs of the Life of Colonel Hutchinson.* Margaret Cavendish, after multiple and contradictory attempts at self-definition, finally concluded her autobiography with an unadorned, relational formula: "I was daughter to one Master Lucas of St. Johns, near Colchester, in Essex, second wife to the Lord Marquis of Newcastle; for my Lord having had two Wives, I might easily have been mistaken, especially if I should dye and my Lord Marry again" (p. 310). And Lady Halkett seems to have found the conclusion to her narrative only when she accepted Sir James and agreed to define herself as his wife; her account may be a quest for a relational (rather than individual) self-definition.

But what signifies more—at least for the institutionalizing of women's autobiography—are the rhetorical maneuvers by which nineteenth-century editors made relational self-definitions not only superior to, but identical with, literary merit. When Sir Egerton Brydges, the editor of Margaret Cavendish's account, states that "her Grace wanted taste," that she "had not the talent of seizing that *selection* of circumstances," that she "knew not what to obtrude, and what to leave out" (pp. 262-63), he refers to her literary productions generally. From this judgment, however, he excludes her biography, the *Life of William Cavendish, Duke of Newcastle,* and presumably her own pendant autobiography. These productions reveal her "great fault" less, Brydges claims, because they are "domestic." Brydges thus implies that the domestic memoirist cannot praise her husband too excessively, that the reader does not expect aesthetic balance anyway, that the evidence of feminine virtue is what really matters in a woman's autobiography.

More subtly, Ann Fanshawe's editor attributes a woman's literary fame to domestic merit. Unlike Cavendish's editor, Fanshawe's praises the style, thought, and reliable historical sense of his authoress: "Celebrated as this country is for female talent and virtue, there is no one with whom Lady Fanshawe may not be compared and gain by the comparison" (pp. viii-ix). But as his link of "talent" and "virtue" hints, the former depends on the latter. The subsequent comments make explicit the point that, in order to achieve a lasting place in the literary canon, a woman writer must be "a bright example to posterity" (p. ix).

The critical responses and rhetorical choices of Victorian editors allow us to sense the immense pressure on contemporary women to make their autobiographies domestic, their self-conceptions relational. These editors express (and helped shape) Victorian assumptions about the proper modes of women's self-writing. One consequence of such assumptions was the rise of the Victorian domestic memoir. Another was the inclusion of domestic patterns—plots of sisterhood, motherhood, conjugal life—in the autobiography of virtually every major Victorian 'woman writer, even when such patterns caused disjunctions in narrative structure.[41] A third was a fundamental confusion in literary history. Victorian women who wrote autobiography came to believe that they had inherited a domestic tradition from their female predecessors. In reality, they inherited it not so much from female predecessors as from male editors who transmitted to them their literary heritage.

If we compare the editorial work of *The Friends' Library* with the archival (re)productions of seventeenth-century women's memoirs, we can sense the contradictions that Victorian women faced when they conceived of writing autobiography. The two traditions implied different ways of constructing the self: one essentially genderless, the other highly gendered; one inner and psychological, the other social and domestic; one religious, the other secular. Women autobiographers might, of course, have aligned themselves with a tradition simply on the basis of this last difference: religious versus secular. But for writers interested in autobiography as literary production, the choice was not so clear-cut, not simply a matter of religious affiliation or secular interest. As a literary form, women's autobiography was institutionalized with the contradictions embedded in it. . . .

Notes

[1] Mary G. Mason, "The Other Voice: Autobiographies of Women Writers," in James Olney, ed., *Autobiography: Essays Theoretical and Critical* (Princeton, N. J.: Princeton University Press, 1980); Estelle C. Jelinek, *The Tradition of Women's Autobiography: From Antiquity to the Present* (Boston: Twayne, 1986); Sidonie Smith, *A Poetics of Women's Autobiography: Marginality and the Fictions of Self-Representation* (Bloomington: Indiana University Press, 1987); and Carolyn G. Heilbrun, *Writing a Woman's Life* (New York: Norton, 1988). Heilbrun's book is not, strictly speaking, a historical study, but it as-

sumes the historical development of a women's tradition in its discussion of certain modern texts as "revolutionary" (Adrienne Rich's autobiographical works), as a "turning point" (May Sarton's *Journal of a Solitude*), or as otherwise exemplifying progress in the genre. Collections that include attempts to define a women's tradition are Estelle C. Jelinek, ed., *Women's Autobiography: Essays in Criticism* (Bloomington: Indiana University Press, 1980); Domna C. Stanton, ed., *The Female Autograph: Theory and Practice of Autobiography from the Tenth to the Twentieth Century* (Chicago: University of Chicago Press, 1987); and Shari Benstock, ed., *The Private Self: Theory and Practice of Women's Autobiographical Writings* (Chapel Hill: University of North Carolina Press, 1988).

[2] Jelinek, *The Tradition of Women's Autobiography*, p. 8. Cf. Susan Stanford Friedman's conclusion to "Women's Autobiographical Selves: Theory and Practice," in Benstock, ed., *The Private Self*, pp. 55-56: "Women's autobiography comes alive as a literary tradition of self-creation when we approach its texts from a psycho-political perspective based in the lives of women. . . . Individualistic [male] paradigms do not take into account the central role collective consciousness of self plays in the lives of women and minorities."

[3] The exclusion of women's autobiographies from major theoretical studies is documented in Jelinek, *The Tradition of Women's Autobiography*, pp. 1-8; Smith, *A Poetics of Women's Autobiography*, pp. 3-19; and Friedman, "Women's Autobiographical Selves," pp. 34-44. About this exclusion, Smith writes: "The poetics of autobiography, as the history of autobiography, thus remains by and large an androcentric enterprise. Despite the critical ferment brought about by feminist critiques of the academy, of disciplinary methodologies, of the canon, the majority of autobiography critics still persist in either erasing woman's story, relegating it to the margins of critical discourse, or, when they treat women's autobiographies seriously, uncritically conflating the dynamics of male and female selfhood and textuality" (p. 15).

[4] See the Introduction to this volume for an account of the term.

[5] Mason, "The Other Voice," p. 210.

[6] Paul de Man, "Autobiography as De-Facement," *Modern Language Notes*, 94 (1979): 920.

[7] I use the term *auto/biography* throughout this essay to designate texts that combine both autobiographical and biographical modes, or collections that include both biographies and autobiographies.

[8] William Evans and Thomas Evans, eds., *The Friends' Library* (Philadelphia: Joseph Rakestraw, 1837-50), 1: 1-2. Besides the rationale provided by the prospectus, it is probably the case that the Evans brothers shared the concern of many Victorian Friends that Quakerism was losing its spiritual center and thus needed models to restore its members to a purer form of faith.

[9] Because Augustine's influence on the tradition of English spiritual autobiography was negligible (or at least indirect) until the nineteenth century, it is more accurate to speak of a "Bunyanesque" tradition. Even this label, meant to acknowledge the crucial influence of *The Pilgrim's Progress* as well as of *Grace Abounding to the Chief of Sinners*, neglects the early contributions of women writers to the formation of the English tradition.

[10] *The Life and Testimony of that Faithful Servant of the Lord, Elizabeth Stirredge*, in Evans and Evans, eds., *The Friends' Library*, 2: 187-212. Stirredge's account was written in the 1690's, first published in 1711, and reissued throughout the eighteenth century.

[11] *A Brief Account of the Life and Travels of Thomas Wilson*, in Evans and Evans, eds., *The Friends' Library*, 2: 319-33.

[12] Richard T. Vann, "The Theory and Practice of Conversion," in *The Social Development of English Quakerism, 1655-1755* (Cambridge, Mass.: Harvard University Press, 1969), pp. 1-46. Howard T. Brinton summarizes the major episodes of the Quaker formula in *Quaker Journals: Varieties of Religious Experience Among Friends* (Wallingford, Pa.: Pendle Hill Publications, 1972).

[13] For the episodes summarized in this paragraph, see in Evans and Evans, eds., *The Friends' Library: The Life of Elizabeth Ashbridge*, 4: 11; *Some Account of the Life of Joseph Pike*, 2: 358; *A Short Account of Alice Hayes, Minister of the Gospel*, 2: 73-74; *Memoirs of the Life and Convincement of Benjamin Bangs*, 4: 224-25; and Wilson, 2: 330.

[14] Hayes, in Evans and Evans, eds., *The Friends' Library*, 2: 71; compare Malachi 3:2-3 and Ezekiel 22:17-22.

[15] Prospectus, Evans and Evans, eds., *The Friends' Library*, 1: 1-2.

[16] See, for example, Cynthia S. Pomerleau's statement that "for seventeenth-century women, much more than men, love acted as a defining force" ("The Emergence of Women's Autobiography in England," in Jelinek, ed., *Women's Autobiography*, p. 25). Pomerleau's judgment results from an emphasis on secular texts and, perhaps, from a neglect of accounts written by male autobiographers.

[17] See Nancy Chodorow, *The Reproduction of Mothering: Psychoanalysis and the Sociology of Gender* (Berkeley: University of California Press, 1978); and Carol Gilligan, *In a Different Voice: Psychological Theory and Women's Development* (Cambridge, Mass.: Harvard University Press, 1982). The models proposed by these two fine studies, highly influential on recent feminist criticism, are problematic when applied to seventeenth-century accounts. Criticism needs to maintain the historical and cultural limits that Chodorow and Gilligan themselves recognize.

[18] Stirredge, in Evans and Evans, eds., *The Friends' Library,* 2: 193. The practice of including "testimonies" (character references) holds for all autobiographers, male and female alike.

[19] Hoskens, *The Life of that Faithful Servant of Christ, Jane Hoskens, A Minister of the Gospel,* in Evans and Evans, eds., *The Friends' Library,* 1: 471.

[20] *Some Account of Circumstances in the Life of Mary Pennington* (London: Harvey and Darton, 1821), pp. 10-13, 68-70. The first half of Pennington's account is a spiritual record left to her daughter, Gulielma Maria Springett, which focuses on the mother's history before marriage and with her first husband; the second half, a family memoir intended for her grandson, focuses on the paternal heritage. One knows only after reading both halves that Mary Pennington had two children—one daughter, one son.

[21] Benjamin Bangs, *Memoirs of the Life and Convincement of that Worthy Friend Benjamin Bangs* (London: Luke Hinde, 1757), p. 48.

[22] The revision in Evans and Evans, eds., *The Friends' Library,* 4: 227, reads: "Although we had often met together before in our journeys, I never so much as mentioned to her; though my spirit was united in a Divine fellowship with her." The original "Word of Courtship" disappears.

[23] See Arnold Lloyd's discussion of Quaker marriage in *Quaker Social History, 1669-1738* (London: Longmans, Green, 1950), pp. 48-65.

[24] In Evans and Evans, eds., *The Friends' Library:* Hayes, 2: 68; Pike, 2: 351; Oxley, *Journal of Joseph Oxley's Life and Travels,* 2: 415. The rationale for autobiography as a spiritual legacy is formulaic, though not universal in the Quaker tradition.

[25] Hayes, in Evans and Evans, eds., *The Friends' Library,* 2: 75, 78. When Hayes first attended Quaker meetings, Smith was quite a cruel husband, locking up her clothes to prevent her attendance and threatening to desert her and the children unless she renounced the Friends.

[26] Stirredge, in Evans and Evans, eds., *The Friends' Library,* 2: 190, 192. The editorial materials surrounding Stirredge's account seem to clarify the question of her motherhood. The "testimonies" mention her late husband but no children; the biographical notice attached by the Hemel Hempstead Friends, however, is signed by a James Stirredge, presumably her son.

[27] Nancy Armstrong, *Desire and Domestic Fiction: A Political History of the Novel* (New York: Oxford University Press, 1987).

[28] *Memoirs of Lady Fanshawe,* ed. E. Harris Nicolas (London: Henry Colburn, 1829).

[29] Some modern historians like Natalie Zemon Davis do, indeed, treat them as a form of history. See her "Gender and Genre: Women as Historical Writers, 1400-1820," in Patricia H. Labalme, ed., *Beyond Their Sex: Learned Women of the European Past* (New York: New York University Press, 1980), pp. 153-82. For my argument, fixing their genre is less important than noticing the autobiographical designation that Victorians chose.

[30] *The Autobiography of Mrs. Alice Thornton of East Newton, Co. York,* ed. Charles Jackson (London: Surtees Society, 1875), p. v.

[31] *The Autobiography of Anne Lady Halkett,* ed. John Gough Nichols (Westminster: Camden Society, 1875), p. i; *Memoirs of Lady Fanshawe,* p. viii; *Autobiography of Mary Countess of Warwick,* ed. T. Crofton Croker (London: Percy Society, 1848), p. xi; *Memoirs of the Life of Colonel Hutchinson . . . to which is prefixed The Life of Mrs. Hutchinson, Written by Herself,* ed. Rev. Julius Hutchinson, 3d ed. (London: Longman, Hurst, Rees, and Orme, 1810), p. xxiv. See also the prefaces to *A Pairt of the Life of Lady Margaret Cunninghame* (Edinburgh: James Ballantyne, 1827) and *A True Relation of the Birth, Breeding, and Life of Margaret Cavendish,* ed. Sir Egerton Brydges (Kent: Johnson and Warwick, 1814).

[32] Mary Beth Rose, "Gender, Genre, and History: Seventeenth-Century English Women and the Art of Autobiography," in Mary Beth Rose, ed., *Women in the Middle Ages and the Renaissance* (Syracuse, N. Y.: Syracuse University Press, 1986), pp. 245, 273. Although Rose initially states that she is "not attempting to establish the extent to which women may be credited with influencing the development of secular autobiography" (p. 247), throughout her essay and especially at its close she refers to women's "contributions" to the genre.

[33] See my "Gender and Autobiographical Form: The Case of the Spiritual Autobiography," in James

Olney, ed., *Studies in Autobiography* (New York: Oxford University Press, 1988), pp. 211-22.

[34] See the index to William Matthews, *British Autobiographies: An Annotated Bibliography of British Autobiographies Published or Written Before 1951* (1955; reprint, Hamden, Conn.: Archon Books, 1968), s.v. "religion." Most of the nineteenth-century women's accounts that Matthews lists as spiritual autobiographies are in fact private diaries to which biographical accounts have been added by an editor.

[35] See Matthews, *British Autobiographies,* s.v. "diplomats' and consuls' wives" and "politicians' wives." As in the seventeenth century, such accounts are written primarily by women from the upper classes.

[36] Matthews, *British Autobiographies,* s.v. "domestic and family life" and "housewives." Women wrote two-thirds of the memoirs listed.

[37] The quest for tradition underlies Elaine Showalter's account of nineteenth-century women's fiction, *A Literature of Their Own: British Women Novelists from Brontë to Lessing* (Princeton, N.J.: Princeton University Press, 1977).

[38] Thornton refers to "the first book of my life" (p. 174), to a "first booke of my widowed condition" (p. 154), to a "2nd booke" (p. 184), and to "my booke of meditations" (p. 142). Her editor simply arranged the entries in chronological order, omitting repetitious material and deleting many of her meditations or thanksgivings for God's mercy.

[39] Presumably, Lady Cunningham thought it appropriate to appeal to her errant spouse in the language of Scripture, although the consequence is a vagueness about her plight and her specific demands. The religious discourse seems to have had little effect on his behavior.

[40] Chodorow, *The Reproduction of Mothering,* pp. 166-69, 173-77. See also Gilligan, *In a Different Voice.*

[41] From the spiritual autobiographies of Francis Power Cobbe and Annie Besant, to the *Bildungsromane* of Charlotte Brontë and Margaret Oliphant, to the artists' autobiographies of Oliphant, Fanny Kemble, Charlotte Riddell, and Mary Cholmondeley, women writers felt the pressure of the domestic memoir. Sometimes, as in Cholmondeley's *Under One Roof,* they turned this pressure into productive literary channels. More often than not, the pressure was counterproductive, as their artistic goals were to circumvent the domestic tradition and reclaim another.

AUTOBIOGRAPHIES CONCERNED WITH RELIGIOUS AND POLITICAL ISSUES

Ann D. Gordon (essay date 1992)

SOURCE: "The Political Is the Personal: Two Autobiographies of Woman Suffragists," in *American Women's Autobiography: Fea(s)ts of Memory*, edited by Margo Culley, The University of Wisconsin Press, 1992, pp. 111-27.

[*In the essay below, Gordon compares the autobiographies of Abigail Scott Duniway and Elizabeth Cady Stanton and argues that both suffragists used their autobiographies to further their political goals.*]

Woman suffragists, like other leaders of women in the nineteenth century, approached the art of autobiography with their public identities well crafted and their public voices tuned closely to a particular pitch of the cultures they sought to influence. In autobiography they might aspire to the definitive variation of their personal story but they did not start afresh. With an acute sense of the historical importance of their work, these leaders knew that they had etched their lives into the history of women and the nation. That record would stand whether or not they retold their story; they would shape its interpretation, fill in its details, but not alter its substance. Because their political goal still eluded women and a political movement still needed its personalities, these leaders created themselves as their followers knew them. To do otherwise would suggest some discomfort with or rejection of their well-known presence, perhaps even some second thoughts about the fight they had waged.

The two best-known autobiographies of suffragists are more particular still. Although they portray women whose social experience, economic fortunes, and personalities differed radically, they are alike in speaking to issues that arose from the leadership of the authors themselves. Frontiers-woman Abigail Scott Duniway (1834-1915) grew up in Illinois and Oregon with no formal education. After marriage to a rancher she seemed destined to replicate her mother's life of heavy domestic labor and frequent childbirth. An accident that disabled her husband forced the family into town where Abigail could support them by teaching school, keeping a millinery shop, and, in time, writing, lecturing, and publishing in the cause of woman's rights. For forty years she dominated the woman's rights movement in the Pacific Northwest, never quite breaking away to achieve a national following but indisputably a regional leader. If the written word can be trusted, she had no sense of humor whatsoever, but excelled in direct debate. Of debate she had considerable experience. Alienated from Easterners and at odds with the woman's temperance movement, Duniway's leadership was fraught with acrimony.[1]

At the other end of the continent, Elizabeth Cady Stanton (1815-1902) knew the privileges of wealth and power in childhood. Her father, Daniel Cady, speculated profitably in lands and practiced law. He served one term in the U.S. House of Representatives and was elevated to a judgeship on the New York State Supreme Court. His daughter received one of the best formal educations available to her generation and learned a considerable amount of law from the constant stream of law students who shared the family's household. After marriage to an antislavery activist, Stanton began to use her connections and talents to define a political career, a career that won her national recognition by the time of the Civil War. Witty and playful, she became a popular figure despite her radical social ideas. A thorough scholar of constitutionalism, she had the ear of politicians even when she could not prevail on them to support her cause.[2]

Their autobiographies are strikingly different in content and narrative voice. Duniway, who published *Path Breaking* in 1914, left no doubt that she intended to vindicate her strategies and tactics by concentrating on the political victories that fell to women under her leadership and by attacking her enemies. The text carries the dual burden of autobiography and, as the subtitle indicates, a "History of the Equal Suffrage Movement in the Pacific Coast States."[3] "I have been importuned . . . to write a history . . . ," she began. "These requests invariably call for statement, in autobiographical form, beginning with the personal history of myself . . ." (1). Far less personal than most of her fiction and seldom pausing for introspection, the book rushes past childhood and marriage in order to record her political work. By the book's midpoint Duniway abandons narrative control over the history in favor of publishing a documentary collection that preserves her most significant speeches.

In *Eighty Years and More,* published in 1898, Elizabeth Cady Stanton was freer of the concern about historical documentation that drove Duniway and more inclined to treat the subject of her individuality. She had prepared in the 1880s three volumes of the *History of Woman Suffrage,* which contained her reminiscences of co-workers, her own interpretations of critical moments and moot principles, and a great many of her addresses. The preface to her autobiography tantalizes with the promise of "the story of my private life as the wife of an earnest reformer, as an enthusiastic housekeeper, . . . and as the mother of seven children, [which] may amuse and benefit the reader" (n.p.). Stanton dwelt on her childhood, reconstructing its environments, entertainments, and pre-

vailing values in great detail, and the style of describing settings and sociability carries through her book. Hers is a chatty, often funny, and very personable work, driven by Stanton's zest for life where Duniway's seems driven by indignation.

When Stanton and Duniway wrote their books, neither of them any longer represented the dominant values and experiences within the movement. The goal of voting had widespread support but not for the reasons that these pioneers had advocated. By going back in time through autobiography they could recapture the roots of their movement and highlight its formative events while reasserting the importance of ideals and strategies that they personally championed.

To discover themselves outside of the movement's center near the end of their lives had a familiar feel, evoking the oppositional roles they had played in their younger days. The creation of audiences for themselves and their ideas had been a large part of their political work and the primary source of their incomes. The start of Stanton's public life in 1848 had coincided with the growth of a new female audience in the northern United States, served by novelists, women's magazines, advice books, and encouraged by religious transformations that allowed women's distinct expressions of conversion and faith. By plunging into this literary marketplace with convictions about individualism and political equality Stanton had helped to diversify the ideals under discussion. By the time Duniway entered this marketplace nearly a generation later around 1868, the competition of ideas was intense. Both women had earned their livings by representing—in both symbolic and political senses—a strong tendency within the audience of women.

That tendency, put simply, applied secular republicanism to the problem of women's degradation. What existed in their society as distinctly female reflected not nature and social adaptation to it but outmoded social structures imposed on a nature that rarely in world history had had opportunity to realize its potential. If women indeed had a nature distinct from men it could not be known until females enjoyed the unfettered individualism that inspired the American political system.[4] Thus, the central tendency in the woman's rights movement argued that gender was a product of an unjust society. But most female activism in the antebellum period took an opposing course and justified itself on the strength of gender difference.

Political conflict among women over the significance of gender became more complex after the Civil War. The numbers of women involved in debating the issues increased, and as women embarked in growing numbers on public work—whether philanthropic or economic—the rival ideas had greater social consequences. By the 1880s, many advocates of a female sphere and moral domain arrived at the conclusion that they needed political power and thus entered the movement so far controlled by advocates of political equality. The woman suffrage movement, thus, at the end of the century contained descendants of both tendencies, and the differences in fundamental philosophy emerged in contests over tactics and strategy.

This political framework may seem remote from the texts of autobiographies, but it provides vital clues for reading these works. Duniway and Stanton spent their adult lives in that contest over first principles, law, and tactics. Their commitments to individualism generated political activity, and their power depended in part on the political fortunes of their ideals. When they turned to the task of writing autobiographies they knew very well the history and current condition of those ideals.

Duniway explains that she began her manuscript in 1905–6 (83). Although she omits to explain why she then set the project aside until 1913–14, the pair of dates pinpoint personal and political events that suggest motives. First, surgery in 1903 very nearly killed her and did leave her deaf in one ear. Moreover, by 1905 conflict over Duniway's identity was of public moment. On the one hand, in its centennial Lewis and Clark Exposition, Oregon honored one of its outstanding pioneers and citizens with Abigail Scott Duniway Day. On the other hand, within the same summer, when the National American Woman Suffrage Association (NAWSA) held its annual convention in Portland at Duniway's invitation, the leaders excluded her from the program and planned a takeover of the state association (Moynihan 210-13). The autobiography at one level explained both identities: the person recognized for her longevity and service to the state and the person at war with major segments of the suffrage movement. Perhaps the regularity of state suffrage campaigns thereafter—1906, 1908, 1910, 1912—precluded the private act of autobiography. Perhaps, too, death seemed more remote as she regained some of her health. But in 1912 Oregon women won the vote, and anything Abigail Scott Duniway said about how the movement should proceed gained new credibility. Then, too, confusion about her significance persisted. The governor turned over to her the job of issuing the proclamation declaring equal suffrage, but many state and national suffragists still denounced Duniway and her views (Moynihan 216). When she resumed the autobiography, she wrote not to celebrate a job well done but to improve an ongoing struggle. Women elsewhere in the United States still battled for the right, while in Oregon women used their new power to campaign for prohibition. The completed book spoke directly to her views on why prohibition should not pass and why woman suffragists did violence to their own history and aspirations by favoring it.

There is no evidence to suggest that Stanton began her reminiscences for such proximate and painful reasons as Duniway. She had, however, taken the measure of her co-laborers in the suffrage cause and found them unwilling to follow her into opposition to their religious degradation that would match their resistance to civil degradation. She approached autobiography first by writing short articles for the *Woman's Tribune,* a suffrage newspaper, where they appeared from April 5, 1889, through July 9, 1892.[5] With the series complete or ended in the *Tribune,* Stanton proceeded to supply the same paper with chapters of the "Woman's Bible, Part I," her witty commentaries on the history of women as revealed in the Bible. These articles appeared as a pamphlet in 1895, prompting the NAWSA to disassociate itself from the *Woman's Bible* in order to keep orthodox women in the movement. Still not ready to return to autobiography, Stanton next wrote "Part II" of the Bible project as a series of articles for the *Boston Investigator.* By 1897 Stanton completed the Bible project and revised and extended the autobiography. The simultaneous creation of these two major works defines her political and historical posture toward the suffrage movement. *Eighty Years* would establish that her own route to secularism paralleled the development of a movement for equal rights and more accurately reflected the history of women's liberation than did the emergence of a suffrage movement which wanted to empower its own religious beliefs and cater to ministerial authority.

Individualists make themselves, or so Stanton and Duniway aver in their construction of prepolitical childhoods. Some quality may have set them apart in their youth, but overall they did what women of their generation and social class did. They reacted to forces external to self, whether Calvinism, frontier insecurities, hierarchical family structures, gender differences, or law. A predisposition toward self-reliance, pitted against an environment that would keep children dependent, made a rebel out of Elizabeth Cady. All the Cady children, Stanton explained, were "disposed to assume the responsibility of their own actions." Although material comforts and opportunities abounded, the household ran on fear, fear as the basis for religious faith and fear as the motive for secular respect. In that atmosphere, "nothing but strong self-will and a good share of hope and mirthfulness could save an ordinary child from becoming a mere nullity" (8). She remembered a distinct childhood, governed by rules which served to introduce life in small doses. In four chapters devoted to the years before her marriage, she recreated in equal amounts the sheer joy of learning, daring, dancing, and laughing and dismal impositions like "the theological dogmas" and single-sex education (24, 33-36). Her description of her own parents and childhood may or may not be objective (and there are virtually no sources against which to check her account), but she highlights historical and cultural conflicts that shaped her life, and the lives of women who would endorse her ideas for change.

The account explains how she defined out of childhood what to change in her society. Her mother, Margaret Cady, has a very small role; like all adults in this childhood, she exemplifies a rigid Calvinism and an anti-democratic authority. That she managed a large staff of servants can be inferred from stories about children's activities. Much more than that cannot be learned. The father personifies law and the codification of inequality. He teaches his daughter about law but bucks responsibility for the shape that law has taken. Further, as a father without surviving sons, he gives voice to the worst of patrilineal culture. He believes that daughters offer less satisfaction than sons and have no need for equal preparation as self-reliant adults. As a wealthy patriarch, he can enforce dependency by his control of wealth.[6]

Duniway could state the principal meaning of her childhood concisely and allowed only eight pages to the topic. Childhood had been the time to learn the burdens of womanhood and consequences of dependence. In physical deformities that she attributed to working at jobs too hard for a child's body, she bore the reminders of its burdens through the rest of her life. Duniway focuses more on her mother than her father. Her father had "an adventurous disposition" which translated into financial dreams and westward migration. But her mother was the ultimate victim: an "invalid" who died on the Oregon Trail. This "busy mother," with a "rapidly increasing family of a dozen," intones, "Poor baby! She'll be a woman some day. Poor baby!" (8). Children die, those that live must work, there's no time for school and rarely occasion to play. Duniway prefaced this sketch of misery with a declaration of her adult ideal about human responsibility and self-dependence. Broaching her opposition to prohibition in the book's introduction, she explains that humans share a "natural inheritance of self-government" and can be taught to live "in voluntary obedience to the God-given right of self-control" (xvii). But unlike Stanton she will not trace the roots of this belief to her childhood influences nor make a rebel of the girl. This family serves simply as the perfect foil for a daughter who will recognize sources of female despair and enter the world to change it.

Marriage changes the conditions of their lives but does not in itself break their dependence. Duniway, in particular, finds in marriage yet another external force that determines her reality. She marries herself off in one sentence: "I met my fate in the person of Mr. Ben C. Duniway" (9); then begins her own burdensome wifehood at an age considerably younger than Stanton at marriage. A world explored in detail in her fiction is here only sketched out in a brief chapter—work to feed and house ranch hands without compa-

rable assistance at her own work, butter sales to raise cash, and births. She calls herself "a general pioneer drudge" and refers to "my life of hopeless toil, amid uncongenial surroundings" (10, 29). A new external force, not self-reliance, takes her out of the kitchen. She becomes a breadwinner because of her husband's inability to support the family. Stanton's rebellion begins before marriage in her discovery of the abolitionist cause and selection of Henry B. Stanton for a mate. It is a partnership for which she takes full responsibility. At first the marriage seems to extend the good side of childhood, offering even greater fields of journey and discovery. It takes her four chapters to recount all the intellectual influences, important people, and travels that occupied her time in the first seven years of her marriage. But she too must accept the reality that Henry defines: his vague and unprofitable career, shifting political ideals, retraining as a lawyer, and ill health that drives them from Boston to Seneca Falls.

It is obvious that there are, in these books, two vastly different sectors of American society, separated by income, education, region, and a host of expectations for self in society. And yet they depict young women moving toward similar personal conversions which in turn draw them into the same political movement. Though their conversions are not "moments" in a life, in which by blinding insight or physical triumph they reach salvation, both authors bow to convention with narratives that try to assign a time and place to their change. Duniway would have it that another woman's fate pushed her into action. Joining a friend in search of justice under Oregon's laws of property, she discovers out of her empathy that women can and should state the terms of their own injustice and lobby for change in the law. At home that evening she "sat on the floor beside his couch," while Benjamin "placed his hand on [her] head" and told her that the inequities in women's lives would continue until women won the right to vote (39-40). The scene safely situates the start of her path breaking within a sentimental domestic tradition and assigns it a philanthropic rather than self-interested purpose.

Stanton narrowed in on her response to domesticity as the catalyst for change. Seven years and several babies after her marriage, when the Stantons moved from Boston to Seneca Falls, her new home seemed "comparatively solitary, and the change . . . was somewhat depressing." The novelty of housewifery had worn off. She had fewer urban conveniences, poor roads, no sidewalks, and "poor servants." Henry "was frequently from home," leaving the work of house and children all to be done by "one brain" (145). She solved her problem by calling a woman's rights convention and demanding the vote. She situates her conversion in an ordinary domesticity that links her to a culture of middle-class women but also registers a sharp complaint about her own downward mobility. Problem and remedy seem oddly out of joint.

The conversion consists of the decision to change society and specifically to change law, while the personal consequences of conversion are to become self-reliant and break the hold of immediate circumstances on their identity. But because both women played critical roles in founding a movement, the path to personal conversion serves as allegory for political change too. In Stanton's text this larger history is more evident and also more important owing to her special claim as originator of the demand for suffrage. This account of her young life puts the conflict over religion at the center of her personality by making her childhood resistance to religious dogma the birthplace of her anti-authoritarianism. Her awakening required constant resistance to what religion taught her, beginning with the "depressing influences" of Scotch Presbyterianism which taught her never to "shadow one young soul with any of the superstitions of the Christian religion" (26). A teenage crisis follows, one brought on by an evangelical revival from which "rational ideas based on scientific facts" (44) save her. While reading the Bible in her late teens, she resists the "popular heresy" taught in every one of its books that the "headship of man" is divinely ordained (34).

From questioning religion she learned to question all arbitrary authority. The habit next spread to law. A child's sense of justice brought to her attention the rule of inequitable law, and in a story she began telling her audiences by 1867, she grasped the concepts of law and law books and planned to attack the problem with scissors. Once her father explained the universe of law and role of lawmakers, this precocious child promised to go to Albany and get the laws changed. The resistance penetrates the realm of mothering. At the heart of her chapter "Motherhood," about learning the job with the first of her seven children, is her struggle to break away from the female traditions and male expertise that she finds irrational and unsuccessful. When she succeeds, she explains, she "trusted neither men nor books absolutely after this, either in regard to the heavens above or the earth below . . ." (120). Perhaps too it spread to marital relations. Although she never describes resistance to *her* husband, the chapters concerned with village life in Senaca Falls recount several amusing stories about teaching wives to resist petty tyrannies in household management. If she would not admit at age eighty to straightening out her own husband, she showed she had an intimate knowledge of unequal marriage relations.

But the most significant use Stanton made of the religious theme was to place it explicitly at the center of her history of the origins of equal rights. She told the story of the World's Anti-Slavery Convention of 1840 as a confrontation over clerical authority and biblical interpretation. On the side of reaction, the British delegates reasoned that "women . . . were excluded by Scriptural texts from sharing equal dignity and author-

ity with men," and when women's participation in the meeting came to a vote, "the clerical portion of the convention was most violent in its opposition." Representing progress, George Bradburn championed the women by telling the ministers that if they were right about the Bible, he should "bring together every Bible in the universe and make a grand bonfire of them," while the American women she met espoused "equality of the sexes and . . . did not believe in the popular orthodox religion" (83).

Further fueling her conversion, there were encounters and associations with other rebels who supplied direction to her anti-authoritarian tendency. From her married life in Boston in the early 1840s she selected the religious influence of Theodore Parker and John Greenleaf Whittier for extended comment, linking herself to the traditions of Unitarianism, transcendentalism, the Free Religious Association, and the groups which shared her resistance. She found the will and courage of the reformer at the home of her good friend and cousin, Gerrit Smith. There among abolitionists she discovered alternatives to her family's aristocratic and patriarchal values, an ideal of human liberty in an unfettered environment, and a culture of reform. "The anti-slavery platform," she proclaimed boldly in 1898, in the era of Jim Crow, "was the best school the American people ever had on which to learn republican principles and ethics" (59).

This metaphor for the origins of "her" movement is also a powerful statement about woman's politics by the time she constructed this text of a young life. Every element of this narrative was in contention within the woman suffrage movement itself. Not even the historical connection between abolitionism and woman's rights could be agreed upon, as evidenced when delegates in 1890 asked that antislavery history no longer be mentioned in speeches at the NAWSA conventions.[8]

Duniway's generation on the East Coast would not merit pioneering status, but she came to maturity and her awakening in time to help launch woman's rights on the West Coast. Among western pioneers of woman's rights, she stood out too for having grown up in the region rather than bringing eastern notions in the migrant's baggage. The relationship between an older, eastern movement and an indigenous, western youngster runs as a theme throughout her text. The brevity of Duniway's prepolitical story in part stems from its familiarity to those who knew her work. She had crafted her political and literary personae from the harsh physical reality of frontier womanhood. In fiction, journalism, stage presence, and political manner, she had distilled her mother's life on the Illinois prairie, her own girlhood there, the new settlements of Oregon in which she married, bore her children, and built her political base. When she turned to write *Path Breaking* she could evoke this vast repertoire with small gems of well-hewn phrases. Recollecting her return home after the birth of a sibling, she describes the timing as "after our mother was able, or felt obliged to call herself able, to resume her many cares" (6), and thus simply captures a painful choice in the universe of the over-worked wife. With similar passing remarks, she por-trays her own frontier physique: "helpless on a bed of illness caused by my own hardships as a pioneer path breaker" (8), "the half-bent farmer's wife" (11). The last domestic details in *Path Breaking,* the last that readers learn about her domestic and economic cir-cumstances, describe her support of her family just before she became a reformer. But preserved in her own misshapen body and physical pain, frontier wom-anhood gave historical legitimacy to her individuality, long after her back needed to bend over the butter churn and the well.

A detailed account of touring the Pacific Northwest with Susan B. Anthony in 1871 sets up the East/West duality. Anthony survives both the experience and the retelling of it quite well. Duniway enjoys anecdotes that show Anthony's initiation into frontier conditions and thus underscore her eastern origins, while Anthony values local initiative and encourages Duniway to de-velop the regional movement. Further along in *Path Breaking,* Duniway scatters allusions to the virtue as-sociated with her own time and place, with being a daughter of the frontier, as if disagreements in her life might be explained by the fact that her enemies lacked her cultural roots. Interfering national suffrage leaders are "Eastern invaders" (67). "Eleventh-hour suffrag-ists" crop up repeatedly, ignorant of history and weak in principles (288). Anna Howard Shaw, Duniway's nemesis from the moment of her debut on the suffrage platform, is introduced as "young, inexperienced" and new (202-3).[9] When her story arrives at the stage of her life during which battles with national leaders pre-dominated, the imagery becomes political argument. Easterners fail to understand the West, while Western-ers learn "by our many Western defeats, under [East-ern] management, that every locality is its own best interpreter of its own plans of work" (211).

Time and space had defined a body of thought and values which in Duniway's mind produced *the* founda-tions for a politics of equal rights. Equal rights were born of relentless labor, dependency, economic uncer-tainty, unequal and inadequate economic opportunities for women, and laws that diminished women's human-ity against all reason. They flourished on a frontier where men and women both understood the meaning of equal opportunity.

With conversions complete, the authors move them-selves to the center of the story as the principal actors. At that point in the narrative family members become bit players, household work recedes, the social and economic environment of life loses its hold on their identities. In what follows, the private life seems hardly private, lacking intimacy, emotional depth, or dirt, while public life intrudes throughout the narrative. Just when modern readers want to know whether all their per-sonal relationships changed as a consequence of their emergence into selfhood and reform, Duniway and Stanton begin to narrate their political work. The nar-rative shift mirrors a new identity, new to history as well as to these specific individuals. Empowered by their decision to change an objective order that has defined them within its construction of a female, there-after they exist primarily in relationship to their role as agents of change. They make, thus, a dual assertion, that female lives are human artifacts subject to change and that the necessary changes result from women's actions. The acts of their own self-creation provide a test case for liberation of the sex.

What Stanton will seek in the last fifty years of her life, she explained in the narrative of youth. From her youthful discoveries, she will teach women to protect the basic principles of American government, to resist orthodoxy and tradition, to develop independent intel-lectual and scientific traditions, to build family life on a foundation of human dignity and equal rights, and to become self-reliant. Her definition of "personal" no longer connotes domestic or familial life but instead the life of herself while making history. The core of *Eighty Years,* nearly two hundred pages covering 1848 to 1880, describes the busiest years of her leadership. While the chapters parallel a history of suffragism, they dwell on feelings, on the personal side of the work, on the inessentials of travel—lost manuscripts, friendships, bad beds and worse food. They provide a portrait of the reformer. The story is organized into clusters of activity and people which are only loosely placed in a chronology. Susan B. Anthony is intro-duced in two chapters following the 1848 convention at Seneca Falls, which locates the start of their friend-ship at the right place, but the chapters exhaust the subject of their half-century collaboration. "Lyceums and Lecturers" places her debut on the commercial lecture platform at its proper point after the 1867 tour of Kansas but then compresses a dozen years of travel and public speaking into its twenty-three pages.

At the point when Stanton recedes from public view due to old age and a preference for writing her ideas rather than speaking them to countless audiences, the narrative shifts again. Time is neatly accounted for by the advent in 1880 of a diary from which she can recreate precise details, and a more sedentary life is reflected in the way that chapters are defined by the places she lived. According to the autobiog-raphy itself, on October 18, 1880, Stanton made the decision to keep a diary and began on her sixty-fifth birthday the next month (323-25). Immediately the text reflects her new source in its specificity and triviality. "On November 12, 1880 . . . it was a bright, sunny day. . . . My thoughts were with my absent children. . . . On November 13 the New York *Tribune* announced. . . . The arrival of Miss Anthony and Mrs. Gage, on November 20 . . ." (325-27). Blocks of time identified by where she was— Toulouse, London, Johnstown, New York—or a major event such as the International Council of Women or the reunion of Troy Seminary graduates divide the text into chapters rather than the themes that shaped her most active years. Here Stanton includes her recreational travels, her reform work in causes other than woman suffragism, and speeches that treat of subjects other than law and constitutionalism. There is something more intimate about these later sections than the more artful constructions of childhood or the historically aware record of campaigning for woman suffrage. This clever crafter of phrase and argument has allowed far more of the detritus of her daily life to fill the space she has allotted to the ongoing agitation of an elderly person.

Religion supplies a narrative thread through all the shifts that Stanton makes, in particular establishing continuity between the formative childhood and the sedentary old age. Anecdotes receive the gloss of religious polemic, as in her visit to the Mormons in 1871 which prompts the statement:

> When women understand that governments and religions are human inventions; that Bible, prayerbooks, catechisms, and encyclical letters are all emanations from the brain of man, they will no longer be oppressed by the injunctions that come to them with the divine authority of "Thus Saith the Lord." (285)

Or in explaining why she resided in a convent in Toulouse for a few months in 1883 she pauses to describe High Mass as "a most entertaining spectacular performance" that "belonged to the Dark Ages"; in sum, "the whole performance was hollow and mechanical" (346). By 1878 the account registers the systematic work "to rouse women to a realization of their degraded position in the Church" (383), including among many other avenues the project to issue the *Woman's Bible*. What seems a simple documentary device stemming from elderly pride, to include in this volume the address she wrote for a celebration of her eightieth birthday in the Metropolitan Opera House, carries the challenges further into her present time. In that address to a broad cross-section of organized, middle-class womanhood, she carefully explained why the battle with churches must be fought if women were to end their dependence. Self-reliance required it.

The principles that Duniway endorsed are not gathered for systematic presentation but rather insinuated throughout the political narrative. The principles underlying her opposition to prohibition dominate because of the immediate need to address an audience on the eve of voting whether to amend the state constitution to prohibit liquor. Liquor, she argues in her introduction, exists as one of the elements of the planet like air, fire, and water. Elements are not legislated out of existence. State power can never make man "safe from his own moral delinquency," short of imprisoning everyone. In this fight, she states, the same conflicts are at work as in the battle to secure equal rights: "the two contending elements of force and freedom." One prohibition is of a piece with the other (xvii-xviii).

In the many references to temperance that occur in the book, she carefully defines her abhorrence of intoxication and her knowledge of the damage it wreaks in the lives of men and women. In the highly compressed section on her childhood, she elects to tell of an uncle who "fell into evil ways" when drunk and then met death at the hands of ruffians (4-5). She admits to an early collaboration with the Temperance Alliance, a group committed to moral suasion, not legislation (62). Among the burdens of a mother she always includes the responsibility to raise sons who will not fall victim to drink. Her dispute is with the "temporary expedients" of "the politico-prohibition movement" (62-64). Sensing "fuel for their pulpits," preachers exploited both the cause and women. "Pettifogging politicians saw their opportunity and began to roar" (54). Women, tired of being "servants without wages," enjoyed earning their own money as lecturers for the cause (206). Morally bankrupt, this temperance movement undermined the cause of equal suffrage at three levels: by challenging the ideal of "moral and individual responsibility" which equal suffrage embodied (62); by positing "an arbitrary government over the inalienable rights of men, to which the average voter quite naturally objects" (106), that is, by alienating voters; and by giving rise to a well-financed, political force opposed to woman suffrage in the form of the liquor lobby.

The record of suffrage work after about 1883 becomes in large part a saga of disasters brought on by this powerful and misguided force. Against it Duniway can only utter the plea she made in a speech in the early seventies: "Make women *free!* Give them the power the ballot gives to you, and the control of their own earnings. . . . " The issue will then be settled at home and on the basis of human strength (63).

There are other principles and tactics that Duniway wants to explain. The use of "equal" rather than "woman" suffrage in her title underlines her opposition to a woman-centered movement based on sexual differences. Whole chapters hang together on the thin thread of political assertion. In the chapter called "Starts a Newspaper," she ostensibly recounts her decision to launch the *New Northwest* in 1872. It opens with explanations about how she and her sisters "had had no reason for hating men"; treats two episodes in which the men of her family came to her aid when hostility to woman suffrage took the form of personal attacks on her; makes the dubious claim that her powerful brother, newspaper editor Harvey W. Scott, was a loving and supportive friend; and then reminisces about businessmen and ministers whose assistance at critical moments made her work possible. This hodge-podge has a theme—the strategical assertion that the "one way by which we may hope to obtain [suffrage] . . . is by and through the affirmative votes of men" (156). It defined her as the antithesis of a newer suffragist who "demand[ed suffrage] as a whip, with which to scourge the real or apparent vices of the present voting classes" (163). Her audiences would recognize an attack on the franchise of moral superiority. The chapter entitled "First Anniversary Meeting," an event of 1872 in Oregon, leaps suddenly to Washington Territory in 1883 because there her tactics succeeded. After explaining why, in Oregon, she did not organize local societies as a basis for popular agitation on the question of suffrage, but before she explains how much criticism her quiet "still hunt" operations warranted over the years, she records how quietly one victory came.

In a sense the whole book works by a similar indirection. Her indignation with fools, her caustic remarks, and insistence on the superiority of her own solutions to troubling problems reveal more of her identity than the selection of details. The intensity of her political recollections as an elderly woman gives the best image of how deeply within the political cause she passed her active years. And the strenuous defense of self measures better than narrative could how deeply troubled she was by the antipathy of her enemies.

In both books, what seems a refusal or inability to construct an identity from the materials of private life may instead be an assertion about identity that would overcome the determining power of gender. Their individualities, indeed their identities, are tied up with how they worked both sides of the divide between politics and family. They portray themselves in new roles, lying between but combining traditional roles of women and men: mothers as lobbyists, wives as political campaigners, housewives as authors, or perhaps more accurately, lobbyists as mothers, and so forth. Duniway goes so far as to merge these outlines explicitly in terms of her three births: a natural one from her mother's womb, a rebirth as wife of Benjamin Duniway and mother to their children, and "my third and latest birth" into the struggle for woman's rights (28). But the best symbol for the middle way that Stanton and Duniway thought they occupied might be the World's Anti-Slavery Convention in 1840, or Stanton's honeymoon. Stanton always, whether writing her life or history, assigned formative experience to this event in the history of woman's rights. She was there not as a delegate but as a bride watching her husband's international debut. By featuring the convention as a major turning point in political history, Stanton assigned to her honeymoon a significance unique in historiography. How much more public can the private become?

Their literary identities made the claim that their new roles were humanly possible and politically desirable to attain. While they contested the debilitating structures grown up around gender differences, Stanton and Duniway had repositioned themselves outside the boundaries of female experience to which they were raised. Further they devoted their lives to destroying spheres both as the means to create a space for their own political work and as the objective for changing laws. The risk of writing about oneself as private, i.e., female, person was that of reinfusing meaning into categories they wanted to shatter. Their own lives had, in real time, continually exhibited new possibilities emergent from nineteenth-century politics and female experience. Thus autobiography should reflect life by insisting that the categories be altered. No preconceived notion of where the line between female selfhood and public discourse might be drawn can capture the dynamic and contested nature of that line in these lives.

Finally there may be miscalculation on their parts. The defining experiences of a woman's movement which required and enabled women to step beyond familial boundaries into public discourse had occurred long before either Stanton or Duniway wrote their books. As elderly, widowed grandmothers with full political careers behind them, they seemed to lose touch with the long-ago struggle to balance conflicting expectations and senses of self. They had made it through the rapids. Memory condensed into pride in their children who grew up amid the confusion. As a personal matter, that, it seemed, was what counted.

But the passage of time had not just dimmed their own recollections or rearranged the importance of life's stages. A period of history had passed. The pioneering work of organizing women's discontent and drawing the connections between personal experience and political power had been done. Whatever sense they had had of the political content in personal life had served its purpose well while they helped to cut the pathway from cookstove to legislative chambers. Two and three generations of women now trod that path, bumping into each other coming and going, tripping over each other's ideas and delusions. Putting their lives out to the service of leadership in 1898 and 1914 called for careful mapping of how this new political mass should move. Like many progressives of their time, they miscalculated the course of change and assumed that the mass of mobilized womanhood had arrived to stay on the political scene. They did not foresee that my generation would want to rediscover the process of awakening an age, that we would have a vital political interest in understanding how private and public lives collide, sometimes to overwhelm and isolate the individual woman and other times to uproot her to be released into collective and political action. Stanton and Duniway died thinking the world had changed.

Notes

[1] An excellent source on Duniway's life, and invaluable aid to my understanding of how her autobiography relates to her life, is Moynihan.

[2] For Stanton's life, I have relied principally on my own work as co-editor of the *Papers of Elizabeth Cady Stanton and Susan B. Anthony*. Readers could consult Lutz or Griffith. Griffith's work, however, confounds autobiographical constructions with objective reality.

[3] I have used the reprint of Duniway's second edition, issued in 1971, and a reprint of Stanton's *Eighty Years and More: Reminiscences, 1815-1897* of the same date. Citations to these texts appear as page numbers within parentheses.

[4] For a discussion of the opposition between two strains of woman's thought in the antebellum era, see DuBois.

[5] Manuscripts of most of the *Tribune* articles are within Stanton's papers at the Library of Congress.

[6] In an undated typescript called "Reminiscences," probably written about the same time that *Eighty Years* appeared, Stanton compresses events from a decade or more of her early life into a single chain of events and accuses her father of withholding a house in Boston for herself and her husband because she insisted on appearing before the New York State legislature. The reliability of this version is doubtful; every element of the story is erroneously dated; before she ever spoke to the legislature, her father had already given her the house at Seneca Falls. There is no way to know if she is nontheless closer to the truth about her own dependence or dramatizing the power of paternal wealth over daughters. (E. C. Stanton, "Reminiscences," in the Political Equality Club of Minneapolis Papers, Division of Archives/Manuscripts, Minnesota Historical Society.)

[7] Duniway is *less* exceptional among her siblings than Stanton, and thus denies more by avoiding the topic of how her family produced her.

[8] See, for example, coverage of the National American Woman Suffrage Association, 22d Annual Convention, in the *Washington Post,* February 19-22, 1890.

[9] Duniway died before Anna Howard Shaw laid claim to the imagery of the frontier in her own co-authored biography.

Works Cited

DuBois, Ellen C. "Politics and Culture in Women's History: A Symposium." *Feminist Studies,* 6 (Spring 1980), 28-36.

Duniway, Abigail Scott. *Path Breaking: An Autobiographical History of the Equal Suffrage Movement in Pacific Coast States.* Introduction by Eleanor Flexner. 1914; rpt. New York: Schocken Books, 1971.

Griffith, Elisabeth. *In Her Own Right: The Life of Elizabeth Cady Stanton.* New York: Oxford University Press, 1984.

Holland, Patricia, G. and Ann D. Gordon, eds. *Papers of Elizabeth Cady Stanton and Susan B. Anthony.* Microfilm ed. Wilmington, DE: Scholarly Resources Inc., 1990.

Lutz, Alma. *Created Equal: A Biography of Elizabeth Cady Stanton.* New York: John Day, 1940.

Moynihan, Ruth Barnes. *Rabel for Rights: Abigail Scott Duniway.* New Haven: Yale University Press, 1983.

Shaw, Anna Howard, with Elizabeth Jordan. *The Story of a Pioneer.* New York: Harper and Bros., 1915.

Stanton, Elizabeth Cady. *Eighty Years and More: Reminiscences, 1815-1897.* Introduction by Gail Parker. 1898; rpt. New York: Schocken Books, 1971.

Nadia Valman (essay date 1995)

SOURCE: "Speculating Upon Human Feeling: Evangelical Writing and Anglo-Jewish Women's Autobiography," in *The Uses of Autobiography*, edited by Julia Swindells, Taylor & Francis, 1995, pp. 98-109.

[*In the essay below, Valman considers the Evangelical Revival and argues that the publication of alleged autobiographies by Jewish women who had converted to Christianity was a means the Evangelicals used to attempt to convert Jews.*]

The two starting points for this paper are the Evangelical Revival of the late eighteenth and early nineteenth centuries and the publication of Sir Walter Scott's *Ivanhoe* in 1819. Following the enormous success of Scott's novel, and in particular his Jewish heroine Rebecca, there was a striking proliferation of fictive Jewesses in popular literature, and my particular interest here will be its conjunction in the mid nineteenth century with texts produced as a result of the Evangelical Revival. After the tradition of Shakespeare's Jessica and Marlowe's Abigail, the figure of the Jewess had always been noted for her eager willingness to renounce her own cultural heritage and embrace the dominant culture, and she now became the subject of a large number of evangelical tracts, narratives of conversion written in novel form. These novels, some historical and some contemporary in setting, were unremarkable to the extent that they were merely further reworkings of the formulaic evangelical story of the regeneration of the sinner for the edification of the unspecified reader. However, they also suggest a more particular context in that they coincided with a wide range of projects to convert English Jews to Protestant Christianity, a campaign which, as Mel Scult has shown in his study of conversionism in Britain, was spectacularly unsuccessful but no less spectacularly supported and invested-in by Victorian middle-class Evangelicals.[1]

This proliferation of activity produced a notable disproportion between the visibility of the Jew—and especially the Jewess—in the public sphere, and their visibility in literary discourse. Novel-readers and theatre-goers would have encountered many fictional versions of the Jew, most of them stereotypes, while conversionist societies, in particular the London Society for the Promotion of Christianity among the Jews, which sponsored nationwide meetings, lectures and publications on the subject, 'had little competition in molding attitudes and ideas about the Jews'.[2] Indeed, demographic statistics suggest that very few contemporary Britons would have ever actually encountered a Jew.[3] In 1756, a century after their readmission to England following the expulsion of 1290, the Jewish population was 8,000, rising to about 27,000 in 1828 and 40,000 in 1860, never more than 0.2 per cent of the population of Britain before the last third of the nineteenth century.[4] Only a very small number of British Jews achieved any kind of public status at this time, and even fewer were women. Thus the figure of the Jewess in literature is primarily a figment of discourse, produced by non-Jewish writers for non-Jewish readers, a figure of imagination, fantasy and desire.

And yet, surprisingly, the first published accounts of Jewish women written by themselves, and in their own voices, were produced within a few years of the publication of *Ivanhoe*. They are clearly products of the Evangelical literary boom, as they are all conversion narratives, stories of Jewish women who renounce family, religion and culture, and convert to Christianity. The first, *Sophia de Lissau, or, a Portraiture of the Jews of the Nineteenth Century: being an outline of the Religious and Domestic Habits of this most interesting nation, with explanatory notes,* was published anonymously in 1826. It turned very rapidly into a family saga, and was followed by the story of Sophia's

sister in *Emma de Lissau* (1828) and an account of the previous generation in *The Orphans of Lissau* (1830). These novels tell the history of a middle-class Jewish family of Polish origin living in England. The family is austere, disciplinarian and pharisaical, and is dominated by a strictly religious Jewish matriarch, Anna de Lissau, who rails against Christians, and England, and torments her daughter Emma mercilessly. The beautiful and pious Sophia, meanwhile, is hopelessly adored by her father's non-Jewish ward, Sydney, and resists his efforts to introduce her to Christianity. Instead she agrees to marry a Jewish man, convinced that his religiosity signifies virtue. However, his fanaticism hides violence and infidelity, and Sophia becomes resigned to suffering, desiring only consolation. She eventually dies a martyr's death, continuing to resist the conversion that would allow narrative closure. However, in the sequel, her sister Emma, encouraged by a female teacher, fulfils her sister's potential and converts.

Madame Brendlah's bizarrely titled *Tales of a Jewess, illustrating the domestic manners and customs of the Jews. Interspersed with original anecdotes of Napoleon* was published in 1838. This is also a conversion story, narrated in the third person, about Judith, Jewish daughter of an eclectic foreigner, a German physician brought up in 'profligate' *ancien régime* France, who changes his religion (to marry a Jewish wife) and his political allegiance after the revolution. Judith begins her assimilation to the Protestant environment at an English boarding school, starts to read the New Testament in secret, and quickly becomes convinced of its truth. She resists an arranged marriage, endures the emotional blackmail of her mother and the persecutions of a rabbi who lives in the household, and is eventually reunited with her Christian childhood sweetheart, with whom she elopes.

The third autobiography I will be considering, *Leila Ada, the Jewish Convert. An Authentic Memoir,* was first published by Leila Ada's editor, Osborn W. Trenery Heighway, in the 1840s and followed by a second and third edition in the 1850s and various offshoots, *Select Extracts from the Diary, Correspondence, etc., of Leila Ada* (1854) and *The Relatives of Leila Ada: with some account of the present persecutions of the Jews* (1856). These posthumously published accounts of a Jewish woman's journey towards Christianity are narrated '*verbatim et literatim*', in her own voice, which debates and struggles with itself in diaries and letters dating from her early teens.[5]

The texts somewhat strenuously stress their authenticity. Leila Ada's editor is anxious to reassure the reader of the purity of the narrative: 'we have everywhere carefully abstained from mixing the language of our own thinkings with the words of that excellent young person who is now with God'.[6] Madame Brendlah states explicitly in *Tales of a Jewess* that the information contained in her narrative is taken from real life:

> Let not the reader expect to find in the following pages, feigned stories, nor tales from the visions of fancy. What is related is mostly founded on facts. If the names of the individuals concerned are altered, it is because it would be unjust to her friends for the Authoress to expose the frailties incidental to human nature; nor would it be decent in her to hold up to ridicule the religious tenets of the Jews, however erroneous she may *now* consider them.

> The Authoress was born a Jewess.[7]

Indeed, details of the extraordinary autobiography outlined by Brendlah in her 'Introduction' bear close resemblance to the life-history of her heroine Judith. The author of the *de Lissau* novels is more coy. Following the heroine's failure to convert in *Sophia de Lissau,* the sequel introduces her sister Emma's story with a renewed stress on its veracity:

> In consequence of various letters and remarks, respecting 'Sophia,' from persons of the first respectability in England and Scotland, addressed to the Author, or communicated to her by her friends, which, though they conveyed a very flattering approbation of that work, yet expressed doubts of its *authenticity,* she thinks it necessary to offer a few brief remarks.

> When she first designed to offer to the public, a sketch of the domestic and religious peculiarities of a people, ever interesting to a reflective mind, and more especially so, to Christians, she found that the *mere* detail, would necessarily be dry and heavy reading. She therefore adopted, (as a vehicle to convey the necessary information,) events with which she was intimately connected, and could therefore detail, with fidelity and accuracy. Many persons have questioned the *truth* of these details. The Author *knows* them to be affecting realities.[8]

The writer argues here that the story was merely a vehicle for presenting information about Judaism, which was the primary purpose of the book. However, almost immediately she goes on to titillate the reader about the origin of the story and the real source of its authenticity:

> In the narrative of 'Emma', (as previously in that of 'Sophia',) dates and names are changed, and anachronisms purposely committed, for substantial reasons. Many events are wholly omitted, to have given *all* the Author *could* have detailed, would have extended the work to twice its present size. The Author has documents in her possession, to which no reference is made in the work, though connected with subjects not uninteresting.[9]

Henry Webb's 'Preface' to the second edition sees further need for reassurance: 'I have known the Author of Emma de Lissau for many years, and have good reasons for believing, that that, which she has written is true'.[10] In *The Orphans of Lissau,* published two years later, which relates the earlier family history of the de Lissaus, the author reveals that 'the following authentic narrative is extracted from the journals of a departed relative'.[11] The 'Recommendatory Preface' to a new edition of the same novel reprinted in the 1850s, however, blurs the distinction between biography and autobiography: 'Her touching and varied narratives are founded on direct information, or the closest personal observation. Some of them, though artificially constructed, describe, with as much precision as prudence dictates, the affecting history of her own conversations and subsequent trials'.[12] Indeed the structure of the author's own preface to *Emma de Lissau* suggests an identification between her sufferings and the sufferings of her heroine:

> Respecting the defective style of composition, visible in the Author's productions, she at once acknowledges it.—Her's [sic] are *native* abilities, if she possesses *any,*—Education has done little for her,—Her reading has been very confined,—added to which disadvantages, 'Emma de Lissau' has been written under much indisposition of body, heightened by the painful anxiety, connected with straitened temporal circumstances. She needs, therefore, the generous allowance of her Christian readers, and confidently believes she shall not be disappointed.

> The narrative closes at the period when Emma became an outcast for the truth's sake, prudential reasons render this needful. The trials of Emma since that period have been of a nature, the details of which, would injure the sacred cause, in the opinion of the world, and perhaps grieve and deter, weak converts among her nation.[13]

A similar gesture is made by Leila Ada's editor, whose oblique references to the persecutory power of Leila's family explain his reluctance to publish further work concerning her; the eventual publication of the book, under such circumstances, becomes additional evidence of its authenticity.[14] The idea of the book produced under stress is an important authenticating device: the respective introductions to the sequel to *Sophia de Lissau* and the subsequent volumes of Leila Ada's work argue that their continuing production is justified by public demand; they are not, they claim, novels written for profit, but on the contrary, narratives written in self-sacrifice for the sake of truth.

I will be suggesting several linked reasons why authenticity seems to be such a key concern for these writers. The first is to do with their cultural context. These texts register a puritan distrust of fiction; they must be considered not only as autobiographies, but as

Evangelical narratives. In drawing a line between her past self represented in the novel and her present self writing the novel, the author names her text as a confession. By publishing her own confession she hopes to multiply it, by revealing her own errors she hopes to illuminate others'. These texts are written not as a testimony of subjectivity, but as argument and evidence for universal truth, evidence which is strengthened by every addition to the genre. They are not about the search for a narrative of the self, but the submission of the self to an already-written narrative. Thus, I would suggest, these texts effectively write autobiography against itself, the individual voice dissolving easily into the universal story.

Yet, at the same time, the autobiographical form's capacity to privilege the individual voice has a particular significance for the Evangelical writer. As Jane Rendall writes, Evangelical theology stressed 'the possibility of salvation through the conversion and rebirth of the individual'.[15] This emphasis on individual consciousness also needs to be contextualized historically in the rise to dominance of Evangelicalism during the social changes of early-nineteenth-century Britain. Catherine Hall has shown how the Evangelical Revival coincided with the formation of the new industrial bourgeois class, and its ideology came to represent the changing consciousness of this class.[16] The theology of individualism also underlies the conservative political stance of the Evangelical movement, which, despite its campaign for the abolition of slavery at the beginning of the century, was not generally in favour of structural change through the redistribution of political power, but advocated reform from within: self-emancipation.[17] This resulted in a very particular understanding of the role of the individual within the nation: 'It was the religious consciousness of England, they argued, which determined her political condition'.[18]

I want to link this individualistic ideology with the form of the novels I have been discussing. Conversionist novels as a genre were produced by the Evangelical preference for self-emancipation through conversion, as opposed to political emancipation and social reform. If enlightenment is the responsibility of the individual not society, the Evangelical writer uses the novel form to underline this emphasis. Autobiography stresses interiority; revelation comes to the heroine of *Tales of a Jewess* in her locked room, in private, silent communion with the Word. Among her Jewish family she experiences 'an instinctive longing to be alone, again to open *that forbidden book,* which she could not overcome'.[19] Leila Ada's memoir embodies this privacy of faith in the self-communing of a private diary, 'a secret correspondence with her own heart'.[20] Her editor explains that 'writing was ever Leila's stronghold. Often when beset with sorrows she found a precious solace in this—partly because it engaged her thoughts; but especially because in it she found a channel for her

earnest feeling'.[21] Yet this exploration of subjectivity seems also to be denied in the search for truth: she resolves 'that I will live only to serve God and for the good of others. Never seek my own pleasure or satisfaction at the expense of that of any one else; but as far as possible I will forget that there is a self to please'.[22] The diary articulates contradictions: both selflessness and extreme introspection, objectivity and subjectivity, and although never intended for publication it somehow made its way into print.

The problem of these paradoxes leads me to what I consider the most important reason for the emphasis on authenticity in these texts—that they are fakes. The gender, religion, culture and life-story of the subjects of these autobiographies are in fact literary strategies. For despite the claims to provide secret insider knowledge, much of the information about Jewish customs in *Tales of a Jewess* and the *Leila Ada* texts is garbled and seems second-hand. There are also more general mistakes, like the claim by Leila's editor Trenery Heighway that her diary and correspondence had to be translated from Hebrew because Jews habitually communicated in that language.[23] Historically, this is wholly unlikely, though it was a commonly held opinion about the Jews. Stylistically, as well, there seems to be little development in 'Leila''s forms of literary self-expression between her early teenagerhood and her adulthood. The *de Lissau* novels, on the other hand, appear to be accurate in the information they offer. However, the anonymous author was in fact Amelia Bristow, later editor of *The Christian Lady's Friend and Family Repository,* one of several conversionist periodicals which devoted considerable attention to documenting and encouraging the conversion of Jews. Like Heighway's and Brendlah's texts, Bristow's narrative is formulaic, showing the awakening of a woman to Christianity through reading the New Testament, her persecution by her family, her inquisition by rabbis and finally her escape or death. Heighway's and Bristow's novels were all reprinted in the late 1850s by the Evangelical publisher Simpkin, Marshall and Co. as part of the 'Run and Read Library, consisting of tales uniting Taste, Humor, and Sound Principles, and written by competent Christian writers with a view to elevate the character of our popular fiction'. The *Jewish Chronicle,* British Jewry's official newspaper, considered the 'Leila Ada' books an obvious conversionist fraud: 'We immediately perceived, from unmistakable evidence, both internal and external, that the book was a fabrication, and as much the invention of the fertile imagination of the author as the innumerable other works of fiction'.[24] The newspaper noted with gleeful irony the successful prosecution of Heighway by his publisher in 1857 for attempting to sell the copyright to another fraudulent memoir, the profits of which were supposed to go to the 'diarist's' poor dependants. The proceedings were reprinted in full, so readers 'may judge of what stuff an author patronised by the conversionists is made, who panders to the morbid taste of a sickly religious public, and in how far credence is to be attached to productions which speculate upon human feelings as the devices of the swindler upon the purse of his neighbour'.[25] Pouring scorn on Heighway's disingenuous profit-making, the *Jewish Chronicle* also recognized that for a reader, Jewish or non-Jewish, without a considerable degree of knowledge and experience of Anglo-Jewish religious and social practice, there are few reasons to question the origins of these texts. This is primarily due to their extremely sophisticated authenticating mechanisms, which use all the apparatus of autobiography, its construction and analysis of subjectivity, and its foregrounding of questions about editorship and authority.

But if Jewish female subjectivity is not what is being explored in these texts, then what is? If we are going to treat these novels as highly self-conscious examples of the *use* of autobiography, how indeed are its features employed, and to what end?

Firstly I want to discuss the reasons why women's autobiography was used as a vehicle for the Evangelical project of the conversion of the Jews. This is a question to some extent of literary precedent. Literary representations of the Jewess had always emphasized her ambiguous, almost intermediate status, her assumed dissatisfaction and therefore less determined adherence to her hereditary religion and culture.[26] The Jewess' physical beauty was conventionally the route to her salvation as it could attract a Christian man who would save her. Thus the female Jew tended to be used to represent a belief in the Hebrews' perpetual potential for redemption and conformity, as opposed to their utter irredeemability and otherness, conventionally signified by the male. I would also suggest that it was the enormous popularity of Scott's *Ivanhoe,* showing a Jewish woman who defiantly refuses to convert, which prompted the subsequent proliferation of Evangelical books about zealously converting Jewesses.

However, I think there are more important political functions of using women's autobiography for this project. These writings appeared in the wake of the granting of political emancipation to Protestant Dissenters and Catholics, and during the campaign by British Jews, who were still barred from public office, the professions and the universities, for similar emancipation. The question of the place of Jews within the British polity was a highly public, contentious issue which struck at the heart of the Protestant and liberal identification of the British state.[27] On the other hand, the novels which I have been discussing frame Jewishness in a very different context; they tell of the lives of middle-class women, and their subject matter is correspondingly domestic. The stories centre around

family relationships, spiritual contemplation, moral reflection: the typical content of the bourgeois domestic novel. The space outside the domestic environment is random and uninterpretable in *Tales of a Jewess,* non-existent in *Sophia de Lissau,* and represented entirely in terms of religious allegory in the diary of Leila Ada (for example her long account of her travels across Europe to Palestine). For the female characters in these novels, being Jewish does not constitute a political identity in the terms of contemporary public debate: Jewishness is manifested entirely in the home, in domestic practices and domestic relations. Thus the autobiographical form's emphasis on interiority focuses the sphere of the domestic novel even further inward. In the diary of Leila Ada in particular, there appears to be no public self at all; Leila exists only through her communion with herself. Using women's autobiography necessitates a different kind of emphasis, determined by contemporary constructions of femininity and the female sphere, and this conjunction enables Evangelical discourse to produce a different account of Jewishness. This is not to say that such representations deliberately avoid reference to the more conventional narrative of the political and social persecution of the Jews. However, in all these novels it is the Jewish *woman* who suffers persecution, and this persecution never takes place outside the domestic sphere. Centring the Jewess in these texts crucially changes the political resonance of the figure of the Jew. The conversionist heroine is the victim not of the anti-semite but of her own family. Persecution is not an external phenomenon, a question of legal and social status, as it is for Scott's heroine Rebecca; instead it is domesticated. The displacement of the political by the personal through the use of autobiography in these Evangelical novels constitutes a significant silence around the relationship between Jews and anti-semitism in British history.

However, autobiography as a form is crucially modified in all these texts. Despite the elaborate devices of authentication, the autobiographical voice is implicitly admitted to be inadequate as a vehicle for information, which, as I showed earlier, Bristow claimed was her primary concern. The personal voice, its introspection lapsing into private language, creates gaps in comprehension which need to be filled for the reader. Cultural difference needs annotation—these texts are unable to sustain their dependence for authority on the individual female voice, and the 'truth' of testimony ultimately shows its limitations. This suggests that the focus in these texts is not only on the account of conversion. The narrators in fact seem as eager to fix their cultural 'origins' as to document the story of their personal development. For this purpose, paratextual commentary appears in all the novels, purporting to explain the arcane. This editorializing takes different forms; in the *de Lissau* series and *Tales of a Jewess* the story is accompanied by a series of scholarly notes which are set apart from the main narrative. In *Tales of a Jewess* the notes soberly and often lengthily debate details of Jewish thought, language and practice and stand in striking contrast to the rembling and irreverent text. Sometimes, however, the voices cross over each other, combining anthropology with judgment:

> The modern Jews are very religious, or rather superstitious, observers of the Sabbath. If a beast by accident fall into a ditch on this day, they do not take him out, as they formerly did, but only feed him there. They neither carry arms, nor gold, nor silver about them; nor are they permitted so much as to touch them. The very rubbing the dirt off their shoes, is a breach of the Sabbath; and their scruples go so far, as even to grant a truce to the fleas.[28]

There is a similar ambivalence in the *Leila Ada* books. Leila's words are introduced by an editor, then commented upon by him throughout, thus annotation is incorporated into the body of the narrative. Her own writings are also supplemented with the testimonies of others who knew her, and often, significantly, the voices of Leila and the editor appear to merge.

Cultural difference had been represented by this form before, notably in Maria Edgeworth's novel on Irishness, *Castle Rackrent* (1800), and Sydney Morgan's *The Wild Irish Girl* (1806), examples of the early-nineteenth-century female genre of the national tale which both use a double narrative structure. However, it is in the editorializing that an ambivalence about the functions of these texts always emerges. Ina Ferris sees the notes in *The Wild Irish Girl* as 'more than scholarly references; they are also political acts, at once vindicating and constructing Irish culture', and thus 'the authorial and narrative worlds in the end confound each other'.[29] Gary Kelly, on the other hand, argues that in *Castle Rackrent* the notes satirize the first-person narrative. In Edgeworth's novel the 'editorial apparatus repeatedly draws attention to the irrational, improvident nature of Irish popular culture, and emphasizes the "otherness" of this culture further by notes on Irish peculiarities of pronunciation and phrasing'.[30] This is precisely the effect in the conversionist texts. Kelly suggests that in *Castle Rackrent* 'the "editor" dominates the text as a whole while operating from its margins . . . and the mere narrative is continually interrupted, controlled, or supervised by the notes, which represent a literate and learned consciousness very different from that of the "illiterate" narrator'.[31]

I would argue that the notes are crucial in modifying autobiography in these texts, in regulating its meaning. Indeed the 'simple, lovely-spirited writings' of 'Leila Ada', who apparently never intentionally wrote for the public, need to be subjected to ventriloquization by a male, Christian editor.[32] Annotation defamiliarizes what autobiography has made familiar. At the same time,

the autobiographical voice defines the function of the notes, drawing their apparently neutral information into a conversionist teleology in which its significance cannot be misinterpreted. And yet, do not the notes also, to some extent, exceed this purpose, *vindicating* as well as constructing Jewishness as in *The Wild Irish Girl?* How useful are the categories of 'fake' and 'authentic'; does it actually matter that these texts are not, like Sydney Morgan's novel, expressions of an ideology of romantic nationalism or cultural preservation, but, on the contrary, written with the purpose of disparaging their subject and relegating it to ancient history?

My concern here is not, in the end, with which register is able to confer authority and regulate meaning. Rather it is with the effects of the difference and interaction between authoritative discourses within these texts. In the narrative of *Tales of a Jewess,* Jewishness is subject to ridicule and inevitable refutation. In the footnotes, which assume a sober, scholarly tone, Jewishness becomes a subject of knowledge. The Western 'Orientalist' production of the Orient through the creation of knowledge about it is replicated here in the codification of knowledge about Jews and Judaism. This was, as Edward Said has argued in his analysis of nineteenth-century Orientalism, an aspect of the power relationship between the Occident and its 'Other'.[33] As the Rev. John Wilson of the Free Church of Scotland's mission, Bombay, wrote in his 'Recommendatory Preface' to Amelia Bristow's novel about Polish Jewry, *The Orphans of Lissau,* 'the more that is known of their present tenets, feelings, observances, and religious and social customs, the more intense will be the interest that is felt in the work of their instruction and enlightenment'.[34]

Robin Gilmour writes of autobiography as paradigmatic for Victorian culture, an introspective version of the age's preoccupations with ancestry. genealogy, links between the present and the past:

> Holding the world together within, finding a coherence in the self which would at the same time impose some meaning and coherence on a rapidly changing world outside: this involved searching for the logic in one's own memories, which is the task of autobiography. The autobiographical pressure which is felt so strongly in Victorian writing of all kinds—fiction, poetry, literary criticism, theology—is an expression of the desire to make sense of an evolutionary universe by discovering evolution in one's own universe of memory.[35]

Describing Jewishness in the texts I have discussed in this paper is in a sense Christian culture searching for its roots, reclaiming its religious origins. Certainly one of the reasons for the new interest in Jews at this time was a return to the puritan tradition of English Protestantism, recognizing 'a kinship which drew inspiration from the Old Testament', regarding Jews not as Christ-killers but as Christ-bearers.[36] However, these texts suggest that for Victorian Evangelicals the production of an evolutionary autobiographical narrative involved identifying, defining and classifying the unfamiliar as well as the familial.

Notes

[1] Mel Scult (1978) *Millennial Expectations and Jewish Liberties: A Study of the Efforts to Convert the Jews in Britain, up to the Mid Nineteenth Century,* Leiden: E.J. Brill, Chapters 6 and 7. The conversion of the Jews was of particular importance to millenarian Evangelicals, who believed that it was necessary as a prelude to the Second Coming.

[2] Scult 1978, p. 126.

[3] For an account of literary representations of the Jew in the novel and the theatre from the seventeenth to the nineteenth century see Edgar Rosenberg (1960) *From Shylock to Svengali: Jewish Stereotypes in English Fiction,* London: Peter Owen.

[4] M. C. N. Salbstein (1982) *The Emancipation of the Jews in Britain: The Question of the Admission of the Jews to Parliament, 1828-1860.* Rutherford, Madison, Teaneck: Fairleigh Dickinson University Press; London and Toronto: Associated University Presses, p. 37.

[5] Osborn W. Trenery Heighway (1853) *Leila Ada, the Jewish Convert. An Authentic Memoir,* third edition, London: Partridge and Oakey, p. viii.

[6] *Ibid.,* p. 207.

[7] Madame Brendlah (1838) *Tales of a Jewess, illustrating the domestic manners and customs of the Jews. Interspersed with original anecdotes of Napoleon.* London: Simpkin, Marshall and Co., p. v.

[8] [Amelia Bristow] (1828) *Emma de Lissau; a Narrative of striking vicissitudes, and peculiar trials; with explanatory notes, Illustrative of the manners and customs of the Jews,* by the author of 'Sophia de Lissau', 'Elizabeth Allen', etc. etc., London: T. Gardiner and Son, pp. iii-iv.

[9] *Ibid.,* p. iv.

[10] [Amelia Bristow] (1829) *Emma de Lissau; a Narrative of Striking Vicissitudes, and peculiar trials: with Notes, illustrative of the manners and customs of the Jews,* by the author of 'Sophia de Lissau', 'Elizabeth Allen', etc. etc., second edition, London: T. Gardiner and Son, p. vi.

[11] [Amelia Bristow] (1830) *The Orphans of Lissau, and other interesting narratives, immediately concerned with Jewish customs, domestic and religious, with explanatory notes,* by the author of 'Sophia de Lissau', 'Emma de Lissau', etc., London: T. Gardiner and Son, p. 4.

[12] [Amelia Bristow] (n.d. [1859]) *The Orphans of Lissau, and other narratives,* by the author of 'Emma de Lissau', 'Sophia de Lissau', etc. etc., new edition, revised, London; Simpkin, Marshall and Co., p. x.

[13] [Bristow] 1828, pp. iv-v.

[14] Osborn W. Trenery Heighway (1854) *Select Extracts from the Diary, Correspondence, &c., of Leila Ada,* London: Partridge, Oakey and Co., pp. vi-vii.

[15] Jane Rendall (1985) *The Origins of Modern Feminism: Women in Britain, France and the United States 1780-1860,* Houndmills: Macmillan, p. 74.

[16] Catherine Hall (1979) 'The Early Formation of Victorian Domestic Ideology', in Sandra Burman (Ed.) *Fit Work for Women,* London; Croom Helm; Canberra: Australian National University Press, pp. 19-20.

[17] Paradoxically, many of the prominent campaigners in the parliamentary campaign for Jewish emancipation later in the century were Evangelicals. However, they were not advocating social reform for its own sake, but, they hoped, as an aid to eventual conversion. See Scult 1978.

[18] Hall 1979, p. 19.

[19] Brendlah 1838, p. 82.

[20] Heighway 1853, p. 7.

[21] Heighway 1854, p. 172.

[22] Heighway 1853, pp. 19-20.

[23] Heighway 1854, p. viii.

[24] 'A Pious Fraud', *Jewish Chronicle,* 15 January 1858, p. 35.

[25] *Ibid.*

[26] This is discussed at greater length in my forthcoming 'Gender and Jewishness in Nineteenth Century British Literature', unpublished PhD thesis, University of London.

[27] See David Feldman (1994) *Englishmen and Jews: Social Relations and Political Culture, 1840-1914,* New Haven: Yale University Press. For an account of the

continuing resonance of this debate in English literature see Bryan Cheyette (1993) *Construction of the Jew in English Literature and Society: Racial Representations 1875-1945,* Cambridge: Cambridge University Press.

[28] Brendlah 1838, p. 213.

[29] Ina Ferris (1991) *The Achievement of Literary Authority: Gender, History, and the Waverley Novels,* Ithaca and London: Cornell University Press, p. 126.

[30] Gary Kelly (1989) *English Fiction of the Romantic Period 1789-1830,* London and New York: Longman, p. 77.

[31] *Ibid.,* p. 78.

[32] Heighway 1854, p. v.

[33] See Edward Said (1991) *Orientalism: Western Conceptions of the Orient,* Harmondsworth: Penguin, 'Introduction'.

[34] [Bristow] n.d. [1859], p. ix.

[35] Robin Gilmour (1993) *The Victorian Period: The Intellectual and Cultural Context of English Literature 1830-1890,* London and New York: Longman, p. 27.

[36] Salbstein 1982, pp. 29-30.

AUTOBIOGRAPHIES BY WOMEN OF COLOR

Genaro Padilla (essay date 1990)

SOURCE: "'Yo Sola Aprendi': Mexican Women's Personal Narratives from Nineteenth-Century California," in *Revealing Lives: Autobiography, Biography, and Gender,* edited by Susan Groag Bell and Marilyn Yalom, State University of New York Press, 1990, pp. 115-29.

[*In the essay below, Padilla explores Mexican women's accounts of life in California before it became part of the United States.*]

> Desde muy niñita, ántes de venir de Mexico, me habían enseñado á leer. . . . Ya cuando era mujercita en California, yo sola aprendí á escribir, valiéndome para ello de los libros que veía— imitaba las letras en cualquier papel que lograba conseguir—tales como cajillas de cigarros vacias, ó cualquier papel blanco que hallaba tirado. Así logré aprender bastante para hacerme entender por escrito cuando necesitaba algo.
>
> (Lorenzana, p. 5)

[When I was a very young girl, before coming from Mexico, I had been taught to read. . . . And so when I was a young woman in California, encouraged by the books I saw, I taught myself to write by copying letters of the alphabet on any piece of paper I could find—such as empty cigarette packets, or any blank sheet of paper I found discarded. In that manner I learned enough to make myself understood in writing when I needed something.]

So Apolinaria Lorenzana remarks in her "Memorias de la Beata" (1878),[1] the account of her life as a nurse and teacher in the mission system of early nineteenth-century California. Doña Lorenzana was one of some forty women whose lives were recorded during the 1870s when Hubert H. Bancroft was collecting personal testimony for his work on California history. She was in her late seventies at the time she collaborated on her "Memorias," feeble in body and therefore discouraged because she felt like a burden to the people around her: poor, dispossessed of large tracts of land she had acquired independently during a lifetime of work and service, completely blind. The world she had known was receding into a past as unrecoverable as her sight. Still, during the late winter of 1878 she was scrawling her mark upon history—I say scrawling because at the end of the narrative, transcribed by Thomas Savage, she literally sealed her life on the last page in a nearly illegible marking of her initials. For an old woman who had lost almost everything, this act of will signified a final utterance of personal identity.

In the 1870s Hubert Howe Bancroft, book-dealer, document collector, and professional historian, solicited scores of personal oral testimonies by "Californios," as the native Hispano-Mexicanos called themselves. These narratives undergird his massive *History of California,* published between 1884 and 1889 in seven volumes, as well as *Pastoral California* (1888), a rather ethnocentric[2] and romanticized history of pre-American California society. As Bancroft himself wrote of the project in *Literary Industries,* he and his field assistants collected some "two hundred volumes of original narrative from memory by as many early Californians, native and pioneers, written by themselves or taken down from their lips . . . the vivid narratives of their experiences."[3] There are, from my count, some 150 Hispano personal narratives, of lengths varying from ten pages to a fair number that are hundreds of pages long. I must confess not only my sense of wonder, but my sense of resurrective power at discovering Bancroft's storehouse of California lives; here are scores of disembodied voices, textualized lives stored away for a time when they might be rescued from obscurity: María Inocente Avila, "Cosas de California"; Juan Bernal, "Memoria de un Californio"; Josefa Carrillo de Fitch, "Narración de una Californiana"; Rafael González, "Experiencias de un soldado"; Pío Pico,

"Narración histórico"; Vincente Sánchez, "Cartas de un Angelino"; Felipa Osuna de Marron, "Recuerdos del pasado"; Pablo Vejar, "Recuerdos de un viejo."

These personal narratives provide a broad field of information on Hispano-Mexicano life before and immediately after the loss of California and much of northern Mexico to the United States in the war of 1846-1848.[4] Given the kind of information Bancroft wished to elicit, the narratives generally describe the significant historical, political, and social events of the day; manners, customs, and education; the social economy, and early relations with the native Indian people and the American immigrants. In the act of testimonial compliance, many of the narrators present a picture of an idyllic pre-American California. Nostalgia is especially conspicuous in the recollections of the social elite; however, even those narratives left by members of the lower classes, men who were soldiers and women who worked in the mission system, produce an image of a generally stable, self-sufficient society—at least before the American invasion and subsequent social transformation. The nostalgic tendency of the narratives must be understood, it seems to me, as a direct result of sociocultural loss, especially since almost all are characterized by a general sense of malaise, evident in those narrative stretches that describe political, economic, and cultural rupture. Nostalgia and attendant bitterness is actually the product of testimonial compliance, in which the recollected past is always at counterpoint with the present.

It is the disjuncture between a valorized pre-American life and the profound sense of loss after the invasion which provided the autobiographical moment when past and present could be reconsidered, conjoined, reconciled to some degree. Whereas for Bancroft the collection of these personal narratives was foundational research for his *History of California* project, for the narrators themselves it was the critical and perhaps only occasion for recreating the life of the self, together with the world inhabited by that self. The reconstitution of pre-American society was less an escapist activity than a strategy, only vaguely conscious of its means for sustaining order, sanity, and purpose in the face of economic and political dispossession, spiritual fragmentation, sadness, and longing. An established way of life was disintegrating, being rubbed out, erased—even at the moment the life was being narrated, transcribed, textualized.

I read these narratives as legitimate autobiographical enunciations, by individuals whose voices have not been merely forgotten but, like the people themselves, suppressed. Rather than affixing a degree of historical truth-value to their testimony or arguing the merits of their representativeness of Hispano-Mexicano culture, my primary concern is to recover the voices of these ghosts. They make their own claim to resurrection simply because, within the confines of oral testimony meant to subordinate their stories to Bancroft's history, these women and men marked their narratives with well-defined personalities. The narratives bequeathed by these individuals may have been used by Bancroft as social history, but it is the ever-present "I" that transforms them from oral history proper into the genre of life-writing we call autobiography. The subtle disclosure of individual experience and the overlay of individual personality upon the description of external sociopolitical realities, as well as the individuating of external events, mark these narratives with distinct autobiographical authority.

As one might expect, of the one hundred and fifty California narratives in the Bancroft collection, fewer than forty are by women. When Bancroft was collecting personal narratives, men who held public office, military officials, soldiers, or traders were called upon to record their *recuerdos* more often than were women. Women's narratives, moreover, were considered either supplemental to the men's or as sources of information for what Bancroft referred to as the "woman's sphere."[5]

Typical of men's autobiographies in general, the men's narratives reconstruct the powerful public identities the Californio patriarchs enjoyed before they lost everything to the Americans. Juan Bautista Alvarado, Pío Pico, Antonio Coronel, Mariano and Salvador Vallejo, and Manuel Castro, along with scores of other once prominent Californios, collaborated on narratives that reconstituted the period from the late eighteenth to the mid-nineteenth century, an era during which they ruled over a vast expanse of geography, native people, as well as their own families. For example, one of the wealthiest and most influential of these patriarchs was Mariano G. Vallejo, whose "Recuerdos históricos y personales tocante a la álta California" (1875) comprise nearly one thousand manuscript pages of personal, familial, social and cultural history.[6] Aristocratic, socially elitist, manipulative and exploitative, these men made for themselves and their families a world predicated upon their unquestioned authority as fathers and husbands.

In such a patriarchal world, male authority is seen as giving purpose and coherence to the family as well as to the larger social community. Respect for, obedience to, honor of, and deference toward the Patriarch were, for Vallejo, signs of familial and general social well-being before the Americanization; after the displacement of the Patriarch, the children fell away from a well-established code of behavior, and the Californio world collapsed upon itself. Once, young men greeted their fathers in the street with respectful address. Young women, once proud of their ability to administer domestic affairs, were in the 1870s interested—according to Vallejo—only in making an impression at the theater and at dances; Vallejo calls them "muñecas incapaces de dirigir el manejo de sus casas" [dolls/ fashionable mannequins incapable of directing the management of their homes]. As he recalls, there were, after the conquest, more "solteronas" [old maids] than ever because men were reluctant to marry, afraid that they would be ruined and dishonored by "mujeres necias y vanidosas" [foolish and vain women] (V.4:336-37).

If for men like Vallejo the good old days of patriarchal authority evoke memories of harmonious filial, martial, and social relations, the women's personal narratives provide a markedly different scenario, especially of personal, communal, and gender-related experience. While there is a general affirmation of the Californio way of life, there is also a tendency to expose the constraints placed upon women within the patriarchy. Many of the narratives were composed by women from prominent families whose reminiscences were recorded primarily because of their relationship to certain influential men; yet, although the women may begin their *memorias* speaking about their husbands, fathers, or brothers, almost invariably the men get lost in the narratives. A few of the most memorable were left by working women who claimed for themselves independence and self-sufficiency; men are absent nearly altogether from these stories. My reading suggests that the California women manipulated the interview process whenever they could in order to comment upon gender-related issues, be it tense relations with parents, especially fathers, or with husbands and the patriarchal system in general. In being asked to remember their lives vis-à-vis men, women often subverted the transcription process in order to mark the narratives with their own distinctly gendered autographs.

Aside from the accounts of political intrigues, revolts against various Mexican officials, and the war with the United States that Bancroft wished to elicit from all his informants, from the women he especially wanted "information on manners and customs of the Californians." He prodded the women to remember social events, their favorite dances and songs, their marriages, children's births—in short, their domestic lives as diminutive reflections of the lives of Hispano men. This directive, ironically, meant that memory was pointed back towards women's activities. Providing basic information on the "woman's sphere" created a space in which a woman could remember *herself* and reconstitute her own life. Whenever topical testimony directed by the interviewer gave way to personally significant reminiscence, the narrative became genuinely autobiographical. This point of convergence between obligatory testimony and a consciously individuated narrative is also often marked by feminine affiliations—women remember themselves in relation to other women. In each of the narratives I have read, then, a distinct female identity emerges that will not be dismissed.

María de las Angustias de la Guerra's *Ocurrencias en California* (1878) offers a lively account of political intrigues and upperclass relations in pre-American Santa Barbara. Much of the narrative records the revolts against the various governors appointed from Mexico City, the pirate Bouchard's raid on Monterey when she was a girl, social balls and comical scandals, and memories of her politically influential father and brothers. As a representative of the Mexican landholding class and a member of one of the leading California families, Angustias de la Guerra generally ratifies patriarchal concerns over land, wealth, political and social status. This is as one might expect, since in reaffirming male class prerogatives, she is reaffirming her own privilege. Yet, Angustias de la Guerra is also scathingly critical of the men in power.

When referring to the early incursions of American "adventurers" surveying California, for example, she seizes the moment to issue an unexpected but sustained critique of the Hispano men's handling of the American threat. Referring to events early in the 1840s, she says that it was obvious, at least to the women, that the Americans in the territory were up to no good. When she and other women make their suspicions about a certain Charles Gillespie known to Manuel Castro, a commanding officer, they are chastised. "Castro told us that we were thinking ill of an invalid gentleman, accusing all the women in general of thinking ill of others, much more than the men. We answered that almost always we more often hit the mark" (de la Guerra, pp. 140-141). As it turned out, Gillespie was an American agent who was instrumental in staging the Bear Flag uprising in Sonoma (June 6, 1846) that led to open warfare between Mexico and the United States.

In a related part of the narrative, she charges that "when the hour came to defend the country against foreign invasion" the military command "performed no more service than the figurehead of a ship." Her sarcastic remarks about the officers are counterpointed by the dramatization of her own part in the struggle against the Americans. She describes an incident (1846) in which a *mexicano,* José Antonio Chavez, who was fleeing for his life from the American troops, was concealed in her home at a time when her husband was away. Although the Americans invade her home, rouse her out of bed—one even points a gun at her—she does not flinch in her resolve to hide Chavez, who is lying under a pile of blankets upon which her infant Carolina is sleeping. In fact, in de la Guerra's account it is women alone who are the main saboteurs: María de la Torre, a neighbor; Manuela and Carolina, her daughters; and various maids are all complicit in the concealment of Chavez. Finally, de la Guerra rather casually mentions that she accomplished all of this after "having given birth to a baby girl a few days before"—this at a time when women were confined to bed for up to forty days after delivery.

*An Old Woman
and
Her Recollections*

Dictated by Doña Eulalia Pérez
who lives at the San Gabriel Mission,
at the advanced age of 139 years

Thomas Savage, for the
Bancroft Library
1877

Title Page for An Old Woman and Her Recollections, *dictated by
Doña Eulalia Pérez.*

The preceding Chavez account, together with her criticism of certain other elements of the patriarchy, constitute enunciations that mark the narrative with her own name and feminine identity, not those of either of her husbands. Nor is her distinctive personality lost in the *a posteriori* versions produced by her male editors. Thomas Savage's introductory notes to the narrative he transcribed, as well as those to the 1956 published translation of her memoirs, all but bury her under the weight of men's names and position. Savage wrote: "Mrs. Ord (née Angustias de la Guerra, and whose first husband was Don Manuel Jimeno Casarín, Secretary of State, Senior member of the Assembly, and several times Governor pro tem, of Cal. & c) is well known as a lady of intelligence. . . . " (de la Guerra, p. 1). The editors of the English translation added: "The historical manuscript, Ord (Angustias de la Guerra), *Ocurrencias en California* was related to Thomas Savage by Mrs. Dr. James L. Ord for the Hubert Howe Bancroft Collection of 1878" (Foreword). María de las Angustias de la Guerra survives only parenthetically in these introductory notes, as well as in much of the solicited narrative, precisely because it was "her connections and position," as Savage noted, that "enabled her to inform herself upon Government affairs"—connections and position vis-à-

vis influential men. Yet, in the entire narrative there is no mention at all of her husband Dr. James L. Ord and only passing remarks on Don Manuel Jimeno Casarín.

Another narrative in which a woman stakes her claim to personal identity other than that of a wife is Eulalia Perez's "Una Vieja y Sus Recuerdos," the acronical story of a woman reputedly 139 years of age when she relates her life as "partera" [mid-wife], "cocinera principal" [head cook], and "llavera" [keeper of the keys], as well as "dueña" [supervisor] of various shops at San Gabriel Mission during the first half of the nineteenth century. In recollecting her life history she reenacts the self-empowering process whereby she, some seventy years earlier, appropriated levels of responsibility within the mission system that, as she makes quite clear in her recollections, granted her authority over numerous men. What presumably begins, for the interviewer at least, as a narrative from which information about the operations of the mission system could be elicited, ends up as a story of a woman, alone with five children, who brought the male-dominated world into conjunction with her own will to be self-sufficient.

Like de la Guerra, her immediate autobiographical utterance is an act of toponymic self-identification: "Yo Eulalia Perez, nacé en el presidio de Loreto en la Baja California. . . . " of her two husbands' names—neither "Guillen" nor "Mariné"—are noted here or anywhere else in her narrative, except where she concedes her brief marital phases with them; not being present in the text, theirs are names without substance. Eulalia Perez's reappropriation of her given name thus constitutes an act of deliberate self-possession, the willing into textual permanence of her own personal existence. It is as though women like Angustias de la Guerra and Eulalia Perez realized that their identities were in danger of being submerged and even effaced by the men to whom they were related and by whom they were censored. Their response to the threat of obscurity was to seize the opportunity provided by the Bancroft oral history project to reconstitute their own lives. There are strikingly discernible moments in each of the narratives when, in the process of reciting the customs and manners Bancroft wanted to record, they rediscover areas of long evaporated personal experience.

Eulalia Perez's location of a distinct identity outside relationships with husbands points to a particularly critical issue in many of the women's narratives. In a word, they reveal no little resentment about marriage expectations. The entire arrangement, from betrothal at an early age to the actual wedding ceremony, was effected almost exclusively between the fathers. The tradition of marrying girls at a young age—between thirteen and fifteen—was a practice that appears especially vexing in many of the women's narratives and is remembered with some bitterness when other momentous life experiences seem forgotten.

María Inocente Pico de Avila, a member of the wealthy and influential Pico family in Los Angeles, defers to her husband's life early in her narrative—"Cosas de California" (1876)—commenting upon his family genealogy, education, military career, and resistance to the American forces. But when remembering their marriage, she suddenly recalls that like other girls she was only beginning to read, write and do arithmetic when taken from school to begin preparation for her *primary* role in life as a wife. As Avila remembers:

> Muchas niñas no concluían ni esos pocos estudios, porque las quitaban sus madres de la escuela casi siempre para casarlas, porque había la mala costumbre de casar á las niñas muy jovencitas, cuando la pedían. Yo estuve en la escuela solo hasta los 14 años; después me llevó mi madre al rancho para enseñarme a trabajar, y a los 15 años y ocho meses me casé. (Pico de Avila, p. 20)

> [Many girls never even finished these few studies, because their mothers nearly always took them from school to marry them off, because there was the bad custom of marrying girls very young, when they were called for. I only stayed in school until my fourteenth year; then my mother took me to the ranch to prepare me to work, and at 15 years and 8 months of age I was married.]

In the men's narratives, as one might expect, the primacy of marriage and the shaping of domestic consciousness in women is regarded as central to the maintenance of social order. In his "Notas históricas sobre California" (1874), Salvador Vallejo, brother of Mariano, remembers, "we [the patriarchs, of course, with mothers as the enforcers of male dictates] taught our girls to be good housewives in every branch of their business; our wives and daughters superintended the cooking and every other operation performed in the house, the result of the training was cleanliness, good living and economy" (S. Vallejo, p. 99). The women's narratives expose such domestic training and early marriage as forms of sexual coercion and social control. Avila's forceful denunciation of "la mala costumbre de casar a las niñas muy jovencitas" ("mala" here signifying "hateful," "callous," "malign" even "evil") is decisively anti-patriarchal. The autobiographical enunciations of the California women, almost without exception, show that they were conscious of the socio-sexual function of early marriage, or marriage at any age, for that matter. For women like Avila, having their schooling abruptly terminated, or being denied a lettered education altogether because of gender, meant having a vital part of the self closed off, stunted.

There were women, of course, who refused to be stunted. Apolinaria Lorenzana, to whom I now return, was one such woman. She had come to Monterey, California, with her mother and a group of orphaned children before she was seven. Lorenzana remembers that the children were distributed among families "como perritos" [like puppies], while she remained with her mother and various other women. Many of the older girls soon married, including her mother, who returned to Mexico with her soldier husband and died soon thereafter. Over a period of seven years, like the other "perritos," she was passed between several families, mostly in soldiers' homes. It was during this period, when she was about fourteen, that she taught herself to write on scraps of paper.

Lorenzana looks back to this moment as the beginning of her independent life as a nurse and teacher. She not only proudly describes how she taught herself to write, but how she shared her knowledge with other young women who were eager to learn in a society that discouraged women's intellectual development. But, as she points out, she did not exclude boys from her lessons: "I taught children of either sex to read at the request of their parents" (MS: 42).

As for marriage, Apolinaria Lorenzana simply chose not to. Nowhere in her narrative does she express the least regret that she had no husband or children, never does she complain of having been lonely. On the contrary, she was highly regarded as a result of her teaching and general care of children, enough so that she had nearly two hundred godchildren, an honor bestowed much more typically upon men, especially *ricos,* than women, especially *solteronas.* As for not taking a husband, she has this to say:

> When I was a girl, there was a young man who often entreated me to marry him. But I did not feel inclined toward matrimony (knowing full well the requirements of that holy institution), and so I refused his offer. He then told me that since I wouldn't marry him, he was leaving for Mexico. So he left. (Lorenzana, p. 43)

Lorenzana says no more about the matter. She does, however, have a great deal to say about her work; in fact, much like Eulalia Perez, whom she knew well, she exults in describing various responsibilities in the mission chain. She remembers overland journeys along the coast of the mission. She vividly relates a story told by Doña María de los Angeles, a woman in her care, about an Indian revolt in which her husband was killed and her children kidnapped. Lorenzana's account of this mother's grief is moving: "The miserable mother neither spoke nor cried, for the anguish had crushed her. I tried to console her, and encouraged her to eat, but she was inconsolable . . . and for the rest of her life she suffered terribly, without cheer—at last she died under the weight of her grief" (Lorenzana, p. 41).

One notices here and throughout the "Memorias" just how much Lorenzana's narrative is women-centered. She gives substance to women, making their desire to learn, their illnesses, and their griefs real and memorable. Lorenzana often maintained contact with women from their infancy to adulthood through multiple generations; for instance, she recalls: "I had in my charge, caring for her from the time she was two or three years old, a girl, whose mother was my goddaughter in both baptism and marriage and for whose three children I was also godmother. At any rate, that girl, who was my first charge, I taught to read, pray, sew, among other things, and when the time came she married and is now the mother of her own family" (Lorenzana, p. 43).

In her late seventies Lorenzana still retains a strong sense of respect from the California community. As Thomas Savage points out in his prefatory remarks to the transcription, "many of the native Californians of both sexes spoke of her in the highest terms of praise . . . as la Beata (the pious)." Yet, there is also a sense of pained resignation at the end of her life. In her own words: "aquí me hallo pobre y desvalida, con escasa salud" [Here I find myself poor and destitute, my health broken]. Her anguish, however, is not merely the result of age, blindness, and infirmity, for as Savage mentions she "appears to be a good old soul, cheerful," but rather because like many Californios—both women and men—she felt displaced, and hence confused, embittered, resentful toward a nation that had made her a stranger in her own land. Remember, here was a woman who was not only psychologically and socially independent, but economically independent as well.

During the many years she worked in the mission, she acquired three separate ranches of her own. Two of these were granted to her by the government, a privilege that was almost never extended to women. The other, situated between the two, she purchased outright. Although Savage notes that she "was loath to speak on this subject, assuring me that she didn't want even to think of it" (Preface), she does say enough to convey a strong sense of proprietary interest in her land; she never intended to sell it and is quite clear about the fact that she was swindled out of it, although like many other *mexicanos,* she is not sure precisely how. It is at this point in the narrative, startled by a twenty-five-year-old nightmare, that she says:

> Es una história larga y no quiero ni hablar de ella. Los otros dos ranchos me los quitáron de algun modo. Así es que después de haber trabajado tantos años, de haber poseído bienes, de que no me desposeí por vento ni de otro modo, me encuentro de la mayor pobreza, viviendo de favor de Dios y de los que me dan un bocado de comer. (Lorenzana, p. 30)

> [It is a long story and I don't even want to discuss it. The other two ranches they somehow took from me. So, that's the way it turns out that after working so many years, after having acquired an estate, which I certainly didn't dispose of by selling or any other means, here I find myself in the greatest poverty, living only by the grace of God and through the charity of those who give me a mouthful to eat.]

Lorenzana discloses no self-pity over her decrepit condition, her loss of sight, nor even her poverty. Evidence of dispiritedness takes the form of sociocultural displacement, present in a majority of the California narratives—in both the women's and the men's. Like nearly all the Californios of her generation, she found herself in the 1870s not only near the end of her life, but at the end of a way of life. With anger and pain apparent in her words, Apolinaria Lorenzana literally inscribes her initials on the final page of her "Memorias" not only as a hedge against her own death, but also, it seems to me, as a gesture of defiance against a form of historical and cultural death.

The women's narratives remind us of just how tenuous existence was in post-1848 society for a people trying to give purpose to the personal life during a time of immense social, political, and cultural upheaval. Life in a stable social world was difficult enough for women. Their narratives make this plain. But what they also make plain is that the American takeover was a trauma that disrupted life for everyone. Bitterness, a profound sense of loss, confusion, and displacement color the women's personal narratives fully as much as the men's. As Lorenzana said over one hundred years ago, the way *mexicanos* in the latter part of the nineteenth century were dispossessed of their land, livelihood, often their dignity and their very voice constitutes a long and troubling story.

Some of the women were so deeply embittered by the events of 1846 that when asked to comment on the war they spoke through clenched teeth. Rosalia Vallejo de Leese, sister to Mariano and Salvador Vallejo, was still so angry three decades after the war that she refused to give more than a brief narrative; what she does remember of the Bear Flag incident of 1846 ends in these words: "those hated men inspired me with such a large dose of hate against their race, that though twenty-eight years have elapsed since that time, I have not yet forgotten the insults they heaped upon me, and not being desirous of coming in contact with them I have abstained from learning their language."[7] She also forbade her children to speak the language of *los estranjeros* in her presence.

Yes, I know, her words here are presented in English, the language of the enemy, but not of her choice, or mine. The document itself was, for some strange reason, transcribed into English even though most of the

California narratives were given and remain in their native Spanish.[8] Even those few texts that have recently been translated will require careful re-reading, since there is evidence of frequent mistranslation. I raise this issue here because it is directly gender-related. To elaborate: Angustias de la Guerra's narrative, one of the handful that have been published in English translation, gives the impression at a crucial juncture that women were not troubled by the American occupation. This happens in Francis Price and William Ellison's translation *Occurrences in California* (1956), where de la Guerra is *made* to say that "the conquest of California did not bother the Californians, least of all the women" (59); what she *did* say was "la toma del país no nos gustó nada á los Californios, y menos á las mujeres"—which should be translated as "the taking of the country did not please the Californios one bit, and least of all the women." Contrary to the mistranslation (was it a willed misreading that made for the mistranslation?) of her comments, de la Guerra's *Ocurrencias* must be read as oppositional narrative. In other words, her narrative as well as those of other California women articulate the fact that they did not welcome the Americans.

Although Bancroft solicited women's personal narratives in order to provide general information on the collective "woman's sphere," the women made the testimonies individually self-reflexive. In each of the narratives I have discussed, a substantive individual identity emerges that warrants autobiographical legitimacy. Apolinaria Lorenzana is distinct from Angustias de la Guerra because both constitute themselves distinctly. Moreover, their narrative lives are contextualized by the sociocultural and gender-related moment that contributed to their historical identities. In that respect, the narratives must be seen as the products of a dialectical process. Since they were collected by men who represented the occupying culture, it is reasonable to assume that Mexican women were engaged in a power struggle within the very interview process. Angustias de la Guerra was sought out for interview because she was related to influential men through whom she had apparently informed "herself upon governmental affairs"; yet by the end of her testimony she had appropriated the narrative process for inscribing her own life. And although at the moment of narration she was "Mrs. Dr. James L. Ord," she did not ratify the American occupation, as perhaps the interviewer had expected. Eulalia Perez was surely approached for interview because she was a curiosity—a woman of 139 years, according to local history; yet she did not relate her life story as a wonder of longevity, but as a story of self-reliance.[9] In each of these narratives there is evidence of evasion, redirection of the past, and reconstitution of a "self" that proceeds beyond interrogatory expectations.

As for the dialectic of gender present in the narratives, while it would be inaccurate to make a gener-

alizing claim that women's narratives roundly criticize the Hispano patriarchal system, they do question masculinist controls within a culture that placed constraints upon their intellectual development, excluded them from the networks of sociopolitical hierarchy, and sought to domesticate their desire for self-sufficiency. Hence, intra-cultural and gender-related commentary of a critical bent is more manifest in the women's narratives than in the men's, where patriarchal customs are self-servingly remembered. Again and again one reads narratives by women who were articulate, intellectually inquisitive, "self"-conscious, and undoubtedly capable of fully independent lives, as demonstrated by Eulalia Perez and Apolinaria Lorenzana.

Patriarchal and testimonial forms of containment, in fact, often provided the impulse to reconstruct individual identity and personal experience in a genuinely self-empowering manner. Angustias de la Guerra reconstructs her own heroism against the insolent *americano* soldiers, and thereby levels a critique at the Californio men; Eulalia Perez marks her consciously planned appropriation of authority in an otherwise male domain; Maria Inocente Pico gives tribute to her husband, but also remembers being yanked out of school to undergo domestic "training" for him; Apolinaria Lorenzana recreates her life not only as nurse and teacher, but as property owner who had to contend with swindling Americans. In each of the narratives women push beyond testimonial expectations to discover or invent the narrative space required for reconsidering their lives within a male-controlled domain, for reassessing the social transformation that affected them as much as their male counterparts, and, ultimately, for celebrating their own lives.

Notes

[1] This and each of the personal narratives to which I refer is housed in the Bancroft Library, University of California, Berkeley. Unless otherwise indicated, references to the manuscripts will be cited by manuscript page (e.g., Lorenzana, p. 5) within the essay. All translations are mine, except those specified in the text.

[2] Bancroft's opening comments in *California Pastoral* (San Francisco, CA: The History Co., 1888) should suffice to make my point here: "Before penetrating into the mysteries of our modern lotus-land, or entering upon a description of the golden age of California, if indeed any age characterized by ignorance and laziness can be called golden. . . . " (p. 1). The text, comprising some 800 pages of ethnographic information on Mexican society before and shortly after 1848, is saturated by this form of ethnocentric consciousness.

[3] *Literary Industries: A Memoir* (San Francisco, CA: The History Co., 1891), p. 285. It should be pointed

out that Bancroft hired numerous assistants to collect the personal narratives. Enrique Cerruti and Thomas Savage were two of the principle collectors who, during a six-year period from 1863-1870, traveled a wide circuit from San Francisco to San Diego transcribing the lives of the Californios. See Savage's "Report on Labors and Archives and Procuring Material for the History of California, 1876-79," and Cerruti's more autobiographical "Ramblings in California" (1874), both in the Manuscript Collection, Bancroft Library, University of California, Berkeley.

[4] For useful accounts of the Mexican-American War, as well as the social, political, and cultural transformations that resulted, see: Rodolfo Acuna, *Occupied America: A History of Chicanos* (New York, NY: Harper & Row, 1981); Albert Camarillo, *Chicanos in a Changing Society: From Mexican Pueblos to American Barrios in Santa Barbara and Southern California, 1848-1930* (Cambridge, MA: Harvard University Press, 1979); Richard Griswold del Castillo, *The Los Angeles Barrio, 1850-1890: A Social History* (Berkeley, CA: University of California Press, 1979); John R. Chavez, *The Lost Land: The Chicano Image in the Southwest* (Albuquerque, NM: University of New Mexico Press, 1984); Leonard Pitt, *The Decline of the Californios: A Social History of the Spanish-Speaking Californians, 1846-1980* (Los Angeles, CA: University of California Press, 1966); Carey McWilliams, *North from Mexico: The Spanish-Speaking People of the United States* (New York, NY: Greenwood, 1968).

[5] In *California Pastoral*, Bancroft wishes to appear as a champion of the women, but given his ethnocentric proclivities and his own patriarchal bent, his sentiments are again immediately suspect. For example, Chapter 10, "Woman and Her Sphere," opens thus: "Women were not treated with the greatest respect: in Latin and in savage countries they seldom are . . ." (p. 305); and then adds: "It was a happy day for the California bride whose husband was American, and happier still for the California husband whose bride was Yankee" (p. 312). Later he delights in comparing Mexican women and their more *beautiful* American sisters, to the merit of neither: "The beauty of women is of shorter duration in Spanish countries than in the United States; but the monster Time behaves differently in the two places. In the states, the sere and yellow leaf of beauty shrivels into scragginess in the extremes of the type; but in Spanish-speaking countries it is not the withering of the gourd of beauty that those have to deplore who sit beneath its shadow with so great delight, but it is the broadening of that shadow. Without altogether endorsing sylph-like forms, it is yet safe to affirm that degrees of beauty in women are not in direct ratio to the degrees of the latitude of their circumference" (p. 324). Otherwise, Bancroft asserts that "among the married women of the common class, there was looseness—

not remarkably so, but they were less strict than American women in this respect" (p. 321).

[6] The "Recuerdos," unlike the Franklinian autobiographical text which charts the rise of the individual from poverty and obscurity, is a history of the individual's fall from power, loss of wealth, and social displacement. For all its troubling class attitudes and contradictions, it is also a consciously subversive narrative which was, by Vallejo's own reckoning, a staunchly revisionist counter-discourse. In a letter to his son, Platon, Vallejo writes: "I shall not stop moistening my pen in the blood of our unfounded detractors, certain accursed writers who have insulted us . . . to contradict those who slander 'tis not vengeance, it is regaining a loss." Madie Brown Emparan, *The Vallejos of California* (San Francisco, CA: University of San Francisco Press, 1968), p. 182.

[7] The Bear Flag rebellion, which initiated the Mexican American War in California, commenced when a group of Americans took Mariano Vallejo, and his brother Salvador, Jacobo Leese, and other Californios prisoner, raised a flag with a bear insignia, and proclaimed their liberation from Mexican rule. Rosalia Vallejo de Leese describes these Americans as "a large group of rough-looking men, some wearing caps made with the skins of coyotes or wolves, some wearing slouched hats full of holes, some wearing straw hats as black as coal. The majority of this marauding band wore buckskin pants . . . several had no shirts, shoes were only to be seen on the feet of the fifteen or twenty among the whole lot." And like Angustias de la Guerra she describes having resisted the Americans, by saving a seventeen-year-old girl from being sexually assaulted by Fremont and his officers. She also bitterly remembers being forced to write a letter to a Captain Padilla, who was riding toward Sonoma with troops, requesting him to return to San Jose; she says "I consented, not for the purpose of saving my life, but being then in the family way I had no right to endanger the life of my unborn baby; moreover, I judged that a man who had gone so far would not stop at anything [Fremont told me he would burn our houses with us inside them] . . . and being desirous of saving trouble to my countrywomen I wrote the fatal letter." "History of the Bear Flag Party," Manuscript Collection, Bancroft Library, p. 5.

[8] Rosalia Vallejo de Leese's narrative "History of the Bear Flag Party" is only some six pages long. A note in the manuscript vaguely mentions that it was recorded by her daughter Rosalia, but it was probably transcribed by Enrique Cerruti, who was the chief collector in the Sonoma area, and whose transcription of Salvador Vallejo's narrative is also recorded in English.

[9] As it turned out, Doña Perez was actually about 104 years old when she narrated her life. Her repute as an

"ancient woman," however, had circulated sufficiently to make her an item of wide curiosity. In fact, at the very end of the narrative, her daughter, María de Rosario, was worried that a member of the family would try to capitalize on her mother's reputed age: "In June of the year 1876 my sister Maria Antonia . . . wanted to make some money by capitalizing on my mother for six weeks, exhibiting her in San Francisco for $5,000 in Woodward Gardens, and afterwards taking her to the exposition in Philadelphia. Fortunately, she had already been taken secretly to Los Angeles." "Una vieja y sus recuerdos," Manuscript Collection, Bancroft Library, p. 34.

Lindon Barrett (essay date 1993)

SOURCE: "Self-Knowledge, Law, and African American Autobiography: Lucy A. Delaney's *From the Darkness Cometh the Light*," in *The Culture of Autobiography: Constructions of Self-Representation*, edited by Robert Folkenflik, Stanford University Press, 1993, pp. 104-24.

[*In the following essay, Barrett explores the definition of self and authority in African-American autobiographies through an examination of the writings of Lucy A. Delaney.*]

The autobiographical text this discussion considers is a recollection of antebellum slave life and of release from chattel slavery. Published some 25 years after the Civil War, Lucy A. Delaney's *From the Darkness Cometh the Light*, subtitled *Struggles for Freedom*, recalls as its climax events from 1844, the year in which Delaney's mother, Polly Berry, sued successfully for Delaney's freedom in a Missouri courtroom.[1] The legal case and judgment for Delaney's freedom turned upon the status of Delaney's mother, who was born free in Illinois, kidnapped as a child, and taken to slaveholding territory. Legally a free woman, Berry could not bear enslaved children in the eyes of the law. Thus, successfully establishing the biological mother-daughter relationship between Berry and Delaney amounted to a demonstration of Delaney's legally free status. Despite the singularity of this movement from slavery to freedom in terms of classic slave narratives, Delaney's recollections bear central characteristics of the classic antebellum text in which, during the years from 1836 to the end of the Civil War, "the stigma traditionally associated with slavery [was transferred] from the slave to the slaveholder."[2] What is significant about Delaney's text is that the working out of these traditional concerns and themes occurs at a very novel site: the American courtroom.

The climax of Delaney's narrative in the setting of an American courtroom tellingly resituates the "scene of writing" so peculiar to African American autobiography. The "scene of writing" in these narratives is the scene in which the autobiographer learns to read, write, or respect fully the power of literacy and discursive conventions. The scene provides a sometimes veiled but always undeniable commentary on the construction of the autobiographical self presented by the narrative. The revision suggested by Delaney's narrative tellingly documents the manner in which each African American autobiographer must in some measure recast the hostile construction of African American identity already undertaken by dominant American society. The courtroom setting in Delaney's narrative dramatizes the convergence of the scriptive and the prescriptive, the private and the public, the individual and the social. Put another way, it dramatizes "a complex political technology" by which the self is represented.[3] This "complex political technology," as *From the Darkness Cometh the Light* reveals, is ultimately implicated in the terms of American law. The critical reader sees in the courtroom scene of writing the African American self as a manifest fiction—a provisional composite of self-declaration and judicial arbitration.

In addition to prompting the critical reader to consider the American courtroom as a primary site for "political and conceptual" determinations (as well as disclosures) of African American identity, Delaney's text prompts recognition of the technological and epistemological fiction of the genre of autobiography.[4] This essay examines these intersecting exposures. It begins by analyzing Delaney's portrayal of the nuclear family and her presentation of her own representativeness vis-à-vis all other African Americans; these subordinate elements of the narrative underscore the exposures of the climactic scenes in the courtroom. The essay concludes by claiming a central place for the American courtroom as a site for the writing of African American identity and autobiography.

The convergence at this site is important for investigations of the situation of the self of African American autobiography, because the foremost concern of African American autobiographies has been the relation between the individual and the communal. Accordingly, the academic study of African American autobiography is perennially concerned with this relation. In 1974, in the introduction to his *Black Autobiography in America*, Stephen Butterfield writes: "The 'self' of black autobiography . . . is not an individual with a private career. . . . The self is conceived as a member of an oppressed social group with ties and responsibilities to the other members."[5] Almost twenty years later it is now routinely acknowledged that there are important distinctions to be made along these lines between autobiographies written by African American women and African American men. These distinctions concern the relation that the narrated subjects of the autobiographies bear to the com munity of African Americans with whom they share their oppression, or in other words the extent to which the narratives are or are not individualistic, celebrating individual struggles and individual triumphs. The now-classic pairing of Frederick Douglass's *Narrative of the Life of Frederick Douglass* and Harriet Jacobs's *Incidents in the Life of a Slave Girl* is taken to exemplify such distinctions. Douglass more fully fashions a mythic tale of individual perseverance and ingenuity, while Jacobs more fully records her indebtedness to and enduring concerns for the familial community in relation to which she defines herself. The pairing brings together strikingly different models of the way in which African American autobiographies present the dramatic actualization or realization of the self, given a set of intellectual, civic, and legal circumstances operating to prevent precisely that.

Needless to say, one recognizes equally important similarities. One critic describes the shared complexities of African American autobiographical projects as follows: "Autobiography as a genre should be the history of individual craziness, but in black autobiography the outer reality in which heroes move is so massive and absolute in its craziness that any one person's individual idiosyncrasies seem almost dull in their normality."[6] African American autobiographies present readers with narratives that are, in terms of the dominant society, unimaginable. In these texts, what is normally taken for granted becomes, as a matter of course, eccentric. These eccentricities involve defying socially assigned identities and undertaking their revision in light of personally proclaimed identities. The autobiographies of Douglass and Jacobs share, in addition to these traits, more widespread characteristics of autobiography. Both suggest, for instance, that the genre offers "not a simple recapitulation of the past; it is also the attempt and the drama of [persons] struggling to reassemble [themselves] in [their] own likeness at a certain moment of [their] history."[7]

Differences and similarities notwithstanding, these estimations of African American autobiography depend upon notions that Candace Lang, in her reprimand of traditional scholars of autobiography, terms a relatively "unskeptical acceptance of the unified, autonomous self." Writing of Georges Gusdorf and James Olney, among others, Lang invites one to see that "few of the critics in question here manifest an entirely unskeptical acceptance of the unified, autonomous self, but virtually none goes so far as to ponder the consequences of a total rejection of that notion of the subject. To do so would constitute . . . a serious and sustained critique of the 'genre' and its ideological foundations."[8] My contention is that the circumstances of African American autobiography prompt such a sustained critique. That critique operates at the level of the ideological foundations of the genre, but it also operates beyond them, putting into question the ideological foundations of

American social custom and law. It thus identifies discursive practices from which African American autobiography must extract itself, practices that it must revise. This critique is suggested, but only suggested, by the pairing of Douglass and Jacobs. The issues setting the two narratives in opposition imply the problematics troubling any definitive declaration of the limits and boundaries of the self. The self, as it turns out, is always a questionable fiction, whether that fiction is exposed in terms of relations to a community, or in terms of narrative complexities that betray a self performing the narration over and against a self being narrated.

African American autobiography stands as a peculiar site at which a critical reader can witness, in diverse realms, the dynamics animating fictions of the self. In addition to observing narrative disturbances fretting a discourse generically premised on the viability of a discrete identity, the reader is privy to disturbances of the enduring national fictions in the United States that propose it is impossible and undesirable, in the words of Abraham Lincoln, to "introduce political and social equality between the white and black races . . . [as a result of] a physical difference between the two, which . . . will probably forever forbid their living together upon the footing of perfect equality."[9] Lucy Delaney's *From the Darkness Cometh the Light* articulates this coincidence of generic and social fictions, providing a fiction of personal identity that also rehearses a systemic fiction of national identity, a coincidence that one might attribute to the terms of all African American autobiography. One is openly prompted by Delaney's narrative to see the autobiographical heroine as multiple and as defined in deeply conflicting ways. Additionally, the climax of the narrative—the courtroom scene that eventually secures Delaney her freedom—graphically conjoins the fictitious self-evidence of autobiography with the imperatives of social and legal systems in the United States that remain hostile to African Americans. The "ideological foundations" of the generic, unitary self and of a racial, gendered, and classed national configuration appear there in powerful complementarity. The equivocal fiction of the self is set in relief against the assumed univocality of an overwhelming system. Accordingly, the official site of the courtroom takes its place as the paramount scene for multiple fictive selves, or what amounts to the same, multiple fictions of the self. The tenuous fiction of the self is inevitable, but is taken as less tenuous at some sites than at others.

Not so oddly, then, the autobiographical self-knowledge to be accrued from reading Delaney's narrative—and by extension all African American autobiography—proves to be the ironic knowledge of another/an Other. For Delaney this odd self-knowledge is a foreign and contrary knowledge imposed by a hostile and dominant other party and is, furthermore, knowledge of an estranged and, at best, marginalized Other that/who must be· understood as one's self. African American autobiographical acts recapitulate the hostile "knowledge" that discounts them in the first place, as well as the marginalized personal and community "knowledge" that, opposingly, promotes them in the first place. For an African American "simply to write the story of his or her own life represent[s] an assault" on the line of reasoning that assumes and perpetuates the construct that African Americans do not live—at the very least— as fully imaginative, significant, intellectual, and complex lives as the dominant American community, "since to make oneself the subject of a narrative presumes both the worth of that self and its interest for a reader."[10] Given this set of circumstances, *From the Darkness Cometh the Light* underscores correspondences between the generic dimensions of a social configuration and the social dimensions of a generic configuration; *From the Darkness Cometh the Light* challenges "ideological foundations" that obscure these conjunctions.

There are two principal ways in which the text imputes the fictive status to the self. The first returns us to the exemplary concerns of *Incidents in the Life of a Slave Girl,* since the construct of the family holds priority in both narratives. Delaney's narrative begins with the abduction of her mother at the age of five from the state of Illinois "across the Mississippi River to the city of St. Louis" and shortly "up the Missouri River [where she is] sold into slavery."[11] Sold and resold as a slave, Polly meets "a mulatto servant, who was as handsome .as Apollo" (p. 11) and eventually the two are married and begin to raise two daughters. With foreshadowing irony, Delaney characterizes her early childhood: "With mother, father, and sister, a pleasant home and surroundings, what happier child than I!" (p. 13). A state of domestic unity and happiness is recuperated from the opening misdeeds of the narrative; however, as one suspects, the archetypal unity and happiness prove ephemeral. The ensuing episodes of Delaney's narrative seem to chronicle a quest to reconvene the blissful family unit.

Delaney recalls that "Though in direct opposition to the will of Major Berry, my father's quondam master and friend Judge Wash tore my father from his wife and children and sold him 'way down South'!" (p. 14). This disbanding of the family marks the beginning of the misfortunes from which Delaney must continually extricate herself. Although the evil of slavery underlies the whole narrative, the disbanding of the family also marks the first of only two occasions when the text calls the evil by its name. Delaney decries "Slavery! cursed slavery . . . [which means] bondage as parts husband from wife, the mother from her children, aye, even the babe from her breast" (pp. 14-15). The terms of this initial and most enduring distress are those of the separation of family member from family member. Conversely, the terms of greatest consolation are

implied to be the return of family members into each other's presence. The narrative is structured so that its penultimate moment appears to effect such success, but the equivocal nature of this success suggests the fictiveness that the notion of family bears in Delaney's autobiography—despite the fact that it determines both the autobiographical narrator's dilemma and her delivery from that dilemma. Years after the initial catastrophe, and years after her own emancipation as well as the emancipation and death of her mother, years after the abolition of "slavery [and] involuntary servitude, except as a punishment for crime whereof the party shall have been duly convicted,"[12] Delaney is haunted by the impulse to redress the longstanding disintegration of her family. She locates her father, and calls her sister Nancy down from Canada, then she writes of her triumph of sorts:

> Forty-five years of separation, hard work, rough times and heart longings, had perseveringly performed its work, and instead of a man bearing his years with upright vigor, he was made prematurely old by the accumulation of troubles. My sister Nancy came from Canada, and we had a most joyful reunion, and only the absence of our mother left a vacuum, which we deeply and sorrowfully felt. Father could not be persuaded to stay with us, when he found his wife dead; he longed to get back to his old associations of forty-five years standing, he felt like a stranger in a strange land, and taking pity on him, I urged him no more, but let him go though with great reluctance. (p. 61)

Delaney's triumph in effect recapitulates the initial loss. The passage begins with "separation" and ends with references to leavetaking, "a strange land," and "reluctance"—the very markers of the distress wrought 45 years earlier. Indeed, the brief mention of "a most joyful reunion" is encircled by references to "the accumulation of troubles" and "a vacuum . . . deeply and sorrowfully felt." It would appear that the configuration of "family," so heavily privileged in depictions of the African American experience by nineteenth-century white writers like Harriet Beecher Stowe, is one that is strangely never sustained or realized at this or any other point in the narrative. The configuration of "family" is an absent term that nonetheless maintains a brooding, fantastic, and highly rhetorical presence. One must remember that the reunion inevitably falls short of the original union it seeks, since the death of Delaney's mother starkly precludes the possibility. Polly never again faces her husband "who was as handsome as Apollo"; the benevolent romance that introduces and privileges the term "family" within the text survives only as a lost, unattainable fiction.

The teasing impossibility of this presiding fiction is underscored by the scenes immediately preceding the narrative's penultimate episode: after the accidental death of her first husband, Frederick Turner, Delaney is importuned by her mother to remember that death proves a better fate than enslavement. The unexpected separation Delaney must endure is not ordained by American law and privilege, as is the arbitrary legal separation of her father from her mother. In her grief Delaney submits to the judgment that the burden of slavery outweighs the burden of death: "I had been taught that there was hope beyond the grave, but hope was left behind when sold 'down souf'" (p. 57). Even in light of further misfortunes, the fiction of the original family unit and the trauma of its fracture presides. Equally, when the four children she bears in her second marriage (to Zachariah Delaney) all die either in childhood or by the age of 24, Delaney reflects that "one consolation was always mine! Our children were born free and died free! Their childhood and my maternity were never shadowed with a thought of separation" (p. 58). No doubt this claim is an odd one to be made by a mother who endures the deaths of two of her children in childhood and two in young adulthood, for the reader is asked to understand that, as she witnessed the death of each child, she is never troubled with "thought[s] of separation," even though that separation might be effected by physical death as opposed to enslavement. The ultimate outrage of American chattel slavery is portrayed in the narrative in terms of the customary priority accorded to the family in nineteenth-century American life. The principal evil of slavery is the arbitrary severing of African American families. So too the narrative represents this arbitrary severing of families as the preeminent despair of Delaney's life. The fiction of the family represents or pursues the fact of Delaney's despair.

The third in the series of deaths enumerated immediately prior to the scene of the curious family reunion is the death of Delaney's mother, her most cherished and longstanding companion. The focus and tone of this passage is substantially different from that registering her distress at her father's forced removal. Delaney remarks that she is pleased her mother "had lived to see the joyful time when her race was made free, their chains struck off, and their right to their own flesh and blood lawfully acknowledged" (p. 59). The death of her mother represents in the narrative not a traumatic separation but an occasion for satisfying and almost calming reflection. As in describing the death of her children, Delaney moves, if not to hyperbole, to measured lyricism:

> Her life, so full of sorrow was ended, full of years and surrounded by many friends, both black and white, who recognized and appreciated her sufferings and sacrifices and rejoiced that her old age was spent in freedom and plenty. The azure vault of heaven bends over us all, and the gleaming moonlight brightens the marble tablet which marks her last resting place, "to fame and fortune unknown," but in the eyes of Him who judgeth us, hers was a heroism which outvied the most famous. (p. 59)

Once again, the reader is asked to overlook the trauma of this separation, while the narrative itself is structured so as never to overlook the imposed separation outlined early in the events of Delaney's life. Strikingly, the episode that immediately follows, Delaney's attempt at a family reunion, returns to the consequences of that early separation.

It is clear that the privileged form of self-definition in Delaney's narrative is the family, yet it is equally clear that within the circumstances of her life and narrative this privileged form operates foremost as a tantalizing fiction. In her life and narrative, Delaney's family disintegrates even as it is invoked. The term enters the narrative to recapitulate its rupture and absence. As Frances Smith Foster comments, "the problem of distinguishing between the individual self and the community self and the desire to present the symbolic nature of one's personal experiences while maintaining one's own inimitability is traditional for autobiographical writers"; nonetheless, for the African American autobiographer "the question is complicated by his [or her] status . . . in the United States." That status is an alien and inferior one that in large part abrogates the prerogatives of self-definition. "The slave narrator," and subsequent writers are aliens "whose assertions of common humanity and civil rights conflict with some basic beliefs" of the society they address.[13] African American autobiographers define themselves in relation to at least two communities, a dominating American community that brooks no identification with African Americans and a community of African Americans with whom they share an imposed singularity. Delaney's narrative outlines ways in which defining oneself beyond these options amounts to pursuing a tantalizing and forever absent fiction. Thus, the privileged term of her narrative, the primary register of her self-evidence proves unprocurable. The central family in her narrative, which the prerogatives of American chattel slavery violate, remains above all in the text what the OED calls "a supposition known to be at variance with fact." Delaney recounts her life and defines her self in terms of a fiction, unfortunately a hostile fiction authored by American law and custom. What is more, the fictive status of her family in both the autobiographical narrative and the "reality" of American life implies an equal fictiveness for the self that reference to this family records. Defining the self in terms of what is ultimately fantastic calls into question its "unified and autonomous" nature, because this fantastic self remains, by definition, "at variance with fact." Presented without fact, the unity and autonomy of the self are not those of a first order reality faithfully recorded by the autobiographical act, but of a fiction manifestly invented by others. The principal sign of Delaney's autobiographical self-presence rests outside her self in what is "known to be at variance with fact," so that the text gives the lie to "the assumption that the . . . [autobiographical] work is the expression (however inadequate) of an anterior idea originating in the writing subject and for which that subject was the sole authority."[14] One must remember that in large part Delaney's persevering fictions represent a struggle with American law and custom for authorship of and authority over the terms of her life. Given the plainness of these circumstances and their attendant fictions, *From the Darkness Cometh the Light* advertises its fictiveness as opposed to its facticity. The autobiography restates the conditions of invention determining autobiographical representation as much as it appears to redact a fixed presence, a unified and autonomous self.

The even larger irony to be noted here is that every African American autobiographer wishes to pursue options of self-definition beyond the two imperatives that allow her or him either no room for resemblance or no room for difference. In the negative relation African Americans are assumed to bear to the dominating American community we are granted conversely an inexorable representativeness in relation to all other African Americans, and the second of the two principal ways in which Delaney's text imputes the fictive status of the self concerns this assumption of representativeness. Following her rehearsal of the partial, belated reunion of her family, Delaney concludes her text with an enumeration of her personal accomplishments, an enumeration immediately recuperated as racial exemplum. Both the brief listing that includes such items as her election as "President of the first colored society, called the 'Female Union,' which was the first ever organized exclusively for women" (p. 62), as well as the narrative in its entirety, are offered in the hopes that either "may settle the problem in your mind, if not in others, 'Can the negro race succeed, proportionately, as well as the whites, if given the same and an equal start?'" (pp. 63-64). Delaney briefly fashions herself as representative of all African Americans and of their potential. Nevertheless, only three paragraphs earlier, she writes:

> There are abounding in public and private libraries of all sorts, lives of people which fill our minds with amazement, admiration, sympathy, and indeed with as many feelings as there are people, so I can scarcely expect that the reader of these episodes of my life will meet with more than a passing interest, but as such I will commend it to your thought for a brief hour. (pp. 61-62)

Delaney acknowledges a vast multiplicity of individuals who are not easily reducible to one another, and acknowledges as well a multiplicity of feelings that may animate any of those individuals. She characterizes herself as acutely aware that for one to read her text is to make a single choice among many and, accordingly, she asks only "for a brief hour" devoted to her own. In effect, at the moment in the text when she

sets her own life as a standard or gauge for millions of other lives she also considers her life in terms of the infinite differences that implicitly make such a substitution impossible. Furthermore, she suggests that not only is it troublesome to imagine one life standing in the place of another or many others, it is equally troublesome to imagine any of the many "feelings" that play their part in any one life somehow standing as indicative of that individual life. Oddly, then, at the same time the impossibilities of representation are briefly considered, the narrative nonetheless claims a representative posture for Delaney. One sees that this representative understanding is openly provisional at best and, therefore, in one further and pronounced way, Delaney's reader witnesses (and witnesses Delaney witnessing) her self as "a supposition known to be at variance with fact."

As with the persistent attention to family, the form of the self being invoked responds to the invocation with rupture and withdrawal. The presented self-evidence underscores its own contrivance. The notion that African Americans are invariably more similar than different, and that one African American may always stand in the place of another, is sometimes a profitable fiction and sometimes is not. The notion remains, in any case, always a fiction, as made clear emphatically and irrevocably by the urbanization of large populations of African Americans early in the twentieth century: "After the war, black intellectuals had to confront the black masses on the streets of their cities. . . . After World War I, the large-scale movement of black people into the cities of the North meant that intellectual leadership and its constituencies fragmented. No longer was it possible to mobilize an undifferentiated address to 'the black people' once an urban black working class was established."[15] The closing paragraphs of Delaney's autobiography comprehend and imply deep conflicts that disturb assumptions of a unitary identity attributed by law or custom to African Americans. Indeed, this is an outcome her narrative shares generally with African American autobiographies. (Of course, this description is necessarily ironic, insofar as it advances a unitary identity.) The conflicts of racial representation are registered in Delaney's text in the terms of her autobiographical self, inasmuch as Delaney equivocally proposes a role for her self in that representative fiction.

In effect, as does the genre in general, Delaney's autobiography leads the critical reader to a meditation on fiction. Importantly, however, suggesting perennial concerns of African American autobiography, the fictions to be imagined and re-imagined in this instance are not simply personal or generic, but also and necessarily social and legal. As much as the scene of writing here is generic, it also is "constitutional" in the social and legal senses of that word—a scene of writing from which one necessarily infers the civic and judicial. Hence, if African American autobiography, this overdetermined scene of writing, always undertakes "a total rejection of the notion of the subject,"[16] then it troubles, by definition—even beyond the ideological foundations of autobiography—the foundations of powerful social and legal practices.

The climactic scenes of Delaney's text powerfully illuminate this imperative and intricate cathexis. Her text lays bare the deeply composite nature and unquestioned priority of these scenes. Although the importance of scenes of writing is well acknowledged within African American autobiographies and the commentaries on them, Delaney's text manifestly draws out and elaborates the non-subjective and systemic nature of this peculiar scene of writing in which she, as African American "subject," discovers her self. The novelty of Delaney's rendition becomes clear if one considers briefly well-known scenes of writing in *Narrative of the Life of Frederick Douglass* and *Incidents in the Life of a Slave Girl.*

In Douglass's text, in keeping with the more individualistic focus attributed to his narrative, the scene is in large part self-centered. Douglass's lessons in literacy provided by Mrs. Auld are stopped by Mr. Auld, since attaining literacy invariably spoils slaves by making them "unmanageable." At this juncture Douglass understands the white man's power to enslave as well as "the pathway from slavery to freedom."[17] He undertakes learning to read and write by tricking and bribing white boys in his neighborhood and by using for practice such communal markers as fences and such markers of his alienation from that community as the discarded schoolbooks of his master's son. The scene of writing outlined here underscores individual acumen, ingenuity, and the remove imposed by hostile, dominating agents. In Jacobs's text, by contrast, the more miscible, promiscuous, or indiscreet nature of the scene of writing is suggested. Initially, Linda Brent's literacy seems a liability, since it means she must endure an additional form of entreaty from Dr. Flint. However, much later in the narrative, Brent writes letters to Flint (from within the garret to which she "escapes") that are mailed and postmarked from New York. She convinces Flint of her successful "escape" to the North, ensuring "he had no suspicion of [her] being any where in the vicinity."[18] The scene of writing sketched here is more mediated; literacy and the construction of texts are taken up by diverse and conflicting hands and acquire their truth or potency by means of circulation and marks of that circulation. Here, one sees how language, literacy, and the construction and interpretation of texts operate "constitutionally"—that is, in a formative but always incomplete manner—to "confer explanatory power with regard to a wide range of evidence."[19] Scenes of writing are scenes in which occur struggles for and determinations of "explanatory power," as well as the

disposition "of evidence." Certainly, the texts of both Douglass and Jacobs suggest this state of affairs; nevertheless, they have been traditionally understood to do so in a manner that privileges the more private interstitial and marginal aspects of their inscriptional scenes.

Conversely, the climactic scenes of Delaney's text place the dynamics of language, literacy, and interpretation as they bear on African American "subjectivity" at the most literal and open site of interpretive activity, the American courtroom. The courtroom is a site at which one is not prompted to understand the scene of writing in terms of inscriptions made between the lines or in intramural spaces. The courtroom neither resembles a garret nor confines its proceedings to the margins of used, discarded sheets of paper. Rather than an interstitial space, it is apparently one in which matters are brought into the open and settled. Moreover, the courtroom is a space in which presentations of "evidence" and conferring of "explanatory power" concerning African American identity have sweeping and enduring repercussions. At the site of the courtroom, statutory law is interpreted and upheld and, all too plainly, the particulars of the presence of African Americans in the United States have been meaningfully determined by statutory law. Scenes of writing in African American autobiographies, in this sense, are the site of struggles for the right of individuals to control this "explanatory power" and to determine the disposition of the "evidence" of their own existence. The setting of Delaney's climactic scene of writing in a courtroom brilliantly allows her text to represent the problematic nature of this struggle. It allows her to stage, via the representation of an autobiographical self, the multiple fictions of selfhood that are the only resort of those for whom the "constitutional" issue of their identity already has been settled without their participation or consent. Just as the "fact" of her family is an elusive fiction, so is the ostensible subject of Delaney's narrative. In the end, what the courtroom scene allows her to represent is the enforced fictionality of any subject defined by the impersonality of the law's "constitutional" power, even when that power is employed on behalf of the freedom of the subject.

It is useful to consider briefly the nature of statutory law.

> Statutory law is a distillation of some of the society's most cherished values, or at least of the class that wields the hegemonic power that produces laws. Statutes are one way, and a solemn and formal one, for the elite that imposes its values on a society to state what those values are and how behavior should conform to them. No other social act performs this function so conspicuously and directly. Statutory law is thus a valuable window on the hopes and fears of a society, of its images of itself, and of the ways it hoped to shape the time to come.[20]

Statutory law represents the convergence and "distillation" of a plurality of discourses, a formalizing of values, practices, and customs. The courtroom is the site at which this synthesis is understood and rehearsed. Historically, this site has provided the most far-reaching determinations of African American identity, an identity that cannot be understood as a "unified and autonomous" subjectivity in light of its determination at a site so open to the influences of diverse pressures, agencies, and convergences. Although "the idea of racial inferiority certainly did not appear in colonial law with the introduction of Negroes," and although "the legal determination of who might be slaves developed slowly," as American colonial law was refined, according to William E. Moore it allowed African Americans identity only as a collective, "not as individuals." Colonial law, in its attempt to confine slavery "to those who quite obviously were different in appearance," and in its attempt to justify itself "on the basis of [African Americans'] inferior background as a people, not as individuals . . . [took] the position that slavery is justified as a status properly attaching to a different and inferior people."[21] Thus, one finds in the colonial courtroom the binding interpretation (promoted by mechanisms of "explanatory power") that African Americans bear little estimable resemblance to any community other than that of African Americans and that African Americans bear little estimable difference from one another. The dilemma of the African American autobiographer—and of African Americans—is part of the story American law has written.

The construction of the African American self in this way has been contested as a fiction by African American rebellions, by expressive cultures (dance, song, oral performance) and, within the concerns of this discussion, by autobiographical texts. To grant that, in the words of Paul Finkelman, a leading scholar of early African American legal history, "slavery must be understood not only as a social, economic, or political institution but also as a legal institution"[22] is not simply to acknowledge the brutalizing determinations of African American identity in the legislature and then in the courtroom; it is to recognize, in addition, the persistent challenges to those determinations, as well as their troublesome ramifications. The fictiveness of the established legal "facts" concerning African Americans requires that interpretations separating fiction from fact be made again and again in the American courtroom. The courtroom remains a site of powerful interventions into these perpetual deliberations.

> The establishment of the legal principle that slavery was a status properly belonging to the Negro, as inherently inferior, went far toward the legal determination of who might be slaves. But because slavery was *not* uniformly the status of Negroes from their first introduction, because not all Negroes were slaves even after slavery was established as being proper to them, and

finally, because anti-miscegenation laws were not in force from the first and not uniformly obeyed thereafter, so that physiological criteria were variable and fallible, for all these reasons the legal criteria of the status of slavery required further elaboration.[23]

This is to say, the identity of African Americans "required further elaboration." Ultimately, however, this conflict between fiction and fact concerning African American identity proved unmanageable even for the "explanatory power" of the antebellum courtroom. Historian Eugene Genovese observes in his review of Paul Finkelman's *An Imperfect Union: Slavery, Federalism, and Comity* that "the 'judicial secession' that Finkelman describes paralleled a moral and ideological secession that struck the deepest sensibilities, and together they prepared the way for the political secession that formally declared the existence of contrasting views of civilization."[24] Equally, one might say the political secession dramatically declared the existence of contrasting views of African Americans in that civilization.

The courtroom, in its interpretation of statutory law, thus stands as a preeminent site for the construction of African American identity. It allows Delaney to dramatize the fictional nature of the forms that identity has been forced to take. Her courtroom scenes heighten the ideological drama of perceiving the fictive nature of the self; they heighten the ideological drama of "a total rejection of that notion of the subject." In the text, Delaney's appearance in court in a suit for her freedom is precipitated by an altercation with her mistress, Mrs. Mitchell. Several times Delaney is entrusted "to do the weekly washing and ironing . . . [even though she] had no more idea how it was to be done than Mrs. Mitchell herself" (p. 24). Delaney is treated as if the particulars of menial servitude are innate, and her failures and protestations to the contrary prompt Mrs. Mitchell to sell her. Delaney flees and hides in the home of her legally free mother, who subsequently "on the morning of the 8th of September 1842 . . . sued Mr. D. D. Mitchell for the possession of her child" (p. 33). The issue brought before the court is who rightfully possesses the child Lucy Ann Berry, and it is precipitated by Delaney's headstrong self-determination—self-determination out of place in a situation in which that determination is a foregone conclusion.

In the courtroom the tale of the illegal abduction of Delaney's mother is rehearsed, and witnesses attest to the fact that Delaney "to the best of [their] knowledge and belief" (p. 40) is her biological child, and hence illegally enslaved. It is important to note that Delaney's defense is not premised on Delaney's personal identity, but on the very law that defines the status of African American slaves—taken as a collective entity—as perpetually the property of their masters. Delaney's defense depends on the condition of her mother, since "a master who owned a female slave owned also her increase."[25] It is the courtroom scene that occurs after the testimonies, however, that is most memorable to Delaney:

> After the evidence from both sides was all in, Mr. Mitchell's lawyer, Thomas Hutchinson, commenced to plead. For one hour, he talked so bitterly against me and against my being in possession of my liberty that I was trembling, as if with ague, for I certainly thought everybody must believe him; indeed I almost believed the dreadful things he said, myself, and as I listened I closed my eyes with sickening dread, for I could just see myself floating down the river, and my heart-throbs seemed to be the throbs of the mighty engine which propelled me from my mother and freedom forever! (p. 40)

The power of the law here resides in the power of Thomas Hutchinson's rhetoric and his construction and interpretation of the "facts" before the court. This power is not negligible, for it challenges Delaney's sense of herself. The words "I could just see myself" introduce a vision of herself that strongly contradicts the identity she is struggling to maintain and to validate by means of legal sanction. Moreover, this vision may well be the one that will receive that sanction. Delaney recalls that "on the day the suit for [her] freedom began . . . the jailer's sister-in-law, Mrs. Lacy, spoke to [her] of submission and patience; but [she] could not feel anything but rebellion against [her] lot" (p. 39). This rebellion matches her earlier one against the "government" of Mrs. Mitchell for, in the dispute over the laundry, Delaney "would not permit [Mrs. Mitchell] to strike her; [Mrs. Mitchell] used shovel, tongs and broomstick in vain, as [Delaney] disarmed her as fast as she picked up each weapon" (p. 27). Nevertheless, that rebellious character dissipates as Hutchinson pleads, and the character in which Mrs. Mitchell would cast her seems confirmed—even in Delaney's own mind. In the arena of the courtroom, Delaney represents herself as having no say concerning who she is to be.

Only when Hutchinson concludes his pleading does Delaney find respite from the "constitutional" power of the law over her identity. "Oh! what a relief it was to me when he finally finished his harangue and resumed his seat! As I never heard anyone plead before, I was very much alarmed, although I knew in my heart that every word he uttered was a lie! Yet, how was I to make people believe? It seemed a puzzling question" (pp. 40-41). Yet that respite is brief. Delaney, in her apprehension, stumbles upon the disconcerting issue that "explanatory power alone does not guarantee the truth of interpretation. Nothing does and nothing could."[26] It is apparent that fictions may assert themselves in any circumstances, in any place, in any construct, even those that may appear most legitimate and convincing. It is also apparent that, as Delaney represents herself, her "self" is essentially a fiction con-

structed by others. It becomes clear that in the courtroom what are determined as facts are for Delaney fictions constructed through the determining technologies of legal discourse.

Confronting Delaney is the overwhelming trouble that "problems of multiple authorship," the competing textual activities of various agents, "have . . . separated the text from its original authors and given it a life of its own."[27] The terms "life" and "text" become interchangeable in this scene and at this point of the narrative. They achieve a strange equivalence, as they do in all autobiographical acts, but with recognizably greater force in African American autobiography. Delaney's autobiographical self-representation exposes the way in which the always preexisting construction of her life in the impersonal text of the law relies on "structures of discourse that so often contribute to the [African American] writers' oppression."[28] The life that is written in this scene is literally not her own. Even though the scene ostensibly produces her freedom, it dramatizes an enduring state of subjugation. Of course, such a predicament or analogous predicaments in the courtroom are not exclusive to African Americans. Nevertheless, it is imperative to see that for African Americans the issue does not involve any precipitating activity on their part. At issue in the case of African Americans are not the complications of precedent actions but an a priori state of being, the determination of an identity on which social existence and relations depend. One immediately understands, then, that African Americans and African American autobiographers must revise or recast in the terms of their lives a story that is already (unacceptably) written—and writ large—by American law and custom. They attempt to write a story already recorded and on which the book, for the most part, has been closed.

Among the issues in the balance is the issue of "authorship," and most particularly self-authorship. Hence, it proves more than incidental that the power to resist and abrogate Hutchinson's interpretations of the "facts"—or, equally, to elaborate an alternative fiction—rests not with Delaney, but with Edward Bates, who acts as her attorney. In this representation of her life, he "represents" her, not just as her advocate, but also as one more practitioner of the law who wields its power to construct and construe her life in accord with its letter.

> Judge Bates arose, and his soulful eloquence and earnest pleading made such an impression on my sore heart, I listened with renewed hope. I felt the black storm clouds of doubt and despair were fading away, and that I was drifting into the safe harbor of the realms of truth. I felt as if everybody *must* believe *him*, for he clnng [sic] to the truth, and I wondered how Mr. Hutchinson could so lie about a poor defenseless girl like me. (p. 41; emphasis in original)

The eloquence and "explanatory power" of Judge Bates are beyond question, as is his role in securing the relief and victory of Delaney. The emphasis falls on his actions and influence, while Delaney appears as merely acted upon. The turning point in the crisis of her self-determination depends upon the force and efficacy of a self constructed by another. In her own rendition of the climax of her quest for and attainment of self-determination, Delaney has no authority, self-authority or any other kind. Indeed, in Delaney's self-representation in this scene she ironically dramatizes her inability to represent herself in any terms but those supplied by those whose law and customs have enslaved her and will also set her "free." The conventional bathos of "a poor defenseless girl like me" underlines her self-representation as a tactic undertaken within a world of always polite fictions that systematically determine the discourse of self-representation and identity for African Americans. Drawn in the courtroom and in anxiety as "a poor defenseless girl," she possesses less proximity to her "self" than Bates or, for that matter, Hutchinson. Delaney, in deference to the commanding power of the competing renditions of her self, is a negligible player at this point, and the irony is underscored rhetorically; "defenseless" is an interesting term to employ in reference to a life that turns precisely on a legal "defense" successfully upheld.

As with the narrative's privileging of the term "family" and its equivocal representation of Delaney's representativeness, the courtroom drama belies the notion of a "unified and autonomous" subject. Delaney represents her identity as decisively and variously constituted by the representations of others. The proceedings of the court as well as the autobiographical act that both renders them and is rendered possible by them expose the fictiveness of such a belief. This autobiographical act and its central terms—the privileging of the family, the claim of representativeness, and the climactic legal drama—also challenge the "ideological foundations" of that belief, the principles determining which fictions do and do not count. Because it alludes to the manifest fiction operating at the site of the courtroom itself, the peroration of Judge Bates forms a further element of this exposition. Bates commends the court as a site at which laws attain their most imposing, and thus inviolate, status, and Delaney transcribes his statement as follows:

> "Gentlemen of the jury, I am a slave-holder myself, but, thanks to the Almighty God, I am above the base principle of holding anybody a slave that has as good right to her freedom as this girl has been proven to have; she was free before she was born; her mother was free, but kidnapped in her youth, and sacrificed to the greed of negro traders, and no free woman can give birth to a slave child, as it is in direct violation of the laws of God and man." (p. 42)

This ultimately successful argument turns on a larger set of ironies. What ultimately secures the court's determination of Delaney's identity is an act of self-definition by her legal representative ("I am a slave-holder myself") enabling a local, limited condemnation of slavery that remains clearly subordinate to an approbation of slavery in general. In his argument the laws of God and man rest surely on Delaney's side, yet the laws of God and man stand as surely behind slavery in general.[29] And to assert thus confidently the unequivocal meaning of divine and human law in this setting is to advance one further fiction. As Bates's activity as an advocate and Delaney's anxiety over whose definition of her identity will prevail attest, the courtroom is a site of equivocation. It is a site at which multiple determinations converge, conflict, and are deliberated. Delaney, furthermore, sets out explicitly a critique of the notion of unquestioned determinacy, a notion that assigns her an identity by a process that her narrative puts into question.

The courtroom would be transformed by Bates's appeal to the uncontestable will of God and to the mandates of man, not of men (not of individuals but of a species), into a site where there is no room for interpretation, since all determination has already been made. Because the courtroom is the site and mechanism of statutory interpretation—of the choosing of a particular meaning because a variety of possibilities presupposes and demands the deliberation—Bates's rhetorical gesture can only be understood as another fiction, "a supposition at variance with the facts." Rather than accepting appeals to unquestioned determinacy, courts make determinations "in the way that all knowledge is secure[d], by virtue of its acceptance within a community of interpretation whose existence is a prerequisite to the production of knowledge itself."[30] In other words, the courtroom gathers representatives of a community in order to determine what the community knows because conflicting interests have put into question what it knows. The knowledge that courts are charged to research, discover, and possess emanates from and returns to the civic and political communities from which the law is constructed.

This point is underscored by the lack of clear legislative origins for the law of American slavery. "Slavery was not established by law in any American colony, but its development by custom was later recognized by legislation."[31] Law and custom interact to the point at which their distinctions blur; upon scrutiny law is premised on custom, while custom manages to manifest itself as law. The two equally enlist one another, as colonial laws of American slavery continually remind us.

> When Rhode Island legislators began the gradual statutory abolition of slavery in their state in 1784, they declared in a preamble that slavery "has gradually obtained [in Rhode Island] by

unrestrained custom and the permission of the laws." This pithily restated the accepted explanations of the legal origins of slavery in the American states. To create slavery by law it was not necessary, as United States Supreme Court Justice John McLean later observed, to pass legislation providing "that slavery shall exist"; and no such statute was ever adopted in any American jurisdiction. Rather, as an anonymous Garrisonian abolitionist maintained in a retrospective survey of the statutory law of slavery in the British American mainland colonies, the legal origins of slavery are found in "the provincial legislative acts, which establish and sanction the custom [of slaveholding] and stamp it with the character of law."[32]

The situation Delaney narrated in her courtroom scene was related to the collective wills, conflicts, machinations, and imaginations of those segments of civic and political communities best able to command "the legal process . . . as an expression of social control."[33] The determined intermingling of custom and law composing the legal process demands that both be understood in relation to one another.

What law, custom, and the court, as it superintends them, struggle to define in Delaney's autobiography is her identity, her self as that self is complicated by being African American in communities in which African Americans are at worst enslaved and at best marginalized. If one understands the climactic courtroom scene of *From the Darkness Cometh the Light* as the autobiography's preeminent scene of writing, one understands—in addition to the manifest fictiveness of self-determining inscriptions—the manner in which some fictions are enforced and thus acquire greater sanction and power than others. Fictions transcend their provisional status always to someone's or some group's interest. In doing so, they acquire a further provisional status that is less discernible. Scenes of writing turn on issues of power, as is made clear by the conclusion Delaney assigns to the courtroom drama. The conclusion of the scene directly represents her continued confinement by a process of "constitutional" definition that always will determine her identity, even after it has defined her as "free." After Bates's peroration, "the case was then submitted to the jury, about 8 o'clock in the evening, and I was returned to the jail and locked in the cell which I had occupied for seventeen months, filled with the most intense anguish" (p. 43). The courtroom is a site at which fictions are fabricated and acquire legal and social sanction, one at which the peculiar situation of African American identity is made clear. The determination of her freedom and of the various forms of her continued subjugation rests with a community that takes it upon itself to measure, imagine, and (re)cast who she must be. Indeed, once American slavery was a fully formed legal institution, "statutory provisions directly or indirectly securing the rights of slaves were scanty. The only positively accorded

right [in the mid-eighteenth century] appears in South Carolina's code of 1740 and Georgia's derivative code of 1755, where blacks could bring suit to test the legality of their enslavement."[34] Equally illustrative of the distinct association courts bear to African American subjectivity is the observation that "these suits, the only type of civil action a slave could take, did not begin until the nineteenth century."[35] Besides criminal prosecution, American courtrooms admitted African Americans primarily to determine their identity.

Hence, the individual scene of writing of the African American autobiographer is always matched by socially and legally prescriptive scenes of writing best imagined in terms of the courtroom, and for these reasons Delaney's autobiography effects an exposition of the concerns of the genre. Delaney seizes and begins to fill for African American autobiography "a prime fictive space"[36] that holds great priority for African Americans in determining the terms of their lives. It would seem that to write African American autobiography is not only to write "from behind the veil" but also to write in the public, yet confining "constitutional" space of American custom and law.

It is fair to say that Delaney's "story undercuts the authority of both points of view presented in the story: the personal and the legal."[37] In Delaney's text "the personal and the legal" converge at the peculiar nexus that is the courtroom, enabling the critical reader to see in the interrelated fictions of the personal and the legal how African American autobiography necessarily challenges the ideological foundations of the genre and the ideological foundations of American life. In undercutting both, Delaney exposes the dual fictions of unity and autonomy in the autobiographical subject and its claim to self-identity. Fictions may assert themselves in any circumstances, in any place, in any construct, even those that may appear most legitimate and convincing. The self is one such fiction, legality another, and the convergence of the two in terms of African American identity another still.

Notes

[1] Lucy A. Delaney, *From the Darkness Cometh the Light, or Struggles for Freedom* (c. 1891), in *Six Women's Slave Narratives,* intro. William L. Andrews (New York: Oxford University Press, 1988).

[2] Marion Wilson Starling, *The Slave Narrative* (Washington, D.C.: Howard University Press, 1988), p. 106.

[3] Michel Foucault, *The History of Sexuality: An Introduction* (New York: Vintage, 1978), p. 127. I am prompted to use this phrase by Teresa de Laurentis's understanding and explanation of it in her essay "The Technology of Gender." De Laurentis suggests that cultural formations and identities such as gender, race,

class are produced by cultural technologies "in the sense in which industrial machinery produces goods or commodities, and in so doing also produces social relations" (*The Technologies of Gender: Essays on Theory, Film, and Fiction* [Bloomington: Indiana University Press, 1987], p. 12).

[4] Mark Tushnet, *The American Law of Slavery, 1810-1860: Considerations of Humanity and Interest* (Princeton, N.J.: Princeton University Press, 1981), p. 229.

[5] Stephen Butterfield, *Black Autobiography in America* (Amherst: University of Massachusetts Press, 1974), pp. 2-3.

[6] Roger Rosenblatt, "Black Autobiography: Life as the Death Weapon," in James Olney, ed., *Autobiography: Essays Theoretical and Critical* (Princeton, N.J.: Princeton University Press, 1980), p. 174. Rosenblatt also makes the observation that "no black American author has ever felt the need to invent a nightmare to make his [or her] point" (p. 172).

[7] Georges Gusdorf, "Conditions and Limits of Autobiography," in Olney, ed., *Autobiography,* p. 43. The terms supplied in brackets, however awkward they may seem, open the possibilities of the genre in ways that the original's gendered nouns and pronouns prohibit.

[8] Candace Lang, "Autobiography in the Aftermath of Romanticism," *Diacritics,* 12 (Winter 1982), p. 5.

[9] Abraham Lincoln, "First Joint Debate, Ottawa, August 21: Mr. Lincoln's Reply," in Robert W. Johannsen, ed., *The Lincoln-Douglas Debates* (New York: Oxford University Press, 1965), p. 52.

[10] Valerie Smith, *Self-Discovery and Authority in Afro-American Narrative* (Cambridge, Mass.: Harvard University Press, 1987), p. 21.

[11] Lucy A. Delaney, *From the Darkness,* p. 10.

[12] Constitution of the United States, Thirteenth Amendment (1865).

[13] Frances Smith Foster, *Witnessing Slavery* (Westport, Conn.: Greenwood Press, 1979), pp. 5-6.

[14] Lang, "Autobiography," pp. 5, 10.

[15] Hazel Carby, *Reconstructing Womanhood: The Emergence of the Afro-American Woman Novelist* (New York: Oxford University Press, 1987), p. 164. At this point in her argument, Carby is considering the vexed dynamics of representation both "in relation to art and creative practices, and as it applies to intellectuals who understand themselves to be responsible for the representation of 'the race,' defining and constructing in their art its representative members and situating themselves as representative members of an oppressed social group" (p. 164).

[16] Lang, "Autobiography," p. 5.

[17] Frederick Douglass, *Narrative of the Life of Frederick Douglass, An American Slave Written by Himself,* ed. Benjamin Quarles (Cambridge, Mass.: Harvard University Press, 1960), pp. 58, 59.

[18] Harriet A. Jacobs, *Incidents in the Life of a Slave Girl, Written by Herself,* ed. Jean Fagan Yellin (Cambridge, Mass.: Harvard University Press, 1987), p. 132.

[19] Walter Benn Michaels, "The Fate of the Constitution," in Sanford Levinson and Steven Mailloux, eds., *Interpreting Law and Literature* (Evanston, Ill.: Northwestern University Press, 1988), p. 391.

[20] William W. Wiecek, "The Statutory Law of Slavery and Race in the Thirteen Mainland Colonies of British North America," in Kermit L. Hall, ed., *The Law of American Slavery* (New York: Garland, 1987), p. 683.

[21] William E. Moore, "Slave Law and the Social Structure," in *The Law of American Slavery,* p. 332.

[22] Paul Finkelman, *Slavery in the Courtroom* (Washington, D.C.: Library of Congress, 1985), p. 14.

[23] Moore, "Slave Law," pp. 338-39.

[24] Eugene D. Genovese, "Slavery in the Legal History of the South and the Nation," in Paul Finkelman, ed., *Law, the Constitution, and Slavery* (New York: Garland, 1989), p. 162.

[25] Moore, "Slave Law," p. 340.

[26] Michaels, "The Fate of the Constitution," p. 391.

[27] Ibid., p. 390. It is important to note that in this and all my uses of quotations from Michaels's "The Fate of the Constitution" I am using the author's prose in the service of a position that he particularly argues against. In its entirety the sentence I am now quoting reads: "Instead, they [theorists who think that texts can be separated from intention] imagine that the passage of time and the problems of multiple authorship have eventually separated the text from its original authors and given it a life of its own." Michaels states that at present "it may seem perverse not only to defend intention but to claim that every interpreter is always and only looking for authorial intention" (p. 390); he writes further that, despite this climate, it is precisely his intention to do so. I repudiate Michaels's stance in regard to autobiography generally and African American autobiography in par-

ticular. Indeed, the issue, or problem, is exactly who the author is. The problem is especially exasperating for the African American autobiographer for whom the terms of life to be written appear (unacceptably) already written.

[28] Smith, *Self-Discovery and Authority,* p. 6.

[29] Perhaps one might even go so far as to say that in this discourse Delaney emerges as an ironic figure in a pro-slavery argument. Certainly, these passages strike a very different chord from, say, the somewhat analogous concluding moment in Harriet Jacobs's *Incidents in the Life of a Slave Girl,* when Jacobs's freedom is purchased.

[30] Kenneth S. Abraham, "Statutory Interpretation and Literary Theory: Some Common Concerns of an Unlikely Pair," in Levinson and Mailloux, eds., *Interpreting Law and Literature,* p. 129.

[31] Moore, "Slave Law," p. 325.

[32] Wiecek, "Statutory Law of Slavery," p. 661.

[33] A. Leon Higginbotham, Jr., *In the Matter of Color: Race and the American Legal Process—The Colonial Period* (New York: Oxford University Press, 1978), p. 13.

[34] Wiecek, "Statutory Law of Slavery," p. 668.

[35] Moore, "Slave Law," p. 342.

[36] Robert B. Stepto, telephone conversations, June 22 and 23, 1991. One might imagine the courtroom as "a prime fictive space" because, in the words of Stepto, "barred from a certain context, especially as it involves voice and telling one's own story," it is inevitable that you finally arrive there.

[37] Brook Thomas, *Cross-examinations of Law and Literature: Cooper, Hawthorne, Stowe, and Melville* (New York: Cambridge University Press, 1987), p. 110.

Patricia Felisa Barbeito (essay date 1998)

SOURCE: "Making Generations in Jacobs, Larsen, and Hurston: A Genealogy of Black Women's Writing," in *American Literature,* Vol. 70, No. 2, June, 1998, pp. 365-95.

[*In the following excerpt, Barbeito examines the impact of slavery and racial politics on "black female sexuality" as explored by Harriet Jacobs in her writings.*]

> *"The important thing is making generations. . . . And that['s] what makes the evidence. And that's what makes the verdict."*

"Procreation. That could also be a slave-breeder's way of thinking."—Gayl Jones, *Corregidora*

The lines from Gayl Jones's *Corregidora* identify a formative trope in black women's writing that links the "making of generations," the black female sexual and procreative body, to a history of slavery. "Making generations" in the context of a history of slavery is both "evidence" and "verdict," a sign and symptom of slavery that generates both a repetition and revision of that history. The lines from Jones's text can also be taken as a commentary on a genealogy of black women's writing in which the procreative black female body emerges as a central and determinative concern. This paper examines the way the trope of "making generations" shapes the work of three women writers—Harriet Jacobs, Nella Larsen, and Zora Neale Hurston—into a distinct literary lineage.

The lineage of black women's writing that places the black female body at the center of the conception of racial politics responds to a critical tradition that has consistently portrayed this race-sex interaction as inherently problematic; issues surrounding the sexual identity and expression of black women have been either considered at odds with and peripheral to the interests of a racial politics or completely subsumed into this politics.[1] Harriet Jacobs's ground-breaking slave narrative, which was enlisted in the abolitionist effort, focuses on the sexual exploitation of women during slavery and directly associates the woman slave's struggle for freedom with the freedom to control her own sexual activity. The treatment of black female sexuality is similarly central and controversial for both Larsen and Hurston.

Nathan Huggins divides the "history making and race building" projects of the Harlem Renaissance into two camps—that of refined civility and that of passion—according to their main strategies, which posited and depended on antithetical conceptions of the Negro as genteel and cultured or natural and primitive.[2] For Huggins, this "schizophrenic" approach to racial identity had the effect of either completely polarizing sex and race or conflating them. The primitive school emphasized a type of atavistic sensuality and exoticism that centered on the black woman as erotic and libidinous, while the genteel school emphasized her controlled virtue and conventional morality.[3] For both Larsen and Hurston, as for Jacobs, the portrayal of black female sexual identity was fraught with the tensions inherent in the interactions of race and sex. Their texts map these tensions and rearticulate them; by interrogating the ways in which the construction of racial identity both informs and suppresses sexual identity, Jacobs, Larsen, and Hurston attempt to reconceptualize the relation of black women's expression to racial politics.

In "A Perilous Passage in the Slave Girl's Life," the tenth chapter of her autobiographical *Incidents in the Life of a Slave Girl, Written by Herself* (1861), Harriet Jacobs, in the voice of her narrator Linda Brent, writes:

> And now, reader, I come to a period in my unhappy life, which I would gladly forget if I could. The remembrance fills me with sorrow and shame. It pains me to tell you of it; but I have promised to tell you the truth, and I will do it honestly, let it cost me what it may. I will not try to screen myself behind the plea of compulsion from a master; for it was not so. Neither can I plead ignorance or thoughtlessness. For years, my master had done his utmost to pollute my mind with foul images, and to destroy the pure principles inculcated by my grandmother. . . . The influences of slavery had had the same effect on me that they had on other young girls; they had made me prematurely knowing, concerning the evil ways of the world. I knew what I did, and I did it with deliberate calculation.[4]

The "perilous passage" obliquely referred to in this chapter is Brent's sexual liaison with an unmarried white man, a Mr. Sands, with whom she has two children. Despite Brent's promises to tell us the truth and her refusal to screen herself, this liaison is consistently represented indirectly; it is an unspecified evil that serves to underscore the evils of slavery. Brent's sexual transgression, the fact that she not only is sexually active outside of wedlock but also acts knowingly and "with deliberate calculation," is thus portrayed as a symptom of slavery. Slavery is an evil that contagiously perverts all relations in the text, sexual and nonsexual.

The implications of Jacobs's figuration of slavery as a sexually polluting disease are most apparent in her portrayal of Brent's relation to her first child. The meaning of Brent's "plunge into the abyss" (53) is revealed when she tells us that she is pregnant. Her male child is "the ever-present witness of [Brent's] shame" both because he is a tangible sign of her lack of virtue and because he implicates her sexual activity in the economy of slavery: "slaveholders have been cunning enough to enact that 'the child shall follow the condition of the *mother*,' not of the *father*; thus taking care that licentiousness shall not interfere with avarice" (76). Slavery is described as a particularly feminine and feminizing disease passed on from mother to child in a way that disrupts conventional genealogies and causes a chaotic disorientation.[5] The "plunge into the abyss," as a sign of what W. E. B. DuBois would have called Brent's double-consciousness—her status as a fallen woman and her redeeming maternity—explicitly links her sexual and procreative experience to a racial divide that renders this experience inherently self-negating and problematic:[6]

> The little vine was taking deep root in my existence, though its clinging fondness excited a mixture of love and pain. When I was most sorely oppressed I found a solace in his smiles. I loved to watch his infant slumbers; but always there was a dark cloud over my enjoyment. I could never forget that he was a slave. Sometimes I wished that he might die in infancy. God tried me. My darling became very ill. . . . I had prayed for his death, but never so earnestly as I now prayed for his life. . . . Alas, what mockery it is for a slave mother to try to pray back her dying child to life! Death is better than slavery. (62)

The child embodies Jacobs's identification of the condition of slavery as a type of death in life.

Incidents in the Life of a Slave Girl presents the reader with an interpretative problem that centers on the status of black female sexuality.[7] Figured as Brent's "plunge into the abyss," black female sexuality is conceived as possessing a dangerous duplicity—it is linked to joy and sadness, life and death—that is reinscribed by sexuality's status as an absent presence in the text. Some readers of Jacobs's text have emphasized her denial of sexual expression and her appeal to conventional morality as an empowering strategy for female self-expression.[8] They consider Jacobs's reticence about sexual matters and her appeal to a redeeming maternity reponses to the popular conception and iconography of the black female body as diseased and sexually voracious.[9] Deborah McDowell summarizes this position in her description of the effect on black women's writing of "the network of social and literary myths perpetuated throughout history about black women's libidinousness":

> Given this historical context it is not surprising that a pattern of reticence about black female sexuality tended to dominate novels by black women. . . . [B]lack women writers responded to the myth of the black woman's sexual licentiousness by insisting fiercely on her chastity. Fighting to overcome their heritage of rape and concubinage, . . . they stripped the characters they created of all sexual desire, imprinting instead the 'purity,' the sexual morality of the Victorian bourgeoisie.[10]

Yet while Jacobs certainly uses the conventions of sentimental fiction to identify slavery as the denial of natural human bonds, she seems to be doing much more than prudishly positing redemptive domestic female virtue as an antidote to the perversions of slavery.[11] As Jean Fagan Yellin points out in her introduction to the narrative, Jacobs relativizes and complicates notions of virtue by clearly linking them to economic and political privilege in this apostrophe to her white female readers: "But, O, ye happy women, whose purity has been sheltered from childhood, who have been free to choose the objects of your affection, whose homes are protected by law" (54). Furthermore, by locating the problem of black female sexuality at the heart of the problem of slavery, she posits the resolution of the tension between the erasure and expression of sexuality as integral to the attainment of personhood and self-expression.[12]

Jacobs's narrative, generally considered a prime example of the slave narrative genre, is also recognized as a particularly female conception of that genre.[13] It differs fundamentally from male slave narratives, which chronicle an ascent from slavery to manhood and freedom through a literal movement from South to North; the male slave's body—his physical wholeness and his "rise" from object to subject—is centered on and subsumed by the attainment of literacy and voice.[14] As Carolyn Porter has pointed out, Jacobs's alienation from both her body and her labor renders this movement northward fraught with the unreconcilable tension between body and voice.[15] Jacobs chronicles a series of "incidents" that mark this tension. The suppression of Brent's body, epitomized in the seven years she spends hidden in a tiny attic, paradoxically enables a voice that repeatedly points to her inability to be truly free. Brent's ascent, her movement from South to North, repeatedly refers to and cannot escape the consequences of her "fall." Even in the North Brent is deprived of a home of her own and finds herself serving the woman who has bought her freedom:

> The dream of my life is not yet realized. I do not sit with my children in a home of my own. . . . But God so orders circumstances as to keep me with my friend Mrs. Bruce. . . . It is a privilege to serve her who pities my oppressed people, and who has bestowed the inestimable boon of freedom on me and my children.

> It has been painful to me, in many ways, to recall the dreary years I passed in bondage. . . . Yet the retrospection is not altogether without solace; for with those gloomy recollections come tender memories of my good old grandmother, like light, fleecy clouds floating over a dark and troubled sea." (201)

Jacobs's narrative does not end by granting Brent the home she seeks; the North does not cancel out and amend the evils of the South.[16] In fact, Jacobs's journey north seems to present only a slightly altered mirror image of the South in the "double-voicedness" that characterizes her prose at the end of her narrative.[17] Jacobs seems to be not only revising men's slave narratives such as Frederick Douglass's but also responding to popular conceptions of North-South

oppositions by collapsing them; her "servitude" in the North mirrors her "bondage" in the South.

Brent ventures North only to return, at least in retrospection, to the South; while the image of her grandmother comforts her with an image of maternal domesticity that she cannot attain even in the North, her grandmother also points to the South's legacy of slavery as a maternal trait that follows Brent everywhere. Jacobs's narrative highlights the problematic status of female sexual expression and thus undercuts the implications of her newly gained "voice." By interrogating the specious opposition between North and South that reduces the black female body to an absent presence in her narrative, she becomes the foremother of a literary tradition centered on the black female body.

Notes

[1] See Bell Hooks's *Ain't I a Woman* (Boston: South End Press, 1981), which discusses this dynamic as it pertains to the position of black women within feminist and race politics.

[2] Nathan Huggins, *Harlem Renaissance* (New York: Oxford Univ. Press, 1971), 157.

[3] Huggins's discussion of Carl Van Vechten's infamous *Nigger Heaven* (1926) and Claude McKay's *Home to Harlem* (1928) highlights the way these texts exoticize and sexualize black identity, in particular that of the black woman. Van Vechten compares his attraction to "Negroes" to the lure of an overpowering drug: he is "*violently* interested in Negroes. . . . I would say violently because it was almost an addiction" (*Harlem Renaissance,* 99, my emphasis). Furthermore, Huggins's reading of Jean Toomer's *Cane* highlights the way in which Toomer condemns the Negro's denial of his Southern heritage by portraying the South as a region of incomplete, stultified, and childless women.

[4] Harriet Jacobs, *Incidents in the Life of a Slave Girl, Written by Herself,* ed. Jean Fagan Yellin (1981; reprint, Cambridge: Harvard Univ. Press, 1987), 53-54. All further references to *Incidents* are to this edition and are cited parenthetically in the text.

[5] Jacobs's association of slavery with feminine disease and pollution draws upon the nineteenth-century obsession with female diseases in medical discourse and popular imagery. See, for example, Sally Shuttleworth's "Female Circulation: Medical Discourse and Popular Advertising in the Mid-Victorian Era," in *Body/Politics: Women and the Discourses of Science,* ed. Mary Jacobus, Evelyn Fox Keller, and Sally Shuttleworth (New York: Routledge, 1990), 47-68, in which Shuttleworth claims that "[w]omanhood itself [was] figured as a form of pathology" (62); and

Carroll Smith-Rosenberg's *Disorderly Conduct: Visions of Gender in Victorian America* (New York: Oxford Univ. Press, 1985). Appropriately, as Carolyn Porter notes, the South was represented as a region of feminized excesses in the popular imagination. This conceptualization of the South involved a conflation of sex and race: "If the North now understood itself to represent the progressive force of the Anglo-Saxon race, while the South embodied blackness and barbarism, the North also saw itself as masculine and the South as a woman" ("Social Discourse and Nonfictional Prose," in *Columbia Literary History of the United States,* ed. Emory Elliott [New York: Columbia Univ. Press, 1988], 356).

[6] W. E. B. DuBois defines double-consciousness as follows: "It is a peculiar sensation, this double-consciousness, this sense of always looking at one's self through the eyes of others, of measuring one's soul by the tape of a world that looks on in amused contempt and pity. One ever feels his twoness,—an American, a Negro; two souls, two thoughts, two unreconciled strivings; two warring ideals in one dark body, whose dogged strength alone keeps it from being torn asunder" (*The Souls of Black Folk* [New York: Bantam Books, 1989], 3).

[7] In her editor's introduction to *Incidents* Yellin writes, "It is difficult to determine the extent to which Linda Brent's characterization of her action as 'a headlong plunge' and a 'great sin' are merely conventional, and the extent to which these articulate a serious endorsement of a sexual standard that condemns her" (xxxi). Indeed, the difficulty of determining Jacobs's stance in relation to the depiction of this "headlong plunge" constitutes one of the most complex questions in her narrative and has led to much debate. For discussions of Jacobs's use of sentimental conventions as a challenge to domestic ideology, see Hazel Carby's *Reconstructing Womanhood: The Emergence of the Afro-American Woman Novelist* (New York: Oxford Univ. Press, 1987); William L. Andrews's "The Changeing Moral Discourse of Nineteenth-Century African American Women's Autobiography: Harriet Jacobs and Elizabeth Keckley," in *De/Colonizing the Subject: The Politics of Gender in Women's Autobiography,* ed. Sidonie Smith and Julia Watson (Minneapolis: Univ. of Minnesota Press, 1992), 225-41; Deborah M. Garfield's "Speech, Listening, and Female Sexuality in *Incidents in the Life of a Slave Girl*," *Arizona Quarterly* 50 (summer 1994): 19-49; and Mauri Skinfill's "Nation and Miscegenation: *Incidents in the Life of a Slave Girl*," *Arizona Quarterly* 52 (summer 1995): 63—79. See also Michelle Burnham's discussion of Jacobs's text as a staging of the political ambiguity of sentimental discourse in "Loopholes of Resistance: Harriet Jacobs' Slave Narrative and the Critique of Agency in Foucault," *Arizona Quarterly* 49 (summer 1993): 53-73.

[8] See, for example, Bruce Mills's discussion of Lydia Maria Child's revisions of Jacobs's text, in which he argues that Child encouraged Jacobs to emphasize the theme of self-sacrificing maternity in the narrative, in "Lydia Maria Child and the Endings to Harriet Jacobs's *Incidents in the Life of a Slave Girl*," *American Literature* 64 (June 1992): 255-72.

[9] See Sander L. Gilman's discussion of the ways nineteenth-century art, medicine, and literature portrayed the black female body as sexually decadent and thus linked to insanity and disease in "Black Bodies, White Bodies: Toward an Iconography of Female Sexuality in Late Nineteenth-Century Art, Medicine, and Literature," in *"Race," Writing, and Difference,* ed. Henry Louis Gates Jr. (Chicago: Univ. of Chicago Press, 1985), 232-61.

[10] Deborah E. McDowell, "'That Nameless . . . Shameful Impulse': Sexuality in Nella Larsen's *Quicksand and Passing*," in *Studies in Black American Literature, Volume III: Black Feminist Criticism and Critical Theory,* ed. Joe Weixlmann and Houston A. Baker Jr. (Greenwood, Fla.: The Penkevill Publishing Company, 1988), 141-42. See also Jacobs's correspondence with Amy Post, which reveals the reason for her misgivings about the revelation of her sexual liaison and the rationale for her purported prudery: "there are some things that I might have made plainer I know—Woman can whisper—her cruel wrongs into the ear of a very dear friend—much easier than she can record them for the world to read—*I have left nothing out but what I thought the world might believe that a Slave Woman was too willing to pour out*—that she might gain their sympathies" (quoted in the appendix to Yellin's edition of the narrative, 242, my emphasis). Jacobs fears that her attempts to appeal to the sensibilities of her readers by portraying herself as a virtuous woman defiled may in fact backfire—she may be considered indecent, too willing to "pour out" her wrongs.

[11] Jacobs emphasizes the fact that because Brent is a slave she is prohibited from marrying the man she truly loves. Brent consequently resolves to escape her tyrannical master's advances by submitting to the advances of another white man, and in a much commented upon passage in the narrative she claims that there is a measure of freedom in choosing this lesser of two evils: "It seems less degrading to give one's self, than to submit to compulsion" (55). In her introduction to the narrative, Jean Fagan Yellin notes that Jacobs draws on the "over-wrought style of popular [seduction] fiction" when she recounts her sexual experiences. According to Yellin, this is but one of the various literary styles Jacobs uses in her narrative, and it is precisely through Jacobs's demonstration of the black woman's inability to conform to rules of proper sexual behavior that Jacobs manages to break the "taboo" of the for-

bidden subject of the "sexual exploitation of women in slavery" (xxxiii). Yellin further writes: "By creating a narrator who presents her private sexual history as a subject of public political concern, Jacobs moves her book out of the world of conventional nineteenth-century polite discourse. In and through her creation of Linda Brent, who yokes her success story as a heroic slave mother to her confession as a woman who mourns that she is not a storybook heroine, Jacobs articulates her struggle to assert her womanhood and projects a new kind of female hero" (xiv).

[12] Hazel Carby defends black women's writing from the charge of prudery by similarly pointing to the political import of their depiction of sexuality in "'On the Threshold of Woman's Era': Lynching, Empire, and Sexuality in Black Feminist Theory," in *"Race," Writing, and Difference,* 301-16.

[13] See Yellin, *Incidents,* xxvi; and Porter, "Social Discourse and Nonfictional Prose," 361-62.

[14] Literary studies of slave narratives include Charles T. Davis and Henry Louis Gates Jr., *The Slave's Narrative* (New York: Oxford Univ. Press, 1985); Deborah E. McDowell and Arnold Rampersad, *Slavery and the Literary Imagination* (Baltimore: Johns Hopkins Univ. Press, 1989); Robert Stepto, *From Behind the Veil: A Study of Afro-American Narrative* (Urbana: Univ. of Illinois Press, 1991); William Andrews, *To Tell a Free Story: The First Century of Afro-American Autobiography, 1760-1865* (Urbana: Univ. of Illinois Press, 1988); and Frances Smith Foster, *Witnessing Slavery: The Development of Antebellum Slave Narratives* (Westport, Conn.: Greenwood, 1979). For a discussion of Jacobs's narrative in the context of black women's autobiographical writing, see Elizabeth Fox-Genovese's "My Statue, My Self: Autobiographical Writings of Afro-American Women," in *Reading Black, Reading Feminist: A Critical Anthology,* ed. Henry Louis Gates Jr. (New York: Meridian, 1990), 176-203.

[15] Porter, "Social Discourse and Nonfictional Prose," 362.

[16] See Sharon Davie's discussion of the significance of the ending of Jacobs's narrative in "'Reader, My Story Ends with Freedom': Harriet Jacobs's *Incidents in the Life of a Slave Girl,*" in *Famous Last Words: Changes in Gender and Narrative Closure,* ed. Alison Booth (Charlottesville: Univ. Press of Virginia, 1993), 86-109.

[17] Gates describes "double-voicedness" as a tradition of parody and hidden internal polemic in African American literature in *The Signifying Monkey: A Theory of African-American Literary Criticism* (New York: Oxford Univ. Press, 1988), 110-13. . . .

AUTOBIOGRAPHIES BY WOMEN PIONEERS

Lillian Schlissel (essay date 1977)

SOURCE: "Women's Diaries on the Western Frontier," in *American Studies,* Vol. XVIII, No. 1, Spring, 1977, pp. 87-100.

[*In the following essay, Schlissel discusses the usefulness of diaries in the study of the impact of Western migration on nineteenth-century women.*]

This book began with a fascination for the diaries of the overland women, with the detail of their lives and the dramatic dimensions of their everyday existence. These were ordinary women who were caught up in a momentous event of history. Between 1840 and 1870, a quarter of a million Americans crossed the continental United States, some twenty-four hundred miles of it, in one of the great migrations of modern times. They went West to claim free land in the Oregon and California Territories, and they went West to strike it rich by mining gold and silver. Men and women knew they were engaged in nothing less than extending American possession of the continent from ocean to ocean. No other event of the century except the Civil War evoked so many personal accounts as the overland passage. Young people and even children kept diaries and felt that their lives, briefly, had become part of history. The mundane events of each day—the accidents and the mishaps and the small victories—had grown significant. In the case of women, suddenly, because of their diaries, their daily lives became accessible, where so much of the life of nineteenth-century women has disappeared from view.

The westward movement was a major transplanting of young families. All the kinfolk who could be gathered assembled to make that hazardous passage together. Women were part of the journey because their fathers, husbands, and brothers had determined to go. They went West because there was no way for them *not* to go once the decision was made.

The emigrants came from Missouri, Illinois, Iowa, and Indiana, and some all the way from New York and New Hampshire. Most of them had moved to "free land" at least once before, and their parents and grandparents before them had similarly made several removals during their lifetime. These were a class of "peasant proprietors." They had owned land before and would own land again. They were young and consumed with boundless confidence, believing the better life tomorrow could be won by the hard work of today. Emblematic of their determination was Barsina French, who fastidiously copied pen-

APRON FULL OF
GOLD

THE LETTERS OF MARY JANE MEGQUIER

FROM SAN FRANCISCO

1849–1856

SECOND EDITION

EDITED & WITH AN INTRODUCTION BY

POLLY WELTS KAUFMAN

INTRODUCTION TO THE FIRST EDITION BY

ROBERT GLASS CLELAND

UNIVERSITY OF NEW MEXICO PRESS

ALBUQUERQUE

Title page for Apron Full of Gold: The Letters of Mary Jane Megquier from San Francisco 1849-1856,
edited by Polly Welts Kaufman

manship and grammatical exercises into her diary as the oxen led her parents' wagon across the empty plains.

The journey started in the towns along the Missouri River between St. Joseph and Council Bluffs. These settlements came to be known as the "jumping-off places." In the winter months emigrants gathered to join wagon parties and to wait for the arrival of kin. It was an audacious journey through territory that was virtually unknown. Guidebooks promised that the adventure would take no more than three to four months time—a mere summer's vacation. But the guidebooks were wrong. Often there was no one in a wagon train who really knew what the roads would bring, or if there were any roads at all. Starting when the mud of the roads began to harden in mid-April, the emigrants would discover that the overland passage took every ounce of ingenuity and tenacity they possessed. For many, it would mean six to eight months of grueling travel, in a wagon with no springs, under a canvas that heated up to 110° by midday, through drenching rains and summer storms. It would mean swimming cattle across rivers and living for months at a time in tents.

Over eight hundred diaries and day journals kept by those who made the overland journey have been published or catalogued in archives, and many more are still in family collections. As a general category, the nineteenth-century diary is something like a family history, a souvenir meant to be shared like a Bible, handed down through generations, to be viewed not as an individual's story but as the history of a family's growth and course through time. Overland diaries were a special kind of diary, often meant to be published in county newspapers or sent to relatives intending to make the same journey the following season. Many of them are filled with information about the route, the watering places, the places where one could feed the cattle and oxen, and the quality of the grasses along the way. Such diaries seldom contain expression of intimate feelings, but there are occasions when emotions flash out, beyond control and sharp.

The story of the Overland Trail has been told many times, and emigrant diaries have been used before in these histories. Merrill Mattes, in his study *The Great Platte River Road,* drew upon some six hundred diaries as he described the Trail from the Missouri to the South Pass of the Rockies.[1] And other historians, among them John Faragher, Howard Lamar, Julie Roy Jeffrey, and John Unruh, have used such diaries as the bases for revisions of different aspects of the West's history.[2] No study, though, has been woven entirely out of the stuff of the women's writing in order to assess whether our picture of this single event of history, the overland experience, is in significant manner altered by the perception of the women.

Working with personal papers—letters and diaries—presents the historian with special problems. As documents, these items are the accounts of singularities. They record the particular moment and the personal response. Therefore it is necessary to determine whether they are merely idiosyncratic and anomalous, or whether they form part of a larger configuration that contains and explains disparate events. Only when the patterns emerge with regularity can one believe the responses are representative.[3]

This narrative is made of the diaries, reminiscences, and letters of 103 women, a random sample among the thousands of women who went West. These are the diaries of white women, many of them daughters of second and third generation American families. Some attempt is made to include the experiences of black women, many of whom went West as slaves. White or black, these women neither directed events nor affected the course of the journey. They were ordinary women in ordinary families, and the question is whether, as their story unfolds, the historical event takes on new dimension.

What I have looked for in reading these diaries were places where the women seemed to see something different than their men saw. What I asked was whether the overland experience, studied so many times before, would be revealed in a new aspect through the writings of women, and whether such perspective as the women bring might prove to be historically valuable.

The first step was to reconstruct from the diaries in fine detail the daily lives of the women, to separate out of the diaries those writings that pertained to the "woman's sphere." In the course of describing the daily life of the women, I came to see the design of the emigrant family and something of the dimensions of its emotional balances and work roles. For while it is true that family history cannot be reconstructed from women's writings alone, nevertheless the women were the shapers of the family, and it is they who provide us with primary access to the internal dynamics of households.

Certain dimensions emerged simply and easily. For example, marriage was the social norm accepted by both men and women, although within the structure of marriage men were considerably more free. Great numbers of men went West, leaving their wives and children at home; women, in contrast, almost always traveled within a family structure.

Most marriages seemed companionable. They were entered into in recognition that farming and particularly the work of making a farm out of a frontier was work that required a large family if it were to succeed. Dynamics within the family, what historian John Faragher has termed the "political economy of sex," was determined by the work of each partner, but the balance of power always followed upon the strong prescriptions of patriarchy.[4] Men were the heads of households, and while frontier women were often called upon to perform "men's work," those additional chores did not yield them any extra perquisites.

On the Overland Trail, women strove to be equal to the demands of the day. They asked no special help or treatment. They responded to the spectacular beauty of the land, and they took keen interest in the economies of the road, recording the costs of ferriage and food supplies. They were as knowledgeable as men about the qualities of grasses for the animals. They understood what was expected of them and endeavored to do their share of the work of each day.

The women on the Overland Trail did the domestic chores: they prepared the meals and washed the clothes and cared for the children. But they also drove the ox teams and collected pieces of dung they called "buffalo chips" to fuel their fires when there was no wood. And when there were no buffalo chips, they walked in clouds of dust behind the wagons, collecting weeds. They searched for wild berries and managed to roll some dough on a wagon seat and bake a pie over hot rocks in order to lift meals out of the tedium of beans and coffee.

For women traveling with small children, the overland experience could be nerve-wracking. Children fell out of the wagons. They got lost among the hundreds of families and oxen and sheep. Children suffered all the usual childhood ills—measles, fevers, toothaches, diarrhea. But on the Trail, children who were drenched by days of heavy rains or burned by hot sun could be especially irritable and hard to care for. Free from supervision, older children were full of excitement and mischief. Their mothers worried constantly that Indians would steal them.

For women who were pregnant, the overland crossing could be a nightmare. One never knew for certain where labor might begin: in Indian territory, or in the mountains, or in drenching rain. One might be alone, with no women to help, and only fear at hand. The birth might be simple, or it might be complicated and tortuous. Among rural Americans of the nineteenth century, pregnancy and impending birth were not reasons to defer the decision to move, not when free land lay at the journey's end.

It has been suggested by historian Howard Lamar and psychiatrist Daniel Levinson that the overland passage played a vital role in the life cycle of men, corresponding to "breaking away," improving, or bettering oneself, the stages that mark a man's life.[5] If experiences attain mythic dimension because some pattern in all the endless variety reverberates against the fixed frame of human needs and yearnings, if the westward migration became an expression of testing and reaching for men, then it surely must have been an "anti-mythic" journey for women. It came when the physical demands of their lives drained their energies into other directions.[6] The severity of the dislocation of the journey can be gauged in the knowledge that about one of every five overland women was seized by some stage of pregnancy, and virtually every married woman traveled with small children. When women wrote of the decision to leave their homes, it was almost always with anguish, a note conspicuously absent from the diaries of men.

The diaries of men and women carry certain predictable characteristics, with men writing of "fight, conflict and competition and . . . hunting," and women writing of their concerns with "family and relational values."[7] But it is not true, as some have concluded, that the diaries of men and of women are essentially alike.[8] Although many women, along with the men, wrote of the splendors of the landscape and the rigors of the road, although many overland diaries seem tediously interchangeable, there are not only important distinctions, but distinctions so profound as to raise the question whether women did not ultimately perceive the westward trek differently. Traveling side by side, sitting in the very same wagons, crossing the continent in response to the call for free land, women did not always see the venture in the clear light of the expectation of success. There were often shadows in their minds, areas of dark reservation and opposition. The diaries of women differ from the accounts of the men in both simple and in subtle ways. In the diaries of the women for example, the Indians are described as helpful guides and purveyors of services far more often than they are described as enemies. Although the women universally feared the Indians, they nevertheless tell, with some amusement, that their farmer-husbands were not always good buffalo hunters, coming back to the wagon parties empty-handed and later trading shirts with the Indians for salmon and dried buffalo meat. The women, in the naturalness of their telling, offer a new perception of the relations between the emigrants and the Indians. Having no special stake in asserting their bravery, having no special need to affirm their prowess, the women correct the historical record as they write of the daily exchanges by which the Indians were part of life of the road.[9]

New configurations continue to appear when one reads the women's diaries closely. One of the commonplaces of rural life was the absence of men for periods that varied from weeks to months and years. Many of the men who traveled the Oregon Trail alone had left behind them their wives and their children, and they might be gone for two years or more. During these periods women were expected to serve as head of the household as well as of the farm or of any commercial enterprise—a mill or a store—that the family owned. On the Overland Trail, when a woman was widowed, she was expected to continue with her children and to file her claim alone. No widow ever placed her wagon and her family under the protection of another family. The expectation was that women would direct the family enterprise independently when need arose. There are indices that in the partiarchal values of rural communities there were interfaces where women were more independent—and independent in more ways—than has been commonly assumed.

In another aspect the women's diaries differ from the diaries written by men. As ritual caretakers of the sick and the dying, the women saw the real enemies of the road as disease and accident. It is in women's diaries that we are reminded that the heaviest emigration of the Overland Trail was accomplished during years of cholera epidemic. As travelers hurried across the continent to the "rag towns" of California and Nevada in order to pan the clear streams for gold, cholera swept over the Trail.

Nowhere in the world could it have been more bleak to be stricken than on an open and unmarked road, to be left by the side of the Trail either to recover or to die. The women write of the deaths and the burials. They tell of typhoid, mountain fever, measles, dysentery and drownings. The women knew that disease and accident killed more emigrants than did Indians. The women, whose job it was to care for the dying, carefully noted the cost of the westward movement in human life. Whereas men recorded the death in aggregate numbers, the women knew death as personal catastrophe and noted the particulars of each grave site, whether it was newly dug or old, whether of a young person or an adult, whether it had been disturbed by wolves or by Indians. The women were the actuaries of the road, tallying the miles with the lives that were lost. One must suspect, finally, that many women judged the heroic adventure of their men as some kind of outrageous folly thrust upon them by obedience to patriarchal ritual.

In their accommodation to the life of the road, the women tried to weave a fabric of accustomed design, a semblance of their usual domestic circle. Out of the disorder of traveling, the women created and held on to some order and routine. Against all odds, they managed to feed their families, do the wash, and care for the scattering children. They strove to calm the quarreling men, to keep a diary record of passing friends and families, to note who took the children when parents died on the road, to note carefully the names on the grave markers. The women even managed to bear new life on the crest of the journey's upheaval.

In the end, a woman who came through the journey felt she had won her own victory. The test of the jour-

ney was whether or not she had been equal to the task of holding her family together against the sheer physical forces that threatened to spin them to the four winds of chance. It was against the continual threat of dissolution that the women had striven. If ever there was a time when men and women turned their psychic energies toward opposite visions, the overland journey was that time. Sitting side by side on a wagon seat, a man and a woman felt different needs as they stared at the endless road that led into the New Country.

Overland women recorded their pride in having preserved the integrity of family life intact in the names they gave to the children born on the Trail. Gertrude Columbia was born on the shores of the surging Columbia River. Alice Nevada drew first breath in the rocky lands of the Sierra Nevada. Gila Parrish was born somewhere along the Gila River in Arizona. Two children lived, and one child died. The New Country, the women knew in a profound way, was a bittersweet promise that took its own toll of hope and of optimism.

In the very commonplace of their observations, the women bring us a new vision of the overland experience; they bring it closer to our own lives. They do not write of trailblazing or of adventure but of those facets of living that are unchanging. In reading their diaries we come closer to understanding how historical drama translates into human experience. Through the eyes of the women we begin to see history as the stuff of daily struggle.

Notes

[1] Merrill J. Mattes, *The Great Platte River Road*, Vol. 25, Publications of Nebraska State Historical Society, 1969.

[2] John M. Faragher, *Women and Men on the Overland Trail* (New Haven, Yale University Press, 1979). Howard R. Lamar, "Rites of Passage: Young Men and Their Families in the Overland Trail Experience, 1843-69," *Soul-Butter and Hog Wash and Other Essays on the American West,* Charles Redd Monographs in Western History, No. 8 (Provo, Utah, Brigham Young University Press, 1978). Julie Roy Jeffrey, *Frontier Women: The Trans-Mississippi West, 1840-1880* (New York, Hill & Wang, 1979). John Unruh, *The Plains Across: The Overland Emigrants and the Trans-Mississippi West, 1840-60* (Chicago, University of Illinois Press, 1979). See also such works as Dale M. Morgan, ed., *Overland in 1846: Diaries and Letters of the California-Oregon Trail*, 2 vols. (Georgetown, California, Talisman Press, 1963); Irene D. Paden, *The Wake of the Prairie Schooner* (New York, Macmillan, 1943); and George R. Stewart, *The California Trail: An Epic with Many Heroes* (New York, McGraw-Hill, 1962).

[3] See Gertrude Ackerman, "Family Papers and the Westward Movement." *Minnesota History* (1939):314-316;

Alice Felt Tyler, "The Westward Movement as Reflected in Family Papers," *Minnesota History* (1943):111-124; Gordon W. Allport, *The Use of Personal Documents in Psychological Science* (New York, The Social Science Research Council, 1942); Louis Gottschalk, Clyde Kluckhohn, and Robert Angell, *The Use of Personal Documents in History, Anthropology and Sociology* (Washington, D.C., Social Science Research Council, 1945).

[4] John M. Faragher, "Women and Men on the Farming Frontier of Illinois: The Political Economy of Sex," unpublished essay.

[5] "For young men [the Overland Trail] was a dramatic rite of passage to mastery and adulthood" Howard R. Lamar, "Rites of Passage," p. 51. Also see Daniel J. Levinson, "The Mid-Life Transition: A Period in Adult Psychosocial Development," *Psychiatry* 40 (1977): 100.

[6] For a valuable discussion of the concepts of life-cycle and historical time, see Tamara K. Hareven, "Family Time and Historical Time," *Daedalus,* 106 (1977), 57-70.

[7] Faragher, *Women and Men on the Overland Trail,* p. 14.

[8] Faragher compared twenty-two men's and twenty-eight women's diaries according to a list of fifty-three selected value-topics, and concluded that "the diaries indicate, first and foremost that these mid-nineteenth century men and women were part of a common culture, that they were, indeed, *more alike than different* [emphasis added]. *Ibid.,* p. 15 and Appendix II, Table AII-3, pp. 202-203. In contrast, this study finds that the value topics of the women significantly *differ* from those that prevail in the diaries of men.

[9] The picture of the relationship between Indian and emigrant as described by the women in their diaries is substantiated by John Unruh in his excellent study *The Plains Across.*

Lillian Schlissel (essay date 1982)

SOURCE: Introduction to *Women's Diaries of the Westward Journey*, Schocken Books, 1982, pp. 10-18

[*In the following excerpt, Schlissel discusses the historical relevance of diaries written by nineteenth-century women pioneers, examining in particular what the diaries reveal about frontier gender roles.*]

For the women who traveled to the western territories in the nineteenth century, the journey brought sharp dislocations. Traditional work patterns were daily overturned with women called upon to do what they had long regarded as "means' work." The consequence was that gender role, class orientation, even self-evaluation, became troubled areas to many women, but particularly to those women who came to the Overland Trail and the frontier experience in their middle years.

In addition, the great migration disrupted those "long-lived, intimate, loving friendship[s]" which women had formed with other women in the settled communities of the East.[1] The diaries and the journals of women on the frontier reveal that the dissolution of bonds with other women contributed heavily to their sense of dislocation. This dissolution of emotional ties aggravated the merely physical hardships women endured on the journey. When these women wrote longingly of the homes they left behind them, "home" meant their close bonds with mothers, sisters and friends, and they grieved over the loss of those relationships which had provided the structure and the emotional support of their lives. This sundering of their emotional life with women and with the familiar world of womanly affairs, one may surmise, lay at the root of the antagonism to men that marks the pages of so many diaries of the journeying women.

In almost all the early stages of frontier life—the Trail itself and the first settlements—women strove to re-establish the traditional norms of sex roles and work patterns. Thus, there are numerous diary accounts of mothers insisting that their young daughters wear sunbonnets and gloves on the wagon trains.[2] Once the settlements were established, wives and mothers, but particularly young girls, found themselves caught between "old" and "new" life styles. The diaries provide remarkable records of ambivalence, of anxiety and sometimes of exultation as women moved toward new expressions of freedom and self-assertion.

In the period immediately preceding the great westward migration a women's world had been ordered by a separation of the sexes. The delineation of "sexual spheres" placed women in life-long contiguities with other women, and allowed them to find high levels of emotional fulfillment within their own group.[3] On the westward journey, women found themselves cast into what was essentially a man's world, the proportion of women to men on the Trail sometimes being no more than one in ten. Once the rigors of the journey were upon them, and the congenial contours of the Great Plains had been passed, women found themselves trudging on foot behind the wagons, in choking clouds of dust, collecting buffalo "chips" for fuel, keeping the cows from wandering off, and the children from accidents. When the men were needed for more pressing chores, the women drove the teams of horses or mules. When the wagons were being inched up the mountain passes of the Rockies, the women worked behind, carrying large rocks to set beneath the wagon wheels to keep them from backsliding. Many diarists fairly exploded with bitterness as the hard journey erased the more graceful tributes by which eastern society had flattered women and hidden the inequalities of their station.[4]

Although the corps of families that emigrated between 1840 and 1860 was a broadly hetergenous cross-section of social, ethnic and economic groups, women within that population had been trained to fairly uniform social roles. Standards of female behavior and female propriety show strong conformity in virtually every literate diary, and those standards were strongly oriented toward middle-class behavior. Thus, the work imposed on women during the six or seven months of travel along the Overland Trail was not merely arduous, but was often felt to be demeaning.

From the first, women understood the westward migration as a masculine enterprise. The decision to make the journey was always a determination made by men. Once it had begun, the two-thousand-mile journey meant that the determination of women's lives,—when to start, when to stop, which trail to follow—was taken from them. One diarist tells how, after months of hard journey, the men went out to survey the area and, still dissatisfied, ordered the march to continue. The women, bone weary, pressed on, waiting for the Pacific Ocean itself to stop the endless travel of the wagon trains.[5]

It became commonplace for women to appraise their condition with anger and despair, and sometimes to feel their very sex had become a burden and a punishment. Abigail Scott Duniway recalls:

> I was born Oct. 22, 1834, just 4 years after my parents wedding day. I being the third in their rapidly increasing family of a dozen. The eldest . . . had died in infancy before the 2nd child . . . was born. . . . I remember when my mother informed me . . . her sorrow over my sex was almost too great to be borne.

> I remember standing at the beside when another little sister came to our crowded home. My mother said, through her tears, "Poor baby, she'll be a woman some day, poor baby, a woman's life is so hard."[6]

For Abigail Duniway, the crossing of the plains was a burden history had no business laying at the door of women, and she always considered the frontier directly responsible for her mother's death. "That long and perilous journey across the Great Plains, over the Oregon Trail. . . . Suffice it to say that our gentle mother fell ill of cholera and died."[7]

Of her own lot as a married woman, Duniway records:

> To bear 2 children in 2 1/2 years from my marriage day, to make thousands pounds of butter every year for market, not including what was used in our free hotel at home; to sew and cook and wash and iron; to bake and clean and stew and fry, to be in short a general woman drudge, and never a penny of my own was a hard lot.[8]

Duniway's plaintive self-appraisal, that she saw herself "a general woman drudge, and never a penny of my own," is the silent interface of scores of other lives.

The physical demands made upon women were not less than those which men endured. The common conditions of heat, flies, dirt, weariness, lack of water, lost cattle, fear of Indian attack and disease, all these men and women shared. But to the women were reserved the travails of pregnancy and childbirth, the rituals of attending the sick and the dying, the care of the crying infants and the irritable children. America Rollins, in 1852, recorded how the wagon train was "called to a halt quite by accident. Mrs. George's child has fallen out of the wagon and both wheels have passed over his body. Called a physician some hopes are entertained of its recovery."[9]

Women became relentless recorders of the physical and mental anguish of the westward journey. "Mrs. Harriman . . . is suffering severely with rheumatism and she seems to be in perfect anguish and cannot move her hands at all today. Cannot take care of her little one, now nearly two years old. It was presented to her on her journey into the Territory, delaying the company only 2 days. . . . Exposure [has] brought the dreadful disease to her. . . . "[10] The excerpt shows the vicissitudes of the travel, but it also reveals a circle of female solicitude and sisterhood. Driven by the exquisite punishment of the Trail, women helped each other, were responsive to each other's needs, and strove to weave the sort of bonding that helped to preserve the old equilibrium. The diaries show that women fought against the dissolution of their customary roles, fought against the awesome demands of the trail, and sought, sometimes with desperation, "to hold together the few fragments of female subculture left. . . . "[11] Thus, continued the same diarist, "I picked a lovely bouquet of prairie flowers and carried it to [Mrs. Harriman] but she couldn't take it into her hands."[12]

While not so strenuous as the labors of the men, women's work brought no time for respite. Occasionally, high-strung women were exhausted by the journey. "Mrs. Spalding was so oppressed with labor, that she could not have the society of even her own little daughter. The child was put in a rude kind of wagon in the morning to be drawn about by the Indian children, while the mother was occupied with her domestic chores. . . . "[13] Often a newborn died on the journey. "Mrs. George Belshaw give birth to a daughter 4 o'clock this morning. [Lived] about 2 weeks."[14] Each careful account of another women's misfortune was a muted protest on the part of the diarist against her own fate.

The most singular pattern that emerges from the frontier diaries comes from the accounts kept by women of the journey's death toll. Recorded with a bookkeeper's care are the numbers of gravesites passed, the carcasses of the dead animals, and the record of the miles crossed. These peculiar records recur in the diaries of women who were unknown to each other, on different adventures and with different destinations. They provide a startling access into the psychology of women, and suggest how disparate were the emotional worlds of men and women on the westward migration.

Mrs. Cecilia McMillen Adams, who kept the diary of her family's journey from Illinois to Oregon in 1852, traced the wagon train's journey as follows:

> Child's grave . . . smallpox . . . child's grave. . . .
> [We] passed 7 new-made graves. One had 4 bodies
> in it . . . cholera. A man died this morning with the
> cholera in the company ahead of us. . . . Another
> man died. . . . Passed 6 new graves. . . . We have
> passed 21 new-made graves . . . made 18 miles. . . .
> Passed 13 graves today. Passed 10 graves. . . .

> June 25: Passed 7 graves . . . made 14 miles;
> June 26: Passed 8 graves;
> June 29: Passed 10 graves;
> June 30: Passed 10 graves . . . made 22 miles;
> July 1: Passed 8 graves . . . made 21 miles;
> July 2: One man of [our] company died.
>   Passed 8 graves made 16 miles;
> July 4: Passed 2 graves . . . made 16 miles;
> July 5: Passed 9 graves . . . made 18 miles;
> July 6: Passed 6 graves . . . made 9 miles;
> July 11: Passed 15 graves . . . made 13 miles;
> July 12: Passed 5 graves . . . made 15 miles;
> July 18: Passed 4 graves . . . made 16 miles;
> July 19: Passed 2 graves . . . made 14 miles;
> July 23: Passed 7 graves . . . made 15 miles;
> July 25: Passed 3 graves . . . made 16 miles;
> July 27: Passed 3 graves . . . made 14 miles;
> July 29: Passed 8 graves . . . made 16 miles;
> July 30: I have kept an account of the dead
>   cattle we passed & the number today is 35;
> Aug. 7: We passed 8 graves with a week . . .
>   made 16 miles;
> Sept. 7: We passed 14 graves this week . . .
>   made 17 miles;
> Sept. 9: We passed 10 graves this week . . .
>   made 16 miles;
> Oct. 1: Have seen 35 graves since leaving
>   Fort Boise
> Oct. 17: Here are 12 graves all together.[15]

Virtually the same kind of tally appears in the diary of Maria Parsons Belshaw, in 1833, as she and her husband journeyed from Indiana to the Oregon Territory:

> Aug. 25: Passed 1 grave . . . we made 12
>   miles;
> Aug. 26: Passed 3 graves . . . 1 dead horse,
>   18 cattle . . . made 13 miles;
> Aug. 27: Passed 5 graves . . . 1 horse, 23
>   cattle . . . made 15 miles;
> Aug. 28: Passed 1 grave . . . 17 cattle . . .
>   made 23 miles;
> Aug. 29: Passed 5 dead cattle . . . made 15
>   miles;
> Aug. 30: Passed 3 graves . . . 6 dead cattle . . .
>   made 6 miles;
> Aug. 31: Passed 9 dead cattle . . . made 15
>   miles;
> Sept. 1: Passed 1 grave . . . 2 dead horses, 21
>   cattle, made 10 miles;
> Sept. 2: Passed 8 graves . . . 19 cattle . . .
>   made 12 miles;
> Sept. 3: Passed 5 graves . . . 8 dead cattle . . .
>   made 20 miles;
> Sept. 4: Passed 2 graves . . . 8 dead cattle . . .
>   made 17 miles;
> Sept. 5: Passed 3 graves . . . 3 dead cattle . . .
>   made 17 miles;
> Sept. 6: Passed 1 graves . . . 3 dead cattle . . .
>   made 17 miles;
> Sept. 7: Passed 2 graves . . . 3 dead cattle . . .
>   made 18 miles;
> Sept. 8: Passed 1 graves . . . 3 dead cattle . . .
>   made 16 miles;
> Sept. 9: Passed 16 graves . . . 1 ox . . . made
>   16 miles;
> Sept. 10: Passed 2 graves . . . 2 horses . . .
>   made 16 miles;
> Sept. 11: Passed 1 graves . . . 4 cattle . . .
>   made 15 miles;
> Sept. 12-14: Passed 15 dead cattle, 3 dead
>   oxen . . . made 32 miles[16]

In some journals the daily accounts of gravesites are transcribed as weekly aggregates, but they are never ignored. Not even births seem to be recorded with such tenacious attention.

Lodisa Frizzell, telling of her family's travel to California in 1852, wrote: "On the 30th day of the wagon train, we passed several graves. . . . I do not think there would be as much sickness as there usually is for we have passed less than 100 fresh graves . . . hope [wolves] will not disturb the graves."[17] A few pages later in the diary, she wrote:

> Saw . . . one old cow, a paper pinned on her head.
> It stated that she had been left to die . . . but
> requested that no one abuse her as she had been one

of the best cows. . . . It called up so many associations to mind that it affected me to tears. . . . [18]

The journal continues: "Passed where they were burying a man; scarce a day but some one is left on these plains. . . . "[19] On the 72nd day of the journey, Frizzell wrote:

> we are hardly half way . . . the heart has a thousand misgivings, and the mind is tortured with anxiety, and often as I passed the fresh-made graves, I have glanced at the side boards of the wagons, not knowing how soon it would serve as a coffin for some one of us.[20]

The diaries reveal some sense of the extent to which the women felt themselves in antagonistic relation with their men. On occasion, opposition broke into open revolt, as in the account of the desparate woman who set fire to the wagons.[21] But more often, the women maintained their silence. These journals, with their relentless record-keeping of the graves passed, were ultimately indictments of men. As wagon trains penetrated the territories of the West, they drew the backward-bending memories of the women and the leaden inertia of their opposing wills. However bravely they started, however they mustered their strength to meet the demands of each day, however they rallied to appreciate the splendors of the new lands, women—particularly those of mature years—were daily in touch with the journey's terrible toll.[22] In their natural roles as child-bearers, in their familial roles as nurses of the sick, and in their social roles as ritual caretakers and mourners for the dead, the women were in close contact with death on the westward journey.

When a family separated from the wagon trail, there were usually two basic patterns which affected women's lives. If her husband chose to farm a section isolated from other settlements, then in the first season the man was a hunter and his wife a forager. Miriam Davis, who settled with her husband and children in Kansas, in 1855, described tying her small children to the legs of a table when she went to the river to search for roots and plants, for fear the children would be bitten by rattlesnakes if they were free to wander.

Of her kitchen, Miriam Davis writes: "It is roofed by the blue dome of heaven. . . . The oven is so small could bake only one loaf at a time . . . wind has blown so hard that I was obliged to lay stones all around the oven to keep the coals under it. . . . Have already labored hard all day and have baked only 2 small loaves of bread, while in a family of seven like ours one can be dispatched at each meal."[23] Housekeeping on the frontier was something like cleaning the Augean stables.

Beyond the purely physical demands was the sense in which frontier labor was judged to be demeaning.

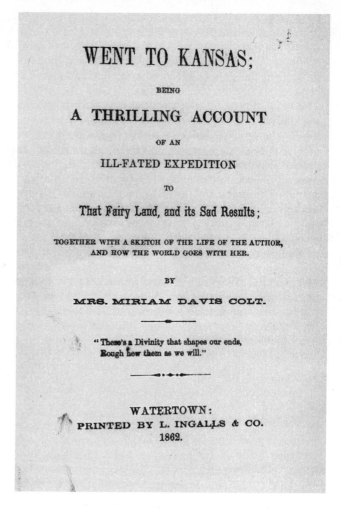

WENT TO KANSAS;

BEING

A THRILLING ACCOUNT

OF AN

ILL-FATED EXPEDITION

TO

That Fairy Land, and its Sad Results;

TOGETHER WITH A SKETCH OF THE LIFE OF THE AUTHOR, AND HOW THE WORLD GOES WITH HER.

BY

MRS. MIRIAM DAVIS COLT.

"There's a Divinity that shapes our ends,
Rough hew them as we will."

WATERTOWN:
PRINTED BY L. INGALLS & CO.
1862.

Title Page for Went to Kansas *by Miriam Davis Colt*

Describing her work during the first year of their settlement, Miriam Davis wrote:

> I have cooked so much out in the hot sun and smoke, that I hardly know who I am, and when I look into the little looking glass I ask "Can this be me?" Put a blanket over my head, and I would pass well for an Osage squaw.[24]

Frontier women vigorously disparaged the sloth and the vagrant habits of the Indians, often in proportion as they felt reduced to comparable conditions. The diarist's observations suggests how direct the relation could be between social dislocation and cultural hostility.[25]

In such isolated frontier circumstances, women hauled water and chopped wood, plowed and hoed, drove horses and mules. The routine led a woman to see herself as having become a squaw or a hired hand. Conversely, "while women did men's work, there is little evidence that men reciprocated."[26] It was virtually unthinkable, even in the isolation of unpeopled territory, for women to ask men to cook or to care for small children. The physical withdrawal from the community did not, in itself, set either men or women free of the gender roles established in the eastern settlements. Quite the opposite; the isolated condition of the first frontier sometimes tended to make those roles even more rigid. Many a frontier wife found that her isolated position led her backward to a more subservient dependence upon her husband's will and fortunes than she had known back East.[27]

If the family settled nearer a community, then a very different pattern emerged. In such cases, the house of the married settler often became a hostel for unmarried men in the vicinity, and a woman had to undertake the care and preparation of food for her family and for as many as 18 or 20 single men. From the letters of Mary Jane Megquier, who accompanied her husband to California during the gold rush and prepared all the meals for the men in the mining camp:

> We have a [hotel]. . . . I make the biscuit, then I fry the potatoes, then broil 2 pounds of steak and as much liver. . . . I bake six loaves of bread, then 4 pies, or a pudding, then we have lamb, beef and pork, baked turnips, beets, potatoes, radishes, salad, and that everlasting soup, every day. . . . I have cooked every mouthful that has been eaten. . . . If I had not the constitution of six horses I [should] have been dead long ago. . . . I am sick and tired of work . . . three nights a week I have to iron. I do not go to bed until midnight and often until 2 o'clock.[28]

Similarly, Mollie Dorsey Sanford, who traveled with her husband to the mines of Colorado, described her lot: "My husband is to do the blacksmithing for the company, and as was arranged I am to cook for the men. My heart sinks within me when I see 18 or 20, and no conveniences at all."[29] Much like Miriam Davis' was Mollie's perception of a woman's life in Colorado. "I feel stiff and lame tonight. Have raised my eyes to look into the glass. I see that Mollie Sanford does not look as fair as Mollie Dorsey did one year ago. Mountain air has given her a browner tinge."[30]

Narcissa Whitman, describing how her mother had to cook and keep house for 10 or more "loose" men, writes:

> I often think how disagreeable it used to be to [her] to do her cooking in the presence of men sitting about the room. This I have to bear ever since I have been here . . . at times it seems as though I cannot endure it any longer . . . the cooking and eating room [is] always filed with 5 or more [men]. They are so filthy they require a great deal of cleaning wherever they go, and this wears out a woman very fast. . . . I hardly know how to describe our feelings at the prospect of a clean comfortable house and one large enough so that I can find a closet to pray in [alone].[31]

Whitman was herself a missionary's wife, and the men in her house were often Indians. In her longing for a closet to pray in alone, Whitman was pleading for a refuge from the world of men. Reared in a society which had prescribed separation of the sexes, she sought a situation in which, if she could not be in the company of other women, she could at least be alone.

In letter-writing, as in prayer, women discovered a legitimate provision for privacy. These scattered and diligent correspondents wove a network by which they strove to maintain their sisterhood. News of parents left at home; news of weddings; news of births and deaths; news of illnesses and prosperities—the network of family and of the community of women was sustained even when the interval between letters was months or years. Virtually every diary I have read in some manner suggests this network of women, with some notation that a sister, a mother, a cousin or a friend has or has not written the news of home and extended family.

Letters were a defence against isolation, a defence against the world of men, and a mode of building a community of sensibility with other women where no real community yet existed. Letter-writing was acceptable behavior which allowed women to absent themselves from the company of men and children, and to secure, however temporarily, "a world of female support, intimacy and ritual," a sense of "continuity in a rapidly changing society."[32]

Once settlements were started, the frontier brought new conditions, and women often found themselves in conflict between their sense of women's proper sphere and the demands of each new day. The diaries indicate that adaptation was anxious and often uneasy. Minor anecdotes, some trivial, some humorous, betray the confusion. Miriam Davis tells that when her husband and children were ill with fever, and the cow had run off, she started on foot to retrieve the animal. A neighbor offered his horse. There, alone on the empty Kansas land, Davis stood wondering whether she dared mount the horse "man fashion!" When at last she did so and brought home the cow, her husband met her at the door of their home, more struck at seeing his wife riding astride than in seeing her return with the cow.[33]

Mollie Dorsey Sanford recalled a similar adventure when she was a young girl, and told how she also set off to retrieve a runaway cow. "It occurred to me how much easier I could get through the tangled underbrush if I were a man, and without letting anyone know of my project, I slipped out into the back shed, and donned an old suit of Father's clothes. . . . "[34] Coming upon a camp of men, Mollie ran home. "When it was all explained, it was very funny to all but Mother, who feared I am losing all the dignity I ever possessed. I know I am getting demoralized. . . . " The girl's judgment of the impediments of long skirts in a world without paved streets violated her mother's vision of propriety and female rectitude; thus, accommodation to the West for girls and women usually meant deviation from received norms and several diaries suggest that the generation-gap between mothers and daughters may have produced sharp differences. Adrietta Hixon recalls "Mother was always reminding me . . . to be [a] lady, but it seemed to me that the requirements were too rigid, for I always liked to run, jump and climb. . . . "[35] Lydia Waters, who crossed the Overland Trail as a young girl, was least troubled by her mother's strictures. She drove the ox team with prideful excitement and recalled climbing hills on the trail; "sometimes my feet would slip off the [tree] limbs and I would be hanging by my arms. You may be sure my skirts were not where they ought to have been then. . . . There were many things to laugh about."[36]

Some women eagerly accepted the challenges of frontier life, built and ran hotels, established mills and saw-mills, were storekeepers, ranch-women and business-women.[37] But there remained an uneasy line between respectability and notoriety. Folklore suggests the frontier's ambivalence toward independent women. The fame of Belle Starr, Calamity Jane, Pickhandle Nan, Madame Moustache and Poker Alice indicates the outer range of tolerance. These flambouyant women were indulged by western society like petted tomboys.[38] But there were other women whose efforts at independence were more uncertain. Learning to crack the whip while driving oxen, as she had seen the men do, left Mary Ellen Todd with "a secret joy in being able to have a power that set things going, [but] also a sense of shame. . . . "[39]

Women who were widowed or single, women whose husbands were given to alcoholism, women whose husbands had abandoned them and their children found independence hard to maintain. Their property rights were ambiguous and poorly protected. Writing of her own life in its legal implications, Abigail Duniway describes being a frontier widow:

> [If] my husband had lived and I had died, he could have spent everything we had earned in twenty years of married life and nobody could have cared what became of my children. . . . My girls and I have sold butter, eggs, poultry, cord wood, vegetables, grains and hay . . . but after I've earned [the money] I can't even buy a pair of shoes without being lectured by the court for my extravagance.[40]

Another woman, whose husband had signed a note for a friend who defaulted, found that both she and her husband were being sued: "I was . . . a legal nonentity, with no voice for self-protection . . . but, when penalty occurred, I was [my husband's] legal representative."[41] A similar story is that of a woman whose husband sold all the household furniture and left her and five children destitute. Prevailing on a townsman to take a mortgage on her house, the woman managed to take in boarders and to support her family. But on the husband's return, he repudiated the mortgage, divorced the wife, and sent the children away. Thus, the rights of women in the territories were a matter of uncertain dimension.[42]

Under the Oregon Donation Land Claim Act of 1850, for example, a woman might claim 320 acres of land, or half a married couple's allotment of 640 acres, but when the Act expired in 1855, it was not re-enacted. The state-by-state legislation by which women could or could not buy and sell in their own names is an area of much-needed research. The legal rights of married or widowed women were far from clear, and one suspects that as historians we know more accurately the rights of slaves under the slave codes of the Old South than we do of the rights of women in the western territories.

During the later stages of the frontier women succeeded in wringing a measure of personal independence from their situation. Women's suffrage made strong headway in the West, with the territorial legislatures of Wyoming and Utah giving women the franchise in 1869 and 1870 and Washington soon following.[43] In addition, western women availed themselves of the right to divorce in higher proportion than did their eastern sisters. The *United States Census Report of 1887-1906* indicates that while the highest marriage rate outside the South prevailed in the Mid-West, so did the highest rate of divorce.[44] The ten states with the greatest number of divorces in relation to population were Washington, Montana, Colorado, Arkansas, Texas, Oregon, Wyoming, Indiana, Idaho and Oklahoma. The ten states showing the lowest rate of divorce were Delaware, New York, New Jersey, North Carolina, Georgia, Pennsylvania, Maryland, Virginia, Massachusetts and Louisiana.[45] Although demographic evidence and statistical data are incomplete, the indications are that divorce and suffrage formed strong lines of self-determination for western women. With all its special hardships, the frontier in its later developments set women free of many eastern conventions. The western experience, which in its initial stages exacerbated the traditional inequalities imposed upon women by custom and by law, seems in later stages to have yielded to newer social and legal forms for women.

The last question to be posed is what happened to those women who were not strong enough to meet the frontier's extravagant demands, to those women who could not sustain the work or the loneliness, the loss of children or the weariness of spirit. The rate of insanity and emotional breakdown on the frontier remains, like other questions, in need of study. Whether the ratio of insanity was greater for women or for men, whether the frontier experience in itself generated pathology, are questions still to be answered.

A director of the Oregon Insane Asylum in 1878 attempted to convince legislators of that state that insanity was more prevalent in the East because foreign immigrants were more susceptible to mental illness and to criminality than were the "native-born" madmen of his own state.[46] While the record is far from clear, interesting issues are raised. The *Reports* of the Insane Asylum of Portland, Oregon, between 1870 and 1890, show that the total number of patients treated in the hospital increased from 260 between 1870-72, to 411 between 1876-78, and that it swelled to 734 between 1884-86. Of this number, the ratio of female to male patients begins at approximately one third and increases within one decade to one half.[47] Regarding the commitment of women to asylums, one suspects that only the most violent acts of madness and the most rigid types of withdrawl prompted their removal from the families and from society.

The statistics for those committed to the Asylum in the 1870's show that all women were either married or widowed, whereas similar tables for the 1880's show that women were both single and divorced, indicating the admission of women who were living widely different life styles. The causes of insanity, as they are offered in the Reports of the Portland Asylum, range from disappointment in love to masturbation.[48]

That pathology on the frontier was commonplace one may gather from an assortment of sources. Sandoz' biography of her father, for example, records that:

Two men and a woman were sent to the insane asylum on the first passenger train East. Down at the edge of the hills a mother of three hung herself. North of Hay Springs a man killed his brother with an ax. . . .[49]

A neighbor on the south table hanged himself in his well curbing and dangled unnoticed for two days in plain sight of the road, so nearly did his head resemble a windlass swinging.[50]

And of course Rolvaag's *Giants in the Earth* provides the classic portrait of the frontier woman for whom loneliness and isolation led from depression to insanity. The frontier diaries contain an occasionally searing notation of loneliness, as in the account of two women who trudged down to the railroad depot to gaze at the faces of people as the moving cars passed through the desolate lands.[51]

Samuel Eliot Morison, writing of America's colonial frontier, tells that:

Anne Hutchinson, a stouter-hearted woman than Anne Bradstreet, "when she came within sight of Boston and looking on the meanness of the place . . . uttered these words, if she had not a sure word that England would be destroyed, her heart would shake." [Governor Bradford] who reported those words said it was very strange that she should say so'—of course a man would! Hawthorne inferred that the horror of wilderness life brought the Lady Arabella Johnson to an early grave; and I suspect some such thing behind the silence of Governor Bradford on the death of his young wife Dorothy, drowned from the Mayflower in Province-town Harbor, after gazing for weeks on the desolate sand dunes of Cape Cod.[52]

The common disposition of Americans has been to view the western experience as the process of taming and civilizing the continent. In this familiar saga, women have figured as the civilizing agents. We have not yet asked whether the wilderness exerted an opposing, a countervailing impulse, one which resisted the incursion of the settlers. We have not asked how the wilderness condition worked *against* the pioneer, or how women, often drawn unwillingly into that wilderness, worked *against* the men. New studies of women on the frontier, by opening inquiry to those ways in which women were vulnerable to the pressures of the frontier, must provide new avenues by which we will begin to see, too, the vulnerability of men.[53] New studies of women, conflicted by new social and sex roles, must also throw light on role conflict in men.

Once we have begun to gather adequate demographic data on marriage and divorce, on insanity and suicide, on illigitimacy and property rights, on gender roles and the subtle attitudes of class identification, only then can we begin to assess the frontier heritage we have assumed all along to have known. The diaries of women on the Overland Trail and on the frontier are a rich source we have just begun to explore.

Notes

[1] The description of the "sororial" relations of women in the first half of the nineteenth century appears in the work of William R. Taylor and Christopher Lasch, "Two 'Kindred Spirits': Sorority and Family in New England 1839-1846," *New England Quarterly,* 36 (1863), 25-41. Charles E. Rosenberg, "Sexuality, Class, and Role in Nineteenth-Century America," *American Quarterly,* 25 (May 1973), 131-53, and the recent published essay by Carroll Smith-Rosenberg, "The Female World of Love and Ritual: Relations Between Women in Nineteenth Century America," *Signs,* I (1975), 1-28, are more rich in conceptual framework and have been valuable in the preparation of this paper.

[2] See Adrietta Applegate Hixon, *On To Oregon! A True Story of a Young Girl's Journey into the West* (Wesler, Idaho, 1947), p. 12.

[3] See, for example, the works of Barbara Welter, "The Cult of True Womanhood: 1820-1860," *American Quarterly,* 18 (Summer, 1966), 151-74; Ann Firor Scott, *The Southern Lady; From Pedestal to Politics, 1830-1930* (1970), chs. 1, 2.; Aileen Kraditor, ed., *Up from the Pedestal* (1968), ch. I; Nancy Cott, ed., *Root of Bitterness* (1972), ch. 3.

[4] Selections of this paper were read at the meeting of the Midcontinent American Studies Association, May, 1975, and it was prepared before the publication of "Women and Their Families on the Overland Trail to California and Oregon, 1842-67," by Johnny Faragher and Christine Stansell, *Feminist Studies,* vol. 2, no. 2/3 (1975), 150-66. Their research, like my own, is based upon diaries and journals of women and many conclusions of the present paper are corroborative of their work. I am indebted to the unpublished dissertation of Dawn Lander Gherman, "From Parlor to Tepee: The White Squaw on the American Frontier," University of Massachusetts, 1975, for its rich bibliography.

[5] "Diary of Maria Parsons Belshaw, 1853," ed. Joseph W. Ellison, in *Oregon Historical Quarterly,* 33 (1932), 332.

[6] Abigail Scott Duniway, *Pathbreaking: An Autobiographical History of the Equal Suffrage Movement in Pacific Coast States* (Portland, Oregon, 1914), 3, 8.

[7] *Ibid.,* 8.

[8] *Ibid.,* 9-10.

[9] Mrs. Ashmun Butler (America E. Rollins), "Diary of the Rogue River Valley, 1852-1854," *Oregon Historical Quarterly,* 41 (December 1940), 340, *cf.* also Mrs. Velina Williams, "Diary of a Trip Across the Plains in 1853," *Oregon Pioneer Association Transactions,* 47th Annual Reunion (1919), 220-226.

[10] Miriam Colt Davis, *Went to Kansas* (Watertown, N.Y., 1862), 56-57.

[11] Faragher and Stansell, 151.

[12] Davis, 57.

[13] Clifford M. Drury, *First White Women Over the Rockies: Diaries, Letters and Biographical Sketches of the Six Women of the Oregon Mission Who Made the Overland Journey in 1836 and 1838,* Vol. I (1963), 211.

[14] Maria Parsons Belshaw, 328.

[15] Mrs. Cecilia McMillen Adams, "Crossing the Plains in 1852," *Oregon Pioneer Association Transactions, 32nd Annual Reunion* (1904), 290-325.

[16] Maria Parsons Belshaw, 321-330.

[17] Lodisa Frizzell, *Across the Plains to California in 1852* (New York Public Library Pamphlet, 1915), pp. 14-16.

[18] *Ibid.,* 2-21.

[19] *Ibid.,* 22.

[20] *Ibid.,* 29.

[21] Faragher and Stansell, 160.

[22] "Men viewed drudgery, calamity, and privation as trials along the road to prosperity. . . . But to . . . women . . . hardship and loss only testified to the inherent folly of the emigration to 'this wild goose chase.'" *Ibid.,* 153.

[23] Miriam Davis, 53.

[24] *Ibid.*

[25] *Cf.* Mary E. Ackley, *Crossing the Plains and Early Days in California* (San Francisco, 1925), 66; "When my washerwoman was ill I would hire an Indian Man to do the rubbing, never a squaw. The squaws were hideous. . . . "

[26] Faragher and Stansell, 155.

[27] "Women's status will be lowest . . . where women are isolated from one another and placed under a single man's authority, in the home." Michelle Zimbalist Rosaldo and Louise Lamphere, eds., *Women, Culture, and Society* (Stanford, 1974), 36.

[28] Mary Jane Megquier, *Apron Full of Gold: Letters from San Francisco, 1849-1856* (Huntington Library, 1949), 33, 46-47.

[29] Mollie Dorsey Sanford, *Journal in Nebraska and Colorado Territories 1857-1866* (Lincoln, Nebraska, 1958), 137.

[30] *Ibid.,* 143.

[31] Drury, 137-138.

[32] Smith-Rosenberg, 28, 11.

[33] Miriam Davis, 110.

[34] Mollie Dorsey Sanford, 53.

[35] Adreitta Hixon, 21.

[36] Lydia Milner Waters, "A Trip Across the Plains in 1855," *Quarterly of the Society of California Pioneers,* 6 (June, 1929), 78.

[37] See *The Saga of "Auntie" Stone and Her Cabin, 1801-95,* "A Pioneer Woman Who Built and owned the first dwelling operated the first Hotel, Built the first dwelling, Erected the first Brick Kiln in the City of Fort Collins," ed., Nolie Mumey (Boulder, 1964).

[38] See *Poker Alice, History of a Woman Gambler in the West.* Nolie Mumey, ed. (Denver, 1951).

[39] Faragher and Stansell, 157.

[40] Abigail Duniway, 14-15.

[41] *Ibid.,* 23.

[42] *Ibid.,* 37-38.

[43] T. A. Larson, "Dolls, Vassals, and Drudges-Pioneer Women in the West," *Western Historical Quarterly,* III (January, 1972), 5.

[44] U.S. Department of Commerce, Bureau of the Census, Bulletin No. 96, *Marriage and Divorce 1887-1906,* 15-18.

[45] *Ibid.,* 19.

[46] Oregon Insane Asylum, Portland, Oregon, *Joint Committee Report,* 1878, 16.

[47] Oregon Insane Asylum, Portland, Oregon, *Reports of the Physicians, 1870-72; 1876-78; 1884-86.*

[48] Joint Committee Report, 1878, 18. Norman Dain's book, *Concepts of Insanity in the United States 1789-1865* and Gerald N. Grob's *Mental Institutions in America: Social Policy to 1875* indicate how comparatively scarce are the necessary materials for the western territories.

[49] Sandoz, *Old Jules* (Lincoln, 1962), 110, and throughout.

[50] *Ibid.,* 166.

[51] See Jane Lippincott, *New Life in New Lands* (1871), 27, also Jane Cazneau (Cora Montgomery), *Eagle Pass* (N.Y., 1852).

[52] Samuel Eliot Morison, *Builders of the Bay Colony* (Boston, 1962), 321.

[53] Richard Slotkin's book, *Regeneration Through Violence, The Mythology of the American Frontier 1600-1860* (1973), provides an excellent treatment of the captivity narratives (ch. 4), but the full subject of
womens' experience on the frontier and in the wilderness has not yet been assayed.

AUTOBIOGRAPHIES BY WOMEN OF LETTERS

Sidonie Smith (essay date 1987)

SOURCE: "Harriet Martineau's Autobiography: The Repressed Desire of Life Like a Man's," in *A Poetics of Women's Autobiography: Marginality and the Fictions of Self-Representation,* Indiana University Press, 1987, pp. 123-49.

[*In the following excerpt, Smith evaluates Harriet Martineau's autobiography and discusses elements specific to Victorian autobiography.*]

> I fully expect that both you and I shall occasionally feel as if I did not discharge a daughter's duty, but we shall both remind ourselves that I am now as much a citizen of the world as any professional *son* of yours could be.

—Harriet Martineau to her mother, July 8, 1833

Charlotte Charke [in her autobiography *A Narrative of the Life of Mrs. Charlotte Charke* written in 1755] dons the clothes and gestures of the man as she sets out on her adventures, virtually erasing the signature of her mother on her life. The fictions of "woman" that she does attend to as she plays the part of the sentimental heroine in her story are undermined by the bravado of the quixote. Centering her narrative attention on the father and the fictions of "man," she plays the prodigal "son," imitating and rebelling against the father as well as against his middle-class proprieties and conventions. Dressed up as a man in both life and text, she manages before her death to offer the reader a luxuriating romp through the margins of transgressive female selfhood. But her romp fails to eventuate in self-illumination that might render it truly subversive. In the end Charke dies a silent death, alone in her poverty and marginality.

In the next century, Harriet Martineau also assumes the role of the "manly" woman, appropriating the prerogatives and privileges of male selfhood; but the dynamics of her "masculine" selfhood are entirely different from those of Charke's. When Martineau takes up the pen to write her autobiography, she looks back on a radically different experience. Having achieved public recognition for her intellectual and political accomplishments, she has secured her place in English life and history. Her writings are widely read; her opinions and advice are anxiously sought by political leaders; her knowledge of other cultures is extensive. An intellectually and financially independent woman, Martineau has become famous in her own right, not because she is someone else's daughter or wife. Thus, when Martineau writes her *Autobiography,* she assumes her authority to speak as an acknowledged figure of the time.

"From my youth upwards," she tells her reader,

> I have felt that it was one of the duties of my life to write my autobiography. I have always enjoyed, and derived profit from, reading that of other persons, from the most meagre to the fullest: and certain qualities of my own mind,—a strong consciousness and a clear memory in regard to my early feelings,—have seemed to indicate to me the duty of recording my own experience. When my life became evidently a somewhat remarkable one, the obligation presented itself more strongly to my conscience: and when I made up my mind to interdict the publication of my private letters, the duty became unquestionable.[1]

The tone of moral rectitude and self-confidence evident in that opening passage pervades both volumes of Martineau's life story. The insecurities, the ambivalent desires of a Charke, of a [Margery] Kempe, or of a [Margaret] Cavendish, are tucked centuries away from the staunch certitudes of Martineau's speaking posture as she reviews her life from the security of a considerable public stature and from the psychological vantage point of self-satisfaction and intellectual confidence, not from the vantage point of failure, destitution, and cavalier rebellion that characterizes Charke's retrospective.

Confidence in the importance of her individual destiny derived from the culture's ideological preoccupations. The romantic poets had created in the reading public an appetite for the exploration of subjective experience, a fascination with psychology also promoted and satisfied by the nineteenth-century novel. Autobiography and biography mirrored that interest in the unfolding of individual destiny. Joining such works as John Stuart Mill's *Autobiography,* Mrs. Gaskell's *Life of Charlotte Brontë,* Brontë's *Jane Eyre,* and Dickens's *David Copperfield,* Martineau's *Autobiography* told in concert with them the evolutionary story of selfhood as it traced the curve of individual experience from a tormented childhood to the autumnal years of personal satisfaction and social integration.[2] Autobiography and biography simultaneously satisfied a reading public fascinated by the story of individualism. "In an increasingly competitive economy," notes Mary Poovey, "individual effort became the mark of past accomplishments and the guarantor of future success; this was the era of the 'self-made man,' when aristocratic privilege could finally be challenged on a wide scale by individuals with talent, opportunity, and the capacity for simple hard work."[3] Further, autobiography responded to the public's desire for information about the lives of

famous people, those larger-than-life "Carlylian" figures whose influence on the unfolding of history was profound. In a time when traditional religious beliefs eroded before the onslaught of scientific discoveries and political and social theories, the writer and artist took on the role of prophet and truth-sayer. Of course, the famous romantics had lived lives of mythical dimensions as they defied social conventions in the name of creativity and freedom. But Victorian literary figures also assumed a prominent place in the English imagination, redefining as they did the way human beings situated themselves in relationship to God, to nature, to history, and to each other.

Martineau does indeed join a distinguished group of writers engaged in the autobiographical project. Yet the list just rehearsed underscores the fact that autobiography proper remained a male preserve. Women writes on the list wrote either biography (Gaskell) or autobiographical novel (Charlotte Brontë), not public autobiography. Women not on the list may have written about themselves but did so in socially acceptable, and more private, forms. As Linda H. Peterson suggests, they "turned to their private journals not because they desired to produce whitehot records of the moment, but because they were judged incapable of writing autobiography in its standard form."[4] Peterson goes on to describe how the arguments about women's unsuitability for the autobiographical enterprise derived from certain notions of woman's intellectual difference, a difference captured clearly in such works as Hannah More's influential *Strictures on the Modern System of Female Education,* published in 1799:

> Women have equal *parts,* but are inferior in *wholeness* of mind, in the integral understanding: that though a superior woman may possess single faculties in equal perfection, yet there is commonly a juster proportion in the mind of a superior man: that if women have in equal degree the faculty of fancy which creates images and the faculty of memory which collects and stores ideas, they seem not to possess in equal measure the faculty of comparing, combining, analysing, and separating these ideas; that deep and patient thinking which goes to the bottom of a subject; nor that power of arrangement which knows how to link a thousand connected ideas in one dependent train, without losing sight of the original idea out of which the rest grow, and on which they all hang.[5]

Descriptions of female difference such as More's reveal a cultural ideology that would have effectively discouraged women from writing in an autobiographical tradition associated in the mid-nineteenth century with an analytic, summative, retrospective practice. Furthermore, as Peterson suggests, women faced other obstacles in thinking about autobiography. The practice demands confidence in the significance of the narrator's life, a confidence that in women was weak or nonexistent, in part because they lacked the wide range of experience open to men and the sense of authority to write at all for public self-display.

"Martineau," writes Peterson, "had no desire to circumvent a primary literary tradition simply because she was a woman or to write autobiographical fiction because it was a typical form of feminine self-expression."[6] On the contrary, she maintained the prerogatives of male intellectuality and embraced the autobiographical purpose and practice in the face of imminent death.[7] Confident in her authority to speak publicly, she offered her narrative as a gift to a public that would know the significance of its heroes, those individuals who best exemplified the optimistic side of the Victorian imagination, its utilitarianism, its positivism, its belief in progress. In fact, conceiving of her life as a model for human development, she imagined herself as representative "man." Despite her confidence, despite her certitude, however, this representative "man" remained keenly aware of her precarious position as unrepresentative "woman." Like Charke, though to nowhere near the same extent, the controversial Martineau had experienced a certain alienation from society. She had been labeled "an ill-favoured dogmatizing, masculine spinster"; and she had been indicted as "[a] *woman* who thinks child-bearing a *crime against society! An unmarried woman* who declaims against *marriage!*"[8] Inevitably, the other story of her life, the muted drama of repression, disrupts the evolutionary line of "masculine" identity. For me, at least, the tension generated by competing fictions of selfhood tinges the stolid, verbose autobiography with a melancholy shadow. Martineau paid a high price for her unconventional life, a price whose effect permeates the very writing of her autobiography. Like Charke before her, she too is betrayed by the story of "man," by the very storytelling demanded of "autobiography."

For Victorians, autobiography commenced in childhood, that distant place of beginnings. Accordingly, the structural pattern that comes to define Martineau's *Autobiography* originates, as it does in so much fiction of the century, in the troubled state of infancy and childhood. Earlier autobiographers lingered far less critically on those years. Kempe never mentions them. Cavendish and Charke briefly describe some details of their early experiences; but both women do so as a way of suggesting the kind of young girls they were—the former raised in the sheltered environment of ideal femininity, the latter anxious to command the powers and attention of youthful male selfhood. Their real narrative interest lies in the experiences of adulthood. In contrast, the nineteenth-century autobiographer became fascinated by the idea that at birth the mind is effectively a *tabula rasa* and that the subsequent development of the "innocent" child depended intimately on environmental influences. The Victorians, Martineau

Harriet Martineau

among them, became acutely aware of the formal qualities of human development, especially important in an age so challenged by theories of evolution. Throughout the seventeenth century the idea of childhood had changed radically as Locke's *Treatise on Education* altered the cultural understanding of human development. Emphasizing the importance of the senses as the original source of ideas and information about the world, Locke questioned the efficacy of educating the child through programs designed to proceed from abstract reasoning.[9] The new consciousness of childhood as a critical time in the development of the adult gained cultural currency through the writings of Rousseau *(Émile, Julie, Confessions)*, followed by the work of English romantics such as Wordsworth (whose *Prelude* "revealed that there *was* an epic dimension to childhood experience") and of German romantics such as Goethe *(Dichtung und Wahrheit* and *Wilhelm Meisters Lehrjahre)*.[10] By the middle of the nineteenth century, stories of childhood fired the public's and the writer's imagination. "If childhood is in one sense a historical 'invention,'" comments Luann Walthur as she explores the representation of childhood in Victorian autobiography, "the Victorian autobiographical childhood is in another sense a literary one, since never before this period had so many English writers been interested in recalling their early lives at length within the form of sustained prose autobiography."[11] But two antithetical representations of childhood emerged: the nostalgic memory of idyllic belonging rendered powerfully in Wordsworth's *Prelude* and the haunting memory of physical and psychological deprivation. Many Victorian autobiographies and novels, galvanized by and grounded in evolutionary tropes, described in powerful scenes the constrictions of loveless and orphaned beginnings. Martineau's is one of those evocations of profound loneliness, remarkably similar to Brontë's *Jane Eyre,* Dickens's *David Copperfield,* Mill's *Autobiography.*

Her narrative of childhood establishes the origins of her desire to repress the vulnerable "woman" within and to live life like a man. Consequently, the early pages of the *Autobiography* invite detailed attention. Since she "really remember[s] little that was not painful at that time of my life" (I:17), the memories that the older woman pieces together recreate a story of intense suffering. The ambiance of a lonely, fearful, emotionally "orphaned" childhood overwhelms the early pages of the narrative, which remain of all the work the most compelling, vivid, memorable. She describes how, as an infant abandoned to a wet nurse, a common practice among the prosperous middle class, she literally starves because the wet nurse has no milk. When her mother discovers the undernourished Martineau, she forces milk on a child who ever after experiences nausea in response to it. (This is the first moment in the text when Martineau's mother is associated with her illnesses, but it will not be the last.) During childhood and adolescence the young Martineau, continuing to receive little nurturance from her mother, responds desperately to the kindnesses of occasional strangers or relatives. Throughout the early pages of the story, Martineau portrays her mother as a strong-willed, distant, capricious, authoritarian figure. At once powerful and oppressive, her mother becomes the locus of emotional deprivation and physical disease.[12] (Of her father, Martineau says almost nothing except when she describes her response to his death.) . . .

Influenced by evolutionary theory, especially by the belief that environment is central in shaping individual destiny, Martineau structures her story of childhood in terms of its relationship to her later intellectual development. Ironically, childhood suffering as it becomes the source of later accomplishment assumes a beneficial aspect. In fact, Martineau joins other Victorian novelists and autobiographers in affirming the ultimate efficacy of suffering.[14] She would not have recommended to parents that they model their relationships with children on her own life; and yet, had she not suffered from self-disgust and from an inner turmoil made more potent for lack of the ability to voice her sense of confusion, pain, and shame, she would not

have sought sustenance in the intellectual life and thus achieved the public reputation she did.

Even more important, the young girl would not have developed the storytelling capacity that serves her intellectual and emotional purposes. Martineau describes how as a young girl she applied her "methodical" mind to the task of "distribut[ing] scripture instructions under the heads of the virtues and vices, so as to have encouragement or rebuke always ready at hand" (I:27). While she pokes fun at herself for the presumption of wrenching the Bible into her own maxims for good living, she nonetheless reveals the pattern-making, or hermeneutical, propensity that characterized her early response to life. Patterns provided a means of control, making life more coherent and tractable, less chaotic and threatening. Through pattern making the child could use her mind to overcome the pains of emotional deprivation. Early patterns of self-expression and identity, as suggested in the discussion of Charke, become paradigmatic. Further, "these self-defining acts," as Paul John Eakin notes, "may be re-enacted as the autobiographical narrative is being written."[15] In Martineau's case, the autobiographical project is another one of those attempts, first identified in the child, to control her life by imposing a pattern on it. In that way she would make her "life" a maxim, an edifying model for others to live and to learn by.

After describing a painful, stifled, repressive childhood and an adolescence spent withdrawing into religion and literature, Martineau goes on to chronicle her public career as an author, focusing on those first electrifying attempts at publication, then detailing the circumstances of her authorship of the Political Economy series, her journeys to America and the Middle East, and her subsequent literary work. Here is the exceptional woman at work, absorbed in a consequential vocation, surrounded in her text as in life with famous personages, involved in exciting adventures. But the *Autobiography* offers more than a retrospective summary of a life's work, more than glimpses at the famous people who surrounded her. Looking forward to death and backward over the past, Martineau finds, as she was wont to do from an early age, a clear pattern, what she calls "the progression of a mind." An evolutionary figure of selfhood, such progression reflected a pattern dear to the Victorian sensibility, one that seemed to satisfy a culture drawn to the idea of human progress, individual and social. In literature that cultural fascination crystallized in the emergence and maturity of what became known as the *Bildungsroman.* For Wilhelm Dilthey, a student of the structures of selfhood in the nineteenth century, the formal qualities of the *Bildungsroman* were specific: "A regulated development within the life of the individual is observed, each of its stages has its own intrinsic value and is at the same time the basis for a higher stage. The dissonances and conflicts of life appear as the necessary growth points through which the individual must pass on his way to maturity and harmony."[16] The structure of Martineau's autobiography parallels that fictive pattern, its idea of progressive selfhood, its developmental plot.

The overall design of the *Autobiography* is purposive. The autobiographer divides her narrative into discrete stages of growth, into chronological periods and sections within them. Characterized by its own unique preoccupations, each stage follows naturally from the previous one and prepares the way for the next. The autobiographer even provides the reader with signposts, projecting forward at certain points in the text, implanting in the story line expectations about the future and, in doing so, testifying to the inevitability of destiny. Moreover, all the difficulties (the hearing problems, the loss of financial security, the tumor that confines her to bed for five years) function as chastening and eventually energizing difficulties. Each successive obstacle has a salutory effect on the line of her life, the development of her ideas, the movement toward mature vision. Each potentially disempowering and imprisoning experience becomes paradoxically a liberating obstacle that leads her to the freedom she desires. Everything fits the hermeneutical framework. . . .

Martineau participated in [the] tradition of self-sacrificing transmission even as she lived life as a man; and she did so in two ways. Her autobiography chronicles a life devoted to "bearing the word" of male philosophers (Jeremy Bentham, Thomas Malthus, Auguste Comte, among others). She literally translated Comte into English so that his word would be accessible to a wider audience. She translated the ideas of Bentham and Malthus into novels more accessible to the masses of people whom she sought to educate. But more than that, her very autobiography serves as a vessel through which she can "bear" the philosophical vision of Comtian positivism and thereby reaffirm the ordination of androcentric selfhood.

But. . . . The patterns of self-interpretation are too tight, too procrustean. "I am disposed to think it probable that I am casting back the light of a later time among the mists of an earlier, and supposing myself sooner capable than I really was of practically distinguishing between a conception and a conviction" Martineau comments at one point (I:82). In that dramatic aside the confident autobiographer qualifies the truthfulness of her story. Drawing on earlier sources to refresh her memory—the article "Literary Lionism," the journals of her American tour, the letters to Atkinson—she reveals the uncertainty of memory as a source of truth. Throughout, she punctuates the narrative with muted references to experiences not included in her official story for

various reasons: She would appear too self-promoting; she has recounted them elsewhere; she considers them inconsequential; propriety demands their omission. In all these ways, Martineau sustains the tentative nature of the autobiographical project, hinting at stories left untold, life left unrepresented, ultimately unmasking the fictive nature of her pattern making.

Actually, Martineau's narrative remains overdetermined. In his study of memory and writing, Philip Davis argues that in most nineteenth-century autobiographies "memory proposes itself as the end of time and therefore aptly summative and conclusive of it. Everything falls into line, becoming in the life's story what, with hindsight, it turned out to be."[33] For those autobiographers who wrote their stories when they believed death to be near, as Martineau did, that tendency is especially pronounced. For someone who, like Martineau, is drawn to the Necessarian Solution, the summative tendency of memory is further exacerbated: Having embraced the ideology of evolutionary progress, the autobiographer looks back on a life that seems destined to have evolved along the lines it did. Thus, as Davis notes, Martineau's *Autobiography* embodies a disturbing fatedness.[34] Since all human desire, emotion, tentativeness, ambivalence have apparently been erased from the text, the self-satisfying acceptance of her destiny takes its toll on the very truthfulness of her "life." The following passage, quoted also by Davis, captures the static nature of Martineau's vision:

> I think I may sum up my experience of this sort by saying that this book [the Atkinson letters] has been an inestimable blessing to me by dissolving all false relations, and confirming all true ones. No one who would leave me on account of it is qualified to be my friend; and all who, agreeing or disagreeing with my opinions, are faithful to me through a trial too severe for the weak are truly friends for life. I early felt this. (II:46-47)

Suppressing the experience of disappointment, betrayal, and loss that must have characterized that period in her life, Martineau insists that there were from the beginning only two kinds of people—the friends and the not-friends. Davis calls the kind of thinking evidenced in such passages "the logic of retrospection," wherein all "interim meanings" are suppressed, giving way to the authority of summative meanings.[35]

Yet that approach toward autobiography served Martineau in profound psychological ways. As already noted, in constructing a story of fatedness, she defended herself against those critics, real and imagined, who charged her with arrogant female transgression. But the same sense of fatedness allows her to overcome the ravages of conventional female selfhood. To explore this aspect of fatedness, let me return to the passage quoted at length above. The language she uses to describe the loss of a fiancé is terse, cold, controlled, entirely void of emotion. "Love" becomes "that matter." Her feelings are an "occasional annoyance, presently disposed of." Mind and manner overcome the emergencies and indeterminacies of passion. Everything, all possible "interim meanings" are contained within the carefully structured language of a system. As Davis suggests, the grammatical past tense assigns everything, including her emotions, to the finality of fact.[36] The Necessarian Solution provided this woman a system of belief through which to subdue, then to escape the entanglements of passion, those swirling and stifling pains and pangs of doubt and shame and self-disgust that kept the child constantly on the edge of desire.[37] The language of autobiographical selfhood betrays the desire to repress all the confusion of life and fire inside. Mind exerts control over emotion, that seething stressful wind of passion, rebellion, and shame. And that control is piercingly evident in the patterns language imposes on the past, in the autobiographer's allegiance to memory rather than to what Davis calls "the provisional nature of time."[38] Martineau's suppression of interim meanings, her desire to repress her passional experience within the public, official story of her life, recapitulates the childhood scene she so vividly recreates in the opening pages of her text: "It never occurred to me to speak of anything I felt most" (I:9). Evading feeling, she develops a fierce need to find patterns for living (by wrenching the Bible into her own maxims, by embracing "solutions"). She flees toward pattern making in order to escape the emotional life. Fundamentally, that escape from the world of emotions becomes an escape from the "feminine" life of feeling and sensitivity, from "female" autobiography as defined by the ideology of gender in the nineteenth century. Embracing the story of a man as she embraces the life of a man, Martineau, like Charke before her, literally gives her self up to the exactions of male autobiography.

Identifying with the "father" and his world of public action, Martineau grounds her authority to write about herself in the fit of her life to the story of male selfhood. In doing so, she suppresses the story of emotional turmoil, the story of sexual difference and desire. Giving her allegiance to the ideology of male selfhood, she silences the "feminine" story of her identity as daughter. Yet the suppressed story of thwarted emotion and desire disturbs the placid surfaces of the stolid and carefully structured narrative of representative man; and it does so through the glimpses of her experience as daughter to her mother. For in the portrait she draws of her mother, Martineau unmasks her ambivalence about domestic life and ideal womanhood by indirectly revealing the underside of domesticity and motherhood. On the one hand, she would be the "ideal" daughter, dutifully imitating the model of filiality dear to her

mother. She emphasizes how much she has enjoyed sewing, an occupation forced on her by her mother in their early days of financial distress. She presents herself as a woman to whom the comfort and retirement of home is sustaining. She describes how, contrary to her wishes, she obeys her mother, returning home after her first successful trip to London. She represents herself as obedient toward her mother, domestically oriented, chaste, self-sacrificing. But this mother is fundamentally a figure of overpowering dominance and gloom. In fact, the last and most fundamental form of imprisonment Martineau suffers and flees is the imprisonment within her relationship as daughter to this mother. Buried inside her official life, therefore, lies a story of rebellion against the tyranny of the mother and the tyranny of female life scripts.

Unlike Cavendish, this daughter presents the mother as a tarnished, rather than as an ideal, figure. Her childhood memories resonate with the vision of a mother remote, capricious, insensitive, harsh. Dramatically, she admits that, when she left home and escaped the daily influence of her mother, her habitual tendency to tell untruths ceased (I:68). And yet she did not really escape the presence of her mother until much later; for when the family loses its money, when her favorite older brother dies, when Martineau begins to support herself from the proceeds of her career as a writer, she and her mother become the new household. Reconfigured in a complex way, the domestic drama casts Martineau as the "husband/son" who supports the household financially while her mother plays the "wife" by assuming responsibility for all domestic arrangements. Critically, the arrangement in part reverses the dynamics of the earlier, parent-child relationship: The mother is dependent on a daughter formerly dependent on her. Moreover, the daughter achieves public recognition and authority "like a man." . . .

In the introduction Martineau announces a theory of autobiography as she defends her decision to have her personal letters burned. "Bear[ing] emphatic practical testimony on behalf of the principles of the privacy of epistolary intercourse," she maintains for a variety of reasons that personal correspondence should be held from public scrutiny. She herself has acted to restore confidence in the integrity of personal correspondence "by a stringent provision in my will against any public use whatever being made of my letters, unless I should myself authorize the publication of some, which will, in that case, be of some public interest, and not confidential letters" (I:3). Establishing a distinction between official and unauthorized versions of selfhood, she suggests at the outset of her story that the work the reader has just begun to read is only one version of the real Martineau, the public version. Revealingly, she acknowledges that public versions are not always the most truthful: "The most valuable conversation, and that which best illustrates character, is that which passes between friends, with their feet on the fender, on winter nights, or in a summer ramble" (I:3). Nonetheless, public versions are the most carefully controlled, the most rational, authoritative, legitimate. They are, that is, the most "masculine."

For Harriet Martineau male autobiography served public and private purposes. If her autobiography denies interim meanings "because she felt her emotions to be pre-empted by the laws of Necessity and silenced by the law of Justice," it defends by proving inevitable the law of Harriet Martineau's evolutionary selfhood.[40] She lived her life like a man because it was inevitable that her life be lived that way. Thus the controversial woman could defend herself publicly before those critics who condemned her for her unfeminine life and personality. Privately, male autobiography, as text and context, provided her a medium through which to escape the emotional vulnerability that characterized the "life" of this psychologically damaged nineteenth-century woman. Repressing the "private," "maternal" story of desire in service to a male ideal of dispassionate intellectuality, Martineau gained control over both her own suffering and subsequent interpretations of her life. She did so at the price of her own passional life.

Notes

[1] *Harriet Martineau's Autobiography,* 2 vols., ed. Maria Weston (Boston: James R. Osgood, 1877), vol. 1, p. 1. Subsequent citations appear in the text.

[2] Critics who discuss Martineau's *Autobiography* comment on the importance of the new understanding of individual psychological development that emerged during the century. See, for instance, R. K. Webb, *Harriet Martineau: A Radical Victorian* (New York: Columbia Univ. Press, 1960); Mitzi Myers, "*Harriet Martineau's Autobiography:* The Making of a Female Philosopher," in *Women's Autobiography: Essays in Criticism,* ed. Estelle C. Jelinek (Bloomington: Indiana Univ. Press, 1980), pp. 53-70; Valerie Kossew Pichanick, *Harriet Martineau: The Woman and Her Work* (Ann Arbor: Univ. of Michigan Press, 1980); Gillian Thomas, *Harriet Martineau* (Boston: Twayne, 1985), p. 123; and Gaby Weiner, "New Introduction" to *Harriet Martineau's Autobiography* (London: Virago Press, 1983), pp. ix-xx.

[3] Mary Poovey, "*Persuasion* and the Promises of Love," in *The Representation of Women in Fiction: Selected Papers from the English Institute, 1981,* ed. Carolyn G. Heilbrun and Margaret R. Higonnet (Baltimore: Johns Hopkins Univ. Press, 1983), p. 153.

[4] Linda H. Peterson, *Victorian Autobiography: The Tradition of Self-Interpretation* (New Haven and London: Yale Univ. Press, 1986), p. 126.

[5] *The Works of Hannah More* (New York: Harper and Brothers, 1854), vol. 1, p. 367, quoted in ibid., p. 127.

[6] Peterson, p. 136.

[7] Martineau wrote her autobiography at furious speed in 1855, thinking death was near. She lived another twenty years but never revised or supplemented her text.

[8] Sir Edward Boyle, *Biographical Essays, 1790-1890* (London: Oxford Univ. Press, 1936), p. 182; E. Boyle, "Miss Martineau's Monthly Novels," *Quarterly Review* 49 (April 1833): 136.

[9] Richard N. Coe, *When the Grass Was Taller: Autobiography and the Experience of Childhood* (New Haven: Yale Univ. Press, 1984), p. 12.

[10] Ibid., p. 38.

[11] Luann Walthur, "The Invention of Childhood in Victorian Autobiography," in *Approaches to Victorian Autobiography,* ed. George P. Landow (Athens: Ohio Univ. Press, 1979), p. 65.

[12] For an extensive discussion of Martineau's willful mother, see Mitzi Meyers, "Unmothered Daughter and Radical Reformer: Harriet Martineau's Career," in *The Lost Tradition: Mothers and Daughters in Literature,* ed. Cathy N. Davidson and E. M. Broner (New York: Ungar, 1980), pp. 70-80. . . .

[14] Walthur, p. 71.

[15] Paul John Eakin, *Fictions in Autobiography: Studies in the Art of Self-Invention* (Princeton: Princeton Univ. Press, 1985), p. 226.

[16] Wilhelm Dilthey, *Das Erlebnis und die Dichtung* (Leipzig, 1913), p. 394, quoted in *The Voyage In: Fictions of Female Development,* ed. Elizabeth Abel, Marianne Hirsch, and Elizabeth Langland (Hanover: Univ. Press of New England, 1983), pp. 5-6. . . .

[33] Davis, p. 240.

[34] Ibid., pp. 242-44.

[35] Ibid., p. 241.

[36] Ibid., p. 244.

[37] "In proportion as the taint of fear and desire and self-regard fell off, and the meditation had fact instead of passion as its subject, the aspiration became freer and sweeter, till at length, when the selfish superstition had wholly gone out of it, it spread its charm through

every change of every waking hour,—and does now, when life itself is expiring" (1:88).

[38] Davis, p. 244. . . .

[40] Davis, p. 243.

Janet Bottoms (essay date 1995)

SOURCE: "Sisterhood and Self-Censorship in the Nineteenth Century," in *The Uses of Autobiography*, edited by Julia Swindells, Taylor & Francis, 1995, pp. 110-27.

[*In the essay below, Bottoms discusses Alice James's attempts to come to terms with life and express herself through her diary.*]

Diary writing is sometimes perceived as a private and spontaneous activity; unstructured, uninhibited, it flows on from day to day, a modest little stream of consciousness. In reality it is very far from this, though the writer may not be fully conscious of the process of selection and structuring which is taking place. When Alice James—sister of Henry, the novelist, and William, the author of *Principles of Psychology*—began her journal she was 40 years old, an invalid and alone, apart from her nurse, having moved to England a few years earlier for what had been intended to be a short visit. Like many other diary writers, therefore, her decision that to write a little every day might 'bring relief as an outlet to that geyser of emotions, sensations, speculations, and reflections which ferments perpetually within my poor old carcass for its sins',[1] was motivated by a desperate sense of isolation.

One of the most noticeable things about her diary, however, is that it is *not* a 'geyser of emotions'. If the first instinct of the diarist is towards freedom of expression, the second instinct is to retreat, for no sooner does pen touch paper than the writer becomes also a reader, and a complex of inhibitions and an inculcated self-consciousness come into play. The diary is very much a woman's form because it is secret—it makes no open claim to notice—and yet to record oneself in this manner is, after all, to make an assertion that one is worthy of record. In many diaries we find that combination of defensive self-mockery and self-assertion which is also to be found in Emily Dickinson's equally 'secret', self-reflexive poetry.

> I'm Nobody! Who are you?
> Are you—Nobody—Too?
> Then there's a pair of us?
> Don't tell![2]

Alice James referred to this poem in her diary while recording how she had been asked whether she had

herself (like her famous brothers) ever written for the press. She repudiated the suggestion vehemently[3] and with scorn, yet her friend and amanuensis Katharine Loring was quite sure that she wanted her diary to be made public eventually.

Secondly, the diarist is a reader *before* she is a writer. Alice James brings together both the writing and reading processes when she speaks of the value of being able to 'get on to my sofa and occupy myself for four hours, at intervals, thro' the day, scribbling my notes and able to read the books that belong to me, in that *they clarify the density and shape the formless mass within*' (*Diary*, 5 May 1890; my emphasis). Apparently it is this need to clarify, to give form, which lies at the root of much diary writing. Some kind of defining shape is constantly being sought and imposed upon contingency—but in this process the diarist is necessarily influenced by the way her or his idea of self has already been constructed, through society and its narratives.

The diarist, then, is both writer and reader, observed and observed, in a way which replicates the life experience of many women. A woman, John Berger has said, learns continually to watch herself because how she appears to others is so important to what is, or at least traditionally has been seen as, her 'success' in life.

> So she comes to consider the *surveyor* and the *surveyed* within her as the two constituent yet always distinct elements of her identity as a woman. . . . Her own sense of being in herself is supplanted by a sense of being appreciated as herself by another.[4]

The diary may be a private form of writing, but it is remarkable how many diarists do, in fact, address themselves to someone or something, to a fantasized reader who is a part of themselves and yet separated in order to give the affirmation, the appreciation which they dare not claim consciously. The way that the reader is conceived of must therefore make a difference to the selecting and shaping process by which experience is translated into written record. Most female diarists imagine a female *alter ego,* but Alice James' 'Dear Inconnu' is male, a fact to which she draws self-mocking attention, and which can surely be understood in the light of the dominant role played in her life by her father and brothers, as well as her 'failure' to acquire the husband who would have given her a social validity. Berger's comment that 'the surveyor of woman in herself is male: the surveyed female' is therefore particularly relevant to Alice James. It is a male view of herself which the diary shows her both adopting and unconsciously wrestling with, and it is for a male-gendered reader that she seems to be 'writing' herself (though there is an unquantifiable extra dimension in the fact that from the beginning of 1891 every entry was dictated through a woman).

Diaries, and women's diaries in particular, are excellent examples of the autobiographical process at work precisely because they are not spontaneous outpourings but are shaped, however unconsciously, and the *Diary* of Alice James is a fascinating example of the inconsistencies and attempts to create something consistent, the self-projection and self-censoring, the compulsion to truth and the 'bracketing' of it, which underlies diary writing for many women. Her 'reader' is defined as male, as I have noted, and in the James family 'male' meant intelligence, wit, and having a 'moral' being and individual identity in a way which being female did not. Henry James senior, an eccentric but respected writer on the philosophy of religion, had developed a theory of moral evolution seen at work in man, for whom an apprehension and experience of evil was a necessary part of his development. Women, on the other hand, were different—their purpose being to inspire and comfort rather than to have a moral consciousness of their own. In this he was encouraged and confirmed by Mrs James, 'the very incarnation of *banality*', according to one contemporary observer,[5] but whom it was an article of faith with all the James children to see as the epitome of self-effacement and maternal devotion.

Consciously at least, the family ideology was not to be questioned—too much emotional capital was invested in it—and nor could a daughter consciously question the priority given to her obviously brilliant brothers. At 18 she subscribed herself in a letter to William, 'Your loving *idiotoid* sister', and at the end of a life marked by an accelerating series of psychological and physical breakdowns, she wrote to him again:

> But you must believe that you greatly exaggerate the tragic element in my commonplace little journey. . . . You must also remember that a woman, by nature, needs much less to feed upon than a man, a few emotions & she is satisfied.[6]

'Matrimony', she had early concluded, 'seems the only successful occupation that a woman can undertake', but matrimony was denied to her, and her hope of being able to find a similar role as the comfort and support of her widowed father was thwarted by his apparently willed death within the year.[7] This was the point at which, as she wrote later in her diary, 'my scaffolding began to fall'—the point at which the 'meaning' of her life as it had been written for and by her until that point seemed to disappear.

Alice's diary was begun six years later, and ended with her death from breast cancer at the age of 43. There are two main aspects to it—a day to day record of ideas and incidents, and, increasingly towards the end, a retrospective view of her life. Naturally, a selecting process is at work in both, but the shaping tools are different. On the first level, she makes use of a defensive irony and ambiguity. Much of her diary is a record of her lively interest in political and social issues and her extensive reading. Her brother Henry wrote to William that her 'vigour of mind and decision of character' as well as her 'brilliant and trenchant conversation' were much admired in England,[8] but Alice herself exhibits a compulsion to avoid any appearance of taking herself seriously.

> I wonder whether, if I had had any education I should have been more, or less, of a fool than I am. It would have deprived me surely of those exquisite moments of mental flatulence which every now and then inflate the cerebral vacuum with a delicious sense of latent possibilities—of stretching oneself to cosmic limits. (*Diary,* 12 December 1889)

She can only safely lay claim to the ability partially to follow in the intellectual footsteps of a man, 'one's mind stretching to the limits of his', and 'such a subtle flattery emanating from his perfection in "putting it" as to make an absolutely ignorant creature like me vibrate, as with knowledge, in response to the truth of his exquisitely subtle perceptions' (*Diary,* 12 June 1889). When this happens, she writes, her whole being is 'vivified with the sense of the *Intelligent* revealed!' but whether she means revealed in him or in herself is left ambiguous. Moreover, in case she appears to be taking herself too seriously, there is always that bolthole word 'flattery': a woman comparing her mental abilities with a man must be either flattering herself, or being flattered.

She depicts herself as a traditional object of comedy—a 'grotesque'.

> Yesterday Nurse and I had a good laugh but I must allow that decidedly she 'had' me. I was thinking of something that interested me very much and my mind was suddenly flooded by one of those luminous waves that sweep out of consciousness all but the living sense and overpower one with joy in the rich, throbbing complexity of life, when suddenly I looked up at Nurse, who was dressing me, and saw her primitive, rudimentary expression (so common here) as of no inherited quarrel with her destiny of putting petticoats over my head; the poverty and deadness of it contrasted to the tide of speculation that was coursing thro' my brain made me exclaim, 'Oh! Nurse, don't you wish you were inside of *me!*'—her look of dismay and vehement disclaimer—'Inside of you, Miss, when you have just had a sick head-ache for five days!'—gave a greater blow to my vanity than that much battered article had ever received. (*Diary,* 12 July 1889)

To be reminded so abruptly that, even when within her she felt 'the potency of a Bismarck', to the world her 'glorious role was to stand for *Sick headache* to mankind!' was enough to make her retreat again into defensive irony.

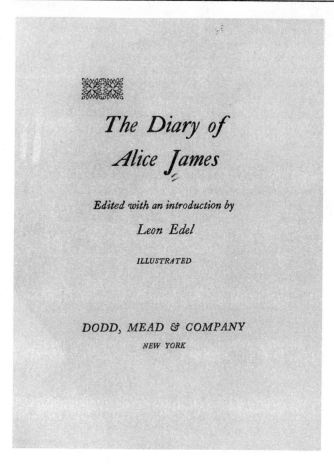

Title page for The Diary of Alice James

To sit by and watch these absurdities is amusing in its way and reminds me of how I used to *listen* to my 'company manners' in the days when I had 'em, and how ridiculous they sounded.

Such comments are a reminder that *irony*—the simultaneous acceptance of and protest against incongruity or injustice—is the weapon of the relatively powerless. It may be turned on other people or the context in which the ironist is unwillingly placed, but if, for reasons of emotional need, she dare not consciously criticize those who are responsible for her situation, she will tend to divide and turn upon her own self. Alice seems to have felt, subconsciously, that if she was to justify herself her critical comments on other people and institutions - a necessary exercise, for her, of the 'acrid strain to stiffen the sinews' (*Diary* 12 January 1890) but an expression of the 'hardness' which she recalls her father deploring in her - she must turn her satirist's eye inwards first of all.

Her comments on the journals of other women writers show a scorn—and a fear—of self-pity. Her physicians having impressed upon her that the way to health was to ignore all her symptoms and emotional moods, 'be they temporarily pleasant or unpleasant',[9] she came to regard the voicing of them as typically female and feeble. The *Journal* of the young Russian artist Marie Bashkirtseff, begun in passionate eagerness at the age of 15 and broken off in despair shortly before she died of tuberculosis at the age of 24, had just been published and was the subject of everyone's conversation. Alice James, however, consciously reading it, noted:

> I imagine her the perverse of the perverse and what part so dreary to read of, or what part so easy to act as we walk across our little stage lighted up by our self-conscious foot-lights (*Diary* 16 June 1890)

She was shocked by the 'futile whining' and 'superlative solemnity' about herself of George Eliot, a writer she had ardently admired. 'What a lifeless, diseased, *self-conscious* being she must have been!' she exclaims in disgust, 'As if it weren't degrading eno[ugh] to have head-aches, without jotting them down in a row to stare at one for all time' (*Diary* 28 May 1889; my emphasis). For Alice James, dignity went hand-in-hand with a sense of humour, and both of them were part of the pride of being a James.

Her record of the past was also highly selective. Her childhood; her enthusiasm for riding; gossipy adolescent friendships; and great tracts of her life as a young woman growing up during the Civil War, or as a Bostonian lady involved in some of the social and educational reform movements of the postwar period are ignored. Instead, what emerges is a gradually evolving narrative of what had come to seem significant to her subjectively conceived self, and here her preferred tool was metaphor. She searched, in her own reading, for images through which to write her 'story'. At first this took the form of unexplored jottings. In the opening pages of the diary she refers to a sketch of the Cobb at Lyme Regis, 'off which dear, sweet Louisa Musgrove jumped', adding enigmatically: 'Think of my being so mentally clumsy as not to have seen her ghost of my own motion' (*Diary* 1 June 1889). Three days later she noted, 'What one reads, or rather all that comes to us is surely only of interest and value in proportion as we find ourselves therein, form given to what was vague, what slumbered stirred to life'. What was it that was given form by the image of Louisa Musgrove's disastrous jump in *Persuasion?* On the face of it there is little similarity between the impetuous, wilful Louisa and 'poor Alice', the Bostonian invalid spinster. Does Louisa stand for 'the expectant', which 'palpitated within' her in childhood, and which took the form of such excitement at a promised visit, on one occasion, that her mother decided she must be denied it in order to bring her back to a more level emotional state?[10] Youth, she commented later in the diary, was the most difficult period of life.

The blank youthful mind, ignorant of catastrophe, stands crushed and bewildered before the perpetual postponement of its hopes, things promised in the dawn that the sunset ne'er fulfils. Owing to muscular circumstances my youth was not of the most ardent, but I had to peg away pretty hard between 12 and 24, 'killing myself,' as some one calls it—absorbing into the bone that the better part is to clothe oneself in neutral tints, walk by still waters, and possess one's soul in silence . . . How I recall the low grey Newport sky in that winter of 62-63, as I used to wander about over the cliffs, my young soul struggling out of its swaddling-clothes as the knowledge crystallized within me of what Life meant for me. (*Diary* 21 February 1890)

Nothing she had written at that earlier period suggests any such knowledge.

Gradually, her autobiographical narrative began to take shape as she discovered the metaphors through which to express it, but it was in looking back that she was enabled to impose structure on her experience—negative suffering transposed into positive control. One of the best examples of the process is in one of her longer autobiographical passages, inspired by her brother William's paper on the 'Hidden Self'. In this he had described how 'the nervous victim "abandons" certain portions of his consciousness', an 'excellent expression' in her view, even though she herself had never been able to abandon her own consciousness enough to get even five minutes' rest.

I have passed thro' an infinite succession of conscious abandonments and in looking back now I see how it began in my childhood, altho' I wasn't conscious of the necessity until '67 or '68 when I broke down first, acutely, and had violent turns of hysteria. (*Diary* 26 October 1890)

In the complete physical collapse which followed the storm, but with her mind 'luminous and active', she saw, as she says, 'distinctly', that life was to be, for her, one long battle between her body and her will, 'a battle in which the former [the female body rather than the "male" intellect or will] was to be triumphant to the end'.

'Owing to some physical weakness, excess of nervous susceptibility', she continues, 'the moral power *pauses; as it were* for a moment, and refuses to maintain muscular sanity, worn out with the strain of its constabulary functions'. The body, it may be noted, is now apparently also criminal. And against what law does it offend?

As I used to sit immovable reading in the library with waves of violent inclination suddenly invading my muscles taking some one of their myriad forms

such as throwing myself out of the window, or knocking off the head of the benignant pater as he sat with his silver locks, writing at his table, it used to seem to me that the only difference between me and the insane was that I had not only all the horrors and suffering of insanity but the duties of doctor, nurse, and strait-jacket imposed upon me, too. (*Diary* 26 October 1890)

The pater, the head—literally and figuratively—was the object of both her bitter resentment and her need to love, of kisses and of violence. She might well have said, with Othello:

Excellent wretch, perdition catch my soul
But I do love thee, and when I love thee not
Chaos is come again.

It was the pater who insisted, all through her life, on writing her as patient and sweet. In her earliest extant letter, at the age of 12, Alice promised him, 'I will try to be good and sweet till you come back, and merit the daisy curtains, and get a chance at your dear old pate again'.[11] Surely it must be better to kill herself rather than to attack such a head. And yet even suicide, as an expression of a rebellion against 'being good', was denied her because when she asked her father whether he thought suicide was a sin, he had replied that it might be seen as a rational response to intolerable suffering, and therefore she had his full permission to end her life when she pleased.[12]

Paralysis, figured as a self-imposed strait-jacket (self-imposed but also 'imposed upon me') was all that was left to her at that period. Later, in her diary, she found the tool which enabled her to face and construct her narrative. In this context, also, she could also appeal for understanding. The language shifts from narrative mode to apostrophe—an appeal to that reader who is both herself and the male 'Inconnu'.

Conceive of never being without the sense that if you let yourself go for a moment your mechanism will fall into pie and that at some given moment you must abandon it all, let the dykes break and the flood sweep in, acknowledging yourself abjectly impotent before the immutable laws. (*Diary* 26 October 1890)

The force of that word 'abject' suggests a powerful self-disgust, and yet the abject victim is also source of the destructive flood—both Maggie and the Floss in spate. This is now no longer an account of that period in the past, her first breakdown, but of the story of her life—the key she has discovered to her own autobiography. 'When all one's moral and natural stock in trade is a temperament forbidding the abandonment of an inch or the relaxation of a muscle, 'tis a never-ending fight.' Anything which might start up those expectant or ambitious feelings again must be guarded against, 'until life becomes one long flight from remote suggestion and complicated eluding of the multi-fold traps set for your undoing'.

Alice's ability to construct her life as a pattern of 'flight' *from* the unfaceable had finally been brought about by her ability to see the goal she is moving *to*. The process of selection involved in diary writing depends very much upon a sense of direction or purpose, and the long autobiographical passage quoted above was written when it had finally become clear to everyone involved that her death was inevitable. This seems to have given her the sense of closure, of a complete narrative structure, within which to place what could now be seen as significant in the past. From wondering what she could possibly 'stand for'—'a collection simply of fantastic *un*productive emotions enclosed within tissue paper . . . all safety valves shut down in the way of "the busy ineffectiveness of women" ' (*Diary* 7 November 1890)—she begins to lay claim to 'a clearer perception of the significance of experience' (*Diary* 23 March 1891).

> One becomes suddenly picturesque to oneself, and one's wavering little individuality stands out with a cameo effect and one has the tenderest indulgence for all the abortive little *stretchings out* which crowd in upon the memory. (*Diary* 1 June 1891)

The significance of a life, like the structure now given to her diary, was to be discovered in its ending. The deaths of acquaintances and relatives now seemed to clarify their lives and make clear what, essentially, they 'stood for', while her own death was seen to rank as her life's work, to rival, finally, her brothers'. In June of 1891 she sums up their achievements in the last year—Henry's novels and plays, William's *Principles of Psychology*—as 'not a bad show for one family! especially if I get myself dead, the hardest job of all' (*Diary* 16 June 1891). Six months later she commented, with exasperation, 'The difficulty about all this dying is that you can't tell a fellow anything about it, so where does the fun come in?' (*Diary* 11 December 1891), but the irony at her own expense and that of others, the cool observation and the 'hard core', remained.

> How wearing to the substance and exasperating to the nerves is the perpetual bewailing, wondering at and wishing to alter things happened, as if all personal concern didn't vanish as the 'happened' crystallizes into history. Of what matter can it be whether pain or pleasure has shaped and stamped the pulp within, as one is absorbed in the supreme interest of watching the outline and the tracery as the lines broaden for eternity. (*Diary* 29 February 1892)

This is the penultimate entry in the diary. On the last day of her life, as her friend Katharine Loring noted,

'Alice was making sentences', and one of the last things she said was to correct the wording of the final entry. As she 'crystallized into history' Alice James succeeded finally in writing her own 'story'.

Notes

[1] L. Edel (Ed.) (1982) *The Diary of Alice James,* Harmondsworth: Penguin, p. 25. All subsequent references to the *Diary* are to this edition.

[2] T. H. Johnson (Ed.) (1975) *The Complete Poems of Emily Dickinson,* London: Faber and Faber, p. 133.

[3] *Diary,* p. 227. Alice James quotes the second stanza of Dickinson's poem, 'How dreary to be somebody . . . ' before recording her vehement rejection of the 'imputation'. After Alice's death, Katharine Loring had copies of the *Diary* privately printed for her brothers, and encouraged its later publication, telling William's daughter, Margaret James Porter, that 'though [Alice] never said so, I understood that she would like to have it published'; R. Yeazell (1981) *The Death and Letters of Alice James,* Berkeley and London: University of California Press, p. 5.

[4] J. Berger (1972) *Ways of Seeing,* Harmondsworth: Penguin, pp. 46-7.

[5] J. Strouse (1980) *Alice James: A Biography,* Boston: Houghton Mifflin, p. 44.

[6] Letter to William James, 6 August 1867; Strouse 1980, pp. 115-16. Letter to William James, 30 July 1891; Yeazell 1981, pp. 186-7.

[7] Letter to her friend, Annie Ashburner, about the artistic ambitions of another young woman, 12 April 1876; Yeazell 1981, p. 72. Mrs James died in January 1882. Alice's aunt, Katharine Walsh, commented that 'her mother's death seems to have brought new life to Alice', and her brother Henry wrote that 'as she is a person of great ability it is an extreme good fortune that she is now able to exert herself'. However, Henry James senior was to die in December of the same year: Katharine Loring wrote to Robertson James, 'He gets over the delay in dying by asserting that he has already died': Strouse 1980, pp. 202, 208.

[8] Henry James to William James, 9 May 1886; Strouse 1980, p. 254.

[9] Alice spent the winter of 1866/67 under the care of Dr Charles Fayette Taylor whose system for the treatment of neurasthenic young women, outlined in *Theory and Practice of the Movement Cure* (1861), included impressing upon the patient that 'she must not regard her symptoms, . . . but should ignore them as much as

possible, taking a course to secure ultimate immunity from them': quoted in Strouse 1980, p. 107.

[10] Strouse 1980, pp. 67-8.

[11] Letter to Henry James senior, 11 March 1860; Yeazell 1981, p. 49. Twenty years on, Alice would write, 'How sick one gets of being "good", how much I should respect myself if I could burst out and make every one wretched for 24 hours . . . If it were only voluntary and one made a conscious choice, it might enrich the soul a bit, but when it has become simply automatic thro' a sense of the expedient—of the grotesque futility of the perverse—it's degrading! And then the dolts praise one for being "amiable!" ': Edel 1982, p. 64.

[12] Strouse 1980, p. 186.

Pam Hirsch (essay date 1995)

SOURCE: "Gender Negotiations in Nineteenth-Century Women's Autobiographical Writing," in *The Uses of Autobiography*, edited by Julia Swindells, Taylor & Francis, 1995, pp. 120-27.

[*In the following essay, Hirsch examines the construction of gender in the autobiographies of Elizabeth Barrett Browning and George Sand.*]

Joanna Russ' provocative book *How to Suppress Women's Writing* has demonstrated the process of 'false categorizing' which operates in order to distract attention away from the woman writer towards her love affair(s).[1] So, for example, the mythology surrounding Elizabeth Barrett has suggested a pale semi-invalid, a Victorian Sleeping Beauty, dreaming unproductively until awoken by the kiss of Robert Browning into mature poethood. In the case of George Sand, similarly, volumes have been written about her love affairs, representing her as a kind of groupie, attaching herself to men of genius. One of the 'uses of autobiography' for both these women was the articulation of their struggles to construct themselves as writing subjects. Their autobiographical writings represent both 'the process of being gendered, and the project of putting that process into discourse'.[2] I am taking it as axiomatic that gender identification is not a fixed and stable given, but always liable to negotiation and renegotiation. To give an example: Elaine Showalter in *A Literature of Their Own* has pointed out that a common trait among nineteenth-century writers was 'their identification with, and dependence upon, the father; and either loss of, or alienation from, the mother'.[3] This cannot be a surprise: the socially dependent but ambitious daughter desired for herself the privileges of freedom of movement and superior education that her father exempli-

fied. However, this identification with the parent of the other sex often became conflicted as the girl moved from childhood to adolescence; the project of rethinking gender identification was often painful, prolonged and possibly never fully resolved.

Elizabeth Barrett's diary written in 1820, when she was 14, is my first example of an aspiring woman writer struggling with these gender negotiations. Her tiny manuscript diary, only five inches by three inches, cut, folded and sewn together in order to fit into her pocket, ready to be fished out when she wanted to write something, could easily have been lost to us. It was discovered by Robert Browning after her death and subsequently entrusted to their son, Pen. After his death it came into the public domain and its very existence reveals both that poetry was the aim and object of her life from an early age, and also, that female ambition was inextricably linked with a conflict of gender.[4]

Briefly, the family politics were as follows: Elizabeth Barrett was the eldest of eleven children living with her parents at 'Hope End' in Ledbury, Herefordshire. As a small child her precocious talent was recognized and rewarded by her father. In her diary she wrote: 'In my sixth year for some lines on virtue which I had penned with great care I received from Papa a ten shilling note enclosed in a letter which was addressed to the Poet Laureat [sic] of Hope End'.[5] Encouraged by paternal approval she continued to turn out masses of apprentice stuff, generally rehashes of works by male authors, such as her 'Battle of Marathon' in imitation of Pope. Of all her siblings, she was closest to her brother Edward, nicknamed Bro', born in 1807, one year after Elizabeth. They spent all their time together—climbing, fishing, horseriding, organizing plays and picnics. She shared Bro''s tutor, Mr McSwiney, and learned Greek with him. But when Bro' left for Charterhouse Mr McSwiney left too. On the last page of the diary there is a striking sense of an ungendered Paradise Lost: 'My past days now appear as a bright star glimmering far, faraway and I feel almost agony to turn from it for ever!' She plotted that when she was grown-up she would 'wear men's clothes and live on a Greek island, the sea melting into turquoise all around it'.[6]

The day Bro' left for school at the age of 13, Elizabeth realized that there was an inescapable difference between being a clever boy and being a clever girl. She was literally 'left behind' at what now seemed the aptly named 'Hope End'. Figuratively she was afraid of being left behind intellectually and was consumed with envy of the previously beloved brother. He wrote to her all the time complaining that she hardly ever wrote back. She assumed, in the teeth of contrary evidence, that Bro' had become expert in Latin at school, and this caused her anguish:

Whenever I am employed in any literary undertaking which requires much depth of thought and learned reference I cannot help feeling uneasy and imagining that if I were conversant with such languages I might perhaps come to a descision [sic] at once on a point which now occupies days in conjecture!! This is tormenting and sometimes agitates me to a painful and almost nervous degree.[7]

Elizabeth's life at home meandered through extended visits to relations, a typically middle-class way of keeping girls occupied, because they had no sustained education to interrupt. If boys' departure to school was a masculine middle-class rite of passage, the equivalent rite of passage for girls (at approximately the same age) was the onset of menstruation, which for the middle-class girl was often accompanied by restraints on girls' outdoor romping. It became apparent to Elizabeth at this point that her mother's life, and not her father's, was the model that she was supposed to be studying. It seems hardly surprising that it was not a life she would choose for herself. Her mother, Mary, had been married in 1805, and had, from then on, produced children with almost monotonous regularity (1806, 1807, 1809, 1810, 1812, 1813, 1814, 1816, 1818, 1820, 1822, 1824). After the birth of her twelfth child Mary Barrett never fully regained her health and in 1828 she died. Thinking back about her mother's life much later, when she herself was contemplating marriage, Elizabeth wrote to her fiancé that her mother was 'one of those women who never can resist; but, in submitting and bowing in on themselves, make a mark, a plait, within—a sign of suffering'.[8] This use of the word 'plait' (now commonly superseded by the word 'pleat') is interesting. Literally it means a crease in any natural structure, thus a 'plait between the brows' simply means a frown. However, its figurative meaning is that of a hidden recess, often carrying with it an association of sinuosity of character. I'd like to suggest that to evoke an image of a 'hidden recess' in close conjunction with a woman unable to 'resist' reveals Elizabeth's fears about the reproductive fate of women. I see that in the same letter she referred to her mother's 'sweet gentle nature, which the thunder a little turned from its sweetness—as when it turns milk'. As Elizabeth's father was nicknamed the Thunderer and 'milk' is yet another image associated with the female body and its reproductive history, it seems that the soon-to-be bride was trying to convey to her lover her acute anxiety that her poet-self could be destroyed by maternity.

But, back in 1820, Elizabeth was in the process of changing from a happy child to an unhappy adolescent. The reasons for this, or at least some of them, can be unpicked from her diary. She had read Mary Wollstonecraft's *A Vindication of the Rights of Women* when she was about 12 years old and I think this text resonates in some of the diary's pronouncements:

My mind, wrote Elizabeth, is naturally independent and spurns that subserviency of opinion which is generally considered necessary to feminine softness. But this is a subject on which I always feel strongly, for I feel within me an almost proud consciousness of independance [sic] which prompts me to defend my opinions and to yield them only to conviction!!! . . . Better, oh how much better, to be the ridicule of mankind, the scoff of society than lose the self respect which tho' this heart were bursting would elevate me above misery—above wretchedness and above abasement!!! It is not—I feel it is not vanity that dictates them! it is not—I know it is not an encroachment on Masculine prerogative but it is a proud sentiment which will never, never allow me to be humbled in my own eyes!!![9]

The tone of the assertion is both defiant and anxious: the anxiety, on the one hand, that vanity is a particularly feminine vice and, on the other, that only masculine minds possess intellectual toughness points to the problem of gendering her writing self. This gender anxiety is repeated in her comment that she had 'made a secret vow never to pause at undertaking any literary difficulty if convinced of its final utility, but manfully to wade thro' the waves of learning, stopping my ears against the enchanted voice of the Syren'.[10] Learning is clearly identified by Elizabeth with the masculine, and femininity, signified by the siren, is represented as the undoer of masculine learning.

It is unclear what happened to her immediately following the writing of this diary. From being a healthy outdoor sort of child Elizabeth fell suddenly into a mysterious invalid state. This has been variously attributed by her biographers to the result of a fall from a pony, a wasting disease of the spine, an undiagnosed case of anorexia, or ME, and so on. Certainly no contemporary doctor seemed able to diagnose her condition. Without wishing to dwell on or develop this argument, one can at any rate note that her invalidism meant that she was not required to fulfil the tasks eldest daughters usually undertook in nineteenth-century middle-class homes, even after the death of her mother. She continued to study, to write, and to meditate on the particular conundrum of what it meant to be a woman and a writer. Bro' was to die in a sailing accident in 1840. In 1846 she married another poet, Robert Browning, who first fell in love with her poetry and then with the woman. Aged 43, despite all the years of invalidism, she gave birth to a healthy son. Many critics have seen *Aurora Leigh* (1857) as her finest work. It is an epic poem, whose form bespeaks her 'masculine' studies, but here she triumphantly makes the 'condition of the poem's very existence the fact that its protagonist is a woman and a poet'.[11] It is, among other things, even in its name 'Aurora', a homage to her contemporary female idol, the French writer, Aurore Dudevant, a.k.a. George Sand, and the poem's insistent 'I . . . I . . . I . . . I . . . I . . . I write' suggests that for Elizabeth Barrett Browning the earlier gendered crisis had been triumphantly resolved.

Elizabeth Barrett's diary was the private meditation of a young girl right at the beginning of her writing career. George Sand's *Histoire de ma Vie,* on the other hand, was the autobiography of a mature writer who had already published thirty novels.[12] She signed a contract in December 1847 to produce, in instalments, a five-volume autobiography. A deal was struck of 130000 francs, money she needed to keep herself, her children and her household at Nohant. This was the most immediate use of *writing* her autobiography. However, *reading* the autobiography, one is ineluctably drawn to psychoanalytic perspectives, because the text 'produces' the reader as analyst. If we accept (like analysts) that the family is the primary locus where the psyche assumes a gender and a history, we feel that what we are being offered by this story is a case study of repetitious family dynamics. Here, I can only sketch in the elements pertinent to my theme very briefly.

On Aurore Dupin's father's side the family were aristocratic, with royal forebears. Her father Maurice was the only son of Claude Dupin de Franceuil and Aurore de Saxe; her mother Sophie Delaborde was the daughter of a Paris birdseller whom Maurice had met when serving as Murat's aide-de-camp during the Napoleonic campaigns. In wedding Sophie, Maurice had defied the wishes of his mother; the older and the younger woman became locked in a deadly sexual rivalry. Maurice's early death in a riding accident made the 4-year-old Aurore the legitimate heir to the family estate of Nohant, in Berry. The two women's rival love for Maurice was now displaced onto the small girl. Aurore de Saxe reasserted old class distinctions and pensioned Sophie off to Paris on an allowance when Aurore was 9, severely restricting Sophie's subsequent visits to Nohant.[13] Aurore persistently and passionately dreamed of the time when she and her mother would be reunited. This mother-want, primarily for a recuperated, ideal mother is a persistent trope in Sand's fictional work.[14]

But the psychic reality for Aurore Dupin at Nohant was an identification with her dead father; he was 'the real author of the story of my life'.[15] In the psychoanalyst R.D. Laing's words: 'the young are introduced to the parts the dead once played'.[16] Aurore was her father's living double: 'My voice, features, manners, taste—everything about me reminded [my grandmother] of her son as a child, to the point where sometimes, while watching me play, she would have a kind of hallucination, call me Maurice and speak of me as her son'.[17]

The identification with the dead father was further reinforced by Deschartes, Maurice's tutor, who took

Aurore at the dead of night to kiss her father's skull in the family grave:

> Having taught only boys, I think [Deschartes] was eager to see me as male and convince himself I was one. My skirts disturbed the seriousness of his teaching, and it is true that when I took his advice and donned the masculine smock, cap, and gaiters, he became ten times more pedantic and crushed me under his Latin, presuming that I could understand it much better.[18]

Because the grandmother's only passion had been the maternal one, it redoubled in intensity towards her granddaughter. To protect her self from being overwhelmed, Aurore took refuge in a 'poetic and fantastic world'.[19] At its centre was the imaginary figure of Corambé, a kind of bisexual muse who was simultaneously the hero/heroine of a continuous novel in her head and also a kind of personal god/goddess. 'Corambé . . . was as pure and charitable as Jesus, as shining and handsome as Gabriel, but . . . it often appeared to me with female features'.[20] Her play and her reveries protected her until Aurore de Saxe, furious because, despite all her efforts, the young girl still wanted to be with her mother, 'settled on the most baleful means of all' to win the struggle.[21] She told Aurore that Sophie had been a garrison wife, an army camp-follower and a prostitute and that if Aurore were to live with her mother, she too would inevitably be prostituted. At the moment of puberty, then, a crucial epoch in the complicated process of gender identification, 14-year-old Aurore was told that her mother was a disgraceful and disgraced woman. The consequences were devastating:

> I no longer knew if I loved or hated anyone, I no longer felt impassioned over anyone or resentful towards anyone. I had what seemed like an enormous burn inside me and a searing emptiness where my heart should have been. I was aware only of a kind of contempt for the whole universe and a bitter disdain for life as it would henceforth be for me: I no longer loved myself. If my mother was detestable and hateful, then I, the fruit of her womb was too . . . I gave up my sweet reveries. No more novel, no more daydreams. Corambé was silent.[22]

Aurore's immediate response was to suffer one of the first of several bouts of anorexia she experienced during her life. She wrote that her 'mute anger' had the effect that her 'stomach rejected all food: my throat tightened, nothing would go down, and I could not repress a secret pleasure in telling myself that death by starvation would occur without my having a hand in it'.[23] She was full of rage against both 'bonne-mamam' (grandmother) and her 'bad mother' (Sophie), but, incapable of stopping loving them, either of them, her rage was turned in on her own body, the female body which she now knew to be deeply unreliable.

In a move which seems strikingly like a punishment for not repudiating her mother, the grandmother sent Aurore to live and be educated in the English Convent in Paris. Although cut off from the outside world she also had two years' respite from the family conflict. Once again Aurore experimented with gender roles. Firstly, she joined the *diables,* that is the group of girls with a reputation for wild escapades, the sort of girls who are often called 'tomboys'. This was succeeded by a sudden perverse reaction, when she became almost pathologically pious, mortifying her flesh. At the end of the two years she decided that she would enter the convent permanently when she reached her majority of 21. Instead, following her grandmother's death in 1821 she finally achieved her desire of being reunited with her mother. Although mother and daughter found it difficult to live with one another after a separation that had effectively established Aurore in a different class to that of her mother, nevertheless, this interregnum appears to have been very important. She wrote: 'If destiny had made me pass immediately from my grandmother's control to that of a husband or a convent, it is possible that . . . I would never have become myself'.[24] It was during this period that she was once more able to conjure up Corambé, that 'eternal poem . . . where I felt myself true to my emotions'.[25]

It is, I think clear from her account that the self she refers to is her writing self, 'George Sand'. This pen-name is in itself curious, an ungendered sign, in that the French masculine form would be 'Georges'. Arguably, her pen-name signals an identification with her 'dream-muse', Corambé, in that it is not securely masculine *or* feminine. In 1822, Aurore married Casimir Dudevant (later Baron Dudevant) and had two children, a son Maurice (named after her father) in 1823 and a daughter Solange in 1828. The marriage broke down quite quickly and in 1831 Aurore decided to live in Paris and make her living from writing. On her first attempt to get impartial advice in Paris she was told: 'a woman shouldn't write . . . don't make books, make babies'.[26] She started to 'pass' as a young man: 'having dressed like a boy during my childhood, then having hunted in smock and gaiters with Deschartes' she had a 'sentry box redingote (the male fashion of the day) made for myself, out of thick grey cloth, with matching trousers and vest. With a grey hat and wide wool tie, I was the perfect little first-year student'.[27] In this outfit she enjoyed the same freedom as young male students; her clothing, she wrote, made her feel 'fearless'. Her cross-dressing and her identification with her soldier-father seem to have been psychologically necessary to safeguard her from a deep-rooted fear of the female.

In her fictional writing, however, she dwelled with great intensity on the problems of growing up female.[28] She used her autobiography to 'prove' that her father had loved her mother. If her father loved her mother, her mother was no longer disgraced. In recuperating the reputation of her mother, she simultaneously attempted to recuperate her own 'daughterliness', which she equated with 'femininity'. Nevertheless, to the reader/analyst, her gender oscillations seem doomed never to be fully resolved. She rarely bonded with other women (except a very few, and those few did not include her daughter). She wrote endlessly, even obsessively, her creative writing operating out of her daydreams, which played and replayed the original family romance. In the case of George Sand, one might say, it was the never-to-be-resolved anxiety and fragility of her gender identification that was one of the most powerful sources of her creative drive.[29]

Notes

[1] Joanna Russ (1983) *How to Suppress Women's Writing,* London: The Women's Press.

[2] Elspeth Probyn (1993) *Sexing the Self: Gendered Positions in Cultural Studies,* London and New York: Routledge, p. 2.

[3] Elaine Showalter (1978) *A Literature of Their Own,* London: Virago, p. 61.

[4] Elizabeth Barrett (1914) *Glimpses into My Own Life and Literary Character,* Boston: The Bibliophile Society.

[5] *Ibid.,* p. 7.

[6] Introduction by H. Buxton Forman to Barrett 1914, p. xxxv.

[7] Barrett 1914, p. 25.

[8] *The Letters of Robert Browning and Elizabeth Barrett 1845-1846* (1969), 2 vols, ed. Elvan Kintner, Cambridge, Mass.: Harvard University Press, vol. II, p. 1012.

[9] Barrett 1914, p. 24.

[10] *Ibid.,* p. 25.

[11] Cora Kaplan's introduction to Elizabeth Barrett (1982) *Aurora Leigh,* London: The Women's Press.

[12] It was written in installments between 1846 and 1854. I will be quoting from: *Story of My Life: the Autobiography of George Sand* (1991), a group translation, edited by Thelma Jurgrau, Albany: State University of New York Press.

[13] See Wendy Deutelbaum and Cynthia Huff (1985) 'Class, Gender and Family System: The Case of George Sand', in Shirley Nelson Garner, Claire Kahane and Madelon Sprengnether (Eds) *The (M)other Tongue: Essays in Feminist Psychoanalytic Interpretation,* Ithaca and London: Cornell University Press.

[14] I have argued this case in my MA 'Scheherezade and her Half-sisters' (University of Essex, 1989) and in Chapter 3 of my PhD thesis 'Barbara Leigh Smith Bodichon and George Eliot: An Examination of Their Work and Friendship' (Anglia Polytechnic University in collaboration with the University of Essex, 1992).

[15] Sand 1991, p. 169.

[16] R. D. Laing (1972) *The Politics of the Family and Other Essays,* New York: Vintage, p. 29. See Freud's essay, 'Creative Writers and Day-Dreaming', in *The Complete Psychological Works of Sigmund Freud* (1959), tr. from the German under the general editorship of James Strachey in collaboration with Anna Freud, London: Hogarth Press, vol. 9, pp. 143-53, in which he writes: 'You will not forget that the stress [my model] lays on childhood memories in the writer's life . . . is ultimately derived from the assumption that a piece of creative writing, like a day-dream, is a continuation of, and a substitute for, what was once the play of childhood' (p. 152). George Sand wrote that the name Corambé was merely a 'fortuitous collection of syllables' (*ibid.,* p. 605). Hélène Deutsch (1946) *Psychology of Women,* London: Research Books, offers this account: 'When Aurore was small and her father was away, her mother tried to teach her the alphabet. The little one showed application and talent. But she had one curious difficulty: the letter "b" did not exist for her . . . it seems to me that the "b" repressed in her childhood is identical with the "bé" that later turned up as the suffix to "coram" [Latin for "in the presence of"]. The whole word could then mean, "in the presence of 'b'". If the "b" repressed in childhood referred to the absent father, whom she hardly knew at the time, then its turning up in Corambé would be quite understandable' (p. 246).

[17] Sand 1991, p. 467.

[18] *Ibid.,* p. 781.

[19] *Ibid.,* p. 60.

[20] Sand 1991, p. 605.

[21] Sand 1991, p. 633.

[22] *Ibid.,* pp. 634-5.

[23] *Ibid.,* p. 824.

[24] *Ibid.,* p. 752.

[25] *Ibid.,* p. 804.

[26] *Ibid.,* p. 915.

[27] *Ibid.,* p. 893.

[28] See Michael Danahy (1982) 'Growing Up Female: George Sand's View in La Petite Fadette', in Natalie Datlof (Ed.) *The George Sand Papers: Conference Proceedings 1978,* New York: AMS Press.

[29] 'Only in artistic dreaming did George Sand realize her aborted femininity', Deutsch 1946, p. 241.

FURTHER READING

Couser, G. Thomas. "Mary Boykin Chesnut: Secession, Confederacy, Reconstruction." In *Altered Egos: Authority in American Autobiography*, pp. 156-88. New York: Oxford University Press, 1989.

> Considers the issues of authenticity and validity in the case of Mary Boykin Chesnut's Civil War diary.

Dodson, Jualynne E. Introduction to *An Autobiography: The Story of the Lord's Dealings with Mrs. Amanda Smith the Colored Evangelist*, by Amanda Smith, pp. xxvii-xlii. New York: Oxford University Press, 1988.

> Argues that Smith's *An Autobiography* provides unique insight into African-American women's roles in the AME Church and Christian Evangelism.

Jelinek, Estelle C. "The Paradox and Success of Elizabeth Cady Stanton." In *Women's Autobiography: Essays in Criticism*, edited by Estelle C. Jelinek, pp. 71-92. Bloomington: Indiana University Press, 1980.

> Explores Stanton's effort to present an ordinary but positive life-story in order to attract readers to her cause.

Myers, Mitzi. "*Harriet Martineau's Autobiography*: The Making of a Female Philosopher." In *Women's Autobiography: Essays in Criticism*, edited by Estelle C. Jelinek, pp. 53-70. Bloomington: Indiana University Press, 1980.

> Describes *Harriet Martineau's Autobiography* as a study of the development of the philosopher's mind.

Ridgers, Brian. "'What I earnestly longed for. . .': Elizabeth Missing Sewell, Writing, Autobiography and Victorian Womanhood." In *The Uses of Autobiography*, edited by Julia Swindells, pp. 138-50. London: Taylor and Francis, 1995.

> Discusses the defining elements of women's Victorian autobiographies.

Smith, Sidonie. "Resisting the Gaze of Embodiment: Women's Autobiography in the Nineteenth Century." In *American Women's Autobiography: Fea(s)ts of Memory*, edited by Margo Culley, pp. 75-110. Madison: University of Wisconsin Press, 1992.

> Argues that nineteenth-century autobiographies reflect the formation of female selfhood.

Symes, Ruth A. "Catharine Cappe of York (1822)." In *The Uses of Autobiography*, edited by Julia Swindells, pp. 128-37. London: Taylor and Francis, 1995.

> Contends that there is a strong connection, which has yet to be explored, between educational writing and autobiography in the early nineteenth century.

Washington, Mary Helen. An Introduction to *A Voice from the South*, by Anna Julia Cooper, pp. xxvii-liv. New York: Oxford University Press, 1988.

> States that African-American women's autobiographies not only challenged white supremacy but also criticized gender relations within the African-American community.

Nineteenth-Century
Literature Criticism

Topics Volume
Cumulative Indexes

Volumes 1-76

How to Use This Index

The main references

Calvino, Italo
1923–1985 .... CLC 5, 8, 11, 22, 33, 39,
73; SSC 3

list all author entries in the following Gale Literary Criticism series:

BLC = *Black Literature Criticism*
CLC = *Contemporary Literary Criticism*
CLR = *Children's Literature Review*
CMLC = *Classical and Medieval Literature Criticism*
DA = *DISCovering Authors*
DAB = *DISCovering Authors: British*
DAC = *DISCovering Authors: Canadian*
DAM = *DISCovering Authors: Modules*
    DRAM: *Dramatists Module;* **MST**: *Most-Studied Authors Module;*
    MULT: *Multicultural Authors Module;* **NOV**: *Novelists Module;*
    POET: *Poets Module;* **POP**: *Popular Fiction and Genre Authors Module*
DC = *Drama Criticism*
HLC = *Hispanic Literature Criticism*
LC = *Literature Criticism from 1400 to 1800*
NCLC = *Nineteenth-Century Literature Criticism*
PC = *Poetry Criticism*
SSC = *Short Story Criticism*
TCLC = *Twentieth-Century Literary Criticism*
WLC = *World Literature Criticism, 1500 to the Present*

The cross-references

See also CANR 23; CA 85-88;
   obituary CA116

list all author entries in the following Gale biographical and literary sources:

AAYA = *Authors & Artists for Young Adults*
AITN = *Authors in the News*
BEST = *Bestsellers*
BW = *Black Writers*
CA = *Contemporary Authors*
CAAS = *Contemporary Authors Autobiography Series*
CABS = *Contemporary Authors Bibliographical Series*
CANR = *Contemporary Authors New Revision Series*
CAP = *Contemporary Authors Permanent Series*
CDALB = *Concise Dictionary of American Literary Biography*
CDBLB = *Concise Dictionary of British Literary Biography*
DLB = *Dictionary of Literary Biography*
DLBD = *Dictionary of Literary Biography Documentary Series*
DLBY = *Dictionary of Literary Biography Yearbook*
HW = *Hispanic Writers*
JRDA = *Junior DISCovering Authors*
MAICYA = *Major Authors and Illustrators for Children and Young Adults*
MTCW = *Major 20th-Century Writers*
NNAL = *Native North American Literature*
SAAS = *Something about the Author Autobiography Series*
SATA = *Something about the Author*
YABC = *Yesterday's Authors of Books for Children*

Beauvoir, Simone (Lucie Ernestine Marie Bertrand) de 1908-1986 CLC 1, 2, 4, 8, 14, 31, 44, 50, 71; DA; DAB; DAC; DAM MST, NOV; WLC
See also CA 9-12R; 118; CANR 28, 61; DLB 72; DLBY 86; MTCW 1, 2

Becker, Carl (Lotus) 1873-1945   TCLC 63
See also CA 157; DLB 17

Becker, Jurek 1937-1997   CLC 7, 19
See also CA 85-88; 157; CANR 60; DLB 75

Becker, Walter 1950-   CLC 26

Beckett, Samuel (Barclay) 1906-1989 CLC 1, 2, 3, 4, 6, 9, 10, 11, 14, 18, 29, 57, 59, 83; DA; DAB; DAC; DAM DRAM, MST, NOV; SSC 16; WLC
See also CA 5-8R; 130; CANR 33, 61; CDBLB 1945-1960; DLB 13, 15; DLBY 90; MTCW 1, 2

Beckford, William 1760-1844   NCLC 16
See also DLB 39

Beckman, Gunnel 1910-   CLC 26
See also CA 33-36R; CANR 15; CLR 25; MAICYA; SAAS 9; SATA 6

Becque, Henri 1837-1899   NCLC 3
See also DLB 192

Beddoes, Thomas Lovell 1803-1849 NCLC 3
See also DLB 96

Bede c. 673-735   CMLC 20
See also DLB 146

Bedford, Donald F.
See Fearing, Kenneth (Flexner)

Beecher, Catharine Esther 1800-1878 NCLC 30
See also DLB 1

Beecher, John 1904-1980   CLC 6
See also AITN 1; CA 5-8R; 105; CANR 8

Beer, Johann 1655-1700   LC 5
See also DLB 168

Beer, Patricia 1924-   CLC 58
See also CA 61-64; CANR 13, 46; DLB 40

Beerbohm, Max
See Beerbohm, (Henry) Max(imilian)

Beerbohm, (Henry) Max(imilian) 1872-1956 TCLC 1, 24
See also CA 104; 154; DLB 34, 100

Beer-Hofmann, Richard 1866-1945 TCLC 60
See also CA 160; DLB 81

Begiebing, Robert J(ohn) 1946-   CLC 70
See also CA 122; CANR 40

Behan, Brendan 1923-1964 CLC 1, 8, 11, 15, 79; DAM DRAM
See also CA 73-76; CANR 33; CDBLB 1945-1960; DLB 13; MTCW 1, 2

Behn, Aphra 1640(?)-1689 LC 1, 30, 42; DA; DAB; DAC; DAM DRAM, MST, NOV, POET; DC 4; PC 13; WLC
See also DLB 39, 80, 131

Behrman, S(amuel) N(athaniel) 1893-1973 CLC 40
See also CA 13-16; 45-48; CAP 1; DLB 7, 44

Belasco, David 1853-1931   TCLC 3
See also CA 104; 168; DLB 7

Belcheva, Elisaveta 1893-   CLC 10
See also Bagryana, Elisaveta

Beldone, Phil "Cheech"
See Ellison, Harlan (Jay)

Beleno
See Azuela, Mariano

Belinski, Vissarion Grigoryevich 1811-1848 NCLC 5
See also DLB 198

Belitt, Ben 1911-   CLC 22
See also CA 13-16R; CAAS 4; CANR 7, 77;

DLB 5

Bell, Gertrude (Margaret Lowthian) 1868-1926 TCLC 67
See also CA 167; DLB 174

Bell, J. Freeman
See Zangwill, Israel

Bell, James Madison 1826-1902   TCLC 43; BLC 1; DAM MULT
See also BW 1; CA 122; 124; DLB 50

Bell, Madison Smartt 1957-   CLC 41, 102
See also CA 111; CANR 28, 54, 73; MTCW 1

Bell, Marvin (Hartley) 1937- CLC 8, 31; DAM POET
See also CA 21-24R; CAAS 14; CANR 59; DLB 5; MTCW 1

Bell, W. L. D.
See Mencken, H(enry) L(ouis)

Bellamy, Atwood C.
See Mencken, H(enry) L(ouis)

Bellamy, Edward 1850-1898   NCLC 4
See also DLB 12

Bellin, Edward J.
See Kuttner, Henry

Belloc, (Joseph) Hilaire (Pierre Sebastien Rene Swanton) 1870-1953 TCLC 7, 18; DAM POET; PC 24
See also CA 106; 152; DLB 19, 100, 141, 174; MTCW 1; YABC 1

Belloc, Joseph Peter Rene Hilaire
See Belloc, (Joseph) Hilaire (Pierre Sebastien Rene Swanton)

Belloc, Joseph Pierre Hilaire
See Belloc, (Joseph) Hilaire (Pierre Sebastien Rene Swanton)

Belloc, M. A.
See Lowndes, Marie Adelaide (Belloc)

Bellow, Saul 1915- CLC 1, 2, 3, 6, 8, 10, 13, 15, 25, 33, 34, 63, 79; DA; DAB; DAC; DAM MST, NOV, POP; SSC 14; WLC
See also AITN 2; BEST 89:3; CA 5-8R; CABS 1; CANR 29, 53; CDALB 1941-1968; DLB 2, 28; DLBD 3; DLBY 82; MTCW 1, 2

Belser, Reimond Karel Maria de 1929-
See Ruyslinck, Ward
See also CA 152

Bely, Andrey   TCLC 7; PC 11
See also Bugayev, Boris Nikolayevich
See also MTCW 1

Belyi, Andrei
See Bugayev, Boris Nikolayevich

Benary, Margot
See Benary-Isbert, Margot

Benary-Isbert, Margot 1889-1979   CLC 12
See also CA 5-8R; 89-92; CANR 4, 72; CLR 12; MAICYA; SATA 2; SATA-Obit 21

Benavente (y Martinez), Jacinto 1866-1954 TCLC 3; DAM DRAM, MULT
See also CA 106; 131; HW; MTCW 1, 2

Benchley, Peter (Bradford) 1940- CLC 4, 8; DAM NOV, POP
See also AAYA 14; AITN 2; CA 17-20R; CANR 12, 35, 66; MTCW 1, 2; SATA 3, 89

Benchley, Robert (Charles) 1889-1945 TCLC 1, 55
See also CA 105; 153; DLB 11

Benda, Julien 1867-1956   TCLC 60
See also CA 120; 154

Benedict, Ruth (Fulton) 1887-1948 TCLC 60
See also CA 158

Benedict, Saint c. 480-c. 547   CMLC 29

Benedikt, Michael 1935-   CLC 4, 14
See also CA 13-16R; CANR 7; DLB 5

Benet, Juan 1927-   CLC 28

See also CA 143

Benet, Stephen Vincent 1898-1943 TCLC 7; DAM POET; SSC 10
See also CA 104; 152; DLB 4, 48, 102; DLBY 97; MTCW 1; YABC 1

Benet, William Rose 1886-1950   TCLC 28; DAM POET
See also CA 118; 152; DLB 45

Benford, Gregory (Albert) 1941-   CLC 52
See also CA 69-72; CAAS 27; CANR 12, 24, 49; DLBY 82

Bengtsson, Frans (Gunnar) 1894-1954 TCLC 48
See also CA 170

Benjamin, David
See Slavitt, David R(ytman)

Benjamin, Lois
See Gould, Lois

Benjamin, Walter 1892-1940   TCLC 39
See also CA 164

Benn, Gottfried 1886-1956   TCLC 3
See also CA 106; 153; DLB 56

Bennett, Alan 1934- CLC 45, 77; DAB; DAM MST
See also CA 103; CANR 35, 55; MTCW 1, 2

Bennett, (Enoch) Arnold 1867-1931 TCLC 5, 20
See also CA 106; 155; CDBLB 1890-1914; DLB 10, 34, 98, 135; MTCW 2

Bennett, Elizabeth
See Mitchell, Margaret (Munnerlyn)

Bennett, George Harold 1930-
See Bennett, Hal
See also BW 1; CA 97-100

Bennett, Hal   CLC 5
See also Bennett, George Harold
See also DLB 33

Bennett, Jay 1912-   CLC 35
See also AAYA 10; CA 69-72; CANR 11, 42; JRDA; SAAS 4; SATA 41, 87; SATA-Brief 27

Bennett, Louise (Simone) 1919- CLC 28; BLC 1; DAM MULT
See also BW 2; CA 151; DLB 117

Benson, E(dward) F(rederic) 1867-1940 TCLC 27
See also CA 114; 157; DLB 135, 153

Benson, Jackson J. 1930-   CLC 34
See also CA 25-28R; DLB 111

Benson, Sally 1900-1972   CLC 17
See also CA 19-20; 37-40R; CAP 1; SATA 1, 35; SATA-Obit 27

Benson, Stella 1892-1933   TCLC 17
See also CA 117; 155; DLB 36, 162

Bentham, Jeremy 1748-1832   NCLC 38
See also DLB 107, 158

Bentley, E(dmund) C(lerihew) 1875-1956 TCLC 12
See also CA 108; DLB 70

Bentley, Eric (Russell) 1916-   CLC 24
See also CA 5-8R; CANR 6, 67; INT CANR-6

Beranger, Pierre Jean de 1780-1857 NCLC 34

Berdyaev, Nicolas
See Berdyaev, Nikolai (Aleksandrovich)

Berdyaev, Nikolai (Aleksandrovich) 1874-1948 TCLC 67
See also CA 120; 157

Berdyayev, Nikolai (Aleksandrovich)
See Berdyaev, Nikolai (Aleksandrovich)

Berendt, John (Lawrence) 1939-   CLC 86
See also CA 146; CANR 75; MTCW 1

Beresford, J(ohn) D(avys) 1873-1947 TCLC 81

CANR 2, 30, 75; CDALB 1968-1988; DLB
2, 8; MTCW 1, 2; SATA 11, 64
Bradford, Gamaliel 1863-1932 **TCLC 36**
See also CA 160; DLB 17
Bradley, David (Henry), Jr. 1950- **CLC 23,
118; BLC 1; DAM MULT**
See also BW 1; CA 104; CANR 26; DLB 33
Bradley, John Ed(mund, Jr.) 1958- **CLC 55**
See also CA 139
Bradley, Marion Zimmer 1930- **CLC 30;
DAM POP**
See also AAYA 9; CA 57-60; CAAS 10; CANR
7, 31, 51, 75; DLB 8; MTCW 1, 2; SATA 90
Bradstreet, Anne 1612(?)-1672**LC 4, 30; DA;
DAC; DAM MST, POET; PC 10**
See also CDALB 1640-1865; DLB 24
Brady, Joan 1939- **CLC 86**
See also CA 141
Bragg, Melvyn 1939- **CLC 10**
See also BEST 89:3; CA 57-60; CANR 10, 48;
DLB 14
Brahe, Tycho 1546-1601 **LC 45**
Braine, John (Gerard) 1922-1986**CLC 1, 3, 41**
See also CA 1-4R; 120; CANR 1, 33; CDBLB
1945-1960; DLB 15; DLBY 86; MTCW 1
Bramah, Ernest 1868-1942 **TCLC 72**
See also CA 156; DLB 70
Brammer, William 1930(?)-1978 **CLC 31**
See also CA 77-80
Brancati, Vitaliano 1907-1954 **TCLC 12**
See also CA 109
Brancato, Robin F(idler) 1936- **CLC 35**
See also AAYA 9; CA 69-72; CANR 11, 45;
CLR 32; JRDA; SAAS 9; SATA 97
Brand, Max
See Faust, Frederick (Schiller)
Brand, Millen 1906-1980 **CLC 7**
See also CA 21-24R; 97-100; CANR 72
Branden, Barbara **CLC 44**
See also CA 148
Brandes, Georg (Morris Cohen) 1842-1927
TCLC 10
See also CA 105
Brandys, Kazimierz 1916- **CLC 62**
Branley, Franklyn M(ansfield) 1915-**CLC 21**
See also CA 33-36R; CANR 14, 39; CLR 13;
MAICYA; SAAS 16; SATA 4, 68
Brathwaite, Edward Kamau 1930- **CLC 11;
BLCS; DAM POET**
See also BW 2; CA 25-28R; CANR 11, 26, 47;
DLB 125
Brautigan, Richard (Gary) 1935-1984**CLC 1,
3, 5, 9, 12, 34, 42; DAM NOV**
See also CA 53-56; 113; CANR 34; DLB 2, 5,
206; DLBY 80, 84; MTCW 1; SATA 56
Brave Bird, Mary 1953-
See Crow Dog, Mary (Ellen)
See also NNAL
Braverman, Kate 1950- **CLC 67**
See also CA 89-92
Brecht, (Eugen) Bertolt (Friedrich) 1898-1956
**TCLC 1, 6, 13, 35; DA; DAB; DAC; DAM
DRAM, MST; DC 3; WLC**
See also CA 104; 133; CANR 62; DLB 56, 124;
MTCW 1, 2
Brecht, Eugen Berthold Friedrich
See Brecht, (Eugen) Bertolt (Friedrich)
Bremer, Fredrika 1801-1865 **NCLC 11**
Brennan, Christopher John 1870-1932**TCLC
17**
See also CA 117
Brennan, Maeve 1917-1993 **CLC 5**
See also CA 81-84; CANR 72

Brent, Linda
See Jacobs, Harriet A(nn)
Brentano, Clemens (Maria) 1778-1842**NCLC
1**
See also DLB 90
Brent of Bin Bin
See Franklin, (Stella Maria Sarah) Miles
(Lampe)
Brenton, Howard 1942- **CLC 31**
See also CA 69-72; CANR 33, 67; DLB 13;
MTCW 1
Breslin, James 1930-1996
See Breslin, Jimmy
See also CA 73-76; CANR 31, 75; DAM NOV;
MTCW 1, 2
Breslin, Jimmy **CLC 4, 43**
See Breslin, James
See also AITN 1; DLB 185; MTCW 2
Bresson, Robert 1901- **CLC 16**
See also CA 110; CANR 49
Breton, Andre 1896-1966**CLC 2, 9, 15, 54; PC
15**
See also CA 19-20; 25-28R; CANR 40, 60; CAP
2; DLB 65; MTCW 1, 2
Breytenbach, Breyten 1939(?)- **CLC 23, 37;
DAM POET**
See also CA 113; 129; CANR 61
Bridgers, Sue Ellen 1942- **CLC 26**
See also AAYA 8; CA 65-68; CANR 11, 36;
CLR 18; DLB 52; JRDA; MAICYA; SAAS
1; SATA 22, 90
Bridges, Robert (Seymour) 1844-1930 **TCLC
1; DAM POET**
See also CA 104; 152; CDBLB 1890-1914;
DLB 19, 98
Bridie, James **TCLC 3**
See also Mavor, Osborne Henry
See also DLB 10
Brin, David 1950- **CLC 34**
See also AAYA 21; CA 102; CANR 24, 70;
INT CANR-24; SATA 65
Brink, Andre (Philippus) 1935- **CLC 18, 36,
106**
See also CA 104; CANR 39, 62; INT 103;
MTCW 1, 2
Brinsmead, H(esba) F(ay) 1922- **CLC 21**
See also CA 21-24R; CANR 10; CLR 47;
MAICYA; SAAS 5; SATA 18, 78
Brittain, Vera (Mary) 1893(?)-1970 **CLC 23**
See also CA 13-16; 25-28R; CANR 58; CAP
1; DLB 191; MTCW 1, 2
Broch, Hermann 1886-1951 **TCLC 20**
See also CA 117; DLB 85, 124
Brock, Rose
See Hansen, Joseph
Brodkey, Harold (Roy) 1930-1996 **CLC 56**
See also CA 111; 151; CANR 71; DLB 130
Brodskii, Iosif
See Brodsky, Joseph
Brodsky, Iosif Alexandrovich 1940-1996
See Brodsky, Joseph
See also AITN 1; CA 41-44R; 151; CANR 37;
DAM POET; MTCW 1, 2
Brodsky, Joseph 1940-1996 **CLC 4, 6, 13, 36,
100; PC 9**
See also Brodskii, Iosif; Brodsky, Iosif
Alexandrovich
See also MTCW 1
Brodsky, Michael (Mark) 1948- **CLC 19**
See also CA 102; CANR 18, 41, 58
Bromell, Henry 1947- **CLC 5**
See also CA 53-56; CANR 9
Bromfield, Louis (Brucker) 1896-1956**TCLC**

11
See also CA 107; 155; DLB 4, 9, 86
Broner, E(sther) M(asserman) 1930- **CLC 19**
See also CA 17-20R; CANR 8, 25, 72; DLB 28
Bronk, William 1918- **CLC 10**
See also CA 89-92; CANR 23; DLB 165
Bronstein, Lev Davidovich
See Trotsky, Leon
Bronte, Anne 1820-1849 **NCLC 71**
See also DLB 21, 199
Bronte, Charlotte 1816-1855 **NCLC 3, 8, 33,
58; DA; DAB; DAC; DAM MST, NOV;
WLC**
See also AAYA 17; CDBLB 1832-1890; DLB
21, 159, 199
Bronte, Emily (Jane) 1818-1848**NCLC 16, 35;
DA; DAB; DAC; DAM MST, NOV, POET;
PC 8; WLC**
See also AAYA 17; CDBLB 1832-1890; DLB
21, 32, 199
Brooke, Frances 1724-1789 **LC 6, 48**
See also DLB 39, 99
Brooke, Henry 1703(?)-1783 **LC 1**
See also DLB 39
Brooke, Rupert (Chawner) 1887-1915 **TCLC
2, 7; DA; DAB; DAC; DAM MST, POET;
PC 24; WLC**
See also CA 104; 132; CANR 61; CDBLB
1914-1945; DLB 19; MTCW 1, 2
Brooke-Haven, P.
See Wodehouse, P(elham) G(renville)
Brooke-Rose, Christine 1926(?)- **CLC 40**
See also CA 13-16R; CANR 58; DLB 14
Brookner, Anita 1928-**CLC 32, 34, 51; DAB;
DAM POP**
See also CA 114; 120; CANR 37, 56; DLB 194;
DLBY 87; MTCW 1, 2
Brooks, Cleanth 1906-1994 **CLC 24, 86, 110**
See also CA 17-20R; 145; CANR 33, 35; DLB
63; DLBY 94; INT CANR-35; MTCW 1, 2
Brooks, George
See Baum, L(yman) Frank
Brooks, Gwendolyn 1917- **CLC 1, 2, 4, 5, 15,
49; BLC 1; DA; DAC; DAM MST, MULT,
POET; PC 7; WLC**
See also AAYA 20; AITN 1; BW 2; CA 1-4R;
CANR 1, 27, 52, 75; CDALB 1941-1968;
CLR 27; DLB 5, 76, 165; MTCW 1, 2; SATA
6
Brooks, Mel **CLC 12**
See also Kaminsky, Melvin
See also AAYA 13; DLB 26
Brooks, Peter 1938- **CLC 34**
See also CA 45-48; CANR 1
Brooks, Van Wyck 1886-1963 **CLC 29**
See also CA 1-4R; CANR 6; DLB 45, 63, 103
Brophy, Brigid (Antonia) 1929-1995 **CLC 6,
11, 29, 105**
See also CA 5-8R; 149; CAAS 4; CANR 25,
53; DLB 14; MTCW 1, 2
Brosman, Catharine Savage 1934- **CLC 9**
See also CA 61-64; CANR 21, 46
Brossard, Nicole 1943- **CLC 115**
See also CA 122; CAAS 16; DLB 53
Brother Antoninus
See Everson, William (Oliver)
The Brothers Quay
See Quay, Stephen; Quay, Timothy
Broughton, T(homas) Alan 1936- **CLC 19**
See also CA 45-48; CANR 2, 23, 48
Broumas, Olga 1949- **CLC 10, 73**
See also CA 85-88; CANR 20, 69
Brown, Alan 1950- **CLC 99**

See also CA 156

Brown, Charles Brockden 1771-1810 **NCLC 22, 74**
See also CDALB 1640-1865; DLB 37, 59, 73

Brown, Christy 1932-1981 **CLC 63**
See also CA 105; 104; CANR 72; DLB 14

Brown, Claude 1937- **CLC 30; BLC 1; DAM MULT**
See also AAYA 7; BW 1; CA 73-76

Brown, Dee (Alexander) 1908- **CLC 18, 47; DAM POP**
See also AAYA 30; CA 13-16R; CAAS 6; CANR 11, 45, 60; DLBY 80; MTCW 1, 2; SATA 5

Brown, George
See Wertmueller, Lina

Brown, George Douglas 1869-1902 **TCLC 28**
See also CA 162

Brown, George Mackay 1921-1996 **CLC 5, 48, 100**
See also CA 21-24R; 151; CAAS 6; CANR 12, 37, 67; DLB 14, 27, 139; MTCW 1; SATA 35

Brown, (William) Larry 1951- **CLC 73**
See also CA 130; 134; INT 133

Brown, Moses
See Barrett, William (Christopher)

Brown, Rita Mae 1944- **CLC 18, 43, 79; DAM NOV, POP**
See also CA 45-48; CANR 2, 11, 35, 62; INT CANR-11; MTCW 1, 2

Brown, Roderick (Langmere) Haig-
See Haig-Brown, Roderick (Langmere)

Brown, Rosellen 1939- **CLC 32**
See also CA 77-80; CAAS 10; CANR 14, 44

Brown, Sterling Allen 1901-1989 **CLC 1, 23, 59; BLC 1; DAM MULT, POET**
See also BW 1; CA 85-88; 127; CANR 26, 74; DLB 48, 51, 63; MTCW 1, 2

Brown, Will
See Ainsworth, William Harrison

Brown, William Wells 1813-1884 **NCLC 2; BLC 1; DAM MULT; DC 1**
See also DLB 3, 50

Browne, (Clyde) Jackson 1948(?)- **CLC 21**
See also CA 120

Browning, Elizabeth Barrett 1806-1861 **NCLC 1, 16, 61, 66; DA; DAB; DAC; DAM MST, POET; PC 6; WLC**
See also CDBLB 1832-1890; DLB 32, 199

Browning, Robert 1812-1889 **NCLC 19; DA; DAB; DAC; DAM MST, POET; PC 2; WLCS**
See also CDBLB 1832-1890; DLB 32, 163; YABC 1

Browning, Tod 1882-1962 **CLC 16**
See also CA 141; 117

Brownson, Orestes Augustus 1803-1876 **NCLC 50**
See also DLB 1, 59, 73

Bruccoli, Matthew J(oseph) 1931- **CLC 34**
See also CA 9-12R; CANR 7; DLB 103

Bruce, Lenny **CLC 21**
See also Schneider, Leonard Alfred

Bruin, John
See Brutus, Dennis

Brulard, Henri
See Stendhal

Brulls, Christian
See Simenon, Georges (Jacques Christian)

Brunner, John (Kilian Houston) 1934-1995 **CLC 8, 10; DAM POP**
See also CA 1-4R; 149; CAAS 8; CANR 2, 37;

MTCW 1, 2

Bruno, Giordano 1548-1600 **LC 27**

Brutus, Dennis 1924- **CLC 43; BLC 1; DAM MULT, POET; PC 24**
See also BW 2; CA 49-52; CAAS 14; CANR 2, 27, 42; DLB 117

Bryan, C(ourtlandt) D(ixon) B(arnes) 1936- **CLC 29**
See also CA 73-76; CANR 13, 68; DLB 185; INT CANR-13

Bryan, Michael
See Moore, Brian

Bryant, William Cullen 1794-1878 **NCLC 6, 46; DA; DAB; DAC; DAM MST, POET; PC 20**
See also CDALB 1640-1865; DLB 3, 43, 59, 189

Bryusov, Valery Yakovlevich 1873-1924 **TCLC 10**
See also CA 107; 155

Buchan, John 1875-1940 **TCLC 41; DAB; DAM POP**
See also CA 108; 145; DLB 34, 70, 156; MTCW 1; YABC 2

Buchanan, George 1506-1582 **LC 4**
See also DLB 152

Buchheim, Lothar-Guenther 1918- **CLC 6**
See also CA 85-88

Buchner, (Karl) Georg 1813-1837 **NCLC 26**

Buchwald, Art(hur) 1925- **CLC 33**
See also AITN 1; CA 5-8R; CANR 21, 67; MTCW 1, 2; SATA 10

Buck, Pearl S(ydenstricker) 1892-1973 **CLC 7, 11, 18; DA; DAB; DAC; DAM MST, NOV**
See also AITN 1; CA 1-4R; 41-44R; CANR 1, 34; DLB 9, 102; MTCW 1, 2; SATA 1, 25

Buckler, Ernest 1908-1984 **CLC 13; DAC; DAM MST**
See also CA 11-12; 114; CAP 1; DLB 68; SATA 47

Buckley, Vincent (Thomas) 1925-1988 **CLC 57**
See also CA 101

Buckley, William F(rank), Jr. 1925- **CLC 7, 18, 37; DAM POP**
See also AITN 1; CA 1-4R; CANR 1, 24, 53; DLB 137; DLBY 80; INT CANR-24; MTCW 1, 2

Buechner, (Carl) Frederick 1926- **CLC 2, 4, 6, 9; DAM NOV**
See also CA 13-16R; CANR 11, 39, 64; DLBY 80; INT CANR-11; MTCW 1, 2

Buell, John (Edward) 1927- **CLC 10**
See also CA 1-4R; CANR 71; DLB 53

Buero Vallejo, Antonio 1916- **CLC 15, 46**
See also CA 106; CANR 24, 49, 75; HW; MTCW 1, 2

Bufalino, Gesualdo 1920(?)- **CLC 74**
See also DLB 196

Bugayev, Boris Nikolayevich 1880-1934 **TCLC 7; PC 11**
See also Bely, Andrey
See also CA 104; 165; MTCW 1

Bukowski, Charles 1920-1994 **CLC 2, 5, 9, 41, 82, 108; DAM NOV, POET; PC 18**
See also CA 17-20R; 144; CANR 40, 62; DLB 5, 130, 169; MTCW 1, 2

Bulgakov, Mikhail (Afanas'evich) 1891-1940 **TCLC 2, 16; DAM DRAM, NOV; SSC 18**
See also CA 105; 152

Bulgya, Alexander Alexandrovich 1901-1956 **TCLC 53**
See also Fadeyev, Alexander
See also CA 117

Bullins, Ed 1935- **CLC 1, 5, 7; BLC 1; DAM DRAM, MULT; DC 6**
See also BW 2; CA 49-52; CAAS 16; CANR 24, 46, 73; DLB 7, 38; MTCW 1, 2

Bulwer-Lytton, Edward (George Earle Lytton) 1803-1873 **NCLC 1, 45**
See also DLB 21

Bunin, Ivan Alexeyevich 1870-1953 **TCLC 6; SSC 5**
See also CA 104

Bunting, Basil 1900-1985 **CLC 10, 39, 47; DAM POET**
See also CA 53-56; 115; CANR 7; DLB 20

Bunuel, Luis 1900-1983 **CLC 16, 80; DAM MULT; HLC**
See also CA 101; 110; CANR 32, 77; HW

Bunyan, John 1628-1688 **LC 4; DA; DAB; DAC; DAM MST; WLC**
See also CDBLB 1660-1789; DLB 39

Burckhardt, Jacob (Christoph) 1818-1897 **NCLC 49**

Burford, Eleanor
See Hibbert, Eleanor Alice Burford

Burgess, Anthony **CLC 1, 2, 4, 5, 8, 10, 13, 15, 22, 40, 62, 81, 94; DAB**
See also Wilson, John (Anthony) Burgess
See also AAYA 25; AITN 1; CDBLB 1960 to Present; DLB 14, 194; DLBY 98; MTCW 1

Burke, Edmund 1729(?)-1797 **LC 7, 36; DA; DAB; DAC; DAM MST; WLC**
See also DLB 104

Burke, Kenneth (Duva) 1897-1993 **CLC 2, 24**
See also CA 5-8R; 143; CANR 39, 74; DLB 45, 63; MTCW 1, 2

Burke, Leda
See Garnett, David

Burke, Ralph
See Silverberg, Robert

Burke, Thomas 1886-1945 **TCLC 63**
See also CA 113; 155; DLB 197

Burney, Fanny 1752-1840 **NCLC 12, 54**
See also DLB 39

Burns, Robert 1759-1796 **LC 3, 29, 40; DA; DAB; DAC; DAM MST, POET; PC 6; WLC**
See also CDBLB 1789-1832; DLB 109

Burns, Tex
See L'Amour, Louis (Dearborn)

Burnshaw, Stanley 1906- **CLC 3, 13, 44**
See also CA 9-12R; DLB 48; DLBY 97

Burr, Anne 1937- **CLC 6**
See also CA 25-28R

Burroughs, Edgar Rice 1875-1950 **TCLC 2, 32; DAM NOV**
See also AAYA 11; CA 104; 132; DLB 8; MTCW 1, 2; SATA 41

Burroughs, William S(eward) 1914-1997 **CLC 1, 2, 5, 15, 22, 42, 75, 109; DA; DAB; DAC; DAM MST, NOV, POP; WLC**
See also AITN 2; CA 9-12R; 160; CANR 20, 52; DLB 2, 8, 16, 152; DLBY 81, 97; MTCW 1, 2

Burton, Sir Richard F(rancis) 1821-1890 **NCLC 42**
See also DLB 55, 166, 184

Busch, Frederick 1941- **CLC 7, 10, 18, 47**
See also CA 33-36R; CAAS 1; CANR 45, 73; DLB 6

Bush, Ronald 1946- **CLC 34**
See also CA 136

Bustos, F(rancisco)
See Borges, Jorge Luis

Bustos Domecq, H(onorio)

See Bioy Casares, Adolfo; Borges, Jorge Luis

Butler, Octavia E(stelle) 1947-   **CLC 38;
    BLCS; DAM MULT, POP**
    See also AAYA 18; BW 2; CA 73-76; CANR
    12, 24, 38, 73; DLB 33; MTCW 1, 2; SATA
    84

Butler, Robert Olen (Jr.) 1945-**CLC 81; DAM
    POP**
    See also CA 112; CANR 66; DLB 173; INT
    112; MTCW 1

Butler, Samuel 1612-1680   **LC 16, 43**
    See also DLB 101, 126

Butler, Samuel 1835-1902 **TCLC 1, 33; DA;
    DAB; DAC; DAM MST, NOV; WLC**
    See also CA 143; CDBLB 1890-1914; DLB 18,
    57, 174

Butler, Walter C.
    See Faust, Frederick (Schiller)

Butor, Michel (Marie Francois) 1926-**CLC 1,
    3, 8, 11, 15**
    See also CA 9-12R; CANR 33, 66; DLB 83;
    MTCW 1, 2

Butts, Mary 1892(?)-1937   **TCLC 77**
    See also CA 148

Buzo, Alexander (John) 1944-   **CLC 61**
    See also CA 97-100; CANR 17, 39, 69

Buzzati, Dino 1906-1972   **CLC 36**
    See also CA 160; 33-36R; DLB 177

Byars, Betsy (Cromer) 1928-   **CLC 35**
    See also AAYA 19; CA 33-36R; CANR 18, 36,
    57; CLR 1, 16; DLB 52; INT CANR-18;
    JRDA; MAICYA; MTCW 1; SAAS 1; SATA
    4, 46, 80

Byatt, A(ntonia) S(usan Drabble) 1936- **C L C
    19, 65; DAM NOV, POP**
    See also CA 13-16R; CANR 13, 33, 50, 75;
    DLB 14, 194; MTCW 1, 2

Byrne, David 1952-   **CLC 26**
    See also CA 127

Byrne, John Keyes 1926-
    See Leonard, Hugh
    See also CA 102; CANR 78; INT 102

Byron, George Gordon (Noel) 1788-1824
    **NCLC 2, 12; DA; DAB; DAC; DAM MST,
    POET; PC 16; WLC**
    See also CDBLB 1789-1832; DLB 96, 110

Byron, Robert 1905-1941   **TCLC 67**
    See also CA 160; DLB 195

C. 3. 3.
    See Wilde, Oscar

Caballero, Fernan 1796-1877   **NCLC 10**

Cabell, Branch
    See Cabell, James Branch

Cabell, James Branch 1879-1958   **TCLC 6**
    See also CA 105; 152; DLB 9, 78; MTCW 1

Cable, George Washington 1844-1925 **T C L C
    4; SSC 4**
    See also CA 104; 155; DLB 12, 74; DLBD 13

Cabral de Melo Neto, Joao 1920-   **CLC 76;
    DAM MULT**
    See also CA 151

Cabrera Infante, G(uillermo) 1929- **CLC 5,
    25, 45; DAM MULT; HLC**
    See also CA 85-88; CANR 29, 65; DLB 113;
    HW; MTCW 1, 2

Cade, Toni
    See Bambara, Toni Cade

Cadmus and Harmonia
    See Buchan, John

Caedmon fl. 658-680   **CMLC 7**
    See also DLB 146

Caeiro, Alberto
    See Pessoa, Fernando (Antonio Nogueira)

Cage, John (Milton, Jr.) 1912-1992 **CLC 41**
    See also CA 13-16R; 169; CANR 9, 78; DLB
    193; INT CANR-9

Cahan, Abraham 1860-1951   **TCLC 71**
    See also CA 108; 154; DLB 9, 25, 28

Cain, G.
    See Cabrera Infante, G(uillermo)

Cain, Guillermo
    See Cabrera Infante, G(uillermo)

Cain, James M(allahan) 1892-1977**CLC 3, 11,
    28**
    See also AITN 1; CA 17-20R; 73-76; CANR 8,
    34, 61; MTCW 1

Caine, Mark
    See Raphael, Frederic (Michael)

Calasso, Roberto 1941-   **CLC 81**
    See also CA 143

Calderon de la Barca, Pedro 1600-1681 **L C
    23; DC 3**

Caldwell, Erskine (Preston) 1903-1987**CLC 1,
    8, 14, 50, 60; DAM NOV; SSC 19**
    See also AITN 1; CA 1-4R; 121; CAAS 1;
    CANR 2, 33; DLB 9, 86; MTCW 1, 2

Caldwell, (Janet Miriam) Taylor (Holland)
    1900-1985**CLC 2, 28, 39; DAM NOV, POP**
    See also CA 5-8R; 116; CANR 5; DLBD 17

Calhoun, John Caldwell 1782-1850**NCLC 15**
    See also DLB 3

Calisher, Hortense 1911-**CLC 2, 4, 8, 38; DAM
    NOV; SSC 15**
    See also CA 1-4R; CANR 1, 22, 67; DLB 2;
    INT CANR-22; MTCW 1, 2

Callaghan, Morley Edward 1903-1990**CLC 3,
    14, 41, 65; DAC; DAM MST**
    See also CA 9-12R; 132; CANR 33, 73; DLB
    68; MTCW 1, 2

Callimachus c. 305B.C.-c. 240B.C. **CMLC 18**
    See also DLB 176

Calvin, John 1509-1564   **LC 37**

Calvino, Italo 1923-1985**CLC 5, 8, 11, 22, 33,
    39, 73; DAM NOV; SSC 3**
    See also CA 85-88; 116; CANR 23, 61; DLB
    196; MTCW 1, 2

Cameron, Carey 1952-   **CLC 59**
    See also CA 135

Cameron, Peter 1959-   **CLC 44**
    See also CA 125; CANR 50

Campana, Dino 1885-1932   **TCLC 20**
    See also CA 117; DLB 114

Campanella, Tommaso 1568-1639   **LC 32**

Campbell, John W(ood, Jr.) 1910-1971 **C L C
    32**
    See also CA 21-22; 29-32R; CANR 34; CAP
    2; DLB 8; MTCW 1

Campbell, Joseph 1904-1987   **CLC 69**
    See also AAYA 3; BEST 89:2; CA 1-4R; 124;
    CANR 3, 28, 61; MTCW 1, 2

Campbell, Maria 1940-   **CLC 85; DAC**
    See also CA 102; CANR 54; NNAL

Campbell, (John) Ramsey 1946-**CLC 42; SSC
    19**
    See also CA 57-60; CANR 7; INT CANR-7

Campbell, (Ignatius) Roy (Dunnachie) 1901-
    1957   **TCLC 5**
    See also CA 104; 155; DLB 20; MTCW 2

Campbell, Thomas 1777-1844   **NCLC 19**
    See also DLB 93; 144

Campbell, Wilfred   **TCLC 9**
    See also Campbell, William

Campbell, William 1858(?)-1918
    See Campbell, Wilfred
    See also CA 106; DLB 92

Campion, Jane   **CLC 95**

See also CA 138

Campos, Alvaro de
    See Pessoa, Fernando (Antonio Nogueira)

Camus, Albert 1913-1960**CLC 1, 2, 4, 9, 11, 14,
    32, 63, 69; DA; DAB; DAC; DAM DRAM,
    MST, NOV; DC 2; SSC 9; WLC**
    See also CA 89-92; DLB 72; MTCW 1, 2

Canby, Vincent 1924-   **CLC 13**
    See also CA 81-84

Cancale
    See Desnos, Robert

Canetti, Elias 1905-1994**CLC 3, 14, 25, 75, 86**
    See also CA 21-24R; 146; CANR 23, 61; DLB
    85, 124; MTCW 1, 2

Canfield, Dorothea F.
    See Fisher, Dorothy (Frances) Canfield

Canfield, Dorothea Frances
    See Fisher, Dorothy (Frances) Canfield

Canfield, Dorothy
    See Fisher, Dorothy (Frances) Canfield

Canin, Ethan 1960-   **CLC 55**
    See also CA 131; 135

Cannon, Curt
    See Hunter, Evan

Cao, Lan 1961-   **CLC 109**
    See also CA 165

Cape, Judith
    See Page, P(atricia) K(athleen)

Capek, Karel 1890-1938   **TCLC 6, 37; DA;
    DAB; DAC; DAM DRAM, MST, NOV;
    DC 1; WLC**
    See also CA 104; 140; MTCW 1

Capote, Truman 1924-1984**CLC 1, 3, 8, 13, 19,
    34, 38, 58; DA; DAB; DAC; DAM MST,
    NOV, POP; SSC 2; WLC**
    See also CA 5-8R; 113; CANR 18, 62; CDALB
    1941-1968; DLB 2, 185; DLBY 80, 84;
    MTCW 1, 2; SATA 91

Capra, Frank 1897-1991   **CLC 16**
    See also CA 61-64; 135

Caputo, Philip 1941-   **CLC 32**
    See also CA 73-76; CANR 40

Caragiale, Ion Luca 1852-1912   **TCLC 76**
    See also CA 157

Card, Orson Scott 1951-**CLC 44, 47, 50; DAM
    POP**
    See also AAYA 11; CA 102; CANR 27, 47,
    73; INT CANR-27; MTCW 1, 2; SATA 83

Cardenal, Ernesto 1925-   **CLC 31; DAM
    MULT, POET; HLC; PC 22**
    See also CA 49-52; CANR 2, 32, 66; HW;
    MTCW 1, 2

Cardozo, Benjamin N(athan) 1870-1938
        TCLC 65
    See also CA 117; 164

Carducci, Giosue (Alessandro Giuseppe) 1835-
    1907   **TCLC 32**
    See also CA 163

Carew, Thomas 1595(?)-1640   **LC 13**
    See also DLB 126

Carey, Ernestine Gilbreth 1908-   **CLC 17**
    See also CA 5-8R; CANR 71; SATA 2

Carey, Peter 1943-   **CLC 40, 55, 96**
    See also CA 123; 127; CANR 53, 76; INT 127;
    MTCW 1, 2; SATA 94

Carleton, William 1794-1869   **NCLC 3**
    See also DLB 159

Carlisle, Henry (Coffin) 1926-   **CLC 33**
    See also CA 13-16R; CANR 15

Carlsen, Chris
    See Holdstock, Robert P.

Carlson, Ron(ald F.) 1947-   **CLC 54**
    See also CA 105; CANR 27

See Chang, Eileen

Channing, William Ellery 1780-1842 **N C L C 17**
  See also DLB 1, 59

Chao, Patricia 1955- **CLC 119**
  See also CA 163

Chaplin, Charles Spencer 1889-1977 **CLC 16**
  See also Chaplin, Charlie
  See also CA 81-84; 73-76

Chaplin, Charlie
  See Chaplin, Charles Spencer
  See also DLB 44

Chapman, George 1559(?)-1634 **LC 22; DAM DRAM**
  See also DLB 62, 121

Chapman, Graham 1941-1989 **CLC 21**
  See also Monty Python
  See also CA 116; 129; CANR 35

Chapman, John Jay 1862-1933 **TCLC 7**
  See also CA 104

Chapman, Lee
  See Bradley, Marion Zimmer

Chapman, Walker
  See Silverberg, Robert

Chappell, Fred (Davis) 1936- **CLC 40, 78**
  See also CA 5-8R; CAAS 4; CANR 8, 33, 67; DLB 6, 105

Char, Rene(-Emile) 1907-1988 **CLC 9, 11, 14, 55; DAM POET**
  See also CA 13-16R; 124; CANR 32; MTCW 1, 2

Charby, Jay
  See Ellison, Harlan (Jay)

Chardin, Pierre Teilhard de
  See Teilhard de Chardin, (Marie Joseph) Pierre

Charles I 1600-1649 **LC 13**

Charriere, Isabelle de 1740-1805 **NCLC 66**

Charyn, Jerome 1937- **CLC 5, 8, 18**
  See also CA 5-8R; CAAS 1; CANR 7, 61; DLBY 83; MTCW 1

Chase, Mary (Coyle) 1907-1981 **DC 1**
  See also CA 77-80; 105; SATA 17; SATA-Obit 29

Chase, Mary Ellen 1887-1973 **CLC 2**
  See also CA 13-16; 41-44R; CAP 1; SATA 10

Chase, Nicholas
  See Hyde, Anthony

Chateaubriand, Francois Rene de 1768-1848 **NCLC 3**
  See also DLB 119

Chatterje, Sarat Chandra 1876-1936(?)
  See Chatterji, Saratchandra
  See also CA 109

Chatterji, Bankim Chandra 1838-1894 **NCLC 19**

Chatterji, Saratchandra **TCLC 13**
  See also Chatterje, Sarat Chandra

Chatterton, Thomas 1752-1770 **LC 3; DAM POET**
  See also DLB 109

Chatwin, (Charles) Bruce 1940-1989 **CLC 28, 57, 59; DAM POP**
  See also AAYA 4; BEST 90:1; CA 85-88; 127; DLB 194, 204

Chaucer, Daniel
  See Ford, Ford Madox

Chaucer, Geoffrey 1340(?)-1400 **LC 17; DA; DAB; DAC; DAM MST, POET; PC 19; WLCS**
  See also CDBLB Before 1660; DLB 146

Chaviaras, Strates 1935-
  See Haviaras, Stratis
  See also CA 105

Chayefsky, Paddy **CLC 23**
  See also Chayefsky, Sidney
  See also DLB 7, 44; DLBY 81

Chayefsky, Sidney 1923-1981
  See Chayefsky, Paddy
  See also CA 9-12R; 104; CANR 18; DAM DRAM

Chedid, Andree 1920- **CLC 47**
  See also CA 145

Cheever, John 1912-1982 **CLC 3, 7, 8, 11, 15, 25, 64; DA; DAB; DAC; DAM MST, NOV, POP; SSC 1; WLC**
  See also CA 5-8R; 106; CABS 1; CANR 5, 27, 76; CDALB 1941-1968; DLB 2, 102; DLBY 80, 82; INT CANR-5; MTCW 1, 2

Cheever, Susan 1943- **CLC 18, 48**
  See also CA 103; CANR 27, 51; DLBY 82; INT CANR-27

Chekhonte, Antosha
  See Chekhov, Anton (Pavlovich)

Chekhov, Anton (Pavlovich) 1860-1904 **TCLC 3, 10, 31, 55; DA; DAB; DAC; DAM DRAM, MST; DC 9; SSC 2, 28; WLC**
  See also CA 104; 124; SATA 90

Chernyshevsky, Nikolay Gavrilovich 1828-1889 **NCLC 1**

Cherry, Carolyn Janice 1942-
  See Cherryh, C. J.
  See also CA 65-68; CANR 10

Cherryh, C. J. **CLC 35**
  See also Cherry, Carolyn Janice
  See also AAYA 24; DLBY 80; SATA 93

Chesnutt, Charles W(addell) 1858-1932 **TCLC 5, 39; BLC 1; DAM MULT; SSC 7**
  See also BW 1; CA 106; 125; CANR 76; DLB 12, 50, 78; MTCW 1, 2

Chester, Alfred 1929(?)-1971 **CLC 49**
  See also CA 33-36R; DLB 130

Chesterton, G(ilbert) K(eith) 1874-1936 **TCLC 1, 6, 64; DAM NOV, POET; SSC 1**
  See also CA 104; 132; CANR 73; CDBLB 1914-1945; DLB 10, 19, 34, 70, 98, 149, 178; MTCW 1, 2; SATA 27

Chiang, Pin-chin 1904-1986
  See Ding Ling
  See also CA 118

Ch'ien Chung-shu 1910- **CLC 22**
  See also CA 130; CANR 73; MTCW 1, 2

Child, L. Maria
  See Child, Lydia Maria

Child, Lydia Maria 1802-1880 **NCLC 6, 73**
  See also DLB 1, 74; SATA 67

Child, Mrs.
  See Child, Lydia Maria

Child, Philip 1898-1978 **CLC 19, 68**
  See also CA 13-14; CAP 1; SATA 47

Childers, (Robert) Erskine 1870-1922 **T C L C 65**
  See also CA 113; 153; DLB 70

Childress, Alice 1920-1994 **CLC 12, 15, 86, 96; BLC 1; DAM DRAM, MULT, NOV; DC 4**
  See also AAYA 8; BW 2; CA 45-48; 146; CANR 3, 27, 50, 74; CLR 14; DLB 7, 38; JRDA; MAICYA; MTCW 1, 2; SATA 7, 48, 81

Chin, Frank (Chew, Jr.) 1940- **DC 7**
  See also CA 33-36R; CANR 71; DAM MULT; DLB 206

Chislett, (Margaret) Anne 1943- **CLC 34**
  See also CA 151

Chitty, Thomas Willes 1926- **CLC 11**
  See also Hinde, Thomas
  See also CA 5-8R

Chivers, Thomas Holley 1809-1858 **NCLC 49**
  See also DLB 3

Choi, Susan **CLC 119**

Chomette, Rene Lucien 1898-1981
  See Clair, Rene
  See also CA 103

Chopin, Kate **TCLC 5, 14; DA; DAB; SSC 8; WLCS**
  See also Chopin, Katherine
  See also CDALB 1865-1917; DLB 12, 78

Chopin, Katherine 1851-1904
  See Chopin, Kate
  See also CA 104; 122; DAC; DAM MST, NOV

Chretien de Troyes c. 12th cent. - **CMLC 10**
  See also DLB 208

Christie
  See Ichikawa, Kon

Christie, Agatha (Mary Clarissa) 1890-1976 **CLC 1, 6, 8, 12, 39, 48, 110; DAB; DAC; DAM NOV**
  See also AAYA 9; AITN 1, 2; CA 17-20R; 61-64; CANR 10, 37; CDBLB 1914-1945; DLB 13, 77; MTCW 1, 2; SATA 36

Christie, (Ann) Philippa
  See Pearce, Philippa
  See also CA 5-8R; CANR 4

Christine de Pizan 1365(?)-1431(?) **LC 9**
  See also DLB 208

Chubb, Elmer
  See Masters, Edgar Lee

Chulkov, Mikhail Dmitrievich 1743-1792 **L C 2**
  See also DLB 150

Churchill, Caryl 1938- **CLC 31, 55; DC 5**
  See also CA 102; CANR 22, 46; DLB 13; MTCW 1

Churchill, Charles 1731-1764 **LC 3**
  See also DLB 109

Chute, Carolyn 1947- **CLC 39**
  See also CA 123

Ciardi, John (Anthony) 1916-1986 **CLC 10, 40, 44; DAM POET**
  See also CA 5-8R; 118; CAAS 2; CANR 5, 33; CLR 19; DLB 5; DLBY 86; INT CANR-5; MAICYA; MTCW 1, 2; SAAS 26; SATA 1, 65; SATA-Obit 46

Cicero, Marcus Tullius 106B.C.-43B.C. **CMLC 3**
  See also DLB 211

Cimino, Michael 1943- **CLC 16**
  See also CA 105

Cioran, E(mil) M. 1911-1995 **CLC 64**
  See also CA 25-28R; 149

Cisneros, Sandra 1954- **CLC 69, 118; DAM MULT; HLC; SSC 32**
  See also AAYA 9; CA 131; CANR 64; DLB 122, 152; HW; MTCW 2

Cixous, Helene 1937- **CLC 92**
  See also CA 126; CANR 55; DLB 83; MTCW 1, 2

Clair, Rene **CLC 20**
  See also Chomette, Rene Lucien

Clampitt, Amy 1920-1994 **CLC 32; PC 19**
  See also CA 110; 146; CANR 29; DLB 105

Clancy, Thomas L., Jr. 1947-
  See Clancy, Tom
  See also CA 125; 131; CANR 62; INT 131; MTCW 1, 2

Clancy, Tom **CLC 45, 112; DAM NOV, POP**
  See also Clancy, Thomas L., Jr.
  See also AAYA 9; BEST 89:1, 90:1; MTCW 2

Clare, John 1793-1864 **NCLC 9; DAB; DAM POET; PC 23**

See also DLB 55, 96

Clarin
See Alas (y Urena), Leopoldo (Enrique Garcia)

Clark, Al C.
See Goines, Donald

Clark, (Robert) Brian 1932-   **CLC 29**
See also CA 41-44R; CANR 67

Clark, Curt
See Westlake, Donald E(dwin)

Clark, Eleanor 1913-1996   **CLC 5, 19**
See also CA 9-12R; 151; CANR 41; DLB 6

Clark, J. P.
See Clark, John Pepper
See also DLB 117

Clark, John Pepper 1935-   **CLC 38; BLC 1;
DAM DRAM, MULT; DC 5**
See also Clark, J. P.
See also BW 1; CA 65-68; CANR 16, 72;
MTCW 1

Clark, M. R.
See Clark, Mavis Thorpe

Clark, Mavis Thorpe 1909-   **CLC 12**
See also CA 57-60; CANR 8, 37; CLR 30;
MAICYA; SAAS 5; SATA 8, 74

Clark, Walter Van Tilburg 1909-1971 **CLC 28**
See also CA 9-12R; 33-36R; CANR 63; DLB
9, 206; SATA 8

Clark Bekederemo, J(ohnson) P(epper)
See Clark, John Pepper

Clarke, Arthur C(harles) 1917- **CLC 1, 4, 13,
18, 35; DAM POP; SSC 3**
See also AAYA 4; CA 1-4R; CANR 2, 28, 55,
74; JRDA; MAICYA; MTCW 1, 2; SATA
13, 70

Clarke, Austin 1896-1974   **CLC 6, 9; DAM
POET**
See also CA 29-32; 49-52; CAP 2; DLB 10, 20

Clarke, Austin C(hesterfield) 1934- **CLC 8, 53;
BLC 1; DAC; DAM MULT**
See also BW 1; CA 25-28R; CAAS 16; CANR
14, 32, 68; DLB 53, 125

Clarke, Gillian 1937-   **CLC 61**
See also CA 106; DLB 40

Clarke, Marcus (Andrew Hislop) 1846-1881
NCLC 19

Clarke, Shirley 1925-   **CLC 16**

Clash, The
See Headon, (Nicky) Topper; Jones, Mick;
Simonon, Paul; Strummer, Joe

Claudel, Paul (Louis Charles Marie) 1868-1955
TCLC 2, 10
See also CA 104; 165; DLB 192

Claudius, Matthias 1740-1815   **NCLC 75**
See also DLB 97

Clavell, James (duMaresq) 1925-1994 **CLC 6,
25, 87; DAM NOV, POP**
See also CA 25-28R; 146; CANR 26, 48;
MTCW 1, 2

Cleaver, (Leroy) Eldridge 1935-1998 **CLC 30,
119; BLC 1; DAM MULT**
See also BW 1; CA 21-24R; 167; CANR 16,
75; MTCW 2

Cleese, John (Marwood) 1939-   **CLC 21**
See also Monty Python
See also CA 112; 116; CANR 35; MTCW 1

Cleishbotham, Jebediah
See Scott, Walter

Cleland, John 1710-1789   **LC 2, 48**
See also DLB 39

Clemens, Samuel Langhorne 1835-1910
See Twain, Mark
See also CA 104; 135; CDALB 1865-1917; DA;
DAB; DAC; DAM MST, NOV; DLB 11, 12,

23, 64, 74, 186, 189; JRDA; MAICYA;
SATA 100; YABC 2

Cleophil
See Congreve, William

Clerihew, E.
See Bentley, E(dmund) C(lerihew)

Clerk, N. W.
See Lewis, C(live) S(taples)

Cliff, Jimmy   **CLC 21**
See also Chambers, James

Clifton, (Thelma) Lucille 1936- **CLC 19, 66;
BLC 1; DAM MULT, POET; PC 17**
See also BW 2; CA 49-52; CANR 2, 24, 42,
76; CLR 5; DLB 5, 41; MAICYA; MTCW
1, 2; SATA 20, 69

Clinton, Dirk
See Silverberg, Robert

Clough, Arthur Hugh 1819-1861   **NCLC 27**
See also DLB 32

Clutha, Janet Paterson Frame 1924-
See Frame, Janet
See also CA 1-4R; CANR 2, 36, 76; MTCW 1,
2

Clyne, Terence
See Blatty, William Peter

Cobalt, Martin
See Mayne, William (James Carter)

Cobb, Irvin S. 1876-1944   **TCLC 77**
See also DLB 11, 25, 86

Cobbett, William 1763-1835   **NCLC 49**
See also DLB 43, 107, 158

Coburn, D(onald) L(ee) 1938-   **CLC 10**
See also CA 89-92

Cocteau, Jean (Maurice Eugene Clement)
1889-1963 **CLC 1, 8, 15, 16, 43; DA; DAB;
DAC; DAM DRAM, MST, NOV; WLC**
See also CA 25-28; CANR 40; CAP 2; DLB
65; MTCW 1, 2

Codrescu, Andrei 1946- **CLC 46; DAM POET**
See also CA 33-36R; CAAS 19; CANR 13, 34,
53, 76; MTCW 2

Coe, Max
See Bourne, Randolph S(illiman)

Coe, Tucker
See Westlake, Donald E(dwin)

Coen, Ethan 1958-   **CLC 108**
See also CA 126

Coen, Joel 1955-   **CLC 108**
See also CA 126

The Coen Brothers
See Coen, Ethan; Coen, Joel

Coetzee, J(ohn) M(ichael) 1940- **CLC 23, 33,
66, 117; DAM NOV**
See also CA 77-80; CANR 41, 54, 74; MTCW
1, 2

Coffey, Brian
See Koontz, Dean R(ay)

Cohan, George M(ichael) 1878-1942 **TCLC 60**
See also CA 157

Cohen, Arthur A(llen) 1928-1986   **CLC 7, 31**
See also CA 1-4R; 120; CANR 1, 17, 42; DLB
28

Cohen, Leonard (Norman) 1934-   **CLC 3, 38;
DAC; DAM MST**
See also CA 21-24R; CANR 14, 69; DLB 53;
MTCW 1

Cohen, Matt 1942-   **CLC 19; DAC**
See also CA 61-64; CAAS 18; CANR 40; DLB
53

Cohen-Solal, Annie 19(?)-   **CLC 50**

Colegate, Isabel 1931-   **CLC 36**
See also CA 17-20R; CANR 8, 22, 74; DLB
14; INT CANR-22; MTCW 1

Coleman, Emmett
See Reed, Ishmael

Coleridge, M. E.
See Coleridge, Mary E(lizabeth)

Coleridge, Mary E(lizabeth) 1861-1907 **TCLC
73**
See also CA 116; 166; DLB 19, 98

Coleridge, Samuel Taylor 1772-1834 **NCLC 9,
54; DA; DAB; DAC; DAM MST, POET;
PC 11; WLC**
See also CDBLB 1789-1832; DLB 93, 107

Coleridge, Sara 1802-1852   **NCLC 31**
See also DLB 199

Coles, Don 1928-   **CLC 46**
See also CA 115; CANR 38

Coles, Robert (Martin) 1929-   **CLC 108**
See also CA 45-48; CANR 3, 32, 66, 70; INT
CANR-32; SATA 23

Colette, (Sidonie-Gabrielle) 1873-1954 **TCLC
1, 5, 16; DAM NOV; SSC 10**
See also CA 104; 131; DLB 65; MTCW 1, 2

Collett, (Jacobine) Camilla (Wergeland) 1813-
1895   **NCLC 22**

Collier, Christopher 1930-   **CLC 30**
See also AAYA 13; CA 33-36R; CANR 13, 33;
JRDA; MAICYA; SATA 16, 70

Collier, James L(incoln) 1928- **CLC 30; DAM
POP**
See also AAYA 13; CA 9-12R; CANR 4, 33,
60; CLR 3; JRDA; MAICYA; SAAS 21;
SATA 8, 70

Collier, Jeremy 1650-1726   **LC 6**

Collier, John 1901-1980   **SSC 19**
See also CA 65-68; 97-100; CANR 10; DLB
77

Collingwood, R(obin) G(eorge) 1889(?)-1943
TCLC 67
See also CA 117; 155

Collins, Hunt
See Hunter, Evan

Collins, Linda 1931-   **CLC 44**
See also CA 125

Collins, (William) Wilkie 1824-1889 **NCLC 1,
18**
See also CDBLB 1832-1890; DLB 18, 70, 159

Collins, William 1721-1759   **LC 4, 40; DAM
POET**
See also DLB 109

Collodi, Carlo 1826-1890   **NCLC 54**
See also Lorenzini, Carlo
See also CLR 5

Colman, George 1732-1794
See Glassco, John

Colt, Winchester Remington
See Hubbard, L(afayette) Ron(ald)

Colter, Cyrus 1910-   **CLC 58**
See also BW 1; CA 65-68; CANR 10, 66; DLB
33

Colton, James
See Hansen, Joseph

Colum, Padraic 1881-1972   **CLC 28**
See also CA 73-76; 33-36R; CANR 35; CLR
36; MAICYA; MTCW 1; SATA 15

Colvin, James
See Moorcock, Michael (John)

Colwin, Laurie (E.) 1944-1992 **CLC 5, 13, 23,
84**
See also CA 89-92; 139; CANR 20, 46; DLBY
80; MTCW 1

Comfort, Alex(ander) 1920-   **CLC 7; DAM
POP**
See also CA 1-4R; CANR 1, 45; MTCW 1

Comfort, Montgomery

See Campbell, (John) Ramsey
Compton-Burnett, I(vy) 1884(?)-1969 CLC 1,
3, 10, 15, 34; DAM NOV
See also CA 1-4R; 25-28R; CANR 4; DLB 36;
MTCW 1
Comstock, Anthony 1844-1915   TCLC 13
See also CA 110; 169
Comte, Auguste 1798-1857   NCLC 54
Conan Doyle, Arthur
See Doyle, Arthur Conan
Conde, Maryse 1937-   CLC 52, 92; BLCS;
DAM MULT
See also Boucolon, Maryse
See also BW 2; MTCW 1
Condillac, Etienne Bonnot de 1714-1780 LC
26
Condon, Richard (Thomas) 1915-1996 CLC 4,
6, 8, 10, 45, 100; DAM NOV
See also BEST 90:3; CA 1-4R; 151; CAAS 1;
CANR 2, 23; INT CANR-23; MTCW 1, 2
Confucius 551B.C.-479B.C. CMLC 19; DA;
DAB; DAC; DAM MST; WLCS
Congreve, William 1670-1729 LC 5, 21; DA;
DAB; DAC; DAM DRAM, MST, POET;
DC 2; WLC
See also CDBLB 1660-1789; DLB 39, 84
Connell, Evan S(helby), Jr. 1924- CLC 4, 6,
45; DAM NOV
See also AAYA 7; CA 1-4R; CAAS 2; CANR
2, 39, 76; DLB 2; DLBY 81; MTCW 1, 2
Connelly, Marc(us Cook) 1890-1980 CLC 7
See also CA 85-88; 102; CANR 30; DLB 7;
DLBY 80; SATA-Obit 25
Connor, Ralph   TCLC 31
See also Gordon, Charles William
See also DLB 92
Conrad, Joseph 1857-1924 TCLC 1, 6, 13, 25,
43, 57; DA; DAB; DAC; DAM MST, NOV;
SSC 9; WLC
See also AAYA 26; CA 104; 131; CANR 60;
CDBLB 1890-1914; DLB 10, 34, 98, 156;
MTCW 1, 2; SATA 27
Conrad, Robert Arnold
See Hart, Moss
Conroy, Pat
See Conroy, (Donald) Pat(rick)
See also MTCW 2
Conroy, (Donald) Pat(rick) 1945- CLC 30, 74;
DAM NOV, POP
See also Conroy, Pat
See also AAYA 8; AITN 1; CA 85-88; CANR
24, 53; DLB 6; MTCW 1
Constant (de Rebecque), (Henri) Benjamin
1767-1830   NCLC 6
See also DLB 119
Conybeare, Charles Augustus
See Eliot, T(homas) S(tearns)
Cook, Michael 1933-   CLC 58
See also CA 93-96; CANR 68; DLB 53
Cook, Robin 1940-   CLC 14; DAM POP
See also BEST 90:2; CA 108; 111; CANR 41;
INT 111
Cook, Roy
See Silverberg, Robert
Cooke, Elizabeth 1948-   CLC 55
See also CA 129
Cooke, John Esten 1830-1886   NCLC 5
See also DLB 3
Cooke, John Estes
See Baum, L(yman) Frank
Cooke, M. E.
See Creasey, John
Cooke, Margaret

See Creasey, John
Cook-Lynn, Elizabeth 1930- CLC 93; DAM
MULT
See also CA 133; DLB 175; NNAL
Cooney, Ray   CLC 62
Cooper, Douglas 1960-   CLC 86
Cooper, Henry St. John
See Creasey, John
Cooper, J(oan) California (?)- CLC 56; DAM
MULT
See also AAYA 12; BW 1; CA 125; CANR 55;
DLB 212
Cooper, James Fenimore 1789-1851 NCLC 1,
27, 54
See also AAYA 22; CDALB 1640-1865; DLB
3; SATA 19
Coover, Robert (Lowell) 1932- CLC 3, 7, 15,
32, 46, 87; DAM NOV; SSC 15
See also CA 45-48; CANR 3, 37, 58; DLB 2;
DLBY 81; MTCW 1, 2
Copeland, Stewart (Armstrong) 1952- CLC 26
Copernicus, Nicolaus 1473-1543   LC 45
Coppard, A(lfred) E(dgar) 1878-1957 TCLC
5; SSC 21
See also CA 114; 167; DLB 162; YABC 1
Coppee, Francois 1842-1908   TCLC 25
See also CA 170
Coppola, Francis Ford 1939-   CLC 16
See also CA 77-80; CANR 40, 78; DLB 44
Corbiere, Tristan 1845-1875   NCLC 43
Corcoran, Barbara 1911-   CLC 17
See also AAYA 14; CA 21-24R; CAAS 2;
CANR 11, 28, 48; CLR 50; DLB 52; JRDA;
SAAS 20; SATA 3, 77
Cordelier, Maurice
See Giraudoux, (Hippolyte) Jean
Corelli, Marie 1855-1924   TCLC 51
See also Mackay, Mary
See also DLB 34, 156
Corman, Cid 1924-   CLC 9
See also Corman, Sidney
See also CAAS 2; DLB 5, 193
Corman, Sidney 1924-
See Corman, Cid
See also CA 85-88; CANR 44; DAM POET
Cormier, Robert (Edmund) 1925- CLC 12, 30;
DA; DAB; DAC; DAM MST, NOV
See also AAYA 3, 19; CA 1-4R; CANR 5, 23,
76; CDALB 1968-1988; CLR 12, 55; DLB
52; INT CANR-23; JRDA; MAICYA;
MTCW 1, 2; SATA 10, 45, 83
Corn, Alfred (DeWitt III) 1943-   CLC 33
See also CA 104; CAAS 25; CANR 44; DLB
120; DLBY 80
Corneille, Pierre 1606-1684   LC 28; DAB;
DAM MST
Cornwell, David (John Moore) 1931- CLC 9,
15; DAM POP
See also le Carre, John
See also CA 5-8R; CANR 13, 33, 59; MTCW
1, 2
Corso, (Nunzio) Gregory 1930-   CLC 1, 11
See also CA 5-8R; CANR 41, 76; DLB 5, 16;
MTCW 1, 2
Cortazar, Julio 1914-1984 CLC 2, 3, 5, 10, 13,
15, 33, 34, 92; DAM MULT, NOV; HLC;
SSC 7
See also CA 21-24R; CANR 12, 32; DLB 113;
HW; MTCW 1, 2
CORTES, HERNAN 1484-1547   LC 31
Corvinus, Jakob
See Raabe, Wilhelm (Karl)
Corwin, Cecil

See Kornbluth, C(yril) M.
Cosic, Dobrica 1921-   CLC 14
See also CA 122; 138; DLB 181
Costain, Thomas B(ertram) 1885-1965 C L C
30
See also CA 5-8R; 25-28R; DLB 9
Costantini, Humberto 1924(?)-1987 CLC 49
See also CA 131; 122; HW
Costello, Elvis 1955-   CLC 21
Costenoble, Philostene
See Ghelderode, Michel de
Cotes, Cecil V.
See Duncan, Sara Jeannette
Cotter, Joseph Seamon Sr. 1861-1949 T C L C
28; BLC 1; DAM MULT
See also BW 1; CA 124; DLB 50
Couch, Arthur Thomas Quiller
See Quiller-Couch, Sir Arthur (Thomas)
Coulton, James
See Hansen, Joseph
Couperus, Louis (Marie Anne) 1863-1923
TCLC 15
See also CA 115
Coupland, Douglas 1961- CLC 85; DAC; DAM
POP
See also CA 142; CANR 57
Court, Wesli
See Turco, Lewis (Putnam)
Courtenay, Bryce 1933-   CLC 59
See also CA 138
Courtney, Robert
See Ellison, Harlan (Jay)
Cousteau, Jacques-Yves 1910-1997 CLC 30
See also CA 65-68; 159; CANR 15, 67; MTCW
1; SATA 38, 98
Coventry, Francis 1725-1754   LC 46
Cowan, Peter (Walkinshaw) 1914-   SSC 28
See also CA 21-24R; CANR 9, 25, 50
Coward, Noel (Peirce) 1899-1973 CLC 1, 9, 29,
51; DAM DRAM
See also AITN 1; CA 17-18; 41-44R; CANR
35; CAP 2; CDBLB 1914-1945; DLB 10;
MTCW 1, 2
Cowley, Abraham 1618-1667   LC 43
See also DLB 131, 151
Cowley, Malcolm 1898-1989   CLC 39
See also CA 5-8R; 128; CANR 3, 55; DLB 4,
48; DLBY 81, 89; MTCW 1, 2
Cowper, William 1731-1800 NCLC 8; DAM
POET
See also DLB 104, 109
Cox, William Trevor 1928-   CLC 9, 14, 71;
DAM NOV
See also Trevor, William
See also CA 9-12R; CANR 4, 37, 55, 76; DLB
14; INT CANR-37; MTCW 1, 2
Coyne, P. J.
See Masters, Hilary
Cozzens, James Gould 1903-1978 CLC 1, 4,
11, 92
See also CA 9-12R; 81-84; CANR 19; CDALB
1941-1968; DLB 9; DLBD 2; DLBY 84, 97;
MTCW 1, 2
Crabbe, George 1754-1832   NCLC 26
See also DLB 93
Craddock, Charles Egbert
See Murfree, Mary Noailles
Craig, A. A.
See Anderson, Poul (William)
Craik, Dinah Maria (Mulock) 1826-1887
NCLC 38
See also DLB 35, 163; MAICYA; SATA 34
Cram, Ralph Adams 1863-1942   TCLC 45

See Malzberg, Barry N(athaniel)
Denby, Edwin (Orr) 1903-1983 **CLC 48**
See also CA 138; 110
Denis, Julio
See Cortazar, Julio
Denmark, Harrison
See Zelazny, Roger (Joseph)
Dennis, John 1658-1734 **LC 11**
See also DLB 101
Dennis, Nigel (Forbes) 1912-1989 **CLC 8**
See also CA 25-28R; 129; DLB 13, 15; MTCW 1
Dent, Lester 1904(?)-1959 **TCLC 72**
See also CA 112; 161
De Palma, Brian (Russell) 1940- **CLC 20**
See also CA 109
De Quincey, Thomas 1785-1859 **NCLC 4**
See also CDBLB 1789-1832; DLB 110; 144
Deren, Eleanora 1908(?)-1961
See Deren, Maya
See also CA 111
Deren, Maya 1917-1961 **CLC 16, 102**
See also Deren, Eleanora
Derleth, August (William) 1909-1971 **CLC 31**
See also CA 1-4R; 29-32R; CANR 4; DLB 9;
DLBD 17; SATA 5
Der Nister 1884-1950 **TCLC 56**
de Routisie, Albert
See Aragon, Louis
Derrida, Jacques 1930- **CLC 24, 87**
See also CA 124; 127; CANR 76; MTCW 1
Derry Down Derry
See Lear, Edward
Dersonnes, Jacques
See Simenon, Georges (Jacques Christian)
Desai, Anita 1937- **CLC 19, 37, 97; DAB; DAM NOV**
See also CA 81-84; CANR 33, 53; MTCW 1, 2; SATA 63
Desai, Kiran 1971- **CLC 119**
See also CA 171
de Saint-Luc, Jean
See Glassco, John
de Saint Roman, Arnaud
See Aragon, Louis
Descartes, Rene 1596-1650 **LC 20, 35**
De Sica, Vittorio 1901(?)-1974 **CLC 20**
See also CA 117
Desnos, Robert 1900-1945 **TCLC 22**
See also CA 121; 151
Destouches, Louis-Ferdinand 1894-1961 **CLC 9, 15**
See Celine, Louis-Ferdinand
See also CA 85-88; CANR 28; MTCW 1
de Tolignac, Gaston
See Griffith, D(avid Lewelyn) W(ark)
Deutsch, Babette 1895-1982 **CLC 18**
See also CA 1-4R; 108; CANR 4; DLB 45;
SATA 1; SATA-Obit 33
Devenant, William 1606-1649 **LC 13**
Devkota, Laxmiprasad 1909-1959 **TCLC 23**
See also CA 123
De Voto, Bernard (Augustine) 1897-1955 **TCLC 29**
See also CA 113; 160; DLB 9
De Vries, Peter 1910-1993 **CLC 1, 2, 3, 7, 10, 28, 46; DAM NOV**
See also CA 17-20R; 142; CANR 41; DLB 6;
DLBY 82; MTCW 1, 2
Dexter, John
See Bradley, Marion Zimmer
Dexter, Martin
See Faust, Frederick (Schiller)

Dexter, Pete 1943- **CLC 34, 55; DAM POP**
See also BEST 89:2; CA 127; 131; INT 131;
MTCW 1
Diamano, Silmang
See Senghor, Leopold Sedar
Diamond, Neil 1941- **CLC 30**
See also CA 108
Diaz del Castillo, Bernal 1496-1584 **LC 31**
di Bassetto, Corno
See Shaw, George Bernard
Dick, Philip K(indred) 1928-1982 **CLC 10, 30, 72; DAM NOV, POP**
See also AAYA 24; CA 49-52; 106; CANR 2,
16; DLB 8; MTCW 1, 2
Dickens, Charles (John Huffam) 1812-1870
**NCLC 3, 8, 18, 26, 37, 50; DA; DAB; DAC;
DAM MST, NOV; SSC 17; WLC**
See also AAYA 23; CDBLB 1832-1890; DLB
21, 55, 70, 159, 166; JRDA; MAICYA;
SATA 15
Dickey, James (Lafayette) 1923-1997 **CLC 1, 2, 4, 7, 10, 15, 47, 109; DAM NOV, POET, POP**
See also AITN 1, 2; CA 9-12R; 156; CABS 2;
CANR 10, 48, 61; CDALB 1968-1988; DLB
5, 193; DLBD 7; DLBY 82, 93, 96, 97, 98;
INT CANR-10; MTCW 1, 2
Dickey, William 1928-1994 **CLC 3, 28**
See also CA 9-12R; 145; CANR 24; DLB 5
Dickinson, Charles 1951- **CLC 49**
See also CA 128
Dickinson, Emily (Elizabeth) 1830-1886
**NCLC 21; DA; DAB; DAC; DAM MST,
POET; PC 1; WLC**
See also AAYA 22; CDALB 1865-1917; DLB
1; SATA 29
Dickinson, Peter (Malcolm) 1927- **CLC 12, 35**
See also AAYA 9; CA 41-44R; CANR 31, 58;
CLR 29; DLB 87, 161; JRDA; MAICYA;
SATA 5, 62, 95
Dickson, Carr
See Carr, John Dickson
Dickson, Carter
See Carr, John Dickson
Diderot, Denis 1713-1784 **LC 26**
Didion, Joan 1934- **CLC 1, 3, 8, 14, 32; DAM NOV**
See also AITN 1; CA 5-8R; CANR 14, 52, 76;
CDALB 1968-1988; DLB 2, 173, 185;
DLBY 81, 86; MTCW 1, 2
Dietrich, Robert
See Hunt, E(verette) Howard, (Jr.)
Difusa, Pati
See Almodovar, Pedro
Dillard, Annie 1945- **CLC 9, 60, 115; DAM NOV**
See also AAYA 6; CA 49-52; CANR 3, 43, 62;
DLBY 80; MTCW 1, 2; SATA 10
Dillard, R(ichard) H(enry) W(ilde) 1937- **CLC 5**
See also CA 21-24R; CAAS 7; CANR 10; DLB 5
Dillon, Eilis 1920-1994 **CLC 17**
See also CA 9-12R; 147; CAAS 3; CANR 4,
38, 78; CLR 26; MAICYA; SATA 2, 74;
SATA-Essay 105; SATA-Obit 83
Dimont, Penelope
See Mortimer, Penelope (Ruth)
Dinesen, Isak **CLC 10, 29, 95; SSC 7**
See also Blixen, Karen (Christentze Dinesen)
See also MTCW 1
Ding Ling **CLC 68**
See also Chiang, Pin-chin

Diphusa, Patty
See Almodovar, Pedro
Disch, Thomas M(ichael) 1940- **CLC 7, 36**
See also AAYA 17; CA 21-24R; CAAS 4;
CANR 17, 36, 54; CLR 18; DLB 8;
MAICYA; MTCW 1, 2; SAAS 15; SATA
92
Disch, Tom
See Disch, Thomas M(ichael)
d'Isly, Georges
See Simenon, Georges (Jacques Christian)
Disraeli, Benjamin 1804-1881 **NCLC 2, 39**
See also DLB 21, 55
Ditcum, Steve
See Crumb, R(obert)
Dixon, Paige
See Corcoran, Barbara
Dixon, Stephen 1936- **CLC 52; SSC 16**
See also CA 89-92; CANR 17, 40, 54; DLB
130
Doak, Annie
See Dillard, Annie
Dobell, Sydney Thompson 1824-1874 **NCLC 43**
See also DLB 32
Doblin, Alfred **TCLC 13**
See also Doeblin, Alfred
Dobrolyubov, Nikolai Alexandrovich 1836-1861 **NCLC 5**
Dobson, Austin 1840-1921 **TCLC 79**
See also DLB 35; 144
Dobyns, Stephen 1941- **CLC 37**
See also CA 45-48; CANR 2, 18
Doctorow, E(dgar) L(aurence) 1931- **CLC 6, 11, 15, 18, 37, 44, 65, 113; DAM NOV, POP**
See also AAYA 22; AITN 2; BEST 89:3; CA
45-48; CANR 2, 33, 51, 76; CDALB 1968-
1988; DLB 2, 28, 173; DLBY 80; MTCW 1,
2
Dodgson, Charles Lutwidge 1832-1898
See Carroll, Lewis
See also CLR 2; DA; DAB; DAC; DAM MST,
NOV, POET; MAICYA; SATA 100; YABC
2
Dodson, Owen (Vincent) 1914-1983 **CLC 79;
BLC 1; DAM MULT**
See also BW 1; CA 65-68; 110; CANR 24; DLB
76
Doeblin, Alfred 1878-1957 **TCLC 13**
See also Doblin, Alfred
See also CA 110; 141; DLB 66
Doerr, Harriet 1910- **CLC 34**
See also CA 117; 122; CANR 47; INT 122
Domecq, H(onorio) Bustos
See Bioy Casares, Adolfo; Borges, Jorge Luis
Domini, Rey
See Lorde, Audre (Geraldine)
Dominique
See Proust, (Valentin-Louis-George-Eugene-)
Marcel
Don, A
See Stephen, SirLeslie
Donaldson, Stephen R. 1947- **CLC 46; DAM POP**
See also CA 89-92; CANR 13, 55; INT CANR-13
Donleavy, J(ames) P(atrick) 1926- **CLC 1, 4, 6, 10, 45**
See also AITN 2; CA 9-12R; CANR 24, 49,
62; DLB 6, 173; INT CANR-24; MTCW 1,
2
Donne, John 1572-1631 **LC 10, 24; DA; DAB;
DAC; DAM MST, POET; PC 1; WLC**

See also CDBLB Before 1660; DLB 121, 151
Donnell, David 1939(?)-   **CLC 34**
Donoghue, P. S.
  See Hunt, E(verette) Howard, (Jr.)
Donoso (Yanez), Jose 1924-1996**CLC 4, 8, 11,
    32, 99; DAM MULT; HLC; SSC 34**
  See also CA 81-84; 155; CANR 32, 73; DLB
    113; HW; MTCW 1, 2
Donovan, John 1928-1992   **CLC 35**
  See also AAYA 20; CA 97-100; 137; CLR 3;
    MAICYA; SATA 72; SATA-Brief 29
Don Roberto
  See Cunninghame Graham, R(obert) B(ontine)
Doolittle, Hilda 1886-1961**CLC 3, 8, 14, 31, 34,
    73; DA; DAC; DAM MST, POET; PC 5;
    WLC**
  See also H. D.
  See also CA 97-100; CANR 35; DLB 4, 45;
    MTCW 1, 2
Dorfman, Ariel 1942-   **CLC 48, 77; DAM
    MULT; HLC**
  See also CA 124; 130; CANR 67, 70; HW; INT
    130
Dorn, Edward (Merton) 1929-   **CLC 10, 18**
  See also CA 93-96; CANR 42; DLB 5; INT 93-
    96
Dorris, Michael (Anthony) 1945-1997   **C L C
    109; DAM MULT, NOV**
  See also AAYA 20; BEST 90:1; CA 102; 157;
    CANR 19, 46, 75; DLB 175; MTCW 2;
    NNAL; SATA 75; SATA-Obit 94
Dorris, Michael A.
  See Dorris, Michael (Anthony)
Dorsan, Luc
  See Simenon, Georges (Jacques Christian)
Dorsange, Jean
  See Simenon, Georges (Jacques Christian)
Dos Passos, John (Roderigo) 1896-1970 **C L C
    1, 4, 8, 11, 15, 25, 34, 82; DA; DAB; DAC;
    DAM MST, NOV; WLC**
  See also CA 1-4R; 29-32R; CANR 3; CDALB
    1929-1941; DLB 4, 9; DLBD 1, 15; DLBY
    96; MTCW 1, 2
Dossage, Jean
  See Simenon, Georges (Jacques Christian)
Dostoevsky, Fedor Mikhailovich 1821-1881
    **NCLC 2, 7, 21, 33, 43; DA; DAB; DAC;
    DAM MST, NOV; SSC 2, 33; WLC**
Doughty, Charles M(ontagu) 1843-1926
    TCLC 27
  See also CA 115; DLB 19, 57, 174
Douglas, Ellen   **CLC 73**
  See also Haxton, Josephine Ayres; Williamson,
    Ellen Douglas
Douglas, Gavin 1475(?)-1522   **LC 20**
  See also DLB 132
Douglas, George
  See Brown, George Douglas
Douglas, Keith (Castellain) 1920-1944 **T C L C
    40**
  See also CA 160; DLB 27
Douglas, Leonard
  See Bradbury, Ray (Douglas)
Douglas, Michael
  See Crichton, (John) Michael
Douglas, (George) Norman 1868-1952 **T C L C
    68**
  See also CA 119; 157; DLB 34, 195
Douglas, William
  See Brown, George Douglas
Douglass, Frederick 1817(?)-1895**NCLC 7, 55;
    BLC 1; DA; DAC; DAM MST, MULT;
    WLC**

See also CDALB 1640-1865; DLB 1, 43, 50,
    79; SATA 29
Dourado, (Waldomiro Freitas) Autran 1926-
    CLC 23, 60
  See also CA 25-28R; CANR 34; DLB 145
Dourado, Waldomiro Autran
  See Dourado, (Waldomiro Freitas) Autran
Dove, Rita (Frances) 1952-**CLC 50, 81; BLCS;
    DAM MULT, POET; PC 6**
  See also BW 2; CA 109; CAAS 19; CANR 27,
    42, 68, 76; DLB 120; MTCW 1
Doveglion
  See Villa, Jose Garcia
Dowell, Coleman 1925-1985   **CLC 60**
  See also CA 25-28R; 117; CANR 10; DLB 130
Dowson, Ernest (Christopher) 1867-1900
    TCLC 4
  See also CA 105; 150; DLB 19, 135
Doyle, A. Conan
  See Doyle, Arthur Conan
Doyle, Arthur Conan 1859-1930**TCLC 7; DA;
    DAB; DAC; DAM MST, NOV; SSC 12;
    WLC**
  See also AAYA 14; CA 104; 122; CDBLB
    1890-1914; DLB 18, 70, 156, 178; MTCW
    1, 2; SATA 24
Doyle, Conan
  See Doyle, Arthur Conan
Doyle, John
  See Graves, Robert (von Ranke)
Doyle, Roddy 1958(?)-   **CLC 81**
  See also AAYA 14; CA 143; CANR 73; DLB
    194
Doyle, Sir A. Conan
  See Doyle, Arthur Conan
Doyle, Sir Arthur Conan
  See Doyle, Arthur Conan
Dr. A
  See Asimov, Isaac; Silverstein, Alvin
Drabble, Margaret 1939-**CLC 2, 3, 5, 8, 10, 22,
    53; DAB; DAC; DAM MST, NOV, POP**
  See also CA 13-16R; CANR 18, 35, 63;
    CDBLB 1960 to Present; DLB 14, 155;
    MTCW 1, 2; SATA 48
Drapier, M. B.
  See Swift, Jonathan
Drayham, James
  See Mencken, H(enry) L(ouis)
Drayton, Michael 1563-1631   **LC 8; DAM
    POET**
  See also DLB 121
Dreadstone, Carl
  See Campbell, (John) Ramsey
Dreiser, Theodore (Herman Albert) 1871-1945
    **TCLC 10, 18, 35, 83; DA; DAC; DAM
    MST, NOV; SSC 30; WLC**
  See also CA 106; 132; CDALB 1865-1917;
    DLB 9, 12, 102, 137; DLBD 1; MTCW 1, 2
Drexler, Rosalyn 1926-   **CLC 2, 6**
  See also CA 81-84; CANR 68
Dreyer, Carl Theodor 1889-1968   **CLC 16**
  See also CA 116
Drieu la Rochelle, Pierre(-Eugene) 1893-1945
    TCLC 21
  See also CA 117; DLB 72
Drinkwater, John 1882-1937   **TCLC 57**
  See also CA 109; 149; DLB 10, 19, 149
Drop Shot
  See Cable, George Washington
Droste-Hulshoff, Annette Freiin von 1797-1848
    NCLC 3
  See also DLB 133
Drummond, Walter

See Silverberg, Robert
Drummond, William Henry 1854-1907**TCLC
    25**
  See also CA 160; DLB 92
Drummond de Andrade, Carlos 1902-1987
    CLC 18
  See also Andrade, Carlos Drummond de
  See also CA 132; 123
Drury, Allen (Stuart) 1918-1998   **CLC 37**
  See also CA 57-60; 170; CANR 18, 52; INT
    CANR-18
Dryden, John 1631-1700**LC 3, 21; DA; DAB;
    DAC; DAM DRAM, MST, POET; DC 3;
    PC 25; WLC**
  See also CDBLB 1660-1789; DLB 80, 101, 131
Duberman, Martin (Bauml) 1930-   **CLC 8**
  See also CA 1-4R; CANR 2, 63
Dubie, Norman (Evans) 1945-   **CLC 36**
  See also CA 69-72; CANR 12; DLB 120
Du Bois, W(illiam) E(dward) B(urghardt) 1868-
    1963   **CLC 1, 2, 13, 64, 96; BLC 1; DA;
    DAC; DAM MST, MULT, NOV; WLC**
  See also BW 1; CA 85-88; CANR 34; CDALB
    1865-1917; DLB 47, 50, 91; MTCW 1, 2;
    SATA 42
Dubus, Andre 1936- **CLC 13, 36, 97; SSC 15**
  See also CA 21-24R; CANR 17; DLB 130; INT
    CANR-17
Duca Minimo
  See D'Annunzio, Gabriele
Ducharme, Rejean 1941-   **CLC 74**
  See also CA 165; DLB 60
Duclos, Charles Pinot 1704-1772   **LC 1**
Dudek, Louis 1918-   **CLC 11, 19**
  See also CA 45-48; CAAS 14; CANR 1; DLB
    88
Duerrenmatt, Friedrich 1921-1990 **CLC 1, 4,
    8, 11, 15, 43; DAM DRAM**
  See also CA 17-20R; CANR 33; DLB 69, 124;
    MTCW 1, 2
Duffy, Bruce 1953(?)-   **CLC 50**
  See also CA 172
Duffy, Maureen 1933-   **CLC 37**
  See also CA 25-28R; CANR 33, 68; DLB 14;
    MTCW 1
Dugan, Alan 1923-   **CLC 2, 6**
  See also CA 81-84; DLB 5
du Gard, Roger Martin
  See Martin du Gard, Roger
Duhamel, Georges 1884-1966   **CLC 8**
  See also CA 81-84; 25-28R; CANR 35; DLB
    65; MTCW 1
Dujardin, Edouard (Emile Louis) 1861-1949
    TCLC 13
  See also CA 109; DLB 123
Dulles, John Foster 1888-1959   **TCLC 72**
  See also CA 115; 149
Dumas, Alexandre (pere)
  See Dumas, Alexandre (Davy de la Pailleterie)
Dumas, Alexandre (Davy de la Pailleterie)
    1802-1870   **NCLC 11; DA; DAB; DAC;
    DAM MST, NOV; WLC**
  See also DLB 119, 192; SATA 18
Dumas, Alexandre (fils) 1824-1895**NCLC 71;
    DC 1**
  See also AAYA 22; DLB 192
Dumas, Claudine
  See Malzberg, Barry N(athaniel)
Dumas, Henry L. 1934-1968   **CLC 6, 62**
  See also BW 1; CA 85-88; DLB 41
du Maurier, Daphne 1907-1989**CLC 6, 11, 59;
    DAB; DAC; DAM MST, POP; SSC 18**
  See also CA 5-8R; 128; CANR 6, 55; DLB 191;

See also AITN 2; CA 81-84; 138; DLB 143; DLBY 81

Eynhardt, Guillermo
See Quiroga, Horacio (Sylvestre)

Ezekiel, Nissim 1924-   **CLC 61**
See also CA 61-64

Ezekiel, Tish O'Dowd 1943-   **CLC 34**
See also CA 129

Fadeyev, A.
See Bulgya, Alexander Alexandrovich

Fadeyev, Alexander   **TCLC 53**
See also Bulgya, Alexander Alexandrovich

Fagen, Donald 1948-   **CLC 26**

Fainzilberg, Ilya Arnoldovich 1897-1937
See Ilf, Ilya
See also CA 120; 165

Fair, Ronald L. 1932-   **CLC 18**
See also BW 1; CA 69-72; CANR 25; DLB 33

Fairbairn, Roger
See Carr, John Dickson

Fairbairns, Zoe (Ann) 1948-   **CLC 32**
See also CA 103; CANR 21

Falco, Gian
See Papini, Giovanni

Falconer, James
See Kirkup, James

Falconer, Kenneth
See Kornbluth, C(yril) M.

Falkland, Samuel
See Heijermans, Herman

Fallaci, Oriana 1930-   **CLC 11, 110**
See also CA 77-80; CANR 15, 58; MTCW 1

Faludy, George 1913-   **CLC 42**
See also CA 21-24R

Faludy, Gyoergy
See Faludy, George

Fanon, Frantz 1925-1961   **CLC 74; BLC 2; DAM MULT**
See also BW 1; CA 116; 89-92

Fanshawe, Ann 1625-1680   **LC 11**

Fante, John (Thomas) 1911-1983   **CLC 60**
See also CA 69-72; 109; CANR 23; DLB 130; DLBY 83

Farah, Nuruddin 1945-   **CLC 53; BLC 2; DAM MULT**
See also BW 2; CA 106; DLB 125

Fargue, Leon-Paul 1876(?)-1947   **TCLC 11**
See also CA 109

Farigoule, Louis
See Romains, Jules

Farina, Richard 1936(?)-1966   **CLC 9**
See also CA 81-84; 25-28R

Farley, Walter (Lorimer) 1915-1989 **CLC 17**
See also CA 17-20R; CANR 8, 29; DLB 22; JRDA; MAICYA; SATA 2, 43

Farmer, Philip Jose 1918-   **CLC 1, 19**
See also AAYA 28; CA 1-4R; CANR 4, 35; DLB 8; MTCW 1; SATA 93

Farquhar, George 1677-1707   **LC 21; DAM DRAM**
See also DLB 84

Farrell, J(ames) G(ordon) 1935-1979 **CLC 6**
See also CA 73-76; 89-92; CANR 36; DLB 14; MTCW 1

Farrell, James T(homas) 1904-1979 **CLC 1, 4, 8, 11, 66; SSC 28**
See also CA 5-8R; 89-92; CANR 9, 61; DLB 4, 9, 86; DLBD 2; MTCW 1, 2

Farren, Richard J.
See Betjeman, John

Farren, Richard M.
See Betjeman, John

Fassbinder, Rainer Werner 1946-1982 **C L C**

20
See also CA 93-96; 106; CANR 31

Fast, Howard (Melvin) 1914- **CLC 23; DAM NOV**
See also AAYA 16; CA 1-4R; CAAS 18; CANR 1, 33, 54, 75; DLB 9; INT CANR-33; MTCW 1; SATA 7; SATA-Essay 107

Faulcon, Robert
See Holdstock, Robert P.

Faulkner, William (Cuthbert) 1897-1962 **CLC 1, 3, 6, 8, 9, 11, 14, 18, 28, 52, 68; DA; DAB; DAC; DAM MST, NOV; SSC 1; WLC**
See also AAYA 7; CA 81-84; CANR 33; CDALB 1929-1941; DLB 9, 11, 44, 102; DLBD 2; DLBY 86, 97; MTCW 1, 2

Fauset, Jessie Redmon 1884(?)-1961 **CLC 19, 54; BLC 2; DAM MULT**
See also BW 1; CA 109; DLB 51

Faust, Frederick (Schiller) 1892-1944(?) **TCLC 49; DAM POP**
See also CA 108; 152

Faust, Irvin 1924-   **CLC 8**
See also CA 33-36R; CANR 28, 67; DLB 2, 28; DLBY 80

Fawkes, Guy
See Benchley, Robert (Charles)

Fearing, Kenneth (Flexner) 1902-1961 **C L C 51**
See also CA 93-96; CANR 59; DLB 9

Fecamps, Elise
See Creasey, John

Federman, Raymond 1928-   **CLC 6, 47**
See also CA 17-20R; CAAS 8; CANR 10, 43; DLBY 80

Federspiel, J(uerg) F. 1931-   **CLC 42**
See also CA 146

Feiffer, Jules (Ralph) 1929-   **CLC 2, 8, 64; DAM DRAM**
See also AAYA 3; CA 17-20R; CANR 30, 59; DLB 7, 44; INT CANR-30; MTCW 1; SATA 8, 61

Feige, Hermann Albert Otto Maximilian
See Traven, B.

Feinberg, David B. 1956-1994   **CLC 59**
See also CA 135; 147

Feinstein, Elaine 1930-   **CLC 36**
See also CA 69-72; CAAS 1; CANR 31, 68; DLB 14, 40; MTCW 1

Feldman, Irving (Mordecai) 1928-   **CLC 7**
See also CA 1-4R; CANR 1; DLB 169

Felix-Tchicaya, Gerald
See Tchicaya, Gerald Felix

Fellini, Federico 1920-1993   **CLC 16, 85**
See also CA 65-68; 143; CANR 33

Felsen, Henry Gregor 1916-   **CLC 17**
See also CA 1-4R; CANR 1; SAAS 2; SATA 1

Fenno, Jack
See Calisher, Hortense

Fenollosa, Ernest (Francisco) 1853-1908 **TCLC 91**

Fenton, James Martin 1949-   **CLC 32**
See also CA 102; DLB 40

Ferber, Edna 1887-1968   **CLC 18, 93**
See also AITN 1; CA 5-8R; 25-28R; CANR 68; DLB 9, 28, 86; MTCW 1, 2; SATA 7

Ferguson, Helen
See Kavan, Anna

Ferguson, Samuel 1810-1886   **NCLC 33**
See also DLB 32

Fergusson, Robert 1750-1774   **LC 29**
See also DLB 109

Ferling, Lawrence
See Ferlinghetti, Lawrence (Monsanto)

Ferlinghetti, Lawrence (Monsanto) 1919(?)- **CLC 2, 6, 10, 27, 111; DAM POET; PC 1**
See also CA 5-8R; CANR 3, 41, 73; CDALB 1941-1968; DLB 5, 16; MTCW 1, 2

Fernandez, Vicente Garcia Huidobro
See Huidobro Fernandez, Vicente Garcia

Ferrer, Gabriel (Francisco Victor) Miro
See Miro (Ferrer), Gabriel (Francisco Victor)

Ferrier, Susan (Edmonstone) 1782-1854 **NCLC 8**
See also DLB 116

Ferrigno, Robert 1948(?)-   **CLC 65**
See also CA 140

Ferron, Jacques 1921-1985   **CLC 94; DAC**
See also CA 117; 129; DLB 60

Feuchtwanger, Lion 1884-1958   **TCLC 3**
See also CA 104; DLB 66

Feuillet, Octave 1821-1890   **NCLC 45**
See also DLB 192

Feydeau, Georges (Leon Jules Marie) 1862-1921 **TCLC 22; DAM DRAM**
See also CA 113; 152; DLB 192

Fichte, Johann Gottlieb 1762-1814 **NCLC 62**
See also DLB 90

Ficino, Marsilio 1433-1499   **LC 12**

Fiedeler, Hans
See Doeblin, Alfred

Fiedler, Leslie A(aron) 1917-   **CLC 4, 13, 24**
See also CA 9-12R; CANR 7, 63; DLB 28, 67; MTCW 1, 2

Field, Andrew 1938-   **CLC 44**
See also CA 97-100; CANR 25

Field, Eugene 1850-1895   **NCLC 3**
See also DLB 23, 42, 140; DLBD 13; MAICYA; SATA 16

Field, Gans T.
See Wellman, Manly Wade

Field, Michael 1915-1971   **TCLC 43**
See also CA 29-32R

Field, Peter
See Hobson, Laura Z(ametkin)

Fielding, Henry 1707-1754   **LC 1, 46; DA; DAB; DAC; DAM DRAM, MST, NOV; WLC**
See also CDBLB 1660-1789; DLB 39, 84, 101

Fielding, Sarah 1710-1768   **LC 1, 44**
See also DLB 39

Fields, W. C. 1880-1946   **TCLC 80**
See also DLB 44

Fierstein, Harvey (Forbes) 1954-   **CLC 33; DAM DRAM, POP**
See also CA 123; 129

Figes, Eva 1932-   **CLC 31**
See also CA 53-56; CANR 4, 44; DLB 14

Finch, Anne 1661-1720   **LC 3; PC 21**
See also DLB 95

Finch, Robert (Duer Claydon) 1900- **CLC 18**
See also CA 57-60; CANR 9, 24, 49; DLB 88

Findley, Timothy 1930- **CLC 27, 102; DAC; DAM MST**
See also CA 25-28R; CANR 12, 42, 69; DLB 53

Fink, William
See Mencken, H(enry) L(ouis)

Firbank, Louis 1942-
See Reed, Lou
See also CA 117

Firbank, (Arthur Annesley) Ronald 1886-1926 **TCLC 1**
See also CA 104; DLB 36

Fisher, Dorothy (Frances) Canfield 1879-1958 **TCLC 87**
See also CA 114; 136; DLB 9, 102; MAICYA;

YABC 1

Fisher, M(ary) F(rances) K(ennedy) 1908-1992
CLC 76, 87
See also CA 77-80; 138; CANR 44; MTCW 1

Fisher, Roy 1930-   **CLC 25**
See also CA 81-84; CAAS 10; CANR 16; DLB
40

Fisher, Rudolph 1897-1934**TCLC 11; BLC 2;**
DAM MULT; SSC 25
See also BW 1; CA 107; 124; DLB 51, 102

Fisher, Vardis (Alvero) 1895-1968   **CLC 7**
See also CA 5-8R; 25-28R; CANR 68; DLB 9,
206

Fiske, Tarleton
See Bloch, Robert (Albert)

Fitch, Clarke
See Sinclair, Upton (Beall)

Fitch, John IV
See Cormier, Robert (Edmund)

Fitzgerald, Captain Hugh
See Baum, L(yman) Frank

FitzGerald, Edward 1809-1883   **NCLC 9**
See also DLB 32

Fitzgerald, F(rancis) Scott (Key) 1896-1940
TCLC 1, 6, 14, 28, 55; DA; DAB; DAC;
DAM MST, NOV; SSC 6, 31; WLC
See also AAYA 24; AITN 1; CA 110; 123;
CDALB 1917-1929; DLB 4, 9, 86; DLBD
1, 15, 16; DLBY 81, 96; MTCW 1, 2

Fitzgerald, Penelope 1916-   **CLC 19, 51, 61**
See also CA 85-88; CAAS 10; CANR 56; DLB
14, 194; MTCW 2

Fitzgerald, Robert (Stuart) 1910-1985**CLC 39**
See also CA 1-4R; 114; CANR 1; DLBY 80

FitzGerald, Robert D(avid) 1902-1987**CLC 19**
See also CA 17-20R

Fitzgerald, Zelda (Sayre) 1900-1948**TCLC 52**
See also CA 117; 126; DLBY 84

Flanagan, Thomas (James Bonner) 1923-
CLC 25, 52
See also CA 108; CANR 55; DLBY 80; INT
108; MTCW 1

Flaubert, Gustave 1821-1880**NCLC 2, 10, 19,**
62, 66; DA; DAB; DAC; DAM MST, NOV;
SSC 11; WLC
See also DLB 119

Flecker, Herman Elroy
See Flecker, (Herman) James Elroy

Flecker, (Herman) James Elroy 1884-1915
TCLC 43
See also CA 109; 150; DLB 10, 19

Fleming, Ian (Lancaster) 1908-1964   **CLC 3,**
30; DAM POP
See also AAYA 26; CA 5-8R; CANR 59;
CDBLB 1945-1960; DLB 87, 201; MTCW
1, 2; SATA 9

Fleming, Thomas (James) 1927-   **CLC 37**
See also CA 5-8R; CANR 10; INT CANR-10;
SATA 8

Fletcher, John 1579-1625   **LC 33; DC 6**
See also CDBLB Before 1660; DLB 58

Fletcher, John Gould 1886-1950   **TCLC 35**
See also CA 107; 167; DLB 4, 45

Fleur, Paul
See Pohl, Frederik

Flooglebuckle, Al
See Spiegelman, Art

Flying Officer X
See Bates, H(erbert) E(rnest)

Fo, Dario 1926-   **CLC 32, 109; DAM DRAM;**
DC 10
See also CA 116; 128; CANR 68; DLBY 97;
MTCW 1, 2

Fogarty, Jonathan Titulescu Esq.
See Farrell, James T(homas)

Folke, Will
See Bloch, Robert (Albert)

Follett, Ken(neth Martin) 1949-   **CLC 18;**
DAM NOV, POP
See also AAYA 6; BEST 89:4; CA 81-84;
CANR 13, 33, 54; DLB 87; DLBY 81; INT
CANR-33; MTCW 1

Fontane, Theodor 1819-1898   **NCLC 26**
See also DLB 129

Foote, Horton 1916-**CLC 51, 91; DAM DRAM**
See also CA 73-76; CANR 34, 51; DLB 26;
INT CANR-34

Foote, Shelby 1916-**CLC 75; DAM NOV, POP**
See also CA 5-8R; CANR 3, 45, 74; DLB 2,
17; MTCW 2

Forbes, Esther 1891-1967   **CLC 12**
See also AAYA 17; CA 13-14; 25-28R; CAP
1; CLR 27; DLB 22; JRDA; MAICYA;
SATA 2, 100

Forche, Carolyn (Louise) 1950- **CLC 25, 83,**
86; DAM POET; PC 10
See also CA 109; 117; CANR 50, 74; DLB 5,
193; INT 117; MTCW 1

Ford, Elbur
See Hibbert, Eleanor Alice Burford

Ford, Ford Madox 1873-1939**TCLC 1, 15, 39,**
57; DAM NOV
See also CA 104; 132; CANR 74; CDBLB
1914-1945; DLB 162; MTCW 1, 2

Ford, Henry 1863-1947   **TCLC 73**
See also CA 115; 148

Ford, John 1586-(?)   **DC 8**
See also CDBLB Before 1660; DAM DRAM;
DLB 58

Ford, John 1895-1973   **CLC 16**
See also CA 45-48

Ford, Richard 1944-   **CLC 46, 99**
See also CA 69-72; CANR 11, 47; MTCW 1

Ford, Webster
See Masters, Edgar Lee

Foreman, Richard 1937-   **CLC 50**
See also CA 65-68; CANR 32, 63

Forester, C(ecil) S(cott) 1899-1966   **CLC 35**
See also CA 73-76; 25-28R; DLB 191; SATA
13

Forez
See Mauriac, Francois (Charles)

Forman, James Douglas 1932-   **CLC 21**
See also AAYA 17; CA 9-12R; CANR 4, 19,
42; JRDA; MAICYA; SATA 8, 70

Fornes, Maria Irene 1930-**CLC 39, 61; DC 10**
See also CA 25-28R; CANR 28; DLB 7; HW;
INT CANR-28; MTCW 1

Forrest, Leon (Richard) 1937-1997   **CLC 4;**
BLCS
See also BW 2; CA 89-92; 162; CAAS 7;
CANR 25, 52; DLB 33

Forster, E(dward) M(organ) 1879-1970 **C L C**
1, 2, 3, 4, 9, 10, 13, 15, 22, 45, 77; DA; DAB;
DAC; DAM MST, NOV; SSC 27; WLC
See also AAYA 2; CA 13-14; 25-28R; CANR
45; CAP 1; CDBLB 1914-1945; DLB 34, 98,
162, 178, 195; DLBD 10; MTCW 1, 2;
SATA 57

Forster, John 1812-1876   **NCLC 11**
See also DLB 144, 184

Forsyth, Frederick 1938-**CLC 2, 5, 36; DAM**
NOV, POP
See also BEST 89:4; ÇA 85-88; CANR 38, 62;
DLB 87; MTCW 1, 2

Forten, Charlotte L.   **TCLC 16; BLC 2**

See also Grimke, Charlotte L(ottie) Forten
See also DLB 50

Foscolo, Ugo 1778-1827   **NCLC 8**

Fosse, Bob   **CLC 20**
See also Fosse, Robert Louis

Fosse, Robert Louis 1927-1987
See Fosse, Bob
See also CA 110; 123

Foster, Stephen Collins 1826-1864 **NCLC 26**

Foucault, Michel 1926-1984   **CLC 31, 34, 69**
See also CA 105; 113; CANR 34; MTCW 1, 2

Fouque, Friedrich (Heinrich Karl) de la Motte
1777-1843   **NCLC 2**
See also DLB 90

Fourier, Charles 1772-1837   **NCLC 51**

Fournier, Henri Alban 1886-1914
See Alain-Fournier
See also CA 104

Fournier, Pierre 1916-   **CLC 11**
See also Gascar, Pierre
See also CA 89-92; CANR 16, 40

Fowles, John (Philip) 1926-**CLC 1, 2, 3, 4, 6, 9,**
10, 15, 33, 87; DAB; DAC; DAM MST;
SSC 33
See also CA 5-8R; CANR 25, 71; CDBLB 1960
to Present; DLB 14, 139, 207; MTCW 1, 2;
SATA 22

Fox, Paula 1923-   **CLC 2, 8**
See also AAYA 3; CA 73-76; CANR 20, 36,
62; CLR 1, 44; DLB 52; JRDA; MAICYA;
MTCW 1; SATA 17, 60

Fox, William Price (Jr.) 1926-   **CLC 22**
See also CA 17-20R; CAAS 19; CANR 11;
DLB 2; DLBY 81

Foxe, John 1516(?)-1587   **LC 14**
See also DLB 132

Frame, Janet 1924-**CLC 2, 3, 6, 22, 66, 96; SSC**
29
See also Clutha, Janet Paterson Frame

France, Anatole   **TCLC 9**
See also Thibault, Jacques Anatole Francois
See also DLB 123; MTCW 1

Francis, Claude 19(?)-   **CLC 50**

Francis, Dick 1920-**CLC 2, 22, 42, 102; DAM**
POP
See also AAYA 5, 21; BEST 89:3; CA 5-8R;
CANR 9, 42, 68; CDBLB 1960 to Present;
DLB 87; INT CANR-9; MTCW 1, 2

Francis, Robert (Churchill) 1901-1987 **C L C**
15
See also CA 1-4R; 123; CANR 1

Frank, Anne(lies Marie) 1929-1945**TCLC 17;**
DA; DAB; DAC; DAM MST; WLC
See also AAYA 12; CA 113; 133; CANR 68;
MTCW 1, 2; SATA 87; SATA-Brief 42

Frank, Bruno 1887-1945   **TCLC 81**
See also DLB 118

Frank, Elizabeth 1945-   **CLC 39**
See also CA 121; 126; CANR 78; INT 126

Frankl, Viktor E(mil) 1905-1997   **CLC 93**
See also CA 65-68; 161

Franklin, Benjamin
See Hasek, Jaroslav (Matej Frantisek)

Franklin, Benjamin 1706-1790   **LC 25; DA;**
DAB; DAC; DAM MST; WLCS
See also CDALB 1640-1865; DLB 24, 43, 73

Franklin, (Stella Maria Sarah) Miles (Lampe)
1879-1954   **TCLC 7**
See also CA 104; 164

Fraser, (Lady) Antonia (Pakenham) 1932-
CLC 32, 107
See also CA 85-88; CANR 44, 65; MTCW 1,
2; SATA-Brief 32

Fraser, George MacDonald 1925- **CLC 7**
See also CA 45-48; CANR 2, 48, 74; MTCW 1
Fraser, Sylvia 1935- **CLC 64**
See also CA 45-48; CANR 1, 16, 60
Frayn, Michael 1933-CLC **3, 7, 31, 47; DAM DRAM, NOV**
See also CA 5-8R; CANR 30, 69; DLB 13, 14, 194; MTCW 1, 2
Fraze, Candida (Merrill) 1945- **CLC 50**
See also CA 126
Frazer, J(ames) G(eorge) 1854-1941TCLC **32**
See also CA 118
Frazer, Robert Caine
See Creasey, John
Frazer, Sir James George
See Frazer, J(ames) G(eorge)
Frazier, Charles 1950- **CLC 109**
See also CA 161
Frazier, Ian 1951- **CLC 46**
See also CA 130; CANR 54
Frederic, Harold 1856-1898 **NCLC 10**
See also DLB 12, 23; DLBD 13
Frederick, John
See Faust, Frederick (Schiller)
Frederick the Great 1712-1786 **LC 14**
Fredro, Aleksander 1793-1876 **NCLC 8**
Freeling, Nicolas 1927- **CLC 38**
See also CA 49-52; CAAS 12; CANR 1, 17, 50; DLB 87
Freeman, Douglas Southall 1886-1953 T C L C **11**
See also CA 109; DLB 17; DLBD 17
Freeman, Judith 1946- **CLC 55**
See also CA 148
Freeman, Mary Eleanor Wilkins 1852-1930 **TCLC 9; SSC 1**
See also CA 106; DLB 12, 78
Freeman, R(ichard) Austin 1862-1943 T C L C **21**
See also CA 113; DLB 70
French, Albert 1943- **CLC 86**
See also CA 167
French, Marilyn 1929-CLC **10, 18, 60; DAM DRAM, NOV, POP**
See also CA 69-72; CANR 3, 31; INT CANR-31; MTCW 1, 2
French, Paul
See Asimov, Isaac
Freneau, Philip Morin 1752-1832 **NCLC 1**
See also DLB 37, 43
Freud, Sigmund 1856-1939 **TCLC 52**
See also CA 115; 133; CANR 69; MTCW 1, 2
Friedan, Betty (Naomi) 1921- **CLC 74**
See also CA 65-68; CANR 18, 45, 74; MTCW 1, 2
Friedlander, Saul 1932- **CLC 90**
See also CA 117; 130; CANR 72
Friedman, B(ernard) H(arper) 1926- **CLC 7**
See also CA 1-4R; CANR 3, 48
Friedman, Bruce Jay 1930- **CLC 3, 5, 56**
See also CA 9-12R; CANR 25, 52; DLB 2, 28; INT CANR-25
Friel, Brian 1929- **CLC 5, 42, 59, 115; DC 8**
See also CA 21-24R; CANR 33, 69; DLB 13; MTCW 1
Friis-Baastad, Babbis Ellinor 1921-1970C L C **12**
See also CA 17-20R; 134; SATA 7
Frisch, Max (Rudolf) 1911-1991CLC **3, 9, 14, 18, 32, 44; DAM DRAM, NOV**
See also CA 85-88; 134; CANR 32, 74; DLB 69, 124; MTCW 1, 2
Fromentin, Eugene (Samuel Auguste) 1820-

1876 **NCLC 10**
See also DLB 123
Frost, Frederick
See Faust, Frederick (Schiller)
Frost, Robert (Lee) 1874-1963CLC **1, 3, 4, 9, 10, 13, 15, 26, 34, 44; DA; DAB; DAC; DAM MST, POET; PC 1; WLC**
See also AAYA 21; CA 89-92; CANR 33; CDALB 1917-1929; DLB 54; DLBD 7; MTCW 1, 2; SATA 14
Froude, James Anthony 1818-1894 NCLC **43**
See also DLB 18, 57, 144
Froy, Herald
See Waterhouse, Keith (Spencer)
Fry, Christopher 1907- CLC **2, 10, 14; DAM DRAM**
See also CA 17-20R; CAAS 23; CANR 9, 30, 74; DLB 13; MTCW 1, 2; SATA 66
Frye, (Herman) Northrop 1912-1991CLC **24, 70**
See also CA 5-8R; 133; CANR 8, 37; DLB 67, 68; MTCW 1, 2
Fuchs, Daniel 1909-1993 **CLC 8, 22**
See also CA 81-84; 142; CAAS 5; CANR 40; DLB 9, 26, 28; DLBY 93
Fuchs, Daniel 1934- **CLC 34**
See also CA 37-40R; CANR 14, 48
Fuentes, Carlos 1928-CLC **3, 8, 10, 13, 22, 41, 60, 113; DA; DAB; DAC; DAM MST, MULT, NOV; HLC; SSC 24; WLC**
See also AAYA 4; AITN 2; CA 69-72; CANR 10, 32, 68; DLB 113; HW; MTCW 1, 2
Fuentes, Gregorio Lopez y
See Lopez y Fuentes, Gregorio
Fugard, (Harold) Athol 1932-CLC **5, 9, 14, 25, 40, 80; DAM DRAM; DC 3**
See also AAYA 17; CA 85-88; CANR 32, 54; MTCW 1
Fugard, Sheila 1932- **CLC 48**
See also CA 125
Fuller, Charles (H., Jr.) 1939-CLC **25; BLC 2; DAM DRAM, MULT; DC 1**
See also BW 2; CA 108; 112; DLB 38; INT 112; MTCW 1
Fuller, John (Leopold) 1937- **CLC 62**
See also CA 21-24R; CANR 9, 44; DLB 40
Fuller, Margaret **NCLC 5, 50**
See also Ossoli, Sarah Margaret (Fuller marchesa d')
Fuller, Roy (Broadbent) 1912-1991CLC **4, 28**
See also CA 5-8R; 135; CAAS 10; CANR 53; DLB 15, 20; SATA 87
Fulton, Alice 1952- **CLC 52**
See also CA 116; CANR 57; DLB 193
Furphy, Joseph 1843-1912 **TCLC 25**
See also CA 163
Fussell, Paul 1924- **CLC 74**
See also BEST 90:1; CA 17-20R; CANR 8, 21, 35, 69; INT CANR-21; MTCW 1, 2
Futabatei, Shimei 1864-1909 **TCLC 44**
See also CA 162; DLB 180
Futrelle, Jacques 1875-1912 **TCLC 19**
See also CA 113; 155
Gaboriau, Emile 1835-1873 **NCLC 14**
Gadda, Carlo Emilio 1893-1973 **CLC 11**
See also CA 89-92; DLB 177
Gaddis, William 1922-1998CLC **1, 3, 6, 8, 10, 19, 43, 86**
See also CA 17-20R; 172; CANR 21, 48; DLB 2; MTCW 1, 2
Gage, Walter
See Inge, William (Motter)
Gaines, Ernest J(ames) 1933- CLC **3, 11, 18,**

86; **BLC 2; DAM MULT**
See also AAYA 18; AITN 1; BW 2; CA 9-12R; CANR 6, 24, 42, 75; CDALB 1968-1988; DLB 2, 33, 152; DLBY 80; MTCW 1, 2; SATA 86
Gaitskill, Mary 1954- **CLC 69**
See also CA 128; CANR 61
Galdos, Benito Perez
See Perez Galdos, Benito
Gale, Zona 1874-1938TCLC **7; DAM DRAM**
See also CA 105; 153; DLB 9, 78
Galeano, Eduardo (Hughes) 1940- **CLC 72**
See also CA 29-32R; CANR 13, 32; HW
Galiano, Juan Valera y Alcala
See Valera y Alcala-Galiano, Juan
Galilei, Galileo 1546-1642 **LC 45**
Gallagher, Tess 1943- CLC **18, 63; DAM POET; PC 9**
See also CA 106; DLB 212
Gallant, Mavis 1922- CLC **7, 18, 38; DAC; DAM MST; SSC 5**
See also CA 69-72; CANR 29, 69; DLB 53; MTCW 1, 2
Gallant, Roy A(rthur) 1924- **CLC 17**
See also CA 5-8R; CANR 4, 29, 54; CLR 30; MAICYA; SATA 4, 68
Gallico, Paul (William) 1897-1976 **CLC 2**
See also AITN 1; CA 5-8R; 69-72; CANR 23; DLB 9, 171; MAICYA; SATA 13
Gallo, Max Louis 1932- **CLC 95**
See also CA 85-88
Gallois, Lucien
See Desnos, Robert
Gallup, Ralph
See Whitemore, Hugh (John)
Galsworthy, John 1867-1933TCLC **1, 45; DA; DAB; DAC; DAM DRAM, MST, NOV; SSC 22; WLC**
See also CA 104; 141; CANR 75; CDBLB 1890-1914; DLB 10, 34, 98, 162; DLBD 16; MTCW 1
Galt, John 1779-1839 **NCLC 1**
See also DLB 99, 116, 159
Galvin, James 1951- **CLC 38**
See also CA 108; CANR 26
Gamboa, Federico 1864-1939 **TCLC 36**
See also CA 167
Gandhi, M. K.
See Gandhi, Mohandas Karamchand
Gandhi, Mahatma
See Gandhi, Mohandas Karamchand
Gandhi, Mohandas Karamchand 1869-1948 **TCLC 59; DAM MULT**
See also CA 121; 132; MTCW 1, 2
Gann, Ernest Kellogg 1910-1991 **CLC 23**
See also AITN 1; CA 1-4R; 136; CANR 1
Garcia, Cristina 1958- **CLC 76**
See also CA 141; CANR 73
Garcia Lorca, Federico 1898-1936TCLC **1, 7, 49; DA; DAB; DAC; DAM DRAM, MST, MULT, POET; DC 2; HLC; PC 3; WLC**
See also CA 104; 131; DLB 108; HW; MTCW 1, 2
Garcia Marquez, Gabriel (Jose) 1928-CLC **2, 3, 8, 10, 15, 27, 47, 55, 68; DA; DAB; DAC; DAM MST, MULT, NOV, POP; HLC; SSC 8; WLC**
See also AAYA 3; BEST 89:1, 90:4; CA 33-36R; CANR 10, 28, 50, 75; DLB 113; HW; MTCW 1, 2
Gard, Janice
See Latham, Jean Lee
Gard, Roger Martin du

See Martin du Gard, Roger

Gardam, Jane 1928-   **CLC 43**
  See also CA 49-52; CANR 2, 18, 33, 54; CLR 12; DLB 14, 161; MAICYA; MTCW 1; SAAS 9; SATA 39, 76; SATA-Brief 28

Gardner, Herb(ert) 1934-   **CLC 44**
  See also CA 149

Gardner, John (Champlin), Jr. 1933-1982   **CLC 2, 3, 5, 7, 8, 10, 18, 28, 34; DAM NOV, POP; SSC 7**
  See also AITN 1; CA 65-68; 107; CANR 33, 73; DLB 2; DLBY 82; MTCW 1; SATA 40; SATA-Obit 31

Gardner, John (Edmund) 1926-   **CLC 30; DAM POP**
  See also CA 103; CANR 15, 69; MTCW 1

Gardner, Miriam
  See Bradley, Marion Zimmer

Gardner, Noel
  See Kuttner, Henry

Gardons, S. S.
  See Snodgrass, W(illiam) D(e Witt)

Garfield, Leon 1921-1996   **CLC 12**
  See also AAYA 8; CA 17-20R; 152; CANR 38, 41, 78; CLR 21; DLB 161; JRDA; MAICYA; SATA 1, 32, 76; SATA-Obit 90

Garland, (Hannibal) Hamlin 1860-1940   **TCLC 3; SSC 18**
  See also CA 104; DLB 12, 71, 78, 186

Garneau, (Hector de) Saint-Denys 1912-1943   **TCLC 13**
  See also CA 111; DLB 88

Garner, Alan 1934-CLC 17; DAB; DAM POP
  See also AAYA 18; CA 73-76; CANR 15, 64; CLR 20; DLB 161; MAICYA; MTCW 1, 2; SATA 18, 69

Garner, Hugh 1913-1979   **CLC 13**
  See also CA 69-72; CANR 31; DLB 68

Garnett, David 1892-1981   **CLC 3**
  See also CA 5-8R; 103; CANR 17; DLB 34; MTCW 2

Garos, Stephanie
  See Katz, Steve

Garrett, George (Palmer) 1929-CLC 3, 11, 51; SSC 30
  See also CA 1-4R; CAAS 5; CANR 1, 42, 67; DLB 2, 5, 130, 152; DLBY 83

Garrick, David 1717-1779   **LC 15; DAM DRAM**
  See also DLB 84

Garrigue, Jean 1914-1972   **CLC 2, 8**
  See also CA 5-8R; 37-40R; CANR 20

Garrison, Frederick
  See Sinclair, Upton (Beall)

Garth, Will
  See Hamilton, Edmond; Kuttner, Henry

Garvey, Marcus (Moziah, Jr.) 1887-1940   **TCLC 41; BLC 2; DAM MULT**
  See also BW 1; CA 120; 124

Gary, Romain   **CLC 25**
  See Kacew, Romain
  See also DLB 83

Gascar, Pierre   **CLC 11**
  See also Fournier, Pierre

Gascoyne, David (Emery) 1916-   **CLC 45**
  See also CA 65-68; CANR 10, 28, 54; DLB 20; MTCW 1

Gaskell, Elizabeth Cleghorn 1810-1865NCLC 70; DAB; DAM MST; SSC 25
  See also CDBLB 1832-1890; DLB 21, 144, 159

Gass, William H(oward) 1924-CLC 1, 2, 8, 11, 15, 39; SSC 12
  See also CA 17-20R; CANR 30, 71; DLB 2;

MTCW 1, 2

Gasset, Jose Ortega y
  See Ortega y Gasset, Jose

Gates, Henry Louis, Jr. 1950-CLC 65; BLCS; DAM MULT
  See also BW 2; CA 109; CANR 25, 53, 75; DLB 67; MTCW 1

Gautier, Theophile 1811-1872   **NCLC 1, 59; DAM POET; PC 18; SSC 20**
  See also DLB 119

Gawsworth, John
  See Bates, H(erbert) E(rnest)

Gay, John 1685-1732   **LC 49; DAM DRAM**
  See also DLB 84, 95

Gay, Oliver
  See Gogarty, Oliver St. John

Gaye, Marvin (Penze) 1939-1984   **CLC 26**
  See also CA 112

Gebler, Carlo (Ernest) 1954-   **CLC 39**
  See also CA 119; 133

Gee, Maggie (Mary) 1948-   **CLC 57**
  See also CA 130; DLB 207

Gee, Maurice (Gough) 1931-   **CLC 29**
  See also CA 97-100; CANR 67; CLR 56; SATA 46, 101

Gelbart, Larry (Simon) 1923-   **CLC 21, 61**
  See also CA 73-76; CANR 45

Gelber, Jack 1932-   **CLC 1, 6, 14, 79**
  See also CA 1-4R; CANR 2; DLB 7

Gellhorn, Martha (Ellis) 1908-1998 CLC 14, 60
  See also CA 77-80; 164; CANR 44; DLBY 82, 98

Genet, Jean 1910-1986CLC 1, 2, 5, 10, 14, 44, 46; DAM DRAM
  See also CA 13-16R; CANR 18; DLB 72; DLBY 86; MTCW 1, 2

Gent, Peter 1942-   **CLC 29**
  See also AITN 1; CA 89-92; DLBY 82

Gentlewoman in New England, A
  See Bradstreet, Anne

Gentlewoman in Those Parts, A
  See Bradstreet, Anne

George, Jean Craighead 1919-   **CLC 35**
  See also AAYA 8; CA 5-8R; CANR 25; CLR 1; DLB 52; JRDA; MAICYA; SATA 2, 68

George, Stefan (Anton) 1868-1933TCLC 2, 14
  See also CA 104

Georges, Georges Martin
  See Simenon, Georges (Jacques Christian)

Gerhardi, William Alexander
  See Gerhardie, William Alexander

Gerhardie, William Alexander 1895-1977   **CLC 5**
  See also CA 25-28R; 73-76; CANR 18; DLB 36

Gerstler, Amy 1956-   **CLC 70**
  See also CA 146

Gertler, T.   **CLC 34**
  See also CA 116; 121; INT 121

Ghalib   **NCLC 39**
  See also Ghalib, Hsadullah Khan

Ghalib, Hsadullah Khan 1797-1869
  See Ghalib
  See also DAM POET

Ghelderode, Michel de 1898-1962CLC 6, 11; DAM DRAM
  See also CA 85-88; CANR 40, 77

Ghiselin, Brewster 1903-   **CLC 23**
  See also CA 13-16R; CAAS 10; CANR 13

Ghose, Aurabinda 1872-1950   **TCLC 63**
  See also CA 163

Ghose, Zulfikar 1935-   **CLC 42**

See also CA 65-68; CANR 67

Ghosh, Amitav 1956-   **CLC 44**
  See also CA 147

Giacosa, Giuseppe 1847-1906   **TCLC 7**
  See also CA 104

Gibb, Lee
  See Waterhouse, Keith (Spencer)

Gibbon, Lewis Grassic   **TCLC 4**
  See also Mitchell, James Leslie

Gibbons, Kaye 1960-CLC 50, 88; DAM POP
  See also CA 151; CANR 75; MTCW 1

Gibran, Kahlil 1883-1931   **TCLC 1, 9; DAM POET, POP; PC 9**
  See also CA 104; 150; MTCW 2

Gibran, Khalil
  See Gibran, Kahlil

Gibson, William 1914-   **CLC 23; DA; DAB; DAC; DAM DRAM, MST**
  See also CA 9-12R; CANR 9, 42, 75; DLB 7; MTCW 1; SATA 66

Gibson, William (Ford) 1948-   **CLC 39, 63; DAM POP**
  See also AAYA 12; CA 126; 133; CANR 52; MTCW 1

Gide, Andre (Paul Guillaume) 1869-1951   **TCLC 5, 12, 36; DA; DAB; DAC; DAM MST, NOV; SSC 13; WLC**
  See also CA 104; 124; DLB 65; MTCW 1, 2

Gifford, Barry (Colby) 1946-   **CLC 34**
  See also CA 65-68; CANR 9, 30, 40

Gilbert, Frank
  See De Voto, Bernard (Augustine)

Gilbert, W(illiam) S(chwenck) 1836-1911   **TCLC 3; DAM DRAM, POET**
  See also CA 104; 173; SATA 36

Gilbreth, Frank B., Jr. 1911-   **CLC 17**
  See also CA 9-12R; SATA 2

Gilchrist, Ellen 1935-CLC 34, 48; DAM POP; SSC 14
  See also CA 113; 116; CANR 41, 61; DLB 130; MTCW 1, 2

Giles, Molly 1942-   **CLC 39**
  See also CA 126

Gill, Eric 1882-1940   **TCLC 85**

Gill, Patrick
  See Creasey, John

Gilliam, Terry (Vance) 1940-   **CLC 21**
  See also Monty Python
  See also AAYA 19; CA 108; 113; CANR 35; INT 113

Gillian, Jerry
  See Gilliam, Terry (Vance)

Gilliatt, Penelope (Ann Douglass) 1932-1993   **CLC 2, 10, 13, 53**
  See also AITN 2; CA 13-16R; 141; CANR 49; DLB 14

Gilman, Charlotte (Anna) Perkins (Stetson) 1860-1935   **TCLC 9, 37; SSC 13**
  See also CA 106; 150; MTCW 1

Gilmour, David 1949-   **CLC 35**
  See also CA 138, 147

Gilpin, William 1724-1804   **NCLC 30**

Gilray, J. D.
  See Mencken, H(enry) L(ouis)

Gilroy, Frank D(aniel) 1925-   **CLC 2**
  See also CA 81-84; CANR 32, 64; DLB 7

Gilstrap, John 1957(?)-   **CLC 99**
  See also CA 160

Ginsberg, Allen 1926-1997CLC 1, 2, 3, 4, 6, 13, 36, 69, 109; DA; DAB; DAC; DAM MST, POET; PC 4; WLC
  See also AITN 1; CA 1-4R; 157; CANR 2, 41, 63; CDALB 1941-1968; DLB 5, 16, 169;

MTCW 1, 2

Ginzburg, Natalia 1916-1991 **CLC 5, 11, 54, 70**
See also CA 85-88; 135; CANR 33; DLB 177;
MTCW 1, 2

Giono, Jean 1895-1970 **CLC 4, 11**
See also CA 45-48; 29-32R; CANR 2, 35; DLB
72; MTCW 1

Giovanni, Nikki 1943- **CLC 2, 4, 19, 64, 117;
BLC 2; DA; DAB; DAC; DAM MST,
MULT, POET; PC 19; WLCS**
See also AAYA 22; AITN 1; BW 2; CA 29-
32R; CAAS 6; CANR 18, 41, 60; CLR 6;
DLB 5, 41; INT CANR-18; MAICYA;
MTCW 1, 2; SATA 24, 107

Giovene, Andrea 1904- **CLC 7**
See also CA 85-88

Gippius, Zinaida (Nikolayevna) 1869-1945
See Hippius, Zinaida
See also CA 106

Giraudoux, (Hippolyte) Jean 1882-1944
TCLC 2, 7; DAM DRAM
See also CA 104; DLB 65

Gironella, Jose Maria 1917- **CLC 11**
See also CA 101

Gissing, George (Robert) 1857-1903**TCLC 3,
24, 47**
See also CA 105; 167; DLB 18, 135, 184

Giurlani, Aldo
See Palazzeschi, Aldo

Gladkov, Fyodor (Vasilyevich) 1883-1958
TCLC 27
See also CA 170

Glanville, Brian (Lester) 1931- **CLC 6**
See also CA 5-8R; CAAS 9; CANR 3, 70; DLB
15, 139; SATA 42

Glasgow, Ellen (Anderson Gholson) 1873-1945
TCLC 2, 7; SSC 34
See also CA 104; 164; DLB 9, 12; MTCW 2

Glaspell, Susan 1882(?)-1948**TCLC 55; DC 10**
See also CA 110; 154; DLB 7, 9, 78; YABC 2

Glassco, John 1909-1981 **CLC 9**
See also CA 13-16R; 102; CANR 15; DLB 68

Glasscock, Amnesia
See Steinbeck, John (Ernst)

Glasser, Ronald J. 1940(?)- **CLC 37**

Glassman, Joyce
See Johnson, Joyce

Glendinning, Victoria 1937- **CLC 50**
See also CA 120; 127; CANR 59; DLB 155

Glissant, Edouard 1928- **CLC 10, 68; DAM
MULT**
See also CA 153

Gloag, Julian 1930- **CLC 40**
See also AITN 1; CA 65-68; CANR 10, 70

Glowacki, Aleksander
See Prus, Boleslaw

Gluck, Louise (Elisabeth) 1943-**CLC 7, 22, 44,
81; DAM POET; PC 16**
See also CA 33-36R; CANR 40, 69; DLB 5;
MTCW 2

Glyn, Elinor 1864-1943 **TCLC 72**
See also DLB 153

Gobineau, Joseph Arthur (Comte) de 1816-
1882 **NCLC 17**
See also DLB 123

Godard, Jean-Luc 1930- **CLC 20**
See also CA 93-96

Godden, (Margaret) Rumer 1907-1998 **C L C
53**
See also AAYA 6; CA 5-8R; 172; CANR 4,
27, 36, 55; CLR 20; DLB 161; MAICYA;
SAAS 12; SATA 3, 36

Godoy Alcayaga, Lucila 1889-1957

See Mistral, Gabriela
See also BW 2; CA 104; 131; DAM MULT;
HW; MTCW 1, 2

Godwin, Gail (Kathleen) 1937- **CLC 5, 8, 22,
31, 69; DAM POP**
See also CA 29-32R; CANR 15, 43, 69; DLB
6; INT CANR-15; MTCW 1, 2

Godwin, William 1756-1836 **NCLC 14**
See also CDBLB 1789-1832; DLB 39, 104,
142, 158, 163

Goebbels, Josef
See Goebbels, (Paul) Joseph

Goebbels, (Paul) Joseph 1897-1945 **TCLC 68**
See also CA 115; 148

Goebbels, Joseph Paul
See Goebbels, (Paul) Joseph

Goethe, Johann Wolfgang von 1749-1832
**NCLC 4, 22, 34; DA; DAB; DAC; DAM
DRAM, MST, POET; PC 5; WLC**
See also DLB 94

Gogarty, Oliver St. John 1878-1957**TCLC 15**
See also CA 109; 150; DLB 15, 19

Gogol, Nikolai (Vasilyevich) 1809-1852**NCLC
5, 15, 31; DA; DAB; DAC; DAM DRAM,
MST; DC 1; SSC 4, 29; WLC**
See also DLB 198

Goines, Donald 1937(?)-1974**CLC 80; BLC 2;
DAM MULT, POP**
See also AITN 1; BW 1; CA 124; 114; DLB 33

Gold, Herbert 1924- **CLC 4, 7, 14, 42**
See also CA 9-12R; CANR 17, 45; DLB 2;
DLBY 81

Goldbarth, Albert 1948- **CLC 5, 38**
See also CA 53-56; CANR 6, 40; DLB 120

Goldberg, Anatol 1910-1982 **CLC 34**
See also CA 131; 117

Goldemberg, Isaac 1945- **CLC 52**
See also CA 69-72; CAAS 12; CANR 11, 32;
HW

Golding, William (Gerald) 1911-1993**CLC 1,
2, 3, 8, 10, 17, 27, 58, 81; DA; DAB; DAC;
DAM MST, NOV; WLC**
See also AAYA 5; CA 5-8R; 141; CANR 13,
33, 54; CDBLB 1945-1960; DLB 15, 100;
MTCW 1, 2

Goldman, Emma 1869-1940 **TCLC 13**
See also CA 110; 150

Goldman, Francisco 1954- **CLC 76**
See also CA 162

Goldman, William (W.) 1931- **CLC 1, 48**
See also CA 9-12R; CANR 29, 69; DLB 44

Goldmann, Lucien 1913-1970 **CLC 24**
See also CA 25-28; CAP 2

Goldoni, Carlo 1707-1793**LC 4; DAM DRAM**

Goldsberry, Steven 1949- **CLC 34**
See also CA 131

Goldsmith, Oliver 1728-1774 **LC 2, 48; DA;
DAB; DAC; DAM DRAM, MST, NOV,
POET; DC 8; WLC**
See also CDBLB 1660-1789; DLB 39, 89, 104,
109, 142; SATA 26

Goldsmith, Peter
See Priestley, J(ohn) B(oynton)

Gombrowicz, Witold 1904-1969**CLC 4, 7, 11,
49; DAM DRAM**
See also CA 19-20; 25-28R; CAP 2

Gomez de la Serna, Ramon 1888-1963**CLC 9**
See also CA 153; 116; HW

Goncharov, Ivan Alexandrovich 1812-1891
NCLC 1, 63

Goncourt, Edmond (Louis Antoine Huot) de
1822-1896 **NCLC 7**
See also DLB 123

Goncourt, Jules (Alfred Huot) de 1830-1870
NCLC 7
See also DLB 123

Gontier, Fernande 19(?)- **CLC 50**

Gonzalez Martinez, Enrique 1871-1952
TCLC 72
See also CA 166; HW

Goodman, Paul 1911-1972 **CLC 1, 2, 4, 7**
See also CA 19-20; 37-40R; CANR 34; CAP
2; DLB 130; MTCW 1

Gordimer, Nadine 1923- **CLC 3, 5, 7, 10, 18,
33, 51, 70; DA; DAB; DAC; DAM MST,
NOV; SSC 17; WLCS**
See also CA 5-8R; CANR 3, 28, 56; INT
CANR-28; MTCW 1, 2

Gordon, Adam Lindsay 1833-1870 **NCLC 21**

Gordon, Caroline 1895-1981**CLC 6, 13, 29, 83;
SSC 15**
See also CA 11-12; 103; CANR 36; CAP 1;
DLB 4, 9, 102; DLBD 17; DLBY 81; MTCW
1, 2

Gordon, Charles William 1860-1937
See Connor, Ralph
See also CA 109

Gordon, Mary (Catherine) 1949- **CLC 13, 22**
See also CA 102; CANR 44; DLB 6; DLBY
81; INT 102; MTCW 1

Gordon, N. J.
See Bosman, Herman Charles

Gordon, Sol 1923- **CLC 26**
See also CA 53-56; CANR 4; SATA 11

Gordone, Charles 1925-1995**CLC 1, 4; DAM
DRAM; DC 8**
See also BW 1; CA 93-96; 150; CANR 55; DLB
7; INT 93-96; MTCW 1

Gore, Catherine 1800-1861 **NCLC 65**
See also DLB 116

Gorenko, Anna Andreevna
See Akhmatova, Anna

Gorky, Maxim 1868-1936**TCLC 8; DAB; SSC
28; WLC**
See also Peshkov, Alexei Maximovich
See also MTCW 2

Goryan, Sirak
See Saroyan, William

Gosse, Edmund (William) 1849-1928 **T C L C
28**
See also CA 117; DLB 57, 144, 184

Gotlieb, Phyllis Fay (Bloom) 1926- **CLC 18**
See also CA 13-16R; CANR 7; DLB 88

Gottesman, S. D.
See Kornbluth, C(yril) M.; Pohl, Frederik

Gottfried von Strassburg fl. c. 1210- **C M L C
10**
See also DLB 138

Gould, Lois **CLC 4, 10**
See also CA 77-80; CANR 29; MTCW 1

Gourmont, Remy (-Marie-Charles) de 1858-
1915 **TCLC 17**
See also CA 109; 150; MTCW 2

Govier, Katherine 1948- **CLC 51**
See also CA 101; CANR 18, 40

Goyen, (Charles) William 1915-1983 **CLC 5,
8, 14, 40**
See also AITN 2; CA 5-8R; 110; CANR 6, 71;
DLB 2; DLBY 83; INT CANR-6

Goytisolo, Juan 1931- **CLC 5, 10, 23; DAM
MULT; HLC**
See also CA 85-88; CANR 32, 61; HW; MTCW
1, 2

Gozzano, Guido 1883-1916 **PC 10**
See also CA 154; DLB 114

Gozzi, (Conte) Carlo 1720-1806 **NCLC 23**

See also CA 124; 130; MTCW 1

Grove, Frederick Philip   **TCLC 4**
See also Greve, Felix Paul (Berthold Friedrich)
See also DLB 92

Grubb
See Crumb, R(obert)

Grumbach, Doris (Isaac) 1918-**CLC 13, 22, 64**
See also CA 5-8R; CAAS 2; CANR 9, 42, 70;
INT CANR-9; MTCW 2

Grundtvig, Nicolai Frederik Severin 1783-1872
NCLC 1

Grunge
See Crumb, R(obert)

Grunwald, Lisa 1959-   **CLC 44**
See also CA 120

Guare, John 1938- **CLC 8, 14, 29, 67; DAM
DRAM**
See also CA 73-76; CANR 21, 69; DLB 7;
MTCW 1, 2

Gudjonsson, Halldor Kiljan 1902-1998
See Laxness, Halldor
See also CA 103; 164

Guenter, Erich
See Eich, Guenter

Guest, Barbara 1920-   **CLC 34**
See also CA 25-28R; CANR 11, 44; DLB 5,
193

Guest, Judith (Ann) 1936- **CLC 8, 30; DAM
NOV, POP**
See also AAYA 7; CA 77-80; CANR 15, 75;
INT CANR-15; MTCW 1, 2

Guevara, Che   **CLC 87; HLC**
See also Guevara (Serna), Ernesto

Guevara (Serna), Ernesto 1928-1967
See Guevara, Che
See also CA 127; 111; CANR 56; DAM MULT;
HW

Guicciardini, Francesco 1483-1540   **LC 49**

Guild, Nicholas M. 1944-   **CLC 33**
See also CA 93-96

Guillemin, Jacques
See Sartre, Jean-Paul

Guillen, Jorge 1893-1984   **CLC 11; DAM
MULT, POET**
See also CA 89-92; 112; DLB 108; HW

Guillen, Nicolas (Cristobal) 1902-1989 **C L C
48, 79; BLC 2; DAM MST, MULT, POET;
HLC; PC 23**
See also BW 2; CA 116; 125; 129; HW

Guillevic, (Eugene) 1907-   **CLC 33**
See also CA 93-96

Guillois
See Desnos, Robert

Guillois, Valentin
See Desnos, Robert

Guiney, Louise Imogen 1861-1920 **TCLC 41**
See also CA 160; DLB 54

Guiraldes, Ricardo (Guillermo) 1886-1927
TCLC 39
See also CA 131; HW; MTCW 1

Gumilev, Nikolai (Stepanovich) 1886-1921
TCLC 60
See also CA 165

Gunesekera, Romesh 1954-   **CLC 91**
See also CA 159

Gunn, Bill   **CLC 5**
See also Gunn, William Harrison
See also DLB 38

Gunn, Thom(son William) 1929-**CLC 3, 6, 18,
32, 81; DAM POET; PC 26**
See also CA 17-20R; CANR 9, 33; CDBLB
1960 to Present; DLB 27; INT CANR-33;
MTCW 1

Gunn, William Harrison 1934(?)-1989
See Gunn, Bill
See also AITN 1; BW 1; CA 13-16R; 128;
CANR 12, 25, 76

Gunnars, Kristjana 1948-   **CLC 69**
See also CA 113; DLB 60

Gurdjieff, G(eorgei) I(vanovich) 1877(?)-1949
TCLC 71
See also CA 157

Gurganus, Allan 1947- **CLC 70; DAM POP**
See also BEST 90:1; CA 135

Gurney, A(lbert) R(amsdell), Jr. 1930- **C L C
32, 50, 54; DAM DRAM**
See also CA 77-80; CANR 32, 64

Gurney, Ivor (Bertie) 1890-1937   **TCLC 33**
See also CA 167

Gurney, Peter
See Gurney, A(lbert) R(amsdell), Jr.

Guro, Elena 1877-1913   **TCLC 56**

Gustafson, James M(oody) 1925-   **CLC 100**
See also CA 25-28R; CANR 37

Gustafson, Ralph (Barker) 1909-   **CLC 36**
See also CA 21-24R; CANR 8, 45; DLB 88

Gut, Gom
See Simenon, Georges (Jacques Christian)

Guterson, David 1956-   **CLC 91**
See also CA 132; CANR 73; MTCW 2

Guthrie, A(lfred) B(ertram), Jr. 1901-1991
CLC 23
See also CA 57-60; 134; CANR 24; DLB 212;
SATA 62; SATA-Obit 67

Guthrie, Isobel
See Grieve, C(hristopher) M(urray)

Guthrie, Woodrow Wilson 1912-1967
See Guthrie, Woody
See also CA 113; 93-96

Guthrie, Woody   **CLC 35**
See also Guthrie, Woodrow Wilson

Guy, Rosa (Cuthbert) 1928-   **CLC 26**
See also AAYA 4; BW 2; CA 17-20R; CANR
14, 34; CLR 13; DLB 33; JRDA; MAICYA;
SATA 14, 62

Gwendolyn
See Bennett, (Enoch) Arnold

H. D.   **CLC 3, 8, 14, 31, 34, 73; PC 5**
See also Doolittle, Hilda

H. de V.
See Buchan, John

Haavikko, Paavo Juhani 1931-   **CLC 18, 34**
See also CA 106

Habbema, Koos
See Heijermans, Herman

Habermas, Juergen 1929-   **CLC 104**
See also CA 109

Habermas, Jurgen
See Habermas, Juergen

Hacker, Marilyn 1942- **CLC 5, 9, 23, 72, 91;
DAM POET**
See also CA 77-80; CANR 68; DLB 120

Haeckel, Ernst Heinrich (Philipp August) 1834-
1919   **TCLC 83**
See also CA 157

Haggard, H(enry) Rider 1856-1925**TCLC 11**
See also CA 108; 148; DLB 70, 156, 174, 178;
MTCW 2; SATA 16

Hagiosy, L.
See Larbaud, Valery (Nicolas)

Hagiwara Sakutaro 1886-1942 **TCLC 60; PC
18**

Haig, Fenil
See Ford, Ford Madox

Haig-Brown, Roderick (Langmere) 1908-1976
CLC 21

See also CA 5-8R; 69-72; CANR 4, 38; CLR
31; DLB 88; MAICYA; SATA 12

Hailey, Arthur 1920-**CLC 5; DAM NOV, POP**
See also AITN 2; BEST 90:3; CA 1-4R; CANR
2, 36, 75; DLB 88; DLBY 82; MTCW 1, 2

Hailey, Elizabeth Forsythe 1938-   **CLC 40**
See also CA 93-96; CAAS 1; CANR 15, 48;
INT CANR-15

Haines, John (Meade) 1924-   **CLC 58**
See also CA 17-20R; CANR 13, 34; DLB 212

Hakluyt, Richard 1552-1616   **LC 31**

Haldeman, Joe (William) 1943-   **CLC 61**
See also CA 53-56; CAAS 25; CANR 6, 70,
72; DLB 8; INT CANR-6

Hale, Sarah Josepha (Buell) 1788-1879**NCLC
75**
See also DLB 1, 42, 73

Haley, Alex(ander Murray Palmer) 1921-1992
**CLC 8, 12, 76; BLC 2; DA; DAB; DAC;
DAM MST, MULT, POP**
See also AAYA 26; BW 2; CA 77-80; 136;
CANR 61; DLB 38; MTCW 1, 2

Haliburton, Thomas Chandler 1796-1865
NCLC 15
See also DLB 11, 99

Hall, Donald (Andrew, Jr.) 1928- **CLC 1, 13,
37, 59; DAM POET**
See also CA 5-8R; CAAS 7; CANR 2, 44, 64;
DLB 5; MTCW 1; SATA 23, 97

Hall, Frederic Sauser
See Sauser-Hall, Frederic

Hall, James
See Kuttner, Henry

Hall, James Norman 1887-1951   **TCLC 23**
See also CA 123; 173; SATA 21

Hall, Radclyffe
See Hall, (Marguerite) Radclyffe
See also MTCW 2

Hall, (Marguerite) Radclyffe 1886-1943
TCLC 12
See also CA 110; 150; DLB 191

Hall, Rodney 1935-   **CLC 51**
See also CA 109; CANR 69

Halleck, Fitz-Greene 1790-1867   **NCLC 47**
See also DLB 3

Halliday, Michael
See Creasey, John

Halpern, Daniel 1945-   **CLC 14**
See also CA 33-36R

Hamburger, Michael (Peter Leopold) 1924-
CLC 5, 14
See also CA 5-8R; CAAS 4; CANR 2, 47; DLB
27

Hamill, Pete 1935-   **CLC 10**
See also CA 25-28R; CANR 18, 71

Hamilton, Alexander 1755(?)-1804 **NCLC 49**
See also DLB 37

Hamilton, Clive
See Lewis, C(live) S(taples)

Hamilton, Edmond 1904-1977   **CLC 1**
See also CA 1-4R; CANR 3; DLB 8

Hamilton, Eugene (Jacob) Lee
See Lee-Hamilton, Eugene (Jacob)

Hamilton, Franklin
See Silverberg, Robert

Hamilton, Gail
See Corcoran, Barbara

Hamilton, Mollie
See Kaye, M(ary) M(argaret)

Hamilton, (Anthony Walter) Patrick 1904-1962
CLC 51
See also CA 113; DLB 191

Hamilton, Virginia 1936-   **CLC 26; DAM**

See also CA 133; CAAS 22; DLB 120

Honig, Edwin 1919-   **CLC 33**
See also CA 5-8R; CAAS 8; CANR 4, 45; DLB 5

Hood, Hugh (John Blagdon) 1928-**CLC 15, 28**
See also CA 49-52; CAAS 17; CANR 1, 33; DLB 53

Hood, Thomas 1799-1845   **NCLC 16**
See also DLB 96

Hooker, (Peter) Jeremy 1941-   **CLC 43**
See also CA 77-80; CANR 22; DLB 40

hooks, bell   **CLC 94; BLCS**
See also Watkins, Gloria
See also MTCW 2

Hope, A(lec) D(erwent) 1907-   **CLC 3, 51**
See also CA 21-24R; CANR 33, 74; MTCW 1, 2

Hope, Anthony 1863-1933   **TCLC 83**
See also CA 157; DLB 153, 156

Hope, Brian
See Creasey, John

Hope, Christopher (David Tully) 1944- **C L C 52**
See also CA 106; CANR 47; SATA 62

Hopkins, Gerard Manley 1844-1889 **N C L C 17; DA; DAB; DAC; DAM MST, POET; PC 15; WLC**
See also CDBLB 1890-1914; DLB 35, 57

Hopkins, John (Richard) 1931-1998   **CLC 4**
See also CA 85-88; 169

Hopkins, Pauline Elizabeth 1859-1930**T C L C 28; BLC 2; DAM MULT**
See also BW 2; CA 141; DLB 50

Hopkinson, Francis 1737-1791   **LC 25**
See also DLB 31

Hopley-Woolrich, Cornell George 1903-1968
See Woolrich, Cornell
See also CA 13-14; CANR 58; CAP 1; MTCW 2

Horatio
See Proust, (Valentin-Louis-George-Eugene-) Marcel

Horgan, Paul (George Vincent O'Shaughnessy) 1903-1995   **CLC 9, 53; DAM NOV**
See also CA 13-16R; 147; CANR 9, 35; DLB 212; DLBY 85; INT CANR-9; MTCW 1, 2; SATA 13; SATA-Obit 84

Horn, Peter
See Kuttner, Henry

Hornem, Horace Esq.
See Byron, George Gordon (Noel)

Horney, Karen (Clementine Theodore Danielsen) 1885-1952   **TCLC 71**
See also CA 114; 165

Hornung, E(rnest) W(illiam) 1866-1921 **TCLC 59**
See also CA 108; 160; DLB 70

Horovitz, Israel (Arthur) 1939-**CLC 56; DAM DRAM**
See also CA 33-36R; CANR 46, 59; DLB 7

Horvath, Odon von
See Horvath, Oedoen von
See also DLB 85, 124

Horvath, Oedoen von 1901-1938   **TCLC 45**
See also Horvath, Odon von
See also CA 118

Horwitz, Julius 1920-1986   **CLC 14**
See also CA 9-12R; 119; CANR 12

Hospital, Janette Turner 1942-   **CLC 42**
See also CA 108; CANR 48

Hostos, E. M. de
See Hostos (y Bonilla), Eugenio Maria de

Hostos, Eugenio M. de
See Hostos (y Bonilla), Eugenio Maria de

See Hostos (y Bonilla), Eugenio Maria de

Hostos, Eugenio Maria
See Hostos (y Bonilla), Eugenio Maria de

Hostos (y Bonilla), Eugenio Maria de 1839-1903 **TCLC 24**
See also CA 123; 131; HW

Houdini
See Lovecraft, H(oward) P(hillips)

Hougan, Carolyn 1943-   **CLC 34**
See also CA 139

Household, Geoffrey (Edward West) 1900-1988 **CLC 11**
See also CA 77-80; 126; CANR 58; DLB 87; SATA 14; SATA-Obit 59

Housman, A(lfred) E(dward) 1859-1936 **TCLC 1, 10; DA; DAB; DAC; DAM MST, POET; PC 2; WLCS**
See also CA 104; 125; DLB 19; MTCW 1, 2

Housman, Laurence 1865-1959   **TCLC 7**
See also CA 106; 155; DLB 10; SATA 25

Howard, Elizabeth Jane 1923-   **CLC 7, 29**
See also CA 5-8R; CANR 8, 62

Howard, Maureen 1930-   **CLC 5, 14, 46**
See also CA 53-56; CANR 31, 75; DLBY 83; INT CANR-31; MTCW 1, 2

Howard, Richard 1929-   **CLC 7, 10, 47**
See also AITN 1; CA 85-88; CANR 25; DLB 5; INT CANR-25

Howard, Robert E(rvin) 1906-1936 **TCLC 8**
See also CA 105; 157

Howard, Warren F.
See Pohl, Frederik

Howe, Fanny (Quincy) 1940-   **CLC 47**
See also CA 117; CAAS 27; CANR 70; SATA-Brief 52

Howe, Irving 1920-1993   **CLC 85**
See also CA 9-12R; 141; CANR 21, 50; DLB 67; MTCW 1, 2

Howe, Julia Ward 1819-1910   **TCLC 21**
See also CA 117; DLB 1, 189

Howe, Susan 1937-   **CLC 72**
See also CA 160; DLB 120

Howe, Tina 1937-   **CLC 48**
See also CA 109

Howell, James 1594(?)-1666   **LC 13**
See also DLB 151

Howells, W. D.
See Howells, William Dean

Howells, William D.
See Howells, William Dean

Howells, William Dean 1837-1920 **TCLC 7, 17, 41**
See also CA 104; 134; CDALB 1865-1917; DLB 12, 64, 74, 79, 189; MTCW 2

Howes, Barbara 1914-1996   **CLC 15**
See also CA 9-12R; 151; CAAS 3; CANR 53; SATA 5

Hrabal, Bohumil 1914-1997   **CLC 13, 67**
See also CA 106; 156; CAAS 12; CANR 57

Hroswitha of Gandersheim c. 935-c. 1002 **CMLC 29**
See also DLB 148

Hsun, Lu
See Lu Hsun

Hubbard, L(afayette) Ron(ald) 1911-1986 **CLC 43; DAM POP**
See also CA 77-80; 118; CANR 52; MTCW 2

Huch, Ricarda (Octavia) 1864-1947**TCLC 13**
See also CA 111; DLB 66

Huddle, David 1942-   **CLC 49**
See also CA 57-60; CAAS 20; DLB 130

Hudson, Jeffrey
See Crichton, (John) Michael

Hudson, W(illiam) H(enry) 1841-1922 **T C L C 29**
See also CA 115; DLB 98, 153, 174; SATA 35

Hueffer, Ford Madox
See Ford, Ford Madox

Hughart, Barry 1934-   **CLC 39**
See also CA 137

Hughes, Colin
See Creasey, John

Hughes, David (John) 1930-   **CLC 48**
See also CA 116; 129; DLB 14

Hughes, Edward James
See Hughes, Ted
See also DAM MST, POET

Hughes, (James) Langston 1902-1967**CLC 1, 5, 10, 15, 35, 44, 108; BLC 2; DA; DAB; DAC; DAM DRAM, MST, MULT, POET; DC 3; PC 1; SSC 6; WLC**
See also AAYA 12; BW 1; CA 1-4R; 25-28R; CANR 1, 34; CDALB 1929-1941; CLR 17; DLB 4, 7, 48, 51, 86; JRDA; MAICYA; MTCW 1, 2; SATA 4, 33

Hughes, Richard (Arthur Warren) 1900-1976 **CLC 1, 11; DAM NOV**
See also CA 5-8R; 65-68; CANR 4; DLB 15, 161; MTCW 1; SATA 8; SATA-Obit 25

Hughes, Ted 1930-1998 **CLC 2, 4, 9, 14, 37, 119; DAB; DAC; PC 7**
See also Hughes, Edward James
See also CA 1-4R; 171; CANR 1, 33, 66; CLR 3; DLB 40, 161; MAICYA; MTCW 1, 2; SATA 49; SATA-Brief 27; SATA-Obit 107

Hugo, Richard F(ranklin) 1923-1982 **CLC 6, 18, 32; DAM POET**
See also CA 49-52; 108; CANR 3; DLB 5, 206

Hugo, Victor (Marie) 1802-1885**NCLC 3, 10, 21; DA; DAB; DAC; DAM DRAM, MST, NOV, POET; PC 17; WLC**
See also AAYA 28; DLB 119, 192; SATA 47

Huidobro, Vicente
See Huidobro Fernandez, Vicente Garcia

Huidobro Fernandez, Vicente Garcia 1893-1948   **TCLC 31**
See also CA 131; HW

Hulme, Keri 1947-   **CLC 39**
See also CA 125; CANR 69; INT 125

Hulme, T(homas) E(rnest) 1883-1917 **T C L C 21**
See also CA 117; DLB 19

Hume, David 1711-1776   **LC 7**
See also DLB 104

Humphrey, William 1924-1997   **CLC 45**
See also CA 77-80; 160; CANR 68; DLB 212

Humphreys, Emyr Owen 1919-   **CLC 47**
See also CA 5-8R; CANR 3, 24; DLB 15

Humphreys, Josephine 1945- **CLC 34, 57**
See also CA 121; 127; INT 127

Huneker, James Gibbons 1857-1921**TCLC 65**
See also DLB 71

Hungerford, Pixie
See Brinsmead, H(esba) F(ay)

Hunt, E(verette) Howard, (Jr.) 1918- **CLC 3**
See also AITN 1; CA 45-48; CANR 2, 47

Hunt, Kyle
See Creasey, John

Hunt, (James Henry) Leigh 1784-1859**NCLC 1, 70; DAM POET**
See also DLB 96, 110, 144

Hunt, Marsha 1946-   **CLC 70**
See also BW 2; CA 143

Hunt, Violet 1866(?)-1942   **TCLC 53**
See also DLB 162, 197

Hunter, E. Waldo

See also SATA 67; SATA-Brief 51

Jones, Thom 1945(?)- **CLC 81**
See also CA 157

Jong, Erica 1942- **CLC 4, 6, 8, 18, 83; DAM NOV, POP**
See also AITN 1; BEST 90:2; CA 73-76; CANR 26, 52, 75; DLB 2, 5, 28, 152; INT CANR-26; MTCW 1, 2

Jonson, Ben(jamin) 1572(?)-1637 **LC 6, 33; DA; DAB; DAC; DAM DRAM, MST, POET; DC 4; PC 17; WLC**
See also CDBLB Before 1660; DLB 62, 121

Jordan, June 1936- **CLC 5, 11, 23, 114; BLCS; DAM MULT, POET**
See also AAYA 2; BW 2; CA 33-36R; CANR 25, 70; CLR 10; DLB 38; MAICYA; MTCW 1; SATA 4

Jordan, Neil (Patrick) 1950- **CLC 110**
See also CA 124; 130; CANR 54; INT 130

Jordan, Pat(rick M.) 1941- **CLC 37**
See also CA 33-36R

Jorgensen, Ivar
See Ellison, Harlan (Jay)

Jorgenson, Ivar
See Silverberg, Robert

Josephus, Flavius c. 37-100 **CMLC 13**

Josipovici, Gabriel 1940- **CLC 6, 43**
See also CA 37-40R; CAAS 8; CANR 47; DLB 14

Joubert, Joseph 1754-1824 **NCLC 9**

Jouve, Pierre Jean 1887-1976 **CLC 47**
See also CA 65-68

Jovine, Francesco 1902-1950 **TCLC 79**

Joyce, James (Augustine Aloysius) 1882-1941 **TCLC 3, 8, 16, 35, 52; DA; DAB; DAC; DAM MST, NOV, POET; PC 22; SSC 3, 26; WLC**
See also CA 104; 126; CDBLB 1914-1945; DLB 10, 19, 36, 162; MTCW 1, 2

Jozsef, Attila 1905-1937 **TCLC 22**
See also CA 116

Juana Ines de la Cruz 1651(?)-1695 **LC 5; PC 24**

Judd, Cyril
See Kornbluth, C(yril) M.; Pohl, Frederik

Julian of Norwich 1342(?)-1416(?) **LC 6**
See also DLB 146

Junger, Sebastian 1962- **CLC 109**
See also AAYA 28; CA 165

Juniper, Alex
See Hospital, Janette Turner

Junius
See Luxemburg, Rosa

Just, Ward (Swift) 1935- **CLC 4, 27**
See also CA 25-28R; CANR 32; INT CANR-32

Justice, Donald (Rodney) 1925- **CLC 6, 19, 102; DAM POET**
See also CA 5-8R; CANR 26, 54, 74; DLBY 83; INT CANR-26; MTCW 2

Juvenal c. 60-c. 13 **CMLC 8**
See also Juvenalis, Decimus Junius
See also DLB 211

Juvenalis, Decimus Junius 55(?)-c. 127(?)
See Juvenal

Juvenis
See Bourne, Randolph S(illiman)

Kacew, Romain 1914-1980
See Gary, Romain
See also CA 108; 102

Kadare, Ismail 1936- **CLC 52**
See also CA 161

Kadohata, Cynthia **CLC 59**

See also CA 140

Kafka, Franz 1883-1924 **TCLC 2, 6, 13, 29, 47, 53; DA; DAB; DAC; DAM MST, NOV; SSC 5, 29; WLC**
See also CA 105; 126; DLB 81; MTCW 1, 2

Kahanovitsch, Pinkhes
See Der Nister

Kahn, Roger 1927- **CLC 30**
See also CA 25-28R; CANR 44, 69; DLB 171; SATA 37

Kain, Saul
See Sassoon, Siegfried (Lorraine)

Kaiser, Georg 1878-1945 **TCLC 9**
See also CA 106; DLB 124

Kaletski, Alexander 1946- **CLC 39**
See also CA 118; 143

Kalidasa fl. c. 400- **CMLC 9; PC 22**

Kallman, Chester (Simon) 1921-1975 **CLC 2**
See also CA 45-48; 53-56; CANR 3

Kaminsky, Melvin 1926-
See Brooks, Mel
See also CA 65-68; CANR 16

Kaminsky, Stuart M(elvin) 1934- **CLC 59**
See also CA 73-76; CANR 29, 53

Kandinsky, Wassily 1866-1944 **TCLC 92**
See also CA 118; 155

Kane, Francis
See Robbins, Harold

Kane, Paul
See Simon, Paul (Frederick)

Kane, Wilson
See Bloch, Robert (Albert)

Kanin, Garson 1912- **CLC 22**
See also AITN 1; CA 5-8R; CANR 7, 78; DLB 7

Kaniuk, Yoram 1930- **CLC 19**
See also CA 134

Kant, Immanuel 1724-1804 **NCLC 27, 67**
See also DLB 94

Kantor, MacKinlay 1904-1977 **CLC 7**
See also CA 61-64; 73-76; CANR 60, 63; DLB 9, 102; MTCW 2

Kaplan, David Michael 1946- **CLC 50**

Kaplan, James 1951- **CLC 59**
See also CA 135

Karageorge, Michael
See Anderson, Poul (William)

Karamzin, Nikolai Mikhailovich 1766-1826 **NCLC 3**
See also DLB 150

Karapanou, Margarita 1946- **CLC 13**
See also CA 101

Karinthy, Frigyes 1887-1938 **TCLC 47**
See also CA 170

Karl, Frederick R(obert) 1927- **CLC 34**
See also CA 5-8R; CANR 3, 44

Kastel, Warren
See Silverberg, Robert

Kataev, Evgeny Petrovich 1903-1942
See Petrov, Evgeny
See also CA 120

Kataphusin
See Ruskin, John

Katz, Steve 1935- **CLC 47**
See also CA 25-28R; CAAS 14, 64; CANR 12; DLBY 83

Kauffman, Janet 1945- **CLC 42**
See also CA 117; CANR 43; DLBY 86

Kaufman, Bob (Garnell) 1925-1986 **CLC 49**
See also BW 1; CA 41-44R; 118; CANR 22; DLB 16, 41

Kaufman, George S. 1889-1961 **CLC 38; DAM DRAM**

See also CA 108; 93-96; DLB 7; INT 108; MTCW 2

Kaufman, Sue **CLC 3, 8**
See also Barondess, Sue K(aufman)

Kavafis, Konstantinos Petrou 1863-1933
See Cavafy, C(onstantine) P(eter)
See also CA 104

Kavan, Anna 1901-1968 **CLC 5, 13, 82**
See also CA 5-8R; CANR 6, 57; MTCW 1

Kavanagh, Dan
See Barnes, Julian (Patrick)

Kavanagh, Julie 1952- **CLC 119**
See also CA 163

Kavanagh, Patrick (Joseph) 1904-1967 **C L C 22**
See also CA 123; 25-28R; DLB 15, 20; MTCW 1

Kawabata, Yasunari 1899-1972 **CLC 2, 5, 9, 18, 107; DAM MULT; SSC 17**
See also CA 93-96; 33-36R; DLB 180; MTCW 2

Kaye, M(ary) M(argaret) 1909- **CLC 28**
See also CA 89-92; CANR 24, 60; MTCW 1, 2; SATA 62

Kaye, Mollie
See Kaye, M(ary) M(argaret)

Kaye-Smith, Sheila 1887-1956 **TCLC 20**
See also CA 118; DLB 36

Kaymor, Patrice Maguilene
See Senghor, Leopold Sedar

Kazan, Elia 1909- **CLC 6, 16, 63**
See also CA 21-24R; CANR 32, 78

Kazantzakis, Nikos 1883(?)-1957 **TCLC 2, 5, 33**
See also CA 105; 132; MTCW 1, 2

Kazin, Alfred 1915- **CLC 34, 38, 119**
See also CA 1-4R; CAAS 7; CANR 1, 45; DLB 67

Keane, Mary Nesta (Skrine) 1904-1996
See Keane, Molly
See also CA 108; 114; 151

Keane, Molly **CLC 31**
See also Keane, Mary Nesta (Skrine)
See also INT 114

Keates, Jonathan 1946(?)- **CLC 34**
See also CA 163

Keaton, Buster 1895-1966 **CLC 20**

Keats, John 1795-1821 **NCLC 8, 73; DA; DAB; DAC; DAM MST, POET; PC 1; WLC**
See also CDBLB 1789-1832; DLB 96, 110

Keene, Donald 1922- **CLC 34**
See also CA 1-4R; CANR 5

Keillor, Garrison **CLC 40, 115**
See also Keillor, Gary (Edward)
See also AAYA 2; BEST 89:3; DLBY 87; SATA 58

Keillor, Gary (Edward) 1942-
See Keillor, Garrison
See also CA 111; 117; CANR 36, 59; DAM POP; MTCW 1, 2

Keith, Michael
See Hubbard, L(afayette) Ron(ald)

Keller, Gottfried 1819-1890 **NCLC 2; SSC 26**
See also DLB 129

Keller, Nora Okja **CLC 109**

Kellerman, Jonathan 1949- **CLC 44; DAM POP**
See also BEST 90:1; CA 106; CANR 29, 51; INT CANR-29

Kelley, William Melvin 1937- **CLC 22**
See also BW 1; CA 77-80; CANR 27; DLB 33

Kellogg, Marjorie 1922- **CLC 2**
See also CA 81-84

Kellow, Kathleen
See Hibbert, Eleanor Alice Burford
Kelly, M(ilton) T(erry) 1947-   CLC 55
See also CA 97-100; CAAS 22; CANR 19, 43
Kelman, James 1946-   CLC 58, 86
See also CA 148; DLB 194
Kemal, Yashar 1923-   CLC 14, 29
See also CA 89-92; CANR 44
Kemble, Fanny 1809-1893   NCLC 18
See also DLB 32
Kemelman, Harry 1908-1996   CLC 2
See also AITN 1; CA 9-12R; 155; CANR 6, 71; DLB 28
Kempe, Margery 1373(?)-1440(?)   LC 6
See also DLB 146
Kempis, Thomas a 1380-1471   LC 11
Kendall, Henry 1839-1882   NCLC 12
Keneally, Thomas (Michael) 1935- CLC 5, 8, 10, 14, 19, 27, 43, 117; DAM NOV
See also CA 85-88; CANR 10, 50, 74; MTCW 1, 2
Kennedy, Adrienne (Lita) 1931-CLC 66; BLC 2; DAM MULT; DC 5
See also BW 2; CA 103; CAAS 20; CABS 3; CANR 26, 53; DLB 38
Kennedy, John Pendleton 1795-1870NCLC 2
See also DLB 3
Kennedy, Joseph Charles 1929-
See Kennedy, X. J.
See also CA 1-4R; CANR 4, 30, 40; SATA 14, 86
Kennedy, William 1928- CLC 6, 28, 34, 53; DAM NOV
See also AAYA 1; CA 85-88; CANR 14, 31, 76; DLB 143; DLBY 85; INT CANR-31; MTCW 1, 2; SATA 57
Kennedy, X. J.   CLC 8, 42
See also Kennedy, Joseph Charles
See also CAAS 9; CLR 27; DLB 5; SAAS 22
Kenny, Maurice (Francis) 1929-   CLC 87; DAM MULT
See also CA 144; CAAS 22; DLB 175; NNAL
Kent, Kelvin
See Kuttner, Henry
Kenton, Maxwell
See Southern, Terry
Kenyon, Robert O.
See Kuttner, Henry
Kepler, Johannes 1571-1630   LC 45
Kerouac, Jack   CLC 1, 2, 3, 5, 14, 29, 61
See also Kerouac, Jean-Louis Lebris de
See also AAYA 25; CDALB 1941-1968; DLB 2, 16; DLBD 3; DLBY 95; MTCW 2
Kerouac, Jean-Louis Lebris de 1922-1969
See Kerouac, Jack
See also AITN 1; CA 5-8R; 25-28R; CANR 26, 54; DA; DAB; DAC; DAM MST, NOV, POET, POP; MTCW 1, 2; WLC
Kerr, Jean 1923-   CLC 22
See also CA 5-8R; CANR 7; INT CANR-7
Kerr, M. E.   CLC 12, 35
See also Meaker, Marijane (Agnes)
See also AAYA 2, 23; CLR 29; SAAS 1
Kerr, Robert   CLC 55
Kerrigan, (Thomas) Anthony 1918-CLC 4, 6
See also CA 49-52; CAAS 11; CANR 4
Kerry, Lois
See Duncan, Lois
Kesey, Ken (Elton) 1935- CLC 1, 3, 6, 11, 46, 64; DA; DAB; DAC; DAM MST, NOV, POP; WLC
See also AAYA 25; CA 1-4R; CANR 22, 38, 66; CDALB 1968-1988; DLB 2, 16, 206;

MTCW 1, 2; SATA 66
Kesselring, Joseph (Otto) 1902-1967CLC 45; DAM DRAM, MST
See also CA 150
Kessler, Jascha (Frederick) 1929-   CLC 4
See also CA 17-20R; CANR 8, 48
Kettelkamp, Larry (Dale) 1933-   CLC 12
See also CA 29-32R; CANR 16; SAAS 3; SATA 2
Key, Ellen 1849-1926   TCLC 65
Keyber, Conny
See Fielding, Henry
Keyes, Daniel 1927-CLC 80; DA; DAC; DAM MST, NOV
See also AAYA 23; CA 17-20R; CANR 10, 26, 54, 74; MTCW 2; SATA 37
Keynes, John Maynard 1883-1946 TCLC 64
See also CA 114; 162, 163; DLBD 10; MTCW 2
Khanshendel, Chiron
See Rose, Wendy
Khayyam, Omar 1048-1131CMLC 11; DAM POET; PC 8
Kherdian, David 1931-   CLC 6, 9
See also CA 21-24R; CAAS 2; CANR 39, 78; CLR 24; JRDA; MAICYA; SATA 16, 74
Khlebnikov, Velimir   TCLC 20
See also Khlebnikov, Viktor Vladimirovich
Khlebnikov, Viktor Vladimirovich 1885-1922
See Khlebnikov, Velimir
See also CA 117
Khodasevich, Vladislav (Felitsianovich) 1886-1939   TCLC 15
See also CA 115
Kielland, Alexander Lange 1849-1906 TCLC 5
See also CA 104
Kiely, Benedict 1919-   CLC 23, 43
See also CA 1-4R; CANR 2; DLB 15
Kienzle, William X(avier) 1928-   CLC 25; DAM POP
See also CA 93-96; CAAS 1; CANR 9, 31, 59; INT CANR-31; MTCW 1, 2
Kierkegaard, Soren 1813-1855   NCLC 34
Killens, John Oliver 1916-1987   CLC 10
See also BW 2; CA 77-80; 123; CAAS 2; CANR 26; DLB 33
Killigrew, Anne 1660-1685   LC 4
See also DLB 131
Kim
See Simenon, Georges (Jacques Christian)
Kincaid, Jamaica 1949- CLC 43, 68; BLC 2; DAM MULT, NOV
See also AAYA 13; BW 2; CA 125; CANR 47, 59; DLB 157; MTCW 2
King, Francis (Henry) 1923-CLC 8, 53; DAM NOV
See also CA 1-4R; CANR 1, 33; DLB 15, 139; MTCW 1
King, Kennedy
See Brown, George Douglas
King, Martin Luther, Jr. 1929-1968 CLC 83; BLC 2; DA; DAB; DAC; DAM MST, MULT; WLCS
See also BW 2; CA 25-28; CANR 27, 44; CAP 2; MTCW 1, 2; SATA 14
King, Stephen (Edwin) 1947-CLC 12, 26, 37, 61, 113; DAM NOV, POP; SSC 17
See also AAYA 1, 17; BEST 90:1; CA 61-64; CANR 1, 30, 52, 76; DLB 143; DLBY 80; JRDA; MTCW 1, 2; SATA 9, 55
King, Steve
See King, Stephen (Edwin)

King, Thomas 1943-   CLC 89; DAC; DAM MULT
See also CA 144; DLB 175; NNAL; SATA 96
Kingman, Lee   CLC 17
See also Natti, (Mary) Lee
See also SAAS 3; SATA 1, 67
Kingsley, Charles 1819-1875   NCLC 35
See also DLB 21, 32, 163, 190; YABC 2
Kingsley, Sidney 1906-1995   CLC 44
See also CA 85-88; 147; DLB 7
Kingsolver, Barbara 1955-CLC 55, 81; DAM POP
See also AAYA 15; CA 129; 134; CANR 60; DLB 206; INT 134; MTCW 2
Kingston, Maxine (Ting Ting) Hong 1940- CLC 12, 19, 58; DAM MULT, NOV; WLCS
See also AAYA 8; CA 69-72; CANR 13, 38, 74; DLB 173, 212; DLBY 80; INT CANR-13; MTCW 1, 2; SATA 53
Kinnell, Galway 1927- CLC 1, 2, 3, 5, 13, 29; PC 26
See also CA 9-12R; CANR 10, 34, 66; DLB 5; DLBY 87; INT CANR-34; MTCW 1, 2
Kinsella, Thomas 1928-   CLC 4, 19
See also CA 17-20R; CANR 15; DLB 27; MTCW 1, 2
Kinsella, W(illiam) P(atrick) 1935- CLC 27, 43; DAC; DAM NOV, POP
See also AAYA 7; CA 97-100; CAAS 7; CANR 21, 35, 66, 75; INT CANR-21; MTCW 1, 2
Kinsey, Alfred C(harles) 1894-1956TCLC 91
See also CA 115; 170; MTCW 2
Kipling, (Joseph) Rudyard 1865-1936 TCLC 8, 17; DA; DAB; DAC; DAM MST, POET; PC 3; SSC 5; WLC
See also CA 105; 120; CANR 33; CDBLB 1890-1914; CLR 39; DLB 19, 34, 141, 156; MAICYA; MTCW 1, 2; SATA 100; YABC 2
Kirkup, James 1918-   CLC 1
See also CA 1-4R; CAAS 4; CANR 2; DLB 27; SATA 12
Kirkwood, James 1930(?)-1989   CLC 9
See also AITN 2; CA 1-4R; 128; CANR 6, 40
Kirshner, Sidney
See Kingsley, Sidney
Kis, Danilo 1935-1989   CLC 57
See also CA 109; 118; 129; CANR 61; DLB 181; MTCW 1
Kivi, Aleksis 1834-1872   NCLC 30
Kizer, Carolyn (Ashley) 1925-CLC 15, 39, 80; DAM POET
See also CA 65-68; CAAS 5; CANR 24, 70; DLB 5, 169; MTCW 2
Klabund 1890-1928   TCLC 44
See also CA 162; DLB 66
Klappert, Peter 1942-   CLC 57
See also CA 33-36R; DLB 5
Klein, A(braham) M(oses) 1909-1972CLC 19; DAB; DAC; DAM MST
See also CA 101; 37-40R; DLB 68
Klein, Norma 1938-1989   CLC 30
See also AAYA 2; CA 41-44R; 128; CANR 15, 37; CLR 2, 19; INT CANR-15; JRDA; MAICYA; SAAS 1; SATA 7, 57
Klein, T(heodore) E(ibon) D(onald) 1947- CLC 34
See also CA 119; CANR 44, 75
Kleist, Heinrich von 1777-1811 NCLC 2, 37; DAM DRAM; SSC 22
See also DLB 90
Klima, Ivan 1931-   CLC 56; DAM NOV

See also CA 25-28R; CANR 17, 50

Klimentov, Andrei Platonovich 1899-1951
  See Platonov, Andrei
  See also CA 108

Klinger, Friedrich Maximilian von 1752-1831
  NCLC 1
  See also DLB 94

Klingsor the Magician
  See Hartmann, Sadakichi

Klopstock, Friedrich Gottlieb 1724-1803
  NCLC 11
  See also DLB 97

Knapp, Caroline 1959-   **CLC 99**
  See also CA 154

Knebel, Fletcher 1911-1993   **CLC 14**
  See also AITN 1; CA 1-4R; 140; CAAS 3;
  CANR 1, 36; SATA 36; SATA-Obit 75

Knickerbocker, Diedrich
  See Irving, Washington

Knight, Etheridge 1931-1991CLC 40; BLC 2;
  DAM POET; PC 14
  See also BW 1; CA 21-24R; 133; CANR 23;
  DLB 41; MTCW 2

Knight, Sarah Kemble 1666-1727   **LC 7**
  See also DLB 24, 200

Knister, Raymond 1899-1932   **TCLC 56**
  See also DLB 68

Knowles, John 1926-   **CLC 1, 4, 10, 26; DA;**
  DAC; DAM MST, NOV
  See also AAYA 10; CA 17-20R; CANR 40, 74,
  76; CDALB 1968-1988; DLB 6; MTCW 1,
  2; SATA 8, 89

Knox, Calvin M.
  See Silverberg, Robert

Knox, John c. 1505-1572   **LC 37**
  See also DLB 132

Knye, Cassandra
  See Disch, Thomas M(ichael)

Koch, C(hristopher) J(ohn) 1932-   **CLC 42**
  See also CA 127

Koch, Christopher
  See Koch, C(hristopher) J(ohn)

Koch, Kenneth 1925-   **CLC 5, 8, 44; DAM**
  POET
  See also CA 1-4R; CANR 6, 36, 57; DLB 5;
  INT CANR-36; MTCW 2; SATA 65

Kochanowski, Jan 1530-1584   **LC 10**

Kock, Charles Paul de 1794-1871 NCLC 16

Koda Shigeyuki 1867-1947
  See Rohan, Koda
  See also CA 121

Koestler, Arthur 1905-1983CLC 1, 3, 6, 8, 15,
  33
  See also CA 1-4R; 109; CANR 1, 33; CDBLB
  1945-1960; DLBY 83; MTCW 1, 2

Kogawa, Joy Nozomi 1935- **CLC 78; DAC;**
  DAM MST, MULT
  See also CA 101; CANR 19, 62; MTCW 2;
  SATA 99

Kohout, Pavel 1928-   **CLC 13**
  See also CA 45-48; CANR 3

Koizumi, Yakumo
  See Hearn, (Patricio) Lafcadio (Tessima Carlos)

Kolmar, Gertrud 1894-1943   **TCLC 40**
  See also CA 167

Komunyakaa, Yusef 1947-CLC 86, 94; BLCS
  See also CA 147; DLB 120

Konrad, George
  See Konrad, Gyoergy

Konrad, Gyoergy 1933-   **CLC 4, 10, 73**
  See also CA 85-88

Konwicki, Tadeusz 1926- CLC 8, 28, 54, 117
  See also CA 101; CAAS 9; CANR 39, 59;

MTCW 1

Koontz, Dean R(ay) 1945-   **CLC 78; DAM**
  NOV, POP
  See also AAYA 9; BEST 89:3, 90:2; CA 108;
  CANR 19, 36, 52; MTCW 1; SATA 92

Kopernik, Mikolaj
  See Copernicus, Nicolaus

Kopit, Arthur (Lee) 1937-CLC 1, 18, 33; DAM
  DRAM
  See also AITN 1; CA 81-84; CABS 3; DLB 7;
  MTCW 1

Kops, Bernard 1926-   **CLC 4**
  See also CA 5-8R; DLB 13

Kornbluth, C(yril) M. 1923-1958   **TCLC 8**
  See also CA 105; 160; DLB 8

Korolenko, V. G.
  See Korolenko, Vladimir Galaktionovich

Korolenko, Vladimir
  See Korolenko, Vladimir Galaktionovich

Korolenko, Vladimir G.
  See Korolenko, Vladimir Galaktionovich

Korolenko, Vladimir Galaktionovich 1853-
  1921   **TCLC 22**
  See also CA 121

Korzybski, Alfred (Habdank Skarbek) 1879-
  1950   **TCLC 61**
  See also CA 123; 160

Kosinski, Jerzy (Nikodem) 1933-1991CLC 1,
  2, 3, 6, 10, 15, 53, 70; DAM NOV
  See also CA 17-20R; 134; CANR 9, 46; DLB
  2; DLBY 82; MTCW 1, 2

Kostelanetz, Richard (Cory) 1940- **CLC 28**
  See also CA 13-16R; CAAS 8; CANR 38, 77

Kostrowitzki, Wilhelm Apollinaris de 1880-
  1918
  See Apollinaire, Guillaume
  See also CA 104

Kotlowitz, Robert 1924-   **CLC 4**
  See also CA 33-36R; CANR 36

Kotzebue, August (Friedrich Ferdinand) von
  1761-1819   **NCLC 25**
  See also DLB 94

Kotzwinkle, William 1938-   **CLC 5, 14, 35**
  See also CA 45-48; CANR 3, 44; CLR 6; DLB
  173; MAICYA; SATA 24, 70

Kowna, Stancy
  See Szymborska, Wislawa

Kozol, Jonathan 1936-   **CLC 17**
  See also CA 61-64; CANR 16, 45

Kozoll, Michael 1940(?)-   **CLC 35**

Kramer, Kathryn 19(?)-   **CLC 34**

Kramer, Larry 1935-CLC 42; DAM POP; DC
  8
  See also CA 124; 126; CANR 60

Krasicki, Ignacy 1735-1801   **NCLC 8**

Krasinski, Zygmunt 1812-1859   **NCLC 4**

Kraus, Karl 1874-1936   **TCLC 5**
  See also CA 104; DLB 118

Kreve (Mickevicius), Vincas 1882-1954TCLC
  27
  See also CA 170

Kristeva, Julia 1941-   **CLC 77**
  See also CA 154

Kristofferson, Kris 1936-   **CLC 26**
  See also CA 104

Krizanc, John 1956-   **CLC 57**

Krleza, Miroslav 1893-1981   **CLC 8, 114**
  See also CA 97-100; 105; CANR 50; DLB 147

Kroetsch, Robert 1927-CLC 5, 23, 57; DAC;
  DAM POET
  See also CA 17-20R; CANR 8, 38; DLB 53;
  MTCW 1

Kroetz, Franz

See Kroetz, Franz Xaver

Kroetz, Franz Xaver 1946-   **CLC 41**
  See also CA 130

Kroker, Arthur (W.) 1945-   **CLC 77**
  See also CA 161

Kropotkin, Peter (Aleksieevich) 1842-1921
  TCLC 36
  See also CA 119

Krotkov, Yuri 1917-   **CLC 19**
  See also CA 102

Krumb
  See Crumb, R(obert)

Krumgold, Joseph (Quincy) 1908-1980 CLC
  12
  See also CA 9-12R; 101; CANR 7; MAICYA;
  SATA 1, 48; SATA-Obit 23

Krumwitz
  See Crumb, R(obert)

Krutch, Joseph Wood 1893-1970   **CLC 24**
  See also CA 1-4R; 25-28R; CANR 4; DLB 63,
  206

Krutzch, Gus
  See Eliot, T(homas) S(tearns)

Krylov, Ivan Andreevich 1768(?)-1844NCLC
  1
  See also DLB 150

Kubin, Alfred (Leopold Isidor) 1877-1959
  TCLC 23
  See also CA 112; 149; DLB 81

Kubrick, Stanley 1928-   **CLC 16**
  See also AAYA 30; CA 81-84; CANR 33; DLB
  26

Kumin, Maxine (Winokur) 1925- CLC 5, 13,
  28; DAM POET; PC 15
  See also AITN 2; CA 1-4R; CAAS 8; CANR 1,
  21, 69; DLB 5; MTCW 1, 2; SATA 12

Kundera, Milan 1929- CLC 4, 9, 19, 32, 68,
  115; DAM NOV; SSC 24
  See also AAYA 2; CA 85-88; CANR 19, 52,
  74; MTCW 1, 2

Kunene, Mazisi (Raymond) 1930- **CLC 85**
  See also BW 1; CA 125; DLB 117

Kunitz, Stanley (Jasspon) 1905-CLC 6, 11, 14;
  PC 19
  See also CA 41-44R; CANR 26, 57; DLB 48;
  INT CANR-26; MTCW 1, 2

Kunze, Reiner 1933-   **CLC 10**
  See also CA 93-96; DLB 75

Kuprin, Aleksandr Ivanovich 1870-1938
  TCLC 5
  See also CA 104

Kureishi, Hanif 1954(?)-   **CLC 64**
  See also CA 139; DLB 194

Kurosawa, Akira 1910-1998   **CLC 16, 119;**
  DAM MULT
  See also AAYA 11; CA 101; 170; CANR 46

Kushner, Tony 1957(?)- **CLC 81; DAM**
  DRAM; DC 10
  See also CA 144; CANR 74; MTCW 2

Kuttner, Henry 1915-1958   **TCLC 10**
  See also Vance, Jack
  See also CA 107; 157; DLB 8

Kuzma, Greg 1944-   **CLC 7**
  See also CA 33-36R; CANR 70

Kuzmin, Mikhail 1872(?)-1936   **TCLC 40**
  See also CA 170

Kyd, Thomas 1558-1594LC 22; DAM DRAM;
  DC 3
  See also DLB 62

Kyprianos, Iossif
  See Samarakis, Antonis

La Bruyere, Jean de 1645-1696   **LC 17**

Lacan, Jacques (Marie Emile) 1901-1981

88; MTCW 1, 2

Lazarus, Emma 1849-1887   **NCLC 8**

Lazarus, Felix
See Cable, George Washington

Lazarus, Henry
See Slavitt, David R(ytman)

Lea, Joan
See Neufeld, John (Arthur)

Leacock, Stephen (Butler) 1869-1944**TCLC 2;**
    DAC; DAM MST
See also CA 104; 141; DLB 92; MTCW 2

Lear, Edward 1812-1888   **NCLC 3**
See also CLR 1; DLB 32, 163, 166; MAICYA;
    SATA 18, 100

Lear, Norman (Milton) 1922-   **CLC 12**
See also CA 73-76

Leautaud, Paul 1872-1956   **TCLC 83**
See also DLB 65

Leavis, F(rank) R(aymond) 1895-1978 **C L C**
    24
See also CA 21-24R; 77-80; CANR 44; MTCW
    1, 2

Leavitt, David 1961-   **CLC 34; DAM POP**
See also CA 116; 122; CANR 50, 62; DLB 130;
    INT 122; MTCW 2

Leblanc, Maurice (Marie Emile) 1864-1941
    TCLC 49
See also CA 110

Lebowitz, Fran(ces Ann) 1951(?)-**CLC 11, 36**
See also CA 81-84; CANR 14, 60, 70; INT
    CANR-14; MTCW 1

Lebrecht, Peter
See Tieck, (Johann) Ludwig

le Carre, John   **CLC 3, 5, 9, 15, 28**
See also Cornwell, David (John Moore)
See also BEST 89:4; CDBLB 1960 to Present;
    DLB 87; MTCW 2

Le Clezio, J(ean) M(arie) G(ustave) 1940-
    CLC 31
See also CA 116; 128; DLB 83

Leconte de Lisle, Charles-Marie-Rene 1818-
    1894   **NCLC 29**

Le Coq, Monsieur
See Simenon, Georges (Jacques Christian)

Leduc, Violette 1907-1972   **CLC 22**
See also CA 13-14; 33-36R; CANR 69; CAP 1

Ledwidge, Francis 1887(?)-1917   **TCLC 23**
See also CA 123; DLB 20

Lee, Andrea 1953-   **CLC 36; BLC 2; DAM**
    MULT
See also BW 1; CA 125

Lee, Andrew
See Auchincloss, Louis (Stanton)

Lee, Chang-rae 1965-   **CLC 91**
See also CA 148

Lee, Don L.   **CLC 2**
See also Madhubuti, Haki R.

Lee, George W(ashington) 1894-1976**CLC 52;**
    BLC 2; DAM MULT
See also BW 1; CA 125; DLB 51

Lee, (Nelle) Harper 1926- **CLC 12, 60; DA;**
    DAB; DAC; DAM MST, NOV; WLC
See also AAYA 13; CA 13-16R; CANR 51;
    CDALB 1941-1968; DLB 6; MTCW 1, 2;
    SATA 11

Lee, Helen Elaine 1959(?)-   **CLC 86**
See also CA 148

Lee, Julian
See Latham, Jean Lee

Lee, Larry
See Lee, Lawrence

Lee, Laurie 1914-1997 **CLC 90; DAB; DAM**
    POP

See also CA 77-80; 158; CANR 33, 73; DLB
    27; MTCW 1

Lee, Lawrence 1941-1990   **CLC 34**
See also CA 131; CANR 43

Lee, Li-Young 1957-   **PC 24**
See also CA 153; DLB 165

Lee, Manfred B(ennington) 1905-1971 **C L C**
    11
See also Queen, Ellery
See also CA 1-4R; 29-32R; CANR 2; DLB 137

Lee, Shelton Jackson 1957(?)-   **CLC 105;**
    BLCS; DAM MULT
See also Lee, Spike
See also BW 2; CA 125; CANR 42

Lee, Spike
See Lee, Shelton Jackson
See also AAYA 4, 29

Lee, Stan 1922-   **CLC 17**
See also AAYA 5; CA 108; 111; INT 111

Lee, Tanith 1947-   **CLC 46**
See also AAYA 15; CA 37-40R; CANR 53;
    SATA 8, 88

Lee, Vernon   **TCLC 5; SSC 33**
See also Paget, Violet
See also DLB 57, 153, 156, 174, 178

Lee, William
See Burroughs, William S(eward)

Lee, Willy
See Burroughs, William S(eward)

Lee-Hamilton, Eugene (Jacob) 1845-1907
    TCLC 22
See also CA 117

Leet, Judith 1935-   **CLC 11**

Le Fanu, Joseph Sheridan 1814-1873**NCLC 9,**
    58; DAM POP; SSC 14
See also DLB 21, 70, 159, 178

Leffland, Ella 1931-   **CLC 19**
See also CA 29-32R; CANR 35, 78; DLBY 84;
    INT CANR-35; SATA 65

Leger, Alexis
See Leger, (Marie-Rene Auguste) Alexis Saint-
    Leger

Leger, (Marie-Rene Auguste) Alexis Saint-
    Leger 1887-1975 **CLC 4, 11, 46; DAM**
    POET; PC 23
See also CA 13-16R; 61-64; CANR 43; MTCW
    1

Leger, Saintleger
See Leger, (Marie-Rene Auguste) Alexis Saint-
    Leger

Le Guin, Ursula K(roeber) 1929- **CLC 8, 13,**
    22, 45, 71; DAB; DAC; DAM MST, POP;
    SSC 12
See also AAYA 9, 27; AITN 1; CA 21-24R;
    CANR 9, 32, 52, 74; CDALB 1968-1988;
    CLR 3, 28; DLB 8, 52; INT CANR-32;
    JRDA; MAICYA; MTCW 1, 2; SATA 4, 52,
    99

Lehmann, Rosamond (Nina) 1901-1990**CLC 5**
See also CA 77-80; 131; CANR 8, 73; DLB
    15; MTCW 2

Leiber, Fritz (Reuter, Jr.) 1910-1992**CLC 25**
See also CA 45-48; 139; CANR 2, 40; DLB 8;
    MTCW 1, 2; SATA 45; SATA-Obit 73

Leibniz, Gottfried Wilhelm von 1646-1716**LC**
    35
See also DLB 168

Leimbach, Martha 1963-
See Leimbach, Marti
See also CA 130

Leimbach, Marti   **CLC 65**
See also Leimbach, Martha

Leino, Eino   **TCLC 24**

See also Loennbohm, Armas Eino Leopold

Leiris, Michel (Julien) 1901-1990   **CLC 61**
See also CA 119; 128; 132

Leithauser, Brad 1953-   **CLC 27**
See also CA 107; CANR 27; DLB 120

Lelchuk, Alan 1938-   **CLC 5**
See also CA 45-48; CAAS 20; CANR 1, 70

Lem, Stanislaw 1921-   **CLC 8, 15, 40**
See also CA 105; CAAS 1; CANR 32; MTCW
    1

Lemann, Nancy 1956-   **CLC 39**
See also CA 118; 136

Lemonnier, (Antoine Louis) Camille 1844-1913
    TCLC 22
See also CA 121

Lenau, Nikolaus 1802-1850   **NCLC 16**

L'Engle, Madeleine (Camp Franklin) 1918-
    CLC 12; DAM POP
See also AAYA 28; AITN 2; CA 1-4R; CANR
    3, 21, 39, 66; CLR 1, 14; DLB 52; JRDA;
    MAICYA; MTCW 1, 2; SAAS 15; SATA 1,
    27, 75

Lengyel, Jozsef 1896-1975   **CLC 7**
See also CA 85-88; 57-60; CANR 71

Lenin 1870-1924
See Lenin, V. I.
See also CA 121; 168

Lenin, V. I.   **TCLC 67**
See also Lenin

Lennon, John (Ono) 1940-1980 **CLC 12, 35**
See also CA 102

Lennox, Charlotte Ramsay 1729(?)-1804
    NCLC 23
See also DLB 39

Lentricchia, Frank (Jr.) 1940-   **CLC 34**
See also CA 25-28R; CANR 19

Lenz, Siegfried 1926-   **CLC 27; SSC 33**
See also CA 89-92; DLB 75

Leonard, Elmore (John, Jr.) 1925- **CLC 28,**
    34, 71; DAM POP
See also AAYA 22; AITN 1; BEST 89:1, 90:4;
    CA 81-84; CANR 12, 28, 53, 76; DLB 173;
    INT CANR-28; MTCW 1, 2

Leonard, Hugh   **CLC 19**
See also Byrne, John Keyes
See also DLB 13

Leonov, Leonid (Maximovich) 1899-1994
    CLC 92; DAM NOV
See also CA 129; CANR 74, 76; MTCW 1, 2

Leopardi, (Conte) Giacomo 1798-1837**N C L C**
    22

Le Reveler
See Artaud, Antonin (Marie Joseph)

Lerman, Eleanor 1952-   **CLC 9**
See also CA 85-88; CANR 69

Lerman, Rhoda 1936-   **CLC 56**
See also CA 49-52; CANR 70

Lermontov, Mikhail Yuryevich 1814-1841
    NCLC 47; PC 18
See also DLB 205

Leroux, Gaston 1868-1927   **TCLC 25**
See also CA 108; 136; CANR 69; SATA 65

Lesage, Alain-Rene 1668-1747   **LC 2, 28**

Leskov, Nikolai (Semyonovich) 1831-1895
    NCLC 25; SSC 34

Lessing, Doris (May) 1919-**CLC 1, 2, 3, 6, 10,**
    15, 22, 40, 94; DA; DAB; DAC; DAM
    MST, NOV; SSC 6; WLCS
See also CA 9-12R; CAAS 14; CANR 33, 54,
    76; CDBLB 1960 to Present; DLB 15, 139;
    DLBY 85; MTCW 1, 2

Lessing, Gotthold Ephraim 1729-1781 **LC 8**
See also DLB 97

See Leino, Eino
See also CA 123
Loewinsohn, Ron(ald William) 1937-**CLC 52**
See also CA 25-28R; CANR 71
Logan, Jake
See Smith, Martin Cruz
Logan, John (Burton) 1923-1987   **CLC 5**
See also CA 77-80; 124; CANR 45; DLB 5
Lo Kuan-chung 1330(?)-1400(?)   **LC 12**
Lombard, Nap
See Johnson, Pamela Hansford
London, Jack   **TCLC 9, 15, 39; SSC 4; WLC**
See also London, John Griffith
See also AAYA 13; AITN 2; CDALB 1865-
1917; DLB 8, 12, 78, 212; SATA 18
London, John Griffith 1876-1916
See London, Jack
See also CA 110; 119; CANR 73; DA; DAB;
DAC; DAM MST, NOV; JRDA; MAICYA;
MTCW 1, 2
Long, Emmett
See Leonard, Elmore (John, Jr.)
Longbaugh, Harry
See Goldman, William (W.)
Longfellow, Henry Wadsworth 1807-1882
**NCLC 2, 45; DA; DAB; DAC; DAM MST,
POET; WLCS**
See also CDALB 1640-1865; DLB 1, 59; SATA
19
Longinus c. 1st cent. -   **CMLC 27**
See also DLB 176
Longley, Michael 1939-   **CLC 29**
See also CA 102; DLB 40
Longus fl. c. 2nd cent. -   **CMLC 7**
Longway, A. Hugh
See Lang, Andrew
Lonnrot, Elias 1802-1884   **NCLC 53**
Lopate, Phillip 1943-   **CLC 29**
See also CA 97-100; DLBY 80; INT 97-100
Lopez Portillo (y Pacheco), Jose 1920-**CLC 46**
See also CA 129; HW
Lopez y Fuentes, Gregorio 1897(?)-1966**C L C
32**
See also CA 131; HW
Lorca, Federico Garcia
See Garcia Lorca, Federico
Lord, Bette Bao 1938-   **CLC 23**
See also BEST 90:3; CA 107; CANR 41; INT
107; SATA 58
Lord Auch
See Bataille, Georges
Lord Byron
See Byron, George Gordon (Noel)
Lorde, Audre (Geraldine) 1934-1992**CLC 18,
71; BLC 2; DAM MULT, POET; PC 12**
See also BW 1; CA 25-28R; 142; CANR 16,
26, 46; DLB 41; MTCW 1, 2
Lord Houghton
See Milnes, Richard Monckton
Lord Jeffrey
See Jeffrey, Francis
Lorenzini, Carlo 1826-1890
See Collodi, Carlo
See also MAICYA; SATA 29, 100
Lorenzo, Heberto Padilla
See Padilla (Lorenzo), Heberto
Loris
See Hofmannsthal, Hugo von
Loti, Pierre   **TCLC 11**
See also Viaud, (Louis Marie) Julien
See also DLB 123
Louie, David Wong 1954-   **CLC 70**
See also CA 139

Louis, Father M.
See Merton, Thomas
Lovecraft, H(oward) P(hillips) 1890-1937
TCLC 4, 22; DAM POP; SSC 3
See also AAYA 14; CA 104; 133; MTCW 1, 2
Lovelace, Earl 1935-   **CLC 51**
See also BW 2; CA 77-80; CANR 41, 72; DLB
125; MTCW 1
Lovelace, Richard 1618-1657   **LC 24**
See also DLB 131
Lowell, Amy 1874-1925   **TCLC 1, 8; DAM
POET; PC 13**
See also CA 104; 151; DLB 54, 140; MTCW 2
Lowell, James Russell 1819-1891   **NCLC 2**
See also CDALB 1640-1865; DLB 1, 11, 64,
79, 189
Lowell, Robert (Traill Spence, Jr.) 1917-1977
**CLC 1, 2, 3, 4, 5, 8, 9, 11, 15, 37; DA; DAB;
DAC; DAM MST, NOV; PC 3; WLC**
See also CA 9-12R; 73-76; CABS 2; CANR
26, 60; DLB 5, 169; MTCW 1, 2
Lowenthal, Michael (Francis) 1969-**CLC 119**
See also CA 150
Lowndes, Marie Adelaide (Belloc) 1868-1947
TCLC 12
See also CA 107; DLB 70
Lowry, (Clarence) Malcolm 1909-1957**TCLC
6, 40; SSC 31**
See also CA 105; 131; CANR 62; CDBLB
1945-1960; DLB 15; MTCW 1, 2
Lowry, Mina Gertrude 1882-1966
See Loy, Mina
See also CA 113
Loxsmith, John
See Brunner, John (Kilian Houston)
Loy, Mina   **CLC 28; DAM POET; PC 16**
See also Lowry, Mina Gertrude
See also DLB 4, 54
Loyson-Bridet
See Schwob, Marcel (Mayer Andre)
Lucan 39-65   **CMLC 33**
See also DLB 211
Lucas, Craig 1951-   **CLC 64**
See also CA 137; CANR 71
Lucas, E(dward) V(errall) 1868-1938 **T C L C
73**
See also DLB 98, 149, 153; SATA 20
Lucas, George 1944-   **CLC 16**
See also AAYA 1, 23; CA 77-80; CANR 30;
SATA 56
Lucas, Hans
See Godard, Jean-Luc
Lucas, Victoria
See Plath, Sylvia
Lucian c. 120-c. 180   **CMLC 32**
See also DLB 176
Ludlam, Charles 1943-1987   **CLC 46, 50**
See also CA 85-88; 122; CANR 72
Ludlum, Robert 1927-   **CLC 22, 43; DAM
NOV, POP**
See also AAYA 10; BEST 89:1, 90:3; CA 33-
36R; CANR 25, 41, 68; DLBY 82; MTCW
1, 2
Ludwig, Ken   **CLC 60**
Ludwig, Otto 1813-1865   **NCLC 4**
See also DLB 129
Lugones, Leopoldo 1874-1938   **TCLC 15**
See also CA 116; 131; HW
Lu Hsun 1881-1936   **TCLC 3; SSC 20**
See also Shu-Jen, Chou
Lukacs, George   **CLC 24**
See also Lukacs, Gyorgy (Szegeny von)
Lukacs, Gyorgy (Szegeny von) 1885-1971

See Lukacs, George
See also CA 101; 29-32R; CANR 62; MTCW
2
Luke, Peter (Ambrose Cyprian) 1919-1995
CLC 38
See also CA 81-84; 147; CANR 72; DLB 13
Lunar, Dennis
See Mungo, Raymond
Lurie, Alison 1926-   **CLC 4, 5, 18, 39**
See also CA 1-4R; CANR 2, 17, 50; DLB 2;
MTCW 1; SATA 46
Lustig, Arnost 1926-   **CLC 56**
See also AAYA 3; CA 69-72; CANR 47; SATA
56
Luther, Martin 1483-1546   **LC 9, 37**
See also DLB 179
Luxemburg, Rosa 1870(?)-1919   **TCLC 63**
See also CA 118
Luzi, Mario 1914-   **CLC 13**
See also CA 61-64; CANR 9, 70; DLB 128
Lyly, John 1554(?)-1606**LC 41; DAM DRAM;
DC 7**
See also DLB 62, 167
L'Ymagier
See Gourmont, Remy (-Marie-Charles) de
Lynch, B. Suarez
See Bioy Casares, Adolfo; Borges, Jorge Luis
Lynch, David (K.) 1946-   **CLC 66**
See also CA 124; 129
Lynch, James
See Andreyev, Leonid (Nikolaevich)
Lynch Davis, B.
See Bioy Casares, Adolfo; Borges, Jorge Luis
Lyndsay, Sir David 1490-1555   **LC 20**
Lynn, Kenneth S(chuyler) 1923-   **CLC 50**
See also CA 1-4R; CANR 3, 27, 65
Lynx
See West, Rebecca
Lyons, Marcus
See Blish, James (Benjamin)
Lyre, Pinchbeck
See Sassoon, Siegfried (Lorraine)
Lytle, Andrew (Nelson) 1902-1995   **CLC 22**
See also CA 9-12R; 150; CANR 70; DLB 6;
DLBY 95
Lyttelton, George 1709-1773   **LC 10**
Maas, Peter 1929-   **CLC 29**
See also CA 93-96; INT 93-96; MTCW 2
Macaulay, Rose 1881-1958   **TCLC 7, 44**
See also CA 104; DLB 36
Macaulay, Thomas Babington 1800-1859
NCLC 42
See also CDBLB 1832-1890; DLB 32, 55
MacBeth, George (Mann) 1932-1992**CLC 2, 5,
9**
See also CA 25-28R; 136; CANR 61, 66; DLB
40; MTCW 1; SATA 4; SATA-Obit 70
MacCaig, Norman (Alexander) 1910-**CLC 36;
DAB; DAM POET**
See also CA 9-12R; CANR 3, 34; DLB 27
MacCarthy, Sir(Charles Otto) Desmond 1877-
1952   **TCLC 36**
See also CA 167
MacDiarmid, HughCLC 2, 4, 11, 19, 63; PC 9
See also Grieve, C(hristopher) M(urray)
See also CDBLB 1945-1960; DLB 20
MacDonald, Anson
See Heinlein, Robert A(nson)
Macdonald, Cynthia 1928-   **CLC 13, 19**
See also CA 49-52; CANR 4, 44; DLB 105
MacDonald, George 1824-1905   **TCLC 9**
See also CA 106; 137; DLB 18, 163, 178;
MAICYA; SATA 33, 100

Macdonald, John
  See Millar, Kenneth
MacDonald, John D(ann) 1916-1986 **CLC 3,**
  27, 44; DAM NOV, POP
  See also CA 1-4R; 121; CANR 1, 19, 60; DLB
  8; DLBY 86; MTCW 1, 2
Macdonald, John Ross
  See Millar, Kenneth
Macdonald, Ross   **CLC 1, 2, 3, 14, 34, 41**
  See also Millar, Kenneth
  See also DLBD 6
MacDougal, John
  See Blish, James (Benjamin)
MacEwen, Gwendolyn (Margaret) 1941-1987
  CLC 13, 55
  See also CA 9-12R; 124; CANR 7, 22; DLB
  53; SATA 50; SATA-Obit 55
Macha, Karel Hynek 1810-1846   **NCLC 46**
Machado (y Ruiz), Antonio 1875-1939 **T C L C**
  3
  See also CA 104; DLB 108
Machado de Assis, Joaquim Maria 1839-1908
  TCLC 10; BLC 2; SSC 24
  See also CA 107; 153
Machen, Arthur   **TCLC 4; SSC 20**
  See also Jones, Arthur Llewellyn
  See also DLB 36, 156, 178
Machiavelli, Niccolo 1469-1527 **LC 8, 36; DA;**
  DAB; DAC; DAM MST; WLCS
MacInnes, Colin 1914-1976   **CLC 4, 23**
  See also CA 69-72; 65-68; CANR 21; DLB 14;
  MTCW 1, 2
MacInnes, Helen (Clark) 1907-1985 **CLC 27,**
  39; DAM POP
  See also CA 1-4R; 117; CANR 1, 28, 58; DLB
  87; MTCW 1, 2; SATA 22; SATA-Obit 44
Mackay, Mary 1855-1924
  See Corelli, Marie
  See also CA 118
Mackenzie, Compton (Edward Montague)
  1883-1972   **CLC 18**
  See also CA 21-22; 37-40R; CAP 2; DLB 34,
  100
Mackenzie, Henry 1745-1831   **NCLC 41**
  See also DLB 39
Mackintosh, Elizabeth 1896(?)-1952
  See Tey, Josephine
  See also CA 110
MacLaren, James
  See Grieve, C(hristopher) M(urray)
Mac Laverty, Bernard 1942-   **CLC 31**
  See also CA 116; 118; CANR 43; INT 118
MacLean, Alistair (Stuart) 1922(?)-1987 **C L C**
  3, 13, 50, 63; DAM POP
  See also CA 57-60; 121; CANR 28, 61; MTCW
  1; SATA 23; SATA-Obit 50
Maclean, Norman (Fitzroy) 1902-1990 **C L C**
  78; DAM POP; SSC 13
  See also CA 102; 132; CANR 49; DLB 206
MacLeish, Archibald 1892-1982 **CLC 3, 8, 14,**
  68; DAM POET
  See also CA 9-12R; 106; CANR 33, 63; DLB
  4, 7, 45; DLBY 82; MTCW 1, 2
MacLennan, (John) Hugh 1907-1990 **CLC 2,**
  14, 92; DAC; DAM MST
  See also CA 5-8R; 142; CANR 33; DLB 68;
  MTCW 1, 2
MacLeod, Alistair 1936- **CLC 56; DAC; DAM**
  MST
  See also CA 123; DLB 60; MTCW 2
Macleod, Fiona
  See Sharp, William
MacNeice, (Frederick) Louis 1907-1963 **C L C**

1, 4, 10, 53; DAB; DAM POET
  See also CA 85-88; CANR 61; DLB 10, 20;
  MTCW 1, 2
MacNeill, Dand
  See Fraser, George MacDonald
Macpherson, James 1736-1796   **LC 29**
  See also Ossian
  See also DLB 109
Macpherson, (Jean) Jay 1931-   **CLC 14**
  See also CA 5-8R; DLB 53
MacShane, Frank 1927-   **CLC 39**
  See also CA 9-12R; CANR 3, 33; DLB 111
Macumber, Mari
  See Sandoz, Mari(e Susette)
Madach, Imre 1823-1864   **NCLC 19**
Madden, (Jerry) David 1933-   **CLC 5, 15**
  See also CA 1-4R; CAAS 3; CANR 4, 45; DLB
  6; MTCW 1
Maddern, Al(an)
  See Ellison, Harlan (Jay)
Madhubuti, Haki R. 1942- **CLC 6, 73; BLC 2;**
  DAM MULT, POET; PC 5
  See also Lee, Don L.
  See also BW 2; CA 73-76; CANR 24, 51, 73;
  DLB 5, 41; DLBD 8; MTCW 2
Maepenn, Hugh
  See Kuttner, Henry
Maepenn, K. H.
  See Kuttner, Henry
Maeterlinck, Maurice 1862-1949   **TCLC 3;**
  DAM DRAM
  See also CA 104; 136; DLB 192; SATA 66
Maginn, William 1794-1842   **NCLC 8**
  See also DLB 110, 159
Mahapatra, Jayanta 1928-   **CLC 33; DAM**
  MULT
  See also CA 73-76; CAAS 9; CANR 15, 33, 66
Mahfouz, Naguib (Abdel Aziz Al-Sabilgi)
  1911(?)-
  See Mahfuz, Najib
  See also BEST 89:2; CA 128; CANR 55; DAM
  NOV; MTCW 1, 2
Mahfuz, Najib   **CLC 52, 55**
  See also Mahfouz, Naguib (Abdel Aziz Al-
  Sabilgi)
  See also DLBY 88
Mahon, Derek 1941-   **CLC 27**
  See also CA 113; 128; DLB 40
Mailer, Norman 1923- **CLC 1, 2, 3, 4, 5, 8, 11,**
  14, 28, 39, 74, 111; DA; DAB; DAC; DAM
  MST, NOV, POP
  See also AITN 2; CA 9-12R; CABS 1; CANR
  28, 74, 77; CDALB 1968-1988; DLB 2, 16,
  28, 185; DLBD 3; DLBY 80, 83; MTCW 1,
  2
Maillet, Antonine 1929- **CLC 54, 118; DAC**
  See also CA 115; 120; CANR 46, 74, 77; DLB
  60; INT 120; MTCW 2
Mais, Roger 1905-1955   **TCLC 8**
  See also BW 1; CA 105; 124; DLB 125; MTCW
  1
Maistre, Joseph de 1753-1821   **NCLC 37**
Maitland, Frederic 1850-1906   **TCLC 65**
Maitland, Sara (Louise) 1950-   **CLC 49**
  See also CA 69-72; CANR 13, 59
Major, Clarence 1936- **CLC 3, 19, 48; BLC 2;**
  DAM MULT
  See also BW 2; CA 21-24R; CAAS 6; CANR
  13, 25, 53; DLB 33
Major, Kevin (Gerald) 1949- **CLC 26; DAC**
  See also AAYA 16; CA 97-100; CANR 21, 38;
  CLR 11; DLB 60; INT CANR-21; JRDA;
  MAICYA; SATA 32, 82

Maki, James
  See Ozu, Yasujiro
Malabaila, Damiano
  See Levi, Primo
Malamud, Bernard 1914-1986 **CLC 1, 2, 3, 5,**
  8, 9, 11, 18, 27, 44, 78, 85; DA; DAB; DAC;
  DAM MST, NOV, POP; SSC 15; WLC
  See also AAYA 16; CA 5-8R; 118; CABS 1;
  CANR 28, 62; CDALB 1941-1968; DLB 2,
  28, 152; DLBY 80, 86; MTCW 1, 2
Malan, Herman
  See Bosman, Herman Charles; Bosman,
  Herman Charles
Malaparte, Curzio 1898-1957   **TCLC 52**
Malcolm, Dan
  See Silverberg, Robert
Malcolm X   **CLC 82, 117; BLC 2; WLCS**
  See also Little, Malcolm
Malherbe, Francois de 1555-1628   **LC 5**
Mallarme, Stephane 1842-1898 **NCLC 4, 41;**
  DAM POET; PC 4
Mallet-Joris, Francoise 1930-   **CLC 11**
  See also CA 65-68; CANR 17; DLB 83
Malley, Ern
  See McAuley, James Phillip
Mallowan, Agatha Christie
  See Christie, Agatha (Mary Clarissa)
Maloff, Saul 1922-   **CLC 5**
  See also CA 33-36R
Malone, Louis
  See MacNeice, (Frederick) Louis
Malone, Michael (Christopher) 1942- **CLC 43**
  See also CA 77-80; CANR 14, 32, 57
Malory, (Sir) Thomas 1410(?)-1471(?) **LC 11;**
  DA; DAB; DAC; DAM MST; WLCS
  See also CDBLB Before 1660; DLB 146; SATA
  59; SATA-Brief 33
Malouf, (George Joseph) David 1934- **CLC 28,**
  86
  See also CA 124; CANR 50, 76; MTCW 2
Malraux, (Georges-)Andre 1901-1976 **CLC 1,**
  4, 9, 13, 15, 57; DAM NOV
  See also CA 21-22; 69-72; CANR 34, 58; CAP
  2; DLB 72; MTCW 1, 2
Malzberg, Barry N(athaniel) 1939- **CLC 7**
  See also CA 61-64; CAAS 4; CANR 16; DLB
  8
Mamet, David (Alan) 1947- **CLC 9, 15, 34, 46,**
  91; DAM DRAM; DC 4
  See also AAYA 3; CA 81-84; CABS 3; CANR
  15, 41, 67, 72; DLB 7; MTCW 1, 2
Mamoulian, Rouben (Zachary) 1897-1987
  CLC 16
  See also CA 25-28R; 124
Mandelstam, Osip (Emilievich) 1891(?)-1938(?)
  TCLC 2, 6; PC 14
  See also CA 104; 150; MTCW 2
Mander, (Mary) Jane 1877-1949   **TCLC 31**
  See also CA 162
Mandeville, John fl. 1350-   **CMLC 19**
  See also DLB 146
Mandiargues, Andre Pieyre de   **CLC 41**
  See also Pieyre de Mandiargues, Andre
  See also DLB 83
Mandrake, Ethel Belle
  See Thurman, Wallace (Henry)
Mangan, James Clarence 1803-1849 **NCLC 27**
Maniere, J.-E.
  See Giraudoux, (Hippolyte) Jean
Mankiewicz, Herman (Jacob) 1897-1953
  TCLC 85
  See also CA 120; 169; DLB 26
Manley, (Mary) Delariviere 1672(?)-1724 **L C**

1, 42
See also DLB 39, 80

Mann, Abel
See Creasey, John

Mann, Emily 1952-   **DC 7**
See also CA 130; CANR 55

Mann, (Luiz) Heinrich 1871-1950   **TCLC 9**
See also CA 106; 164; DLB 66, 118

Mann, (Paul) Thomas 1875-1955 **TCLC 2, 8, 14, 21, 35, 44, 60; DA; DAB; DAC; DAM MST, NOV; SSC 5; WLC**
See also CA 104; 128; DLB 66; MTCW 1, 2

Mannheim, Karl 1893-1947   **TCLC 65**

Manning, David
See Faust, Frederick (Schiller)

Manning, Frederic 1887(?)-1935   **TCLC 25**
See also CA 124

Manning, Olivia 1915-1980   **CLC 5, 19**
See also CA 5-8R; 101; CANR 29; MTCW 1

Mano, D. Keith 1942-   **CLC 2, 10**
See also CA 25-28R; CAAS 6; CANR 26, 57; DLB 6

Mansfield, Katherine **TCLC 2, 8, 39; DAB; SSC 9, 23; WLC**
See also Beauchamp, Kathleen Mansfield
See also DLB 162

Manso, Peter 1940-   **CLC 39**
See also CA 29-32R; CANR 44

Mantecon, Juan Jimenez
See Jimenez (Mantecon), Juan Ramon

Manton, Peter
See Creasey, John

Man Without a Spleen, A
See Chekhov, Anton (Pavlovich)

Manzoni, Alessandro 1785-1873   **NCLC 29**

Map, Walter 1140-1209   **CMLC 32**

Mapu, Abraham (ben Jekutiel) 1808-1867
NCLC 18

Mara, Sally
See Queneau, Raymond

Marat, Jean Paul 1743-1793   **LC 10**

Marcel, Gabriel Honore 1889-1973 **CLC 15**
See also CA 102; 45-48; MTCW 1, 2

Marchbanks, Samuel
See Davies, (William) Robertson

Marchi, Giacomo
See Bassani, Giorgio

Margulies, Donald   **CLC 76**

Marie de France c. 12th cent. - **CMLC 8; PC 22**
See also DLB 208

Marie de l'Incarnation 1599-1672   **LC 10**

Marier, Captain Victor
See Griffith, D(avid Lewelyn) W(ark)

Mariner, Scott
See Pohl, Frederik

Marinetti, Filippo Tommaso 1876-1944
TCLC 10
See also CA 107; DLB 114

Marivaux, Pierre Carlet de Chamblain de 1688-1763   **LC 4; DC 7**

Markandaya, Kamala   **CLC 8, 38**
See also Taylor, Kamala (Purnaiya)

Markfield, Wallace 1926-   **CLC 8**
See also CA 69-72; CAAS 3; DLB 2, 28

Markham, Edwin 1852-1940   **TCLC 47**
See also CA 160; DLB 54, 186

Markham, Robert
See Amis, Kingsley (William)

Marks, J
See Highwater, Jamake (Mamake)

Marks-Highwater, J
See Highwater, Jamake (Mamake)

Markson, David M(errill) 1927-   **CLC 67**
See also CA 49-52; CANR 1

Marley, Bob   **CLC 17**
See also Marley, Robert Nesta

Marley, Robert Nesta 1945-1981
See Marley, Bob
See also CA 107; 103

Marlowe, Christopher 1564-1593 **LC 22, 47; DA; DAB; DAC; DAM DRAM, MST; DC 1; WLC**
See also CDBLB Before 1660; DLB 62

Marlowe, Stephen 1928-
See Queen, Ellery
See also CA 13-16R; CANR 6, 55

Marmontel, Jean-Francois 1723-1799   **LC 2**

Marquand, John P(hillips) 1893-1960 **CLC 2, 10**
See also CA 85-88; CANR 73; DLB 9, 102; MTCW 2

Marques, Rene 1919-1979   **CLC 96; DAM MULT; HLC**
See also CA 97-100; 85-88; CANR 78; DLB 113; HW

Marquez, Gabriel (Jose) Garcia
See Garcia Marquez, Gabriel (Jose)

Marquis, Don(ald Robert Perry) 1878-1937
TCLC 7
See also CA 104; 166; DLB 11, 25

Marric, J. J.
See Creasey, John

Marryat, Frederick 1792-1848   **NCLC 3**
See also DLB 21, 163

Marsden, James
See Creasey, John

Marsh, (Edith) Ngaio 1899-1982 **CLC 7, 53; DAM POP**
See also CA 9-12R; CANR 6, 58; DLB 77; MTCW 1, 2

Marshall, Garry 1934-   **CLC 17**
See also AAYA 3; CA 111; SATA 60

Marshall, Paule 1929- **CLC 27, 72; BLC 3; DAM MULT; SSC 3**
See also BW 2; CA 77-80; CANR 25, 73; DLB 157; MTCW 1, 2

Marshallik
See Zangwill, Israel

Marsten, Richard
See Hunter, Evan

Marston, John 1576-1634 **LC 33; DAM DRAM**
See also DLB 58, 172

Martha, Henry
See Harris, Mark

Marti, Jose 1853-1895   **NCLC 63; DAM MULT; HLC**

Martial c. 40-c. 104   **PC 10**
See also DLB 211

Martin, Ken
See Hubbard, L(afayette) Ron(ald)

Martin, Richard
See Creasey, John

Martin, Steve 1945-   **CLC 30**
See also CA 97-100; CANR 30; MTCW 1

Martin, Valerie 1948-   **CLC 89**
See also BEST 90:2; CA 85-88; CANR 49

Martin, Violet Florence 1862-1915 **TCLC 51**

Martin, Webber
See Silverberg, Robert

Martindale, Patrick Victor
See White, Patrick (Victor Martindale)

Martin du Gard, Roger 1881-1958 **TCLC 24**
See also CA 118; DLB 65

Martineau, Harriet 1802-1876   **NCLC 26**
See also DLB 21, 55, 159, 163, 166, 190;

YABC 2

Martines, Julia
See O'Faolain, Julia

Martinez, Enrique Gonzalez
See Gonzalez Martinez, Enrique

Martinez, Jacinto Benavente y
See Benavente (y Martinez), Jacinto

Martinez Ruiz, Jose 1873-1967
See Azorin; Ruiz, Jose Martinez
See also CA 93-96; HW

Martinez Sierra, Gregorio 1881-1947 **TCLC 6**
See also CA 115

Martinez Sierra, Maria (de la O'LeJarraga) 1874-1974   **TCLC 6**
See also CA 115

Martinsen, Martin
See Follett, Ken(neth Martin)

Martinson, Harry (Edmund) 1904-1978 **CLC 14**
See also CA 77-80; CANR 34

Marut, Ret
See Traven, B.

Marut, Robert
See Traven, B.

Marvell, Andrew 1621-1678   **LC 4, 43; DA; DAB; DAC; DAM MST, POET; PC 10; WLC**
See also CDBLB 1660-1789; DLB 131

Marx, Karl (Heinrich) 1818-1883   **NCLC 17**
See also DLB 129

Masaoka Shiki   **TCLC 18**
See also Masaoka Tsunenori

Masaoka Tsunenori 1867-1902
See Masaoka Shiki
See also CA 117

Masefield, John (Edward) 1878-1967 **CLC 11, 47; DAM POET**
See also CA 19-20; 25-28R; CANR 33; CAP 2; CDBLB 1890-1914; DLB 10, 19, 153, 160; MTCW 1, 2; SATA 19

Maso, Carole 19(?)-   **CLC 44**
See also CA 170

Mason, Bobbie Ann 1940- **CLC 28, 43, 82; SSC 4**
See also AAYA 5; CA 53-56; CANR 11, 31, 58; DLB 173; DLBY 87; INT CANR-31; MTCW 1, 2

Mason, Ernst
See Pohl, Frederik

Mason, Lee W.
See Malzberg, Barry N(athaniel)

Mason, Nick 1945-   **CLC 35**

Mason, Tally
See Derleth, August (William)

Mass, William
See Gibson, William

Master Lao
See Lao Tzu

Masters, Edgar Lee 1868-1950 **TCLC 2, 25; DA; DAC; DAM MST, POET; PC 1; WLCS**
See also CA 104; 133; CDALB 1865-1917; DLB 54; MTCW 1, 2

Masters, Hilary 1928-   **CLC 48**
See also CA 25-28R; CANR 13, 47

Mastrosimone, William 19(?)-   **CLC 36**

Mathe, Albert
See Camus, Albert

Mather, Cotton 1663-1728   **LC 38**
See also CDALB 1640-1865; DLB 24, 30, 140

Mather, Increase 1639-1723   **LC 38**
See also DLB 24

Matheson, Richard Burton 1926-   **CLC 37**

See also CA 110; 111; CANR 63; DLB 2; INT 111; MTCW 2

Millin, Sarah Gertrude 1889-1968   **CLC 49**
See also CA 102; 93-96

Milne, A(lan) A(lexander) 1882-1956**TCLC 6, 88; DAB; DAC; DAM MST**
See also CA 104; 133; CLR 1, 26; DLB 10, 77, 100, 160; MAICYA; MTCW 1, 2; SATA 100; YABC 1

Milner, Ron(ald) 1938-**CLC 56; BLC 3; DAM MULT**
See also AITN 1; BW 1; CA 73-76; CANR 24; DLB 38; MTCW 1

Milnes, Richard Monckton 1809-1885 **N C L C 61**
See also DLB 32, 184

Milosz, Czeslaw 1911- **CLC 5, 11, 22, 31, 56, 82; DAM MST, POET; PC 8; WLCS**
See also CA 81-84; CANR 23, 51; MTCW 1, 2

Milton, John 1608-1674 **LC 9, 43; DA; DAB; DAC; DAM MST, POET; PC 19; WLC**
See also CDBLB 1660-1789; DLB 131, 151

Min, Anchee 1957-   **CLC 86**
See also CA 146

Minehaha, Cornelius
See Wedekind, (Benjamin) Frank(lin)

Miner, Valerie 1947-   **CLC 40**
See also CA 97-100; CANR 59

Minimo, Duca
See D'Annunzio, Gabriele

Minot, Susan 1956-   **CLC 44**
See also CA 134

Minus, Ed 1938-   **CLC 39**

Miranda, Javier
See Bioy Casares, Adolfo

Mirbeau, Octave 1848-1917   **TCLC 55**
See also DLB 123, 192

Miro (Ferrer), Gabriel (Francisco Victor) 1879-1930   **TCLC 5**
See also CA 104

Mishima, Yukio 1925-1970**CLC 2, 4, 6, 9, 27; DC 1; SSC 4**
See also Hiraoka, Kimitake
See also DLB 182; MTCW 2

Mistral, Frederic 1830-1914   **TCLC 51**
See also CA 122

Mistral, Gabriela   **TCLC 2; HLC**
See also Godoy Alcayaga, Lucila
See also MTCW 2

Mistry, Rohinton 1952-   **CLC 71; DAC**
See also CA 141

Mitchell, Clyde
See Ellison, Harlan (Jay); Silverberg, Robert

Mitchell, James Leslie 1901-1935
See Gibbon, Lewis Grassic
See also CA 104; DLB 15

Mitchell, Joni 1943-   **CLC 12**
See also CA 112

Mitchell, Joseph (Quincy) 1908-1996**CLC 98**
See also CA 77-80; 152; CANR 69; DLB 185; DLBY 96

Mitchell, Margaret (Munnerlyn) 1900-1949 **TCLC 11; DAM NOV, POP**
See also AAYA 23; CA 109; 125; CANR 55; DLB 9; MTCW 1, 2

Mitchell, Peggy
See Mitchell, Margaret (Munnerlyn)

Mitchell, S(ilas) Weir 1829-1914   **TCLC 36**
See also CA 165; DLB 202

Mitchell, W(illiam) O(rmond) 1914-1998**CLC 25; DAC; DAM MST**
See also CA 77-80; 165; CANR 15, 43; DLB 88

Mitchell, William 1879-1936   **TCLC 81**

Mitford, Mary Russell 1787-1855   **NCLC 4**
See also DLB 110, 116

Mitford, Nancy 1904-1973   **CLC 44**
See also CA 9-12R; DLB 191

Miyamoto, Yuriko 1899-1951   **TCLC 37**
See also CA 170; DLB 180

Miyazawa, Kenji 1896-1933   **TCLC 76**
See also CA 157

Mizoguchi, Kenji 1898-1956   **TCLC 72**
See also CA 167

Mo, Timothy (Peter) 1950(?)-   **CLC 46**
See also CA 117; DLB 194; MTCW 1

Modarressi, Taghi (M.) 1931-   **CLC 44**
See also CA 121; 134; INT 134

Modiano, Patrick (Jean) 1945-   **CLC 18**
See also CA 85-88; CANR 17, 40; DLB 83

Moerck, Paal
See Roelvaag, O(le) E(dvart)

Mofolo, Thomas (Mokopu) 1875(?)-1948 **TCLC 22; BLC 3; DAM MULT**
See also CA 121; 153; MTCW 2

Mohr, Nicholasa 1938-**CLC 12; DAM MULT; HLC**
See also AAYA 8; CA 49-52; CANR 1, 32, 64; CLR 22; DLB 145; HW; JRDA; SAAS 8; SATA 8, 97

Mojtabai, A(nn) G(race) 1938- **CLC 5, 9, 15, 29**
See also CA 85-88

Moliere 1622-1673**LC 10, 28; DA; DAB; DAC; DAM DRAM, MST; WLC**

Molin, Charles
See Mayne, William (James Carter)

Molnar, Ferenc 1878-1952   **TCLC 20; DAM DRAM**
See also CA 109; 153

Momaday, N(avarre) Scott 1934- **CLC 2, 19, 85, 95; DA; DAB; DAC; DAM MST, MULT, NOV, POP; PC 25; WLCS**
See also AAYA 11; CA 25-28R; CANR 14, 34, 68; DLB 143, 175; INT CANR-14; MTCW 1, 2; NNAL; SATA 48; SATA-Brief 30

Monette, Paul 1945-1995   **CLC 82**
See also CA 139; 147

Monroe, Harriet 1860-1936   **TCLC 12**
See also CA 109; DLB 54, 91

Monroe, Lyle
See Heinlein, Robert A(nson)

Montagu, Elizabeth 1720-1800   **NCLC 7**

Montagu, Mary (Pierrepont) Wortley 1689-1762   **LC 9; PC 16**
See also DLB 95, 101

Montagu, W. H.
See Coleridge, Samuel Taylor

Montague, John (Patrick) 1929- **CLC 13, 46**
See also CA 9-12R; CANR 9, 69; DLB 40; MTCW 1

Montaigne, Michel (Eyquem) de 1533-1592 **LC 8; DA; DAB; DAC; DAM MST; WLC**

Montale, Eugenio 1896-1981**CLC 7, 9, 18; PC 13**
See also CA 17-20R; 104; CANR 30; DLB 114; MTCW 1

Montesquieu, Charles-Louis de Secondat 1689-1755   **LC 7**

Montgomery, (Robert) Bruce 1921-1978
See Crispin, Edmund
See also CA 104

Montgomery, L(ucy) M(aud) 1874-1942 **TCLC 51; DAC; DAM MST**
See also AAYA 12; CA 108; 137; CLR 8; DLB 92; DLBD 14; JRDA; MAICYA; MTCW 2;

SATA 100; YABC 1

Montgomery, Marion H., Jr. 1925-   **CLC 7**
See also AITN 1; CA 1-4R; CANR 3, 48; DLB 6

Montgomery, Max
See Davenport, Guy (Mattison, Jr.)

Montherlant, Henry (Milon) de 1896-1972 **CLC 8, 19; DAM DRAM**
See also CA 85-88; 37-40R; DLB 72; MTCW 1

Monty Python
See Chapman, Graham; Cleese, John (Marwood); Gilliam, Terry (Vance); Idle, Eric; Jones, Terence Graham Parry; Palin, Michael (Edward)
See also AAYA 7

Moodie, Susanna (Strickland) 1803-1885 **NCLC 14**
See also DLB 99

Mooney, Edward 1951-
See Mooney, Ted
See also CA 130

Mooney, Ted   **CLC 25**
See also Mooney, Edward

Moorcock, Michael (John) 1939-**CLC 5, 27, 58**
See also Bradbury, Edward P.
See also AAYA 26; CA 45-48; CAAS 5; CANR 2, 17, 38, 64; DLB 14; MTCW 1, 2; SATA 93

Moore, Brian 1921- **CLC 1, 3, 5, 7, 8, 19, 32, 90; DAB; DAC; DAM MST**
See also CA 1-4R; CANR 1, 25, 42, 63; MTCW 1, 2

Moore, Edward
See Muir, Edwin

Moore, G. E. 1873-1958   **TCLC 89**

Moore, George Augustus 1852-1933**TCLC 7; SSC 19**
See also CA 104; DLB 10, 18, 57, 135

Moore, Lorrie   **CLC 39, 45, 68**
See also Moore, Marie Lorena

Moore, Marianne (Craig) 1887-1972**CLC 1, 2, 4, 8, 10, 13, 19, 47; DA; DAB; DAC; DAM MST, POET; PC 4; WLCS**
See also CA 1-4R; 33-36R; CANR 3, 61; CDALB 1929-1941; DLB 45; DLBD 7; MTCW 1, 2; SATA 20

Moore, Marie Lorena 1957-
See Moore, Lorrie
See also CA 116; CANR 39

Moore, Thomas 1779-1852   **NCLC 6**
See also DLB 96, 144

Morand, Paul 1888-1976   **CLC 41; SSC 22**
See also CA 69-72; DLB 65

Morante, Elsa 1918-1985   **CLC 8, 47**
See also CA 85-88; 117; CANR 35; DLB 177; MTCW 1, 2

Moravia, Alberto 1907-1990**CLC 2, 7, 11, 27, 46; SSC 26**
See also Pincherle, Alberto
See also DLB 177; MTCW 2

More, Hannah 1745-1833   **NCLC 27**
See also DLB 107, 109, 116, 158

More, Henry 1614-1687   **LC 9**
See also DLB 126

More, Sir Thomas 1478-1535   **LC 10, 32**

Moreas, Jean   **TCLC 18**
See also Papadiamantopoulos, Johannes

Morgan, Berry 1919-   **CLC 6**
See also CA 49-52; DLB 6

Morgan, Claire
See Highsmith, (Mary) Patricia

Morgan, Edwin (George) 1920-   **CLC 31**

See also CA 5-8R; CANR 3, 43; DLB 27
Morgan, (George) Frederick 1922-   **CLC 23**
    See also CA 17-20R; CANR 21
Morgan, Harriet
    See Mencken, H(enry) L(ouis)
Morgan, Jane
    See Cooper, James Fenimore
Morgan, Janet 1945-   **CLC 39**
    See also CA 65-68
Morgan, Lady 1776(?)-1859   **NCLC 29**
    See also DLB 116, 158
Morgan, Robin (Evonne) 1941-   **CLC 2**
    See also CA 69-72; CANR 29, 68; MTCW 1;
    SATA 80
Morgan, Scott
    See Kuttner, Henry
Morgan, Seth 1949(?)-1990   **CLC 65**
    See also CA 132
Morgenstern, Christian 1871-1914   **TCLC 8**
    See also CA 105
Morgenstern, S.
    See Goldman, William (W.)
Moricz, Zsigmond 1879-1942   **TCLC 33**
    See also CA 165
Morike, Eduard (Friedrich) 1804-1875**NCLC
    10**
    See also DLB 133
Moritz, Karl Philipp 1756-1793   **LC 2**
    See also DLB 94
Morland, Peter Henry
    See Faust, Frederick (Schiller)
Morley, Christopher (Darlington) 1890-1957
    TCLC 87
    See also CA 112; DLB 9
Morren, Theophil
    See Hofmannsthal, Hugo von
Morris, Bill 1952-   **CLC 76**
Morris, Julian
    See West, Morris L(anglo)
Morris, Steveland Judkins 1950(?)-
    See Wonder, Stevie
    See also CA 111
Morris, William 1834-1896   **NCLC 4**
    See also CDBLB 1832-1890; DLB 18, 35, 57,
    156, 178, 184
Morris, Wright 1910-1998**CLC 1, 3, 7, 18, 37**
    See also CA 9-12R; 167; CANR 21; DLB 2,
    206; DLBY 81; MTCW 1, 2
Morrison, Arthur 1863-1945   **TCLC 72**
    See also CA 120; 157; DLB 70, 135, 197
Morrison, Chloe Anthony Wofford
    See Morrison, Toni
Morrison, James Douglas 1943-1971
    See Morrison, Jim
    See also CA 73-76; CANR 40
Morrison, Jim 1943-   **CLC 17**
    See also Morrison, James Douglas
Morrison, Toni 1931-**CLC 4, 10, 22, 55, 81, 87;**
    BLC 3; DA; DAB; DAC; DAM MST,
    MULT, NOV, POP
    See also AAYA 1, 22; BW 2; CA 29-32R;
    CANR 27, 42, 67; CDALB 1968-1988; DLB
    6, 33, 143; DLBY 81; MTCW 1, 2; SATA
    57
Morrison, Van 1945-   **CLC 21**
    See also CA 116; 168
Morrissy, Mary 1958-   **CLC 99**
Mortimer, John (Clifford) 1923-**CLC 28, 43;**
    DAM DRAM, POP
    See also CA 13-16R; CANR 21, 69; CDBLB
    1960 to Present; DLB 13; INT CANR-21;
    MTCW 1, 2
Mortimer, Penelope (Ruth) 1918-   **CLC 5**

See also CA 57-60; CANR 45
Morton, Anthony
    See Creasey, John
Mosca, Gaetano 1858-1941   **TCLC 75**
Mosher, Howard Frank 1943-   **CLC 62**
    See also CA 139; CANR 65
Mosley, Nicholas 1923-   **CLC 43, 70**
    See also CA 69-72; CANR 41, 60; DLB 14,
    207
Mosley, Walter 1952-   **CLC 97; BLCS; DAM**
    MULT, POP
    See also AAYA 17; BW 2; CA 142; CANR 57;
    MTCW 2
Moss, Howard 1922-1987   **CLC 7, 14, 45, 50;**
    DAM POET
    See also CA 1-4R; 123; CANR 1, 44; DLB 5
Mossgiel, Rab
    See Burns, Robert
Motion, Andrew (Peter) 1952-   **CLC 47**
    See also CA 146; DLB 40
Motley, Willard (Francis) 1909-1965   **CLC 18**
    See also BW 1; CA 117; 106; DLB 76, 143
Motoori, Norinaga 1730-1801   **NCLC 45**
Mott, Michael (Charles Alston) 1930-**CLC 15,**
    34
    See also CA 5-8R; CAAS 7; CANR 7, 29
Mountain Wolf Woman 1884-1960   **CLC 92**
    See also CA 144; NNAL
Moure, Erin 1955-   **CLC 88**
    See also CA 113; DLB 60
Mowat, Farley (McGill) 1921-**CLC 26; DAC;**
    DAM MST
    See also AAYA 1; CA 1-4R; CANR 4, 24, 42,
    68; CLR 20; DLB 68; INT CANR-24; JRDA;
    MAICYA; MTCW 1, 2; SATA 3, 55
Mowatt, Anna Cora 1819-1870   **NCLC 74**
Moyers, Bill 1934-   **CLC 74**
    See also AITN 2; CA 61-64; CANR 31, 52
Mphahlele, Es'kia
    See Mphahlele, Ezekiel
    See also DLB 125
Mphahlele, Ezekiel 1919-1983   **CLC 25; BLC**
    3; DAM MULT
    See also Mphahlele, Es'kia
    See also BW 2; CA 81-84; CANR 26, 76;
    MTCW 2
Mqhayi, S(amuel) E(dward) K(rune Loliwe)
    1875-1945**TCLC 25; BLC 3; DAM MULT**
    See also CA 153
Mrozek, Slawomir 1930-   **CLC 3, 13**
    See also CA 13-16R; CAAS 10; CANR 29;
    MTCW 1
Mrs. Belloc-Lowndes
    See Lowndes, Marie Adelaide (Belloc)
Mtwa, Percy (?)-   **CLC 47**
Mueller, Lisel 1924-   **CLC 13, 51**
    See also CA 93-96; DLB 105
Muir, Edwin 1887-1959   **TCLC 2, 87**
    See also CA 104; DLB 20, 100, 191
Muir, John 1838-1914   **TCLC 28**
    See also CA 165; DLB 186
Mujica Lainez, Manuel 1910-1984   **CLC 31**
    See also Lainez, Manuel Mujica
    See also CA 81-84; 112; CANR 32; HW
Mukherjee, Bharati 1940-**CLC 53, 115; DAM**
    NOV
    See also BEST 89:2; CA 107; CANR 45, 72;
    DLB 60; MTCW 1, 2
Muldoon, Paul 1951-**CLC 32, 72; DAM POET**
    See also CA 113; 129; CANR 52; DLB 40; INT
    129
Mulisch, Harry 1927-   **CLC 42**
    See also CA 9-12R; CANR 6, 26, 56

Mull, Martin 1943-   **CLC 17**
    See also CA 105
Muller, Wilhelm   **NCLC 73**
Mulock, Dinah Maria
    See Craik, Dinah Maria (Mulock)
Munford, Robert 1737(?)-1783   **LC 5**
    See also DLB 31
Mungo, Raymond 1946-   **CLC 72**
    See also CA 49-52; CANR 2
Munro, Alice 1931-   **CLC 6, 10, 19, 50, 95;**
    DAC; DAM MST, NOV; SSC 3; WLCS
    See also AITN 2; CA 33-36R; CANR 33, 53,
    75; DLB 53; MTCW 1, 2; SATA 29
Munro, H(ector) H(ugh) 1870-1916
    See Saki
    See also CA 104; 130; CDBLB 1890-1914; DA;
    DAB; DAC; DAM MST, NOV; DLB 34,
    162; MTCW 1, 2; WLC
Murdoch, (Jean) Iris 1919-**CLC 1, 2, 3, 4, 6, 8,**
    11, 15, 22, 31, 51; DAB; DAC; DAM MST,
    NOV
    See also CA 13-16R; CANR 8, 43, 68; CDBLB
    1960 to Present; DLB 14, 194; INT CANR-
    8; MTCW 1, 2
Murfree, Mary Noailles 1850-1922   **SSC 22**
    See also CA 122; DLB 12, 74
Murnau, Friedrich Wilhelm
    See Plumpe, Friedrich Wilhelm
Murphy, Richard 1927-   **CLC 41**
    See also CA 29-32R; DLB 40
Murphy, Sylvia 1937-   **CLC 34**
    See also CA 121
Murphy, Thomas (Bernard) 1935-   **CLC 51**
    See also CA 101
Murray, Albert L. 1916-   **CLC 73**
    See also BW 2; CA 49-52; CANR 26, 52, 78;
    DLB 38
Murray, Judith Sargent 1751-1820 **NCLC 63**
    See also DLB 37, 200
Murray, Les(lie) A(llan) 1938-**CLC 40; DAM**
    POET
    See also CA 21-24R; CANR 11, 27, 56
Murry, J. Middleton
    See Murry, John Middleton
Murry, John Middleton 1889-1957 **TCLC 16**
    See also CA 118; DLB 149
Musgrave, Susan 1951-   **CLC 13, 54**
    See also CA 69-72; CANR 45
Musil, Robert (Edler von) 1880-1942 **TCLC
    12, 68; SSC 18**
    See also CA 109; CANR 55; DLB 81, 124;
    MTCW 2
Muske, Carol 1945-   **CLC 90**
    See also Muske-Dukes, Carol (Anne)
Muske-Dukes, Carol (Anne) 1945-
    See Muske, Carol
    See also CA 65-68; CANR 32, 70
Musset, (Louis Charles) Alfred de 1810-1857
    NCLC 7
    See also DLB 192
My Brother's Brother
    See Chekhov, Anton (Pavlovich)
Myers, L(eopold) H(amilton) 1881-1944
    TCLC 59
    See also CA 157; DLB 15
Myers, Walter Dean 1937-   **CLC 35; BLC 3;**
    DAM MULT, NOV
    See also AAYA 4, 23; BW 2; CA 33-36R;
    CANR 20, 42, 67; CLR 4, 16, 35; DLB 33;
    INT CANR-20; JRDA; MAICYA; MTCW
    2; SAAS 2; SATA 41, 71; SATA-Brief 27
Myers, Walter M.
    See Myers, Walter Dean

Myles, Symon
See Follett, Ken(neth Martin)

Nabokov, Vladimir (Vladimirovich) 1899-1977
**CLC 1, 2, 3, 6, 8, 11, 15, 23, 44, 46, 64;
DA; DAB; DAC; DAM MST, NOV; SSC
11; WLC**
See also CA 5-8R; 69-72; CANR 20; CDALB
1941-1968; DLB 2; DLBD 3; DLBY 80, 91;
MTCW 1, 2

Nagai Kafu 1879-1959   **TCLC 51**
See also Nagai Sokichi
See also DLB 180

Nagai Sokichi 1879-1959
See Nagai Kafu
See also CA 117

Nagy, Laszlo 1925-1978   **CLC 7**
See also CA 129; 112

Naidu, Sarojini 1879-1943   **TCLC 80**

Naipaul, Shiva(dhar Srinivasa) 1945-1985
CLC 32, 39; DAM NOV
See also CA 110; 112; 116; CANR 33; DLB
157; DLBY 85; MTCW 1, 2

Naipaul, V(idiadhar) S(urajprasad) 1932-
**CLC 4, 7, 9, 13, 18, 37, 105; DAB; DAC;
DAM MST, NOV**
See also CA 1-4R; CANR 1, 33, 51; CDBLB
1960 to Present; DLB 125, 204, 206; DLBY
85; MTCW 1, 2

Nakos, Lilika 1899(?)-   **CLC 29**

Narayan, R(asipuram) K(rishnaswami) 1906-
CLC 7, 28, 47; DAM NOV; SSC 25
See also CA 81-84; CANR 33, 61; MTCW 1,
2; SATA 62

Nash, (Frediric) Ogden 1902-1971   **CLC 23;
DAM POET; PC 21**
See also CA 13-14; 29-32R; CANR 34, 61; CAP
1; DLB 11; MAICYA; MTCW 1, 2; SATA
2, 46

Nashe, Thomas 1567-1601(?)   **LC 41**
See also DLB 167

Nashe, Thomas 1567-1601   **LC 41**

Nathan, Daniel
See Dannay, Frederic

Nathan, George Jean 1882-1958   **TCLC 18**
See also Hatteras, Owen
See also CA 114; 169; DLB 137

Natsume, Kinnosuke 1867-1916
See Natsume, Soseki
See also CA 104

Natsume, Soseki 1867-1916   **TCLC 2, 10**
See also Natsume, Kinnosuke
See also DLB 180

Natti, (Mary) Lee 1919-
See Kingman, Lee
See also CA 5-8R; CANR 2

Naylor, Gloria 1950- **CLC 28, 52; BLC 3; DA;
DAC; DAM MST, MULT, NOV, POP;
WLCS**
See also AAYA 6; BW 2; CA 107; CANR 27,
51, 74; DLB 173; MTCW 1, 2

Neihardt, John Gneisenau 1881-1973 **CLC 32**
See also CA 13-14; CANR 65; CAP 1; DLB 9,
54

Nekrasov, Nikolai Alekseevich 1821-1878
NCLC 11

Nelligan, Emile 1879-1941   **TCLC 14**
See also CA 114; DLB 92

Nelson, Willie 1933-   **CLC 17**
See also CA 107

Nemerov, Howard (Stanley) 1920-1991 **C L C
2, 6, 9, 36; DAM POET; PC 24**
See also CA 1-4R; 134; CABS 2; CANR 1, 27,
53; DLB 5, 6; DLBY 83; INT CANR-27;

MTCW 1, 2

Neruda, Pablo 1904-1973 **CLC 1, 2, 5, 7, 9, 28,
62; DA; DAB; DAC; DAM MST, MULT,
POET; HLC; PC 4; WLC**
See also CA 19-20; 45-48; CAP 2; HW; MTCW
1, 2

Nerval, Gerard de 1808-1855 **NCLC 1, 67; PC
13; SSC 18**

Nervo, (Jose) Amado (Ruiz de) 1870-1919
TCLC 11
See also CA 109; 131; HW

Nessi, Pio Baroja y
See Baroja (y Nessi), Pio

Nestroy, Johann 1801-1862   **NCLC 42**
See also DLB 133

Netterville, Luke
See O'Grady, Standish (James)

Neufeld, John (Arthur) 1938-   **CLC 17**
See also AAYA 11; CA 25-28R; CANR 11, 37,
56; CLR 52; MAICYA; SAAS 3; SATA 6,
81

Neville, Emily Cheney 1919-   **CLC 12**
See also CA 5-8R; CANR 3, 37; JRDA;
MAICYA; SAAS 2; SATA 1

Newbound, Bernard Slade 1930-
See Slade, Bernard
See also CA 81-84; CANR 49; DAM DRAM

Newby, P(ercy) H(oward) 1918-1997 **CLC 2,
13; DAM NOV**
See also CA 5-8R; 161; CANR 32, 67; DLB
15; MTCW 1

Newlove, Donald 1928-   **CLC 6**
See also CA 29-32R; CANR 25

Newlove, John (Herbert) 1938-   **CLC 14**
See also CA 21-24R; CANR 9, 25

Newman, Charles 1938-   **CLC 2, 8**
See also CA 21-24R

Newman, Edwin (Harold) 1919-   **CLC 14**
See also AITN 1; CA 69-72; CANR 5

Newman, John Henry 1801-1890   **NCLC 38**
See also DLB 18, 32, 55

Newton, (Sir) Isaac 1642-1727   **LC 35**

Newton, Suzanne 1936-   **CLC 35**
See also CA 41-44R; CANR 14; JRDA; SATA
5, 77

Nexo, Martin Andersen 1869-1954 **TCLC 43**

Nezval, Vitezslav 1900-1958   **TCLC 44**
See also CA 123

Ng, Fae Myenne 1957(?)-   **CLC 81**
See also CA 146

Ngema, Mbongeni 1955-   **CLC 57**
See also BW 2; CA 143

Ngugi, James T(hiong'o)   **CLC 3, 7, 13**
See also Ngugi wa Thiong'o

Ngugi wa Thiong'o 1938-   **CLC 36; BLC 3;
DAM MULT, NOV**
See also Ngugi, James T(hiong'o)
See also BW 2; CA 81-84; CANR 27, 58; DLB
125; MTCW 1, 2

Nichol, B(arrie) P(hillip) 1944-1988 **CLC 18**
See also CA 53-56; DLB 53; SATA 66

Nichols, John (Treadwell) 1940-   **CLC 38**
See also CA 9-12R; CAAS 2; CANR 6, 70;
DLBY 82

Nichols, Leigh
See Koontz, Dean R(ay)

Nichols, Peter (Richard) 1927- **CLC 5, 36, 65**
See also CA 104; CANR 33; DLB 13; MTCW
1

Nicolas, F. R. E.
See Freeling, Nicolas

Niedecker, Lorine 1903-1970   **CLC 10, 42;
DAM POET**

See also CA 25-28; CAP 2; DLB 48

Nietzsche, Friedrich (Wilhelm) 1844-1900
TCLC 10, 18, 55
See also CA 107; 121; DLB 129

Nievo, Ippolito 1831-1861   **NCLC 22**

Nightingale, Anne Redmon 1943-
See Redmon, Anne
See also CA 103

Nightingale, Florence 1820-1910   **TCLC 85**
See also DLB 166

Nik. T. O.
See Annensky, Innokenty (Fyodorovich)

Nin, Anais 1903-1977 **CLC 1, 4, 8, 11, 14, 60;
DAM NOV, POP; SSC 10**
See also AITN 2; CA 13-16R; 69-72; CANR
22, 53; DLB 2, 4, 152; MTCW 1, 2

Nishida, Kitaro 1870-1945   **TCLC 83**

Nishiwaki, Junzaburo 1894-1982   **PC 15**
See also CA 107

Nissenson, Hugh 1933-   **CLC 4, 9**
See also CA 17-20R; CANR 27; DLB 28

Niven, Larry   **CLC 8**
See Niven, Laurence Van Cott
See also AAYA 27; DLB 8

Niven, Laurence Van Cott 1938-
See Niven, Larry
See also CA 21-24R; CAAS 12; CANR 14, 44,
66; DAM POP; MTCW 1, 2; SATA 95

Nixon, Agnes Eckhardt 1927-   **CLC 21**
See also CA 110

Nizan, Paul 1905-1940   **TCLC 40**
See also CA 161; DLB 72

Nkosi, Lewis 1936- **CLC 45; BLC 3; DAM
MULT**
See also BW 1; CA 65-68; CANR 27; DLB 157

Nodier, (Jean) Charles (Emmanuel) 1780-1844
NCLC 19
See also DLB 119

Noguchi, Yone 1875-1947   **TCLC 80**

Nolan, Christopher 1965-   **CLC 58**
See also CA 111

Noon, Jeff 1957-   **CLC 91**
See also CA 148

Norden, Charles
See Durrell, Lawrence (George)

Nordhoff, Charles (Bernard) 1887-1947
TCLC 23
See also CA 108; DLB 9; SATA 23

Norfolk, Lawrence 1963-   **CLC 76**
See also CA 144

Norman, Marsha 1947- **CLC 28; DAM DRAM;
DC 8**
See also CA 105; CABS 3; CANR 41; DLBY
84

Normyx
See Douglas, (George) Norman

Norris, Frank 1870-1902   **SSC 28**
See also Norris, (Benjamin) Frank(lin, Jr.)
See also CDALB 1865-1917; DLB 12, 71, 186

Norris, (Benjamin) Frank(lin, Jr.) 1870-1902
TCLC 24
See also Norris, Frank
See also CA 110; 160

Norris, Leslie 1921-   **CLC 14**
See also CA 11-12; CANR 14; CAP 1; DLB 27

North, Andrew
See Norton, Andre

North, Anthony
See Koontz, Dean R(ay)

North, Captain George
See Stevenson, Robert Louis (Balfour)

North, Milou
See Erdrich, Louise

Northrup, B. A.
See Hubbard, L(afayette) Ron(ald)
North Staffs
See Hulme, T(homas) E(rnest)
Norton, Alice Mary
See Norton, Andre
See also MAICYA; SATA 1, 43
Norton, Andre 1912-   **CLC 12**
See also Norton, Alice Mary
See also AAYA 14; CA 1-4R; CANR 68; CLR
50; DLB 8, 52; JRDA; MTCW 1; SATA 91
Norton, Caroline 1808-1877   **NCLC 47**
See also DLB 21, 159, 199
Norway, Nevil Shute 1899-1960
See Shute, Nevil
See also CA 102; 93-96; MTCW 2
Norwid, Cyprian Kamil 1821-1883 **NCLC 17**
Nosille, Nabrah
See Ellison, Harlan (Jay)
Nossack, Hans Erich 1901-1978   **CLC 6**
See also CA 93-96; 85-88; DLB 69
Nostradamus 1503-1566   **LC 27**
Nosu, Chuji
See Ozu, Yasujiro
Notenburg, Eleanora (Genrikhovna) von
See Guro, Elena
Nova, Craig 1945-   **CLC 7, 31**
See also CA 45-48; CANR 2, 53
Novak, Joseph
See Kosinski, Jerzy (Nikodem)
Novalis 1772-1801   **NCLC 13**
See also DLB 90
Novis, Emile
See Weil, Simone (Adolphine)
Nowlan, Alden (Albert) 1933-1983   **CLC 15;**
DAC; DAM MST
See also CA 9-12R; CANR 5; DLB 53
Noyes, Alfred 1880-1958   **TCLC 7**
See also CA 104; DLB 20
Nunn, Kem   **CLC 34**
See also CA 159
Nye, Robert 1939-   **CLC 13, 42; DAM NOV**
See also CA 33-36R; CANR 29, 67; DLB 14;
MTCW 1; SATA 6
Nyro, Laura 1947-   **CLC 17**
Oates, Joyce Carol 1938-CLC 1, 2, 3, 6, 9, 11,
15, 19, 33, 52, 108; DA; DAB; DAC; DAM
MST, NOV, POP; SSC 6; WLC
See also AAYA 15; AITN 1; BEST 89:2; CA
5-8R; CANR 25, 45, 74; CDALB 1968-
1988; DLB 2, 5, 130; DLBY 81; INT CANR-
25; MTCW 1, 2
O'Brien, Darcy 1939-1998   **CLC 11**
See also CA 21-24R; 167; CANR 8, 59
O'Brien, E. G.
See Clarke, Arthur C(harles)
O'Brien, Edna 1936- CLC 3, 5, 8, 13, 36, 65,
116; DAM NOV; SSC 10
See also CA 1-4R; CANR 6, 41, 65; CDBLB
1960 to Present; DLB 14; MTCW 1, 2
O'Brien, Fitz-James 1828-1862   **NCLC 21**
See also DLB 74
O'Brien, Flann   **CLC 1, 4, 5, 7, 10, 47**
See also O Nuallain, Brian
O'Brien, Richard 1942-   **CLC 17**
See also CA 124
O'Brien, (William) Tim(othy) 1946- **CLC 7,**
19, 40, 103; DAM POP
See also AAYA 16; CA 85-88; CANR 40, 58;
DLB 152; DLBD 9; DLBY 80; MTCW 2
Obstfelder, Sigbjoern 1866-1900   **TCLC 23**
See also CA 123
O'Casey, Sean 1880-1964CLC 1, 5, 9, 11, 15,

88; DAB; DAC; DAM DRAM, MST;
WLCS
See also CA 89-92; CANR 62; CDBLB 1914-
1945; DLB 10; MTCW 1, 2
O'Cathasaigh, Sean
See O'Casey, Sean
Ochs, Phil 1940-1976   **CLC 17**
See also CA 65-68
O'Connor, Edwin (Greene) 1918-1968CLC 14
See also CA 93-96; 25-28R
O'Connor, (Mary) Flannery 1925-1964 C L C
1, 2, 3, 6, 10, 13, 15, 21, 66, 104; DA; DAB;
DAC; DAM MST, NOV; SSC 1, 23; WLC
See also AAYA 7; CA 1-4R; CANR 3, 41;
CDALB 1941-1968; DLB 2, 152; DLBD 12;
DLBY 80; MTCW 1, 2
O'Connor, Frank   **CLC 23; SSC 5**
See also O'Donovan, Michael John
See also DLB 162
O'Dell, Scott 1898-1989   **CLC 30**
See also AAYA 3; CA 61-64; 129; CANR 12,
30; CLR 1, 16; DLB 52; JRDA; MAICYA;
SATA 12, 60
Odets, Clifford 1906-1963CLC 2, 28, 98; DAM
DRAM; DC 6
See also CA 85-88; CANR 62; DLB 7, 26;
MTCW 1, 2
O'Doherty, Brian 1934-   **CLC 76**
See also CA 105
O'Donnell, K. M.
See Malzberg, Barry N(athaniel)
O'Donnell, Lawrence
See Kuttner, Henry
O'Donovan, Michael John 1903-1966CLC 14
See also O'Connor, Frank
See also CA 93-96
Oe, Kenzaburo 1935- CLC 10, 36, 86; DAM
NOV; SSC 20
See also CA 97-100; CANR 36, 50, 74; DLB
182; DLBY 94; MTCW 1, 2
O'Faolain, Julia 1932-   CLC 6, 19, 47, 108
See also CA 81-84; CAAS 2; CANR 12, 61;
DLB 14; MTCW 1
O'Faolain, Sean 1900-1991 CLC 1, 7, 14, 32,
70; SSC 13
See also CA 61-64; 134; CANR 12, 66; DLB
15, 162; MTCW 1, 2
O'Flaherty, Liam 1896-1984CLC 5, 34; SSC 6
See also CA 101; 113; CANR 35; DLB 36, 162;
DLBY 84; MTCW 1, 2
Ogilvy, Gavin
See Barrie, J(ames) M(atthew)
O'Grady, Standish (James) 1846-1928T C L C
5
See also CA 104; 157
O'Grady, Timothy 1951-   **CLC 59**
See also CA 138
O'Hara, Frank 1926-1966 CLC 2, 5, 13, 78;
DAM POET
See also CA 9-12R; 25-28R; CANR 33; DLB
5, 16, 193; MTCW 1, 2
O'Hara, John (Henry) 1905-1970CLC 1, 2, 3,
6, 11, 42; DAM NOV; SSC 15
See also CA 5-8R; 25-28R; CANR 31, 60;
CDALB 1929-1941; DLB 9, 86; DLBD 2;
MTCW 1, 2
O Hehir, Diana 1922-   **CLC 41**
See also CA 93-96
Okigbo, Christopher (Ifenayichukwu) 1932-
1967 CLC 25, 84; BLC 3; DAM MULT,
POET; PC 7
See also BW 1; CA 77-80; CANR 74; DLB 125;
MTCW 1, 2

Okri, Ben 1959-   **CLC 87**
See also BW 2; CA 130; 138; CANR 65; DLB
157; INT 138; MTCW 2
Olds, Sharon 1942-   **CLC 32, 39, 85; DAM**
POET; PC 22
See also CA 101; CANR 18, 41, 66; DLB 120;
MTCW 2
Oldstyle, Jonathan
See Irving, Washington
Olesha, Yuri (Karlovich) 1899-1960 **CLC 3**
See also CA 85-88
Oliphant, Laurence 1829(?)-1888   **NCLC 47**
See also DLB 18, 166
Oliphant, Margaret (Oliphant Wilson) 1828-
1897   **NCLC 11, 61; SSC 25**
See also DLB 18, 159, 190
Oliver, Mary 1935-   **CLC 19, 34, 98**
See also CA 21-24R; CANR 9, 43; DLB 5, 193
Olivier, Laurence (Kerr) 1907-1989 **CLC 20**
See also CA 111; 150; 129
Olsen, Tillie 1912-CLC 4, 13, 114; DA; DAB;
DAC; DAM MST; SSC 11
See also CA 1-4R; CANR 1, 43, 74; DLB 28,
206; DLBY 80; MTCW 1, 2
Olson, Charles (John) 1910-1970CLC 1, 2, 5,
6, 9, 11, 29; DAM POET; PC 19
See also CA 13-16; 25-28R; CABS 2; CANR
35, 61; CAP 1; DLB 5, 16, 193; MTCW 1, 2
Olson, Toby 1937-   **CLC 28**
See also CA 65-68; CANR 9, 31
Olyesha, Yuri
See Olesha, Yuri (Karlovich)
Ondaatje, (Philip) Michael 1943-CLC 14, 29,
51, 76; DAB; DAC; DAM MST
See also CA 77-80; CANR 42, 74; DLB 60;
MTCW 2
Oneal, Elizabeth 1934-
See Oneal, Zibby
See also CA 106; CANR 28; MAICYA; SATA
30, 82
Oneal, Zibby   **CLC 30**
See also Oneal, Elizabeth
See also AAYA 5; CLR 13; JRDA
O'Neill, Eugene (Gladstone) 1888-1953TCLC
1, 6, 27, 49; DA; DAB; DAC; DAM DRAM,
MST; WLC
See also AITN 1; CA 110; 132; CDALB 1929-
1941; DLB 7; MTCW 1, 2
Onetti, Juan Carlos 1909-1994   **CLC 7, 10;**
DAM MULT, NOV; SSC 23
See also CA 85-88; 145; CANR 32, 63; DLB
113; HW; MTCW 1, 2
O Nuallain, Brian 1911-1966
See O'Brien, Flann
See also CA 21-22; 25-28R; CAP 2
Ophuls, Max 1902-1957   **TCLC 79**
See also CA 113
Opie, Amelia 1769-1853   **NCLC 65**
See also DLB 116, 159
Oppen, George 1908-1984   **CLC 7, 13, 34**
See also CA 13-16R; 113; CANR 8; DLB 5,
165
Oppenheim, E(dward) Phillips 1866-1946
TCLC 45
See also CA 111; DLB 70
Opuls, Max
See Ophuls, Max
Origen c. 185-c. 254   **CMLC 19**
Orlovitz, Gil 1918-1973   **CLC 22**
See also CA 77-80; 45-48; DLB 2, 5
Orris
See Ingelow, Jean
Ortega y Gasset, Jose 1883-1955   **TCLC 9;**

See also CA 110; 153; DLB 10

Pinero, Miguel (Antonio Gomez) 1946-1988
CLC 4, 55
See also CA 61-64; 125; CANR 29; HW

Pinget, Robert 1919-1997   **CLC 7, 13, 37**
See also CA 85-88; 160; DLB 83

Pink Floyd
See Barrett, (Roger) Syd; Gilmour, David;
Mason, Nick; Waters, Roger; Wright, Rick

Pinkney, Edward 1802-1828   **NCLC 31**

Pinkwater, Daniel Manus 1941-   **CLC 35**
See also Pinkwater, Manus
See also AAYA 1; CA 29-32R; CANR 12, 38;
CLR 4; JRDA; MAICYA; SAAS 3; SATA
46, 76

Pinkwater, Manus
See Pinkwater, Daniel Manus
See also SATA 8

Pinsky, Robert 1940-CLC 9, 19, 38, 94; DAM
POET
See also CA 29-32R; CAAS 4; CANR 58;
DLBY 82, 98; MTCW 2

Pinta, Harold
See Pinter, Harold

Pinter, Harold 1930-CLC 1, 3, 6, 9, 11, 15, 27,
58, 73; DA; DAB; DAC; DAM DRAM,
MST; WLC
See also CA 5-8R; CANR 33, 65; CDBLB 1960
to Present; DLB 13; MTCW 1, 2

Piozzi, Hester Lynch (Thrale) 1741-1821
NCLC 57
See also DLB 104, 142

Pirandello, Luigi 1867-1936TCLC 4, 29; DA;
DAB; DAC; DAM DRAM, MST; DC 5;
SSC 22; WLC
See also CA 104; 153; MTCW 2

Pirsig, Robert M(aynard) 1928-CLC 4, 6, 73;
DAM POP
See also CA 53-56; CANR 42, 74; MTCW 1,
2; SATA 39

Pisarev, Dmitry Ivanovich 1840-1868 NCLC
25

Pix, Mary (Griffith) 1666-1709   **LC 8**
See also DLB 80

Pixerecourt, (Rene Charles) Guilbert de 1773-
1844   **NCLC 39**
See also DLB 192

Plaatje, Sol(omon) T(shekisho) 1876-1932
TCLC 73; BLCS
See also BW 2; CA 141

Plaidy, Jean
See Hibbert, Eleanor Alice Burford

Planche, James Robinson 1796-1880NCLC 42

Plant, Robert 1948-   **CLC 12**

Plante, David (Robert) 1940-   CLC 7, 23, 38;
DAM NOV
See also CA 37-40R; CANR 12, 36, 58; DLBY
83; INT CANR-12; MTCW 1

Plath, Sylvia 1932-1963 CLC 1, 2, 3, 5, 9, 11,
14, 17, 50, 51, 62, 111; DA; DAB; DAC;
DAM MST, POET; PC 1; WLC
See also AAYA 13; CA 19-20; CANR 34; CAP
2; CDALB 1941-1968; DLB 5, 6, 152;
MTCW 1, 2; SATA 96

Plato 428(?)B.C.-348(?)B.C.   **CMLC 8; DA;**
DAB; DAC; DAM MST; WLCS
See also DLB 176

Platonov, Andrei   **TCLC 14**
See also Klimentov, Andrei Platonovich

Platt, Kin 1911-   **CLC 26**
See also AAYA 11; CA 17-20R; CANR 11;
JRDA; SAAS 17; SATA 21, 86

Plautus c. 251B.C.-184B.C.   **CMLC 24; DC 6**

See also DLB 211

Plick et Plock
See Simenon, Georges (Jacques Christian)

Plimpton, George (Ames) 1927-   **CLC 36**
See also AITN 1; CA 21-24R; CANR 32, 70;
DLB 185; MTCW 1, 2; SATA 10

Pliny the Elder c. 23-79   **CMLC 23**
See also DLB 211

Plomer, William Charles Franklin 1903-1973
CLC 4, 8
See also CA 21-22; CANR 34; CAP 2; DLB
20, 162, 191; MTCW 1; SATA 24

Plowman, Piers
See Kavanagh, Patrick (Joseph)

Plum, J.
See Wodehouse, P(elham) G(renville)

Plumly, Stanley (Ross) 1939-   **CLC 33**
See also CA 108; 110; DLB 5, 193; INT 110

Plumpe, Friedrich Wilhelm 1888-1931TCLC
53
See also CA 112

Po Chu-i 772-846   **CMLC 24**

Poe, Edgar Allan 1809-1849 NCLC 1, 16, 55;
DA; DAB; DAC; DAM MST, POET; PC
1; SSC 34; WLC
See also AAYA 14; CDALB 1640-1865; DLB
3, 59, 73, 74; SATA 23

Poet of Titchfield Street, The
See Pound, Ezra (Weston Loomis)

Pohl, Frederik 1919-   **CLC 18; SSC 25**
See also AAYA 24; CA 61-64; CAAS 1; CANR
11, 37; DLB 8; INT CANR-11; MTCW 1, 2;
SATA 24

Poirier, Louis 1910-
See Gracq, Julien
See also CA 122; 126

Poitier, Sidney 1927-   **CLC 26**
See also BW 1; CA 117

Polanski, Roman 1933-   **CLC 16**
See also CA 77-80

Poliakoff, Stephen 1952-   **CLC 38**
See also CA 106; DLB 13

Police, The
See Copeland, Stewart (Armstrong); Summers,
Andrew James; Sumner, Gordon Matthew

Polidori, John William 1795-1821 NCLC 51
See also DLB 116

Pollitt, Katha 1949-   **CLC 28**
See also CA 120; 122; CANR 66; MTCW 1, 2

Pollock, (Mary) Sharon 1936-CLC 50; DAC;
DAM DRAM, MST
See also CA 141; DLB 60

Polo, Marco 1254-1324   **CMLC 15**

Polonsky, Abraham (Lincoln) 1910- CLC 92
See also CA 104; DLB 26; INT 104

Polybius c. 200B.C.-c. 118B.C.   **CMLC 17**
See also DLB 176

Pomerance, Bernard 1940-   **CLC 13; DAM**
DRAM
See also CA 101; CANR 49

Ponge, Francis (Jean Gaston Alfred) 1899-1988
CLC 6, 18; DAM POET
See also CA 85-88; 126; CANR 40

Pontoppidan, Henrik 1857-1943   **TCLC 29**
See also CA 170

Poole, Josephine   **CLC 17**
See also Helyar, Jane Penelope Josephine
See also SAAS 2; SATA 5

Popa, Vasko 1922-1991   **CLC 19**
See also CA 112; 148; DLB 181

Pope, Alexander 1688-1744 LC 3; DA; DAB;
DAC; DAM MST, POET; PC 26; WLC
See also CDBLB 1660-1789; DLB 95, 101

Porter, Connie (Rose) 1959(?)-   **CLC 70**
See also BW 2; CA 142; SATA 81

Porter, Gene(va Grace) Stratton 1863(?)-1924
TCLC 21
See also CA 112

Porter, Katherine Anne 1890-1980 CLC 1, 3,
7, 10, 13, 15, 27, 101; DA; DAB; DAC;
DAM MST, NOV; SSC 4, 31
See also AITN 2; CA 1-4R; CANR 1, 65;
DLB 4, 9, 102; DLBD 12; DLBY 80; MTCW
1, 2; SATA 39; SATA-Obit 23

Porter, Peter (Neville Frederick) 1929- C L C
5, 13, 33
See also CA 85-88; DLB 40

Porter, William Sydney 1862-1910
See Henry, O.
See also CA 104; 131; CDALB 1865-1917; DA;
DAB; DAC; DAM MST; DLB 12, 78, 79;
MTCW 1, 2; YABC 2

Portillo (y Pacheco), Jose Lopez
See Lopez Portillo (y Pacheco), Jose

Post, Melville Davisson 1869-1930 TCLC 39
See also CA 110

Potok, Chaim 1929-   CLC 2, 7, 14, 26, 112;
DAM NOV
See also AAYA 15; AITN 1, 2; CA 17-20R;
CANR 19, 35, 64; DLB 28, 152; INT CANR-
19; MTCW 1, 2; SATA 33, 106

Potter, (Helen) Beatrix 1866-1943
See Webb, (Martha) Beatrice (Potter)
See also MAICYA; MTCW 2

Potter, Dennis (Christopher George) 1935-1994
CLC 58, 86
See also CA 107; 145; CANR 33, 61; MTCW
1

Pound, Ezra (Weston Loomis) 1885-1972
CLC 1, 2, 3, 4, 5, 7, 10, 13, 18, 34, 48, 50,
112; DA; DAB; DAC; DAM MST, POET;
PC 4; WLC
See also CA 5-8R; 37-40R; CANR 40; CDALB
1917-1929; DLB 4, 45, 63; DLBD 15;
MTCW 1, 2

Povod, Reinaldo 1959-1994   **CLC 44**
See also CA 136; 146

Powell, Adam Clayton, Jr. 1908-1972CLC 89;
BLC 3; DAM MULT
See also BW 1; CA 102; 33-36R

Powell, Anthony (Dymoke) 1905-CLC 1, 3, 7,
9, 10, 31
See also CA 1-4R; CANR 1, 32, 62; CDBLB
1945-1960; DLB 15; MTCW 1, 2

Powell, Dawn 1897-1965   **CLC 66**
See also CA 5-8R; DLBY 97

Powell, Padgett 1952-   **CLC 34**
See also CA 126; CANR 63

Power, Susan 1961-   **CLC 91**

Powers, J(ames) F(arl) 1917-CLC 1, 4, 8, 57;
SSC 4
See also CA 1-4R; CANR 2, 61; DLB 130;
MTCW 1

Powers, John J(ames) 1945-
See Powers, John R.
See also CA 69-72

Powers, John R.   **CLC 66**
See also Powers, John J(ames)

Powers, Richard (S.) 1957-   **CLC 93**
See also CA 148

Pownall, David 1938-   **CLC 10**
See also CA 89-92; CAAS 18; CANR 49; DLB
14

Powys, John Cowper 1872-1963CLC 7, 9, 15,
46
See also CA 85-88; DLB 15; MTCW 1, 2

Powys, T(heodore) F(rancis) 1875-1953
TCLC 9
See also CA 106; DLB 36, 162

Prado (Calvo), Pedro 1886-1952 **TCLC 75**
See also CA 131; HW

Prager, Emily 1952- **CLC 56**

Pratt, E(dwin) J(ohn) 1883(?)-1964 **CLC 19;**
DAC; DAM POET
See also CA 141; 93-96; CANR 77; DLB 92

Premchand **TCLC 21**
See also Srivastava, Dhanpat Rai

Preussler, Otfried 1923- **CLC 17**
See also CA 77-80; SATA 24

Prevert, Jacques (Henri Marie) 1900-1977
CLC 15
See also CA 77-80; 69-72; CANR 29, 61;
MTCW 1; SATA-Obit 30

Prevost, Abbe (Antoine Francois) 1697-1763
LC 1

Price, (Edward) Reynolds 1933-**CLC 3, 6, 13,**
43, 50, 63; DAM NOV; SSC 22
See also CA 1-4R; CANR 1, 37, 57; DLB 2;
INT CANR-37

Price, Richard 1949- **CLC 6, 12**
See also CA 49-52; CANR 3; DLBY 81

Prichard, Katharine Susannah 1883-1969
CLC 46
See also CA 11-12; CANR 33; CAP 1; MTCW
1; SATA 66

Priestley, J(ohn) B(oynton) 1894-1984**CLC 2,**
5, 9, 34; DAM DRAM, NOV
See also CA 9-12R; 113; CANR 33; CDBLB
1914-1945; DLB 10, 34, 77, 100, 139;
DLBY 84; MTCW 1, 2

Prince 1958(?)- **CLC 35**

Prince, F(rank) T(empleton) 1912- **CLC 22**
See also CA 101; CANR 43; DLB 20

Prince Kropotkin
See Kropotkin, Peter (Aleksieevich)

Prior, Matthew 1664-1721 **LC 4**
See also DLB 95

Prishvin, Mikhail 1873-1954 **TCLC 75**

Pritchard, William H(arrison) 1932- **CLC 34**
See also CA 65-68; CANR 23; DLB 111

Pritchett, V(ictor) S(awdon) 1900-1997 **C L C**
5, 13, 15, 41; DAM NOV; SSC 14
See also CA 61-64; 157; CANR 31, 63; DLB
15, 139; MTCW 1, 2

Private 19022
See Manning, Frederic

Probst, Mark 1925- **CLC 59**
See also CA 130

Prokosch, Frederic 1908-1989 **CLC 4, 48**
See also CA 73-76; 128; DLB 48; MTCW 2

Propertius, Sextus c. 50B.C.-c. 16B.C.**C M L C**
32
See also DLB 211

Prophet, The
See Dreiser, Theodore (Herman Albert)

Prose, Francine 1947- **CLC 45**
See also CA 109; 112; CANR 46; SATA 101

Proudhon
See Cunha, Euclides (Rodrigues Pimenta) da

Proulx, Annie
See Proulx, E(dna) Annie

Proulx, E(dna) Annie 1935- **CLC 81; DAM**
POP
See also CA 145; CANR 65; MTCW 2

Proust, (Valentin-Louis-George-Eugene-)
Marcel 1871-1922 **TCLC 7, 13, 33; DA;**
DAB; DAC; DAM MST, NOV; WLC
See also CA 104; 120; DLB 65; MTCW 1, 2

Prowler, Harley

See Masters, Edgar Lee

Prus, Boleslaw 1845-1912 **TCLC 48**

Pryor, Richard (Franklin Lenox Thomas)
1940- **CLC 26**
See also CA 122; 152

Przybyszewski, Stanislaw 1868-1927**TCLC 36**
See also CA 160; DLB 66

Pteleon
See Grieve, C(hristopher) M(urray)
See also DAM POET

Puckett, Lute
See Masters, Edgar Lee

Puig, Manuel 1932-1990**CLC 3, 5, 10, 28, 65;**
DAM MULT; HLC
See also CA 45-48; CANR 2, 32, 63; DLB 113;
HW; MTCW 1, 2

Pulitzer, Joseph 1847-1911 **TCLC 76**
See also CA 114; DLB 23

Purdy, A(lfred) W(ellington) 1918-**CLC 3, 6,**
14, 50; DAC; DAM MST, POET
See also CA 81-84; CAAS 17; CANR 42, 66;
DLB 88

Purdy, James (Amos) 1923-**CLC 2, 4, 10, 28,**
52
See also CA 33-36R; CAAS 1; CANR 19, 51;
DLB 2; INT CANR-19; MTCW 1

Pure, Simon
See Swinnerton, Frank Arthur

Pushkin, Alexander (Sergeyevich) 1799-1837
NCLC 3, 27; DA; DAB; DAC; DAM
DRAM, MST, POET; PC 10; SSC 27;
WLC
See also DLB 205; SATA 61

P'u Sung-ling 1640-1715 **LC 49; SSC 31**

Putnam, Arthur Lee
See Alger, Horatio, Jr.

Puzo, Mario 1920-1999 **CLC 1, 2, 6, 36, 107;**
DAM NOV, POP
See also CA 65-68; CANR 4, 42, 65; DLB 6;
MTCW 1, 2

Pygge, Edward
See Barnes, Julian (Patrick)

Pyle, Ernest Taylor 1900-1945
See Pyle, Ernie
See also CA 115; 160

Pyle, Ernie 1900-1945 **TCLC 75**
See also Pyle, Ernest Taylor
See also DLB 29; MTCW 2

Pyle, Howard 1853-1911 **TCLC 81**
See also CA 109; 137; CLR 22; DLB 42, 188;
DLBD 13; MAICYA; SATA 16, 100

Pym, Barbara (Mary Crampton) 1913-1980
CLC 13, 19, 37, 111
See also CA 13-14; 97-100; CANR 13, 34; CAP
1; DLB 14, 207; DLBY 87; MTCW 1, 2

Pynchon, Thomas (Ruggles, Jr.) 1937-**CLC 2,**
3, 6, 9, 11, 18, 33, 62, 72; DA; DAB; DAC;
DAM MST, NOV, POP; SSC 14; WLC
See also BEST 90:2; CA 17-20R; CANR 22,
46, 73; DLB 2, 173; MTCW 1, 2

Pythagoras c. 570B.C.-c. 500B.C. **CMLC 22**
See also DLB 176

Q
See Quiller-Couch, SirArthur (Thomas)

Qian Zhongshu
See Ch'ien Chung-shu

Qroll
See Dagerman, Stig (Halvard)

Quarrington, Paul (Lewis) 1953- **CLC 65**
See also CA 129; CANR 62

Quasimodo, Salvatore 1901-1968 **CLC 10**
See also CA 13-16; 25-28R; CAP 1; DLB 114;
MTCW 1

Quay, Stephen 1947- **CLC 95**

Quay, Timothy 1947- **CLC 95**

Queen, Ellery **CLC 3, 11**
See also Dannay, Frederic; Davidson, Avram
(James); Lee, Manfred B(ennington);
Marlowe, Stephen; Sturgeon, Theodore
(Hamilton); Vance, John Holbrook

Queen, Ellery, Jr.
See Dannay, Frederic; Lee, Manfred
B(ennington)

Queneau, Raymond 1903-1976 **CLC 2, 5, 10,**
42
See also CA 77-80; 69-72; CANR 32; DLB 72;
MTCW 1, 2

Quevedo, Francisco de 1580-1645 **LC 23**

Quiller-Couch, SirArthur (Thomas) 1863-1944
TCLC 53
See also CA 118; 166; DLB 135, 153, 190

Quin, Ann (Marie) 1936-1973 **CLC 6**
See also CA 9-12R; 45-48; DLB 14

Quinn, Martin
See Smith, Martin Cruz

Quinn, Peter 1947- **CLC 91**

Quinn, Simon
See Smith, Martin Cruz

Quiroga, Horacio (Sylvestre) 1878-1937
TCLC 20; DAM MULT; HLC
See also CA 117; 131; HW; MTCW 1

Quoirez, Francoise 1935- **CLC 9**
See also Sagan, Francoise
See also CA 49-52; CANR 6, 39, 73; MTCW
1, 2

Raabe, Wilhelm (Karl) 1831-1910 **TCLC 45**
See also CA 167; DLB 129

Rabe, David (William) 1940- **CLC 4, 8, 33;**
DAM DRAM
See also CA 85-88; CABS 3; CANR 59; DLB
7

Rabelais, Francois 1483-1553**LC 5; DA; DAB;**
DAC; DAM MST; WLC

Rabinovitch, Sholem 1859-1916
See Aleichem, Sholom
See also CA 104

Rabinyan, Dorit 1972- **CLC 119**
See also CA 170

Rachilde 1860-1953 **TCLC 67**
See also DLB 123, 192

Racine, Jean 1639-1699 **LC 28; DAB; DAM**
MST

Radcliffe, Ann (Ward) 1764-1823**NCLC 6, 55**
See also DLB 39, 178

Radiguet, Raymond 1903-1923 **TCLC 29**
See also CA 162; DLB 65

Radnoti, Miklos 1909-1944 **TCLC 16**
See also CA 118

Rado, James 1939- **CLC 17**
See also CA 105

Radvanyi, Netty 1900-1983
See Seghers, Anna
See also CA 85-88; 110

Rae, Ben
See Griffiths, Trevor

Raeburn, John (Hay) 1941- **CLC 34**
See also CA 57-60

Ragni, Gerome 1942-1991 **CLC 17**
See also CA 105; 134

Rahv, Philip 1908-1973 **CLC 24**
See also Greenberg, Ivan
See also DLB 137

Raimund, Ferdinand Jakob 1790-1836**NCLC**
69
See also DLB 90

Raine, Craig 1944- **CLC 32, 103**

See Hartmann, Sadakichi

Sade, Donatien Alphonse Francois, Comte de 1740-1814   **NCLC 47**

Sadoff, Ira 1945-   **CLC 9**
See also CA 53-56; CANR 5, 21; DLB 120

Saetone
See Camus, Albert

Safire, William 1929-   **CLC 10**
See also CA 17-20R; CANR 31, 54

Sagan, Carl (Edward) 1934-1996 CLC 30, 112
See also AAYA 2; CA 25-28R; 155; CANR 11, 36, 74; MTCW 1, 2; SATA 58; SATA-Obit 94

Sagan, Francoise   **CLC 3, 6, 9, 17, 36**
See also Quoirez, Francoise
See also DLB 83; MTCW 2

Sahgal, Nayantara (Pandit) 1927-   **CLC 41**
See also CA 9-12R; CANR 11

Saint, H(arry) F. 1941-   **CLC 50**
See also CA 127

St. Aubin de Teran, Lisa 1953-
See Teran, Lisa St. Aubin de
See also CA 118; 126; INT 126

Saint Birgitta of Sweden c. 1303-1373 C M L C 24

Sainte-Beuve, Charles Augustin 1804-1869 **NCLC 5**

Saint-Exupery, Antoine (Jean Baptiste Marie Roger) de 1900-1944 TCLC 2, 56; DAM NOV; WLC
See also CA 108; 132; CLR 10; DLB 72; MAICYA; MTCW 1, 2; SATA 20

St. John, David
See Hunt, E(verette) Howard, (Jr.)

Saint-John Perse
See Leger, (Marie-Rene Auguste) Alexis Saint-Leger

Saintsbury, George (Edward Bateman) 1845-1933   **TCLC 31**
See also CA 160; DLB 57, 149

Sait Faik   **TCLC 23**
See also Abasiyanik, Sait Faik

Saki   **TCLC 3; SSC 12**
See also Munro, H(ector) H(ugh)
See also MTCW 2

Sala, George Augustus   **NCLC 46**

Salama, Hannu 1936-   **CLC 18**

Salamanca, J(ack) R(ichard) 1922-CLC 4, 15
See also CA 25-28R

Sale, J. Kirkpatrick
See Sale, Kirkpatrick

Sale, Kirkpatrick 1937-   **CLC 68**
See also CA 13-16R; CANR 10

Salinas, Luis Omar 1937-   **CLC 90; DAM MULT; HLC**
See also CA 131; DLB 82; HW

Salinas (y Serrano), Pedro 1891(?)-1951 **TCLC 17**
See also CA 117; DLB 134

Salinger, J(erome) D(avid) 1919-CLC 1, 3, 8, 12, 55, 56; DA; DAB; DAC; DAM MST, NOV, POP; SSC 2, 28; WLC
See also AAYA 2; CA 5-8R; CANR 39; CDALB 1941-1968; CLR 18; DLB 2, 102, 173; MAICYA; MTCW 1, 2; SATA 67

Salisbury, John
See Caute, (John) David

Salter, James 1925-   **CLC 7, 52, 59**
See also CA 73-76; DLB 130

Saltus, Edgar (Everton) 1855-1921 **TCLC 8**
See also CA 105; DLB 202

Saltykov, Mikhail Evgrafovich 1826-1889 **NCLC 16**

Samarakis, Antonis 1919-   **CLC 5**
See also CA 25-28R; CAAS 16; CANR 36

Sanchez, Florencio 1875-1910   **TCLC 37**
See also CA 153; HW

Sanchez, Luis Rafael 1936-   **CLC 23**
See also CA 128; DLB 145; HW

Sanchez, Sonia 1934-   **CLC 5, 116; BLC 3; DAM MULT; PC 9**
See also BW 2; CA 33-36R; CANR 24, 49, 74; CLR 18; DLB 41; DLBD 8; MAICYA; MTCW 1, 2; SATA 22

Sand, George 1804-1876NCLC 2, 42, 57; DA; DAB; DAC; DAM MST, NOV; WLC
See also DLB 119, 192

Sandburg, Carl (August) 1878-1967CLC 1, 4, 10, 15, 35; DA; DAB; DAC; DAM MST, POET; PC 2; WLC
See also AAYA 24; CA 5-8R; 25-28R; CANR 35; CDALB 1865-1917; DLB 17, 54; MAICYA; MTCW 1, 2; SATA 8

Sandburg, Charles
See Sandburg, Carl (August)

Sandburg, Charles A.
See Sandburg, Carl (August)

Sanders, (James) Ed(ward) 1939-   **CLC 53; DAM POET**
See also CA 13-16R; CAAS 21; CANR 13, 44, 78; DLB 16

Sanders, Lawrence 1920-1998CLC 41; DAM POP
See also BEST 89:4; CA 81-84; 165; CANR 33, 62; MTCW 1

Sanders, Noah
See Blount, Roy (Alton), Jr.

Sanders, Winston P.
See Anderson, Poul (William)

Sandoz, Mari(e Susette) 1896-1966   **CLC 28**
See also CA 1-4R; 25-28R; CANR 17, 64; DLB 9, 212; MTCW 1, 2; SATA 5

Saner, Reg(inald Anthony) 1931-   **CLC 9**
See also CA 65-68

Sankara 788-820   **CMLC 32**

Sannazaro, Jacopo 1456(?)-1530   **LC 8**

Sansom, William 1912-1976 CLC 2, 6; DAM NOV; SSC 21
See also CA 5-8R; 65-68; CANR 42; DLB 139; MTCW 1

Santayana, George 1863-1952   **TCLC 40**
See also CA 115; DLB 54, 71; DLBD 13

Santiago, Danny   **CLC 33**
See also James, Daniel (Lewis)
See also DLB 122

Santmyer, Helen Hoover 1895-1986 **CLC 33**
See also CA 1-4R; 118; CANR 15, 33; DLBY 84; MTCW 1

Santoka, Taneda 1882-1940   **TCLC 72**

Santos, Bienvenido N(uqui) 1911-1996 C L C 22; DAM MULT
See also CA 101; 151; CANR 19, 46

Sapper   **TCLC 44**
See also McNeile, Herman Cyril

Sapphire
See Sapphire, Brenda

Sapphire, Brenda 1950-   **CLC 99**

Sappho fl. 6th cent. B.C.-   **CMLC 3; DAM POET; PC 5**
See also DLB 176

Saramago, Jose 1922-   **CLC 119**
See also CA 153

Sarduy, Severo 1937-1993   **CLC 6, 97**
See also CA 89-92; 142; CANR 58; DLB 113; HW

Sargeson, Frank 1903-1982   **CLC 31**

See also CA 25-28R; 106; CANR 38

Sarmiento, Felix Ruben Garcia
See Dario, Ruben

Saro-Wiwa, Ken(ule Beeson) 1941-1995 C L C 114
See also BW 2; CA 142; 150; CANR 60; DLB 157

Saroyan, William 1908-1981CLC 1, 8, 10, 29, 34, 56; DA; DAB; DAC; DAM DRAM, MST, NOV; SSC 21; WLC
See also CA 5-8R; 103; CANR 30; DLB 7, 9, 86; DLBY 81; MTCW 1, 2; SATA 23; SATA-Obit 24

Sarraute, Nathalie 1900-CLC 1, 2, 4, 8, 10, 31, 80
See also CA 9-12R; CANR 23, 66; DLB 83; MTCW 1, 2

Sarton, (Eleanor) May 1912-1995 CLC 4, 14, 49, 91; DAM POET
See also CA 1-4R; 149; CANR 1, 34, 55; DLB 48; DLBY 81; INT CANR-34; MTCW 1, 2; SATA 36; SATA-Obit 86

Sartre, Jean-Paul 1905-1980CLC 1, 4, 7, 9, 13, 18, 24, 44, 50, 52; DA; DAB; DAC; DAM DRAM, MST, NOV; DC 3; SSC 32; WLC
See also CA 9-12R; 97-100; CANR 21; DLB 72; MTCW 1, 2

Sassoon, Siegfried (Lorraine) 1886-1967C L C 36; DAB; DAM MST, NOV, POET; PC 12
See also CA 104; 25-28R; CANR 36; DLB 20, 191; DLBD 18; MTCW 1, 2

Satterfield, Charles
See Pohl, Frederik

Saul, John (W. III) 1942-CLC 46; DAM NOV, POP
See also AAYA 10; BEST 90:4; CA 81-84; CANR 16, 40; SATA 98

Saunders, Caleb
See Heinlein, Robert A(nson)

Saura (Atares), Carlos 1932-   **CLC 20**
See also CA 114; 131; HW

Sauser-Hall, Frederic 1887-1961   **CLC 18**
See also Cendrars, Blaise
See also CA 102; 93-96; CANR 36, 62; MTCW 1

Saussure, Ferdinand de 1857-1913 **TCLC 49**

Savage, Catharine
See Brosman, Catharine Savage

Savage, Thomas 1915-   **CLC 40**
See also CA 126; 132; CAAS 15; INT 132

Savan, Glenn 19(?)-   **CLC 50**

Sayers, Dorothy L(eigh) 1893-1957 TCLC 2, 15; DAM POP
See also CA 104; 119; CANR 60; CDBLB 1914-1945; DLB 10, 36, 77, 100; MTCW 1, 2

Sayers, Valerie 1952-   **CLC 50**
See also CA 134; CANR 61

Sayles, John (Thomas) 1950-   **CLC 7, 10, 14**
See also CA 57-60; CANR 41; DLB 44

Scammell, Michael 1935-   **CLC 34**
See also CA 156

Scannell, Vernon 1922-   **CLC 49**
See also CA 5-8R; CANR 8, 24, 57; DLB 27; SATA 59

Scarlett, Susan
See Streatfeild, (Mary) Noel

Scarron
See Mikszath, Kalman

Schaeffer, Susan Fromberg 1941-CLC 6, 11, 22
See also CA 49-52; CANR 18, 65; DLB 28; MTCW 1, 2; SATA 22

Schary, Jill
See Robinson, Jill

Schell, Jonathan 1943- **CLC 35**
See also CA 73-76; CANR 12

Schelling, Friedrich Wilhelm Joseph von 1775-
1854 **NCLC 30**
See also DLB 90

Schendel, Arthur van 1874-1946 **TCLC 56**

Scherer, Jean-Marie Maurice 1920-
See Rohmer, Eric
See also CA 110

Schevill, James (Erwin) 1920- **CLC 7**
See also CA 5-8R; CAAS 12

Schiller, Friedrich 1759-1805 **NCLC 39, 69;
DAM DRAM**
See also DLB 94

Schisgal, Murray (Joseph) 1926- **CLC 6**
See also CA 21-24R; CANR 48

Schlee, Ann 1934- **CLC 35**
See also CA 101; CANR 29; SATA 44; SATA-
Brief 36

Schlegel, August Wilhelm von 1767-1845
NCLC 15
See also DLB 94

Schlegel, Friedrich 1772-1829 **NCLC 45**
See also DLB 90

Schlegel, Johann Elias (von) 1719(?)-1749L C
5

Schlesinger, Arthur M(eier), Jr. 1917-**CLC 84**
See also AITN 1; CA 1-4R; CANR 1, 28, 58;
DLB 17; INT CANR-28; MTCW 1, 2; SATA
61

Schmidt, Arno (Otto) 1914-1979 **CLC 56**
See also CA 128; 109; DLB 69

Schmitz, Aron Hector 1861-1928
See Svevo, Italo
See also CA 104; 122; MTCW 1

Schnackenberg, Gjertrud 1953- **CLC 40**
See also CA 116; DLB 120

Schneider, Leonard Alfred 1925-1966
See Bruce, Lenny
See also CA 89-92

Schnitzler, Arthur 1862-1931**TCLC 4; SSC 15**
See also CA 104; DLB 81, 118

Schoenberg, Arnold 1874-1951 **TCLC 75**
See also CA 109

Schonberg, Arnold
See Schoenberg, Arnold

Schopenhauer, Arthur 1788-1860 **NCLC 51**
See also DLB 90

Schor, Sandra (M.) 1932(?)-1990 **CLC 65**
See also CA 132

Schorer, Mark 1908-1977 **CLC 9**
See also CA 5-8R; 73-76; CANR 7; DLB 103

Schrader, Paul (Joseph) 1946- **CLC 26**
See also CA 37-40R; CANR 41; DLB 44

Schreiner, Olive (Emilie Albertina) 1855-1920
TCLC 9
See also CA 105; 154; DLB 18, 156, 190

Schulberg, Budd (Wilson) 1914- **CLC 7, 48**
See also CA 25-28R; CANR 19; DLB 6, 26,
28; DLBY 81

Schulz, Bruno 1892-1942**TCLC 5, 51; SSC 13**
See also CA 115; 123; MTCW 2

Schulz, Charles M(onroe) 1922- **CLC 12**
See also CA 9-12R; CANR 6; INT CANR-6;
SATA 10

Schumacher, E(rnst) F(riedrich) 1911-1977
CLC 80
See also CA 81-84; 73-76; CANR 34

Schuyler, James Marcus 1923-1991 **CLC 5,
23; DAM POET**
See also CA 101; 134; DLB 5, 169; INT 101

Schwartz, Delmore (David) 1913-1966**CLC 2,
4, 10, 45, 87; PC 8**
See also CA 17-18; 25-28R; CANR 35; CAP
2; DLB 28, 48; MTCW 1, 2

Schwartz, Ernst
See Ozu, Yasujiro

Schwartz, John Burnham 1965- **CLC 59**
See also CA 132

Schwartz, Lynne Sharon 1939- **CLC 31**
See also CA 103; CANR 44; MTCW 2

Schwartz, Muriel A.
See Eliot, T(homas) S(tearns)

Schwarz-Bart, Andre 1928- **CLC 2, 4**
See also CA 89-92

Schwarz-Bart, Simone 1938- **CLC 7; BLCS**
See also BW 2; CA 97-100

Schwob, Marcel (Mayer Andre) 1867-1905
TCLC 20
See also CA 117; 168; DLB 123

Sciascia, Leonardo 1921-1989 **CLC 8, 9, 41**
See also CA 85-88; 130; CANR 35; DLB 177;
MTCW 1

Scoppettone, Sandra 1936- **CLC 26**
See also AAYA 11; CA 5-8R; CANR 41, 73;
SATA 9, 92

Scorsese, Martin 1942- **CLC 20, 89**
See also CA 110; 114; CANR 46

Scotland, Jay
See Jakes, John (William)

Scott, Duncan Campbell 1862-1947 **TCLC 6;
DAC**
See also CA 104; 153; DLB 92

Scott, Evelyn 1893-1963 **CLC 43**
See also CA 104; 112; CANR 64; DLB 9, 48

Scott, F(rancis) R(eginald) 1899-1985**CLC 22**
See also CA 101; 114; DLB 88; INT 101

Scott, Frank
See Scott, F(rancis) R(eginald)

Scott, Joanna 1960- **CLC 50**
See also CA 126; CANR 53

Scott, Paul (Mark) 1920-1978 **CLC 9, 60**
See also CA 81-84; 77-80; CANR 33; DLB 14,
207; MTCW 1

Scott, Sarah 1723-1795 **LC 44**
See also DLB 39

Scott, Walter 1771-1832 **NCLC 15, 69; DA;
DAB; DAC; DAM MST, NOV, POET; PC
13; SSC 32; WLC**
See also AAYA 22; CDBLB 1789-1832; DLB
93, 107, 116, 144, 159; YABC 2

Scribe, (Augustin) Eugene 1791-1861 **N C L C
16; DAM DRAM; DC 5**
See also DLB 192

Scrum, R.
See Crumb, R(obert)

Scudery, Madeleine de 1607-1701 **LC 2**

Scum
See Crumb, R(obert)

Scumbag, Little Bobby
See Crumb, R(obert)

Seabrook, John
See Hubbard, L(afayette) Ron(ald)

Sealy, I. Allan 1951- **CLC 55**

Search, Alexander
See Pessoa, Fernando (Antonio Nogueira)

Sebastian, Lee
See Silverberg, Robert

Sebastian Owl
See Thompson, Hunter S(tockton)

Sebestyen, Ouida 1924- **CLC 30**
See also AAYA 8; CA 107; CANR 40; CLR
17; JRDA; MAICYA; SAAS 10; SATA 39

Secundus, H. Scriblerus

See Fielding, Henry

Sedges, John
See Buck, Pearl S(ydenstricker)

Sedgwick, Catharine Maria 1789-1867**NCLC
19**
See also DLB 1, 74

Seelye, John (Douglas) 1931- **CLC 7**
See also CA 97-100; CANR 70; INT 97-100

Seferiades, Giorgos Stylianou 1900-1971
See Seferis, George
See also CA 5-8R; 33-36R; CANR 5, 36;
MTCW 1

Seferis, George **CLC 5, 11**
See also Seferiades, Giorgos Stylianou

Segal, Erich (Wolf) 1937- **CLC 3, 10; DAM
POP**
See also BEST 89:1; CA 25-28R; CANR 20,
36, 65; DLBY 86; INT CANR-20; MTCW 1

Seger, Bob 1945- **CLC 35**

Seghers, Anna **CLC 7**
See also Radvanyi, Netty
See also DLB 69

Seidel, Frederick (Lewis) 1936- **CLC 18**
See also CA 13-16R; CANR 8; DLBY 84

Seifert, Jaroslav 1901-1986 **CLC 34, 44, 93**
See also CA 127; MTCW 1, 2

Sei Shonagon c. 966-1017(?) **CMLC 6**

S<eacute>jour, Victor 1817-1874 **DC 10**
See also DLB 50

Sejour Marcou et Ferrand, Juan Victor
See S<eacute>jour, Victor

Selby, Hubert, Jr. 1928-**CLC 1, 2, 4, 8; SSC 20**
See also CA 13-16R; CANR 33; DLB 2

Selzer, Richard 1928- **CLC 74**
See also CA 65-68; CANR 14

Sembene, Ousmane
See Ousmane, Sembene

Senancour, Etienne Pivert de 1770-1846
NCLC 16
See also DLB 119

Sender, Ramon (Jose) 1902-1982 **CLC 8;
DAM MULT; HLC**
See also CA 5-8R; 105; CANR 8; HW; MTCW
1

Seneca, Lucius Annaeus c. 1-c. 65 **CMLC 6;
DAM DRAM; DC 5**
See also DLB 211

Senghor, Leopold Sedar 1906-**CLC 54; BLC
3; DAM MULT, POET; PC 25**
See also BW 2; CA 116; 125; CANR 47, 74;
MTCW 1, 2

Senna, Danzy 1970- **CLC 119**
See also CA 169

Serling, (Edward) Rod(man) 1924-1975 **C L C
30**
See also AAYA 14; AITN 1; CA 162; 57-60;
DLB 26

Serna, Ramon Gomez de la
See Gomez de la Serna, Ramon

Serpieres
See Guillevic, (Eugene)

Service, Robert
See Service, Robert W(illiam)
See also DAB; DLB 92

Service, Robert W(illiam) 1874(?)-1958**TCLC
15; DA; DAC; DAM MST, POET; WLC**
See also Service, Robert
See also CA 115; 140; SATA 20

Seth, Vikram 1952-**CLC 43, 90; DAM MULT**
See also CA 121; 127; CANR 50, 74; DLB 120;
INT 127; MTCW 2

Seton, Cynthia Propper 1926-1982 **CLC 27**
See also CA 5-8R; 108; CANR 7

See also CA 93-96; CANR 63
Smith, Pauline (Urmson) 1882-1959 **TCLC 25**
Smith, Rosamond
See Oates, Joyce Carol
Smith, Sheila Kaye
See Kaye-Smith, Sheila
Smith, Stevie   **CLC 3, 8, 25, 44; PC 12**
See also Smith, Florence Margaret
See also DLB 20; MTCW 2
Smith, Wilbur (Addison) 1933-   **CLC 33**
See also CA 13-16R; CANR 7, 46, 66; MTCW 1, 2
Smith, William Jay 1918-   **CLC 6**
See also CA 5-8R; CANR 44; DLB 5; MAICYA; SAAS 22; SATA 2, 68
Smith, Woodrow Wilson
See Kuttner, Henry
Smolenskin, Peretz 1842-1885   **NCLC 30**
Smollett, Tobias (George) 1721-1771 **LC 2, 46**
See also CDBLB 1660-1789; DLB 39, 104
Snodgrass, W(illiam) D(e Witt) 1926- **CLC 2, 6, 10, 18, 68; DAM POET**
See also CA 1-4R; CANR 6, 36, 65; DLB 5; MTCW 1, 2
Snow, C(harles) P(ercy) 1905-1980 **CLC 1, 4, 6, 9, 13, 19; DAM NOV**
See also CA 5-8R; 101; CANR 28; CDBLB 1945-1960; DLB 15, 77; DLBD 17; MTCW 1, 2
Snow, Frances Compton
See Adams, Henry (Brooks)
Snyder, Gary (Sherman) 1930- **CLC 1, 2, 5, 9, 32; DAM POET; PC 21**
See also CA 17-20R; CANR 30, 60; DLB 5, 16, 165, 212; MTCW 2
Snyder, Zilpha Keatley 1927-   **CLC 17**
See also AAYA 15; CA 9-12R; CANR 38; CLR 31; JRDA; MAICYA; SAAS 2; SATA 1, 28, 75
Soares, Bernardo
See Pessoa, Fernando (Antonio Nogueira)
Sobh, A.
See Shamlu, Ahmad
Sobol, Joshua   **CLC 60**
Socrates 469B.C.-399B.C.   **CMLC 27**
Soderberg, Hjalmar 1869-1941   **TCLC 39**
Sodergran, Edith (Irene)
See Soedergran, Edith (Irene)
Soedergran, Edith (Irene) 1892-1923 **T C L C 31**
Softly, Edgar
See Lovecraft, H(oward) P(hillips)
Softly, Edward
See Lovecraft, H(oward) P(hillips)
Sokolov, Raymond 1941-   **CLC 7**
See also CA 85-88
Solo, Jay
See Ellison, Harlan (Jay)
Sologub, Fyodor   **TCLC 9**
See also Teternikov, Fyodor Kuzmich
Solomons, Ikey Esquir
See Thackeray, William Makepeace
Solomos, Dionysios 1798-1857   **NCLC 15**
Solwoska, Mara
See French, Marilyn
Solzhenitsyn, Aleksandr I(sayevich) 1918- **CLC 1, 2, 4, 7, 9, 10, 18, 26, 34, 78; DA; DAB; DAC; DAM MST, NOV; SSC 32; WLC**
See also AITN 1; CA 69-72; CANR 40, 65; MTCW 1, 2
Somers, Jane
See Lessing, Doris (May)

Somerville, Edith 1858-1949   **TCLC 51**
See also DLB 135
Somerville & Ross
See Martin, Violet Florence; Somerville, Edith
Sommer, Scott 1951-   **CLC 25**
See also CA 106
Sondheim, Stephen (Joshua) 1930- **CLC 30, 39; DAM DRAM**
See also AAYA 11; CA 103; CANR 47, 68
Song, Cathy 1955-   **PC 21**
See also CA 154; DLB 169
Sontag, Susan 1933- **CLC 1, 2, 10, 13, 31, 105; DAM POP**
See also CA 17-20R; CANR 25, 51, 74; DLB 2, 67; MTCW 1, 2
Sophocles 496(?)B.C.-406(?)B.C.   **CMLC 2; DA; DAB; DAC; DAM DRAM, MST; DC 1; WLCS**
See also DLB 176
Sordello 1189-1269   **CMLC 15**
Sorel, Georges 1847-1922   **TCLC 91**
See also CA 118
Sorel, Julia
See Drexler, Rosalyn
Sorrentino, Gilbert 1929- **CLC 3, 7, 14, 22, 40**
See also CA 77-80; CANR 14, 33; DLB 5, 173; DLBY 80; INT CANR-14
Soto, Gary 1952- **CLC 32, 80; DAM MULT; HLC**
See also AAYA 10; CA 119; 125; CANR 50, 74; CLR 38; DLB 82; HW; INT 125; JRDA; MTCW 2; SATA 80
Soupault, Philippe 1897-1990   **CLC 68**
See also CA 116; 147; 131
Souster, (Holmes) Raymond 1921- **CLC 5, 14; DAC; DAM POET**
See also CA 13-16R; CAAS 14; CANR 13, 29, 53; DLB 88; SATA 63
Southern, Terry 1924(?)-1995   **CLC 7**
See also CA 1-4R; 150; CANR 1, 55; DLB 2
Southey, Robert 1774-1843   **NCLC 8**
See also DLB 93, 107, 142; SATA 54
Southworth, Emma Dorothy Eliza Nevitte 1819-1899   **NCLC 26**
Souza, Ernest
See Scott, Evelyn
Soyinka, Wole 1934- **CLC 3, 5, 14, 36, 44; BLC 3; DA; DAB; DAC; DAM DRAM, MST, MULT; DC 2; WLC**
See also BW 2; CA 13-16R; CANR 27, 39; DLB 125; MTCW 1, 2
Spackman, W(illiam) M(ode) 1905-1990 **C L C 46**
See also CA 81-84; 132
Spacks, Barry (Bernard) 1931-   **CLC 14**
See also CA 154; CANR 33; DLB 105
Spanidou, Irini 1946-   **CLC 44**
Spark, Muriel (Sarah) 1918- **CLC 2, 3, 5, 8, 13, 18, 40, 94; DAB; DAC; DAM MST, NOV; SSC 10**
See also CA 5-8R; CANR 12, 36, 76; CDBLB 1945-1960; DLB 15, 139; INT CANR-12; MTCW 1, 2
Spaulding, Douglas
See Bradbury, Ray (Douglas)
Spaulding, Leonard
See Bradbury, Ray (Douglas)
Spence, J. A. D.
See Eliot, T(homas) S(tearns)
Spencer, Elizabeth 1921-   **CLC 22**
See also CA 13-16R; CANR 32, 65; DLB 6; MTCW 1; SATA 14
Spencer, Leonard G.

See Silverberg, Robert
Spencer, Scott 1945-   **CLC 30**
See also CA 113; CANR 51; DLBY 86
Spender, Stephen (Harold) 1909-1995 **CLC 1, 2, 5, 10, 41, 91; DAM POET**
See also CA 9-12R; 149; CANR 31, 54; CDBLB 1945-1960; DLB 20; MTCW 1, 2
Spengler, Oswald (Arnold Gottfried) 1880-1936 **TCLC 25**
See also CA 118
Spenser, Edmund 1552(?)-1599 **LC 5, 39; DA; DAB; DAC; DAM MST, POET; PC 8; WLC**
See also CDBLB Before 1660; DLB 167
Spicer, Jack 1925-1965 **CLC 8, 18, 72; DAM POET**
See also CA 85-88; DLB 5, 16, 193
Spiegelman, Art 1948-   **CLC 76**
See also AAYA 10; CA 125; CANR 41, 55, 74; MTCW 2
Spielberg, Peter 1929-   **CLC 6**
See also CA 5-8R; CANR 4, 48; DLBY 81
Spielberg, Steven 1947-   **CLC 20**
See also AAYA 8, 24; CA 77-80; CANR 32; SATA 32
Spillane, Frank Morrison 1918-
See Spillane, Mickey
See also CA 25-28R; CANR 28, 63; MTCW 1, 2; SATA 66
Spillane, Mickey   **CLC 3, 13**
See also Spillane, Frank Morrison
See also MTCW 2
Spinoza, Benedictus de 1632-1677   **LC 9**
Spinrad, Norman (Richard) 1940-   **CLC 46**
See also CA 37-40R; CAAS 19; CANR 20; DLB 8; INT CANR-20
Spitteler, Carl (Friedrich Georg) 1845-1924 **TCLC 12**
See also CA 109; DLB 129
Spivack, Kathleen (Romola Drucker) 1938- **CLC 6**
See also CA 49-52
Spoto, Donald 1941-   **CLC 39**
See also CA 65-68; CANR 11, 57
Springsteen, Bruce (F.) 1949-   **CLC 17**
See also CA 111
Spurling, Hilary 1940-   **CLC 34**
See also CA 104; CANR 25, 52
Spyker, John Howland
See Elman, Richard (Martin)
Squires, (James) Radcliffe 1917-1993 **CLC 51**
See also CA 1-4R; 140; CANR 6, 21
Srivastava, Dhanpat Rai 1880(?)-1936
See Premchand
See also CA 118
Stacy, Donald
See Pohl, Frederik
Stael, Germaine de 1766-1817
See Stael-Holstein, Anne Louise Germaine Necker Baronn
See also DLB 119
Stael-Holstein, Anne Louise Germaine Necker Baronn 1766-1817   **NCLC 3**
See also Stael, Germaine de
See also DLB 192
Stafford, Jean 1915-1979 **CLC 4, 7, 19, 68; SSC 26**
See also CA 1-4R; 85-88; CANR 3, 65; DLB 2, 173; MTCW 1, 2; SATA-Obit 22
Stafford, William (Edgar) 1914-1993 **CLC 4, 7, 29; DAM POET**
See also CA 5-8R; 142; CAAS 3; CANR 5, 22; DLB 5, 206; INT CANR-22

56; DLB 15, 160; JRDA; MAICYA; MTCW
1, 2; SATA 2, 32, 100; SATA-Obit 24

Toller, Ernst 1893-1939 **TCLC 10**
See also CA 107; DLB 124

Tolson, M. B.
See Tolson, Melvin B(eaunorus)

Tolson, Melvin B(eaunorus) 1898(?)-1966
CLC 36, 105; BLC 3; DAM MULT, POET
See also BW 1; CA 124; 89-92; DLB 48, 76

Tolstoi, Aleksei Nikolaevich
See Tolstoy, Alexey Nikolaevich

Tolstoy, Alexey Nikolaevich 1882-1945 **TCLC 18**
See also CA 107; 158

Tolstoy, Count Leo
See Tolstoy, Leo (Nikolaevich)

Tolstoy, Leo (Nikolaevich) 1828-1910 **T C L C 4, 11, 17, 28, 44, 79; DA; DAB; DAC; DAM MST, NOV; SSC 9, 30; WLC**
See also CA 104; 123; SATA 26

Tomasi di Lampedusa, Giuseppe 1896-1957
See Lampedusa, Giuseppe (Tomasi) di
See also CA 111

Tomlin, Lily **CLC 17**
See also Tomlin, Mary Jean

Tomlin, Mary Jean 1939(?)-
See Tomlin, Lily
See also CA 117

Tomlinson, (Alfred) Charles 1927- **CLC 2, 4, 6, 13, 45; DAM POET; PC 17**
See also CA 5-8R; CANR 33; DLB 40

Tomlinson, H(enry) M(ajor) 1873-1958 **TCLC 71**
See also CA 118; 161; DLB 36, 100, 195

Tonson, Jacob
See Bennett, (Enoch) Arnold

Toole, John Kennedy 1937-1969 **CLC 19, 64**
See also CA 104; DLBY 81; MTCW 2

Toomer, Jean 1894-1967 **CLC 1, 4, 13, 22; BLC 3; DAM MULT; PC 7; SSC 1; WLCS**
See also BW 1; CA 85-88; CDALB 1917-1929; DLB 45, 51; MTCW 1, 2

Torley, Luke
See Blish, James (Benjamin)

Tornimparte, Alessandra
See Ginzburg, Natalia

Torre, Raoul della
See Mencken, H(enry) L(ouis)

Torrey, E(dwin) Fuller 1937- **CLC 34**
See also CA 119; CANR 71

Torsvan, Ben Traven
See Traven, B.

Torsvan, Benno Traven
See Traven, B.

Torsvan, Berick Traven
See Traven, B.

Torsvan, Berwick Traven
See Traven, B.

Torsvan, Bruno Traven
See Traven, B.

Torsvan, Traven
See Traven, B.

Tournier, Michel (Edouard) 1924- **CLC 6, 23, 36, 95**
See also CA 49-52; CANR 3, 36, 74; DLB 83; MTCW 1, 2; SATA 23

Tournimparte, Alessandra
See Ginzburg, Natalia

Towers, Ivar
See Kornbluth, C(yril) M.

Towne, Robert (Burton) 1936(?)- **CLC 87**
See also CA 108; DLB 44

Townsend, Sue **CLC 61**

See also Townsend, Susan Elaine
See also AAYA 28; SATA 55, 93; SATA-Brief 48

Townsend, Susan Elaine 1946-
See Townsend, Sue
See also CA 119; 127; CANR 65; DAB; DAC; DAM MST

Townshend, Peter (Dennis Blandford) 1945- **CLC 17, 42**
See also CA 107

Tozzi, Federigo 1883-1920 **TCLC 31**
See also CA 160

Traill, Catharine Parr 1802-1899 **NCLC 31**
See also DLB 99

Trakl, Georg 1887-1914 **TCLC 5; PC 20**
See also CA 104; 165; MTCW 2

Transtroemer, Tomas (Goesta) 1931- **CLC 52, 65; DAM POET**
See also CA 117; 129; CAAS 17

Transtromer, Tomas Gosta
See Transtroemer, Tomas (Goesta)

Traven, B. (?)-1969 **CLC 8, 11**
See also CA 19-20; 25-28R; CAP 2; DLB 9, 56; MTCW 1

Treitel, Jonathan 1959- **CLC 70**

Tremain, Rose 1943- **CLC 42**
See also CA 97-100; CANR 44; DLB 14

Tremblay, Michel 1942- **CLC 29, 102; DAC; DAM MST**
See also CA 116; 128; DLB 60; MTCW 1, 2

Trevanian **CLC 29**
See also Whitaker, Rod(ney)

Trevor, Glen
See Hilton, James

Trevor, William 1928- **CLC 7, 9, 14, 25, 71, 116; SSC 21**
See also Cox, William Trevor
See also DLB 14, 139; MTCW 2

Trifonov, Yuri (Valentinovich) 1925-1981 **CLC 45**
See also CA 126; 103; MTCW 1

Trilling, Lionel 1905-1975 **CLC 9, 11, 24**
See also CA 9-12R; 61-64; CANR 10; DLB 28, 63; INT CANR-10; MTCW 1, 2

Trimball, W. H.
See Mencken, H(enry) L(ouis)

Tristan
See Gomez de la Serna, Ramon

Tristram
See Housman, A(lfred) E(dward)

Trogdon, William (Lewis) 1939-
See Heat-Moon, William Least
See also CA 115; 119; CANR 47; INT 119

Trollope, Anthony 1815-1882 **NCLC 6, 33; DA; DAB; DAC; DAM MST, NOV; SSC 28; WLC**
See also CDBLB 1832-1890; DLB 21, 57, 159; SATA 22

Trollope, Frances 1779-1863 **NCLC 30**
See also DLB 21, 166

Trotsky, Leon 1879-1940 **TCLC 22**
See also CA 118; 167

Trotter (Cockburn), Catharine 1679-1749 **L C 8**
See also DLB 84

Trout, Kilgore
See Farmer, Philip Jose

Trow, George W. S. 1943- **CLC 52**
See also CA 126

Troyat, Henri 1911- **CLC 23**
See also CA 45-48; CANR 2, 33, 67; MTCW 1

Trudeau, G(arretson) B(eekman) 1948-
See Trudeau, Garry B.

See also CA 81-84; CANR 31; SATA 35

Trudeau, Garry B. **CLC 12**
See also Trudeau, G(arretson) B(eekman)
See also AAYA 10; AITN 2

Truffaut, Francois 1932-1984 **CLC 20, 101**
See also CA 81-84; 113; CANR 34

Trumbo, Dalton 1905-1976 **CLC 19**
See also CA 21-24R; 69-72; CANR 10; DLB 26

Trumbull, John 1750-1831 **NCLC 30**
See also DLB 31

Trundlett, Helen B.
See Eliot, T(homas) S(tearns)

Tryon, Thomas 1926-1991 **CLC 3, 11; DAM POP**
See also AITN 1; CA 29-32R; 135; CANR 32, 77; MTCW 1

Tryon, Tom
See Tryon, Thomas

Ts'ao Hsueh-ch'in 1715(?)-1763 **LC 1**

Tsushima, Shuji 1909-1948
See Dazai Osamu
See also CA 107

Tsvetaeva (Efron), Marina (Ivanovna) 1892-1941 **TCLC 7, 35; PC 14**
See also CA 104; 128; CANR 73; MTCW 1, 2

Tuck, Lily 1938- **CLC 70**
See also CA 139

Tu Fu 712-770 **PC 9**
See also DAM MULT

Tunis, John R(oberts) 1889-1975 **CLC 12**
See also CA 61-64; CANR 62; DLB 22, 171; JRDA; MAICYA; SATA 37; SATA-Brief 30

Tuohy, Frank **CLC 37**
See also Tuohy, John Francis
See also DLB 14, 139

Tuohy, John Francis 1925-
See Tuohy, Frank
See also CA 5-8R; CANR 3, 47

Turco, Lewis (Putnam) 1934- **CLC 11, 63**
See also CA 13-16R; CAAS 22; CANR 24, 51; DLBY 84

Turgenev, Ivan 1818-1883 **NCLC 21; DA; DAB; DAC; DAM MST, NOV; DC 7; SSC 7; WLC**

Turgot, Anne-Robert-Jacques 1727-1781 **L C 26**

Turner, Frederick 1943- **CLC 48**
See also CA 73-76; CAAS 10; CANR 12, 30, 56; DLB 40

Tutu, Desmond M(pilo) 1931- **CLC 80; BLC 3; DAM MULT**
See also BW 1; CA 125; CANR 67

Tutuola, Amos 1920-1997 **CLC 5, 14, 29; BLC 3; DAM MULT**
See also BW 2; CA 9-12R; 159; CANR 27, 66; DLB 125; MTCW 1, 2

Twain, Mark TCLC 6, 12, 19, 36, 48, 59; SSC 34; WLC
See also Clemens, Samuel Langhorne
See also AAYA 20; DLB 11, 12, 23, 64, 74

Tyler, Anne 1941- **CLC 7, 11, 18, 28, 44, 59, 103; DAM NOV, POP**
See also AAYA 18; BEST 89:1; CA 9-12R; CANR 11, 33, 53; DLB 6, 143; DLBY 82; MTCW 1, 2; SATA 7, 90

Tyler, Royall 1757-1826 **NCLC 3**
See also DLB 37

Tynan, Katharine 1861-1931 **TCLC 3**
See also CA 104; 167; DLB 153

Tyutchev, Fyodor 1803-1873 **NCLC 34**

Tzara, Tristan 1896-1963 **CLC 47; DAM POET**

West, C. P.
See Wodehouse, P(elham) G(renville)

West, (Mary) Jessamyn 1902-1984 CLC 7, 17
See also CA 9-12R; 112; CANR 27; DLB 6;
DLBY 84; MTCW 1, 2; SATA-Obit 37

West, Morris L(anglo) 1916- **CLC 6, 33**
See also CA 5-8R; CANR 24, 49, 64; MTCW
1, 2

West, Nathanael 1903-1940 **TCLC 1, 14, 44;**
SSC 16
See also CA 104; 125; CDALB 1929-1941;
DLB 4, 9, 28; MTCW 1, 2

West, Owen
See Koontz, Dean R(ay)

West, Paul 1930- **CLC 7, 14, 96**
See also CA 13-16R; CAAS 7; CANR 22, 53,
76; DLB 14; INT CANR-22; MTCW 2

West, Rebecca 1892-1983 **CLC 7, 9, 31, 50**
See also CA 5-8R; 109; CANR 19; DLB 36;
DLBY 83; MTCW 1, 2

Westall, Robert (Atkinson) 1929-1993 **CLC 17**
See also AAYA 12; CA 69-72; 141; CANR 18,
68; CLR 13; JRDA; MAICYA; SAAS 2;
SATA 23, 69; SATA-Obit 75

Westermarck, Edward 1862-1939 **TCLC 87**

Westlake, Donald E(dwin) 1933- **CLC 7, 33;**
DAM POP
See also CA 17-20R; CAAS 13; CANR 16, 44,
65; INT CANR-16; MTCW 2

Westmacott, Mary
See Christie, Agatha (Mary Clarissa)

Weston, Allen
See Norton, Andre

Wetcheek, J. L.
See Feuchtwanger, Lion

Wetering, Janwillem van de
See van de Wetering, Janwillem

Wetherald, Agnes Ethelwyn 1857-1940 **TCLC**
81
See also DLB 99

Wetherell, Elizabeth
See Warner, Susan (Bogert)

Whale, James 1889-1957 **TCLC 63**

Whalen, Philip 1923- **CLC 6, 29**
See also CA 9-12R; CANR 5, 39; DLB 16

Wharton, Edith (Newbold Jones) 1862-1937
TCLC 3, 9, 27, 53; DA; DAB; DAC; DAM
MST, NOV; SSC 6; WLC
See also AAYA 25; CA 104; 132; CDALB
1865-1917; DLB 4, 9, 12, 78, 189; DLBD
13; MTCW 1, 2

Wharton, James
See Mencken, H(enry) L(ouis)

Wharton, William (a pseudonym) **CLC 18, 37**
See also CA 93-96; DLBY 80; INT 93-96

Wheatley (Peters), Phillis 1754(?)-1784 **LC 3,**
50; BLC 3; DA; DAC; DAM MST, MULT,
POET; PC 3; WLC
See also CDALB 1640-1865; DLB 31, 50

Wheelock, John Hall 1886-1978 **CLC 14**
See also CA 13-16R; 77-80; CANR 14; DLB
45

White, E(lwyn) B(rooks) 1899-1985 **CLC 10,**
34, 39; DAM POP
See also AITN 2; CA 13-16R; 116; CANR 16,
37; CLR 1, 21; DLB 11, 22; MAICYA;
MTCW 1, 2; SATA 2, 29, 100; SATA-Obit
44

White, Edmund (Valentine III) 1940- **CLC 27,**
110; DAM POP
See also AAYA 7; CA 45-48; CANR 3, 19, 36,
62; MTCW 1, 2

White, Patrick (Victor Martindale) 1912-1990

CLC 3, 4, 5, 7, 9, 18, 65, 69
See also CA 81-84; 132; CANR 43; MTCW 1

White, Phyllis Dorothy James 1920-
See James, P. D.
See also CA 21-24R; CANR 17, 43, 65; DAM
POP; MTCW 1, 2

White, T(erence) H(anbury) 1906-1964 **C L C**
30
See also AAYA 22; CA 73-76; CANR 37; DLB
160; JRDA; MAICYA; SATA 12

White, Terence de Vere 1912-1994 **CLC 49**
See also CA 49-52; 145; CANR 3

White, Walter
See White, Walter F(rancis)
See also BLC; DAM MULT

White, Walter F(rancis) 1893-1955 **TCLC 15**
See also White, Walter
See also BW 1; CA 115; 124; DLB 51

White, William Hale 1831-1913
See Rutherford, Mark
See also CA 121

Whitehead, E(dward) A(nthony) 1933- **CLC 5**
See also CA 65-68; CANR 58

Whitemore, Hugh (John) 1936- **CLC 37**
See also CA 132; CANR 77; INT 132

Whitman, Sarah Helen (Power) 1803-1878
NCLC 19
See also DLB 1

Whitman, Walt(er) 1819-1892 **NCLC 4, 31;**
DA; DAB; DAC; DAM MST, POET; PC
3; WLC
See also CDALB 1640-1865; DLB 3, 64; SATA
20

Whitney, Phyllis A(yame) 1903- **CLC 42;**
DAM POP
See also AITN 2; BEST 90:3; CA 1-4R; CANR
3, 25, 38, 60; JRDA; MAICYA; MTCW 2;
SATA 1, 30

Whittemore, (Edward) Reed (Jr.) 1919- **C L C**
4
See also CA 9-12R; CAAS 8; CANR 4; DLB 5

Whittier, John Greenleaf 1807-1892 **NCLC 8,**
59
See also DLB 1

Whittlebot, Hernia
See Coward, Noel (Peirce)

Wicker, Thomas Grey 1926-
See Wicker, Tom
See also CA 65-68; CANR 21, 46

Wicker, Tom **CLC 7**
See also Wicker, Thomas Grey

Wideman, John Edgar 1941- **CLC 5, 34, 36,**
67; BLC 3; DAM MULT
See also BW 2; CA 85-88; CANR 14, 42, 67;
DLB 33, 143; MTCW 2

Wiebe, Rudy (Henry) 1934- **CLC 6, 11, 14;**
DAC; DAM MST
See also CA 37-40R; CANR 42, 67; DLB 60

Wieland, Christoph Martin 1733-1813 **N C L C**
17
See also DLB 97

Wiene, Robert 1881-1938 **TCLC 56**

Wieners, John 1934- **CLC 7**
See also CA 13-16R; DLB 16

Wiesel, Elie(zer) 1928- **CLC 3, 5, 11, 37; DA;**
DAB; DAC; DAM MST, NOV; WLCS
See also AAYA 7; AITN 1; CA 5-8R; CAAS
4; CANR 8, 40, 65; DLB 83; DLBY 87; INT
CANR-8; MTCW 1, 2; SATA 56

Wiggins, Marianne 1947- **CLC 57**
See also BEST 89:3; CA 130; CANR 60

Wight, James Alfred 1916-1995
See Herriot, James

See also CA 77-80; SATA 55; SATA-Brief 44

Wilbur, Richard (Purdy) 1921- **CLC 3, 6, 9,**
14, 53, 110; DA; DAB; DAC; DAM MST,
POET
See also CA 1-4R; CABS 2; CANR 2, 29, 76;
DLB 5, 169; INT CANR-29; MTCW 1, 2;
SATA 9

Wild, Peter 1940- **CLC 14**
See also CA 37-40R; DLB 5

Wilde, Oscar 1854(?)-1900 **TCLC 1, 8, 23, 41;**
DA; DAB; DAC; DAM DRAM, MST,
NOV; SSC 11; WLC
See also CA 104; 119; CDBLB 1890-1914;
DLB 10, 19, 34, 57, 141, 156, 190; SATA
24

Wilder, Billy **CLC 20**
See also Wilder, Samuel
See also DLB 26

Wilder, Samuel 1906-
See Wilder, Billy
See also CA 89-92

Wilder, Thornton (Niven) 1897-1975 **CLC 1,**
5, 6, 10, 15, 35, 82; DA; DAB; DAC; DAM
DRAM, MST, NOV; DC 1; WLC
See also AAYA 29; AITN 2; CA 13-16R; 61-
64; CANR 40; DLB 4, 7, 9; DLBY 97;
MTCW 1, 2

Wilding, Michael 1942- **CLC 73**
See also CA 104; CANR 24, 49

Wiley, Richard 1944- **CLC 44**
See also CA 121; 129; CANR 71

Wilhelm, Kate **CLC 7**
See also Wilhelm, Katie Gertrude
See also AAYA 20; CAAS 5; DLB 8; INT
CANR-17

Wilhelm, Katie Gertrude 1928-
See Wilhelm, Kate
See also CA 37-40R; CANR 17, 36, 60; MTCW
1

Wilkins, Mary
See Freeman, Mary Eleanor Wilkins

Willard, Nancy 1936- **CLC 7, 37**
See also CA 89-92; CANR 10, 39, 68; CLR 5;
DLB 5, 52; MAICYA; MTCW 1; SATA 37,
71; SATA-Brief 30

William of Ockham 1285-1347 **CMLC 32**

Williams, Ben Ames 1889-1953 **TCLC 89**
See also DLB 102

Williams, C(harles) K(enneth) 1936- **CLC 33,**
56; DAM POET
See also CA 37-40R; CAAS 26; CANR 57;
DLB 5

Williams, Charles
See Collier, James L(incoln)

Williams, Charles (Walter Stansby) 1886-1945
TCLC 1, 11
See also CA 104; 163; DLB 100, 153

Williams, (George) Emlyn 1905-1987 **CLC 15;**
DAM DRAM
See also CA 104; 123; CANR 36; DLB 10, 77;
MTCW 1

Williams, Hank 1923-1953 **TCLC 81**

Williams, Hugo 1942- **CLC 42**
See also CA 17-20R; CANR 45; DLB 40

Williams, J. Walker
See Wodehouse, P(elham) G(renville)

Williams, John A(lfred) 1925- **CLC 5, 13; BLC**
3; DAM MULT
See also BW 2; CA 53-56; CAAS 3; CANR 6,
26, 51; DLB 2, 33; INT CANR-6

Williams, Jonathan (Chamberlain) 1929-
CLC 13
See also CA 9-12R; CAAS 12; CANR 8; DLB

5
Williams, Joy 1944- **CLC 31**
See also CA 41-44R; CANR 22, 48
Williams, Norman 1952- **CLC 39**
See also CA 118
Williams, Sherley Anne 1944-**CLC 89; BLC 3;**
DAM MULT, POET
See also BW 2; CA 73-76; CANR 25; DLB 41;
INT CANR-25; SATA 78
Williams, Shirley
See Williams, Sherley Anne
Williams, Tennessee 1911-1983**CLC 1, 2, 5, 7,**
8, 11, 15, 19, 30, 39, 45, 71, 111; DA; DAB;
DAC; DAM DRAM, MST; DC 4; WLC
See also AITN 1, 2; CA 5-8R; 108; CABS 3;
CANR 31; CDALB 1941-1968; DLB 7;
DLBD 4; DLBY 83; MTCW 1, 2
Williams, Thomas (Alonzo) 1926-1990 **C L C**
14
See also CA 1-4R; 132; CANR 2
Williams, William C.
See Williams, William Carlos
Williams, William Carlos 1883-1963**CLC 1, 2,**
5, 9, 13, 22, 42, 67; DA; DAB; DAC; DAM
MST, POET; PC 7; SSC 31
See also CA 89-92; CANR 34; CDALB 1917-
1929; DLB 4, 16, 54, 86; MTCW 1, 2
Williamson, David (Keith) 1942- **CLC 56**
See also CA 103; CANR 41
Williamson, Ellen Douglas 1905-1984
See Douglas, Ellen
See also CA 17-20R; 114; CANR 39
Williamson, Jack **CLC 29**
See also Williamson, John Stewart
See also CAAS 8; DLB 8
Williamson, John Stewart 1908-
See Williamson, Jack
See also CA 17-20R; CANR 23, 70
Willie, Frederick
See Lovecraft, H(oward) P(hillips)
Willingham, Calder (Baynard, Jr.) 1922-1995
CLC 5, 51
See also CA 5-8R; 147; CANR 3; DLB 2, 44;
MTCW 1
Willis, Charles
See Clarke, Arthur C(harles)
Willis, Fingal O'Flahertie
See Wilde, Oscar
Willy
See Colette, (Sidonie-Gabrielle)
Willy, Colette
See Colette, (Sidonie-Gabrielle)
Wilson, A(ndrew) N(orman) 1950- **CLC 33**
See also CA 112; 122; DLB 14, 155, 194;
MTCW 2
Wilson, Angus (Frank Johnstone) 1913-1991
CLC 2, 3, 5, 25, 34; SSC 21
See also CA 5-8R; 134; CANR 21; DLB 15,
139, 155; MTCW 1, 2
Wilson, August 1945- **CLC 39, 50, 63, 118;**
BLC 3; DA; DAB; DAC; DAM DRAM,
MST, MULT; DC 2; WLCS
See also AAYA 16; BW 2; CA 115; 122; CANR
42, 54, 76; MTCW 1, 2
Wilson, Brian 1942- **CLC 12**
Wilson, Colin 1931- **CLC 3, 14**
See also CA 1-4R; CAAS 5; CANR 1, 22, 33,
77; DLB 14, 194; MTCW 1
Wilson, Dirk
See Pohl, Frederik
Wilson, Edmund 1895-1972**CLC 1, 2, 3, 8, 24**
See also CA 1-4R; 37-40R; CANR 1, 46; DLB
63; MTCW 1, 2

Wilson, Ethel Davis (Bryant) 1888(?)-1980
CLC 13; DAC; DAM POET
See also CA 102; DLB 68; MTCW 1
Wilson, John 1785-1854 **NCLC 5**
Wilson, John (Anthony) Burgess 1917-1993
See Burgess, Anthony
See also CA 1-4R; 143; CANR 2, 46; DAC;
DAM NOV; MTCW 1, 2
Wilson, Lanford 1937- **CLC 7, 14, 36; DAM**
DRAM
See also CA 17-20R; CABS 3; CANR 45; DLB
7
Wilson, Robert M. 1944- **CLC 7, 9**
See also CA 49-52; CANR 2, 41; MTCW 1
Wilson, Robert McLiam 1964- **CLC 59**
See also CA 132
Wilson, Sloan 1920- **CLC 32**
See also CA 1-4R; CANR 1, 44
Wilson, Snoo 1948- **CLC 33**
See also CA 69-72
Wilson, William S(mith) 1932- **CLC 49**
See also CA 81-84
Wilson, (Thomas) Woodrow 1856-1924**TCLC**
79
See also CA 166; DLB 47
Winchilsea, Anne (Kingsmill) Finch Counte
1661-1720
See Finch, Anne
Windham, Basil
See Wodehouse, P(elham) G(renville)
Wingrove, David (John) 1954- **CLC 68**
See also CA 133
Wintergreen, Jane
See Duncan, Sara Jeannette
Winters, Janet Lewis **CLC 41**
See also Lewis, Janet
See also DLBY 87
Winters, (Arthur) Yvor 1900-1968 **CLC 4, 8,**
32
See also CA 11-12; 25-28R; CAP 1; DLB 48;
MTCW 1
Winterson, Jeanette 1959-**CLC 64; DAM POP**
See also CA 136; CANR 58; DLB 207; MTCW
2
Winthrop, John 1588-1649 **LC 31**
See also DLB 24, 30
Wirth, Louis 1897-1952 **TCLC 92**
Wiseman, Frederick 1930- **CLC 20**
See also CA 159
Wister, Owen 1860-1938 **TCLC 21**
See also CA 108; 162; DLB 9, 78, 186; SATA
62
Witkacy
See Witkiewicz, Stanislaw Ignacy
Witkiewicz, Stanislaw Ignacy 1885-1939
TCLC 8
See also CA 105; 162
Wittgenstein, Ludwig (Josef Johann) 1889-1951
TCLC 59
See also CA 113; 164; MTCW 2
Wittig, Monique 1935(?)- **CLC 22**
See also CA 116; 135; DLB 83
Wittlin, Jozef 1896-1976 **CLC 25**
See also CA 49-52; 65-68; CANR 3
Wodehouse, P(elham) G(renville) 1881-1975
CLC 1, 2, 5, 10, 22; DAB; DAC; DAM
NOV; SSC 2
See also AITN 2; CA 45-48; 57-60; CANR 3,
33; CDBLB 1914-1945; DLB 34, 162;
MTCW 1, 2; SATA 22
Woiwode, L.
See Woiwode, Larry (Alfred)
Woiwode, Larry (Alfred) 1941- **CLC 6, 10**

See also CA 73-76; CANR 16; DLB 6; INT
CANR-16
Wojciechowska, Maia (Teresa) 1927-**CLC 26**
See also AAYA 8; CA 9-12R; CANR 4, 41;
CLR 1; JRDA; MAICYA; SAAS 1; SATA
1, 28, 83; SATA-Essay 104
Wolf, Christa 1929- **CLC 14, 29, 58**
See also CA 85-88; CANR 45; DLB 75; MTCW
Wolfe, Gene (Rodman) 1931- **CLC 25; DAM**
POP
See also CA 57-60; CAAS 9; CANR 6, 32, 60;
DLB 8; MTCW 2
Wolfe, George C. 1954- **CLC 49; BLCS**
See also CA 149
Wolfe, Thomas (Clayton) 1900-1938**TCLC 4,**
13, 29, 61; DA; DAB; DAC; DAM MST,
NOV; SSC 33; WLC
See also CA 104; 132; CDALB 1929-1941;
DLB 9, 102; DLBD 2, 16; DLBY 85, 97;
MTCW 1, 2
Wolfe, Thomas Kennerly, Jr. 1930-
See Wolfe, Tom
See also CA 13-16R; CANR 9, 33, 70; DAM
POP; DLB 185; INT CANR-9; MTCW 1, 2
Wolfe, Tom **CLC 1, 2, 9, 15, 35, 51**
See also Wolfe, Thomas Kennerly, Jr.
See also AAYA 8; AITN 2; BEST 89:1; DLB
152
Wolff, Geoffrey (Ansell) 1937- **CLC 41**
See also CA 29-32R; CANR 29, 43, 78
Wolff, Sonia
See Levitin, Sonia (Wolff)
Wolff, Tobias (Jonathan Ansell) 1945- **C L C**
39, 64
See also AAYA 16; BEST 90:2; CA 114; 117;
CAAS 22; CANR 54, 76; DLB 130; INT 117;
MTCW 2
Wolfram von Eschenbach c. 1170-c. 1220
CMLC 5
See also DLB 138
Wolitzer, Hilma 1930- **CLC 17**
See also CA 65-68; CANR 18, 40; INT CANR-
18; SATA 31
Wollstonecraft, Mary 1759-1797 **LC 5, 50**
See also CDBLB 1789-1832; DLB 39, 104, 158
Wonder, Stevie **CLC 12**
See also Morris, Steveland Judkins
Wong, Jade Snow 1922- **CLC 17**
See also CA 109
Woodberry, George Edward 1855-1930
TCLC 73
See also CA 165; DLB 71, 103
Woodcott, Keith
See Brunner, John (Kilian Houston)
Woodruff, Robert W.
See Mencken, H(enry) L(ouis)
Woolf, (Adeline) Virginia 1882-1941**TCLC 1,**
5, 20, 43, 56; DA; DAB; DAC; DAM MST,
NOV; SSC 7; WLC
See also Woolf, Virginia Adeline
See also CA 104; 130; CANR 64; CDBLB
1914-1945; DLB 36, 100, 162; DLBD 10;
MTCW 1
Woolf, Virginia Adeline
See Woolf, (Adeline) Virginia
See also MTCW 2
Woollcott, Alexander (Humphreys) 1887-1943
TCLC 5
See also CA 105; 161; DLB 29
Woolrich, Cornell 1903-1968 **CLC 77**
See also Hopley-Woolrich, Cornell George
Wordsworth, Dorothy 1771-1855 **NCLC 25**

See also DLB 107

Wordsworth, William 1770-1850 **NCLC 12, 38; DA; DAB; DAC; DAM MST, POET; PC 4; WLC**
See also CDBLB 1789-1832; DLB 93, 107

Wouk, Herman 1915-   **CLC 1, 9, 38; DAM NOV, POP**
See also CA 5-8R; CANR 6, 33, 67; DLBY 82; INT CANR-6; MTCW 1, 2

Wright, Charles (Penzel, Jr.) 1935-**CLC 6, 13, 28, 119**
See also CA 29-32R; CAAS 7; CANR 23, 36, 62; DLB 165; DLBY 82; MTCW 1, 2

Wright, Charles Stevenson 1932-   **CLC 49; BLC 3; DAM MULT, POET**
See also BW 1; CA 9-12R; CANR 26; DLB 33

Wright, Frances 1795-1852   **NCLC 74**
See also DLB 73

Wright, Jack R.
See Harris, Mark

Wright, James (Arlington) 1927-1980**CLC 3, 5, 10, 28; DAM POET**
See also AITN 2; CA 49-52; 97-100; CANR 4, 34, 64; DLB 5, 169; MTCW 1, 2

Wright, Judith (Arandell) 1915-**CLC 11, 53; PC 14**
See also CA 13-16R; CANR 31, 76; MTCW 1, 2; SATA 14

Wright, L(aurali) R. 1939-   **CLC 44**
See also CA 138

Wright, Richard (Nathaniel) 1908-1960 **C L C 1, 3, 4, 9, 14, 21, 48, 74; BLC 3; DA; DAB; DAC; DAM MST, MULT, NOV; SSC 2; WLC**
See also AAYA 5; BW 1; CA 108; CANR 64; CDALB 1929-1941; DLB 76, 102; DLBD 2; MTCW 1, 2

Wright, Richard B(ruce) 1937-   **CLC 6**
See also CA 85-88; DLB 53

Wright, Rick 1945-   **CLC 35**

Wright, Rowland
See Wells, Carolyn

Wright, Stephen 1946-   **CLC 33**

Wright, Willard Huntington 1888-1939
See Van Dine, S. S.
See also CA 115; DLBD 16

Wright, William 1930-   **CLC 44**
See also CA 53-56; CANR 7, 23

Wroth, LadyMary 1587-1653(?)   **LC 30**
See also DLB 121

Wu Ch'eng-en 1500(?)-1582(?)   **LC 7**

Wu Ching-tzu 1701-1754   **LC 2**

Wurlitzer, Rudolph 1938(?)-   **CLC 2, 4, 15**
See also CA 85-88; DLB 173

Wycherley, William 1641-1715**LC 8, 21; DAM DRAM**
See also CDBLB 1660-1789; DLB 80

Wylie, Elinor (Morton Hoyt) 1885-1928
TCLC 8; PC 23
See also CA 105; 162; DLB 9, 45

Wylie, Philip (Gordon) 1902-1971   **CLC 43**
See also CA 21-22; 33-36R; CAP 2; DLB 9

Wyndham, John   **CLC 19**
See also Harris, John (Wyndham Parkes Lucas) Beynon

Wyss, Johann David Von 1743-1818**NCLC 10**
See also JRDA; MAICYA; SATA 29; SATA-Brief 27

Xenophon c. 430B.C.-c. 354B.C.   **CMLC 17**
See also DLB 176

Yakumo Koizumi
See Hearn, (Patricio) Lafcadio (Tessima Carlos)

Yamamoto, Hisaye 1921-   **SSC 34; DAM**

MULT
Yanez, Jose Donoso
See Donoso (Yanez), Jose

Yanovsky, Basile S.
See Yanovsky, V(assily) S(emenovich)

Yanovsky, V(assily) S(emenovich) 1906-1989
CLC 2, 18
See also CA 97-100; 129

Yates, Richard 1926-1992   **CLC 7, 8, 23**
See also CA 5-8R; 139; CANR 10, 43; DLB 2; DLBY 81, 92; INT CANR-10

Yeats, W. B.
See Yeats, William Butler

Yeats, William Butler 1865-1939**TCLC 1, 11, 18, 31; DA; DAB; DAC; DAM DRAM, MST, POET; PC 20; WLC**
See also CA 104; 127; CANR 45; CDBLB 1890-1914; DLB 10, 19, 98, 156; MTCW 1, 2

Yehoshua, A(braham) B. 1936-   **CLC 13, 31**
See also CA 33-36R; CANR 43

Yep, Laurence Michael 1948-   **CLC 35**
See also AAYA 5; CA 49-52; CANR 1, 46; CLR 3, 17, 54; DLB 52; JRDA; MAICYA; SATA 7, 69

Yerby, Frank G(arvin) 1916-1991 **CLC 1, 7, 22; BLC 3; DAM MULT**
See also BW 1; CA 9-12R; 136; CANR 16, 52; DLB 76; INT CANR-16; MTCW 1

Yesenin, Sergei Alexandrovich
See Esenin, Sergei (Alexandrovich)

Yevtushenko, Yevgeny (Alexandrovich) 1933-
CLC 1, 3, 13, 26, 51; DAM POET
See also CA 81-84; CANR 33, 54; MTCW 1

Yezierska, Anzia 1885(?)-1970   **CLC 46**
See also CA 126; 89-92; DLB 28; MTCW 1

Yglesias, Helen 1915-   **CLC 7, 22**
See also CA 37-40R; CAAS 20; CANR 15, 65; INT CANR-15; MTCW 1

Yokomitsu Riichi 1898-1947   **TCLC 47**
See also CA 170

Yonge, Charlotte (Mary) 1823-1901**TCLC 48**
See also CA 109; 163; DLB 18, 163; SATA 17

York, Jeremy
See Creasey, John

York, Simon
See Heinlein, Robert A(nson)

Yorke, Henry Vincent 1905-1974   **CLC 13**
See also Green, Henry
See also CA 85-88; 49-52

Yosano Akiko 1878-1942   **TCLC 59; PC 11**
See also CA 161

Yoshimoto, Banana   **CLC 84**
See also Yoshimoto, Mahoko

Yoshimoto, Mahoko 1964-
See Yoshimoto, Banana
See also CA 144

Young, Al(bert James) 1939-**CLC 19; BLC 3; DAM MULT**
See also BW 2; CA 29-32R; CANR 26, 65; DLB 33

Young, Andrew (John) 1885-1971   **CLC 5**
See also CA 5-8R; CANR 7, 29

Young, Collier
See Bloch, Robert (Albert)

Young, Edward 1683-1765   **LC 3, 40**
See also DLB 95

Young, Marguerite (Vivian) 1909-1995 **C L C 82**
See also CA 13-16; 150; CAP 1

Young, Neil 1945-   **CLC 17**
See also CA 110

Young Bear, Ray A. 1950-   **CLC 94; DAM**

MULT
See also CA 146; DLB 175; NNAL

Yourcenar, Marguerite 1903-1987   **CLC 19, 38, 50, 87; DAM NOV**
See also CA 69-72; CANR 23, 60; DLB 72; DLBY 88; MTCW 1, 2

Yurick, Sol 1925-   **CLC 6**
See also CA 13-16R; CANR 25

Zabolotsky, Nikolai Alekseevich 1903-1958
TCLC 52
See also CA 116; 164

Zamiatin, Yevgenii
See Zamyatin, Evgeny Ivanovich

Zamora, Bernice (B. Ortiz) 1938-   **CLC 89; DAM MULT; HLC**
See also CA 151; DLB 82; HW

Zamyatin, Evgeny Ivanovich 1884-1937
TCLC 8, 37
See also CA 105; 166

Zangwill, Israel 1864-1926   **TCLC 16**
See also CA 109; 167; DLB 10, 135, 197

Zappa, Francis Vincent, Jr. 1940-1993
See Zappa, Frank
See also CA 108; 143; CANR 57

Zappa, Frank   **CLC 17**
See also Zappa, Francis Vincent, Jr.

Zaturenska, Marya 1902-1982   **CLC 6, 11**
See also CA 13-16R; 105; CANR 22

Zeami 1363-1443   **DC 7**

Zelazny, Roger (Joseph) 1937-1995 **CLC 21**
See also AAYA 7; CA 21-24R; 148; CANR 26, 60; DLB 8; MTCW 1, 2; SATA 57; SATA-Brief 39

Zhdanov, Andrei Alexandrovich 1896-1948
TCLC 18
See also CA 117; 167

Zhukovsky, Vasily (Andreevich) 1783-1852
NCLC 35
See also DLB 205

Ziegenhagen, Eric   **CLC 55**

Zimmer, Jill Schary
See Robinson, Jill

Zimmerman, Robert
See Dylan, Bob

Zindel, Paul 1936-**CLC 6, 26; DA; DAB; DAC; DAM DRAM, MST, NOV; DC 5**
See also AAYA 2; CA 73-76; CANR 31, 65; CLR 3, 45; DLB 7, 52; JRDA; MAICYA; MTCW 1, 2; SATA 16, 58, 102

Zinov'Ev, A. A.
See Zinoviev, Alexander (Aleksandrovich)

Zinoviev, Alexander (Aleksandrovich) 1922-
CLC 19
See also CA 116; 133; CAAS 10

Zoilus
See Lovecraft, H(oward) P(hillips)

Zola, Emile (Edouard Charles Antoine) 1840-1902**TCLC 1, 6, 21, 41; DA; DAB; DAC; DAM MST, NOV; WLC**
See also CA 104; 138; DLB 123

Zoline, Pamela 1941-   **CLC 62**
See also CA 161

Zorrilla y Moral, Jose 1817-1893   **NCLC 6**

Zoshchenko, Mikhail (Mikhailovich) 1895-1958
TCLC 15; SSC 15
See also CA 115; 160

Zuckmayer, Carl 1896-1977   **CLC 18**
See also CA 69-72; DLB 56, 124

Zuk, Georges
See Skelton, Robin

Zukofsky, Louis 1904-1978**CLC 1, 2, 4, 7, 11, 18; DAM POET; PC 11**
See also CA 9-12R; 77-80; CANR 39; DLB 5,

165; MTCW 1
Zweig, Paul 1935-1984   **CLC 34, 42**
See also CA 85-88; 113
Zweig, Stefan 1881-1942   **TCLC 17**
See also CA 112; 170; DLB 81, 118
Zwingli, Huldreich 1484-1531   **LC 37**
See also DLB 179

Literary Criticism Series
Cumulative Topic Index

This index lists all topic entries in Gale's *Classical and Medieval Literature Criticism, Contemporary Literary Criticism, Literature Criticism from 1400 to 1800, Nineteenth-Century Literature Criticism,* and *Twentieth-Century Literary Criticism.*

Topic Index

Topic Index

NCLC Cumulative Nationality Index

Nationality Index

ISBN 0-7876-2878-6

90000

9 780787 628789